Footprint

Australia Handbook

Andrew Swaffer, Katrina O'Brien & Darroch Donald

Everything we do is overshadowed by the pure silence of the interior, by hallucinatory clouds of cockatoos, by water grinding against rock, by the chatter of mangroves clicking and tut-tutting in the tide, by the silhouette of Uluru, the spread fingers of Sydney Harbour, the honeycomb of coral reefs spawning, seen and unseen.

Tim Winton, *Down to Earth* (1999)

1st edition

Australia

See colour maps at back of book

1 South Coast
Soaring karri forests meet granite coasts and snowy beaches

2 Ningaloo Reef
Wade off the beach into a haven for marine wildlife

3 Pilbara
Where incredibly deep, tight gorges meet expansive views of red and gold ranges

4 East Kimberley
The superb Ord River and the incomparable beehive Bungles

5 Uluru and Kata Tjuta
The world's biggest and most mesmerising rock

6 Kakadu
Ancient rock art and the perfectly picturesque Twin Falls

7 Flinders Ranges
Saturating colour and remarkable, rugged walks

8 Kangaroo Island
A wildlife wonderland

9 Great Ocean Road
The twelve apostles and a surprise around every twisting corner

10 High Country
An adventurer's playground with breathtaking views

Timor Sea

Darwin · Jabiru **6**

The Kimberley

Katherine

Indian Ocean

Kununurra **4**
Lake Argyle
Derby · Purnululu (Bungle Bungles) NP

Broome

NORTHERN

Glibb River Rd

Port Hedland

Great Sandy Desert

Tanami Track

2 Exmouth

3 ◆
Karijini NP

Newman

WESTERN AUSTRALIA

Kings Canyon

Yulara **5**

Outback Highway

Shark Bay

Kalbarri NP ◆

Mount Magnet

Geraldton

Kalgoorlie-Boulder

SOUTH

Eucla

Perth

Esperance

Great Australian Bight

Margaret River

Albany **1**

Southern Ocean

N

0 km 300
0 miles 300

⑪ Wilsons Promontory
A bushwalking wilderness with pure white beaches

⑫ Port Arthur
The most tangible reminder of modern Australia's penal beginnings

⑬ Cradle Mountain
A jagged peak standing guard over Australia's best walking track

⑭ Sydney Harbour
One of the world's great sights, sparkling like crushed diamonds

⑮ Lightning Ridge
Win the lottery by finding the elusive black opal

⑯ Silverton
Mad Max meets Priscilla, Queen of the desert in the back of beyond

⑰ Byron Bay
Surf's up in the New South Wales coastal capital of cool

⑱ Fraser Island
The 4WD adventure of a lifetime on the largest sand island in the world

⑲ Mossman Gorge
Aboriginal Dreamtime and rainforest paradise

⑳ Great Barrier Reef
Tropical island fantasy

Contents

A foot in the door

Right In outback NSW, eroded ridges of sand are proof that, as infrequent as it may be, when it rains, it really rains
Below The cool, crystal-clear waters of Lake Mackenzie in the heart of Fraser Island – the world's largest sand island – off the coast of Queensland, provide the perfect spot for a swim
Previous page Surfers eye the waves and queue up to enter the fray at the surfing mecca of Coolangatta

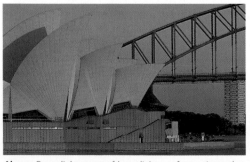

Above Dawn light on two of Australia's most famous icons, the Sydney Opera House and Harbour Bridge
Right Reflections of half-submerged paperbark trees in the early morning light at Yellow Waters, Kakadu

Introducing Australia

Popular images of Australia are as varied as they are strange: the shimmering sails of Sydney Opera House; the brooding red hulk of Uluru; the paint-daubed Aboriginal; the cute koala and peculiar platypus; and the vast emptiness of the outback. They're all here, but the Australian experience is far more subtle and profound than that. The 'Great Southern Land' offers beauty and diversity in spades, the world's oldest living culture and the very last word in weird wildlife. Then, of course, there's the size of the place. The word 'big' doesn't even begin to cover it. Australia is so outrageously outsized that trying to squeeze it all into one visit is about as feasible as fitting a basketball player with a pair of toddler's shoes. Here in Australia, size matters.

Australia is a land of extremes, of scarcity and excess. Some of the best things about the country, its space, sunshine and wildlife, can also be its worst, but it is exactly this element of the untameable that makes Australia an exciting destination. The place is huge, about the same size as the USA or Europe, yet is one of least densely populated countries in the world. But although there's plenty of room to spread out, most people live on the edge of the continent by the sea. Not only that, but if you drew a line from Adelaide to Brisbane you would find eighty five percent of Australians living in that southeastern corner. Head inland and nothing comes between you and the horizon but a bright infinite sky because Australia is also the flattest, lowest and driest continent on earth. It is an ancient landscape, eroded down into low-rounded ranges and vast plains, subject to blinding heat and flash floods. In the solitude of the outback or on the never-ending beaches you can always find space and lose time.

Big is beautiful

Much of inland Australia contains desert or arid plains of a stark and minimalist beauty, but around the edges of the continent there are surprisingly diverse landscapes. In the Northern Territory golden escarpment walls rise above emerald green wetlands, while over the border Queensland's idyllic tropical islands and coral bays are better known than its rainforest-cloaked mountains. New South Wales and Victoria both have snow fields as well as surf beaches, and the jagged peaks of Tasmania's central plateau have little in common with the hospitable nature of the rolling green hills below. South Australia has pretty cultivated valleys, such as the Barossa, as well as the vast dazzling salt pan of Lake Eyre. In the west, tall karri forests and tranquil granite-framed bays are separated by thousands of kilometres from the magnificent red ranges of the Pilbara and Kimberley in the north.

Out & about   The outback is as much an idea as a place. The notion that magical peace and freedom is to be found outdoors and away from civilization goes deep into the Australian psyche. Of course to be really intimate with the great outdoors you've got to fall asleep in a swag looking at the stars and wake to the dawn chorus of cockatoos, or pitch a tent in a forest and watch a quoll flash past in the firelight. Other good ways to get outback are either to work on an outback 'station', or join a four-wheel drive adventure trip into one of the spectacular national parks or along one of the great outback tracks. Another possibility, though requiring much care and planning, is to tackle one of the great outback walking trails such as the Larapinta in the central MacDonnells or the Heysen in South Australia. The country's best walking, however, is not in the arid centre but the glorious hill country of the Great Dividing Range, Victoria's Grampians and, the very best of all, Tasmania's incredible Wilderness World Heritage Area.

Previous owners   It may seem like a wilderness out there, without roads, crops, buildings or even ruins, but the truth is that the Australian landscape has been managed, altered and cared for by its indigenous people for an unimaginable length of time. Australian Aboriginals are thought to have lived in the country for around 60,000 years and despite the turmoil and change wrought by dispossession, their culture has survived to the present day. In a world that is over consuming its resources, it is well worth listening to people whose culture is based around an inextricable link between land and people; caring for both in the present to ensure they exist in the future. You can learn about this fascinating and very different culture in many ways; perhaps by looking at rock art in Northern Australia, or contemporary Aboriginal art in a Melbourne gallery, listening to a didjeridu performance or an Aboriginal band. Possibly the best way is to take a tour with Aboriginal people who wish to show you their country, but all such encounters will enrich a visit to Australia.

Left A lone ghost gum at Stubbs Waterhole, Welcome Pound, Arkaroola, in the Flinders Ranges

Below Tiwi Aboriginal women searching for turtle eggs on Melville Island, Northern Territory

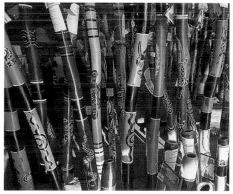

Left The former outback mining settlement of Silverton, near Broken Hill, NSW, has given up its ghosts to a community of hardy artisans

Above The weird and wonderful didjeridu, that ancient Aboriginal instrument which creates the sound so synonymous with Australia

Next pages Uluru (Ayers Rock) remains an extraordinary, brooding presence throughout the day

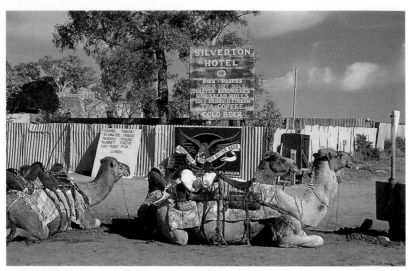

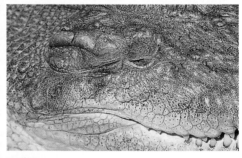

Top Camel Train resting at Silverton
Above Road sign in Victoria warns of koalas and kangaroos crossing
Above right The saltwater crocodile, one of the largest and most fearsome creatures on earth
Right A koala takes a well-earned break from all the hugging and attention in a Queensland wildlife sanctuary
Next page The sheer sandstone cliffs of the Blue Mountains, near Sydney

Go wild in the country

It is a strange paradox that such a harsh and unforgiving country should possess such absurdly cute, soft and fluffy animals, which produce even more appealing mini versions of themselves out of a built-in pocket. The kangaroo and koala are the best known of over a hundred species of marsupials unique to Australia, such as the wombat, tasmanian devil, bilby, numbat, quoll and bandicoot. The country's birds are magnificent too, from the elegant wetlands waders like the dancing brolga and the stately jabiru to the magnificent eagles and raucous parrots, whose piercing screech may be the price they have paid for their vivid beauty. Of course some Australian wildlife has a more deadly appeal, like the poisonous snakes, spiders and marine creatures, or the powerful 'saltie' crocodile, but as long as you keep your distance these need only bite or sting your imagination.

Close encounters

Many native Australian animals are under intense pressure from introduced species and habitat degradation. Tragically, many species have now vanished forever. Those that remain, however, are surprisingly visible – if you know where to look. Outside the cities kangaroos, wallabies and emus are commonly seen from the road, if not on the road. Sightings of many other animals in the wild may involve a little planning and patience, but do not think you can only see them in wildlife parks. Platypus, penguins, seals, wombats, whales, dolphins and koalas can all be seen in southern Australia, and whale sharks, turtles, manta rays, crocodiles, and dugongs are found in the northern half of the country. Unbelievably, these are just a few of the creatures that can be seen, often without great effort or expenditure.

Thrills & spills

Australia isn't just about seeing, but doing. This is one of the world's great adventure destinations, where almost anything and everything is possible. As well as walking and four-wheel driving you can cycle, ski, trail-bike, horse-ride or even skate your way around. Even the most rugged mountains and gorges can be climbed and explored by the well-prepared, and if you've a taste for getting below ground there are cave systems in every state. For an eagle-eye view you can take to the skies in all manner of aircraft, from gliders to hang gliders, balloons to microlights. You can leap out of a plane strapped to a parachute, or off a platform attached to a bungy. Explore the bays and rivers in kayaks or rafts, or even behind a boat on water-skis. Off the coast, try your hand at surfing or its hard-to-master associates, windsurfing or kitesurfing. If you like the idea of some wind in your sails, but want to stay dry, then jump on a yacht or a tall ship and sail the coasts and islands. Finally, take the plunge and snorkel or dive under the waves to see some of Australia's marine life, reefs and wrecks.

Essentials

Planning your trip

Where to go

See map on page 908 to get some idea of the scale of this vast country

Australia is the world's biggest island nation. So big an island that it isn't even accorded the status of the world's biggest (the title is usually given to Greenland), but rather the smallest continent. It is vast; larger in area than Western Europe and the equivalent of the contiguous United States. If you have no more than one or two weeks for a visit, dismiss the idea of trying to see too much of it, and certainly of attempting to see every state.

Where you choose to visit will primarily be determined by the time of year. Broadly speaking, the far north from October to April is extremely hot, humid and monsoonal. Cairns still gets visitors who want to see the Great Barrier Reef, and some enthusiasts extol the delights of Kakadu and the Kimberley in 'the wet', but most visitors will want to enjoy the glorious summer weather in the southern regions and avoid the humidity up north. A visit during May to September not only opens up the north, but also allows an itinerary to range almost anywhere in the country.

One to two week trip

If you've only a few days on your way through, pick a city as a base and check out its hinterland. Perhaps also take a three-night excursion (by air) to one of the other centres. The following are suggested 'short breaks' to suit the various times of year. **January** Hobart and the Tasman Peninsula. **February** Sydney for the Mardi Gras, and the New South Wales (NSW) east coast. **March** Melbourne, Wilsons Prom or Great Ocean Road. **April** Perth and the west coast. **May** Alice Springs and Uluru. **June** Darwin and Kakadu. **July** Brisbane, Cairns and the Great Barrier Reef. **August** Kununurra and the east Kimberley. **September** Adelaide, Kangaroo Island or the Flinders Ranges. **October** Sydney, Blue Mountains and coastal parks. **November** Melbourne for the Festival, AFL Grand Final and Melbourne Cup. **December** Perth and the Cape-to-Cape region.

A **two-week** visit allows a trip based around two to three centres, concentrating on flying. Alternatively it broadens the scope to a swift exploratory road-trip. Some of the best of these in the warmer months include: from Sydney to Melbourne, a Tasmanian circuit or the southwest of Western Australia (WA). In the winter months Sydney to Cairns, Alice Springs to Uluru or Darwin via Kakadu, and Perth to Broome make excellent trips. Two weeks could also allow a more specific and detailed exploration of some of the country's harder-to-get-to gems, such as the Pilbara and Kimberley areas of WA, the wilderness areas of Tasmania, Queensland's (QLD) York Peninsula or the 'high country' of NSW and Victoria (VIC).

Three to four week trip

This is the minimum amount of time a visitor from Europe or the USA should contemplate. A trip of this length allows a visitor to see one of the smaller states, say Tasmania, Victoria or Northern Territory (NT), in some detail and jump on one or two extended tours. Three to four weeks is also sufficient time to base a trip around three centres, say Perth, Alice Springs and Sydney for someone on a round-the-world air ticket. Perth to Darwin can just about be contemplated in this time frame, as can Darwin to Adelaide or Melbourne to Cairns.

Longer trips

Visits measured in months rather than weeks really start to open Australia up to the visitor, and will give you the chance to see a variety of terrain, culture and climate that will paint a much more accurate picture of the country. Four months is the minimum amount of time you should consider for either of the eastern or western 'circuits', though at least six months for each will allow a far more rewarding trip.

Twenty great Aussie adventures

- Canoe or raft the awesome **Ord** and **Franklin Rivers**
- Climb the ramparts of Wilpena Pound in the beautiful **Flinders Ranges**
- Complete the three great day walks of Central Australia: around Uluru, through the **Valley of the Winds** at Kata Tjuta and around the rim of **Kings Canyon**
- Explore the plunging gorges of the **Karijini**, perhaps tackling sections of the fabled '**Miracle Mile**'
- Gain an understanding of Aboriginal people and their culture by staying with then at places like the **Iga Warta** in the Flinders Ranges or **Lombadina** near Broome
- Head for the Ningaloo Reef to snorkel amongst teeming **fish**, swim with **whale sharks** and dive with **manta rays**
- Lace up your boots at majestic **Cradle Mountain** and hike the **Overland Track** to **Lake Street Clair**
- Saddle up and emulate the mountain men and women of the high country in the **Snowy Mountains** and the **Victorian Alps**
- Sleep outside in a comfy **swag** with only the **stars** and a **billy** on the fire for company
- Take a good look around **Kakadu National Park**
- Get to grips with 4WD amidst the stunning scenery of **Fraser Island**, the world's largest sand island
- Sit next to a huge turtle laying its eggs on the beach at **Mon Repos**, near Bundaberg
- Be the first to see the Australian dawn from the summit of **Mount Warning** in the Byron Bay hinterland
- Come face to face with an 'old wife' or a 'bucket mouth', **snorkelling** off a coral cay in Queensland
- Be dwarfed by a potato cod while diving the **SS Yongala** wreck off **Townsville**
- Go night spotting in **wet tropics rainforest** and come face to face with possums
- Take a balloon flight at dawn over the **Hunter Valley vineyards**
- Watch dolphins surfing off the beach at **Cape Byron**
- Go island hopping by floatplane, yacht or kayak around the beautiful **Whitsundays**
- Wander through the bizarre, 190,000-year-old **Undara Lava Tubes** in Queensland's outback

1. Eastern circuit – Sydney – via coast – **Brisbane** – via coast – Townsville – offshoot to Cairns – Townsville – **Tennant Creek** – offshoot to **Darwin** and Kakadu circuit – **Katherine** – Tennant Creek – **Alice Springs** – Erldunda – **Yulara (Uluru)** – Erldunda – **Adelaide** – Grampians – Warrnambool – via coast – **Melbourne** – **Canberra** – Bathurst – Sydney

2. Western Circuit – Perth – **Kalbarri** – Overlander – offshoot to **Monkey Mia** – Overlander – **Exmouth** – Tom Price – **Karijini** – **Broome** – via highway – **Kununurra** – **Katherine** – offshoot to **Darwin** and Kakadu circuit – Katherine – **Alice Springs** – Erldunda – **Yulara (Uluru)** – Erldunda – **Adelaide** – Port Augusta – **Albany** – via coast – **Margaret River** – via coast – Perth.

Record of the history of the indigenous **Aboriginal** peoples is often conspicuous by its absence. The state museums and galleries usually have sections devoted to Aboriginal culture, but Aboriginal cultural centres, some within Aboriginal communities and some in National Parks, are often the most interesting and enlightening of formal sources. The best of these are at Uluru and Cooinda in Kakadu.

Sights *Entry to National Trust properties is free to members from UK, USA, Canada, New Zealand, Japan and Netherlands*

Essentials

The preservation and display of the 'European' history in Australia is, as to be expected, much more extensive. The major museums and art galleries of the state capitals are superb, and well worth the time spent wandering their halls and galleries. As in many countries a National Trust has been developed to buy and manage buildings of historic and cultural importance.

Some of the world's earliest National Parks and Reserves were declared in Australia. They generally constitute natural areas of ecological, cultural or simply aesthetic importance (often a combination of all three), and can claim to encompass almost all of Australia's most startling natural attractions. They range from a few hectares to the size of small countries and the degree of public access allowed is as variable. National Parks are generally managed by the state in which they are situated, except for some of those in the NT, by a state government parks agency. In some states there is an entry fee to each park, in others entry is free to some or all. Where entry fees are charged it is usually possible to obtain a state-wide pass lasting from four weeks to a year. See state introductions for further details. There is no national pass.

When to go

Details of school and bank holidays on page 54. *If planning a trip of three months or more, try to make spring or autumn the core of your stay; this will allow maximum geographical travelling potential and will avoid the major tourist periods*

One of the joys of Australia is that at any time of year there are considerable chunks of territory where the weather is just about right. The converse, of course, is that those particular about their destination need good timing. The peak season, broadly speaking, in the southern third of the country is mid-December through to the end of January. This is high summer and school holidays, and also when the airlines hike up their fares from Europe and North America. Practically every form of accommodation on the coast, from Shark Bay in the west, right around the south to the Gold Coast in the east, gets booked out – months in advance in the most popular spots. In the centre and north of the country winter is the most popular time, with dry, warm weather the norm. The northwest of WA (Pilbara and Kimberley), 'red centre' (Alice Springs and Uluru), Top End (Darwin and Katherine) and the QLD coast get particularly busy May-September. Generally, accommodation and tourist sites stay open year-round, the exceptions being in the far north in summer (December-March), and Tasmania (TAS) and some coastal parts of VIC in winter (May-July). The exceptions to the standard tourist seasons are: **skiing** in the mountainous areas of NSW, VIC and TAS from June-September; **walking** the glorious hill ranges of South Australia (SA), which is simply too hot and dangerous from November-March; and **whale-watching**, possible at many southern coastal spots from March-October.

Watch out for **school holidays**, when some areas get completely booked out. They vary from state to state (see www.australia.com for details), but broadly speaking they cover the whole of **January**, a week or two around **Easter**, a couple of weeks in **June-July** and another couple during **September**.

Climate
Being a southern hemisphere continent, the seasons, such as they are, are reversed (Christmas on the beach is the classic image for those from the northern hemisphere)

As a general rule, the further north you travel, and the further in time from July, the hotter it gets. And hot means very hot: days over 40°C regularly occur in high summer in the arid regions, and even cities as far south as Perth and Adelaide often get '30-over-30' (over 30°C for 30 consecutive days). In the north of the country summer (November-April) is characterized by high humidity, heat, tremendous monsoonal rainfall and occasional, powerful cyclones (the Australian equivalent of hurricanes). Australia is the driest continent, excluding Antarctica, and virtually nowhere further than 250 km inland gets more than an average of 600 mm (24 in) of rain a year. About half the continent, in a band across the south and west, gets less than 300 mm and much of it is desert. The only areas that get significant rainfall (in excess of 1,600 mm) spread over more than 160 days a year are bits of the north QLD coast, the western coastal areas of VIC, the southwestern highlands in TAS and the southwest tip of WA.

◀◀

Australian Tourist Commission offices

Auckland, Level 13, 44-48 Emily Place, T09 9152826.

Bangkok, Unit 1614,16th floor, River Wing East, Empire Tower, 195 South Sathorn Road, Yannawa, Sathorn, 10120, T02 6700640.

Frankfurt, Neue Mainzer Strasse 22, D 60311, T069 274 00622.

Hong Kong, Suite 1501 Central Plaza, 18 Harbour Road, Wanchai, T2802 7700.

London, Gemini House, 10-18 Putney Hill, SW15 6AA, T020-8780 2229.

Los Angeles, 2049 Century Park East, Suite 1920, CA 90067, T310 2294870.

Singapore, 101 Thomson Road, 26-05 United Square, 307591, T2554555.

Sydney, Level 4 80 William Street, Woolloomooloo NSW 2011, T02 9360 1111.

Tokyo, c/o Australian Business Centre, New Otani Garden Court Building 28F, 4-1 Kioi-cho Chiyoda-ku, 102-0094, T03 5214 0720.

The whole picture is complicated by *ENSO* (El Niño Southern Oscillation). This global climatic effect has a profound influence on the Australian climate. It starts out in the eastern Pacific every two to eight years, with an abnormal increase in the temperature of the surface layers of the ocean bringing violent, destructive storms to the normally arid western coast of South America. As a counter to this the surface ocean off eastern Australia is cooler than usual, lowering evaporation and cloud formation. Naturally low rainfall is decreased yet further and the net effect on much of the southern and eastern parts of the continent are drought, desiccation and sometimes horrific bushfires. There were early signs of a new ENSO developing as this guide was going to press.

Tours and tour operators

There are a host of companies offering general interest or special interest tours. Most are district, state or multi-centre based. The main two national, coach-based, tour operators are *AAT Kings*, www.aatkings.com, and *APT*, www.aptouring.com.au The main Australian travel agents are: *Flight Centre*, T131600, www.flightcentre.com.au; *Harvey World Travel*, T132757, www.harveyworld.com.au; *JetSet*, T136384, www.jetset.com.au; and *STA*, T131776, www.statravel.com

Australian based operators are detailed within states

Absolute Australia, 180 Varick Street, New York, T212 627 8258, www.absoluteaustralia.com Have a diverse range of specialist trips to Australia with expert guides. *Earthwatch Research and Exploration*, PO Box 75, Maynard, MA 01754, USA, T978 461 0081, www.earthwatch.org Run excellent eco-tourism trips to Australia in combination with conservation research on Australian wildlife. There are offices in USA, UK and Australia.

American tour operators

Travelbag, 3-5 High Street, Alton, GU34 1TL, UK, T0870 9001350, www.travelbag.co.uk Reputable UK based firm offering a good range of general and tailor-made trips to Australia at reasonable prices.

British tour operators

Several operators combine the role of bus and tour company. These will typically drive from A to B, taking from twice to five times as long as a scheduled bus service, and stopping at many of the key sights along the way. Some offer tickets that allow travellers to 'jump-on, jump-off' as they wish during a set period. The more adventurous tours will include 4WD routes and bush camping. For more information see Backpacker buses, page 42.

Essentials

▶▶ **Government tourism and environment agencies**

The *Australian Tourist Commission* is based at Level 4, 80 William Street, Woolloomooloo NSW, T02 9360 1111, www.australia.com and www.aussie.net.au **Parks Australia**, www.ea.gov.au/parks, manage the ACT and Kakadu, Watarrka and Uluru-Kata Tjuta national parks.

ACT Canberra Tourism, T02 6205 0666, www.canberratourism.com.au **Environment ACT**, 12 Wattle Street, Lyneham, T02 6207 9777, www.environment.act.gov.au **National Trust of Australia (ACT)**, T02 6273 4744, www.act.nationaltrust.org.au

NSW Tourism New South Wales, T02 9931 1111, www.visitnsw.com.au / www.tourism.nsw.gov.au **National Parks and Wildlife Service**, T1300-361967, www.npws.nsw.gov.au **National Trust of Australia (NSW)**, T02 9258 0123, www.nsw.nationaltrust.org.au

NT Northern Territory Tourist Commission, T08 8999 3900, www.nttc.com.au **Parks and Wildlife Commission**, T08 8999 5511, www.nt.gov.au/paw **National Trust of Australia (NT)**, T08 8981 2848, www.northernexposure.com.au/trust

QLD Tourism Queensland, T07 3406 5400, www.queensland-holidays.com.au

Queensland Parks and Wildlife *Service,* 160 Ann Street, Brisbane, T07 3227 8186, www.env.qld.gov.au **National Trust of Australia (QLD)**, T07 3229 1788, www.nationaltrustqld.org

SA South Australian Tourist Commission, T08 8303 2222, wwww.southaustralia.com **Parks and Wildlife Service**, T08 8336 0924, www.parks.sa.gov.au **National Trust of Australia (SA)**, T08 8212 1133, admin@nationaltrustsa.org.au

TAS Tourism Tasmania, T03 6230 8169, www.discovertasmania.com **Parks and Wildlife Service**, T1300-368550, www.parks.tas.gov.au **National Trust of Australia (TAS)**, T03 6344 6233, www.tased.edu.au/tasonline/nattrust

VIC Tourism Victoria, T03 9653 9777, www.visitvictoria.com **Parks Victoria**, T03 8627 4699, www.parkweb.vic.gov.au **National Trust of Australia (VIC)**, T03 9654 4711, www.nattrust.com.au

WA Western Australia Tourist Commission, T08 9220 1700, www.westernaustralia.net **Dept of Conservation and Land Management** ('CALM'), T08 9334 0333, www.calm.gov.au **National Trust of Australia (WA)**, T08 9321 6088, www.ntwa.com.au

Finding out more

The *Australian Tourist Commission*, **www.australia.com**, and its state equivalents (see box on previous page) can be of great help, and there is also a wealth of all sorts of information to be found on the Federal and government websites (**www.fed.gov.au**). For general stats on all aspects of Australian life check out the website of the *Australian Bureau of Statistics*, **www.abs.gov.au** You can access the national database of telephone numbers and their accompanying addresses at www.whitepages.com.au The *Yellow Pages* also has its own site at www.yellowpages.com.au

Before you travel

Visas
Travellers on a tourist visa are not allowed to work while in Australia

Visas are subject to change, so it is essential to check with your local Australian Embassy or High Commission. All travellers to Australia, other than New Zealand citizens, must have a valid visa to enter Australia. These must be arranged prior to travel (allow two months) and cannot be organized at Australian airports. **Tourist visas**, are free, and available from your local Australian Embassy or High Commission, or in some countries, in

Overseas embassies and consulates in Australia ◀◀

Belgium, 12a Trelawney Street, Woollahra, NSW, T02-9327 8377.

Canada, Level 5, 111 Harrington Street, Sydney, T02-9364 3000; 123 Camberwell Road, Hawthorn East, VIC, T03-9811 9999; 267 St Georges Terrace, Perth, T08-9322 7930.

Denmark, 19 Phillimore Street, Fremantle, WA, T08-9335 5122.

France, 31 Market Street, Sydney, T02-9261 5779; 492 St Kilda Road, Melbourne, T03-9820 0921; 46 Stanley Street, Nedlands, WA, T08-9386 9366.

Germany, 13 Trelawney Street, Woollahra, NSW, T02-9328 7733; 480 Punt Road, South Yarra, VIC, T03-9864 6888; 16 St Georges Terrace, Perth, T08-9325 8851.

Italy, 12 Grey Street, Deakin, ACT, T02-6273 3333; 31 Labouchere Road, South Perth, T08-9367 8922.

Japan, 52 Martin Place, Sydney, T02-9231 3455; 221 St Georges Terrace, Perth, T08-9321 7816.

Netherlands, 500 Oxford Street, Bondi Junction, Sydney, T02-9387 6644; 199 St Kilda Road, Melbourne, T03-9867 7933; 77 Hay Street, Subiaco, Perth, T08-9381 3539.

New Zealand, Level 10, 55 Hunter Street, Sydney, T02-9223 0222.

Norway, 17 Hunter Street, Yarralumla, ACT, T02-6273 3444.

South Africa, State Circle, Yarralumla, ACT, T02-6273 2424.

Spain, 15 Arkana Street, Yarralumla, ACT, T02-6273 3555.

Sweden, Level 5, 350 Kent Street, Sydney, T02-9262 6433.

Switzerland, 500 Oxford Street, Bondi Junction, Sydney, T02-8383 4000; 420 St Kilda Road, Melbourne, T03-9867 2954.

United Kingdom, Sap House, Akuna Street, Canberra, T02-6257 2434; (trade and commercial) Level 16, The Gateway, 1 Macquarie Place, Sydney, T02-9247 7521; (emergencies only) 77 St Georges Terrace, Perth, T08-9221 5400.

USA, 19-29 Martin Place, Sydney, T02-9373 9200; 553 St Kilda Road, Melbourne, T03-9526 5900; 16 St Georges Terrace, Perth, T08-9231 9400.

---

electronic format (an **Electronic Travel Authority** or ETA) from their websites, and from selected travel agents and airlines. Passport holders eligible to apply for an ETA include those from Austria, Belgium, Canada, Denmark, Finland, France, Germany, Greece, Hong Kong, the Irish Republic, Italy, Japan, Netherlands, Norway, Spain, Sweden, Switzerland, the UK and the USA. Tourist visas allow one (or in some cases) multiple visits of up to three months within the year after the visa is issued. Six-month, multiple-entry tourist visas are also available to visitors from certain countries.

The **Australian Department of Immigration and Multicultural Affairs** (DIMA, T1800-040070, see also www.immi.gov.au/visitors) provides further details of Australian immigration and visa requirements. Once in Australia it may be possible to extend your tourist visa. Contact DIMA well in advance if you think that overstaying may be necessary.

Working holiday visas
Also see 'Working in Australia', page 32. Application forms can be downloaded from the embassy website or from www.immi.gov.au

This visa, which also must be arranged before travelling to Australia, is available to people between 18 and 30 from certain countries that have reciprocal arrangements with Australia. These include Canada, Denmark, Germany, Irish Republic, Japan, Norway, Sweden and the UK. The working holiday visa allows multiple entry for one year from first arrival, and allows the holder to gain casual employment. It is granted on the condition that the holder works for no more than three months for a single employer. The visa, for which there is a charge, is issued by your local Australian Embassy or High Commission.

Vaccinations

No vaccinations are required or recommended for travel to Australia unless travelling from a **yellow-fever** infected country in Africa or South America. Check with your local Australian Embassy for further advice. A **tetanus** booster is recommended if you have one due.

Essentials

▶▶ **Australian embassies and High Commissions**

A full list can be found at
www.immi.gov.au
Canada, *7th Floor, Suite 710,*
50 O'Connor St, Ottawa, Ontario,
T613 2360841, www.ahc-ottaw.org
France, *(and visa processing for*
Luxembourg and Belgium),
4 rue Jean Rey, 75724 Paris, C
edex 15, www.austgov.fr
Germany, *(and visa processing for*
Switzerland, Denmark and Norway)
Friedrichstrasse 200, 10117 Berlin, T030
8800880, www.australian-embassy.de
Irish Republic, *2nd Floor, Fitzwilton House,*
Wilton Terrace, Dublin 2, T01 6761517,
www.australianembassy.ie
Italy, *Corso Trieste 25, 00198 Rome, T06*
852721, www.australian-embassy.it
Japan, *2-1-14 Mita, Minato-Ku, Tokyo, T03*
5232 4111, www.australia.or.jp

Netherlands, *Carnegielaan 4, 2517 KH The*
Hague, T070 3108200,
www.australian-embassy.nl
New Zealand, *7th Floor, Union House,*
132-138 Quay St, Auckland, T09 3032429,
www.australia.org.nz
South Africa, *292 Orient Street, Pretoria,*
Arcadia 0001, T012 3423740,
www.australia.co.za
Spain, *Plaza Descubridor Diego de Ordás,*
3, 28003 Madrid, T091 441 5025,
www.embaustralia.es
Sweden, *Sergels Torg 12, 11th Floor, 111 57*
Stockholm, T08 613 2900, www.austemb.se
United Kingdom, *Australia House, The*
Strand, London, WC2B 4LA, T0207
3794334, www.australia.org.uk
USA, *1601 Massachusetts Av, NW 20036,*
Washington D.C., T202 7973000,
www.austemb.org

Insurance
If you are unfortunate enough to have something stolen, make sure you get a copy of the police report, as you will need this to substantiate your claim

It's a very good idea to take out some form of travel insurance, wherever you're travelling from. This should cover you for theft or loss of possessions and money, the cost of medical and dental treatment, cancellation of flights, delays in travel arrangements, accidents, missed departures, lost baggage, lost passport and personal liability and legal expenses. Also check on inclusion of 'dangerous activities' if you plan on doing any. These generally include climbing, diving, skiing, horse-riding, parachuting, even trekking. You should always read the small print carefully. Not all policies cover ambulance, helicopter rescue or emergency flights home. Find out if your policy pays medical expenses direct to the hospital or doctor, or if you have to pay and then claim the money back later. If the latter applies, make sure you keep all records.

Insurance companies
There are a variety of policies to choose from, so it's best to shop around. Your travel agent can advise on the best deals available

Reputable student travel organizations often offer good value policies. Travellers from North America can try the ***International Student Insurance Service*** (ISIS), which is available through ***STA***, T800 7770112, www.sta-travel.com Other recommended travel insurance companies include ***Access America***, T800 2848300, ***Travel Insurance Services***, T800 9371387, and ***Council Travel***, T888-COUNCIL, www.counciltravel.com Companies worth trying in Britain include ***Direct Travel Insurance***, T0190 3812345, www.direct-travel.co.uk, the ***Flexicover Group***, T0870 9909292, www.flexicover.net.uk, and ***Columbus***, T020 7375 0011. Note that some companies will not cover those over 65. The best policies for older travellers are offered by ***Age Concern***, T01883 346964.

What to take
If you do forget some essential item you'll be able to find everything you could possibly need in the major Australian cities. Special respect must be paid to the Australian **sun**. A decent wide-brimmed hat is essential, as is factor 30 sun-cream (usually cheapest in Australian supermarkets). Light, long-sleeved tops and trousers cut down the necessity for quite as much sun-cream, help keep out the mosquitoes and keep you warmer in the early evening when the temperature can drop markedly. Anywhere in the southern two-thirds of the country can get cold in winter – very cold in Victoria and Tasmania – so a few key warm clothes are also a good idea.

Travel tips

- Buy your suntan lotion and sunblock after you arrive – they are cheaper. Camera film and developing is cheaper too
- Set your watch to Aussie time as soon as you leave, sleep in Aussie night-time hours. Whatever you do, do not go to sleep after you arrive until at least mid-evening
- Internal flights can be cheaper if pre-purchased
- Check the Australia tourist board website at australia.com
- Book a couple of nights'

accommodation before you arrive to save you looking for a bed after a 24-hour flight
- Take photocopies of important documents and tickets. Store one separately in your luggage and leave the other with an easily contactable family member or friend
- It's a long, long flight: pop a toothbrush and toothpaste in your handbag or pocket
- If your luggage is at all overweight get to the check-in desk good and early

Essentials

If you're planning on doing some **walking** or **trekking**, come as prepared as you would do for wetter climes. The weather can change rapidly, particularly in the hill country of Victoria and Tasmania, and some of the Tasmanian trails can get extremely boggy. Good boots can also provide some protection in the very rare but dangerous instance of snake bite. Getting lost is a strong possibility on longer treks so bring (and know how to use) a compass and acquire appropriate local maps (see page 48). Most walking and camping equipment (other than boots) can usually be hired in the larger cities. A sleeping bag is useful in hostels and caravan parks, particularly outside the major cities, as linen is not always supplied. In summer a sheet sleeping bag and pillow case will usually suffice. Other useful items include a comfortable day bag, strong waterproof sandals, decent penknife (with bottle and can opener), a padlock and short length of light chain for securing your bag, LED head torch, single-use underwater camera, foldaway water bottle (such as the *Platypus*), plastic lunchbox and a travel alarm clock.

The limits for duty-free goods brought into the country include $400 ($200 for under 18s) worth of goods not including alcohol or tobacco, 1,125 ml of any alcoholic drink (beer, wine or spirits), and 250 cigarettes, or 250 g of cigars or tobacco. There are various import restrictions, many there to help protect Australia's already heavily hit ecology. Some may unexpectedly affect the inbound tourist. These primarily involve dangerous items, live plants and animals, plant and animal materials (including all items made from wood) and foodstuffs. If in doubt, avoid bringing animals, plants or seeds at all, confine wooden and plant goods to well-worked items (such as handles, picture frames, straw hats) and bring processed food only (even this may be confiscated, though *Marmite* is accepted with a knowing smile). Even muddy walking boots may attract attention. Declare any such items for inspection on arrival if you are unsure.

Customs regulations & tax
See website www.customs.gov.au for more details

There are strict prohibitions when leaving the country. Plant and animal life, including derivative articles and seeds, cannot be taken from the country. Australia's cultural heritage is also protected, and though a dot-painting or didjeridu will be fine to take home, some art works and archaeological items are definitely not. T02-6271 1610 or see www.dcita.gov.au, for details.

Almost all goods in Australia are subject to a **Good and Services Tax** (the GST) of 10%. Visitors from outside Australia will find certain gift shops can deduct the GST on production of a valid departure ticket.

Money

The local currency is the Australian dollar ($), divided into 100 cents (c). Coins come in denominations of $0.5, $0.10, $0.20, $0.50, $1 and $2. Banknotes, which are plastic and not ruined by an inadvertent soaking, come in denominations of $5, $10, $20, $50 and $100. The currency is not legal tender in New Zealand, and New Zealand dollars are not legal tender in Australia. **Exchange rates** (August 2002): 1 Aus$ = US$1.81, £2.78, €1.78.

Banks, ATMs & credit cards
Bank opening hours are Monday-Friday, from around 0930 to 1630

The four major banks are the *Commonwealth*, *National*, *ANZ* and *Challenge/Westpac*. Banks are usually the best places to change money and cheques, though bureaux de change tend to have slightly longer opening hours and often open at weekends. Most hotels, shops, tourist operators and restaurants in Australia accept the major credit cards (*Access/Mastercard*, *Visa* and *Amex*), though some places may charge for using them. They will be less useful in more remote areas and smaller establishments such as B&Bs, which will sometimes only accept cash. Always check when booking. You can withdraw cash from most ATMs (cashpoints) with a cash card or credit card issued by most of the major international banks, though cards connected with building societies are more rarely accepted. Most credit cards can also be used at banks, post offices and bureaux de change to withdraw cash. *EFTPOS* (the equivalent of *switch* in the UK) is a way of paying for goods and services with a cash card. Most establishments now operate EFTPOS and will also allow cash to be taken as part of a transaction. Unfortunately EFTPOS only works with cash cards linked directly to an Australian bank account. In many country areas EFTPOS is the only way to obtain cash, so long term visitors should consider opening a local bank account.

Travellers' cheques
Commission when cashing cheques is usually 1% or a flat rate. Avoid changing money or cheques in hotels as rates are usually poor

The safest way to carry money is in travellers' cheques, though travellers' dependence on them is fast becoming superseded by the prevalence of credit cards and general ATMs. Travellers' cheques are available for a small commission from all major banks and specialist outlets, *American Express (Amex)*, *Thomas Cook* and *Visa* being the most commonly accepted. Make sure to keep a record of the cheque numbers and the cheques you've cashed separate from the cheques themselves, so that you can get a full refund of all uncashed cheques should you lose them. Cheques are generally accepted for exchange in banks, large hotels, post offices and large gift shops. Some insist that at least a portion of the amount is in exchange for goods or services.

Money transfers

If you need money urgently, the quickest way to have it sent to you is to have it wired to the nearest bank via *Western Union*, T1800-337377, www.travelex.com.au Charges apply but on a sliding scale, costing proportionally less to wire out more money. Money can also be wired by *Amex* or *Thomas Cook*, though this may take a day or two, or transferred direct from bank to bank, but this can take several days.

Costs
By European, North American and Japanese standards Australia is an inexpensive place to visit

Accommodation, particularly outside the major cities is good value, though prices can rise uncomfortably in peak seasons. **Eating out** can be very cheap. There are some restaurants in Melbourne and Sydney, comparable with the best in London or New York, where $150 is enough to cover dinner for two, including wine, and other establishments, hardly less enjoyable, where the bill will be half that. **Transport**, though cheaper than in Europe, varies considerably in price and can be a major factor in your travelling budget. Beer is about $4-6 a throw in pubs and bars, as is a neat spirit or glass of wine. Beer is a lot cheaper from bottle shops, particularly if bought by the case (or 'slab'). Wine will generally be around 1½ times to double the price in restaurants as it would be from a bottleshop. The general cost of living in Australia is reckoned to be a little cheaper than in the USA and up to 40% cheaper than the UK.

◀◀

Comparison of budget travel costs

The following table compares the costs of various ways of travelling. It is based on the approximate cost for two people travelling together, includes food (cooking rather than eating out), tours ($200 per week each without own transport, $100 otherwise), and where appropriate bus passes, fuel, AAA cover and insurance (not travel), depreciation and maintenance, and the purchase of camping equipment ($300). It assumes campers and campervanners will bushcamp for free approximately half the time. For one person travelling alone the bus pass options are almost always the cheapest, unless you're planning a very long trip. The relative merits of each form of travel are, of course, not limited to cost alone.

*1 **Aus Experience** and stay in hostels*
*2 **McCaffertys/Greyhound** (by Explorer or km pass) and stay in hostels*
3 Hire a campervan
4 Hire a car and stay in hostels
5 Hire a car and camp
6 Buy a car and stay in hostels
7 Buy a car or van and camp

	1	2	3	4	5	6	7
26 weeks/ 16,000 km	$23,700	$23,250	$22,890	$25,730	$19,390	$21,400	$15,060
16 weeks/ 13,000 km	$15,220	$14,770	$14,430	$16,150	$12,360	$13,820	$10,030
12 weeks/ 10,000 km	$11,440	$11,080	$10,850	$12,140	$9,370	$10,830	$8,060
8 weeks/ 7,000 km	$7,610	$7,440	$7,270	$8,120	$6,380	$7,040	$6,090
4 weeks/ 3,500 km	$3,790	$3,780	$3,640	$4,060	$3,340	$4,590	$3,870
2 weeks/ 2,000 km	$2,000	$1,920	$1,990	$2,200	$1,990	$3,100	$2,890

The **minimum** budget required, if staying in hostels or campsites, cooking for yourself, not drinking much and travelling relatively slowly is about $50 per person per day, but this isn't going to be a lot of fun. Going on the odd tour, travelling faster and eating out occasionally will raise this to a more realistic $70-100. Those staying in modest B&Bs, hotels and motels as couples, eating out most nights and taking a few tours will need to reckon on about $150-250 per person per day. Costs in the major cities and, significantly, Yulara, will be 20-50% higher. Non-hostelling single travellers will have to pay more than half the cost of a double room and should budget on spending around 60-70% of what a couple would spend.

Discounts & bargaining

Many forms of transport and most tourist sites and tours will give discounts to all or some of the following: students, backpackers, the unemployed, the aged (all grouped as 'concessions' in this guide) and children. Discounts range from as little as 5% off to as much as 50%, depending on the operator, with children usually being given the highest discount.

Proof will normally be required of anyone asking for a discount. A passport will usually suffice for children or the aged. There are various official youth/student ID cards available, including the widely recognized **International Student ID Card** (ISIC), **Federation of International Youth Travel Organizations** (FIYTO) card, **Euro 26 Card** and **Go-25 Card**. Each also conveys subsidiary benefits to simply getting discounts, such as emergency medical coverage and 24-hour hotlines. The cards are issued by student travel agencies and hostelling organizations (see page 38). Backpackers will find a *YHA* or *VIP* membership card just as useful.

There is little bargaining to be done in Australia, except for accommodation and tours in off-seasons when some establishments and operators will bend an ear to a fair offer.

Tipping   Tipping is not considered the norm in Australia, but a discretionary 5-10% tip for particularly good service will be much appreciated. Staff in service industries, such as waiters, are paid an award wage based on the assumption that they will not receive tips.

Getting there

Air

As Australia is an island nation, and a considerable distance from anywhere except Indonesia and Papua New Guinea, the vast majority of visitors to Australia come by air. There are international flights direct to all state capitals except Hobart, and it is quite possible to have different points of arrival and departure that complement your intended itinerary. If there is not a direct flight to your primary choice there will usually be a same-day connection from Sydney, Melbourne or Perth.

It is usually possible to book internal Australian flights when booking your international ticket, at lower prices than on arrival. Some do not even require a stated departure and arrival point. If you have any plans to fly within Australia check this out with your travel agent prior to booking.

Buying a ticket   There are now enormous numbers of high street, phone and internet outlets for buying your plane ticket. This can make life confusing but the competition does mean that dogged work can be rewarded in a very good deal. Fares will depend on the season, with prices much higher during December-January unless booked several months in advance. Mid-year tends to see the cheapest fares, though bargains can be found at any time outside the peak period. *Qantas*, www.qantas.com.au, is Australia's main international airline, though will rarely be the cheapest option, and flies from a considerable number of international capitals and major cities. Most other major airlines have flights to Australia from their home countries or Europe.

The internet is seen as one of the best ways of finding that bargain ticket, but it really only comes into its own if you are looking for a straight return or single fare to a single destination city. If you are considering a multi-destination journey and/or Australian itinerary it is worth checking out two or three agents in person.

One-way flight tickets are not necessarily a lot more expensive than half a return fare, especially if the exchange rate is favourable to your currency. If you are contemplating a lengthy trip and are undecided about further plans, or like the idea of being unconstrained, then a single fare could be for you. Note, however, that Australian immigration officials can get very suspicious of visitors arriving on one-way tickets, especially on short term visas. Anyone without long-term residency on a one-way ticket will certainly need to show proof of substantial funds – enough for your stay and onward flight. Discuss your circumstances with your local Australian Embassy or High Commission before committing to a one-way ticket.

Round-the-World (RTW) tickets can be a real bargain, particularly if you stick to the most popular routes, sometimes working out even cheaper than a return fare. RTWs start at around £750 (€ 1,125) or US$1,500, depending on the season. Perth and Sydney are usually easy to include on a RTW itinerary.

Airlines flying from Europe

Air New Zealand, www.airnz.co.uk

Qantas, www.qantas.co.uk

Emirates, www.emirates.com

British Airways, www.britishairways.com

Discount travel agents in Britain and Ireland

Council Travel, 28a Poland Street, London W1V 3DB, T020 7437 7767, www.destinations-group.com

Ebookers, www.ebookers.com Comprehensive travel ticket booking website.

Expedia, www.expedia.com Another web-only travel site, also with lots of background information.

STA Travel, 86 Old Brompton Road,

London SW7 3LH, T020 7361 6161, www.statravel.co.uk Specialists in student discount fares, IDs and other travel services. Also branches in most major cities and many college campuses.

Trailfinders, 194 Kensington High Street, London W8 6FT, T020 7938 3939, www.trailfinders.co.uk Particularly good on personalized itineraries and adventure travel.

When trying to find the best deal, make sure you check the route, duration of the journey, stopovers, departure and arrival times, restrictions and cancellation penalties. Many of the cheapest flights are sold by small agencies, most of whom are honest and reliable, but there may be some risks involved with buying tickets at rock-bottom prices. Avoid paying too much money in advance and check with the airline directly to ensure you have a reservation.

Flights from Asia There are direct **Qantas** flights from **Bangkok** to Melbourne and Sydney, from **Jakarta** to Perth and Sydney, from **Osaka** to Brisbane and Sydney, and from **Hong Kong** and **Tokyo** to Brisbane, Cairns, Melbourne, Perth and Sydney. Most other Asian flights connect with services from **Singapore**. From here there are direct flights to Adelaide, Brisbane, Cairns, Darwin, Melbourne, Perth and Sydney. Flights to Darwin, Cairns and Perth are usually marginally cheaper than to the other state capitals.

Flights from Europe The main route, and the cheapest, is via **Asia**, though fares will also be quoted via **North America** or **Africa**. The Asia route, including stops, usually takes from 20 to 30 hours. There are direct **Qantas** flights from **London Heathrow** to Darwin, Melbourne, Perth and Sydney with same-day connections to most other major cities. Flights from Belfast, Birmingham, Dublin, Edinburgh, Glasgow, Newcastle and Manchester connect with some of these, or with flights from Frankfurt and Paris. There are flights from **Frankfurt** via Singapore to Brisbane, Cairns, Darwin, Melbourne, Perth and Sydney, and from **Paris** to Perth and Sydney. There are also flights to Sydney from **Athens** and **Rome** via Bangkok and **Zurich** via Singapore. Flights from most other major European cities connect with London or Frankfurt. None fly non-stop, however, so it's worth checking out what stopovers are on offer – this might, after all, be your only chance to see Kuala Lumpur. Stopovers of a few nights do not usually increase the cost of the ticket appreciably. The cheapest return flights, off-season, will be around £500 (€ 750), with stand-by prices rising to at least £800 around Christmas. Flights to Perth are usually marginally cheaper than to the other state capitals.

Flights from New Zealand There are direct **Qantas** flights from Auckland, Christchurch and Wellington to Brisbane, Melbourne and Sydney. **Air New Zealand**, www.airnewzealand.co.nz, and **Freedom Air**, www.freedom.co.nz, are the other two main carriers, both offering routes that **Qantas** do not. Expect to pay a minimum of NZ$400-500 for a return to Sydney.

▶▶ Airlines flying from North America

Air New Zealand, www.airnz.co.uk   *Air Canada*, www.aircanada.ca
United, www.ual.com   *Singapore Airlines*, www.singaporeair.com

Discount travel agents in North America

Air Brokers International, 323 Geary St, Suite 4111, San Francisco, CA 94102, T800 8833273, www.airbrokers.com. Consolidator and specialist on RTW and Circle Pacific tickets.
Council Travel, 205 E 42nd St, New York, NY 10017, T800-COUNCIL, www.counciltravel.com. Student/budget agency with branches in many US cities.
Discount Airfares Worldwide On-Line, www.etn.nl/discount.htm. A hub of consolidator and discount agent links.

International Travel Network/Airlines of the Web, www.itn.net/airlines. Online information and reservations.
STA Travel, 5900 Wiltshire Boulevard, suite 2110, Los Angeles, CA 90036, T800 7770112, www.sta-travel.com Discount/youth travel.
Travel CUTS, 187 College St, Toronto, ON M5T 1P7, T800 6672887, www.travel cuts.com. Student discount fares, IDs and other travel services.
Travelocity, www.travelocity.com. Online consolidator.

Flights from the Americas There are direct *Qantas* flights from Los Angeles to Brisbane, Melbourne and Sydney, and from Vancouver and New York to Sydney. The Cost of a standard return in the high season from Vancouver starts from around US$2,200, from New York from US$2,000 and from Los Angeles from US$1,700. There are also direct flights from Buenos Aires to Sydney.

Flights from South Africa There are direct *Qantas* flights from Johannesburg to Perth and, more expensively, Sydney. *South African Airways*, www.saa.co.za, also fly direct.

Departure tax There are currently a number of various departure taxes levied by both individual airports (such as noise tax) and the government. One of these is a $10 contribution to funds for workers adversely affected by the collapse of the Ansett group of airlines in 2001. All departure taxes will be included in the cost of your ticket.

Touching down

Tourist information

Tourist offices – known as **Visitor Information Centres** (VICs) – can be found in all but the smallest Australian towns. Their locations, phone numbers, website or email addresses and opening hours are listed in the relevant sections of this guide. In most larger towns they are open daily 0900-1700. Smaller offices may close at weekends, but given that many are run entirely by volunteers – something to bear in mind when someone struggles to find an obscure piece of information – the level of commitment to the visitor is impressive. Most will provide a free town map.

Disabled travellers

Also see www.australia.com and state sections Disabled travellers to Australia will find that although there are a good range of facilities meeting their needs, they can be spread quite thinly, especially outside of the major cities. All buildings with independent access have to meet certain government

Touching down

Business hours are generally 0830-1700 Monday-Friday. Banks may close at 1600 but stores may stay open later and generally also open 0900-1300 Saturday, if not all day Saturday and Sunday. Many convenience stores and supermarkets are open daily. Late night shopping in larger towns and cities is generally either Thursday or Friday.

Electricity The current in Australia is 240/250v AC. Plugs have 2 or 3 blade pins and adapters are widely available.

Emergencies For police, fire brigade or ambulance dial 000.

Laundry Most larger towns have coin operated launderettes. The average cost is about $5 for a wash and tumble dry. Most large hotels, hostels, B&Bs and caravan parks also have laundry facilities.

Official language English.

Time Australia covers three time zones: Western Standard GMT+8 hours (WA); Central Standard GMT+9½ hours (SA, NT); Eastern Standard GMT+10 hours (all other states) ACT, NSW, VIC, SA and TAS operate daylight saving, putting their clocks forward one hour between October and March. Most national institutions work to Eastern Standard Time.

Smoking Illegal in restaurants, cafés and pubs where eating is a primary activity, and on public transport.

Toilets Even the smallest country town will have free public toilets, usually in the public parks or often adjacent to the tourist office or town hall. They are also found at most bus and train stations, national parks and roadhouses. For a comprehensive round-up see www.toiletmap.gov.au

Useful phone numbers Police, fire, ambulance T000. AAA breakdown T131111.

Water Generally safe to drink from the tap, though not always pleasant. Water is a precious resource in this, one of the driest countries in the world – use sparingly.

Weather For national forecasts T1900 926113, www.bom.gov.au

Weights and measures The metric system is universally used in Australia.

standards, but the standards actually in place can vary a lot. High profile sights and attractions, and even parks generally have good access. The key to successful travel, just as with able-bodied travellers, is planning, and there are several national and state organizations who can give considerable help with this, including **ACROD**, 33 Thesiger Court, Deakin ACT 2600, T02 6282 4333, the national industry association for disability services, and **NICAN**, PO Box 407, Curtin, ACT 2605, T02-6285 3713, who provide information on recreation, tourism, sport and the arts. The state automobile associations (see box, page 45) can also be very helpful with finding accommodation. Many organizations are equipped for handling TTY (telephone typewriter) calls. For further information contact **Telstra Disability Services**, GPO Box 4997WW, Melbourne VIC 3000, T1800-068424. The **Australian Communication Exchange** (ACE) offers a free service for TTY users, relaying messages between a TTY and a hearing phone user. ACE can be contacted on T07 3815 7600. Publications on disabled travel in Australia include the guide boook **Easy Access Australia – A Travel Guide to Australia** by Bruce Cameron (updated 2000, ISBN 095775101X).

Getting there & around

As with many major airlines **Qantas**, T9957 7103 or T1800-652660 (both TTY) has considerable experience with disabled passengers. If you have to be accompanied by a support person on any internal flight, they offer the passenger and the nominated carer a 50% discount off the full-economy or business-class fare. A Carer Concession Photo ID is required, however. Contact **NICAN** for further details. Guide dogs may be brought into Australia, but are subject to quarantine, with occasional exceptions. Contact the **Australian Quarantine & Inspection Service**, Edmund Barton Building, Kings Avenue, Barton, ACT 2600, T02-9832 4025, for further details. The interstate railways (see page 43) generally have facilities for the disabled but public transport in many states is not yet well designed for disabled travellers unless you have assistance. The major interstate bus operators are pleased to accommodate disabled travellers but prefer notice, though few coaches are equipped with lifts or lowered floors. The *TT-Line* ferry between TAS and VIC has a handful of specially designed cabins. Not all hire car companies have adapted vehicles available, but the big operators, including *Avis* and *Budget* (see box on page 47) do. Disabled overseas parking permits may be used in all states except NSW and VIC. In NSW you will need to apply for a permit at a *Roads and Traffic Authority* office, T02-9218 6670, or for VIC you need to organize a permit with *VicRoads*, T03-9854 2666, at least one month prior to arrival. Each state's permits are valid nationally. A list of Bed & Breakfasts with particularly good facilities for the disabled can be found at www.babs.com.au

Gay and lesbian travellers

The gay community in Australia is vibrant, vocal and visible. Sydney is the undoubted capital of gay and lesbian Australia, hosting in February the annual *Gay and Lesbian Mardi Gras* (see page 117), the biggest event of its kind in the world, and incidentally one of the biggest and most watched events in the country. Melbourne also has a very active gay and lesbian scene, and its added reputation as one of Australia's two principal gourmet cities also makes it a very popular destination. Outside of the major cities, however, discrimination is not unknown and public displays of affection may not be enthusiastically received by the locals. The *International Gay & Lesbian Travel Association* (IGLTA), T02-9818 6669, has several members in Australia happy to help with travel and accommodation advice. There are several national magazines keeping lesbians and gays in touch with what's going on, including *Lesbians on the Loose* and *DNA*. One of the most comprehensive websites is **www.gayaustraliaguide.com** Dedicated to lesbian and gay friendly accommodation is **www.qbeds.com**

Photography

Australia presents endless photo opportunities and you will find a good camera is about essential as a sun hat or a pair of Speedos. Given the harsh light in Australia, if you are at all serious about photography and getting good results and have a digital or manual SLR (Single Lens Reflex) camera then a polarising filter is essential. You after all need sun glasses, so essentially, so does your camera. An orange 80A filter to warm up landscapes is also recommended. Film is expensive in Australia so you are advised to stock up before coming to Australia (especially in the USA) or at duty free shops on arrival. For daytime shooting with transparency film ASA50-200 Fuji or Kodakachrome 64 or 200 is recommended. For print photography Kodak ASA100 is fine. For creative night shooting you will need a sturdy tripod but this may go beyond luggage capacity. If you are carrying an expensive camera and have travel insurance make sure it is properly covered. This may involve an added premium and special listing. Happy hunting.

Working in Australia

A working holiday visa will be required for casual work, see page 23

Those travelling on a working holiday visa can seek paid employment during their visit to Australia, on the condition that they work for no employer for longer than three months. The easiest work to get, though not to do, is generally fruit harvesting or packing. The pay isn't sensational, though hard workers can do alright, but it's sociable and can be fun. The main harvest periods are February-May (NSW, TAS, VIC, SA) and May-October (north WA), with picking of various crops going on year-round in QLD. If you do plan to rely on harvesting it can pay to bring a small tent as accommodation can become problematic.

◀◀

National employment organizations

How big is your footprint?

Agricultural work and station stays Employment National, T1300- 720126, www.employment national.com.au, can provide good advice on where in the country to find seasonal work, and have local agencies helping find specific employment. **Visitoz**, T07-4168 6106, www.visitoz.org, put you in touch with outback stations looking for workers; **Willing Workers on Organic Farms**, T03- 5155 0218, www.wwoof.com.au, specialize in matching travellers with their 1,400 affiliated farms and stations. The $45 membership gets you a guide book on the scheme, friendly advice and insurance against accidental injury.

Conservation holidays Conservation Volunteers, T1800-032501, www.conservationvolunteers.com.au, organize volunteer conservation projects around Australia. Costs are currently $23 per day, including accommodation, food and work-related travel. There is no cost for day volunteers, who are asked to bring their own lunch and drink.

Essentials

Other outdoor work can be found at farms and stations, though you will usually only receive board, lodging and 'pocket money'. Although unpaid, working on a conservation project can be extremely rewarding, a lot of fun and is a great way of meeting the locals. In the cities work opportunities are often tipped firmly in favour of women. Some temp agencies will take on travellers if they have decent resumes. The hospitality industry (hotels, pubs and bars) is the biggest employer of casual workers. Those with the right qualifications will usually find medical employment quite easy to come by, as are au pair positions, again for those with the right experience.

Jobs are advertised in local newspapers and on the internet, though the best place to start is by going round the notice boards of the local backpacker hostels, or contacting them in advance. If working is going to form a major part of your travels, or you are thinking of emigrating to Australia, then consider a publication such as **Living and Working in Australia** by **Laura Veltman** (updated 2000, ISBN 1857036700).

Responsible tourism

All over the world the responsible traveller sticks to the creed of 'take nothing but photographs and leave nothing but footprints'. Of course this should apply to Australia too, where there are also some unique considerations. One of Australia's main attractions is the natural environment and its wildlife, and there are many opportunities for eco-tourism.

All state national park agencies (see list, page 22) promote a minimal impact bushwalking code aimed at protecting the environment, which is also a useful guide for minimising your footprint in other natural environments.

Fire is a critical issue in Australia's hot dry environments where only a spark is needed to create a fire that can get out of control and destroy an area the size of a small country in a day or two, perhaps threatening lives and property. For this reason, in some areas, there are total fire bans, either for a seasonal period or on days when a high risk of fire is predicted. In extreme circumstances a national park, scenic attraction or walking trail may be closed because the risk of fire is so high. Fire bans or restrictions usually apply in summer (November-March) in the south and during the late Dry season in the north (July-November). Check fire restrictions before travel with the nearest parks, shire, police or tourist office as they may affect your preparations; for example on days of Total Fire Ban you may not even use a camping stove and will have to take food that doesn't need cooking. Campers should always carry a fuel stove for cooking as many national parks or public reserves forbid campfires or the collection of wood or both. Fallen timber and hollow logs are an important habitat for wildlife.

▶▶ How big is your footprint?

- *Follow the minimal impact bushwalking code for walking and camping. Details can be obtained from any park office. Choose a responsible operator. The Ecotourism Association of Australia, T07 3229 5550, www.ecotourism.org.au promotes ecologically sustainable and responsible tourism and runs an accreditation programme for tour operators.*
- *Try not to drive at dawn, dusk or at night, both to avoid killing native animals and for your own safety.*
- *Water is a precious resource in Australia*

- don't waste it or pollute it. In dry conditions camp away from waterholes so that animals are not afraid to approach the water.
- *Make sure you are well prepared for the local conditions. Carrying sufficient water, food and fuel and appropriate clothing or equipment may save your life and avoid danger, expense and inconvenience for those who might otherwise have to rescue you.*
- *If you have to pass through gates in national parks or on private property the rule is 'leave them as you find them'.*

It is also good practice to keep your walking or camping gear clean between different environments, particularly in areas affected by dieback, a fungus called *Phytophthora cinnamomi* that attacks the roots of plants so that they die of thirst. It is spread when soil or roots are moved, possibly via your boots, car or tent. Dieback areas are usually closed to the public but boot-cleaning stations are provided for high-risk walking tracks. TAS and WA are badly affected, QLD, VIC and NSW less so, but care is still needed.

Travellers in Australia will also come across 'sacred sites', areas of religious importance to indigenous people, and naturally it is important to respect any restrictions that may apply to these areas. Permission is usually required to enter an Aboriginal community and you may be asked to comply with restrictions, such as a ban on alcohol. If you visit a community, or travel through Aboriginal land, respect the privacy of Aboriginal people and never take photographs without asking first.

If you want to know more about environmental issues or get involved in conservation contact the **Australian Conservation Foundation**, T02 9212 6600, www.acfonline.org.au, or **The Wilderness Society**, T03 6234 9799, www.wilderness.org.au The quarterly wilderness adventure magazine **Wild** is also a good source of information on current environmental issues and campaigns. Available at newsagents or see www.wild.com.au

Safety

See also Health page 63 Australia certainly has its dangers, but with a little common sense and basic precautions they are relatively easy to minimize or avoid entirely. The most basic but important precautions, at any time or place, are against the effects of the sun. UV levels can soar in Australia, with safe exposure limits as low as three minutes. A bad burn has ruined many a holiday, and unhealthy exposure in young people particularly can lead to much worse in later life. Always have a wide-brimmed hat, high factor sunscreen (suntan lotion) and sunglasses to hand, and consider wearing light, long-sleeved or legged clothing. As well as sunburn, **heat-stroke** is also a danger, a common result of too much heat and too little fluid. Visitors should also take care in four other principal situations:

In **urban areas**, as in almost any city in the world, there is always the possibility of muggings, alcohol-induced harassment or worse. The usual simple precautions apply, like keeping a careful eye and hand on belongings, not venturing out alone at night and avoiding dark, lonely areas.

Essentials

Taking care in the bush

Before bushwalking seek advice about how to access the start and finish of the track, the terrain you are planning to traverse, how long it will take given your party's minimum fitness level, the likely weather conditions, and prepare accordingly. Park rangers and the police are good sources of information. Learn about the various local poisonous snakes, their seasonal habits, tell-tale wound marks and symptoms, and the correct procedure for treatment. Plan, if possible, to walk in the early morning, a magical time to go walking in Australia, or late afternoon when the famous golden glow often takes hold just before sunset. These are also the best times for viewing wildlife. Take a decent map of the area, a compass (which you know how to use!), and a first-aid kit. Take full precautions for the sun, but also be prepared for wet or cold weather. Take plenty of water, in hot weather at least one litre for every hour you plan to walk (a frozen plastic bottle will ensure cold water for some time). On long distance walks take something to purify stream and standing water as giardia is present in some areas. Wear stout walking shoes and socks, even in hot weather. Tell someone where you are going and when you plan to get back. Avoid striding through long grass, try to keep to tracks where snakes will be easily visible. If grass or low scrub does obscure some of the path, make plenty of noise as you walk. If you need to squat to go to the toilet, or are collecting firewood, bash the undergrowth for a good area around your position. Avoid confrontations with snakes. If they see, smell or hear you first it's a safe bet you'll never know they were there. If you do see one, however, give it a wide berth and there'll probably be no trouble. If you do get bitten by either a spider or snake stay calm and still, apply pressure to the bite area and wind a compression bandage around it (except for redback bites). Try to remain as still as possible and keep the limb immobile, using a splint if necessary. Seek urgent medical attention. A good description of the offending creature, and residual venom on the victim's skin, will help medical staff with swift identification and so treatment. Anti-venom is available for most spider and snake bites. Avoid walking alone, and keep walking partners in sight. Keep to paths and avoid cliff edges and other dangers indicated by signs.

The principal dangers on country **roads** are not actually from other drivers. Fatigue is the cause of many Australian accidents, as are large native and stock animals wandering onto roads. **Hitch-hiking** is not recommended. For more information on road safety contact one of the *AAA* associations (see box on page 46).

On the **beach** there is little to trouble the holidaymaker who sticks to the shore and swims between the flags on patrolled beaches, but swimmers must be aware of hidden dangers. The principal one is the rip, a strong, off-shore undertow that can sweep even waders off their feet, submerge them and drown them astonishingly quickly. Always look out for signs indicating common rip areas, and ask locals if at all unsure. See the *Surf Life Saving Australia* website, www.slsa.asn.au, for more information. Much publicized, but out of all proportion, is the danger from **sharks**. It is true that there are a handful of shark attacks in Australian waters each year, and usually one or two are fatal, but this must be balanced against the number of times someone goes for a swim or surf each year – hundreds of millions. There are several other sea creatures far more likely to do you harm. Biggest of these are the Estuarine **crocodiles** ('salties') of the north. If given the opportunity they will ambush and eat any animal or person careless enough to stray near or into their river, estuary or mangrove swamp. Always check whether a waterhole or river is likely to be a crocodilian home, and if in doubt assume it is. Australian coastal waters are also home to a host of fish, jellyfish, octopus, urchins, coral and even molluscs that can inflict extremely painful and sometimes lethal stings and bites.

▶▶ Taking care in the water

*Before swimming in the sea, rivers and pools, always seek **local advice** about tides and rips, crocodile haunts, and the likely presence of poisonous or dangerous fish, jellyfish and other marine creatures. Park rangers and the police are good sources of information. If you have time **learn** about the various local poisonous marine creatures, their tell-tale wound-marks and symptoms, and the correct procedure for treatment. Tell someone onshore you are going for a swim. While snorkelling or diving – **do not touch**, either creatures or coral. Even minor coral scratches can lead to nasty infections, and it doesn't do the coral any good either. Wear a wetsuit or t-shirt and shorts even if the water is warm. This will lessen the effect of any sting and help protect against the sun. Wear plenty of waterproof **sunscreen**, and reapply frequently. If **wading** around in shallow water, particularly near coral reefs, always wear a pair of old trainers or waterproof sandals. A large number of the little beasties that can do you serious harm tend to do so because you've trodden on them. Avoid swimming **alone**, and keep swimming partners in sight. If you are bitten or stung get out of the water, carefully remove any spine or tissue, seek advice as to appropriate immediate **treatment** and apply it, and quickly seek medical help.*

Visitors are also likely to want to venture out into the country (the 'bush'). Once again, there are numerous creatures, mostly snakes, spiders and scorpions that possess very poisonous bites. Most will only do so, however, if trodden on, cornered or harassed. The most common poisonous spider is the tiny, shy redback, which has a shiny black body with distinct red markings. Fond of nooks and crannies it regularly sets up shop under rocks or in garden sheds and garages. Outside toilets are also a fave – a habit of checking under seats is a good one to get into. Far more dangerous, though restricted to the Sydney area only, is the Sydney funnel-web, a larger and more aggressive customer entirely, and this one simply loves outdoor loos! There are dozens of venomous snake species in Australia. Few are actively aggressive and even those only during certain key times of year, such as mating season, but all are easily provoked and for many an untreated bite can be fatal. Thanks to anti-venom, deaths are now rare, but those that do occur are often due to a species of brown snake, common throughout mainland Australia. Also widespread across the southern half of the country are tiger snakes. The taipan group of species includes some of the world's most venomous, and are common in the tropical north of Australia. The main dangers while bush-walking, however, are dehydration, from a lack of water, heat-stroke, and getting lost. Careful preparation will easily negate these.

Emergency services
Dial 000 for the emergency services

The three main professional emergency services are supported by several others, including the **State Emergency Service** (SES), **Country Fire Service** (CFS), **Surf Life Saving Australia** (SLSA), **Sea-search and Rescue**, and **St John's Ambulance**. The **CFS** provides invaluable support in fighting and controlling bush fires. The **SES** has both a local role, prominent in co-ordinating and supplying personnel for search and rescue operations, and on a larger scale during times of regional difficulty or disaster. Many visitors to Australia who get into difficulties in a country area soon find themselves being ably assisted by an orange-clad SES rescuer. In country areas they are often the first on the scene of an accident or incident, from vehicle collisions to heat-stroke. All these services, though professionally trained, are mostly provided by unpaid volunteers.

Accommodation price codes

Accommodation prices in this guide are graded with the letters below and are based on the cost for one night during the high season, including breakfast if a B&B, but not dinner. Many places, even smaller B&Bs and hostels, will offer substantial discounts during low season or for longer stays. Very few establishments with doubles and twin rooms at a **C** grade or higher will have single-only rooms, and will normally charge 75-100% of the normal cost for a double or twin. Where rooms or units sleep more than two people a nominal extra charge will sometimes be levied for a third and fourth person. Scaled grades, for example '**B-C**', indicate a range of rooms of varying standards or styles. We have tried to include choices from each category, though this is not always possible. Except sometimes in the smaller towns, all places listed are recommended as offering relatively good value, quality and standards of service within their respective price category.

LL	$300 or over for a double or twin
L	$200-299 for a double or twin
A	$150-199 for a double or twin
B	$110-149 for a double or twin
C	$80-109 for a double or twin
D	$25-39 for a single or dorm, $50-79 for a double or twin
E	$16-24 for a single or dorm, $31-49 for a double or twin
F	$15 or under for a single or dorm, $30 or under for a double or twin

Essentials

Where to stay

Booking accommodation in advance is highly recommended, especially in peak seasons. Note that single rooms are relatively scarce. Twin or double rooms let to a single occupant are rarely half the price, and you may even be charged the full cost for two people. Establishments of all types are quite likely to have air-conditioning (a/c). Check whether they do when booking, and if they don't ask how they keep their rooms cool. There are rooms without air-conditioning all over Australia that are almost impossible to sleep in during hot weather.

Hotels and other places to sleep are identified by a ▪ symbol on maps See also 'Working in Australia', page 32

Hotels, motels and resorts

At the top end of the scale, usually only in the biggest cities or prime tourist areas, are some impressive international-standard hotels and resorts. Very few are based on pre-existing historical buildings, and simply offer luxurious surroundings and facilities, attentive service and often outstanding locations. Rooms will typically start in our **L** range. Also only in the main cities are a few less expensive hotels in the **A-B** range. Most 'hotels', and virtually all outside of the capital cities, are pubs with upstairs or external accommodation. If upstairs a room is likely have access to shared bathroom facilities and a tea and coffee making area. Often above the main bar, these rooms can be noisy. A light breakfast may be included. External rooms are usually standard en-suite motel units. The quality of pub-hotel accommodation varies considerably, but is usually a budget option (**C-D**), often the only one if you are travelling alone and want a single room. Linen is almost always supplied.

Motels in Australia are usually depressingly anonymous, but dependably clean and safe, and usually the cheapest form of accommodation offering en-suite rooms. Designed around the business traveller, most have dining facilities and free, secure parking. Some budget motels will fall into our **D** range, most will be a **B-C**. Linen is always supplied.

Motels

▶▶ Bed and breakfast state websites

NSW & ACT	www.bedandbreakfastnsw.com
NT	www.bed-and-breakfast.au.com
QLD	www.bnb.au.com
SA	www.sabnb.org.au
TAS	www.tasmanianbedandbreakfast.com
VIC	www.innhouse.com.au /
WA	www.australianbnbs.com

B&Bs and self-catering

Check whether linen is supplied in self-catering accommodation

The **Bed and breakfast** is a relatively new concept in Australia, and in some ways quite different from the British model. The major difference is that they are rarely a budget option, almost all falling into our **B-C** ranges, and offering very comfortable accommodation in usually upmarket, sometimes historic houses. Rooms are usually en suite or have access to a private bathroom. Bathrooms shared by more than two rooms are very rare. Hosts are usually friendly and informative, and a good source of local knowledge. Some B&Bs, even more removed from the classic model, are actually a semi or fully self-contained cottage or cabin with breakfast provisions supplied in the fridge. The larger ones, with full kitchens, are self-catering in all but name. As well as self-contained cottages and houses, **self-catering** options are also provided by tourist parks and hostels, though there are some resorts and motels with apartment style units. Some will insist on a two-night minimum stay.

National parks & farms/ stations
See box, page 22, for National Park authority contact details

Some National Parks and rural cattle and sheep stations have old settlers' or workers' homes that have been converted into tourist accommodation, usually self-contained. They are often magical places to stay and include many old light-house keepers' cottages and shearers' quarters. Stations may also invite guests to see, or even get involved in the day's activities. Unfortunately many are set up for parties of six or more and consequently quite expensive for one or two. Transport to them can also be difficult. Linen is often not supplied in this sort of accommodation.

Hostels

For those travelling on a tight budget, there is a large network of hostels offering cheap accommodation (**D-F**). These are also popular centres for backpackers and provide a great opportunity for meeting fellow travellers. Most will have at least one double room and possibly singles, sometimes with linen. All hostels have kitchen and common room facilities, some considerably more. A few, particularly in cities, will

Main Australian YHA membership and travel offices

Adelaide, 135 Waymouth Street, T08-8414 3000, yha@yhasa.org.au

Alice Springs, Pioneer YHA, corner Parsons Street and Leichardt Terrace, T08- 8952 8855, alicepioneer@yhant.org.au

Brisbane, 154 Roma Street, T07-3236 1680, membership@yhaqld.org or travel@yhaqld.org

Cairns, 20-24 McLeod Street, T07-5051 1368.

Darwin, 69 Mitchell Street, T08-8981 2560,

darwintravel@yhant.org.au

Hobart, 28 Criterion Street, T03-6234 9617, yhatas@yhatas.org.au

Melbourne, 83-85 Hardware Lane, T03-9670 9611, travel@yhavic.org.au

Perth, 236 William Street, T08-9227 5122, enquiries@yhawa.com.au or travel@yhawa.com.au

Sydney, 422 Kent Street, T02-9261 1111, yha@yhansw.org.au

offer freebies including breakfast and pick-ups. Many are now open 24-hours, even if the front desk is closed at night. Standards vary considerably, and it's well worth asking other travellers about the hostels at your next port of call. Most are effectively independent, even most *YHAs* are simply affiliates, but the best tend to be those that are owner-managed. Of several hostel associations *YHA* (www.yha.org.au) and *NOMADS* (T1800-819883, www.nomadsworld.com, no membership fee) seem to keep the closest eye on their hostels, ensuring a consistency of quality. The *YMCA* and *YWCA* (T1800-249124, www.travel-ys.com), are usually a clean and quiet choice in the major cities. The list of 'clean, small and friendly' hostels on www.bpf.com.au, also offers dependably good choices. International visitors can obtain a **Hostelling International Card** (HIC) from any *YHA* hostel or travel centre. For this you get a handbook to *YHA* hostels nation-wide and around $3 off every night's *YHA* accommodation. Some transport and tourist establishments will also offer discounts to HIC holders.

Camping, roadhouses and campervans

Almost every town will have at least one caravan park, partly because a small but significant number of Australians live in them permanently. Almost all will have unpowered and powered sites, varying from $5-20, for campers, caravans and campervans, an ablution block and usually a camp kitchen or BBQs. Many will also have a range of permanently sited caravans (on-site vans) and cabins. On-site vans are usually the cheapest option (**E-F**) for couples or small families looking for a self-catering option. Cabins range from a little to a lot more expensive (**C-D**). Top of the range cabins will have televisions, en-suite bathrooms, separate bedrooms with linen and well-equipped kitchens.

Caravan & tourist parks
Joining a park association will get you a discount in all parks that are members of that association

Where Australian towns are more than 100 km apart there will usually be roadhouses on the route. They vary from simple fuel stops and small stores to mini-resorts with caravan park and motel accommodation, small supermarkets, post offices, daytime cafés, evening restaurants and bars. They will often have single and double rooms in what look like converted shipping containers known as *ATCOs* or *dongers*.

Roadhouses

Some National Parks allow camping, mostly in designated areas only, with a few allowing limited bush camping. Facilities are usually minimal. Most have basic toilets, fireplaces and perhaps tank water; some have BBQs and shower blocks, few have much more. The key to enjoyable camping in National Parks is to be well-prepared. Payment is often at a self-registration station (usually around $3-10 per person or tent), so have small denomination notes and a variety of change ready. Also have plenty of change for electric or gas BBQs which often require $0.20, $0.50 or $1 coins (though some are free). In most cases it is preferable to bring your own gas stove and in many parks this is

Camping in National Parks
See page 22 for National Park authority details.
Park notes/maps are available at tourist/parks offices, entrance point or park websites

Essentials

▶▶ **Caravan and Tourist Park Associations**

Big 4, T1800-632444,
www.big4.com.au
Cosy Cabins (TAS), T03-6245 9220,
www.cosycabins.com

Family Parks of Australia, T1800-682492,
www.familyparks.com.au
Top Tourist Parks, T08-8363 1901,
www.toptourist.contact.com.au

---

compulsory. However, if there are fireplaces you can bring your own wood and firelighters. Collecting wood within a park is prohibited, partly because logs and twigs are an important habitat for native animals. No fires may be lit, even stoves, during a Total Fire Ban period. Even if water is supposedly available it is not guaranteed so taking a supply can be a wise move, as is taking your own toilet paper. **Bush camping** in National Parks is strongly regulated, with due regard to the environment. The key rules are to be particularly careful with fire, complying with bans when in place, camp at least 20 m from any water hole or course, and to disturb the environment as little as possible. Nothing must be left behind, and nothing removed, even rocks. Toilet waste should be carefully buried, at least 100 m from any water hole or course, and some parks will even insist that this should be removed along with your rubbish.

Bush & roadside camping
See also 'Taking care in the bush', p x
Publications describing free roadside and bush camping places widely available

Bush camping outside National Parks is usually only allowed with the permission of the owner of the land, though there are many spots, with a variety of owners, where camping is expressly allowed. A few are managed by forestry agencies and other local authorities, and there may be a small fee. On rare occasions there may be the basic facilities of toilets, water and fireplaces. Out of courtesy and regard for the environment, follow the rules for camping as if you were in a National Park. All major highways have parking bays dotted along them and some allow overnight stays in caravans or campervans. Even if expressly forbidden, always stop for a sleep if the choice is between that or driving while very tired.

Campervans
Also see next section, 'Getting around'

A popular choice for many visitors wishing to get out of the major cities is to hire or buy a vehicle in which you can sleep. They combine the costs of accommodation and transport in one package, although you will still need to book into caravan parks for power and ablutions. They range from the popular *VW Kombi* to enormous vans with integral bathrooms, and can be hired from as little as $30 per day to as much as $500. A decent van for two people at around $100 per day combines reasonable economy with great freedom and convenience. High-clearance, 4WD campervans are also available from most of the major hire companies, and increase travel possibilites yet further. If you are in Australia for a few months consider buying one. Kombis can usually be had for around $2,500. An even cheaper, though much less comfortable alternative is to buy a panel van or large station wagon (estate car) that is big enough to lay out a sleeping mat and bag in.

Getting around

View and print-off road and street maps for all the major Australian regions, cities and towns at www.arta.com.au

Public transport in and around the **state capitals**, based on a variety of bus, tram and train networks, is generally good and efficient, and often easier than driving. Many of the larger non-capital cities also have metropolitan bus services, but some can be curiously regardless of tourist traffic and there is many an important outlying attraction poorly served by public transport, or even missed off the bus routes completely. Some cities are compact enough for this to be a minor irritation, others are so spread out that the visitor must invest in an expensive tourist bus service or taxis to get around. In such places staying at a hostel or B&B with free or low-cost bicycle hire can save a lot of money.

Main interstate and state airlines

National Qantas, *T131313*, www.qantas.com.au **Virgin Blue**, *T136789*, www.virginblue.com.au
NSW QantasLink, *T131313*, www.qantas.com.au in conjunction with **Hazelton** 131713, www.hazelton.com.au are the principal air carriers in NSW offering regular services between the main coast and outback centres
NT/WA Air North, *T08 8920 4000*, www.airnorth.com.au
QLD QantasLink, *T131313*, www.qantas.com.au in conjunction with

Macair 131313, www.macair.com.au are the principal air carriers offering regular services between the main coast and outback centres. Smaller regional charters and airlines cover most Great Barrier Islands
VIC/SA/TAS/NSW Kendell, *T131300*, www.kendell.com.au
TAS Tasair, *T03 6248 5088*, www.tasair.com.au
WA Skywest, *T131300*, www.skywest.com.au **Northwest Regional Airlines**, *T08 9192 1369*, www.northwestregional.com.au

Essentials

Outside the cities by far the best way of seeing Australia is under your own steam, or with a tour operator with an in-depth itinerary. The further from the capitals you go, the more public transport becomes patchy and irregular. Each state, except NT and the northern halves of WA and QLD, has a state transportation service based on a combination of bus, and sometimes train, networks. Some of these services helpfully connect up at border towns, but it is not always so and an unwise assumption to make.

If short on time and long on funds, flying can save a lot of time and effort, both interstate and within the larger states, and in some cases is the only realistic option. A few routes also pass over spectacular landscapes and coastlines, and the flight alone can be worth the fare. Most other interstate options involve long-distance buses, and on a very few routes, trains.

Air

Air travel within Australia is traditionally relatively expensive because of the distances, low population and limited competition. Each state capital has an international airport, and almost every country town and outback station in Australia has at least an airstrip. For many outlying communities air transport is the only practical means of long distance travel, and some are a very long distance from anywhere. Between them **Qantas** and **Virgin Blue** link most of the state capitals to each other and to many of the larger provisional towns, cities and main tourist destinations. If one of them does operate a route they are likely to offer the cheapest fare, usually between $100-700 one-way depending on distance and the popularity of the route. In addition there are several regional airways operating smaller planes on specialist routes. For up-to-date information on whether a destination is served by a scheduled or charter flight contact the local VIC.

Note that many provincial airports may not be staffed when you arrive. Check with the airline or local VIC regarding transport from the airport to the town

Bus

State and interstate bus services form the backbone of travel within Australia, and usually offer the most cost-effective way of constructing an interstate itinerary. The main operator is **Travel Coach**, which now manages the two previously independent companies **Greyhound Pioneer** and **McCafferty's**. Their network generally follows all of the main interstate highways on mainland Australia with offshoots including Cairns, Exmouth, Kakadu, and Yulara, and three routes between Sydney and Adelaide. As well as scheduled routes and fares they offer two varieties of jump-on, jump-off passes. The **Explorer Pass** commits you to a set one-way or circular route and is valid between 30 and 365 days. There are a couple of dozen options including **Sydney-Cairns** at around

A range of services can be found at www.buslines.com.au The interstate companies are complemented by statewide bus/train networks in each state except NT. See state sections for details

▶▶ Main interstate and state bus companies

Mainland McCafferty's/Greyhound, T132030, www.mccaffertys.com.au Although buses and routes for these two carriers are still separately badged, they have merged and are managed as a single concern.
NSW/VIC/SA Firefly, T1800 631164 or 03 9317 9312, www.fireflyexpress.com.au
NSW and QLD McCafferty's/Greyhound, T132030, www.greyhound.com.au and **Premier Motor Service**, T131410, www.premierms.com.au are the principal long distance, interstate coach service providers in NSW and QLD, but there are many other smaller regional companies.

Most are listed under the relevant destinations. **Countrylink** T132232, www.countrylink.nsw.gov.au also offer coach services to some centres in conjunction with rail schedules between NSW and QLD.
SA Premier Stateliner, T08 8415 5555, www.adelaidemetro.com.au
TAS Tassie Link, 03 6272 7300, www.tigerline.com.au **Redline**, T1300 360000, redline@tasredline.com.au
VIC V~Line, T136196, www.vlinepassenger.com.au
WA **Westrail**, T131053, www.wagr.gov.wa.au

$300, a **western circuit** ($1,000) and an **eastern circuit** ($1,200). Slightly more expensive per km is the more flexible **Kilometre Pass**. This allows you to travel anywhere on the network over the course of a year, travelling a maximum total of km, agreed and paid for in advance. A 2,000 km pass is $281, concessions $253, with each extra 1,000 km costing around $100. *Firefly* are one of the few interstate alternatives, with good value fares between Sydney and Melbourne, and Melbourne and Adelaide.

Bus travel advice If travelling by bus around Australia, always check the journey duration and time of arrival. Some routes can literally take days, with just a couple of short meal stops. Although many coaches are equipped with videos, ensure you have plenty of reading material for long journeys. It's also a good idea to have a lightweight blanket to hand, socks, a pillow, snacks, drinks, toothbrush and ear-plugs. As the buses run around the clock there's a good chance that you will arrive in the late evening or the early hours of the morning. Check this in advance and if it is the case, book accommodation ahead and, if possible, pre-arrange transfer transportation or at least have a decent map of the town to hand and know where you are going. Try to avoid walking around any town alone late at night. Also double-check times of connections. Many a traveller's arrangements have been disrupted by discovering, all too late, that the connecting bus was on a different day than assumed. Many of the 'transport' sections in this guide do indicate departure times and days of the major services. These are, of course, subject to change and should *not* be relied upon as definitive.

Backpacker buses In addition to the traditional bus services, which principally focus on getting you from A to B, there are now several operators who make the assumption that the most important part of your trip is the journey. These companies, loosely termed backpacker buses though open to anyone, combine the roles of travel operator and tour guide. They take longer than scheduled services (from twice to five times as long in some cases), and this is a good indicator of just how much they get off the highway and take you to those interesting, hard to get to places. They are well worth considering if you don't have your own transport. In terms of style and what is included they vary greatly, and it is important to clarify this prior to booking. Some offer transport and commentary only, others include accommodation and some meals, a few specialize in taking the 4WD routes and camping in the bush. The latter are not for everyone, but for many will provide an experience you'll never forget. Depending on what's included they cost between $75 and $150 per day. A few, including *Oz Experience*, which completes the

Main backpacker bus companies

NSW/QLD/VIC/SA/NT *Oz Experience,*
T1300 300028, www.ozexperience.com
NSW/NT/SA/WA *Travelabout,* T08 9244
1200, www.travelabout.au.com
WA/NT/SA/TAS *Adventure Tours,* T08
8936 1311, www.adventuretours.com.au
NSW/QLD *Wonderbus* T02 9555 9800,
www.wonderbus.com.au offer good tours of
the Blue Mountains and a day trip to Port
Stephens and the Hunter Valley vineyards.
The Adventure Company, 1st Floor, 13
Shields St, T40514777,
www.adventures.com.au and **Billy Tea Bush
Safaris,** T40320055, www.billytea.com.au are
both Cairns-based adventure tour operators
offering a good range of day and multi-day
trips in Far North Queensland.

NSW/VIC/SA *Autopia Tours,* T1800
000507 or 03 9326 5536,
www.autopiatours.com.au; *Wild-Life
Tours,* T03 9534 8868,
www.wildlifetours.com.au
NT/SA/VIC *Wayward Bus,* T1800 882823
or 08 8410 8833,
www.waywardbus.com.au; *Groovy
Grape,* T1800 661177,
www.groovygrape.com.au
SA/WA *Nullarbor Traveller,* T1800
816858, info@the-traveller.com.au
TAS *Under Down Under,* T1800 064726
or 03 6369 5555,
www.underdownunder.com.au
WA *Easyrider,* T9226 0307,
www.easyriderbp.com.au

full 'eastern circuit' with offshoots to Cairns, Kakadu and Yulara, offer jump-on, jump-off packages, and are priced more on distance. Oz Experience have many options incorporating a **Qantas** flight for part of the journey. The popular option of flying Sydney to Cairns and returning by bus is $630. The eastern circuit, including a flight between Darwin and Cairns, is around $1,600.

A few agents, including **Student Uni Travel**, T02-9232 8444, www.sut.com.au, and **Bus/plane
Travellers Contact Point**, T02-9221 8744, www.travellers.com.au, specialize in putting **itineraries**
together travel itineraries incorporating bus, plane and train. Not linked to any one travel operator, they can offer a high degree of flexibility.

Train

There is no comprehensive rail network in Australia. The main tracks run across the continent from Sydney to Perth, up through the centre from Melbourne to Alice Springs (currently being extended to Darwin), and up the east coast from Melbourne to Sydney/Brisbane. There are also limited local lines operated by the state bus companies of NSW, VIC, SA and WA, and integrated into their general schedules. This has the consequence that many state journeys alternate between bus and train. Tickets are available at coach and bus stations and via the various telephone booking numbers (see box, page 42).

There are five major interstate services. The XPT is operated twice daily (one overnight) **Interstate**
by **Countrylink** between Sydney and Melbourne (11 hours, from $55 to $231 for a **services**
sleeper) and Sydney and Brisbane *Adult fares get
considerably cheaper
   The other services, operated by **Trainways**, T1800 888480 or (rail only), T132147 if booked in advance*
(holiday packages and passes), www.gsr.com.au, run less often and try to create a flavour of nostalgia, promoting them as adventures in themselves. Some love these journeys, enjoying the serenity of watching the landscape gradually change in relative comfort. Others find the journeys too cramped, noisy and boring to recall the glory days of rail travel. The **Indian Pacific** connects Perth with Sydney via Port Augusta. An unbroken trip takes three days and nights. The **Ghan** connects Alice Springs to

Adelaide. The journey takes about 20 hours, with optional onward legs to Melbourne or Sydney. This was the original Australian outback rail track, and named after the Afghans (most were actually Indians) who had helped open the route. The **Overland** connects Adelaide and Melbourne (10 hours). There are three ticket levels on the Indian Pacific and Ghan. The '*Gold Kangaroo*' passenger gets a small sleeping cabin, all meals in the finely decked out 'Gold' dining car, and a very pleasant lounge. If you do want to get a feel of travelling in a bygone era, then this is the way to go. '*Red Kangaroo*' passengers have separate lounge and dining car (meals not included), and have the choice between a cabin or day/nighter seat (a real ordeal for some). The seat-only prices are roughly equivalent with interstate buses, with the red cabins about 2½ times the cost and gold cabins 3½ times. Concessions are good value, particularly for the long-distance, 'red' seats (Sydney to Perth for as little as $207!). The Great Southern Railway Backpacker Pass ($350) allows unlimited travel in a 'red' day/nighter seat on the Ghan, Indian Pacific and Overland for 6 months. Pass holders must be members of a recognised backpacker organization (eg *YHA*). Upgrades to sleeping berths are allowed, but surcharges apply.

Ferry

Australia is not a single landmass, and the main continent has a halo of islands ranging from the insignificant to one bigger than many independent countries, Tasmania. There are ferries to most of the inhabited islands, and most of these carry vehicles. The most popular can get booked well ahead in peak periods so plan carefully. The longest, and most expensive trip by far is the one from Victoria to **Tasmania** and it is well worth considering flying unless you have your own vehicle and are planning a long trip. Much the same can be said for **Kangaroo Island** in SA, where tours from Adelaide also offer a more economic, if usually far too brief option. **King** and **Flinders Islands** in the Bass Strait have quite limited ferry services and for these flying is also usually the better option. Most other ferry trips generally offer better value than flying, and do not often take much longer.

Car, motorbike and bicycle

www.travel mate.com.au is a useful website for driving tips in Australia

For maximum flexibility there is no substitute in Australia for having your own transport. Cars, campervans, motorbikes and bicycles can all be hired or bought with little difficulty. As a general rule of thumb consider buying a car for travelling for periods over two months (see box on page 27). Long-term bicycle hire for touring is rarely available, and cyclists should plan to bring their own bike and gear, or buy in Australia. If hiring or buying a car always consider the option of a campervan. These can sometimes be had for little more than the cost of a standard car, the savings on accommodation can be considerable, and itineraries are even less constrained.

Traffic congestion is rarely an issue in Australia, and only the Sydney and Melbourne metropolitan areas have anything like the traffic problems of most nations. Congestion on country roads and highways is practically unheard of. This means that driving itineraries can be based on covering a planned distance each day, up to, say 100 km for each solid hour's driving.

The key factor in planning transport is distance. Driving or cycling outside of the main cities is relatively stress-free, but the distances can be huge. The trip from Adelaide to Perth involves a 1,000-km stretch with only roadhouses for company, spaced about 100 km apart, and not a single town. Straight sections regularly exceed 20 km. The scenery for passengers can be wonderful, but the driver can get very bored – and sleepy. There are a lot of single-vehicle accidents in Australia, and many are simply a result of drivers falling asleep.

State motoring organizations

NSW NRMA, T132132, www.nrma.com.au
NT AANT, T08-8981 3837
QLD RACQ, T131905, www.racq.com.au
SA RAA, T1800-630878, www.raa.net

TAS RACT, T13 1111 (24 hrs), www.ract.com.au
VIC RACV, T131955, www.racv.com.au
WA RAC, T131703, www.rac.com.au

Essentials

Another important factor in country driving is large animals. Kangaroos and emus can appear on roads seemingly out of nowhere, particularly at dawn and dusk, and sheep and cattle frequently stray onto unfenced roads, especially at night. Collisions with animals are the other major cause of single-vehicle accidents. Such collisions are not simply irritations. Hitting a kangaroo, emu or sheep will probably write-off the vehicle and cause injury. Hitting a camel or cattle is considerably worse. This means that you should drive *only* in full daylight, an important consideration when planning a self-drive itinerary.

On country roads you will also meet road trains. These haulage trucks can be over 50 m long including up to four separate trailers strung along behind the main cab. Overtaking them obviously entails great care – wait for a good long stretch before committing yourself. If you are on a single track bitumen road or an unsealed road you are well advised to pull right over when one comes the other way. Not only can dust cause visibility to hit zero, but you will also minimize the possibility of stones pinging up and damaging your windows.

The other major factor when planning is the type of roads you may need to use. Almost all the main interstate highways are now sealed, though there are a few exceptions. Many country roads are unsealed, usually meaning a gravel or sand surface. When recently *graded* (levelled and compacted) they can be almost as pleasant to drive on as sealed roads, but even then there are reduced levels of handling and increased stopping distances. After grading, unsealed roads deteriorate over time. Potholes form, they can become very boggy, even impassable, when wet, and corrugations usually develop. These are regular ripples in the road surface, perpendicular to the road direction, and can go on for tens of km. Small ones simply cause an irritating judder, large ones can reduce tolerable driving speeds to 10-20 kmph. Generally, the bigger the wheel size, and the longer the wheel-base, the more comfortable journeys over corrugations will be. Most designated unsealed roads can be negotiated with a 2WD, low-clearance vehicle, but the ride will be a lot more comfortable, and safer in a 4WD, high-clearance one. Note that most hire-car companies will not allow their 2WD vehicles to be driven on unsealed roads. High-clearance, 4WD cars and campervans are available from most of the major hire companies.

Fuel costs are approximately half that in Britain, twice that in the US, fluctuating between $0.75-1 a litre in city centres and $0.90-1.35 a litre outside the main cities. Allow at least $10 for every estimated 100 km (62 miles)

Some unsealed roads are designated as 4WD-only or tracks, though definitions of some differ according to the map or authority you consult. In dry weather and after recent grading the Mereenie Loop and Oodnadatta Tracks, for example, can be driven in well-prepared 2WD cars. At other times they cannot, without serious risk of accident, vehicle or tyre damage or getting bogged. If in any doubt whatsoever, stick to the roads you are certain are safe for your vehicle, and you are sufficiently prepared for. With careful preparation and the right vehicles (convoys are always recommended), however, traversing the major outback tracks can be an awesome experience. Note that hire-companies have strict terms on the use of their 4WD vehicles. Many can only be used on sealed or graded unsealed roads and not taken down 4WD tracks or off-road. Always check with the hire company where you can and cannot take your vehicle, and also what your liability will be in the case of an accident.

▶▶ Campervan hire companies

The following are campervan specialists, though the major car hire companies also have campervans available (see page 47). **Mainland** Apollo, T1800-777779, www.apollocamper.com.au
Backpacker, T1800-670232, www.backpackercampervans.com
Britz, T1800-331454 , www.britz.com **Getabout**, T02-9380 5536, www.getaboutoz.com
Maui, T1300- 363800,

www.maui-rentals.com
NQ, T1800- 079529, www.nqrentals.com
Eastern states Abbeys, T1800-888401.
Wicked, T1800-246869, www.wickedcampers.com.au Both offer budget vans.
WA/NT/TAS Trailmaster, T1800-651202, www.trailmaster.com.au
TAS Autorent, T03-6391 8677
Tasmanian Campervan Hire, T1800- 807119.

Prepare carefully before driving to remote areas. Even if there are regular roadhouses, it is wise to carry essential spares and tools such as fan belts, hoses, gaffer tape, a tyre repair kit, extra car jack, extra spare wheel and tyre, spade, decent tool kit, oil and coolant, and a fuel can with fuel. A short course in vehicle maintenance before you travel can also save much grief. Membership of a state breakdown organization is highly recommended, as is informing friends, relatives or the police of your intended itinerary. Above all carry plenty of spare water, at least 10 litres per person, 20 if possible.

Rules & regulations To drive in Australia you must have a current driving licence. Foreign nationals also need an international drivers licence, available from your national motoring organization for a small fee. Each Australian state issues its own licences. If driving in any one state for more than three months check with police whether that state requires a local licence. In all of Australia you drive on the left. Speed limits vary between states, with maximum urban limits of 50-60 kmph and maximum country limits of 100-120 kmph (unrestricted in the NT). Penalties for speeding include a fine, and police usually allow less than 5 kmph over the limit as leeway – the safest bet in all respects is to stay under the limit. Seatbelts are compulsory for drivers and all passengers. Driving while under the influence of alcohol or drugs is illegal over certain (very small) limits and penalties are severe.

Motoring organizations *The general breakdown number for all associations is T131111* Every state has a breakdown service affiliated to the **Australian Automobile Association** (AAA), www.aaa.asn.au, which your home country organization may have a reciprocal link with. To join in Australia you need to join one of the state associations (see box on previous page). Note that you will only be covered for about 100 km (depending on scheme) of towing distance.

Vehicle hire *Also see box on page 46 Some companies will offer one-way hire on certain models and under certain conditions* Prices for car rental vary considerably according to where you hire from (it's cheaper in the state capitals, though small local companies sometimes have good deals), what you hire and the mileage/insurance terms. You may be better off making arrangements in your own country for a fly/drive deal through one of the main multi-national companies. Watch out for kilometre caps; some may be as low as 100 km per day. The minimum you can expect to pay in Australia is around $200 a week for a small car. Drivers need to be over 21. Note that at peak times it can be impossible to get a car at short notice. Also many companies will dispose of a booked car within as little as half an hour of you not showing up for an agreed pick-up time. If you've booked a car but are going to be late ensure that you contact them before the pick-up time. For advice on hiring or buying **motorcycles** anywhere in Australia, try **Garners**, Melbourne, T03-9326 8676, www.garnersmotorcycles.com.au

Major car hire companies

Australia Avis, T136333,
www.avis.com **Budget**, T1300 362848,
www.budget.com.au **Delta-Europcar**,
T1800-811541, www.deltacars.com.au **Hertz**,
T133039, www.hertz.com **Thrifty**,
T1300-367227, www.rentacar.com.au
Britain Avis, T0990-900500 **Budget**,
T0800-181181 **Delta-Europcar**,
T8457-222525 **Hertz**,

T0990-996699 **Thrifty**, T0990-168238.
New Zealand Avis,
109-5262847 **Budget**,
T09-3752222 **Hertz**, T09-3676350.
North America Avis, T800 3311084,
www.avis.com **Budget**, T800 5270700,
www.budgetrentacar.com **Hertz**, T800
6543001, www.hertz.com **Thrifty**, T800
3672277, www.thrifty.com

◀◀

Essentials

Buying a vehicle
Buying a vehicle in Australia is a relatively simple process provided you have somewhere you can give as an address

Cars and vans are relatively inexpensive and ones that should go the distance can be picked up for as little as $2,500, or $6,000 for a 4WD. Paying more definitely increases peace of mind, but can increase your exposure to losses when you sell it. You should expect to lose about a third on selling. If you're dealing with a second-hand car dealer you may be able to agree a 'buy-back' price – thus saving the hassle, risk and time of selling it once you're done. Another factor in favour of dealers is that they usually offer some sort of warranty. The alternatives are fellow travellers, hostel notice boards, and the classified pages of local newspapers. The principal advantage to buying privately is cost and vehicles being sold by desperate travellers in a hurry to close a deal can be real bargains. The state motoring organizations offer vehicle checks for around $100 and these are well worth considering if you have little mechanical knowledge yourself. Most cars in Australia are either locally made or imported from Asia. European and American vehicles are relatively thin on the ground and so usually more expensive and harder to find spares for. An older vehicle may well need a little 'tlc' during your custodianship so the availability of spares should be a serious consideration. They are most easily come by for the Australian built Fords and Holdens, though Toyota parts are also common.

Every car is registered with the authorities within the state it is first purchased, and the registration papers must be transferred at each sale, again in the state of sale. If a car is re-sold in a different state it has first to be re-registered in that state. You will need to formally complete the transfer of registration with the transport department, presenting them with the papers, the receipt (you will have to pay a stamp duty tax proportional to the sale price, usually about 5%), plus in some states a certificate of roadworthiness. The latter may be provided by the seller or you may have to have the vehicle checked yourself at a suitable garage. Registration must be renewed, within the state the vehicle was last sold, every 6 or 12 months. In some states vehicles must also be checked annually for roadworthiness.

Third-party personal injury insurance is included in the registration and by law no other insurance is required. It is foolish, however, not to at least invest in third party vehicle and property insurance, and even in comprehensive cover if you could not afford to lose the entire value of your vehicle.

Hitching

Hitchhiking, while not strictly illegal in most states, is not advised by anyone. The tragic events near Barrow Creek in 2001, plus the infrequent but suspicious disappearances of people around the country, demonstrate that there will always be the odd twisted soul around who will randomly assault or abduct people for their own evil ends. This is not to say that hitching is more dangerous in Australia than any other country, indeed it is probably safer than most, but simply to say that, yes, bad things happen.

Maps

View and print off touring and street maps at www.arta.com.au

Several publishers produce country-wide and state maps. Regional maps are also available and the most useful for general travel. The best and cheapest of these are generally published by each state's motoring organization (see box, page 46).

AUSLIG, the national mapping agency, are publishing 54 x 54 km topographic maps, at 1:100,000 scale, of every such size area in Australia, recommended for any long-distance trekking or riding. Most areas are now in print, but if not black and white copies can be obtained. For a map index, place name search, details of distributors or mail order, contact T1800 800173, www.auslig.gov.au *AUSLIG* also publish a 1:250,000 series, covering the whole country, useful for those heading outback on 4WD trips. If you're thinking of tackling one of the major outback tracks, such as the Great Central Road, Tanami, Birdsville or Strzelecki, then get hold of the appropriate map published by *Westprint*, T03 5391 1466, www.westprint.com.au, the acknowledged experts in this field.

Specialist map shops

Adelaide *The Map Shop*, T08 8231 1911, www.mapshop.net.au **Brisbane** *World Wide Maps and Guides*, 187 George St, T3221 4330, www.worldwidemaps.com.au **Darwin** *Maps NT*, T08 8999 7032. **Hobart** *Tasmanian Map Centre*,T03 6231 9043, www.on tas.com.au/map-supplies **Internet** (Australia) www.travelguidewarehouse.com (London) *Stanfords*, T020 7836 1321, www.stanfords.co.uk **Melbourne** *Map Land*, T03 9670 4383, www.mapland.com.au **New York** *Rand McNally* 150E 52nd Street, Midtown East, T212 758 7488. **Perth** *Perth Map Centre*, T08 9322 5673, www.perthmap. com.au **Sydney** The *Travel Bookshop* at 175 Liverpool Street, T9261 8200, or *Dymocks* 350 George Street, 261 George Street, and 34 Hunter Street, T1800 688 319, www.dymocks.com.au

Keeping in touch

Internet

Internet access, and thus email, is widely available. Many hostels, hotels and cafés have dedicated internet booths, though these are usually the most expensive option with connection a stiff $2 for 10-15 minutes. Internet cafés usually use standard PCs, as do some hostels, and so can charge via a sliding scale and offer specials such as 'all-night lock-ins'. State governments are keen for their citizens to have access to the internet and some have set up schemes to allow cheap, or even free access. Based either in libraries or dedicated centres, they are usually also accessible to visitors.

Post

Most post offices are open Monday-Friday 0900-1700, and Saturday 0900-1230. Many now operate out of a shop. Postage for a postcard, greeting card or 'small' letter anywhere in

Australia is $0.45 and should arrive within three days of posting. Small letters must be less than 130 x 240 mm, 5 mm thick and 250 g in weight. Postage of large letters starts at $0.98. Airmail for postcards and greetings cards is $1 anywhere in the world, small letters (under 50 g) are $1 to southeast Asia and the Pacific, $1.50 beyond. Parcels can be sent either by sea, economy air (often a good trade-off option between speed and cost) or air. For more information contact **Australia Post** on T131318, www.auspost.com.au

Most public payphones are operated by *Telstra*, www.telstra.com.au, the nationally-owned telecommunications operator. They are fairly widespread in towns and cities, though much less so in country areas. Most payphones take all coins or phonecards, available from newsagents and post offices. Some also take credit cards.

A phonebox call within Australia requires $0.40, or $0.50 in some non-*Telstra* public phones. If you are calling locally (within approximately 50 km) this will last as long as you like. STD calls, outside the local area, will use up that $0.40 in the first 43 seconds if calling before 1900, and 78 seconds after 1900. Subsequent same-time blocks cost $0.40 each. Calls from private phones vary according to the owners plan, the time of day and distance. Generally calls are cheapest between 1900 and 0700 and at weekends. To check if a number is local to you, or the likely cost of a STD or international call, dial T1800 113011.

There are no separate phone codes for towns or cities. Instead each state has a phone code: **02** for ACT/NSW; **03** for VIC/TAS; **07** for QLD; **08** for NT/SA/WA and by some quirk Broken Hill. You do not need to use the state code unless the state you are calling has a different code from the state you are in. Any number prefixed by 1800 is free to the caller; 13 and 1300 incur the flat $0.40 charge; and most premium numbers start 190.

Well worth considering if you are here for any length of time is a pre-paid mobile phone. *Telstra* and *Vodaphone* give the best coverage and their phones are widely available from as little as $50, including some call-time. Calls are more expensive of course, though there are some good plans on offer for calling between mobiles

To call Australia from overseas, dial the international prefix (011 from the USA and Canada, 00 from the UK and New Zealand) followed by 61, then the state phone code minus the first 0, then the 8-digit number. You can access the national database of telephone numbers and their accompanying addresses at www.whitepages.com.au The *Yellow Pages* also has its own site at www.yellowpages.com.au

To call overseas from Australia diall 0011 followed by the country code. Country codes include: **Republic of Ireland** 353; **New Zealand** 64; **South Africa** 27; the **USA** and **Canada** 1; the **UK** 44. By far the cheapest way of calling overseas is to use an international pre-paid phonecard (though they cannot be used from a mobile phone, or from some of the blue and orange public phones). Available from city post offices and newsagents, every call made with them initially costs about $1 (a local call plus connection) but subsequent per minute costs are a fraction of *Telstra* or mobile phone charges.

Telephone
Service difficulties:132203 International service difficulties: 1221 Directory enquiries: 1223 International Directory enquiries: 1225

Essentials

Media

The *Sydney Morning Herald* and Melbourne's *The Age* are considered influential newspapers and have a national readership. Aside from these it is difficult to buy a state paper from outside that state. There is only one national newspaper and this is the respected broadsheet, *The Australian*, published Monday-Friday and *The Weekend Australian*, published Saturday. The *Financial Review* is published Monday-Saturday. Australians are avid consumers of magazines and even the smallest newsagent will carry a bewildering range on every subject from brides to surfing. Australia's main current affairs magazine is *The Bulletin*, including a section of Newsweek, published weekly. There are Australian editions of international magazines such as *Vogue*, *Elle*, and *Harpers Bazaar*. Every corner shop and supermarket sells a weekly dose of celebrity gossip in the magazines, *New Idea*, *Woman's Day* and *New Weekly*.

Newspapers & magazines
Each state has its own daily and Sunday newspaper and some of the larger states have two

Foreign newspapers & magazines

Foreign newspapers are widely available in larger newsagents in the cities and towns. It is also possible to buy special weekly editions of British papers such as the *Daily Telegraph* and *The Guardian*. There are Asian editions of *Time* and *The Economist*. Foreign magazines are stocked everywhere although foreign language editions will only be available in one or two large city newsagents.

TV & radio

There are five main television channels in Australia; the publicly funded ABC and SBS and the independent commercial stations, Channel 7, Channel 9 and Channel 10. The commercial stations serve up very similar fare of American sitcoms and Australian news and drama but Channel 10 is the most lowbrow and has the heaviest imported content. The ABC aims for Australian content of high quality and also imports many BBC programs. SBS is an excellent channel focusing on the culture, current affairs, sport and film of many different nationalities. This channel has by the far the best world news, in depth and non parochial, shown daily at 1830.

The ABC network also broadcasts several national radio channels: *Radio National* features news, current affairs, arts, culture and music; *Classic FM* plays mostly classical music; and *Triple J* is aimed at a young, 'alternative' audience. ABC *Regional Radio* covers local issues in country regions. There are also many local commercial radio stations in each city and in some regional areas that broadcast a mix of news, talk-back, and music.

Food and drink

Restaurants and other places to eat are identified by a ● symbol on maps

The quintessential image of Australian cooking may be of throwing some meat on the barbie but the truth is that Australia has a dynamic and vibrant cuisine all of its own. Until at least the 1950s and 1960s Australian cooking was basically bland English; in other words meat, potatoes and three veg boiled into a pale, limpid and sorry state. However as Australian society became increasingly multicultural the food of the Chinese, Thai, Vietnamese, Italian, Greek and Lebanese immigrants began to seep into the Australian consciousness. Australia developed a fusion cuisine that takes elements from many cultures and mixes them into something new and original. A typical dish might be something like Sydney restaurant *Rockpool*'s Asian noodle salad with Australian abalone, flavored with truffle oil, ginger and scallion; a blend of Asian and Italian flavours with fresh local seafood.

Freshness is the other striking quality of this cuisine called **Modern Australian**. The food is super fresh, achieved by using produce from the local area, and cooked in a way that preserves the food's intrinsic flavour. The food is allowed to shine for itself without being smothered in heavy or dominating sauces. The ingedients used make it distinctive too. Native animals are used, such as kangaroo, emu and crocodile, and native plants that Aboriginal people have been eating for thousands of years such as quandong, wattle seed or lemon myrtle leaf.

While you are rubbing your hands with anticipation – a word of warning. This fantastic food is mostly restricted to cities and large towns. There are pockets of foodie heaven in the country, like the Barossa or Yarra Valleys, but these are usually associated with wine regions and are the exception rather than the rule.

Australian icons

There are a few special foods that Australians produce and treasure. The meat pie is the favourite Australian fast food, about the size of your palm and filled with mince or steak and gravy. If you are tempted your best bet is a fresh one from a bakery rather than a mass-produced one (sealed in a little plastic bag) that sits in a shop's warming oven all day. Fish and chips are also popular and these are often good in Australia because the fish is fresh and only light vegetable oils are used for frying.

Eating categories

In this guide places to eat are divided into four categories: **expensive** *(over $35 a head),* **mid-range** *($25-35 a head),* **cheap** *($15-25 a head),* **seriously cheap** *(under $15 a head). These prices are based on a two-course meal (entrée plus main course) without drinks. Note that desserts are usually cheaper than entrées. We have tried to include choices from each category, though this is not always possible. Except sometimes in the smaller towns, all places listed are recommended as offering relatively good value, quality and standards of service within their price category.*

Vegemite is a dark and sticky yeast extract that looks a bit like axle grease and is spead on bread. Australian kids are almost weaned on it and conceive a passion for it that lasts a lifetime. It is the Aussie equivalent of British Marmite, though fans of one usually detest the other. Note that there *is* a brand called Marmite in Australia, but it's *not* the same as the British brand. Bring your own or look out for the repackaged and imported My Mate. *Tim Tams* are a thick chocolate biscuit, very similar to the Brits' Penguin, and reputedly the best selling snack in the country. What Brits call crisps, Aussie's call chips ('hot chips' are, well, hot chips or fries), with *Twisties* a very Australian favourite.

Damper is a loaf of bread that is made out of nothing more than flour, salt and water and usually baked out bush in the ashes of a campfire. Nothing beats warm damper slathered with jam and butter. Another Australian product of baking is the lamington; a block of sponge that has been dipped in chocolate and rolled in coconut. The pavlova is a classic Australian desert, although it is never consumed without an argument about whether the Australians or the New Zealanders invented it. Both claim it was created for the visit of Russian ballerina, Anna Pavlova. The 'pav' is like a cake-sized meringue, served topped with whipped cream and fresh fruit.

Where to eat

Traditional restaurants, serving Australia's home-grown fusion cuisine or cuisines from all over the world, are common even in smaller towns. Chinese and Thai restaurants are very common, with other cuisines appearing only in the larger towns and cities. In Melbourne and Sydney, the undisputed gourmet capitals of Australia, you will find the very best of Modern Australian as well as everything from Mexican to Mongolian, Jamaican to Japanese. Both corporate hotels and motels and traditional pubs will almost all have attached restaurants or serve counter meals. Only a few will have a more imaginative menu or better quality fare than the local restaurants. A very few restaurants are not licensed for the consumption of alcohol. Some are licensed for BYO only, in which case you take your own wine or beer and the restaurant provides glasses. There is usually a corkage fee in such establishments, but it still works out cheaper than drinking alcohol in fully licensed premises. European-style cafés are only rarely found outside of the cities and bigger towns. As in many western countries the distinction between cafés, bistros and restaurants is becoming extremely blurred.

Fast food junkies fear not. Australians have taken to **fast food** as enthusiastically as anywhere else in the world. Alongside these are **food courts**, found in the shopping malls of cities and larger towns. These have several takeaway options, usually including various Asian cuisines, surrounding a central space equipped with tables and chairs. Also in the budget bracket are the **delis** and **milk bars**, also serving hot takeaways, together with sandwiches, cakes and snacks.

If you **cook for yourself** you'll find just about everything in an Aussie supermarket that you would find in Europe or the USA, and at very reasonable prices. *Coles* and *Woolworths* are the main supermarket chains. An excellent meal for two can easily be put together for under $20. With a few utensils it is possible to have a BBQ almost anywhere, due to the wealth of public facilities.

Essentials

▶▶ **The Aussie barbie**

"Throw another prawn on the barbie". The image is very familiar to travellers well before they arrive, and for once this is no myth. Aussies love a BBQ, and many households will have a couple a week as a matter of course, as well as assuming that any day out will include a barbie somewhere along the way. Public BBQs are common, often found in town and national parks, and beach foreshores. Sometimes they're free, otherwise a $0.20, $0.50 or $1 coin will get you 15-30 minutes of frying time. There are never any utensils, so you'll need to be prepared. At private BBQs, bringing your own meat and alcohol is the norm, with hosts usually providing salads, bread and a few extra sausages ('snags').

Wine

Several operators offer dedicated wine-tasting tours, including Venture Winetours Australia, www.venturewine tours.com.au, Wine Tours Australia/NZ, www.winetours australia-nz.com, and Avalon Wine Tours, www.avalon-tours.com

Australian wine will need no introduction to most readers, as it is now imported in huge quantities into Europe and the USA. Many of the labels you might be familiar with, including *Penfolds* and the giant of the industry, *Jacob's Creek*, are produced in South Australia, but there are dozens of recognized wine regions right across the southern third of Australia, and several in the process of development. The industry has a creditable history in such a young country, with several wineries boasting a tradition of a century or more. The 'Mediterranean' climate of much of the south of the country is very favourable for grape-growing, and the soil, relatively poor though it is, is sufficient to produce a high-standard grape. The price of wine, however, is unexpectedly high given the relatively low cost of food and beer. Australia now has many wineries in these dozens of regions, ranging in size from the vastness of *Jacob's Creek*, to one-person operations. **Cellar doors** range from modern marble and glass temples to venerable, century-old former barns of stone and wood. Some will open for a couple of hours on a Saturday afternoon, others every day from 0900-1700. In some you'll be lucky to get half a dry cracker to go with a sip, others boast some of the best restaurants in the country. A few are in small town high streets, others are set in hectares of exquisitely designed and maintained gardens. The truly wonderful thing is that this mix of styles is found within most of the regions, making a day or two's tasting expedition a scenic and cultural delight as well as an epicurean one.

Pubs, bars & beer

Pubs are the best places to meet the locals

The typical Aussie pub is a solid brick and wood affair with wide first floor verandahs extending across the front, and sometimes down the sides as well. These usually have separate public and lounge bars, a bottleshop (off-license) off to the side, and increasingly a separate 'bar' full of pokies (slot machines or one-armed bandits). The public bar often doubles as a *TAB* betting shop. Pubs and bars in Australia vary as much in style as anywhere in the western world. Some pubs are rough as guts and a stranger venturing in is guaranteed a hard stare. Others go out of their way to make a visitor feel welcome. Some haven't seen a paintbrush since the day they were built, others have been beautifully renovated in styles ranging from modern to authentic outback, saloon to Irish.

The vast majority of beer drunk by Australians is lager, despite many being called 'ale' or 'bitter'. The big brands such as **VB** and **Carlton** (VIC), **Tooheys** (NSW), **West End** (SA) and **Swan** (WA) can be very homogenous but equally refreshing on a hot day. If your palate is just a touch more refined hunt out some of the products of the smaller breweries such as **Matilda Bay** and **Little Creatures** (WA), **Coopers** (SA), **Cascade** and **Boags** (TAS). Beer tends to be around 4-5% alcohol, with the popular and surprisingly pleasant tasting 'mid' varieties about 3½%, and 'light' beers about 2-2½%. Drink driving laws are strict, and the best bet is to not drink alcohol at all if you are driving. As well as being available on draught in pubs, beer is also available from bottleshops (or 'bottle-o's') in cases (or 'slabs') of 24-36 cans ('tinnies' or 'tubes') or bottles ('stubbies') of 375 ml each. This is by far the cheapest way of buying beer (often under $1 per can or bottle).

Australia's great wine regions

*There are several wine regions that will delight almost anyone's senses. Some offer beautiful scenery as well as excellent wines. Others have long and intriguing histories, a few have attracted communities of artists, and others still have proved fertile not just for grapes but produce as diverse as cheese and chocolate, honey and mustard. In NSW the **Hunter Valley** provides one of the best vineyard experiences in the world with over 100 wineries, world class B&Bs and a range of tours from cycling to horse-drawn carriage. Victoria's **Yarra Valley** would be a contender for the country's most picturesque. In SA the **Clare Valley** is serenely beautiful and cultured, while the adjacent **Barossa** is famous for its history, charm and Maggie Beer. WA's area known as **Margaret River** can boast some of the state's best beaches, waves tailor-made for surfers, a string of fascinating cave systems and a rich Epicurean and art culture.*

Essentials

Entertainment

As in most 'western' nations, much of the country's entertainment is provided by its pubs and bars. Not only are they a social meeting point but many put on regular live music, DJs, karaoke and quiz nights. Most also double as mini gambling dens, restricted to a *TAB* betting shop in some states, also incorporating pokie machines (one-armed bandits) in others. In some medium-sized towns they also operate a club or discotheque. True nightclubs will only be found in the cities and larger towns, and then usually only open a few nights of the week. They do generally charge an entrance fee, usually around $5-15, though entry will commonly be free on some mid-week nights or before a certain time.

The **cinema** is popular in Australia and some will have outdoor screens with either deckchair seating or drive-in slots. Expect to pay around $13 for an adult ticket, but look out for early week or pre-1800 specials. Every big city in the country has its major **casino**, with those in Sydney, Melbourne, Brisbane and Perth on prodigious scales. Most are open 24 hours a day and, as well as offering gaming tables and rank upon rank of pokies, also have live music venues and good-value food halls and restaurants. Other indoor pursuits found in most large towns and cities include **10-pin bowling**, **bingo**, **karting**, **snooker** and **pool** halls, and large recreational centres offering everything from **swimming** to **squash**, **basketball** to **badminton**.

Shopping

Tourist shops exploit the cute and cuddly factor of Australian native mammals to the limit so most tourist merchandise seems to consist of soft toy kangaroos and koalas and brightly coloured clothing featuring the same creatures. Other typical items perpetuate the corny Australian stereotypes. Beware of hats strung with corks; they are not comfortable and you'll only look foolish.

However corkless hats are a popular and practical souvenir, particularly the distinctively Australian *Akubra* hats, made from felt in muddy colours. Along the same lines, stockman's clothing made by *RMWilliams* is also popular and very good quality. Three of the company's best sellers are elastic-sided boots, moleskins, soft brushed-cotton trousers cut like jeans, and the *Driza-bone*, a long oilskin raincoat with a fixed shoulder cape which keeps one 'dry as a bone'. Australian surfwear is sought after worldwide and is a good buy while in the country. Most shopping streets will have at least one surfwear shop. Look for labels such as *Ripcurl, Quiksilver, Mambo* and *Billabong*.

Essentials

Australia is a good place to shop for **jewellery**. There are many talented craftspeople making exquisite metal and bead work and the country produces unique and precious gems such as opal, pearl and diamonds. The widest range will be available in the cities but, as in most countries, products are often cheapest at the source and a wonderful momento of place. Look for opals in Coober Pedy, pearls in Broome and pink, champagne and cognac coloured Argyle diamonds in the Kimberley.

Aboriginal art & souvenirs
See also Aboriginal culture section in Background chapter

In the tourist shops Aboriginal art designs are as ubiquitous as cuddly toys and printed on everything from t-shirts to teatowels. Some of these designs can be beautiful but be aware that many articles have no link to Aboriginal people and do not benefit them directly – check the label. *Desert Designs* is a successful label printing the stunning designs of the Great Sandy Desert artist Jimmy Pike on silk scarves and sarongs. It is possible to buy genuine Aboriginal art and craft but it is more commonly available in country areas close to Aboriginal communities or from Aboriginal owned or operated enterprises. This applies more to craft items such as didjeridu and scorched carvings than paintings and of course there are reputable vendors everywhere but if in doubt ask for more information. Art and crafts bought from reputable sources ensures that the money ends up in the artist's pocket and supports Aboriginal culture, skills and self-reliance.

Many people are keen to buy an Aboriginal dot painting, usually acrylic on canvas, but this can be a daunting shopping experience. Also note that there are different styles of Aboriginal art, often depending on the region the artist comes from. For example the x-ray paintings on bark only come from Arnhem Land. The best Aboriginal paintings sell for many thousands but there are also many thousands of average paintings sold for a few hundred dollars. A good painting will cost at least $800-1,500. Simple works on canvas can be as little as $100 and make good souvenirs. Take your time and have a good look around. Visit public and private galleries where you can see work of the highest quality – you may not be able to afford it but you'll learn something of what makes a good piece of Aboriginal art. Some of the qualities to look for are fine application, skilful use of colour and a striking design. The major cities all have commercial galleries selling Aboriginal art. Alice Springs has a particularly impressive range of galleries and work but Darwin and Kakadu are also good places to buy art. Work can also sometimes be bought direct from the community. Some of the best outlets are the *Uluru-Kata Tjuta Cultural Centre*, the former mission at Hermannsburg, Manyallaluk near Katherine, the *Bowali Visitor Centre* and *Warradjan Cultural Centre* in Kakadu, *Injaluk Arts Centre* and *Buku Larrngay Mulka Art Centre* in Arnhem Land, *Desart* and *Papunya Tula* in Alice Springs.

Holidays and festivals

Bank holidays

As a general rule of thumb, businesses open every day will close on Christmas Day, and perhaps a couple of other public holidays. Attractions open only on weekends generally also tend to open on public holidays (except Christmas Day) with Sunday hours. Most public holidays are recognized nationwide, but each state also has 2-4 public holidays of its own.

School holidays

School holidays can play a major role in what is and isn't possible for the international traveller. In the southern states the Christmas and Easter holidays see many traditional Australian holiday destinations completely booked out, in some cases for months in advance, and in the north the same thing can happen in the winter break. Holidays vary from state to state, but broadly speaking they cover the whole of January, a week or two around Easter, a couple of weeks in June or July and another couple in September or October. See state sections for more details.

National public holidays

New Years Day	1 Jan 2003	1 Jan 2004
Australia Day	27 Jan 2003	26 Jan 2004
Good Friday	18 Apr 2003	9 Apr 2004
Easter Monday	21 Apr 2003	12 Apr 2004
Anzac Day	25 Apr 2003	26 Apr 2004
Queens Birthday (Oct in WA)	9 Jun 2003	14 Jun 2004
Christmas Day	25 Dec 2003	27 Dec 2004
Boxing (Proclamation) Day	26 Dec 2003	28 Dec 2004

In addition to these there are several state public holidays. See state sections for details.

Festivals & events
Details of local festivals are given under individual towns. See www.australia.com for exact forthcoming dates

Victoria's festivals and events are concentrated in **Melbourne** but there are a few outside the city worth looking out for. The **Port Fairy Folk Festival** is held in early March and attracts over 40,000 people and some seriously good national and international musicians. **South Australia** proudly calls itself the Festival State, and not without good reason. Every major town boasts a string of festivals and activities around the year, none more so than the capital, **Adelaide** which seems to have something going on every weekend and more besides. There are small regional festivals held throughout **Tasmania** every month of the year so there should be something on during your visit. The best known Tasmanian event is the **Sydney to Hobart yacht race**, starting in Sydney on Boxing Day and reaching Hobart a few days later. At the same time the city holds the **Taste of Tasmania festival**; a celebration of Tasmanian food and wine celebrated on the Hobart waterfront and incorporating lots of live entertainment. While the **Northern Territory** cannot claim to have the high profile and high-budget events of the more populated areas in the south it does have some interesting festivals and events that range from completely bonkers to unusual experiences that may be among the highlights of your trip. Most events are held during the Top End Dry or Central Australian winter and spring. **Pine Creek** hosts a Didj festival on the first Sunday in May. The **Barunga Festival** is held around Katherine in early June, when Aboriginal communities get together to compete in sporting and cultural events. During the last weeks of August and early September, the **Festival of Darwin** enlivens the city with arts and cultural events. At the end of the August, Alice Springs hosts the bizarre **Henley-on-Todd regatta** in a dry riverbed. In **Western Australia**, most major events and festivals are held in and around Perth. The city's **International Arts Festival** includes local and international theatre, opera, dance, visual arts, film and music and is held every January-February.

Sport and special interest travel

If you're a real adrenaline junkie then Australia can offer quite a range of heart-stopping activities, most of them involving moving quickly over water, even faster over snow, slowly but precariously over or under rock, or with gut-wrenching inevitability through nothing but fresh air. One of the world's great adventure countries, Australia is well set up for, and can offer a tremendous range of activities. Many of the best Australian experiences are offered by specialist tour and hire operators, and if you have some specific goals it is essential to check out your options carefully in advance as the time of year and availability of spaces can make a big difference as to what is possible. *Wild Magazine* has a good website, **www.wild.com.au**, and publishes quite a few walking and adventure guides. The website **www.breakloose.com.au** enables you to search for tour and hire operators, by both state and type of activity. It's not comprehensive or qualitative, and tends to give telephone numbers instead of web links, but can be a good starting point.

Walking and trekking

See also 'Taking care
in the bush', page 35 A certain amount of walking is necessary to see many of the country's great natural sights, but Australia can also boast a great range of short, day and overnight walks, mostly in the many national parks. Surprisingly there are even long routes in the north of the country, such as the 50-km **Jatbula Trail** in Nitmiluk National Park and the 220-km **Larapinta Trail** in the West MacDonnell Ranges, though they should only be tackled in winter. WA has two long-distance tracks, also best during Autumn-Spring, the 960-km **Bibbulmun** from Perth to Albany that traverses the state's magnificent southern coasts and forests, and the 140-km **Cape-to-Cape** track from Dunsborough to Augusta. The other major 'hot country' route is SA's 1,500-km **Heysen Trail**, designed, like the Bibbulmun, to traverse some of best scenery the state has to offer.

Bush, mountain and coastal walking trails are most widespread in the south east of the country. Victoria has some superb tracks, both in the hill country of the **Grampians**, **Dandenongs** and the **Alps**, and along much of the coast. NSW/QLD also boasts extensive trails. In NSW the **Blue Mountains** and **Warrumbungle National Parks** are particularly recommended while in Queensland the 32km four day/three night **Thorsborne Trail** on Hinchinbrook Island between Townsville and Cairns is a classic (book well ahead). For many walkers, however, Australian trekking reaches its zenith in Tasmania where the **Overland Track**, from Cradle Mountain to Lake St Clair, has reached legendary status, and trails such as the **South West Track** and the **Bay of Fires** offer very different but exhilarating and challenging alternatives. **Bushwalking clubs** are a good source of local advice and often welcome visitors on their regular expeditions. For a comprehensive list of clubs see www.bushwalking.org.au The best series of books on walking in Australia has been penned by indefatigable walker **Tyrone T Thomas**. Find a listing, descriptions of a few key walks and some bush-walking tips on his website: **members.ozemail.com.au/~tyronet**

Many of Australia's natural ecologies are particularly sensitive to human activity and you should take care to disturb as little as possible and follow the adage 'take nothing but photographs, leave nothing but footprints'. All the state conservation authorities have a minimal impact bushwalking code, published on their websites and printed on the park notes for all the national parks. Most of the longer walks, and some even as short as two hours, have a walker registration system in place – essentially ensuring that if you get lost or injured someone will come looking. If there is no such system in place make sure someone (it can be the local park ranger or the police) knows where you are going and how long you plan to be.

Climbing, abseiling and canyoning

Although much of Australia is flat as a tack there are a few fabulous climbing spots, with most of the recognized routes in the eastern half of the country in the **Great Dividing Range**, but there are other great climbs. In Victoria, **Mount Buffalo** offers challenging granite climbs on tors, boulders and the long face of Mount Buffalo Gorge, while the **Grampians** and **Mount Arapiles** offer some of the best climbing in the country, an almost infinite number of sandstone routes at all levels. SA's Flinders Ranges has a fine site at **Moonarie**, on the edge of Wilpena Pound, and WA has a lot of incredibly ancient and rugged rock country, pioneered in the south by climbers in **Albany**, the **Cape-to-Cape** region and **Kalbarri**. The state that has the most to offer in a relatively compact area is Tasmania. Hobart's **Mount Wellington** and the Tasman Peninsula's **Totem Pole** have great climbs close to civilization, but there are also very challenging remote climbs on mountains such as **Federation Peak** and **Ben Lomond**. To find out more look out for *Climbing Australia: The Essential Guide* by Greg Pritchard or see www.climbing.com.au, which picks out the country's top sites and has a directory of climbing operators, many of whom offer abseiling as a one-day tour.

Canyoning is a sport almost exclusively restricted to the Great Dividing Ranges of NSW, and involves a combination of climbing, abseiling, wading and swimming through the canyons and gorges of the Blue Mountains and Manning Valley.

Horse riding

Horses were a major factor in the British colonial expansion from their early footholds, particularly in the south and east, and for a century or more were an essential requirement for pioneering pastoralists. On many stations they are still in active use, giving boundary riders the scope and range that vehicles still cannot yet muster. Off the stations recreational riding is hugely popular and private ownership considerable. In consequence the country has a great number of both horse-riding schools and station stays offering recreational rides, and you would be hard pressed to travel far in the more populated regions without finding one. Rides can be from 30 minutes to several days duration.

The great Australian image of the horse-riding cattleman was shaped by Banjo Paterson's electrifying poem, *The Man from Snowy River*, and it is indeed in the high country between Mansfield, in Victoria, and Canberra that the most awesome Australian horse riding can be experienced.

Cycling and mountain biking

Bicycles are commonly available for hire in cities and major towns, but facilities are scarce otherwise. Huge as the country is, cycling around it is a popular pastime and some states, notably Victoria with their Rail Trails, are actively promoting the activity. If you plan to do most of your touring on a bike you will need to either bring your own or buy in Australia, as long-term hire facilities are virtually non existent (there's a notable exception in Tasmania). One alternative is to join a cycle-based tour, such as those organized by *Remote Outback Cycles*, www.cycletours.com.au, in the western states or *Boomerang Bicycle Tours*, ozbike@ozemail.com.au, over east.

Wildlife and birdwatching

The unique Australian wildlife experience is one that goes far beyond the cuddling of koalas, feeding friendly kangaroos and coming face-to-face with a potato cod on the Great Barrier Reef. Almost everywhere you go wildlife surrounds you and can be observed; from huge bats in Sydney's Botanical Gardens to Tiger Quolls bottoms up in the dish washing tub of New England National Park. The concept that almost all of it, beyond the humble roo, is out to clamp its jaws, fangs or stinging tentacles in to you is greatly over exaggerated and certainly not helped with international Reality TV stars like the Crocodile Hunter. True there are many venomous and potentially dangerous creatures out there, but nothing a bit of common sense and respect won't protect you from. In summary, provided you retain an open mind as well as open eyes you will return home with an armoury of interesting memories, stories and photographs that will confirm the fact that Australia is one of the best places to encounter wildlife on the planet.

Fishing

One of Australia's favourite hobbies, fishing is in some areas the only recreational activity available to locals and is pursued with an almost religious obsession. As you head north surfboards begin to disappear from vehicle roof racks only to be replaced by the 'tinnies', short aluminium boats that allow the fishing family to go where they please.

Essentials

▶▶ **Tracking down wildlife**

Many of the following creatures, though widespread are not always easy to see. With patience sightings are virtually 'guaranteed' in their natural environment at the following places (tours and entry fees sometimes apply):
Dolphins Monkey Mia and Bunbury (WA), Port Phillip Bay (VIC), Tin Can Bay and Tangalooma Dolphin Resort on Moreton Island (QLD)
Dugong Hinchinbrook Island National Park (QLD)
Eagles and kites northern WA and the Top End of NT, NSW Outback especially along the Barrier Highway to Broken Hill
Echidnas Kangaroo Island (SA)
Fairy or Little penguins Penguin Island (WA), Kangaroo Island and Victor Harbor (SA), Melbourne and Phillip Island (VIC), Bruny Island, Bicheno and Stanley (TAS) and even occasionally in Sydney Harbour (NSW)
Flying Foxes Botanical Gardens, Sydney, Grafton and Bellingen (NSW), Cape Tribulation (QLD)
Kangaroos Murramarang and Sturt National Parks (NSW)
Koalas Kangaroo Island (SA), Great
Ocean Road and Raymond Island (VIC), Pilliga State Forest, Coonabarabran and Port Macquarie (NSW), Magnetic Island (QLD)
Platypus Burnie (TAS), Great Ocean Road (VIC), Bombala (NSW), Eungella National Park and Yungaburra, Atherton Tablelands (QLD)
Quokkas Rottnest Island (WA)
Saltwater Crocodiles Hinchinbrook, Daintree and Cape York (QLD)
Seals and sealions Leeman and Jurien Bay (WA), Kangaroo Island and Streaky Bay (SA), Cape Bridgewater, Phillip Island and Croajingalong (VIC), Montague Island, Narooma (NSW)
Tasmanian Devils Northwest coast of TAS
Turtles Coral Bay, Exmouth and Port Hedland (WA), Mons Repos, Bundaberg and Heron Island, Great Barrier Reef (QLD)
Whales Albany, Augusta and Dunsborough (WA), Head of Bight and Victor Harbour (SA), Warrnambool (VIC), Eden (NSW), Hervey Bay (QLD)
Wombats Wilson's Promontory (VIC), Narawntapu National Park (TAS), Thredbo River, Snowy Mountains (NSW)

Inland fishing, mostly for barramundi in the north and the feral trout in the south, requires a license in some states, though beach and sea fishing do not. Whatever the case tour operators and hire companies will usually organize that for you. Excellent off-shore sportsfishing is widely available as a day tour, usually for around $150-200. There are several excellent websites on recreational fishing in Australia, with location reports and details of tour operators and retailers, including **www.fishnet.com.au** and **www.sportsfishaustralia.com.au**

Surfing, windsurfing, kitesurfing and waterskiing

If an Aussie lives near the beach there's a fair bet they'll be a surfer; if they're inland and anywhere near water then waterskiing will probably be the go. This makes for a great many local clubs, tuition and equipment hire. Surfing is generally best in the southern half of the country with famous, and often jealously guarded spots in places as far flung as **Kalbarri** and **Margaret River** in WA, **Cactus Beach** near Ceduna in SA, **Bells Beach** in VIC and **Woollongong**, **Newcastle**, **Port Macquarie** and, of course, **Byron Bay** in NSW, and **Coolangatta**, **North Stradbroke Island**, **Maroochy** and **Noosa** in QLD. Windsurfing and kitesurfing are also widespread, though are arguably at their best in WA where windy west coast cities such as **Fremantle** and **Geraldton** draw enthusiasts from all over the world.

There are quite a few websites dedicated to surfing, one of Australia's national obsessions, including **www.surfinfo.com.au**, which links to a great many surfie retail and travel businesses, and **www.realsurf.com**, which has condition reports from all the major spots around the country. There's also a lot of information to be found at **www.windsurfing.org**, with club, holiday and tuition details on the state pages. Dedicated surfies will want to get hold of a copy of **Mark Warren's** *Atlas of Australian Surfing*.

Canoeing, kayaking and rafting

Australia may be the driest continent but there are actually quite a few opportunities for a river paddle, mostly around the north, east and south coasts and, most notably, in Tasmania. Canoeing down the **Ord River** in WA's Kimberley is one of the finest river experiences Australia has to offer, if very tranquil, and the **Katherine Gorge** is another top spot. The **Perth Hills** can generate a bit of white water in winter, though the rivers flowing down from the Victorian **High Country** and the **Snowy Mountains** of NSW are the chief mainland destinations for those after a rough and exciting ride. In Tassie the **Franklin River** is considered the apogee of the Australian canoeing and rafting experience, while sea-kayaking around the **Tasman Peninsula** is an altogether different though still awesome experience.

The Australian Canoeing website, **www.canoe.org.au**, concentrates on competitive canoeing, but some of the state links, such as Tasmania, have good river descriptions and links to commercial operators.

Diving

Australia is famous for the **Great Barrier Reef**, and for decades backpackers have made a beeline there to earn their diving spurs. Increasingly travellers are also heading for the west coast to learn to dive on the lesser known **Ningaloo Reef**, off Exmouth. These are by no means the only good diving areas around this immense coast, however, which can boast a wealth of diverse options from kelp forests and encrusted jetties to wrecks old and new, much of it in the more temperate southern regions.

The websites **www.diveoz.com.au** and **www.scubaaustralia.com.au**, both have some very useful general information as well as fairly comprehensive, though not qualitative, state-by-state directories including sites, dive centres and charter boats. **www.divedirectory.net** have details of several multi-day diving trips, including the Great Barrier Reef and looking for Great White sharks off SA (April-September). Travellers basing their trip on diving around the Australian coast should pick up a copy of *Diving Australia* by **Coleman and Marsh** to decide what sites will best suit them.

Golf

Almost every town in Australia has at least one golf course, even in the outback, though the feel of the greens may not be too familiar, and most welcome visitors. The very best courses are, unsurprisingly, close to Sydney, Melbourne and Brisbane, with high concentrations on the **Mornington Peninsula** and the **Sunshine** and **Gold Coasts**. The list of the top 50 public access courses to be found on the excellent and very comprehensive website **www.ausgolf.com.au**, features a lot in QLD, but for the last couple of years has ranked **Joondalup** in Perth (www.joondalupresort.com.au) and **The Dunes** in Rye, VIC (www.thedunes.com.au) as the top two.

Gliding, hang-gliding and microlighting

Gliding is particularly popular in inland towns, often bordering the wheatbelts, where there is a rich harvest of sunny days and strong thermals, most common in the south west of WA, along the Murray River in SA, and out on the broad plains of inland NSW. The gliding clubs in these areas, usually small and run by club members and volunteers, are excellent places to earn your gliding wings and a comprehensive list of them can be found at **www.gfa.org.au**, the website of the Gliding Federation of Australia, T03-9379 7411.

Hang-gliding, while still requiring thermals for extended flights, makes use of elevated areas for take-off and so is most popular in upland and elevated coastal areas. A few operators offer hang-gliding and paragliding lessons, and a very few simple one-off flights. Most of these are based on the central QLD coast, the northern NSW coast (particularly in **Byron Bay**), and the west coast and high country of VIC (notably in **Bright**), with a handful in the Adelaide and Perth Hills. You'll find a listing at **www.hgfa.asn.au**, the website of the Hang-gliding Federation of Australia, T02 6947 2888.

Flying in microlights, effectively hang-gliders with engines and wheels and also known as 'trikes', and ultralights, similar but more aeroplane-like, is a fast growing activity in Australia where weather and space make it an ideal sport, or simply a way of getting around. A few operators around the country offer scenic flights in two-seat versions, but if you're interested in getting more involved contact one of the local clubs listed at **members.ozemail.com.au/~aerial**

Parachuting and bungy jumping

Some people don't just want to get up in the air in some kind of aircraft but also want to fling themselves out of it once they're up there. Many of the several dozen skydiving clubs in Australia offer short, usually one-day courses in parachuting (also known as 'skydiving'), including a jump or two, and some cut out much of the training by organizing tandem jumps where you're strapped, facing forward, to the chest of the instructor. If a quick thrill is all you're after then the latter is the better option as it usually involves 30-60 seconds of freefall, by far the most exhilarating part of the experience, and costs around $250-300. A list of skydiving clubs affiliated to the Australian Parachute Federation, T02-6281 6830, can be found at **www.apf.asn.au**

If you fancy jumping out into thin air without a parachute then bungy jumping, essentially leaping off a platform with an elastic rope tied around your ankles, is just about the safest option going. A J Hackett first brought the sport to the world's attention over a decade ago, but the thrill has yet to pall. Hackett, **www.ajhackett.com.au**, still operates the original Aussie jump in Cairns, but there are now also opportunities to make the big leap at several spots on the southern QLD coast, plus in Sydney, Melbourne and Perth. A list of them can be found at **www.bungee-experience.com**

Skiing and snowboarding

Yes it does get cold enough, and sometimes even snows enough in Australia to ski and snowboard, but only in a few places in the **Victorian Alps**, just over the border in the **Snowy Mountains** of NSW, and at **Ben Lomond** in Tasmania. The season is short (around June-September at best) and the slopes are not considered world-class, but that's not to say that there aren't some decent runs, particularly in the top 'Alpine' resorts, and a lot of fun is had by around a million snow-loving Aussies every year. Check out the comprehensive website **www.ski.com.au**, for current conditions and travel deals.

For most, the concept of snow and skiing anywhere in Australia-a continent best known for its heat and surfing- is something of a surprise if not a complete novelty. But snow it does especially on the 'Roof of Australia'-the Snowy Mountains at the southern terminus of the Great Dividing Range in NSW-where the skiing resorts of **Thredbo**, **Perisher** and **Mount Selwyn** attract thousands in increasing numbers every year, between the months of June and September. If you do go, Thredbo and Perisher in particular will reveal excellent facilities and skiing and, if nothing else, provide the opportunity to built a snowman or had a snowball fight in one of the most arid continents on earth. Details for all resorts and facilities can be found in the Snowy Mountains section, in the NSW chapter. With many mountains pushing 2,000 m the **Victorian High Country** gets a dependable snow covering for a couple of months each year between mid-June and September. Several ski and snow resorts take advantage of this. Mount Stirling, Dinner Plain and Lake Mountain have little downhill excitement except toboggan runs, but are all good destinations for the dedicated cross-country skier, particularly the latter. There are learner slopes at the three major resorts but beginners can get away with paying a bit less by heading for **Mount Baw Baw** or **Mount Buffalo**, though a relatively low altitude at both means a tighter window of opportunity. Intermediates will find **Falls Creek** has the greatest variety of runs and it also has the best snow-making facilities, making it a good bet if the natural stuff is thin on the ground. Its proximity to the **Bogong High Plains** makes it another top spot for cross-country. The most challenging runs are at **Mount Hotham** with its difficult steep slopes and powder, and this resort also has its own airport, making it a good package destination from Melbourne or Sydney. The best all-round resort is **Mount Buller**, with the quickest road access from Melbourne, best day-visitor facilities as well as good 'après', and a large range of runs for all abilities. For all resorts book accommodation well in advance for the ski season. Weekends and the July school holidays are the busiest periods.

Spectator sport

It's enough to make an Englishman spit. Any sport Australia takes seriously it does well at. This supremacy makes for a glorious opportunity for visitors to Australia. If you choose to be a spectator at a sport the Aussies really get into, then you're in for a treat: world-class competition at relatively low prices.

This is the classic down-under game, to the casual observer a free-for-all that defies the gods in causing as few broken necks as it does. A derivative of the rough football that was being played in Britain and Ireland in the late 1700s it shares some affinities with Gaelic Football, and indeed Ireland and Australia do meet to contest an 'international rules' cup.

Australian rules football
Also called 'Aussie rules' or just plain 'footy'

As with rugby and soccer, it's a winter game, with most leagues playing between March and September. The game is contested on a huge oval pitch, up to 200 m long, between two teams of 18 players each. At each end of the pitch four high posts denote the goal-mouth, and it is through these that the teams attempt to get the oval-shaped ball. If the ball goes directly between the central two posts a *goal* is scored and six points awarded, if it goes between one of the central posts and an outer post, or is touched by the defending team on the way then a *behind* is scored and a single point awarded. Players may kick or *hand pass* the ball in any direction, but not throw it. To hand pass is to punch the ball from the palm of one hand with the clenched fist of the other. If the ball is kicked over 10 m and cleanly caught then the catcher can call a *mark*. He can't be tackled and has time to kick the ball toward goal or a team-mate unmolested. The game is split into four quarters, each lasting 25 minutes. Scoring is usually regular, and winning teams with an excess of 100 points are not unusual.

The national league, the *AFL*, www.afl.com.au, is followed most closely, in fact obsessively, though there are enthusiastic state and local amateur leagues right around the country. Most of the clubs are in and around Melbourne, where the game was invented, but the national league also has top-flight teams from Adelaide, Brisbane, Perth and Sydney. The most exciting place to see an AFL match is at one of the country's great stadiums such as the *MCG* in Melbourne, *Subiaco Oval* in Perth or the *Gabba* in Brisbane. After a series of round-robin and knock-out rounds the season culminates in the AFL Grand Final, always held at the MCG in September. A good way of getting into the spirit of the game is by watching Channel 9's mad-cap *Footy Show*.

Rugby League & Union
The website www.rugby.com.au, is a guide to Australian League and Union codes

If Victoria is the bastion of AFL, then the big game on the eastern seaboard is **Rugby League**. The main league is the **NRL**, www.nrl.com.au, and like the AFL the season's Grand Final is in September. New South Wales and Queensland select teams to play 'state of origin' crunch matches every year and a full Australian side (the *Kangaroos*) is also regularly put together for international matches and tours. Needless to say, Australia is extremely good and can often claim to be the best in the world.

Rugby Union traditionally had much less of a grass roots following until the national side, the *Wallabies*, won the Rugby World Cup in 1991. In the decade since they can claim to have always rated in the world's top five teams, and frequently vie with arch rivals, the New Zealand *All Blacks*, for status as world's best. Aside from the World Cup (which they won in 1999) and regular international tours, the Wallabies compete in an annual three-way competition (the '**Tri Nations**') against South Africa and New Zealand. The winners of the Aussie vs Kiwi games gain possession of the much-prized **Bledisloe Cup**, which has been contested by the two countries since 1931.

Cricket
For round-ups on Australian and international news see www.cricket.org

Once the Footy seasons ends around September a large number of minds switch to cricket, just another major international team sport at which Australians just happen to be, more-or-less, better than anyone else. If you're a fan of the sport then we hardly need tell you this, or that the Melbourne Cricket Club ('MCG') is the spiritual home of the sport in Australia. Their website, www.mcg.org.au, is a very good place to catch up on what's going on in Australian cricket. The national side is involved in an annual series against England (the Ashes) plus a few series against some of the major cricketing countries.

Horse racing
One of the best and well-maintained independent racing websites is www.racing australia.net

Australians are mad about the gee-gees. There are horse racing or *pacing* (horse and trap) tracks all over the country, in all but the tiniest towns, and there are usually a dozen or so meetings every day, and dozens of races to satisfy the most dedicated of punters. Most of the country's betting is via the state *TAB*s, a pooling system similar to the UK's *Tote*. There are some high street TABs, but most can be found in the public bars of the nation's pubs. The country's most prestigious meeting is the **Spring Carnival** in Melbourne in November. Held at a couple of courses the big race is the **Melbourne Cup** at Flemington, a race that is held in serious regard in the international calendar.

Motor sport
For round-ups on Australian and international news see www.motorsm.com/ oz_motoring

Australian motor sport's Mecca is Bathurst, home of the *Bathurst 1000* every October, an all-afternoon effort to be the first to cover the hallowed 1,000 km, a sort of Australian *Le Mans*. The major domestic series is the *Super V8 Supercars*, a touring car championship held at various tracks between March-December. Featuring strongly on the international scene, Melbourne hosts the first *Formula 1 Grand Prix* of the season in early March, and major motorbike fixtures are held on nearby Phillip Island.

Netball & basketball
Australia's biggest participant sport is netball. The big national competition is the *Commonwealth Bank Trophy*, which is competed for by city and town-based teams between April-August. The website for Australian netball is www.netball.asn.au

As eagerly watched, though with far humbler expectations on the international scale is basketball. The *National Basketball League* title, www.nbl.com, is competed for between October-March, and the *Women's National Basketball League*, home.vicnet.net.au/~wnbl, between November-March.

Swimming

It doesn't seem fair. Australia doesn't just have one or two international standard swimmers, they have a small poolful. Ian Thorpe (the 'Thorpedo', size 16 feet), Grant Hackett and Michael Klim are all giants on the international scene, often only having each other for serious competition. For this the reason the Australian National Championships are the best domestic competition in the world to go and see. They're held in March, see www.ausswim.telstra.com.au, for details.

Tennis
For round-ups on tennis news see www.tennis australia.com.au

Unlike their swimmers Australia has for a long time had to depend on just one or two brilliant players to keep the male flag flying, and the women's game is surprisingly weak. The boys have got their timing down to a tee: just as Pat Rafter finds he may have to hang up his racquet, along comes Leyton Hewitt, possibly the most exciting player on the international circuit since John McEnroe. Australia hosts one of the world's four Grand Slam competitions, the *Australian Open*, www.ausopen.org, in January. By now you'll have guessed that it's held in Melbourne.

Health

Australia is known as the 'lucky country' and in health terms it is. There are few nasty diseases and the health care facilities are of a very high standard.

Australia has a national, government funded health care scheme called *Medicare*. This, together with the supporting private network, is reckoned to be one of the best health care systems in the world, so you can rest easy with the thought that if you suffer an unexpected accident or illness you should be well looked after. Public hospitals are part of Medicare, a large number of pharmaceutical products are funded or subsidized by the scheme, and most doctors are registered so that their services can also be funded or subsidized by the scheme. Doctors who invoice Medicare directly, so charging the patient nothing on examination, are said to bulk bill. Those that don't bulk bill charge the patient who then has to reclaim the charge from Medicare. Large cities usually have clinics where you can walk in without an appointment. The *Travellers Medical and Vaccination Centre* ('TMVC' or 'The Travel Doctor') operates several clinics around the country.

Australia has reciprocal arrangements with a handful of countries which allow citizens of those countries to receive free 'immediately necessary medical treatment' under the Medicare scheme. The arrangements with New Zealand and the Republic of Ireland provide visitors to Australia with free care as a public patient in public hospitals and subsidized medicines under the Pharmaceutical Benefits Scheme. In addition to these benefits, visitors from Finland, Italy, Malta, the Netherlands, Sweden and the UK also enjoy subsidized out-of-hospital treatment (ie visiting a doctor). Most visitors under the arrangement are covered for their entire stay. Visitors from Malta and Italy, however, are covered for a maximum of six months. If you qualify under the reciprocal arrangement, contact your own national health scheme to check what documents you will require in Australia to claim Medicare. All visitors to Australia are, however, strongly advised to take out medical insurance for the duration of their visit. You do not need to pre-register with Medicare to be entitled to the benefits, but can register on your first visit to a doctor or hospital. Charges can be reclaimed either via the post or in person at a Medicare office, which can be found in all major towns and cities.

Essentials

Essentials

▶▶ Useful health organizations and websites

World Health Organization,
www.who.ch and www.who.int
Australia Travellers Medical and
Vaccination Centre, T02-9221 7133
(Sydney), www.tmvc.com.au and

www.traveldoctor.com.au
UK Medical Advisory Services for
Travellers, T0207 6314408, www.masta.org
USA US Centers for Disease Control &
Prevention, T888 232 3228, www.cdc.gov

There are two main threats to health in Australia. One is global warming, and with that the spread of more tropical diseases such as Dengue Fever. The second are the ever present, poisonous snakes and spiders. Check loo seats, boots and the area around you if you're a visiting the bush.

Before you go

Ideally, you should see your GP or travel clinic at least six weeks before your departure for general advice on travel risks, malaria and vaccinations. Make sure you have travel insurance, get a dental check (especially if you are going to be away for more than a month), know your own blood group and, if you suffer a long-term condition such as diabetes or epilepsy, make sure someone knows or that you have a Medic Alert bracelet/necklace with this information on it.

Items to take with you
For longer trips involving jungle treks taking a clean needle pack, clean dental pack and water filtration devices are common-sense measures

Mosquito repellents may be useful in sub-tropical areas such as Darwin. Remember that DEET (Di-ethyltoluamide) is the gold standard. Apply the repellent every 4-6 hours but more often if you are sweating heavily. If a non-DEET product is used check who tested it. Validated products (tested at the London School of Hygiene and Tropical Medicine) include Mosiguard, Non-DEET Jungle formula and non-DEET Autan. If you want to use citronella remember that it must be applied very frequently (ie hourly) to be effective. If you are a popular target for insect bites or develop lumps quite soon after being bitten, carry an Aspivenin kit. This syringe suction device is available from many chemists and draws out some of the allergic materials and provides quick relief.

Sun Block The Australians have a great campaign, which has reduced skin cancer. It is called Slip, Slap, Slop. Slip on a shirt, Slap on a hat, Slop on sun screen. **Pain killers** Paracetomol or a suitable painkiller can have multiple uses for symptoms but remember that more than eight paracetmol a day can lead to liver failure. **Ciproxin (Ciprofloaxcin)** A useful antibiotic for some forms of travellers diarrhoea (see below). **Immodium** A standby for those diarrhoeas that occur at awkward times (ie before a long coach/train journey or on a trek). It helps stop the flow of diarrhoea and is of more benefit than harm. **Pepto-Bismol** Used a lot by Americans for diarrhoea. It certainly relieves symptoms but like Immodium it is not a cure for underlying disease. Be aware that it turns the stool black as well as making it more solid. **MedicAlert** These simple bracelets, or an equivalent, should be carried or worn by anyone with a significant medical condition.

Diarrhoea & intestinal upset
These are less likely to occur in Australia compared to travel in Asia

Symptoms Diarrhoea can refer either to loose stools or an increased frequency; both of these can be a nuisance. It should be short lasting but persistence beyond two weeks, with blood or pain, require specialist medical attention. **Cures** Ciproxin (Ciprofloaxcin) is a useful antibiotic for bacterial traveller's diarrhoea. It can be obtained by private prescription in the UK which is expensive, or bought over the counter in Australian pharmacies. You need to take one 500 mg tablet when the diarrhoea starts and if you do not feel better in 24 hours, the diarrhoea is likely to have a non-bacterial cause and may be viral (in which case there is little you can do apart from keep yourself

Vaccinations

◀◀

Vaccination	Obligatory	Recommended
Polio	Yes	If nil in last 10 years
Tetanus	Yes	If nil in last 10 years (but after 5 doses you have had enough for life)
Hepatitis A		The disease can be caught easily from food/water
Typhoid	Not necessary for Australia	Yes if nil in last 3 years but will be required if travelling through Southeast Asia on your way back home
Japanese Encephalitis	Not required for Australia but see note above regarding Southeast Asia	

Yellow Fever does not exist in Australia. However, the authorities may wish to see a certificate if you have recently arrived form an endemic area in Africa or South America. Officially, Australia has no *rabies* but there is a very similar virus called Lyssa virus and the vaccine protects against it

rehydrated and wait for it to settle on its own). The key treatment with all diarrhoeas is rehydration. Try to keep hydrated by taking the right mixture of salt and water. This is available as Oral Rehydration Salts (ORS) in ready-made sachets or can be made up by adding a teaspoon of sugar and a half teaspoon of salt to a litre of clean water. Drink at least one large cup of this drink for each loose stool. You can also use flat carbonated drinks as an alternative. Immodium and Pepto- Bismol provide symptomatic relief. **Prevention** The standard advice is to be careful with water and ice for drinking. Ask yourself where the water came from. If you have any doubts then boil it or filter and treat it. There are many filter/treatment devices now available on the market. Food can also transmit disease. Be wary of salads (what were they washed in, who handled them), re-heated foods or food that has been left out in the sun having been cooked earlier in the day. There is a simple adage that says wash it, peel it, boil it or forget it. Also be wary of unpasteurized dairy products, these can transmit a range of diseases from brucellosis (fevers and constipation), to listeria (meningitis) and tuberculosis of the gut (obstruction, constipation, fevers and weight loss).

Underwater health

Symptoms If you go diving make sure that you are fit do so. The **British Scuba Association** (BSAC), Telford's Quay, South Pier Road, Ellesmere Port, Cheshire CH65 4FL, United Kingdom, T01513-506200, F01513-506215, www.bsac.com, can put you in touch with doctors who do medical examinations. Protect your feet from cuts, beach dog parasites (larva migrans) and sea urchins. The latter are almost impossible to remove but can be dissolved with lime or vinegar. Keep an eye out for secondary infection. **Cures** Antibiotics for secondary infections. Serious diving injuries may need time in a decompression chamber. **Prevention** Check that the dive company know what they are doing, have appropriate certification from BSAC or Professional Association of Diving Instructors (PADI), Unit 7, St Philips Central, Albert Road, St Philips, Bristol, BS2 0TD, T0117-3007234, www.padi.com, and that the equipment is well maintained.

Sun protection

Symptoms White Britons are notorious for becoming red in hot countries because they like to stay out longer than everyone else and do not use adequate sun protection. This can lead to sunburn, which is painful and followed by flaking of skin. Aloe

Essentials

Essentials

vera gel is a good pain reliever for sunburn. Long-term sun damage leads to a loss of elasticity of skin and the development of pre-cancerous lesions. Many years later a mild or a very malignant form of cancer may develop. The milder basal cell carcinoma, if detected early, can be treated by cutting it out or freezing it. The much nastier malignant melanoma may have already spread to bone and brain at the time that it is first noticed. **Prevention** Sun screen. SPF stands for Sun Protection Factor. It is measured by determining how long a given person takes to "burn" with and without the sunscreen product on. So, if it takes 10 times longer to burn with the sunscreen product applied, then that product has an SPF of 10. If it only takes twice as long then the SPF is 2. The higher the SPF the greater the protection. However, do not just use higher factors just to stay out in the sun longer. 'Flash frying' (desperate bursts of excessive exposure), as it is called, is known to increase the risks of skin cancer. Follow the Australians' with their Slip, Slap, Slop campaign.

Dengue fever   **Symptoms** This disease can be contracted throughout Australia. In travellers this can cause a severe 'flu-like illness which includes symptoms of fever, lethargy, enlarged lymph glands and muscle pains. It starts suddenly, lasts for 2-3 days, seems to get better for 2-3 days and then kicks in again for another 2-3 days. It is usually all over in an unpleasant week. The local children are prone to the much nastier haemorrhagic form of the disease, which causes them to bleed from internal organs, mucous membranes and often leads to their death. **Cures** The traveller's version of the disease is self limiting and forces rest and recuperation on the sufferer. **Prevention** The mosquitoes that carry the Dengue virus bite during the day unlike the malaria mosquitoes. Which sadly means that repellent application and covered limbs are a 24 hour issue. Check your accommodation for flower pots and shallow pools of water since these are where the dengue-carrying mosquitoes breed.

Hepatitis   **Symptoms** Hepatitis means inflammation of the liver. Viral causes of the disease can be acquired anywhere in Australia. The most obvious symptom is a yellowing of your skin or the whites of your eyes. However, prior to this all that you may notice is itching and tiredness. **Cures** Early on, depending on the type of hepatitis, a vaccine or immunoglobulin may reduce the duration of the illness. **Prevention** Pre-travel hepatitis A vaccine is the best bet. Hepatitis B (for which there is a vaccine) is spread through blood and unprotected sexual intercourse, both of these can be avoided. Unfortunately there is no vaccine for hepatitis C or the increasing alphabetical list of other Hepatitis viruses.

Tuberculosis   Australia has the fourth lowest level in the world for this disease and is well protected by health screens before people can settle there. The bus driver coughing as he takes your fare could expose you to the mycobacterium. **Symptoms** Cough, tiredness, fever and lethargy. **Cures** At least 6 months treatment with a combination of drugs is required. **Prevention** Have a BCG vaccination before you go and see a doctor early if you have a persistent cough, cough blood, fever or unexplained weight loss.

Snakes & other poisonous things   A bite itself does not mean that anything has been injected in to you. However, a commonsense approach is to clean the area of the bite (never have it sutured early on) and get someone to take you to a medical facility fast. It is better to be taken because the more energy you expand the faster poisons spread around the body. Do not try to catch the snake or spider. You will only get more bites and faster spread of poison for your troubles. For some snake bites a knowledgeable first aider can provide appropriate bandaging and if a poison is on-board specialist anti-venoms will be administered by an experienced doctor.

Sex is part of travel and many see it as adding spice to a good trip but spices can sometimes be unpalatable. Think about the sexual souvenirs any potential new partner may have picked up or live with. The range of visible and invisible diseases is awesome. Unprotected sex can spread HIV, Hepatitis B and C, Gonorrhea (green discharge), chlamydia (nothing to see but may cause painful urination and later female infertility), painful recurrent herpes, syphilis and warts, just to name a few. You can cut down the risk by using condoms, a femidom or avoiding sex altogether. Commercial sex workers in Australia have high levels of HIV. If you do stray, consider getting a sexual health check on your return home, since these diseases are not the sort of gift people thank you for.

Further information

Essentials

Foreign and Commonwealth Office (FCO) (UK), www.fco.gov.uk This is a key travel advice site, with useful information on the country, people, climate and lists the UK embassies/consulates. The site also promotes the concept of 'Know Before You Go'. And encourages travel insurance and appropriate travel health advice. It has links to the Department of Health travel advice site, see below.

Department of Health Travel Advice (UK) www.doh.gov.uk/traveladvice This excellent site is also available as a free booklet, the T6, from Post Offices. It lists the vaccine advice requirements for each country.

Medic Alert (UK), www.medicalalert.co.uk This is the website of the foundation that produces bracelets and necklaces for those with existing medical problems. Once you have ordered your bracelet/necklace you write your key medical details on paper inside it, so that if you collapse, a medical person can identify you as someone with epilepsy or allergy to peanuts etc.

Blood Care Foundation (UK), www.bloodcare.org.uk The Blood Care Foundation is a Kent-based charity "dedicated to the provision of screened blood and resuscitation fluids in countries where these are not readily available." They will dispatch certified non-infected blood of the right type to your hospital/clinic. The blood is flown in from various centres around the world.

Public Health Laboratory Service (UK) www.phls.org.uk This site has up-to-date malaria advice guidelines for travel around the world. It gives specific advice about the right drugs for each location. It also has useful information for those who are pregnant, suffering from epilepsy or planning to travel with children.

Centers for Disease Control and Prevention (USA) www.cdc.gov This site from the US Government gives excellent advice on travel health, has useful disease maps and details of disease outbreaks.

World Health Organization www.who.int The WHO site has links to the WHO Blue Book (it was Yellow up to last year) on travel advice. This lists the diseases in different regions of the world. It describes vaccination schedules and makes clear which countries have Yellow Fever Vaccination certificate requirements and malarial risk.

Tropical Medicine Bureau (Ireland) www.tmb.ie This Irish-based site has a good collection of general travel health information and disease risks.

Fit for Travel (UK) www.fitfortravel.scot.nhs.uk This site from Scotland provides a quick A-Z of vaccine and travel health advice requirements for each country.

British Travel Health Association (UK) www.btha.org This is the official website of an organization of travel health professionals.

NetDoctor (UK) www.Netdoctor.co.uk This general health advice site has a useful section on travel and has an "ask the expert", interactive chat forum.

Travel Screening Services (UK) www.travelscreening.co.uk This is the author's website. A private clinic dedicated to integrated travel health. The clinic gives vaccine, travel health advice, email and SMS text vaccine reminders and screens returned travellers for tropical diseases.

Books *The Travellers Good Health Guide* by **Dr Ted Lankester** by ISBN 0-85969-827-0. *Expedition Medicine* (The Royal Geographic Society) Editors **David Warrell and Sarah Anderson** ISBN 1 86197 040-4. *International Travel and Health World Health Organization Geneva* ISBN 92 4 158026 7. *The World's Most Dangerous Places* by **Robert Young Pelton, Coskun Aral and Wink Dulles** ISBN 1-566952-140-9.

Leaflets *The Travellers Guide to Health* (T6) can be obtained by calling the *Health Literature Line* on T0800 555 777. Advice for travellers on avoiding the risks of HIV and AIDS (Travel Safe) available from **Department of Health**, PO Box 777, London SE1 6XH. The Blood Care Foundation order form PO Box 7, Sevenoaks, Kent TN13 2SZ T44-(0)1732-742427.

New South Wales

From the outback landscapes of Broken Hill to the surf of Sydney's Bondi Beach; the 'Premier State', as New South Wales is dubbed, is the most visited, populous and historically significant in Australia. Ever since that day in 1778, when the First Fleet sailed into Jackson Bay, Sydney, the fate of the city, the state and the entire nation was sealed. Since then **Sydney** has grown to become a truly world-class city boasting two of the nation's greatest icons – the Opera House and Harbour Bridge. North and south of Sydney, the New South Wales coastline stretches 1000 km from Ben Boyd National Park to Tweed Heads and provides an endless chain of magnificent beaches and scenic headlands. To the north is a series of happening towns like Nelson Bay, Port Macquarie and – most famous of all – the surfing Mecca of **Byron Bay**, while to the south the lesser known, but no less attractive coastal towns of Jervis Bay, Batemans Bay and Narooma act as the gateway to the greatest concentration of national parks in the state. Inland are the vineyards of the **Hunter Valley**, and beyond the Great Divide, the outback takes over, its vast emptiness interrupted only by the occasional interminable road to fascinating outposts like **Broken Hill**.

There are over 580 national parks and nature reserves in NSW all containing their own particular attractions, from the tame, surf loving kangaroos of **Murramarang** to 40,000 year-old Aboriginal skeletons in **Mungo National Park**. New South Wales also has its fair share of bizarre, man-made 'big things' to add to that great Australian Inventory, including the 'Big Guitar' in Tamworth, the 'Big Banana' in Coffs Harbour and the 'Big Merino' in Goulburn.

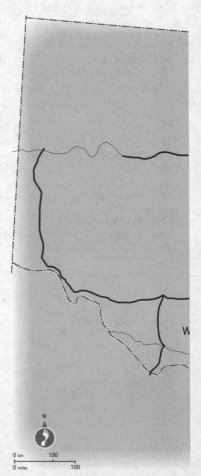

N

0 km   100
0 miles   100

Things to do in New South Wales

1 Book a balcony seat at the world famous *Doyle's Seafood Restaurant* in Watson's Bay, Sydney, then book another balcony seat at the **Opera House.**
2 Spend a weekend at a world-class B&B, wine tasting in the **Hunter Valley.**
3 Try fossicking for opals in the outback mining town of **Lightning Ridge** or stay at an underground motel in **White Cliffs.**
4 Ride that wave off the beach at **Cape Byron**, or watch wild dolphins instead.
5 Roll up, roll up…at the annual Cannabis Festival in **Nimbin.**

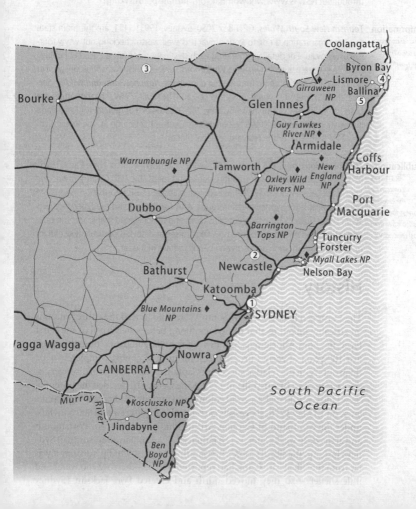

Ins and outs

Getting there & around
Note the line gauge differs to that of Queensland so between the two (NSW Countrylink) provide coach connections to Brisbane for onward travel

The entire state is well served by air, coach and rail services. *QantasLink*, T131313, www.qantas.com.au, in conjunction with *Hazelton*, T131713, www.hazelton.com.au, and *Virgin Blue*, T136789, www.virginblue.com.au, are the principal **air** carriers. *Kendell Airlines*, T131300, also offer services from Adelaide to Broken Hill. All are listed under the relevant destinations. *McCafferty's/Greyhound*, T132030, and *Premier Motor Service*, T131410, www.premierms.com.au, are the main long distance, interstate **coach** services, but there are many other smaller regional service providers. Most are listed under the relevant destinations. *Countrylink*, T132232, www.countrylink.nsw.gov.au, offer **rail** and rail/coach services state-wide. The main *Countrylink Travel Centre* in Sydney is located at the Central Railway Station, Eddy Av, T9955 4237. *Great Southern Rail*, T132147, www.gsr.com.au, operate services from Sydney to Perth ('Indian Pacific') via Broken Hill and Adelaide and Sydney to Alice Springs ('The Ghan') via Melbourne and Adelaide. *Countrylink* operate the 'XPT' (11 hrs, twice daily, 1 overnight) between Sydney and Melbourne and a continued northbound service from Sydney to Brisbane. A useful website for general travel throughout NSW is www.webwombat.com.au/transport/nsw.htm

Information
Regional and parks offices are all listed in the travelling text

Tourism New South Wales, GPO Box 7050, Sydney, T9931 1111, are the main state tourism organization. Prior to your arrival it is well worth checking out www.tourism.nsw.gov.au For detail surrounding each destination consult the Fairfax Publications sponsored travel website *Walkabout*, www.walkabout.fairfax.com.au For National Parks and camping information consult the *National Parks and Wildlife Service* (NPWS) website, www.npws.nsw.gov.au The main QPWS headquarters are based at 43 Bridge St, Hurstville, Sydney, T02-9585 6444. For general National Parks Information contact the NPWS National Parks Centre, 102 George St, The Rocks, Sydney, T1300-361967, or the relevant regional offices.

Publications & maps
Look out for the excellent Cartoscope maps, available free from most regional VICs

The Travel Bookshop, 175 Liverpool St, Sydney (southern edge of Hyde Park), T9261 8200, is a good source of information, books and maps. The *UBD Country Towns and Street Directory: New South Wales* has excellent maps and basic information. A separate book is available for Sydney and surrounds. *AAA Tourism* publish the *Experience New South Wales Guide* ($16) which contains town and regional road maps, accommodation listings and brief descriptions on things to see and do. It is particularly useful for motor parks information and is always handy to have in the car.

History

The European history of New South Wales and indeed the entire nation is inextricably linked to that of Sydney. Long before the arrival of the 'First Fleet' the Eora Aboriginals had thrived for many millenia, though it took just 100 years of early European colonization to almost completely wipe them out. With the relative success of Captain Cook's voyage of discovery of the eastern coast of Australia in 1770, King George III decided the potential 'new lands' would make a good colony, and initially an ideal jail. Eight years later, on 13 May 1778, six vessels carrying about 300 crew and 800 convicts, under the command of Captain Arthur Phillip, set sail from Portsmouth and arrived, 36 weeks later, on 18 January 1779, at Botany Bay, south of Sydney Harbour, the site of Cook's first landing. Much to Phillip's dismay it was far from the 'ideal' site Cook had reported it to be – there was no water and little shelter – so they moved north and entered Port Jackson (Sydney

Harbour) named in 1770 by Cook. Finding it eminently more suitable, Phillip named it Sydney Cove after British Secretary of State Viscount Sydney and Phillips himself was quickly sworn in as the first Governor of the newly proclaimed state of New South Wales.

Initial attempts at settlement proved disastrous, since the crew were ill prepared, poorly supplied and unskilled in utilizing local resources. The hopeless new penal colony struggled on trying unsuccessfully to grow crops and teetering on the brink of starvation until 1790 when the discovery of more favourable soils further up the harbour at Parramatta turned despair to hope. For the next two decades Sydney and its surrounds developed and grew with the arrival of more convicts and the parole of others. With the departure of the weary new governor, power hungry soldiers (known as the New South Wales Corps) left in charge of the convicts took advantage of the administrative vacuum and the sheer distance from the homeland, by granting each other rights to secure tracts of land and use convict labour for its development.

In the absence of money rum became the currency of choice, earning the new 'mafia' the nickname, the 'Rum Corps'. England's first attempt to restore official order in the form of Captain Bligh (from *'Mutiny of the Bounty'* fame) failed and it took the new governor Lachlan Macquarie to restore order to a colony he described as adhering to a system of 'infantile imbecility'. A great planner and a fair man, Macquarie was instrumental in the transformation of the established colony from an insignificant port built on the base of local exploitation to a progressive society earning international recognition. By the mid-1800s new farms and settlements dotted the region and explorers Lawson, Blaxland and Wentworth had found a way through the seemingly impenetrable Blue Mountains, opening up the west of the state to agriculture and settlement. In 1840 the transportation of convicts (many of whom had by now been relocated from Sydney to Port Macquarie) to New South Wales was finally abolished.

The discovery of gold near Bathurst west of the Blue Mountains in the 1850s, and mineral finds in Broken Hill, dramatically increased the population of the state and almost doubled that of Sydney to around 370,000 by 1890. It was not all progressive and positive however, with the inevitable inequalities in wealth creating a whole range of social problems from rampant disease and deprivation to widespread alcoholism and crime. The problems of racial disharmony and the continued annihilation of the Aboriginals and their culture also remained a major problem throughout the state and the developing nation as a whole.

With the creation of the Commonwealth of Australia in 1901 and a new capital – Canberra – in 1927, Sydney and New South Wales took a back seat in the affairs of the nation. Two world wars came and went and immigration increased rapidly. Sydney in particular was becoming a truly cosmopolitan city proud of its lifestyle, helped by two of Australia's most famous icons – the Sydney Harbour Bridge, completed in 1932, and the Opera House, in 1973. Slowly, Sydney, was becoming one of the best loved and most dynamic cities in the world. With massive amounts of money being spent on the city in preparations to stage the 2000 Olympics and their subsequent and undeniable success, the image of the city, the state and the nation was further enhanced.

New South Wales

Sydney

Phone code 02
Colour map 3, grid C4
Population: 4 million
875 km from
Melbourne
292 km from Canberra
1,154 km from
Broken Hill
984 km from
Brisbane
2,685 km from
Cairns

Many adjectives and superlatives have been used to describe Sydney, but the feeling produced on seeing this city for the first time go beyond mere words. Seasoned travellers often complain that the world's great cities can seem a trifle disappointing and their icons can seem smaller in reality than the imagination. But not so Sydney. That first sighting of its majestic harbour from Circular Quay, with the grand Opera House on one side and the mighty Harbour Bridge on the other, is one that always exceeds expectations. Aussie writer and TV personality Clive James aptly described it as looking 'like crushed diamonds'. The 2000 Olympics only added to the city's growing reputation. Vast amounts of money were spent on inner-city rejuvenation, transportation and state-of-the-art sports venues, all of which provided the infrastructure and the stage for what many agree were the best games yet. Afterwards, things just went back to normal in a city whose inhabitants know that their lifestyle is one of the best in the world. Sydney is absolutely world-class and has a whole lot to offer the tourist. With such remarkable and instantly recognizable icons, so many fascinating museums and art galleries, top-class restaurants and beaches, world renowned festivals and cultural events, 24-hour entertainment and a whole host of exciting activities, the list just goes on and on.

Ins and outs

Getting there
Information and flight arrivals/departures, T9667 6065, www.sydney airport.com.au Due to the US terrorist attacks the locker service at Sydney Airport International Terminal is currently unavailable

Air Sydney's **Kingsford Smith Airport** is 9 km south of the city centre. Given a major overhaul for the 2000 Olympic Games its negotiation is pretty straightforward and the facilities are excellent. There is a **Tourism New South Wales information desk** in the main arrivals concourse where help is at hand to organize transport and accommodation bookings, flight arrival information and airport facilities, T9667 6065, www.sydneyairport.com Additionally, The Sydney Airport **Help Desk** is in the centre of the terminal (Departures). Volunteer **Airport Ambassadors** identified by gold jackets are also on hand to answer any questions. Other airport facilities include ATM's, *Thomas Cook* and *Travelex Foreign Exchange*, car hire, a post office and even a medical centre. The Airport is open from 0400-2300 daily. The **Domestic Terminal** a short distance west of the International Terminal has also been fully modernized and is serviced by *Airport Express* (No 300 or 350) readily and regularly available outside both terminals. Check the eligibility for *Qantas Seamless Transfer Service* with your airline. You may also book a bus with various operators including *Kingsford Smith Transport*, T02-9666 9988 for just $3. The *Airport Link Rail*, with stations in the domestic and international terminals, is another way to move around within the airport area.

Public transport to the city centre is available within a short walk of the terminal building. The *Airport Express*, T131500, services the city centre (daily 0500-2300) including the Central Railway Station, Circular Quay and Wynyard bus and rail stations (300, $7, child $3.50, return $12, tickets from the driver) with connecting services to Kings Cross, Bondi, Coogee (No 350) and Darling Harbour, Glebe (No 352). There is a ticket booth in the main bus area. **Taxis** are available outside the terminal (south). A trip to the city centre takes about 30 mins and costs about $25. Various other independent shuttle operators and courtesy accommodation shuttles also operate door-to-door from outside the terminal building, including *Kingsford Smith Transport*, T9666 9988, which runs anywhere in the city. One-way $8 for adults and $13 return, $4 for children (between the ages of 4 and 12). Every 20-30 mins. There is also a **rail link** every 10-15 mins to the city ($10). The airport station is open from 0500-2400 (0100 Fri-Sun).

Greater Sydney

New South Wales

To Maroota, Wisemans
Ferry, St Albans, Darugh
& Yengo National Parks

Glenorie

Northern Rd

Berowra

Galston

Galston Rd

Mount
Ku-ring-gai
Berowra
Valley

Mt
Colah

Pacific Highway

Sydney Newcastle Freeway

Hawkesbury River

Cowan Creek

Bobbin
Head

Ku-ring-gai Chase
National Park

Brisbane Water
National Park

Broken Bay

Barrenjoey
Head

West
Head

Basin
Beach

Palm Beach
Whale
Beach

Avalon
Beach

Pittwater

Mona Vale

Hornsby

Mona Vale Rd

Narrabeen
Beach

COLLAROY

Hills Motorway

PARRAMATTA

Homebush Bay
Olympic Park

Western Motorway

To Featherdale Wildlife Park,
Sydney Wonderland & Penr'th

NORTH
SYDNEY

BALMORAL
MOSMAN

NEUTRAL BAY
CREMORNE

Sydney
Harbour

WATSONS
BAY

MANLY

North Head
Middle Head
South Head

LILYFIELD
LEICHARDT

GLEBE

Sydney

BONDI

Bondi Beach

South Western Motorway

Kingsford
Smith Airport

Eastern Dist

BRONTE
CLOVELLY
COOGEE

Botany Bay

La Perouse

Botany Bay
National Park

Kurnell

Botany Bay
National Park

LOFTUS

ENGADINE

Princes Highway

AUDLEY

CRONULLA

Bundeena

Heathcote

Royal
National Park

South
Pacific Ocean

Waterfall

Southern Freeway

Wattamolla Beach

Garie Beach

To Burning Palms Beach & Otford

N

0 km   2

0 miles   2

New South Wales

Bus The **Sydney Coach Terminal** can be found at the Central Railway Station, Shop 4-7, Eddy Av, T9212 3433, open daily 0600-2230. There is a left luggage facility and showers are available in the terminal. *McCafferty's/Greyhound*, T132030, and *Premier Motor Service*, T133410, are the main interstate and state coach companies offering regular daily schedules to most of the main centres. *Firefly Express*, 482 Pitt St, TT9211 1644, www.fireflyexpress.com.au, operate a daily/overnight Melbourne to Sydney or Sydney to Melbourne service and drop off/pick up at their 482 Pitt St terminal. *Murray's*, T132259, offer a 'Canberra Express' service 3 times a day from the main coach terminal at Eddy Av.

Train All interstate and NSW State destination trains arrive and depart from the **Central Railway Station** on Eddy Av, just south of the city centre. There is an information booth and ticket offices on the main platform concourse. *Countrylink* are the main interstate operators operating with a combination of coach and rail to all the main interstate and NSW destinations, T132232 (daily 0630-2200), bookings@countrylink.nsw.gov.au The *Countrylink Travel Centre* is at the railway station, T9955 4237; Town Hall Station, T9379 4076; Wynyard Station, T9224 4744; Circular Quay, T9224 3400; and Bondi Junction T9377 9377. First class and economy fares vary so you are advised to shop around and compare prices with the various coach operators. Ask about their **Discovery Pass** which offers unlimited journeys on the rail and coach network, including Brisbane, 14 days $165, 6 months $330. The **East Coast Discovery Pass** gives you 6 months economy class travel, one way, either north or south with unlimited stopovers, Melbourne $93.50, Cairns $247.50. The railway station also houses the main interstate city coach terminal (*McCafferty's/Greyhound*) and from there, or Pitt St and George St, you can pick up regular city and suburban buses. *The Airport Express* also stops outside the train station (coach terminal). For information T131500, www.sydneytransport.net.au *Great Southern Rail*, T132147, www.gsr.com.au, operate services from Sydney to Perth ('Indian Pacific') via Broken Hill and Adelaide and Sydney to Alice Springs ('The Ghan') via Melbourne and Adelaide. *Countrylink* operate the 'XPT' (11 hrs, twice daily, 1 overnight) between Sydney and Melbourne and Sydney to Cairns.

Sydney Ferries

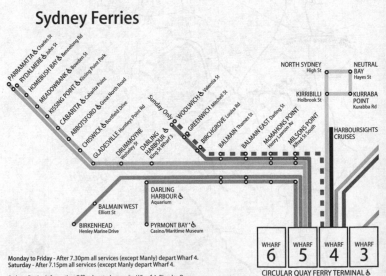

Monday to Friday - After 7.30pm all services (except Manly) depart Wharf 4.
Saturday - After 7.15pm all services (except Manly depart Wharf 4.

Sydney Ferries information Office located opposite Wharf 4, Circular Quay.

Suburban Travel Passes

*There are numerous popular travel pass systems in operation through the STA. The new and very attractive **DayTripper Pass** gives all-day access to Sydney's trains, bus and ferries within the suburban area for $13, child $6.50. Tickets can be purchased at any rail, bus or ferry sales or information outlet or on the buses themselves.*
***TravelPass** allows unlimited, weekly, quarterly or yearly combined travel throughout designated zones or sections. A seven-day pass for example, covering the inner (orange) zone costs $33, child $16.50.*

*For the toursit staying only a few days however, the best bet is the **The Sydney Pass** which offers unlimited travel on ferry and standard buses as well as the Sydney and Bondi Explorer routes and the four STA Harbour Cruises. They are sold as a three-day ($90, child $45), five-day ($120, child $60) or seven-day ($140, child $70). Return Airport Express transfers are also included and family conssesions apply. Note that discount, 10-trip '**TravelTen**' (bus) and '**FerryTen**' passes are also available and recommended.*

Getting around

Public transport in Sydney is generally both efficient and convienient. The great hub of public transportation in the city centre revolves around **Circular Quay** at the base of the CBD. It is from there that most ferry (**Sydney Ferries**), suburban rail (**CityRail**) and bus (**Sydney Buses**) services operate. **State Transit** (STA) own and operate the principal suburban ferry and bus services. Other principal terminals are **Wynyard** on York St for northbound bus and rail services, **Town Hall** on George St, and the **Central Railway Station**. All have information booths supplying on the spot train and bus information. For information about all public transport in Sydney, T131500 (daily 0600-2200). Prior to arrival it is well worth checking out www.131500.com.au For discount travel passes see box on page 77. Once in the city, ferry and rail route maps are available from information centres. The free 'Sydney Public Transport Directory' is available from the Sydney VIC.

Car Travelling by car around Sydney is a nightmare with numerous tolls, expensive parking and omnipresent parking wardens. There really is no need to see the sights by car but if you must take lots of change. For car, campervan rental companies and second-hand purchase see page 47. The **NRMA** are located at 74-76 King St, CBD, T132132.

Train Sydney's 24-hr double-deckered train services are a convienient way to reach the city centre and outlying areas, or to link in with bus and ferry services. Fares start at $1 and savings of up to 40% can be made with 'Off-Peak Tickets' which operate after 0900 on weekdays. Further savings can be made with the TravelPass and Sydney Pass (see box on page 77). Children travel half-price and there are also family concessions. There are coloured routes with the green/purple City Circle (Central, Town Hall, Wynyard, Circular Quay, St James and the Museum) and blue Eastern Suburbs Line (Central, Town Hall, Martin Place, Kings Cross, Edgecliff, Bondi Junction) being the most convenient. Tickets and information are available at all major stations. For information about suburban trains in Sydney, T131500, www.131500.com.au

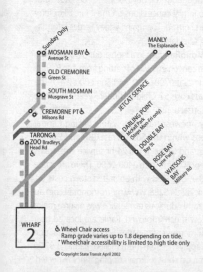

Sunday Only

MOSMAN BAY &
Avenue St

OLD CREMORNE
Green St

SOUTH MOSMAN
Musgrave St

CREMORNE PT &
Milsons Rd

TARONGA
ZOO Bradleys
Head Rd &

MANLY
The Esplanade &

JETCAT SERVICE

DARLING POINT
McKell Park
(Dogs Mon-Fri only)

DOUBLE BAY
Bay St.

ROSE BAY
Lyne Park

WATSONS BAY
Military Rd

WHARF
2

& Wheel Chair access
Ramp grade varies up to 1.8 depending on tide.
* Wheelchair accessibility is limited to high tide only

© Copyright State Transit April 2002

Bus The STA (**Sydney Buses**) are the principal operators with the standard buses being blue and white, the Airport Express a very Aussie green and yellow, the **Sydney Explorer** red and the **Bondi Explorer** blue. Standard bus fares start at $1.50 to $4.60 depending on distance and susequent zone. If you intend to travel regularly by bus a **Travel Ten** ticket is recommended ($11-39) while further savings can be also be made with the **TravelPass** and **Sydney Pass** system (see box, page 77). The **Explorer** buses cost $30 for the full return trip ($50 2-days). There is an on-board commentary and you can hop on and off at will. Both leave at regular intervals from Circular Quay. For all of the above bus fares children travel half-price and there are also family concessesions. Note most 'Explorer' buses operate between 0840 and1722 only. The local (green) **Olympic Explorer** offers trips around the Homebush Bay site and links with ferry services from Circular Quay ($20 with ferry, $10 without), while the weekend (blue and yellow) **Parramatta Explorer** leaves every 20 mins from the RiverCat ferry terminal in Parramatta, $10 (ex Rivercat). Note that children travel half-price and there are also family concessions on most fares. For **information** about suburban buses in Sydney, T131500, www.131500.com.au Note that drivers do not automatically stop at bus stops. If you are alone you must signal the driver, or at night gesticulate wildly.

Ferry A trip on one of Sydney's harbour ferries is a wonderful experience and an ideal way to see the city, as well as reach many of the major attractions and suburbs. A short return voyage from the busy **Circular Quay** terminal to the zoo, Mosman or Cremorne on the North Shore, during both day and night is highly recommended. The principal operator is *Sydney Ferries* who operate the 'green and golds' and also the fast *JetCats* to Manly and *RiverCat* to Homebush Bay/Parramatta. Several independent companies also operate out of Circular Quay offering a wide range of cruises as well as suburban transportation and water taxis. *Hegarty's Ferries*, T9206 1167, operates daily services from Circular Quay to Milson's Point, Lavender Bay, McMahon's Point, Jeffrey St and Beulah St. *Matilda*, T9264 7377, offer a range of cruise options and The Rocket to Darling Harbour/Lane Cove. For water taxi services see Taxis below. Like the buses, ferry fares are priced according to zone and start at a single trip for $4.20. If you intend to travel regularly by ferry a **FerryTen** ticket (from $26.30) is recommended, while further savings can also be made with the **TravelPass** and **Sydney Pass** system, (see box, page 77). Various travel/entry combo tickets are offered to the major harbourside sights including Taronga Zoo (Zoo Pass $25, child $12.50) and Sydney Aquarium (Aquarium Pass $23.40, child $10.70). Various Cruises are also on offer throughout the day (see page 100). Note that children travel half-price and there are also family concessions on most fares. For ferry information T131500, www.sydneytransport.com.au The main Sydney Ferries Information Centre can be found opposite Wharf 4, Circular Quay.

Metro MonoRail and LightRail The **MonoRail** runs in a loop around Darling Harbour and South Western CBD and provides a convenient way of getting from A to B. They run every 3-5 mins, Mon-Thu 0700-2200, Fri/Sat 0700-2400, and Sun 0800-2200. The standard fare (1 loop) is $3.50 while a Day Pass costs $7. Children under 5 years travel free and discounts are available to some major attractions.

The new **LightRail** network is Sydney's newest transport system linking Central Station with Lilyfield, via a number of stops within the South West CBD and Darling Harbour, as well as the Casino, Fish Market and Glebe. It is a 24-hr service with trains every 10-15 mins from 0600-2400 and every 30 mins from 2400-0600. There are 2 fare zones starting at a single journey at $2.20. A Day Pass with unlimited stops costs $8. Children travel at half price. For information, T8584 5288, www.metromonorail.com.au

Land and Water Taxis Sydney's once rather dubious taxi service was given a major revamp for the 2000 Olympics and it is now much improved. Ranks are located near every railway station, at Circular Quay and numerous spots in the CBD, otherwise hail one as required. From 2200-0600 higher tariffs apply. The minimum (hailed) flagfall is $2.20 with about a $1.10 charge per km thereafter. On short journeys tipping is not expected.

Plastic fantastic

The **SeeSydneyCard** is a **pre-paid tourist credit card** giving unlimited admissions to a wide variety of attractions, activities and tours and additionally offers reductions at some restaurants and shops. The card also includes optional public transport and comes with a free full colour guidebook and maps. There are two types of card, adult and children (5-15 years). Adult cards range from one-day for $49 (with transport $62) to a week at $149 ($207) and children one-day $29 (with transport $35.50) to a week at $89 ($118). For more information and purchasing contact the major VICs or T92551788, www.seesydneycard.com

There are several companies including **Combined**, T8332 8888, **ABC**, T132522, **Premier**, T131017, **Legion**, T131451, and **RSL**, T132211. **Water taxis** operate all over the harbour with most being based on the western edge of Circular Quay. The main operators are **Taxis Afloat**, T9955 3222, **Harbour Shuttle**, T9810 5010, and **About Taxis**, T9555 1155.

Bicycle Travel by bike within the city centre is not recommended. The suburbs are a little less manic, but theft is also a problem. Several companies offer bike hire from about $30 per day or $170 per week, including **Bicycles in the City**, 722 George St, T9281 6977, who offer not only bike hire but maps and touring information. Other hire companies include **Inner City Cycles**, 151 Glebe Point Rd, Glebe, T9660 6605; **Woolly's Wheels**, 82 Oxford St, T933 12671, and the **Manly Cycle Centre**, 36 Pittwater Rd, Manly, T9977 1189. For general advice contact **Bicycle NSW**, Level 2, 209 Castlereagh St, T9283 5200, www.ozemail.com.au/~bikensw For 'Sydney Cycle Ways' maps and additional information contact the **RTA**, T9218 6816.

Beyond the Visitor Information booth at the airport international arrivals terminal, the first stop for any visitor should be the **Sydney Visitors Centre**, T9255 1788, F9241 5010, www.sydneyvisitorcentre.com, at 106 George St, The Rocks. Open 0900-1800 daily. The centre provides a comprehensive service which includes information, brochures, maps and reservations for hotels, tours, cruises, restaurants and other city-based activities. The centre can book stand-by accommodation (discounted rates), but this is a face-to-face service only, alternatively visitors can contact some hotels and tour/activity operators via the free-to-use phones. There is another principal VIC at **Darling Harbour**, T19022 60568, www.darlingharbour.com It offers much the same in services as the Rocks centre but has an emphasis on sights and activities within Darling Harbour itself. Note neither centre issues public transport tickets. Manly, Parramatta, Homebush Bay and Bondi also have **local information centres** and these are listed in the relevant texts while small manned **information booths** are located on the corner of Pitt St and Alfred St, Circular Quay; opposite St Andrews Cathedral near the Town Hall on George St and on Martin Pl, near Elizabeth St.

Information
Sydney websites include:
www.visitnsw.com.au
www.sydney.city
search.com.au,
www.discover
sydney.com.au

There are several **independent travel offices** designed mainly to cater for backpackers including: **Travellers Contact Point**, 7th Floor, 428 George St, T9221 8744, sydney@travellers.com.au, www.travellers.com.au (open Mon-Fri 0900-1800, Sat 1000-1600), which also offers mail-forwarding and employment advice; **Backpackers World**, Central Station, 482 Pitt St, and Level 3 Imperial Arcade, 83 Castlereagh St, T18006 76763, www.backpackersworld.com.au; **YHA Travel Centre**, Sydney Central YHA, T9281 9444, and 422 Kent St, T9261 1111, travel@yhansw.org.au; **Student Uni Travel**, Level 8, 92 Pitt St, T9232 8444, www.sut.com.au Most of these offices also have internet facilities. The **Australian Travel Specialists** cater for the full range of traveller and have offices throughout the city, including one at Wharf 6, Circular Quay, T9555 2700.

Sydney centre

New South Wales

To North Sydney

Sydney Harbour Bridge

Sydney Opera House

Walsh Bay

Dawes Point Park

45

A

13

22

Hickson Rd
Pottinger St
Lower Fort St
Bradley Highway
Hickson Rd
George St

53

37   THE ROCKS

Sydney Harbour Tunnel

Government House

Clydebank

9   Windmill St
52
Argyle Pl

Rocks Toy Museum
3
54
Sydney Visitors Centre
Cadmans Cottage

Argyle St
Argyle St

Sydney Observatory

2

Museum of Contemporary Art

40
17   28

Circular Quay Ferry Terminal

Susannah Place

Circular Quay Station

Opera Quays
Macquarie St

1

B

High St
Kent St
12

SH Ervin Gallery

14

Cahill Expressway

Alfred St
12

Justice & Police Museum

8

Customs House

Darling Harbour

Hickson Rd

Cumberland St
Gloucester St
Harrington St

9

Grosvenor St

Bridge St
Lotus St

Museum of Sydney
30

Royal Botanical Gardens

8

Jamison St
39

Tropical Centre

Margaret St

Spring St
Bent St
O'Connell St
George St
Hunter St
Pitt St
Phillip St
Bligh St

Chiefly Square
20

State Library of New South Wales

Macquarie St

C

Pyrmont Bay

King's St Wharf

Wynyard Station

7

Martin Place Station

NSW Parliament House

Cahill Expressway

The Domain
34

National Maritime Museum

48

Erskine St
Clarence St
Carrington St
York St
Kent St
Sussex St

Martin Pl

NRMA

Martin Place

i

Sydney Hospital

Art Gallery of New South Wales

To Sky City Casino

Sydney Aquarium

King St

44

Royal Mint

Art Gallery Rd

Sir John

Harbourside

35

AMP (Centrepoint) Tower

James Rd

Hyde Park Barracks
St James Station

M

Darling Park

14

Archibald Fountain

St Mary's Cathedral

PYRMONT

Cockle Bay

15

Market City
State Theatre

M   City Centre

11

Hyde Park

College St

D

M   Convention

16

38

Queen Victoria Building
46

Park Plaza

Cockle Bay Wharf

Druitt St
Town Hall

Park St

Western Distributor

IMAX

20

St Andrew's Cathedral

Town Hall Station

Park St

Australian Museum

51

William St

Riley St
Crown St

Western Distributor

Bathurst St

Museum Station

Castlereagh St
Elizabeth St

Tumbalong Park

42

Liverpool St

Anzac War Memorial

Francis St

Stanley St

Darling Dr

Chinese Garden of Friendship

13

M   World Square

24

21

Exhibition Centre

Pier St
1

CHINATOWN

Goulburn St

Oxford St
Palmer St

E

6

57

Wentworth Av

Poplar St
Pelican St

Powerhouse Museum & Motor World

Haymarket

17

Hay St

Campbell St

55

Taylor Square

M

7   3

ULTIMO   HAYMARKET

Paddy's Market

26
M

56

Capital Square

Hay St

Campbell St

Denham St

Macarthur St
Harris St

18

George St

Reservoir St

Smith St

Ann St

Mary Ann St

Ultimo Rd

Quay St

4

Rawson Pl

35

18

Central

Bourke St

Albion St

10
5

SURRY HILLS

Thomas St

Coach Terminal

L

Eddy Av

Fitzroy St

F

Central Station

Commonwealth St
Belmore St
Bettevue St

Detail map
A Kings Cross,
page 93

1

Broadway

Regent St

Lee St

2   Central

Kippax St
Foveaux St

3

36   29
21

Related map
Manly, page 98

New South Wales

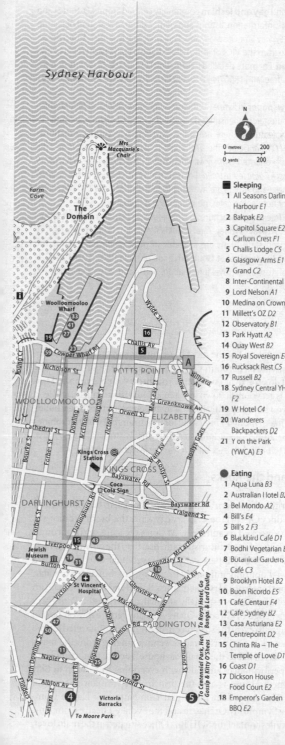

Sydney Harbour

Mrs Macquarie's Chair

Farm Cove

The Domain

Woolloomooloo Wharf

POTTS POINT

WOOLLOOMOOLOO

ELIZABETH BAY

Kings Cross Station

KINGS CROSS

Coca Cola Sign

DARLINGHURST

Jewish Museum

St Vincent's Hospital

PADDINGTON

Victoria Barracks

To Moore Park

To Centennial Park, Hot Gossip & Kitty O'Shea's

To Royal Hotel, Go Bunga & Lord Dudley

Sleeping
1 All Seasons Darling Harbour *E1*
2 Bakpak *E2*
3 Capitol Square *E2*
4 Carlton Crest *F1*
5 Challis Lodge *C5*
6 Glasgow Arms *E1*
7 Grand *C2*
8 Inter-Continental *B3*
9 Lord Nelson *A1*
10 Medina on Crown *F3*
11 Millett's OZ *D2*
12 Observatory *B1*
13 Park Hyatt *A2*
14 Quay West *B2*
15 Royal Sovereign *E4*
16 Rucksack Rest *C5*
17 Russell *B2*
18 Sydney Central YHA *F2*
19 W Hotel *C4*
20 Wanderers Backpackers *D2*
21 Y on the Park (YWCA) *E3*

Eating
1 Aqua Luna *B3*
2 Australian Hotel *B2*
3 Bel Mondo *A2*
4 Bill's *E4*
5 Bill's 2 *F3*
6 Blackbird Café *D1*
7 Bodhi Vegetarian *E2*
8 Botanical Gardens Café *C3*
9 Brooklyn Hotel *B2*
10 Buon Ricordo *E5*
11 Café Centaur *F4*
12 Café Sydney *B2*
13 Casa Asturiana *E2*
14 Centrepoint *D2*
15 Chinta Ria – The Temple of Love *D1*
16 Coast *D1*
17 Dickson House Food Court *E2*
18 Emperor's Garden BBQ *E2*

19 Fishface *E4*
20 Forty One *C3*
21 Fuel *F3*
22 Guillaume at Bennelong *A3*
23 Harry's Café de Wheels *C4*
24 Hyde Park Café *E2*
25 Indian Home Diner *F4*
26 Kam Fook Seafood *E2*
27 Manta Ray *C4*
28 MCA Café *B2*
29 MG Garage *F3*
30 MOS Café *C3*
31 Oh, Calcutta *E4*
32 Orphee *F5*
33 Otto *C4*
34 Pavillion on the Park *C3*
35 Pitt St Mall *D2*
36 Prasit's Thai Takeaway *F3*
37 Quay *A2*
38 QVB Building *D2*
39 Restaurant VII *B2*
40 Rockpool *B2*
41 Shimbashi Soba on the Sea *C4*
42 Tetsuya's *F2*
43 Una's *E4*
44 Vivo *C2*
45 Wharf *A2*
46 Zenergy *D2*

Pubs & bars
47 Albury Hotel *F4*
48 Cargo *C1*
49 Durty Nelly's *F4*
50 Grand Pacific Blue Room *F4*
51 Hard Rock Cafe *D3*
52 Hero of Waterloo & Harbour View Hotel *A2*
53 Mercantile *A2*
54 Orient *B2*
55 Oxford Hotel *E3*
56 Paddy McGuires *E2*
57 Scruffy Murphys *E2*
58 Scubar *F2*
59 Woolloomooloo Bay Hotel *C4*

Ⓛ LightRail Station
Ⓜ MonoRail Station

Sydney has a thriving **gay and lesbian** community centred around Oxford St and Darlinghurst. For more information, listings and venues simply ask around or pick up the free street press *'Sydney Star Observer'* and *'Capital Q'*. The free leaflet *'CBD Access Map Sydney'* available from the VICs or information booths is a very useful map and guide for the **disabled**. For more detailed information contact the *Disability Council of NSW*, T9211 2866 (freecall T1800 044 848) or *Disability Services Australia*, T9791 6599, www.dsa.org.au

The main daily **newspaper** in Sydney is the excellent *Sydney Morning Herald* which has comprehensive entertainment listings daily (see the pull-out *Metro* section on Friday) and regular city features. There are some excellent, free **tourist brochures** including the *'Sydney Official Guide'*, the *'This Week in Sydney'*, *'Where Magazine'*, the very interesting suburb-oriented *'Sydney Monthly'* and for the backpacker *'TNT'* (NSW Edition) or the *'Backpack Guide to Australia'*. For entertainment look out for *The Revolver* and *3-D World*. All these and others are available from the principal VIC's, city centre information booths or from some cafes, newsagents and bookshops.

Maps Most of the free tourist brochures have useful maps but for more detail purchase a copy of the Sydway *'Sydney Tourist Guide Map'* ($6). Comprehensive city street (UBD) region and state maps are available in most major bookshops. The *Travel Bookshop* at 175 Liverpool St (southern edge of Hyde Park), T9261 8200, is also a good source of Australian travel information, books and maps. Open Mon-Fri 0900-1800, Sat 1000-1700.

Sights

Sydney is without doubt one of the most beautiful cities in the world and the main reasons for this are its harbour, Opera House and Harbour Bridge. The first thing you must do on arrival, even before you throw your bags on a bed and sleep off the jet lag, is get yourself down to Circular Quay, day or night, and let it blow you away. If you have a specific interest in museums and historical buildings consider the *Ticket Through Time* (valid for three months) which combines many of the major attractions administered by the Historic Houses Trust. ■ *$23, children $10, family $40. Ask the VIC for the leaflet and details*

Circular Quay and the Rocks

Sydney Opera House
A performance will cost anywhere from $30-180 depending on its prestige and your seat

Bookings are essential

Even the fiercest critics of modern architecture cannot fail to be impressed by the magnificent Sydney Opera House. Every day, since this bizarre edifice was created people have flocked to admire it. At times the steps and concourse seem more like the nave of some futuristic cathedral than the outside of an arts venue, with hordes of worshippers gazing in reverential awe. The Opera House is best viewed not only intimately from close up, but also from afar. Some of the best spots are from Mrs Macquarie's Point (end of the Domain on the western edge of farm Cove) especially at dawn, and from the *Park Hyatt Hotel* on the eastern edge of Circular Quay. Also any ferry trip west bound from Circular Quay will reveal the structure in many of its multifaceted forms.

The Opera House has five performance venues ranging from the main, 2,690 capacity Concert Hall to the small Playhouse Theatre that, combined, host about 2,500 performances annually with everything from Bach to Billy Connolly. The Opera House is also the principal performance venue for Opera Australia, The Australian Ballet and Contemporary Dance Companies, the Sydney Symphony Orchestra and the Sydney Theatre Company. For the latest schedules contact the SOH Box Office situated in the main foyer,

T9250 7777, bookings@soh.nsw.gov.au, www.soh.nsw.gov.au ■ *Mon-Sat 0900-2030*. There are also three **tours** and performance packages available. The Front of House Tour provides an insiders view of selected theatres and foyers; The Backstage Pass, as the name suggests, takes you behind the scenes and there is also the historical 'Bennelong Walk'. The tours are available on a regular basis between 0900-1700 daily and take about 45 minutes with some having to fit round actual performances or rehearsals. Prices range from $15.40-25.20. The Performance Package combines a range of performance, dining and tour options. The Guided Tour Office is located on the Lower Concourse, T9250 7209. An SOH store selling official souvenirs, cafés, bars and a restaurant are also located within the complex.

Circular Quay
Look out for the 'Writers Walk' which is a series of plaques on the main concourse with quotes from famous Australian writers

As well as being a major hub of transportation Circular Quay is also a bustling venue from which to soak up the impressive sight of the Opera House, the Harbour Bridge and the manic activity of the inner harbour. The quay also provides the main walkway from the historic and commercial Rocks area to the Opera House and the Botanical Gardens beyond. It is a great place to linger, take photographs or pause to enjoy the many bizarre street performers that come and go with the tides. At the eastern edge of the quay the new **Opera Quays** façade provides many tempting, if expensive, cafés and restaurants as well as an art gallery and a cinema, www.operaquays.com.au There are three other notable attractions skirting the edges of Circular Quay. The **Justice and Police Museum**, housed in the former 1856 Water Police Court, features a magistrates court and former police cells, as well as a gallery, and historical displays, showcasing the antics and fate of some of Sydney's most notorious criminals. ■ *Sat/Sun 1000-1700, daily in Jan, $7, children $6.60, T9252 1144, www.hht.nsw.gov.au Corner of Albert St and Phillip St*. Nearby, facing the quay, is the former 1840 **Customs House** which now houses several exhibition spaces, café/bars and popular *Café Sydney* (see page 109). The Object Galleries (third floor) lends itself to craft and design, while on the fourth floor, the City Exhibition Space showcases historical and contemporary aspects of the city with a 1:500 model of the CBD being its main attraction. At the southwestern corner of Circular Quay it is hard to miss the rather grand Art Deco **Museum Of Contemporary Art**. Opened in 1991 it maintains a collection of some of Australia's best contemporary works, together with works by renowned international artists like Warhol and Hockney. The museum also hosts regular national and international exhibitions. Overlooking the quay the in-house *MCA Café* is a popular spot for lunch or a coffee (see page 109). ■ *Daily 1000-1700, free with a small charge for some visiting exhibitions, tours available Mon-Fri 1100-1400, Sat/Sun 1200-1330, T9241 5892, www.mca.com.au*

A little further towards the Harbour Bridge is **Cadman's Cottage** that now sits looking somewhat out of place overlooking the futuristic Cruise liner terminal. The cottage built in 1816 is the oldest surviving residence in Sydney and was originally the former base for Governor Macquarie's boat crew, before playing host to the Sydney Water Police. The cottage is named after the coxswain of the boat crew, John Cadman, who was sent to Australia for stealing a horse. The cottage is now the base for the **Sydney Harbour National Park Information Centre**, which is the main booking office and departure point for a number of harbour and island tours (see page 100). A small historical exhibition is housed in the lower level. ■ *Mon-Fri 0900-1630, Sat/Sun 1000-1630. Free. T9247 5033, www.npws.nsw.gov.au, 110 George St.*

The Rocks

The Rocks is a great place to spend a morning or afternoon simply wandering about, sightseeing, shopping or eating out. For more information visit the Sydney VIC, or www.rocksvillage.com

Straddling the Bradfield Highway, which now carries a constant flow of traffic across the Harbour Bridge, the historic Rocks village was the first site settled by European convicts and troops as early as 1788. Despite being given a major facelift in recent decades and managing to leave its reputation as the haunt of prostitutes, drunks and criminals to the history books, it still retains much of its original architectural charm and now serves as one of Sydney's most popular modern day tourist attractions. Both old and new is married, quite successfully, in an eclectic array of shops, galleries arcades, cafés and some mighty fine pubs and restaurants. The **Rocks Market**, held every weekend, is perhaps the most popular in Sydney featuring a fine array of authentic arts, crafts, bric-a-brac and souvenirs. By far the best way to see the Rocks properly is to join the official **Rocks Walking Tour**, which is an entertaining and informative insight into both past and present. ■ *Bookings can be made at the Sydney VIC, 106 George St, or at the Walks Office, Shop K4, Kendall La. Tours take 90 mins, departing at 1030, 1230 and 1430 weekdays and 1130 and 1400 weekends. $16, children $10.70, family $41.25, T9247 6678, bookings recommended.* For live entertainment head for the **Rocks Square** in the heart of the village where you'll find jazz, classical or contemporary/traditional music every day from 1200-1400.

The **Rocks Toy Museum** is housed in the former 1854 Coachhouse, 2-6 Kendall Lane, T9181 2311. It boasts over 3,000 toys spanning two centuries. Also in Kendall Lane is the **Puppet Theatre** with free shows at 1100, 1230 and 1400 weekends (daily during school holidays). To escape the crowds, head up Argyle Street, and the steps to Cumberland Street, taking a quick peek at the historic row of cottages at **Susannah Place** (58-64 Gloucester Street, west side, below the popular *Australian* hotel and pub. ■ *Sat/Sun 1000-1700, $7, T9241 1893*), before walking through the pedestrian walkway to **Observatory Park**, which offers some fine views of the bridge and is home to the **Sydney Observatory**, Australia's oldest. There is an interesting exhibition covering early aboriginal and European astronomy. ■ *Daily 1000-1700. Evening tour $10, children $5, family $25. T9217 0485.* Almost next-door is the **S.H. Ervin Gallery**, at the National Trust Centre, with a reputation for hosting some fine, small-scale exhibitions. ■ *Tue-Fri 1100-1700, Sat/Sun 1200-1700, T9258 0122.* From Observatory Park it is a short walk further along Argyle Street to enjoy a small libation and a bite to eat at the *Lord Nelson*, Sydney's oldest pub (see page 113) before perhaps walking north down Lower Fort Street to **Dawes Point Park** with its dramatic bridge perspectives. At 43 Lower Fort Street, you may like to dip into **Clydebank**, a restored mansion with its period furnishings and collection of former Rocks memorabilia. ■ *$8, T9241 4776.*

The Harbour Bridge

From below the best views of the bridge can be enjoyed from Hickson Rd and Deans Point (south side) and Milson's Point (north side)

From near or far, above or below, day or night, the Harbour Bridge is impressive and imposing. The 'Coat hanger', as it is often called, was opened in 1932, taking nine years to build, and it remains the second longest single span bridge in the world, with New York's Bayonne Bridge beating it by about a spanner's length. The deck supports eight lanes of traffic (accommodating around 150,000 vehicles a day), a railway line and a pedestrian walkway, which forms a crucial artery to the North Shore and beyond. For over six decades the best views from the bridge were accessed by foot from its 59-m high deck, but now the **'Bridge Climb'** experience, which ascends the 134-m high, 502-m long span, has become one of the city's 'must-do' activities (see page 99). Not as thrilling, but far cheaper are the views on offer from the top of the **Southeastern Pylon Lookout**, which can be accessed from the eastern walkway and Cumberland Street, the Rocks. The pylon also houses the **Harbour Bridge Exhibition**. ■ *Daily 1000-1700. $2. T9218 6888.*

Sydney harbour is scattered with a number of interesting islands most of which hold some historical significance. **Fort Denison**, just east of the Opera House, is the smallest, and by far the most notorious. Its proper name is Pinchgut Island – so called because it was originally used as an open-air jail and a place where inmates were abandoned for a week and supplied with nothing except bread and water. In 1796, the Governor of NSW left a sobering warning to the new penal colony by displaying the body of executed murderer Francis Morgan from a gibbet on the island's highest point. The island was later converted to a fort in the 1850s (for fear of a Russian invasion during the Crimean war). There is a café and tours are available. ■ *Breakfast Tour, Sat 0630-0900, Tue-Thu 650-0915. $37, children $33. Heritage Tour, Mon-Fri 1130-1505 and 1500-1710, Sat 0900-1140, 1130-1515 and 1500-1640, Sun 0910-1200, 1130-1500 and 1440-1650. $22, children $18. (for more information and bookings, see below).* A little further east, off Darling Harbour, is **Clark Island**, a popular picnic retreat. East again, off Rose Bay, is Shark Island, so called because of its shape. It served as a former animal quarantine centre and public reserve, before becoming part of the Sydney Harbour National Park in 1975. West of the bridge is the largest of the harbour's islands, **Goat Island**, site of a former gunpowder station and barracks. This provides the venue for a range of **tours** including the *Gruesome Tales Tour* (■ *Sat 1800-2130, $24.20, adults only*) which recounts the island's grisly past, and the *Water Rats Tour* (■ *Wed 1200-1415 and 1350-1615, $19.80, children $15.40, family $61.60*), which is a look behind the scenes of one of Australia's most famous TV soap series featuring the antics of the Sydney water police. ■ *A standard Heritage Tour departs Mon, Fri, Sat and Sun, 1300-1515. $19.80, children $15.40, family $61.60.*

Harbour Islands

For all island access, tour information and bookings contact the Sydney Harbour National Park Information Centre, Cadman's Cottage, 110 George St, The Rocks, T9247 5033, www.npws. Nsw.gov.au Mon-Fri 0900-1630, Sat/Sun 1000-1630

City centre

The Museum of Sydney (MOS) was opened in 1995 and is a clever and imaginative mix of old and new. Built on the original site of Governor Phillip's former 1788 residence and incorporating some of the original archaeological remains, it contains uncluttered and well presented displays that explore the history and stories surrounding the creation and development of the city, from the first indigenous settlers, through the European invasion and up to the modern day. Art is an important aspect of this museum and as well as dynamic and temporary exhibitions incorporating a city theme there are some permanent pieces, the most prominent being the intriguing 'Edge of the Trees', a sculptural installation. Shop and café on site. ■ *Daily 0930-1700, $7, children $3, family $17, T9251 5988, www.hht.nsw.gov.au, 37 Philip St, City Centre. Recommended*

Museum of Sydney

The 30-ha Botanical Gardens offer a wonderful sanctuary of peace and greenery only a short stroll east of the city centre. It boasts a fine array of mainly native plants and trees; an intriguing pyramid shaped Tropical House, roses and succulent gardens, rare and threatened species and decorative ponds, as well as a resident colony of wild **flying foxes** (fruitbats). There is a **Visitors Centre** and shop located near Art Gallery Road in the southeastern corner of the park. There you can pick up a self-guided tour leaflet or join a free organized **tour** at 1030 daily. A specialist **Aboriginal tour** exploring the significance of the site to the Cadigal (the original Aboriginal inhabitants) and the first European settler's desperate attempts to cultivate the site is available on request ($16.50, T9231 8134). The *Gardens Café and Restaurant* is right in the heart of the gardens and is one of the best places to observe the bats. ■ *0700-sunset, free. Tropical Centre daily 1000-1600, $5. T9231 8111.*

Royal Botanical Gardens & Macquarie Point

New South Wales

From the Botanical Gardens it is a short stroll to **Macquarie Point**, which offers one of the best views of the Opera House and Harbour Bridge. Mrs Macquarie's chair is the spot where the first Governor's wife came to reflect upon the new settlement. One can only imagine what her reaction would be now. ■ *Maquarie Point is on the Sydney Explorer Bus route, stop No 5.*

The Art Gallery of New South Wales & The Domain

The Art Gallery as a whole is due for expansion in late 2002

At the southeastern edge of the Botanical Gardens and fronting The Domain is the Art Gallery of New South Wales, Australia's largest. Housed inside its grand façade are the permanent works of many of the country's most reverred contemporary artists as well as a collection of more familiar international names like Monet and Picasso. In stark contrast the **Yiribana Gallery** is a major highlight, showcasing a fine collection of Aboriginal and Torres Strait Islander works. There are authentic half-hour dance and music performances in the gallery Tuesday-Saturday at 1200. The main gallery also features a dynamic programme of major visiting exhibitions. Be sure not to miss the quirky and monumental matchsticks installation by the late Brett Whitely, the city's most celebrated artists, behind the main building. More of his work can be seen at the Brett Whitely Museum, 2 Raper Street, Surry Hills, T9225 1881 (see page 94). ■ *The Art Gallery of NSW is open daily 1000-1700, free (small charge for some visiting exhibitions), T9225 1744, www.artgallery.nsw.gov.au, Art Gallery Rd, The Domain. The Gallery is on the Sydney Explorer Bus route, stop 6.* The **Domain**, the pleasant open park sitting between the Art Gallery and Macquarie Place, was declared a public domain in 1810. It is often used as a free concert venue especially over Christmas and during the Sydney Festival.

Macquarie Street

Macquarie St is on the Sydney Explorer Bus route, stop No 4

Macquarie Street forms the eastern fringe of the CBD and is Sydney's most historic street and the site of many important and impressive buildings. Heading north to south, near the Opera House, in its own expansive grounds, is **Government House**, a Gothic revival building completed in 1837. The interior contains many period furnishings and features giving an insight into the lifestyle of the former NSW Governors and their families. ■ *Fri-Sun 1000-1500 (grounds daily 1000-1600). Guided tours only within the house, departing every ½ hr from 1030. Free. T9931 5222.* Further up Macquarie Street, facing the Botanical gardens, is the **State Library of New South Wales**. Its architecture speaks for itself, but housed within its walls are some very significant historical documents, including most of the diaries of the First Fleet. Also worth a look is the foyer floor of the **Mitchell Library** entrance, one of three Melocco Brothers mosaic floor decorations in the city. The library also hosts visiting exhibitions that are almost always worth visiting and offers an on-going programme of films, workshops and seminars. Shop and café on site. ■ *Mon-Fri 0900-2200, Sat 1100-1700. $16 for visiting exhibitions. T9273 1414, www.slnsw.gov.au*

Next door, the original north wing of the 1816 **Sydney Hospital** (formerly known as the Rum Hospital) is now the **NSW Parliament House**. Free tours are offered when Parliament is not in session, and when it is; you can visit the public gallery. The south wing of the hospital gave way to the **Royal Mint** (known as the 'Rum Hospital') in 1854 during the gold rush. The **Hyde Park Barracks**, on the northern edge of Hyde Park, were commissioned in 1816 by Governor Macquarie to house male convicts before being utilized later as an orphanage and an asylum The renovated buildings now house a modern museum displaying the history of the Barracks and the work of the architect Francis Greenway. Guided tours are available, with the unusual option of staying overnight in convict hammocks. Café on-site. ■ *Daily 0100-1700. $7, children $3, family $17. T9223 8922, www.hht.nsw.gov.au*

Hyde Park is a great place to escape the mania of the city and includes the historic grandeur of the 1932 **Archibald Fountain** and 1934 **Anzac War Memorial**. It's also great for people-watching. At the northeastern edge of the park, on College Road, is **Saint Mary's Cathedral**, which is well worth a look inside. It has an impressive and wonderfully peaceful interior, with the highlight being the Melocco Brothers mosaic floor in the crypt. ■ *The crypt is open daily from 1000-1600 and there are free tours on Sun afternoons after mass, T9220 0400.* A little further south along College Road is the **Australian Museum**, established in 1827, but doing a fine job of keeping pace with the cutting edge of technology, especially the modern Biodiversity and Indigenous Australians Displays. Also housed in the museum is the magnificent Chapman Mineral Collection. Also try to coincide your visit to the Indigenous Australian section with the live didjeridu playing and very informative lectures given by aboriginal staff. Children will love the very impressive Search and Discover section. ■ *0930-1700, $8, children $3, family $19 (special exhibitions extra), T9320 6000, www.austmus.gov.au Explorer Bus route, stop 7.*

Hyde Park & surrounds
Explorer Bus route, stop No 15

The **AMP (Centrepoint) Tower** has, since 1981, been a recognizable landmark across the city. The 2,239-tonne golden turret is also known as 'Ned's Helmet' after Ned Kelly's protective headgear. The view from Australia's highest building is mighty impressive. As well as enjoying the stunning vistas from the tower's **Observation Deck**, you can also experience a virtual 'Great Australian Expedition' **tour**, or dine in one of two **revolving restaurants**. ■ *Observation Deck open Sun-Fri 0900-2230, Sat 0900-2330. $16.50, children $11.10, family $45.75, virtual tour extra, T9231 1000 (restaurant bookings T8223 3801), www.centreponit.com.au, 100 Market St.* While you are on Market Street it is worth taking a peek at the impressive interior of the 1929 **State Theatre**. Much of its charm is instantly on view in the entrance foyer, but it is perhaps the 20,000-piece glass chandelier and Wurlitzer organ housed in the auditorium that steals the show. ■ *Self-guided tours are available Mon-Fri-1130-1500. $12, concession $8, T9373 6655, 49 Market St.* Just around the corner from the State Theatre on George Street, taking up an entire city block, is the grand **Queen Victoria Building**. Built in 1898 to celebrate Queen Victoria's Golden Jubilee and to replace the original Sydney Markets, the QVB (as it is known) is a prime **shopping** venue, containing three floors of boutique outlets, but the spectacular interior is well worth a look in itself. At the northern end is the 4-tonne **Great Australian Clock**, the world's largest hanging animated turret clock. It is a stunning creation that took four years to build at a cost of $1.5 mn. Once activated with a $4 donation (which goes to charity) the clock comes alive with moving picture scenes and figurines. At the southern end is the equally impressive **Royal Clock**, with its English historical theme, including the execution of King Charles I. There are also a number of good galleries, historical displays, restaurants and cafés throughout the complex. ■ *Mon-Wed, Fri/Sat 0900-1800, Thu 0900-2100 Sun 1100-1700 (some restaurants and cafés remain open after hours). Guided tours available Mon-Sat 1130 and 1430, Sun 1200 and 1430. T9265 6869.* Information desks on the Ground Floor and Level 2 Dome Area, www.qvb.com.au Across the street from the QVB is the **Town Hall**, built in 1888. It also has an impressive interior the highlight of which is the 8,000-pipe organ, reputed to be the largest in the world. Self-guided tour brochure available in the foyer. ■ *Daily 0900-1700. Free. T9265 9007, corner of George St and Druitt St.* Next door to the Town Hall is the newly renovated **St Andrew's Cathedral**, built between 1819 and 1868. There are regular choir performances and entry is free (T9265 1661).

The Central Business District & Chinatown
Given the high price of entry to the Observation Deck alone, it goes without saying that you should keep an eye on the weather forecast and pick a clear day

The QVB, Town Hall and St Andrew's Cathedral are on Sydney Explorer bus stop 14

New South Wales

New South Wales

Further along George Street and occupying the southwestern corner of the CBD is the Haymarket district and **Chinatown**. The Chinese have been an integral part of Sydney culture since the Gold Rush of the mid 1800s, though today Chinatown is also the focus of many other Asian cultures, including Vietnamese, Thai, Korean and Japanese. The district offers a lively diversion, with its heart being the Dixon Street pedestrian precinct, between the two **pagoda gates** facing Goulburn Street and Hay Street. Here, and in the surrounding streets, you will find a wealth of Asian shops and restaurants. At the northwestern corner of Chinatown is the **Chinese Garden of Friendship**, which was gifted to NSW by her sister Chinese province, Guangdong, to celebrate the Australian Bicentenary in 1988. It contains all the usual beautiful craftsmanship, landscaping and aesthetics. ■ *Daily 0930-dusk. $4.50, children $2, families $10. T9281 6863.* In stark contrast is **Paddy's Market** on the corner of Hay Street and Thomas Street, which is one of Sydney's largest, oldest and liveliest markets. It is also one of the tackiest. ■ *Fri, Sat, Sun 0900-1630. T1300 361 589, www.paddysmarkets.com.au*

Darling Harbour

Sydney Aquarium

For more information call or visit the VIC at the south end of Cockle Bay, next door to Imax, T9281 0788, www.darling harbour.com.au

This modern, well-presented aquarium, has over 650 species, but it's not all about fish. On show are imaginative arrays of habitat arenas, where saltwater crocodiles, frogs, seals, penguins and platypuses. The highlight of the aquarium is the Great Barrier Reef Oceanarium: a huge tank that gives you an incredible insight into the world's largest living thing. Of course, many visit the aquarium to come face-to-face with some of Australia's deadliest sea creatures, without getting their feet, if not their underwear, wet. There is no doubt that such beauty and diversity has its dark side, as the notorious box-jellyfish, cone shell, or rockfish will reveal. ■ *0900-2000. $22, children $10, family $48. Aquarium Pass with ferry from Circular Quay, $23, child $10.70. T9262 2300, www.sydneyaquarium.com.au Aquarium Pier. Explorer bus stop 23.*

National Maritime Museum

The Maritime Museum is easily reached by foot across the Pyrmont Bridge, or by Monorail, LightRail or the Sydney Explorer bus, stop No 20

The National Maritime Museum, designed to look like the sails of a ship, offers a fine mix of old and new. For many, its biggest attractions are without doubt the warship **MHS Vampire** and submarine **HMAS Onslow**, the centrepiece of a fleet of old vessels sitting outside on the harbour. Both can be thoroughly explored with the help of volunteer guides. The interior of the museum contains a range of displays exploring Australia's close links with all things nautical, from the early navigators and the **First Fleet**, to the ocean liners (that brought many waves of immigrants), commerce, the navy, sport and leisure. Other attractions include a café, shop, sailing lessons and a range of short cruises on a variety of historical vessels. Don't miss the beautifully restored, 1874 square rigger, The *James Craig* which is moored to the north of the museum at Wharf 7. After completion she will set sail again offering another historic cruise option. ■ *Daily 0930-1700. Tickets range according to the number of attractions and range from the basic gallery pass at $10 to the Super Pass at $20, children $6-10, family $25-45. T9298 3777, www.anmm.gov.au, 2 Murray St.*

Sky City Casino   Set back off the harbour and facing the city is the Sky City Casino. Even if you are not a gambler the complex is worth a visit, especially at night, when the many and varied water features that are incorporated in its curvaceous design spring to life in a water and light spectacular. The casino is open 24 hours and there are also two theatres, a nightclub, restaurants, cafés and bars, a hotel and a health club, T9777 9000, www.starcity.com.au

For any one interested in sea creatures, the spectacle of the Sydney Fish Market is highly recommended. Every morning from 0530, nearly 3,000 crates of seafood are sold to a lively bunch of 200 buyers using a computerized auction clock system. The best way to see the action and more importantly the incredible diversity of species is to join a tour group, which will give you access to the auction floor. Normally the general public are confined to the viewing deck high above the floor. Also within the market complex are cafés, some excellent seafood eateries and a superb array of open markets where seafood can be bought at competitive prices. ■ *Tours operate Mon-Fri from 0700, T9552 2180, www.sydneyfishmarket.com.au To get there by car entry is from Bank St Pyrmont. Other possibilities include Sydney Light Rail or bus routes 443 from Circular Quay and 501 from Town Hall.*

Sydney Fish Market
The best time to get to the market is about 0600. Things start to wind up about 1000

With nearly 400,000 items collected over 120 years, the Powerhouse is Australasia's largest museum. Housed in the former Ultimo Power Station, there is an impressive range of memorabilia from aircraft to musical instruments, mainly with an emphasis on Australian innovation and achievement, and covering a wide range of general topics from science and technology to transportation, social history, fashion and design. Shop and café on site. ■ *Daily 1000-1700. $9, children $3, family $20. T9217 0100, www.phm.gov.au 500 Harris St, Ultimo. Access by Monorail, LightRail or Sydney Explorer bus, stop No 17.* Only a short walk from the Powerhouse Museum is **Motor World**, where car buffs can drool over more than 150 rare and everyday vehicles, motorcycles and automotive memorabilia. ■ *Wed-Sun 1000-1700. $10, children $5, family $20. T9552 3375. 320 Harris St, Pyrmont.*

Powerhouse Museum & Motor World
Half a day is barely enough to cover the Powerhouse

Next door to the Darling Harbour VIC, on the Cockle Bay waterfront, is the eight-storey **IMAX** theatre, which shows several one-hour films, with some in 3D, alternately from 1000 daily. ■ *1000-2200. $16.20, children $10.80, family $38. T9281 3300, www.imax.com.au Explorer bus stop No 22.* Facing Tumbalong Park in the southern section of Darling Harbour, and next door to the Chinese Garden, is **Australia's Northern Territory and Outback Centre**. This is little more than a glorified souvenir shop with a free 30-minute live show. If you intend going to the Northern Territory there is also a specialist travel shop and booking agent. ■ *Daily 1000-1800. Performances Tue-Fri 1300, 1500 and 1700, Sat/Sun 1300, 1400, 1500 and 1700. T9283 7477, www.outbackcentre.com.au* Darling Harbour is spectacular at night when the **Waterscreens** show springs to life with a light and music spectacular, using multicoloured lasers that are projected onto two, fine mist fountains in the middle of Cockle Bay. Shows alternate using classical, jazz and popular music and the animated images are excellent. ■ *Wed-Sun every half hour from 1930.*

Other Darling Harbour attractions

The Inner West

Straddling Johnstons Bay and connecting Darling Harbour and Pyrmont with the peninsula suburb of Balmain is Sydney's second landmark bridge, the Anzac Bridge, opened in 1995. It is a modern and strangely attractive edifice, which makes an admirable attempt to compete with the mighty Harbour Bridge. Just beyond its spoke-like suspensions, the former working-class suburb of Balmain has undergone a quiet metamorphosis from a nondescript moth to a vibrant butterfly in search of the tourist dollars. The main drag of Darling Street now boasts a small but eclectic range of gift shops, modern cafés, restaurants and pubs which provide a pleasant half-day escape from the

Balmain

New South Wales

city centre. Try the cosy *Sir William Wallace Hotel*, 31 Cameron Street, T9555 8570, or the more traditional and historic 1857 *Dry Dock Hotel*, corner of Cameron Street and College Street, T9555 1306. There's a popular Saturday market in the grounds of St Andrew's Church, on the corner of Darling Street and Curtis Street. ■ *Starts 0800-1600. Balmain can be reached by bus from the QVB, numbers 441-444, or by ferry from Circular Quay, Wharf 5.*

Glebe & Newtown

Glebe can be reached by bus from George St in the city, numbers 431 or 434 Newtown can be reached by bus from Loftus St (Circular Quay) or George St in the city: Nos 422, 423, 426-428. The Newtown Railway Station is on the Inner West/Bankstown (to Liverpool) lines

To the southwest of Darling Harbour, beyond Ultimo, and seperated by the campus of **Sydney University** (Australia's oldest), are Glebe and Newtown. **Glebe** prides itself in having a New Age village atmosphere, where a cosmopolitan, mainly student crowd sits in the laid-back cafés, browses old-style bookshops or bohemian fashion outlets, or seeks the latest therapies in alternative health shops. The Saturday market provides an outlet for local crafts people to sell their work as well as a mix of bric-a-brac, clothes and New Age essentials. ■ *Mon-Sat 1100-1230, Sun 1100-1145. Grounds of Glebe Public School, Glebe Point Rd, T9660 2370.* South beyond the university is **King Street**, the hub of Newtown's idiosyncratic range of shops, cafés and restaurants. Here you can purchase anything from a black leather cod-piece to an industrial size brass buddah, dribble over the menus of a vast range of interesting eateries, or simply sit over a latte, feeling hopelessly boring and conservative. A few hour's exploration, Sunday brunch or an evening meal in Newtown's King Street is highly recommended. Don't miss **Gould's Secondhand Bookshop** at 32 King Street, which is an experience in itself. Other interesting second-hand shops await you at the southern end of Kings Street, beyond the railway station.

Leichardt

Leichardt can be reached by bus from the QVB in the city, Nos 440 or 445

Although receiving less attention than the eccentricities of Glebe and Newtown Leichardt is a pleasant suburb, famous for its **Italian** connections and subsequently its eateries and cafés. There are numerous places to enjoy a fine expresso, gelato or the full lasagne with Norton Street being the main focus. Some of the most popular venues include *Bar Italia,*169 Norton Street, T9560 9981, *Sorriso,* 70 Norton Street, T9572 9915, *Elio,* 159 Norton Street, T9560 9129, *Café Corso at the Italian Forum*, T9569 2997, and *Frattini,* 122 Marion Street, T9569 2997.

Further West

Homebush Bay Olympic Park

Although the vast swathes of Sydney's Western Suburbs remain all but an urban and ethnic jungle for the vast majority of tourists, there are a few major and minor sights worth a mention. Topping the list is of course the multi-million dollar **Homebush Bay Olympic Park** with its mighty stadium, the centrepiece of a vast array of architecturally stunning sports venues and public amenities. **Telstra Stadium** (formerly Stadium Australia) was the main focus of the games, being the venue for the opening and closing ceremonies, as well as track and field and soccer events. Although the Olympic flame has long been extinguished, it remains an important national venue for international and national rugby union, rugby league, Aussie rules football and soccer matches. ■ *Tours are conducted hourly and daily from 1000-1600, T8765 2300, www.stadiumaustralia.com.au* Next door is the state-of-the-art **Sydney Superdome** that hosted basketball and gymnastics during the games and now offers a huge indoor arena for a range of public events from music concerts to Australia's largest agricultural show, the Royal Easter Show. ■ *Guided tours available daily from 1000-1600, T8765 4321.* Perhaps the most celebrated venue during the games was the **Sydney International Aquatic Centre** where the triumphant Aussie swimming team took on the world and won in the wake of such stars as Thorpe ('Thorpedo') and Klim. The complex continues to hold international swimming and diving events and is now open to the public, T9752 3666. The Olympic Park has many other state-of-the-art sports facilities and is surrounded by superb parkland. **Bicentennial Park** is a 100-ha mix of dryland and conservation wetland and a popular spot for walking, jogging, birdwatching or simply feeding the ducks. Guided nature tours are available, T9763 1844.

■ *For information on facilities and activities within Olympic Park call or visit the Homebush Bay Olympic Park Visitors Centre at 1 Herb Elliot Av, near the Olympic Park Railway Station. It has maps, displays, tour details and Olympic Games information. Daily 0900-1700, T9714 7888, www.oca.nsw.gov.au There is also a VIC in Bicentennial Park, T9763 1844. Daily 0930-1630. Homebush Bay is about 14 km west of the city centre and is best reached by train (Western Line) from the city, or alternatively by Rivercat, from Circular Quay (Wharf 5) to Homebush Bay Wharf. The Olympic Explorer Bus leaves every 15 mins between 0920-1700 daily from the VIC, Herb Elliot Av, $10, children $5, T131500. The Olympic Explorer links with ferry services from Circular Quay.*

About 6 km further west from Homebush is **Parramatta**, often dubbed the city within the city, a culturally diverse centre which boasts some of the nation's most historic sites. When the First Fleeters failed in their desperate attempts to grow crops in what is now Port Jackson in the city centre, they penetrated the upper reaches of the Parramatta River and established a farming settlement, first known as Rose Hill before reverting to its original Aboriginal name. The oldest European site is **Elizabeth Farm**, a 1793 colonial homestead built for John and Elizabeth Macarthur, former pioneers in the Australian wool industry. The homestead contains a number of interesting displays and is surrounded by a recreated 1830s garden. ■ *Daily 1000-1700, $7, children $3, family $17, T9635 9488. 70 Alice St, Rosehill.* Also of interest is the 1799 **Old Government House** in Parramatta Park. It is Australia's oldest public building and houses a fine collection of Colonial furniture. ■ *Mon-Fri 1000-1600, Sat/Sun 1100-1600, $12, T9635 8149.* **Experiment Farm Cottage**, 9 Ruse Street, T9635 5655, is the site of the colonial government's first land grant to former convict James Ruse in 1791. The cottage itself dates from 1834. ■ *Tue-Fri 1030-1530, Sat/Sun 1130-1530, $5.* The **Parramatta River** which quietly glides past the city is without doubt its most attractive natural attraction and it features in a number of heritage walking trails. These and many other historical details are displayed at the **Parramatta Heritage and Visitors Information Centre**, 346a Church Street. ■ *Mon-Fri 1000-1700, Sat/Sun 1000-1600 T9630 3703, www.parracity.nsw.gov.au* Parramatta can be reached by train direct from the city centre (Western Line) or bus route 520 from Circular Quay. The best way to make a day of your visit is to take the 50 minute *Parramatta Rivercat* journey from Wharf 5 Circular Quay. It winds its way up the Inner Harbour offering great views back across the city and ventures past the Homebush Bay Olympic Park. The *Parramatta Explorer Bus* is a specialist service that explores the historical aspects of the city at weekends between 1000-1600. It stops at both the Rivercat Terminal and the main railway station, $10, child $5, T9630 3703.

Featherdale Wildlife Park, in Doonside, has the largest private collection of native Australian Wildlife in the country with over 2,000 animals roaming free in the park. You can also hand-feed kangaroos, wallabies and emus and of

Parramatta & around
The free brochure 'Discover Parramatta 2002', that is available from the local or Sydney VICs is also very useful

course cuddle a koala. The on-site shop is also excellent. ■ *Daily 0900-1700, $15, children $7.50, family $38, T9622 1644. 217 Kildare Road. Recommended. By car go via the M4 and turn off onto Reservoir Rd. After 4 km turn left onto Kildare Rd. Alternatively take the train from the city (Western Line) to Blacktown then bus 725 from the station.* Other face-to-face wildlife encounters can be had at The **Australian Wildlife Park** which is part of **Wonderland Sydney**, a vast amusement park with many highly staged aspects of Australiana from boomerang throwing to sheep mustering. ■ *Daily 0900-1700, Wildlife Park only $16.50 (Wonderland $44), children $9.90 ($29.70), family $47.50, T9830 9100, www.wonderland.com.au Wallgrove Rd, Eastern Creek. Take the Wallgrove exit off the M4 westbound or Wonderlink a transport and entry combo, T131500. The Wonderland Express also offers transits from major hotels, T9830 9187.*

Penrith Sitting at the base of the Blue Mountains and beside the Nepean River, Penrith offers a number of exciting water-based activities which have been augmented with the creation of the Penrith Whitewater Stadium used for the canoe/kayak slalom venue for the 2000 Olympics. Rafting sessions are now available to the public. Phone for details and directions, T4730 4333. The **Sydney International Regatta Centre** has two purpose built facilities used for the rowing and canoeing events of the 2000 Olympics. Much more user-friendly is the **Cables Waterski Park,** near the VIC, which offers cable-towed water skiing, waterslides and pools. ■ *For more information contact the VIC, Panthers Carpark, Mulgoa Rd, Penrith, T4732 7671, wwwpenrithvalley.com.au Daily 0900-1630.*

The Inner East

Kings Cross & surrounds
You need to have your wits about you as petty theft is common and be ready for the largely unwanted attention of omnipresent drunks

Even before arriving in Sydney you will have probably heard of Kings Cross, the notorious hub of Sydney nightlife and the long-established focus of sex, drugs and rock and roll. Situated near the navy's Woolloomooloo docks 'The Cross' (as it's often called) has been a favourite haunt of visiting sailors and Sydneysiders for years. The main drag, **Darlinghurst Road**, is the focus of the action, while Victoria Road is home to a rash of Backpacker hostels. At the intersection of both and the top of William Street, which connects The Cross with the city, is the huge **Coca Cola sign**, a popular meeting point. The best time to visit The Cross is in the early hours when the bars, the clubs and ladies of the night are all in full swing. It is enormously popular with backpackers and Sydneysiders alike and can provide a great (and often memorable) night out. It is also a great place to meet people, make contacts, find work and even buy a car. Admist all the mania there are a number of notable and more sedate sights in and around Kings Cross. **Elizabeth Bay House** is a revival style estate that was built by popular architect John Verge for Colonial secretary Alexander Macleay in 1845. The interior is restored and faithfuly furnished in accordance with the times and the house has a great outlook across the harbour. ■ *Tue-Sun 1000-1630, $7, children $3, family $17, T9356 3022. 7 Onslow Av, Elizabeth Bay.*

To the northwest of Kings Cross, through the quieter and more upmarket sanctuary of Potts Point, is the delightfully named suburb of **Woolloomooloo**. 'Woo' is the main east coast base for the Australian Navy and visiting sailors also weigh anchor here, heading straight for the Kings Cross souvenir shops. Other than the warships and a scattering of lively pubs, it is the **Woolloomooloo Wharf** and a pie cart that are the major attractions. The new wharf has a rash of fine restaurants which are a popular dining alternative to the busy city centre. If the wharf restaurants are beyond your budget, nearby is one of Sydneys best cheap eateries. **Harry's Café de Wheels**, near the wharf entrance, is something of an instituton, selling its own $3 range of meat, mash, pea and gravy pies. The cart is open almost 24 hours a day. Kings Cross can be reached by foot from the city via William Street or Woolloomooloo. By bus *Sydney Explorer* stop No 9, Elizabeh Bay House stop 11, Wooloomooloo stop No 13 (0840-1722 only) or regular bus services Nos 311, 323-325, 327, 333 or by train Illawarra Line from

New South Wales

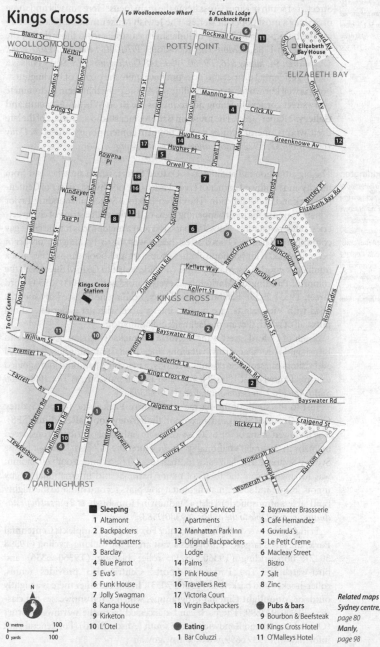

Kings Cross

Sleeping
1 Altamont
2 Backpackers Headquarters
3 Barclay
4 Blue Parrot
5 Eva's
6 Funk House
7 Jolly Swagman
8 Kanga House
9 Kirketon
10 L'Otel
11 Macleay Serviced Apartments
12 Manhattan Park Inn
13 Original Backpackers Lodge
14 Palms
15 Pink House
16 Travellers Rest
17 Victoria Court
18 Virgin Backpackers

Eating
1 Bar Coluzzi
2 Bayswater Brassserie
3 Café Hernandez
4 Govinda's
5 Le Petit Creme
6 Macleay Street Bistro
7 Salt
8 Zinc

Pubs & bars
9 Bourbon & Beefsteak
10 Kings Cross Hotel
11 O'Malleys Hotel

Related maps
Sydney centre, page 80
Manly, page 98

Town Hall or Martin Place. Between 2400 and 0430. Nightride buses replace trains, but check times and stops between 0600-2200 (T131500).

New South Wales

Darlinghurst & Surry Hills

Darlinghurst and Surry Hills can be reached by foot from the city via William St, Liverpool St or Oxford St or by bus Nos 311-399

The lively suburb of Darlinghurst fringes the city to the west, Kings Cross to the north and Surry Hills to the south. Both Darlinghurst and Surry Hills offer some great **restaurants** and **cafés** with Darlinghurst Road and Victoria Street, just south of Kings Cross being the main focus. Here you will find some of Sydney's most popular eateries. The **Jewish Museum** has displays featuring the holocaust and history of Judaism in Australia from the arrival of the First Fleet in 1788. ■ *Mon-Thu 1000-1600, Fri 1000-1400, Sun 1100-1700, $7, children $4, family $16, T9360 7999. 148 Darlinghurst Rd.* Surry Hills is a mainly residential district and does not have quite the pizzaz of Darlinghurst, but it is well known for its very traditional Aussie pubs that seem to dominate every street corner One thing not to miss is the **Brett Whitley Museum and Gallery**, 2 Raper Street. The museum is the former studio and home of the late Brett who is one of Sydney's most popular contemporary artists. ■ *Daily 1000-1600, $7, T9225 1881, info@brettwhiteley.org*

Paddington

For a full listing of galleries pick up a free 'Art Find' brochure from one of the galleries or the Sydney VIC. A stroll down Glenmore Rd to the crossroads of Goodhope and Heeley St will reveal some of the best of them

The big attraction in Paddington is **Oxford Street**, which stretches east from the city and southwest corner of Hyde Park to the northwest corner of Centennial Park and Bondi Junction. The city end Oxford Street, surrounding Taylor Square, is one of the most happening areas of the city with a string of cheap eateries, cafés, restaurants, clubs and bars. It is also a major focus for the city's gay community. Then as Oxford street heads west in to Paddington proper it becomes lined with boutique clothes shops, art and book shops, cafés and a number of good pubs. Many people coincide a visit to Oxford Street with the colourful **Paddington Market**, held every Saturday from 1000 (395 Oxford Street, T9331 2923). Behind Oxford Street, heading north, are leafy suburbs lined with Victorian terrace houses, interspersed with **art galleries** and old **pubs**, all of which that are the hallmark of Paddington.

South of Oxford Street is the **Victoria Barracks** which has been a base to British and Australian Army battalions since 1848. It remains fully functional and visitors can see a flag-raising ceremony, a marching band and join a guided tour on Thursdays at 1000. There is also a small museum. ■ *Thu 1000-1400 Sun 1000-1500 (museum only), free, T9339 3303.*

Just to the south of the Barracks in **Moore Park** is the famous **Sydney Cricket Ground (SCG)** and, next door, the **Sydney Football Stadium (SFS)**. The hallowed arena of the SCG is a veritable cathedral of cricket, considered by many as Australia's national sport. In winter the SCG is taken over by the Sydney Swans, Australian rules football team. The Sydney Football Stadium was for many years the focus of major national and international, rugby union, league and soccer matches but it now plays second fiddle to the mighty (and far less atmospheric) Telstra Stadium in Homebush. ■ *Tours of both stadiums are available to the public, T9380 0383.*

Fringing the two stadiums and former Fox Studios Complex is **Centennial Park**, the city's largest. It provides a vast arena for walking, cycling (T9398 5027), horse-riding (T9360 7521), roller blading (T9360 6356) and bird-watching. The Parklands Sports Centre also provides tennis, roller-hockey and basketball (T9662 7033). In late summer there is a nightly outdoor **Moonlight Cinema** programme, which often showcases old classics; T1900-933899. The park can be accessed from the northwest corner (Oxford Street) and Randwick to the south (Alison Road). For general park information T9339 6699, www.cp.nsw.gov.au

Paddington can be reached by foot from the southeast corner of Hyde Park in the city via Oxford Street. By bus 378-382, or the *Bondi and Bay Explorer* (stop No 14) from Circular Quay and Railway Square.

Further East

Watson's Bay, on the leeward side of **South Head**, which guards the mouth of Sydney Harbour, provides an ideal city escape and is best reached by ferry from Circular Quay. As well as being the home to one of Sydney's oldest and most famous seafood restaurants – **Doyles** – it offers some quiet coves, attractive swimming beaches and peninsula walks. The best beaches are to be found at **Camp Cove** about 10 minutes walk north of the ferry terminal. A little further north is **Lady Bay Beach**, which is very secluded and a popular naturist beach. The best walk in the area is the 1-2 hour jaunt to the 1858 **Hornby Lighthouse** and South Head itself, then south to the **HMAS Watson Naval Chapel** and the area known as **The Gap**. The clifftop aspect provides greats views out towards the ocean and north to North Head and Manly.

> **Watson's Bay**
> *Reached by ferry from Circular Quay Wharfs 2 and 4, or by bus 342 and 325 from Circular Quay*

The area also boasts some interesting historical sites. Camp Cove was used by Governor Phillip as an overnight stop before reaching Port Jackson in the Inner Harbour. **Vaucluse House** on Wentworth Road, south of Watson's Bay, was built in 1827 and is a fine example of an early colonial estate. ■ *Tue-Sun 1000-1630, $7, children $3, family $17, T9388 7922.* Many people spend a morning exploring Watsons Bay before enjoying a leisurely lunch at *Doyles,* which sits just above the beach and ferry terminal on Marine Parade. Nextdoor to *Doyles* is the *Watsons Bay Hotel,* a more casual affair offering equally good views of the city skyline and a superb outdoor BBQ area offering a range of fresh seafood. If you intend to dine at *Doyles,* bear in mind it is hugely popular, so book well ahead, T9337 2007.

Bondi Beach is by far the most famous of Sydney's many ocean beaches. Its hugely inviting stretch of sand is a prime venue for surfing, swimming and sunbathing and the epitome of Sydney lifestyle. Behind the beach, Bondi's bustling waterfront and village offers a tourist trap of cafés, restaurants, bars, surf and souvenir shops. For years Bondi has been a popular suburb for alternative lifestylers and visiting backpackers keen to avoid the central city. It is also the place to see or be seen by all self-respecting beautiful people. If you intend swimming at Bondi note that, like every Australian beach, it is subject to dangerous rips so always swim between the yellow and red flags, clearly marked on the beach. Watchful lifeguards, also clad in yellow and red, are on hand. Bondi Beach is the focus of wild celebrations on Christmas Day with one huge beach party, usually culminating in a mass naked dash into the sea.

> **Bondi, Bronte & Coogee beaches**

To the south of Bondi Beach and best reached by a popular **coastal walk-way**, is the small oceanside suburb of **Bronte**. This little enclave offers a smaller, quieter and equally attractive beach with a number of very popular cafés frequented especially at the weekend for brunch. A little further south still is **Clovelly**, which has another sheltered beach especially good for kids. Many people finish their walk at **Coogee**, which has a fine beach and bustling waterfront. Although playing second fiddle to Bondi, it is also a popular haunt for backpackers or couples keen to stay near the beach and outwith the city centre. Bondi can be reached by car from the city, via Oxford Street, by the *Bondi and Bay Explorer,* or bus services 321, 322, 365, 366, 380. By rail first get to Bondi Junction (Illawara Line) then take the bus (numbers above). Coogee is serviced by bus 372-374 and 314-315.

New South Wales

The North Shore

New South Wales

North Sydney & surrounds

At night, the ferry trip across the harbour to the city from Cremorne Wharf is almost worth the trip in itself

On the northern side of the Harbour Bridge a small stand of highrise buildings with neon signs heralds the mainly commercial suburb of **North Sydney**. There is little here for the tourist to justify a special visit, but nearby, the suburb of **McMahons Point**, and more especially **Blues Point Reserve**, on the shores of Lavender Bay, offers fine city views. Another good vantage point is right below the bridge at **Milsons Point**. There is a lookout point which looks straight across to Circular Quay and the Opera House almost in the shadow of the bridge. Milsons Point is also home to the seldom used Luna Park, a former fun park, which has become another icon of the inner harbour. Another attraction is the old **Sydney Olympic Pool** next door to Luna Park, which offers spectacular city views, T9955 2309. Kirribilli is a serene little suburb lying directly to the east of the bridge. Admiralty House and **Kirribilli House**, the Sydney residences of the Governor General and the Prime Minister sit overlooking the Opera House on Kirribilli Point. Both are closed to the public and are best seen from the water. Beyond Kirribilli, are the residential suburbs and secluded bays of **Neutral Bay** and **Cremorne**.

Mosman & Balmoral

Mosman has a very pleasant village feel and its well-heeled residents are rightly proud. Situated so close to the city centre, it has developed into one of the most exclusive and expensive areas of real estate in the city. However, don't let this put you off. Mosman in unison with its equally comfy, neighbouring, beachside suburb of Balmoral, are both great escapes by ferry from the city centre and offer some fine eateries, designer clothes shops, walks and **beaches**, plus one of Sydney's 'must-see' attractions, **Taronga Zoo**. Mosman is best reached by ferry from Circular Quay (Wharf 4) to the Mosman Bay where a bus awaits to take you up the hill to the commercial centre. Alternatively take buses 238, 250 or, for Mosman and the zoo, 247 from Wynyard Station in the CBD.

Taronga Zoo

First opened in 1881 in the grounds of Moore Park, south of Centennial Park, Paddington, before being relocated to Bradley's Head, Mosman in 1916, Taronga has all the usual suspects of the zoological world, but also has the huge added attraction of perhaps the best location and views of any city zoo in the world. You will almost certainly need a full day to explore the various exhibits on offer and there are plenty of events staged throughout the day to keep both adults and children entertained. The best of these is the Kodak **Bird Show** which is staged twice daily in an open-air arena overlooking the city. ■ *Daily 0900-1700. $21, children 11.50, family $38.50. A Zoo Pass combo ticket which includes ferry transfers and zoo entry costs $25, child $12.50. Taronga is best reached by ferry from Circular Quay (Wharf 2). Ferries go back and forth every half hour Mon-Fri from 0715-1845, Sat 0845-1845 and Sun 0845-1730. Note that Taronga is built on a hill and the general recommendation is to take the waiting bus from the zoo wharf up to the main entrance then work your way back down to the lower gate. Alternatively for a small additional charge on entry you can take a scenic gondola ride to the main gate. If you are especially interested in wildlife it pays to check out the dynamic programme of specialist public tours on offer. The 'Night Zoo' tour after hours is especially popular. T1900 920 218 (tours T9969 2455), www.zoo.nsw.gov.au*

Balmoral Beach is one of the most popular and sheltered in the harbour. Here, more than anywhere else in the city, you can observe Sydneysiders enjoying something that is quintessentially Sydney and Australian – the early morning, pre-work dip. Balmoral Beach overlooks **Middle Harbour**, whose waters infiltrate far into suburbs of the North Shore. On **Middle Head**, which juts out in to the harbour beyond Mosman, you will find one of Sydney's best and most secluded naturist beaches – **Cobblers Beach**. The atmosphere is friendly and the crowd truly cosmopolitan, though the less extrovert among you should probably avoid the peninsula on the eastern edge of the beach. The beach is served several times a day by a refreshments boat which stocks soft drinks and ice cream. Access is via a little known track behind the softball pitch near the end of Military Road. You can also walk to the tip of **Middle Head**, where old wartime fortifications look out across North Head and the harbour entrance, or enjoy the walk to the tip of **Bradleys Head**, below the zoo, with its wonderful views of the city. Park your car at the Ashton Park car park about 1 km before the zoo wharf and find the track to the west, skirting the water's edge. Alternatively just follow the path, east from the zoo's lower entrance.

Walks & beaches
The NSW National Parks and Wildlife Service offer guided tours to Bradleys Head on the 1st and 3rd Sun of each month at 1330-1530 and to Middle Head on the 2nd and 4th Sun of the month from 1030-1230, $13.20, children $9.90

Manly and the Northern Beaches

Manly is by far the most visited suburb on the North Shore and is practically a self-contained holiday resort, offering an oceanside sanctuary, away from the manic city centre. The heart of the community sits on the neck of the **North Head** peninsula, which guards the entrance of Sydney Harbour. **Manly Beach**, which fringes the ocean or eastern edge of the suburb, is very much the main attraction. At its southern end, an attractive oceanside walkway connects Manly Beach with two smaller, quieter alternatives, **Fairy Bower Beach** and **Shelly Beach**. As you might expect, Manly comes with all the tourist trappings, including an attractive tree-lined waterfront, fringed with cafés, restaurants, souvenir and surf shops and a wealth of accommodation options.

Manly

Connecting Manly Beach with the ferry terminal and **Manly Cove** (on the western or harbour side) is the **Corso**, a fairly tacky pedestrian precinct lined with cheap eateries, bars and souvenir shops. Its only saving grace being the **market** held at its eastern end every weekend. The Manly Visitors **Information Centre** is located on the forecourt, next to the ferry terminal and is an ideal first stop. It is well stocked with leaflets and the staff are enthusiastic and helpful (■ *Daily 1000-1600, T9977 1088, www.manly.nsw.gov.au* **Internet** *is available at the* Manly Internet and Travel Centre, *35 Belgrave Square, T99762070, or* Manly Computers, *1/27 Sydney Road*.

Just to the west of the ferry terminal is West Esplanade with a quiet swimming beach (with shark net) that is ideal for kids. At the western are Oceanworld and the Manly Art Gallery and Museum. **Oceanworld** is a long established aquarium and worth a visit if you have children. The star attraction is the sharks, along with various other 'dangerous' Australian creatures. ■ *Regular tours are available and the sharks are fed on Mon, Wed and Fri at 1100. Daily 1000-1730, $16, children $8, family $25, T9949 2644, www.oceanworldmanly.com* The **Manly Art Gallery and Museum** showcases an interesting array of permanent historical items with the obvious emphasis on all things 'beach', while the gallery offers both permanent and temporary shows of contemporary art and photography. It also hosts the **Manly Arts Festival** held annually around September. ■ *Tue-Sun 1000-1700, $3.50, children $1.10, T9949 1776.*

The tip of **North Head**, to the south of Manly is well worth a look, if only to soak up the **views** across the harbour and out to sea. The cityscape is especially

New South Wales

stunning at dawn. Just follow Scenic Drive to the very end. The **Quarantine Station**, taking up a large portion of the peninsula, was used from 1832 to harbour ships known to be carrying diseases like smallpox, bubonic plague, cholera and spanish influenza and to protect the new colony from the spread of such nasties. The station closed in 1984 and is now administered by the NSW Parks and Wildlife Service. ■ *Daily tours are available Mon,Wed,Fri,Sat and Sun at 1310, $11, children $7.70. More popular still is the daily 3-hr Ghost Tour at 1930 which includes supper, Wed $22, Fri-Sun $27.50. A 2-hr kids' version at 1800 is also available, $13.20, T9247 5033. Bookings recommended. Bus 135 from Manly wharf.* Although it is closed to the public, the Sydney **Water Pollution Control Station**, on the peninsula's northeastern corner, is worth a mention, not just because it boasts a street called **Poo Avenue**, but as one of the last remaining Sydney strongholds of the **long nosed bandicoot**, an eternally appealing, rat-sized marsupial, that once thrived throughout the region.

Manly offers a wealth of other **activities** including cycling, sea kayaking, roller-blading, diving and of course surfing. The VIC lists outlets and hire prices. Manly also hosts a major **Jazz Festival** in October and a **Food and Wine Festival** in June. The-10 km **Manly Scenic Walkway** from Manly to Spit Bridge is an excellent scenic harbour walk. It starts from the end of West

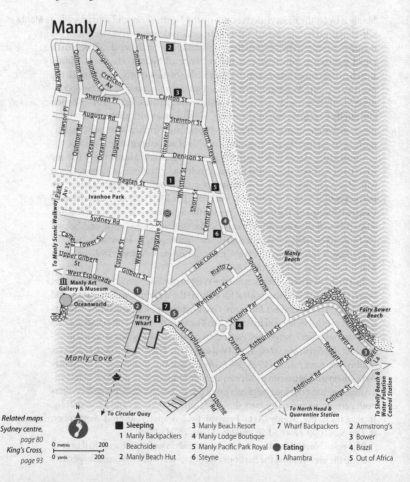

Manly

N

To Circular Quay

■ **Sleeping**	3 Manly Beach Resort	7 Wharf Backpackers
1 Manly Backpackers	4 Manly Lodge Boutique	
Beachside	5 Manly Pacific Park Royal	● **Eating**
2 Manly Beach Hut	6 Steyne	1 Alhambra

2 Armstrong's
3 Bower
4 Brazil
5 Out of Africa

0 metres 200
0 yards 200

Esplanade and takes from three to four hours. You can catch a 144 or 143 bus back to Manly from the Spit, T131500. Before you attempt this walk try to get hold of the NSW Parks and Wildlife Service 'Manly Scenic Walkway' leaflet from the Sydney or Manly VICs or Sydney Harbour National Parks Office, Cadman's Cottage, The Rocks, T92475033. ■ The best way to reach Manly is by ferry from Circular Quay (wharfs 2 and 3). Ferry $5, children $2.50, 30 mins; Jet Cat $6.30, 15 mins. Both leave on a regular basis daily. Alternatively take bus 151 or 171 from Wynyard in the city, T131500.

The coast north of Manly is indented by numerous bays and fine beaches that stretch 10 km to **Barrenjoey Head** at Broken Bay and the entrance to the Hawkesbury River harbour. Perhaps the most popular of these are **Narrabeen**, **Avalon** and **Whale Beach**, but there are many to choose from. Narabeen has the added attraction of a large lake, used for sailing, canoeing and windsurfing, while Avalon and Whale Beach, further north, are smaller, quite picturesque and more sheltered. A day trip to the very tip and Barrenjoey Head is recommended and the area is complemented by **Palm Beach**, a popular weekend getaway with some fine restaurants. There are many water activities on offer in the area focused mainly on **Pittwater**, a large bay on the sheltered western side of the peninsula. Day **cruises** up the **Hawkesbury River** ($30, children $15), or shorter excursions to **The Basin** (pretty beaches and camping areas in the Ku-ring-Gai Chase National Park) are also available from the Palm Beach Public Wharf, T9997 4815. The Barrenjoey Boathouse has boats and kayaks for hire, T9974 4229, and a Dive Centre, T9974 4261. You can even fly into Pittwater from Sydney harbour by **floatplane**, T1300 656787, www.sydneybyseaplane.com The most popular walk in the area is to the summit of Barrenjoey Head and the historic **lighthouse**, built in 1881. The views both north and south are spectacular. Access is from the Barrenjoey Boathouse car park and via the northern end of Station Beach (western side). Whether just for a day-trip or a weekend stay get hold of the free 'Northern Beaches Visitors Guide' from the Sydney VIC. It is an excellent **information** booklet covering just about everything from accommodation to shopping, anywhere north of Manly to Barrenjoey Head, www.sydneynorthernbeaches.com.au The L90 bus from Wynard in the city goes via all the main northen beaches suburbs to Palm Beach, every 30 minutes daily.

The North of Manly to Palm Beach
Palm Beach has been made especially famous by the popular Aussie soap opera 'Home and Away'

New South Wales

Activities

The most high-profile activity in the city is the award-winning **Bridge Climb**, which involves the ascent of the 134-m Harbour Bridge span. The three-hour climb can be done day or night and in most weather conditions besides electrical storms. Before setting out you are suitably garbed and given a thorough safety briefing. Many say that as well as the stunning views from the top it is the excitement of getting there that is most memorable. Although it is fairly easy-going and is regularly done by the elderly, the sight and noise of the traffic below adds a special edge. Note that you cannot take your own camera on the trip – for safety reasons – but photographs of your group will be taken at the top. Bridge Climb headquarters is at 5 Cumberland Street, The Rocks. ■ 0700-1900. Climbs during the week cost from from $125, children $100, weekends $150, children $125. Night climbs during the week cost from $150, children $125, at weekends $170, children $150. T8274 7777, www.bridgeclimb.com

With all there is to see in Sydney visitors rarely have time to partake in specialist activities beyond the beach. However the city does offer a number of attractive possibilities, mostly based on or around the harbour

Cruises

There are numerous good value Harbour Cruises on offer with most being based at Circular Quay. Trips vary from a sedate cruise on a replica of the Bounty to paddle steamers and fast catamarans

There are three principal companies offering a wide range of cruises on mainly modern craft; *Captain Cook* (T9206 1111, cruise@captaincook.com.au), *Sydney ferries*, based at Circular Quay, T9997 4815, and *Matilda*, based at Aquarium Wharf, Darling Harbour. Other companies offering cruises on older or specialist vessels include the replica of *The Bounty* (T9247 1789, www.thebounty.com.au), *The Vagabond* (T9660 0388, www.vagabond.com.au), *Ocean Spirit* (T9660 0207, www.oceanspirit.com.au), *The Majestic* (T9552 2722, www.bluelinecruises.com.au), and the 1874 *James Craig* (T9298 3870). Majestic also own and operate the *Sydney Showboat Paddlesteamer* fleet which are replicas of the original vessels that used to ply the harbour in the 1800s. *The Americas Cup Spirit* is a fairly new edition to the harbour fleet. She is an International America's Cup Class yacht from the 1992 San Diego Challenge. The three-hour cruise offers an exhilarating introduction to the world of yacht racing, T9660 9133. No sailing experience is necessary. There are also excellent cruise options up the Hawkesbury River from Palm Beach, north of Sydney, with *Sydney Ferries*. The *Harbour Jet* and *Jet Cats* also cruise to Manly or up to Parramatta, T131500, www.sydneytransport.net.au If you are looking for a cruise with a difference, contact *Aussie Duck*, T131007, www.aussieduck.com

Diving

Although diving is best at the Barrier Reef, if you are heading north to Queensland, NSW and Sydney there is some good diving. The southern beaches, La Perouse and the Botany Bay National Park offer the best spots. There are dive shops in the city and companies offering tuition and trips. These include the popular *Dive Centre* bases at both Manly (10 Belgrave Street, T9977 4355) and Bondi (192 Bondi Road, T9369 3855), www.divesydney.com They offer shore, boat and shark dives from $40 (own gear), $80 (hire) and Open Water Certificates from $270. Pro Dive, 478 George Street, T9264 6177, offer similar local trips and training and stock a good range of equipment.

Fishing

The VIC has listings of other charters based in Sydney, many of which also offer Whale-watching trips from June to October

Despite all the harbour activity, both the **fishing** and the water quality in Sydney Harbour is said to be pretty good, with species like flathead, whiting and trevally being regularly caught, especially downstream from the Harbour Bridge. Offshore, the fishing obviously improves dramatically and Sydney is home to its own fishing fleet that regularly catch such exotics as marlin and tuna. There are a number of fishing charters available including *Charter One*, T04-0133 2355, www.charterone.com, based in Manly. Trips range from a three-hour jaunt from $65 to full-day $125, including tackle hire. *Quayside Charters*, T9555 2600, are based at Circular Quay. Others include *Fishfinder*, T4446 4466, *Bounty Hunter*, 378 Pitt Street, T9661 9430, and *Gemini*, T04-1822 8729.

Surfing

The best spots in Sydney are of course Bondi and Manly but most of Sydney's beaches offer great possibilities

Surfing is of course a national pastime in Australia with most kids learning to ride the waves from a very early age. For those wishing to learn *Manly Surf School*, based at the North Steyne Surf Club, Manly Beach, T9977 6977, www.manlysurfschool, offer good value daily classes from 1100-1300, from $45 for one lesson to five-day lessons from $150. The *Dripping Wet Surf Company*, Shop 2/93-95 North Steyne, Manly, T9977 3549, offer boards, body boards, flippers and wetsuits for hire. Board hire costs from $12 per hour. *Aloha Surf*, 44 Pittwater Road, Manly, T9977 3777, offer similar rates. In Bondi try the *Bondi Surf Company*, 2/72 Campbell Parade, T9365 0870. For up-to-date surf conditions. Check the website www.wavecam.com.au *Aussie Surf Adventures* are another company that offer multi-day surf trips and intensive lessons from Sydney to Byron Bay, T1800 113 044, www.surfadventures.com.au (five days, from $500).

Swimming is of course a popular pastime in Australia and given Sydney's **Swimming**
climate, can be enjoyed in the sea almost year round. South of the Heads the
beaches at Bondi, Bronte, Clovelly and Coogee are hugely popular while to
the north, Manly, Collaroy, Narrabeen, Avalon, Ocean Beach and Palm
Beach are also good spots. Lifeguards patrol most beaches in summer and
you are strongly advised to swim between the yellow and red flags. These are
clearly staked out along the beach and placed according to conditions. At
times when the surf is unusually high beaches may be closed for swimming
altogether. Most of the city beaches also have safe, open-air, salt-water
swimming pools to provide added safety, especially for children. Indoor
heated pools are not a rarity in Sydney and three in particular offer great
facilities. Topping the list is the *Sydney Aquatic Centre*, at the Homebush
Bay Olympic Park. ■ *Mon-Fri 0500-2145, Sat/Sun 0600-1945, T9752 3666.*
Right in the centre of town is the *Cook Phillip Park Aquatic Centre*, 6 College
Street, next to Hyde Park. ■ *$4.50, children $3.30. T9326 0444.* Much older
but offering the best view in town is the *Sydney Olympic Pool*, that sits almost
below the Harbour Bridge, on Alfred Street, Milson's Point, North Shore.
■ *$3.80, children $1.80. T9955 2309.* The *McCallum Pool* is a smaller outdoor public pool on Cremorne Point (off Milson's Road). It also offers great
views across the harbour.

Inevitably perhaps Circular Quay and Darling Harbour are home to a couple **Other**
of **jet boating** companies that zip up and down the inner harbour. At Circular **watersports**
Quay *Oz Jetboating* rule the roost and are based at east Circular Quay, T9660
6111, www.ozjetboating.com They offer 30-minute trips departing daily
from 1000, from $30, children $20, family $90. Based at the western shore of
Cockle Bay in Darling Harbour, *Harbourjet* offer trips from 35 minutes for
$35, to one hour 20 minute trips from $75, T9929 7373, www.harbourjet.com
au Sydney Harbour offers some of the best **sailing** in the world. On Boxing
Day every year, at the start of the Sydney to Hobart race the inner harbour
becomes a patchwork of colourful spinnakers given to the mercy of the winds.
Sydney Mainsail, T9979 3681, www.sydneymainsail.com.au, offer
three-hour trips three times daily with highly experienced skippers. The *Australian Spirit Sailing Company*, T9878 0300, www.austspiritsailingco.com.au,
also offer similar trips. The National Maritime Museum is also a good place to
enquire, being the base for *Sydney by Sail*, which runs introductory lessons
from $54 for 1½ hours, T9280 1110. The office is based below the lighthouse.
Other possibilities include the *Australian Sailing School and Club*, The Spit,
Mosman, T9960 3077, the *Eastsail, D'Albora Marina,* New Beach Road,
Ruschcutters Bay, T9327 1166, and the *Balmoral Windsurfing and Sailing
School,* 2 The Esplanade, Balmoral Beach, T9960 5344. Pittwater to the north
of Sydney is also a hugely popular spot for sailing and offers numerous oppor-
tunities. Get hold of a copy of the '*Northern Beaches Visitors Guide*' from the
VIC for listings.

   Sea kayaking is a great way to see the harbour and explore the backwaters
and bays of the inner suburbs. The Middle Harbour, which branches off
between Middle Head and Clontarf, snakes over 10 km into the
lesser-known North Shore suburbs and is especially good. It also offers a
much quieter environment and more wildlife. It is not entirely unusual to
see the odd sea eagle or fairy penguin. Kayaks can be hired from the *Sydney
Kayak Centre*, Spit Road, Spit Bridge, T9969 4590. *Sydney Harbour Kayaks*,
3/235 The Spit Road, Mosman T9960 4389, info@4shk.com, also offer
guided trips. In Manly try *Q.Craft*, Shop 3/200 Pittwater Road, Manly

T9976 6333, www.qcraft.com.au **Typical prices are from $15 per hour or full-day from $70.** *Country Road Adventures*, T1300-130561, www.countryroad.net.au, offer excellent guided day-trips up the vast Hawkesbury River harbour from $110. If **wind surfing** is your thing, or you'd like to learn, try the *Balmoral Windsurfing and Sailing School*, 2 The Esplanade, Balmoral Beach, T9960 5344. The 90-minute **Whitewater rafting** sessions at the Olympic Whitewater Stadium in Penrith (50 km) are a great day out. Phone for details and directions, T4730 4333.

Airborne activities

Seeing the city from above can be exhilarating and provide an entirely different aspect, especially of icons like the Opera House

There are a number of fixed-wing and helicopter **scenic flight** companies including *Sydney Heli-Aust*, T9317 3402, www.heliaust.com.au They are based at the airport but offer pick-ups from the city. An interesting alternative are the scenic flights offered by *Palm Beach Seaplanes*, based in Rose Bay (eastern harbour suburbs) and Palm Beach (Pittwater), T1300 656 787, www.sydneybyseaplane.com.au A 15-minute flight around the harbour will cost you from $95, children $50, while a 90-minute trip taking in the harbour, beaches and Blue Mountains costs from $620, children $310. If you want to see the northern beaches from the air and to arrive in Palm Beach by style the one-way trip will cost you a hefty $435. There are a number of scenic flight companies based at Bankstown Airport, T9796 2300. These include *Sydney Air Scenics*, T9790 0628, and *Dakota National Air*, T9791 9900. You can also try your courage at **sky diving** in and around Sydney. Companies include *Simply Skydive*, CM12, Mezzanine, Centrepoint, City, T9231 5865, info@simplyskydive.com.au *Atomic Dog*, T1300 655 622, *NSW Tandem Skydive*, 20 Allandale Road, T1800-000759, and the *Sydney Skydiving Centre* based out at Bankstown Airport, T9791 9155. Jumps start from about $265. Still with spectacular views in mind but far more sedate is **Ballooning**. There are two Sydney-based companies, *Cloud 9*, T96867777, cloud9balloons@bigpond.com, and *Balloon Aloft*, T1800 028 568, www.balloonaloft.com, that offer early morning flights over the outer suburbs or in the Hunter Valley from $245, children $160.

Land-based activities

Beyond jumping on a ferry, **walking** is by far the best way to explore the city. The VIC has a number of free walking brochures including the detailed '*Go Walkabout*' produced by Sydney Ferries, '*Sydney harbour Foreshore Walks*', '*Historical Sydney*', '*Sydney Sculpture Walk*' and the '*Manly Scenic Walkway*'. *Aboriginal Discoveries* is an aboriginal owned and operated outfit that offer day, half-day and 1½-hour guided tours and cruises covering some of Sydney's most significant Aboriginal sites, T9568 6880. **Skating** is very popular, especially along the beachfronts of Manly and Bondi, in Centennial Park and around Farm Cove in the Botanical Gardens. Hire will cost you about $11 per hour with $6 extra for every hour after that or around $20 for all-day hire. Skates can be hired from *Action Inline*, Shop 3/93-95 North Steyne (corner of Pine Street), Manly, T9976 3831, www.actionskate.com.au, or *Manly Blades*, Shop 2/49 North Steyne, Manly, T9976 3833, www.manlyblades.com.au In Bondi try *Bondi Boards and Blades*, 148 Curlewis Street, T9365 6555. And for Centennial Park *Total Skate*, 36 Oxford Street, T9380 6356.

Essentials

Sleeping

As one of Australia's main tourist attractions as well as the main arrival point for most international travellers, Sydney has a wealth of accommodation of all types and to suit all budgets. Most of the major luxury hotels are located around Circular Quay, Darling Harbour and the northern CBD (Central Business District). Numerous serviced apartments are also on offer in the CBD but you are advised to book early *Medina* have several establishments throughout the city, T9360 1699, www.medinaapartments.com.au Other more moderately priced hotels, motels and small boutique hotels are scattered around the southern city centre and inner suburbs. It is worth considering this option as many in the suburbs provide an attractive alternative to the busy city centre. Pub rooms are another alternative but standards vary and costs are generally quite high (from $80). For details T1800-786550, www.pubstay.com.au There are a few good Bed and Breakfast establishments in the city and these can be studied in detail through the **Bed and Breakfast** Council of NSW, T4984 1799, www.bedandbreakfast.org.au If you are intending to stay in Sydney for a few weeks then you should consider Flatting (flat share). The best place to look is in the '*Flats to Let*' section of the *Sydney Morning Herald* on Sat or on hostel or café notice boards. Expect to pay no less than $120 per week with the inner suburbs being even more expensive. As you might expect, there are few motor camps or campsites in the city and few hostels have camping facilities. The nearest and best motor parks are listed below. The web is a fine place to research the many types of accommodation on offer before your arrival.

■ *On maps*
If you have not pre-booked any accommodation on arrival, the Sydney VIC in The Rocks is a good place to start. At anytime in the peak season (Oct-Apr) and especially over Christmas, the New Year and during major sporting or cultural events, pre-booking is generally recommended for all types of accommodation

For those who can afford it, or as a one-off special occasion the hotels surrounding Sydney Cove, Circular Quay offer, even in view alone, one of best hotel stays in the country (if not the world). The **LL** *Park Hyatt*, 7 Hickson Rd, T9241 1234, is a firm favourite and given its waterside location, overlooking the Sydney Opera House and in the shadow of the Harbour Bridge, this is hardly surprising. It offers all the usual mod cons and has a fine restaurant on the ground floor, which is the ideal spot to watch the activity on the harbour and the sunset play on the Opera House. The full-scale replica of the Bounty is also moored right outside. For something a little less commercial and very classy try the **LL** *Observatory Hotel*, 89 Kent St, T9256 2222. Although not so well placed as the competition it is nicely appointed and deservingly popular. The historic **LL-L** *Lord Nelson Pub and Hotel*, corner of Kent St and Argyle St, The Rocks, T9251 4044, hotel@lordnelson.com.au, has some very pleasant, new and affordable, en suites above the pub. The added attraction here is the home-brewed beer, food and general ambience. The pub closes fairly early at night, so noise is generally not a factor. Recommended. Slightly cheaper, yet still offering views of the harbour and also retaining a historic ambiance, right in the heart of The Rocks, is the **L** *Russell Hotel*, 143A George St, T9241 3543, www.therussell.com.au, which offers a good range of singles, en suites standard rooms and suites and has an appealing rooftop garden.

Circular Quay & the Rocks

At the northern edge of the CBD, fringing Circular Quay, there are several more of the reliable chain **hotels** that still offer a peek across the harbour. These include the impressive and well facilitated **LL-L** *Hotel Inter-Continental*, 177 Macquarie St, T9230 0200, and the **LL-L** *Quay West*, 98 Gloucester St, T9240 6000. Well placed right next to the Chinese Gardens and Chinatown and at the southeastern corner of Darling Harbour is the cheaper **L** *All Seasons Darling Harbour*, 17 Little Pier, T8217 4000. For **pub/hotel stays** within the city centre try either the **A** *Grand Hotel*, 30 Hunter St, T9232 3755, or the **L-A** *Glasgow Arms Hotel*, 527 Harris St, Ultimo, T9211 2354. Although most of the city centre

City Centre & Darling Harbour
Darling Harbour itself is surrounded by large modern hotels most of which offer fine views down into Cockle Bay and across the CBD

New South Wales

backpacker hostels are to be found in Haymarket, one of the newest and the best is to be found right in the heart of the city. The all new **B-D** *Wanderers Backpackers*, 477 Kent St, T9267 7718, www.wanderersonkent.com.au, is large, spacious and well-facilitated, with fine doubles, twins and dorms. There are no kitchen facilities but with a cheap café and bar on the ground floor and a rash of eateries all around this is of little concern. It is very well run and also has to be the only backpackers with a stand-up solarium. Recommended. Another newly refurbished budget establishment in the heart of the city is **A-E** *Millett's OZ*, Level 1, 161 Casltlereagh St, T9283 6599, www.wakeup.com.au It has nicely appointed doubles/twins, some with en suite, and a range of dorms. It also has a newly established café, bar, travel desk and employment information.

New South Wales

Haymarket & City centre South

Around Haymarket the hotels become cheaper and begin to be replaced by hostels. The **LL** *Carlton Crest Hotel*, 169 Thomas St, T/F9281 6888, is one exception and is noted for its interesting architecture and popular pre-theatre restaurant. It also offers fine views back across the city centre, especially from its rooftop outdoor pool. Right next door to the Capitol Theatre is the friendly boutique hotel, the **L** *Capitol Square*, corner of Campbell St and George St, T9211 8633, www.goldspear.com.au It has cosy en suite rooms, a good restaurant and is one of the best affordable 4-star hotels in the city centre. Pitched somewhere between a budget hotel and a hostel is the **L-D** *Y on the Park (YWCA)* , 5-11 Wentworth Av, T9264 2451, T1800-994994, www.ywca-sydney.com.au It welcomes both male and female clients, has a good range of clean, modern, spacious and quiet rooms and boasts all the usual facilities. It is also well placed between the city centre and social hub of Oxford St.

There are plenty of **hostels** in and around Haymarket some good, some shocking so shop around. The two **A-E** *Hotel Bakpak* hostels, opposite each other at 412 Pitt St, Freecall T1800-013186 (the newest), and 417 Pitt St, Freecall T1800-813 522, www.bakpakgroup.com, are popular (mainly due to their position) and offer a good range of clean, modern rooms most with en suite, TV, fridge and telephone. The services which include tour bookings, and onward travel are also very good. Further south is the vast **C-D** *Sydney Central YHA*, corner of Pitt St and Rawson Pl, T9281 9111, sydcentral@yhansw.org.au, which is even more popular and ideally placed next to Central Station and the main interstate bus depot. The huge heritage building, has over 500 beds split into a vast range of dorms, doubles and twins, with some en suite. Naturally, it also offers all mod cons including, pool, sauna, café, bar, internet, mini-mart, TV rooms and employment and travel desks. A good 10-min walk further south of Central Station, down Chalmers St and across Prince Alfred Park, is the **A-E** *Alfred Park Private Hotel*, 207 Cleveland St, T9319 4031, hotels@g-day.aust.com A cross between a budget hotel and a backpackers, offering peace and quiet. It is well kept and very clean, offering tidy dorms, and spacious singles, doubles and twins. Modern facilities and free guest parking.

Glebe & Newtown

Glebe is especially popular as an alternative backpackers venue offering a village-type atmosphere with interesting cafes, shops and pubs all within easy walking distance. There are also one or two good mid-range options and an excellent B&B

LL-L *Trickett's Luxury B&B*, 270 Glebe Point Rd, T9552 1141, is a beautifully restored Victorian mansion, decorated with antiques and Persian rugs and offering spacious, nicely appointed en suites. Halfway between a small hotel and a quality hostel is the **L-D** *Alishan International Guesthouse*, 100 Glebe Point Rd, T9566 4048, www.alishan.com.au It is a spacious, renovated Victorian mansion with spotless doubles, twins and family en suites, all with TV and fridge. Shared accommodation is also available and overall the facilities are excellent. A great value budget option, especially for couples looking for a place away from the city centre. Nearby, is the equally good **B-D** *Wattle House*, 44 Hereford St, T9552 4997, www.wattlehouse.com.au A lovingly restored Victorian house, with a very cosy, homely feel and friendly owners. It also has great double rooms and is especially popular for those looking for a quieter more intimate place to stay. Book well in advance. Recommended. The **D-E** *Glebe Point YHA*, 262 Glebe Point Rd, T9692 8418, glebe@yhansw.org.au, is a popular place with a nice atmosphere, offering fairly small twin and 4-share dorms and modern facilities throughout. BBQs on the roof are a speciality. Regular shuttle in to the city and transport departure points. Almost next door the **B-E** *Glebe Village Backpackers*, 256 Glebe Point Rd, T9660 8133, Free call T1800 801 983, glebevillage@bakpak.com.au, is a large working backpacker's favourite. It offers a range of dorms and a few basic doubles and is friendly, laid-back and of course prides itself on finding work for guests. In-house café, pick-ups and regular day tours to beaches and other locations.

Newtown has yet to blossom with tourist accommodation. One budget option offering a good range of en suites, standard rooms and dorms is the **A-E** *Billabong Gardens*, 5-11 Egan St, Newtown, T9550 3236, Free call T1800-806419, www.billabonggardens.com.au There is also a fully equipped kitchen, lounge with TV, internet and a heated pool

Kings Cross, Potts Point & Woolloomooloo

There is no shortage of hotels in Kings Cross and its surrounding suburbs, with everything from the deluxe 5-star to the basic and affordable

At the top end and recommended is the very chic and modern **LL** *W Hotel*, 6 Cowper Wharf Rd, Woolloomooloo, T9331 9000. Also recommended is the newly renovated, classy **L** *The Barclay*, 17 Bayswater Rd, Kings Cross, T9358 6133, barclayhotel@bigpond.com Heading north away from the mania of Kings Cross proper is one of the cheapest standard hotels, the **A** *Manhattan Park Inn*, 8 Greenknowe Av, T9358 1288, www.parkplaza.com.au The **LL-A** *Victoria Court*, 122 Victoria St, Potts Point, T9357 3200, www.VictoriaCourt.com.au, is a delightful and historic boutique hotel in a quiet location. It comes complete with period antiques, well appointed en suites, fireplaces and 4-poster beds. The courtyard conservatory is excellent. Recommended. Nearby the **B** *Challis Lodge*, 21-23 Challis Av, T9358 5422, challislodge@wheretostay.com.au, is another historic mansion, cheaper and therefore less salubrious, yet with a good range of singles, twins and doubles, some with en suites. If you are looking for an affordable apartment with a great view across the harbour try the **L-A** *Macleay Serviced Apartments*, 28 Mcleay St, Potts Point, T9357 7755, macleay@nectar.com.au

Backpacker hostels The **C-E** *Funk House*, 23 Darlinghurst Rd, T9358 6455, goodtimes@funkhouse.com.au Set right on Darlinghurst Rd this is definitely one for the younger party set. Zany artworks don the walls and doors. 3-4 bed dorms and double/twins all with fridge, TV and fan. Lots of freebies. Their almost legendary rooftop BBQ's are a great place to meet others. Good job search assistance. The **C-E** *Jolly Swagman*, 27 Orwell St, T9358 6400, www.jollyswagman.com.au Another buzzing hostel set in the heart of the action. Very professionally managed with all the usual facilities. TV, fridge and fan in most rooms. Excellent travel desk and job search assistance. Social atmosphere. 24-hr check in, fast internet and free beer on arrival. **C-E** *Eva's*, 6-8 Orwell St, Potts Point, T9358 2185, www.evasbackpackers.com.au/www.nomadsworld.com This is another, clean well managed hostel that offers a distinctly homely feel. Arty rooms with some en suites. Rooftop space used for social BBQ's and offering great views across the city. Similarly The **C-D** *Kanga House*, 141 Victoria St, T9357 7879, offers a warm welcome and if you are lucky you may be able to secure a room with a view of the Opera House. **C-E** *The Virgin Backpackers*, 144 Victoria St, T9357 4733, www.vbackpackers.com.au Quite modern and chic the 'V' offers good facilities, a nice balance between the lively and quiet. Tidy doubles and twins with TV and fridge and dorms. Well-travelled, helpful managers internet café with good cheap meals. **C-E** *The Original Backpackers Lodge*, 160-162 Victoria St, T9356 3232, www.originalbackpackers.com.au Possibly the best hostel in Kings Cross if not the city and certainly one of the best facilitated and managed. The historic house is large and homely, nicely appointed and comfortable, offering a great range of double, twin, single, triple and dorm rooms all with TV, fridge and fans (heated in winter). There is a great open courtyard in which to socialize or enjoy a BBQ. Cable TV. The staff are always on hand to help with onward travel, job seeking or things

With over 35 hostels in and around Kings Cross the choice is vast. Most are located along Victoria St, Orwell St or on the main drag, (and in the heart of the action) Darlinghurst Rd. Others are scattered in quieter locations around the main hub, especially towards Potts Point

to see and do. Recommended. Book ahead. **C-E** *Travellers Rest*, 156 Victoria St, T9358 4606. Well-established hostel especially popular with long-stayers. Dorm, single twin and doubles some with TV, fridge, fan, phone and kettle. Attractive weekly rates. **B-E** *Backpackers Headquarters*, 79 Bayswater Rd, T9331 6180. Immaculately kept and well run, the layout is a little odd but otherwise it is a fine choice in a quiet location, yet close to the action. **C-E** *The Pink House*, 6-8 Barncleuth Square, T/F9358 1689, thepinkh@qd.com.au, is an historic mansion offering a proper house, homely feel that is lacking in many of the other Kings Cross hostels. It is mainly because of that deservingly popular, especially for those tired of the party scene. Lots of quiet corners and a shady courtyard in which to find peace of mind. Large dorms and some good doubles, Cable TV and free internet. **C-E** *The Palms* (Nomads), 23 Hughes St, T9357 1199, has a good friendly atmosphere and a very social courtyard out front. All rooms have TV and fridge. **C-E** *Rucksack Rest*, 9 McDonald St, Potts Point, T/F9358 2348, is a long established private hostel. It is basic and a little tired looking but good value, in a quiet location. Good double rooms. The **C-D** *Blue Parrot*, 87 Mcleay St, Potts Point, T9356 4888, is located towards Potts Point and is a new player on the scene. As such, it has all new fixtures and fittings which is an attraction in itself.

Darlinghurst, Paddington & Surry Hills
Separated only by a river of traffic Darlinghurst offers a fine alternative to Kings Cross and is still within a zebra crossing away

There are 3 very good, contemporary and immensely chic boutique hotels. **LL** *L'Otel*, 114 Darlinghurst Rd, T9360 6868, www.lotel.com.au, is very classy yet given its minimalist décor perhaps not everyone's cup of tea. Very hip and very much a place for the modern couple. Excellent personable service and a fine restaurant attached. Across the road the **LL** *Hotel Altamont*, 207 Darlinghurst Rd, T9360 6000, www.altamont.com.au, is no less classy, yet supports a more traditional décor with beautiful spacious deluxe rooms with wooden floors and fittings. Recommended. A little further south on Darlinghurst Rd (229) is the **LL** *Kirketon*, T9332 2011, www.kirketon.com.au Modern, chic and minimalist with a bar and restaurant to match. For something more traditional look no further than the **A** *Royal Sovereign Hotel*, corner of Liverpool St and Darlinghurst Rd, T9331 3672, www.darlobar.com.au The newly refurbished range of rooms above the popular 'Darlo' bar are spotless and great value. Shared bathroom facilities. Paddington and Surry Hills do not have a huge range of options. If you are looking for good apartments then try the **LL** *Medina on Crown*, 359 Crown St, Surry Hills, T9360 6666, www.medinaapartments.com.au They are expensive but, like the sister establishments throughout the city, very tidy. For quiet backpacker options try the **C-E** *Oxford on Oxford*, 146 Oxford St, Woollahra, T9328 4450, www.oxfordonoxford.com.au, or the **C-E** *Kangaroo Bakpak*, 665 South Dowling St, Surry Hills, T9319 5915.

Bondi Beach
The older, well-established beachfront hotels in Bondi look a little garish but their interiors will not dissapoint, and they are, as boasted, only yards from the world famous beach

The largest and most spectacular is the **LL** *Swiss Grand*, corner Campell Pde and Beach Rd, T9365 5666, www.swissgrand.com.au Luxury all suite hotel and offers all mod cons, excellent views, a fine restaurant, gaming bar and an interesting foyer. The rooftop pool is stunning and a great escape from the hordes on the beach. Occassionally offers good value 'Getaway' deals that are great for couples. Slightly less obvious and intimate is **LL-L** *Ravesi's*, corner Campell Pde and Hall St, T9365 4422, www.ravesis.com.au It has pleasant, good value 3-star standard rooms, standard suites and luxury split level suites, most with balconys overlooking all the action. The newly refurbished balcony restaurant is one of the best in the area. The **L-A** *Hotel Bondi*, 178 Campell Par, T9130 3271, www.hotelbondi.com.au, is a little more traditional, with a popular public bar downstairs, a good café and a nightclub/performance space, 'Zinc' where you can 'shake your pants' to live bands and DJ's or take part in pool competitions most nights. The **L-A** *Bondi Beachside Inn*, 152 Campbell Pde, T9130 5311, www.bondiinn.com.au, is another beachfront option, pitched somewhere between a hotel and motel, offering tidy rooms and suites with kitchenettes and ocean views to match the more expensive hotels. Good for families or couples. If you are looking for a quiet motel within walking distance of the beach the **A** *City Beach Motor Inn*, 99 Curlewis St, T9365 3100, is a good choice having very neat, newly refurbished or new units, some with spa. Breakfast on request. Secure parking.

There are almost a dozen backpackers in Bondi. One of the most popular is **C-D** *Indy's Bondi Beach Backpackers*, 35A Hall St, T9365 4900, www.indys.com.au It is modern, friendly and has all the usual facilities, including doubles and twins with TV, fridge and fans and a very comfy cable TV room. It has a lively social atmosphere and its sheer range of free hires, from surfboards to roller blades, are an added attraction. Recommended. **C-E** *Lamrock Lodge Backpackers*, 19 Lamrock Av, T9130 5063, www.lamrocklodge.com.au Offers new, modern facilities and all rooms, dorm, single, twin and double have cable TV, fridge, kitchenette and microwave. Good value. Recommended. Perched on the hill, overlooking the beach as you descend in to Bondi proper is the **B-E** *Noah's Bondi Beach Backpackers*, 2 Campbell Par, T9365 7100, www.noahs.com.au It is a large place and popular due to its position and price. As such it is certainly not the quietest. Former hotel rooms converted to dorms, twins and doubles (some with ocean view). Rooftop BBQ area offers great views.

LL-A *Coogee Bay Boutique Hotel*, 9 Vicar St, T9665 0000, www.coogeebayhotel.com.au Very pleasant, newly refurbished, boutique style rooms in addition to good traditional pub-style options. Well appointed, en suite, have ocean views and are good value. The hotel itself is also a main social focus in Coogee both day and night. Recommended. There are several backpacker hostels in Coogee. The largest is the beachside **C-E** *Surfside Backpackers*, 186 Arden St, T9315 7888, www.surfsidebackpackers.com.au It is a very social place with a solid reputation and all the usual facilities. Just as good, but smaller and with more character are the two houses (Wizard of Oz and Beachside) that combined form the **B-E** *Coogee Beachside Backpackers*, 1/8/172 Coogee Bay Rd, T9315 8511, www.sydneybeachside.com.au The rooms, especially the doubles are excellent. Good facilities, friendly staff with good work contacts. 5-min walk to the beach. Ask about flat shares if you intend to stay long-term. Another quieter, personable option is **B-D** *Beachouse Private Hotel*, 171 Arden St, T9665 1162. Lone travellers, especially girls are well looked after. Free breakfast.

Coogee
Coogee is steadily growing in popularity as a viable and often cheaper alternative base to Bondi Beach

The quiet yet central suburb of **Kirribilli**, across the water from The Opera House, is an excellent place to base yourself, with a short, cheap and spectacular ferry trip to the CBD. There is very little in the way of accommodation but that is part of its charm. **B-D** *Glenferrie Lodge*, 12A Carabella St, T9955 1685, www.glenferrielodge.com.au, is a vast, 68-room Victorian mansion under new management and looks set to explode on to the quality budget accommodation scene. The range of shared, single, twin or doubles are superb with some having their own balconies. Cheap dinners are on offer nightly. Very friendly. Nearby you might also like to try the cheaper **C-E** *Kirribilli Court Private Hotel*, 45 Carabella St, T9955 4344, www.kirribillicourt.com.au

Inner North Shore & Manly

Being a well established resort within the city there is no shortage of accommodation in **Manly**. The VIC on the Forecourt beside the ferry wharf have detailed listings, maps and can help arrange bookings, T9977 1088, www.manly.nsw.gov.au There are several hotels from the luxury to the pub traditional. The beachside **LL** *Manly Pacific Park Royal*, 55 North Steyne, T9977 7666, www.parkroyal.com.au, is the most luxurious offering all mod cons, ocean views, a rooftop pool and a good restaurant. The **L** *Manly Lodge Boutique Hotel*, 22 Victoria Par, T9977 8655, www.manlylodge.com.au, is a more homely option and is both popular and good value. Recommended. The **L-D** *Steyne Hotel*, corner of Ocean Beach and The Corso, T9977 4977, stay@steynehotel.com.au, is an older, cheaper and traditional pub style hotel with standard, deluxe and backpacker rooms, including breakfast. For a motel option try the 3-star **L-E** *Manly Beach Resort*, 6 Carlton St, T9977 4188, www.manlyview.com.au All

New South Wales

New South Wales

rooms are en suite and breakfast is included. Backpacker style accommodation also available. Pool and spa. Although also serving as a backpackers the **L-D** *Manly Beach Hut*, 7 Pine St, T9977 8777, www.manlybeachhut.com.au, offers some quality, good value twins and doubles for couples or the more mature independent traveller as well as shared accommodation. There are about a dozen or so pure backpacker establishments in Manly. The busy **B-D** *Manly Backpackers Beachside*, 28 Raglan St, T9977 3411, manlybackpack@bigpond.com.au, is well-rated with some en suite doubles and small dorms. The cheaper and arty **C-E** *Wharf Backpackers*, 48 East Esplanade (right opposite the ferry terminal), T9977 2800, is also popular. The VIC has full listings.

Northern Beaches   Two backpackers stand out along the northern beaches. The superb **B-E** *Collaroy YHA* (Sydney Beachhouse), 4 Collaroy St, Collaroy Beach, T9981 1177, www.sydney beachouse.com.au, is the hilton of Sydney backpackers and offers tidy dorms, twins, doubles and family rooms (some en suite) and great over all facilities, including a heated pool, spacious kitchen, dining areas, TV rooms, free equipment hire and organized day trips. Even free digiridoo lessons. It deserves its reputation as one of the best backpackers in the city. Recommended. Book ahead Catch the L90 or L88 bus from Central, Wynyard or QVB. The remote **C-E** *YHA Pittwater*, via Halls Wharf, Morning Bay, via Church Pt, T9999 2196, pittwater@rivernet.com.au, is a real getaway, located in the Kuringai National Park and accessible only by ferry. It has dorms and a few doubles. Plenty of walking and water-based activities or simple peace and quiet. Phone for details, take all your supplies and book ahead. **Plam Beach** has plenty of excellent B&Bs especially suited to couples or families. **LL** *Jonah's*, 69 Bynya Rd, Palm Beach, T9974 5599, is a luxury boutique hotel and restauurant set high on the hill overlooking Ocean Beach. It offers 7 very cosy rooms with great views. The restaurant is French Mediterranean and recommended. For detailed accommodation listings get hold of the comprehensive *'Northern Beaches Visitors Guide'*, www.sydneynorthernbeaches.com.au, from major VICs or contact the *Palm Beach and Peninsula Bed and Breakfast Group*, T9973 4732.

Motor parks & campsites
There are plenty of campsites and motor parks surrounding Sydney but within the inner city convenient parks are hard to find

One of the best however is the 3-star **C-E** *Lane Cove River Caravan Park*, Plassey Rd, North Ryde, T9888 9133, lccp@npws.nsw.gov.au   Although nothing spectacular it offers powered and non-powered sites and a few basic yet comfortable cabins 14 km north of the city centre, in a bush setting and within the bounds of the Lane Cove National Park. The site is owned and operated by the National Parks and Wildlife Service. In Narrabeen, 26 km north of Sydney and near the beach is the 4-star **A-D** *Sydney Lakeside Narrabeen*, Lake Park Rd, T9913 7845, www.sydneylakeside.com.au   It has a good range of quality villas, bungalows as well as powered and non-powered sites. In Ramsgate, 17 km south of the city centre, near the airport and on public transport routes is the 3-star **A-D** *Grand Pines Tourist Park*, 112 Alfred St, Ramsgate, T9529 7329, www.thegrandpines.com.au   It offers deluxe en suite and standard cabins and powered sites but no tents are allowed.

Eating

● *On maps*   When it comes to quality and choice there is no doubt that Sydney is on a par with any major city in the world and with over 3,000 restaurants to choose from you have to wonder where on earth to start. As a general rule you will find the best of the fine dining establishments specializing in Modern Australian cuisine in and around **Circular Quay**, **The Rocks**, the **CBD** and **Darling Harbour**, however pockets of international speciality abound, from chow mein in **Chinatown** to pasta in **Paddington**. Sydney's thriving café culture is generally centred around the suburbs of **Darlinghurst**, **Glebe**, **Newtown** and the eastern beaches of **Bondi** and **Bronte**. There are plenty of detailed *'Eating Out'* guides to be found in the major bookshops and the eating section of the site, www.sydney.citysearch.com.au, is also very helpful.

Expensive Housed within one of the smaller 'shells' of the Opera House complex is the newly renovated *Guillaume at Bennelong Restaurant*, T9250 7578. Recent reports suggest this 'icon within the icon' will more than live up to its former excellent reputation. Open dinner Mon-Sat and lunch on Fri. Housed within the notorious 'Toaster' is *Aqua Luna*, 2/18, Opera Quays, East Circular Quay, T9251 3177. A slick looking establishment, known for its fine Italian cuisine, views and lively distinctly trendy atmosphere. Open Mon-Fri for lunch and daily for dinner. In the heart of The Rocks *The Rockpool*, 107 George St, T92521 8888, is a firm favourite, offering highly imaginative cuisine with a Euro/Asian edge. Open for lunch Mon-Fri and dinner Mon-Sat. Equally popular is *Bel Mondo*, Level 3, Argyle Stores, 18 Argyle St, T9241 3700. Set in a former warehouse, it offers fine Italian cuisine and again a good wine list. Open for lunch Tue-Fri and daily for dinner. Closer to the water and offering views of the bridge and the Opera House is the Euro-influenced *Quay*, Upper Level, Overseas Passenger Terminal, Circular Quay West, T9251 5600. Open for lunch Mon-Fri and dinner daily.

Mid-range Set high above Circular Quay at the top of Customs House, and offering superb views and al fresco dining is the *Café Sydney*, Level 5, 31 Alfred St, T9251 8683. The food is traditional Modern Australian; it has a nice atmosphere and also offers occasional live jazz. Open daily for lunch, Mon-Sat for dinner. For a taste of Aussie, an even better atmosphere and all the classic Australian beers, try the *Australian Hotel*, 100 Cumberland St, T9247 2229. Good value, good al fresco and menu, which includes pizza, croc, emu and roo steaks. Open daily for lunch and dinner. Off the beaten track and a firm local favourite is the *Wharf Restaurant*, Pier 4, Hickson Rd, Walsh Bay, T9250 1761. Located at the end of one of the historic Walsh Bay piers it has a great atmosphere and wonderful views of the busy harbour. Modern Australian. Open for lunch and dinner Mon-Sat.

Cafés The Museum of Contemporary Art *MCA Cafe*, 140 George St, T9241 4253, is ideally located next to all the action on Circular Quay. It is a bit expensive but worth it and the seafood is excellent. Open for lunch Mon-Fri and breakfast and lunch Sat/Sun.

Expensive *Tetsuya's*, 729 Kent St, T9267 2900, is without doubt one of Sydney's best restaurants. Chef Tetsuya Wakuda is world famous for his Japanese/Mediterranean creations. The restaurant has only recently been relocated to new and extremely swish premises. Book well in advance and if you can afford it, try the 12-course degustation dinner. Open for lunch Fri/Sat and dinner Tue-Sat. *Forty One*, Level 41, Chiefly Tower, Chiefly Sq, T9221 2500, is very popular, classy, congenial and has excellent city views. Modern Australian. Open for lunch Mon-Fri and dinner Mon-Sat. Again book well in advance. *Restaurant VII*, 7 Bridge St, T9252 7777, is one of the newest upmarket restaurants in Sydney, earning a good reputation and offering imaginative Japanese cuisine with a French influence. Excellent attention to detail and great cuisine, but you will pay for it!

Mid-range *Pavilion on the Park*, 1 Art Gallery Rd, The Domain, T9232 1322, sits opposite the Art Gallery and is the perfect escape from the city centre, offering al fresco dining with an eclectic Modern Australian menu. Perfect for lunch after a tour of the gallery. *Casa Asturiana*, 77 Liverpool St, T9264 1010, is well known for its Mediterranean (Spanish) cuisine and its tapas in particular. Lots of atmosphere and regular live music. Open daily for lunch and dinner The *Brooklyn Hotel*, corner of George St and Grosvenor St, T9247 6744, is well known for its meat dishes, especially steak and has plenty of inner city pub atmosphere. Open for lunch Mon-Fri.

Cheap There are numerous underground food courts in the city centre offering a huge range of takeaway options for under $10, from pasta and burgers to wraps and chow mien. Good venues include the *Pitt St Mall*, *Centrepoint* and the *QVB Building*. Just beside the QVB, down Druitt St, is *Zenergy* (68), T9261 5679, which is great for healthy vegetarian wraps and sandwiches. To escape the crowds at lunchtime, grab what you need and head for Hyde Park, which is a great place to chill out on the grass and watch the world go by.

Circular Quay & the Rocks
On the eastern side of the Quay you will find mid-range and expensive options with lots of atmosphere and memorable views under the concourse of the Opera House and within 'The Toaster'

City Centre
The sheer chaos and noise that surrounds you in the CBD is enough to put anyone off eating. A retreat to the Botanical Gardens or Hyde Park is recommended, especially armed with a tasty takeaway

New South Wales

Cafés *Hyde Park Cafe*, corner of Elizabeth St and Liverpool St, T9264 8751, is in a great spot for escaping the crowds, breakfast, light lunches, coffee and people-watching. Open daily from 0700-1630. Below the Museum of Sydney is the congenial *MOS Cafe*, corner of Bridge and Phillip St, T9241 3636 offering imaginative and value Modern Australian for lunch. Open for lunch and dinner Mon-Fri from 0700 and Sat/Sun 0800-1800. *Vivo*, 388 George St, T9221 1169, is right in the heart of the action offering a refreshingly wide choice at affordable prices and good coffee. For sublime tranquillity amidst the Botanical Gardens try the *Botanical Gardens Cafe*, Mrs Macquarie Rd, T9241 2419. The bat colony might not be everybody's cup of tea but for environmentalists and botanists it's really hard to beat. Open daily 0830-1800.

Haymarket & Darling Harbour

Haymarket is home to Chinatown, while Darling Harbour provides a great spot for lunch and dinner surrounded by plenty to see and do

Expensive *Coast*, Roof Terrace, Cockle Bay Wharf, Darling Park, 201 Sussex St, T9267 700, offers a fine range of Modern Australian dishes and has a formal, yet relaxed atmosphere and great views across Darling Harbour. Great for lunch (Mon-Fri, Sun) or dinner (daily). **Mid-range** *Chinta Ria – The Temple of Love*, Roof Terrace, Cockle Bay Wharf, 201 Sussex St, T9264 3211. With a name like that who can resist? Great aesthetics, buzzing atmosphere with quality Malaysian cuisine. Open daily for lunch and dinner. *Bodhi Vegetarian Restaurant*, Ground Floor, Capitol Square, George St, T9212 2828, is considered one of the best places in town for Asian Vegan cuisine. Its Yum Cha is almost legendary. Open daily 1000-1700. *Emperor's Garden Seafood*, 96 Hay St, Haymarket, T9211 2135. One of the most reliable of the Chinatown restaurants, always bustling, offering great service and value for money. Open daily 0800-0100. The *Emperor's Garden BBQ*, 213 Thomas St, T9281 9899, is a great place for duck and suckling pig. Open daily 0900-0100. *Kam Fook Seafood Restaurant*, Level 3, Market City, Hay St, Haymarket, T9211 8988, is a huge establishment and the epitome of Chinatown, great for the claustrophobics and seafood, but not for the faint hearted or the vegetarian. **Cheap** The *Dickson House Food Court*, corner of Little Hay St and Dixon St, has a wealth of cheap Asian takeaways with generous meals for under $6. The *Blackbird Cafe*, Mid Level, Cockle Bay Wharf, T9283 7385, is deservingly popular, congenial, laid back and good value with a huge selection from pasta to steak.

Glebe & Newtown

Glebe is home to many laid-back cafes and good pubs and in many ways the same applies to Newtown, except that Kings St has no end of attractive little restaurants offering everything from curry to charred emu. Both venues are also great for soaking up that lazy Sun morning atmosphere

Expensive *Boathouse on Blackwattle Bay*, Ferry Rd, Glebe, T9518 9011. A quality up-market (yet informal) seafood restaurant offering refreshingly different harbour views than those sought at Circular Quay and Darling Harbour. Here you can watch the lights of Anzac Bridge or the comings and goings of Sydney's fishing fleet while tucking in to the freshest seafood. Open for lunch and dinner Tue-Sun. **Mid-range** *Flavour of India*, 142A Glebe Point Rd, Glebe, T9692 0662. Quite simply Glebe's best Indian restaurant with lots of character, great service and value for money. *Thai Pothong*, 294 King St, Newtown, T9550 6277. On a street with more Thai restaurants than you can shake a chopstick at, the Thai Pothong stands head and shoulders above the rest. Good value, good choice and good service. Open for lunch Tue-Sun and daily for dinner. **Cheap** *Iku*, 25A Glebe Point Rd, Glebe, T9692 8720. The first of what is now a chain of fine vegetarian and macrobiotic vegan cafes under the 'Iku' banner, offering a delicious array of options. Open Mon-Fri 1130-2100, Sat/Sun 1130-2100. *Toxteth Hotel*, 345 Glebe Point Rd, Glebe T9660 2370, is a modern, traditional Australian pub serving mountainous plates of good pub grub at very reasonable prices. Open daily from 1100. *Thanh Binh*, 111 King St, Newtown, T9557 1175. Good value Vietnamese offering delicious dishes from simple noodles to venison in curry sauce. Open for lunch Thu-Sun, daily for dinner.

Cafés *Badde Manors*, 37 Glebe Point Rd, Glebe, T9660 3797. Something of institution in Glebe for many years this favourite student hangout can always be relied on for atmosphere and character, which is more than can be said for the service. Open daily from 0730 till late. A few doors down is *Well Connected*, 35 Glebe Point Rd, Glebe, T9566 2655, which was one of the city's first internet cafes. Laid-back with a whole floor upstairs full of sofas dedicated to surfing the web. Not a bad cup of coffee either. Open 0700-2400 daily. *Fishcafe*, 239 King St, Newtown, T9519 4295. A charming little café and one of Newtown's best and most popular haunts, especially for breakfast and good coffee. Open daily from 0730-2300. *Cinque*, 261 King St, Newtown, T9519 3077. Another popular café located next to the Dendy Cinema and a small bookshop. Great all day breakfasts, coffee. Open daily 0730-late.

Kings Cross, Potts Point & Wooloo mooloo
This section of the 'Inner East' offers a truly eclectic range of choices, from the numerous fast food outlets of Kings Cross to the chic and expensive options to be found along The Wharf at Wooloomooloo, which is growing in reputation as one of the best for fine dining in the city

Expensive *Bayswater Brasserie*, 32 Bayswater Rd, Kings Cross, T9357 2177. Always a reliable choice and immensely popular for its laid-back, yet classy atmosphere and imaginative Modern Australian cuisine. Open Mon-Thu 1700-2300, Fri 1200-2300, Sat 1700-2300. *Otto*, 8 The Wharf, Cowper Wharf Rd, Wooloomooloo T9368 7488. Very trendy, quality Italian with all the necessary trimmings including extrovert waiters. Next door the *Manta Ray*, 7 The Wharf, Cowper Wharf Rd, Wooloomooloo, T9332 3822, is an equally classy (and expensive) seafood restaurant. Some say one of the best in the city. Open for lunch Mon-Fri and dinner daily. **Mid-range** *Shimbashi Soba on the Sea*, 6 The Wharf, Cowper Wharf Rd, Wooloomooloo, T9357 7763. A fine Japanese restaurant that just adds to the sheer choice and quality to be found on the Wharf strip in 'Woolie'. Good mix of pure Japanese cuisine with more familiar meat and poultry dishes. Good value. Open daily 1100-2200. *Macleay Street Bistro*, 73 Macleay St, Potts Point, T9358 4891. Well-established local favourite and good value, with a wide-ranging blackboard menu. **Cheap** *Govinda's* 112 Darlinghurst Rd, Kings Cross, T9380 5155. Restaurant and cinema combo offering great value 'all-you-can-eat' vegetarian buffet along with the movie ticket. *Harry's Café de Wheels*, Cowper Wharf, Wooloomooloo. Harry's is something of a Sydney Institution, offering the famously yummy pies with pea toppings and gravy. One is surely never enough, as the photos of satisfied customers will testify. Open from 0700-0200 Sun-Thu and 0700-0300 Fri/Sat.

Cafés *Café Hernandez*, 60 Kings Cross Rd, Kings Cross, T9331 2343. Great, eccentric 24-hr café serving Spanish fare, great coffee and with lots of character. In contrast *Zinc*, 77 Macleay St, T9358 6777, is not every 'Joe's' cup of tea being very trendy, but there is no denying its ever increasing popularity, especially for breakfast, T9358 6777.

Darlinghurst, Paddington & Surry Hills
Darlinghurst and Paddington dominate the city's café scene

Expensive *Salt*, 229 Darlinghurst Rd, Darlinghurst, T9332 2566. Very trendy, class establishment with a clientele to match, offering some of the best Modern Australian in the city. Open for lunch Mon-Fri and dinner daily. *Buon Ricordo*, 108 Boundary St, Paddington, T9360 6729. Lively Italian that enjoys a citywide reputation. Open for lunch Fri-Sat and dinner Tue-Sat. *MG Garage*, 490 Crown St, Surry Hills, T9383 9383. Classic cars meet costly cuisine in this unique place with expensive autos surrounding the tables. Open for lunch Mon-Fri and dinner Mon-Sat. Book ahead.

Mid-range *Fishface*, 132 Darlinghurst Rd, Darlinghurst, T9332 4803. Admirably secures the best base for fish and other seafood dishes in and around the inner east. Excellent fish and chips. Open daily for dinner. *Oh, Calcutta*, 251 Victoria St, Darlinghurst, T9360 3650. An award winning Indian restaurant and by far the best in the inner east. Book ahead. Open for lunch Fri and dinner Mon-Sat. *Royal Hotel*, 237 Glenmore Rd, Paddington, T9331 5055. One of the best choices at the increasingly popular Five Ways crossroads in Paddington. A grand old pub with gracious yet modern feel. Excellent Modern Australian cuisine is served upstairs in the main restaurant or on the prized veranda. Perfect for a lazy afternoon. Open for lunch and dinner from 1200. *Go Bungai*, 8 Heeley St, Five Ways, Paddington, T9380 8838. Fine little Japanese restaurant with a loyal following, yet nicely off the beaten track. A secluded courtyard adds to its appeal. *Fuel*, 476 Crown St, Surry Hills, T9383 9388. Little sister to the *MG Garage Restaurant* (see above), offering more affordable but equally good bistro-style cuisine. Especially popular for weekend brunch. Open daily from 0800 for breakfast, lunch and dinner.

New South Wales

Cheap *Prasit's Thai Takeaway*, 395 Crown St, T9332 1792. Great value Thai restaurant and take away and the locally recommended cheap option in Surry Hills. Don't automatically expect to get a seat however. Plenty of vegetarian options. Open for lunch and dinner Tue-Sun. *Indian Home Diner (Paddington)*, 86 Oxford St, T9331 4183. You really can't go wrong here with the usual great value (if mild), Indian combo dishes and on this occasion, a small courtyard out back. *Orphee*, 210 Oxford St, Paddington, T9360 3238, is a great French-style restaurant with a lovely atmosphere. Open Mon-Sat from 1000 and Sun 0800, closes around 1800.

Cafés *Bar Coluzzi*, 322 Victoria St, Darlinghurst, T9380 5420. A well-established café that consistently gets the vote as one of Sydney's best. The character, the truly cosmopolitan clientele and the coffee are the biggest draw as opposed to the food. Open daily from 0500-1900. *Bill's*, 433 Liverpool St, Darlinghurst, T9360 9631. One of the city's top breakfast cafés with legendary scrambled eggs. Small and at times overcrowded but that's part of the experience. Open for breakfast and lunch daily from 0730-1500. There is also an equally fine *Bill's 2*, at 359 Crown St, Surry Hills, T9360 4762. *Le Petit Creme*, 118 Darlinghurst Rd, Darlinghurst, T9361 4738. Superb little French number with all the classics, from baguettes to cavernous bowls of café au lait. Great omelettes for breakfast or lunch. Open daily from 0800. *Una's*, 340 Victoria St, Darlinghurst, T9360 6885. Local favourite offering generous hangover cure breakfasts and Euro influenced lunches, including schnitzel and mouth watering strudel. Open daily from 0730-late. *Café Centaur*, 19 Oxford St, Paddington, T9560 3200. A pleasant quiet little café in a great bookshop that will delay your touristical wanderings for hours. Light fare, delectable sweets and good coffee. Open daily 1000-2330. *Hot Gossip*, 438 Oxford St, Paddington T9332 4358. A well-established 'Paddo' café with retro 50s furnishings and an interesting clientele. Good food, healthy smoothies and a great cake selection. Open daily 0730-late.

East Beaches
As well as Bondi, the suburbs of Bronte and Coogee are also top spots

Expensive *Doyle's on the Beach*, 11 Marine Par, Watson's Bay, T9337 2007. Sydney's best known restaurant for years. It has been in the same family for generations and has an unfaltering reputation for superb seafood, atmosphere and harbour/city views that all combine to make it a one of the best dining experiences in the city, if not Australia. If you can, book well ahead and ask for a balcony seat. Sunday afternoons are especially popular and you could combine the trip with a walk around the heads. Open daily for lunch and dinner. Book ahead. *Hugo's*, 70 Campbell Par, Bondi Beach, T9300 0900. A well established favourite in Bondi, offering a combination of classy atmosphere, quality Modern Australian cuisine and fine views of the iconic beach. Open daily for dinner, Sat/Sun for breakfast and lunch). **Mid-range** *Sean's Panorama*, 270 Campbell Par, Bondi Beach, T9365 4924. Modern Australian with a Euro edge. Open for lunch Sat/Sun and dinner Wed-Sat. *Aqua Bar*, 266 Campbell Par, Bondi Beach, T9130 6070. Healthy options, laid-back atmosphere. Open daily 0630-1530. *Watson's Bay Hotel*, 1 Military Rd, Watson's Bay, T9337 4299. Located right next door to the famous Doyle's, Watson's offers some stiff competition in the form of quality, value seafood al fresco, with lots of choice. You can even cook your own. Great for a whole afternoon especially at the weekend. **Cheap** *Coogee Bay Hotel*, corner of Coogee bay Rd and Arden St, T966 5000. The most popular spot in Coogee day or night with multiple bars, huge open air eating, value pub-grub and live entertainment.

Cafés *Sejuiced*, 487 Bronte Rd, T9389 9538. Has competition on both sides, but is consistently the café of choice on the 'Bronte strip'. Favourite breakfast spot at weekends and a great start (or finish) to the cliff-top walk between Bronte and Bondi. Open daily 0700-1830. *Love in a Cup*, 106 Glenayr Av, Bondi Beach, T9365 6418. Best-kept secret in Bondi, off the beaten track and very popular with the locals, especially for breakfast/brunch. Good value and good coffee. Open Mon-Sat 0700-1700, Sun 0800-1700. *Le Paris-Go Cafe*, 38 Hall St, T9130 8343. Very bohemian, laid back and popular, with good vegetarian options and all day breakfasts.

Expensive *Armstrong's*, Manly Wharf, T9976 3835, well positioned on the wharf overlooking the beach, good value Modern Australian and locally recommended. Open daily for lunch and dinner. *Watermark*, 2A The Esplanade, Balmoral Beach, T9968 3433. Set in a beautiful location overlooking a beautiful beach, *Watermark* is well off the beaten track, but a wee gem, offering great Modern Australian with a seafood speciality. Also good for breakfast (open daily from 0800). **Mid-range** *Out of Africa*, 43 East Esplanade, Manly, T9977 0055. Good value, authentic African cuisine with all the expected furnishings. It seems oddly out of place in Manly, but remains refreshingly different. Open for dinner Mon-Sun, lunch Thu-Sun. Equally good is the Spanish/Mediterranean fare on offer at the *Alhambra*, 54 West Esplanade, Manly, T9976 2975. Tapas are its speciality. Open daily for lunch and dinner. *Bower Restaurant*, 7 Marine Par, T9977 5451. Located right at the end of Marine Parade with memorable views back towards Manly Beach. Great spot for breakfast. Open daily for breakfast and lunch, Thu and some weekends for dinner. **Cheap** There is no end of cheap takeaways along the concourse between the ferry wharf and Manly Beach. Elsewhere the *Mosman Yacht Club*, opposite the Mosman Ferry Terminal, T9969 1244, is a little known option offering club prices in a classy setting overlooking the marina and properties you could probably never afford! In Mosman itself the *Mosman RSL*, 719 Military Rd, T9969 7255, has 3 levels including a great value restaurant and al fresco bistro overlooking the main street and across the city.

Cafés *Brazil*, 46 North Steyne, Manly, T9977 3825. Set right in the heart of the action overlooking Manly Beach. Standard Modern Australian and good coffee, but gets a bit busy in the evenings. Open daily from 0800 until late. The *Bathers Pavilion Cafe*, 4 The Esplanade, Balmoral Beach, T9969 5050, is ideally located in the historic pavilion overlooking Balmoral Beach, superb spot for breakfast, or for lunch, with quality of food to match. Open daily from 0700.

Manly & the Eastern North Shore
Manly is blessed with numerous restaurants and cafés and a wide range of choice

New South Wales

Pubs and bars

Sydney has some fine pubs both in the city centre and suburbs to suit most tastes. Most are the traditional, street corner Australian hotels, but there are lots of modern, trendy establishments, pseudo Irish pubs and truly historic alehouses on offer. Note that, unlike Europe, you will find that most antipodeans do not buy 'rounds'. Also note that many pubs especially those along Oxford St and in Kings Cross attract a cosmopolitan and happy mix of straight and gay clients. *Sydney Pub Trek* is a very messy backpacker based pub-crawl on Thu nights with plenty of price reductions, from $25, T9235 0999.

● *On maps*

From Circular Quay the best place to start is with a swift half in the *Orient*, 89 George St, T9251 1255, which is an old favourite set in the heart of Sydney's oldest precinct. From the Orient negotiate the steady climb up to Cumberland St (the steps are located on the right, before the bridge behind the Argyle Stores) and reward yourself with an obligatory Australian beer in the *Australian Hotel*, 100 Cumberland St, T9247 2229. You may also like to sample a kangaroo, emu or crocodile steak for dinner. Then, from the Australian, go under the Bradfield Highway, via the pedestrian tunnel, past Observatory Park and down to Argyle St. On the corner of Argyle and Kent (top end) is the historic *Lord Nelson*, T9251 4044. The Nelson is Sydney's oldest pub and within its hallowed, nautically-themed walls, it brews its own ales and also offers some fine pub grub and accommodation. Just around the corner from The Nelson is the smaller and characterful *Hero of Waterloo*, 18 Lower Fort St, T9252455, which can be a bit of a squeeze but is always entertaining. If you can drag yourself away from there, head towards the bridge (truly spectacular view) and under it again, to rejoin George St, perhaps stopping in the newly refurbished *Harbour View Hotel*, 18 Lower Fort St, before catching last orders in the chaotic Irish pub the *Mercantile*, 25 George St, T9247 3570. The 'Merc' is often busy, but offers a fairly decent pint of guiness as well as great live traditional music until late.

The Rocks
The best single drinking venue in Sydney is undoubtedly The Rocks, where history, aesthetics, atmosphere and most importantly darn good beer combine to guarantee a great night out

New South Wales

City Centre   *Scruffy Murphys*, on the corner of Gouldburn St and George St, T9211 2002, is a popular, well-established Irish pub that always draws the crowds. It's a great place to meet people and the live bands and beers are good, but there really is very little Irish about it. Open well into the early hours. A little further down George St, and in contrast, another Irish offering, *Paddy McGuires*, on the corner of George and Hay, T9212 2111, has just been refurbished and offers pleasant surroundings in which you can actually have a decent conversation or sample a fine range of beers. The pub food is good and there is also live entertainment on offer most nights. *Scubar*, corner of Rawson Pl and Rawson Lane, T9212 4244, www.scubar.com.au, is a popular backpacker oriented pub that offers cheap beer, pizzas, pool, big TV screens and popular music until late. Cockle Bay and Kings St Wharf in Darling Harbour have some very hip bars with outdoor seating areas. In the Kings St Wharf look out for the laid-back *Cargo Bar*, 52-60 The Promanade, T9262 1777.

City East   **Paddington** has a number of excellent pubs. *Durty Nelly's*, 9 Glenmore Rd, Paddington, T9360 4467, is the smallest, the best and most intimate Irish pub in the city, offering, nice aesthetics and a grand congenial jam session on Sun evenings (last orders 2330). Further down Glenmore Rd (crossroads with Goodhope St and Heeley St) is the *Royal Hotel*, T9331 2604, which has a large atmospheric public bar downstairs and a fine restaurant on the 2nd floor. Deep in the Paddington suburbs on the fringes with Woollahra is the grand historic rabbit warren called the *Lord Dudley*, 236 Jersey Rd, T9327 5399, www.lorddudley.com.au There is also some great, if expensive, pub-grub on offer (last orders 2330). Recommended. Back on **Oxford St** is another Irish offering, the *Kitty O'Sheas*, 384 Oxford St, T9360 9668. It is a large place and very popular especially at weekends when live bands play. If you need to escape the mêlée, try the bar upstairs. If old traditional pubs are not to your taste you might like to try the more cutting edge establishments where the music and atmosphere that the cosmopolitan and mixed gay and straight (but always trendy) clientele hold dear. Some great examples are the *Grand Pacific Blue Room*, corner of Oxford St and South Dowling St, T9331 7108, *The Oxford Hotel*, 134 Oxford St, T9331 3467, or the *Albury Hotel*, 6 Oxford St, T9361 6555.

   Kings Cross is perhaps a little overrated when it come to pubs. *O' Malley's Hotel*, 228 William St, T9357 2211, is the local Irish offering with good live bands, but is by no means the best Irish pub in the city (last orders around 0200). Almost next door and in the shadow of the huge Coca Cola sign is the bizarre interior of the *Kings Cross Hotel*, 248 William St, T9358 3377, which is a rowdy backpacker favourite open well into the early hours. Further up Darlinghurst Rd (24) is the American-style *Bourbon and Beefsteak*, T9358 1144, which attracts all types and is open 24 hrs. Nearby in Woolloomooloo is the *Woolloomooloo Bay Hotel*, 2 Bourke St, T9357 1177, which has karaoke nights and regular DJs. When you can no longer pronounce their name is definitely time to go home! Between the city and Kings Cross and just off William St is the old favourite the *Hard Rock Café*, 121 Crown St, T9331 1116, with the suspended automobiles, electric guitars and band memorabilia that have now been the trademark of the global outlets for 30 years. Roll in for their 'two-for-one-drinks', Mon-Fri from 1700-1900.

   In **Bondi** the *Hotel Bondi*, 178 Campell Par, T9130 3271, has a lively bar with live bands and a nightclub attached, while in **Coogee** try the multiple bars and live music at the beachside *Coogee Bay Hotel*, 9 Vicar St, T9665 0000.

City West   **Glebe** has 2 great pubs. The 'World Famous' *Friend In Hand Pub*, 58 Cowper St, T9660 2326, looks more like a venue for an international garage sale, but oozes character and also offers a bar café and Italian restaurant. Look out the Cockatoo does bite! In the heart of Glebe the *Toxteth Hotel*, 345 Glebe Point Rd, T9660 2370, is a far more modern, traditionally Australian affair. It is always pretty lively, has pool competitions and serves mountainous plates of good pub grub. In Newtown the *Kuleto's Cocktail Bar*, 157 Kings St, T9519 6369, offers something completely different.

Entertainment

There is always a wealth of things to entertain in Sydney. For the latest information and reviews check the '*Metro*' section in the Fri '*Sydney Morning Herald*'. '*The Beat*' and the '*Sydney City Hub*' are free weeklies that are readily available in restaurants, cafés, bars and bookshops in and around the city centre. On the net consult the websites already listed on page 79, or try www.sydney.sidewalk.com.au The usual ticket agent is **Ticketek**, Sydney Entertainment Centre, Harbour St, Haymarket, T9266 4800, www.ticketek.com.au They produce their own monthly events magazine '*The Ticket*'. **Ticketmaster**, T136100, also deal with theatre tickets. Discounted tickets can often be secured on the same day from **Halftix**, Darling Park, 201 Sussex St, T9286 3310. Bookings can also be made over the net, www.halftix.com.au

In the City Centre the **Slip Inn**, 111 Sussex St, T9299 4777, is a trendy night spot with 3 rooms and a courtyard that fills with the young and beautiful, who let rip to a mix of house and rave. *Good Vibrations* on a Sat is especially popular, and with a name like that, so it should be. Free entry before 2200. The **Globe**, corner of Park St and Elizabeth St, T9264 4844. Open daily 1100-2200, Fri/Sat 1100-0600, Fri $10, Sat $15, is the place to go to get the funk out of yer face. **Gas**, 477 Pitt St, Haymarket, T9211 3088, is one of the best venues for dance music in the city with excellent, clued-up DJs revving up the crowds to a range of soul, funk, hip-hop, house and R&B, especially on Fri/Sat. Open 2200-0400, $15-25. Nearby, though essentially a pub, cocktail bar and restaurant, the **Civic Hotel**, 388 Pitt St (corner of Gouldburn St), T8267 3181, is a traditional weekend haunt for a cosmopolitan crowd who repeatedly come to enjoy old anthems and classics. Under $10. The new **Tank Nightclub**, 3 Bridge La, and the **Chinese Laundry**, 3 Slip St, T9299 1700, both have a solid reputation, $10-15.

Around Circular Quay is the ever-popular **Basement**, 29 Reiby Pl, Circular Quay, T9251 2797, www.thebasement.com.au and **Jacksons on George**, 176 George St, T9247 2727, which is a huge club spread over 4 floors with 5 bars, dining, dancing, live bands and pool, open 24 hrs. **Darling Harbour** is home to **Home**, Cockle Bay Wharf, T9266 0600, which is one of the country's largest, state of the art nightclubs. Here, on 4 levels, you can get on down to house and trance. Every Sat there is a kinkidisco, which sounds appealing. Open 2200-0600, $15. Nearby, in the Star City Complex, 80 Pyrmont Rd, T9566 4755, is the highly trendy **Cave Nightclub**. It offers good dance and R&B combo, and far more girls than guys. **Oxford St**, is, of course, a major focus for nightlife and the main haunt for the gay and lesbian community. The **Goodbar**, 11A Oxford St, T9360 6759, is a well-established club and an old favourite amongst Sydneysiders, from the sexy young things to the sexually confused and the odd forgot-how-to-be-sexy fossils. Mixed music and good value in every respect, $6. Further up towards Taylor Sq is **Arq**, 16 Flinders St, T9380 8700. It has 2 large dance floors, plenty of space and a good balcony from which to watch a friendly crowd of both straight and gay.

Kings Cross is the main focus for travellers, particularly backpackers, but is not necessarily the best venue in town. True, a great night out (and certainly an experience) is on offer, but recent drug busts in some clubs have given the place a slightly dodgy edge. There are quite a few popular clubs most of which keep entry costs down to attract the backpacker crowd. The newly refurbished **World**, 24 Bayswater Rd, T9357 7700, is a laid-back club set in grand surrounds and offering mainly UK house music, Fri-Sat $5 after 2200. Almost next door is **Zen**, 22 Bayswater Rd, T9358 4676, which is another new revamp and as the name suggests, this time has an Oriental theme. Again it concentrates on progressive house music. Fri nights are especially good. The **Icebox**, 2 Kellet St, T9331 0058, offers more hardcore house and rave. Open 2200-500, From $5-15.

Nightclubs
For the latest in club information and special events get hold of the free 3-D World magazine, available in many backpackers, cafes or the clubs themselves, www.threed world.com.au

New South Wales

Cinema

For listings see the Sydney Morning Herald or call Movieline, T9218 2421. For details of the huge 8-storey high Imax Theatre in Darling Harbour (see page 89)

In the city centre most of the major conventional cinema complexes are to be found along George St between Town Hall and Chinatown. These include *Greater Union*, 525 George St, T9267 8666, *Hoyts*, at 505, T9273 7431, and the *Village*, at 545, T9264 6701. *Dendy* are based at 19 Martin Pl, T9233 8166, and 2 East Circular Quay, T9247 3800. Elsewhere on Oxford St is the *Academy Twin* (3A), T9361 4453, the *Chauvel*, corner of Oxford St and Oatley Rd, T9361 5398, and *Verona*, Level 2, 17 Oxford St, T9360 6296. The Chauvel in particular showcases more retro, foreign or fringe films.The *Hayden Orpheum Cinema*, 180 Military Rd, Cremorne, T9908 4344, on the North Shore, is a wonderful Art Deco cinema which offers a fine alternative to the modern city cinemas. A movie ticket will cost from $13, children $10. Half-price tickets are often offered on Tue nights. *Moonlight Cinema*, Centennial Park, T1900 933 899, movies@moonlight.com.au (23 Nov-23 Feb) and the *Open Air Cinema* at the Royal Botanical Gardens near Mrs Macquarie's Chair (summer only) offer older classics under the stars. Take a picnic and plenty of cushions.

Contemporary music

There are plenty of mainstream music and the major CD stores in the city centre. For second-hand stores and alternative music shops try Kings St in Newtown, Oxford St in Paddington and Glebe Point Rd in Glebe

Australian   You will almost certainly hear the bizarre and extraordinary tones of the didjeridu somewhere during your explorations be it the buskers on Circular Quay or in the many souvenir shops in the city. For live performances of traditional Aussie instruments try the **Australia's Northern Territory and Outback Centre**, 28 Darling Walk, Darling Harbour (Tue-Sun 1300, 1500 and 1700) or the *Reds Australian Restaurant*, 12 Argyle St, The Rocks, T9247 1011, daily with dinner 1745 and 1930. The *Didj Beat Didjeridoo Shop* in the Clocktower Square Mall, T9251 4289, just across the road, is also a great venue to hear impromtu performances by the staff.

Folk   All the Irish pubs offer folk jam nights early in the week and live bands from Wed to Sun. For some of the best try the *Merchantile Hotel*, 25 George St, The Rocks, *Scruffy Murphys*, corner of Gouldburn St and George St, T9211 2002, *Kitty O'Shea's*, 384 Oxford St, T9360 9668, and *O'Malley's Hotel*, 228 William St Kings Cross, T9357 2211. Two excellent quieter options are *Paddy McGuires*, on the corner of George and Hay, T9212 2111, and *Durty Nelly'* (the best), on Glenmore Rd off Oxford St, which is a more intimate Irish pub offering low key jam sessions on Sun afternoons.

Jazz and blues   *Soup Plus*, 383 George St, T9299 7728, *The Basement*, 29 Reiby Pl, Circular Quay, T9251 2797, www.thebasement.com.au, and the *Harbourside Brasserie*, Pier One, The Rocks, T9252 3000, are the major local jazz venues. For daily details of jazz gigs tune into the *Jazz Gig Guide* at 0800 on *Jazz Jam*, 89.7FM Eastside Radio, Mon-Fri. The *Sydney Jazz Club* can be contacted on T9798 7294. *Zambezi Blues Room*, 481 Kent St (behind Town Hall Square), T9266 0200, is a fine venue and free.

Rock   The 3 main rock concert venues are the massive state-of-the-art *Sydney SuperDome*, in the Homebush Bay Olympic Park, T8765 4321, www.superdome.com.au, the 12,000-seat *Sydney Entertainment Centre*, 35 Harbour St, City, T9320 4200, and the *Metro*, 624 George St, T9287 2000. Tickets for a major international band will cost anything from $60 to $90.

Comedy

National or international comedy acts are generally hosted by the smaller theatres, like the *Lyric* and the *Belvoir* (see Performing Arts below). *Club Luna* at the Basement, 29 Reiby St, T9251 2797, is excellent on Sun nights, from $13. A number of inner city hotels have comedy nights once a week including the *Exchange Hotel*, corner of Beattie St and Mullins St, Balmain, T9810 6099 (Wed, from $5); and the *Marlborough Hotel*, 145 King St, Newtown, T9519 1222 (Tue, from $5), both of which are recommended. Another long-established venue is the *Unicorn Hotel*, 106 Oxford St, Paddington, T9360 3554 (Mon, from $7). Other venues with more regular acts are the *Comedy Store*, Bent St, Fox Studios, T9357 1419 (Tue-Sat, from $10-27), the *Laugh Garage*, 1st Floor, Macquarie Hotel, corner of Gouldburn St and Wentworth Av, T9560 1961 (Thu-Sat, from $11-22), and the *Comedy Cellar*, 1 Bay St, Ultimo, T9212 3237.

Gambling is big business in Australia with an estimated $10-12 bn being spent annually. **Gambling**
Given the population of 19 million that figure is indeed staggereing and makes Australians the most avid gamblers on earth. You will find that almost every traditional Australian Hotel and pub in Sydney has the omnipresent rows of hyperactive pokies (slot
machines), which to the uninitiated, need a Phd in bankruptcy and visual literacy skills to
play (whatever happened to a row of lemons or cherries?) The main focus for trying your
luck in Sydney is the *Star City Casino*, 80 Pyrmont St, a coins roll from Darling Harbour,
T9777 9000, www.starcity.com.au It is a vast arena with 200 gaming tables, 1,500 pokies
and lots of anxious faces. Open 24 hrs. Smart casual dress mandatory.

Sydney has a thriving gay and lesbian community that has reached legendary status **Gay & lesbian**
through the *Mardi Gras Festival* held every Feb, which culminates in the hugely popular *For more info*
parade through the city on the 1st Sat of Mar, www.mardisgras.com.au The main focus *and venues look*
for social activity is **Oxford St**, especially at the western end between Taylor Sq and Hyde *out for the free gay*
Park, while **Newtown**, in the inner west, is home to Sydney's lesbian scene. There are *papers 'Capital Q'*
many clubs and cafés that attract a casual mix of both straight and gay. Some of the more *(weekly) and the*
gay-oriented bars are *Albury Hotel*, *Beauchamp Hotel* and *Oxford Hotel* on Oxford St, *'Sydney Star*
and the *Newtown Hotel*, 174 Kings St, Newtown. Some popular nightclubs for men are *Observer' available*
Midnight Shift, 85 Oxford St, and *The Barracks*, 1 Flinders St. *DCM*, 33 Oxford St, T9267 *at most gay friendly*
7380, and the *Taxi Club*, 40 Flinders St, Darlinghurst, attract a mixed crowd. For counsell- *restaurants, cafés*
ing and referal call the Gay and Lesbian line T1800-805379. 1600-2400 daily. AIDS Coun- *and bookshops,*
cil of NSW (ACON) T9206 2000, www.bigayguy.com/need.htm *The Bookshop*, 207 *especially on Oxford St*
Oxford St, T9331 1103, is also a good source of information.

Naturally the focus for the performing arts in Sydney is the **Sydney Opera House**. It offers **Performing**
5 venues, the Concert Hall, the Opera Theatre, the Drama Theatre, the Playhouse and the **arts**
Studio. The Concert Hall is the largest venue and home to the **Sydney Symphony
Orchestra**. The Opera House is the home of **Opera Australia**, the **Australian Ballet** and
the **Sydney Dance Company**. The Drama Theatre is a performing venue for the Sydney
Theatre Company while the Playhouse is used for small cast plays, more low key performances, lectures and seminars. **The Studio** is used for contemporary music and performance. Prices and seats range from about $28 to $180. For details call the Opera
House box office, T9250 7250, www.soh.nsw.gov.au
    The beautiful and historic *State Theatre*, 49 Market St, City, T9022 6258,
www.statetheatre.com.au, offers a dynamic range of specialist and mainstream performances and cinema. Similarly the lovingly restored *Capitol*, 13 Campbell St, T9320 5000,
offers a diverse range of performances, while the *Theatre Royal*, MLC Centre, 108 King St,
T136166, is noted for its musicals and plays. The *Lyric Theatre* and the *Showroom*, at the
Star City complex, 80 Pyrmont St, T9777 9000, offer theatre, concerts, comedy, dance and
musicals. From around $40-80 for a major performance. The *Wharf Theatre*, Pier 4
Hickson Rd, The Rocks, is a second home (after the Opera House) for the Sydney Theatre
Company, and the *Bangarra Aboriginal Dance Company*, T9250 1777. The *Wharf Restaurant* next door is a superb for pre-performance dining and 'Behind the Scenes Tours'
are available, T9250 1777, $5. The *Belvoir Theatre*, 25 Belvoir St, Surry Hills, T9699 3444, is
another less well known venue offering a good range of performances. The *City Recital
Hall*, Angel Pl, City, T9231 9000, www.cityrecitalhall.com.au, offers a program of regular
classical music performances from around $35. The newly refurbished *Sydney Conserva-
torium of Music*, near the Botanical Gardens, off Mcquarie St, T9351 1222, info@green
way.usyd.edu.au, also hosts occassional live performances. The *Sydney Entertainment
Centre*, 35 Harbour St, City, T9320 4200, is one of the city's largest and most modern performance venues, hosting a wide range of acts, shows, fairs and sporting events.
Bangarra are a contemporary Aboriginal dance group and are based at Wharf 4, Walsh
Bay, The Rocks, T9251 5333, www.bangarra.ozemail.com.au

New South Wales

New South Wales

Festivals

New Year: Every New Year kicks in with spectacular fireworks and celebrations that centre around The Rocks and the Harbour Bridge. Other good vantage points include Milsons Point, The Opera House and Cremorne Point. **Jan**: The *Sydney Festival and Fringe Festival* takes place through most of the month. It is a celebration of the arts including the best of Australian theatre, dance, music and visual arts and is held at many venues throughout the city. For many the highlights are the free open air concerts in the Domain, including *Opera in the Park* and *Symphony under the Stars* (check www.sydneyfestival.org.au). The 26th sees the annual *Australia Day* celebrations with the focus being a flotilla of vessels flying the flag on the harbour (www.australia day.com.au). Without doubt the most famous Sydney event is the legendary *Gay and Lesbian Mardi Gras Festival and Parade* held each **Feb** for a month. It is an opportunity for the gay community to celebrate, entertain and shock. The highlight is a good shake of the pants and cod pieces (or very lack of them) during the spectacular parade from Liverpool St to Anzac Par (held at the end of the festival), T9557 4332 (www.mardi gras.com.au). **Mar**: the *Royal Agricultural Easter Show* is held every **Easter** and now uses the state of the art facilities at Olympic Park as a venue. **Apr**: The 25th sees the annual *Anzac Day* service at the Martin Place Cenotaph and a parade down George St. **May**: the annual *Sydney Morning Herald Half Marathon* is a great attraction, especially when it involves crossing the Harbour Bridge. *Australian Fashion Week* celebrations showcase some of the country's top designers. There is also another fashion week in Nov to preview the best of the winter collections. **Jun**: *Sydney Film Festival*, a 2 week fest for film buffs featuring over 150 features from 40 countries, T9660 3844, www.sydneyfilmfestival.org.au   **Aug**: *Sun-Herald City to Surf*, a 14-km race from Bondi Beach to the City Centre, T1800-555514. **Sep**: *Festival of The Winds* at Bondi Beach is a colourful festival of kites and kite flying, while the avid sports fans fight over tickets and take several days drinking leave for the Rugby League and Rugby Union *Grand Finals*. **Oct**: the weekend *Manly Jazz Festival* is a gathering of Australia's best along with some fine foreign imports. Stages located in several public arenas including the beachfront and the Corso, as well as hotels, restaurants and bars, T9977 1088. **Nov**: *Sydney to the Gong* (Wollongong – 80 km) cycle race. For details contact Bicycle NSW, T9283 5200, www.oze mail.com.au/~bikensw **Dec**: Christmas *Carols by Candlelight* is the main festive public celebration of song in the Domain, while the wild and wicked grab a beer glass and a patch of sand at the *Bondi Beach Christmas Party*, which usually ends up as a mass streak into the waves. Far more serious is the *Sydney to Hobart* sailing race, which departs from the inner harbour, winds allowing, every **Boxing Day**.

Shopping

Most shops' opening hours are from 0900-1730 on weekdays. At weekends shops shut slightly early. Thursday shopping is until 2100. Pick up 'Sydney Shopping, The Official Guide' from the VIC, or call the City Info Line on T9265 9007, or visit the website www.sydney-shopping.com.au

Sydney can offer a superb, world-class shopping experience. The most popular shopping venues are naturally to be found in the city centre, but many of the suburban high streets also support a wide range of interesting outlets and colourful weekend markets. In the city most of the large department stores, arcades, malls and specilist boutiques are to be found along **George St** and in the area around **Pitt St Mall, Castlereagh St** and **King St**. Not to be missed is the magnificent **Queen Victoria Building** (QVB), T9264 9209, www.qvb.com.au, which is a vast and historic eddifice in which the levels of retail therapy are almost legendary (see also page 87). Nearby, connecting George St (412) with Pitt St is the smaller, yet no less attractive and historic **Strand Arcade**, T9232 4199, www.strandarcade.com.au, which was originally built in 1892. On **Market St** there are 3 great Sydney institutions, the characterful department stores of *Grace Bros*, T9238 9111, www.gracebros.com.au, *David Jones*, T9266 5544, www.davidjones.com.au, and *Gowings*, T9287 6394, www.gowings.com.au The suburbs of **Newtown** (Kings St) and

Glebe (Glebe Point Rd) have some fascinating shops selling everything from cod pieces to second-hand surfboards. **Double Bay**, **Mosman** and **Paddington** (Oxford St) are renowned for their stylish boutique clothes shops and *The Rocks* is definitely the place to go for a didjeridu or cuddly koala. For factory outlets try the vast *Birkenhead Point Outlet Centre*, Roseby St, Drummoyne, T9181 3922, and for the largest of the suburban malls the *Warringah Mall*, Pittwater Rd, Brookvale, North Shore, T9905 0633.

For the best in authentic and original Aboriginal art try: *The Aboriginal and Tribal Art Centre*, 1st Floor, 117 George St, The Rocks, T9247 9625. Open daily 1000-1700; *The Coo-ee Emporium and Aboriginal Art Gallery*, 98 Oxford St, Paddington, T9332 1544. Open Mon-Sat 1000-1800, Sun 1100-1700; the *Hogarth Galleries* nearby, at 7 Walker La, T9360 6839; and *The Gavala Aboriginal Art Centre*, Shop 377, Harbourside, Darling Harbour, T9212 7232. Further afield the *Boomalli Aboriginal Artists Co-operative*, 191 Parramatta Rd, Annandale, T9560 2541, is also recommended. There are many art galleries showcasing some of the best Australian contemporary artists with most being in *The Rocks* or *Paddington*. Try to get hold of the free *'Art Find'* brochure from one of the galleries or the Sydney VIC. *Ken Done* is one of the most famous Sydney-based artists. He has a colourful style which you will either love or hate. His main outlet is at 123 George St, The Rocks, T9247 2740, www.gallery@done.com.au For some panoramic Australian photographs check out the *Ken Duncan Gallery*, George St, The Rocks (opposite the VIC) or the ubiquitous *Peter Lik Gallery* in the QVB, George St, www.peterlik.com.au

Aboriginal art, contemporary fine art & photography
Look out for the National Indigenous Arts Advocacy Association Label of Authenticity. The Traveller Consumer Helpline also has details, T1300-552001

From the iconic *Akubra hats* (minus the gimmick of corks) and *RM Williams* boots to the *Driza-Bone* oilskin coats, you'll find all the main brands and outlets in Sydney. Generally speaking these world-famous brands and products are all beautifully made and well worth the money. A pair of RM's boots for example will, provided you look after them, last a lifetime. RM Williams clothing outlets can be found at 389 George St and Shop 1-2 Chiefly Plaza, corner of Hunter St and Phillip St, www.rmwilliams.com.au *Akubra Hats* and *Drizabones* can be found at the *Goodwood Saddlery*, 237-239 Broadway, T9660 6788, open Mon-Fri 0900-1730, Thu until 2000, Sat 0900-1700, Sun 1000-1600, or *Strand Hatters* in the Strand Arcade, 412 George St, T9231 6884. For unique Australian crafts try the *Craft Australia Boutique* in David Jones department store, Market St, 4th Floor, T9266 6276. *Object*, on the 3rd Floor of the Customs House, 31 Alfred St, near Circular Quay, T9247 9126, www.object.com.au, also showcase the best in authentic Australian crafts. For a good range of souvenir-based products the many outlets in **The Rocks** (and weekend Rocks Market) are a good source along with *Australia's Northern Territory and Outback Centre*, 28 Darling Walk, Darling Harbour, T92837477, www.outbackcentre.com.au You can purchase didjeridu and boomerangs all over the city but perhaps the best outlet is the *Didj Beat Didgeridoo Shop* in the Clocktower Square Mall, The Rocks, T9251 4289. It has over 2,000 'didjies' on show. A free 1-hr workshop is offered with your purchase (from $55-1,500) and they also stock a good selection of original Aboriginal art. Open 1000-1830 daily, www.didjibeat.com.au

Australiana

Dymocks are the major player with outlets throughout the city. The largest (and apparently the largest bookshop in Australasia) is at 428 George St, with other outlets at 350 George St, 261 George St, and 34 Hunter St, T1800 688 319, www.dymocks.com.au Open Mon-Wed/Fri 0900-1800, Thu 0900-2100, Sat/Sun 0900-1700. For Travel Guides and maps the *Travel Bookshop* at 175 Liverpool St (southern edge of Hyde Park), T9261 8200, F92618481, is also a good source of information, books and maps. Open Mon-Fri 0900-1800, Sat 1000-1700. For smaller more traditional bookshops or second-hand try the two *Gleebooks* shops, (new books at 49 Glebe Point Rd, T9660 2333, and Childrens and Secondhand at 191, open 7 days), and *Sappho Books* at 165 Glebe Point Rd, T9552 4498. Open 7 days 1000-2200. Paddington's Oxford St is also home to 2 good

Bookshops

New South Wales

independent stores, *Ariel* (42), T9332 4581, and *Berkelouw's Books* (19), T9360 3200. The latter also sells a great range of second-hand books and has the added attraction of a café. Both are open until late. The largest and most bizarre second-hand bookshop in the city is the 'lost world'of *Goulds Book Arcade*, 32 Kings St, Newtown.

Clothes   You will find all the major labels in the major central city shopping streets, arcades and department stores. **Oxford St** in Paddington and also the suburbs of **Double Bay** and to a lesser extent **Chatswood**, are renowned for their boutique clothes stores and Australian designer labels. Names and labels to look for include Helen Kaminski, Collette Dinnigan, Morrissey, Bare, Isogawa and Bettina Liano. For designer bargains try the **Market City** above Paddy's Markets in Haymarket. Finally, if you are looking for something different then head for **Kings St** in Newtown.

Food & wine   If you are a novice or even a seasoned wine buff, before purchasing any Australian labels you might benefit from a trip to the *Australian Wine Centre*, 1 Alfred St, Circular Quay, T9247 2755, www.wine.ptylimited.com.au The staff are very knowledgable and are backed by a great collection of over 1,000 wines. They also offer a worldwide delivery service. Open daily. For a taste of Australian foods take a look at the food hall in the elegant *David Jones* department store, Market St, T9266 5544. Even if you don't like seafood a trip to the **Sydney Fish Markets**, Pyrmont is fascinating with the shoal of stalls setting up their displays of Australia's best from about 0800 (see page 89). For late night food shopping the Coles Express supermarket, corner of George St and King St, and at the Wynard Station and Kings Cross are open 0600-2400 daily.

Jewellery   Given the fact Australia produces over 90% of the worlds opals it is not surprising to find a wealth of specialists dealing in their almost surreal beauty and worth. Some of the best include *Flame Opals*, 119 George St, T9247 3446, wwwflameopals.com.au Open Mon-Fri 0900-1845, Sat 1000-1700, Sun 1130-1700, *Opal Minded*, 36-64 George St, T9247 9885. Open daily 1000-1800, *Australian Opal Cutters*, Suite 10, 4th Floor, 250 Pitt St, T9261 2442, and *Gems from the Heart*, Shop 33 in the QVB, George St, T9261 2002. To ensure authenticity and good workmanship only purchase opals from retailers who are members of the *Australain Opal and Gem Industry Association Ltd* (AOGIA) or the *Jewellers Association of Australia*. Pearls from the great Australian 'pinctada maxima' oyster, from gold to snow white, are also big business in Sydney and for some of the best and biggest look no further than *Bunda*, Shop 42, Ground Floor, QVB, George St, T9261 2210.

Markets   There are plenty of weekend markets held in the inner city that offer a range of new and
For more information   second-hand clothes, arts, crafts and foods. The most popular is **The Rocks Market** held
on markets see under   every Sat/Sun at the top end of George St. This is supplemented on Sun with an unclut-
Sights section   tered open-air, market on the **Opera House** concourse, which concentrates mainly on arts, crafts and souvenirs. The biggest market in the city centre is the gloomy and fairly tacky **Paddy's Markets** in Haymarket which is open Thu-Sun. Good inner suburbs markets include the **Paddington Market** held every Sat in the grounds of the church at 395 Oxford St; **Balmain Market** at St Andrews Church, corner of Darling St and Curtis St, also on Sat; the **Glebe Market**, in the grounds of Glebe Public Schools, Glebe Point Rd every Sun, and the beachside **Bondi Markets** on Campbell Par, also held every Sun. The fascinating **Sydney Fish Markets** held every morning in Pyrmont.

Outdoor   **Kent St** is the place to start looking for camping and outdoor equipment. *Paddy Pallin* (507), T9264 2685, www.paddypallin.com.au, *Mountain Equipment* (491), T9264 5888, www.mountainequipment.com.au and *Patagonia* (497), T9264 2500, are all near to each other. *Adventure Sports Australia* are based at 722 George St, T9281 6977. For *Rent-A-Tent* outlets call T998 74924, in Hornsby Heights, or T9653 1631 in Galston.

Sport

Most of the sporting venues are to be found at the **Homebush Bay Olympic Park** (see page 90). Even without any special events the facilities are still worth seeing. The **Telstra** Stadium (T8765 2300, www.stadiumaustralia.com.au) is now the main focus of national and international rugby union, rugby league, Aussie rules football and soccer matches, but lacks the atmosphere of the former venue, the Sydney Football Stadium (SFS) in Moore Park, Paddington. Next door to the SFS is the **Sydney Cricket Ground** **(SCG)**, the main venue for national and international cricket matches. A day spent here watching a 1-day international cricket match is truly memorable, more for the antics off-field than on. In winter the SCG is taken over by the Sydney Swans, **Australian Rules** Football team, which has a local, though no less fanatical following. Tours of both stadiums are available to the public, T9380 0383.

Sydney is the obvious venue for some of the most important major national and international sporting events in Australia. The huge success of the 2000 Olympic Games has also left the city legacy of some superb sporting venues

Swimming is of course another major sport in Australia with the national team now being consistently the best in the world. Again Olympic Park and the ultra-modern **Sydney Aquatic Centre** is the primary focus. It is also open to the public, T9752 3666. Homebush also hosts regular major tennis, hockey, basketball and athletic events. **Surfing** is of course another major national sport with Sydney's ocean beaches being a year-round venue. Triathlons and Surf Lifesaving Team competitions are also a regular feature of the sand and surf. **Sailing** is also hugely popular and Sydney Harbour hosts a number of minor events, with the most noted exception being the start of the **Sydney to Hobart** race every Boxing Day. To join a spectator ferry that follows the 18-ft sailing skiffs taking part in the Formula One races every weekend from Oct-Apr, contact the **Sydney Flying Squadron**, T9955 8350 (Sat), or the **Australian Sailing League**, T9363 2995 (Sun). Fees apply. Test Rugby, Aussie Rules and Test Cricket match tickets are often very hard to come by and any attempt must be made well in advance. A ticket will cost from $40 to $70 for a cricket test match and $40-100, for a rugby Grand Final. The usual ticket agent is *Ticketek*, T9266 4800, www.ticketek.com.au If you cannot secure tickets or don't rate your chances securing a spare ticket outside the venue (often possible), joining the throngs of Sydneysiders in the city pubs can be just as enjoyable and atmospheric.

Directory

Banks The major banks have ATMs on all the major shopping and eating streets. **Foreign Exchange** is readily available on the arrivals concourse of Sydney Airport. In the city there are many outlets around Circular Quay and along George St including *Thomas Cook*, QVB Walk, Shop 64, T9264 1133, *Visa Customer Centre*, 91 George St, The Rocks, T1800-180 900 (open 1000-1800), and *American Express*, 124 and 50 Pitt St, T9239 9226.

Car hire Offices at the airport (Arrivals south) include *Avis*, T9667 0667, *Hertz* T9669 2444, *Thrifty* T9317 4161, *Budget* T132848, *National*, T9207 9409, and *Red Spot*, T9317 2233. In the city try *Avis*, *Budget* and *Ascot* centred on or around William St, Darlinghurst. Cheaper more localized companies include *Dollar*, Sir John Young Cres, T9223 1444, and *Bayswater Rentals*, 180 William St, Kings Cross, T9360 3622. Rates start from about $55 per day. **Campervan hire** *Maui*, Free call T1300-363800; www.maui-rentals.com.au, *Britz*, Free call T1800-331454, www.britz.com.au **Car and campervan dealers (second-hand)** *Travellers Auto Barn*, 177 William St, Kings Cross, T1800-674374, www.travellers-autobarn.com.au, *Kings Cross Car Market*, Ward St Car Park, Kings Cross, T1800-808188, www.carmarket.com.au (good buy and sell venue)

Communications Internet is widely available throughout the city centre with the southern end of George St and Pitt St (between Liverpool and Hay) and the western end of Oxford St (between Crown and College) having numerous outlets. *Global Gossip* have outlets at 34 Wentworth Av, 770 George St in the CBD, and 317 Glebe Point Rd, Glebe. Most backpackers offer their own internet facilities and outlets in the outer

New South Wales

suburbs and are listed in the Sleeping section. Expect to pay from $3 to $8 per hr (be careful to confirm your start and finish time with the person on duty; overcharging or convienient 'rounding up' seems to be common). There are **Post Shops** dotted around the city marked with the prominent red and white circular logo The main General **Post Office** is located at 159 Pitt St (Martin Pl), T131318. Open Mon-Fri 0815-1730, Sat 1000-1400. **Post Restante** is based at the George Street branch, 310 George St (across the road from the Wynyard Station entrance). Log your name into the computer to see if any mail awaits. The city centre post restante code is NSW 2001. Open Mon-Fri 0830-1700. Most internet outlets, newsagents and grocery stores advertise a copious number of allegedly 'spectacularly cheap' international phone cards, claiming to have rates to far flung countries for as little as $0.09 per min. Be careful of these claims, since most are based on weird off-peak times and are dependent on the location from which you call. Read the small print and avoid cards that require you to pay $0.40 at a public phone to connect with the company (ie without a direct national 1800 number). These can be more trouble than they are worth especially once you are out of the city. Set rates in phone booths in internet outlets are a good bet, but lack privacy.

Laundry *City Laundromat*, Millennium Tower, corner of Sussex St and Bathhurst St, T9264 6661. **Library** *State Library of NSW* (see page 86), *Sydney City Library*, 456 Kent St, T9265 9470. Open Mon-Fri 0800-1900, Sat 0900-1200.

Medical services *St Vincent's Hospital* Victoria St, Darlinghurst, T9339 1111, *Royal North Shore Hospital*, Pacific Highway, St Leonard's, T9926 7111, *Prince of Wales Hospital*, High St, Randwick, T9382 2222, *Sydney Children's Hospital*, T9382 1111. **After Hours Dental Emergency** 144/313 Harris St, Pyrmont, T9660 3322.

Police Emergency T000, general enquiries T9690 4960. *City of Sydney Police Station*, 192 Day St, T9265 6499.

Around Sydney

*One of the wonderful things about Australia's largest city is that you are never too far away from water or parks and nature reserves. To the west, a mere 70 km delivers you to the fringes of some of the state's largest and most celebrated national parks, all within the Greater Blue Mountains region. Even closer to home is the **Ku-ring-gai Chase National Park** to the north and **The Royal National Park** to the south, sitting at either end of the city like two great green book ends.*

Botany Bay National Park
15-30 km south of Sydney Vehicle entry to the park costs $6

Botany Bay holds a very special place in Australian (European) history as the site of Captain Cook's first landing in April 1770. The landing site is near what is now **Kurnell** on the southern shores of Botany Bay, which along with **La Perouse** on the northern shore, comes under the auspices of the 458-ha Botany Bay National Park. As well as possessing highly significant historical sites for both the European and Aboriginal cultures it presents plenty of walking opportunities and ocean views. In the southern sector of the park the **NPWS Botany Bay National Park Discovery Centre**, Cape Solander Drive, T9668 9111, is a good source of park and walks information and hosts a interesting display surrounding Cook's landing as well as the usual natural history aspects. ■ *Mon-Fri 1100-1500, Sat/Sun 1000-1630.*

Within the small **northern sector** of the park, around **La Perouse** on the northern headland, you can take a tour of **Bare Island Fort**, erected amidst wartime paranoia and the perceived threat of foreign invasion. ■ *Guided tours on Sat/Sun. $7.70, child $5.50. T9247 5033.* Also located on the headland is the **La Perouse Museum and Visitors Centre**, on the actual site of the first landing of the First Fleet in 1788. The museum explores the great historical event and the fate of French explorer Captain La Perouse, as well as local Aboriginal and European heritage. ■ *Wed-Sun 1000-1600. $5.50, child $3.30. T9311 3379. Cable Station, Anzac Par.* The **southern sector** is larger and hosts the **NPWS Discovery Centre** (see above) and the best walks including the short (1 km) **Monument Track** and the more demanding **Coast Walk** to Bailey lighthouse.

Transport Access to the northern sector is via Anzac Par. *Sydney Buses*, T131500, offer regular daily **bus** services from Railway Sq (No 393) or Circular Quay (No 394) in Sydney's CBD. To get to the southern sector by **car**, follow the Princes Highway south, take a left on to The Boulevarde, and then follow Captain Cook Dr. By **train** from Sydney's Central Station, take *CityRail*, T131500, to Cronulla (Illawarra line), then *Kurnell Bus*, T9523 4047, No 987 to the park gates.

Royal National Park
Colour map 3, grid C4
32 km south of Sydney

Vehicle entry costs $10 per day

The 15,080-ha Royal National Park was the first national park in Australia gazetted in 1879. As well as providing over 100 km of walking tracks, many taking in terrific ocean views, there are some beautiful beaches and other activities ranging from swimming to scuba diving. However, the park is subject to the constant threat of fire and more than once in the last decade the Royal has been almost completely (but temporarily) destroyed by bush fires. The main hub of human activity centres around historic **Audley** at the park's northern entrance, where you will find the **NPWS Royal National Park Visitors Centre**. ■ *Daily 0830-1630. Farnell Av, T9542 0648.*They can provide park maps, detailed information on walks and all other activities. Ranger guided walks are often available. There is car and caravan based camping (F)available at Bonnie Vale.

Wattamolla, Garie and Burning Palms are three beautiful **beaches** and the choice of **walks** ranges from the 500-m (wheelchair-accessible) Bungoona Track to the 26-km **Coast Track** (Bundeena to Otford) which guarantees some glorious coastal views and on occasion (from June-September) the odd whale sighting. You can hire rowboats and canoes at the **Audley Boatshed**, near the visitors centre for a leisurely paddle up Kangaroo Creek. Mountain bikes are also available for hire but trail routes are limited and there is good surfing at the patrolled **Garie Beach**. Several freshwater pools also provide sheltered swimming with the **Deer Pool** (near Marley Beach) being the most popular.

Transport By **car** from Sydney take the Princes Highway south and follow signs for Audley (left, at Loftus on Farnell Av and McKell Av). By **train** take *CityRail* (Illawarra line) from Central Station to Loftus (4 km from Audley), Engadine, Heathcote, Waterfall or Otford. You can also alight at Cronulla and take the short crossing by **ferry** to Bundeena at the park's northeastern corner, T9523 2990, from $3.

Ku-ring-gai Chase National Park
Colour map 3, grid C4
26 km north of Sydney

Vehicle entry costs $10 per day

Though a few wealthy Sydney entrepreneurs might see Ku-ring-gai Chase as little more than 14,883-ha of wasted prime real estate, the rugged sandstone country that fringes the mighty Hawkesbury River, with its stunning views and rich array of native wild animals and plants, is thankfully safe from further suburban encroachment and has been since it was designated as a National Park in 1894. As well as the stunning views across Pittwater and Broken Bay (the mouth of the Hawkesbury River), from the **West Head Lookout**, the park offers some lovely bush walks, secluded beaches and regionally significant Aboriginal rock art. It is also a great place to see that much celebrated state flower, the warratah, in bloom. The park is named after the Guringai (Ku-ring-Gai) Aboriginals who occupied the region for over 20,000 years

New South Wales

New South Wales

before the arrival of the Europeans. The **NPWS Bobbin Head Information Centre**, Bobbin Inn, Bobbin Head Road (western side of the park), T9472 8949 (daily 1000-1600), or the **Kalkari Visitors Centre**, Chase Road (between Mount Colah and Bobbin Head), T9457 9853 (daily 0900-1700), can supply walks, camping information and maps. The former also has a gift shop. Ranger guided walks are often available.

Without doubt the highlight of the park is the **West Head Lookout**, high above the peninsula overlooking **Broken Bay** and the mouth of the **Hawkesbury River**. To the north is the beginning of the central coast and Brisbane Water National Park, while to the west is the tip of the northern beaches and the historic Barrenjoey Lighthouse. West Head is criss-crossed with walking tracks that start from West Head Road. Aboriginal rock art can be seen along the **Basin Track** (which falls to the Basin Beach **campsite** and the arrival/departure point of the Palm Beach ferry) and the 3½-km **Red Hand Track** (Aboriginal Heritage Track). **Bobbin Head** at the western end of the park is a popular base for water-based activities. Here, too, is the VIC, which can supply details on walks. A great place to stay is the **C-E** *Pittwater YHA*, T9999 2196.

Transport By **car** access is via Bobbin Head Rd, via the Pacific Highway (from the south) or from Ku-ring-Gai Chase Rd via F3 Freeway (from the north). Access to the eastern side (West Head Rd and West Head Lookout) is from Mona Vale Rd, Northern Beaches. The nearest public transport (western side) by **train** is with *CityRail*, T131500 (Northern Line), from Central Station to Berowa, Mt Ku-ring-gai and Mt Colah, then walk to Bobbin Head (3-6 km). A better alternative is to catch a **bus** (No L90) to Palm Beach (eastern side) then catch the **ferry** to Basin Beach. Ferry Cruises also run to Bobbin Head (see Northern Beaches section, Sydney).

Blue Mountains

Colour map 3, grid C4   The 'Blues', as they are affectionately known, form part of the Great Dividing Range, 70 km, or two hours, west of Sydney and contain no less than five national parks covering a total area of 10,000 sq km. They are not really mountains at all, but a network of eroded river valleys, gorges, and bluffs, that have formed over millions of years. The result is a huge wonderland of natural features, from precipitous cliffs, to dramatic waterfalls and canyons, not to mention the most dramatic limestone caves on the continent.

Once the home of the Daruk Aboriginals, the Blue Mountains were seen by the first Europeans merely as a highly inconvenient barrier to the interior and for almost a quarter of a century they remained that way, before finally being traversed in 1813 by explorers Blaxland, Wentworth and Lawson. To this day the impenetrable geography still limits transportation and essentially the same two convict-built roads and railway line completed over a century ago reach west through a string of settlements from Glenbrook to Lithgow on the other side. For decades the 'Blues' have been a favourite weekend or retirement destination for modern-day Sydney escapees, who welcome the distinctly cooler temperatures and the colourful seasons that the extra elevation creates. But superb scenery and climate aside, the Blue Mountains also present some excellent walking opportunities, as well as other, more fearsome activities like abseiling, canyoning and rock climbing. Given the region's popularity there are also a glut of good restaurants and a wide range of accommodations from showpiece backpackers to romantic hideaways.

Greater Blue Mountains National Parks

The Blue Mountains region contains five national parks which cover an area of 10,000 sq-km, with half of that being considered 'wilderness area'. The largest, at an expansive 4,876 sq km (and the second largest in the state after Kosciuszko National Park) is **Wollemi National Park**, to the north of the Bells Line of Road. It incorporates the state's most extensive officially recognized wilderness area and is very rugged and inaccessible. As well as its complex geology, topography, Aboriginal art sites and botanical features it is also home to a rich variety of birds. Of all the parks in the region it is the one for the well-prepared modern-day explorer. There are basic NPWS campsites at Wheeny Creek, Colo Meroo, Dun's Swamp and Newnes. Main access is from Putty Road 100 km northwest of Sydney or via Rylstone.

The most famous and accessible park is the 2,470-sq-km **Blue Mountains National Park**, straddling the Great Western Highway and a string of mountain villages and towns, from Glenbrook in the east to Lithgow in the west. Only recently expanded in the 1980s, it contains natural features that range from deep canyons and forested valleys to pinnacles and waterfalls, as well as a rich abundance of flora and fauna. Although now receiving over one million visitors a year, much of the park remains extremely inaccessible, with over 500 sq km considered official wilderness area. Sadly, the Blue Mountains, like so many national parks in NSW, has suffered in recent years from the temporary impact of widespread bush fires. There are basic NPWS campsites at Euroka Clearing near Glenbrook, Ingar near Wentworth Falls and Perry's Lookdown near Blackheath. You can also camp anywhere within 500 m from roads and facilities. Access is from many points east and west off the Great Western Highway, or from the Bells Line of Road 70 km west of Sydney.

Next up is the beautiful 680-sq-km **Kanangra-Boyd National Park**, to the southwest of Katoomba. Fringed by the Blue Mountains National Park on all but one side it contains a similar geology and topography but is particularly famous for two natural features, the **Jenolan limestone caves** and the **Kanangra Walls** (a series of outstanding bluffs). Both are well worth visiting, with the latter considered one of the great walks in the region. There is a basic NPWS campsite at Boyd River. Access is via Mount Victoria and the Jenolan Caves 180 km west of Sydney.

To the southeast of Kanangra-Boyd and the Blue Mountains National Parks is the 860-sq-km **Nattai National Park**. It touches the region's largest body of water, **Lake Burragorang**, and contains the region's largest populations of eastern grey kangaroos as well as many rare plants and animals. There is basic NPWS camping near the lake. Access is 110 km south of Sydney between the Warragamba Dam and Wombeyan Caves Road.

The smallest national park in the group is the 12,000-ha **Gardens of Stone National Park** north of Lithgow. Adjoining Wollemi it is most noted for its prominent and shapely limestone outcrops and sandstone escarpments. Birdlife is once again prolific. There are no campsites. Access is 30 km north of Lithgow via Mudgee Road.

For detailed **information** on all the national parks above contact or visit the NPWS Heritage Centre in Blackheath, T4787 8877, or the NPWS offices in Richmond, Bowman's Cottage, 370 Windsor Street, T4588 5247.

Ins and outs

Although public transport to and around the Blue Mountains is generally good you are advised to take your own vehicle or hire one, allowing you to make the most of the numerous viewpoints and sights within the region. **Trains** are generally the best way to arrive independently and leave Sydney's Central Station (*Countrylink* and/or *CityLink* platforms) on the hour daily well into the evening, stopping at all major towns

Getting there

New South Wales

through the Blue Mountains to Mt Victoria and beyond, T132232. The journey to Katoomba takes about 2 hrs and costs around $15 day-return. *CityRail*, T131500, in conjunction with *Fantastic Aussie Tours*, T1300-300915, also offer a number of rail/coach tour options with *Blue MountainsLink* operating Mon-Fri and *Blue Mountains ExplorerLink* operating daily. Price includes return transport and tour on arrival in Katoomba. *McCaffery's/Greyhound*, T132030, offer standard daily coach transportation on the westbound run to Dubbo. Numerous **coach** companies also offer day sightseeing tours from Sydney. Backpackers should ask any of the main hostels which are currently offering the best deals and which are currently recommended. Some may allow overnight stops. For others the main accredited VIC in Sydney can assist with the extensive choice and bookings. Most of the buses leave from Circular Quay. *Aerocity Shuttles*, T4782 1866, offer direct links from Sydney Airport.

Getting around
For transport details, see Katoomba or the relevant locations

The route through the Blue Mountains is generally easily negotiable. From the west (Sydney) you take the M4 ($2 toll), eventually crossing the **Neapean River**, before it forms the **Great Western Highway** at **Glenbrook** (65 km). Then, beginning the ascent of the main plateau and following the same route as the railway line, you pass through Blaxland, Springwood, Faulconbridge and Woodford, before arriving at **Wentworth Falls**. It is in Wentworth that you essentially reach the top of the main plateau at an average height of just above 1,000 m. From Wentworth Falls the road then continues west through the northern edges of **Leura** and **Katoomba**, then north, through the heart of **Blackheath** and **Mt Victoria**. From Mt Victoria you then begin the descent to **Lithgow** (154 km). The rather peculiarly named **Bells Line of Road** provides another access point across the mountains from **Windsor** on the east to Mt Victoria on the Great Western Highway (77 km). Katoomba is the largest of the towns and is generally accepted as providing the best amenities.

Information

The main accredited VICs are in **Glenbrook, Katoomba** and **Lithgow** on the Great Western Highway (west to east) and **Oberon** (west, near the Jenolan Caves). The main *NPWS* office is at the Heritage Centre, near Govetts Leap, **Blackheath**. All these are listed under the relevant section. If approaching from the east, stop at the Glenbrook VIC to begin with and stock up with the free visitors guide and maps. All regional centres also offer a free accommodation bookings service. The NPWS stock a wide range of books covering the numerous walks within the national parks, as well as topographical maps. There are also detailed guides and books available in most major bookshops in Sydney.

Glenbrook to Wentworth Falls
Distance 37 km

Proud of its European roots and its railway heritage, the pretty village of **Glenbrook**, just beyond the **Nepean River**, acts as the unofficial gateway to the Blue Mountains. The **Glenbrook Visitors Information Centre** is located just off the Great Western Highway in Glenbrook, T1300-653408, www.bluemountainstourism.org.au ■ *Mon-Fri 0900-1700, Sat and Sun 0830-1630.* Along with Katoomba this is the main tourism administration and information centre for the Blue Mountains. The **NPWS Conservation Hut**, at the end of Fletcher Street (off Falls Road), T4757 3827, can provide walks information and has a small shop and café.

Fringing the village, south of the highway, is the southern section of the **Blue Mountains National Park** and access to numerous attractions, including the **Red Hands Cave**, a fine example of Aboriginal rock art. The distinctive hand stencils made on the cave wall are thought to be over 1,600 years old. You can reach the caves either by road or by foot (8 km return) from the Glenbrook Creek causeway, just beyond the park entrance. There are also shorter walks to the **Jellybean Pool** and the **Euroka Clearing**, a basic NPWS

New South Wales

campsite and the ideal spot to see grey kangaroos, especially early or late in the day. Fees apply, T4588 5247. For a map of the park and its attractions call in at the Glenbrook VIC. To reach the park gate ($5 per day, walkers free), take Ross Road behind the VIC onto Burfitt Parade and then follow Bruce Road. The lookouts at **The Bluff**, at the end of Brook Road (slightly further east off Burfitt, then Grey), are also worth a look. North of the highway in Glenbrook you can also follow signs to the **Lennox Bridge** the oldest in Australia, built by convicts in 1833. Nearby, in **Knapsack Park**, the Marge's and Elizabeth **Lookouts** provide great views back towards the western suburbs and Sydney.

Beyond Blaxland and Springwood is the small settlement of **Faulconbridge**, home to the **Norman Lindsay Gallery and Museum**. Lindsay (1879-1969) is just one of many noted artists that have found the Blue Mountains conducive to their creativity and his studio remains very much the way he left it. ■ *Daily 1000-1600. $8, child $4. T4751 1067. 14 Norman Lindsay Cres.* For most, it is the stunning **lookouts** across **Wentworth Falls** and the **Jamieson Valley** that offer the first memorable introduction to the dramatic scenery of the Blue Mountains – assuming the weather is clear, of course. The car park is the starting point for some superb walking tracks, best of which is the four-hour **Wentworth Pass Walk** which crosses the top of the falls, and then descends precariously down to the valley floor. Then, if that were not enough, the track skirts the cliff base, through rainforest, before climbing back up via the dramatic **Valley of the Waters** gorge to the **Conservation Hut** (see above). From there it's an easy walk back to the car park. Another excellent walk is the five-hour **National Pass Walk** which follows a cutting halfway up the cliff, carved out in the 1890s. Both walks involve steep sections around cliff edges and laddered sections, but if you have a head for heights either one is highly recommended. Give yourself plenty of time and make sure you get maps from the Conservation Hut before setting out. Some improvements are being made to both tracks and the base section of the Wentworth Pass can also be a little vague at times, so go prepared and don't forget your camera. For something less demanding, try the **Den Fenella Track**, which will take you to some good lookouts, then you can return or preferably keep going (west) to the Conservation Hut along the **Overcliff Track**. Better still, is the magical **Undercliff Track** to **Princes Rock Lookout**.

Sleeping and eating Wentworth has plenty of good **B&Bs** offering a quieter alternative to those in Leura and Katoomba. The VIC in Glenbrook or Katoomba can advise and book ahead. The **café** in the Conservation Hut (see above) offers light snacks and good coffee. Open daily 0900-1700.

Although the pretty village of Leura plays second fiddle to Katoomba, the two essentially merge into one. Possessing a distinct air of elegance, the residents of Leura are proud of their village and in particular their gardens. **Everglades Gardens** provide the best horticultural showpiece and has done since the early 1930s. ■ *Daily 1000-1700. $6, child $2. T4784 1938. 37 Everglades Av.* The **Leuralla and NSW Toy and Railway Museum** is well worth a look, for kids and parents alike. ■ *Daily 1000-1700. $6, child $2. T4784 1169, Olympian Par.* A short stroll west of the museum is the **Gordon Falls Lookout**, which is also worth a look. There are several other walks and lookouts around the cliff fringes in Leura with the best being the short 500-m walk to the aptly named **Sublime Lookout**, which offers arguably the best view of the Jamieson Valley and **Mount Solitary**. Follow signs from Gladstone Road, west of The Mall.

Leura
Population: 4,000
107 km west of Sydney 3 km east of Katoomba

New South Wales

Leura has many excellent historic B&Bs and self-contained cottages and the VIC can provide full listings

Sleeping and eating The **LL** *Manderley*, 157 Megalong St, T4784 3252, www.blue mts.com.au/manderley, and the more affordable **L-A** *Peartree Cottage*, Holmes St, T9489 9195, www.bluemts.com.au/cottages, are 2 fine self-contained options, while the **LL-L** *Peppers Fairmont Resort*, 1 Sublime Point Rd, T4782 5222, www.peppers.com.au, has a fine reputation and offers luxuriously appointed rooms and suites, as well as a res-taurant, bar, pool, spa and massage. It is also very handy for the golf course. Of the many fine restaurants and cafés in Leura is the *Silk's Brasserie*, 128 The Mall, T4784 2534, offer-ing fine modern Australian cuisine. Open daily for lunch and dinner (book ahead).

Katoomba and around

Colour map 3, grid C4
Population: 18,000
122 km west of Sydney 43 km southeast of Lithgow

Considered the capital of the Blue Mountains, the erstwhile mining town of Katoomba offers an interesting mix of old and new and a truly cosmopolitan ambience. As well as the wealth of amenities and activities based in the town, many come here simply to see the archetypal, two-dimensional postcard image of the Blue Mountains transformed into the real thing from the famous **Three Sisters** lookout at Echo Point.

Ins & outs

Getting there Katoomba **train station**, T4782 1902, acts as the main transport hub within the town and is located off Main St, at the northern end of Katoomba St. Trains leave Sydney's Central Station on a regular basis. *Countrylink*, T132232, offer daily ser-vices to/from Sydney hourly. *CityRail*, T131500, with *Fantastic Aussie Tours*, T1300-300915, also offer a number of rail/coach tour options with *Blue MountainsLink*, operat-ing Mon-Fri and *Blue Mountains ExplorerLink*, operating daily. Prices include return transport and a tour on arrival in Katoomba. *Greyhound/McCafferty's*, offer standard daily **coach** transportation on the westbound run from Sydney to Dubbo, stopping behind the train station near the Gearin Hotel, Great Western Highway.

Getting around Once you get to Katoomba there are a number of operators offer-ing general local transportation or specialist sightseeing trips further afield. The *Blue Mountains Explorer Double-Decker Bus*, T4782 4807, www.explorerbus.com.au, offers a local service with 27 stops around Katoomba and Leura, hourly between 0930 and 1730. An unlimited jump-on/off day pass costs $25, child $12.50. Alternatively, the *Blue Mountains Bus Co*, T4782 4213, offer a standard *Hail 'n' Ride* service around Katoomba, Leura and Wentworth Falls, Mon-Fri from 0745-2025, Sat 0800-1530, Sun 0915-1530, from $2. *Mountainlink,* 285 Main St, T1800-801577, operate a 29-stop trolley bus tour around the main sights of Katoomba and Leura, with an all day unlim-ited stop travel pass, daily from 1015-1615, for $12. *Fantastic Aussie Tours*, 283 Main St, T4782 1866, www.fantastic-aussie-tours.com.au, offer a wide range of tour-based options from coach and 4WD adventure tours. **Car hire** is available from *Thrifty*, 80 Megalong St, Leura, T4784 2888. **Bike hire** is available from *Cycletech*, 182 Katoomba St, T4782 2800, from $19-50 per day. *Katoomba Radio Cabs*, T4782 1311, operate a 24-hr taxi service between Mt Victoria and Wentworth Falls.

Information and orientation The new **Katoomba Visitors Information Centre** is located at Echo Point, T1300-653408, www.bluemountainstourism.org.au Open daily 0900-1700. There is a *Backpackers Travel Centre* at 283 Main St, T4782 5342. Main St itself runs parallel with the Great Western Highway and forms a junction with Katoomba's main **Katoomba St** which then runs due south to Lilianfels Av, and Echo Point Rd, terminating at **Echo Point**, the VIC and the **Three Sisters** Lookout.

Sights & walks

A steady stream of tourist traffic floods consistently and relentlessly down Katoomba's main drag towards **Echo Point** to enjoy the Blue Mountains' most famous view, the **Three Sisters**. It is little wonder the place is so popular, since here you can appreciate the true grandeur of the Blue Mountains. Built precariously 170 m above the valley floor, the lookout seems to defy gravity. The only downside is the constant stream of people. Dawn and sunset are far better times to visit. From the lookout it is possible to walk around to the stacks and descend the taxing **Giant Stairway Walk** (30 minutes) to the valley floor. From there you join the **Federal Pass Track**, back through the forest

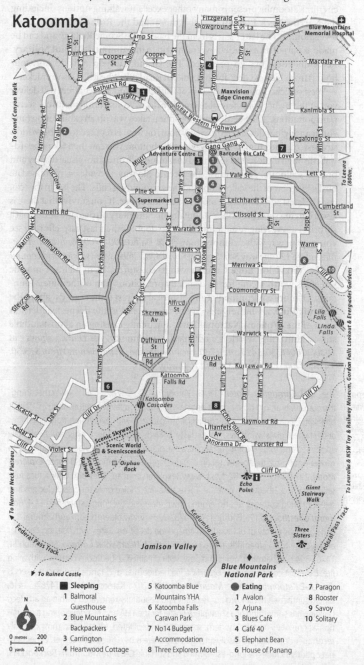

Katoomba

	Sleeping	5	Katoomba Blue		Eating	7	Paragon
1	Balmoral		Mountains YHA	1	Avalon	8	Rooster
	Guesthouse	6	Katoomba Falls	2	Arjuna	9	Savoy
2	Blue Mountains		Caravan Park	3	Blues Café	10	Solitary
	Backpackers	7	No14 Budget	4	Café 40		
3	Carrington		Accommodation	5	Elephant Bean		
4	Heartwood Cottage	8	Three Explorers Motel	6	House of Panang		

below the cliffs to the **Katoomba Cascades** and **Orphan Rock**. As the name suggests it is a single pillar that became separated from the nearby cliff over many centuries of erosion. From Orphan Rock it is a short walk to a choice of exits: the hard option, on foot, up the 1,000-step Furbers Steps, or for the less adventurous, the **Scenic Railway**. Give yourself three hours for the complete circuit. Katoomba presents many other excellent walking options, including the **Narrow Neck Plateau** (variable times) and the **Ruined Castle** (12 km, seven hours). The latter starts from the base of the Scenic Railway and can be made as part of an extended overnight trip to the summit of **Mount Solitary**. Recommended, but go prepared. The **Grand Canyon** walk (5 km, four hours) from Neates Glen, Evans Lookout Road, Blackheath, is also a cracker.

West of Echo Point the junction of Cliff Drive and Violet Street will deliver you at the highly commercial **Scenic World**, with its various unusual scenic transportations. The **Scenic Railway** option takes you on an exhilarating (and vomit-inducing) descent to the valley floor; on what is reputed to be the world's steepest 'inclined funicular railway'. At the bottom you can then take a board-walk through the forest to see an **old coal mine** with an audio-visual display and bronze sculpture. In contrast, the **Scenic Skyway** provides a more sedate bird's-eye view of the valley floor and the surrounding cliffs. The last in the trio, and the latest addition, is the modern **Scenicscender**. If you survive that there is also a **cinema** showing a Blue Mountains documentary on demand and (what a surprise) a revolving restaurant, which no doubt is their last gasp effort to see you on your way with an empty stomach. ■ *Daily 0900-1700, Railway and Scenicsender $12 (one way $6), Skyway $10. T4782 2699, www.scenicworld.com.au*

The **Maxvision Edge Cinema** with its six-storey, 18-m high, 24-m wide screen, is worth seeing for its distinctly precipitous film of the Blue Mountains. Of more environmental and historical interest is the segment about the **Polemic Pine**, an entirely new species discovered in the deepest wilderness areas of the **Wollemi National Park**, apparently causing an almost audible stir within the world's botanical community. ■ *Daily, shows at 1030/1200/1330/1425 and 1730, (new release films in the evening) from $13.50, T4782 8900. 225 Great Western Highway.*

Sleeping

There is plenty of choice. The VIC has full listings and provide a free bookings service. Note prices are higher at weekends and you are advised to book ahead at any time of year, especially winter

The **LL-L** *Carrington Hotel*, 15-47 Katoomba St, T4782 1111, www.thecarrington.com.au, is an old classic, built originally in 1882 and lavishly refurbished in 1998. It offers an elegant, historic and congenial atmosphere, with everything from open fires and stained glass windows, to a classy billiards room. The rooms are beautifully appointed and there is a fine restaurant, a bar, nightclub and a spa. Recommended. For a **motel** option try the locally recommended and unconventional **L-B** *Three Explorers Motel*, 197 Lurline St, T4782 1733, www.3explorers.com.au They also offer a nice fully self-contained 2-bedroom cottage. There are a fine choice of historic B&Bs, lodges and self-contained cottages in and around town including the long-established **LL-L** *Balmoral Guesthouse*, 196 Bathurst Rd, T4782 2264, www.bluemts.com.au/balmoral It is large and has plenty of old world charm, period decor, en suites with spa, log fires, bar and is close to all amenities. More modern is the **L** *Heartwood Cottage*, 56 Station St, T4782 3942, a charming, quiet and cosy, self-contained, 2-bedroom cottage with a log fire. Excellent complimentary breakfast. Pitched both at mid-range and backpackers is the **A-E** *Katoomba Blue Mountains YHA*, 207 Katoomba St, T4782 1416, bluemountains@yhansw.org.au Recently and beautifully renovated within an art-deco building it is something of a showpiece hostel for the YHA and fast developing a reputation as one of its best. Its modern, spacious, well facilitated, friendly and most certainly recommended. Trips are gladly arranged and there is bike hire and internet. Other budget options include the long-established and sociable **C-E** *Blue Mountains Backpackers*,

190 Bathurst St, T1800-624226, the owners of which also run the Katoomba Adventure Centre, so there is plenty of good advice surrounding local activities, especially walks. **C-E** *No14 Budget Accommodation*, 14 Lovel St, T4782 7104, www.bluemts.com.au/no14, is another alternative providing a peaceful, relaxed atmosphere in a old former guesthouse with double/twin, single and family rooms. The **A-E** *Katoomba Falls Caravan Park*, Katoomba Falls Rd, T4782 1835, is well located and offers standard cabins, powered and non-powered sites and a camp kitchen.

Eating
Katoomba and the Blue Mountains generally pride themselves in offering some classy restaurants and fine cuisine. For the more expensive restaurants you are advised to book ahead

Expensive *Solitary*, 90 Cliff Dr, T4782 1164, is a very classy award winner with a fine reputation offering imaginative modern Australian cuisine and fine views across the Jamieson Valley. Open lunch Sat/Sun and public/school holidays and dinner Tue-Sat. *The Avalon*, 18 Katooma St, T4782 5532, is a more relaxed but classy restaurant located upstairs in the town's old art-deco theatre. It is especially noted for its generous servings and its valley views. **Mid-range** *The Savoy*, 26 Katoomba St, T4782 5050, is locally recommended for good value and especially for its conventional and kangaroo steak dishes. Open daily form 1100-2000. *Arjuna*, 16 Valley Rd, T4782 4662, is the best Indian restaurant in the region and the views are almost as hot as the curry. Open Thu-Mon from 1800 (book ahead). Also offering a fine view is *The Rooster Restaurant* in the *Jamieson Guest House*, 48 Merriwa St, T4782 1206. It is an old favourite that serves good value French-influenced cuisine. Open daily for dinner and for lunch Sat/Sun. The accommodation is also very good. **Cheap** The *House of Panang*, 183 Katoomba St, T4782 6222, is a good value, no-nonsense Malaysian restaurant. For a great breakfast in a relaxed atmosphere try *Café 40*, 40 Katoomba St, T4782 4063. Open daily 0700-2200. The *Elephant Bean*, 159 Katoomba St, T4782 4620, is another fine café and recommended for lunch. Open Wed-Mon 0800-1500. For vegetarian food look no further than the *Blues Café*, 57 Katoomba St, T4782 2347. Open daily from 0900-1700. Finally if you have a sweet tooth you just cannot afford to miss out on a Katoomba institution, the art deco *Paragon*, 65 Katoomba St, T4782 2928. Open daily 0800-1700.

Tours & activities

Walking, rock-climbing, canyoning, mountain biking and abseiling are the big 5 major activities in the Blue Mountains and several Katoomba based operators offer supervised package deals. Other options include horse riding, 4WD adventures and numerous day tours to several major attractions like the **Jenolan Caves** or the stunning **Kanangra-Boyd National Park**. The VIC has full listings. Local operators include the very clued-up and eco-friendly folks at the *Katoomba Adventure Centre*, 1 Katoomba St, T1800-624226, www.kacadventures.com.au, offering great advice on independent walking as well as numerous adventure options, including abseiling from $99, canyoning (repelling) from $99, rock climbing from $109 and adventure walks (recommended) from $64. Others companies include *High 'N' Wild*, 3/5 Katoomba St, T4782 6224, www.high-n-wild.com.au, who offer good mountain biking trips. The *Australian School of Mountaineering*, 182 Katoomba St, 14782 2014, www.ausmtn.com.au, offer hardcore professional rock climbing and bush craft trips (amongst others) and the reputable *Blue Mountains Adventure Company*, 84a Bathurst Rd, T4782 1271, www.bmac.com.au, are another worth looking at. *Blue Mountain Horse Riding Adventures*, T4787 8688, www.megalong.cc, in the Megalong Valley west of Kato- omba, offer hour/half/full and multi day horse rides from $22. Their 'Pub Ride' holds infinite appeal. *Getabout 4WD Adventures*, T9831 8385, www.getabout.com.au, offer professional 4WD tours with a tag-along option allowing you to take your own vehicle. For eco tours ask about the 'Ranger Guided Walks' and activity adventures with the NPWS at the Heritage Centre at Govetts Leap, Blackheath. Tim Tranter's *Tread Lightly Eco-tours*, T4788 1229, www.treadlightly.com.au, are also a good option. Camping equipment/adventure activity supplies and hire from *Katoomba Adventure Centre*, 1 Katoomba St, T1800-624226, and *Paddy Pallin*, 166 Katoomba St, T4782 4466.

New South Wales

Directory   Most **bank** branches with ATMs are located along Katoomba St. **Communications** Internet available at *Barcode 6ix Café*, 6 Katoomba St, T4782 6896. Open daily 0900-2100, or the *Katoomba Adventure Centre*, 1 Katoomba St, T1800-624226. **Post Office** behind Katoomba St, on Pioneer Pl. Open Mon-Fri 0900-1700. **Medical services** *Blue Mountains Memorial Hospital*, Great Western Highway (1 km east of the town centre), T4784 6500. **Police** 217 Katoomba St, T4782 8199.

Medlow Bath, Blackheath & Mount Victoria   From Katoomba the Great Western Highway heads north through the pretty villages of Medlow Bath, Blackheath and Mount Victoria. Although, not as commercial as their bustling neighbour all provide excellent accommodation, restaurants and are fringed both north and south by equally stunning views and excellent walks. To the east is the easily accessible **Megalong Valley**, particularly well known for its horse trekking, while to the west, in contrast, is the **Grose Valley**. The **Evans** and **Govetts Leap** Lookouts east of Blackheath, provide the best easily accessible viewpoints, but there are also some lesser-known spots well worth a visit. The **NPWS Blue Mountains Heritage Centre** is near the terminus of Govetts Leap Road, Blackheath. ■ *Daily 0900-1630. T4787 8877, www.npws.nsw.gov.au* They stock extensive national parks and walks information and also sell books, guides, maps and gifts.

In **Medlow Bath** is the historic **Hydro Majestic Hotel**, built in 1903 and the longest building in Australia at the time. Though a hotel in its own right, its original function was as a sanatorium, offering all manner of health therapies, from the sublime – mud baths and spas – to the ridiculous – strict abstinence from alcohol. At the time the rarefied air in the Blue Mountains was hailed as a cure-all for city ills and people flocked to the Hydro. Today, although the mud baths (and thankfully the prohibition) have gone, the hotel still provides fine accommodation and a great spot for afternoon tea.

Blackheath is a sleepy little village with a lovely atmosphere, enhanced in autumn when the trees take on their golden hues. There are two lookouts well worth visiting. The first, **Evans Lookout**, is accessed east along Evans Lookout Road and provides the first of many viewpoints across the huge and dramatic expanse of the Grose Valley. One of the best walks in the region, **The Grand Canyon Trail**, departs from Neates Glen, off Evans Lookout Road (5 km, five hours). From there you descend through the rainforest and follow Greaves Creek through moss-covered rock tunnels and overhangs, before climbing back up to Evans Lookout. Recommended. The other lookout, **Govetts Leap**, is a stunner and has the added attraction of the **Bridal Veil Falls**, the highest (but not necessarily the most dramatic), in the Blue Mountains. Just before the lookout car park is the **NPWS Heritage Centre**, which is worth a visit providing walks information, maps, guide and gifts. The **Fairfax Heritage Track**, built to accommodate wheelchairs, links the centre with the lookout. From Govetts Leap you can walk either north to reach Pulpit Rock or south to Evans Lookout via the falls.

Although Govetts and Evans are both stunning, three other superb lookouts await your viewing pleasure and can be accessed from Blackheath. These are often missed, but no less spectacular. The first, **Pulpit Rock**, can be reached by foot from Govetts (1½ hours, 2½ km) or better still, by 2WD via Hat Hill Road. The lookout, which sits on the summit of a rock pinnacle, is accessed from the car park by a short 500-m walk. From the same car park then continue north (unsealed road) to **Anvil Rock**, being sure not to miss the other short track to the bizarre geology of the **wind eroded cave**. Perry Lookdown is 1 km before Anvil Rock and a path from there descends into the valley to connect with some demanding walking trails. Also well worth a visit is the aptly-named **Hanging Rock**, which will, on first sight, take your breath away. Watch your footing and do not attempt to climb to the point, as tempting as it may be. It is a favourite abseiling spot, but only for the well equipped and utterly insane. Like all the other lookouts on the southern fringe of the Grose Valley, sunrise is by far the best time to visit. The rock can be reached along a rough, unsealed track (Ridgewell Road), on the right, just beyond Blackheath heading north. It is best suited to 4WD but if you don't have your own transport most local 4WD tours go there.

The **Megalong Valley**, accessed on Megalong Valley Road west of Blackheath town centre, provides a pleasant scenic drive and is one of the most accessible and most developed of the wilderness Blue Mountains valleys. The **Megalong Australian Heritage Centre** offers a whole range of activities from horse trekking and 4WD adventures, to livestock shows. Accommodation is also available and there is a bistro restaurant. ■ *Daily 0730-1800. Horse trekking from $22. T4787 8688, www.megalong.cc.au*

New South Wales

The **LL** *Hydro Majestic Hotel*, Great Western Highway, Medlow Bath, T4788 1002, www.hydromajestic.com.au, is worth staying in purely for the historical aspect, the architecture and especially the views. Recently renovated, it offers luxury rooms and suites (some with spa and valley views) plus all the amenities you might expect. The **LL-L** *Jemby-Rinjah Eco Lodge*, 336 Evans Lookout Rd, T4787 7622, www.jembyrinjah lodge.com.au, offers either 1- or 2-bedroom, self-contained, modern cabins (one with a Japanese hot tub), log fires, all in a beautiful bush setting close to the lookout and walks. Dinner, bed and breakfast packages are also available. The **L-B** *Glenella Guesthouse*, 56 Govetts Leap Rd, T4787 8352, is a well known surprisingly affordable, historic guesthouse, with a reputable restaurant attached, plus all the comforts including sauna, open fires and cable TV. In Mt Victoria the historic **LL-C** *Imperial Hotel*, 1 Station St, T4787 1878, www.bluemts.com.au/hotelimperial, is reputedly the oldest tourist hotel in Australia. Beautifully restored it is a fine place to soak up the history and offers a wide range of well-appointed rooms from the traditional to the 4-poster with double spa. Breakfast included, good restaurant, bar and live entertainment at the weekends. For camping try the **A-E** *Blackheath Caravan Park*, Prince Edward St, which is in a quiet suburban bush setting and within walking distance of the village. On-site vans, powered and non-powered sites, BBQ and kiosk, but no camp kitchen. Other than the *Glenella Guesthouse* and the *Imperial* (see above) there are several notable eateries in Blackheath. The very classy French-style *Cleopatra*, 118 Cleopatra St, T4787 8456, is actually a guesthouse, but has won so many awards for its cuisine; it is often dubbed the 'restaurant with accommodation'. It is expensive but worth it. Open Tue-Sun for dinner, lunch on Sun. A more affordable but equally well-known Blackheath institution is *Vulcans*, 33 Govetts Leap Rd, T4787 6899, whose only drawback is the limited opening from Fri-Sun for lunch and dinner.

Sleeping & eating
The villages north of Katoomba all provide excellent accommodation away from the bustle of the Blue Mountains capital. The VIC has full listings

Medlow Bath, Blackheath and Mt Victoria are all on the main local bus/train routes to/from Katoomba. The train station is in the centre of town off the Great Western Highway and on Station St, off the Great Western Highway in Mt Victoria.

Transport
See Katoomba for operator listings

Lithgow marks the western boundary of the Blue Mountains and was founded in 1827 by explorer Hamilton Hume. An industrial town and Australia's first producer of steel, its main tourist attraction is the remarkable **Zig Zag Railway** 10 km east in Clarence as well as a scattering of historical buildings. The town also acts as the gateway to the Jenolan Caves and Kanangra-Boyd National Park to the south and the wilderness **Wollemi National Park**, to the north. Wollemi is one of the largest and the most inaccessible wilderness areas in NSW, a fact

Lithgow
Colour map 3, grid C4
Population: 11,500
161 km from Sydney
For details of the Zig Zag Railway
see page 135

that was highlighted in no uncertain terms in 1994 with the discovery of the Wollemi Pine, a species that once flourished over sixty million years ago. The exact location of the small stand of trees is kept secret. As well as its botanical treasures Wollemi National Park and its fringes are also a birdwatchers paradise and for once, this is a place where nature is getting a little of its own back, quite literally, by quietly repossessing the two former industrial towns of **Newnes** and **Glen Davis**. The Lithgow **VIC** is at 1 Cooerwull Road (off the Great Western Highway, at the western end of town), T6353 1859, www.tourism.lithgow.com (■ *Daily 0900-1700*).They supply town maps and have accommodation listings. For national park details, directions and maps call at the **NPWS** Heritage Centre in Blackheath (see above).

There are three fairly low-key museums in the town. The **State mine and Heritage Park and Railway** outlines the town's proud links with coal mining and the railway. ■ *Sat/Sun 1000-1600. T6353 1513, State mine Gully Rd (off Atkinson St)*. The **Lithgow Small Arms Museum**, that recalls the history of a local small arms factory. ■ *Sat/Sun 1000-1600. $4, child $2, T6351 4452*. The **Eskbank House Museum** is a Georgian homestead built in 1842, complete with period furnishings and Lithgow pottery. ■ *Thu-Mon 1000-1600. $2, T6351 3557. Corner of Inch St and Bennett St*.

Of far more natural historical appeal are the derelict villages of **Newnes** and **Glen Davis**, to the north of Lithgow, between the scenic **Gardens of Stone National Park** and the western fringe of the Wollemi National Park. Both were once thriving villages supporting a population of thousands that worked in the two large oil-shale refineries during the early 1900s. South of Newnes an added attraction is the old 400-m rail tunnel that was once part of a busy line that connected the shale plants with Clarence Station. Now left dark and forbidding, the tunnel is the silent home of **glow worms** (gnat larvae), which light up its walls like a galaxy of stars. All along the unsealed roads to both Newnes and Glen Davis look out for the prolific birdlife, from huge wedge-tailed eagles and raucous flocks of sulphur-crested cockatoos to tiny, iridescent fairy wrens.

See Katoomba section
for operator listings

Transport Lithgow is on the main local and westbound bus/train route to/from Katoomba and Sydney. The train station is on Main St, *Countrylink*, T132032, and *CityRail*, T131500, both offer regular daily services east and west.

Jenolan Caves
Colour map 3, grid C4
Population: 7,000
190 km west
of Sydney
60 km south
of Lithgow

The Jenolan Caves on the northern fringe of the Kanangra-Boyd National Park, south of Lithgow, comprise nine major (and 300 in total) limestone caves considered to be amongst the most spectacular in the southern hemisphere. After over 160 years of exploration and development, (since their discovery in 1838 by pastoralist James Whalan), the main caves are now well geared up for your viewing pleasure with a network of paths and electric lighting to guide the way and to highlight the bizarre subterranean features. As well as **guided cave tours**, some other caves have been set aside for **adventure caving**, and above ground, there is a network of pleasant **bush trails**. If you are short of time the **Lucas Cave** and **Temple of Baal Cave** are generally recommended. The **Chiefly Cave** is the most historic and along with the **Imperial Cave** it has partial wheelchair access. The **River Cave** is said to be one of the most demanding. On your arrival at the caves you immediately encounter the **Grand Arch** a 60-m wide, 24-m high cavern that was once used for camping and even live entertainment to the flicker of firelight. Nearby the historic and congenial **Caves House** has been welcoming visitors since 1898. ■ *The main caves can only be visited by guided tour, daily from 1000-2000. 1 hr $15, child $10; 2 hrs $27.50. 3-cave-combo from $38.50, child $26.50. T6359 3311, www.jenolancaves.org.au*

Information The main accredited VICs in **Katoomba** and **Oberon** (30 km northwest of Jenolan), 137-139 Oberon St, T6336 0666 (Mon-Fri 0830-1630, Sat/Sun 1000-1600) can both supply the detail and assist with accommodation and activity bookings. The *NPWS Blue Mountains Heritage Centre*, in Blackheath, T4787 8877 (see above), stock extensive national parks and walks Information. For specific detail on the caves, tours and activities contact the *Jenolan Caves Reserves Trust*, T6359 3311, www.jenolancaves.org.au

Sleeping and eating The grand and multi-facilitated **LL-F** *Jenolan Caves Resort*, T6359 3322, www.jenolancaves.com.au, includes the Caves House that offers a range of rooms and suites, as well as self-contained cottages and campsite. Also restaurant, bistro, bar and a host of activities. A cheaper alternative is the **L-A** *Jenolan Cabins*, Porcupine Hill, 42 Edith Rd, T6335 6239, www.bluemts.com.au/JenolanCabins Each self-contained cabin accommodates 6 with one queen size and bunks. The owners also operate local tours, www.bluemts.com.au/Jenolan4WD

There is plenty of accommodation in and around Jenolan, from the historic Caves House and quiet self-contained cottages, to basic campsites

There is no public transport to the Jenolan Caves, but numerous tour operators in Katoomba and Sydney run day tours. A basic day tour to the caves will cost about $70 exclusive of caves tour, $80 with one cave inspection and $150 with one cave inspection and a spot of adventure caving. The VICs in Katoomba or Sydney have full details.

Transport

Bells Line of Road is named after Archibald Bell, who discovered the 'second' route through the Blue Mountains to Lithgow from Sydney, in 1823, at the age of 19 . Starting just west of Richmond in the east, then climbing the plateau to fringe the northern rim of the Grose Valley, it provides a quieter, more sedate, scenic trip across the Great Divide and is particularly well renowned for its **gardens** (best viewed in spring and autumn) and also for its spectacular **views**. Just beyond the village of Bilpin, west of Richmond, the huge basalt outcrop of **Mount Tomah** (1,000 m) begins to dominate the scene and supports the 28-ha cool-climate annexe of the Sydney **Botanical Gardens**. Opened in 1987 the garden's rich volcanic soils nurture over 10,000 species, including a huge quantity of tree ferns and rhododendrons. Although the gardens are well worth visiting in their own right, it is the views, the short walks and the restaurant that make it extra special. ■ *Daily 1000-1600. $6. T4567 2154, www.rbgsyd.nsw.gov.au* Just beyond Mount Tomah (right) is the **Walls Lookout**, with its expansive views across the Grose Valley. It requires a one-hour return walk from the Pierces Pass Track car park but the effort is well worth it. Back on the Bells Line of Road and just a few kilometres further west is the junction (north, 8 km) to the pretty village of **Mount Wilson** which is famous for its English-style open gardens. These include Linfield Park (on Mount Irvine Road, $3) and Nooroo (■ open Sep-Nov and Apr-May, $3, T4756 2018, Church Lane). Also of interest is the **'Cathedral of Ferns'** at the northern end of the village. The Wynnes and Du Faurs **Lookouts** can also be reached from Mount Wilson and are signposted, east and west of the village centre. Back on the Bells Line of Road you can continue west to Clarence (16 km) and Lithgow (29 km). In Clarence you will find the **Zig Zag Railway** a masterpiece of engineering originally built between 1866 and 1869. Operated commercially up until 1910 as a supply route to Sydney it now serves as a tourist attraction with lovingly restored steam trains making the nostalgic 8-km (1½ hours) journey from Clarence to Bottom Points (near CityRail's Zig Zag Station). ■ *Steam trains leave Clarence on Wed/Sat/Sun at 1100/1300 and 1500. On other weekdays the less exciting motorized trains take over and leave at the same time. $14, child $11. T6353 1795, www.zigzagrailway.com.au Request drop off if you are arriving by CityRail from Sydney/Katoomba at the Zig Zag Station.*

Bells of Line Road
Distance 77 km between Windsor and Lithgow

New South Wales

North Coast

The North Coast of New South Wales, stretching almost 900 km from Sydney to Tweed Heads, is, to many travellers, an outdoors utopia; an endless string of beautiful beaches, bays, and headlands, crystal clear waters and national parks, with the constant soundtrack of rolling surf. Such appeal, however, has its costs, and the weak-willed traveller may suffer from severe option paralysis. As a general guide, from north to south, extended stops in Nelson Bay (Port Stephens), Myall Lakes National park, Port Macquarie, South West Rocks, Coffs Harbour, Angourie, Bundjalung National Park, and of course, Byron Bay, are all recommended. Also, try to break up the journey with the odd trip inland, especially to Bellingen, the Dorrigo and New England National Parks and the numerous other superb national parks in the Rainbow Region, inland from Byron Bay.

Sydney to Newcastle
Distance 163 km

The coastal region from Sydney (Broken Bay) to Newcastle is referred to as the **Central Coast** and is essentially by-passed by the Sydney-Newcastle Freeway (Hwy1). The region's largest settlement, **Gosford** (on the Pacific Highway) acts very much as a satellite town to Sydney and holds few attractions in itself. There are however two good national parks in the region (Brisbane Water and Bouddi), along with some fine **beaches** and a wealth of **inland lakes** and harbours, providing some excellent walking, boating, fishing, swimming and surfing. But though a hugely popular weekend getaway, it's best to treat the area as an extended day trip from Sydney and press on towards Newcastle, Port Stephens, or the Hunter Valley. There are accredited VICs in Gosford, Terrigal, Woy Woy and The Entrance. ■ *For general information and bookings, T4385 4430, www.cctourism.com.au Most are open daily Mon-Sat 0900-1700, Sun 0900-1400.* The **NPWS** have an office in Gosford, Suites 36-38, 207 Albany Street North, T432 44911 (■ *Mon-Fri 0900-1700*).

The two major tourist attractions in the central coast lie just west of the Pacific Highway Gosford Junction (13 km west of Gosford). The **Australian Reptile Park and Wildlife Sanctuary** is the first of many wildlife parks encountered between Sydney and Cairns. Recovering well from a recent fire, this particular park carves its niche by concentrating on everyone's favourite reptiles and spiders, as well as wombats, roos and koalas. ■ *Daily 0900-1700. $17, child $8, family $44. T4340 1146, www.reptilepark.com.au Signposted from the Pacific Highway turn-off to Gosford.* Nearby, **Old Sydney Town** tries hard to faithfully represent the quiet and quaint little colonial seaside settlement of **Sydney Cove** between 1788 and 1810. Over 150 ha of parkland, complete with replica historic buildings, sets the scene for various displays of early crafts, trades and methods of transportation, as well as re-enactments of pistol duels and floggings. Café and pub on-site. ■ *Wed-Sun 1000-1600. $24, child $13.50. T4340 1104. Signposted off the Pacific Highway Turn- Gosford turn-off.*

There are three **national parks** in the region, two of which are within 20 km of Gosford. To the southeast, fringing the northern arm of the Hawkesbury River Inlet, the sandstone landscapes of **Brisbane Water National Park** host a few examples of Aboriginal art and a good lookout, both of which are accessed via Woy Woy Road off the Pacific Highway at Kariong. Further east the more popular **Bouddi National Park** offers coastal scenery, **walks** and secluded beaches. The NPWS office in Gosford supply details surrounding both parks and there is a small information centre at Maitland Bay in the Bouddi National Park. Vehicle entry is $6 at Putty Beach, T4368 2277. North of Bouddi are more great **surf beaches**, including **McMasters**, **Avoca** and **Terrigal**.

The Central Coast also has a wealth of saltwater lakes and harbours with **Brisbane Waters** south of Gosford and **Tuggerah Lake** north of Terrigal being the largest. North of that the Central Coast Region gives way to **Lake Macquarie** which stretches all the way to Newcastle and is four times the size of Sydney Harbour. Sailing is popular here, with a wide range of other water sports also being well represented. The VICs have full details. The waterways also naturally attract lots of birds, with groups of friendly **pelicans** being a common sight, especially at Memorial Park, The Entrance, daily at 1530.

The small and friendly **B-E** *Terrigal YHA*, 12 Campbell Cr, Terrigal, T4385 3330, is in a beachside location and offers dorm, double/twin, single and family room options (some cabin with en suite), internet, free use of surf/body boards. Regional motor parks include the well-placed and well-facilitated **LL-D** *Blue Lagoon Beach Resort*, Bateau Bay Rd, Blue Lagoon (9 km north of Terrigal), T4332 1447, www.bluelagoonbeachresort.com.au For more solitude you might consider the **NPWS campsites** in the Bouddi National Park. Car-based camping is available at **F** *Putty Beach* (no campervans), with toilets, BBQs and no water, while backpack camping is available at **F** *Little and Tallow Beaches*.

Sleeping

The Central Coast is a popular weekend getaway from Sydney

Booking is advised and the VICs can provide full listings

The region can be accessed by car, bus, train, ferry and floatplane. Long-distance **coach** company *McCafferty's/Greyhound*, T132030, stop in Gosford outside the train station and provide daily services. *Busways*, T4392 6666, and *Red Bus*, T4325 1781, are the 2 main **local bus** companies offering an extensive daily service. Many stop at the **train station** in Gosford, located behind the VIC on Mann St. *Cityrail*, T131500, offer services to Sydney and Newcastle, while *Countrylink*, T132232, provide state-wide. *Central Coast Airbus*, T1300-367470, provides daily shuttle services to Sydney Airport. A small local **ferry** crosses Broken Bay between Palm Beach and Wagstaff or Ettalong, Mon-Fri, T9918 2747, and www.palmbeachferry.com.au For **floatplane** services between Sydney and the Central Coast, T1300-656787, www.sydneybyseaplane.com

Transport

Newcastle

Newcastle has had a lot of bad press, but don't believe everything you may have heard or read. This is, or was, one of the most industrialized cities in Australia, and its main street is about as charming as Kabul suburb, but it actually has a lot to offer. In the CBD are the attractive façades of some of the most historic buildings in Australia and to the east lie some of the best surf beaches in the State. Having said that, if you're thinking of using it merely as a stopover on the way north, you would be far better to head for Port Stephens and Nelson Bay 50 km further north.

Colour map 3, grid C5
Population: 270,000
150 km north of Sydney
348 km south of Brisbane

Getting there and around Newcastle **airport**, T4965 1925, is 24 km north of the city centre. *Qantas*, T4929 5821, Newcastle@Qantas.com.au, is the main operator. *Coastal Air Services*, T1800-262782, www.coastalairsservice.com, also operate a fleet of **amphibious aircraft** from Sydney. *Thrifty*, T4942 2266, *Hunter Valley Connections*, T4934 6163, and *All Travel*, T4955 6777, all provide **shuttles** to the airport from $36 one-way. The main **train station** is at the far end of Hunter St. *Cityrail*, T131500, offer regular daily services to Sydney. *Countrylink*, T4962 9438, have a travel centre at the station (open daily 0900-1700) and luggage storage is also available. Note, state-wide service connections are from Broadmeadow, 5 mins west of the station. Long distance **coaches** stop next door to the train station. *McCafferty's/Greyhound*, T132030, offer daily Sydney and north/southbound services. The *Countrylink Travel Centre* acts as booking agents. *Port Stephens Coaches*,

Ins & outs

New South Wales

T4982 2940, www.psbuses.nelsonbay.com, also provide daily services to Sydney and Port Stephens. If you intend to pass through the Great Lakes Region and Myall National Park, *Great Lakes Coaches* (Kings Bros), T4983 1560, offer daily **regional bus** services between Taree and Sydney, via Tuncurry Forster, Bluey's Beach, Hawks Nest and Newcastle. *Newcastle Bus and Ferry*, T131500, provide local bus and ferry services. Fares start at $2.50 and allow an hour's unlimited travel with an all day pass costing $7.40. Bus/Ferry and Train/Bus/ferry passes are also available from $33 per week. *Ferry Services*, T131500, link central Newcastle (Queens Wharf) with Stockton from 0515-2400 Mon-Sat, 0830-2200 Sun, $1.80, child $0.90 one-way, tickets on board. **Bike hire** is unavailable in Newcastle. **Taxi**, T4979 3000.

Information The **VIC** is in Wheeler Pl, opposite the Civic Rail Station, 363 Hunter St, T4974 2999, www.newcastletourism.com Open Mon-Fri 0900-1700, Sat/Sun 1000-1530. The NPWS do not have an office in Newcastle.

Sights The city's fine **viewpoints** are a good place to start. The **Obelisk** on Ordnance Street, above the city centre, offers good views across the city, the harbour and out to sea, where fleets of huge vessels wait offshore to enter the harbour. Fine coastal vistas are afforded from **Fort Scratchley** on Nobby's Road, (base of the lighthouse peninsula at the mouth of the harbour) which also houses the local **Maritime and Military Museum**. ■ *Tue-Fri 1000-1600, Sat/Sun 1200-1600. Free. T4929 2588.* Newcastle can boast some very fine and gracious **historical buildings**, including the 1892 **Christ Church Cathedral** (Church Street), the 1890 **Courthouse** (Bolton Street) and several classics on and around Hunter Street and Watt Street, including the **post office** (1903), the **railway station** (1878) and **Customs House** (1877). The VIC can supply a self-guided **heritage walk** leaflet, but by far the best way to experience the city's historical sights is on board the **Newcastle Tram** that departs from the railway station on the hour daily from 1000-1500, 45 minutes, from $10, child $6.50, T4963 7954. There area number of good galleries and museums in the

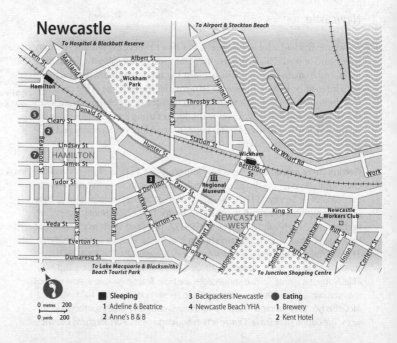

Newcastle

To Airport & Stockton Beach

To Hospital & Blackbutt Reserve

Sleeping		3 Backpackers Newcastle	Eating
1 Adeline & Beatrice		4 Newcastle Beach YHA	1 Brewery
2 Anne's B & B			2 Kent Hotel

0 metres 200
0 yards 200

city with the **Regional Museum** (■ *Tue-Sun 1000-1700. Free. T4974 1400, 787 Hunter St*) and the **Newcastle Regional Art Gallery** (■ *Tue-Sun 1000-1700. Free. T4974 5100, Laman St*) both being worthy of investigation.

The **beaches** on the eastern fringe of the city are superb and well known for their excellent **surfing**, swimming (patrolled in summer) and fishing. The main **Newcastle Beach** is at the end of Church Street. To the north of that a rocky platform has been utilized to create the man-made **Ocean Baths** before the sand returns to form **Nobby's Beach** and the peninsula known as **Nobby's Head**. **Bar** and **Merewether Beaches**, south of the city centre, also provide their fair share of world-class surf breaks. **Lake Macquarie**, fringing the southern city suburbs, forms a huge saltwater harbour and provides another favourite spot for water-based activities. The **Lake Macquarie Visitors Information Centre**, 72 Pacific Highway, Blacksmiths, T4972 1172, www.lakemac.com.au, can offer detailed local information. The 180-acre **Blackbutt Reserve**, 10 km west of the city centre, has some good bush walks and wildlife exhibits with the inevitable koala feeding daily at 1400-1500. ■ *Daily 0700-1700. Free. T4952 1449. Off Carnley Av, New Lambton (bus No 232/363).*

Tours & activities

Other than the obvious attraction of the city's beaches and its convenience as a base from which to secure a tour of the **Hunter Valley Vineyards**, Newcastle has reluctantly given over the region's activity capital status to Port Stephens and Nelson Bay. Many of the activities on offer there (and listed in that section) are also on offer from Newcastle. Particularly exciting are the various 4WD, ATV and horse trekking trips along the dune landscapes of **Stockton Beach**, which stretches over 30 km to Anna Bay, just south of Port Stephens. Several rusting **shipwrecks** add to its appeal. The VIC can supply full listings of local activities including the many Hunter Valley tour operators. *Shadows*, T4990 7002, offer an interesting and entertaining day trip (0930-1630) aimed at younger folk and on board an old double-decker bus, from $35. For **surf**

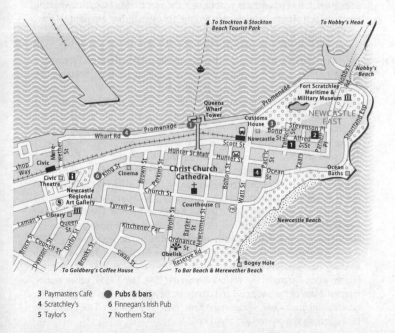

3 Paymasters Café
4 Scratchley's
5 Taylor's

● **Pubs & bars**
6 Finnegan's Irish Pub
7 Northern Star

information and equipment **hire** contact Pacific Dreams, 7 Darby Street, T4926 3355, or for something new Surfoplane, a sort of cross between a lilo and a surfboard, 39 Darby Street, T4929 1244, www.surfoplane.com **Surfest** held annually in March is an internationally recognized competition and celebration of the art of staying upright.

Sleeping

■ *On map*
A good range of accommodation is on offer throughout the city and bar public holidays there is seldom need to book well in advance

The much-loved historic terrace houses **LL-L** *Adeline & Beatrice*, on Telford St, Newcastle East, T4929 4575, are proving a popular self-contained option, suitable for families, close to the historic precincts and city beaches, as is the **LL-L** *Anne's B&B*, at Ismebury, 3 Stevenson Pl, T4929 5376, just around the corner. Of the handful of **hostels** in the city, the **B-E** *Newcastle Beach YHA*, 30 Pacific St (corner of King St), T4925 3544, is something of a showpiece for the organization, being housed in a gracious heritage building, complete with chandeliers, ballroom, large open fireplaces and leather armchairs. Given its charm it is deservingly popular and offers numerous spacious dorms and doubles and the odd family and single room. The facilities are impressive and also on offer is internet, free use of surf/boogie boards. They seem to have the finger very much on the pulse of local activities, events and entertainment and an added attraction are the weekly all-you-can-eat BBQs and $4 pizza nights. 3 km west, the less grandiose and more intimate, suburban **C-E** *Backpackers Newcastle*, 42-44 Denison St, Hamilton, T4969 3436, www.newcastlebackpackers.com.au, offers a fine alternative, with a nice laid-back, friendly atmosphere close to Hamilton's lively eat streets. It offers large dorms and double/twins and spacious adequate facilities. There is even a bath! Internet, free surf lessons (with $10 board hire). Of the numerous **motor parks** in the area, the well-facilitated **B-E** *Stockton Beach Tourist Park*, Pitt St, Stockton, T4928 1393, is recommended. Bear in mind however it is a 21-km car ride from the city centre, or alternatively, a short passenger ferry ride from the city centre ($1.80 per trip, or $33 weekly, combination bus/ferry pass). This is part of the charm but may not suit everyone. If you insist on using the car the **E-F** *Blacksmiths Beach Tourist Park*, Gommera St, Blacksmiths (29 km south on Hwy111), is one of many outlying alternatives. It is in a beachside position near the inlet to Lake Macquarie affording guests the best of both aquatic worlds. No cabins or camp kitchen, but plenty of powered and non-powered sites and BBQ facilities.

Eating

● *On map*

The main venues for fine dining in Newcastle are **Queens Wharf** and the **Promenade** beside the River. About 3 km to the west in the suburb of Hamilton, **Beaumont St**, dubbed the 'city's best eat street', provides the widest selection of lively and affordable café, pub and international options. **Darby St** off Hunter St and **Pacific St** in Newcastle East are also worth looking at. On the Promenade (200 Wharf Rd), **Scratchley's** has become something of a regional institution over the last decade combining excellent cuisine (comprising mainly seafood and steak) with great views across the river, T4929 1111, www.scratchleys.com.au Open daily for lunch, Mon-Sat for dinner. Book ahead. Just a little further east the Queens Wharf buildings offer some other good alternatives including the more affordable *Brewery Restaurant*, 150 Wharf Rd, T4929 5792. It is also one of the city's best nightspots and during the day provides a great al fresco balcony from which to watch the ferries and the huge ships ply the river. Open for breakfast Sat/Sun 0800-1100, lunch and dinner Mon-Sat. 2 good café options (from east to west) are: the historic and characterful *Paymasters Café*, 18 Bond St, Newcastle East, T4925 2600 and the locally popular *Goldberg's Coffee House*, 137 Darby St, T4929 3122, with its shady courtyard and old English pub feel (open daily 0700-2400). Of the many options along Beaumont the *Taylor's Restaurant* (54), T4962 1553, comes recommended. Many of the traditional and often historic pubs in the city provide quality, quantity and good value, including the *Kent Hotel*, 59 Beaumont, T4961 3303. The Kent also hosts jazz on weekend afternoons.

The *Civic Theatre*, opposite the VIC, 387 Hunter St, T4929 1977, is an excellent regional theatre hosting some of the best travelling shows and plays in the country. For up-to-date listings visit www.civictheatrenewcastle.com.au, or consult the *Newcastle Herald* on Thu. The city centre cinemas are located at 183 King St, T4926 2233 (Union), 31 Wolfe St, T4929 5019 (Showcase) and 299 Hunter St (Kensington). Tue night is cheap night. When it comes to pubs there are plenty to choose from. For something traditional try the *Great Northern* or *Kent* on Beaumont St and for something new *Finnegan's Irish Pub*, corner of Darby St and King St. For dancing, the 'hip' *Brewery Hotel and Bar* on The Promenade (Queens Wharf), or the more down to earth *Newcastle Workers Club*, corner of King St and Union St, are locally recommended. Both stay open well into the early hours, most nights.

Entertainment
● *On map*

Banks Most branches with ATMs are along the Hunter St Mall. **Car hire** *Thrifty*, 113 Parry St, T4961 1141. *ARA*, 86 Belford St, T4962 2488, from $40 per day. **Communications** Internet VIC Hunter St. Also, free with a purchase at the *Regional Museum Café*, 787 Hunter St (see above) or at the *Regional Library* on Laman St, T4974 5300. Open Mon-Fri 0930-1700, Tue 0930-200, Sat 0930-1700. Book ahead. **Post Office** 96 Hunter St. Open Mon-Fri 0830-1700. **Medical services** *John Hunter Hospital*, New Lambton, T4923 6000. **Police** Corner of Church St and Watt St, T4929 0999.

Directory

Nelson Bay (Port Stephens)

Port Stephens is a name loosely used to describe both the large natural harbour (Port Stephens) 50 km north of Newcastle and the string of foreshore communities that fringe its southern arm and (in particular) the beautiful **Tomaree Peninsula**. The recognized capital among these communities is **Nelson Bay**, which is fast developing into a prime New South Wales coastal holiday destination and provides the ideal first base or stopover heading north up the coast from Sydney. Other than the tremendous beauty of the place there are an ever-increasing number of activities on offer.

Colour map 3, grid C5
Population: 30,000
57 km north
of Newcastle,
300 km south
of Port Macquarie

Getting there and around The nearest **airport** is at Newcastle, 30 km south of Nelson Bay (see page 137). *Baydreamer*, T4982 0700, offer shuttles, while *Port Stephen's Coaches*, T4982 2940, www.psbuses.nelsonbay.com, offer regular bus services between the airport and Port Stephens. Long distance **coaches** stop on Stockton St in Nelson Bay. *Port Stephens Coaches* provide **local bus** services and a daily Sydney service. Another alternative is to use the Newcastle bound services (see Newcastle section), then catch the regular daily service from Newcastle to Port Stephens, with *Port Stephen's Coaches*. Similar connections can be made by train via Newcastle. If you intend to pass through the Great Lakes Region and Myall National Park, *Great Lakes Coaches* (Kings Bros), T4983 1560, offer **regional bus** services between Taree and Sydney, via Tuncurry Forster, Bluey's Beach, Hawks Nest and Newcastle. **Ferry** services, T4981 3798, then link Nelson Bay with Tea Gardens, daily 1000/1200/1430/1630, $17, child $9 return. **Bike hire**, 63 Shoal Bay Rd, T4981 4121. **Taxi**, T131008.

Ins & outs

Information The Port Stephens **VIC** is next to the Marina on Victoria Par, T4981 1579, www.portstephens.org.au Open daily 0900-1700. The **NPWS**, 12B Teramby Rd (Marina Complex), T4984 8200, hunter@npws.nsw.gov.au, can provide national parks and camping information.

If you do nothing else around Nelson Bay area, the 30-minute climb to the summit of **Tomaree Head**, at the far east end of Shoal Bay is a must, especially at sunrise or sunset, for the fantastic views. The best beaches in the area fringe the national park east and south of Nelson Bay. To the east **Shoal Bay** is closest

Sights

New South Wales

to all amenities, while farther east still, within the national park boundary, **Zenith Beach**, **Wreck Beach** and **Box Beach** all provide great surfing, solitude and scenery. About 2 km south of Shoal Bay, the glorious beach that fringes **Fingal Bay** connects **Point Stephens** with the mainland. You can access the headland and its fine walking tracks at low tide. South of Fingal Bay (though not connected to it by road) **One Mile Beach** is another regional gem, while **Samurai Beach** just north of that, is the local naturist beach. West of One Mile Beach **Boat Harbour** gives way to **Anna Bay**, which forms the northern terminus of **Stockton Beach**. This endless swathe of sand extends over 30 km all the way down to Newcastle and is well worth a visit simply to see the endless sweep of dunes. If you have **4WD** you can 'let rip' but a permit must be obtained from the council (or the VIC), T4980 0255 ($5). *Tag-Along Tours*, T4984 6112, offer guided trips taking your own vehicle.

There is a healthy suburban population of **koalas** in the region with the best place to see them being the fringes of Tomaree National Park or wooded areas of the Tilligerry Peninsula (Lemon Tree Passage, accessed via Lemon Tree Passage Road, off Nelson Bay Road, 30 km south of Nelson Bay). If you are unsuccessful you can always satisfy the desire to see them at **Oakvale Farm and Fauna World**, opposite the Lemon Tree Passage and Nelson Bay Road Junction, though it's mainly geared towards children. ■ *Daily 1000-1700. $11,child $6.50. T4982 6222*. While you are in the area you may also be tempted to visit **Tanilba House**, one of the oldest homesteads in Australia, built by convicts in 1831. ■ *Wed/Sat/Sun 1030-1630. From $5.50, child $2. T4982 4866*. Still on the historic theme, but closer to Nelson Bay, is the **Nelson Head Inner Lighthouse** set just above Little Bay, 1½ km east of the town centre. On offer are guided tours, great views and a small café. ■ *Daily 1000-1600, T4984 9758*. Little Bay is also great place to see pelicans as they wait patiently for fisherman's handouts late on in the day.

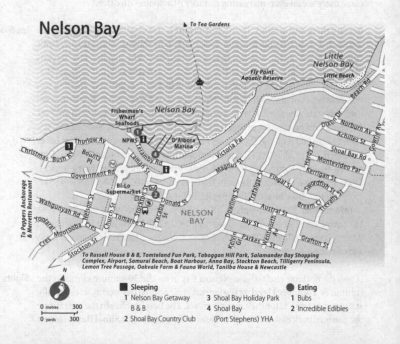

Nelson Bay

To Russell House B & B, Tomteland Fun Park, Taboggan Hill Park, Salamander Bay Shopping Complex, Airport, Samurai Beach, Boat Harbour, Anna Bay, Stockton Beach, Tilligerry Peninsula, Lemon Tree Passage, Oakvale Farm & Fauna World, Tanilba House & Newcastle

0 metres 300
0 yards 300

■ Sleeping		● Eating
1 Nelson Bay Getaway	3 Shoal Bay Holiday Park	1 Bubs
B & B	4 Shoal Bay	2 Incredible Edibles
2 Shoal Bay Country Club	(Port Stephens) YHA	

Hotel options include the classy and indulgent **LL** *Peppers Anchorage*, Corlette Point Rd, T4984 2555, www.peppers.com.au, which offers luxurious rooms and suites (some with spa), a heated pool, sauna, massage, open fires, gym and the *Merretts Restaurant* (mainly good seafood). Cheaper hotel options include the friendly **L-A** *Shoal Bay Country Club Hotel*, Shoal Bay Rd, T4981 1555, www.shoalbaycountryclub.com.au, which looks over the bay and is handy to all amenities. It has apartments, suites, family and standard rooms (all en suite) with B&B or Dinner B&B, pool a la carte and casual dining and a lively bar. There are several good B&Bs in the region. The friendly **LL-L** *Nelson Bay Getaway B&B*, 31 Thurlow Av, T4984 4949, www.nelsonbaygetaway.com.au, offers both B&B and self-contained, spas and is the closest to the town centre, while the popular **LL** *Russell House B&B*, 114 Salamander St, T4984 4246, combines old world charm with luxury, offering beautifully appointed suites (one with a 4 poster bed), in-house massage and a great traditional cooked breakfast. Of the hostels in the region the eco-friendly **A-E** *Samurai Beach Bungalows*, corner of Frost Rd and Robert Connell Cl, Anna Bay, T4982 1921, samurai@nelsonbay.com, is recommended. Although on the bus route it is some distance from Nelson Bay (5 km), but its position amidst bush at the edge of the Tomaree National Park, gives it a great relaxed atmosphere to add to its undeniable character. The range of accommodation options from dorm to en suite double bungalows (with TV and mini kitchen). The general facilities are also excellent and the odd, resident, koala and supervised (harmless) snake encounter is also on the cards. Free sand, surf and boogie board hire, bike hire (free with 3-night stay) and pick-ups. Recommended. The other alternative, with far less character, is the beachside, motel-style **C-E** *Shoal Bay (Port Stephens) YHA*, 59 Shoal Bay Rd, Shoal Bay, T4981 0982. En suite dorms, doubles and family rooms close to all amenities. For a good **motor park**, look no further than the excellent **LL-E** *Shoal Bay Holiday Park*, Shoal Bay Rd, T4981 1427, shoalbay@beachsideholidays.com.au It is beachside, modern, and friendly, close to all amenities and offers the full range of accommodation options, including camping. Great camp kitchen.

Sleeping
■ *On map*
There is plenty of choice in and around Nelson Bay, from resorts and modern self-contained apartment blocks to tidy B&Bs and koala-infested hostels. Book ahead at peak holiday periods. The VIC has full listings

New South Wales

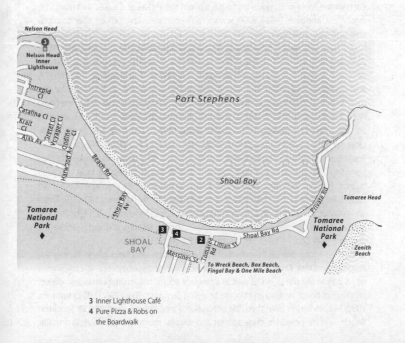

3 Inner Lighthouse Café
4 Pure Pizza & Robs on the Boardwalk

Eating
● *On map*

For something different consider the dinner cruise options with *Moonshadow* (see activities above). On dry land most of Nelson Bays eateries are to be found in the D'Albora Marina Complex on Victoria Par. There you will find an award winning, fine dining option at *Robs on the Boardwalk*, T4984 4444. Open daily 1000-late. It's fully licensed and comes recommended, especially for seafood. *Merretts Restaurant* in the *Peppers Anchorage* (see above) also has a good reputation for à la carte and seafood. Cheaper options include *Pure Pizza*, upstairs in the Marina Complex, T4984 2800. It offers dine in and free deliveries, (open daily 1100-late). Then there's *Bubs*, T4984 3917 (open daily from 1100-1800), located a short stroll further west, for good fish and chips. *Fisherman's Wharf Seafoods*, T4984 3330, opposite, provides fresh seafood straight off the boats, should you prefer to cook your own. For good coffee and sandwiches head for *Incredible Edibles*, Shop 6 Nelson Sq, Donald St, T4981 4511, and for great harbour views the *Inner Lighthouse Café*, Nelson Head, above Little Beach, T4984 9758. Open daily 1000-1600.

Tours & activities

There is an ever-increasing range of mainly water-based activities on offer in and around Nelson Bay and Port Stephens, with the town Marina being the base for most operators. The VIC opposite has a comprehensive list of daily tours and excursions and can assist with bookings. Note tour schedules are reduced across the board in winter. For something removed from the seemingly omnipresent dolphin watching, try the trip to the uninhabited **Broughton Island** off the Myall Coast. It is a beautiful place and part of the Myall Lakes National Park.

Dolphin-watching (year round) and **whale-watching** (Jul-Oct) are top of the agenda. *Moonshadow*, Shop 3/35 Stockton St, T4984 9388, www.moonshadow.com.au, are the biggest operator with the largest, fastest and most comfortable vessels ('Supercats'). They offer daily wildlife cruises (from $18-39), trips to Broughton Island off the Myall Coast (from $59) and also twilight dinner and entertainment trips around the Port, from 1900, $55. *Spirit of the Bay*, T4984 1004, offer a similar range of trips on a smaller vessel (launch) with a boom net, spa, bar (and a waterslide!), from $20-55. For a cheaper option, try the *Tamboi Queen* which has been plying the Ports waters for over 30 years. It also has a boom net and a bar. Cruises start from $14, family $38. *Imagine*, T4984 9000, www.imagineportstephens.com.au, offer comfortable and less crowded cruises on board a sail catamaran, from $20-50 (Broughton Island, from $50. Recommended). In contrast, for a **jet boat** ride contact *X-Jet*, T4997 2555, from $40, child $20. The most intimate encounters with local pods of dolphin are of course most likely on a **sea-kayaking** trip. *Blue Water Sea Kayaking*, T4981 5177, www.seakayaking.com.au, can oblige with guided day or sunset trips, and for the more experienced, excursions further afield around Broughton Island and up the Myall River. Tours start from $35 (1½ hrs) and they offer pick-ups. Recommended. Local trips are also offered by *Sea Kayak Adventure Tours*, T4982 7158, from $35. To get really close up with a whole array of interesting sea creatures *Pro Dive*, D'Albora Marina, Teramby Rd, T4981 4331, prodive@hunterlink.net.au, offer **dive** and snorkelling trips from $40-160. The depth of Port Stephens creates some interesting local sub aqua habitats highlighted within the **Fly Point Aquatic Reserve**, just 1 km east of the town centre. Broughton Island also provides some excellent diving (from $80-130). There are many other charter options for **fishing** as well as independent yacht, houseboat and jet ski hire companies. The VIC has details. **Surfing lessons** and surf gear hire are available with *Eon*, T4984 9796, from $33 (hire from $33, 2 hrs).

Pitched (quite literally) somewhere between water and land based trips is the amphibious *Duck Dive*, T4981 5472, www.duckdive.nelsonbay.com It combines a novel way to see the sights as well as a range of additional activities including diving, snorkelling, boom netting and boogie boarding. Departs 0900/1200/1500 in summer, 1030/1400 in winter from the Little Beach Boat Ramp, from $40, child $30. **Stockton Beach** with its incredible dune habitat and wrecks, south of Nelson Bay, is a major playground for 4WD and ATV tours. There are numerous (very similar) options with *Dawson's Scenic 4WD Tours*, T4982 0980, *Port Stephens 4WD Adventure Tours*, T04 2784 6475, *Horizon Safaris*, T4982 6266, and *Port Stephens 4WD Tours*, T4982 7277, all providing fun and excitement with 1 hr to full-day trips from $14-50. Lunch and sand boarding are often included. *Port Stephens Dune Adventures*, T0500-550066, www.bushmobile.com.au, offer a 6x6, yellow, go anywhere monstrosity. The 1½-hr, standard Dune Adventure (all weather) 1100/1230 with sand boarding and a spot of horseshoe tossing costs $20, child $15. The extended 2½-3 hr trip taking in 'Tin City' (a hidden ramshackle settlement, threatened by the encroaching sand) costs from $30, child $20. *Sand Safaris*, T4965 0215, www.sandsafaris.com.au, offer an award winning, 2½-3 hr, 20-30 km trip on ATVs, with sand boarding included, from $99, child $54. This option provides an element of exhilaration and independence lacking on the other tours. Recommended. Alternatively, depending on your experience, a far less predictable mount awaits with *Beach and Bush Riding Adventures*, 2630 Nelson Bay Rd, T4965 1387.They are the **horse trekking** operator located closest to the dunes, offering trips of 1-3 hrs, from $30. Other operators include *Sahara Trails*, T4981 9077 (from $25, accommodation also available), and *Rambling Sands* (very flexible with trips), Janet Par, off Nelson Bay Rd, Salt Ash, T4982 6391. *Hades*, T4967 5969, and *Baydreamer*, T4982 0700 (good value), offer more conventional road tours to local and regional sights, including the Hunter Valley vineyards (from $40).

Banks Most of the major branches with ATMs are to be found along Stockton St or Magnus St, Nelson Bay. **Car hire** *Nelson Bay Rent-A-Car*, 28 Stockton St, Nelson Bay, T4984 2244, or *Avis*, Newcastle Airport, T4965 1612. **Communications** Internet *Tomaree Library*, Salamander Shopping Centre, T4982 0670. Open Mon/Wed/Fri 1000-1800, Tue/Thu 1000-2000, Sat 0930-1400. **Post Office** Corner of Stockton St and Magnus St. Open Mon-Fri 0900-1700.

Directory

The 40,453-ha Barrington Tops National Park encompasses a 25-km long plateau extending between a series of extinct volcanic peaks in the Mount Royal Ranges, north of the Hunter Valley. Rising to a height of 1,577 m at **Polblue Mountain**, the plateau forms one of the highest points on the Great Dividing Range and contains a diverse range of habitats from rainforest to alpine meadows with numerous waterfalls and great views. The high elevation also results in unpredictable weather year-round and an annual rainfall of over 2 m, with sub-zero temperatures and snow in winter. The park hosts a diverse range of species including lyrebirds, bandicoots and spotted tailed quolls. At the very least you are almost certain to encounter kangaroos as well as small squadrons of elegant and very vocal black cockatoos. The scenery and wildlife alone make a day-trip well worthwhile, though given the many excellent B&Bs, campsites, walks and activities available you may well be tempted to extend your stay.

Barrington Tops National Park
Colour map 3, grid C5
80 km northwest of Newcastle
150 km southwest of Port Macquarie

Getting there From the south and east the park and the 2 main fringing communities of Dungog and Gloucester are best accessed from **Bucketts Way Rd (Highway 2)** that heads northwest off the Pacific Highway 33 km north of Newcastle. Alternatively, the northern sector of the park (and Gloucester) can be accessed west off the Pacific Highway at Nabiac, 160 km north of Newcastle. If you have a 2WD and are limited for time, the drive up the Gloucester River Valley to **Gloucester Tops** is recommended. This drive (unsealed) climbs through the varied vegetation types, offers great views down the valley and provides a few good short walks to a waterfall and views at the terminus. Take the Gloucester Tops Rd off Bucketts Way Rd, 10 km south of Gloucester. The climb to the plateau begins at the park boundary and the lovely Gloucester River Camping Area (see below). The northern sector of the park offers a more extensive

78-km scenic drive (mostly unsealed) from **Gloucester to Scone** via Scone Rd and then Barrington Tops Rd, west of Gloucester, though the best views from **Carey's Peak** and its surrounding campsites can only be reached by 4WD south off Forest Rd, just west of the **Devils Hole Camping Area**. The southern sector of the park is accessed 40 km northwest of **Dungog**, via **Salisbury** and the **Williams River Valley Rd**. There are 3 campsites, several viewpoints and picnic areas beyond the Williams River Day Use Area. The only way to access the park by public transport is with the *Forster Bus Service* (No 308), T6554 6431, which accesses Gloucester, Mon-Fri, from Forster-Tuncurry. Note entry to the park costs $7.50 per day.

Information The **NPWS** office, Church St, Gloucester, T6538 5300, Gloucester@ npws.nsw.gov.au, is the nearest to the park. Open Mon-Fri 0830-1700. There is also an office in Nelson Bay, Port Stephens (see above). For web information visit www.barrington.com.au The main regional VIC handling Barrington Tops information is the Great Lakes VIC in **Forster** (see below). There are local VICs in **Dungog**, 191 Dowling St, T4992 2212, dungogvc@midac.com.au (open Mon-Fri 0900-1700, Sat/Sun 0900-1500) and **Gloucester**, Denison St, T6558 1408, gsc@midcoast.com.au (open daily 0930-1630). Look out for the free *'Barrington Tops World Heritage Area'* brochure.

The local VICs have full accommodation listings including the numerous quaint B&Bs that surround the park. The NPWS can also supply details of the many campsites within it

Sleeping and eating The basic **F** *Gloucester River Camping Area*, Gloucester Tops Rd, T6538 5300, is in a fine riverside spot at the park boundary and comes complete with tame kangaroos but no showers. No bookings required. Far more comfortable accommodation is available at the award-winning **LL** *Barrington Guest House*, T4995 3212, wwwbarrington-g-h.com.au, set in a private wildlife refuge, 40 km west of Dungog near Salisbury. Meals and activities from bush walking to horse riding are included and it is considered the finest luxury option in the region. The new, self-contained **LL** *Allyn Riverside Cabins*, T4982 1921, located 3 km from the Park (35 km north of East Gresford) are also recommended, offering queen rooms, spa, handmade furniture and decks overlooking the river. Cheaper is the **A-B** *Barringtons Country Retreat*, Chichester Dam Rd, 23 km north of Dungog, T4995 9269, www.thebarring tons.com.au, a bush resort offering comfortable lodges, an à la carte (BYO) restaurant, pool, spa and organized activities, including horse riding.

Myall Lakes National Park

Colour map 3, grid C5 100 km north of Newcastle 161 km south of Port Macquarie

The Myall Lakes National Park, or Great Lakes as they are known, combine beautiful coastal scenery with a patchwork of inland lakes, waterways and forest, which combine to create one of the best-loved eco-playgrounds in NSW. Only four hours north of Sydney and one hour and 20 minutes from Newcastle, the only drawback is its inevitable popularity in summer holidays and at weekends. However, given the sheer scale of the area – 21, 367 ha of park of which half is water – it seems there is always somewhere to escape the crowds. The main settlements fringing the national park are **Tea Gardens** and **Hawks Nest** that sit on the northeastern shores of **Port Stephens** to the south, **Bulahdelah** on the Pacific Highway to the west and, back on the coast, the popular surf spots of **Bluey's Beach** and **Pacific Palms** to the north. If you have at least two days the order of destination and route below, from Tea Gardens in the south to Pacific Palms in north, or vice versa is recommended.

Ins & outs

Getting there and around *Great Lakes Coaches* (Kings Bros), T4983 1560, offer **regional bus** services between Taree and Sydney via Tuncurry Forster, Bluey's Beach, Hawks Nest and Newcastle. *Forster Bus Service*, T6554 6431, offer daily **local bus** services around the twin towns and south as far as Pacific Palms, Bluey's Beach and Smith

Lake (weekdays). **Ferry** services, T4981 3798, link Tea Gardens (The wharf opposite the Tea Gardens Hotel) with Nelson Bay daily 1000/1200/1430/1630, $17, child $9 return. Boat hire is readily available in Forster, Tea Gardens and Hawks Nest. **Houseboats** can be hired from *Myall Lakes Houseboats*, Bulahdelah, T4997 4221, *Luxury Houseboats*, Myall Marina, Bulahdelah, T1800-025908, www.luxuryhouseboat.com.au, or *Luxury Afloat*, Marine Dr, Tea Gardens, T4997 0307.

Information The Great Lakes **Visitors Information Centre** in **Forster** is the main one for the region, and there are smaller local VICs in **Tea Gardens**, Myall St, T4997 0111 (open daily 1000-1600), **Bulahdelah**, corner of Pacific Highway and Crawford St, T4997 4981 (open daily 0900-1700), and **Pacific Palms**, Boomerang Dr, Bluey's Beach, T6554 0123 (open daily 1000-1600). All hold NPWS parks and camping information with the nearest **NPWS** office being in Nelson Bay, T4984 8200. For navigation, be it by foot, by car or by paddle The *Great Lakes District Map* ($6) is not only recommended but also almost essential. For web information visit www.greatlakes.org.au

New South Wales

The little-known but fast developing coastal settlements of Tea Gardens and Hawks Nest, on the northeastern shores of Port Stephens, serve not only as excellent holiday destinations in themselves, but as the main southern gateway to the Myall Lakes National Park. The twin towns offer a wealth of activities from surfing to **koala spotting**, but most come here simply to escape the crowds and to relax. The place to be is **Bennetts** (Ocean Beach) at the southeastern end of Hawks Nest. From there you can access the **Yaccaba Walk** (3 km return) that climbs the summit of the **Yaccaba Headland** affording some memorable views across the mouth of Port Stephens and the numerous offshore islands. To reach Bennetts Beach, cross the bridge from Tea Gardens on Kingfisher Avenue, turn right on Mungo Brush Road, then left to the end of Booner Street. Another excellent, but far more demanding walk is the **Mungo Track** which follows the Myall River through coastal forest to the **Mungo Brush Campsite** (15 km one-way). It starts on the left off Mungo Brush Road, 600 m past the national park boundary. The detailed booklet '*Walkers Guide to The Mungo Track*' breaks the entire walk into sections with additional alternatives, and is available from the Tea Gardens VIC, NPWS or Hawks Nest Real Estate on Tuloa Avenue. Look out for koalas along the way, especially late in the day. **Dolphin watching** cruises, diving, golf, **fishing** charters, boat, **sea kayak**, canoe and surf ski hire are all readily available in the twin towns. The Tea Gardens VIC has full listings (see above). The *Hawks Nest Service Station*, Tuloa Avenue, T4997 1486, hires **bikes**.

Tea Gardens & Hawks Nest
Population. 2,200 75 km north of Newcastle 112 km south of Forster-Tuncurry

Sleeping and eating The friendly **A** *Tea Gardens Hotel Motel*, on the waterfront, corner of Maxwell St and Marine Dr, Tea Gardens, T4997 0203, offers regular value deals especially on doubles with free breakfast. The **A-E** *Hawks Nest Caravan Park*, Booner St, Hawks Nest, T1800-072244, www.hawksnestcaravan.com.au, is in a good position next to Bennetts Beach and the town centre. **L-E** *Jimmy's Beach Caravan Park*, Coorilla St, T4997 0466, has a better range of cabins. For eating Marine Parade in Tea Gardens is the place to sample local fare with the *Oyster Hut*, T4997 0579, offering fresh, locally harvested oysters, and the *Tea Gardens Hotel* and *Waterfront Seafood Restaurant*, affordable mains for lunch and dinner. In Hawks Nest, *Beaches Café*, corner of Booner and Tuloa St, T4997 1022, is both convenient and a local favourite.

Marine Dr in Tea Gardens and Mungo Brush Rd / Booner St in Hawks Nest host the twin town's main amenities including post offices, eateries, service stations and supermarkets. The Post Offices act as bank agents

From Hawks Nest Mungo Brush Road heads north, parallel with the **Myall River**, to meet the southern boundary of the Myall National Park (4½ km). From there the road remains sealed and cuts through the **littoral rainforest** and coastal heath for 15 km to the **Mungo Brush Campsite** beside the

Hawks Nest to Bulahdelah

Bombah Broadwater, the second largest of the Great Lakes. Before reaching Mungo Brush consider stopping and walking the short distance east to the deserted beach. There are a number of 4WD tracks, which provide a walkway if you only have 2WD. **Dark Point** is a good option and can be accessed via 4WD track, about 5 km north of the southern boundary at Robinson's Crossing (4½ km return). It is an interesting rocky outcrop that is the only significant feature along the 44 km of beach between Hawks Nest and Seal Rocks. It is an interesting spot and the site of a **midden** used by the Worimi Aboriginal peoples for centuries. This particular example is thought to be at least 2,000 years old. Lying almost tantalizingly offshore lies **Broughton Island** (accessed by day trip from Nelson Bay).

From Mungo Brush the road skirts the northern shores of Bombah Broadwater, turning inland, past increasingly thick stands of **paperbark trees**, to reach the Bombah Point **ferry** crossing (daily every 30 minutes 0800-1800, $3). The large yet unobtrusive **LL-F** *Myall Shores Eco-tourism Resort* dominates Bombah Point and provides a range of accommodation from luxury waterfront villas, en suite cabins, budget bungalows to shady powered and non-powered sites. There is also a small licensed restaurant, a café/bar, fuel, a small store, boat and canoe hire. Prices rocket at peak holiday times and at any time in the high season, book ahead. T4997 4495, resort@myallshores.com.au From Bombah Point 16 km of partly sealed roads takes you to the small community of **Bulahdelah** and the Pacific Highway. Bulahdelah has a helpful VIC and is the main venue for **houseboat** hire for the region (see above).

Bulahdelah, Seal Rocks & Sanbar   About 4 km north of Bulahdelah is the Lakes Way, the main sealed access road through the Great Lakes region, which heads east, eventually skirting **Myall Lake**, the largest of the Lakes. But before reaching the lake you may consider the short diversion 5 km north along Stoney Creek Road (Wang Wauk Forest Drive, 38 km) into the southern fringe of the Bulahdelah State Forest to see '**The Grandis**', a towering 76-m flooded gum reputed to be the highest tree in NSW. It's no sequoia but still worth a look. Back on The Lakes Way between Myall Lake and Smiths Lake, Seal Rocks Road (unsealed) heads 11 km southeast to reach the coast and the pretty beachside settlement of Seal Rocks, a sublime little piece of wilderness and the jewel in the Myall. Other than the superb beach and short rainforest and headland walks, the 2-km stroll to the **Sugarloaf Point Lighthouse** past the **Seal Rocks Blow Hole** is well worth it. The views from the lighthouse (no public access to the interior) are excellent and **Lighthouse Beach** to the south is more than inviting. **Seal Rocks**, lying just offshore, serve as a favourite dive site and are home home to numerous grey nurse sharks. Back on The Lake Way another recommended diversion (3 km east) ventures to **Sandbar**, 1 km past the turn-off to Smiths Lake village. Here you will find some excellent, quiet **beaches** (500 m walk), good bird watching along the sandbar and many lakeside activities based at the delightful caravan park. The lakeside **L-E** *Sandbar Caravan Park*, T6554 4095, sandbar@paspaley.com.au, offers self-contained cabins, powered and non-powered sites, BBQ, kiosk, fuel, canoe and bike hire and golf course. The **A-E** *Seal Rocks Camping Reserve*, Kinka Road, T4997 6164, overlooks the main beach and offers a handful of self-contained cabins, powered and non-powered sites.

Pacific Palms & Bluey's Beach   About 4 km north of Smiths Lake is the small community of **Pacific Palms**, on the southern shores of **Lake Wallis**, and 2 km east are the delightful little beachside communities of Bluey's Beach, Boomerang Beach and Elizabeth Beach which are something of a local **surfing** Mecca. **Bluey's Beach** itself is idyllic and further north, beyond Boomerang Point, **Boomerang Beach** only marginally less attractive. Further north the rather unfortunately named Pimply Rock and **Charlotte Head** give way to **Elizabeth Beach**, which is an absolute gem. *Sun and Surf*, Boomerang Drive, Pacific Palms, T6554 0929, www.sunandsurf.com.au, offer **surfing lessons** from $35 per hour, and board hire from $30 (half day). *Pacific Palms Windsurfing* (Tiona Park), T6554 0309, offer **windsurfing lessons** from $40 per hour. *Pacific Palms Kayaking Tours*, T6554 0079, tours@ppkayaktours.com.au, explore the local coast by **sea kayak** and get to places otherwise inaccessible on half, full day or overnight trips from $33. Birders will enjoy the early morning outings on offer with *Birdwatching Breakfasts*, T6554 0757, from $30, child $15, or the extended half or full day rainforest, hinterland and rainy day **tours** under their *Boomerang Forest Tours* banner, T6554 0757, ppmartin@gl.hardnet.com.au The local VIC on Boomerang Dr (see above) has full listings for holiday lets and B&Bs in the four communities. **L-B** *Bluey's by the Beach*, 184 Boomerang Drive, Pacific Palms, T6554 0665, blueys@midcoast.com.au, is a good motel option with nine tidy units, and outdoor pool and spa, all within a short stroll from the beach. Campervans are best accommodated at **L-F** *Moby's Beachside Retreat*, Redgum Road (off Boomerang Drive), T6554 0292, which is the closest to the surf beaches, however campers should look to **NPWS Ruins and Green Cathedral campsites** north of Elizabeth Beach off The Lakes Way (see Forster section below). **Boomerang Drive** (Bluey's Beach) offers a wide range of low-key amenities including a supermarket, newsagent, service station, pharmacy, and a few **eateries** including the basic **Pacific Palms Takeaway**, T6554 0452.

Forster-Tuncurry

The twin coastal towns of Forster-Tuncurry, which straddle **Wallis Lake** and the Cape Hawke Harbour, are a favourite domestic holiday destination and provide the northern gateway to the superb **Great Lakes Region**. Although the town itself has some fine **beaches** and numerous, mainly **water-based activities**, it is the lakes, beaches and forests of the **Booti Booti** and **Myall Lakes National Park**s to the south that are the headline attraction. As one of the most appealing coastal regions between Sydney and Byron Bay, a few days here is highly recommended.

Colour map 3, grid C5
Population: 21,000
140 km north of
Newcastle,
120 km south of
Port Macquarie

Information The Great Lakes Visitors Information Centre, beside the river on Little St, Forster, T6554 8799, www.greatlakes.org.au, serves Forster-Tuncurry and the Great Lakes (Myall) Region as far south as Tea Gardens and Hawks Nest. Open daily 0900-1700. To find your way around the twin towns and region ask for the free *Cartoscope Great Lakes Region Map*. The *Great Lakes District Map* ($6) is also recommended if you intend to explore the Myall Lakes and National Park fully. The VIC also supplies NPWS camping and national parks information. **Internet** is available at *Leading Edge Computers*, on the corner of Head St and Beach St, T6555 7959 or the YHA.

Ins & outs

Forster Beach sits at the mouth of the Hawke Harbour Inlet, just north of Forster's main drag, Head Street, but better beaches lie further east. **Pebbly Beach**, which is only a short walk along the coast from Forster Beach (or alternatively accessed by car, just beyond the junction of Head Street and MacIntosh Street), is a great spot for families and despite the name, does possess some sand. At the eastern end of town is **One Mile Beach**, the town's favourite and a real gem, offering great views and good surfing at its northern end. It is best accessed via Boundary Street, south off Head Street/Bennetts

Sights

New South Wales

Head Road, then east down Strand Street. **Bennetts Head** also provides good views south along the One Mile Beach. **Booti Booti National Park** is well worthy of investigation. At the park's northern fringe, head east along Minor Road (just south of Forster, off The Lakes Way) and climb to the top of **Cape Hawke** where there is a superb lookout tower (40 minutes return). **McBride's Beach** sits in splendid near-isolation and is the ideal place to escape for the day, provided you are up for the 20-minute walk from the parking area just west of the lookout car park. To the south **Seven Mile Beach** stretches to **Booti Hill**, **The Ruins** and **Charlotte Head**. The Ruins has a good NPWS **campsite** and the southern edge of the park offers some excellent walks, with the 7 km track from The Ruins to Elizabeth Beach being recommended. **Elizabeth Beach** is another absolute gem and may detain you for days. On the western side of Lakes Way **Wallis Lake** provides saltwater swimming, fishing, boating and numerous picnic sites.

Sleeping

The VIC has full listings of the many motels, resorts, apartment blocks and caravan parks in the Forster-Tuncurry area

Overlooking Forster Beach is the tidy **L** *Tudor House Lodge*, 1 West St, T6554 8766, with standard doubles, ocean view suites, complimentary breakfast and a good in-house bar/restaurant. The **A-C** *Great Lakes Motor Inn*, 24 Head St, T6554 6955, is modern, well-facilitated and within walking distance of the Forster beaches and town centre. Back on Head St (43) you will find the **C-E** *Dolphin Lodge YHA*, T6555 8155, dolphin_lodge@hotmail.com It's quiet, friendly and offers tidy motel-style double/twin/single rooms and dorms, well equipped kitchen, free use of boogie boards, bike hire and internet. 500 m from the beaches, VIC and long-distance bus terminal. The centrally placed **L-E** *Forster Beach Caravan Park*, Reserve Rd, T6554 6269, is right beside the Harbour Inlet and Forster Beach and is within walking distance of Forster town centre. It has a good range of cabins and BBQs but lacks much privacy and has no camp kitchen. Further south (2 km) is the better facilitated, but less conveniently located **L-F** *Smugglers Cove Holiday Village*, 45 The Lakes Way, T6554 6666. The best bet if you do not wish to be in town is **NPWS Ruins** campsite at beneath Booti Hill at what is known as the 'Green Cathedral' about 20 km south. It is in a great position, beach or lakeside, with good coastal and forest walks. Self-registration, hot showers, but no fires allowed, T6554 0446.

Eating

The great rivals for the title of best fish and chips are the well-established *Lobby's*, T6554 6225, and the newer *Beach St Seafoods*, T6557 5300, both on Beach St. When it comes to facilities and service The Beach wins hand down but for value for money, it has to be Lobby's. Alternatively, you will find more value seafood and pub-grub at the popular local, the *Lakes and Ocean Hotel*, corner of Little St and Lake St, T6555 4117. For fine dining, the intimate *Oyster Rack*, Oyster Bar and Restaurant in the Pacific Arcade off Memorial Av, T6557 5577, is popular, while almost next door, for Italian, the *Divino*, T6557 5033, is good value. Open daily lunch 1100-1500, dinner from 1800. For a great Aussie institution try a pie and peas from *Harry's Café de Wheels*, corner Beach St and Memorial Dr. Open daily until late.

Tours & activities

There are plenty of water-based activity and boat hire operators in Forster with most tendering for your custom along Little St and the lakeside

Dolphin Watch Cruises, Fisherman's Wharf, T6554 7478, are the only local operators permitted to put people in the water (in a boom net) with dolphins, from $38, child $15. *'Amaroo'*, Lakeside, T04 1933 3445, and *'Free Spirit'*, Tikki Boatshed (opposite the VIC), T6559 2899, also offer general lake cruises and dolphin watching, from $20. There are several excellent dive sites in the region, including Seal Rocks, The 'S.S. Satara' wreck dive, Bennetts Head and the 'Pinnacles', which are all well known for their grey nurse sharks. Idol Bay is also home to 'Aggro', the inquisitive loggerhead turtle. There are several local dive operators, including *Underwater Adventures*, Fisherman's Wharf, T6554 7478, which reputedly have the best boat and offer a good range of packages.

Action Divers, Shop 4, 1-5 Manning St, Tuncurry, T6555 4053, www.actiondivers.com.au, offer value for money, with full gear hire from $38, single dives from $44 and a good trip to Seal Rocks from $95. *Joy C*, Little St, T6554 6321, and *Double-D Deep Sea*, T6554 7189, both offer entertaining half or full-day fishing trips. *Great Lakes Seaplanes*, T6555 8771, offer scenic floatplane flights, often spotting dolphins and whales, from $40-90. All manner of watercraft, from BBQ boats to canoes, can be hired along the waterfront. The *Tikki Boatshed*, 15 Little St, T6554 6321, is one of the major players and are based opposite the VIC.

Long distance **buses** stop outside the VIC on Little St. The VIC also acts as booking agents. *McCafferty's/Greyhound*, T132030, offer services from Sydney or Port Macquarie. *Great Lakes Coaches* (Kings Bros), T4983 1560, also offer services between Taree and Sydney via Tuncurry Forster, Bluey's Beach, Hawks Nest and Newcastle. The **train** station is at Taree. *Countrylink*, T132232, offer daily services north and south. Kings Bros (above) or Eggins, Elizabeth St, Taree, T6552 2700, provide links between the station and Forster. *Forster Bus Service*, T6554 6431, offer daily **local bus** services around the twin towns and south as far as Pacific Palms, Bluey's Beach and Smith Lake (weekdays). *Budget* **car rentals**, Traveland Forster Shopping Centre, Breeze Par, T6555 5700.

Transport

New South Wales

Taree, 33 km north of Forster-Tuncurry, is a pleasant riverside town and commercial centre for the picturesque **Manning Valley** and Manning River District. **Houseboats** and dinghies can be hired along Crescent Avenue. The 160-m, sheer drop, **Ellenbourgh Falls**, near the Bulga State Forest provides a good day trip and can be reached by mainly unsealed roads (46 km), northwest, beyond Wingham. Back on the coast the **Crowdy Bay National Park** can be accessed (unsealed) from Moorland off the Pacific Highway, 30 km north of Taree. There are some good **NPWS campsites** at Kylie's Beach, Indian Head and **Diamond Head**, T6586 8300. Alternatively, a good way to sample the coastal scenery is to take the short diversion east, to Crowdy Head and Harrington (23 km north of Taree). Although **Harrington** is pleasant enough, and offers some good fishing and bird watching around the Harrington Inlet, press on further north to the tiny fishing village of **Crowdy Head**. Although it provides very little in the way of amenities, the views from the pocket-sized lighthouse on the headland are memorable, followed perhaps with a swim or a stroll along the beach at the base of **Crowdy Bay**.

Forster-Tuncurry to Port Macquarie
Distance 124 km

Back on the Pacific Highway take the road to Laurieton from Kew, 51 km north of Taree. Just before Laurieton itself, take the road to the summit of **North Brother** through the **Dooragan National Park**. The views up and down the coast on a clear day are stunning. Below, Laurieton and its neighbouring settlements of North Haven and Dunbogan – collectively known as **Camden Haven** – merge and fringe the **Queens** and **Watson Taylor Lake** inlets. Boating and fishing are, not surprisingly, hugely popular with *Camden Haven River Cruises*, based at the Dunbogan Boat Shed, 46 The Boulevard, T6559 6978, providing a range of cruise options. Boats can also be hired from the **Boat Shed**, T6583 6300. The **Kattang Nature Reserve** on the headland beside Dunbogan offers some good picnic spots and short coastal walks offering more great views. From Laurieton it is another 30 km through the lazy beachside settlements of Bonny Hills and Lake Cathie to Port Macquarie. The Manning Valley **VIC** is on the Pacific Highway (on 21 Manning River Drive), at the northern approach into Taree, T1800-182733, www.retreat-to-nature.com Daily 0900-1700. There is another VIC in **Kew** (Pacific Highway), T1300-303154, www.port macquarie.com.au ■ *Daily 0900-1700*. Kings Bros, *6 Denham St, Port Macquarie, T6583 3079, access the eastern beaches to Laurieton daily (No 331).*

Port Macquarie

Colour map 3, grid C5
Population: 34,000
399 km north
of Sydney,
589 km south
of Brisbane

Officially declared as possessing the best year-round climate in Australia, and blessed with a glut of superb beaches, engaging historical sights, suburban nature reserves full of wildlife and a huge variety of mainly water-based activities, the former penal colony of Port Macquarie is surely one of the best holiday destinations anywhere in NSW. The strange thing is that most foreign visitors pass it by as they rush north on the Pacific Highway to the more high-profile destinations like Byron Bay.

Ins & outs

Getting there and around   Port Macquarie **Airport** is 3 km west of the town centre on Boundary Rd (off Hastings River Dr), T6583 4382. *QantasLink*, T131313, and *Hazelton*, T131713, offer daily services to Sydney. Long distance buses stop at the **bus terminal** on Hayward St. *Premier Motor Service* have a booking office at the terminal, T6583 1488. Open Mon-Fri 0830-1700, Sat 0830-1200. *McCafferty's/Greyhound*, T132030, also offer daily state-wide services. *Keans Coaches*, T1800-043 339, run a service from Port Macquarie to Scone (via the Waterfall Way, Dorrigo/Bellingen/Armidale and Tamworth) 3 times a week, Tue/Thu/Sun. The nearest **train** station is at Wauchope 19 km west of the city, T132232. The connecting bus to Port Macquarie is included in the fare. *Kings Bros*, 6 Denham St, T6583 3079, www.kingsbrosbus.com.au, offer both **local and regional bus** services to Wauchope and Kempsey, with connections to Coffs Harbour and Armidale 3 times a week. To access the eastern beaches, take a No 331. **Taxi**, T65810081. **Bike hire** is available from *Graham Seers*, Shop 1, Port Marina, Park St, T6583 2333, from $22 per day.

Orientation and information   Port Maquarie is 10 km east of the Pacific Highway along the **Oxley Highway**. The **Port Macquarie Visitors Information Centre** is located right in the heart of town on the corner of Clarence St and Hay St, T6581 8000, www.portmacquarieinfo.com.au Open Mon-Fri 0830-1700, Sat/Sun 0900-1600. The **NPWS** have an office at 152 Horton St, T6586 8300, port@npws.nsw.gov.au Open Mon-Fri 0830-1700.

Sights

For a full tour of the historic sites pick up the free 'Port Macquarie's Heritage' leaflet from the VIC

Allman Hill on Stewart Street is home to the settlements first cemetery (used until 1824). The gravestones will reveal the obvious hardships and life expectancies. The site of the first gaol is at **Gaol Point Lookout** just off Stewart Street and the 1869 **Courthouse**, where the completely disproportionate punishments were dished out, is on the corner of Clarence Street and Hay Street. It 'served' the community for over 117 years and is now faithfully refurbished. If you are lucky you may time your visit with a period uniform re-enactment with cannon firing, held on the occasional Saturday at 1130. Ask for up-coming dates from the VIC. ■ *Mon-Sat 1000-1600. $2, child $0.50. T6584 1818.* Across the road is the **Historical Museum**, which is housed in a former convict-built store (1835). It contains 14 rooms of historical artefacts. ■ *Mon-Sat 0930-1630, Sun 1300-1630. $4, child $2. T6583 1108.* The **Maritime Museum** is worth a look with the emphasis very much on wrecks. It is housed in former pilot station cottages built in 1896. ■ *Mon-Sat 1100-1500. $2. T6583 1866, 6 William St.* **St Thomas's Church**, on the corner of Hay Street and William Street, is the fifth oldest Anglican Church still in use in Australia and was built by convict labour through the late 1820s. Buried beneath one of the pews is Captain Rolland, the former gaol supervisor. He died, believe it or not, from sunstroke and was buried inside to prevent his body being exhumed by his many enemies, torn limb from limb, and displayed around the town. ■ *Mon-Fri 0930-1200/1400-1600. Entry by donation. T6584 1033.*

Port Macquarie

New South Wales

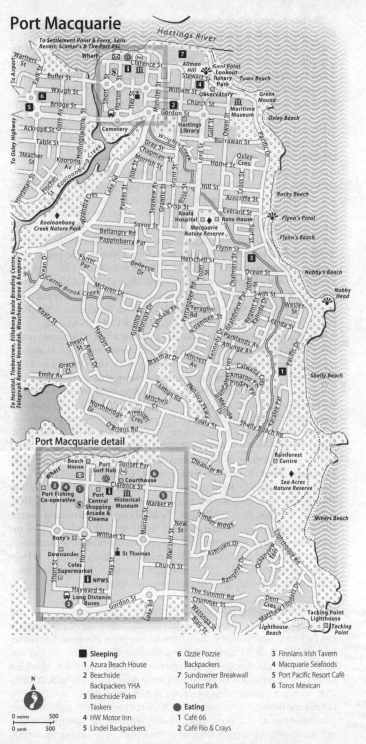

Port Macquarie detail

■ **Sleeping**	6 Ozzie Pozzie	3 Finnians Irish Tavern
1 Azura Beach House	Backpackers	4 Macquarie Seafoods
2 Beachside	7 Sundowner Breakwall	5 Port Pacific Resort Café
Backpackers YHA	Tourist Park	6 Toros Mexican
3 Beachside Palm		
Taskers	● **Eating**	
4 HW Motor Inn	1 Café 66	
5 Lindel Backpackers	2 Café Rio & Crays	

N

0 metres 500
0 yards 500

The beaches that fringe the eastern suburbs of the town from the Hastings River mouth, south to Tacking Point and beyond are simply superb, offering some excellent swimming, fishing, surfing, walks and views. Even north of the town the great swathe of **North Beach**, stretching 15 km to **Point Plomer**, fringed by the diverse coastal habitats of **Limeburners Creek Nature Reserve**, provides almost total solitude. Access is via the Settlement Point ferry ($2) on the North Shore. **Town Beach**, at the eastern end of the town centre, is convenient for swimming and is patrolled in summer. There is good surfing at the northern end. South, beyond Green Mound, **Oxley Beach** and **Rocky Beach** are less accessible. Beyond those, **Flynn's Beach** and **Nobby's Beach** are two other favourite spots with good swimming as well as fossicking and snorkelling on the extensive rock platforms. **Flynn's Point** and **Nobby Head** also provide great views. South of Nobby Head the coastal fringe gives way to **Shelly Beach** and the Sea Acres Nature Reserve, a superb tract of rainforest (see below). As well as an excellent boardwalk there is a track through the rainforest from the terminus of Beach Road (off Pacific Drive) to Lighthouse Road. **Miners Beach**, reached by a coastal path from the same car park, is a favourite spot for naturists. At the terminus of Lighthouse Road is **Tacking Point** and the pocket-sized **Tacking Point Lighthouse** built in 1879. From there you are afforded great views south, along **Lighthouse Beach** towards Bonny Hills and North Brother Hill. The best way to see the beaches is by foot, following the coastal paths and initially Pacific Drive, south from Town Beach. From Tacking Point, then head back up to Pacific Drive and catch the bus 331 back to the town centre.

Port Macquarie claims to be the koala capital and a healthy suburban population clings precariously to the area's nature reserves and parks. Numerous road signs bear testament to this. In town one of the best places to spot wild koala is the 72-ha coastal **Sea Acres Nature Reserve**, south of the town centre along Pacific Drive. There, a sublime piece of rainforest is preserved with a 1.3 km boardwalk providing the ideal observation point. The boardwalk starts and finishes at the **Rainforest Centre**, which houses an interesting range of displays, a café and shop. Guided tours available. Recommended. ■ *Daily 0900-1630. $10, children under 7 free, family $27. T6582 3355*. If you are out of luck and there is not a furry set of ears in sight, then try the **Koala Hospital** in the **Macquarie Nature Reserve** on Lord Street. ■ *Feeding daily at 0800 and 1500. Donation. T6584 1522*. **Roto House**, a restored settlers' homestead, built in 1890, is also located in the grounds of the reserve. ■ *Mon-Fri 1000-1600, Sat/Sun 1000-1300. Free. T6584 2180*. The **Billabong Koala Breeding Centre**, provides copious koala-petting opportunites (1030/1330/1530), as well as the usual array of natives including wallabies, wombats and rainbow lorikeets in six acres of landscaped gardens. Café, BBQ and picnic facilities provided. ■ *Daily 0900-1700. $9.50, child $6. T6585 1060, 61 Billabong Dr, 10 km from the town centre on the western side of the Pacific Highway overpass.*

Sleeping

■ *On map*
The VIC has full accommodation listings and help with bookings (freephone · T1300-303155)

Book ahead in the high season and holiday periods

LL-L *Sails Resort*, 20 Park St, T6583 3999, www.sailsresort.com.au, is the town's top resort offering suites and units some with spa, pool, bar, good restaurant and sports facilities. For a really chic motel in the ideal position, look no further than the **LL-L** *HW Motor Inn*, 1 Stewart St, T6583 1200, www.hwmotorinn.com.au The rooms are very well appointed with most offering views across the river mouth and Town Beach. In town and handy to the eastern beaches is the modern **L** *Azura Beach House*, 109 Pacific Dr, T6582 2700, www.azura.com.au, offering en suites, heated pool and spa. Out of town the **LL** *Telegraph Retreat*, 126 Federation Way (35 km northwest), T6585 0670, www.telegraphretreat.com.au, is a lovely, classy, old-style self-contained country house with well-appointed suites, spa, pool and great cuisine. Complimentary pick-ups available.

Hostels The suburban, family-run **B-E** *Beachside Backpackers YHA*, 40 Church St, T6583 5512, is the closest hostel to the beaches, offering dorms, twins and family rooms, spacious facilities, free bikes, body/surf boards (free boogie board lessons), small gym, internet, Telegraph Retreat pick-ups from the bus station. Further west the friendly, family-run **C-E** *Lindel Backpackers*, 2 Hastings River Dr, T6583 1719, lindel@midcoast.com.au, is an historic house with lots of character, dorms, twins and doubles, pool, 24-hr kitchen and TV room, free use of boogie boards, fishing gear, bikes, pool table, internet and pick-ups. Nearby, the more modern, activity-oriented **C-E** *Ozzie Pozzie Backpackers*, 36 Waugh St, T6583 8133, www.nomadsworld.com, is making its mark and well in tune with travellers needs, with good facilities, dorms, doubles/twins, internet, pick-ups, free use of boogie boards, bikes and fishing gear.

Motor parks There are plenty of motor parks in the area with the vast **L-E** *Sundowner Breakwall Tourist Park*, right beside the river mouth, town centre and Town Beach, 1 Munster St, T6583 2755, www.sundowner.net.au, hard to beat for position. The staff are a bit aloof but it is well-facilitated, with a pool and camp kitchen. A good alternative is the **L-E** *Beachside Palms Taskers*, 14 Flynn St, T6583 1520. It is just a short walk to Flynn's Beach and the Peppermint Park and Fantasy Glades amusement parks. Pool and BBQ, but no camp kitchen. Remote **NPWS camping** is available at Big Hill and Point Plomer in the Limeburners Creek Nature Reserve, T6586 8300.

Expensive Both *Cray's*, beside the wharf at 74 Clarence St, T6583 7885 (open daily for lunch and dinner), and *Scampi's*, at the Port Marina, Park St, T6583 7200 (open daily from 1800), are the best venues for quality seafood. Cray's also serves good steak. **Mid-range** *Café 66*, 66 Clarence St, T6583 2484, is recommended for Italian and is open daily for breakfast and lunch and Tue-Sun for dinner. The long-established *Toros Mexican*, 22 Murray St, T6583 4340, is good value and does a wicked fajita. The lively *Café Rio*, 74 Clarence St, T6583 3933, offers more traditional fare and good coffee. Out of town the *Verandah*, 764 Fernbank Creek Rd (corner of Pacific Highway), T6582 8320, is a small, award-winning French/Mediterranean restaurant at the *Cassegrain Winery*, with a congenial atmosphere and nice views across the vines. Open for lunch from 1030-1600 daily. For good pub grub try *Finnians Irish Tavern*, 97 Gordon St, T6583 4646. **Cheap** For great fish and chips look no further than *Macquarie Seafoods*, corner of Clarence St and Short St, T6583 8476. Open daily 1100-2100. *The Port RSL*, 1 Bay St, T6580 2300, offers both value for money, outdoor and fine dining (Tue-Sat) as well as a family restaurant and live entertainment. The *Port Pacific Resort Café*, 14 Clarence St, T6583 8099 offers all-you-can-eat breakfasts for $10.50. If you are looking to cook your own, the *Port Fishing Co-operative* is beside the wharf.

Eating
● *On map*
Seafood rules in Port Macquarie from the full plate of oysters to humble fish and chips. The main outlets can be found at the Wharf end of Clarence St. The regional vineyards are also worth considering, especially for lunch

The **cinema** is at the corner of Clarence St and Horton St, T6583 8400. There are 3 main nightclubs in the Port: *Roxy's*, on William St. Open Wed-Sat 2000-0400, which attracts a young crowd; the popular *Beach House*, on the Green, Horton St, T6584 5692, open nightly, free entry until 2300, then $5 (free all night Thu), jazz on Sun afternoons; and the *Downunder*, next to Coles, which has karaoke on Wed and attracts a slightly older crowd. Open 2000-0300. There is also live entertainment at the very modern and happening *Port RSL*, Settlement City, Bay St, T6580 2300, every Fri/Sat. For low-key night try *Finnians Irish Tavern*, 97 Gordon St. They stage live bands at the weekend.

Entertainment
● *On map*
For up-to-date entertainment listings pick up the free, weekly 'Hastings Happenings' at the VIC

Water based Most of 'The Port's' activities are of course water-based with almost everything on offer from sedate river cruises to surf lessons. The **Wharf** at the western end of Clarence St is a good place to start. There you will find *Port Macquarie River Cruise* (Port Venture), T6583 3058. They carry over 200 passengers onboard the 'M.V. Venture' offering a scenic 2-hr **River Cruise**, 1000/1400, most days, from $20, child $8; 5-hr **BBQ Cruise** 1000 Wed, from $37, child $18, and a 4-hr BBQ Cruise, 1000 Mon, from $35, child

Tours & activities

$15. Also based at the Wharf are *Waterbus Everglades Tours*, T1300-555890, who offer daily river cruises to an oyster farm 1000/1400, from $22, child $9, 5-hr Everglades and Butter Factory Cruise, Tue, 0930, from $50, child $33, and a 4½-hr cruise to Wauchope and Timbertown, Wed 1000, from $38, child $25. *'The Pelican'* is a 30-ft **steamboat** offering a very sedate and value range of cruises, from $20, T1865 2171. Independent **boat and canoe hire** is also available at the Wharf with Hastings *River Boat Hire*, T6583 8811, *Jordan's Boat Hire* in the Caravan Park on Settlement Point Rd (North Shore), T6583 1005, and at Settlement Point itself, T6583 6300. All shapes and sizes of craft are on offer, starting at about $20 for 2 hrs. *C-Spray*, at the northern end of the Wharf, Short St, T6584 1626, also offer **jet ski hire** from $40 for 15 mins. *Port water Sports*, T1223 4509, offer **parasailing**, from $55. For **offshore fishing** charters contact *Odyssey*, T6582 2377, www.odysseycharters.com.au, or *Canopus*, T6585 5474, from $95 half day. *Port Macquarie Estuary Sportsfishing*, T6582 2545, offer full or half day **estuary fishing** from $77, and *Castaway*, T6582 5261, run **beachfishing** trips. **Surfing lessons** are available with *Dawn Light*, T6584 1477, dawnlight@turboweb.net.au, from $30 per hr. There are a number of **dive operators** including *Port Diving Academy*, Shop 7 Port Marina, T6584 6062, portdivingacademy@tsn.cc, offering equipment hire, courses and weekend packages with 5 boat dives from $220 and midweek packages with 8 boat dives for certified divers, from $350. *Rick's Dive School*, T6584 7759 offer courses starting at $220.

In the air *Alltime Skydive*, T6584 3655, skydive@midcoast.com.au, offer 10,000 ft tandem **skydives** from $290. The *High Adventure Air Park*, Pacific Highway, Johns River, T1800-063648, www.highadventure.com.au, offer an exciting range of activities including tandem **hang gliding** (from $195), **paragliding** (30 mins from $185) and 45-min **microlight** flights from $130. *Johnston Aviation*, T1800-025935, *Coastwings*, T6584 1130, and *Wingaway Air*, T6584 1155 all offer fixed-wing **scenic flights** from $35. *Seaplane Joy and Charter*, T1250 7698, offer **float plane** trips from $45-273 while for true adrenaline try the *Fighter Flight Centre*, T6583 9788, www.fighterflightcentre.com, 35 mins from $450-1,950. *Port Aero Transport and Training*, T6583 4198, can also offer scenic flights where you take the controls (albeit briefly) on your own, from $55.

Land-based The **Camel Safaris** on Lighthouse Beach are a local favourite, T6583 7650. Rides are from 20 mins to 1 hr, from $15/$28, child $10/$18, with breakfast from $33. *Centre of Gravity*, 52 Jindalee Rd, T6581 3899, offer **indoor rock climbing**, with walls from 5-11 m, bouldering, caves and ladders, from $15 with instruction. Phone for varying seasonal opening hours. You can go for a full day's **abseiling**, up to 45 m, with *Edge Experience*, T6585 3531. You can blat about on an **ATV** with the all new *ATV Quad Bike Tours*, T6582 3065. **Mountain biking** with *Hastings Valley Mountain Bike Riders*, T6583 3633, from $12 (plus hire). **Horse trekking** with *Cowarra Forest Trails* in Wauchope, T6585 3531, 1 hr from $30. **Wine tours** There are a number of excellent wineries in the region. The VIC can supply details of the **North Coast Wine Trail**, which takes in 5 of the best. *Macquarie Mountain Tours*, offer various regional tours including a wine tasting tour on Thu/Sat/Sun afternoons from $29, T6582 3065. **Bus tours** The *Port Explorer*, T6581 2181, offers informative bus tours of the town, from $16, child $15 and as far afield as Bellingen and Dorrigo, from $42, child $36.

Directory **Bank** All major branches with ATMs can be found along Clarence and Horton St. **Car hire** *Budget*, corner of Gordon St and Hollingworth St, T6583 5144, *Hertz*, 102 Gordon St, T6583 6599. **Communications** Internet *Port Surf Hub Internet Lounge*, 57 Clarence St, T6584 4744. Open daily until late. Or the *Hastings Library*, corner of Grant St and Gordon St, T6581 8755. Open Mon-Fri 0930-1800, Sat 0900-1200. **Post Office** Corner of Clarence and Horton. Open Mon-Fri 0900-1700. **Medical services** *Port Macquarie Base Hospital*, Wright Rd, T6581 2000. **Police** 2 Hay St, T6583 0199. **Travel Agencies** *Port Macquarie Travel Agency*, 110 William St, T6583 1422, porttvl@bigpond.com

Port Macquarie to Coffs Harbour

Although a pleasant place with a few notable attractions, **Kempsey** serves mainly as a temporary stop before heading further north or east to the coast, the Hat Head National Park and Crescent Head. The **VIC**, South Kempsey Park, (off Pacific Highway), T1800-642480, www.kempsey.midcoast.com.au, offers full accommodation listings for Kempsey and Crescent Head as well as NPWS national parks information. (Monday-Friday 0900-1700, Saturday/Sunday 1000-1600). The **Macleay River Museum** is next door to the VIC and includes a replica of a pioneer settlers cottage. ■ *Daily from 1000-1600, T6562 7572.* The **Wingay Aboriginal Culture Park** offers plenty of cultural insight including traditional bush tucker, boomerang throwing and didjeridu playing. Entertaining and informative tours are also on offer with genuine Aboriginal guides. ■ *Daily. $7. T6566 2332, Danger St.* Although tiny **Crescent Head** does not have the same appeal as South West Rocks and Smoky Cape (37 km further north), it does offer a quiet escape with some fine beaches with good **surfing**. To the south of the village, the **Limeburners Creek Nature Reserve** has a number of coastal walks featuring Aboriginal sites. Basic NPWS camping is available at both, T6586 8300. The basic **A-F** *Crescent Head Holiday Park*, is on Pacific Street, east of the village centre, T6566 0261. It offers a good range of cabins, powered and non-powered sites, BBQ, but no camp kitchen. *Kings Bros*, T6562 4724 run a Kempsey (Belgrave Street) to Crescent Head (Country Club) **bus** service (No 345), Monday to Friday at 0835/1230.

Kempsey & Crescent Head
Colour map 3, grid B5
Population: 9,000
49 km north of Port Macquarie
167 km south of Mackay

South West Rocks is the best-kept secret on the NSW north coast. Compared to Byron Bay, it has everything except the footprints. Long swathes of golden sand, great fishing and swimming, a cliff top lighthouse, stunning views and a superb local national park – Hat Head – combine to make South West Rocks the ideal place to kick back for a few days. For here once, you can even watch dolphins surfing as opposed to people. The South West Rocks **VIC** is housed in the one of two historic **Boatman's Cottages** on Ocean Drive, next to the caravan park (end of Gregory Street), T6566 7099, www.kempsey.midcoast.com.au ■ *Open daily 1000-1600.* There is a small **maritime museum** attached. The Kempsey VIC (see above) is another good source of information on the southern approach. They also hold NPWS national parks information.

From Clybucca, on the Pacific Highway, 19 km north of Kempsey, Highway 12, flirts with the **Macleay River Delta** to the small fishing port of Jerseyville, before branching north to South West Rocks and east to **Arakoon** and the **Smoky Cape**. South West Rocks sits at the southern bank of the Mcleay River mouth and western end of **Trail Bay**, where the colourful, wave-eroded **rocks** form a perfect playground for swimmers and snorkellers. At the eastern end of Trial Bay the charming settlement of Arakoon fringes the **Arakoon State Recreation Area** and **Laggers Point** which is the site of **Trial Bay Gaol** , built in 1886 and now housing a small museum. ■ *Daily 0900-1700. $4. T6566 6168.* At the terminus of Wilson Street, at the eastern end of Arakoon, is **Little Bay**. The car park also provides access to the **Graves Monument** walking track (2 km return) which provides memorable views back across Trial Bay and the Trail Bay Goal. **Gap Beach**, accessed a little further south is another fine spot, especially for the more adventurous surfer. South of Arakoon (3 km) Lighthouse Road provides access to the northern fringe of the **Hat Head National Park**, **Smoky Beach** and the Smoky Cape Lighthouse. The 1891 **lighthouse** is one of the tallest and oldest in NSW, and provides stunning **views**, south to Crescent Head and north down to the beckoning solitude of **North Smoky Beach**.

South West Rocks, Hat Head & The Hat Head National Park
Colour map 3, grid B5
Population: 3,500
94 km north of Port Macquarie
123 km south of Coffs Harbour

New South Wales

South of South West Rocks (accessed via Hat Head Village Road and Kinchela) the small village and headland of **Hat Head**, sits in the heart of the national park, separating the long swathes of Smoky Beach north and Killick Beach, to the south. The village has a caravan park, limited amenities and provides **walking** access to **Hat Hill**, Korogoro Point, Connor's Beach and the Hungry Hill Rest Area. The immediate area is renowned for its excellent **dive** sites including the 120-m **Fish Rock Cave**, home to many species including wobbygongs and rays. *South West Rocks Dive Centre*, 5/98 Gregory St, T6566 6474, www.southwestrocksdive.com.au, offer both trips and accommodation. The entrance to the Macleay River also offers some good **snorkelling**, but only at peak tide. *Trail Bay Fishing Charters*, T2725 6556, offer **fishing** and **whale/dolphin-watching** trips and Osprey, T6566 6612 **river trips** (Boatshed via Gordon Young Drive, 5 km west off Gregory Street).

Sleeping The most unusual accommodation in the area has to be the former keepers quarters at the **L** *Smoky Cape Lighthouse*, T6566 6301, www.smokycapelighthouse.com.au Totally refurbished in the interior it provides self-contained or B&B options, modern facilities, a 4-poster and stunning views south across the national park. Book well in advance. Recommended. The busy and beautifully placed **A-E** *Horseshoe Bay Beach Park*, Livingstone St, T6566 6370, overlooks the river, ocean and the sheltered Horseshoe Bay Beach, within yards of the town centre. It offers cabins, on-site vans and powered sites (some en suite). Hugely popular with locals so book well in advance. **D** *Arakoon State Recreation Area*, T6566 6168, on Laggers Point, beside the Trail Bay Goal, is the best spot for camping. There are **NPWS campsites** at the **F** *Smoky Rest Area*, near the lighthouse, and the **F** *Hungry Rest Area*, south of Hat Head village. Pit toilets, no water and fires permitted. Self-registration, fees apply, T6584 2203.

Eating In Arakoon, overlooking the Trail Bay Goal and beach, the *Trial Bay Kiosk*, T6566 7100, provides a superb location, al fresco dining and quality but fairly pricey fare. Good breakfasts and coffee. Open daily for breakfast and lunch 0800-1600 and Thu/Fri/Sat for dinner. Back in South West Rocks *Geppy's*, corner of Livingstone St and Memorial Av, T6566 6196, is well known for good seafood, Italian and modern Australian cuisine. Live jazz and blues on Wed. Cheaper options include the locally recommended *Pizza on the Rocks*, on Prince of Wales Av, T6566 6626, or the *Seabreeze Hotel Bistro*, at the top of Livingstone St, T6566 6205.

Transport *Kings Bros*, T6562 4724, run a Kempsey (Belgrave St) to South West Rocks (Livingstone St) **bus** (No 350), Mon-Fri, 0740/1130/1530. *Rocks Travel*, Shop 1/3 Livingstone St, T6566 6770, www.rockstravel.com.au, aid with onwards travel. **Taxi**, T6566 6677.

Nambucca Heads
Colour map 3, grid B5
Population: 6,000
131 km north of Port Macquarie
53 km south of Coffs Harbour

Nambucca is a popular domestic holiday destination on the east coast and has been for years. Much quieter than Coffs Harbour, it provides a good place to escape the crowds and is blessed with some glorious **beaches** and **lookouts**. The picturesque Nambucca River also provides some good fishing and boating opportunities. The Nambucca Heads **VIC** is on the Pacific Highway at the southern entrance to Nambucca Heads (Riverside Drive), T6568 6954, www.nambuccatourism.com.au ■ *Daily 0900-1700*. **Internet** is available at the *Bookshop and Internet Café*, corner of Bowra Street and Ridge Street, T6568 5855. ■ *Daily 0900-1700*.

Nambucca's elevated position gives the town some excellent views up and down the coast. The **Rotary** and **Captain Cook Lookouts** on Parkes Street (east off Bowra and right off Ridge Street) offer fine views south to South West Rocks, across the river mouth and down over **Shelly Beach**. Further north (at the end of Liston Street, beyond Ridge Street) the **Lions Lookout** looks north and below to the **Main Surfing Beach**. No doubt the views will tempt you down to the beaches, which are patrolled in summer and provide some good **surfing**. The sea wall at the river mouth ('Vee Wall') is good for **fishing** and **dolphin-watching**. Although the locals snorkel here do not be tempted as the currents are notorious. River **boats and canoes** can be hired from the *Nambucca Boatshed*, Wellington Drive, T6568 5550, and *Beachcomber Marine*, Riverside Drive, T6568 6432. Canoes can also be hired for exploring the **Warrel Creek**, from the *Scotts Head Caravan Park*, 1 Short Street, T6569 8122.

The **Vee Wall** is covered in messages and insights from visitors and makes for some colourful, if repetitive reading. Far more imaginative is the 60-m mosaic **wall** outside the police station in Bowra Street. Inland from Nambucca the historic villages of Macksville and Bowraville are worth a look. The **Bowraville Folk Museum** is considered one of the best folk museums in the state. ■ *Wed/Fri 1000-1230, Sat/Tue 1000-1500, Sun 1100-1500. $1.10, child $0.55, T6564 8200, High St.* The **Pub With No Beer** in Taylors Arm (26 km) is a congenial, historic local made famous by folk singer Slim Dusty. It does in fact sell beer and also a quality lunch, T6564 2101.

Sleeping The **A-C** *Max Motel*, 4 Fraser St, T6568 6138, has tidy rooms with 2 offering superb views across the river mouth. Within walking distance of the beach is the friendly and good value **A-C** *Beilby's Beach House B&B*, 1 Ocean St, T6568 6466, beilbys@midcoast.com.au, which has well appointed single/double/twin/quad and family rooms with en suites, showers or shared bathrooms, complimentary breakfast, bikes, boogie/surf board, fishing gear hire, internet and a great pool. The only **backpackers** in town is the quiet, motel-style **C-E** *Nambucca Backpackers Hostel*, 3 Newman St, T6568 6360. It has dorms, doubles, twins, singles, and fully self-contained units and can take the odd tent. Good discounts in the low season. Organized trips, free bike, boogie/surf board, snorkel gear, hire, internet and pick-ups from the bus stop. The best **motor park** in the town is the **L-F** *White Albatross Holiday Resort*, right next to the Nambucca River mouth and Vee Wall (end of Wellington Dr), T6568 6468. It has just about everything from luxury units with spa, to on-site vans and campsites. Good camp kitchen and excellent bistro/bar.

Eating For seafood and steak the *Boatshed Seafood Brasserie*, overlooking the river (1 Wellington St), T6568 9292, is recommended. Open daily for lunch from 1200-1430 and for dinner from 1800. At the end of Wellington St the *V Wall Tavern Bistro and Bar*, T6568 6394, is an award-winner and popular with the locals. For great value try the modern *RSL*, Nelson St, T6568 6288. It is especially good for budget meals on Thu/Sun. For good coffee, breakfasts and light lunches, head for the friendly *Star Fish Café*, 5 Mann St, T6569 4422. Open daily 0800-1700.

Transport The long-distance **bus** terminal is located near the VIC and supermarket on the Pacific Highway. *McCafferty's/Greyhound*, T132030, and *Premier*, T133410, all provide drop offs. *King Bros Buses*, T1300-555 611, run between Nambucca Heads and Bellingen several times daily, Mon-Fri, from $5.40, child $5. *Newmans*, T6568 1296, stop outside the police station on Bowra St and offer daily services to Coffs Harbour. *Keans Coaches*, T1800-043339, run a service from Scone to Port Macquarie and Coffs Harbour (via the Waterfall Way and Dorrigo/Belligen) 3 times a week, Mon/Wed/Fri returning Tue/Thu/Sun. The **train** station is 3 km northwest of the town centre, via Railway Rd (off Bowra). *Countrylink*, T132232, offer state and interstate services. *Nambucca World Travel*, Shop 16 Nambucca Plaza, T6569 4411, act as the local bus and rail booking agents.

New South Wales

Bellingen
Colour map 3, grid B5
Population: 3,000
160 km north of
Port Macquarie
38 km south of
Coffs Harbour

Sitting neatly on the banks of the **Bellinger River**, in the heart of the **Bellinger Valley**, the pleasant country village of Bellingen – or 'Bello' as it's affectionately known by the locals – is renowned for its artistic and alternative community, its markets, music festivals and laid-back ambience. It's a great place to pause for breath before continuing further inland to explore the superb national parks of Dorrigo and New England, or the resumption of the relentless journey northwards up the coast. The **VIC** is beside the Pacific Highway, in Uranga just south of the Bellingen turn-off, T6655 5711, www.bellin gen.nsw.gov.au/tourism/ bellingen.html (■ *Mon-Sat 0900-1700, Sun 1000-1400*). *Bellingen Travel*, 42 Hyde Street, Bellingen, T6655 2055, can also offer some local information and can assist with travel bookings and enquiries. **Internet** is available free at the *Bellingen Library*, Hyde Street (■ *Tue-Fri 1030-1730*) or at the *Bellingen Environment Centre*, 1 Church Street Lane (just off Church Street) T6655 2599 (■ *Mon-Fri 0900-1715*).

The Old Butter Factory, Doepel Lane, T6655 9599 (■ *Daily 0930-1700*), on the eastern approach to the village, and the unmistakable **Yellow Shed**, 2 Hyde Street, T6655 1189 (■ *Daily 0900-1700*), are the two main arts and crafts outlets in the village. The Old Butter Factory also has a café and offers a range of relaxation and healing therapies including iridology, massage and a float tank. The colourful Bellingen craft and produce **market** is considered one of the best in the region and is held in the local park on the third Saturday of the month. The village also hosts a top quality **Jazz Festival** in mid August, T6655 9345, and the equally popular **Global Carnival**, which is an entertaining celebration of world music held in the first week of October. Bat lovers should take a look at the large **flying fox (fruit bat) colony** on Bellingen 'Island', beside the river, within easy walking distance from the centre of the village. The best place to view the colony is from the Bellingen Caravan Park on Dowle Street (cross the Bridge off Hyde, on to Hammond then turn right into Dowle), while the best time to observe them en masse is around dusk when they head off in search of food. Even during the day it is an impressive sight as they hang like a thousand Christmas decorations from almost every tree.

Bellingen offers a fine base from which to explore the numerous excellent rainforest **walks** of the Dorrigo National Park (see below). The river also offers some exciting opportunities; either by **canoe** or on a **river cruise**. *Bellingen Canoe Adventures*, T6655 9955, www.bellingen.com/canoe, offer half-day guided trips from $44, full day trips from $88, a sunset tour from $66 and independent hire from $11 per hour, while *Water Rat River Cruises*, based in Uranga, T6655 6439, offer sedate cruises of the lower reaches, from $25. *On the Wallaby*, 18 Hammond Street, T6655 4388, offer half and full-day **4WD eco-tours** of the Bellinger Valley and Dorrigo Plateau and also wildlife **nightspotting** from $30. *Gambarri Aboriginal Tours*, T6655 4195, offer local guided tours with lots of cultural insight, activities and entertainment, from $50.

Sleeping The **L** *Monticello Countryhouse*, 11 Sunset Ridge Drive (2 km), T6655 1559, www.bellingen.com/monticello, and **L** *Bliss Lodge*, 355 Martells Rd (12 km southeast), T6655 9111, www.blissholidays.com.au, are both popular B&Bs, within easy reach of the village. The slightly cheaper **L-A** *Rivendell Guest House* is situated right in the heart of town on Hyde St (12), T6655 0060. The **L** *Fernridge Farm Cottage*, 1673 Waterfall Way (4 km west), T6655 2142, fernridge@bellingen.com.au, provides peaceful, cosy, self-contained accommodation in a 19th-century 'Queenslander' cottage on a 120 ha alpaca farm. The **A-B** *Bellinger Valley Motor Inn*, 1381 Waterfall Way, T6655 1599, provides a good motel option within walking distance of the village centre, with pool, spa and in-house restaurant. The **B-F** *Bellingen YHA Backpackers*, 2 Short St, T6655 1116, belloyha@midcoast.com.au, consistently receives rave reviews and deservingly so. Housed in a beautifully maintained two-storey historic homestead in the heart of the village, with large decks overlooking the river valley, it oozes character and has a great social, laid-back atmosphere. It has a range of dorms, double/twins and family rooms and camping facilities. Internet, musical instruments, hammocks and entertaining trips to Dorrigo National Park are all on offer and donning the hallways are tasteful nude photographs of over 300 guests willing to get genuinely creative and arty. The basic **C-F** *Bellingen Caravan Park*, beside the bat colony on Dowle St, T6655 1338, has on-site vans, powered and non-powered sites but no camp kitchen.

Eating For fine dining *No2 Oak St,* T6655 9000, is recommended. Housed in a 1910 heritage cottage it offers an excellent and innovative menu. Book ahead. Open Tue-Sat, from 1800. There are plenty of excellent cafés in the village. The *Cool Creek Café*, on Church St, has a nice atmosphere, is good value and offers occasional live music. Closed Tue/Wed. Next door, the *Good Food Shop* is great for sandwiches, while the *Swiss Patisserie and Bakery* offers some irresistible cakes and sweets. Elsewhere, overlooking the river valley, *Lodge 241*, 121 Hyde St, T6655 2470, is a café and gallery combined offering fine local cuisine and good coffee. Open daily 0800-1700. For good value, wholesome pub-grub and live music, try *Diggers Tavern*, 30 Hyde St, T6655 0022. Open Wed-Sat for lunch and Wed-Sun for dinner. For gourmet pizza try *Café Bare Nature*, 111 Hyde St, T6655 1551. Open Mon-Fri from 1430, Sat/Sun from 1130.

Transport The long-distance buses do not detour to Bellingen, the nearest stop is either Nambucca Heads or Uranga. *King Bros Buses*, T1300-555611, run between Nambucca Heads Uranga, Coffs Harbour and Bellingen several times daily, Mon-Fri, from $5.40, child $5. The nearest **train** station is in Uranga, *Countrylink*, T132232.

From Bellingen the **Waterfall Way** follows the Bellinger River upstream, passing through some beautiful countryside, before making the steep, 1000-m climb through the lush, subtropical slopes of the **Dorrigo National Park** to emerge at the crest of the **Dorrigo Plateau** and the former timber town of **Dorrigo**, gateway to the World Heritage listed **Dorrigo National Park**. Further west the Waterfall Way resumes its scenic course through gorgeous green rolling hills towards the **New England National Park** and Armidale. The Dorrigo Visitors Information Centre on Hickory Street in the centre of Dorrigo, T6657 2202, www.dorrigo.com.au, offers local accommodation listings. ■ *Daily 1000-1600*. The **NPWS Dorrigo National Park Rainforest Visitors Centre**. Dome Road, T6657 2309, supplies national parks, walks and some local information, but the real attraction here is its position at the edge of the escarpment, with fantastic views across the forested slopes of the Bellinger Valley towards the coast, greatly enhanced with the slightly shaky 100-m **Skywalk** that sits like a jetty out across the rainforest canopy. The visitors centre itself has some good interpretative displays and a small café. The main office and shop can provide the necessary detail on the excellent rainforest walks ■ *Daily 0900-1700. Free. T6657 2309*. From the Rainforest Centre it is a short, scenic 10-km drive along the edge of the escarpment to the **Never Never Picnic Area**, starting point for a network of rainforest walks. Before heading into Dorrigo township itself, it is worth taking the short 2-km drive to **Griffith's Lookout**, with its memorable views across the Bellinger Valley. The road to the lookout is signposted about 1 km south of Dome Road off the Waterfall Way. Just north of Dorrigo (1½ km), the **Dangar Falls** are impressive after heavy rain.

Dorrigo & the Dorrigo National Park

Colour map 3, grid B5
Population: 1,000
188 km north of Port Macquarie
66 km southwest of Coffs Harbour

New South Wales

Sleeping, eating and transport L *Ridgetop Hideaway*, 193 Old Coast Rd (5 km northwest), T6657 2243, www.dorrigo.com/hideaway, and **A** *Fernbrook Lodge*, 4705 Waterfall Way (6 km west), T6657 2573, fernbrooklodge@midcoast.com.au, both offer great views and are recommended. The **B-C** *Historic Dorrigo Hotel* in the centre of town (corner of Hickory St and Cudgery St), T6657 2016, offers traditional pub rooms at affordable prices. Comfortable budget (B&B) accommodation is offered at **A-E** *Grace-mere Grange*, 325 Dome Rd (2 km from the Rainforest Centre), T6657 2630, helenp@omcs.com.au   The **C-F** *Dorrigo Mountain Resort* on the southern edge of the town on the Waterfall Way, T6657 2564, has standard self-contained cabins, powered and non-powered sites, BBQs, but no camp kitchen. For fine dining try *Misty's*, 33 Hickory St, T6657 2855 (open Thu-Sun from 1800). For pub grub the hotel is an old classic and for coffee and light snacks the *Art Place Gallery*, 20 Cudgery St, T6657 2622 (open daily 1000-1630), or *The Good, the Bad and the Healthy*, also on Cudgery St, T6657 2304. *Kings Bros*, T1300-555622, offer coach tours to Dorrigo from Coffs Harbour.

Coffs Harbour

Colour map 3, grid B6
Population: 23,000
558 km north of Brisbane
426 km south of Brisbane

Roughly halfway between Sydney and Brisbane, and the only spot on the NSW coast where the Great Dividing Range meets the sea, Coffs Harbour is a favourite domestic holiday resort and the main commercial centre for the northern NSW coast. Surrounded by rolling hills draped by lush banana plantations and pretty beaches it's a fine spot to kick back for a couple of days. The main activities are centred around the town's attractive **marina**, where regular fishing, whale and dolphin-watching cruises are on offer, together with highly popular **diving** and snorkelling trips to the outlying **Solitary Islands**. The island group and surrounding coast is considered to have one of the most diverse marine biodiversities in NSW. Other principal attractions include **Muttonbird Island**, which guards the entrance to the harbour and offers sanctuary to thousands of burrowing seabirds and, in complete contrast, the distinctly kitschy **Big Banana** complex, on the northern edge of the town.

Ins & outs   **Getting there**   Coffs Harbour **Airport** is about 3 km south of the town centre off Hogbin Dr. *Qantaslink*, T131313, and *Hazelton Airways*, T131713, offer regular daily services to Sydney, Brisbane and Newcastle. A taxi into town costs about $7. The **train station** is at the end of Angus McLeod St (right off High St and Camperdown St), near the harbour jetty. *Countrylink*, T132232, offer daily services to Sydney and Brisbane. Long distance **buses** stop beside the VIC on Elizabeth St. *McCafferty's/Greyhound*, T132030, and *Premier*, T133410, offer daily interstate services. *Keans Coaches*, T1800-043 339, run a service from Coffs Harbour (via the Waterfall Way and Dorrigo/Belligen/Armidale and Tamworth) 3 times a week, Tue/Thu/Sun

Getting around   *King Bros*, T1300-555 611, are the local suburban **bus** company with daily, half-hourly services from 0715-1730. To get from Park Av in the town centre to the jetty, take the No 365E. *Ryan's Buses*, T6652 3201, offer local services to Woolgoolga and Grafton. **Bikes** can be hired from *Bob Wallis Bicycle Centre*, corner Collingwood St and Orlando St, T6652 5102, from $20 per 24 hrs ($50 deposit). *Coastal Power Bikes* rent out scooter/bike hybrids, free delivery, T6650 9064. **Taxi**, T131008.

Information   The Coffs Harbour **VIC** is at the southern end of the town, corner of Elizabeth St and Maclean St, T6652 1522, www.coffstourism.com.au/www.coffs coast.com.au Open daily 0900-1700. Ask for the free *'Coffs Coast Visitors Guide'* and the regional *Cartoscope Tourist Map* The **NPWS** have an office by the harbour, 32 marina Dr, T6652 0900, coffs.coast@npws.nsw.gov.au   Open Mon-Fri 0900-1700.

New South Wales

The harbour is hemmed in by the town's three main beaches: **Park Beach**, which straddles Coffs Creek to the north, **Jetty Beach**, beside the harbour, and **Boambee Beach** to the south. Park Beach is the most popular generally and is regularly patrolled in summer. Jetty Beach is considered the safest. There are also numerous other, excellent beaches, stretching 20 km north all the way to **Woolgoolga**. Linked to the mainland by the marina's 500-m sea wall is **Muttonbird Island Nature Reserve**, home to thousands of breeding **wedge-tailed shearwaters** (muttonbirds) that nest in a warren of burrows across the entire island. The birds are best viewed just after dusk, when they return in number to feed their mates or chicks. Keep a lookout for **humpback whales**, which are spotted offshore from June to September.

The **Regional Botanical Gardens** are at the end of Hardacre Street (off High Street) and networked with a series of boardwalks (■ *0900-1700 daily. Donations. T6652 3820*) and **Coffs Harbour Creek Walk** (5½ km) starts from Coff Street (just off Grafton) fringes both the gardens and the creek, and ends at Englands Park and Orlando Street and the **Pet Porpoise Pool** (■ *From $17, child $8, family $52. Dolphin swimming Sat only. T6652 2164*). For those who have not yet seen **wild kangaroos** keep your eyes open (especially towards dusk) in the landscaped areas beside the highway and opposite the zoo. Also north of the town is the new **Legends Surf Museum**, with over 120 classic boards on display as well as the odd canoe and photos. ■ *Daily. $5, T6653 6536. Gauldrons Rd, left off the Pacific Highway.*

Coff's best known attraction is, rather worryingly, the **Big Banana**, just north of the town on the Pacific Highway, which fronts a banana plantation that hosts a number of activities from a train plantation tour to a lookout, toboggan rides, ice skating and lots of souvenir kitsch. ■ *Daily 0900-1600, free entry, rides from $5 and tours, from $12, child $7.50, T6652 4355, www.bigbanana.com.au*

Sights
Although the main drag through Coffs Harbour might suggest the town lacks any charm, a dramatic improvement is instantly revealed towards the coast

The **LL-L** *Allambie Apartments*, 22 Camperdown St, T6652 6690, www.stayin coffs.com.au, offer superb views, pool and spa. For sheer luxury the **LL** *Friday Creek Retreat*, 267 Friday Creek Rd, Upper Orara, T6653 8221, www.fridaycreek.com.au, offer 9 superb fully self-contained cottages with spas, open fires, hammocks and great views, free bike hire, complementary breakfast and dinner by arrangement. The **hostels** in Coffs Harbour are lively places and very activity- and party-oriented. The friendly **C-E** *Coffs Harbour YHA*, 110 Albany St, T6652 6462, is in a suburban setting halfway between the town centre and the beach, offering dorms, doubles, twins and family rooms, pool, internet, cable TV and free bikes, surf/body boards and pick-ups. Further towards the beach, at 312 High St, the **C-F** *Aussitel Backpackers*, T6651 1871, is a highly social place with emphasis on discounted activities and its own attractive dive packages being a speciality. Dorms, twins and doubles, large kitchen, common area, internet, pool, bikes, surf/body boards, wetsuits, etc. At the northern end of town, within a stone's throw from the Park Beach Shopping Plaza, is the purpose-built, motel-style **C-E** *Coffs Harbour Backpackers* (Barracuda), 19 Arthur St, T6651 3514, www.barracuda backpack-ers.com.au, offering dorms, doubles/twins (most en suite). It's laid-back, social and again very activity oriented with attractive discounts and its own organized outings, pool, spa, internet, free equipment hire and pick-ups. Links with the other hostels for social pub/club outings. There are plenty of **motor parks** in the area with the best-located north of the town. The **A-E** *Emerald Beach Holiday Park*, Fishermans Dr, Emerald Beach, 18 km north of Coffs, has luxury villas, standard cabins, on-site vans, powered and shaded non-powered sites in bush setting with shop, café and pool. The beach is only yards away and is simply superb, with headland walks nearby. Recommended. If you must stay in Coffs itself the newly-renovated **L-F** *Park Beach Caravan Park* on Ocean Par, T6651 2465, is the best facilitated and beachside.

Sleeping
■ *On map*
The VIC has full listings for self-contained apartments, resorts, B&Bs and motels. There are lots of motels and resorts along the Pacific Highway on the north and south approaches and along the waterfront on Ocean Parade

New South Wales

New South Wales

Eating
● *On map*

For a good breakfast, coffee and lunch locals swear by the *Foreshore Café* on the Jetty Strip, 394 High St, T665 23127. Open daily. Another relaxed alternative nearby is the *Shearwater Restaurant* overlooking Coffs Creek, 321 High St, T6651 6053. Open daily for breakfast, lunch and dinner (Wed-Sun) from 0800. For fine dining, beyond the classy restaurants in the main resorts, seafood at the Marina complex is recommended. A pre-dinner walk to Muttonbird Island can be followed by quality al fresco dining at the award-winning *Tide and Pilot Brasserie*, Marina Dr, T6651 6888. Open daily for breakfast, lunch and dinner from 0700. Nearby the *Coffs Harbour Fisherman's Co-op*, 69 Marina Dr, T6652 2811, is the place for fish and chips. Open daily until 1800. Elsewhere, the *Star Anise*, 93 Grafton St, T6651 1033, is earning a good reputation for its innovative modern Australian cuisine. For cheaper deals around town try the value pub-style food *Rainforest Bar and Grill*, corner of Pacific Highway and Bray St, T6651 5488. Open daily for lunch and dinner. The Ocean Front Brasserie in the *Coffs Harbour Deep Sea Fishing Club*, Jordan Esplanade, T6651 2819, is also good value and offers great views across the harbour. Open daily 1200-1430/ 1800-2030.

Entertainment
● *On map*

Coffs tries hard to show the backpacker party set a good time with the *Plantation*, *Coffs Harbour*, and *Fitzroy Hotels* on Grafton St, all offering cheap drinks, pool and

Coffs Harbour

Sleeping ■
1 Allambie Apartments
2 Aussitel Backpackers
3 Coffs Harbour YHA
4 Park Beach Caravan Park

Eating ●
1 Coffs Harbour Deep Sea Fishing Club
2 Coffs Harbour Fisherman's Co-op
3 Foreshore Café
4 Shearwater
5 Star Anise
6 Tide & Pilot Brasserie

regular live entertainment. The latter remains open well into the wee hours. In the centre of town (Grafton St) is the local nightclub *Heat*, 1st Floor, 15 City Centre Mall ($8 cover). The town's modern cinema complex is located in the Bray St Complex just off the Pacific Highway (corner of Bray St), T6651 5568. The *Greenhouse Tavern* directly opposite is more of a modern pub with great live music and a good atmosphere especially at the weekends.

Cruising and fishing *Spirit of Coffs Harbour Cruises*, Shop 5, Marina, T6650 0155, www.spiritofcoffs.com.au, offer a range of cruise options, from a 3-hr Solitary Island trip/dolphin spotting, departing 0930 Mon/Wed/Fri/Sat/Sun, from $35, child $20: Whale-watching (mid May-mid Nov), from $35 and a 4-hr Luncheon/Waterslide Cruise, departing 0930 Tue/Thu, from $45, child $25. *Pacific Explorer*, T6652 7225, www.pacificexplorer.com.au, offer a sedate half-day island/dolphin- and whale-watching cruise on board their sailing catamaran, with snorkelling and boom netting departing 0900 and 1330, from $49, child $35. *Blue Wing*, T6651 1611, also offer value whale-watching trips in season twice daily at 0830 and 1330, from $44, couple $40 and child $25. *Bluefin II*, T04-2866 8072: *Adriatic III*, T6651 1277, and the classy *Cougar Cat 12*, T6651 6715, all offer entertaining fishing trips from around $70 for a half-day and big game fishing, from $140.

Diving The **Solitary Islands** offer some fine dive sites and a wealth of marine life, including lots of grey nurse sharks, 90 species of coral, 280 species of fish and the densest colonies of anemones and anemone fish (clown fish) in the world. Coffs Harbour is also one of the cheapest places to get certified on the NSW coast. The *Jetty Dive Centre*, 398 High St, T6651 1611, www.jettydive.com.au, offer small group Padi Certification from $185, introductory dives from $137 and snorkelling trips from $50. *Pacific Blue*, 40 Marina Dr, T6652 2033, pacificblue@bigpond.com.au, offer Padi Certification from $175, 1-day introductory from $115, half-day snorkelling from $55 and certified half-day trips from $75 (with gear $105). *ScubaCrew*, T1800-330335, offer a 4-day/4-night packages culminating in 4 ocean dives, through the Aussitel Backpackers, from $230.

Horse trekking *Valery Trails*, T6653 4301, is an outfit suited to all located 13 km south of Coffs Harbour. They offer 1 hr/2 hr/breakfast; BBQ, moonlight and camp ride-outs from $35. *Busland Trail Rides*, based at Halfway Creek, 50 km north of Coffs Harbour, T6649 4487, bushland trails@ozemail.com.au, offer 2 hr-breakfast, family and twilight rides, full-day rides on request. Closer to Coffs, The *Wyndyarra Estate*, Island Loop Rd, Upper Orara, T6653 8488, offer similar rides and 'Swim with the Horses' rides, from $30 with pick-ups.

Tours & activities
The VIC has full activity listings and can offer good advice

The Marina Booking Centre based at the marina also act as booking agents for most regional activities and cruises, T6651 4612. Open daily. For general activity information visit www.coffs central.com.au

New South Wales

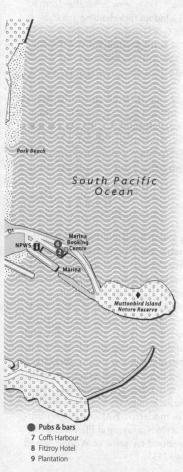

Park Beach

South Pacific Ocean

Marina Booking Centre

NPWS

Marina

Muttonbird Island Nature Reserve

● **Pubs & bars**
7 Coffs Harbour
8 Fitzroy Hotel
9 Plantation

Tours There are plenty of local tour operators from private 4WD adventures to coach trips. The well-established *Mountain Trails 4WD Tours*, T6658 3333, offer everything from day-long trips to Bellingen the Dorrigo National Park and a gold mine, from $85; Historical and Aboriginal tours, from $55 and also nocturnal wildlife spotting trips. *Blue Tongue*, T6651 8566, offer entertaining town and locality tours from $25, Dorrigo, from $50 and South West Rocks (south) from $60 (recommended).

Whitewater rafting, sea kayaking and surf rafting *Liquid Assets*, T6658 0850, liquidassets1@yahoo.com.au, offer an exhilarating range of aquatic adventures, including half- or full-day whitewater rafting, on the Goolang River (grade 3) and the **Nymbodia River** which is a scenic grade 3-5, from $80; sea kayaking, half-day from $40; surf rafting, half-day from $40 and Flat water kayaking in the **Bongil Bongil National Park**, half-day from $40. A 'Big Day Out' sea kayak, surf rafting and whitewater rafting combo costs from $135. Recommended. *WoW Rafting*, T6654 4066, www.wowrafting.com.au, offer a 1-day 9 km trip down the Nymbodia with 25 rapids from $153 and a 2-day trip with 75 rapids. All meals, camping included, from $325. *Whitewater Rafting*, T6653 3500, www.wildwateradventures.com.au, offer similar 1-2 day trips for the same price and extended 4-day and Queensland adventures, from $560.

Other activities *Coffs City Skydivers*, T6651 1167, www.coffsskydivers.com.au, offer **tandem skydiving**, 10,000 ft, from $275. **Indoor rock climbing** is available at Coffs Rock indoor climbing wall, GDT Secombe Cl (off Orlando), T66516688, from $13. Open Wed/Thu 1300-2000, Sat/Sun 1200-1700. **Surfing lessons** are offered with the *East Coast Surf School*, T6651 5515, www.eastcoastsurfschool.com.au, at Diggers Beach (near the Big Banana), 1030-1230, from $35, private lessons, from $50 per hr.

Directory   **Banks** All major branches with ATMs can be found on the Mall or along Grafton St and Park Av. **Car hire** *Coffs Harbour Rent-A-Car*, Shell Roadhouse, corner of Pacific Highway and Marcia St, from $44 per-day, T6652 5022, *Thrifty*, T6652 8622, *Hertz*, airport, T66511899. **Communications** Internet *The Internet Room*, Shop 21, Jetty Village Shopping Centre, T6651 9155. Open Mon-Fri 0900-1800, Sat/Sun 1000-1600 or The *Jetty Dive Centre*, 398 High St, T66511611. **Post Office** Palms Centre Arcade, Vernon St. Open Mon-Fri 0830-1700, Sat 0830-1200.

Coffs Harbour to Byron Bay

Wooli, Minnie Water & Yuragyir National Park (Southern Section)
Colour map 3, grid B6
Population: 550
105 km north of Coffs Harbour,
210 km south of Byron Bay

Some 70 km north of Coffs Harbour the Wooli Road heads east towards the coast and the two sleepy beachside settlements of **Wooli** and **Minnie Water**. Either provide a relaxing base from which to explore the surrounding, southern section of the **Yuragyir National Park**, renowned for its rich variety of wildlife, secluded beaches and, in the spring, its vivid displays of wild flowers. Just offshore the **Solitary Islands Marine Park** offers some fine **diving** and is considered to have one of the most diverse marine bio-diversities in NSW. *Wooli Deepsea Tours*, T6649 7100, offer dive and snorkelling trips as well as fishing, island sight seeing and whale/dolphin watching. Maps, accommodation listings and national parks **information** can all be secured at The Grafton VIC (see below). Wooli is the larger of the two settlements and has a general store (with Eftpos), service station, newsagents, motel, hotel and two caravan parks. Minnie Water (15 km north of Wooli) has a store, service station and the modern **C-F** *Minnie Water Caravan Park*, T6649 7693. There is basic **F** NPWS camping at Illaroo and Diggers Camp (see above). If you enjoy seafood try some of Wooli's famed oysters at the *Wooli Oyster Supply*, T6649 7537.

An elegant provincial city on the banks of the Clarence River, Grafton is renowned for its graceful old buildings and tree-lined streets, but attracts few visitors. Grafton was founded on the cedar cutting industry in the mid-1800s and is named after the grandfather of Governor Fitzroy. City maps, accommodation and activity listings can be found at the **VIC** (just off the Pacific Highway, in South Grafton), T6642 4677, crta@nor.com.au ■ *Daily 0900-1700*. For national parks information contact the **NPWS** office on Level 3, 49 Victoria Street, T6641 1500. ■ *Mon-Fri, 0900-1700*. **Internet** is available at *Grafton Health Foods*, 75 Prince Street. ■ *Mon-Fri, 0800-1700, Sat 0900-1300*. The **Grafton Regional Gallery** is one of the best regional galleries in NSW and is housed in one of Grafton's finest historical buildings, **Prentice House**, built in 1880. The courtyard café is a great place for a relaxed lunch. ■ *Tue-Sun, 1000-1600, donation, T6642 3177. 158 Fitzroy St*. Also worth a visit is the **Shaeffer House Museum** which occupies a historic homestead and displays a wide range of exhibits tracing the history of the city and Clarence River Valley. ■ *Tue-Thu and Sun, 1300-1600, T6642 5212, 192 Fitzroy St*. **Susan Island**, which sits mid-river in the heart of the city, is partly a nature reserve and home to the largest colony of **flying foxes** (fruit bats) in the southern hemisphere. The *Clarence Islander Rivercat*, 22 Mary Street, T6642 5957, can take groups across to the island by private charter. **River cruises** are offered by *Great Time Cruises*, Prince Street Wharf, from $10, T6642 3456. Better still, hire your own **house-boat** and do some real river cruising, through *Clarence Riverboats*, T6647 6232.

Sleeping and eating The VIC has full accommodation listings. The most modern and best facilitated motor park is the **A-E** *Gateway Village Tourist Park*, 598 Summerland Way (north of the CBD on the Casino Rd), T6642 4225. It has deluxe villas, on-site vans, en suite/standard powered and non-powered sites, pool but no camp kitchen. The **A-E** *Crown Hotel Motel*, 1 Prince St, T6642 4000, and **D** *Roaches Hotel*, 85 Victoria St, T6642 2866, both offer good budget and standard rooms. There are few good restaurants, with the art gallery café (open Mon-Fri 1000-1600), local hotels and motels being the best bet. *Victoria's Restaurant* in the Clarence Motor Inn, 51 Fitzroy St, T6643 3444, has a good local reputation.

Transport Long-distance **buses** stop in South Grafton. *Premier Motor Service*, T133 410, offer daily services between Sydney and Brisbane. The **train** station is on Through St, South Grafton (just off the Pacific Highway). *Countrylink* have an office in the station, T6640 9438. *King Brothers Bus Service*, T6646 2019, daily services from Grafton- Yamba- Maclean-Iluka. There is a regular **city bus** service operating on an hourly circuit, T6642 3111, and the public can also travel on school buses to outlying areas. **Taxi**, T6642 4633.

The coastal fishing town of **Yamba**, 13 km east of the Pacific Highway (just before the Clarence River bridge), on the southern bank of the Clarence River mouth, is famed for its prawn industry and **surf beaches**. Serving mainly as a **domestic holiday destination** it offers the opportunity to spend two or three days away from the mainstream tourist resorts along the north coast. **Main Beach**, below Flinders Park is the most popular, but **Turners Beach**, between the main breakwater and lighthouse, **Covent Beach**, between Lovers Point and Main Beach, and **Pippie Beach**, the most southerly, are equally beautiful. The **Clarence River Delta** and **Lake Wooloweyah** (4 km south) all provide a wealth of boating, fishing and cruising opportunities. The **Yamba-Illuka ferry** shuttles back and forth daily to Iluka, providing access to some sublime beaches, bluffs, a stunning rainforest nature reserve and the wilderness Bundjalung National Park (see below).

Grafton
Colour map 3, grid B6
Population: 18,500
86 km north of Coffs Harbour, 162 km south of Byron Bay.

Grafton is also the gateway to some excellent canoeing and rafting opportunities. The VIC has details

New South Wales

Yamba, Angourie & Yuragyir National Park (Northern Section)
Colour map 3, grid B6
Population: 5,000
169 km north of Coffs Harbour, 132 km south of Byron Bay

South of Yamba (5 km) is the small, picturesque village of **Angourie**, with its spectacular ocean views and world-class (advanced) **surf breaks**, best seen from the Angourie **Lookout**. The **Blue Pool**, reached via a walking track from the car park at the eastern end of the Crescent, is a deep freshwater pool and a favourite spot for swimming. The northern section of the **Yuraygir National Park** encompasses the Angourie Point headlands, Woody Bluff, Shelly, Plumbago and Red Cliff headland, which are linked by sand dunes and glorious beaches. There are plenty of **walking** opportunities including Angourie Lookout to Angourie Point and Back Beach (unofficial naturist beach). A gravel road links the Lakes Boulevarde Road to the Mara Creek car park. From there an excellent 10-km (three hours) walking track leads to Lake Arragan and Brooms Head (Recommended). Walk-in **camping** is available at Shelly and Lake Arragan. Maps, accommodation listings and national parks **information** can all be found at the **Lower Clarence Visitor Centre**, Ferry Park (just off the Pacific Highway 5 km south of the Clarence River bridge), T6645 4121, crta1@nor.com.au ■ *Daily 0900-1700.*

Sleeping and eating The excellent 5-star **LL-E** *Blue Dolphin Holiday Resort*, Yamba Rd, T6646 2194, offers luxury/standard self-contained cabins, en suite/standard powered and non-powered sites, café, pool and camp kitchen. The **LL-A** *Surf Motel*, 2 Queen St, T6646 1955, is a modern, well-appointed motel option right next to Main Beach. The *Restaurant Castalia*, 1/15 Clarence St, T6646 1155, offers good modern Australian fare. Open Wed-Sat for lunch and dinner. The *Pacific Hotel*, overlooking the ocean, 18 Pilot St, also offers budget accommodation and value bistro meals, daily, T6646 2491. For breakfast and coffee try the *Beachwood Café/Restaurant*, 16 Clarence St, T6646 9258. Open daily.

Tours and activities *Action Adventures*, Yamba, T04-3846 1137, are a professional outfit offering scenic sea kayaking, half day from $65 and full day from $100. The *Yamba Surfing Academy*, T6646 2971, can provide surfing lessons from beginner to advanced.

Transport The **Iluka-Yamba ferry** departs daily from the River St Wharf at 0930/1100/1515/1645, from $4. River Cruises depart 1100 Wed/Fri/Sun, from $16, chid $8, and there is also an Evening BBQ Cruise on offer at 1645 Wed, from $25, child $12.50 (book ahead), T6646 6423. *King Brothers Bus Service*, T6646 2019, provide daily services from Yamba-Maclean-Iluka-Grafton.

Iluka & the Bundjalung National Park

Colour map 3, grid B6
Population: 2,200
156 km north of Coffs Harbour, 119 km south of Byron Bay
Give yourself at least 2-3 days to explore the Iluka area; you won't regret it

Just north of the **Clarence River** and Chatsworth, on the Pacific Highway, Iluka Road heads east (14 km) terminating at the northern mouth of the Clarence and the sleepy fishing village of **Iluka**. Other than the superb coastal scenery of the southern sector of the **Bundjalung National Park**, and one of the best campsites on the northern NSW coast at **Woody Head**, the big attraction in Iluka is the **World Heritage Rainforest Walk** through the **Iluka Nature Reserve**. The 136-ha reserve contains the largest remaining stand of litoral rainforest in NSW – a rich forest habitat unique to the coastal environment supporting a huge number of associated species. The 2½ km rainforest walk can be tackled either from the north at the **Iluka Bluff** car park (off the main Iluka Road opposite the golf club) or from the caravan park at the eastern edge of the village (Crown Street). **Iluka Beach** is another fine quiet spot reached via Beach Road (just head east from the end of Iluka Road). Further north just beyond Iluka Bluff, **Bluff Beach** and **Frazer's Reef** are also popular for swimming and fishing. On the southern bank of the Clarence River mouth, Iluka's twin fishing village of **Yamba** and its equally good (if busier) beaches can be reached by ferry from the end of Charles Street (see below). North of Iluka and Woody Head the 18,000-ha wilderness of **Bundjalung National Park** with its 38 km of beaches, litoral rainforest, heathlands, unusual rock formations, lagoons, creeks and swamps is an explorer's paradise. Sadly, access from the south is by **4WD** only ($16 permit), or on foot. There is better access from the north along the 21 km unsealed road (Gap Road off the Pacific Highway, 5 km south of Woodburn) to the Black Rocks campsite. Maps, accommodation listings and national parks **information** are available at the **Lower Clarence Visitor Centre** (see above).

Sleeping F *(NPWS) Woody Head Campsite*, beside the beach off Iluka Rd (14 km east of the Pacific Highway and 4 km north of Iluka), T6646 6134, is simply superb. It has non-powered sites, toilets, water, hot showers, boat ramp and fires permitted, plus 3 cabins with cooking facilities. The information office and reception is open daily 0900-1000 (book well ahead). The far more basic NPWS *Black Rocks Campsite*, located beside the beach in the heart of the national park, is harder to access, but another alternative. Iluka itself also has 3 basic caravan parks.

Transport The Iluka-Yamba ferry departs daily from the Boatshed and Marina at the end of Charles St, Iluka at 0845/1015/1430 and 1600, from $4. River Cruises depart 1145 Wed/Fri/Sun, from $14, child $7 and there is also an Evening BBQ Cruise on offer at 1715 Wed, from $25, child $12.50 (book ahead), T6646 6423. *King Brothers Bus Service*, T6646 2019, provide daily services from Yamba-Maclean-Iluka-Grafton.

From Woodburn, 92 km north of Grafton, the coastal road to Evans Head and back through the Broadwater National Park, presents another welcome break from the relentless Pacific Highway. Straddling the mouth of the **Evans River** and separating the two coastal national parks of Bundjalung to the south and Broadwater to the north, the mainly fishing and prawning settlement of Evans Head is in an idyllic position and offers a fine spot for a picnic, fishing or a swim. The **Main Beach** access is beside the Surf Club at the end of Booyong Street, which is off Woodburn Street. Also not to be missed is the view looking north from the **Razorback Lookout**, which is accessed across the river, then left, at the end of Ocean Drive. Further explorations can be made off Ocean Drive (Chinaman's Beach Road) to **Chinaman's Beach** and Snapper Point a favourite spot for serious surfers at the edge of the **Dirrawong Headland Reserve** and the Bundjalung National Park. From the northern edge of Evans Head (Beech Road) you can then drive through the heart of **Broadwater National Park** to rejoin the Pacific Highway at Broadwater (8 km). The Salty Lagoon walking track (3 km return) is 2 km north of Evans Head, while 2½ km south of Broadwater, the Broadwater Lookout offers the best views across the park.

Evans Head & Broadwater National Park
Population: 2,000
192 km north of Coffs Harbour, 62 km south of Byron Bay

For most people their only memory of Ballina is the **'Big Prawn'**, a gigantic crustacean on top of a service station on the town's southern approach. Shame really, since Ballina is a pleasant enough coastal service centre and domestic holiday town, with fine **beaches**, scenic headlands and a good range of accommodation. The **VIC** is on the corner of River Street and Las Balsas Plaza, T6686 3484, balinfo@balshire.org.au/www.tropicalnsw.com.au ■ *Mon-Fri 0900-1700, Sat/Sun 0900-1600.* Next door is the small **Ballina Naval and Maritime Museum**, home to the 1973 Las Balsas Trans Pacific Expedition Raft (Ballina to South America). ■ *Daily 0900-1600, entry by donation, T6681 1002. Regatta Av.* **Internet** is available at the *Ballina Ice Creamery and Internet Café*, 178 River Street, T6686 5783. ■ *Open Mon-Fri 0930-1800, Fri/Sat 0930-2100.*

Ballina
Colour map 3, grid B6
Population: 16,000
210 km north of Coffs Harbour, 30 km south of Byron Bay

Ballina's best beaches are to be found at the eastern end of town across North Creek and the **Richmond River** in East Ballina. **Shelly Beach** and **Lighthouse Beach** both offer good swimming, surfing and can be reached via Compton Street (just beyond the bridge, off Hill Street). On the way, **Shaws Bay Lagoon**, next to the river, also provides a pleasant swimming spot. *Summerland Surf School*, 51 Ocean Drive, Evans Head, T6682 4393, www.surfingaustralia.com.au, can oblige with surfing lessons for both beginners or the advanced. The '*M.V. Bennelong*' offers an interesting range of scenic and historical cruises on the Richmond River, T6688 8266. *Richmond River Cruises*, T6687 7940, also offer weekly cruises. Much more exhilarating are the fast launch **dolphin-watching** tours offered by *Ballina Ocean Tours*, 24 Smith Drive, T6686 3999, www.ballinaoceantours.ballina.net.au *Jack Ransom Cycles*, 16 Cherry Street, T6686 3485, rents bikes. *Forgotten Country Eco-Tours*, T6687 7845, offer entertaining and informative guided rainforest walks and gold-panning, canoeing, horse riding and whitewater rafting by arrangement.

Sleeping and eating Comfort with a traditional, historical edge can be secured at the **LL-L** *Ballina Manor*, 25 Norton St, T6681 5888, www.ballinamanor.com.au, while the more modern and cheaper **L-A** *Ballina Heritage Inn*, 229 River St, T6686 0505, has motel-style singles, doubles and family rooms, with spas and a pool. For backpackers and budget travellers the quiet, motel-style **E** *YHA Ballina Travellers Lodge*, 36 Tamar St, T6686 6737, lenballina@ozemail.com.au, offers dorm rooms, doubles/twins with all amenities, close to the town centre. There are plenty of caravan parks in and around town with the 4-star, **A-F** *Ballina Lakeside Holiday Park*, Fenwick Dr, East Ballina, T6686 3953, offering the full range of accommodation and facilities, close to the eastern beaches and alongside Shaws Bay Lagoon. For fine dining, the *Beaches Restaurant* in the Ballina Beach Resort, T6686 8888, is locally recommended with its regional cuisine and al fresco dining. Open daily for breakfast, lunch and dinner. In East Ballina, *Shelly's on the Beach Café*, Shelly's Beach Rd, T6686 9844, offers value traditional Australian cuisine and great ocean views. Open daily for breakfast and lunch, from 0730-1500. For down to earth value try the *Ballina RSL* at the western end of River St, T6686 2544. It offers both à la carte and bistro-style meals and hosts live bands every Fri and Sat nights, plus Jazz every Sun from 0800 (all you can eat breakfast also on Sun from 0800). For good beer, traditional pub-grub and a congenial atmosphere try *Paddy McGinty's Irish Pub*, 56 River St, T6686 2135.

Transport Ballina **Airport** is 3 km to the east of the town off Southern Cross Dr and is served from Sydney daily by *QantasLink*, T131313, and *Hazelton Airways*, T131713. *Byron Bay Airbus*, T6681 3355 (from $25 one-way). Long distance **buses** stop outside the unmistakable 'Big Prawn', 3½ km south of the town centre. *McCafferty's/Greyhound*, T132030, *Premier Motor Service*, T133410, all offer daily services to Sydney and Brisbane while Lismore-based company *Kirklands*, T6622 1499, offer daily services to Lismore, the Gold Coast, Byron Bay and Brisbane. *Blanch's Buses*, T6686 2144, offer local bus services between Byron Bay (Mullumbimby) and Ballina (No 640), Lismore (Nos 661/611) and Evans Head (#660). There are several **car hire** companies based at the airport including *Avis*, T6686 7650, and *Budget*, T6681 4031. Ballina **Taxi** service, T6686 9999.

Lennox Head
Population: 2,400
226 km north of Coffs Harbour, 21 km south of Byron Bay

The small, beachside settlement of Lennox Head, 11 km north of Ballina and 20 km south of Byron Bay, is world famous for the long **surf breaks** that form with welcome repetition at the terminus of **Seven Mile Beach** and Lennox Point. Either with or without a board the village offers a quieter, alternative destination in which to spend a relaxing couple of days, away from the tourist hype of Byron Bay. Just south of the village the namesake heads offer excellent views north to Cape Byron and are considered a prime spot for both hang gliding and dolphin- or whale-spotting. The Lennox Reef below the heads known as 'The Moat' is also good for snorkelling. At the northern end of the village **Lake Ainsworth** is a fine venue for freshwater swimming, canoeing and windsurfing. The *Lennox Head Sailing School* beside the lake on Pacific Pde, T6687 6010, hires water sports equipment and offers lessons. The lake edge also serves as the venue for the coastal **markets** that are held on the second and fifth Sundays of the month.

Sleeping and eating The **C-E** *Lennox Head Beachouse YHA*, 3 Ross St, T6687 7636, backpack@spot.com.au, is a purpose-built hostel with a great laid-back, friendly atmosphere, near the beach and Lake Ainsworth. It offers dorms and small doubles and free use of surf/boogie boards, bikes and fishing gear. Free sailing and windsurfing lessons can also be arranged and there is a natural therapies (massage) clinic on-site and legendary chocolate cake. For campers and campervans the **B-E** *Lake Ainsworth Caravan Park*, Pacific Par, T6687 7249, is ideally located next to the lake and offers en suite/standard cabins, powered and non-powered sites but no camp kitchen. Activities include windsurfing, sailing and canoeing. *Sullivan's Restaurant* in the Headland Beach Resort is recommended. Other more affordable options and cafés can be found beachside, at the junction of Pacific Par and Byron St, including *Ruby's Bar and Restaurant*, 17 Pacific Par, T6687 5769. Closed Mon.

Transport Long-distance **buses** stop on Ballina St including *Premier Motor Service*, T133410. *Blanch's Buses*, T6686 2144 offer local bus services between Byron Bay and Ballina (No 640). You can flag them down along Pacific Par.

Byron Bay

Anything goes in 'Byron'. This is a town that would love to have its own passport control to prevent entry to anyone remotely conservative, or who thinks surfing is something you do in front of a computer. It's not all drop-outs, though. Some well-respected artists, writers and poets have made Byron home and so have a number of film stars. Only three decades ago Byron Bay was little more than a sleepy, attractive coastal enclave. Few strayed off the main highway heading north except those alternative lifestylers who found it an ideal escape and the land prices wonderfully cheap. But news spread and its popularity exploded. Now Byron is number one on the tourist itinerary between Sydney and Queensland, but to its credit has avoided the worst excesses of commercialism and crass tourist development.

Colour map 3, grid B6
Population: 6,000
790 km north of Sydney, 173 km south of Mackay

Getting there The closest **airports** to Byron Bay are Coolangatta, 90 km to the north (see page 270) and Ballina, 31 km south. Both are served by *QantasLink*, T131313. The *Airporter Shuttle*, T04-1460 8660, and *Byron Bay International*, T6685 7447, serve Coolangatta from $66 one-way. *Byron Bay Airbus*, 16681 3355, serve Ballina, from $25 one-way. The long-distance **bus** stop is located right in the heart of town on Jonson St. *McCafferty's/Greyhound*, T132030, and *Premier Motor Services*, T133410, offer daily inter-state services north/south. *Kirklands*, T1300-367 077, offer services to Brisbane, Ballina, Lismore and Coolangatta. *Byron Bay Bus and Backpacker Centre*, 84 Jonson St, T6685 5517, act as the local booking agents. The **train** station is also located right in the heart of town, just off Jonson St. *Countrylink*, T132232, offer daily services south to Sydney and beyond and north (with bus link) to *Queensland Rail*, T132232, to Brisbane.

Ins & outs

Getting around *Blanch's Buses*, T6686 2144, offer local **bus** services within Byron Bay (No 637) and also south to Ballina via Lennox Head (No 640) and north to Mullumbimby (No 640). For **bike hire** contact *Byron Bay Bicycles*, 93 Jonson St, T6685 6067, *Byron Bay Bike Hire* (free delivery), T0500-856985, or *Rockhoppers*, Shop1/87 Jonson St, T0500-881881, from $25 per day. **Motorcycles** can be hired from *Ride On*, 105 Jonson St, T6685 6304, from $110 per-day. Byron bay **Taxi**, T6685 5008.

Information The **Byron Bay Visitors Information Centre** is beside the main stop, 80 Jonston St, T6680 8558, www.byron-bay.com.au Open daily 0900-1700. For backpackers the *Byron Bus and Backpacker Centre*, T6685 5517, also on Jonson St, acts as travel /activity booking agents and offers car rental and locker storage. Daily from 0700.

Sights   The main attraction in Byron beyond its hugely popular social and creative scene, are of course the surrounding **beaches** and the superb scenery of the **Cape Byron Headland Reserve**. There are over 37 km of beach around Byron and seven world-class surf beaches stretching from Belongil Beach in the west to Broken Head in the south.

Only metres from the town centre **Main Beach** is the main focus of activity. It is also patrolled and the safest for families or surfing beginners. West of Main Beach, **Belongil Beach** stretches about 1 km to the mouth of Belongil Creek. About 500 m beyond that (accessed via Bayshore Drive) is a designated **naturist beach**. East of the town centre, Main Beach merges with **Clark's Beach**, which is no less appealing and generally much quieter. Beyond Clark's Beach and the headland called **The Pass** (which is a favourite surf spot) Watego's and Little Watego's Beaches fringe the northern side of Cape Byron providing more surf breaks and some dramatic coastal scenery with Cape Byron looming above. South of the Cape, **Tallow Beach**

Byron Bay

To Julian Rocks

Byron Bay

Main Beach

To Belongil Beachouse, Belongil Beach, Pacific Highway, Lismore & Tweed Heads

To Garden Burees, Arts Factory, Pighouse Flicks & Old Pigpery

To Summerhouse, Broken Head & Nature Reserve

Shirley St
Shirley La
Wordsworth St
Somerset St
Burns St
Butler St
Jonson St
Byron Images
Cocomangas
Soundwaves
Byron Foreign Exchange
Sunday Arts & Crafts
Byron Bus & Backpacker Centre & Global Gossip
Plaza Shopping Centre
Bay St
Bay La
Lawson St
Fletcher St
Byron St
Marvell St
Middleton St
Carlyle St
Kingsley St
Tennyson St
Cowper St
Marvell St
Gilmore St
Massinger St
Kipling St
Paterson La
Paterson St
Daniels St
Paterson St North

N
Not to scale

Sleeping	
1 Amigo's Byron Bay Guesthouse	
2 Aquarius Backpackers Motel	
3 Backpackers Inn	
4 Bamboo Cottage	9 Clark's Beach Caravan Park
5 Beach	10 First Sun Holiday Park
6 Byron Bay Bunkhouse	11 Holiday Village Backpackers
7 Byron Bayside Motel	12 J's Bay Hostel
8 Cape Byron Hostel (YHA)	

stretches about 9 km to **Broken Head**. It is a great spot to escape the crowds, but is unpatrolled. Several walks also access other more remote headland beaches within the very pretty **Broken Head Nature Reserve**. In the heart of Byron Bay itself, the small and clearly visible rocky outcrop known as **Julian Rocks** provides a favourite snorkelling and diving spot and is especially noted for its visiting manta rays.

Cape Byron, named after the grandfather of the famous 19th-century poet Lord Byron, is Australia's easternmost point. Crowning the headland is the **Byron Bay Lighthouse**, built in 1901. As well as the dramatic coastal views east over Byron Bay and south down Tallow Beach to Broken Head, the headland provides some excellent **walking** opportunities, with the track down from the lighthouse to Little Watego's Beach being the most popular. Humpback **whales** can often be seen offshore, during their annual migrations in mid winter and early summer, while **dolphins** and the occasional manta ray can be spotted in the clear waters below the cliffs year round. ■ *The lighthouse precinct is open between 0800-1930 (1730 in winter). Lighthouse tours (40 mins) are available Tue/Thu at 1100/1230 and 1400, Sat/Sun 1000/1100/1230/1400/ 1530, from $8, child $6. T6685 5955. Note that free parking is limited and a charge of $4 is levied to enter the lighthouse car park.*

The town has a number of **galleries** worth seeing including the *Colin Heaney Glass Blowing Studio*, 6 Acacia Street (■ *Daily, T6685 7044*) and *Byron Images*, on the corner of Lawson Street and Jonson Street, www.johnderrey.com.au Byron also hosts an arts and crafts **market** on the first Sunday of the month (Butler Street). The VIC has full gallery listings and a tour to meet local artists and see their work and studios is offered by *Studio Arts Tours*, T6680 9797, from $30 (two hours), $55 (3½ hours) $98 full day.

New South Wales

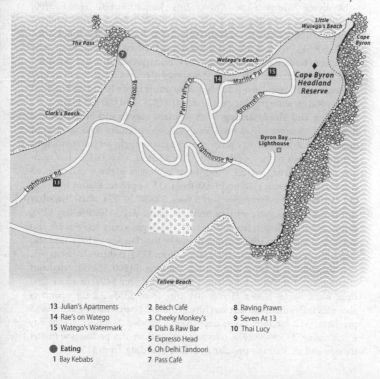

13 Julian's Apartments
14 Rae's on Watego
15 Watego's Watermark

● **Eating**
1 Bay Kebabs

2 Beach Café
3 Cheeky Monkey's
4 Dish & Raw Bar
5 Expresso Head
6 Oh Delhi Tandoori
7 Pass Café

8 Raving Prawn
9 Seven At 13
10 Thai Lucy

Tours & activities   Surfing is the most popular pastime, though diving and mountain biking are also recommended. *Rockhoppers*, Shop1/87 Jonson Street, T0500-881881, are one of the largest operators, offering an attractive range of single or combination activity packages, from mountain biking to wake boarding.

Diving   The **Julian Rocks Marine Reserve**, 2½ km from the shore, is listed in Australia's 'top ten' dive sites, with over 400 species of fish including sharks and manta ray, with turtles and dolphins often joining the party. If you are not a certified diver a snorkelling trip to the rocks is recommended. *Sundive*, opposite the Court House on Middleton Street, T6685 7755, offer courses, trips with gear (from $75) and snorkelling from $45 (0830/1100/1400). *The Byron Bay Dive Centre*, 9 Marvel Street, T6685 8333, www.byronbaydivecentre.com.au, offer a similar range of trips.

Health and massage   Byron Bay also supports a large number of massage, yoga practitioners and health therapists. Look out for the free 'Body and Soul' brochure at the VIC for full listings and prices.

Mountain biking   *Rockhoppers*, Shop1/87 Jonson Street, T0500-881881, both offer day-long biking adventures on hinterland rainforest trails, taking in the Minyon Falls, from $69-80. *Wanderlust Eco-Adventures*, T6685 7266, also offer biking adventures with more sedate family-oriented tours.

Paragliding and Hang gliding   *Poliglide*, T04-2866 6843, www.poli glide.com.au, offer tandem paragliding from $165 and day-long introductory courses from $220. *Skylimit*, T6684 3711, skylimit@mul lum.com.au, and *Flight Zone*, T6685 8768, offer tandem hang gliding and microlight flights and courses, from $70.

Sea kayaking   *Dolphin*, T6685 8044, www.dolphinkayaking.com.au, also offer good trips departing at 0900 and 1400 daily from $40. Recommended.

Skydiving   *Skydive Cape Byron*, 2/84 Jonson Street, T6685 5990, www.skydive-cape-byron.com.au, are a reputable outfit, offering tandems from 8,000 ft (from $229) to 12,000 ft (from $299). *Byron Bay Skydiving Centre*, T1800-800840, www.skydivebyronbay.com.au, based west of town near Brunswick Heads, is owned by Australian World representative and 'skysurfer' Ray Palmer. He and his colleagues offer a range of professional services including tandems. The views from the jump zone across Byron Bay to the headland and beyond are stunning. Jumps from 8,000 ft ($253)-10,000 ft ($341).

Surfing and kite boarding   With so many superb surf breaks around Byron and subsequently so many local professionals there is no shortage of opportunity to learn. Most operators offer a guarantee to get you standing or will refund your money. *Style Surfing*, T6685 5634, www.byron- bay.com/ byronbaystylesurfing, offers a four-hour beginners package or advanced courses daily at 0900, 1100 and 1300, from $33, or private lessons from $50 per 1½ hours. The *Byron Bay Surf School*, T1800-707274, www.byronbay surfschool.com.au, have various packages (three-day $110, five-day $150, private two-hour lesson from $85). *Surf Angels*, girl's only sessions are also available. *Kool Katz*, T6685 5169, are one of the cheapest in town and also guarantee to get you standing four hours, from $25 and three-day from $65. For real enthusiasts or serious learners, *Surfaris*, T1800-634951, www.surf aris.com.au, offer a week long Sydney-Byron trip (from $499) or a four-day/ three-night Byron-Noosa-Hervey Bay trip, from $365. All the operators above also offer **independent surf hire** with short boards starting at about $5 per hour, $12 for four hours and around $20 for 24 hours. *Byron Bay Kiteboarding*, T1300-888938, offer half, two or three-day packages to master the new and increasingly popular art of **kite boarding**, from $150.

Tours *Grasshoppers Nimbin Eco-Explorer Tour*, run by Rockhoppers, T0500-881 881, is recommended if you want experience Nimbin from the 'right angle', from $35. Recommended. Transport to the Nimbin backpackers is also an additional option. *Jim's Alternative Tours*, T6685 7720, www.byron-bay.com/jimstours, also offers a wide array of entertaining options from simple lighthouse or market trips to dolphin watching and national park eco-tours. Day tour departs Monday-Saturday at 0900, from $30. The hinterland region west of Byron present a number of worthy attractions with the most aesthetically pleasing being the **Nightcap** and **Mount Warning National Parks**, which encompass part of what was once a huge volcano. Its remaining core, **Mount Warning** (1,157 m), offers visitors a challenging climb to the summit, to be the first in Australia that day to see the sunrise. *Rockhoppers*, T0500-881881, offer guided Sunrise Tuesday/Wednesday/Sunday (with breakfast), or Day Treks to the summit from $49. The small historic village of **Bangalow** has a pleasant laid-back atmosphere, a scattering of art galleries, antique and gift shops. It also hosts a good market on the fourth Sunday of each month.

Walking The **Nightcap, Border Ranges** and **Mount Warning National Parks** all present some excellent walking opportunities. *Byron Bay Walking Tours*, T6687 1112, walknorth@mullum.com.au, offer a range of guided day-trips from the eco-based to historic, taking in both coast and hinterland. Trips range from a basic 8 km day walk along the Evans River (from $65), and an 11-km trip to see the Minyon Falls (from $50), to a part guided, part self-guided 20-km walk through the rugged Nightcap National Park, from $70.

Other activities *Byron Boat Charters*, based at The Pass, Brooke Drive, T6685 6858, offer a range of cruise and activity options, including **dolphin/whale-watching**, **fishing**, snorkelling and general water-based sightseeing, from $35. *Rockhoppers*, T0500-881881, offer day-long '**triple challenge**' waterfall abseiling, rappelling and canyoning adventures in the hinterland rainforest, from $119. For something completely different you might like to try the **flying trapeze** and circus school activities at the *Byron Bay Beach Resort*, Bayshore Drive, T6685 8000, from $25.

Sleeping

■ *On map*

While researching options from afar, or on arrival you are advised to check out the excellent service and free directories available from Byron Bay Accommodation in the VIC, 80 Jonson St, T6680 8666, www.byronbayaccom .net.au Pre-booking is advised at all times

Hotels and motels The **LL** *Rae's on Watego*, overlooking Watego's Beach, T6685 5366, www.raes.com.au, is the most luxurious hotel in Byron and was voted in *Conde Naste Traveller Magazine* (and others) as being in the top 50 worldwide. Although location has a lot to do with that accolade, the place itself is superb and cannot be faulted. It has an in-house restaurant that is also excellent and open to non-guests. More affordable, the **LL** *Beach Hotel*, Bay St, T6685 6402, www.beachhotel.com.au, is the perfect place to be if you like to be in the heart of all the action. It has tidy, spacious rooms and suites (some with spa and ocean views), only yards from the beach and the bar/restaurant downstairs, which is the social hub of the town. Of the many motels the 3-star **A** *Byron Bayside Motel*, 14 Middleton St, T6685 6004, bbaymtl@norex.com.au, is well placed in the heart of town, modern, clean and good value.

Apartments, B&Bs and guesthouses All the following are listed and advertised through Byron Bay Accommodation and recommended. At the upper end of the market, east of the town centre, near the lighthouse the **LL-A** *Julian's Apartments*, 124 Lighthouse Rd, T66809697, has modern, well-appointed en suites close to the beach. Nearby, **LL** *Watego's Watermark*, 29 Marine Par, T6685 8999, wategoswatermark@ byron-bay.com.au, is in the ideal location only metres from the best surf beach, 5 great 'minimalist' rooms, with balcony views and very friendly hosts. Near the town centre the **LL** *Garden Burees*, 19 Gordon St, T6685 5390, www.byron-bay.com/gardenburees, offers something very different with 2-storey, self-contained Bali/Pacific bungalows, beautifully appointed, with spas, in a quiet bush setting. Vegetarian restaurant and massage therapy on site. Out of town, south, the luxurious and beautifully appointed **LL-L** *Nirvana Lodge B&B*, 4 Beach Rd, Broken Head (5 km), T6685 4549, hbrook@bigpond.com.au, has a spa/en suite and en suite close to Broken Head Beach and Nature Reserve. **LL** *Summerhouse*, 9 Coopers Shoot Rd, T6685 3090, www.thesummerhouse.com.au The views take some beating. They offer 3 luxury suites with spa. Some excellent, cheaper options, include **A-B** *Amigo's Byron Bay Guesthouse*, on the corner of Kingsley St and Tennyson St, T6680 8662, with en suite double, double with shared bathroom, bike and body board hire and massage. Another alternative is the **A** *Bamboo Cottage*, 76 Butler St, T6685 5509, bamboocottage@byron-bay.com.au, has a tidy single, twin, double and triple in a quiet garden setting close to all amenities.

Hostels For the quintessential 'alternative' Byron experience The **A-F** *Arts Factory*, Skinners Shoot Rd (via Burns St, off Shirley St), T6685 7709, www.omcs.com.au/ artsfactory takes some beating. It offers a wide range of 'funky' accommodation from the 'Love Shack' and 'Island Retreats', to 'The Gypsy Bus', tepees and campsites. Excellent amenities, pool, sauna, internet, café (plus vegetarian restaurant nearby), bike hire, tours desk and unusual arts, relaxation or music-based activities, including didjeridu making, drumming and yoga. The Pighouse cinema is also next-door. It may not be everybody's cup of tea, but for an experience it is recommended. Also east of the town centre and in contrast to the Arts Factory is the **LL-D** *Belongil Beachouse*, Childe St (Kendal St, off Shirley St), T6685 7868, www.belongilbeachouse.com.au It offers a wide range of modern, well appointed options from dorms and private double/twins with shared facilities, to luxury motel-style rooms with spas, or 2-bedroom self-contained cottages. Quiet setting across the road from the beach. Balinese style café and float/massage therapy centre on site. Internet, bike, body/surf board hire and courtesy bus. Recommended. There are plenty of choices in the town itself. The **A-E** *Aquarius Backpackers Motel*, 16 Lawson St, T6685 7663, www.aquarius-backpack.com.au, is a large and lively complex offering dorms, doubles and spa suites (all en suite, with 'proper beds'), pool, good value licensed café/bistro, internet, free boogie boards, bikes, pool tables and courtesy bus. Just around the corner the popular **A-E** *Cape Byron Hostel (YHA)*, T6685 8788, offers modern, clean dorms, double and twins (some en suite, a/c) centred around a large courtyard with pool. Well managed and friendly. Good kitchen facilities, café, free BBQ nights, large games room, internet and tours desk. Dive shop next door. Just south of the town centre at 116 Jonson St, the **A-E** *Holiday Village Backpackers*, T6685 8888, offers modern dorms, doubles and motel-style apartments (some en suite with TV), large courtyard with pool, spa, well equipped kitchen, All-you-can-eat BBQs, internet, free surf/body boards, scuba lessons, bike hire. If the above are booked up other alternatives include the spotless **C-E** *J's Bay Hostel*, 7 Carlyle St, T6685 8853, jbay@nor.com.au, the very laid-back **C-E** *Byron Bay Bunkhouse*, 1 Carlyle St, T6685 8311, www.byronbay-bunkhouse.com.au, and the beachside **C-E** *Backpackers Inn*, 29 Shirley St, T668 58231, www.byron-bay.com/backpackersinn.

Motor parks The local council operate 4 local caravan parks. All are usually busy and should be booked well in advance. The most convenient to the town centre and Main Beach is the **L-E** *First Sun Holiday Park*, Lawson St (200 m west of the Main Beach Car Park), T6685 6544, www.bshp.com.au/first It offers a range of self-contained/standard cabins, powered and non-powered sites and camp kitchen. Further west, right beside Clark's Beach, is the **L-E** *Clark's Beach Caravan Park*, off Lighthouse Rd, T6685 6496. Again it offers self-contained and standard cabins, powered and shady non-powered sites, no camp kitchen just BBQs. Further afield and much quieter is the **L-E** *Broken Head Caravan Park*, Beach Rd, Broken Head (8 km), T6685 3245. Its appeal is its friendly atmosphere, beachside position and proximity to the Broken Head Nature Reserve. It has cabins, powered and non-powered sites, small shop, BBQ but no camp kitchen.

Expensive *Fins* at the Beach Hotel, T6685 5029, is a seafood restaurant specializing in fresh, organic produce. Open daily from 1830, bookings essential. The *Dish Restaurant and Raw Bar*, corner of Jonson St and Marvell St, T6685 7320, has innovative international and Australian cuisine. **Mid-range** For seafood the award-winning *Raving Prawn* in Feros Arcade, Jonson St, T6685 6737, is recommended (open Mon-Sat from 1800, daily in summer). For Asian *Oh Delhi Tandoori*, 4 Bay La (upstairs in the Bay Lane Arcade), T6680 8800 (open daily 1200-2200) and *Thai Lucy*, Bay La, T6680 8083 (open Mon-Sun 1200-1500 and 1730-2200), both offer excellent dishes, good value and lots of atmosphere, but book ahead. For breakfast, lunch and dinner the *Beach Hotel Bistro*, Bay La, never fails to lure in the crowds and wins hands down for atmosphere (open for lunch and dinner from 1200-2100). **Cheap** *Bay Kebabs* at the bottom of Bay La, T6685 5596, offers generous and good value kebabs. Open daily from 1000 until late. Backpacker specials (as little as $6) are regularly on offer at *Cheeky Monkey's*, 115 Jonson St, T6685 5886, in order to tempt you to stay late at the bar and nightclub (open from Mon-Sat, 1900-0300). For lots of atmosphere and something a little different, try the *Old Piggery* vegetarian wood-fired pizza restaurant ('noshery'), next door to the cinema and Arts Factory Backpackers, 1 Skinners Shoot Rd. Open daily from 1800. **Cafés** *Expresso Head*, 111 Jonson St, T6680 9783, has good coffee and is popular with the locals. Across the road the *Seven At 13*, T6685 7478, in the Woolies Plaza, Jonson St, offers pure, modern organic cuisine in a pleasant al fresco setting (open daily for breakfast, lunch and dinner). You will find a refreshing coffee and generous breakfasts at *Belongil Beach Café* on Childe St, T6685 7144 (open daily 0800-2200), and in the other direction, the *Beach Café*, Clarks Beach, T6685 7598. A little further still is the *Pass Café*, off Lighthouse Rd (end of Clark's Beach), T6685 6074.

Eating
●*On map*
Although Jonson St and the various arcades host some good restaurants and cafés most folk gravitate towards Bay La where you will find plenty of atmosphere

The huge bar at the *Beach Hotel*, T6685 6402, facing the beach off Bay St is the place to see and be seen and is popular both day and night, with the lively atmosphere often spilling out into the beer garden. Live bands Thu-Sun. *Cocomangas*, 32 Jonson St, has Retro 80s on Wed and Disco Funk and House on Sat. Open 2100-0300, free entry before 2330. There are 2 other nightclubs in The Plaza off Jonson St, with the rather tired and loud *Carpark Nightclub*, in The Plaza, Jonson St (open until 0300) and the far less frantic and congenial *Verve* Nightclub, internet café and bar, tucked in the corner, T6685 6170, www.vervenightclub.com.au The atmospheric and very comfortable *Pighouse Flicks*, Arts Factory, Gordon St (Via Butler), T6685 5828, www.piggery.com.au, acts as the local cinema showing both foreign, arts and mainstream films nightly. Meal/movie deals are available in unison with the Old Piggery vegetarian restaurant next door.

Entertainment
The best festival in Byron is the popular Blues and Roots Festival held every Easter weekend, www.blues fest.com.au

Byron offers a wealth of 'alternative' and arts/crafts oriented shops. For a lasting image of Byron, try John Derrey's photography work at *Byron Images*, corner Lawson St and Jonson St, T6685 8909, www.johnderry.com.au *Byron Bay Camping and Disposals*, Plaza, Jonson St, T6685 8085, can oblige should you need camping gear and supplies.

Shopping

Banks Most major branches with ATMs along Jonson or Lawsons St. Foreign Exchange is readily available including *Byron Foreign Exchange*, Shop 3/5-7 Byron St, T6685 7787. Open daily 0900-1800. **Car hire** *Byron Car Hire*, T6685 6345, from $40 per-day. *Byron Bus*, Transit Centre, T6685 5517. *Byron Odyssey*, T1800-771244, from $39 per-day. **Car servicing** *Bayside Mechanical*, 12 Banksia Dr, T6685 8455. **Communications** Interne *Global Gossip*, 84 Jonson St, T6680 9140. Open daily 0800-2400, or *Soundwaves*, 58 Jonson St. Open daily 0900-2100. **Post Office** 61 Jonston St. Open Mon-Fri 0900-1700. Postcode 2481. **Medical** *Byron Bay Hospital*, T6685 6200. **Police** Corner of Shirley St and Butler St, T6685 9499. **Travel Agents** *Backpackers World*, Shop 6 Byron St, T6685 8858. *Backpackers Travel Centre*, Cavanbah Arcade, Jonson St, T6685 7085. *Jetset Travel*, corner of Jonson St and Marvell St, T6685 6554.

Directory

New South Wales

New South Wales

Byron Lismore Hinterland

West of Byron Bay and the far north coast of New South Wales, the dramatic peak of Mount Warning lures the visitor inland. For others, the 'trip' inland is fuelled with the desire to experience that altogether different type of 'high' in a scattering of bohemian, arty villages, famous for their alternative lifestyle. This very pleasant, scenic area, often called the Northern Rivers, or, more aptly, the **Rainbow Region**, stretches from **Murwillumbah** in the north to **Kyogle** in the west, Lismore and **Ballina** in the south and Byron Bay on the coast to the east. While Byron serves as the most popular tourist destination, **Lismore** is the largest town and region's commercial capital, with the small villages of **Nimbin**, **Channon** and **Dunoon**, amongst others, providing the alternative edge. Geologically the region is dominated by the Mount Warning Shield **volcano** and its vast **Caldera** (crater), which is the largest of its type in the southern hemisphere. The huge volcano, which erupted about 23 million years ago, produced a flat shield-shaped landform with its highest point rising almost twice that of **Mount Warning** (1,157 m), which is all that remains today of the original magma chamber and central vent. The region is rich in dramatic geological features. Around the rim and fringing plateaus lush rainforest covered landscapes have risen form the ashes, while the floor of the Caldera acts as a vast watershed for the **Tweed River** that gives itself up to the ocean at the border of New South Wales and Queensland. There are nine **national parks** in the area, including Mount Warning and **Nightcap**, presenting some of the best scenery and walking opportunities.

Lismore
Colour map 3, grid B6
Population: 29,000
47 km west of Byron
Bay, 32 km south
of Nimbin

The attractive city of Lismore is the capital and commercial centre for the Northern Rivers (Rainbow) Region and far north New South Wales. Straddling the banks of the Richmond River, and hosting the Southern Cross University as well as a wealth of creative talent, Lismore offers a pleasant combination of rural beauty and youthful exuberance. It is also a fine base from which to explore the many outlying, **alternative lifestyle villages**, famous for their weekend **markets**, and some of the state's best **national parks**.

Getting there and around   Lismore **Airport**, T6622 2798, is located 2 km southwest of the city centre off the Bruxner Highway and is served from Sydney by *Hazelton Airlines*, T131713, www.hazelton.com.au The local and long-distance **bus** *Transit Centre* is on the corner of Molesworth St and Magellan St, T6621 8620 (open Mon-Fri 0730-1830, Sat 0730-1330, Sun 0730-0830/1600-1700). *Kirklands*, T6622 1499, www.kirklands.com.au, offer regular daily services locally and throughout the region, including Byron Bay and Brisbane. *McCafferty's/Greyhound* and *Premier Motor Service* offer daily interstate services between Sydney and Brisbane. The *Nimbin Byron Shuttle Bus*, T6680 9189, departs Lismore at 1100 and returns at 1500 ($16 return). Lismore's **train station** is across the river from the bus transit centre on Union St. *Countrylink* offer State-wide services including the fast XPT service to Sydney, with regional coach transfers/connections (including the Gold Coast).

   Information   The VIC is at the corner of Ballina St and Molesworth St, just south of the city centre, T6622 0122, www.liscity.nsw.gov.au Open Mon-Fri 0930-1600, Sat/Sun 1000-1500. The VIC also hosts the small but informative *Indoor Rainforest and Heritage Display*, $1. **Internet** is available at *Lismore Internet Services*, 4/172 Molesworth St, T6622 7766. Open Mon-Fri 0900-1700 or the *Lismore Regional Library*, Carrington St, T6621 2464. Open Mon-Wed 0930-1700, Thu/Fri 0930-1930, Sat 0900-1200. Bookings required.

Rainbow Region markets

⏪

*One of the great tourist attractions in the Rainbow Region are its colourful weekend markets that operate in a circuit throughout the region, primarily on Sundays. The **Byron Bay Market** is held in the Butler Street Reserve on the first Sunday of the month, T6687 7181.*

***Lismore** hosts a regional Organic Produce Market at the Lismore Showgrounds every Tuesday between 0700-1000, T6628 2391, there is a Car Boot Market at the Shopping Square on the first and third Sunday of the month, T6628 7333, and the Lismore Showground Markets every second Sunday, T662 28028. The excellent **Channon Craft Market** kicks off in Coronation Park on the second Sunday, T6688 6433, while the Aquarius Fair Markets, in **Nimbin** (Cullen Street) are on the third and fifth Sunday, T6689 1183. The **Bangalow Village Market** held in the local showgrounds on the fourth Sunday is also worth a visit, T6687 1911. The regional VICs list additional venues.*

The **Lismore Regional Art Museum** is one of the oldest in the State and is housed in the 1908 art nouveau Trench Building, 131 Molesworth Street. It showcases permanent international, Australian and local collections as well as a diverse range of travelling exhibitions. ■ *Tue-Fri 1000-1600, Sat/Sun 1030-1430, donation, T6622 2209.* There are several attractive nature reserves in the area many of which contain the last remnants of the 'Big Scrub' – the collective name given to the extensive rainforest that once dominated the region – as well as some interesting fauna. The **Boat Harbour Nature Reserve** (6 km northeast on the Bangalow Road) is a fine example and also supports a colony of flying foxes (fruit bats), while The **Tucki Tucki** Nature Reserve, 15 km south on Wyrallah Road, has the added attraction of a thriving colony of koalas. Late afternoon is the best time to view them in the wild. The '*M.V. Bennelong*' offers an interesting range of scenic and historical **cruises** on both the Richmond and Wilson Rivers with a 3½-hour lunch cruise (1100-1430), from $35, child $17.50 and a day long cruise, downstream to Ballina (1000-1700), from $70, child $35, T6688 8266.

Sleeping and eating   C-E *Currendina Lodge*, 14 Ewing St (just east of the CBD), T6621 6118, currendi@nor.com.au, serves as the local friendly backpackers, offering tidy dorms, singles, doubles and family rooms with all the standard amenities and courtesy pick-ups. There are 4 caravan parks in and around town with the **C-F** *Lismore Palms*, 42-58 Brunswick St (northern, Bangalow Rd approach), T6621 7067, being the best facilitated with cabins, on-site vans, powered and non-powered sites, pool and camp kitchen. If you like Japanese food try the award-winning *Café Millennium*, 78 Uralba St, T6622 0925. Open lunch Tue-Fri 1130-1430, dinner Wed-Sat from 1800, BYO. *Hector's Place*, 34 Molesworth St, T6621 6566, is in a fine spot overlooking the river and offering modern Australian (open lunch Tue-Fri 1200-1400, dinner Tue-Sat from 1800), while for traditional Irish pub-grub amidst a congenial friendly atmosphere, try *Mary Gilhooley's* on the corner of Keen St and Woodlark St, T6622 2924 (open for lunch and dinner Mon-Sat). If that is too expensive try the more traditional *Northern Rivers Hotel*, 33 Terania St, T66215797.

Up until the 1970s, the sleepy, dairy village of Nimbin had changed little since its inception by the first European settlers over a century before. Then, in 1973 the Australian Union of Students (AUS) chose the Nimbin Valley as the venue for the 'experimental and alternative' **Aquarius Festival**. The concept was to create 'a total cultural experience, through the lifestyle of participation' for Australian creatives, students and **alternative lifestylers**. Nimbin never

Nimbin
Population: 300
70 km from Byron Bay,
384,000 km from the moon

got over the invasion and its more enlightened long-term residents have been joined by a veritable army of society's drop-outs, man. The **Nimbin Tourist Connexion** at the northern end of Cullen Street acts as the local VIC. It offers bus, train and accommodation bookings, has internet access and village maps, T6689 1764. ■ *Mon-Fri 1000-1700, Sat 1200-1430, Sun 1000-1700.*

The colourful main street of Nimbin (Cullen Street), is the single collective 'sight' in the village. Amidst a rash of laid-back cafés, alternative health and arts and craft shops, is the 'must-see' **Nimbin Museum** which presents a truly original, creative, historical and often humorous interpretation of the village, its inhabitants and Australia as a whole. ■ *0900-1700 daily, $2 donation,* T6689 1123, *62 Cullen St.* On the other side of Cullen Street, the loudly advertised **Hemp Embassy** is also worth a look. ■ *Free, T6689 1842.* As well as supporting the multifarious uses of hemp, the Nimbin Valley is also well known for fruit growing and permaculture. For the visitor the **Djanbung Gardens Permaculture Centre** offers garden tours, herbal crafts, environmental workshops and an organic café. ■ *Daily 1000-1200, Tue-Fri 1000-1500 (tours Tue/Thu 1030, Sat 1100), T6689 1755. 74 Cecil St.*

Sleeping and eating Nimbin is a popular haunt for backpackers keen to experience the spirit of Nimbin and you are invited to 'Live the Nimbin Dream' at the good value and suitably laid-back **C-F** *Rainbow Retreat Backpackers*, 75 Thorburn St, T6689 1262, www.skybusiness.com/rainbowretreat Not surprisingly, it provides a range of highly unconventional accommodation options from Malay-style huts to VW Kombis, dorms and secluded campsites, all set in a quiet 18-acre site near the edge of the village. Both the facilities and atmosphere are excellent with regular musical jam sessions, visiting chefs, $5 meals, international and alternative practitioners and performers, not to mention the odd platypus in the creek or harmless python up a tree. Overall, it provides the ideal way to experience the true spirit of Nimbin. *Peterpan* in Byron provide free transport, T1800 252 459. Recommended. The **C-F** *Nimbin Caravan and Tourist Park*, 29 Sibley St, T6689 1402, has basic facilities, on-site vans, powered and non-powered sites, within easy walking distance of the village. Cullen Street hosts a number of alternative eateries with the *Rainbow Café* being the oldest. The *Bush Theatre*, T6685 5074, located at the northern end of Cullen St is another popular venue, combining a cinema and a café and offering the occasional good value movie/meal deal. Open Fri/Sat 1930, Sun 1830.

Transport If you are based in Byron Bay, the best way to see the village and its surrounds is to join one of the various day-tour operators. The *Grasshoppers Nimbin Eco-Explorer Tour*, run by Rockhoppers, T0500 881 881 (from $35), is recommended. Other operators include *Jim's Alternative Tours*, T6685 7720, and *Mick's Bay and Bush Tours*, T6685 6889. The *Nimbin Byron Shuttle Bus*, T6680 9189, operates Mon-Sat, departing from Jonson St Byron Bay at 1000, returning at 1430, from $25 return.

Nightcap National Park & the Whian Whian State Forest

Colour map 3, grid B6
50 km northeast of Lismore, 40 km west of Byron Bay
Nightcap National Park receives the highest mean rainfall in the State

The world heritage 8,145-ha Nightcap National Park is located on the southern rim of the Mount Warning shield volcano caldera, northeast of Lismore and west of Byron Bay. Adjacent is the Whian Whian State Forest Park. Combined the two present a wealth of volcanic features including massifs, pinnacles and cliffs eroded by spectacular waterfalls and draped in lush rainforest. Some unique wildlife also resides in the park including the red-legged pademelon (a kind of wallaby), the Fleay's barred frog and the appealingly named wompoo fruit-dove. The main physical features of the park are **Mount Nardi** (800 m), which is 12 km east of Nimbin; Terania Creek and the **Protestors Falls** 14 km north of The Channon and the Whian Whian State Forest and the 100-m **Minyon Falls**, 23 km southwest of Mullumbimby. The 30 km **Whian Whian**

Scenic Drive (unsealed), which can be accessed beyond the Minyon Falls, traverses the forest park and takes visitors through varied rainforest vegetation and scenery including the memorable **Peates Mountain Lookout**.

Popular long walking tracks include the moderate to hard, 7½-km, **Minyon Loop**, which starts from the Minyon Falls Picnic Area and takes in the base of the falls and the escarpment edge, and the moderate to hard, 16-km, **Historic Nightcap Track**, which follows the former pioneer trails between Lismore and Mullumbimby. Other, shorter and easier possibilities are the 3-km **Mount Matheson Loop** and 4-km **Pholis Gap** walks, which both start from Mount Nardi, and the 1½-km **Big Scrub Loop** which starts from the Gibbergunyah Range Road in Whian Whian State Forest. It is said to contain some of the best remnant rainforest in the region. The **Protestors Falls** (named after a successful six-week protest to prevent logging in the late 1970s) are reached on a 1½-km return track from the Terania Creek Picnic Area. **Camping** is available at Rummery Park, 2 km north of the Minyon Falls, T6662 4499.

The little village of Mullumbimby offers a fine stop or diversion on the way to Lismore, Minyon Falls or the Nightcap National Park. The **Crystal Castle** south of Mullumbimby on Monet Drive has a fine display of natural crystals, gardens and a café, as well as crystal healing, a tarot card reading or massage. ■ *Daily 1000-1630, free, T6684 1196, www.crystalcastle.net.au* The friendly, basic **F** *Maca's Camp Ground* is 12 km west of Mullumbimby amidst rainforest and a macadamia nut orchard (free nuts to campers!), T668 45211.

Mullumbimby
Population: 2,900
18 km northwest
of Byron Bay

Other than its stunning scenery and rich flora and fauna, the great lure of Mount Warning is the pilgrimage **summit walk** to see the first rays of sunlight to touch the Australian mainland. The moderate to hard, 4.4-km ascent starts from the Breakfast Creek Picnic Area, 17 km southwest of Murwillumbah, at the terminus of Mount Warning Rd (6 km). To ensure you reach the summit for **sunrise** you are advised to set off about 2½ hours beforehand. For the less energetic the **Lyrebird Track** crosses Breakfast Creek before winding 200 m through palm forest to a rainforest platform. To learn more about the Aboriginal mythology surrounding the mountain and its diverse wildlife, you might like to join either the sunrise or daytime summit walking **tours** on offer from Byron Bay. Access to the park is via Mount Warning Road, 11 km south of Murwillumbah on the main Kyogle Rd. Camping is available at the privately run **B-E** *Mt Warning Caravan Park* about 3 km up Mount Warning Road, T6679 5120. It has cabins, on-site vans, powered and non-powered sites and a camp kitchen.

Mount Warning National Park
Colour map 3, grid B6
17 km west of
Murwillumbah,
80 km north
of Lismore
Mount Warning was
named by Captain
Cook in 1770 to warn
mariners of the
dangers of the
approaching
Barrier Reef

The pleasant, sugar cane town of Murwillumbah sits on the banks of the **Tweed River**, roughly half way between Byron Bay and the Queensland border at Tweed Heads and at the eastern edge of the vast **Mount Warning** shield volcano caldera. It serves as the gateway to the Northern Rivers (or Rainbow) Region with its villages famed for their alternative lifestylers and superb **national parks**, including Mount Warning, Nightcap, Lamington, Springbrook and the Border Ranges. For many the main attraction is the dawn ascent of Mount Warning. The **VIC** shares its office with the NPWS and the **World Heritage Rainforest Centre**, on the corner of Pacific Highway and Alma Street, T6672 1340. Combined they offer insight and information surrounding the region and the parks. ■ *Mon-Sat 0900-1630, Sun 0930-1600.* Most folk 'head for the hills', but if you can spare an hour or so the small **Tweed Regional Art Gallery**, on Tumbulgum Road is worth a look. ■ *Wed-Sun 1000-1700, T6670 2790.* **RitzRail** T1300-795795, www.ritzrail.com.au, offer a range of

Murwillumbah
Colour map 3, grid A6
Population: 8,000
35 km south of Tweed
Heads, 49 km
north of Byron Bay

standard and luxury train trips to Byron Bay and Lismore. The Blue Ribbon Byron Bay Explorer combines a scenic rail journey and coach tour of Byron.
■ *Departs Murwillumbah Mon/Tue/Thu, from $90,child $35.*

Sleeping and eating The award-winning **LL** *Crystal Creek Rainforest Retreat*, Brookers Rd, T6679 1591, www.crystalcreekrainforestretreat.com.au, is located on the edge of the Numinbah Nature Reserve about 23 km west of Murwillumbah, is excellent, with 7 well-appointed self-contained bungalows, spa baths, excellent cuisine, local forest walks and even the odd hammock across the creek. Transfers from Murwillumbah are by arrangement. Recommended. In Murwillumbah itself is the historic **C-E** *Mt Warning/Murwillumbah YHA*, 1 Tumbulgum Rd (first right across the bridge, 200 m, directly across the river from the VIC), T6672 3763, mbahyha@norex.com.au Relaxing, friendly and homely place next to the river and overlooking Mt Warning. Dorms and double/twins, free use of canoes and transport to Mt Warning if you stay 2 nights. If you intend to climb Mt Warning campers or campervans are well accommodated at the **B-E** *Mt Warning Caravan Park* (see Mt Warning NP above). The *Imperial Hotel*, on the Main St offers value pub-style lunches and dinners.

Transport Northbound buses and trains stop in Murwillumbah. The **train station** is opposite the VIC and is served by *Countrylink*, T132232. Long distance and local **bus** company *Kirklands*, T1300-367077, and interstate *McCafferty's/Greyhound* stop outside *Tweed Valley Travel*, corner of Main St and Queen St, T6672 1031.

New England

Despite the many English place names and the cool, 'un-Australian' climate, with its resultant, vivid autumnal colours, New England is as Australian as Uluru or the Opera House. From the industrial city of **Newcastle** *the Hunter River becomes more and more scenic, with rolling hills draped in vineyards backed by wilderness forest, given over to the vast* **Wollombi National Park**. *The* **Lower Hunter Valley** *is home to dozens of* **wineries**, *which provide one of the finest 'winery' experiences in the world. Beyond the Hunter Valley the New England Highway turns north and vineyards give way to* **horse studs** *surrounding the pleasant country town of* **Scone**, *Australia's capital for all things equestrian and the western gateway to the* **Barrington Tops National Park**. *It's all ten-gallon stetsons and cowboy boots in* **Tamworth**, *the extraordinary* **Country and Western** *music capital of Australia. Having picked a fine time to leave Tamworth, you head north, past the former haunts and hunting grounds of bushranger (highwayman)* **Captain Thunderbolt** *towards* **Armidale**, *a pleasant historic town and the perfect base to explore the waterfalls and views of the* **Oxley Rivers** *and* **New England National Park**. *North of Armidale place names like Glencoe and Ben Lomond attest to the region's strong Scottish links, celebrated and maintained in the historic town of* **Glen Innes**.

Hunter Valley

Colour map 3, grid C4
The best time to visit is perhaps in autumn for the colours. Try to aim for midweek, when accommodation is cheaper. Feb-Mar is harvest time

For most people, the Hunter River Valley is synonymous with **world-class vineyards** and fine wine, though, ironically, the true heritage of the Hunter is **coal**, which was extracted from the region's rich subterranean seams as early as 1801. In fact the Hunter River was originally called **Coal River**, before being renamed along with the valley in 1797 in honour of John Hunter the then Governor of NSW. Wine has been the region's raison d'etre since the first tentative attempts at grape-growing in the 1830's. The climate and the soils proved ideal and the region has never really looked back. Now there are over **100 vineyards** in the region, producing mainly shiraz, semillons and chardonnays, and ranging from large scale producers and internationally recognized labels, to low-key boutiques.

Getting there The nearest major **airport** is in Newcastle (see page 137). Newcastle-based *Hunter Valley Shuttles*, T4936 2488, or *All Travel Connections*, T4955 6777, offer shuttle services from the airport to Hunter Valley. *Coastal Air Services*, T1800-262782, www.coastalairservices.com.au, also operate a fleet of amphibious aircraft from Sydney (or coast) to the Hunter Valley. Long distance **coach** companies *MaCafferty's/Greyhound* and *Keans*, T4990 5000, stop at all major towns along the New England Highway, with daily services from Sydney. *Rover Coaches*, 231 Vincent St, Cessnock, T4990 1699, offer services between Newcastle and Cessnock. The nearest **train station** is Maitland which links with Newcastle and Sydney's *Cityrail* services. *Countrylink* offer state-wide services to Queensland via Scone.

    Getting around Organized tours are by far the best way to visit the vineyards (see below). A good alternative is by bike. You can secure independent hire with *Grapemobile*, corner of McDonalds Rd and Palmers La, Pokolbin, T0500-804039, from $30 per day. *Vineyard Shuttle Service*, T4998 7779, based in Cessnock, offer local **transfers** or call a conventional **taxi**, T4990 1111.

    Orientation and Information The Hunter Valley is 2 distinct regions, the **Lower Hunter Valley** and the **Upper Hunter Valley,** with the vast majority of vineyards (over 80) being located in the Lower region. Both are bisected by the **Hunter River** and the New England Highway that heads west (then north) off the Sydney/Newcastle Freeway and Pacific Highway near Newcastle. The Lower Hunter Valley encompasses a region extending from Newcastle on the coast, through **Maitland**, to **Singleton**, with **Cessnock** to the south, considered the 'capital' of the Lower Hunter's vineyards. The Upper Hunter Valley vineyards extend from Singleton to **Scone** with most centred around **Denman** and **Musswellbrook** and are all comprehensively signposted around Cessnock. You are strongly advised to pick up the free detailed maps from the VIC. The principal VIC is the newly located **Hunter Valley (Wine Country Tourism) Visitors Information Centre**, Allendale Rd (next to Cessnock Airport, 2 km north of the town centre), T4990 4477, www.winecountry.com.au Open Mon-Fri 0900-1700, Sat 0930-1700, Sun 0930-1530. They are well set up to provide detailed vineyards information as well as accommodation and tour bookings. To get started, pick up a copy of the free and comprehensive **Visitors Guide** and **Regional Map**. Other local VICs in the region include **Maitland**, corner of High St and New England Highway, T1300-652320, www.visitmaitland.com.au (open daily 0900-1700) **Singleton**, 33 George St, T6571 5888 (open Mon-Fri 0900-1700, Sat/Sun 0930-1630), and, in the Upper Hunter, **Muswellbrook**, 87 Hill St, T6541 4050, www.muswellbrook.org.au (open daily 0900-1700). For information on Wollemi National Park contact the **NPWS**, 137 Kelly St, Scone, T6545 9588, or **Bulga**, T6574 5275.

Lower Hunter Valley
The VIC has comprehensive details (including regional maps)

With over 60 vineyards in the Lower Hunter choosing which to visit is not easy. It's best to mix some of the large, long-established wineries and labels with the smaller boutique affairs. But though many of the 'big guns' are well worth a visit, you will find a more, relaxed and personalized service at the smaller establishments. The following are recommended and often considered the 'must-sees' but by no means is it a comprehensive list. Of the large long-established vineyards (over a century) **Tyrells**, **Draytons** and **Tullochs** (all in Pokolbin), are all recommended, providing fine wine and insight into the actual winemaking process. **Lindemans** and **McGuigans** (again in Pokolbin) and **Wyndhams** in Branxton, are three of the largest and most well-known labels in the region, offering fine vintages and a broad range of facilities. McGuigans and Wyndhams also offer guided tours. Of the smaller boutique wineries **Oakvale**, **Tamburlaine** and **Pepper Tree** (with its class restaurant and former convent guesthouse an added attraction) are also recommended. Then, for a fine view as well as vintage, head for the **Audrey Wilkinson Vineyard**, DeBeyers Rd, Pokolbin.

It seems no vineyard region comes complete without colourful **hot air balloons** gently drifting above the vines and the Hunter is no exception. There are three companies all offering competitive prices and sunrise flights, usually with about one hour in the air and a cooked breakfast and champagne inclusive of the price. *Balloon Aloft*, based in Rothbury, have been adding colour to the skies for over 20 years, T4938 1955, from around $225 ($250 at weekends). If this is too mundane, then try a **tandem skydive**. *Hunter Valley Tandem Skydiving*, T4990 1000, www.tandemskydive.com, can oblige, from around $275 (budget accommodation also available). Other regional activities on offer include abseiling, ATV safaris, **horse trekking**, wildlife tours and even **rally driving**. If you get sick of wine, then there's the **Hunter Valley Chocolate Company**, Shop 5 Hunter Valley Gardens Village, Pokolbin, T4998 7221 (■ *Daily 0930-1730*), or the **Hunter Valley Cheese Factory**, McGuigans Wine Hall, McDonald's Road, Pokolbin, T4998 7744 (■ *Daily 0900-1700*).

There are dozens of B&Bs, guesthouses, self-contained cottages and restaurants set amongst the vineyards, mainly around Pokolbin and Rothbury. Prices tend to increase at weekends, on public holidays and during special events. If you want to avoid driving between your accommodation and restaurant Vineyard Shuttle Service, T4998 7779/ T4991 3655, can oblige

Sleeping and eating The following establishments are considered just a few of the 'Hunter classics' or are listed for being unusual or convenient. The **LL** *Peppers Convent*, Halls Rd, Pokolbin, T4998 7764, www.peppers.com.au, is a renovated convent, with 17 rooms all beautifully appointed with a tariff to match. It also has all the usual extras, including pool, spa and the obligatory open fires. Nearby, is the rustic, and equally expensive *Robert's Restaurant*, T4998 7330, www.robertsatpeppertree.com.au (open daily for lunch and dinner, bookings essential). It is considered by many to be the best in the region. Not to be confused with the Peppers Convent, is the equally delightful **LL** *Peppers Guesthouse*, Ekerts Rd, T4998 7596, www.peppers.com.au It too is a stone's throw from a popular, top-class restaurant the *Chez Pok*, T4998 7596, offering local fare with a French, Asian and Italian edge. Open daily for breakfast, lunch and dinner, again, bookings essential. The **LL** *Casuarina Restaurant and Country Inn*, Hermitage Rd, T4998 7888, www.casuarina-group.com.au, combines fine accommodation with fine dining. It offers 9 exquisite, beautifully appointed, themed suites from the 'French Bordello' to the 'British Empire'. The restaurant offers superb cuisine with a Mediterranean/Asian focus (open daily for dinner, bookings essential). Slightly more down to earth is the **LL** *Hunter Valley Gardens Lodge and Harrigan's Irish Pub and Accommodation*, corner of Broke Rd and McDonald's Rd, T4998 7600, www.hgv.com.au, offering excellent suites and guest rooms, with all facilities, including, of course, a fine pint of Guinness. There is then a choice of the à la carte *Seasons Restaurant* (open daily) or the 'cook your own' Australian fare BBQ or wood-fired pizzas in the pub. Nearby, *The Cellar Restaurant*, Broke Rd, T4998 7584 (open daily for lunch, Mon-Sat for dinner), is also highly regarded. If you love horses as well as wine and want to combine trekking with comfortable, value, 'Barnstay' accommodation, the **B** *Wollombi Horse Riding and Barnstay*, Singleton Rd, T4998 3221, can oblige. Of the lowly, much maligned motels in the region **LL-L** *The Hunter Country Lodge*, 220 Cessnock-Branxton Rd, North Rothbury, T4938 1744, www.hunter countrylodge.com.au, is a quirky motel/restaurant combo. The unusual and colourfully decorated *Shakey Tables Restaurant* adds to the charm (open daily). In and around Cessnock some of the old traditional hotel/pubs can offer attractive rates, perfectly comfortable accommodation and value dining, including the **A-B** *Bellbird Hotel*, 388 Wollombi Rd, T4990 1094, www.bellbird.com **L-E** *Valley Vineyard Tourist Park*, Mount View Rd (2 km west of Cessnock town centre), T4990 2573, is the best of the motor parks, with a range of cabins, powered and non-powered sites, pool and camp kitchen.

Events and festivals The highlight of the Hunter's busy events calendar is the wonderfully hedonistic and convivial *Lovedale Long Lunch*, held over a weekend every **May**. Other events include the musical extravaganzas of the *Jazz in the Vines* Festival and *Opera in the Vines*, both held in **Oct**.

Beyond Singleton, the delights of the Lower Hunter's vineyards gives way to the more traditional rural landscapes of the Upper Hunter Valley, dotted with unsightly coalmines and electricity pylons. Thankfully, once you roll into **Denman** or **Musswellbrook**, the historic and congenial atmosphere returns and vineyards once again dominate the landscape. There are about a dozen wineries in the Upper Hunter with **Arrowfield** (between Denman and Jerry's Plains, T6576 4041, www.arrowfieldwines.com.au), and **Rosemount**, (Rosemount Road, near Denman, T6549 6450), being the oldest and most highly regarded. Both are fine labels and offer daily tastings. The *Rosemount Restaurant* is also highly regarded. ■ *Open Tue-Sun for lunch and morning teas, T6547 2310.* Other notable vineyards include **Reynolds**, Yarraman Road, T6547 8052, www.reynoldswine.com.au, and **Cruickshanks**, 2656 Wybong Road, T6547 8149, www.cruickshanks.com.au, both in Wybong.

Upper Hunter Valley
The VICs in Cessnock or Musswellbrook can provide all the information, the maps and have full accommodation listings

Dubbed the 'horse capital of Australia', Scone (pronounced 'Scoon') is surrounded by over 65 studs. Every year the town hosts the **Scone Horse Festival** each May. This busy 10-day event incorporates a busy program of events, including local parades celebrating the heritage of the horse in Australia, stud sales and the prestigious **Scone Cup**, a race that sees the regional best running in 'the richest day of racing in rural NSW', with over $400,000 worth in prize money. Half- or full-day **stud tours** are available with *Upper Hunter Tours*, T6547 2442, www.upperhuntertours.com.au (historical homestead and winery tours are also available). The really adventurous might like to try an eight-day **cattle drive** with *Mountain Cattle Drives*, Guy Gallen, T6546 5246, cattle@trendnet.com.au, from $499. The town is also often used as a base from which to explore the **Barrington Tops National Park** (50 km to the east) and the more low-key wineries of the Upper Hunter Valley. Some 20 km north of the town the **Burning Mountain Nature Reserve** has a subterranean coal seam that has been steadily burning for over 5,000 years. Directions and detailed information, including a 3½-km self-guided walks leaflet is available from the VIC. The helpful **VIC** is at the northern end of the town, on the left, just off Kelly Street (corner of Susan Street), T6545 1526, www.horsecapital.com.au ■ *Daily 0900-1700.* The *Scone Cyber Centre*, T6545 3703, offers internet access and is housed in the same building with the same opening hours.

Scone
Colour map 3, grid C4
Population: 3,500
270 km north of Sydney, 696 km south of Brisbane
For information about the annual horse festival, visit, www.sconehorse festival.com
For national parks information, T6543 3533

Sleeping The VIC can provide full accommodation listings. The modern and very classy **LL-L** *LeCamah Hill Guesthouse*, Bunnan Rd (10 km), T6545 1181, www.lecamah.com.au, offers peace and quiet, luxury king-sized suites, cabins with shared facilities and fine dining. The friendly **C-E** *Scone YHA*, 1151 Segenhoe Rd (from Scone follow Gundy Rd southeast off Kelly, 9 km), T6545 2072, provides congenial budget accommodation in a former schoolhouse. Dorms and 2 double/family rooms, well-equipped kitchen and comfy lounge, free eggs for brekkie, no internet. There are 3 basic motor parks in Scone, including the **C-F** *Scone Caravan Park*, 50 Kelly St (northern end of town), T6545 2024. Basic cabins, en suite powered and non-powered sites, no camp kitchen.

Transport Long distance **coaches** stop outside *Harvey World Travel*, on Kelly St (166), T6545 1855. They also act as booking agents. *McCafferty's/Greyhound* operate daily services to and from Sydney and Brisbane along the New England Highway.

New South Wales

Keans Coaches, T1800-043339, run a service from Scone to Port Macquarie and Coffs Harbour (via the Waterfall Way and Dorrigo/Bellingen) 3 times a week, Mon/Wed/Fri, returning Tue/Thu/Sun. The **train station** is located on Susan St, around the corner from the VIC. *Countrylink*, T132232, offer daily services to Tamworth and Sydney.

Tamworth

Colour map 3, grid B4
Population: 32,000
414 km north of Sydney, 573 km south of Brisbane

Tamworth is a legend in its own cowboy boots. It is Australia's equivalent to Nashville and the country's much celebrated capital of **Country and Western** (C&W) music. Every January the city hosts the **Australian Country Music Festival**, a mighty 10-day event that also incorporates Australia Day celebrations and sees the population of Tamworth swelling to almost 200,000. A time for locals and visitors alike to don their ten gallon hats and tasselled suede jackets and to 'line-dance' the nights away and whoop and holler in appreciation of the recipients of the much lauded **Golden Guitar Awards**. The **VIC** is on the corner of Peel Street and Murray Street, T6755 4300, www.tamworth. nsw.gov.au (■ Open Mon-Fri 0830-1635, Sat/Sun 0900-1700).

Just behind the **Giant Golden Guitar** on the southern approach to the city (New England Highway) is the **Golden Guitar and Gallery of Stars Wax Museum** – Tamworth's tribute to its C&W heritage. At the rear of the complex is the souvenir hub of the town. A place where you can purchase everything from the latest C&W hit CDs to ten-gallon hats and even ten-gallon boxer shorts. Adjacent to the shop is the wax work museum where well-known stars croon with joy, guitars in hand. This is tourist kitsch at its very best (or worst) but worth a look. ■ *Daily 0900-1700, $6, child $4, T6765 2688, www.big.goldenguitar.com.au* The VIC can provide an official 4.7-km **Heritage Walks** leaflet. The **Australian Country Music Foundation Museum** serves as the repository for the nation's contribution to C&W with displays about home grown 'legends' and a photographic account of the Golden Guitar Awards. A small theatre also screens historic Aussie videos and performances. ■ *Mon-Sat 1000-1400, $5.50, child $3.30, T6766 9696. 96 Brisbane St.*

Tamworth also acts as the gateway to that unique form of Aussie education – the **Jackeroo** and **Jilleroo Schools**. A multi-day residential course will have you riding a mount like The Man from Snowy River, shearing a sheep, mustering stock, cracking a whip, 'swinging a Billy' and castrating a bull in no time. And those are just a few of the daytime activities. A minimum five-day course costs around $375 (11-day $650). The YHA (see below) is a fine place to enquire and they can also act as the staging point to the various operators. For a broad based **city tour** not necessarily over-burdened with C&W, try *Keith's Tam Tours*, half or full day, T6765 5896.

Sleeping *If you intend visiting the city for, or during the festival, you must book well in advance (sometimes even years)* Although not the most luxurious pad in town, the famous **L-A** *Alandale Motel*, corner of New England Highway (6 km south of city centre), T6765 7922, has a swimming pool shaped like a guitar with a base displaying the Australian flag. The **LL-L** *Powerhouse Boutique Hotel*, Armidale Rd (New England Highway), T6766 7000, www.powerhousehotel.com.au, is considered the most luxurious modern motel/hotel in the town, with deluxe suites, and serviced apartments, licensed restaurant, pool, spa, sauna and gym. If you are travelling alone the more traditional **C** *Tamworth Hotel*, 147 Marius St, T6766 2923, offers convenience and value with a historical edge, they only offer single rooms. The VIC has listings for the numerous B&Bs in and around town. One of the best and most centrally placed however is **LL-L** *Beethoven's B&B*, a restored and renovated heritage home at 66 Napier St, T6766 2735. The only backpackers in the city is the spotless, no-nonsense **C-E** *Country Backpackers Hostel (YHA)*, 169 Marius St (opposite the train station), T6761 2600. It is a little lacking in character, but the owners are caring and it is perfectly comfortable with dorms, double/twins and family rooms, internet and free breakfast. The hostel also serves as a staging post to the various Jackeroo and Jilleroo Schools. No bookings available during the C&W Festival and certainly not a party hostel. There are 2 good motor parks in town, the **B-E** *Austin Tourist Park*, Armidale Rd (4 km southeast of the city centre), T6766 2380, and the **B-E** *Paradise Caravan Park*, next to the VIC on Peel St, T6766 3120. Both have cabins, powered and non-powered sites, a pool, kiosk and BBQs, but no camp kitchen.

Eating For the full 18 oz try the themed *Stetson's Steakhouse and Saloon BBQ*, Craigends La, T6762 2238. Open Mon-Sun from 1800. Tamworth has 2 very 'Sydney-style' cafés: The *Old Vic* , 261 Peel St, T6766 3435 (open Mon-Wed 0730-1800, Thu-Sat 0730-2200, Sun 1000-1600), serves fine light meals and coffee, while the *Inland Café* , 407 Peel St, T6761 2882, is similar but also serves a good breakfast and dinner. Open Mon-Wed 0700-1800, Thu-Sat 0700-2300, Sun 0900-1700. For good coffee and a quick surf of the web try *The Coffee Bean* , Shop 18, Tamworth Arcade, Peel St, T6766 3422. Open 0900-1700. *Cha, Cha, Cha Restaurant*, Jenkins St Guesthouse, in the former gold mining town of Nundle (56 km southwest), T6769 3026. Open lunch Sat/Sun, dinner Thu-Sat). A regional favourite. For cheap counter meals try the various traditional pubs, including the historic *Tamworth Hotel*, Marlus St, T6766 2923 (open lunch Mon-Sun, dinner Thu-Sat, from 1830-2130). Coles supermarket is located in the K-Mart Plaza, corner of Peel St and White St. Open late daily except Sat/Sun.

Entertainment The hub of year-round C&W live entertainment is the *Tamworth RSL*, Kable Av, T6766 4661, offering a weekly C&W jamboree every Thu, plus live music Fri/Sat/Sun. *The Pub*, on the corner of Gunnedah Rd and Dampier St, also hosts live bands on Fri. Younger folk generally focus their attentions on the *Imperial Hotel*,on the corner of Marius St and Brisbane St. For the latest entertainment listings contact the VIC.

Transport Tamworth **Airport** is located 7 km west of the city centre along the Oxley Highway. Since the loss of Impulse Airlines check with the VIC for latest service providers. Long distance **coaches** stop at the VIC. *McCafferty's/Greyhound* offer daily services to and from Sydney, Brisbane and Dubbo. *Keans*, T1800-043339, offer services to Port Macquarie and Coffs Harbour (via Armidale and the Waterfall Way) on Mon/Wed/Fri, returning Tue/Thu/Sun. *Harvey World Travel*, Shop 1, 445 447 Peel St, T6766 1277, act as local **booking agents**. The **train station** is off Marius St, just to the northwest of the city centre. *Countrylink* have a travel office at the station, T6766 2357 (Reservations T132232). Open Mon-Fri 0830-1730, Sat 0830-1200. *Hannafords Coaches*, 15 Stewart Av, T6765 9596, offer local bus services (timetables and route maps from the VIC). **Taxi**, T6766 1111.

Directory Most major **bank** branches with ATMs are located along Peel St. *The Travel Group*, 402A Peel St (next to the PO) offer currency exchange, T6766 6344. **Car hire** *Budget*, on the corner of White St and Marius St, T132727, *Avis*, T6760 7404. **Communications** Internet *Coffee Bean*, Shop 18, Tamworth Arcade, Peel St, T6766 3422, or the city library, 203 Marius St, T6755 4457. **Post Office** The Clock Tower, on the corner of Peel St and Fitzroy St. Open Mon-Fri 0900-1700.

Located in the heart of the New England Tablelands and dubbed Australia's highest city (980 m), Armidale possesses an unusually cool climate and is subsequently best known for its distinct seasons and **autumn colours**, as well as its gracious **historical buildings**. The **Autumn Festival** in April is, literally, the city's most colourful event. Unlike many other regional centres located between the classical 'outback' and the coast, Armidale successfully maintains a lively cultural scene greatly energized by the youthful and academic influences of the

Armidale
Colour map 3, grid B5
Population: 25,000
567 km north of Sydney, 467 km south of Brisbane

New South Wales

city's **New England University**, established in 1838. The **VIC** is at the main bus terminal, 82 Marsh Street, T1800 627 736, www.new-england.org/armidale/ ■ *Open Mon-Fri 0900-1700, Sat 0900-1600, Sun 1000-1600.* Their free Visitor Guide has city and regional maps. The VIC and **NPWS**, 85-87 Faulkner Street, 6776 0000, can supply national parks information. The two-hour **Heritage Trolley Tour** on one of the city's original, restored electric trolley buses proves a popular way to see some of the major historical sights. ■ *It departs from the VIC at 1000 Mon-Fri and 1030 Sat/Sun, donation. Book at the VIC.* Armidale is also the perfect base from which to explore several excellent **national parks** (see next page).

Sleeping and eating The VIC has full listings of the many motels and B&Bs in the region. The centrally located, heritage listed (1918) **LL-L** *Lindsay House*, 128 Faulkner St, T6771 4554, www.lindsayhouse.com.au, is the most up-market B&B in the region, furnished with period French and Victorian furniture and offering 8 luxury suites and a licensed restaurant. The slightly cheaper **L** *Comeytrowe B&B*, 184 Marsh St, T6772 5869, is another fine B&B and heritage-listed home, close to all amenities. On the eastern fringe of the city, the **A-E** *Pembroke Tourist and Leisure Park*, 39 Waterfall Way, T6772 6470, doubles as a YHA with a rather characterless bunkhouse, but the full use of park facilities makes up for it. Doubles housed in on-site vans. There are also standard cabins, shaded en suite, powered and non-powered sites, camp kitchen and internet. Besides the **Beardy St Mall**, there is not a huge amount of choice in and around Armidale. The *Deer Park Motor Inn*, 72 Glen Innes Rd, T6772 9999 (closed Sun), or the *Moore Park Inn*, Uralla Rd, T6772 2358, both have good restaurants and are locally recommended for affordable fine dining. Back in the Mall there are many cheap or affordable breakfast or lunch options, including the bustling locals favourite *Rumours Café*, T6772 3084, and for value pub-meals the *New England Hotel*, corner of Beardy St and Dangar St, T6772 7622.

Tours and activities *Waterfall Way Tours*, T6772 2018, www.waterfallway.com.au, offer informative eco-tours to the region's national parks, from $40 and are locally recommended. *Gumnuts Wilderness Adventures*, T1800-333963, www.gumnuts.com.au, based near Gara Gorge, offer more generalized waterfalls and wilderness trips but also host an entertaining wildlife night spotting trip (including dinner), from $50.

Transport Armidale Airport is just off the New England Highway on the southwestern approach to the city. *QantasLink*, T131313, and *Hazelton*, T131713, offer daily services from Sydney. QantasLink also fly daily to Brisbane. The **train station** is located at the western end of Brown St, southwest of the city centre. *Countrylink* offer daily services to and from Sydney. Long distance **coaches** stop beside the VIC on Marsh St. *McCafferty's/Greyhound* operate daily services to and from Sydney and Brisbane via the New England Highway. *Keans Coaches*, T1800-043339, run a service from Scone to Port Macquarie and Coffs Harbour (via the Waterfall Way and Dorrigo/Bellingen) 3 times a week, Mon/Wed/Fri, returning Tue/Thu/Sun. *Edwards Coaches*, 2 Drew St, T6772 3116, are the **local bus** operator (timetables from the VIC). **Bike hire** is available from *Armidale Bicycle Centre*, 244 Beardy St, T6772 3718, from $22 per day. **Taxi** T131008.

Oxley Rivers National Park
Colour map 3, grid B5
40 km east and south of Armidale

The World Heritage listed Oxley Rivers National Park takes in the dramatic **gorges** and **waterfalls** of the **Macleay River** watershed. The two major attractions are the dramatic 260-m **Wollomombi and Chandler Falls** that plunge in to the Wollomombi Gorge 40 km east of Armidale and **Dangars Gorge** (and Falls) to the southeast. The main body of the park however is fairly inaccessible and lies about 50 km southeast of Armidale. If you are short for time the Wollomombi Falls and Gorge are certainly worth a visit with the falls **lookout** only 1 km from the main road and a 100-m walk from the car park. The **Gara Gorge** section of the park, 18 km from Armidale (southeast on Castledoyle Road) also offers some great **swimming holes**. The VIC or NPWS office in Armidale both stock the relevant leaflets and **information**, www.npws.nsw.gov.au Basic car-based (**F**) **camping** is available at Wollomombi Gorge, Long Point, Dangars Gorge, Budds Mare, Aspley Falls and Tia Falls. **Youdales Hut** in the southern sector of the park is another good site for camping. The NPWS also have a historic **homestead** at East Kunderang that provides comfortable, modern, self-contained accommodation. It is remote (112 km southeast of Armidale) but accessible by 2WD. For details, T6776 4260.

New England National Park is a 71,207-ha gem. What makes it so special are not only its sense of wilderness and rich biodiversity, but its **breathtaking views** with the stunning vistas from **Point Lookout** being the most popular, accessible and truly memorable. What adds a very atmospheric and unpredictable edge to this viewpoint is its height, which at over 1,564 m, often results in a shroud of mist or worse still, sheets of rain. But if you can afford a couple of days the camping, the views and the varied **walks** around Point lookout are well worthwhile. Just north of Point Lookout Road, Round Mountain Road (8 km) ventures into the heart of **Cathedral Rock National Park**. The main feature here are the magnificent **granite tors** (Cathedral Rocks) and in spring, vivid displays of **wildflowers**. The 6-km **Cathedral Rock Track** (from the Barokee Rest Area) provides a circuit track with a 200-m diversion to the 'rocks'. Basic car-based (**F**) **camping** is available at the Thungutti campsite, just past the park boundary along Point Lookout Road (2½ km from the lookout). It has basic facilities, water, a good sheltered BBQ area and firewood. Other accommodation options along Point Lookout Road include three self-contained NPWS Cabins ($29-51 per person per night, minimum two night stay). Call for details and book well ahead, T6657 2309. L *Moffat Falls Cottage*, T6775 9166, www.moffatfalls.com.au, is another comfortable self-contained option with a wood fire and two bedrooms on Point Lookout Road. There is basic car-based (**F**) camping available at the Barokee Rest Area in the Cathedral National Park.

Heading north from Armidale a number of place names including Ben Lomond and Glencoe offer a rather obvious clue that you have entered 'Celtic Country', an area settled predominantly by Scots pioneers from 1838. **Glen Innes**, 97 km north of Armidale, is considered the capital of 'Celtic Country' and hosts the annual **Australian Celtic Festival** every May. Local activities include fishing and '**fossicking**', or panning for gems like emeralds, topaz and sapphires. The VIC can point you in the right direction and also provide equipment hire and 'ethics'. You can also go on an organized **pub-crawl** around Glen Innes – on horseback! *Great Aussie Pub Crawls on Horseback*, T6732 1599, offer trips stopping off at historic village pubs. Recommended. Glen Innes also serves as a great base from which to explore a wealth of local nature reserves and **national parks**, with Washpool, Gibraltar Range, Warra, Guy Fawkes, Kings Plains and Capoompeta National Parks all less than 100 km from the town. The **NPWS** office on Church Street (68), T6732 5133, can provide directions, walks, camping and general information. The **VIC** on Church Street, T6732 2397, www.GlenInnessTourism.com (■ *Mon-Fri 0900-1700, Sat/Sun 0900-1500*) can provide town maps and assist with accommodation bookings. The **B-E** *Craigieburn Tourist Park*, 2 km south of the town centre on the New England Highway, T6732 1283, is well-facilitated with standard cabins,

New England & Cathedral Rocks National Parks
Colour map 3, grid B5
85 km east of Armidale, 107 km west from Urunga (Pacific Highway)
The VIC in Armidale or NPWS offices in Armidale or the Dorrigo Rainforest Centre, T6657 2309, www.npws.nsw.gov.au, both stock the relevant leaflets and information surrounding the park, its walks, camping and self-contained accommodation

Armidale to the Queensland border
Distance: 200 km

powered and non-powered sites and a camp kitchen. For eating try the bush tucker on offer at the *Cooramah Aboriginal Cultural Centre*, New England Highway, corner of McKenzie Street, T6732 5960. *Greyhound/McCafferty's*, coaches pass through daily on the Melbourne-Brisbane run, stopping at the VIC. The **train station** is at the western end of Wentworth Street, off Grey Street. *Countrylink* offer daily north/southbound services.

Surrounded by contrasting mountain and rural scenery, the small town of **Tenterfield**, 189 km north of Armidale, is best known as the venue for **Sir Henry Parkes's** famous Federation speech in 1889 that became the precursor to Australian Federation two years later. The VIC can provide information surrounding the town's main historical sights. Far more infamous was legendary local bushranger, Captain Thunderbolt, who had a **hideout** close to town. Access is via Mount Lindsay Road, 11 km. Tenterfield is also often used as a base and stopping off point for exploratory trips to the **Boonoo Boonoo** and **Bald Rock National Parks**. The main feature of Boonoo Boonoo are the 210-m **Boonoo Boonoo Falls**, while Bald Rock is a 'mini Uluru' and the largest granite rock in Australia. The two-hour **summit walk** rewards you with fine 360° views of the surrounding granite country. Both parks provide basic **camping** and are accessed via Mount Lindsay Road northeast of the town centre. The Tenterfield **VIC** is located at the corner of Rouse Street and Miles Street, T6736 1082, www.tenter field.com, (■ *Mon-Fri 0900-1700, Sat/Sun 0900-1600*). The heritage-listed **C-E** *Tenterfield Lodge and Caravan Park*, 1½ km west of the town centre, on Manners Street, T6736 1477, tenterfieldlodge@ozemail.com.au has standard cabins, powered and non-powered sites as well as comfortable backpacker dorms and doubles, with a self-catering kitchen. *McCafferty's/Greyhound* pass through the town daily on the Melbourne-Brisbane. The **train station** is on Railway Avenue, 1 km west of the city centre. *Countrylink* offer daily north/southbound services.

Hume Highway and the Riverina

Distance: 559 km from Sydney to Albury

The Hume Highway (Highway 31) provides the fastest road link to Melbourne, a distance of 879 km. The journey, which is not particularly scenic, can be done in one day, but if time allows, the Hume Highway presents just a few worthy stops along the way. The more attractive alternative route to Victoria is via the coastal road (Princes Highway), which is much slower, but far more scenic and more interesting. West of the Hume Highway, the southwest region of NSW seldom features on international tourist agendas. The reality is that the coastal, outback and northern regions of NSW offer far more in the way of tourist attractions and activities, and many travellers simply do not have the time.

Sydney to Goulburn
Distance: 177 km

The country towns and villages of Mittagong, Bowral, Moss Vale and Bundanoon – collectively known as the **Southern Highlands** – are a welcome respite from the oppressive heat of the coast or outback. In **Mittagong** you can stock upon regional information at the **Southern Highlands VIC** (T1300- 657559, www.southern-highlands.com.au Daily 0800-1730). Some 63 km journey west are the impressive **Wombeyan Limestone Caves**. ■ *Daily (all caves open at weekends). Self-guided: $12, child $8. Guided: 1½ hrs, $15, child $10. 2-cave: $26, adventure from $24, T4843 5976, www.jenolan caves.org.au Via Wombeyan Caves Rd.* Just south of Mittagong (3 km) is **Bowral**, the boyhood home of Sir Donald Bradman, 'The Don'. The **Bradman Museum** is on St Jude Street, T4862 1247, www.bradman.org.au ■ *Daily 1000-1700, $7.50, child $3.50.*

Beyond the rural centre of **Moss Vale** you then arrive at the northern fringe of **The Morton National Park** in the quaint 'highland' village of **Bundanoon**, which is distinctly proud of its Scottish heritage, celebrated **Highland Gathering** in April. The entrance to the northern sector of the **Morton National Park** is only 1 km from the village and there are 14 designated walks and 11 km of cycle tracks that take in numerous good lookouts, several waterfalls and a glow worm dell (marked path at the end of Williams Street). There are plenty of cosy B&Bs in and around the town and the VIC in Mittagong can provide full listings. The **C-F** *Bundanoon YHA*. Railway Avenue (on the left, southbound), T4883 6010, bundyha@hinet.net.au It is an excellent choice, with very friendly owners and set in a spacious former Edwardian Guesthouse. The facilities are excellent and include a well-equipped kitchen, dining hall and reading room. There is also plenty of information surrounding local walks and you can camp in the grounds or use the facilities for day-use ($3).

Goulburn, Australia's first inland city, is now a thriving agricultural commercial centre with many **historical buildings** and fine **gardens** which have helped earn it the title of 'The City of Roses'. A **Rose Festival** is held annually in March. Most visitors, however, 'flock' here to see the 15 m high concrete sheep, the '**Big Merino**', on Hume Street (near the junction with Landsdowne Street) on the southwestern edge of the city. The **VIC** is at 201 Sloane Street (signposted from the Hume Highway Goulburn By-pass exit, north), T4823 4492, www.goulburn.gov.nsw.au ■ *Daily 0900-1700*. They can provide a self-guided **Heritage Trail** leaflet. The **Goulburn Brewery** is reputed to be Australia's oldest. ■ *Tours daily from 1100, $6.50, T4821 6071. 23 Bungonia St.*

Goulburn
Colour map 2, grid B6
Population: 22,000
177 km south of Sydney, 382 km north of Albury

Sleeping and eating For a gracious B&B the **LL** *Bishopthorpe Manor Country Guesthouse*, Bishopthorpe La, off Clinton St (6 km southwest of the city centre), T4822 1570, bmanor@interact.net.au It's a lovely peaceful mansion, with spacious gardens, well-appointed rooms or suites, open fires and all the comforts. The **C-E** *Tattersalls Hotel*, 76 Auburn St, T4821 3088, has basic pub-style budget accommodation with a bar, bistro and internet. If you are just passing through in a camper van the **B-E** *Governor's Hill Carapark*, Sydney Rd (next to Governors Hill Reserve about 3 km north of the city centre), T4821 7373, is the best facilitated with cabins, on-site vans, powered and non-powered sites, BBQ but no camp kitchen. Far more scenic (**F**) NPWS camping is available in the Bungonia State Recreation Area (36 km east), T4844 4277. If you are looking for lunch the *Rimbolin Café*, 380 Auburn St, T4821 7633, is a good option (open lunch Wed-Sun, dinner Thu-Sat), while for a cosy evening meal, the centrally located *Fireside Restaurant*, Market St, T4821 2727 is locally recommended. Open for lunch Tue-Fri (Sun in winter) and dinner Tue-Sat.

Transport Long distance coaches stop either at the **railway station** near the VIC, Sloane St, or outside the Big Merino on Hume Rd. *McCafferty's/Greyhound* offer daily services on the Sydney/Melbourne and Canberra routes. *Fearnes Coaches*, T6921 2316, offer services to Wagga Wagga, Sydney and Canberra. *Countrylink* offer frequent, daily north/southbound **rail** services.

The twin cities of Albury and Wodonga straddle the **Murray River** which forms the border of NSW and Victoria. Given its strategic position on the Hume Highway and sitting roughly half way between Melbourne and Sydney, the twin towns are used most often through necessity rather than design, as a convenient stopover between the two state capitals. The Gateway (Albury-Wodonga) **Visitors Information Centre** is on the Victoria side of

Albury
Colour map 2, grid B4
Population: 42,000
563 km south of Sydney, 300 km north of Melbourne

the river on Lincoln Causeway, T6041 3875/T1800 800 743, www.tourism alburywodonga.com.au ■ *Daily 0900-1700. They can supply full accommodation listings and twin-city maps.*

One of the town's most beautiful historical buildings is the grand, Italianate-style **railway station**, at the eastern end of Smollett Street. It once played a very important role in the development of the city, since travellers travelling between the two states would inevitable have to change trains due to differences in track gauges (a problem that still exists between NSW and Queensland). The VIC can provide a self-guided **Heritage Trail** leaflet outlining other sites and buildings of historical interest. Some of Albury's best attractions lie outside the city. To the east, via Bellbridge, is the man made **Hume Lake**, which presents a bizarre landscape of flooded gum forests. The dark silhouettes of the tree trunks that can be seen from many points along its 340 km of shoreline are an amazing sight, especially at dawn or at dusk. Various canoe trips and other water-based activities are available on the lake and the VIC can provide full details. North of the city (12 km) is the rather gimmicky **Ettamogah Pub** which attempts to recreate the Aussie cartoon world of Ken Maynard. Off-kilter walls, caricatures and even a Fosters beer truck on the roof all add to the fun. Obviously, you can of course enjoy a pint of the real thing in the pub and there is also a café and restaurant on-site. ■ *Sun-Thu 1000-2100, Fri/Sat 1000-2300.* The VIC has details of the many fine **vineyards** in the region, most of which lie on the Victorian side of the river. **River cruises** are available on the lovingly restored *Cumberoona Paddlesteamer*, one hour 1000 and 1400, $13, child $5, 1½ hours 1200, $15, child $7. Western end of Hovell Street.

Sleeping and eating B *Albury Hotel Motel*, 491 Kiewa St, T6021 3599, has good en suites and the added attraction of an in-house Irish pub. Of the many motels the **LL-A** *Sundowner Albury Paddlesteamer*, located right beside the river, the border and the bridge on the Hume Highway, T6041 1711, www.sundownermotorinns.com.au, is a good option. It is upmarket, in a nice position and is well facilitated with restaurant, pool, spa and sauna. The friendly. **C-E** *Albury Backpackers*, 452 David St (near the train station), T6041 1822, is also well located, well facilitated and has dorms and doubles, bike hire and organizes canoeing trips from Sep-May. The *New Albury Hotel*, 491 Kiewa St, T6021 3599, has a good value pub restaurant in its Irish bar (open daily for lunch and dinner) and an à la carte restaurant on the 1st floor. Open Wed-Fri for lunch/dinner and just dinner on Sat.

Transport The **airport** is located east of the city on Borella Rd (Riverina Highway). *Qantas*, T131313, *Kendell*, T131300, and *Hazelton*, T131713, all offer daily flights to Sydney and Melbourne. A **taxi** to the city centre will cost about $10. The impressive **train** station is at the far east end of Smollett St, off Young and has a *Countrylink Travel Centre*, T6041 9555. Open Mon-Fri 0900-1700, Sat 0930-1600. *Countrylink* offer twice daily north and southbound services to Sydney and Melbourne. Most long distance **buses** stop outside the train station including *McCafferty's/Greyhound*, servicing Melbourne, Sydney, Canberra and Dubbo. Victorian company *V-Line*, T136196, also offer services west along the Murray to Mildura and north to Canberra.

The Riverina Region

The Murray River, which forms the border between NSW and Victoria, is one of the nation's longest rivers, stretching almost 1,000 km from the Snowy Mountains to **Wentworth**, where it merges with the Darling River (the longest) near the border with South Australia. Sadly, the Murray is less than mighty. In recent years, like the Darling River, much of the supply is being sapped by regional agricultural practices. Though seldom placed very high on the travelling agenda, especially for international tourists, the Riverina Region does present the cash-strapped backpacker the chance to find fruit picking work.

Wagga Wagga sits west of Gumley Gumley, south of Berry Jerry, north of Walla Walla (and Burrumbuttock) and east of Grong Grong. With names like that you could only be in one country – Australia. Wagga (as it is called) is the commercial capital of the Riverina region and hardly a tourist destination but it is quite a lively place being home to the Charles Sturt University. The **VIC** is beside the Murrumbidgee River close to the centre of the city on Tarcutta Street, T6926 9261, www.wagga.nsw.gov.au Daily 0900-1700. The city's impressive **Botanical Gardens** are set in the extensive **Willans Hill Reserve**, south of the city centre. ■ *Daily 0900-1700, free.*

Wagga Wagga
Colour map 2, grid B4
Population: 43,000
196 km north of Albury Albury

Sleeping and eating There are plenty of motels with most located along Edward St (Sturt Highway). The **LL-A** *Manor Guesthouse*, 38 Morrow St, next to the lagoon and Baylis St, offers 7 good rooms and is ideally located, T6921 5962. The best-facilitated motor park is the **B-E** *Easts Van Park Riverview*, 93 Hammond Av, T6921 4287, on the eastern approach to town. The best placed however is the **C-E** *Wagga Wagga Beach Caravan Park*, at the end of Johnston St in the city centre, beside the river, T6931 0603. Neither park has a camp kitchen but both have kiosks. *Romanos Rugby Bar and Bistro*, corner of Sturt St and Fitzmaurice St, T6921 2013, or the *Victoria Hotel*, 55 Baylis St, T6921 5233, both offer value pub-style food.

Transport The **airport** is located east of the city centre via the Sturt Highway. *Qantas*, T131313, *Hazelton* and *Kendell* provide regular services to Melbourne and Sydney. The **train** station is at the southern end of Baylis St, off Edwards Rd (Sturt Highway). *Countrylink* offer services to Albury and Sydney. City based **coach** company *Fearnes Coaches*, 264 Hammond Av, T6921 2316, offer local regional services and state-wide services to Canberra and Sydney. *McCafferty's/Greyhound* offer services to Albury (Melbourne), Sydney and Dubbo. **Taxi**, T6921 4242.

Like the nation's capital, Canberra, Griffith was designed by the famous American architect **Walter Burley Griffin**. This modern, thriving city is the result of the extensive **Murrumbidgee River Irrigation Scheme**, initiated in the early 1900s. Now a green oasis, Griffith is hyped as the capital of 'Food and Wine Country'. The city also has a strong Italian connection that only adds to its culinary reputation. The **VIC** is on the corner of Banna Avenue and Jondaryan Avenue in the city centre, T6962 4145, griffithvc@griffith.nsw.gov.au ■ *Daily 0900-1700*. The **NPWS** have an office at 200 Yambil Street, T696 68100. ■ *Mon-Fri 0900-1700*. **Internet** is available at the **Library**, 233 Banna Avenue, T6962 2515. ■ *Mon-Fri 0900-1700, Sat 0900-1230*. *Pickers Plus*, 20 Olympic Street, T6964 0080, can assist with finding **fruit-picking** work. There are over 12 **vineyards** around Griffith and the region now produces over 70% of the NSW annual output. The main varieties are Semillon, Shiraz and Chardonnay. The VIC has full details and can provide a map.

Griffith
Colour map 2, grid B4
Population: 23,000
262 km northwest of Albury, 196 km northwest of Wagga Wagga

Sleeping and eating There are plenty of **motels** with the **L-A** *Yambil Inn Motel*, 155 Yambil St, T6964 1233, being one of the best in a central location. The very basic **E** *Griffith International Hostel*, 112 Binya St, T6964 4236, hostel@griffithinternational.com.au, offers budget no frills dorm accommodation. A better option for groups (and fruit-pickers) are the basic **bunkhouses** at the **B** *Griffith Tourist Caravan Park*, 919 Willandra Av (south of the city centre via Jondaryan Av T6964 2144. When it comes to **eating** the VIC puts out an excellent *'Griffith Eating Guide'* that will point you in the right direction. One of the most reputable restaurants in the city is *L'Oasis*, 150 Yambil St, T6964 5588, offering award winning modern Australian fare. Local wines are offered by the glass. Open Tue-Sat 1130-1430 and 1800-2200.

Transport The **airport**, T6964 5600, is 5 km from the city centre. *Hazelton* provide regular services to Sydney. A **taxi** into the city, T6964 1444, will cost about $10. Griffith is well served by long distance **coaches** with *Countrylink*, *McCafferty's/Greyhound* and *V-Line* offering services to Albury (Melbourne), Sydney and Dubbo. Coaches stop at the *Mobil Roadhouse*, 121 Banna Av. Local company *Hoys,* T5831 2880, also offer a comfortable daily coach/train transfer to Melbourne. *Griffith Travel and Transit*, 177 Banna Av, T6962 7199, can assist with bookings

Snowy Mountains

*Though the idea of anything covered in snow may seem totally incongruous to most people's image of Australia, the Snowy Mountains are as much a part of the country as the Great Barrier Reef or the cuddly koala. The 'Snowies', as they are called, contain the highest elevations of the Great Divide (including the continent's highest peak, the 2,228-m **Mount Kosciuszko**) which are protected by **Kosciuszko National Park** (pronounced 'Kozzie-usko'), the state's largest. The park offers a fragile sanctuary to numerous rare plant and animal species. In spring, vivid displays of wild flowers carpet the slopes where the snows have melted and, in autumn, the bark of the gnarly snow gums take on a range colourful hues beyond compare. Although **Cooma**, in the **Monaro Plains** south of Canberra, is often considered the capital of the 'Snowies', it is the mainly winter resort of **Jindabyne**, on the eastern fringe of the national park, that gladly hosts the bulk of tourist traffic.*

Cooma
Colour map 2, grid B5
Population: 7,000
114 kms south
of Canberra

Often considered the capital of the region, Cooma is best known for having served as the principal headquarters for the mighty **Snowy Mountains Hydro-electric Scheme**, which involved the combined skills of over 100,000 workers from 30 countries and took 25 years to complete. The legacy is a proud, cosmopolitan community that is ultimately responsible for the provision of 70% of Eastern Australia's renewable energy. Though quiet for much of the year, once the winter snows have fallen upon the mountaintops, the population in town swells, as skiers flood in to take advantage of the cheaper accommodation and services compared to those in the more commercial resorts of Jindabyne and Thredbo. The **VIC** is next to Centennial Park on Sharp Street, T6450 1742/1800 636 525, www.visitcooma.com.au ■*Daily 0900-1700*. Internet is available at *APA Computers*, 92 Commissioner St, T6452 2555. The **Snowy Mountains Authority Information Centre**, 2 km north of the town, controls the operations of the **Hydro-electric Scheme** and can provide all the detail surrounding the remarkable engineering feat. The centre can also provide information of the various facility **tours** throughout the region, including both surface and subterranean power stations. Ask for a copy of the free **'self-guided drive'** leaflet. ■ *Mon-Fri 0800-1700, Sat/Sun 0800-1300, free, T6453 2004, www.snowyhydro.com.au Yulin Rd, off the Monaro Highway.* There are a number of reputable **horse trekking** companies, including *Yarramba Trail Rides*, Dry Plains Road, Cooma, T6453 7204, offering rides suitable for beginners from one hour/one-day or longer. Slightly further afield, near Adaminaby, are *Reynella Kosciuszko Rides*, Reynella Kingston Road, T1800-029909,

Skiing the Snowies

Generally speaking, skiing the Snowies is of course a strictly winter affair with snow conditions being variable and only really guaranteed in July, August and early September. Standard skiing and snowboarding are both equally popular and well catered for, but the terrain also lends itself to **cross country** skiing. The main ski fields are based at **Perisher Valley**, T1300-655822, www.perisher blue.com.au, and **Thredbo**, T1800-020589, www.thredbo.com.au Other less high profile (and cheaper) fields are located at **Charlotte Pass** (above Perisher) and **Mount Selwyn**, T1800-641064, www.selwynsnow.com.au Thredbo has the best atmosphere and is designed like a true Alpine village, while the others at higher elevations are more subject to the vagaries of the weather. Jindabyne is the main satellite town and offers the broadest range of accommodation and amenities and is cheaper than Thredbo, while Cooma to the east, is cheaper still. **Group packages** are often the best way to go, with the accommodation agents in Jindabyne offering organizational assistance. A useful website is www.snowholidays.com.au Sample **prices** at Perisher are: One Day Mountain (lifts) Pass, $77, child $42, with lesson $104, child $94. Equipment **hire** prices vary, with standard skis/poles/boots starting at about $55, child $35, per day. Snowboard and boots cost about $64, child $50 per day. All the major resorts have hire shops and full amenities at the fields and there are numerous independent ski hire companies in Jindabyne. The VIC has full listings. The individual resorts all issue their own **snow reports** (see the contact numbers above). **Snow chains** can be rented from most of the major service stations in town.

www.reynellarides.com.au, specializing in multi-day rides in the true '*Man from Snowy River*' tradition. *Litchfield Farm*, 20 km east on the Carlaminda Road (off Bomballa, then left on Dangelong), T6453 3231, offer free horse riding as part of their farm stay accommodation package. Sheep shearing demos are an added highlight. **Ski hire** is available with *Cooma Ski Rentals*, 173 Sharp St, T1800 355 899, www.coomaskirentals.com.au, and *The Ski Co*, 167 Sharp St, T1800 686 125, www.skico.com.au

Sleeping There are plenty of motels along Sharp St with the **L-A** *Kinross Inn*, 15 Sharp St, T6452 3577, being the most upmarket motel close to the town centre. The **C** *Royal Hotel*, corner of Sharp St and Lambie St, T64522132, is a more affordable heritage hotel offering pleasant single to family rooms with shared bathrooms, log fire, balcony and in-house restaurant. The **B-C** *Bunkhouse Motel*, 28 Soho St, T6452 2983, offers shared accommodation and basic self-contained motel units with double/twin and singles, at just above standard backpacker hostel prices. The **D** *Alpine Country Guest House*, 32 Maisse St, T6452 1414, info@alpineguesthouse.com.au, also offers backpacker accommodation. The only **motor park** in the town is the well-facilitated **A-E** *Snowtels Caravan Park*, Snowy Mountains Highway (at the western end of town), T6452 1828, offering self-contained cabins, flats, powered and non-powered sites, camp kitchen and also ski-hire.

The VIC can provide full accommodation listings and can also assist with bookings. Pre-booking in the winter holiday season is advised

Transport The transport links to and from Cooma (and west to the Snowies) tend to wax and wane with the seasons, so it pays to check with the VIC for the most up-to-date operators and schedules. *Countrylink*, T132232, offer daily **coach** services to/from Sydney, Canberra and Jindabyne, while *V-Line*, T136196, offer services to Melbourne departing Mon/Thu/Sat and arriving Tue/Fri/Sun. *Summit Coaches*, T6297 2588, also offer services to/from Canberra and Jindabyne on Mon/Wed/Fri/Sun. All buses stop at the

Snowstop Village on Sharp St. *Harvey World Travel* opposite the VIC, 114 Sharp St, T645 24677, cooma@harveyworld.com.au, act as coach and **flight** booking agents and can provide further information. There is a commercial **airport** in Cooma. *Qantas Link*, T131313, are the main service provider. For shuttle transfers to the slopes in winter, T1800 352 957. **Car hire** is available with *Thrifty*, 60 Sharp St, T6452 5300.

Jindabyne

Colour map 2, grid B5
Population: 4,500
176 km south
of Canberra,
62 km west of Cooma,
34 km east of Thredbo
and 30 km east of
Perisher Valley

Jindabyne, at the eastern fringe of the Kosciuszko National Park, is one of a number of regional centres that had to be relocated in the 1960s during the creation of the Snowy Mountains Hydro-electric Scheme. Now rebuilt and revitalized, it is the main satellite town to the ski resorts of the Thredbo and Perisher Valleys. At a height of 930 m, in winter, the town retains a distinctive nip to the air that only adds to the anticipation of skiing, while in summer it's the perfect base for walking and exploring the many lesser known delights of NSW largest national park, Kosciuszko.

Ins & outs
Road services vary
depending on the
season. Check with the
VIC before booking

Getting there The nearest commercial **airport** is at Cooma. *Qantas Link*, T131313, are the main service provider. For shuttle transfers in winter, T1800-352957. In winter Jindabyne is well served from Canberra and Cooma. *Countrylink* offer daily **coach** services to/from Sydney, Canberra via Cooma, while *V-Line* offer services to/from Melbourne departing Mon/Thu/Sat and arriving Tue/Fri/Sun. *Summit Coaches*, T6297 2588, also offer services to/from Canberra and Cooma on Mon/Wed/Fri/Sun.

Getting around Road transport varies greatly so the best bet is to consult the VIC on your arrival to find out the very latest and cheapest methods to reach the fields. There is one method literally set in stone: The **Skitube**, located at Bullock's Flat, 20 km east of Jindabyne (Alpine Way), connects the Thredbo Valley with the Perisher Resort and the summit of Blue Cow Mountain. The 8-km alpine-style train ride, through Australia's longest tunnel (6.3 km), acts as a year-round tourist attraction, as well as a convenient way to reach the ski fields. It operates daily on the hour from 0900-1500 with reduced hours in summer, from $26, child $15 return, T1300 655 844, www.perisher blue.com.au *Snowy Mountains Taxi*, T64572444. For **bike hire** see Activities below.

Information and orientation The *NPWS Snowy Region Visitors Centre* is located east of the main shopping centre in town, just off Kosciuszko Rd, T6450 5600, www.snowymountains.com.au Open daily 0830-1700. As well as all the usual tourist information services, the staff can provide national parks and up-to date weather information, sell detailed maps and issue the necessary park day-use and camping permits. There are also heritage and natural history displays, a shop, café and small theatre. **Internet** is available at the *Snowy Mountains Backpackers* (see below) or the *Video shop* at the end of Snowy River Av, opposite the post office.

Activities

In winter **skiing** and **snowboarding** dominate all mountain activities, but year round and especially in summer, there is still plenty on offer. **Mountain biking** is big business in the 'Snowies'. *RawNRG*, T6457 6282, www.Raw NRG.com.au, based in Thredbo, offer a range of options from full or half day to 'Ride 'n' Stay' packages. Independent hire of quality bikes costs from $60 a day. Given the number of major rivers in the area, **white-water rafting** is a popular pursuit. *Rapid Descents*, T1800-637486, www.rapiddescents.com.au, offer one and two day trips down the Upper Murray River, from $143 and a 'Ride 'n' Raft' option, combining rafting with mountain biking. **Horse trekking** is another very popular. *Snowy River Adventures*, T6456 5033, www.snowyriver adventures.com.au, based in Paupong, south of Jindabyne, offer a wide range of options and are very flexible. The best treks involve several days (two-day/one

New South Wales

night) and are all-inclusive, from $445). Other operators are listed under the Cooma section (see above). **Fishing** in the Snowies is legendary and there are several companies in Jindabyne or Thredbo that offer guided trips, including *High Country*, T6456 2989, www.highfly.com.au, half day from $175, full day $275. They also offer fly casting lessons from $30 per hour. **Lake Jindabyne** is obviously popular in summer for water sports. Small motorboats and canoes can be hired from the *Snowline Caravan Park*, Thredbo Road Junction, T6456 2099, www.snowline.com.au Almost next-door *The Paddy Pallin Adventure Shop*, T6456 2922, offer an attractive range of activity options, from white-water canoeing to **snowshoe walking**. They also hire all sorts of gear from bikes to boots. *Snowy Mountains Backpackers*, T1800-333468, www.topofoz.com.au, also offer an excellent range of activity packages that include all the above, as well as adventure walks, abseiling and fishing.

Sleeping

Almost right next door to the Skitube is the **LL** *Novotel Lake Crackenback Resort*, Alpine Way, T6456 2960, novotel@jindabyne.snowy.net.au It is a fully- equipped lakeside resort with modern self-contained units overlooking the lake, good restaurant, pool, sauna and sports facilities. The luxurious **LL** *Silvertop Lodge Retreat*, Weston's Rd, T6456 1426, www.silvertoplodgecom.au, is a modern, peaceful, all mod cons lodge with 4 doubles and a family room, huge open fire and excellent cuisine. Further up the valley the **LL-A** *Pender Lea Chalets*, Alpine Way, T64562088, www.penderlea.com.au, offer a wide range of options from a mobile home, a rustic (renovated) hut and a bed sitter, through to fully self-contained luxury cottages and chalets, all set in its own 1133 ha property. Horse riding is an added attraction. In Jindabyne itself the **LL-A** *Banjo Patterson Inn*, at the eastern end of town, on Kosciuszko Rd, T6456 2372, is a well established favourite with a good range of rooms from standard to self-contained luxury with spa, restaurant and nightclub. For budget B&B accommodation the **C** *Mad Moose Guest House*, 21 Monyang St, T6456 1108, moose@snowy.net.au, is good fun and good value while the modern. Purpose-built **B-E** *Snowy Mountains Backpackers*, behind the VIC on Gippsland St, T6456 1500, www.snowybackpackers.com.au, is recommended. It has dorms, doubles/twins and family rooms and all the usual facilities, including internet, a café and well-organized activities. There are several motor parks. The most convenient to town and the best facilitated, is the **L-E** *Jindabyne Holiday Park*, next to the lake, off Kosciuszko Rd, T6456 2249. It offers self-contained cabins, powered and non-powered sites, camp kitchen and ski and canoe hire. Further afield the **LL-E** *Kosciuszko Mountain Retreat*, Sawpit Creek (14 km, east up the Perisher Valley), T6456 2249, www.kosireat.com.au, is in a great bush setting with lots of wildlife and local walks. For a great basic camping experience look no further than the **F** *NPWS Thredbo Diggings campsite* up in the Thredbo Valley. It is in a beautiful riverside location with tame kangaroos and wombats.

Prices increase between late Jun and mid-Sep and you are advised to book well ahead during that period. The VIC can assist with general listings while the Kosciuszko Accommodation Centre (Snowy River Travel), Shop 29, Nugget's Crossing (above the shopping arcade), T6456 2022, www.skione.net.au, can assist with holiday lettings and self-contained apartments. Other useful websites include www.jinda byne.com.au, www.jindabyne sports.com.au and www.high country.com.au

Eating & entertainment

For fine dining and a pleasant break from the town bustle try the *Duffers Ridge Restaurant* overlooking the lake at the *Novotel Crackenback Resort*, Alpine Way, T6456 2960 (25 km). Open daily 0700-late. In the town itself the café in the VIC does a good breakfast, while *Il Largo*, 19 Nuggets Crossing, T6456 1171, is good for pizza (plus takeaways) and also has à la carte. Open daily from 1700 (seasonal). For good value and a bit of atmosphere try the *Banjo Patterson Inn*, at the western end of town on Kosciuszko Rd, T6456 2372. The main supermarket is in the Nugget's Crossing Shopping Centre. Open daily until late. Most of 'Jindy's' nightlife revolves around the *Jindabyne Hotel*, Kosciuszko Rd, T6456 2203, which also offers counter meals and live music at the weekends in the high season, or the *Brumbie Bar and Bistro*, corner of Kosciuszko Rd and Kalkite St, just west of the Nugget's Shopping Centre, T64562526. Open 1200-0300 Mon-Sat, 1200-2400 Sun.

Most eateries are located along Kosciuszko Rd within the Nuggets Crossing Shopping Centre, or the shopping mall to the west of the VIC

Kosciuszko National Park

Colour map 2, grid B5

At 600,000 ha, The Kosciuszko National Park is the largest in New South Wales and certainly one of the most beautiful. Home to the continent's highest peak, the 2,228-m **Mount Kosciuszko**, the famous **Snowy River** and the country's best skiing resorts, it offers a year round playground for a host of activities from skiing and mountain biking, to fishing and walking. More importantly, with much of the park being wilderness, it also offers sanctuary to many rare native plants and animals from possums to snow gums.

New South Wales

Ins & outs   **Getting there**   From the south and west, access is via Jindabyne to Perisher Valley (Mt Kosciuszko) and the **Alpine Way** to Thredbo. From Thredbo the Alpine Way then runs to the southwestern access point at Khancoban. From the north the park is accessed via the **Snowy Mountains Highway** south of Tumut.

     Information   You will find all the necessary parks information at the *NPWS Snowy Region Visitors Centre*, just off Kosciuszko Rd in Jindabyne, T6450 5600, www.snowy mountains.com.au   Open daily 0830-1700. As well as all the usual tourist information services, the staff can provide national parks and up-to-date weather information and sell detailed maps. They can also issue all the necessary park day-use and camping permits. Pick up a copy of the free NPWS *'Kosciuszko Today'* newspaper which outlines all the most popular and accessible walks. Other NPWS centres are located at **Khancoban**, (the park's southwestern access point) corner of Scott Av and Mitchell Av, T6076 9373 (open daily 0830-1600), and **Tumut** (northern access point), Old Butter Factory, Adelong Rd, T6947 1849. Open daily 0900-1600. Vehicle access ranges from $15 for 1 day, to $60 for 4. Motorcycles cost $6 per day. There are several camping sites with the best being the delightful, riverside, Thredbo Diggings site on the way to Thredbo (25 km).

Perisher Valley
Colour map 2, grid B5
Population: 2000
35 km west
of Jindabyne

At a height of 1,680 m the Perisher Resort is the largest in the Southern Hemisphere and incorporates the **Perisher Valley**, **Mount Blue Cow**, **Smiggin Holes** and **Guthega**. There are 50 lifts and over 90 runs from advanced to beginner as well as trails suitable for cross country skiing. For detailed skiing **information** T1300-655822, www.perisherblue.com.au The resort is very well facilitated with plenty of mainly upmarket accommodation, eateries and ski hire/retail outlets. An All Day Lift Pass costs from $77, child $42 (6-14 years) which includes access to all the Valley's ski fields. Lessons start at about $60. Hire prices for skis/boots/poles starts at $37, child $30 and for snowboards/boots $54, child $40. The VIC in Jindabyne or website above has full accommodation listings and prices. Access is via the Kosciuszko Road west of Jindabyne. The road is fully sealed but snow chains may be required in winter. The main service stations in Jindabyne offer chain hire from $20. National park day vehicle fees apply, from $15. Shuttle services by road vary from season to season. Contact the VIC for the latest schedules. The other transport alternative is the **Skitube**.

Charlotte Pass
& Mount
Selwyn
Colour map 2, grid B5
Population: nominal
42 km west of
Jindabyne (Mt Selwyn
89 km northwest
of Cooma)

At 1,760 m **Charlotte Pass** marks the end of the Kosciuszko Road and the start of various high **alpine walks** including the 12½-km one-way walk to the summit of Australia's highest mountain. In winter the Charlotte Pass Ski field is the most remote with four lifts and a scattering of chalets and lodges. The area is also particularly good for cross-country skiing. In summer it is a top spot for mountain walks. In the heart of the national park, halfway between Tumut and Cooma, are the **Mount Selwyn** ski fields (1490 m), which are the cheapest, but the least well facilitated. There are about a dozen lifts and runs particularly suitable for children and families. Cross-country trails are also plentiful. *The Selwyn*

Snow World Centre, T6454 9488, offers indoor and outdoor activities for kids, with attractive half or full day programs. For information surrounding Charlotte Pass refer to Perisher Valley sources. The Bavarian-style **LL-A** *Kosciuszko Chalet*, T6457 5245, www.charlottepass.com.au, is Australia's highest resort. It is only open in winter but is a very congenial oasis in the snow, which is all but guaranteed right from the front door, from June-October. For Mount Selwyn information, T1800-641 064, www.selwynsnow.com.au An All Day Lift Pass at Mount Selwyn costs from $44, child $42 (under 15 years). Hire prices for skis/boots/poles, from $28 per day and for snowboards/boots $44. Lift pass an lesson deals from around $70. The VIC in Jindabyne or Tumut, T6947 7025, can assist with accommodation listings and bookings.

Wandering around the Alpine-style mountain village resort of Thredbo in either winter or spring feels most un-Australian. Set in a beautiful river valley and shadowed by the Crackenback Mountain Range, it feels a million miles from the sun-baked outback, the surf beaches or bustling east coast cities. Sadly, in the mind of most Australians, the name Thredbo is eternally associated with a tragic event in August 1997, when a landslip devastated the village and claimed 18 lives. Thredbo however prefers to put that episode behind it and today it is considered a very progressive village and the best ski resort in the country. The excellent and independent **VIC** is at 6 Friday Drive, just opposite the river and bridges to the ski fields, T6459 4294, www.thredbo.com.au Open daily winter 0800-1800, summer 0900-1600. Internet is available at *Ski@Cyber Café*, Lower Concourse, Alpine Hotel, T6457 7333.

Thredbo
*Colour map 2,
grid B5
Population: 2000
32 km west of
Jindabyne, 71 km
east of Khancoban*

New South Wales

Activities When it comes to skiing Thredbo is considered the best venue in the country. Not only is the resort exceptionally well facilitated, but also the fields themselves are also highly regarded with numerous lifts taking you to a wide range of runs. Night skiing is also available. A Lift-only Day Pass costs from $77, child $42, while a Lift and Lesson Pass costs from $103, child $69. There are plenty of ski hire outlets in the village, or at the main lift terminals. Hire prices for skis/boots/poles starts at $50, per day and for snowboards/boots $58. In summer Thredbo also offers a whole host of activities from alpine walking and fishing, to mountain biking and golf. Most of the local operators have outlets in the Valley Ski Terminal. The VIC can also provide a detailed leaflet. The Valley Chairlift stays open in summer allowing walkers and sightseers to reach the higher elevations. Thredbo offers walkers the shortest route to the summit of Mount Kosciuszko (6½ km one-way, lookout 2 km one-way). The ski lift ($21, child $10.50 return, 0900-1630) takes out 1,930 m leaving only 298 m of elevation. Guided summit, sunset and night walks are also available.

Sleeping and eating For sheer style and atmosphere the **LL-A** *House of Ullr* is best, while for value try the **A-C** *Currawong Lodge*, and for families and location the **LL** *River Inn*. For bookings and more information contact the VIC. The **E** *Thredbo YHA*, 8 Jack Adams Pathway, T6457 6376, thredbo@yhasw.org.au, is a purpose-built lodge with tidy dorms, doubles and a studio apartment (winter only). It retains a congenial, social atmosphere and all the lodge-style essentials like a log fire and cosy common areas, large kitchen and internet. Bookings for the winter season should be made well in advance and are by ballot if necessary. For camping in summer the **F** *NPWS Thredbo Diggings* campsite (10 km east is highly recommended). There are over 20 cafés and restaurants in the village some of which are highly regarded. For fine dining with a great view (Modern Australian cuisine) try the *Credo*, Riverside

*The VIC has
accommodation
listings*

*Thredbo
Accommodation
Services, T9894 4044,
www.thredboppropertie
s.com.au, can also be
of assistance for
self-contained
apartments and
holiday lettings*

Cabins, T6457 6844. Open nightly from 1800. Similarly, **Sante**, Village Square, T6457 6083 (open nightly from 1800), offers good Modern Australian. For choice and atmosphere all day try **Altitude 1380**, in the Alpine Hotel Concourse, T6457 6190. And for value pub-food **The Pub**, Village Square, T6459 4200. Open daily from 1000. For nightlife the **Schuss Bar**, in the Alpine Hotel is recommended and open until 0300 in season.

Transport Road services vary depending on the season. Check with the VIC for the latest operators and schedules. In winter a regular shuttle bus service operates between Jindabyne and Thredbo, T6456 7340, for more information. In winter Jindabyne is well served from Canberra and Cooma. **McCaffery's/Greyhound**, T132030, **Murray's**, T132251, and **Lever Coaches**, T6262 3266, all offer regular **coach** services to/from Sydney and Canberra via Cooma and Jindabyne.

The Alpine Way
103 km from Khancoban to Jindabyne

The Alpine Way stretches from Goulburn to Albury, with the 100 km section that straddles the Kosciuszko National Park from Jindabyne to Khancoban being the most scenic. In winter this is one of the very few sealed roads in the entire nation that can be blocked by snow. From Thredbo, heading west, the road climbs to its highest point (1,580 m) at **Dead Horse Gap**. This is a favourite starting point for mountain biking and also for hikers wishing to follow the **Thredbo River Track** back down to Thredbo. From Dead Horse Gap the road winds its way down below the tree line to **Pilots Lookout**, from where you can glimpse **Pilot Mountain** (1,828 m) and beyond that, Victoria. At the rather chilly Tom Groggin **campsite** you then cross the **Murray River**. Next stop is the **Scammel Spur Lookout** where you can enjoy the vista across to the Main Range of the Snowy Mountains. Beyond that you reach the eastern boundary of the national park. From the huge '**Murray 1' Power Station**, it is a further 8 km to **Khancoban**, a pleasant little village that acts as the southeastern gateway to the park and the ski resorts. There is a **NPWS office** in the village, corner of Scott Avenue and Mitchell Avenue, T6076 9373 (■ *Daily 0830-1600*) where you can purchase vehicle entry and camping permits if entering the park from the west.

Yarrangobilly Caves
If you are short for time one of the Glory Caves and the Jersey Cave are recommended

The biggest attraction in the largely wilderness northern sector of the Kosciuszko National Park are the ancient Yarrangobilly Caves, consisting of two main caves; the **North Glory Cave** (358 m) reached through the impressive **Glory Arch**, and the **Glory Hole Cave**, which at 470 m is the longer of the two. Other smaller caves include the **Jillabenan** (73 m and wheelchair accessible) and the **Jersey** (135 m). All the caves are well furnished with stalactites and stalagmites boasting such names as 'Dogs Tooth', 'Judges Wig' and 'The Wedding Cake'. An added attraction is the 27° **thermal pool** originally built in 1861 (free) as well as a network of surface bush walks that take in the river, valley views and a natural limestone arch. Guided cave **tours** are available at least three times daily (1-1½ hours, from $12, child $8). Self-guided tours, adventure caving options and NPWS camping are also available. For bookings and further information call at the **Information Centre**, opposite Caves House, T6454 9597, yarrangobilly@npws.nsw.gov.au ■ *Daily 0830-1600*. The caves and the visitors centre are located 4.7 km off the Snowy Mountains Highway, 77 km south of Tumut and 106 kms north of Cooma.

New South Wales

South Coast

*Few visitors have any idea that this little corner of NSW is just as beautiful as anywhere else in the state. Overshadowed by the hype of Sydney and coast north to Queensland, it has pretty much been left alone. But the south coast has, incredibly, over 35 **national parks** and nature reserves, more than any other region in the state, if not the continent. And most of those are above the waterline. The South Coast is a also major shareholder in the Australian East Coast's lucrative market of beautiful unspoiled **beaches** and stunning **coastal scenery**. South of **Wollongong** and **Kiama** the south coast is split into three quite distinct regions: the **Shoalhaven Coast** which extends from **Nowra** to **Bateman's Bay**; the **Eurobodella Coast** which stretches from Batemans Bay to **Narooma**; and the **Sapphire Coast** which idles its way to the Victorian border.*

Provided you don't look south from the city, Wollongong is actually a very attractive city and without doubt its greatest assets are its beaches, its **harbour** (with its **historic lighthouse**) and behind that, **Flagstaff Point** headland and the **Wollongong Foreshore Park**. Either side of Flagstaff Point over 17 patrolled **beaches** stretch from the Royal National Park in the north to Bass Point in the south all providing excellent opportunities for sunbathers, swimmers and surfies. The **VIC** is behind the City Art Gallery, on the corner of Crown Street and Kembla Street, T4227 5545, www.tourism wollongong.com.au (■ *open Mon-Frid 0900-1700, Sat 0900-1600, Sun 1000-1600*). In the heart of the city the **Wollongong City Gallery** is definitely worth a visit. Considered one of the best and one of the largest regional galleries in NSW it offers a wide range of mediums and an exciting program of local, regional and interstate exhibitions. ■ *Tue-Fri 1000-1700, Sat/Sun 1200-1600, free, T42287500, www.wcg.1earth.net.au Corner of Kembla St and Burelli St.*
For train enthusiasts the **Cockatoo Run** is a scenic mountain railway that climbs through the Illawarra Ranges from Wollongong to Robertson in the Southern Highlands. ■ *Wed/Sun 1055. From $40, child $30 (lunch $25), T42275545, www.3801limited.com.au (bookings required).* South of the city centre, in the suburb of Berkeley, is Wollongong's most unique attraction – the **Nan Tien Buddhist Temple**, the Southern Hemisphere's largest Buddhist temple which is open to visitors and offers a varied programme of weekend workshops and very tidy modern en suite accommodation (see Sleeping below). ■ *Tue-Sun 0900-1700, free T42720500. Berkeley Rd, Berkeley. Public transport to the Temple is with Premier Illawarra Bus Company (route 34), Marine Dr, from $3.20, concession $1.60.*
Wollongong offers some excellent **surfing** with the best breaks said to be on North Beach (just north of Flagstaff Point) and Bulli Beach (12 km north of the city centre). *Pines Surfriders*, T0500-824860, www.surfinfo.com.au, operate out of North Beach. Also worth looking at are *Adrenaline Sports Skydiving*, T4225 8444, www.sportsskydiving.com.au, from $275, and the *Hangdog Climbing Gym*, 130 Auburn Street, T4225 8369, www.hangdog.com.au ■ *Mon-Fri 1000-2100, Sat/Sun 0900-1800, from $10 per day.* Stanwell Park and the Illawarra Ranges north of Wollongong are also the venue of the *Sydney Hang Gliding Centre*, T4294 4294, www.hanggliding.com.au, and also the base for Australian champion *Tony Armstrong*, T04-1793 9200, www.hanggliding.nu, who will take you up tandem, from $155.

Wollongong & around
Colour map 2, grid B6
Population: 219,000
79 km south of Sydney, 441 km from Victoria

New South Wales

The Illawarra Ranges that flank Wollongong inland have some excellent viewpoints that are well worth seeing, such as the **Mount Keira Lookout** in the Illawarra Escarpment State Recreation Area (left on Clive Bissell Road), and **The Bulli Lookout** (right), both off Highway 1 (Ousley Road), just north of the city. There are numerous fine beaches north of the city. **Bulli Beach** is perhaps the best, but it is literally a case of taking your pick, all the way from the city centre to **Otford** at the southern edge of the **Royal National Park**. Another great local attraction just to the south of the city and beyond the stark industrial landscapes of Port Kembla, is **Lake Illawarra**. Essentially a saltwater harbour, sheltered from the ocean by a narrow strip of land it provides a heaven for a wide range of watersports, from sailing to kayaking. The *Boat Shed*, in Windang (near the harbour entrance) rents boats, canoes and kayaks, T4296 2015.

Sleeping and eating For something completely different you might like to consider the **A** *Pilgrim Lodge*, at the Nan Tien Buddhist Temple, Berkeley Rd, Berkeley, T4272 0500, www.australiatravel.com.au/nantien, offering comfortable, modern en suite doubles, triples and family rooms, with meals if required. Specialist meditation weekend packages are also available. There is a dearth of backpackers in the city with the rather tired, but perfectly friendly and welcoming **C-E** *Keiraleagh Backpackers*, 60 Kembla St, T42286216, backpack@primus.com.au, set in a spacious old guest house with dorms, doubles and singles, adequate facilities and internet. Wollongong is very well served with restaurants and cafés with seafood being a speciality. The well established and locally recommended seafood restaurant *The Beach House*, 16 Cliff Rd, T4228 5410, is open for lunch and dinner daily from 1200. Almost next door another fine seafood and modern Australian option is the *Silver Boat Bar and Restaurant*, T4229 9991, with its classy ambience and more wide ranging menu clearly giving the Boat House some stiff competition. Open from 1200 daily for lunch and dinner. Just around the corner the chic *Stingray Café*, Shop 5, 1-5 Bourke St, T4225 7701, is another local favourite with modern Australian and al fresco dining. Open Mon-Fri from 1000, Sat/Sun from 0800. For cheaper eateries Keira St or Corrimal are the best bet with. *The Food World Gourmet Café*, 148 Keira St, T42259655, offering great value Chinese.

Transport The **train station** is west of the city centre at the end of Burrelli St and Station St. CityRail offer regular daily services to/from Sydney to Bomaderry. Long distance coaches stop at the **Wollongong City Coach Terminal**, corner of Keira St and Campbell St, T4226 1022 (open Mon-Fri 0745-1730, Sat 0745-1415). *McCafferty's/Greyhound*, T132030, and *Premier Motor Services*, T133410, offer daily services to Sydney (Brisbane) and Canberra (Melbourne) via the Princes Highway. *Murray's*, T132251, also offer a daily service to Canberra and Narooma via Batemans Bay. **Taxi** Wollongong Radio Cabs, T4229 9311.

Kiama & around

Colour map 2, grid B6
Population: 12,000
106 km south of Sydney, 403 km from the Victorian border

Just to the south of Lake Illawarra, the pretty coastal town of Kiama is the first of many that are encountered time and again on the journey between Wollongong and the Victorian border. The **VIC** is on Blowhole Point, Blow Hole Point Road, T4232 3322, www.kiama.com.au ■ *Daily 0900-1700*. The centre of activity revolves around Blowhole Point, crowned by its 1887 **lighthouse**. Depending on conditions the surging waves can plough into the **blowhole** with awesome power creating a thunderous roar and spout of mist as if issued from some livid subterranean dragon. To the north of Blowhole Point is **Pheasant Point**, with its **rock pool** and north again **Bombo Beach**, a favourite amongst the local surf set. South, beyond the **Mount Pleasant Lookout** on the Princes Highway is **Werri Beach** (good for surfing), then via Crooked River Drive, the headland villages of **Gerringong** and Gerroa. From the **Kingsford Smith Lookout** in Gerroa (that pays tribute to Australia's most famous aviator), it is hard to resist the temptation to explore the vast swathe of **Seven Mile Beach**, which beckons from below the rooftops. Inland, via the little village of **Jamberoo** (10 km), is the **Minnamurra Rainforest**, which forms part of the **Budderoo National Park**. There, the popular **NPWS Minnamurra Rainforest Centre** acts as a base for explorations of the forest and the **Minnamurra Falls**. ■ *Daily 0900-1700, $10 vehicle entry, $4.40 if by coach or public bus, café and shop, T42360469. Right off Mountain Rd, heading west from Jamberoo, signposted.* Further west (8 km) is the **Barren Grounds Nature Reserve**, a 'hanging swamp' mixed with rainforest and sandstone escarpments that combined, creates a superb habitat for birds. The reserve also offers great coastal views from the **Illawarra Lookout** accessed via Griffiths Trail. Beyond the Barren Grounds Reserve (10 km) you can seek more great views, pleasant walks and aquatic cascades at the **Carrington Falls** within the northwestern sector of the national park. Left off Mountain Road on Carrington Falls Road, signposted.

Sleeping and eating Budget beds are available at The **C-D** *Grand Hotel*, corner of Manning St and Bong Bong St, T4232 1037, or you can head a little further south still, to Gerringong and the **C-E** *Nestor House YHA*, Fern St, T4232 1249. It is fairly basic offering 3 small dorms and 2 family rooms, but is well located just a short stroll from Seven Mile Beach. There are plenty of pleasant cafés and affordable eateries in Kiama with most located along Terralong and Collins St or beside the harbour. For fine dining try the seafood and ocean views at *Cargo's Restaurant*, on the Wharf, T4233 2771 (open daily for lunch and dinner). More affordable options include the locally popular and colourful *Ritzy Gritz New Mexican Grill*, T4232 1853 (open daily), or Chachi's Italian, T4233 1144, both on Collins St (closed on Tue). The *Mango Moon Thai Restaurant*, 68 Manning St, 14233 1668, is excellent, very popular, but also quite small, so book ahead. Open for dinner Tue-Sun.

There are plenty of motels in Kiama and numerous motor parks in beachside locations. The VIC can provide full listings

Transport The **train** station is off Bong Bong Rd in the centre of town. *CityRail,* T131500, offer regular daily services from Sydney. Long distance **coaches** also stop in the centre of town on Terralong St, or at the Bombo Railway Station 1½ km north. *Premier* and *McCafferty's/Greyhound* offer daily services between Canberra (Melbourne) and Sydney (Brisbane). *Kiama Coaches*, T4232 3466, offer services from the Bong Bong Rd train station to the Minnamurra Rainforest, daily at 1005, from $10, concession $5 return. **Bike hire** is available with *Kiama Cycles and Sports*, 27 Collins St, T4232 3005. **Taxi**, T4237 7505.

Roughly halfway between Kiama and Nowra is the delightful little village of Berry, which is well worth a stretch of the legs to take a closer look. Almost impossible to miss is the bizarre façade and interior of the **B-E** *Great Southern Hotel Motel*, T4464 1009. Not only is there a small fleet of rowboats on the roof and a signpost laden with markers to all conceivable destinations, there's also, next door, a bottle shop completely decked in shiny hubcaps. But it doesn't end there. Inside the bar is decked with a wide array of objects including a centrepiece **First World War torpedo** set proudly above the pool table. During the great Pacific nuclear testing hiatus in the mid-1990s, said torpedo was actually rammed at admirable speed into the gates of the French Embassy in Canberra atop a VW beetle. There are plenty of nice cafés and restaurants along Berry's main drag and if the pub food in the Southern Hotel is not sufficient, then try the more formal surrounds of the award winning Coach House Restaurant in the **C** *Berry Hotel*, 120 Queen Street, T4464 1011.

Berry
Colour map 2, grid B6
Population: 1,600
128 km south of Sydney, 375 km north of the Victorian border

New South Wales

**Nowra &
Bomaderry**
Colour map 2, grid B6
Population: 24,000
144 km south of
Sydney, 362 km north
of the Victorian border

Beyond Berry you reach the **Shoalhaven River** and the twin towns of Boma-derry and Nowra. From here you are entering the South Coast proper and an area known as **Shoalhaven**, which extends from **Nowra** to **Bateman's Bay**. Although the town of Nowra is a fairly unremarkable introduction to the South Coast, just to the east and especially around **Jervis Bay** and beyond its true magic begins to be revealed, with some of the best beaches and national parks in the state. The Shoalhaven **VIC** is on the southern bank of the Shoalhaven River, just off the Princes Highway, T4421 0778, www.shoalhaven.nsw.gov.au ■ *Daily 0900-1630*. Pick up a copy of the comprehensive *'All you need to know'* Shoalhaven Guide which also contains town and regional maps. The **NPWS** have an office at 55 Graham Street, T4423 2170. **Paringa and Nowra Park**, to the west of Nowra town centre fringes the riverbank and offers a pleasant riverside walk that takes in the 46 m **Hanging Rock Lookout** and a number of unadvertised climbing sites. *Shoalhaven River Cruise*, T2998 1007, offer three-hour trips (with lunch or afternoon tea) either upstream to Bangalee or down to Greenwell Point, at the mouth of the river, on Wednesday 1330, and Sunday 1000 or 1330. Departs from the Nowra Wharf, Wharf Street, just east of the bridge. South of Nowra (8 km) **Australia's Museum of Flight** is the country's largest aviation museum covering the nation's considerable contribution since before the Wright Brothers first powered flight in 1903. ■ *Daily 1000-1600, $10, child $5, T44241920, wwww.museum-of-flight.org.au*

Sleeping and eating The VIC can provide full accommodation listings. For budget accommodation, options include the friendly **C-D** *M&Ms Guest House*, 1A Scenic Dr, just west of the VIC, T4422 8006, www.mmguesthouse.com.au, offering large dorms, double/twins and singles, open fire, pool tables and a complimentary breakfast. The powered and non-powered sites with a difference try the riverside camping facilities next to the **E-F** *Nowra Animal Park*, Rockhill Rd (via Illaroo Rd and McMahon's Rd, off Princes Highway), Bomaderry, T4421 3949. For fine dining it's hard to beat the *Boatshed Restaurant*, 10 Wharf Rd (south bank below the bridge), T44212419. Open Tue-Sat from 1800. In the town centre Kinghorne St is the main drag and the best place to cruise the menus.

Transport The Bomaderry **train** station sees the termination of the line from Sydney. *CityRail*, T131500, offer daily services via Kiama and Wollongong. Numerous long distance **coach** and local **bus** companies base their operations from the bus terminal on Stewart Pl. *Premier McCafferty's/Greyhound* offer daily services between Canberra (Melbourne) and Sydney (Brisbane). *Kennedy's Coaches*, T44217596, offer weekday services through the Kangaroo Valley to Moss Vale. **Bike hire** is available with *Shoalhaven Bike Hire*, T04-1260 3831. **Taxi**, T4421 0333.

**Kangaroo
Valley &
Fitzroy Falls**
Population: 350
15 km northwest
of Bomaderry

Kangaroo Valley is becoming increasingly popular as a tourist destination in its own right, with a scattering of interesting local attractions and activities as well as the inevitable craft shops and cafés and a rash of cosy B&Bs all offering the perfect country getaway. *Kangaroo Valley Safaris*, T4465 1502, www.kangaroovalleycanoes.com.au, offer an exciting range of self-guided **canoeing** options on the Kangaroo and Upper Shoalhaven Rivers, from $25-55, while *The Man from Kangaroo Valley*, T4465 1912, www.kangaroovalleyhorseriding.com.au, offer a variety of trail rides. The perfectly pleasant **A-F** *Kangaroo Valley Tourist Park*, Moss Vale Road (1 km north of the village), T4465 1310, offers standard cabins, powered and non-powered sites, camp kitchen and canoe hire. North of Kangaroo Valley Moss Vale Road hits the northern fringes of the 189,481-ha **Morton National**

Park. The **Fitzroy Falls** are just one of the park's many spectacular features, only a short 10-minute stroll from the **Visitors Centre** off the Moss Vale Road. ■ *Daily 0900-1730, vehicle entry $3, café, T4887 7270. Kennedy's Coaches*, T44217596, offer weekday services through the Kangaroo Valley from Nowra to Moss Vale.

Jervis Bay is a deep, sheltered bay that sits neatly in the embrace of the **Beecroft Peninsula** to the north and the exquisite **Booderee National Park** to the south. It is blessed with stunning coastal scenery, beautiful white beaches, a marine park with **world-class dive sites** and even a resident pod of over 60 playful dolphins, all of which combine to earn it the quiet reputation as the jewel of the NSW South Coast. Local information is available from **Huskisson Trading Post**, 3 Tomerong Road, Huskisson, T4441 5241, www.jervisbaytourism.com.au ■ *Daily 0900-1700.*

Jervis Bay
Colour map 2, grid B6
200 km south of Sydney, 349 km north of the Victorian border

The old ship building town of **Huskisson** (known as 'Husky') and its neighbour **Vincentia** are the two main settlements on Jervis Bay and together form the gateway to the bay's principal mainly water-based activities of boating, fishing, diving and **whale- and dolphin-watching**. The diving in the **Jervis Bay Marine Park** in particular is said to be second only to the Great Barrier Reef and is well known for its variant species and water clarity. Huskisson has three companies offering whale (June-November) and **dolphin watching** (year round) as well as standard bay cruises. *Dolphin Watch*, 50 Owen Street (main drag), T4441 6311, www.dolphinwatch.com.au, *Dolphin Explorer*, 62 Owen Street, T4441 5455, and *Seaspray*, 47 Owen Street, T4441 5012. *Pro Dive*, 64 Owen Street, T4441 5255, www.prodivejervisbay.com.au, are a very knowledgeable, professional operation offering a range of **diving** options and courses. **Bike hire** also available. *Sea Kayak Jervis Bay*, T4443 3858, www.shoal.net.au/~Jbkayaks, offer half/full/weekend and multi day **sea kayaking** trips in Jervis Bay or further afield, while *Bay and Beyond*, T447 8777, bayandbeyond@ozemail.com.au, offer local half/full/twilight tours, as well as independent hire.

Sleeping and eating There are a scattering of up-market B&Bs, motels, pub-hotels, budget and motor park options in and around Huskisson and the Trading Post VIC can supply the full details. The **LL-L** *Paperbark Lodge and Camp*, 605 Woollamia Rd, T44416066, info@paperbarkcamp.com.au, is an excellent eco-tourist set up in a quiet bush setting with luxury en suite tent units, outdoor camp fire, good on-site restaurant, tours and activities. Recommended (book ahead). More conventional, but no less charming, are the 3 luxury (but value) fully self-contained cottages at. **LL-L** *Parma Farm*, an 1874 National Trust property, near Falls Creek, Parma Rd, T4447 8098, www.jervisbay beachandfarmescapes.com.au. Cheaper options in town include the **A** *Bayside Motor Inn*, corner of Hawke St and Bowen St, T4441 5500, and the traditional pub rooms in the well located **C** *Husky Pub*, Owen St, T4441 5001. For fine dining (out of town) the *Gunyah Restaurant*, at the Paperbark Camp (see above, open daily for dinner) is recommended while for no-nonsense, value pub food head for the *Husky Pub* (see above).

Transport *Nowra Coaches* T4423 5244, operate regular daily **bus** services between Nowra, Huskisson, Vincentia and Wreck Bay. For **bike hire** contact Pro Dive (see above).

Booderee National Park (formerly known as the Jervis Bay National Park) takes up almost the entire southern headland of Jervis Bay and is without doubt, one of the most attractive coastal national parks in NSW. Owned and administered not by the NPWS, but independently (and very successfully), by a collaboration of Parks Australia and the Wreck Bay Aboriginal

Booderee National Park
Colour map 2, grid B6

New South Wales

Community, it offers a wealth of fine, secluded beaches, bush walks, stunning coastal scenery and a rich array of wildlife. The **Visitors Information Centre** at the entrance to the park can supply detailed information about the park, its attractions, walks, amenities and its scattering of great campsites. ■ *Daily 0900-1600, T44430977, www.booderee.np.gov.au Jervis Bay Rd*. Not to be missed are **Green Patch Beach**, the further flung **Cave Beach** (good surf spot) and **Summercloud Bay**. The walking track to **Steamers Beach** (2.3 km) is also recommended although there are many fine options to choose from. Another unique attraction in the park is the 80-ha **Booderee Botanic Gardens** that were created in 1952 as an annex of the Australian National Botanic Gardens in Canberra. There are over 1,600 species centred around the small freshwater Lake McKenzie, with most being coastal plants more suited to the local climate. There are a number of short walks and **nature trails**. ■ *Mon-Fri 0800-1600, Sat/Sun 1000-1700, free with park entry fee*.

Getting there and information Access is via Jervis Bay Rd off the Princes Highway and south of Huskisson and Vincentia. The Day park-use fee for a vehicle is $10, by bus/taxi $3. There are good campsites with hot showers at Green Patch, while the similarly facilitated Bristol Point is designed for groups. Camping with cold showers is available at Cave Beach but there is a 250-m walking-only track to the site from the car park. All the campsites have groups of tame kangaroos and rosellas. Campsites of various sizes range in price from $12-17.50 for five, to $52 for groups of 20. Note the camping fee does not include vehicle entry so that does add extra costs, but it is well worth it! For bookings, T4443 0977. Book well ahead during public holidays. There is a general store in Jervis Bay Village off Jervis Bay Rd, within the park boundary. Open 0700-2100 (1900 outside school holidays).

Ulladulla
Colour map 2, grid B6
Population: 8,500
246 km south of
Sydney, 294 km north
of the Victorian border

The fairly unattractive fishing port of Ulladulla and its neighbour Mollymook, to the north, combine to form the largest settlement between Nowra and Batemans Bay. Most visitors to the town use it as a base for surfing, diving, boating, canoeing and fishing along the coast or on the local lakes. Another attraction is the ascent of Pigeon House Mountain, which lies in the southern sector of the Morton National Park about 20 km to the west of town. Just to the north of Ulladulla, the historic village of **Milton** is a popular spot for arts and crafts, hosting some good galleries, cafés and accommodation. The **VIC** is in the Civic Centre, just off the Princes Highway, in the centre of town, T4455 1269 (■ *Mon-Fri 1000-1700, Sat/Sun 0900-1700*). For local cruise operators and fishing charter and tackle hire, contact the VIC. *Ulladulla Dive and Adventure*, 211 Princes Highway, T4455 3029, www.ulladulladive.com.au Half day introductory 'Discover Scuba Trips', cost from $75, snorkelling lessons from $25 and full PADI certification courses from $350. You can even hire a 'dive buddy' from $50. The stunning views from the sandstone plateau of **Pigeon House Mountain** are well worth the climb.

Sleeping and eating The VIC has full listings for motels and B&Bs. The. **C-E** *South Coast Backpackers*, 63 Princes Highway, T44540500, suffers a bit from its busy roadside position but is otherwise comfortable, well facilitated and welcoming. There are plenty of motor parks in the region and it is worth taking a look at what is on offer in the VIC to secure the best beachside location. The best-facilitated park closest to town (2 km) is the. **LL-E** *Beach Haven Holiday Resort*, Princes Highway (south), T44552110. It has all the usual facilities including a heated pool and camp kitchen. For fine dining and imaginative modern Australian cuisine *Cookaburra's Shop*, 2/10 Watson St, T4454

1443, is recommended (open Tue-Sat for dinner from 1800, reduced hours in winter), while for seafood try the *Harbourside Restaurant*, beside the harbour, 84 Princes Highway, T4455 3377. Open daily for lunch and dinner.

The 11,978-ha Murramarang National Park is most famous for its tame and extremely laid-back population of Eastern grey **kangaroos**. Here they not only frequent the campsites, and the foreshore, but on occasion are even said to cool off in the surf. The park is a superb mix of forest and coastal habitat that offers a host of activities from swimming, surfing and walking to simple socializing with the resident marsupials. The beaches and campsites **Pebbly Beach** and **Depot beach** are the most popular spots, but **Durras North**, south of Depot Beach and **Pretty Beach** to the north are also top spots. There is a network of coast and forest walks available including the popular **'Discovery Trail'** off North Durras Road, which skirts the edge of **Durras Lake**. There is also a fine coastal track connecting Pretty Beach with Pebbly Beach. Access to Pebbly Beach is via Mount Agony Road (unsealed) right of the Princes Highway 10 km north of Batemans Bay. Depot Beach and Durras North are accessed via North Durras Road off Mount Agony Road. Pretty Beach and the Murramarang Aboriginal Area is accessed via Bawley Point and Kioloa on Murramarang Road (sealed) off the Princes Highway 16 km south of Ulladulla. Day-use vehicle entry costs $6, pedestrians free.

Murramarang National Park
Colour map 2, grid B6
10 km north of Batemans Bay

Sleeping The **F** NPWS campsite at Pebbly Beach (often busy) has just been renovated and is therefore well facilitated, with hot showers and fire sites, T4478 6006. A warden collects fees daily. **L-F** Depot Beach has cabins, powered and non-powered sites with modern facilities, T44786582, **C-F** Pretty Beach also offers powered and non-powered sites with similar facilities, T44572019. **LL-E** *Murramarang Resort*, on Banyandah St in South Durras, T4478 6355, is also a top spot and although not in the park itself it has its own tame kangaroos and some sublime coastal scenery. There is a choice of luxury cabins, en suite/standard powered and non-powered sites, pool, bar/restaurant, camp kitchen, organized activities and canoe/bike hire.

The **Eurobodalla** coastal region stretches from Batemans Bay in the north to Narooma in the south. The bustling seaside resort of Batemans Bay provides an ideal stopover along the coastal Princes Highway. The very helpful **VIC** is about 750 m south of the river, on the corner of Princes Highway and Beach Road, T44726900, www.naturecoast-tourism.com.au ■ *Daily 1900-1700. Free*. Most of the Bay's **beaches** are located southeast of the town centre and if you have time it is worth heading that way. Tomakin and Broulee offer the best surf and fishing sites and **jet skis** can be hired on Coriggan's Beach, T04-1052 6594. *Surfcentral*, T4472 3811, info@surf-central.com.au, offers surfing lessons, three hours from $45. On the river you can take a leisurely three-hour cruise upstream to the historic riverside village of **Nelligen** (30 minutes stop over) on the locally built *Clyde Princess*, at 1100, daily, from $22, child $11 (lunch options available), T4478 1005. The area offers some excellent **sea kayaking**. *Batemans Bay*, T4471 1135, www.batemansbayseakayaks.com.au, are a very professional set up and offer good half or full day and 'Sunset Tours', from $25-105. Likewise, you will be well looked after on four legs, **horse trekking** with *Billy Joes Trail Rides* offering one, two and three hour trail rides and camping trail rides from $25. There are numerous excellent **dive** sites around the Bay with the *Dive Shop*, 5/33 Orient St, T4472 9930, providing access, trips and gear hire.

Batemans Bay
Colour map 2, grid B6
Population: 10,000
298 km south of Sydney, 146 km east of Canberra, 247 km north of the Victorian border

New South Wales

Sleeping The VIC has full accommodation listings. For tidy motel accommodation try either the **LL-A** *Bridge Motel*, 29 Clyde St (200 m west of the bridge), T4472 6344 or the **A** *Country Comfort Motel*, on the corner of Princes Highway and Canberra Rd (just north of the bridge), T4472 6333. Backpackers and those in camper vans should head for the **A-E** *Shady Willows Holiday Park*, Old Princes Highway, corner of South St, T4472 4972, www.shadywillows.com.au It incorporates a YHA with dorm or on-site vans for couples, fully equipped kitchen, pool, internet and bike hire. Several other motor parks are located beachside along Beach Rd southeast of the city centre but the latter is within a short stroll. The best place for camping are the NPWS sites in the congenial kangaroo infested Murramarang National Park (see above). Seafood and fish and chips are the big favourites in the Bay. For fine dining *Jameson's on the Pier*, Old Punt Rd (just north and west of the bridge), T4472 6405, can always be relied on for excellent seafood as well as classy modern Australian (lunch and dinner, closed Mon) while for fresh fish and chips with the seagulls look no further than *The Boatshed* on the waterfront.

Transport Long distance **coaches** stop outside the Promenade Plaza on Orient St or Post Office on Clyde St. *Premier*, *McCafferty's/Greyhound* and *Priors* offer daily services between Canberra (Melbourne) and Sydney (Brisbane). *Murray's*, T132251, also offer services to Canberra, north to Nowra and south to Narooma. *Harvey World Travel*, 39 Orient St, T4472 9990, can assist with bookings.

Narooma
Colour map 2, grid B6
Population: 3,500
345 km south of Sydney, 177 km north of the Victorian border

Nestled on a headland in the glistening embrace of the **Wagonga River Inlet** and surrounded by rocky beaches, national parks and the odd accessible island, Narooma has all the beauty and potential activities for which the South Coast is famous. The **VIC** is at the northern end of town off the Princes Highway, T4476 2881, www.naturecoast-tourism.com.au ■ *Daily 0900-1700*. The biggest attraction is **Montague Island**, about 8 km offshore. Officially declared a nature reserve and administered by the National Parks and Wildlife Service, Montague Island has an interesting Aboriginal and European history and is crowned by a historic lighthouse built in 1881. But perhaps its greatest appeal are the colonies of **fur seals** and seabirds (including about 10,000 pairs of **fairy penguins**) that make the island home. Between October and December **humpback whales** can also be seen on their annual migration. The **NPWS** provide four-hour guided tour at 0930 and a 3½-hour evening tour at dusk. All tours are weather permitting and numbers are limited, from $69, child $50. Tours depart from the town wharf on Blue Water Drive. Book at the VIC. *Island Charters*, T4476 1047, offer independent sightseeing, fishing or dive charters, from $90. Back on the mainland the immediate coastline offers a number of interesting features including **Australia Rock**, which as the name suggests, looks like the outline of Australia. It is however not the rock that plays with the imagination but a hole in its middle. Access is via Bar Rock Road beyond the golf course, right at the river mouth on Wagonga Head. Further south **Glasshouse Rocks** are another interesting geological formation. On the western side of town the Wagonga Inlet presents opportunities for fishing and **river cruises**. The knowledgeable crew aboard the 90-year-old *Wagonga Princess*, T44762665, offer three-hour cruises up the river with an emphasis on wildlife and history.

Sleeping Though out of town the delightful **A** *Priory at Bingie*, Priory La, Bingie (26 km north) T4473 8881, www.bingie.com.au is a great B&B in a stylish modern home, offering 3 nice doubles, plenty of peace and quiet and great ocean views. South of Narooma (10 km) **A** *Mystery Bay Cottages*, 121 Mystery Ray Rd, Mystery Bay (3 km off the Princes Highway), T4473 7431, are a good self-contained option. In Narooma itself there are plenty of samey motels for which the VIC has full listings. At the northern end of the town just before the bridge (left) is the **C-E** *Bluewater Lodge YHA*, 8 Princes Highway, T4476 4440, which offers dorms, double/twins and family rooms in self-contained cabins, bike/canoe hire and internet.

Transport Long distance **coaches** stop in the town centre on Princes Highway, with services between Canberra (Melbourne) and Sydney (Brisbane). *Murray's* also offer services to Canberra and north to Nowra

From Narooma to the Victorian border is a region known as the **Sapphire Coast**. Just south of Narooma, in the shadow of Mount Dromedary, are the quaint and historic villages of **Central Tilba** and **Tilba Tilba**. Now classified by the National Trust, they boast many historic cottages and also offer some of the South Coast's best cafés and arts and crafts outlets. Ask for a self-guided heritage leaflet from the VIC in Narooma. They can also provide listings for numerous cosy B&Bs in and around the two villages. The **Tilba Valley Vineyard** (off the Princes Highway, 5 km north of Tilba Tilba), was established in 1978 and produces Shiraz, Semillon and Chardonnay. It offers tastings and has a small tavern-like restaurant. ■ *Daily from 1000, T4473 7308.*

The two Tilbas & Mount Dromedary
Population: 100
18 km south of Narooma

Just beyond the junction of Princes Highway and The Bermagui Road (towards Bermagui) is the **Umbarra Aboriginal Cultural Centre**, which offers a range of interesting local Aboriginal cultural tours and cruises to sites including **Mount Dromedary** (Gulaga), Mystery Bay and Lake Wallaga. ■ *Mon-Fri 0900-1700, Sat/Sun 0900-1600, from $50 T4473 7232, umbarra@acr.net.au* The small seaside village of Bermagui is 10 km further south. There's a good beach at **Horseshoe Bay**, though the best **surf breaks** are on Beares Beach to the south or Moorehead's Beach on the northern side of the harbour. *Surf Schools Australia*, T6493 3456, offer surfing lessons, from $30. The volunteer-run **VIC** is just opposite Horseshoe Bay on Lamont Street, T6493 3054, www.sapphirecoast.com.au They can provide full accommodation and fishing charter boat listings and local maps. ■*Open Mon-Fri 1000-1600, Sat/Sun 1000-1300.*

Bermagui
Colour map 2, grid B5
Population: 1,300
375 km south of Sydney, 155 km north of the Victorian border

Bega's town's biggest tourist draw is its famous **cheese factory**. ■ *Daily 0900-1700, free, T6491 7777, www.begacheese.com.au Lagoon St.* To the north and west of Bega is the 79,459 ha **Wadbilliga National Park**, a wilderness region of rugged escarpment and wild rivers. Along the road to the **Brogo River Dam** you can stay at the **LL-L** *Fernmark Inn*, 610 Warrigal Range Road, Brogo, T6492 7136, www.fernmark.com.au, with its worldly themed en suites and fine cuisine. It is the perfect base from which to explore the park's rivers, which is perhaps best done by canoe. *Brogo Wilderness Canoes*, T6492 7328, www.acr.net.au/~brogocanoes, offer trips (including overnight camping), from $15 (full day from $30). From Bega you can then head straight for Merimbula or take a diversion to the coastal village of **Tathra**, where you can laze on the beach or explore the many pleasant features in the **Bournda National Park**. The 10-km **Kangarutha Track** from Tathra South to **Wallagoot Lake** is recommended. NPWS **camping** is available at Hobart Beach (off Sapphire Coast Drive, south of Tathra), T6495 4130. There is a small **VIC** off the Princes Highway in the centre of the town, T6492 2045, begatic@acr.net.au They can supply full accommodation listings.

Brogo, Bega & Tathra
Colour map 2, grid C5
Population: 4,000
446 km south of Sydney, 100 km north of the Victorian border

Merimbula
Colour map 2, grid C5
Population: 4,500
457 km south of
Sydney, 70 km north
of the Victorian border

Merimbula serves as the capital of the Sapphire Coast and receives most of its tourist traffic. Surrounded by fine beaches and bisected by **Merimbula Lake** (which is actually a saltwater inlet), it offers plenty to see and do, with **Main Beach**, south of the lake being the most popular for swimming and bodyboarding. The lake itself is a great venue for boating, wind surfing and fishing. The surrounding coast also offers some good diving and is the happy home of a resident pod of **dolphins**. From September-December migrating whales join the party making cruising the town's speciality. A two-hour Dolphin Cruise with *Merimbula Marina*, T6495 1686, will cost around $30-60. *Sinbad Cruises* offer cruises on the Pambula River and **Pambula Lake** from $27, child $18 (lunch $38/$22). The VIC has full details of **diving** and fishing charters, boat hire, **horse trekking** and scenic flights. *Cycle 'N' Surf*, 1B Marine Par, T6495 2171, hire bikes, surf/body boards and fishing tackle. The **VIC** is on the northern bank of Merimbula Lake on Beach Street, T64974908, www.sapphirecoast.com.au ■ *Daily 0900-1700*. The **NPWS** have a great Discovery Centre, on the corner of Sapphire Coast and Merimbula Drives, offering detailed parks and regional walks information, natural history displays, maps and gifts, T6495 5000. ■ *Open 0830-1630*.

Sleeping and eating There are plenty of motels and self-contained apartments in town and the VIC has full details. The **C-E** *Wandarrah Lodge YHA*, 8 Marine Pde, T64953503, wanlodge@asitis.com.au, is excellent and purpose-built, providing modern en suite dorms, double and family rooms, a well equipped kitchen, 2 lounges, internet, free breakfast and bike, surf/bodyboard hire. Recommended. There are plenty of **motor parks**. East of the town centre near Short Point the **L-E** *Merimbula Holiday Park*, Cliff St (east via Main St), T64951269, is one of the best placed for peace and quiet, while right in the thick of things and near Main Beach, is the well facilitated **LL-E** *South Haven Caravan Park*, Elizabeth St (just south of the bridge), T64951304. Market St (main drag) and Beach St (VIC) host numerous affordable cafés and restaurants. Further afield, the *Wharf Restaurant* overlooking the inlet at the Merimbula Aquarium, Lake St, T64954446, is locally recommended, especially for lunch. Open daily for lunch and Wed-Sat for dinner.

Transport Merimbula **airport** is located 1 km south of the town. *Regional Express Airlines*, T131713, offer services to Sydney and Melbourne. Long distance **coaches** stop at the Ampol Service Station in the town centre. *Premier* and *McCafferty's/Greyhound*, offer daily services between Melbourne and Sydney (Brisbane). *V-Line*, T136196, and *Sapphire Coast Express* both offer additional services to Melbourne. *Edwards Buses*, T6495 4166, offer local weekday services to Bega, Eden and Pambula. *Summerland Travel*, 16 The Plaza, T6495 1008, act as local booking agents. **Bike hire** is available from *Cycle 'N' Surf*, 1B Marine Par, T6495 2171, from $3 per hr ($12 per day).

Eden & Boydtown
Colour map 2, grid C5
Population: 3,000
501 km south of
Sydney, 47 km north
of the Victorian border

In the coastal village of Eden is the **Killer Whale Museum**, which offers a fascinating insight into the villages whaling, pioneering and fishing history. ■ *Mon-Sat 0915-1545, Sun 1115-1545, $6, child $2*, T64962094. *Imlay St. Cat Balou*, T6496 2027, offer half day **whale-watching** trips (October-November) from **Snug Cove** on Twofold Bay, from $25. Diving and fishing charters are also available and the **VIC** can provide listings, at the main roundabout in town (Princes Highway), T64961953, www.sapphirecoast.com.au ■ *Mon-Fri 0900-1600, Sat/Sun 0900-1200*.

Sleeping The spacious and historic **LL-L** *Crown and Anchor B&B*, 239 Imlay St, T6496 1017, www.acr.net.au/~crownanchor, is a delightful place (a former hotel originally built in 1845) with lots of character and great views across Towfold Bay. Nearby the

A *Twofold Bay Motel*, 164 Imlay St, T6496 3058, has tidy units (some with spa) and great views. To the south in Boydtown the **A-B** *Seahorse Inn*, just off the Princes Highway (8 km), T6496 1361, is a historic hotel named after the steamship on which Ben Boyd arrived in Australia. Built in the 1840s and full of character it offers tidy rooms (some en suite) and of course a good bar and restaurant. The **L-E** *Garden of Eden CV Park* is 2 km north of the village centre off the Princes Highway, T1800-224460. Cabins, powered and non-powered sites, pool and BBQ but no camp kitchen.

Transport Long distance **coaches** stop at the Caltex Roadhouse on the Princes Highway. *Premier* and *McCafferty's/Greyhound* have daily services between Melbourne and Sydney. *V-Line* and *Sapphire Coast Express*, both offer additional services to Melbourne. *Edwards Buses* do local weekday services to Merimbula, Bega and Pambula

Sheer wilderness, beautiful coastal scenery, sublime walks, strange, colourful geological features, great campsites and even a remote lighthouse all combine to make the Ben Boyd National Park one of the best coastal parks in NSW. The 9,490-ha park straddles Twofold Bay and the fishing village of Eden. In the northern section of the park, the main feature are 'The Pinnacles', a conglomerate of white and orange, sand and clay that has eroded into strange pinnacle formations over many thousands of years. They can be reached on a short 500-m-circuit walk from the car park off Haycock Road (2 km, partly sealed and signposted off the Princes Highway). To the north, at the end of Edrom Road (16 km signposted off the Princes Highway) is **Boyd's Tower**, which though very grand, never served its intended purpose as a lighthouse. Below the tower a clearing looks down to clear azure waters and the strange volcanic convolutions of the red coastal rocks. Another diversion off Edrom Road, to the west, takes you to the remains of the **Davidson Whaling Station** created in 1818 and the longest-running shore-based station in Australia (ceasing operations in 1930). Further south off Edrom Road an unsealed, badly rutted road leads to the delightful and wildlife rich Bittangabee campsite (15 km, then 5 km on the left). Back on the main track the **Disaster Bay Lookout** is worth a look before it terminates at the 'must-see' **Green Cape Light Station** (21 km). Surrounding by strange rust coloured rocks, pounded by surf and home to laid-back kangaroos, it is a wonderful place to find some solitude. **City Rock** which is accessed down a short badly rutted track (1 km, signposted) off the lighthouse road is also well worth seeing. The wave action against the rock platform is dramatic and it is a favourite haunt for sea eagles. The superb but demanding (30 km) 'Light to Light' **Walking Track** connects the Green Cape light station with Boyd's Tower, passing the Bittangabee and **Saltwater Creek** campsites along the way. It offers one of the best and most remote coastal walks in NSW.

Ben Boyd National Park
Colour map 2, grid C5
556 km south of Sydney, 35 km north of the Victorian border

New South Wales

Getting there and sleeping Access to the park is off Princes Highway (signposted). Roads within the park are both sealed and unsealed. Unsealed sections are badly rutted, but negotiable by 2WD in dry conditions. Day-use vehicle entry to the park costs $6. The **NPWS** office in Merimbula (see above), T64955001, can provide detailed information on the park, its walks and its campsites. Basic (but delightful) camping is available at Saltwater Creek and Bittangabee Bay. Self-registration, fees apply. There is also modern, self-contained accommodation available in the lighthouse (book well ahead). Other local options are the self-contained en suite cabins at the **L-A** *Wonboyn Lake Resort* 1 Oyster La (19 km off Princes Highway), T6496 9162, www.wonboynlakesresort.com.au, or the cabins, powered and non-powered sites at the **A-E** *Wonboyn Cabins and Caravan Park*, Wonboyn Rd, T64969131, www.wonboyncabins.com.au

Central and Northwest NSW

Bathurst
Colour map 3, grid C3
Population: 30,000
203 km west of Sydney, 209 km southeast of Dubbo

Australia's oldest inland settlement, the gracious and historic, former gold mining town of Bathurst is best known these days for its **racing circuit**. The **VIC** is at 28 William Street, T6332 1444/1800 681 000, www.bathurstcity.com ■ *Daily 0900-1700*. Ask for the comprehensive, free, *'Bathurst and District Visitors Guide'* that contains a city **map** and the full list of local attractions and activities. They also stock self-guided **walks** leaflets outlining the best of the city's historic landmarks. The **NPWS** have an office and **shop** at Level 2, 203-209 Russell Street, T6332 9488. ■ *Mon-Fri 0900-1700*. Two of the most notable old buildings are the 1870 baronial mansion **Abercrombie House**, 311 Ophir Road (■ *Open for guided tours Sun, 1500, $5.50, T6332 1444*) and the **Chiefly Home**, 10 Busby Street, (■ *Tue-Sat 1400-1600, Sun 1000-1200, $3, T6332 1444*) once the former residence of the city's most famous son, former Australian Prime Minister Ben Chiefly. *Wambool Aboriginal Cultural Tours*, 28 William Street, T6332 1444, offer a bush tucker lunch followed by an entertaining trip to the **Abercrombie Caves** near Trunkey Creek (70 km south). The undeniable highlight there is the Grand Arch reputedly one the largest features of its kind in the southern hemisphere. ■ *The caves are open daily 0900-1600 (guided tours at 1400), from $13.50. Camping is also available, T6368 8603.*

Sleeping and eating The VIC has full listings of the many motels, B&Bs and self-contained options. The **C** *Bathurst Explorers Motel*, 357 Stewart St (main drag 1 km west of the city centre), T6331 2966, www.lisp.com.au/~explorer offers good budget rooms and has attractive breakfast and dinner deals. The best facilitated **motor park** is the **A/E** *East's Bathurst Holiday* Park, on Sydney Rd, Kelso (5 km east of the city centre), T6331 8286. It offers standard cabins, en suite and standard powered and shady non-powered sites, pool and BBQ but no camp kitchen. Bathurst is home to many chic and often historic restaurants and cafés, including the congenial *Lamplighters*, 126 William St, T6331 1448. Open lunch Mon-Fri, dinner nightly.

Transport Bathurst **Airport**, T8087 4128, is 4 km east of the city centre. *Hazelton*, T131713 offer regular services to/from Sydney. A taxi T6331 1511/131008 to the centre of the city costs about $8 National World Travel, 70 William St, T6331 2333, can assist with bookings. The train station is located 1 km south of the city centre at the end of Keppel St, off Havannah St. Countrylink XPT, T132232, provide daily services east to Sydney and west to Dubbo and beyond. There is a Countrylink Travel Centre at the station, T6332 4844. Long distance bus companies include *McCafferty's/Greyhound*, T132030, that stop at the train station and offer services northwest (Dubbo/Coonabarabran/Brisbane via the Mitchell and Newell Hwys), east to Sydney via the Blue Mountains, and west (to Adelaide via Dubbo, Broken Hill and the Barrier Highway). Rendell's Coaches, T68842411, also offer services to/from Sydney and Canberra

Orange
Colour map 3, grid C3
Population: 31,000
276 km west of Sydney, 153 km southeast of Dubbo

Often dubbed **Australia's Colour City**, Orange offers a cooler climate and a verdant landscape and over 100 parks and has a wealth of gardens that present a palette of golden hues in autumn. The town's most famous son was **Banjo Patterson** who penned *'Waltzing Matilda'*; Australia's much loved and 'unofficial' national anthem. The **VIC**, Civic Square, Byng Street, T6393 8226, www.orange.nsw.gov.au, has full accommodation, activity listings and can provide town and regional maps. ■ *Daily 0900-1700*. The **Ophir Reserve** on Summer Hill Creek, is the site of Australia's first gold discovery in 1851.

Although the great rush has long gone, the reserve still hosts a working mine that produced gold used for the Sydney 2000 Olympic Gold Medals.

Dubbo is one of NSW fastest growing inland cities and the commercial capital for the west of the state. Its biggest attraction is the sizeable **Western Plains Zoo**, the sister to the world famous Taronga Zoo in Sydney. Set in 300 ha of parkland it provides home to over 1,000 species, many endangered, and most roaming free. Given the heat in the middle of the day, the best time to visit is early in the morning by joining one of the guided **Early Morning Zoo Walks** beginning at 0645 (Saturday/Sunday and Wednesday/Friday/Saturday/Sunday during public holidays). This provides a better insight into the zoo and includes breakfast for $10 extra (child $7.70). The walk alone costs $3 on top of the usual admission charge. Note there is also **accommodation** available at the zoo (see below). ■ *0900-1600, $22, child $12 (bike hire $11, buggy $44), T6882 5888, www.zoo.nsw.gov.au Obley Rd (4 km south off Newell Highway).* The **VIC** is at the northeastern fringe of the city, on the corner of Macquarie Street and the Newell Highway, T6884 1422, www.dubbotourism.com.au ■ *Daily 0900-1700.* They can also provide city maps and discounted tickets to the zoo.

Dubbo
Colour map 3, grid C3
Population: 40,000
414 km west of Sydney
Dubbo is derived from the Aboriginal word meaning 'red earth'
If you intend to venture forth by car, most probably to Broken Hill, be sure to check the vehicle and join the NRMA

Sleeping and eating The most unique place to stay in the city are the **LL** *Zoofari Lodges*, a cluster of African-style tented lodges in the zoo grounds. The package includes 2-day entry to the zoo guided tours meals and bike hire, T1300-720018, dmilling@lisp.com.au Most of the **motels** are located along the main highways into town and Cobra St, south of the city centre. There are a scattering of **B&Bs** in and around the city including the **L-A** *Westbury B&B and Restaurant*, corner of Brisbane St and Wingewarra St, T6884 9445, westburydubbo@bigpond.com For cheap and cheerful traditional pub rooms try the **C** *Castlereagh Hotel*, corner of Talbragar St and Brisbane St, T6882 4877, tariff includes breakfast. The **C-E** *Dubbo YHA*, 87 Brisbane St, T6882 0922, is both friendly and well facilitated, offering small dorms, double/twins, singles, family rooms, internet, bike hire and a cheeky pet parrot. It is just a short stroll from the train station and city centre. Some of the upmarket motels have good but rather pricey **restaurants**, including the *Ashwood Country Club and Motel*, corner of Newell Highway and East St, T6881 8700, or the *Countryman*, 47 Cobra St, T6882 7422. In the city itself the *RSL Club and Motel*, corner Brisbane St and Wingewarra St, T6884 9009, and *Amaroo Hotel*, 83 Macquarie St, T6882 3533, both offer the usual value bistro meals. For breakfast, lunch and good coffee (and internet) look no further than the *Grapevine Café*, 144 Brisbane St, T6884 7354.

There are plenty of beds in Dubbo with a glut of quality, but very samey motels, some of which offer zoo packages. The VIC has full listings

Transport Dubbo **Airport** is located 7 km northwest along the Mitchell Highway. *Qantas*, T131313, fly to/from Sydney daily and Brisbane (direct) twice a week. *Hazelton*, T131713, also fly to/from Sydney daily and most major regional centres including Broken Hill. *Western Plains Travel*, 1/18 Talbagar St, T6882 2833, act as airline booking agents. A **taxi** (24-hrs) T131008, to the city centre costs around $14. Long distance **bus/train** combination services (*Countrylink*, T6884 2511) stop at the **train station** on Talbragar St. Onward services include Lightning Ridge, Bourke and Coonabarabran. *Countrylink* XPT trains service Sydney, while other interstate services head west to Adelaide/Broken Hill and south to central, southern NSW and Melbourne. *McCafferty's/Greyhound* stop at the Shell Station, junction of the Newell and Mitchell Hwys and offer services north (Coonabarabran/Brisbane via the Newell Highway), east to Sydney via the Blue Mountains, south (Melbourne via the Newell Highway) and west (to Adelaide via Broken Hill and the Barrier Highway). *Rendell's Coaches*, T6884 2411, also offer services to/from Sydney and Canberra.

Public transport in Dubbo is poor and practically non-existent to the zoo. Get hold of the free 'Dubbo City Bikeway Map' from the VIC

New South Wales

Coonabarabran

Colour map 3, grid B4
Population: 3,000
158 km north of
Dubbo, 182 km west
of Tamworth

High on the Western Plains of NSW, on the verge of true outback country, the small rural town of **Coonabarabran** – or 'Coona' – is labelled *Australia's Astronomy Capital*. The **Sliding Spring Observatory**, 28 km west of the town on the fringe of the Warrumbungle National Park, is the largest optical telescope in Australia. ■ *The centre is open daily 0930-1600, but not at night when its official functions take precedence, from $5.50, child $3.50, T6842 6211, www.slidingspringexploratory.com.au National Park Rd.* The **VIC** is on the southern end of the town on the Newell Highway, T6842 1441, www.lisp.com.au/coonabarabran ■ *Daily 0900-1700.* The **NPWS**, 56 Cassilis Street, T6842 2124 stocks national parks and forest parks information.

Coona serves as the gateway to the **Warrumbungle National Park**, considered by many as one of the best in the state. The stark and jagged volcanic peaks of the 21,000-ha park provide an intriguing landscape, networked with over 30 km of walking tracks that some consider being among the best on offer anywhere in NSW. The primary focus for visitors is the **Grand High Tops**, where the various tracks, ranging from easy 1-km half-day bush rambles, to multi-day treks with strenuous climbs. As well as its stunning geology the park also plays host to a rich assortment of wildlife classics from koalas to emus, many of which can be spotted with a little luck from the various tracks. If you are planning on doing some serious walking get hold of the NPWS *'Warrumbungles Walks Guide'* ($5). There is a NPWS **visitors centre** located in the heart of the park (signposted) off the John Renshaw Parkway 35 km west of Coonabarabran. ■ *Daily 0830-1600, T6825 4364.* As well as providing detailed information and issuing the obligatory $6 car entry (Day Use) fee, you can secure **rock-climbing** and **camping** permits ($5-11, per night, exclusive of Day Use Permit). There are a number of **NPWS campsites** with the most popular, accessible and best-facilitated being **E-F** *Camp Blackman* (powered sites, showers) and **E-F** *Camp Elongery* (non-powered using the latter facilities). Both are signposted north off John Renshaw Parkway, 37 km west of Coonabarabran.

Narrabri

Colour map 3, grid B4
Population: 6,500
118 km north of
Coonabarabran

Narrabri is linked with clear night skies and the **Australia Telescope**, which links up with the scopes in Coonabarabran and Parkes to give a wider coverage of the heavens. There is an interesting visitors centre with various heavenly displays and audio-visual presentations and when not in use the staff will let you take a closer look at the dishes. ■ *Daily 0800-1600 (staff available Mon-Fri only), free, T6790 4070. 20 km west of Narrabri on Yarrie Lake Rd (off the Newell Highway).* **Mount Kaputar National Park**, 20 km east of Narrabri, offers some excellent walking opportunities and stunning views. The park's main geological attraction are the **Sawn Rocks**, an odd basalt formation. They can be reached north of Narrabri then east off the Newell Highway (signposted and unsealed). The **VIC** is off the Newell Highway (between Tibbereena Street and the Narrabri Creek), T6792 3583, www.tournarrabri.nsw.gov.au ■ *Mon-Fri 0900-1700, Sat/Sun 0900-1300.* The **NPWS** have an office at 100 Maitland Street, T6799 1740. ■ *Mon-Fri 0830-1700.*

Lightning Ridge

Colour map 3, grid B3
Population:
2,000-10,000
355 km northwest of
Dubbo, 767 km
northwest of Sydney
For the flights info
contact the VIC

Located just about in the middle of nowhere, near the Queensland border, 767 km from Sydney, Lightening Ridge attracts almost 100,000 visitors a year, all searching for the elusive **black opal**. The **VIC** is on Morilla Street, T6829 1466, www.lightningridge.net.au ■ *Open daily.* It has details of what is on offer. The **Big Opal** has daily underground tours, demonstrates cutting, and has a showroom and its own fossicking area. ■ *Daily 0900-1700, $12, child $4, T6829 0247.* The **Spectrum Mine** has an underground showroom, film presentation and its own fossicking area. ■ *Daily 0900-1700, $4, T6829 0581. Bald Hill Rd.*

The **Walk In Mine**, is a genuine working mine offering underground tours, showrooms and audio-visual. ■ *Daily 0900-1730, $7, child $3 T6829 0473.* *Black Opal Tours*, T6829 0368, blackopaltours@lightningridge.net.au, offer tours from two/three/five hours with fossicking included. Hot, dusty and perhaps unsuccessful, you can then find solace with a dip in the 42° **Bore Baths** on Pandora Street. ■ *Daily 24 hrs, free, T6829 0429.*

Sleeping and eating **A-B** *Wallangulla Motel*, corner of Morella St and Agate St, T6829 0542, offers some spa rooms and the **B** *Black Opal Motel*, on Opal St, T68290518. The **B** *Lightning Ridge Hotel/Motel*, Onyx St, T6829 0304, offers log-cabin style units and a pool, as well as powered and non-powered sites. It also has a restaurant (open Thu/Fri/Sat) and a bistro open daily. The **B** *Tram-O-Tel*, on Morilla St, T6829 0448, has the added attraction of its own fossicking sites.

The town is pretty well facilitated and has plenty of beds, mainly in standard 2-star hotels with the obligatory air-con rooms

Outback NSW

The outback of New South Wales provides the most accessible opportunity to experience the true Australian 'outback' – a word pregnant with meaning, imagery and expectation. If you come from cold lands, urban places, green neighbourhoods, then prepare to be blown away. Outback NSW offers some of the best that Australia has to offer, from surreal landscapes and historic mining towns, to abundant wildlife and even underground homes. If you are in doubt, are inclined to stick to the populous and the coast – think again. At the very least try to visit Broken Hill without doubt one of the best destinations in the state.

From Bathurst the Mitchell Highway heads northwest through Dubbo and Nyngan then continues for almost 200 km to the most outback of towns – Bourke. In fact, the northwestern corner of New South Wales has been affectionately called the **Back O' Bourke** and Bourke has been its capital. Although not high on the tourists agenda the town provides a very typical **outback experience**. The **VIC** is on Anson Street, T6872 2280, www.backobourke.com.au ■ *Daily 0900-1700.* They can provide full accommodation and activity listings, regional and town maps. The **NPWS** office at 51 Oxley Street, T6872 2744, stock national parks information. The VIC also offers very useful, self-guided 'Mud Map Tours' that take in local sites and regional routes, taking in everything from historic buildings and stunning views to Aboriginal rock art. Two of the most noted sites are **Mount Oxley** (309 m, 28 km east, then south) and the **Gundabooka National Park** (50 km, south) with its rust coloured 385 million year old rocks, Aboriginal rock art and, again, fine views. Consult the VIC before making the trip to Mount Oxley. The NPWS office can also provide additional detail. **Brewarrina**, 97 km east of Bourke is noted for its ancient rock **fishing traps** created in the Barwon River by the Ngemba Aboriginals thousands of years ago. There is also an **Aboriginal Cultural Museum** in the town that can provide additional insight. ■ *Mon-Fri 0900-1700, T6839 2868. Bathurst St.*

Bourke
Colour map 3, grid B2
Population: 3,500
364 km northwest of Dubbo, 780 km northwest of Sydney
For roads information T6872 1222
For breakdown assistance NRMA, 12 Richards Street, T6870 1062

Sleeping and eating The classy **A-B** *Darling River Motel*, 74 Mitchell St, T6872 2288, provides some of the best in motel accommodation, while the basic but value **B-C** *Port of Bourke Hotel*, 32 Mitchell St, T6872 2544, offers traditional budget hotel/pub rooms and decent counter and bistro meals. The riverside **C-E** *Kidman's Caravan Park*, Cunamulla Rd (7 km north of town centre), T6872 1612, offers standard cabins, powered and non-powered sites and camp kitchen.

New South Wales

▶▶ **Barrier Highway Petrol Stops and travelling times**

Dubbo and Broken Hill both have 24 hour service stations. Nyngan, Cobar and Wilcannia have service stations open from 0700 until around 2100. There are also roadhouses at Emmdale between Cobar and Wilcannia and Little Topar between Wilcannia and Broken Hill. Note some service stations also provide 24 hour credit card or BP card services. For specific details contact the VICs before departure. The trip from Dubbo to Broken Hill can be done comfortably in 9-10 hours.

Transport *Countrylink*, T132232, provide **coach/rail** services to Sydney via Dubbo, arriving Sun/Tue/Thu/Fri, departing Wed/Fri/Sat. Buses stop outside the VIC on Anson St. By **air** Hazelton, T131713, offer services to Sydney via Dubbo on Mon/Tue/Wed/Fri and from Sydney Tue/Wed/Thu/Fri/Sat. **Taxi**, T6836 2684. The **Mitchell Highway** presents no travelling hazards, other than the usual sheer desolation and kangaroos and the **Kidman Highway**, between the town and Cobar (159 km), is fully sealed. As with anywhere 'outback' it is strongly advised not to travel at night, or for an hour either side of dawn or dusk, due to the risk of hitting kangaroos.

Barrier Highway
753 km from Dubbo to Broken Hill For breakdown assistance contact the local NRMA accredited garage in Cobar, corner Lewis St and Louth Rd, T6836 4007

From Dubbo the Mitchell Highway continues west 165 km to the small, fairly unremarkable town of **Nyngan**. From there it continues 199 km northwest to Bourke, while the Barrier Highway heads 588 km west to Broken Hill and, eventually, Adelaide. Continuing west from Nyngan you gradually either feel a sense of relief or perhaps a tinge of fear, as all things urban begin to dissipate and the outback begins. Next stop (for petrol or otherwise) is a mere 132 km and **Cobar** a small copper mining town. If you intend to have an overnight stop on your journey to Broken Hill then Cobar is recommended as opposed to Wilcannia, further west. The helpful **VIC** is located on the main drag (Barrier Highway) at the eastern end of town, T6836 2448. ■ *Mon-Fri 0830-1700, Sat/Sun 0900-1700*. There are plenty of **motel** rooms with some of the best available at the **L-A** *Sundowner Motel*, 67 Barrier Highway, T6836 2304. For a cheaper motel option try the **B** *Copper City Motel*, 40 Lewis Street (corner Barrier Highway and Lewis Street), T6836 2404. Both have restaurants.

Wilcannia, 260 km west of Cobar, is nothing more than a pit stop. From Wilcannia it is well worth taking the diversion to spend a night and a day in **White Cliffs**, 98 km north. This **opal mining** settlement is so hot and inhospitable the residents have to live underground to keep cool, creating White Cliffs greatest attraction, its **underground homes**. Local information is available at **VIC** in the General Store on the corner of Johnston Street and Keraro Road, T809 16611. They can provide a 'Mud Map' for a fascinating self-guided tour. Alternatively, local *Ross Jones*, T8091 6607, can provide an entertaining insight. You don't need to be a guest to have a guided tour of **L** *PJ's Underground B&B*, Dugout 72 Turley's Hill, T8091 6626, www.babs.com.au/nsw/pj.htm, which has 5 well-appointed rooms, spa and offer either B&B or dinner B&B options. The larger, less homely, yet no less unique **A** *White Cliffs Underground Dug-out Motel*, Smith's Hill, T8091 6647, offers 32 units, with triples/doubles/twins and singles, a restaurant, pool and a spa. The 93-km road between Wilcannia (Barrier Highway) and White Cliffs is partly sealed and suitable for 2WD. For the latest road conditions T8091 5155. There is no scheduled public transport to White Cliffs, but a number of tour operators offer trips from Broken Hill.

Broken Hill or 'Silver City' (as it is dubbed) is a green oasis in the outback and the most famous mining town in Australia, its gracious, dusty streets looking like something out of an Aussie version of Hollywood's 'Wild West'. As well as all the obvious historical and mine based attractions Broken Hill is also home to a thriving arts community and numerous colourful galleries. Numerous tour operators also eagerly await to escort you to see the almost surreal settlement of Silverton, as well true outback adventures to some superb regional national parks and lake systems. All in all Broken Hill is simply a 'must see' and admirably lives up to its other less familiar label; 'Gateway to the Outback'.

Broken Hill
Phone code: 08
Colour map 2, grid A2
Population: 21,000
1160 km west of
Sydney, 753 km west
of Dubbo, 508 km
northeast of Adelaide

Getting there Broken Hill **Airport** is located 4 km southwest of the town via Bonanza St, T8087 4128. A **taxi**, T8088 1144/131008 to/from the airport to the city centre costs about $10. *Hazelton* fly from Sydney every day except Sat. *Qantas* also offer regular services. *Kendell* also offer daily services to/from Adelaide. Long distance coaches stop at the **coach terminal**, T8087 2735, beside the VIC (see above). *McCafferty's/*

Broken Hill is Central
Standard Time.
All other towns in
the region operate
on Eastern
Standard Time

New South Wales

Broken Hill

To Mutawintji National Park
Jack Absalom Studio

To Living Desert & Sculpture Symposium
Pro Hart Studio
To White's Art & Mining Museum, Silverton Hotel & Daydream Mine
To Broken Hill City Caravan Park

School of the Air
To Lake View Caravan Park & The Base B & B

Library
Pol

To Historical Photo Gallery, Airport & Royal Flying Doctor Service

Delprats Mine
Miners Memorial
Line of Lode

Street names: McCulloch St, Uranium St, Radium St, Fisher St, McGowen St, Zebina St, Brazil St, Bagot St, Williams St, Chapple St, Lane St, Iodide St, Cobalt St, Mica St, Beryl St, Argent St, Crystal St, Sulphide St, Oxide St, Iodide St, Union St, Brown St, Wyman St, Cummins St, Sulphide St, Bromide St, Morgan St, Chloride St, Kaolin St, Thomas St, Bowen St, Wicks St, Marks St, Bromide St, Cobalt St, Wolfram St, Kaolin St, Blende St, Garner St, Gossan St, Wright St, Warnock St, Williams St, Jones St, Hill St, Cowan St, O'Farrell St, Galena St, Harvey St, Smith St, Talc St, Mercury St, Beryl St, Federation Way, Murray Dr

Inset map
Silver City Mint & Arts Centre
Broken Hill City Art Gallery
Trades Hall
Town Hall
Court House (Pol)
Library
Railway, Mineral & Train Museum
NPWS
Geocentre
Chloride St, Beryl St, Blende St, Sulphide St, Argent La, Bromide St, Crystal St

N
0 metres 500
0 yards 500

■ **Sleeping**	● **Eating**
1 Charles Rasp Motel	8 YHA Tourist Lodge
2 Gateway Motel	1 Batina's
3 Imperial	2 Black Lion Pub
4 Mario's Palace	3 MacGregors Café
5 Mine Host Motel	4 McPhees
6 Old Vic B & B	5 Ruby's
7 Theatre Royal	

▶▶ **Driving in the outback**

*Driving in the outback obviously presents some special considerations that go beyond mere common sense. The simple things like checking the tyre pressures, taking maps, plenty of water and, on long journeys, extra food and fuel goes without saying. Mobile phones are recommended but bear in mind coverage is very limited. Monitoring petrol is also very important and perhaps new to drivers used to more urban environments. Joining that particular state's Automobile Association and breakdown service is also highly recommended. You will encounter numerous wildlife road kills that merely underline their prevalence, especially accidents involving kangaroos. True they are both fast and agile, but their brains, sadly, do not match the size of their testicles and they tend to run straight towards headlights, instead of avoiding them. Travelling at dawn or dusk and an hour or so either side, when kangaroos are most active, should be avoided. Give 'road trains' and articulated trucks plenty of room and take care on overtaking – though it is far more likely to be the other way around. Never set off along unsealed roads without a detailed map and compass. Also, if you are travelling east to west, or vice versa, bear in mind that the position of the sun late in the day may cause problems. Above all, if you do break down or run out of petrol, unless a property is clearly visible and accessible (and you are not alone), **do not leave your car.** Also, as an extra precaution and paranoia aside, if you are picked up, discreetly jot down the registration number of the 'saviours' car and place it on the dash of your own along with the intended destination. Also on wilderness treks it always pays to inform someone of your itinerary before setting out.*

Greyhound offer 3 weekly services on the Dubbo (Sydney) to Adelaide route. The **train** station is located on the eastern fringe of the city centre along Crystal St, T8087 1400. *Countrylink* and *Great Southern Railways*, T132147, offer combined 'India-Pacific' or 'Ghan' services between Sydney and Perth (via Adelaide) twice weekly. *Traveland*, 350 Argent St, T8087 1969, act as rail, coach and air **booking agents**. For recorded **road condition** details, T8082 6660.

Getting around Murton Staff, 563 Chapple La, T8087 3311, provide **bus** services around town Mon-Fri (but not to Silverton). **Car hire** *Avis*, 121 Rakow St, T8087 7532, *Hertz* VIC, T8087 2719. Prices for 2WD start at $50, 4WD from $100 per day. **Bike hire** *Town and Country Cycles*, 411 Argent St, T8087 2475, from $12 per day.

The **Broken Hill Visitors Information Centre** is located next to the coach terminal, corner of Blende St and Bromide St, T8087 6077, www.murrayoutback.org.au, www.brokenhill.nsw.gov.au, www.brokenhillcity.com.au (daily 0830-1700). Ask for the excellent and comprehensive '*Broken Hill Accessible Outback Guide*', which contains city and regional **maps**. The **NPWS** office, 183 Argent St, T8088 5933, stock outback national parks information. Mon-Fri 0830-1700.

The VIC can supply a detailed, self-guided heritage walk and trail leaflet and also organizes 2-hr guided tours on Mon/Wed/Fri at 1000 (book ahead, donation)

The **Line of Lode** Visitors Centre and Miners Memorial reflects the transformation of Broken Hill from a mining town of the present to the past and occupies its highest point upon the mullock heaps immediately to the east of the town centre. Dominating the skyline is the dramatic **Miners Memorial** shaped like a cross when viewed from above, its interior walls are lined with the names and causes of death of over 800 miners who paid the ultimate price. ■ *Daily 0900-2200, access to memorial $2.50, child free, T80871345, www.lineoflode brokenhill.org.au* From the town centre follow signs from the eastern end of Iodide Street. Surface **tours** (two hours) are also available of the former South Mine nearby, Sunday-Friday at 1000,1400 and 1900, Saturday 1000 and 1400,

$12. Book at the Line of Lode VIC or town VIC. Perched on the mullock heap just below the Line of Lode is **Delprats Mine**, a BHP original that offers two-hour underground tours 200 m below the surface. ■ *Tours Mon-Fri 1030, Sat 1400, $34, child $26, T8088 1604. Book ahead at the VIC or arrive at the mine, via Crystal St and Iodide St 15 mins prior to tour time.* In contrast the **Daydream Mine**, 28 km west of Broken Hill, is an 1882 original with a walk-in mine, once, believe it or not, mined by children as well as adults. ■ *Tours on the hour from 1000-1500, $12.10, child $5.50, T8088 5682, www.daydream mine.com.au Signposted off the Silverton Rd, west (Horsington Dr).*

Broken Hill has a thriving **arts community** creating very diverse works inspired by the landscapes, colours, light and perspectives of the surrounding outback. Many notable names including ex miner **Pro Hart** (108 Wyman Street) and **Jack Absalom** (638 Chapple Street) have led the creative charge and have their studios in the city. The **Broken Hill City Art Gallery** is the oldest regional gallery in NSW and has a fine mix of local and national works. Its showpiece is the much loved 'Silver Tree' a highly unusual sculpture created by German artist Henry Steiner in 1879 and commissioned by the city's founder, Charles Rasp. It comprises of 20 figures including Aborigines, kangaroos, sheep and a drover on horseback. ■ *Mon-Fri 1000-1700, Sat/Sun 1300-1700, $3, T8088 5491. Corner of Blende St and Chloride St.* Many visitors are drawn inextricably to the highly commercial **Silver City Mint and Arts Centre** to see what world's largest acrylic painting on canvas, which may come as a disappointment. The rest of the gallery contains many artworks, some good, some not so good, but all very expensive! There are also jewellery and mineral displays. ■ *Daily 1000-1600, free (big painting an extortionate $5), T8088 6166, 66 Chloride St.* Even more of a lure to visitors (and rightly so) is the **Living Desert and Sculpture Symposium**, a collection of sandstone sculptures commissioned in 1993 and located on the summit of a hill, 12 km northwest of the town. The most popular piece is a strange, yet dramatic cubist piece that catches the setting sun through a hole, perfectly upon the horizon. Sunset is the most popular time to visit but a far quieter time to visit is at dawn. There are two car parks, one that requires a short uphill walk (10 minutes) or the upper car park for which you will need a key from the VIC (deposit). Otherwise free. Follow Nine Mile Road, northwest, at the end of Kaolin Street in the city centre. Recommended.

Broken Hill is also home to the **School of the Air**, which covers an astonishing 800,000 sq km and has 82 students and around 10 teaching staff. You can visit the school and sit quietly to listen to proceedings, which is highly entertaining. ■ *Mon-Fri during term time. Bookings must be made the day before at the VIC and you must be seated by 0820 – or there will be trouble, $3.30, VIC will provide directions.* Less interesting but still worth a look if you have the time is the **Royal Flying Doctor Service**, visitors centre. ■ *Mon-Fri 0900-1700, Sat/Sun 1100-1600, $3, T8080 1777. Aerodrome 5 km southwest of town via Bonanza St*

Sleeping The **A** *Gateway Motel*, 201 Galena St, T8088 7013, or the **L-A** *Charles Rasp Motel*, 158 Oxide St, T8088 1988, are 2 of the most modern and best facilitated motels in town, while the **A** *Mine Host Motel*, 120 Argent St, T8088 4044, is one of the best placed. Of the traditional hotel/pubs the **C** *Theatre Royal Hotel*, 347 Argent St, T8087 3318, is a good budget option while the **LL** *Imperial Hotel*, 88 Oxide St, T8087 7444, imperial@pcpro.net.au, has been recently renovated providing 5 excellent en suite rooms with shared facilities and a very pleasant historic feel. Also worth a look if nothing else is **C** *Mario's Palace Hotel*, 227 Argent St, T8088 4044, which was used in the film 'Priscilla Queen of The Desert' in 1993. Its utterly lurid decorations and murals are something very unique and will prove hard to forget. Of the B&Bs the **B-C** *The Base B&B* on the eastern approach to Broken Hill, Barrier Highway, T8087 7770, is very pleasant good value and ideal for families, while the **C** *The Old Vic B&B*, 230 Oxide St, T8087 1169, is well placed in town and is, again, congenial and good value. Deservingly popular for both budget style motel accommodation and back-packers is the friendly, family run **C-F** *YHA Tourist Lodge*, 100 Argent St, T8088 2086, mcrae@pcpro.net.au It offers dorms, doubles/twins with spacious facilities, pool and bike hire. The owners are very active in the community and local gurus when it comes to town and regional sights and activities advice. The **C-E** *Broken Hill City Caravan Park*, Rakow St (Adelaide Rd), T8087 3841, is the best facilitated motor park in town with all the usual accommodation and a camp kitchen, while the **C-E** *Lake View Caravan Park*, 1 Mann St, T8088 2250, has the best views and good new 2-bed-room flats, kitchen facilities and units for the disabled.

Eating & entertainment Without doubt the best place to eat in town is MacGregor's café in the Line of Lode Visitors Centre perched high above the city centre. It is licensed and open from 0900-2200 daily serving imaginative fare and great coffee, but nothing beats the view. T8087 1318 (Book ahead). Back in the city centre, *Batina's Restaurant*, in the Hilltop Motor Inn is recommended for fine dining, 271 Kaolin St, T8088 2999. For breakfast try **Ruby's**, 393 Argent St, T8087 1188. Open daily from 0800. There are plenty of budget options with the local hotel/pubs and social clubs being the best bet, including *Mc Phees* in the Sturt Club, 321 Blende St, T8087 4541. Open for à la carte Mon-Sat from 1800 and counter meals Tue-Fri 1200-1400 (nothing over $7). The *Black Lion Pub*, 34 Bromide St, T8087 4801, is a popular drinking hole with the locals and has a **nightclub** than goes off on a Fri and Sat until 0300. For lunch and a great evening out don't forget the superb *Silverton Hotel* in Silverton (25 km). See below.

There are numerous tours on offer from Broken Hill from scenic flights and 4WD to local mine tours and even camel rides. The VIC has full details

Tours A fine way to experience the outback is of course from the air. *Crittenden Air*, based at the airport, T8088 5702, can oblige with local flights above Silverton and Broken Hill, or extended trips further afield to the Sturt National Park or Lake Eyre. Of the 4WD tours a guided trip to see the Aboriginal rock art in the **Mutawintji National Park** and/or the opal mining settlement of White Cliffs (both from about $150) is recommended, but there are many additional locations and tours, from half and full day trips to multi-day adventures with accommodation included. *Tri State*, T8088 2389, www.tristate.com.au, *Broken Hills Outback Tours*, T8088 3813, www.outbacktours.net.au, *Silver City*, T8087 6956, sctbhq@ruralnet.net.au (mainly local tours): and *Goanna Safari*, T8087 6057, www.goanna-safari.com.au, are all reputable operators with a good range of options. Local site trips cost from $20-25, a day tour from $100-150 and multi day trips anything up to $2,000. As well as standard regional tours *Corner Country*, T8087 5142, www.cornercountryadventure.com.au, offer some very attractive outback 4WD adventure packages, one of which is a 20-day wilderness tour, on which you can take your own 4WD vehicle from $1,945. Recommended.

Directory All major **bank** branches with **ATMs** are located along Argent St. **Car hire** *Avis*, 121 Rakow St, T8087 7532, *Hertz* VIC, T8087 2719. **Communications** Internet is free at the Library, on the corner of Blende St and Chloride St, T8088 3317. Open Mon-Wed 1000-2000, Thu/Fri 1000-1800, Sat 1000-1300, Sun 1300-1700. Book ahead. Or the *Net Centre*, Unihope Centre, 265-271 Oxide St, T8087 8506. Open Mon-Fri 1000-1800, Sat 1000-1600. **Post Office** On the corner of Argent St and Chloride St, T8082 5230. Open Mon-Fri 0900-1700. **Medical services** Hospital, 174 Thomas St, T8088 0333. **NRMA** T131111. **RAA** T8087 2643. **Police** 252 Argent St, T8087 0299.

The tiny former mining town of **Silverton**, just a short journey from Broken Hill is a surreal place, atypically 'outback' with wide, red, dusty roads and some mighty eccentric residents. Right in its heart (and indeed forming it these days) is the famous **Silverton Hotel** T8088 5313, (■ *Daily 0830-2130*). The village and the surrounding landscape is so typically outback it has featured in numerous magazine advertisements, television commercials and as the backdrop to some well known films, including '*Mad Max II*'. To this day, the hotel – which in itself featured in the film '*A Town Like Alice*' – still plays host to Max fanatics. As well as the hotel which does a good lunch, has a fine atmosphere (ask if you can 'take the test') and self-contained accommodation, there are a number of galleries in town, including the **Peter Brown Gallery** (■ *Daily 0900-1700*), with its stylized ostriches and VW beetles and the **Horizon Gallery**, T8088 5331, www.brokenhillartists.com.au Beyond Silverton it is well worth taking the short 8-km drive to the **Mundi Mundi Lookout**, best visited at sunset or sunrise when the colours take on the warming hues of reds, oranges and browns. Don't be surprised if you see the odd camel around Silverton. They belong to the Silverton **Camel Farm** where treks and safaris are offered from $5 (15 minutes), $40 (two hours), T8088 5316. **D-F** *Penrose Park*, located just north of the town has basic bunkhouse accommodation and campsites with hot water and gas BBQs, T8088 5307. Note there is no public transport to Silverton but it is on the agenda of most Broken Hill tour operators. There is also no fuel on sale in Silverton – well none that isn't made from hops and a bit of yeast, that is!

Some 130 km northeast of Broken Hill are the rugged red sandstone gorges, caves and tranquil rock holes of the **Mutawintji National Park**, which protects part of the Byngnano Ranges northeast of Broken Hill. Home to an abundance of wildlife and also the domain of some very well preserved **Aboriginal ceremonial sites and rock art**, it is a place well worth visiting. The best way to experience Mutawintji (or Mootwingee as it is also known) is on a **guided tour**. Many operators cover the park from Broken Hill, however it is possible to join tours organized by the Local Aboriginal Land Council leaving Wednesday and Saturday (April-November) from the **Homestead Creek** camping ground within the park. The **camping** area, nestled in amongst the river gums, has cold water, toilets and fireplaces. $5 fee per night, child $3. The national park road is accessed off the Silver City Highway, north from Broken Hill. The roads are gravel and generally easily accessible by 2WD, except after rain. For updates T8082 6660, and for more parks information contact the NPWS office in Broken Hill.

Menindee, 110 km southeast of Broken Hill, was the first town on the Darling River, the longest river system on the continent, and is surrounded by a freshwater **lakes system** that is over seven times the size of Sydney Harbour. Bordering the lakes is the **Kinchega National Park**, focus of some superb scenic drives. Two of the most notable historic sights in the region are the remains of the **Kinchega Woolshed** and the **Maidens Hotel**, where Burke and Wills stayed before heading ever northwards. The lakes themselves also support numerous water-based activities. There are plenty of NPWS **campsites** and independent places to stay, as well as fuel and food outlets within Menidee itself. The VIC and NPWS office in Broken Hill (or local rangers office, Menindee, T8091 4214) can supply all the information and the road to Menindee is sealed. Menindee operates on Eastern Standard Time, 30 minutes ahead of Broken Hill

**Tibooburra
& The Sturt
National Park**
Colour map 5, grid C5
Population: 200
334 km north of
Broken Hill
Check road conditions
before departure,
T8082 6660 (or the
VIC). The area
operates on
Eastern Standard
Time, 30 mins ahead
of Broken Hill

Not for the faint hearted is the long, hot and dusty trail north of Broken Hill to Tibooburra – the gateway to **'Corner Country'** and the Sturt National Park. Although gold was once the great lure to these parts, these days, it is the great adventure to reach the **'Corner Stone'** a lonely spot in the desert that marks the junction of NSW, Queensland and South Australia. The mighty 3,500-sq km wilderness of the **Sturt National Park** is named after explorer Charles Sturt who came here with his long-suffering party in 1844 in search of an 'inland sea'. The park is a fascinating place, famous for its deep red hues and its healthy population of **red kangaroos**. The park is essentially split into two halves, the aptly named 'Jump-ups' and the Grey Range. Further west are the red dunes of the **Strzelecki Desert** and to the east the expansive Gibber Plains. Other interesting features include Aboriginal and European settler history and the great **Dingo Fence**-the world's longest, that was erected by the Queensland Government to stop the invasion of rabbits. **Tibooburra** has hotels, motels a caravan park, fuel and a general store. The NPWS also have basic campsites within the park. Before setting out anywhere off the main highway consult the NPWS on Briscoe Street, in Tibooburra, T8091 3308. The VIC in Broken Hill can also supply accommodation listings. The road to Tibooburra is 50% sealed. Fuel is available at Packsaddle (174 km) and Milparinka (293 km, or 40 km south of Tibooburra).

**Mungo
National Park**
Colour map 2, grid A2
320 km south of
Broken Hill, 104 km
north of Mildura

The Mungo National Park in far southwest New South Wales is one of the most significant archaeological and geomorphic sites in Australia, notable for the strangely shaped sand ridges and craters (a lunette) called the **Walls of China**. In the 1960s the same weathering revealed human remains that proved to over 40,000 years old and therefore the oldest known skeleton of Homo sapiens on earth. Other finds included burial and cremation sites, shell middens and a range of early tools. Gazetted as part of the Willandra Lakes World Heritage Area by UNESCO in 1981 the parks timeless atmosphere and strange features (best seen at sunrise or sunset) present a superb place to contemplate the beauty of the outback and your very own place in space and time. The **Mungo National Park Visitors Centre** is located at the southwest entrance of the park and provides maps and displays on the park's natural and human history. Directions and details are also provided for an excellent 60 km self-drive tour of the park. The **E** *Mungo Shearer's Quarters*, next to the centre have been converted to provide basic bunk-style accommodation with shared facilities. Bookings can be made through the Buronga National Parks Office, T03 5023 1278. Good camping facilities are available in the park at Belah Camp, located about halfway around the self-drive tour. Alternatively, the **A-E** *Mungo Lodge*, T5029 7297, mungoldg@ruralnet.net.au, located on the Mildura Road, 2 km from the park entrance provides self-contained cabins, en suite cabins, camping facilities and a licensed restaurant. Mungo National Park is best accessed from Buronga (100 km) just north of Mildura on the border with Victoria or south of Pooncarie on the road to Menindee (Broken Hill).

Australian Capital Territory

In Australia, a continent of over seven million square kilometres, six states and two territories, you wonder if the ACT (as it is known) suffers a bit from 'little man's syndrome'. At just over two thousand square kilometres, it is 343 times smaller than New South Wales and a whopping 1084 times smaller than Western Australia. So, how is it that puny ACT was chosen as the nation's capital? It all began in 1901 with the official federation of the colonies. Australia was without a national capital. For a while, Sydney and Melbourne squared to see who should prevail, but after a duel that lasted more than seven years, the federal government, temporarily based in Melbourne, eventually threw in the towel, called a draw and decided to create a new territory and a new capital roughly half way between the two. Once a suitable area of land had been found near the Snowy Mountains, they initiated an international competition to find the right architect for the job of designing the new capital. The winner, an American called Walter Burley Griffin, won with a rather bold design, incoroporating a series of geometrical shapes similar to the layouts of Washington D.C. and Paris. In 1913 work began in earnest and despite a few major setbacks, including Griffin's departure in 1920, the Depression, Second World War and some lunatic who thought 'Sydmelbane' would be an approriate name for the new city, the new capital began to take shape. In 1927 the federal politicians sat for the first time in the new (now old) Parliament House and ever since, the city, the capital and the territory (as small as it is) has grown from strength to strength.

Things to do in ACT

1   Take a look around the city's incredible **National Museum of Australia**, which just has to be seen to be believed.

2   Pay your respects at the **Australian War Memorial**, like something out of a James Bond movie.

3   Go over the heads of the country's politicans at the **New Parliament Building**, the only seat of government with a grass roof you can walk on.

4   Take a hike in summer in the beautiful **Namadgi National Park**, or in winter, when much of it is covered in snow, go cross-country skiing.

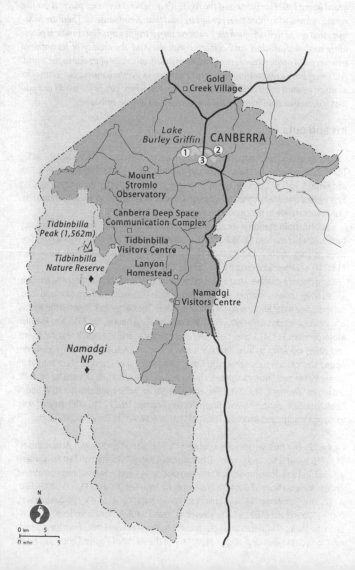

Canberra

Colour map 2, grid B5
Population: 313,000
Phone code: 02
306 km south of
Sydney, 655 km
from Melbourne

Derived from the Aboriginal word 'Kamberra' meaning 'meeting place', Australia's great capital is perhaps the most completely planned and truly modern city in the world, though sadly one of the most underrated. It has been described in many ways – mostly derogatory – with adjectives like artificial, boring and mundane to the fore. Thanks to architect **Walter Burley Griffin's** *deliberately spacious and perhaps overly well-facilitated layout of endless parks, tree-lined circular roads, lakes and highways almost as wide as they are long, the city lacks a certain intimacy. Also, it is too modern to have developed a real sense of history and suburban character, or even a seamy underbelly, and is infested with politicians and civil servants, but surely that is no reason to dismiss it. But if you can ignore all that you may have heard about little Canberra and the ACT, it's actually a very nice place. A bit like rural England, with more trees per square yard than Kew Gardens. There are highways that are so well designed they've never seen a traffic jam. The climate is pleasantly cool, with distinct and colourful seasons. And the quality of its national treasures and architecture is comparable with any other city of its size in the world. ACT may have a reputation similar to Country and Western music, but it can offer as much as most other cities in Australia. Besides, where else in the world can you watch a kangaroo nibbling on the lawn outside a Chinese embassy?*

Ins and outs

Getting there Canberra's international **airport** is about 8 km east of the city centre via Morshead Dr, T6275 2236, www.canberraairport.com.au *QantasLink*, T131313, *Virgin Blue*, T136789, and *Kendell,* T131300, provide regular interstate services to most main centres including Sydney, Brisbane, Melbourne and Adelaide. *Deane's Buslines*, T6299 3722, operate a regular Airliner shuttle to the city centre. A taxi will cost around $15.

Canberra **train station** is located in the suburb of Kingston, 6 km south of the city centre, off Cunningham St, T6257 1576. *Countrylink*, T132232, offer regular daily services to/from Sydney and Melbourne (train/coach). *Action* bus route 39 or $80, T131710, or *Deane's* bus route 830, T6299 3722.

Long distance **coaches** stop at the *Jolimont Tourist Centre*, 65 Northbourne Av, Civic T6249 6006. Lockers, internet, showers, travel bookshop, visitors information and road, rail and airline ticket booking agents are all available. The centre itself (if not all the agents and facilities) is open daily 0600-2330. *McCafferty's/Greyhound*, T132030, and *Premier Motor Services*, T133410, offer daily state and interstate services to most regional towns and cities, including Sydney (Brisbane), Melbourne and Adelaide. *McCafferty's/Greyhound* also provide daily services to Cooma, Jindabyne and Thredbo. Shop around in winter for the best Snowy Mountains packages, some of which are all inclusive of ski lift passes, etc. *Murray's*, T132251, offer a daily service to Sydney and also the NSW South Coast to Narooma and Nowra via Batemans Bay. *Fearnes*, T6921 2316, offer daily services to Wagga Wagga, and *Rendells*, T6884 2411, a daily service to Bathurst and Dubbo.

Getting around Canberra's city **bus** services are operated by the orange and brown *Action Buses,* T131710, www.action.act.gov.au The main interchange is located on East Row where you will find an information office between platforms 1 and 2. Fares operate on a zone system and cost from $2.30-4.40. Buses operate Mon-Sat 0700-2000, Sun 0700-1800. A *'Discover Canberra'* all-day unlimited travel pass costs $9.40 (off-peak travel, 0900-1630 and after 1800, all day weekends costs $5.40). *Action* also offer a free shuttle to the National Museum and Screensound Australia every 15 mins from the car park next to Rydges Lakeside, Civic, or platform 7 at the Jolimont Tourist Centre, between

1045-1600. *Deane's Buses*, T6299 3722, offer regular daily services to Queanbeyan the railway station and airport. *City Sightseeing*, T05-0050 5012 offer a 24 hr 14-stop, hop on-hop off, open top **double-decker tour** with commentary, from $25.

Cycling is a great way to get around the city, with numerous purpose-built cycleways and a fairly flat topography. The VIC can supply more detail and maps. **Bike hire** is available from *Mr Spokes Bike Hire and Café*, Barrine Dr, Acton (beside Lake Burley Griffin).

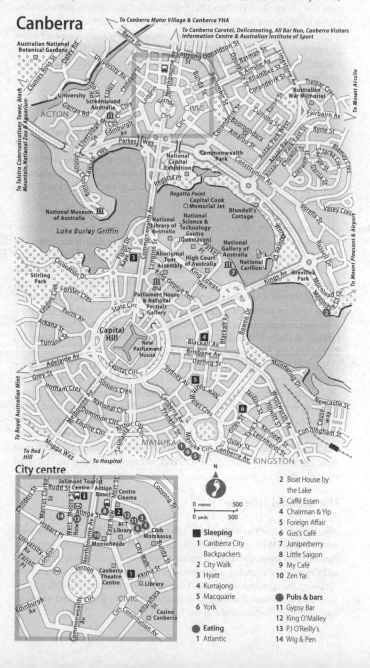

Canberra

Australian Capital Territory

City centre

	Sleeping	2 Boat House by the Lake
	1 Canberra City Backpackers	3 Caffé Essen
	2 City Walk	4 Chairman & Yip
	3 Hyatt	5 Foreign Affair
	4 Kurrajong	6 Gus's Café
	5 Macquarie	7 Juniperberry
	6 York	8 Little Saigon
		9 My Café
	Eating	10 Zen Yai
	1 Atlantic	
		Pubs & bars
		11 Gypsy Bar
		12 King O'Malley
		13 PJ O'Reilly's
		14 Wig & Pen

Open Wed-Sun only, T6257 1188, from $10 per hr. *Row and Ride,* T6254 7838, also hire bikes from $35 for a half day. Sightseeing by car is also fairly straight forward, provided you have a detailed map available free from the VIC. **Taxi** *Canberra Cabs*, T132227.

Information & orientation The **Canberra Visitors Information Centre** is located 3 km north of the city centre, 330 Northbourne Av, T6205 0044, www.canberratourism.com.au/ www.aroundcan-berra.com.au Open Mon-Fri 0900-1700, Sat/Sun 0830-1700. There are also small information booths based at the *Jolimont Tourist Centre*, 65 Northbourne Av, and the airport. All can provide detailed information and detailed city maps. For accommodation bookings and assistance, T1800-100660. For ACT parks and nature reserve information contact *Environment ACT*, 12 Wattle St, Lyneham, T6207 9777, www.environment.act.gov.au

Sights

Canberra offers a great deal to see and do. Many of the sights are an architectural wonder in themselves, never mind having fascinating contents, often of major national importance. If you can, give yourself about three days, but if you are short for time don't miss the National Museum, the New Parliament Building, the Mount Ainslie Lookout and for background, the National Capital Exhibition. The VIC has full listings.

Lookouts Perhaps a fine start to any exploration is with one or more of the excellent lookouts close to the city centre. This will give you an immedite impression of the fascinating perspectives and layout of the city as a whole. Top of the heap (almost literally) is the 195-m **Telstra Communications Tower** on **Black Mountain**, just to the west of the city centre. Like some jagged hypodermic, it is in itself hardly an attractive sight, but the views are certainly worth seeing. There are three public viewing areas as well as a restaurant and an exhibition, 'Making Connections', which showcases the history of Aussie telecommunications. ■ *Daily 0900-2200. $3.30,child $1.10. T1800-806718 (restaurant T6248 6162). Black Mountain Dr, off Clunies Ross St.*

Black Mountain itself hosts a number of nature walks. Superb perspectives of the War Memorial, Anzac Parade and the Old and New Parliament Buildings awaits from the 843 m summit of **Mount Ainslie**, east of the city centre. You may even encounter the odd confused looking kangaroo. To get there, follow Fairbairn Avenue to Mount Ainslie Drive. There are other good lookouts from lower elevations across Lake Burley Griffin from **Mount Pleasant** (just below Mount Ainslie off Morshead Drive) and over the New Parliament Building and the city centre from **Red Hill**, just south of Parliament Hill at the end of Melbourne Avenue.

The National Triangle

Also known as the **Parliamentary Triangle**, this area which is encompassed within **Parkes Way** and **Lake Burley Griffin** to the north, **Kings Avenue** to the east and **Commonwealth Avenue** to the west, contains most of the city's and the nation's most important national buildings and cultural institutions. Although the temptation is to head straight for the triangle's crowning glory, the **New Parliament Building** at its southern apex, try to resist and start your tour instead at the National Capital Exhibition.

The National Capital Exhibition building provides a good starting point for a city tour, imaginatively outlining the fascinating history of the nation's capital, from its indigenous links to the intriguing landscaped metropolis we see today. Interactive displays, audio-visuals and static displays all combine to instil an insatiable desire to explore the real thing. There is also well stocked gift shop and a restaurant. Guided walking tours are available. ■ *Daily 0900-1700. Free. T6257 1068, www.nationalcapital.gov.au Regatta Point, Commonwealth Park, Parkes.* Just below the exhibition building in the lake the **Captain Cook Memorial Jet** bursts in to life daily with a spout that reaches up to 150 m ■ *1000-1200, 1400-1600 year round and 1900-2100 in summer.*

National Capital Exhibition
The views across Lake Burley Griffin are memorable

On the shores of the lake, just east of the National Capital Exhibition centre is Blundell's Cottage and the prominent almost art-deco National Carillon. Blundell's Cottage is the former home of the Campell family (1860) the owners of the 32,000 acre Duntroon Estate, that once encompassed the land that is now under water. The cottage is furnished faithfully to the times with the emphasis being a 'hands-on' experience. ■ *Daily 1100-1600. $2, child $1. T6257 1068. Wendouree Dr.* Further east along Wendouree Drive the National Carillon, built to celebrate the 50th anniversary of the capital, houses dozens of bronze bells that ring out classical and well known popular melodies from 1245-1330 weekdays and from 1445-1530 on weekends. ■ *Lunchtime tours at 1245 Mon/Wed/Fri. $8, child $4. Twilight performances also take place from 1745-1830 on Thu in summer. T62571068.*

Blundell's Cottage and the National Carillon

Immediately opposite the National Carillon, on the southern bank of the lake, is the celebrated National Gallery of Australia. Although lacking the grand façade of other national galleries worldwide, it more than compensates with its interior. Cavernous galleries display an impressive collection of artworks and a wide range of media, from the ancient works of the Aboriginals, to state of the art 'works' using the latest digital video techniques. Don't miss the distinctly 'misty' sculpture garden outside. Obviously, the gallery is usually the first to host the most significant national and international travelling exhibitions for which there is a charge (around $20, concession $12). There is also a good shop, café and an excellent independent restaurant overlooking the sculpture garden. ■ *Daily 0900-1700. Free. Guided tours at 1100 and 1400, Audio tours ($6) on request. T6240 6502, www.nga.gov.au Parkes Pl, free parking.*

National Gallery of Australia

Next door to the National gallery is the imposing High Court of Australia, which first sat (in Canberra) in 1980. Although a far cry from the notoriously biased and unjust judiciary of Australia's colonial past the highest court in the land is still the scene of some fearsome court battles, which can be viewed from a public gallery. The Public Hall also displays various historical items and a small theatrette featuring a short film about the Court's judicial work. ■ *Mon-Fri 0945-1630. Free. T6270 6811. Parkes Pl.*

High Court of Australia

Questacon claims to provide the ultimate experience in 'hands-on' science and technology and as such is a great venue to take budding Newtons and Einsteins. There are literally dozens of exhibits to push, press, blow, lift, squeeze (you name it) and there are plenty of very patient and cheery 'explainers' close by, to do just that. If you're out of your depth, fear not, for you can always head for the 'Cybercity' display for a brain transplant. The 'Earthquake House' is always popular (did the Earth move for you?). ■ *Daily 0900-1700. $10, child $5. T1800-020603, www.questacon.edu.au*

National Science and Technology Centre (Questacon)

Australian Capital Territory

National Library of Australia Librarys are usually about as much fun as an entire evening listening to Mongolian nose flute music. But this place is different; full of of infinite learning and interest, from precious historic documents and photographs to original musical scores. Still not convinced? Well how about some interesting films; 'Charlie' the robotic book trolley, or even a fun behind-the-scenes tour? All followed by a good rummage in the excellent bookstore and a coffee in the café. Book borrowing may never be quite the same again! ■ *Mon-Thu 0900-2100, Fri/Sat 0900-1700, Sun 1330-1700. Free (and free internet). T6262 1111, www.nla.gov.au, Parkes Pl.*

Old Parliament House, The Aboriginal Tent Embassy & the National Portrait Gallery Facing Lake Burley Griffin, in the heart of the National triangle, is the **Old Parliament House** completed in 1927 at triple the initial estimate. At the time, as the official seat of government, it was the most important building in the capital and in essence its raison d'être. The hub of the nation's complex political life for over six decades (before the flash New Parliament House took over in 1988) it now serves as a political museum and also houses the **National Portrait Gallery**, which acts as a visual who's who of Australia's great and good. ■ *Daily 0900-1700. $2, child $1. Shop and Café/bar. T6270 8222. King George Terr.* Immediately outside the Old Parliament building is the **Aboriginal Tent Embassy** which speaks for itself and which serves as a pertinent reminder that the Aboriginal people of Australia were living here for tens of thousands of years before the first acre of land was ever purchased, or brick of any parliament house or embassy was ever laid.

New Parliament House The New Parliament House, completed in 1988, is without doubt the architectural showpiece of Canberra and surely right up there along with the other great Australian man-made wonders, like Sydney's Opera House and Harbour Bridge. Where else in the world is there a building that has its lawn on the roof and (as the travel writer Bill Bryson so aptly pointed out) a Christmas tree stand instead of a chimney. Once you have trampled all over it and taken in the angles, perspectives and views (watched discreetly by armed police patrols) you can then turn to matters of the interior. As well as more fascinating architecture the interior's publically accessible areas host precious Australian art and craft, including **Arthur Boyd**'s impressive *Shoalhaven Tapestry*. When Parliament is sitting, access is allowed to 'Question Time' in the House of Representatives and begins at 1400. Tickets are free and bookings can be made through the 'Seargent of Arms' office. General guided tours are offered every half hour from 0900. ■ *Daily 0900-1700. T6277 5399. Capital Hill, free parking available.*

Outside the Triangle

Royal Australian Mint While the prospect of a visiting a factory that can spew out more dough in half an hour than you earn in a year may seem utterly depressing, a trip to the Australian mint can still prove entertaining. With an expression of deep longing you can view the minting process, then learn about the history of Australian currency production and design. The mint's coin collection is also interesting and will reveal the background to the production of the Holey Dollar and the search for the 1930 pennies worth $6000 each. You can also mint your own $1 coin. ■ *Mon-Fri 0900-1600, Sat/Sun 1000-1600. Free. T6202 6891, www.ramint.gov.au Denison St, Deakin.*

The new and remarkable National Museum of Australia is a shining example of how museums have changed dramatically in recent years, from staid, dusty repositories to exciting state of the art institutions, offering an utter bombardment of all the senses. The National Museum in Canberra, sitting proudly and defiantly on the shores of Lake Burley Griffin, is simply superb. The new museum attempts to present a range of exciting displays and themed galleries that convey all things 'Aussie' and can answer just about every conceivable question you may have wanted to ask about the country. It really is all there – and beautifully designed and presented. Bear in mind, however, that it is not a venue or an attraction to be given an hour or two on your average sightseeing day. Give it a whole day and arrange something completely banal before and after your visit, otherwise your head might explode. ■ *Daily 0900-1700. Free (admission charge to some specialist and travelling displays), restaurant, café, shop and free parking. T1800-026132, www.nma.gov.au Lawson Cres, Acton.*

National Museum of Australia

Though more usually places for sombre reflection and therefore often dismissed on any 'up beat' city tour, you might forego the opportunity to visit the Australian War Memorial in Canberra. But in reality it is well worth a visit and not all doom and gloom. Sitting below Mount Ainslie and an appropriatly bold architectural statement at the end of **Anzac Parade**, its gracious design, large well presented museum and dramatic perspectives, offer a more poignant tourist experience and moment to reflect on the many names listed under the petals of a poppy. Tours avialable. ■ *Daily 0900-1700. Free. T6243 4211, www.awm.gov.au Anzac Pde.*

Australian War Memorial

Formerly the National Film and Sound Archive founded in 1984, Screensound serves as the nation's historical repository for moving image and recorded sound. There are over two million items dating back to the late 1800s, from films and video equipment to scripts and stills. It is all very absorbing and offers a nice change from the static displays of other museums. And although not in three dimensions, there is of course an opportunity to see a very young looking Mel Gibson. ■ *Daily 0900-1700. Free, T6248 2000. McCoy Circuit.*

Screensound Australia

With the almost religious attitude to sport in Australia these days, the Australian Institute of Sport presents the perfect opportunity to see what all the fuss is about, as well as providing a less than subtle reminder that it is time renew the gym membership and go on a diet. Opened in 1981 to provide state of the art training facilities for Australia's elite, visitors are given the opportunity to join a resident athlete on a 90-minute tour to see some of the champions or 'wannabes' in action, view aspects of the nation's sporting history (including the 2000 Olympics) and even try your hand at wheelchair basketball, virtual rowing, or golf. ■ *Tours Mon-Fri 1020/1130/1430, Sat/Sun 1000/1130/ 1300/1430. $12, child $6, T6214 1444, www.aisport.com.au/tours Leverrier Cres, Bruce.*

Australian Institute of Sport

With so many trees and parks in Canberra the concept of a botanical gardens seems a bit ridiculous, since the city, is, in essence, one huge botanical garden. But if you want to learn more about Australian flora or just need to escape all those city 'suits', then head for the National Botanical Gardens in the suburb of Acton. There are over six thousand species on view and the Visitors Centre on-site can provide all the necessary information and point you in the right direction. Guided tours are also available and there is a good bookshop and café. ■ *Daily 0900-1700. Free. T6250 9540.*

Australian National Botanical Gardens

National Zoo & Aquarium Although the word 'national' is a case of having ideas above your station, Canberra's zoo provides a fine experience for kids and an interesting combination of terrestrial and aquatic species. On display are all the usual favourites, including natives, like fairy penguins, kangaroos and koala, as well as the more exotic species, like tigers and bears. Are there any sharks? You betcha! ■ *Daily 0900-1700. $15.50, child $9.50. T6287 1211. Scrivener Dam, Lady Denman Dr, Yarralumla.*

Essentials

Sleeping

There is no need to book ahead, except during festivals and public holidays. The VIC has listings and offer a bookings service, T1800100660, www.canberra tourism.com.au/ getaways

Hotels and apartments Without doubt the most famous and aesthetically remarkable hotel in Canberra is the **LL** *Hyatt Hotel*, Commonwealth Av, Yarralumla, T6270 1234, www.canberra.hyatt.com.au Built in 1924 the heritage-listed building is surrounded by landscaped gardens and has beautifully appointed rooms and suites, all supplemented with facilities you might expect for its 5-star rating. Even if you are not staying there the Art-Deco-influenced foyer is worth a peek. More affordable is the **LL** *Hotel Kurrajong*, 8 National Circuit, Barton T6234 4444, www.hotelkurrajong.com.au, which is considered one of the capital's best boutique hotels. It is well positioned between the lively suburb of Manuka and the National Triangle in Kingston and also offers a good range of rooms as well as dinner, bed and breakfast packages. Nearby another fine establishment is the stylish **LL** *The York*, 31 Giles St, Kingston, T62952333, offering very classy fully serviced apartments and a good café. Still in Kingston, but coming down in price, is the **L-A** *Macquarie Hotel*, 18 National Circuit, T62732325, which offers tidy standard rooms and also budget doubles. Cheaper still and in the city centre, but entirely lacking in character is the **A-D** *City Walk Hotel*, 2 Mort St, City centre T62570124. It also offers dorms at backpacker prices.

Hostels The new and very tidy **A-D** *Canberra City Backpackers*, 7 Akuna St, City centre, T6229 0888, www.canberrabackpackers.com.au, is the closet hostel to the city centre and sits somewhere between a hostel and a budget hotel. Subsequently, it does charge more you're your average hostel but it is certainly worth it. Plenty of rooms from dorm to en suite doubles, kitchen, bar, pool, spa, you name it! Recommended. Doubtless, somewhat peeved with the latter is the current ruler of the roost the **C-E** *Canberra YHA*, 191 Dryandra St, O'Connor, T6248 9155, which although some distance from the city centre (4 km), is still a good choice and cheaper than the latter. It is well established and well facilitated offering dorms, doubles and twins with all the usual amenities, including self-contained kitchens, courtesy shuttle, internet, bike rental and help organizing sightseeing and other activities. The Action 35 bus stops right outside.

Motor parks Close to the YHA is the **L-E** *Canberra Motor Village*, Kunzea St, O'Connor (4 km from the city centre) T6247 5466. It is well facilitated, practically self-contained and next to the Canberra Nature Park, but camping is expensive and there are problems parking a vehicle near the tent. Otherwise it is fine. Campers would be better heading for the **L-E** *Canberra Carotel*, just off the Federal Highway 7 km north via Northbourne Av, Watson, T6241 1377. It offers motel units, on-site vans and plenty of space for camping, with powered and non-powered sites, pool, shop and BBQ, but no camp kitchen. For bush camping refer to the Namadgi National Park (below).

Eating Canberra is not particularly well known for its restaurants but it boasts some excellent eateries from classy á la carte establishments to cheap takeaways. Something different to consider are the cafés and restaurants attached to the various galleries and museums, especially for lunch. The suburb of Manuka is also a great venue particularly in the evening, or for brunch, and retains its own lively atmosphere.

City centre Mid-range For value Chinese cuisine with an Aussie edge, look no further than the *Chairman and Yip*, 108 Bunda St, T6248 7109 (open for lunch Mon-Fri and dinner nightly) and for Thai the *Zen Yai*, 117 London Circuit, T6262 7594. Open Mon-Sat. In the Garema Arcade there is plenty of choice. *Café Essen*, Bunda St, T6248 9300, is the place for coffee and also does wholesome and healthy light meals. Nearby, *Gus's Cafe*, Shop 8, Garema Arcade, Bunda St, T6248 8118, is an equally popular city centre café and especially good for breakfast. Open from 0730 daily.

Cheap *Little Saigon*, corner of Alinga and Northbourne, T6230 5003, is a good value Vietnamese and a firm favourite with students and backpackers

South of the City centre Expensive In the heart of the lively and popular streets of Manuka is the *Foreign Affair*, (upstairs) 8 Franklin St, T6239 5060, which is generally considered to be the city's best Italian restaurant. It is pitched nicely between the formal and laid-back and is locally recommended. Nearby, slightly more formal and equally good, yet with a more wide-ranging European influence is *Atlantic*, 20 Palmerston La, Manuka, T6232 7888. Located within in the National Triangle and sculpture garden of the National Art Gallery the *Juniperberry Restaurant*, T6240 6665, is deservingly popular (especially for lunch) and set in a peaceful position over looking the pond and surrounding sculptures. Open daily for lunch, Thu-Sat for dinner. Book ahead.

Mid-range/cheap The *Boat House by the Lake*, Grevillea Park, Menindee Dr, Barton, T6273 5500, is in a superb position next to Lake Burley Grifffin, which is no doubt why it is so popular. But the modern Australian cuisine also contributes to its numerous awards. *My Cafe*, Shop 1, Manuka Arcade, Manuka T6295 6632 is a long established favourite, with a laid-back social atmosphere and al fresco dining. It is especially good for Sunday brunch and coffee. Open daily from 0800 until late. In the suburb of O'Connor near the YHA and Caravan Park the congenial and trendy *Delicateating* MacPherson St, O'Connor Shops, T6247 1314, is ideal for a pre-drinks meal being right next door to the *All Bar Nun* pub (see below)

No surprise to find Canberra has its fair share of Irish pubs, which are centrally located. **Bars &** Given the student and civil servant population they have a lively atmosphere and a good **Nightclubs** mix of clientele. The *King O'Malley*, 131 City Walk, T6257 0111, is the largest and most centrally located near the city Malls. Great spot for people watching. Open daily from 1100. The other equally lively effort is *P.J. O'Reilly's*, Corner of West Row and Alinga St, T6230 4752. Open Mon-Fri 1100-late, Sat/Sun 1200-late. Nearby, the Anglified *Wig and Pen*, Alinga St, T6248 0171 has equal character and is especially good on a Fri. Further afield in O'Connor *All Bar Nun*, McPherson St, O'Connor Shops, T6257 9191, is less formal and a lesser known favourite. Restaurants and cafes next door add to its atmosphere. Back in the city centre, the lively *Gypsy Bar*, 131 City Walk, T6247 7300, is recognized as a major live music venue for jazz, blues and rock with the occasional comedy night. Open Mon-Fri from 1700, Sat from 1900. When it comes to dancing well in to the wee hours, try *Club Mombassa*, 128 Bunda St, T04-1960 9106. Open Wed-Sun from 2000, or *Mooseheads*, 105 London Circuit, T6257 6496. Open Mon-Sat 1130-0500.

Cinema The *Centre Cinema*, corner of Mort St and Bunda St, T6249 7979, is the most **Entertainment** centrally placed, offering the best mainstream films. Tue night is discount night. *Electric Shadows* Boulevarde Building, Akuna St, T6247 5060, is the venue for alternative and foreign language films. **Theatre** The centrally located*Canberra Theatre Centre*, Civic Sq, T6243 5711, www.canberratheatre.org.au, offers several live entertainment venues under one roof and a dynamic, ecclectic range of shows from dance to Shakespeare. In line with Sydney and Melbourne the capital has its very own **casino**, the*Casino Canberra*, 21 Binara St, T6257 7074. Open daily 1200-0600. The main performance ticket agency in the capital is *Canberra Ticketing*, T6257 1077.

Australian Capital Territory

Festivals & events Over **Christmas** and **New Year**, Exhibition Park hosts the entertaining *Summernats Car Festival* a sort of burn-rubber extravaganza. Lovingly restored early models as well as the inevitable souped-up performance cars and hot rods all combine to create a veritable 'petrol-head' heaven, T6241 8111, www.summernats.com.au Not satisfied with that, the city puts Bathurst to shame with the *GMC 400 Shell Championship* performance car races, in **Jun**, T6205 0666, www.gmc400.com.au, and the *Canberra Rally* in **May**, T6205 0692, www.roc.com.au Far more sedate and ecclectic is *Festival Canberra* held each **Mar** which is developing in to a major multicultural event. Its undeniable highlight is the hugely popular *Balloon Fiesta*, when a multicoloured flock of inflatables take off from the National Triangle and float across the city, T6207 6477, www.multiculturalfestival.com.au Given the distinctly bontanical nature of the city, its not surprising that it hosts a spring floral bonanza in **Sep** to mid **Oct** when Floriade brings even more colour to the capital than the balloons, T6205 0044, www.floriadeaustralia.com.au

Shopping **Books and maps** For mainstream books (and coffee) try *Angus and Robertson*, 16 Petrie Plaza, T6257 6855. For **second-hand** *Winchbooks of Canberra*, 12/25 Kembla St, Fyshwick, T6280 5304, and for **travel** books and maps *Map World*, Jolimont Tourist Centre, 65 Northbourne Av, T6230 4097.

Tours & activities If you have time and want a break from the sightseeing opportunities in the nation's capital, there are a few additional activities on offer. One of the most popular trips and some light relief for tired feet may be a cruise on Lake Burley Griffin. *Southern Cross Cruises* T04-1882 8357, offer an all day, hop on-hop off cruise for $11, child $6.60, with stops at the National Museum, Questacon or Commonwealth Park. Lunch and dinner cruises are also available. Departs every hr (1125-1725) from Regatta Point, near the National Capital Exhibition Building on Regatta Pl. *The Grand Australian Touring Co*, T1800-886633, www.grandaustraliantourco.com.au, offer standard coach tours of the city and also venture further afield to the Snowy Mountains, from $49-80. *Murray's Coaches*, T132251, also offer slightly cheaper city coach tour options, from $31-76. **Scenic flights** in a balloon or fixed-wing aircraft offer the ideal way to see the remarkable layout of the city. *Dawn Drifters*, T6285 4450, www.dawndrifters.com.au, and *Balloon Aloft*, T6285 1540, www.balloonaloft.com.au, both offer dawn balloon flights over the city, from $170 (weekend from $215). *Airport Flying School* corner of Nomad Dr and Widgeon Rd, Canberra Airport, T6248 6292, offer 40-min joy flights from $88 (for 3) and 30 min 'Trial Introductory Flights' from $77. The Snowy Mountain National Park rivers offer some exciting opportunities for **white-water rafting**. *Rapid Descents*, T1800-637486, www.rapiddescents.com.au, can oblige with day, 2-day or multi day trips from $143. Recommended. *Real Fun*, T6278 7838, www.realfun.com.au, also offer rafting from $149 and also canyoning ($95) and abseiling ($79) at the Ginninderra Falls.

Directory **Banks** All major bank branches with ATMs are centred around the city centre on London Circuit, Ainslie Av and Alinga St. **Foreign exchange** *American Express*, corner of City Walk and Petrie Plaza, Centrepoint, T1300-139060. *Thomas Cook*, 19 Canberra Centre, Bunda St, T6257 9984. **Car hire** *Avis*, 15 Bourke Rd, T1800-225533. *Britz Campervans*, Ashley St, Braybrook, T1800-331454. *Hertz*, Canberra Airport, T6249 6211. *Rumbles Rent A Car*, 11 Paragon Mall, Gladstone St, Fyshwick, T6280 7444. *Thrifty*, T1300-367227 (from $46 -90 per day). **Communications** Internet is available in the *Joilmont Tourist Centre*, 65-67 Northbourne Av, and the *On Line Café*, Waldorf Arcade, 2 Akuna St, T6262 7427. **Post Office** is on Alinga St, T62091680, open 0815-1730 Mon-Fri, 0830-1200 Sat/Sun. **Embassies and consulates** British High Commission, T6257 5857. **Canada**, Commonwealth Av, T6273

3285. **Germany**, 119 Empire Cct, T6270 1911. **Ireland** 20 Arkana St, T6273 3022. **Netherlands**, 120 Empire Cct, T6220 9400. **New Zealand**, Commonwealth Av, T6270 4211. **South Africa**, State Circle, T6273 2424. **Sweden**, 5 Turrana St, T6270 2700. **USA**, 21 Moonah Pl, T6214 5600. **Library** National Library, Parkes Pl, T6262 1111. Open Mon-Thu 0900-2100, Fri-Sat 0900-1700, Sun 1330-1700 and the ACT Public Library, Civic, East Row, T6205 9000. Open Mon-Thu 1000-1730, Fri 1000-1900, Sat 0930-1700. **Medical services** *Canberra Hospital*, Yamba Dr, Garran, T6244 2222. **Police** T6256 7777. **Travel Agents** *STA Travel* Civic Mall, Garema Pl, T6247 8633.

Around Canberra

As if there was not enough to see and do in Canberra itself, the rest of the territory offers a few attractions that may lure your beyond the city boundary. It is interesting to note that almost half of ACT is taken up by the Namadgi National Park, which is the epitome of the territory's beautiful natural assets.

South of Canberra

Although there is an observatory in Canberra that offers various displays and public viewing (**Canberra Space Dome**, Hawdon Place, Deniston, T62485333) the region's 'big guns' are located south of the city higher up on the fringe of the Namadgi National Park. Mount Stromlo, 15 minutes west of the city, is the site of the **Mount Stromlo Observatory and Exploratory**. The actual observatory, which is the oldest in Australia, was built in 1924 and has been searching the skies for celestial bodies ever since. The **Visitors Centre**, or Exploratory, opened in 1997 and offers the visitor some insight in to general astronomy as well as the specifics of the Mount Stromlo facility. ■ *Daily 0930-1630. Guided tours of the Astronomy Hall and the 74-in telescope are available, from $6, child $3.50, and there is an additional option of a slide show, from $2.50, child $1.10. Shop and good café. T6125 0232. Off Cotter Rd, Weston Creek.* Further south is the **Canberra Deep Space Communications Complex**, a fine array of paraboloids that have played a key-role in inter-galactic space communications for decades. It was here in 1969 that Armstrong's famous statement 'That's one step for man, one giant leap for mankind' first hit the earth. A more palpable display is a 3-billion year old piece of moon rock. Other displays cover details of more recent NASA Shuttle missions and the voyages of the robotic 'Cassini' and 'Galileo' space probes. ■ *Daily 0900-1700. Free. T6201 7880, www.cdscc.nasa.gov Via Cotter Rd, then Paddy's River Rd, Tidbinbilla.*

Mount Stromlo Observatory & the Canberra Deep Space Communication Complex

Just south of the Deep Space Complex is the Tidbinbilla Nature Reserve, that encompasses a valley of gum forest and rocky outcrops on the fringes of the Namadgi National Park and slopes of the 1562 m Tidbinbilla Peak. Frequented by a rich array of native species, including kangaroos, wallabies, koala, lyrebirds and emus, the reserve presents a fine opportunity to view at least some of them in large enclosures, or along a range of pleasant walks from five minutes to three hours that take in an ancient Aboriginal rock shelter and expansive views. The **Tidbinbilla Visitors Centre** is located near the entrance to the reserve and can supply all the detail. ■ *Daily. $8.50 per day per car, pedestrian $3. Café. T6205 1233.*

Tidbinbilla Nature Reserve

Namadgi National Park   The vast 106,000 ha Namadgi National Park protects a beautiful and fragile sub-alpine wilderness of the **Australian Alps** and covers almost half of the ACT. Rocky outcrops, valleys and forests of candlebarks and snow gum combine to form a region rich in aesthetics and rare wildlife. In summer the park provides a great venue for **walking**, with over 170 km of tracks, while in winter, when much of the park is covered in snow, the only tracks are those made by cross-country skis. The **Namadgi National Park Visitors Centre** hosts a range of introductory displays and can provide walks and camping information. The 3 km walk to the summit of **Mount Franklin** will reward you with great views across Canberra. ■ *Mon-Fri 0900-1600, Sat/Sun 0900-1630. T6207 2900, south of Tharwa (2 km) on Naas Rd.*

Lanyon Homestead   Built in 1835 and located beside the Murrumbidgee River, Lanyon is one of the nation's most celebrated 19th century homesteads. Added to the attraction of the historical displays, gardens and period furnishings is the **Nolan Gallery**, dedicated to the life and works of famous Australian painter Sidney Nolan. His renderings of the famous bushranger Ned Kelly are particularly well known. ■ *Tue-Sun 1000-1600, Sat 1000-1700. $6, child $3. T6237 5136. Tharwa Dr.*

North of Canberra

Gold Creek Village in the suburb of Nicholls (12 km north of the city center) is a rather strange conglomerate of very contrasting attractions centered on the historic **Ginninderra Schoolhouse** built in 1883. **The National Dinosaur Museum** boasts 10 full sized replica skeletons of the once mighty beasts along with various skulls, fossils and minerals from all around the globe. ■ *Daily 1000-1700. $9, child $6. T1800-356000.* In stark contrast is **Cockington Green**, a detailed 1/12th scale replica of an English village complete with figures and miniature landscapes. Elsewhere other buildings, from German castles to Indonesian temples add to the collection. Another new edition is a 34-room dolls house. ■ *Daily 0930-1630. $11.50, child $6. T1800-627273.* **The Australian Reptile Centre** presents the opportunity to get up close and personal with a whole host of Australian species, from the suburban blue-tongued lizard to the infamous thorny devil. There is also the opportunity to handle a very passive python (oo-er, missus!). ■ *Daily 1000-1700. $8, child $4. T6253 8533.* Then bring yourself back to the real world with a stroll through **'Bird Walk'**, a large walk-in aviary with over 500 birds of 54 different species including numerous Australian parrots. ■ *1000-1630. $6.50, child $3.50. T6230 2044.* Gold Creek and all the above attractions are off Gold Creek Rd, which is off the Barton Highway.

Queensland

As if Australia were not big enough, along comes a state about the size of Mexico, with more must-see attractions than you could shake a bottle of tequila at. It's just not fair, is it? Heading north from New South Wales, you pass the forest of high rises strung along the infamous Gold Coast, before emerging in the relaxing embrace of the state's relaxed capital, **Brisbane**. Beyond 'Brizzie' the aptly named Sunshine Coast tempts you with more magnificent beaches, before the peerless **Fraser Island** – the world largest sand island – only deepens your love affair with the Australian coastline. Beyond Townsville, the capital of North Queensland, the tropical landscape becomes ever greener while, inland, the arid outback lies in wait for the more intrepid of travellers. Offshore, the **Great Barrier Reef**, that incredible world beneath the waves, draws visitors from the mainland like kids to a particularly well-stocked sweet shop. For most, the endlessly entertaining city of **Cairns** marks the end of the road, but further north the reef continues to amaze and the tropical rainforests of **Daintree** and **Cape Tribulation** contain one of the richest biodiversities on earth. The **Atherton Tablelands**, meanwhile, prove it's not all blistering heat and humidity. Those in search of the ultimate Aussie adventure can make the thrilling (and brave) 4WD trip all the way up to the **Cape York**, at the very tip of this vast continent.

Things to do in Queensland

1. Get up for dawn in the **Atherton Tablelands** to catch a glimpse of a duck-billed platypus.
2. Cheer for the fastest creepy-crawly, at the annual Cockroach races, on Australia Day in **Brisbane**.
3. Handle a snake, or a baby croc, at the **Billabong Wildlife Sanctuary**.
4. Listen to classical music and hear the incredible acoustics deep underground in the **Capricorn Caves**, near Rockhampton.
5. Write unbearably smug postcards home while sunbathing on a tropical **Barrier Reef Island**.
6. Learn how to open a coconut by the beach at **Cape Tribulation**.
7. Feed wild dolphins by hand at the **Tangalooma Wild Dolphin Resort** on Moreton Island National Park.

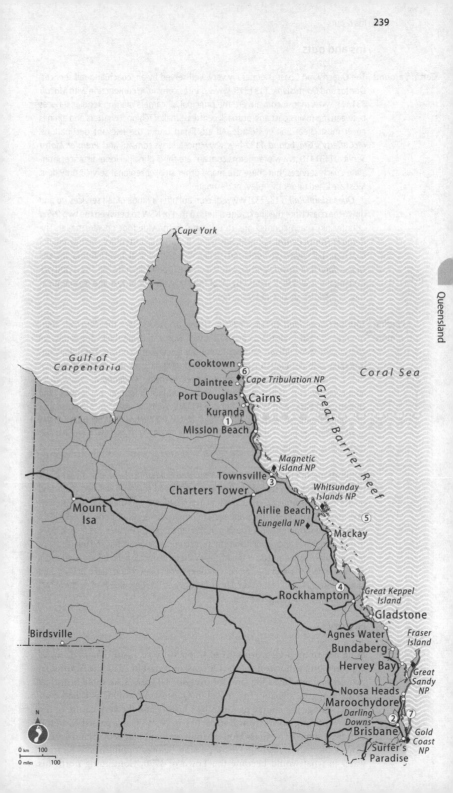

Queensland

Cape York

Gulf of
Carpentaria

Coral Sea

Cooktown
Daintree ⑥ *Cape Tribulation NP*
Port Douglas Cairns
Kuranda ①
Mission Beach

Great Barrier Reef

*Magnetic
Island NP*
Townsville
Charters Tower ③

*Whitsunday
Islands NP*
Airlie Beach ⑤
Eungella NP
Mackay

Mount
Isa

Rockhampton ④ *Great Keppel
Island*
Gladstone

Birdsville

Agnes Water *Fraser
Island*
Bundaberg

Hervey Bay *Great
Sandy
NP*

Noosa Heads
Maroochydore
*Darling
Downs* ②⑦
Brisbane *Gold
Coast NP*
Surfer's
Paradise

N

0 km   100
0 miles   100

Ins and outs

Getting around The Queensland Coast is generally very well served by air, coach and rail services. *Qantas* and *QantasLink*, T131313, www.qantas.com.au, in conjunction with *Macair* 131313, www.macair.com.au, are the principal air carriers offering regular services between the main coast and outback centres. Smaller regional charters and airlines cover most Great Barrier Islands. All are listed under the relevant destinations. *McCafferty's/Greyhound* T131499, www.mccaffertys.com.au, and *Premier Motor Service*, T131410, www.premierms.com.au are the 3 principal long distance, inter-state coach services, but there are many other smaller regional service providers. Most are listed under the relevant destinations.

Queensland Rail, T132232, www.qr.com.au, offer a range of rail services up and down the coast Note the line gauge differs to that of NSW so between the two (NSW Countrylink) coach connections to Brisbane are provided for onward travel. The *Roma St Transit Centre*, Roma St, Brisbane, T3236 3035, hosts offices for most major coach and rail service providers and is a fine source of general travel information. The *Queensland Rail Travel Centre* is located on the Ground Floor, T3235 1331. Outback Queensland is also well served by all of the above but stopovers and less frequent travel schedules are obviously the norm.

Finding out more *Tourism Queensland*, GPO Box 328, Brisbane, T07-3535 3535, is the main state tourism organization. Prior to you arrival it is well worth studying their comprehensive website, www.tq.com.au Another useful site is www.qttc.com.au For details surrounding each destination and general travel information within Australia consult the Fairfax Publications sponsored travel website *Walkabout*, www.walkabout.com.au For National Parks and camping information consult the **Queensland Parks and Wildlife Service** (QPWS) website, www.env.qld.gov.au or the **Department of Natural Resources**, www.dnr.qld.gov.au The main QPWS headquarters are based in Brisbane, 160 Ann St, T07-3227 8186. Other regional and parks offices are all listed in the travelling text.

Publications and maps *World Wide Maps and Guides*, 187 George St, T3221 4330, www.worldwidemaps.com.au, in Brisbane are a good source of detailed maps and guides for both Australia and Queensland. The *UBD Country Towns and Street Directory: Queensland* has excellent maps and basic information. A separate book is available on Brisbane and surrounds. *AAA Tourism* publish the *Experience Queensland Guide* ($16) that contains town and regional road maps, accommodation listings and brief descriptions on things to see and do. It is particularly useful for motor parks information and is always handy to have in the car. For camping within Queensland National Parks and State Forests get hold of the *Camping in Queensland* booklet published by the QPWS and Department of Natural Resources.

History

Long before the well-worn sails of Captain Cook's ship '*The Endeavour*' appeared on the horizons of the Queensland coast in 1770, the Aboriginal peoples had inhabited the land for over 40,000 years. Like some historical battleship, guns blazing, his arrival in Queensland would, as it had elsewhere, change the course of Australia's history and the very nature of the land. Venturing north from Botany Bay in NSW, Cook passed Moreton Bay, then named The Glass House Mountains and Magnetic Island (after a strange anomaly in readings) in the passing, before stopping briefly for fresh water in what would become the Town of 1770. Continuing north his encounter with the Great Barrier Reef proved almost disastrous when he ran aground near Cape Tribulation and was forced to stop for two months to make repairs at the mouth of a river he named the 'Endeavour'. In so doing he effectively established Cooktown, the first temporary European settlement in Australia – something the remote township remains very proud of.

Three decades after the establishment of the new penal colony in Sydney Cove, and with its future firmly based on the arrival of free immigrants, the Governor decided it was necessary to move the most notorious convicts elsewhere. In 1823 Surveyor-General John Oxley was dispatched north to find a suitable location and successfully established a new penal colony in Moreton Bay. A short time later the colony was moved up river (earlier named Brisbane by Oxley) in effect creating the settlement of the same name and what would later become the capital and largest city in the state. In 1842 the penal colony was officially closed and Queensland followed NSW in opening up to free settlement. Given the geography and the climate in Queensland and keen resistance from local Aboriginals, further exploration and settlement of the state progressed slowly but despite that Queensland became a separate colony in 1859 with its own parliament sitting in Brisbane for the first time in 1860. Through the same decade sugar and cotton plantations were established and a huge influx of Kanakas (Pacific Islanders) and Chinese came to work the cane fields. With the discovery of gold in Gympie in 1867 and The Palmer River in the far north in 1872, the population exploded, so much so that restrictions on immigration were passed shortly after federation of the Australian colonies in 1901. In 1902 Brisbane was proclaimed a city and with further lucrative mineral discoveries throughout the state, especially in Mount Isa, the economy grew from strength to strength. After the second World War Queensland joined NSW and the nation in the struggle to find their own identity, but its popularity as the 'holiday state' was becoming increasingly apparent. With the fertile seeds of tourism already planted firmly on the Gold Coast, and the advent of the aqualung sweeping open the curtains across the Great Barrier Reef in the 1950s, it seemed that its popularity was sealed. Thankfully the state government and the authorities have realised that the key to Queensland's continued success as a tourist destination lies in the unique environment and its precious bio-diversity. Queensland is without doubt on the cutting edge of global eco tourism and now has the opportunity to show the world that environmental conservation and tourism can indeed prosper in harmony.

Brisbane

For a former penal settlement that developed into a fairly anonymous state capital and created the disco sensation 'The Bee-Gees', Brisbane has come an awfully long way. Ever since the city hosted Expo 88 it seems that both the progressive desire for improvement and atmosphere of informal pride have never left and the city has gone from strength to strength. As Australia's only true tropical city, Brisbane enjoys an almost perfect climate. Wherever you go, al fresco restaurants, cafés and outdoor activities dominate, with the most obvious being the South Bank parklands. As the site for Expo 88 they are now the city's greatest tourist magnet. Complete with numerous cultural attractions and even its own inner city beach, South Bank represents, in many ways, the very essence of modern-day Brisbane.

Phone code: 07
Colour map 3, grid A6
Population: 1,300,000
984 km north of Sydney, 1710 km south of Cairns

Queensland

Brisbane

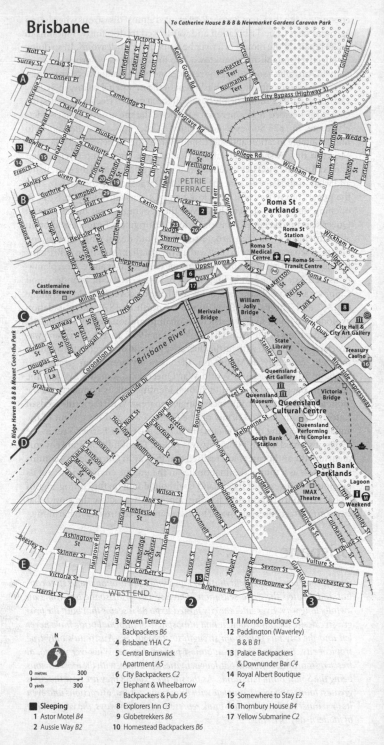

Sleeping
1 Astor Motel *B4*
2 Aussie Way *B2*

3 Bowen Terrace
 Backpackers *B6*
4 Brisbane YHA *C2*
5 Central Brunswick
 Apartment *A5*
6 City Backpackers *C2*
7 Elephant & Wheelbarrow
 Backpackers & Pub *A5*
8 Explorers Inn *C3*
9 Globetrekkers *B6*
10 Homestead Backpackers *B6*

11 Il Mondo Boutique *C5*
12 Paddington (Waverley)
 B & B *B1*
13 Palace Backpackers
 & Downunder Bar *C4*
14 Royal Albert Boutique
 C4
15 Somewhere to Stay *E2*
16 Thornbury House *B4*
17 Yellow Submarine *C2*

Queensland

Queensland

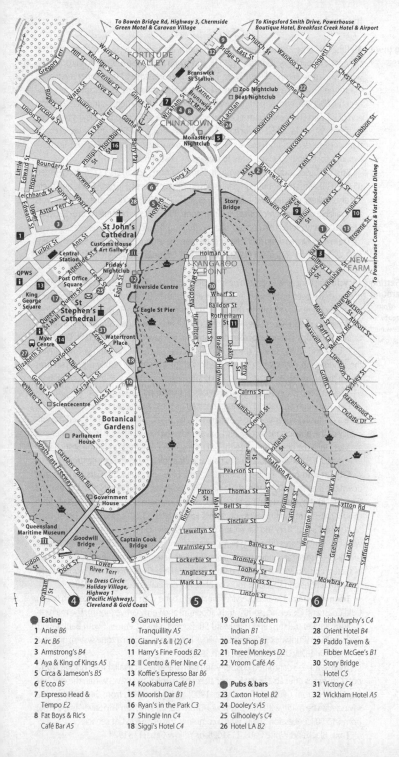

● Eating

1 Anise B6
2 Arc B6
3 Armstrong's B4
4 Aya & King of Kings A5
5 Circa & Jameson's B5
6 E'cco B5
7 Expresso Head & Tempo E2
8 Fat Boys & Ric's Café Bar A5
9 Garuva Hidden Tranquillity A5
10 Gianni's & Il (2) C4
11 Harry's Fine Foods B2
12 Il Centro & Pier Nine C4
13 Koffie's Expresso Bar B6
14 Kookaburra Café B1
15 Moorish Dar B1
16 Ryan's in the Park C3
17 Shingle Inn C4
18 Siggi's Hotel C4
19 Sultan's Kitchen Indian B1
20 Tea Shop B1
21 Three Monkeys D2
22 Vroom Café A6

● Pubs & bars

23 Caxton Hotel B2
24 Dooley's A5
25 Gilhooley's C4
26 Hotel LA B2
27 Irish Murphy's C4
28 Orient Hotel B4
29 Paddo Tavern & Fibber McGee's B1
30 Story Bridge Hotel C5
31 Victory C4
32 Wickham Hotel A5

Ins and outs

Getting there
See also page 254

Air Brisbane's international and domestic **airports** are 16 km and 18 km northeast of the city centre respectively. *Qantas*, T131313, and *Virgin Blue*, T136789, offer daily domestic services to main centres. *Flight West*, T131300, and *Sunstate* (Qantas) offer services to Gladstone, Townsville and other outback or coastal destinations. Trains and buses connect the CBD with both airport terminals: *Airtrain*, T3215 5000 departs from Central (top end of Edward St), Roma (Transit Centre) and Brunswick St (Fortitude Valley) 4 times per hr, from $9, child $4.50. *Coachtrans* (*SkyTrans* service), T3236 1000, www.coach trans.com.au, departs from the Roma St Transit Centre every ½ hr (0500-2100), from $9. Pick-ups cost about $2 extra. A taxi to the airport cost about $27.

Bus All buses stop at the Roma St Transit Centre, Roma St, T3236 3035 (open 0530-2030). Most major bus companies have offices on Level 3 (Coach Deck) and there are also lockers, internet and information desk, T3229 5918. Food outlets and showers are available on Level 2. *McCafferty's/Greyhound*, T132030, and *Premier Motor Services*, T133410, www.premierms.com.au, offer north/southbound interstate services.

Train The *Queensland Rail* Travel Centre is on the Ground Floor, Roma St Transit Centre, T3235 1331, for enquiries T132232 (0600-2000). *Citytrain* offer links to the Gold Coast.

Getting around
For all public transport enquiries T131230, www.trans info.qld.gov.au

Bicycle Brisbane is well geared up for cyclists with over 350 km of city cycleways. Most of these have been established around the edge of the CBD along the riverbank, providing an excellent way to take in the sights and to get from A to B. The VIC supply a free *'Brisbane Bicycle Maps'* booklet. For details of bike hire, see page 255. **Bus** The central Queen Street Bus Station is located downstairs in the Myer Centre, Queen St. City *'Circle 333'* (blue and white) service the city centre circuit, *'Citybus'* (white and yellow) service the suburbs and *'Cityexpress'* (blue and yellow stripes) offers half hourly express services within the Greater Brisbane area, T131230. Fares work on a 5-zone system from $1.80-3.80, concession $0.90-1.90. For details of **bus tours**, see page 254.

Car Although Brisbane is not as congested as most Australian cities, the CBD does have a confusing system of one-way streets an merciless traffic wardens. Given the efficiency of the public transport system you are advised to park the car in a non-metered area and take the bus or ferry into the CBD. Kangaroo Point (just under the Story Bridge on the South Bank) is a good spot to park and cross by ferry to the city centre.

CityCat and ferry Brisbane's famous, sleek blue and white **CityCats** glide up and down the river from Bretts Wharf (Hamilton) in the east to the University of Queensland (St Lucia) in the west, stopping at selected wharfs on both sides of the river, daily from 0550-2230. The round trip takes about 2 hrs. Fares start at $1.60. A 'Day Rover Ticket' costs $8.40, child $4.20. 'Ten Trip Saver' and 'Off-Peak Saver' tickets also apply in conjunction with city bus services. The **City Ferry** operates an 'inner city' and 'cross river' service (every 15-20 mins) at various points along the river. Fares are determined by the number of sectors crossed and start at $1.60. Tthe *'Brisbane River Experience Guide'*, highlights the main attractions and specialist tours on offer. For general enquiries, T131230.

Train *Citytrain*, T132232, services greater Brisbane with networks to Ipswich (west), Gold Coast and Cleveland (south) and Caboolture and Ferny Grove (north). The main city stations are Central (top end of Edward St), Roma (Transit Centre), South Bank (South Brisbane) and Brunswick St (Fortitude Valley). Fares are based on a zone system and start at $1.65, 'One-Day Unlimited Pass', from $8.60.

There is a 1-2-3 combined bus, ferry and train travel ticket available. *Brisbane Transport City buses* offer an 'Off Peak Saver' ticket with unlimited travel within the city centre, Mon-Fri from 0900-1530 and after 1900, all day Sat/Sun, from $4.60. Additional savings can be made with the 'Day Rover' (from $8.40) and 'Ten Trip Saver' (save 20%), from $13.80, concession $6.90, which combines travel on CityCat services.

Taxi Black and White Cabs, T131008, or Yellow Cabs, T131924.

Brisbane's compact CBD (and indeed much of the city) is built around the **Brisbane River**, which in itself provides a convenient way to get from A to B. The hub of activity centres around the shopping malls and precincts of **Queen** St and **Adelaide St**, with the main **transit centre** located 1 km west on **Roma St**. The **South Bank** complex, which is a short walk across either the **Victoria Bridge** or new **Goodwill** (pedestrian) **Bridge** is the city's most famous tourist attraction. Northerly access to the CBD is via Bowen Bridge Rd (Highway 3). Easterly access (airport) is via Kingsford Smith Dr. **Fortitude Valley** (Brunswick St), the **West End** (Melbourne St, across the Victoria Bridge from the CBD) and **Petrie Terr** (via the northern river bank and North Quay) are the main inner city suburbs, all well known for their restaurants, cafés and nightlife. If you are feeling at all lost, or simply want a spectacular view of the city, head for the lookout at **Mt Coot-tha** (8 km), which is signposted off Milton Rd (west of the CBD from Roma St).

Orientation

The *Queen Street Mall Visitors Information Centre*, corner of Albert St and Queen St, T3006 6290, www.brisbanetourism.com.au, offers free city maps and can assist with accommodation bookings. Open Mon-Thu, 0900-1700, Fri 0900-1900, Sat 0900-1600, Sun 1000-1600. (After-hours T3221 8411) The main daily newspaper in Southern Queensland is the *Courier Mail*. The free *'This Week In Brisbane'* booklet is also useful. The **QPWS** main office is at 160 Ann St, T3227 8186. Open Mon-Fri 0830-1700.

Information

History

Aboriginal tribes frequented the mainland and Moreton Bay islands for over 40,000 years before the first Europeans settled in 1824. Like many east coast frontier settlements, it was first established as a penal colony to keep captive the convicts sent to Australia to pay for their, often petty, crimes. The first explorations of the area were made in 1823 by the explorer John Oxley at the behest of the then governor of NSW, Sir Thomas Brisbane. Ironically, their first human contact was with a small gang of escaped convicts on Moreton Island, who secured some reprieve by showing Oxley a source of freshwater. The first settlement was established on the coast at Redcliffe, but moved shortly afterwards to a better site up river (now christened 'The Brisbane') at North Quay. The initially notorious penal colony soon grew into an established colony that went from strength to strength in the 20th century. Shrugging off its non-progressive reputation in recent decades, Brisbane has enjoyed phenomenal growth, greatly accelerated with the hosting of important events like the Commonwealth Games in 1982, Expo 88 and the 2001 Goodwill Games. Although the source of the name Brisbane is obvious, there are many lesser-known place names that remain from Aboriginal beginnings, including Toowong, Indooroopilly and Mount Coot-tha (meaning 'place of native honey').

Sights

At the top (northwest) end of Albert Street, which bisects Queen Street (facing King George Square), is **City Hall**, with its 92 m Italian renaissance clock tower. Built in 1930, it became known as the 'Million Pound Town Hall' due to its huge and controversial construction cost. Once satisfying the irresistible urge to ride the old lift and see the view from to the top, the interior of the building is also worth a look, housing the **City Art Gallery** and grand ballroom. Guided tours are by arrangement. ■ *Lift: Mon-Fri 1000-1500, Sat 1000-1400. Gallery: daily 0900-1700. Free. T3403 8888.* Around the corner on George Street and the riverbank is the grand 19th century façade of the former Treasury Building, now the city's **Treasury Casino** (open 24 hours, T3306 8888). To the west, beside

City centre
One of the best ways to experience the main historical sights is to join the Brisbane Historical Walking Tour (see page 254)

the City Botanical Gardens, is the 1868 French renaissance-style **Parliament House**, which was commissioned when Queensland was declared a separate colony in 1859. ■ *Free tours are available 5 times daily Mon-Fri and you can also watch proceedings when the house is in session. Open Mon-Fri 0900-1700, free, T3406 7111.* Nearby is the **Old Government House** (1862) which houses the HQ of the National Trust. ■ *Daily 1000-1630. Free. T3229 1788.* Further north, beyond the chic restaurants of **Waterfront Place**, Eagle Street Pier and the Riverside Centre, is **Customs House**. Built in 1889, it is like a miniature version of St Paul's Cathedral in London, exuding an elegant Victorian charm. There is also a small **art gallery** and brasserie. ■ *Guided tours Mon- Fri by arrangement. Gallery: daily 1000-1700. Free. T3365 8999.* Directly opposite Customs House is perhaps the city's best-known landmark, the **Story Bridge**, built between 1935 and 1940. Close to Customs House are Brisbane's two main **cathedrals**, the Gothic-style **St John's Cathedral** (uncompleted since 1901), 373 Ann Street, and **St Stephen's Cathedral** (1874), Charlotte Street. Both are open to the public daily and provide a welcome sanctuary from the bustle of the city. The **Sciencentre** houses an entertaining and educational range of interactive exhibits that will keep the little Einsteins or the merely inquisitive amused for hours. ■ *Daily 1000-1700. $8, child $6. T3220 0166, www.sciencentre. qld.gov.au, 110 George St.*

South Bank Overlooking the highrises on the southern bank of the Brisbane River is the superb 17-ha 'oasis in the city' known as South Bank. Built primarily as the showpiece for Expo 88, the 1 km stretch of parkland remains as a fascinating and functional recreational space and includes riverside walks, shops, restaurants, open air markets and a swimming lagoon with its very own beach. At the northwestern end, straddling Melbourne Street, is the **Queensland Cultural Centre**, which comprises the State Library, Queensland Museum, Queensland Art Gallery and The Queensland Performing Arts Complex. The **Queensland Art Gallery** is considered Brisbane's premiere cultural attraction, displaying an impressive collection of Aboriginal, European, Asian and contemporary Australian art. It also hosts major visiting or special exhibitions. ■ *Guided tours are available Mon-Fri 1000/1300/1400, Sat 1100/1400/1500, Sun 1100/1300/1500. Daily 1000-1700. Free (except for special exhibitions), T3840 7303, www.qag.qld.gov.au* Broadside to the art gallery is the **Queensland Museum**, which features prehistoric and natural history displays, as well as the inevitable, though absorbing, collections of indigenous and early European artefacts. ■ *Daily 0930-1700. Free (except special exhibitions). T3840 7555, www.Qmuseum.qld.gov.au*

On the opposite side of Melbourne Street is the multifarious **Queensland Performing Arts Complex**, housing the Lyric Theatre, Concert Hall, Cremorne Theatre and Optus Playhouse. Combined, they offer an exciting and ongoing programme of performance events from plays and ballet to modern dance, musicals and opera. T3840 7444. Further entertainment on a grand scale is also available at the **IMAX Theatre**, with its 8-storey screen. ■ *Screenings 3 times daily, from 1000-2200. $16.20, child $12. T3844 4222, www.imax.com.au* At the southeastern end of the South Bank is the **Queensland Maritime Museum**, which houses all the usual relics. Most of the larger vessels, including the Second World War frigate *Diamantina*, sit forlornly in the adjacent dry dock. ■ *Daily 0930-1630. $5.50, child $2.80. T3844 5361.* The frigate is best viewed from the new and futuristic **Goodwill Bridge**, the latest addition to the South Bank skyline, built in celebration of the 2001 Goodwill Games offers a convenient route back to the CBD via the Botanical Gardens.

There is a **Visitors Information Centre** located in the heart of the South Bank parkland, just behind the lagoon complex. ■ *Mon-Sat 0900-1800, Fri 0900-2200. T3867 2051, www.south-bank.net.au* This area is also the venue for the South Bank **markets** held every Friday night, Saturday and Sunday and the **'Al Fresco Cinema'** in February-March (Wednesday-Saturday).

The **Brisbane City Botanical Gardens** fringes the river on the southeastern edge of the CBD. First established in 1858 as an experimental garden using convict labour, it has since matured to become a fine showpiece of both native and non-native species. There is a short mangrove boardwalk that affords views across the river and a café. ■ *Guided tours are available Tue-Sun, 1100/1300.* In stark contrast is the new **Roma Street Parklands**, at the opposite end of the CBD. Only recently completed and lauded as the world's largest subtropical garden in a city centre, it offers a superb mix of horticultural displays, landscaping, architecture and artworks. Several walks of varying distance take you round numerous interesting features, from fossils to bottle trees. Self-guided walking brochures are available from the Activity Centre next to the Roma Street Rail Station. ■ *Daily dawn to dusk, free, T3006 4545, www.romastreetparkland.com.au*

Botanical Gardens & Roma Street Parklands

Queensland

Further afield is **Mount Coot-tha Park and Botanical Gardens**, reached via Milton Road (off Roma Street). At the base of the hill are 'the other' Botanical Gardens, considered Queensland's best, featuring over 20,000 specimens of 5000 species. To show off this impressive inventory there are 52 ha with numerous features that include a herbarium, tropical dome, bonsai house, and water lily ponds. Within the grounds there is also a Planetarium (T3403 8888) and the *Lakeside Restaurant*. ■ *Daily 0830-1730. Free. Guided tours daily 1100/1300 or pick up a free self-guided leaflet. 13403 8888. Restaurant daily 0900-1700.* Set high above the gardens is the **Mount Coot-tha Lookout**, which offers superb views across the city and out across Moreton Bay to Moreton, North Stradbroke and Bribie Islands. The *Summit Restaurant* and *Kuta Café* (see Eating section) provide an ideal place for lunch or dinner while soaking up the sun and the city views. Backing on to the lookout complex is the **Mount Coot-tha Forest Park** which consists of 1500 ha of open eucalypt forest, networked with walking tracks and containing over 350 weird and wonderful native species. ■ *Getting there by bus: take the No 471 from Adelaide St (stop 44, opposite City Hall), from $5.20 return, T131230.* Or, join the 'City Sights' or 'City Nights Tours' (see page 254). Mount Coot-tha Forest Park is just part of the vast 30,000 ha **Brisbane Forest Park** that backs on to the city, boasting an astonishing range of wildlife and over 30 km of walking tracks. There are also opportunities for horse trekking, mountain biking and bush camping. The park headquarters and **information** centre is located at 'The Gap' on Nebo Road, west of the city centre, T3300 4855. At the same location is the **Walk-about Creek Wildlife Centre**, that features some of the forest wild inhabitants including platypuses and lungfish. ■ *Daily 0900-1630. $3.50, child $2.*

Mount Coot-tha Park
For detailed information about the park, pick up a copy of the 'Brisbane Bushland' and 'Brisbane Parkland' Experience Guides, available free from the VIC, or visit the website, www.brisbaneforest park.com.au

Almost anywhere east of the Great Divide in Queensland, you're never far from an opportunity to cuddle a koala. Brisbane is no different with the Lone Pine Koala Sanctuary, the oldest and the largest in the world. Having opened in 1927 and now housing around 130 of these adorable creatures, it offers a fine introduction, or reminder, of how unique Australia's wildlife really is. Also on display are the equally ubiquitous wombats, echidnas and kangaroos.

Lone Pine Koala Sanctuary & Alma Park Zoo

▶▶ A day at the races (Aussie style)

Twenty years ago (or so the story goes) two Brisbanites were sitting in a bar arguing about whose suburb had the biggest, fastest cockroaches. Unable to reach a settlement, the following day, they captured their very best and raced them. And with that the annual 'Cockroach Races' were born. Now, every Australia Day (26 January) the Story Bridge Hotel in Kangaroo Point hosts the infamous and truly unique 'cocky' races. Of course the races, along with many other events' is merely an excuse to get utterly inebriated. Picture the scene for a second. Small grandstands surround a central ring, bursting with rowdy punters, many with faces painted in national colours and supporting flags (often as the only item of clothing). The race is called and from deep within the throngs of celebrants the sound of badly played bagpipes heralds the arrival of the teams and their roaches. The crowd gives way and the scene is set. On the count of three a plastic container, held in the middle of the ring, is lifted and off the roaches zip in all directions. The crowd goes wild. The squeamish scream as the insects run under bags, shoes and into sandwiches. If the winner can ever be caught, it is identified and the winning team is announced. Then it's drinks all round and more...'Aussie, Aussie, Aussie' until we all fall down. To say it is an experience is an understatement and needless to say, if your visit coincides, it is recommended (but don't plan on doing anything the following day, except maybe checking the contents of your shoes). T3391 2266, www.storeybridgehotel.com.au

■ *Daily 0800-1700. $15, child $10. T3378 1366, www.koala.net.au Jesmond Rd, Fig Tree Pocket (southwest via Milton Road and the western Freeway 5). To get there by bus take the No 430 from the 'koala platform' in the Myer Centre, Queen St. $3.40, child $1.70 single. Alternatively the Mirimar Boat Cruise departs daily from North Quay at 1000, T3221 0300, from $25, child $15 (not including admission, returns at 1500).*

Playing second fiddle to Lone Pine is the **Alma Park Zoo** in Dakabin (30 km north of the city centre off Boundary Road, Bruce Highway). It also features koalas and roos, as well as other non-natives, including deer and water buffalo. ■ *0900-1700. $20, child $10. T3204 6566, www.almaparkzoo.com.au Alma Zoo can be reached by train on the Caboolture line from Roma Street (daily 0902) where a courtesy bus will pick you up.*

Australian Woolshed & Castlemaine Brewery The **Australian Woolshed** claims to offer a 'a real outback experience without leaving Brisbane' with working dog and sheep shows, whip-cracking, farmyard animal feeding and milking and yes, more bloody koalas! It is actually quite entertaining, even the buffet lunch, which involves a strange bushman in an Akubra hat swinging a 'billy' (a sort of tea pot), which apparently improves the taste. ■ *Daily 0730-1600, $15.70, child $10.40, T3872 1100, www.auswoolshed.com.au Samford Road, Ferny Hills (north west of the city centre, via Ashgrove).* One place you will certainly not find any koalas or roos (sober ones anyway) is the **Castlemaine Perkins Brewery**, established in 1878 and maker of that famous Aussie brand XXXX. ■ *Brewery tours (45 mins) are available Mon/Tue/Wed 1100/1330/1600 (Wed night tour including food), from $8.50. Samples included. 'BBQ and Beer' tour Wed 1830, from $18.50. T3361 7597, tour.guides@lion-nathan.com.au Milton Rd (south off Roma St).*

Essentials

Hotels and apartments Most of the big chains are represented, but for something a little bit different try the **LL** *Royal Albert Boutique Hotel* Corner of Albert St and Elizabeth St, T3291 8888, www.atlantisproperties.com.au, art-deco style, with deluxe rooms, suites and self-contained apartments. Across the river on Kangaroo Point, the modern and chic **LL-A** *IL Mondo Boutique Hotel*, 25 Rotherham St, T3392 0111, www.ilmondo.com.au, offers 1-2 bedroom, self-contained apartments in relative peace. It is within walking distance of all the action via a typical Brizzie ferry ride from the Holman St Wharf. In-house Mediterranean al-fresco restaurant and a lap pool. The **L-A** *Central Brunswick Apartment Hotel*, 455 Brunswick St, Fortitude Valley, T3852 1411, www.centralbrunswickhotel.com.au, is modern, friendly and ideally placed for the 'Valley' action. One of the best value (and certainly the best placed) of the budget hotel options is the friendly **A** *Explorers Inn*, 63 Turbot St, T3211 3488, www.powerup.com.au/~explorer It offers tidy (if small) doubles/twins/family rooms and singles and has a cheap but cheerful restaurant/bar. It is only 500 m from the transit centre and Queen St. Recommended.

B&Bs Brisbane has a good selection of B&Bs, some of which present an ideal opportunity to experience a traditional 'Queenslander' house. In Kelvin Grove (2 km northwest) **L-A** *Catherine House*, 151 Kelvin Grove Rd, T3839 6988, www.babs.com.au/catherine, is a large Victorian colonial home with 3 beautifully appointed rooms, a self-contained flat, pool and spacious gardens. In Paddington (2 km west) the **L-A** *Paddington (Waverley) B&B*, 5 Latrobe Terr, T3369 8973, is a traditional Queenslander with 4 rooms, 2 standard en suites and 2 self-contained suites, right on the main café/restaurant strip. Within walking distance of the CBD is **L** *Thornbury House*, 1 Thornbury St, 13832 5985, www.babs.com.au/qld/thornbury.htm Another traditional Queenslander with 5 recently refurbished rooms, all traditionally furnished with private bathrooms and a self-contained apartment. About 4 km south of the city the **L-A** *Ridge Haven B&B*, 374 Annerley Rd, Annerley, 13391 7702, ridgehaven@uq.net.au, is an award-winning Queenslander with 3 very tidy en suites set in a quiet, leafy surroundings.

Motels There are numerous motels on the main highways north and south in to town. On the northern approaches the **A-B** *Chermside Green Motel*, 949 Gympie Rd, Chermside (9 km from the city), T3359 1041, chermside@futureweb.com.au, is modern, friendly, with an in-house restaurant and only a short walk from the huge Westfield Shopping Complex. In the CBD, the **A-B** *Astor Motel*, 193 Wickham Terr, T3831 9522 has tidy modern units and suites close to all amenities.

Hostels City centre Just 500 m southwest of the transit centre, Upper Roma St offers 3 good options. Pick of the bunch is **C-E** *City Backpackers*, 380 Upper Roma St, T3211 3221, offering spotless en suite doubles and dorms, modern kitchen, roof decks, pool, internet and a great bar. It's a very social place that can throw a great party at the weekend, is ideal if you are travelling alone and has excellent security. Almost next door is the **B-E** *Brisbane YHA*, 392 Upper Roma St, T3236 1004. It offers plenty of clean, modern dorms, standard/en suite double/twins, good kitchen, restaurant, internet and good activities/information desk, but it lacks the same casual social atmosphere of its neighbour. Nearby, is the older **C-E** *Yellow Submarine*, 66 Quay St, T3211 3424. It's a rather tired but characterful multi-level homestead, with dorms and doubles, good kitchen, free BBQs (Sun) and a pool. Friendly, casual, social atmosphere and the staff can also help find work. Right in the heart of the CBD is the noisy **C-E** *Palace Backpackers*, Corner of Ann St and Edward St, T3211 2433. It is a large elegant and historic landmark building that has been fully revamped, offering large dorms, doubles and small singles with all amenities including cable TV café and the rowdy in-house *Down Under Bar and Grill*. Not a place for the shy and retiring sort.

Sleeping

Brisbane boasts more than 12,000 beds from large 5 star hotels and modern apartment blocks to numerous backpacker and budget options

The only thing really lacking are good motor parks within easy reach of the city centre

Queensland

Although there are plenty of hostels you are still advised to book a budget bed at least 2 days in advance

Fortitude Valley There are plenty of choices in and around 'The Valley' offering some peace and quiet, but still within walking distance of its popular 24-hr cafés, pubs and nightclubs. **B-F** *Elephant and Wheelbarrow Backpackers*, 230 Wickham St, T3252 4136. Above the popular British-style pub. It has cheap 'n' cheerful dorms, quads/doubles/triples, internet, cable TV, good kitchen and free breakfast. Further south in New Farm (off Brunswick St) the small, characterful, 2-storey **C-E** *Globetrekkers*, 35 Balfour St, T3358 1251, globetrekkers.net.au, is both cosy and homely, with dorms, doubles, free internet and off street parking. Owner, artist, traveller, and all round good guy Dennis is usually on hand to offer advice and point you in the right direction. Recommended. Nearby, on the same side of Brunswick, the **C-E** *Bowen Terrace Backpackers*, 365 Bowen Terr, New Farm, T3254 0458, ceclarke@bigpond.com.au, is also quiet and friendly, with a B&B feel, offering good value singles, twins/doubles (some en suite and bath) with TV, fridge and small kitchen. No internet. Still in New Farm, the **C-E** *Homestead Backpackers*, 57 Annie St, T3254 1609 is one of the Valley's liveliest, offering tidy 3/4/7 dorms, doubles (some en suite), internet, pool, off street parking and a list of 'freebies' from pick-ups, bike hire, day trips to Mt Coot-tha and organized socials with other backpackers.

South and West South of the river the **C-E** *Somewhere to Stay*, corner Brighton Rd and Franklin St, West End, T3846 4584, www.somewheretostay.com.au, offers basic to standard dorms, singles, double/twins with nice views (some with TV and en suite), plus lots of youthful energy. Good kitchen, pool, free pick-ups, organized tours, internet. Needs a good clean. West of the CBD, and handy to Caxton St nightlife and Paddington, is the tidy 1872 colonial house, **C-E** *Aussie Way*, 34 Cricket St, T3369 0711, offering small dorms, singles and doubles, pool, quiet verandas, free pick-ups and internet.

Motor parks On the northern approach, 12 km from the CBD, the **L-E** *Caravan Village*, 763 Zillmere Rd (off Gympie Rd), T3263 4040, www.caravanvillage.com.au, is the best bet, offering a wide range of options from luxury cabins, en suite/standard powered and non-powered sites, pool, store, internet and an excellent camp kitchen. The closest motor park to the city (6 km northwest) is the fairly basic **B-F** *Newmarket Gardens Caravan Park*, 199 Ashgrove Av, (off Enoggera Rd), T3356 1458. It has some tidy cabins, powered and non-powered sites in a quiet suburban setting, BBQs but no camp kitchen. Close to main bus route and shops. South of the city (15 km), the **L-F** *Dress Circle Holiday Village*, 10 Holmead Rd (Logan Rd exit off S.E. Freeway), T3341 6133, is the best upmarket option, close to shops and the main highways. It has luxury apartments, cottages, standard cabins, powered and non-powered sites, pool and a camp kitchen.

Eating

Try the famed Moreton Bay Bugs (a delicious and very weird looking crab) For cheaper options in the city centre try the numerous food courts and outlets along the Queen St Mall or one of the city centre pubs (see opposite)

They say Brizzie can offer the best of most things and its culinary experiences are no exception. The choice is vast. Outside the city centre and the **Riverside** (Eagle St) areas the suburbs of **Fortitude Valley**, **New Farm** (east), **South Bank**, the **West End** (south of the river) and **Paddington** (west) are well worth looking at.

City centre Some of Brisbane's hotels are well known for their exceptional fine dining, including multi-award winners, *Siggi's*, in the Stamford Plaza, corner of Edward St and Margaret St, T3221 1999, *Ryan's in the Park*, in the *Conrad International*, T3306 8899, and *Armstrong's*, *Inchcolm Hotel*, 73 Wickham Terr, T3832 4566 (open breakfast daily, dinner Mon-Sat, lunch Mon-Fri). The latter was founded by one of Brisbane's most famous chefs, Russell Armstrong, and is especially well known for its wine list and Asian-style seafood dishes. On Adelaide St, *Jameson's*, (475), T3831 7633, and *Circa*, (483), T3832 4722 (open lunch Tue-Fri, dinner Mon-Sat) are recommended, with Jameson's renowned for its Japanese influences. On Edward St, *Gianni's*, (12), T3221 7655, offers a Spanish influence and extensive wine cellar. Nearby, *Il (2)* 2 Edward St, T3210 0600, offers meat and seafood dishes (open dinner Mon-Sat, lunch Mon-Fri). The *Riverside and Eagle St Pier* have plenty of options with great river views, including the famous *Pier Nine*, Eagle St Pier, T3229 2194, with its superb seafood, and *Il Centro*, Shop 6, Eagle St Pier, T3221 6090, which is renowned for its stunning sand crab lasagne.

Fortitude Valley, New Farm and east The Valley and New Farm offer a truly vast and eclectic range of mainly affordable options from the Asian restaurants that surround **Chinatown** and the **24 hr café/bars** on Brunswick St Mall, to the new and the chic along Brunswick St and James St, in New Farm. Of the Asian choices on Wickham St and the Chinatown Mall, many swear by the large *King of Kings*, (169), T3852 1122, or for Japanese the *Aya*, (149), T3257 2399. Another great favourite in the Valley is the recently relocated *Garuva Hidden Tranquillity Restaurant and Bar*, 324 Wickham St, T3216 0124. It offers imaginative international cuisine with great decor, sitting on comfy floor cushions. In New Farm, *Arc*, 561 Brunswick St, T3358 3600, is renowned for its modern Australian dishes, while *Anise*, 697 Brunswick St, T3358 1558, is a small and congenial wine bar/restaurant. On the edge of New Farm Park and the river, the *Vat Modern Dining*, in the Powerhouse Centre, is also great for a lazy lunch, T3358 8600. East of Fortitude Valley the *Breakfast Creek Hotel*, 2 Kingsford Smith Dr, T3262 5988, is famous for its ambience and enormous steaks (see Pubs & bars on next page).

South and west One of Brisbane's best restaurants is to be found in the West End. The award winning *E'cco*, 100 Boundary St, T3831 8344, offers simple yet delicious modern Australian dishes. For something different the *Moorish Dar*, 267 Given Terr, Paddington, T3369 0111, offers upmarket, café-style dining with a French/Arabesque influence surrounded by Moorish crafts. Recommended. Also on Given Terr, the *Sultan's Kitchen Indian Restaurant*, (163), T3368 2194, is a friendly, good value curry house. For a really cheap feed well into the wee hours try *Harry's Fine Foods*, corner Petrie Terr and Caxton St. The *Summit Restaurant*, T3369 9922, at Mt Coot-tha is another Brisbane classic with its superb views across the city and Moreton Bay (open daily for lunch/dinner and on Sun for brunch). Next door, the *Kuta Café* offers lighter meals.

Cafés The main focus for Brisbane's casual, al fresco café scene are the **Brunswick St Mall** in Fortitude Valley, the **South Bank** parklands, the West End (**Boundary St** and **Petrie Terr/Paddington** (Caxton and Given Terr). One exception is the quaint *Shingle Inn*, 254 Edward St, T3221 9039, an 'olde-world' teashop with marvellous brews and sweets to die for. Also, for good coffee, keep your eyes open for the *Merlo* brand. *Merlo's*, in the Queensland Art Gallery, is one favourite outlet. Nearby, the South Bank parklands also has many cafés and outdoor eateries to satisfy the midday munchies or provide that sought after caffeine fix. In Fortitude Valley, the Brunswick St Mall has a rash of good options, many of which are open late or even 24 hrs. *Ric's Café Bar*, T3854 1772, and *Fat Boys*, T3252 3789, are 2 favourites. Further south down Brunswick St, the *Vroom Café*, corner of James St and Dogget St, Fortitude Valley, T3257 4455, offers good food and interesting decor, while *Koffie's Expresso Bar* (726), T3254 1254, is good for value and breakfasts. In Paddington, the *Kookaburra Café*, 280 Given Terr, T3369 2400, is well known for its excellent pizza, while the *Tea Shop*, 231 Given Terr, T3876 6088, serves a good value breakfast. The West End is a popular café haunt, especially for weekend brunches with *The Three Monkeys*, 28 Mollison St, T3844 6045. Along Boundary St, *Expresso Head* (169), T3844 8324, and *Tempo*, (181A), T3846 3161, are both recommended.

Pubs & bars Brisbane has a lively and varied pub scene with everything from the historic and traditional Australian to the pseudo Irish and gay friendly

City centre For a traditional street corner Australian try the *Orient Hotel*, corner of Queen St and Ann St, T3839 4625, well known for its live music (Thu-Sat, open nightly until 0300). The *Victory*, corner of Edward St and Charlotte St, T3221 0444, is also an old Brisbane favourite with local (free) live bands Thu-Sun and a good beer garden. There are a glut of Irish pubs throughout the city with *PJ O'Briens*, 127 Charlotte St, T3210 6822, *Gilhooley's*, 283 Elizabeth St, T3221 8566, and the new and classy *Irish Murphy's*, Treasury Chambers, corner of George St and Elizabeth St, T3221 4377, www.irish murphy's.com, all proudly flying the flag in the city centre. Backpackers tend to focus on the *Downunder Bar*, beneath the Palace Backpackers, 308 Edward St, T3002 5740, open nightly until 0300.

Queensland

Fortitude Valley *Dooley's* in the Valley, 394 Brunswick St, T3252 4344, is another Irish offering with live music most nights, while the new *Elephant and Wheelbarrow*, 230 Wickham St, T3252 4136, presents some stiff opposition. The *Wickham Hotel*, Wickham St, T3852 1301, is a well-known gay bar with live music, drag shows and dancing at the weekend.

Petrie Terr and Paddington On the corner of Petrie Terr and Caxton St, the *Hotel LA*, T3368 2560, attracts the loud and pretentious and, if you can get past the 'fashion police' on the door, it will accommodate you well into the wee hours. Further down Caxton St, is the huge *Caxton Hotel*, (38) T3369 5544, with a good restaurant attached (open daily until 0200-0500). In Paddington the *Paddo Tavern*, 186 Given Terr, T3369 0044, is another vast offering and a firm suburban favourite, with adorable barmaids, a fine beer garden and comedy club and there's *Fibber McGee's* Irish bar/restaurant (entertainment nightly). Although a bit of a trek, the 111 year-old *Breakfast Creek Hotel*, 2 Kingsford Smith Dr, T3262 5988, is something of a Brisbane institution. It retains a distinct colonial/art deco feel, has a large Spanish beer garden and serves up the best steaks in town. Over in Kangaroo Point is the *Story Bridge Hotel*, 200 Main St, T3391 2266, www.storeybridgehotel.com.au, a firm favourite at any time, but most famous for hosting the annual Australia Day 'cockroach races' and the Australian Festival of Beers in Sep.

Entertainment

For up-to-date listings and entertainment news consult the Courier Mail on Wed/Sat or the free street press publications, Rave, ShowBriz, Time Off and Scene

Performing Arts The *Queensland Performing Arts Complex* on the South Bank (see Sights section) is the main focus of the city's cultural entertainment. The busy on-going programme includes West End and Broadway musicals, touring productions and Queensland's own ballet, opera, orchestra, theatre and music companies. For programme details check the local press or call *Qtix*, T136246 (Mon-Sat 0900-2100), www.qtix.com.au./ www.qpac.com.au Brisbane's New Farm Park also hosts the newly restored theatre and performance space, the *Powerhouse Complex*, 119 Lamington St, T3358 8600, while *La Boite Theatre*, 57 Hale St, Petrie Terr, T3369 1622, offers mainly Australian themed plays.

Live Music As well as its ever-changing, yet healthy night club scene, **Fortitude Valley** (alias 'The Valley') is the best place to check out the latest local talent, with its many pubs hosting bands from Thu-Sat. Brisbane has a wealth of Irish pubs (see above) with most offering occasional folk jam sessions and regular live bands at the weekend. *Irish Murphy's* is recommended. The *Brisbane Jazz Club*, 1 Annie St, Kangaroo Point, T3391 2006, has a loyal following with regulars playing on Sat/Sun, from 2030 ($7 cover). Other pubs around **Kangaroo Point**, including the *Story Bridge*, 200 Main St, T3391 2266, also host jazz sessions mainly on Sun afternoons. *Jazzy Cat*, 56 Mollison St, West End, T3846 2544, www.jazzycat.com.au, is another good venue.

Nightclubs The *Riverside Centre* (Eagle St, City) and *Petrie Terr* are the main club and dance venues. **In Fortitude Valley** look out for the *Zoo*, 711 Ann St, (Wed-Sat until about 0200). Also *Ric's*, 321 Brunswick St, (Sun-Thu until 0100, Sat/Sun until 0500, free entry), the *Monastery*, 621 Ann St, and the *Beat*, 677 Ann St. **At Riverside**, *Friday's*, 123 Eagle St, (Sun-Thu until 0300, Fri/Sat until 0500). **In the city**, backpackers gravitate towards the *Downunder Bar* (*Palace Backpackers*), 308 Edward St, City, T3002 5740, (nightly until 0300). In Petrie Terr and Paddington try the *Paddo Tavern* and *The Hotel LA* (see Pubs & Bars).

Casino The Brisbane *Treasury Casino* is housed in the grand, former Treasury Building on North Quay and is open 24 hrs. As well as the usual pokies and gaming tables it has 5 restaurants and 7 bars, T1800-506888 Dress is smart casual and the minimum age is 18.

Cinema Other than the huge *Imax* Theatre (see Sights) the city centre hosts *Dendy*, 346 George St, T3211 3244, and 2 *Hoyt's* Cinemas, one at the Myer Centre, 91 Queen St, and another at 197 Queen St. In Fortitude Valley, the *Centro*, 39 James St, T3852 4488, and more alternative *Village Twin*, 701 Brunswick St, T3358 2021 are other options. Tue night is discount night.

Comedy Several pubs host comedy clubs and evenings, featuring the best of local or visiting talent. They include the *Paddo Tavern*, (Wed/Thu/Fri/Sat), 186 Given Terr, Paddington, T3369 4466 and The *Dockside Comedy Bar*, (Thu-Sat), Ferry St, Kangaroo Point, T3391 1110.

Brisbane has a brash and lively gay scene that mainly centres around the pubs and clubs in 'The Valley' and Spring Hill. In the Valley, The *Wickham Hotel*, Wickham St, T3852 1301, and *The Beat*, Ann St, T3852 2661, are especially popular, while in Spring Hill the *Options* Nightclub (Spring Hill Hotel) and the *Sportsman's Hotel*, Leichardt St are other favourite haunts. Street press publications to look out for are *'Brothersister'* or *'Queensland Pride'*.

Gay & lesbian

The year begins with a bang with the *New Year* celebrations and fireworks display over the river beside the South Bank parklands. This is repeated with even more zeal on **26 Jan** - *Australia Day* - with other hugely popular and bizarre events, including the annual **cockroach races** and even a little **'frozen chicken bowling'** (like you do!). Over **Easter** the *Brisbane to Gladstone Yacht Race*, leaves Shorncliffe, while the *Caxton Seafood and Wine Festival* arrives at the western suburb of Paddington. **May** sees the *Queensland Racing Festival* and **Jun** the annual *Queensland Day* celebrations. Fortitude Valley's Chinatown and Brunswick St become the focus for the lively *Valley Festival* in **Jul**, with the *Brisbane International Film Festival* at the end of month. The last week of **Aug** sees the start of the 2-week *Riverfestival*, which celebrates the 'city's lifeblood' with food, fire and festivities, echoed in **Sep** with the *National Festival of Beers* (Australia's biggest) held at the *Story Bridge Hotel*. The *Livid Festival* in **Oct** is Brisbane's biggest live music event with numerous city venues hosting the best of local talent and visiting bands. An up-to-date events listing is available at www.brisbanetourism.com.au

Festivals & events

The city also hosts a few good **markets** including the South Bank markets on Fri night/Sat/Sun, the **Riverside and Eagle St Pier** markets (Sun) and the **'Valley'** markets (Brunswick St) on Sat. For **maps and travel books** look no further than *World Wide Maps and Guides*, 187 George St, T3221 4330, www.worldwidemaps.com.au For mainstream **bookshops** you will find major outlets in around Queen St, including *Angus and Robertson Bookworld*, 52 Queen St, T3229 8899 (also in the Myer Centre, Level A and Post Office Sq) and *The American Book Store*, 173 Elizabeth St, T3229 4677. For second-hand books try *Bent Books*, 205A Boundary St, West End, T3846 5004, or *Emma's Bookshop*, across the road at 132 Boundary St, T3844 4973 (also has internet). For **camping** and outdoor equipment *City Camping Disposals*, 157 Elizabeth St, should supply all your needs. **Stones Corner** in East Brisbane offers the best discount shopping area, with numerous factory and seconds outlets.

Shopping
Brisbane is without doubt the Queensland Capital for retail therapy, with over 1500 stores and 650 shops in and around Queen St alone

There are 3 famous sporting venues in Brisbane: the **'Gabba'** in Woolloongabba (cricket and Aussie football); the **ANZ Stadium** in Nathan (home to rugby league's Brisbane Broncos) and **Ballymore** in Herston (home of rugby union State side, the Queensland Reds). For bookings and tickets contact *Ticketmaster*, T3221 7894, or *Ticketek*, T131931.

Sport

Ballooning *Fly Me To The Moon*, T3423 0400, www.flymetothemoon.com.au, offer flights right over the city with champagne breakfast, Mon-Fri, from $198 (Sat/Sun $218). Other companies include *Champagne Breakfast Flights*, T3397 0033, www.possumairtours.com.au, which take you out over the city to the Moreton Bay Islands, 0600/1730, from $230.

Tours & activities
There are a vast array of tours on offer. The VIC has full listings

Bicycle *Hotel Cycle Tours*, T04-0800 3198, daily 1400/1930, from $30, child $25.

Bus Brisbane Transport's *CitySights* and *CityNights* tours are a great way to see the inner city and the views from Mt Coot-tha, with the added bonus of free bus and CityCat

Queensland

travel on the tour day. The tour itself lasts 1 hr, from $20, child $15, T131230. Tours leave every 45 mins from Post Office Square, from 0900-1545. (CityNights at 1830-2100 Nov-Feb and 1800-2030 Mar-Oct). Recommended. Numerous bus companies offer a wide range of day tours around the region from the Gold and Sunshine Coasts to Fraser Island and The Southern Queensland National Parks, including *Coachtrans* (Gold Coast, Sunshine Coast and hinterlands) from $55; T3236 4165, www.daytours.com.au; *Flight Deck Tours* (City, Moreton Bay and Gold Coast) from $40, T01 4873 5141; *Australia Day Tours* (most places) from $60-80, T3236 4155, www.daytours.com.au and *Grayline* (the same) from $37, T1300-360776. Brochures can be picked up at the various company offices at the Roma St Transit Centre.

Cruises *Club Crocodile Paddle steamers* (formerly known as the *Kookaburra River Queens*), T3221 1300, www.clubcroc.com.au, have become a familiar sight on the river offering a range of sightseeing/dining options. Lunch 1½ hrs, Mon-Fri 1145, from $36. Dinner 2½ hrs, Mon-Thu 1900, Fri-Sat 1845, Sun 1800, from $52.50. Sunday breakfast with live jazz 0730-1030. *The Island* is Brisbane's biggest party boat, departing from Pier 5, Queens Wharf, North Quay, T3211 9090, (bookings essential).

Culinary You can practically eat your way around the city, and sample a 'Moreton Bay Bug' with **Culinary Tour** expert Jan Power, T3268 3889, or combine fine dining with **art gallery tours** with *Art Tours*, T3899 3686, www.artours.coaus.com.au, from $55.

Rock climbing and abseiling The cliffs on the south side of the river between the maritime Museum and Kangaroo Point offer excellent opportunities for climbing and abseiling. *Worthwild*, T3395 6450, and *Careflight*, T5598 0222, offer classes from $70.

Rollerblading *Blade Sensations* offer guided roller blade tours including the unusual *Full Moon Skate* which, sadly, does not mean you skate in the buff, but see the city at night, departs 2000, T3844 0606. *Skatebiz*, 101 Albert St, T3220 0157, offers independent hire, from $11 for 2 hr. Group skating Wed 2000, tours Sun from $10.

Shopping Even the shopaholics are well catered for with *Brisbane Warehouse Shopping Tours*, T3821 0438.

Skydiving *Brisbane Skydiving Centre*, T1800-061555, www.brisbaneskydive. com.au, offer tandems with Australian team member Brian Scoffell over Brisbane city or Willowbank, from $220 (over the city $290). *Ripcord Skydivers*, T3399 3552, www.ripcord-skydivers.com.au, offer similar deals.

Walking Brisbane's river, city parks and surrounding forest parks all offer excellent walking opportunities from short mangrove boardwalks and literary trails to multi-day hikes. The VICs and QPWS office can supply all the details. Local history expert Brian Ogden leads visitors on a journey into Brisbane's interesting past with 1 hr and 2 hr **historical walking tours**, Sat 0830/1130, Wed 1900, Mon 0930 (2 hr tour including 30 min guided tour of St John's Cathedral), from $11, T3217 3673, www.ogdenswalkingtours.com.au Not for the superstitious is the entertaining **Ghost Tour** of Brisbane, T3844 6606, www.ghost-tours.com.au, Tue-Thu/Sat 1100-1700, from $25-61.

Transport
See also page 244
Bus For a good deal to the Gold Coast, catch the Gold Coast Conrad *Jupiter's Casino Bus*, T3222 4067 (departs Roma St Transit Centre daily 0900, returns 1500, Sat/Sun 1100, returns 1700). For $10 you will be transported to Jupiter's Casino where you will then receive a $5 lunch voucher and $5 gaming voucher. *Coachtrans*, T3236 1000, offer 4 daily services to the Gold Coast (including the airport) and 'Unlimited Travel Passes' for city sights, airport and Gold Coast. *Crisps Coaches*, T3236 5266, offer south and westbound services from Brisbane to Toowoomba/Moree, from $29 single and Brisbane to Tenterfield, from $36 single. *Sun Air*, T5478 2811, *Sunshine Coast Sunbus*, T5450 7888, and *Suncoast Pacific*, T3236 1901 (latter recommended for Noosa), offer regular daily services to the Sunshine Coast. *Brisbane Bus Lines*, T3355 0034, also service the Sunshine Coast and South Burnett Region.

Train **Northbound services** The 'Tilt Train' is the new express service between Brisbane-Rockhampton (6 mins) and is the service recommended for those travelling to Noosa via Nambour or Hervey Bay via Maryborough (free bus connection), departs Sun-Fri 1030 and 1700 (Rockhampton$82/Namour $22/Bundaberg $52 single). The 'Sunlander' (Brisbane-Cairns) departs 0855 Tue/Thu/Sat (Cairns from $201 single). The 'Spirit of the Tropics' (Brisbane-Townsville) departs 1340 Tue/Sat (Townsville from $180 single). The 'Queenslander' (Brisbane-Cairns) is a luxury service departing Sun 0855, from $558. **Westbound services** The 'Westlander' (Brisbane-Charleville) departs 1920, Tue/Thu (Charleville from $116 single); The 'Spirit of the Outback' (Brisbane-Longreach) departs 1825 Tue/Fri (Longreach from $180 single).

Airlines *Qantas*, T131313 (247 Adelaide St, T3238 2953). **Banks** All major bank branches with ATMs are represented in the city centre especially in the Malls Queen, Edward St and Eagle St. **Currency Exchange** *Thomas Cook*, Bowman House, 276 Edward St, T3221 9422. *American Express*, 131 Elizabeth St, T3229 2729. **Bike hire** *Brisbane Bicycle*, 87 Albert St, T3229 2433, from $20 per day ($100 deposit for overnight hire); or *Hotel/Valet Cycle Hire*, T04-0800 3198 (tours also available). **Car/Van hire** *Able*, Transit Centre, T131429; *Avis* 133 Albert St, T3221 2900; *Budget* 105 Mary St, T3220 0699; *Britz* camper vans, 647 Kingsford Smith Dr, T3630 1151; *Maui*, 647 Kingsford Smith Dr, T1300-363800. **Chemist** *Day and Night*, 245 Albert St, T3221 8155. **Communications** Internet *International Youth Service Centre*, 2/69 Adelaide St, T3229 9985 (open daily 0800-2400), or the *State Library*, South Bank, T3840 7666, 30 mins free, book a day in advance (open Mon-Thu 1000-2000, Fri-Sun 1000-1700) If you are staying north of the city, *Dymocks* in the Westfield Shopping Centre, Chermside, has free internet with a café purchase. **Post Office** The central Post office is at 261 Queen St (opposite Post Office Sq). Post shops: 44 Roma St, 27 Adelaide St, Wintergarden and Queen St Malls. Open Mon-Fri 0830-1730 (Mall post shops open Fri until 1900 and Sat 0900-1600/Sun 1030-1600). **Post Restante** Queen St, T3405 1448. Open Mon-Fri 0900-1700. **Medical services** *Mater Hospital* (24 hr) Raymond Terr, Woolloongabba, T3840 8111. *Roma St Medical Centre*, Transit Centre, T3236 2988. *Travellers Medical Service*, Level 1, 245 Albert St, T3211 3611. **Police** corner of Queen St and Albert St and opposite the Roma St Transit Centre, T3364 6464. Emergency T000. *RACQ* 261 Queen St, T3361 2394. **Travel Agents** *Backpackers Travel Centre*, 138 Albert St, T3221 2225. *YHA Queensland*, 154 Roma St, T3236 1680. *Flight Centre*, 170 Adelaide St, T3221 8900. **Work** *Work Travel*, Level 3, Transit Centre, Roma, T3236 4899. Centrelink, T132850

Directory

Moreton Bay and Islands

The sand islands of Moreton Bay present a superb 'island experience' and opportunity to escape the clamour and hype of the Gold Coast and Brisbane. Although much smaller than Fraser's land and hosting marginally less dramatic or variant scenery, the true beauty of the Moreton group lies in the fact that they are so easily accessible and so remarkably unspoilt. Of the 300-odd islands scattered throughout the bay, the two largest and most popular are **Moreton Island** *and* **North Stradbroke Island***. Moreton, which lies 37 km northeast of the mouth of the Brisbane River, is almost uninhabited and famous for its* **4WD** *opportunities, its* **shipwrecks** *and its pod of* **friendly dolphins***. Further south, North Stradbroke (or 'Straddie') is the largest of the islands and a true island resort, with three easily accessible, laid-back communities, world-class* **surf beaches***, awesome coastal scenery and the very real possibility of seeing breaching whales, dolphins and manta rays.*

Colour map 3, grid A6

Bayside Resorts Although the islands are the obvious lure of Moreton Bay, several of the coastal settlements (essentially suburbs of Brisbane), offer a more relaxed base from which to explore both the islands and the city, as well as presenting some exciting opportunities for sailing, diving and other watersports. North of the Brisbane River mouth is Sandgate, Brighton and Redcliffe. **Redcliffe**, 36 km northeast of Brisbane, is a picturesque peninsula suburb with a broad range of accommodation, several safe swimming beaches, numerous watersports and activities and also serves as the northerly access point to Moreton Island (see page 259). The **Redcliffe Visitors Information Centre** is located at Pelican Park, Hornibrook Esplanade. ■ *Daily 0900-1600 T3284 3500, www.redcliffe. qld.gov.au* They stock maps and can assist with general information and accommodation/activity bookings.

South of the Brisbane River the main coastal settlements are Wynnum, Manly, Cleveland and Redland Bay. **Manly** is another popular holiday destination and as the host to one of the largest **marinas** in the Southern Hemisphere, offers some excellent **sailing** opportunities. *WAGS* (Wednesday Afternoon Gentleman's Sailing) offer free afternoon sailing, (book before 1230) T3396 8666. The **B-E** *Moreton Bay Lodge*, 45 Cambridge Parade, T3396 3020, offer budget dorms, singles, doubles and family rooms with good views and a café/wine bar. *Manly Eco Tours*, T3396 9400, offer an excellent range of bay cruises, from full day island explorations (from $71, child $35), to Sunday breakfast (from $28) and boom netting parties (from $13.50). Helena Island tours also depart from Manly (see below). The well-organized **Wynnum Manly VIC** is located in the heart of the town at 43A Cambridge Parade, T3348 3524. ■ *Daily 1000-1500*. They stock maps and can assist with general information and accommodation/activity bookings. **Cleveland** and **Redland Bay** to the south of Manly serve as the main departure points to North Stradbroke Island. ■ *Contact Redlands VIC, 152 Shore St West, Cleveland, T3821 0057, redlandstourism@redland.net.au Mon-Fri 0830-1700, Sat/Sun 0900-1600.*

North Stradbroke Island

Colour map 3, grid A6
Population: 3,000
30 km southeast of Brisbane

North Stradbroke, or **'Straddie'** as it is affectionately known, is the largest, most inhabited and most accessible of the Moreton Bay Islands by ferry. Separated from its southerly neighbour, South Stradbroke, by a fierce cyclone in 1896, it has become a magical, though overlooked, tourist attraction. In many ways it is similar to Fraser Island, offering diverse and unspoilt **coastal scenery** and a rich biodiversity so typical of 'sand islands'. The three pleasant and picturesque villages of Dunwich, Amity Point and Point Lookout offer a broad range of accommodation, play host to some excellent **beaches** and host a wealth of waterbased activities, **surfing** being the obvious speciality.

Ins & outs **Getting there** Water taxis and vehicular ferries depart from Toondah Harbour, **Cleveland** or Banana St in **Redland Bay**. To reach the Cleveland ferry terminal by car from Brisbane, follow signs from Highway 1 to Old Cleveland Rd, then follow Finucane Rd right through the centre of Cleveland to Toondah Harbour. From the Gold Coast take the Bryants Rd/Cleveland exit, off the Pacific Highway and follow signs to Redland Bay or Cleveland. By **train**, from Brisbane, take Citytrain to Cleveland from the Roma St Transit Centre, where a bus (National Bus, T3245 3333) will provide pick-ups to the ferry terminal, T131230. *Stradbroke Ferries*, T3286 2666, operate both passenger (water taxi) and vehicle services. The Water Taxi departs every hr Mon-Fri 0600-1915, Sat 0630-1800, Sun 0800-1800, from $12, child $5.50 return. The vehicle ferry also

Brisbane & Moreton Bay

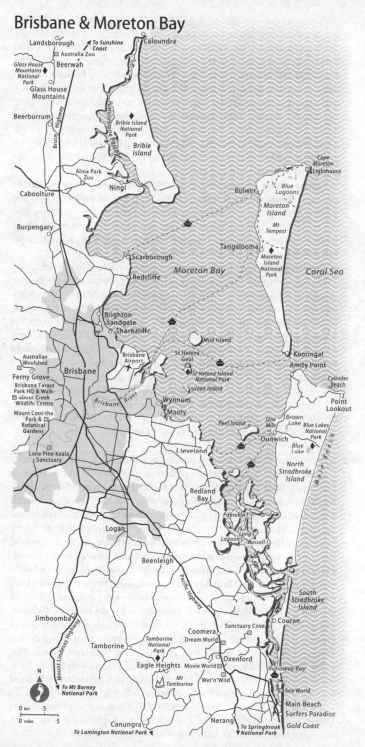

Queensland

departs every hr, Mon-Fri 0530-1830, Sat 0530-1830, Sun 0530-1930, from $86 return (passenger $10, child $5 return, bikes $4). The crossing for both services takes 30 mins. The *North Stradbroke Flyer*, T3286 1964, also offers a fast passenger service, 9 times daily from 0630-1830, from $12 return. They also offer half-day tours to the island (from $129, child $85) Their bus 'Bessie' meets the Cleveland train. **Redland Bay services** To reach the Redland Bay ferry terminal **by car** from Brisbane, or the Gold Coast, follow signs from the Pacific Highway to Bryants Rd exit and follow signs to Redland Bay. *Island's Transport*, T3829 0008, www.islandstransport.com.au, operate both passenger and vehicle services. They departs every 2 hrs, Mon-Fri 0500-1730 (Fri also 1900), Sat/Sun 0700-1730, from $11, child $5.50 return. The vehicle ferry also departs every hr, Mon-Fri 0530-1830, Sat 0530-1830, Sun 0530-1930, from $82 return. The crossing for both services takes about 45 mins.

Getting around All major roads on 'Straddie' are sealed and it has its own **bus** service, *North Stradbroke Bus Services*, T3409 7151. Buses meet every scheduled ferry arrival or departure and operate between Dunwich, One Mile, Amity and Point Lookout, Mon-Fri 0715-1945, Sat/Sun 0715-1830. The return fare from Dunwich to Point Lookout is around $8. For a **taxi**, T3409 9800. Note many mainland car rental companies will not permit their vehicles on the island.

Orientation North Stradbroke is a wedge-shaped island about 36 km in length and 11 km at its widest point. There are only 3 small settlements. **Dunwich** provides the main arrival point and is on the west mid-section of the island. **Amity Point** sits on the northwest corner 17 km from Dunwich (off **East Coast Rd** along Beehive Rd and Claytons Rd), while **Point Lookout**, the main focus for today's tourist accommodation, sights and activities, is 21 km away on the northeast corner. Point Lookout's main drag, East Coast Rd, runs parallel with **Cylinder Beach** and terminates at the picturesque **Point Lookout Peninsula**. Beyond that is **Main Beach**, stretching for 34 km to the island's southern tip.

Information General information is available from the VICs in Brisbane, Manly or Cleveland. On the island itself, The Stradbroke VIC is located 300 m from the ferry wharf on Junner St, Dunwich, T3409 9555, www.redland.net.au/redlandstourism Open Mon-Fri 0830-1700, Sat/Sun 1100-1500. They stock island maps and can assist with general information and accommodation/activity bookings.

Sights If you only have one or two days on the island the place to be is **Point Lookout**, with its golden surf beaches and dramatic headland. At the terminus of East Coast Road (opposite the café) is the start of the **North Gorge Headlands Walk** (1 km one-way). Before you set off take a look at **Frenchman's Bay** below, which gives you a flavour of the dramatic scenery to come. Follow the track to **The Gorge**, a narrow cleft in the rock that is pounded endlessly by huge ocean breakers. Further on **Whale Rock** provides an ideal viewpoint from which to spot migrating **humpback whales** between June-October. **Manta rays, turtles** and **dolphins** are also a familiar sight. At the far end of the walk the vast swathe of **Main Beach** comes into view. Stretching 34 km down the entire length of the island's east coast, it offers some excellent four-wheel driving, fishing, surfing and a few mosquito-infested campsites. **Cylinder Beach**, back along East Coast Road, provides the best recreational spot with great surf breaks and safe swimming. If you do swim always stick to patrolled areas and between the flags. Other attractions on the island include **Blue Lakes National Park**, which is reached via Trans Island Road, from Dunwich. The lake itself (2½ km walk from the car park) is freshwater and fringed with melalucas and eucalypts, providing the perfect spot for a cool swim. To reach Main Beach from there requires 4WD. There is a small **museum** in Dunwich, 15-17 Welsby Street, T3409 9699, that explores the island's rich aboriginal and early settler history. ■ *Wed/Sat. $2.20, child $0.50.*

Queensland

L-A Sunsets at Point Lookout, 6 Billa St, T3409 8829, is one of the few B&Bs with 3 en suites overlooking Home Beach. **A** Amity Bungalows, 33 Ballow St, Amity Point, T3409 7126, www.amitybungalows.com.au, offer 3 well-appointed 1-2 bedroom, self-contained (thatched) bungalows that sleep up to 6. For budget beds try the basic **C-E** Stradbroke Island Guesthouse (above and part of the Dive Shop), 1 East Coast Rd, T3409 8888, www.stradbrokeislandscuba.com.au Internet and Pick-ups from Brisbane. The best-facilitated **motor park**/campsite in Lookout Point is the **B-F** Stradbroke Tourist Park, Dickson Way, T3409 8127. It offers deluxe villas (with spa), en suite/standard cabins, powered and non-powered sites, BBQ but no camp kitchen. There are other basic **E** campsites at Adder Rock and Cylinder Beach in Point Lookout, Amity Point and Dunwich. Camping is also allowed anywhere along the Main Beach foreshore, T3409 9555.

Sleeping
The vast majority of accommodation is based in Point Lookout. The VIC has full listings and pre-booking is recommended in the summer, and on public/school holidays. For holiday rentals and resort information call Raine and Horne, T3409 8213

The Straddie Beach Hotel, T3409 8188, overlooking Cylinder Beach, is a popular spot for value pub meals and has a large outdoor deck space (Open daily for breakfast lunch and dinner from 0730). For something a little more intimate try The Stonefish Restaurant, T3409 8549, on Mintee St, near the headland (open daily from 0800, dinner Wed-Sun). Another alternative is the congenial, al fresco dining at La Focaccia Italian, T3409 8778, Meegera Pl (off Mooloomba/East Coast Rd). Open daily from 0900. Also recommended is Danny's Chinese at the Local Bar, East Coast Rd, T3409 8519. There are **grocery shops** at the Centre Point Shopping Centre, Endeavour St and Mintee St. Open 0700-2100.

Eating

There are several **cruise** and **fishing charters**, including Point Lookout (Mal Starkey), T3409 8353, from $110 and Captain Silver, T3409 8636 (daily at 1000 from One Mile Jetty, Dunwich). The Stradbroke Island Scuba Centre, 1 East Coast Rd, Point Lookout, T3409 8888, www.stradbrokeislandscuba.com.au, offers daily boat dives at 0900/1130/1330, with manta ray, turtle and dolphin spotting, from $110 (including gear). Snorkelling and dive courses are also available. Dive Oceantechniques, 451 Esplanade, T3396 3003, oceantec@stradinet.aunz.com, offer courses, boat dives and eco sightseeing tours, from $45. Straddie Adventures, T3409 8414, straddie@ozemail.com.au, offer backpacker based tours and activities, including sand boarding from $28, Sea kayaking and snorkelling from $33 and half day 4WD tours from $50. Kingfisher Tours, T3409 9502, www.straddiekingfishertours.com.au, and Beach Island Tours, (Tour de Straddie) T3409 8098, both offer 4WD tours. Stradbroke Island Tours, T3409 8051, specialize in wildlife and eco-based trips, from $30.

Tours & activities
The VIC has a free detailed activities and operator broadsheet

Banks The Post Offices in Dunwich, Amity and Point Lookout all act as Commonwealth Bank agents. EFTPOS is available in most shops and holiday resorts. There is an **ATM** at the Stradbroke Island Beach Hotel, Point Lookout. **Communications** Internet Stradbroke Island Guesthouse, 1 East Coast Rd, Point Lookout, T3409 8888. **Post Office** Dunwich, Point Lookout (Megerra Pl), Amity Point. Postcode 4183.

Directory

Moreton Island

Moreton Island, which lies to the north of the Stradbroke Islands, is often considered the jewel of the Moreton group, due to its lack of habitation and unspoilt beauty. At 38 km in length and almost 20,000 ha, it is another 'sand mass' offering long empty beaches, dunes, forest, lagoons and heath lands with abundant wildlife. Other than the sheer beauty and solitude, the greatest attractions are its **4WD opportunities**, fishing, camping, **wreck-snorkelling/diving** and above all, for its world famous pod of bootlenose **dolphins** that put in a nightly appearance at the island's only resort, **Tangalooma**. The dolphins have had a close relationship with humans for centuries, ever since Aboriginal fisherman rewarded them for seeking and herding shoals of fish.

Colour map 3, grid A6
Population: 270
37 km northeast of Brisbane

Queensland

Ins & outs   **Getting there and around**   For those without a 4WD vehicle the best way to reach the island is through the *Tangalooma Resort*, which offers accommodation packages, day trips, island tours and independent transfers, T1300-652250, www.tanga-looma.com.au (excellent website). Their launch leaves from the terminal on the northern bank of the Brisbane River, at the end of Holt St (off Kingsford Smith Dr, just beyond the Gateway Bridge) and departs Sun-Fri 0930, from $35, child $18 (1¼ hr). A courtesy coach operates from the *McCafferty's/Greyhound* Bus Bay 26, Level 3, Roma St Transit Centre in Brisbane city centre at 0900. There are no sealed roads on Moreton and access is by 4WD only ($30 fee for one month). The vehicular/passenger barge *Combie Trader*, T3203 6399, www.moreton-island.com.au, offers regular services from Scarborough (Redcliffe) to Bulwer on the island's northwest coast, from around $150 return. The *Moreton Venture*, T3895 1000, www.moretonventure.com.au, runs from Howard Smith Dr, Lytton, to Kooringal at the island's southern tip. *Heliquest*, T3880 2229, www.heliquest.com.au offer **helicopter** access.

Sights & tours   The main attractions and activities on the island that are accessible without a 4WD are the resort itself (which served as a former **whaling station** between 1952-1962), the **Tangalooma Desert** (a large sand blow near the resort), the **Blue Lagoons** (on the northeast coast), a group of 15 deliberately sunken **shipwrecks** (which provide excellent snorkelling 2 km north of the resort) and, of course, the immensely popular, nightly **dolphin viewing and feeding** at the resort wharf. This is one of the best wild dolphin encounters in the world. The resort offers full/half-day tour options, dolphin feeding/watching and an excellent range of island excursions and activities from sand boarding, snorkelling and diving to scenic helicopter flights. Daily **whale-watching** cruises are also available June-October, from $95, child $55. Their website, www.tanga-looma.com.au, offers all the detail and is a fine introduction to both the resort and the island. *Dolphin Wild*, T5497 5628, www.dolphinwild.com.au, also offer day cruises to Moreton from Redcliffe, from $129,child $70. If you do have the freedom of the island with a 4WD, Cape Moreton at the northwestern tip of the island is worth a visit to see the 1857 **lighthouse** – the oldest in Queensland. **Mount Tempest** (285 m) dominates the heart of the island and is reputed to be the highest coastal sand dune in the world (5 km strenuous walk).

Sleeping   The **LL-D** *Tangalooma Wild Dolphin Resort*, T1300-652250, www.tanga-
& eating   looma.com.au, is a fine resort offering a wide range of beachside accommodations from luxury self-contained apartments and standard rooms/units to new backpacker/budget beds, a restaurant, bistro/bar café, pools and an environmental centre. Recommended. **QPWS campsites** are available at The Wrecks, Ben-Ewa and Comboyuro Point on the west coast and Blue Lagoon and Eagers Creek on the east. The Wrecks campsite is about a 2 km walk from the resort. Each has toilets, and limited supplies of water, cold showers. Fees apply ($3.85 per night), T3408 2710, moreton_is.qpws@bigpond.com.au

Other Moreton   **South Stradbroke Island**, which is the most southerly of the Moreton group,
Bay islands   sits just to the north of Main Beach on the Gold Coast and provides an ideal island getaway. The island is largely uninhabited apart from two resorts. The luxurious **LL** *Couran Cove Resort*, T5597 9000, www.couran.com.au, on the island's west coast offers a range of day tours, with various activities from $55, child $30. **L-A** *South Stradbroke Island Resort*, T5577 3311, www.southstradbrokeislandresort.com.au, offers more basic facilities, numerous water-based activities and caters for day visitors. ■ *The Couran Cove launch offers scheduled daily services from their own terminal at the*

Runaway Bay Marina, 247 Bayview Street, Runaway Bay Marina, T5597 9000. Daily scheduled services to the South Stradbroke Island Resort are also available from the Runaway Bay Marina, (Gate C), T5577 3311. Day Cruises to the latter are also available from Cavill Avenue, Surfers Paradise.

Bribie Island is the most northerly of the Moreton group and closest to the mainland. It is also the only island in the bay that is accessible by car. As such it is fairly well developed with a good infrastructure, amenities and mainly water-based activities. The vast majority of development is located at the southern end of the island, while the north is mainly given over to national and conservation parks. These areas are relatively quiet and unspoilt and provide plenty of opportunity to explore the many wildlife-rich areas. The **Pumicestone Passage**, which separates the island from the mainland, is also a fine venue for bird, turtle and dolphin watching. There are four designated **QPWS campsites**, fees apply, T3408 8451. The **Bribie Island Visitors Information Centre**, Benabrow Avenue, (on the island) T3408 9026, can assist with general information, accommodation/activity listings and bookings. Open Monday-Friday 0900-1600, Saturday 0900-1500, Sunday 0930-1300. From Brisbane travel north via The Bruce Highway to the Caboolture turn-off, then head 26 km east, via Ningi to the bridge at the southern tip of the island.

St Helena Island National Park lies 7 km off the mainland near the mouth of the Brisbane River. Often labelled Australia's Alcatraz, it was first utilized as a **penal colony** as early as 1867 and continued to house prisoners until 1932. With many remnants of the former notorious gaol remaining, as well as an information centre, displays and artefacts, it offers an interesting insight into the harsh treatment of the former convicts, many of whom later helped to put Brisbane on the map. Access is only possible by joining a guided day cruises or **theatrical ghost tours** (book ahead) weekend evenings, from Manly, with *A.B. Sea Cruises*, T3396 3994, www.abseacruises.com.au, from $50.

The Darling Downs

*About 100 km west of Brisbane, across the Great Dividing Range, are The Darling Downs blessed with a cooler, wetter climate and make an an ideal escape from the heat and the hype of the southern Queensland coast. The rich, fertile soils have for decades provided the State with much of its agricultural wealth and a legacy of pleasant, historic and still prosperous rural settlements. Largest amongst them (and one of the largest inland towns in Queensland) is **Toowoomba**, whose leafy streets, parks and gardens have earned it the label of Queensland's 'garden city'. South of Toowoomba is the equally pleasant town of **Stanthorpe**, which sits on the border with New South Wales and in the heart of the **Granite Belt**, an area renowned for its fruit growing and **vineyards**. Straddling both the border and the Great Divide there are also some beautiful national parks, including **Girraween**, Bunya Mountains, Crows Nest, and Mount Barney.*

Toowoomba has lost much of its historical charm, yet is still a pleasant enough place, thanks to its position high on the edge of an escarpment, its broad tree-lined streets and an almost unseemly number of city **parks and gardens**. There are over 150 parks and gardens, including the oldest, **Queens Park** (which incorporates the **Botanical Gardens**) on Lindsay Street, which becomes a blaze of colour in the spring and summer in preparation for the city's most popular annual event, **The Carnival of Flowers**, held every September (last full week). On the outskirts of the city (east and signposted from

Toowoomba
Colour map 3, grid A5
Population: 90,000
Postcode: 4350
122 km west of Brisbane

Queensland

the Warrego Highway) is the **Picnic Point** Lookout, which offers memorable views from the escarpment, across the Lockyer Valley and **Tabletop Mountain**. The **Toowoomba Visitors Information Centre**, 86 James Street (Corner of Kitchener/Warrego Highway), T4639 3797, www.qldsouthern downs.org.au, open daily 0830-1700, can supply town maps and assist with accommodation and activity enquiries and bookings. The **QPWS** has an office at 158 Hume Street, T4639 4599. **Internet** is available at *Coffee on Line*, 148 Margaret Street, T4639 4686.

Sleeping and eating Toowoomba has numerous motels and a smattering of good B&Bs. The Irish **A** *Shamrock Hotel/Motel*, 604 Ruthven St, T4632 2666, is clean and friendly with standard units (some with spa) and a good bar. **C-E** *Mrs Bee's B&B*, 11 Boulton Terr, T4639 1659 is a cosy, budget B&B and YHA affiliate. Of the many motor parks around town the **B-E** *Garden City Caravan Park*, 34A Eiser St (3 km south of the city centre), T4635 1747, and the **B-F** *Jolly Swagman Caravan Park*, 47 Kitchener St, T4632 8735 provide the best facilities. The Garden City has cooking facilities. Most of the town's eateries can be found on **Margaret St** in the city centre.

Transport Bus *McCafferty's/Greyhound*, T131499, and *Crisps Coaches*, T3236 5266, offer regular daily services to Brisbane, stopping at the bus station at 30 Neil St (1 block east of Ruthven St), T4690 9888.

Stanthorpe
Colour map 3, grid A/B5
Population: 5,000
Postcode: 4380
220 km south of Brisbane

The pretty town of Stanthorpe is the commercial centre of the **Granite Belt**, a region renowned for fruit growing and Queensland's best **vineyards**. In spring and summer it becomes a popular base for those wishing escape the heat of the coast and spend a few days exploring the various wineries or **national parks** that bloom in vivid displays of wild flowers. With such a rich heritage dating back to the 1850s, Stanthorpe's **museum** is well worth a visit displaying a weird and wonderful array of interesting artefacts. ■ *Wed-Fri 1000-1600, Sat 1300-1600. $3, child $1, T4681 1711. 12 High St (1 km north of the town centre).* The **Regional Art Gallery** is also worth a look. ■ *Mon-Fri 1000-1600, Sat 1300-1600, Sun 1000-1300. Free, T4681 1874, attached to the library on Locke St.* The VIC has full listings and details of the dozen or so vineyards in the region that are centred mainly around Ballandean, 15 km south of the town. A good start for independent investigations is the **Heritage Wines Estate** at Cottonvale (15 km north on the New England Highway). ■ *Open for sales and tastings, daily 0900-1700, T4684 1263.* The **Stanthorpe Wine Company**, 291 Granite Belt Drive, Thulimbah, T4683 2011 are also worth a visit, offering a broader view of Queensland wines and winemaking. The **Grape Escape**, T4681 4761, offer comprehensive six-hour tours of vineyards throughout the Granite Belt, from $60. Stanthorpe celebrates both its agriculture and climate with three seasonal **festivals**: the **Apple and Grape Festival** is held every even numbered year, the **Spring Wine Festival** every October and the chilly **Brass Monkey Festival** held throughout the winter months. The **Visitors Information Centre** is located at 28 Leslie Parade, T4681 2057. ■ *Open Mon-Fri 0830-1700, Sat/Sun 0900-1600, www.qldsoutherndowns.org.au*

Sleeping and eating There is a good range of accommodation in the area but the rural guesthouses and vineyard B&Bs are recommended. The VIC has full listings. 2 of the best and most upmarket are near the village of Ballandean (15 km south and handy for the national parks). **L** *Smiths B&B*, Zambelli Rd, Ballandean, T4684 1139, and the charming **LL-L** *Vineyard Cottages*, New England Highway, T4684 1270, www.vineyard-cottages.com.au The best-facilitated motor park in town is the **B-E** *Top of Town Caravan*

Park, 10 High St (1 km north of the town centre), T4681 4888, that also offers **backpacker** accommodation. For eating, the classy and friendly Italian *Il Cavallino*, 136 High St, T4681 1556, or *Anna's* 1 O'Mara Terr, T4681 1265, are recommended.

Transport The **bus** station is on Maryland St (Mobil Petrol Station), T4681 1434. *Crisps Coaches*, T3236 5266, offer daily services to Brisbane

What makes the 12,000 ha Girraween National Park so special is its dramatic landscape of massive **granite outcrops**, tors, and precariously balanced rocks, and (in spring and summer) its vivid displays of **wild flowers**. There are 17 km of **walking** tracks, most of which start from the parks **information centre**, at the end of Pyramids Road (off the New England Highway, 26 km south of Stanthorpe), T4684 5157. Generally they culminate with geological odysseys and range in length from a laid-back 1 km stroll to the **Granite Arch**, to the more demanding 10½ km (return) ascent of **Mount Norman**. The park's rich and varied wildlife includes wombats, spotted quolls, possums, parrots and lyrebirds. There are good camping facilities at Bald Rock Creek and Castle Rock at the end of Pyramids Road. Hot showers, toilets and fire-places are available, but no powered sites. Fees apply. Note the average altitude is 900 m so it can be cold. For more information on Girraween National Park, or the neighbouring **Sundown** and **Crows Nest National Parks**, call in to the Brisbane **QPWS** office, or ask at the **information centre**, Pyramids Road, Girraween NP, T4684 5157.

Girraween National Park
Colour map 3, grid B5
260 km south of Brisbane

Gold Coast

With almost five million visitors a year, the bold and brash Gold Coast is the most popular domestic holiday destination and Australia's answer to the Spanish costas. For lovers of the beach lifestyle, hedonists, theme park junkies and shopaholics, it is heaven, but those who baulk at the mere mention of such things should at least give it a chance. One of the most obvious appeals is the sheer range of activities on offer; from jumping out of an aeroplane to sitting beneath a beach umbrella watching the world go by. Also, only an hour away from all the action, is one of the Gold Coast's greatest assets and the 'Green behind the Gold', in the form of the Springbrook and Lamington National Parks, two of Queensland's best.

Colour map 3, grid A6
Population: 400,000
100 km north of Byron Bay, 78 km south of Brisbane

Ins and outs

By air The Gold Coast **Airport** is near Coolangatta, 22 km south of Surfers, T5589 1100. *Qantas*, T131313, *Virgin Blue*, T136789, *Freedom Air*, T1800-122000, and *Flight West*, T132392, all offer domestic services (and/or international connections). *Gold Coast Tourist Shuttles*, T5574 5111, and *Surfside Buses*, T131230, offer local transfers, from $14, child $7. For Brisbane Airport contacts see page 255. *Con-x-ions*, T5591 2525, *Coachtrans*, T5506 9777, *Murray's*, T132259, and *Active Tours*, T5597 0344, all offer regular shuttles between Brisbane City and/or Airport to the Gold Coast, from about $50, child $26.

Getting there

   By bus The long-distance **bus** terminal is located on the corner of Beach Rd and Remembrance Dr. Most of the major coach companies have offices within the complex (open 0600-2200). *Premier Motor Services*, T133410, and *MacCafferty's/Greyhound*, T5538 2700, offer daily inter-state services. *Coachtrans*, T131230, www.coach trans.com.au, are recommended for Brisbane City/Airport transfers. *Kirklands*, T1300-367077, www.kirklands.com.au, and *Suncoast Pacific*, T5531 6000, offer regular services to Byron Bay and the NSW coast.

Queensland

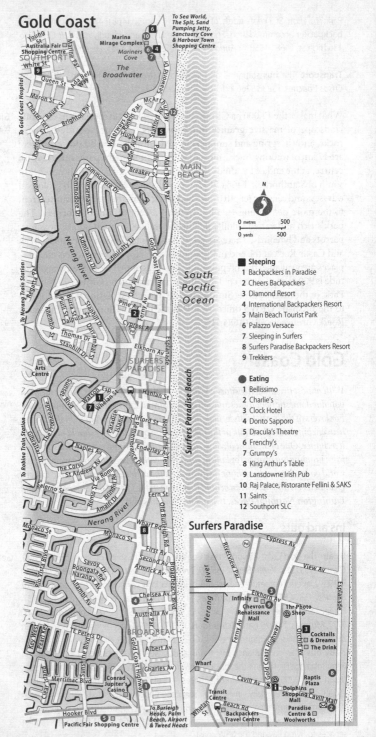

Gold Coast

Queensland

Sleeping
1 Backpackers in Paradise
2 Cheers Backpackers
3 Diamond Resort
4 International Backpackers Resort
5 Main Beach Tourist Park
6 Palazzo Versace
7 Sleeping in Surfers
8 Surfers Paradise Backpackers Resort
9 Trekkers

Eating
1 Bellissimo
2 Charlie's
3 Clock Hotel
4 Donto Sapporo
5 Dracula's Theatre
6 Frenchy's
7 Grumpy's
8 King Arthur's Table
9 Lansdowne Irish Pub
10 Raj Palace, Ristorante Fellini & SAKS
11 Saints
12 Southport SLC

Surfers Paradise

By train Both Robina and Nerang **train** stations, located about 15 km/10 km southwest/west of Surfers are served by *Airtrain*, T131230, from Brisbane (with connections to Brisbane airport), from $50, child $30. *Airtrain Connect*, T5574 5111, and *Surfside Buslines* (Nos 2 and 22) then offer road transport to the coast.

Getting around the Gold Coast is generally very easy, with 24 hr local bus transport, numerous companies offering theme park/airport transfers and car, moped, and bike hire. *Surfside Buslines*, T131230, www.gcshuttle.com.au, offer a 3-14 day 'Freedom Pass', from $40, child $20, which includes a return airport transfer and unlimited theme park/local services. A 1-14 day 'Gold Pass', from $15, child $8, allows unlimited local and theme park transfers, T5574 5111. Also Brisbane City/Airport Transfers with 3-7 day unlimited theme park/local transport from $95. *Airtrain*, T131230, offer suburban services, theme park and airport transfers ($13) between 0830-2245 (main trunk services from Coolangatta to Southport 24 hrs). For other theme park transfers contact *Con-x-ions*, T5591 2525, www.con-x-ion.com.au, *Active Tours*, T5597 0344, or *Coachtrans*, T131230. **Taxis** *Regent-Gold Coast*, T131008. **Bike Hire** is available from *Red Rocket Rent-A-Car*, Shop 9,The Mark Orchid Av, T5538 9074. **Mopeds** can be hired from a number of central outlets including *Yahoo*, 80 Ferny Av, T5592 0227, from $25 ($150 deposit), *Rent-A-Jeep*, Corner Palm and Ferny Av, T5538 6900, hire small jeeps from $69 per day.

Getting around

The **Gold Coast Visitors Information Centre** is an incredibly small affair in the Cavill Av Mall, Surfers Paradise, T5538 4419, www.goldcoasttourism.com.au Open Mon-Fri 0830-1730, Sat 0900-1700, Sun 0900-1530. Try to get a copy of the official *'Gold Coast Holiday Guide'* (Gold Coast Tourism Bureau). The nearest **QPWS** office is near the Tallebudgera Bridge, 1711 Gold Coast Highway, Burleigh Heads, T5535 3032. They stock detailed information surrounding the national parks of the Gold Coast Hinterland.

Information

Queensland

Surfers Paradise

Surfers Paradise is where it all began. Over 40 years ago the Surfers Paradise Hotel opened its doors, giving rise to the endless forests of apartment blocks, shopping malls and exclusive real estate properties we see today. Attractive and thrilling for many, abhorrent to some, Surfers has (and is) everything the average warped imagination can throw up. Other than the obvious attractions of the beach, the surf and the shopping malls, it provides endless entertainment 24 hours a day and serves as the gatehouse to more activities than anywhere else in Australia. Surfers is essentially quite small with most of the action centred in and around the **Cavill Avenue Mall** and adjacent nightclub strip, **Orchid Avenue**.

Surfers Paradise Beach is of course the big draw. If you can, take a stroll at sunrise along the 500 m sand pumping jetty at the end of **The Spit**, north of Sea World (opens at 0600). For $1 you can walk out to the end and take in the memorable view of the entire beach and the glistening high rises all the way to Tweed Heads. Between Surfers Paradise and The Spit, **Main Beach** fringes the southern shores of **The Broadwater** and the Nerang River Inlet. Like an assemblage of huge white tepees, the **Marina Mirage** shopping complex contains some of the best restaurants in the region, most of which offer al fresco dining overlooking **Mariners Cove**, the departure point for most scenic cruises and helicopter scenic flights. Amongst the commercial vessels, the sumptuous launches and ocean-going yachts of the wealthy herald the presence of one of the Gold Coast's newest and most luxurious hotels, the very elegant and distinctly 'watery' *Versace*.

Sights

Theme parks The Gold Coast is often labelled as Australia's Theme Park capital. The stalwarts are Sea World, Dreamworld and Movie World, with other less high-profile parks, like Wet'n'Wild providing 'splashtacular' (or simply 'tackular') back up. Entry for each is expensive, from $33-$54, but that usually includes all the rides and attractions, which provides a very full day of entertainment. The VIC can help you secure the latest discounts (around 12%) and packages on offer, including multi-day trips and transfers. A '3-Park Pass' costs from $141, child $91, which makes no saving on the individual ticket sales but does allow one free return visit. **Sea World** is one of the world's best theme parks. The main attractions are the incredible dolphin and seal shows, the shark feeding, thrill rides and water-ski stunts, and despite the recent (and controversial) addition of polar bears, there is no doubting Sea World's dedication to conservation and welfare. Another great and innovative attraction at Sea World is the ability to swim with the dolphins, in a new seal/dolphin interactive program, which is highly recommended. There are a range of options, one for kids that involves a shallow water experience with the seals (from $40) and dolphins (from $45) and several for adults seals from $80 and dolphins from $110. Book well in advance. ■ *Daily 1000-1700, from $54, child $35. T5588 2205, www.seaworld.com.au Sea World Dr, Main Beach, (1 km).* **Movie World** is perhaps the most popular of all the theme parks. Overall, it is a very exciting and stimulating mix of sights, sounds and action that requires at least one full day. ■ *Daily 1000-1730, $54, child $35. T5573 8485, www.movieworld.com.au Pacific Highway, Oxenford, (21 km).* The big attraction at **Dream World** is the adrenaline pumping rides, some of which are reputed to be the fastest and tallest in the world. ■ *Daily 1000-1700, $54, child $35. T5588 1122, www.dream world.com.au Parkway Coomera, Pacific Highway (25 km)* The aptly named **Wet'n'Wild** offers practically every way imaginable to get soaked, from tubes and slides, to fake waves. ■ *Daily 1000-1700, $33, child $21. T5573 2255, www.wetnwild.com.au Pacific Highway, Oxenford, (21 km).*

Tours and activities Other than the beach, shopping and the theme parks, Surfers presents a mind-bending array of additional activities. Just about everything that can be done legally on land, in the air or on the water can be done here: from skydiving to getting married on a floating church. For **surf board hire** try the *Beach Club House*, 189 Paradise Centre, Cavill Avenue, T5526 7077, from $40 per day and for surfing lessons either professionals Brad Holmes, T5539 4068, or Cheyne Horan, T1800-227873. Perhaps the best thing you can do around here is a rainforest tour to the stunning **Lamington** and **Springbrook National Parks**, only an hour's drive inland from the chaos. *Bushwacker Eco Tours*, T5525 7237, www.bushwacker-ecotours.com.au, offer both day walk/tours and night spotting to Springbrook, from $50. The resorts on **South Stradbroke Island** also offer a suitable coastal escape (see page 260). The VIC on Cavill Avenue has full listings and the latest prices. For anything water-based, including self-hire, shop around at the **Cruise Terminal**, at Mariners Cove (Main Beach) or the wharf at the western end of Cavill Avenue, T5538 3400.

Sleeping With almost 5 mn visitors a year the Gold Coast is well geared up for accommodation of all types to suit all budgets. But even with the 55,000 beds currently available you are advised to book in advance. Prices fluctuate wildly between peak and off peak seasons. Stand-by deals and packages are always on offer so you are advised to shop around and research thoroughly. **Resorts** and **motels** naturally predominate with almost 200 high-rises offering very similar self-contained apartments. Choosing one is a nightmare.

The best advice is to decide exactly what you are looking for, and then consult the various accommodation agents for advice. Booking at least 7 days in advance will usually work out cheaper. If you arrive in the city without bookings you can also simply drive around until you see one you like, then make enquiries, but beware, this will take up valuable time, may be more costly and most are heavily booked in the peak season. The free *Qantas* and *Sunlover* 'Gold Coast' brochures available from travel agents are also an excellent source of illustrated listings. Accommodation agents include the *Gold Coast Accommodation Service*, Shop 1, 1 Beach Rd, Surfers, T5592 0067, www.goldcoastaccommodationservice.com.au, and *In Transit*, Bus Transit Centre, Beach Rd, T5592 2911, intrans@fan.net.au As you'd expect the Gold Coast is home to numerous hotel chains and sumptuous 5-stars, the best of which is the **LL** *Palazzo Versace*, Sea World Dr, Main Beach, T5509 8000, www.palazzoversace.com.au, which is simply unbelievable. For something less ostentatious there's the **L-A** *Diamond Resort*, 19 Orchid Av, T5570 1011, which has no nonsense en suite units, pool and spa.

Hostels Again the choice is vast with most very similar and offering gimmick discount deals, party nights activities and pick-ups. **L-E** *Sleeping in Surfers*, 26 Whelan St, T5592 4455, www.sleepinginn.com.au, similar facilities to the cheaper hostels below but with a wider choice of room options from dorms and singles to doubles, twins and self-contained units with TV and living room. It can also throw a good party. Further north is the **B-E** *Cheers Backpackers*, 8 Pine Av, T5531 6539, which is the largest in town with a wide selection of rooms, including en suite doubles, pool, spa, a spacious bar and beer garden, free internet and good meal deals. The **C-E** *Surfers Paradise Backpackers Resort*, 2837 Gold Coast Highway, T5592 4677, www.surfersparadisebackpackers.com.au, is a purpose-built place on the border of Surfers and Broadbeach. It offers tidy en suite dorms, units (some self-contained with TV) and good facilities, including well equipped kitchen, bar, free laundry, pool, sauna, gym, volley ball pitch, TV/games room, internet, party and activity tours, pick-ups and off street parking. **C-E** *Backpackers in Paradise*, 40 Whelan St, just west of the Transit Centre, T5538 4344. Lively, colourful, friendly and good facilities, with dorms and 3 spacious doubles (en suite), café, bar, pool, internet, tours desk and a comfy TV lounge with a huge screen. In Main Beach overlooking the Mirage Marina and Mariners Cove is the YHA affiliated **C-E** *International Backpackers Resort*, 70 Sea World Dr, T5571 1776, www.british arms.com.au It offers modern facilities, has its own British pub next door and is within yards of the beach. Internet and courtesy bus into Surfers. In Southport 2 km north of Surfers, is **C-E** *Trekkers*, 22 White St, T5591 5616, www.trekkersbackpackers.com.au, which is without doubt the best backpackers in the region. It offers cosy rooms including en suite doubles with TV, nice pool and garden. Great atmosphere, friendly, family run business with the emphasis on looking after each guest rather than the turnover.

Motor parks The Gold Coast City Council operate a number of excellent facilities up and down the coast. Look out for their free *Gold Coast City Council Holiday Parks* brochure or visit www.gctp.com.au In the Surfers area look no further than the **A-E** *Main Beach Tourist Park*, Main Beach Pde, T5581 7722. It offers cabins, en suite/standard powered and non-powered sites, with good facilities and camp kitchens, all nestled quietly amongst the high-rises and across the road from the main beach.

Eating

In Surfers itself, the many, mainly cheap or affordable restaurants are located along the Cavill Mall, along The **Esplanade**, Gold Coast Highway or in the new **Chevron Renaissance Mall**. Elsewhere it is worth looking at the more upmarket affairs along **Tedder Av** or the **Marina Mirage** in Main Beach. Further north **Sanctuary Cove** is a fine spot for lunch. To the south, **Burleigh Heads** provides excellent views, while the many **surf lifesaving clubs** offer great value, views and are undoubtedly in the spirit of the Gold Coast experience. For something different consider the **dinner cruises** on offer from Mariners Cove, T5557 8800, the *Dracula's Theatre Restaurant* in Broadbeach, T5575 1000, or the

Queensland

Olde English surrounds of the *King Arthur's Table*, Raptis Plaza, Cavill Av, T5526 7855.

Expensive The Marina Mirage Complex has some superb al fresco possibilities including *SAKS*, T5591 2755, *Ristorante Fellini*, T5531 0300, and *The Raj Palace*, T5531 1600. Also well worth the trip are *Oskars*, T5576 3722 (mainly seafood) and Italian restaurant, *Daniele*, T5535 0822, both with excellent coastal views at Burleigh Heads.

Mid-range The various restaurant/cafes in the *Chevron Renaissance Mall*, Gold Coast Highway, all share tempting menus in pleasant Mediterranean-style surroundings. Also in the mall is the *Landsdowne Irish Pub*, T5531 5599, that offers the traditional wholesome pub food at reasonable prices. At the northern entrance to the Mall the *Clock Hotel*, T5539 0344, also enjoys a good reputation as a top lunch venue. Tedder Av in Main Beach is a quieter location with some good al fresco options, including *Saints*, T5528 4286, open daily for breakfast lunch and dinner. Further north around Mariners Cove and the Marina Mirage Complex, you will find *Grumpy's Wharf Restaurant*, T5532 2900, and *Frenchy's*, T5531 3030, both of which offer affordable seafood with a casual atmosphere and pleasant views. In Broadbeach, directly opposite Jupiter's Casino, *Bellissimo* Italian Restaurant, T5570 3388, is earning a fine reputation and has live music Fri/Sat. Nearby, the *Donto Sapporo*, 2763 Gold Coast Highway, T5539 9933, is considered one of the best Japanese restaurants in city.

Cheap There is no end of cheap and cheerful eateries in and around Cavill Av. The food court in the *Dolphins Shopping Mall* is a favourite for the ubiquitous all-you-can-eat Asian eateries. *Charlie's Restaurant*, Cavill Av Mall, T5538 5285, offers decent meals 24 hr, and a good breakfast. The many **surf lifesaving clubs** (SLCs) along the coast offer great value meals, including the *Southport SLC*, McArthur Pde, Main Beach, T5591 5083, and the *Palm Beach SLC*, 7th Av and Jefferson La, Palm Beach, T5534 2180. Self-caterers will find the *Woolworths* supermarket, Lower Level, Paradise Centre. *Coles* is located in the Chevron Renaissance Mall.

Entertainment The scope for a good night out is limitless. If you are staying at any of the hostels you will be well looked after by the staff and will only need to go with the flow. The great club crawl is a perennial fave with free drinks and the odd free meal thrown in (and no doubt thrown up later). For those not staying at a hostel the best thing to do is to ask the staff or locals at your accommodation or the nearest hostel. Organized 'night-spot' tours are available, but these may prove too constricting (ask at the VIC). **Orchid Av**, off the Cavill Av Mall is the main focus for clubbing with most staying open well into the wee hours. Dress is smart casual, carry ID and plenty cash. Entry generally ranges from $5-10, which is manageable, but the drinks (especially the obligatory cocktails) are expensive. *Cocktails and Dreams* and *The Drink*, both on Orchid Av, have a good reputation but they are 2 of many. For a more sophisticated night out try the *Lansdowne Irish Pub* in the Chevron Renaissance Mall, T5531 5599. Live music every Fri/Sat. The *Conrad Jupiter's Casino* offers 2 floors of gaming tables and pokies, 24 hrs. Off Hooker Blvd, off Gold Coast Highway, Broadbeach.T5592 1133. There is a **cinema** and **theatre** at the **Arts Centre**, 135 Bundall Rd, T5588 4000, and other mainstream cinemas in the shopping centres at *Pacific Fair*, Broadbeach, T5572 2666, *Australia Fair*, Southport, T5531 2200, and the 14 cinema complex at Harbour Town, corner Gold Coast Highway and Oxley Dr, north of Southport, T5529 1734.

Festivals & events
For a detailed calendar of events visit www.goldcoast tourism.com.au

The Gold Coast hosts a number of exciting annual events most of which involve lots of money, fireworks and parties, races and sporting spectaculars. **Jan** kicks off with *Conrad Jupiter's Magic Millions*, a 10-day horseracing and ladies' fashion event. *Australian Ladies Golf Masters*, is held in **Feb** at the beautiful Royal Pines course, attracting some of the world's best golfers. In **Mar** the beach becomes the main focus with the *Australian Surf Life Saving Championships*, the Gold Coast's most famous event. It attracts over 7000 national and international competitors, all trying to outdo each other, for the pretigious *Iron Man* or *Iron Woman* trophy. In **Jun** Coolangatta revs it up with the 10-day *Wintersun Festival* that sees Australia's biggest 50s and 60s rock'n'roll event combined with the nation's largest display of hot rods and custom cars. 'Americana' comes to the coast on **4 Jul** with an *All Star America Football* competition. **Jul** also sees the *Gold Coast Marathon* – considered Australia's premier long-distance running event. In mid-winter is the ever-popular *Honda Indy 300*, when the streets of Surfers squeal to the sound of racing cars and the evenings to the heady beat of parties, parades and the mardi gras. Numerous **food festivals** are also held throughout the year, including the *Gold Coast Food Festival* in **Sep**, the *Broadbeach Festival* in **Oct** and the *Gold Coast Signature Dish Competition* in **Dec**.

Not surprisingly the Gold Coast offers some golden shopping opportunities. The main **Shopping** shopping centres are *Pacific Fair* in Broadbeach (which is the largest in Queensland) and *Australia Fair* in Southport. In the heart of Surfers, The *Paradise Centre* in Cavill Av is a focus for mainly tourist-based products, with the *Marina Mirage* in Main Beach and *Sanctuary Cove* being a little bit more upmarket. The *Harbour Town Shopping Complex*, corner Gold Coast Highway and Oxley Dr, north of Southport, is well known for its bargain shopping, T5529 1734. The beachfront markets held every Sun at the eastern end of Cavill Av are one of many taking place regularly up and down the coast.

Banks All major branches with **ATMs** and **Currency Exchange** are located in and **Directory** around the Cavill Mall-Gold Coast Highway intersection. *Thomas Cook*, Cavill Av, T5592 1166. **Car hire** *Avis*, T5536 3511, *Budget* T5536 5377, *Hertz* T5536 6133 and *Thrifty* T5536 6955 all have outlets at the Gold Coast Airport. Numerous companies are located in and around Surfers Paradise, with prices starting from about $30 per day. **Chemist** *Day and Night*, Piazza On Boulevard (ANA Hotel) 3221 Gold Coast Highway, Surfers, T5592 2299. Open 0700-2200. **Internet** *1 hr Photo Shop*, 3189 Gold Coast Highway, T5538 4973. Open daily 0900-2100. *Email Centre*, Next door to Shooters, Orchid Av, T5538 7500. Open daily 0830-2400. **Hospital/Medical** *Gold Coast Hospital*, 108 Nerang St, Southport, T5571 8211. Paradise Medical Centre, Paradise Centre, T5592 3999 (24 hr) **Petrol 24 hr** *Shell* (2824) and *Caltex* (2885) Gold Coast Highway. **Police** 68 Ferny Av, Surfers, T5570 7888 **Post Office** Cavill Av Paradise Mall, T5539 4144. Open Mon-Fri 0830-1730, Sat 0900-1200. Postcode 4217. **RACQ** T5532 0311 **Travel Agencies** *Backpackers Travel Centre*, Transit Centre, 8 Beach Rd, Surfers, T5538 0444

From Surfers Paradise south, the stands of high-rise apartment blocks gradu- **Surfers** ally diminish through the resorts of **Broadbeach** and **Burleigh Heads**. The **Paradise to** latter is one of the few breaks in the seemingly endless swathe of golden sand **Currumbin** and offers some world-class **surf breaks** and several good **walking tracks** through the **Burleigh Heads National Park**. West of Burleigh Heads the **David Fleay Wildlife Park** is home to all the usual suspects, including koalas, crocodiles, kangaroos, cassowaries and some of the less well known, like bilbies, brolgas and dunnarts. Overall it offers a fine introduction to Australia's native species and is especially well known for its nocturnal platypus displays, breeding successes and care of sick and injured wildlife. ■ *Daily 0900-1700, $13, child $6.50. T5576 2411*. Signposted 3 km west of Gold Coast Highway on Burleigh Heads Road. South of Burleigh Heads the **Currumbin Wildlife Sanctuary** is another wildlife park, that has for many years been the most popular. One of the more unique aspects of Currumbin is the small train that takes you in to the heart of the park, where you can then investigate the various animal enclosures with everything from Tasmanian devils to tree kangaroos. But without doubt the highlight of the day is the infamous rainbow lorikeet feeding. To either partake or spectate at this highly colourful and entertaining 'avian-human interaction spectacular' is truly memorable and thoroughly recommended. The great feeding frenzy takes place twice daily at 0800 and again at 1600. Given that 80% of Australia's native wildlife is nocturnal, the **'Wildnight' tour** program is also well worth considering. It also includes an Aboriginal dance display (Monday/Wednesday/Saturday 1930-2145). ■ *Daily 0800-1700, $17, child $9.50. T5534 1266, www.currumbin-sanctuary.org.au Just off the Gold Coast Highway, Currumbin.*

Coolangatta

Colour map 3, grid A6
Population: 60,000
100 km from Brisbane

Welcome to the real 'surfer's paradise'. What the eponymous city is to hype and shopping malls, Coolangatta is to surfing. Its greatest attractions are undoubtedly its **beaches** and, more importantly, the mighty surf that breaks upon them. And for those who don't know one end of a surfboard from the other, this is one of the best places in the world to watch in awe.

Ins & outs
The twin towns of Coolangatta and Tweed Heads straddle the New South Wales/ Queensland border

Getting there and around Air The Gold Coast airport is only 2 km from Coolangatta (see page 263). **Bus** *Premiere Motor Services*, T133410, and *McCafferty's/Greyhound* T5538 2700, offer daily inter-State services, while *Coachtrans*, T131230, www.coachtrans.com.au, offer regular shuttles up and down the coast, to Brisbane and to/from the airport. *Kirklands*, T1300-367077, www.kirklands.com.au, and *Suncoast Pacific*, T5531 6000, offer regular services to Byron Bay and the NSW coast. All long-distance buses stop outside the main booking agent, *Golden Gateway Travel*, 29 Bay St, T5536 1700. *Surfside Buslines*, T131230, www.gcshuttle.com.au, are the main suburban bus company with regular links north to Surfers. For a taxi, T5536 1144.

Queensland does not recognise daylight saving between Oct-Mar, which means it is 1 hr behind NSW during that time

Information The **Gold Coast (Coolangatta) Visitors Information Centre** is located at Shop 14B, Coolangatta Pl, corner Griffith St and Warner St, T5536 7765, www.goldcoasttourism.com.au Open Mon-Fri 0800-1700, Sat 0800-1600, Sun 0900-1300. There is a town map in the useful, free brochure 'Tweed-Coolangatta Visitors Guide'. **Internet** is available at the *Coolangatta Internet Café*, beneath Montezuma's, corner Griffith St and Warner St, T5599 2001 (open Mon-Fri 0900-1900, Sat 0900-1800, Sun 1200-1600) or *PB's Internet Café*, Shop 2 Griffith Plaza, Griffith St, T5599 4536, open Mon-Fri 0830-1900, Sat/Sun 0900-1800.

Sights
Coolangatta is fringed with superb beaches that surround the small peninsula known as **Tweed Heads**. The tip of the peninsula, named **Point Danger** by Captain Cook in 1770, provides a good vantage point from which to spectate, and **Duranbah Beach**, which flanks the sea wall at the mouth of the **Tweed River**, is a popular surf spot. To the left is **Snapper Rocks**, perhaps the most popular surf break in the southern Gold Coast and by far the best place to watch the surfers. Just to the west of Snapper Rocks is the pretty little beach called **Rainbow Bay**, which is the first of the beaches that combines both good surfing with safe swimming. Continuing west, Rainbow Bay is then separated from Greenmount Beach by a small headland that offers fine views from **Pat Fagan Park**. **Greenmount Beach** then merges with **Coolangatta Beach**, both of which are idyllic, excellent for swimming and enormously popular with families. At the western end of Coolangatta Beach, **Kirra Point** also provides great views back down Greenmount and Coolangatta beaches and north, beyond **North Kirra Beach**, to Surfers Paradise. If you can drag yourself away from the beaches there is yet another fine viewpoint at the **Tom Beatson Outlook** on Mount Toonbarabah. From there, looking north, the

twin towns of Coolangatta and Tweed Heads (which is in NSW) and the Tweed River are laid out before you, while to the west you can see the prominent volcanic peak of **Mount Warning**. To get there from the centre of Coolangatta and Griffith Street, head south down Dixon, then straight ahead up Razorback Road. For **surfing supplies and rentals** try *Pipedream*, 24/72 Griffith Street, T5599 1164, and *Zumo*, Shop 233 McLean Street, T5536 8502. For surfing lessons try either Brad Holmes, T5539 4068, or Cheyne Horan, T1800-227873. *The Gold Coast Surf Schools Australia*, T5520 0848, can also point you in the right direction. The Tweed River also offers some good **cruising** opportunities. Operators include *Perfector*, T5524 2422, www.catchacrab.com.au, and *Tweed Endeavour*, T5536 8800, www.goldcoastcruising.com *The Blue Juice Diving Centre*, 33 Machinery Drive, T5524 3683, offer local dive trips, courses and equipment sales.

Beyond the beaches and the views there are two main tourist attractions in the immediate area. The **Minjungbal's Aboriginal Historic Site**, corner Kirkwood Road and Duffy Street, offers an insight in to the life and times of the local tribe. ■ *Open daily, $6, T5524 2109*. **Tropical Fruit World** near Kingscliff is reputed to house the world's largest selection of tropical fruits. Although that may sound far from a-'peel'-ing, it is actually quite entertaining and educational, and just about guarantees to introduce you to at least one fruit you have never heard of, seen or tasted before. ■ *Daily from 1000-1700, $25, child $15.T6677 7222, www.tropicalfruitworld.com.au Turn off the Pacific Highway on to Duranbah Rd, 10 mins south of the Gold Coast Airport.*

A-E *Kirra Beach Tourist Park* is located on Charlotte St, off Coolangatta Rd, T5581 7744, offering powered/non-powered sites, cabins, camp kitchen and salt water pool. There are 2 backpackers in the area: **C-E** *Coolangatta YHA*, 230 Coolangatta Rd, T5536 7644, is located near the airport and facing the busy Pacific Highway. It offers tidy dorms, doubles/twins, pool, bike and surfboard hire, internet, with a *Coachtrans* service direct to the hostel. Much closer to the beach and the town centre is the **B-D** *Sunset Strip Budget Resort*, 199-203 Boundary St, T5599 5517. It is an old hotel with unit style singles, doubles, twins, quads and family rooms with shared bathrooms, excellent kitchen facilities, large pool and within yards of the beach. Basic but spacious, good value. Fully self-contained 1 and 2 bedroomed holiday flats are also available. No internet. Recommended. Another accommodation option worth considering is a fully self-contained houseboat with which to cruise the extensive reaches of the Tweed River. *Boyd's Bay House Boats*, T5523 4795, www.goldcoasthouseboats.com.au, can oblige, from around $745 for the most basic vessel per week in the high season. For an affordable dinner most folk are lured by the fine and fishy fare of the *Fisherman's Cove Seafood Taverna*, in the Calypso Resort, Griffith St, T5536 7073. *Raffles Coffee Shop*, 152 Griffith St, T5536 3880, is good for lunch, coffee and light snacks (try a pancake with real maple syrup). For more healthy snacks and sandwiches the *Bayleaf Café*, 1/40 Griffith St, T5536 5636, is recommended, while for breakfast the *Uno Café* on Marine Pde, T5599 5116, provides the best value.

Sleeping & eating

Gold Coast Hinterland

Less than an hour's drive from the Gold Coast are perhaps its greatest attractions: the national parks of Lamington and Springbrook and Mount Tamborine. Labelled 'the Green Behind the Gold', they provide their own natural wonders in the shape of pristine subtropical rainforest, waterfalls, walking tracks and stunning views. Note that the weather here too can be dramatically different, with much more rain and the coolest temperatures in the State. The main Gold Coast **QPWS** office is near the Tallebudgera Bridge, 1711 Gold Coast Highway, Burleigh Heads, T5535 3032. They stock detailed information surrounding all the national parks throughout the region. Alternatively, a walking track guide with map and details are available from the information offices at **Binna Burra**, T5533 3584, and **Green Mountains** (O'Reilly's), T5544 0634. Open Monday, Wednesday-Friday 0900-1100, 1300-1530. Tuesday-Friday 1300-1530. For vineyard information visit www.goldcoastwinecountry.com.au

Lamington National Park
Colour map 3, grid A6
60 km southwest of Surfers Paradise,
110 km south of Brisbane

The 20,500 ha Lamington National Park sits on the border of Queensland and New South Wales and comprises densely forested valleys and peaks straddling the McPherson Range and an ancient volcanic area known as the **Scenic Rim**, about 60 km inland from the Gold Coast. The park is essentially split into two sections: the **Binna Burra** to the east and the **Green Mountains** (O'Reilly's) to the west. Combined, they offer a wealth of superb natural features, over 100 km of **walking tracks** and some exotic residents, including the regent bower bird and the lyrebird.

The **Green Mountains** were first settled in 1911 by the **O'Reilly** family, who took up a number of small dairy farms before consolidating their assets in 1915 with the establishment of their now internationally famous guesthouse. Other than the sense of escape and the rainforest experience, its most popular draw is its **treetop canopy walkway**, which is an ideal way to see the rainforest habitat. There are also some excellent **walking tracks** that range from 1-20 km, offering spectacular views and numerous waterfalls. Guided tours are available, along with a broad range of accommodation options. There is a QPWS campsite nearby (see below). The **Binna Burra** section of the park is the most accessible from the Gold Coast and, like the Green Mountains, also offers a wealth of excellent rainforest **walking** opportunities and plays host to the *Binna Burra Mountain Lodge*, T5533 3758. Guided tours are available through the lodge and there is a QPWS information centre and campsite, T5533 3584.

Sleeping and eating The **LL** *Binna Burra Mountain Lodge*, Binna Burra Rd, Beechmont (via Nerang), T1800-074260, www.binnaburralodge.com.au, offers well appointed en suite cabins with fireplace (some with spa), activities, meals included. **LL-L** *O'Reilly's Rainforest Guesthouse*, Lamington National Park Rd (via Canungra), T5544 0644, www.oreillys.com.au, offers a range of room options from luxury suites to standard, pool, sauna, spa and restaurant. Package includes meals and some tours. There are QPWS campsites at both Binna Burra and Green Mountains (200 m from O'Reilly's) with water, hot showers and toilets. Fees apply, book ahead through the ranger/information centres at each location.

Transport The most accessible section of Lamington NP is **Binna Burra**, 35 km southwest of Nerang on the Pacific Highway. From Brisbane you can travel south via Nerang or via Mt Tamborine and Canungra. The **Green Mountains** (O'Reilly's) section is accessed from **Canungra**. If you do not have your own transport, there are numerous tour operators that provide trips daily to Lamington, including *Mountain Trek Adventures*, T0500-844100, sherpa@bigvolcano.com.au The VICs have full listings. Alternatively, *O'Reilly's Mountain Coach Company*, (Green Mountains section), T5524 4249, offer transportation to and from the Gold Coast to O'Reilly's Resort, daily from $39, child $22 return. The *Binna Burra Mountain Lodge* (see below) also have their own bus service, (Binna Burra section), T5533 3758, from both the Gold Coast and Brisbane, from $44, child $22 return.

The Springbrook National Park (2954 ha) is the most accessible to the coast and sits on the northern rim of what was once a huge volcano centred on Mount Warning. The park is split in to three sections: Springbrook Plateau, Natural Bridge and the Cougals. Like Lamington, they combine to offer a rich subtropical rainforest habitat of ancient trees and gorges, interspersed by creeks, waterfalls and an extensive system of **walking tracks**. In addition, the park is well known for its many excellent views including Canyon, Wunburra, Goomoolahara and the aptly named **'Best of All'**. Other attractions include the **Natural Arch** (1 km walk) – a cavernous rock archway that spans Cave Creek – and the 190 m **Purling Brook Falls** (4 km walk). The Natural Arch also plays host to a colony of **glowworms** (best viewed at night). For detailed information about the park, including accommodation listings, try to get hold of the *Springbrook Mountain Handbook* from the Gold Coast VICs, or from the **Springbrook Mountain Information Centre**, Springbrook Mountain Homestead and Observatory, 2319 Springbrook Road, T5533 5200, www.maguires.com/spring There is also information available at the old **schoolhouse**, Springbrook Road. Springbrook, T5533 5147. Open daily 0800-1600.

Sleeping The characterful and cosy **LL-L** *Mouses Houses*, 2807 Springbrook Rd, Springbrook, T5533 5192, www.mouseshouse.com.au, are recommended. The small **C-E** *Springbrook Mountain Lodge YHA*, 317 Repeater Station Rd, Springbrook (near the 'Best of All' lookout), T5533 5366, offers a fine retreat and has one dorm and 4 double/twins. There is a **QPWS** campsite at Purling Brook Falls.

Transport Springbrook is 29 km south from Mudgeeraba on the Pacific Highway. The Natural Bridge section of the park is accessed from the Nerang to Murwillumbah Rd. Several tour operators offer day trips to Springbrook from both Brisbane and the Gold Coast including *Scenic Hinterland Tours*, Tue/Thu/Sun, T5531 5536 and *Bushwackers Eco Tours*, (day and night tours), T5525 7237.

Springbrook National Park
Colour map 3, grid A6
31 km southwest of Surfers Paradise, 100 km south of Brisbane

Mount Tamborine is a name that is used loosely to describe the 17-section **Tamborine National Park** and the picturesque settlements of **Mount Tamborine**, Tamborine Village and Eagle Heights, 47 km west of Surfers Paradise. They offer an attractive escape from the coast with fine coastal views, walking tracks, vineyards, B&Bs, teahouses and arts and craft galleries. One of the most popular sections is the **Witches Falls**, first designated as a national park in 1908 making it Queensland's oldest. Other popular spots include **Cedar Creek** section, with its pleasant 3 km walk to some pretty waterfalls, or the **Joalah** section, where, if you are lucky, you may see – or more probably hear – one of its best known residents, the mimicking lyrebird.

Mount Tamborine
Colour map 3, grid A6
47 km west of Surfers Paradise, 80 km south of Brisbane

Transport Tamborine is accessed via the Oxenford-Tamborine Rd (Oxenford turn-off) or the Nerang-Tamborine Rd (Nerang turn-off) both on the Pacific Highway. There is no public transport to Mt Tamborine, but various tours are available. *O'Reilly's Mountain Coach Company*, T5524 4249, offer transportation to and from the Gold Coast (via Mt Tamborine) to O'Reilly's Resort in the Lamington National Park.The VICs can supply information and accommodation details, while the **QPWS** at Burleigh Heads (Gold Coast) or the Doughty Park Information Centre, off Main Western Rd, North Tamborine, T5545 3200, stock walks and national parks information. There are no **QPWS** campsites.

Queensland

Queensland

Sunshine and Fraser Coasts

*The Sunshine and Fraser Coasts are synonymous with sand, surf and sunshine. Just an hour north of Brisbane, the spellbinding volcanic peaks known as the **Glass House Mountains** herald your arrival in the aptly-named Sunshine Coast. To the east, on the coastal fringe, is **Maroochy**, with its popular, mainly domestic, holiday resorts of **Maroochydore** and Mooloolaba, bathed in over 300 days of sunshine a year. With the promise of even better things, the vast majority of international tourists sacrifice a visit to Maroochy and head north, to the much-lauded resort of **Noosa Heads**, without doubt the most popular resort on the coast and one of the most sought-after postal codes in Australia. If you can manage to drag yourself away from the coast, the **hinterland** promises a wealth of refreshing and unusual attractions, from dramatic displays of crocodile dentistry at the **Australia Zoo** to the fascinating markets at **Eumundi**. North of Noosa the coastal strip succumbs to the vast expanses of the **Great Sandy Region**, the largest coastal sand mass in the world. The mainland (**Cooloola**) section of the Great Sandy National Park is well worthy of investigation but only serves as an aperitif to the delicious main course just offshore, to the north. Like a huge trigger cocked off the mainland **Fraser Island**, the largest coastal sand island in the world, is southern Queensland's tourist trump card. With its unique and often unexpected range of habitats, natural features and rich biodiversity, all of which can only be fully explored by 4WD, Fraser presents the opportunity for a truly memorable expeiences.*

Noosa

Colour map 3 grid A6
Population: 65,000
145 km north of Brisbane, 187 km south of Hervey Bay

To some the former surfing backwater of Noosa is now little more than an upmarket suburb of Brisbane, yet it possesses one of the finest surf beaches in Queensland, a climate that is 'beautiful one day perfect the next', and is also fringed by two magnificent unspoilt national parks. In the last three decades, the string of coastal communities known loosely as 'Noosa', have rapidly metamorphosed to become one of the most desirable holiday resorts and residential areas on the entire east coast of Australia, but if you turn a blind eye to the pretentiousness of Noosa it makes a worthwhile stop on your way north.

Ins & outs   **Getting there** The nearest **airport** is the Maroochydore (Sunshine Coast) Airport, www.suncoast-airport.com.au, 6 km north of Maroochydore. *Qantas (Sunstate)*, T131313, provide daily services from Brisbane. Local northbound bus services stop at the airport and a taxi to Noosa Heads will cost about $55. *Henry's*, 12 Noosa Dr, T5474 0199, www.henrys.com.au, offer express (non-stop) services between Brisbane Airport/ Maroochydore Airport and Noosa Heads 7 times daily, from $27.50. *Sunshine Shuttle*, T04-1250 7937, offer similar services (Brisbane from $44 one-way) The long-distance bus terminal is located on the corner Noosa Pde and Noosa Dr, on the Noosa Heads. *McCafferty's/Greyhound*, T131499, and *Suncoast Pacific*, T5443 1011, offer daily north/southbound services. *Suncoast Pacific* also offer regular services to Tin Can Bay. *Harvey World Travel*, Shop 2, Lanyana Way, Noosa Heads, T5447 4077, and *Palm Tree Tours*, Bay Village, Hastings St, T5474 9166, act as local booking agents. The nearest train station is at **Cooroy**, T132232. *Sunbus* offer services from there to Noosa Heads (route 12).

Getting around requires a lot of planning, patience and a good map   **Getting around** *Sunbus*, T131230, are the local bus company offering services to the Noosa Heads/Tewantin, (No 10), north/southbound to the Sunshine Coast (No 1), west to Eumundi/Cooroy/Nambour (No 12). **Bike hire** is available from *Noosa Bike Tours and Hire*, T5474 3322, www.noosabikehire.com, delivery and pick-ups and *Mammoth*

Cycles, corner Gympie Terr and Thomas St, Noosaville, T5474 3322, both from $20 per day. To explore the Great Sandy National Park (Cooloola) there are several **4WD hire** companies that oblige, including *Henry's*, 12 Noosa Dr, T5474 0199, www.henrys.com.au; *Thrifty*, Noosa Dr, T136139, and *Coastal 4WD Hire*, T1300-726001. Henry's also hire 'fun-tops' from $44 per day. The Tewantin **car ferries** cross the Noosa River (end of Moorindil St) and provide access to the Great Sandy National Park (Cooloola). It operates from Nov-Jan, Sun-Thu 0430-2230, Fri/Sat 0430-0030 and Feb-Oct Mon-Thu 0600-2230, Fri 0600-0030, Sat 0500-0030, Sun 0500-2230, from $4. **Taxi**, *Sunshine Coast Taxis*, T131008.

Information and orientation The name Noosa actually refers to a string of settlements that border the **Noosa River** and fringe the **Noosa Heads National Park**. Noosa Heads forms the main focus for activity, hosting the main surf beach on **Laguna Bay** and tourist shops, accommodation and restaurants along **Hastings St**. Noosa Junction and **Sunshine Beach Rd** provides the main commercial shopping area. With so many vague boundaries, finding your way around the area is difficult . Your first stop should be the Noosa **Visitors Information Centre** on Hastings St, Noosa Heads, T5447 4988, www.noosa.com.au Open daily 0900-1700. The centre has a very helpful 24 hr touch screen display and the free *'Noosa Guide'* has detailed road and locality maps.

Sights

The main surf beach of **Laguna Bay** backs onto Hastings Street, Noosa Heads. To the east is the pretty 454-ha **Noosa National Park** which offers sanctuary from the beach and some fine walks. The most popular of these is the 2.7 km **Coastal Track** that starts beside the **information office** at the end of Park Road, T5447 3243. The track takes in a number of idyllic bays and headlands, before delivering you at **Alexandria Bay**. Along the way you may see koalas. From there you can return the way you came, explore the interior of the park, continue south to the very plush northern suburbs of **Sunshine Beach**, or simply spend the day on the beach in relative isolation. Note that all the beaches that fringe the national park are unpatrolled and swimming is not recommended. The **Noosa River** runs both west and south from Noosa Heads in a tangled mass of tributaries to join **Lake Weyba** (south) and **Lakes Cooroibah** and **Cootharaba** (west and north). Gympie Terrace (Noosaville) runs along the southern bank of the river and is the focus for most river and lake based activities. To the north of the river is the vast expanse of the **Great Sandy National Park (Cooloola)**, stretching northwards to Rainbow Beach and Fraser Island. It offers some excellent four-wheel driving, walking, fishing and canoeing opportunities. Access to the park is from beyond **Boreen Point** (Lake Cootharaba) or Noosa North Shore (via the car ferry in Tewantin) and is by **4WD only**. The **Eumundi Markets** held in the historic village of Eumundi (23 km west) on Saturday mornings, provide a popular day trip from Noosa.

Sleeping

Noosaville Of the various motels in Noosaville the **A-C** *Noosa Riverfront Motel*, 277 Gympie Terr, T5449 7595, offers good value. It's very friendly and close to all amenities. The **C-E** *Noosa Backpackers Resort*, 9-13 William St, T5549 8151, www.noosabackpackers.com.au is the main backpacker option west of Noosa Heads. It offers tidy 4 bed dorms, en suite doubles, pool, cheap meals, cable TV and internet. Nearby is the best motor park/camping option in the area the **E-F** *Noosa River Caravan Park*, Russell St, T5449 7050. Hugely popular given its riverside location and views, it offers powered and non-powered sites and BBQ. Book at least 2 days in advance

    Noosa Heads The spacious **C-E** *Halse Lodge YHA*, Halse La, T5447 3377, wwwhaselodge.com.au, is only a short walk from the long distance bus stop. It is a historic 1880s Queenslander offering a good range of rooms from 6/4 dorms to doubles,

Noosa is very much like a mini Gold Coast without the high rises, yet with the same almost inexhaustible range of 4-star resort complexes, self-contained holiday apartments and backpacker options

Queensland

twins and triple all with shared bathrooms, bistro/bar, large quiet deck and social areas, good tour and activities desk, surf/body board hire. Just over the hill near Noosa Junction is the **C-E** *Koala Beach Resort*, 44 Noosa Dr, T5447 3355, www.koala-backpackers.com, that offers fairly tired motel-style en suite dorms and doubles. It does however have its finger on the pulse and is considered the liveliest and most social of the backpackers, with a popular bar/ bistro, pool and internet.

Sunshine Beach D-E *Melaluka/Costa Bella*, Selene St, T5447 3663, www.melaluka.com.au Offers spotless and spacious apartment style budget rooms with shared facilities close to the beach. Recommended.

Near **Boreen Point** the **C-F** *Gagaju*, T5474 3522, www.travoholic.com/gagaju/ is a characterful eco-backpackers-cum-bush camp, located between Lakes Cooroibah and Cootharaba, on the Noosa River. Everything is built from recycled timber with dorms, doubles and powered/non-powered, shaded campsites (campfires allowed), full kitchen facilities, TV lounge room and excellent in-house half-, 1- and 3-day **canoe trips** on the river. Pick-ups are offered from Noosa Heads. Next to **Lake Weyba L** *Eumarella Shores*, Eumarella Rd, T544 91254, offers something well removed from the resorts and tourist hype. Fully self-contained colonial and log cabin style cottages sleeping 2-6 in a bush setting over looking the lake, also horse trekking.

Eating   There are almost 150 restaurants in the Noosa area with 30 along Hastings St alone, some featuring top national chefs. Other than the expensive offerings on **Hastings St**

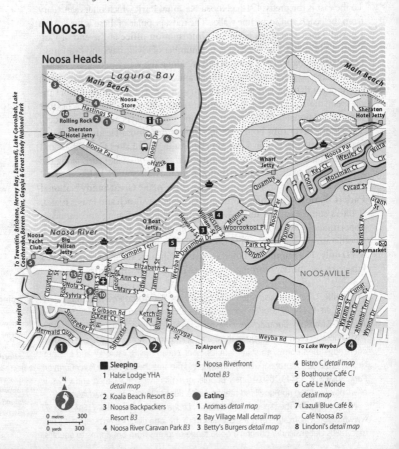

Noosa

Noosa Heads

■ **Sleeping**
1 Halse Lodge YHA
   detail map
2 Koala Beach Resort *B5*
3 Noosa Backpackers
   Resort *B3*
4 Noosa River Caravan Park *B3*

5 Noosa Riverfront
   Motel *B3*

● **Eating**
1 Aromas *detail map*
2 Bay Village Mall *detail map*
3 Betty's Burgers *detail map*

4 Bistro C *detail map*
5 Boathouse Café *C1*
6 Café Le Monde
   detail map
7 Lazuli Blue Café &
   Café Noosa *B5*
8 Lindoni's *detail map*

in Noosa Heads, the main focus for eateries is along **Gympie Terr** and **Thomas St** in Noosaville. The best budget options are to be found along lower Noosa Dr and Sunshine Beach Rd in **Noosa Junction**.

Noosa Heads One of the most popular on Hastings St is *Café Le Monde*, T5449 2366, with its large covered, sidewalk courtyard and live entertainment. It serves generous international and imaginative vegetarian dishes and is also popular for breakfast. Open daily 0630-late. Of the Italian restaurants in Noosa, *Lindoni's*, Hastings St, T5447 5111, has the finest reputation, a nice atmosphere and entertaining staff. Open daily 1800-2230. Tucked away on the beachfront the classy *Bistro C*, T5447 2855, offers a good traditional menu and a welcome escape from the main drag overlooking the beach. Open from 0700-2130 daily. Back on Hastings St, the *Sierra*, 10 Hastings St, T5447 4800, is a very popular café with rather crammed seating, but a laid-back atmosphere, good coffee and good value breakfasts. More spacious and modern is *Aromas*, 32 Hastings St, T5474 9788, which also serves an excellent coffee and provides a great spot to watch the world go by. Open daily 0700-late. *Noosa Heads Surf Lifesaving Club*, 69 Hastings St, T5447 5395, is cheap and offers great sea views. The *Bay Village Mall*, on Hastings St, has a food court with several cheap options. Towards Noosa Junction, on Noosa Dr, the *Noosa Reef Hotel*, T5447 4477, offers fine views, value for money and is especially good for families. Nearby, the *Lazuli Blue Café*, 9 Sunshine Beach Rd, T5448 0055, offers all-you-can-eat vegetarian buffets for $8.50, while *Café Noosa*, 1 David Low Way, T5447 3949, is a popular dine-in/take away pizzeria, offering all the usual toppings from $12.20. An old favourite in town is *Betty's Burgers*, that is now trading from a caravan beside the beach at the end of Hastings St. The $2 burgers are almost legendary.

Noosaville Gympie Terr and Thomas St in Noosaville present all sorts of slightly more affordable options including the excellent and healthy *Thai Breakers*, corner Gympie Terr and The Cockleshell, T5455 5500. Open daily from 0630-1500/1700-2130. The *Natural Thai*, Shop 1/10 Thomas St, T5449 0144, is equally good, with excellent service. Across the road, the small BYO *Max's Native Sun*, No1 Islander Resort, Thomas St, T544 71931, offers something different in quiet and casual surrounds, specializing in duck dishes. Open Tue-Sat from 1800. The *Magic of India*, T5449 7788, just a few doors down, is reputed to be the best Indian takeaway in Noosa. Open dine-in Tue-Sun from 1730. Along Gympie Terr, the colourful *Seawater Café*, (197) T5449 7215, offers generous and affordable seafood platters, fish and chips and is open daily for breakfast, lunch and dinner. Nearby, the *Boathouse Café*, (142), T5474 4444, has a loyal following with its casual but stylish Mediterranean dishes. Open Wed-Sat 1000-late, Sun 1000-1900. Live entertainment Sun 1530-1830.

Queensland

Boreen Point The *Jetty Restaurant*, T5485 3167, over looking Lake Cootharaba, offers a fine escape from the Noosa hype and is deservingly popular, especially for lunch. It has a mainly traditional menu that changes daily. Nearby the *Apollonian Hotel*, Laguna St, Boreen Point, T5485 3100, is also well known for its delicious Sunday spit-roasts.

Sunshine Beach *Sunshine Beach Surf Club* (Spinnakers), corner Duke St and Belmore Terr, T5474 5177, offers value for money and great sea views.

Entertainment The in-house bar at the *Koala Beach Resort*, 44 Noosa Dr, T5447 3355, is considered the liveliest under 30s haunt in town, with the Reef Hotel's *Reef Bar* further up the hill (towards Noosa Heads) taking the overflow after closing at around 2400. On the upper level of the Bay Village Mall, on Hastings St, is the fairly unremarkable and pretentious dance and live band venue, *Rolling Rock*. Open 2100-0300 daily, smart/casual, $5 cover. Of the regular pubs the new *Irish Murphy's*, corner Sunshine Beach Rd and Noosa Dr, T5455 3344, offers the usual ambience, gimmicks, pub grub and fine, over-priced traditional beers. The main *Noosa Cinema*, is located on Sunshine Beach Rd, Noosaville, T1300-366339.

Tours & activities

There are plenty of mainly water-based activities in and around Noosa from surf lessons to river cruises, as well as the more unusual like multi-day canoe trips and camel rides

Camel Safaris *Camel Safaris*, T5442 4397, based on Noosa North Shore, have a fleet of dromedaries offering safaris of 1-2 hrs along Forty Mile Beach (Great Sandy National Park/Cooloola) from $42. **Cruises and boat hire** There are numerous operators that offer sedate cruises up and down the Noosa River from Noosa Heads to Tewantin and beyond. The main ferry terminals are (from west to east): Harbour Marine Village, (Gympie Terr, Noosaville), the O Boat Jetty, the Big Pelican, the Noosa Yacht Club and, at Noosa Heads, the Sheraton Hotel jetty. *Noosa Ferry Cruise*, T5478 0040, run regular services between all these stops, daily, from 0920-1930, from $8.50, child $3.50, family $20 one way. An 'All day pass' costs $12.50. *Noosa Sound Cruises*, T5447 3466, offer morning, or sunset jazz cruises from only $20. *Noosa River Cruises*, T5449 7362, offer a 5-hr trip to Lake Cootharaba daily from $60, while *Cooloola Cruises*, T5449 9177, offer a similar cruise, with an additional 4WD combo that takes in the main sights of the Great Sandy National Park (Cooloola), from $95, child $62. Recommended. For much faster action try the (small group) *Ecstasea Safaris*, T5447 2726, half-day from $65, or *Oceanrider*, T1800-001386, who will hurtle you at over 50 knots (that's fast!) around Noosa Heads and up the Noosa River for 75 mins, from $60. At the other extreme you might like to take your sweetheart out for a quiet *Gondola Cruise*, T04-1292 9369, 1 hr from $90 (including seafood dinner, from $110). There are numerous boat hire operators along the riverbank (Gympie Terr) where you can hire U-Drive Boats, BBQ Boats, speed boats, kayaks and jet skis (from $55, for 30 mins).

Diving *Noosa Blue Water Dive*, Boatshed, Gympie Terr, T5447 1300, offer 4-day open water courses from $399 and half-day charters from $99. **Fishing** *M.V. Trekka*, T5442 4919, offer half/three-quarter/full day deep-sea fishing from $95. *Noosa River Fishing and Crab Tours*, T04-0720 6062, and *Mud Crab Adventures*, T04-0283 4001, offer half-day finger nipping adventures, from $70. **Flight-seeing** *Noosa and Maroochy Flying Services*, T5450 0516, www.noosaaviation.com.au, offer a wide range of scenic flights from coastal trips to Fraser Island and reef safaris, from $45-$439. For something different try the *Dimona Motor Glider Flights* (cross between a light aircraft and a glider), based at the Sunshine Coast Airport, Maroochy, T5478 0077. **Horse trekking** The rather dubiously named *Clip Clop Horse Treks*, Eumarella Road, Lake Weyba, T5449 1254, offer a wide range of options from 2 hr treks to 6-day adventures. Full day from $150. *Bush and Beach*, T5447 1369, based on Noosa North Shore, offers 1-2 hr rides suitable for beginners.

Parasailing and kite surfing *Fly High Para flying*, T0500-872123, offer short flights from Main Beach, while *Kitesurf*, T5455 6677, and *Wind 'N' Sea*, T04-1472 7765 will introduce you to the new and exciting experience of kite surfing from $95 for 2 hrs. **Sea**

Queensland

kayaking and lake/river canoeing The *Elanda Point Canoe Company*, T5485 3165, www.elanda.com.au, offer a wide range of exciting adventures on the waterways of the Great Sandy National Park (Cooloola), from half-day (from $68), 2-day backpacker special (from $198), to 5-day/4-night (from $880). Independent hire is also available. Recommended. *Noosa Ocean Kayaking Tours*, T04-1878 7577, offer sea kayaking around the Noosa National Park, from $45 (2 hrs) and river trips, from $40 (2 hrs). Independent hire is also available, from $35 per day. **Surfing** There are tons of '*Learn to Surf*' operators. All are generally very professional and run by pros and/or experts. 2 hr session from about $35. Companies include *Wavesense*, T5474 9076; *Learn to Surf*, (with world champ Merrick Davies) T04-1878 7577; and for girls only the *Girls Surf School*, T04-1878 7577. *Noosa Longboards*, Shop 4, 64 Hastings St, T5447 2828, hire long/short surfboards and body boards, from $25/$15/$10 per hr. **Spas** *Newland*, 28 Sunshine Beach Rd, T5474 8212, the *Noosa Spa* (South Pacific Resort), T5447 1424, and the 'mobile' *State of Health Company*, T04-1218-1396, can oblige, from $55-$70 per hr. **Sky diving** *Sunshine Coast Skydivers*, Caloundra Airport, T0500-522533, are a large and reputable operator providing daily 12-15,000 ft Tandems from $260 (Excellent Backpacker deals). *Skydive Ramblers*, T04-0799 6400, also have a drop zone on Coolum Beach.

Tours *Noosa 4WD Eco Tours*, T5449 1400, offer full and half-day tours to the Great Sandy National Park (Cooloola) and beyond from $70. *Laguna Bay Tours*, T1800-114434, offer a wide range of day tours Mon/Wed/Fri to the Great Sandy National Park (Cooloola), Sunshine Coast Hinterland, including Australia Zoo (from $35), the Blackall Range and the Eumundi Markets (from $10). *Fraser Island Adventure Tours*, T5444 6957, offer an exciting day trip to Fraser Island, taking in the main sights of the Great Sandy National Park (Cooloola) along the way, from $130, child $90. *Fraser Island Trailblazers Tours*, T1800-626673, www.trailblazertours.com.au (Noosa Backpackers Resort) offer a good value 3-day Camping Safari, via the Great Sandy National Park (Cooloola section), from $245.

Banks Most major branches/ATMs are on Hastings St, Noosa Heads or Sunshine Beach Rd, Noosa Junction. **Currency Exchange** at *Harvey World Travel*, Shop 2 Lanyana Way, Noosa Heads, T5447 4077. **Car hire** *Avis*, corner Hastings St and Noosa Dr, T5447 4933 (from $43), *Budget*, Bay Village, Hastings St, Noosa Heads, T5447 4588. **Communications** Internet *Travel Bugs*, Shop 3/9, Sunshine Beach Rd, Noosa Junction, T5474 8530. Open daily 0800-2200. *Koala Backpackers*, 44 Noosa Dr, Noosa Junction. **Post Office** 91 Noosa Dr. Open Mon-Fri 0830-1730, Sat 0830-1230. Post Restante, T5447 3280. **Medical services** *Noosa Hospital*, 111 Goodchap St, T5455 9200. *Noosaville Medical Centre*, corner Thomas St and Mary St, T544 24922. Open Mon-Thu 0800-2000, Fri-Sun 0800-1800. **Police** 48 Hastings St, T5474 5255.

Directory

Maroochy

The name Maroochy loosely refers to an area of the Sunshine Coast that encompasses a string of popular **coastal holiday resorts** from **Caloundra**, on the northern fringe of Moreton Bay, to Noosa Heads. The largest of these, **Maroochydore**, the principal business and commercial capital, sits neatly on the southern shore of the **Maroochy River** estuary. To the south Maroochydore practically merges with the neighbouring resorts of **Alexandra Heads** and **Mooloolaba**. Famous for its long stretches of unspoiled beach and, of course its climate, the region attracts mainly domestic holiday makers from Brisbane. Beyond the beaches and the rivers there is not exactly a wealth of attractions, but with some excellent **surfing**, fishing and a growing number of adrenaline pumping activities, it may tempt you to stray off the beaten track. The name Maroochydore is thought to have derived

Colour map 3, grid A6
Population: 112,000
110 km north
of Brisbane

Queensland

Queensland

from the aboriginal words 'marutchi' and 'murukutchidha' which combined mean 'the 'waters of the black swans'. These graceful birds, along with the equally large, yet contrasting white pelicans, are a common sight on the Maroochy River.

Ins & outs

Getting there Air Maroochydore (Sunshine Coast) airport, www.suncoast-airport.com.au, 6 km north of Maroochydore, is serviced by *Qantas (Sunstate)*, T131313, several times daily from Brisbane. Local northbound bus services stop at the airport and a taxi to Maroochydore will cost about $15. *Henry's*, 12 Noosa Dr, T5474 0199, www.henrys.com.au, offer express (non-stop) services between Brisbane and Maroochydore Airports and Noosa Heads, 7 times daily, from $27.50. *Sunshine Shuttle*, T04-1250 7937, and *Sun-Air*, T5478 2811, offer similar services (Brisbane from $33 one-way). **Bus** The long-distance bus terminal is located in the Scotlyn Fair Shopping Centre, First Av, Maroochydore, T5443 1011. *McCafferty's/Greyhound*, T132030, and *Suncoast Pacific*, T5443 1011, offer daily north/southbound services. **Train** The nearest train station is at **Nambour**, T132232. Sunbus offer regular services from there to Maroochy (Nos 2, 1A) and Noosa (No 1).

Getting around *Sunshine Coast Sunbus*, T131230, are the local bus company, offering services to the Noosa Heads/Tewantin, (No 1), north/southbound throughout the Sunshine Coast (No 1), west to Eumundi/Cooroy/Nambour (Nos 2, 1A). The main bus stop in Maroochydore is at the Sunshine Plaza, Horton Pde. **Bike hire** is available from *Skate Biz*, 150 Alexandra Pde, Alexandra Headlands, T5443 6111, from $22 per day, and *Mooloolaba Bike Hire*, 25 First Av (behind the Sirocco Resort), T5477 5303, from $20 per day. Tandems can be hired from the Maroochy VIC. **Taxi** *Sunshine Coast Taxis*, T131008.

Information The main regional VIC is the **Maroochy Visitors Information Centre**, corner Sixth Av and Aerodrome Rd, Maroochydore, T5479 1566, www.maroochytourism.com.au Open Mon-Fri 0900-1700, Sat/Sun 0900-1600. There is also a small booth in Mooloolaba, corner First Av and Brisbane Rd, T1800-882032, www.mooloolababeach.com.au, (open Mon-Sun 0900-1700) and an office in **Caloundra**, 7 Caloundra Rd, T5491 0202. All can supply free street maps. **Internet** is available at the *Maroochy Internet Café*, Shop 7, King St, T5479 5061, and *The Mooloolaba Internet Café*, Shop 2/22 River Esp, T5477 5695.

Sights

The main tourist attractions, other than the region's surf beaches, centres around **The Mooloolaba Harbour and Wharf**. There, **Underwater World**, promises a fine introduction to Queensland's aquatic creatures and features an 80 m transparent tunnel that burrows through a massive oceanarium, containing over 20,000 fish, including rays and nurse and leopard sharks. If you wish you can take the plunge and dive with them for about 30 minutes (non-diver from $110, certified from $83). ■ *Daily 0900-1800, from $22, child from $13, T5444 8488, www.underwaterworld.com.au Parklyn Pde, Mooloolaba*. The main focus of Mooloolaba's beach based activity, centres around **The Esplanade**. In Maroochydore the **Maroochy River** is the big attraction, offering a range of water sports activities (see below). One of the most striking features of the river are its resident pelicans and black swans. Upstream the **Maroochy Waters Wetlands Sanctuary** features boardwalks through melaleuca swamps and mangroves that fringe the river. Access is from Sports Road, Bli Bli. North of Maroochydore **Mount Coolum** (208 m) offers a challenging walk, fine coastal views and, incredibly, is home to over 700 species of plants (the whole of the UK has only about twice that!). One hour one-way. Access is off Tanah Street, which is off David Low Way, Coolum.

Maroochydore Of the many resorts The **LL-L** *Argyle on the Park*, 31 Cotton Tree Pde, T5443 3022, is recommended, offering all the usual comforts in a fine position overlooking the river and close to the beach. Most motels are located on the main drags (David Low Av and Alexandra Pde) north and south of the town. The **L-A** *Beach Motor Inn*, 61-65 Sixth Av, T5443 7044, has nice units and is metres from the beach. **C-E** *Cotton Tree Beachouse Backpackers* is in a fine position overlooking the river at 15 Cotton Tree Pde, T5443 1755, www.cottontreebackpackers.com It is a laid-back, friendly place with a distinctly B&B feel, offering tidy dorms, double/twins, internet and free use of surfboards, kayaks and boogie boards. In a more suburban position at 24 Schirmann St (off Cotton Tree and O'Connor), is the **C-E** *Maroochydore YHA*, T5443 3151. It's a quiet, friendly place that looks after its visitors, offering motel-style unit dorms, small double/twins, 1 family room, large kitchen, pool, internet and free use of surf boards, canoes and fishing gear. Courtesy pick-ups, bike hire and cheap, in-house tours to the Glass House Mountains and beyond. There are plenty of **motor parks** in the area with the 4-star **L-E** *Maroochy Palms Holiday Village*, 319 Bradman Av, T5443 8611, www.maroochypalms.com.au being recommended. Cheaper alternatives for vans and campers are the beach/riverside **E** *Pincushion*, Cotton Tree Pde, T1800-461917 and the **E** *Seabreeze* corner of Melrose Pde and Sixth Av, T5443 1167.

Mooloolaba Of the few motels the modern **L-A** *Mooloolaba Motel*, 46 Brisbane Rd, T5444 2988, is well positioned with spacious 1-2 bedroom units and a pool. Inland, near Buderim, the **L-A** *Aquila Guest House*, 21 Box St (off King), T5445 3681, www.guesthousequeensland.com.au, offers superb aesthetics both inside and out, 4 deluxe en suites, gourmet breakfast and fine views. The main **backpackers** in 'Mooloo' is the modern but rather impersonal **B-E** *Mooloolaba Beach Backpackers*, 75 Brisbane Rd, T5444 3399, offering standard and en suite dorms, standard and en suite doubles with TV and a/c, pool and internet. The **E** *Mooloolaba Beach Caravan Park*, Parklyn Pde, T5444 1201, has powered and non-powered sites close to the beach.

Sleeping & eating
The entire coastal strip is dotted with resorts offering comfortable 4-star self-contained apartment blocks with palm tree fringed pools and spas. The VIC has full listings, T1800-660044

Booking is advised during school and public holidays

Rusty's Mexican Restaurant, 68 Sixth Av, T5443 1795, is a long established favourite. Open daily from 1800. In **Mooloolaba**, the **Esplanade** and **Wharf** (Parklyn Pde) are the main restaurant/café spots offering a wide array of options. One of the best is the *Mooloolaba Surf Club*, Esplanade, T5444 1300, that offers good value for money and great views across the beach. Open Mon-Thu 1000-2200, Fri/Sat 1000-2400, Sun 0800-1000. Live entertainment every Thu-Sun in the afternoon. When it comes to fine dining *Harry's Restaurant*, Lindsay Rd, Buderim, T5445 6661 (8 km west of Mooloolaba), is a fine choice, offering modern Australian cuisine in a 120-year-old homestead in a quiet setting.

Eating
Most of Maroochydore's restaurants and cafés are located between Aerodrome Rd and the Esplanade

Abseiling *Adventures Sunshine Coast*, Mooloolaba, T5444 8824, offer abseiling, rock climbing and rap jumping (and wilderness canoeing), half-day from $69, full from $99, 2-day camp from $245. (no experience necessary). **Cruising** From the sedate to the bum-breaking: *Harbour River Canal Cruises*, The Wharf, Mooloolaba, T5444 7477, offer leisurely trips up the Mooloolaba River 1100/1300/1430, from $13, child $4, while *Ocean Sprinter*, T5444 6766, offers an exhilarating 50 mins blast about the bays in a rigid inflatable, from $50. **Diving** *Scuba World*, next door to Undersea World, Parklyn Pde, Mooloolaba, T5444 8595, offer shark diving, from $83 and trips to the Gneerings/Murphy Reefs and Mudjimba Island for certified divers only. **Flight seeing** *Suncoast Helicopters*, Caloundra Airport, T5499 6900, offer a range of scenic flights from the coast to the Glass House Mountains from $85-$135. **Jet Skiing** The Maroochy River and coast is becoming a top venue for Jet Ski adventures. *Jet Ski Hire and Tours*, T04-1263 7363, www.jetskihiretours.com.au, offer independent hire from $75 (30 mins), 2½ hrs Breakfast Tours, from $150 per ski and Offshore Tours, from $160 per ski. Skis can also be hired independently in Mooloolaba from *Ocean Jet Ski Hire*, Mooloolaba Beach, Parklyn Pde, T04-1237 3356.

Tours & activities

Queensland

Sea kayaking The *Aussie Sea Kayak Company*, Shop 9, The Wharf, Mooloolaba, T5477 5335, www.aussieseakayak.com.au, offer everything from sedate 2-hr sunset paddles from $40, to extended trips to Fraser Island and The Whitsundays. **Sky diving** *Sunshine Coast Skydivers*, Caloundra Airport, T0500-522533, are a large and reputable operator providing daily 12-15,000 ft Tandems from $260 (excellent backpacker deals). *Skydive Ramblers*, T04-0799 6400, also have a drop zone in Coolum Beach. **Surfing** The Sunshine Coast almost rivals that of the Gold Coast for surfing with numerous breaks with such evocative names as 'The White House', 'The Groyne', 'Geriatrics Reef', 'Dead Man's' and 'The Cheese Factory'. There are numerous surf shops and hire outlets including *Surf Dog*, 12/110 Sixth Av, Maroochydore, T5475 4565, *Bad Company*, Shop 5/6-8 Aerodrome Rd, Maroochydore, T5443 2457, and *Beach Beat*, 164 Alexandra Pde, Alexandra Head, T5443 2777. Boards cost from $25-$40 per day. **Tours** *Cruise Maroochy Eco Tours*, T5476 5745, are a good outfit offering a wide range of nature-based cruises, including a nocturnal adventure, from 30 mins-5½ hrs, from $33, child $21. **Water-skiing, wake boarding and skurfing** *The Ski and Skurf Cable Ski Park*, 325 David Low Way, Bli Bli (12 km north of Maroochydore), is a purpose built, lake complex, offering skiing and boarding, from $25 for 2 hrs.

Sunshine Coast Hinterland

With a name like 'Sunshine Coast' it is hardly surprising that the vast majority of travellers take the title literally and head straight for the beach. But although the swathes of golden sand will not disappoint, if you allow some time to explore the hinterland you will find a wealth of other attractions, including some strange sights such as giant 'walk-in' fruits, and television's infamous 'Crocodile Hunter'.

Ins & outs The VICs in **Noosa**, T5447 4988, and **Maroochydore**, T5479 1566, www.maroochytourism.com.au, can provide information on the major attractions of the Sunshine Coast hinterland, along with accommodation listings and location maps. The *Montville*, T5478 5544, www.montvillage.com.au and *Maleny*, T5499 9033, information centres offer more localized information. If you are exploring from the south the **Caboolture Visitors Information Centre**, BP Caboolture North Travel Centre, Bruce Highway, Burpengary, T1800-833100, can also be of assistance. Open daily 0830-1700. There is a **QPWS** office on Sunday Creek Rd, Kenilworth, T5446 0925. The VIC also offer a comprehensive *'Art and Craft Gallery Trail'* leaflet.

Eumundi & around The historic 19th century former timber town of **Eumundi**, 1 km off the Bruce Highway and 23 km west of Noosa (on Noosa Road), is pretty enough even without its famous markets. But if your timing is right, a visit to this creative extravaganza is well worth it. Every Saturday and (to a lesser extent) Wednesday mornings, the village becomes a bustling conglomerate of over 300 fascinating arts, crafts and produce stalls. It seems everything is on offer, from kites and bandanas to neck massages and boomerangs. The markets kick off at about 0700 and start winding up about 1500. The best time to go is on Saturday early before the day heats up and the tourist buses arrive. It can get busy and a little stressful. Numerous tours are on offer from Noosa or Brisbane (see below). A fine place to have breakfast is *Chuckles Café*, 2/77 Memorial Drive (across the road from the markets), T5442 8152. Open from 0600-1700.

In the small town of **Yandina**, 15 km south of Eumundi (1 km west off the Bruce Highway) is the *Ginger Factory*, which is the largest of its type in the world. Here you can witness the manufacturing process, watch cooking demonstrations, ride the 'Cane Train' and of course, purchase various end products. ■ *Daily 0900-1700, free. T5446 7096. 50 Pioneer Road, Yandina.* The historic 1853 *Yandina Station Homestead*, 684 Yandina Creek Rd, T5446 6000 (towards the coast via the Yandina-Coolum Road), is one of the best restaurants in the region. Open lunch Friday-Sunday from 1200, dinner Friday/Saturday from 1800. Recommended.

The Blackall Range Tourist Drive through the **Blackall Range** from Nambour to the Glass House Mountains is highly recommended, offering everything from national parks with waterfalls and short rainforest walks, to fine coastal views and cosy B&Bs. From Yandina (Nambour Road) or the Bruce Highway, head west just north of Nambour on the Nambour-Mapleton Road. **Nambour** itself is a busy agricultural service centre for the sugar cane and pineapple industries. The latter is celebrated at the rather kitschy *Big Pineapple Complex* (10 km south and 1 km west of the Bruce Highway) where you can enter the 15 m 'Big Pineapple'. ■ *Daily 0900-1700. Free, T5442 1333.* Back on the Nambour-Mapleton Road you begin the ascent up the Blackall Range to reach the pleasant little town of **Mapleton**. As well as its own great views and attractive B&Bs, Mapleton is the gateway to The **Mapleton Falls National Park**. The heady views of the 120 m falls can be accessed 17 km west on Obi Obi Road. Nearby, the 1.3 km Wompoo Circuit walk winds through rainforest and eucalypts providing excellent views of the Obi Obi Valley. From Mapleton the road heads south along the range through **Flaxton** village and the **Kondalilla National Park**. This 327 ha park is accessed and signposted 1 km south of Flaxton and offers views of the 90 m Kondalilla Falls, from the 2 km Picnic Creek trail and the 2.7 km Kondalilla Falls circuit, that winds its way down through rainforest to the base of the falls. Neither of the parks offers camping facilities.

First settled by fruit growers in 1887, historic **Montville**, 5 km south of Flaxton, is the main tourist hub along the Blackall Range. Replete with European-style historic buildings, chic cafés, galleries and souvenir shops, it is nonetheless unspoiled and provides a pleasant stop for lunch or a stroll. Nearby, **Lake Baroon** also offers a pleasant spot for a picnic. From Montville the road continues south taking in the **Gerrard** and **Balmoral Lookouts** which offer memorable coastal views from Noosa Heads in the north, to Caloundra and Bribie Island in the south. Turning inland you then encounter the equally pretty **Maleny**, which like Montville, offers many interesting arts and crafts galleries, good B&Bs and a winery. At the far end of the town turn left down the narrow Maleny-Stanley Road to access Mountain View Road (left). Heading back towards the coast you are then almost immediately offered the first stunning views of the **Glass House Mountains** to the south, from **McCarthy's Lookout**. A few kilometres further on is the 41-ha **Mary Cairncross Scenic Reserve**, the legacy of 19th century environmentalist Mary Cairncross, where you can also admire the views, visit the park's environmental centre or take a stroll through the rainforest (1.7 km), T5499 9907. From the Cairncross Reserve, the road descends the Blackall Range towards **Landsborough**, which is the northern gateway to the spellbinding Glass House Mountains.

The 13 volcanic peaks of the Glass House Mountains are utterly absorbing. Gradual weathering by both wind and water has, over the last 20 million years, created the distinctive mountain peaks named collectively in the

Blackall Range Tourist Drive

Glasshouse Mountains National Park

passing by Captain Cook in 1770 (who it is believed thought the peaks looked similar to Glass furnaces in his native Yorkshire). The highest peak is **Mount Beerwah** (556 m), while everybody's favourite has to be the distinctly knobbly **Mount Coonowrin** (377 m). Although the best views are actually from Old Gympie Road (runs north to south, just west of Landsborough, Beerwah and Glass House Mountains Village) there is an official **lookout** on the southern edge of the park (3 km west off Old Gympie Road). When it comes to bush walking and summit climbing, **Mount Ngungun** (253 m) is the most accessible (Fullertons Road of Old Gympie Road or Coonowrin Road), while **Mount Tibrogargan** (364 m) and Mount Beerwah also offer base viewpoints and two to three hour rough summit tracks. Sadly, pointy Mount Coonowrin is closed to public access due to the danger of rock falls. There is no camping allowed in the park. Several companies offer walking and climbing adventures (see below).

Australia Zoo Of all Queensland's many wildlife attractions, **Australia Zoo** attracts the biggest crowds. The reason for this, of course, is its association with TV's Crocodile Hunter (alias Steve Irwin), to whom the zoo is official home base. The zoo houses over 550 native and non native species ranging from insomniac wombats to enormous 20 ft pythons. The biggest attraction of the park is the **crocodile feeding**, enthusiastically demonstrated daily at 1330, though, to the disappointment of many, not by Steve himself. But though the whole effect is akin to a circus, and the sheer megalomania can be wearing, especially in the shop, the range of wildlife is impressive and the animals are well looked after. ■ *Daily 0830-1600, $16.50, child $8.50, family $40. T5494 1134, www.crocodilehunter.com.au Glass House Mountains Rd, Beerwah. Free transportation available from Noosa (Wed/Sat/Sun) and Maroochy, Mooloolaba and Caloundra (daily). Phone for details.*

Sleeping & eating

There are numerous excellent B&Bs in the region. The regional and local VICs have full listings

A *Montville Mountain Inn*, Main St, Montville, T5442 9499, www.mont villeinn.com.au Recommended. **LL** *Eyrie Escape B&B*, 316 Brandenburg Rd, Bald Knob, Mooloolah, T5494 8242, www.eyrie-escape.com.au Incredible views. There are a small number of motor parks scattered around the area, including the **B-E** *Lilyponds Holiday Park*, 26 Warruga St, Mapleton, T5445 7238, and the **C-E** *Glass House Mountains Tourist Park*, Glass House Mountains Rd, Beerburrum, T5496 0151.

There are also many fine restaurants and cafés. The *Tree Tops Gallery Restaurant*, Kondalilla Falls Rd, near Flaxton, T1800-087330, www.treehouses.com.au (also has excellent cabin style accommodation), *Poets Café*, 167 Main St, Montville, T5478 5479, and *King Ludwig's German Restaurant and Bar*, T5499 9377, overlooking the Glass House Mountains on Glass House Mountains Rd, are all excellent.

Tours & activities

The Glass House Mountains Adventure Company, T5474 9166, offer a day's **summit climbing** combined with a trip to the Australia Zoo from $100, half-day from $49. *Skydrifter*, Glass House Mountains, T5438 7003, offer **balloon** flights over the mountains, from $175-$240. *Storeyline Tours*, T5474 1500, and *Noosa Hinterland Tours*, T5474 3366, both offer a range of tours to hinterland attractions including the Eumundi Markets (from $12) and the Australia Zoo, from $32. *Tropical Coastal Tours*, T5474 9200, do the Eumundi market run from Noosa, from $12, child $7 return. *Off Beat Tours*, T5473 5135, www.offbeattours.com.au, are a reputable outfit offering 4WD eco tours of the region, from $11.

Rainbow Beach and the Great Sandy National Park (Cooloola Section)

With access limited to 4WD only from Noosa (Tewantin) from the south, and a 76 km diversion from Gympie on the Bruce Highway, from the north, the mainland (Cooloola Coast) section of the **Great Sandy National Park** and its delightful neighbouring coastal communities of **Rainbow Beach** and **Tin Can Bay** are all too often missed by travellers in their eagerness to reach Hervey Bay and Fraser Island. As well as the numerous and varied attractions and activities on offer within the 56,000 ha park, including huge **sand blows**, ancient **coloured sands** and weathered **wrecks**, Tin Can Bay offers an opportunity to feed wild **dolphins**, and Rainbow Beach an ideal rest stop off the beaten track, as well as southerly access to **Fraser island**.

Colour map 4, grid C6
Population: 850
144 km north of Noosa, 110 km south of Hervey Bay

Getting there Road Rainbow Beach is 76 km east of the Bruce Highway at Gympie. Alternative access is by 4WD only from Tewantin, 3 km east of Noosaville, (Noosa River ferry 0600-2200, from $4). *Polley's Coaches*, T5482 2700, offer twice daily (weekday) services from Gympie to Tin Can Bay and Rainbow Beach. *Fraser Explorer Tours*, T5447 3845, www.fraser-is.com, are a good option if you are visiting Fraser Island from Noosa. Their 2/3-day tour has the added attraction of taking in the sights of the Cooloola section of the Great Sandy National Park on the way, from $170-$304. For Fraser Island ferry services see Fraser Island section.

Ins & outs

Information For general visitor information in the area, contact the **Cooloola Visitors Information Centre**, Bruce Highway, Kybong (15 km south of Gympie), T5483 5554, www.cooloola.org.au Open daily 0900-1700. There is also an independently run VIC, 8 Rainbow Beach Rd, Rainbow Beach, T5486 3227. Open daily. For more information regarding Tin Can Bay, T5486 4855, www.tincanbaytourism.org.au The **QPWS**, Rainbow Beach Rd, T5486 3160, have detailed information on the Great Sandy National Park (including Fraser Island) and issue camping/RAM Fraser Island permits. Open daily 0700-1600.

Along with Fraser Island, the Great Sandy National Park forms the largest sand mass in the world. For millennia sediments washed out from the river courses of the New South Wales coast have been steadily carried north and been deposited in vast quantities. Over time this virtual desert has been colonized by vast tracts of mangrove and rainforest and a rich variety of wildlife. Perhaps the most incredible feature of the park are the magnificent coloured sands extending from Rainbow Beach to Double Island Point. Over 200 m high in places and eroded into ramparts of pillars and groves, the sands' colourful palette of over 40 hues, from blood red to brilliant white, glow in the rays of the rising sun. They are also steeped in Aboriginal legend. According to the Kabi tribe who frequented the area long before the Europeans, the mighty sands were formed and coloured by the Rainbow Spirit who was killed there in his efforts to save a beautiful maiden.

Sights

Other features of the park include the **Carlo Sand Blow** just south of Rainbow Beach, which is a favourite haunt for hang gliders, and the wreck of the cargo ship 'Cherry Venture' which ran aground in 1973. The views from the **lighthouse** on Double Island (which is actually a headland, falsely named by Captain Cook in 1770) will also live long in the memory. All the features of the park can be explored by a network of 4WD and **walking** trails, while other popular activities include horse trekking, and fishing. At the southern end of the park (accessed from Noosa) **Lakes Cootharaba** and

Queensland

Cooroibah are also popular for boating and canoeing. Located at the northern edge of the park the laid-back, yet fast developing seaside village of **Rainbow Beach** provides an ideal base from which to explore the park and as a stepping-stone to Fraser Island. **Inskip Point**, 14 km north, serves as the southerly access point to the great island paradise. **Tin Can Bay**, located west of Rainbow Beach on the banks of the Tin Can Bay Inlet, is a popular base for fishing and boating, but by far its biggest attraction is the visiting pod of **wild dolphins** that gathers every morning at 0800 around the Northern Point boat ramp for feeding. For more details, T5483 5554.

Sleeping One of the most unusual and attractive places to stay in the area is on board your own **houseboat** which gives you free access around the Great Sandy Strait and western shores of Fraser Island. *Luxury Afloat Houseboats*, Norman Pt, Tin Can Bay, T5486 4864, www.luxuryafloat.com.au, and *Rainbow Beach Houseboats*, T5486 3146, www.sunfish.com.au/rbhb/htm, have a range of craft and packages. Alternatively, for yachts, try *Fraser Island Rent-A-Yacht*, Tin Can Bay marina, T5486 4814, www.rent-a-yacht.com.au   Prices for houseboats range from about 3 nights midweek from $660 to 7 nights from $1540 (low season) to $825/$1925 (high season).

Back on terra firma, in **Rainbow Beach**, is **L** *Rainbow Shores Resort*, Rainbow Shores Dr, T5486 3999, www.rainbowshores.com.au, a fine eco-resort set in native bush and close to the beach, with fully self-contained villas, bungalows and apartments, a pool and in-house activities. There are 2 backpackers in the village. The newest is the modern, purpose-built **C-E** *Rocks Backpackers Resort*, Spectrum St, T5486 3711, that offers en suite singles, doubles and dorms, bar/restaurant, pool and internet. Located a little further from the centre is the **E** *Rainbow Beach Backpackers*, 66 Rainbow Beach Rd, T5486 3288, rainbowbeachback@excite.com.au, which is small but comfortable, dorms, doubles and internet. For a motor park, try the 3-star **B-E** *Rainbow Waters Holiday Park*, Carlo Rd, T5486 3200, set in 23 acres of parkland next to the water, with self-contained cabins, powered and non-powered sites, kiosk but no camp kitchen.

In **Tin Can Bay**, at the top of the range you will find the **L-A** *Dolphin Waters Holiday Apartments*, 40 Esplanade, T5486 2600, that has 10 modern 1 and 2 bedroom self-contained apartments and a salt water pool. A cheaper option is the **C** *Sandcastle Motel*, Tin Can Bay Rd, T5486 4555. There are 3 motor parks in the area including the **D-E** *Golden Trevally Caravan Park*, Trevally St, T5486 4411, that offers en suite/standard powered and non-powered sites. The **Great Sandy National Park (Cooloola)** hosts 20 varied **QPWS** campsites. The main site is the Freshwater camping area, 20 km southeast of Rainbow Beach. It provides water, showers and toilets, but fires are banned. Access is by 4WD only. Booking centre open Mon-Fri 1300-1500, T5449 7959, otherwise contact the QPWS office in Rainbow Beach.

Tours *Safari Tours*, T5486 3154 offer day or overnight trips to Fraser Island and the Great Sandy National Park (Cooloola). If you want to go it alone, *Aussie Adventure 4WD*, T5486 3599, hire 2-9 seat 4WD vehicles.

Hervey Bay

Colour map 4, grid C6
Population: 33,000
290 km north
of Brisbane

What it lacks in beauty and soul, Hervey Bay more than makes up for in numbers of visitors. People flock here for two reasons: it is considered by many to be the **whale watching** capital of the world and is also the main gateway to the phenomenal **Fraser Island**. But though Hervey Bay tries hard to appeal on its own and keep people on the mainland for more than a day or a night, it's all in vain and the town has become one of Queensland's most muddled and soulless tourist transit centres.

Getting there Air Hervey Bay is served by *Qantas (Sunstate)*, T131313, and *Flight West*, T131300. The airport is 2 km south of Urangan off Elizabeth St/Booral Rd at the eastern end of the city. Taxis meet all scheduled flights. The long-distance **bus** terminal is located in the Bay Central Shopping Centre, Boat Harbour Rd, Pialba, T4124 4000. *McCafferty's/Greyhound*, T132030, and *Premier Motor Services*, T133410, offer daily services north/south. *Suncoast Pacific*, T5443 1011, and *Kirklands*, T1300-367077, offer services to Tin Can Bay and *Polley's Coaches*, T5482 2700, offer onward transfers to Rainbow Beach. The nearest **train** station is in Maryborough, (Lennox St) T4123 9264. Queensland Rail's, '**Spirit of the Tropics**', '**Sunlander**', '**Capricornian**' and fast '**Tilt Train**' (Brisbane to Rockhampton) offer regular services north and south, T132232. The *Trainlink* bus service connects with every Tilt Train for transfers to and from Hervey Bay. *Hervey Bay Travel Centre*, 15 Torquay Rd, T4128 1900, act as booking agents.

Ins & outs
Hervey Bay is on the coast, 34 km east of the Bruce Highway and Maryborough

Getting around *Bay Bus and Coach*, T4128 6411, run local hail and ride **bus** services between Maryborough and Hervey Bay, taking in a circuit of the town through Pialba, along the Esplanade to Urangan and back via Boat Harbour Dr. They operate Mon-Fri every 2 hours from 0600-1900 and Sat 0720-1800. **Bike hire** is available from *Rayz Pushbikes*, T04-1764 4814, from $12 per day. Free delivery and pick-up. Open daily 0700-1700. **Taxi** T131008

Information and orientation Hervey Bay is essentially a beachfront conglomerate of suburbs, from **Point Vernon** in the west, through **Pialba, Scarness** and **Torquay** to **Urangan** in the east. Almost all major amenities are to be found along the **Esplanade** from the junction with Main St in Pialba to Elizabeth St, Urangan. The main Fraser Island ferry and whale-watching terminal is just south of Dayman Point in Urangan. Independent VICs are commonplace and often biased towards certain tours or operators. For bias-free information visit the accredited *Maryborough Fraser Island Visitors Information Centre* at the BP South Tourist Complex on the Bruce Highway, before heading for the coast, T4121 4111, www.frasercoast.org.au Open daily 0900-1700. Or, alternatively, stick to the smaller, local VICs in Hervey Bay, corner Urraween Rd, T4124 2912, www.herveybaytourism.com.au Open Mon-Fri 0830 1700, Sat/Sun 0900-1700. The nearest **QPWS** office is in Maryborough, corner of Alice St and Lennox St, T4121 1800. Open Mon-Fri 0830-1700.

If you have any time to kill between whale-watching and getting to Fraser Island, Hervey Bay tries hard to lure you with a few low-key attractions. **Natureworld**, on the corner of Maryborough Road and Fairway Drive, T4124 1733, is a small but entertaining animal park, with all the usual natives including wombats, fruit bats, roos and, of course, cuddly koalas. Guided tours kick off at 1130, the koala show at 1200 and snake handling at 1230. Courtesy bus and café. ■ *Daily 0900-1700, from $13.50, child $6.50, family $35.* Continuing the eco-theme is **Neptune's Reefworld**, on the corner of Pulgul Street and Kent Street, Urangan, T4128 9828, with coral displays, turtles, stingrays and reef sharks. ■ *Daily from 0915, from $14, child $8 (shark feed 1400, swim with the sharks from $40, free pick ups).* The fearless can also try **Vic Hislop's Great White Shark Expo**, on the corner of the Esplanade and Elizabeth Street, Urangan, T4128 9137. ■ *Daily 0830-1800, $12, child $5.*

Sights

Queensland

Sleeping

True to its transitory demand, Hervey Bay offers plenty of accommodation options with a very heavy emphasis on backpackers and caravan parks

During the whale-watching season and during public holidays you are advised to book ahead

One option often overlooked and ideal given the presence of Fraser Island and the Great Sandy Strait, are **houseboats**. Several companies can oblige, including *Self Sail Holidays*, Great Sandy Straits Marina, Urangan T4125 3822, www.selfsail.com.au, *Luxury Afloat Houseboats*, Norman Pt, Tin Can Bay, T5486 4864, www.luxuryafloat.com.au, and for yachts, Fraser island *Rent-A-Yacht*, Tin Can Bay marina, T5486 4814, www.rent-a-yacht.com.au Prices range from about 3 nights midweek from $660 to 7 nights from $1540 (low season) to $825/$1925 (high season).

Back on terra firma, is the **LL-L** *Great Sandy Straits Marina Resort* in Urangan, T4128 9999, greatsandyresort@bigpond.com.au Set in a position overlooking the bay it offers fully self-contained units with, pool, sauna, spa and bike hire. Off the busy Esplanade, is the **L** *Wanderer Villas*, corner Ann St and Truro St, T4128 9048, hwanderer@hervey.com.au, offering well appointed villas, pool and spa. Motels flourish in Hervey Bay. They range from the 4-star **L-A** *Beachside Motor Inn*, 298 Esplanade, T4124 1999, www.beachsidemotorinn.com.au to the **A-B** *Reef Motel*, 410 Esplanade, T4125 2744. Of the few B&Bs in the city, the **A** *Bay B&B*, 180 Cypress St, T4125 6919, and the more expensive **A** *Oceanic Palms B&B*, 50 King St, T4128 9562, are handy for the boat harbour.

With over 15 backpackers in the city and more on the way, the choice is huge and competition fierce. Many of the large chain backpackers like **C-E** *Beaches*, 195 Torquay Terr, T4124 1322, **C-E** *Palace*, 184 Torquay Rd, T4124 5331 and *Koala*, 408 Esplanade, T4125 3601, all offer the usual party hype and Fraser Island tour/accommodation package deals. Other alternatives include the excellent **A-E** *Colonial Backpackers Resort* YHA, corner Pulgul St and Boat Harbour Dr, T4125 1844, www.coloniallogcabins.com, offering a fine range of options from luxury villas and 1- 2 bedroom cabins, to en suite doubles and dorms, a good bistro/bar, pool, spa, internet, bike hire and tours desk. It is also the closest to the boat harbour. Back in the heart of town and in welcome contrast to the party-hard establishments, is the characterful and friendly **C-E** *Woolshed*, 181 Torquay Rd, T4124 0677, with an exquisite range of nicely decorated (and very different) dorms and twin/double cabins and rooms with all the usual facilities and internet. Recommended. Across the road is **C-E** *Friendly Hostel*, 182 Torquay Rd, T4124 4107, friendlyhostel@hotmail.com It is small and comfortable and more like a B&B, with tidy dorms, doubles/twins with well-equipped kitchen facilities.

Hervey Bay

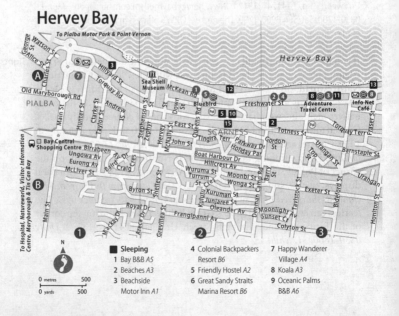

Sleeping		
1 Bay B&B *A5*	4 Colonial Backpackers Resort *B6*	7 Happy Wanderer Village *A4*
2 Beaches *A3*	5 Friendly Hostel *A2*	8 Koala *A3*
3 Beachside Motor Inn *A1*	6 Great Sandy Straits Marina Resort *B6*	9 Oceanic Palms B&B *A6*

There are numerous motor parks to choose from with the decision as usual coming down to location and/or facilities. For an excellent range of options and facilities try the **A-E** *Happy Wanderer Village*, 105 Truro St, Torquay, T4125 1103, hwanderer@hervey.com.au It offers good value fully self-contained duplex villas, studio/standard units, cabins, on-site vans (shared amenities), en suite/standard powered sites and non-powered sites, pool, camp kitchen. Backpacker cabins are also available. Recommended. There are 3 basic, 3-star motor park/campsites (beachside) along the Esplanade, at **Pialba**, T4128 1399, **Scarness**, T4128 1274, and **Torquay**, T4125 1578.

Eating

Most of the mainly mid-range options and cheap eateries are to be found along the Esplanade in Torquay, Scarness and Pialba

Expensive Many of the upmarket resort complexes have restaurants offering fine dining, including the popular *Sails Restaurant*, corner Fraser St and The Esplanade, T4125 5170, with its wide range of seafood, Asian and traditional Australian dishes. Open lunch Thu/Fri 1200-1430, dinner Mon-Sat 1800-late. **Mid-range** *Beach House Hotel*, 344 Esplanade, Scarness, T4128 1233, is deservingly popular for both lunch and dinner, offering a good range of pub/café style options overlooking the beach. They also have live entertainment and pool tables. Also in Scarness is *Le Café*, 325a Esplanade, T4128 1793. Classy surroundings, value for money and good coffee. Open for breakfast, lunch and dinner, from 0645 Tue-Sun. Between Scarness and Torquay, the *Black Dog Café*, corner Esplanade and Denman Camp Rd, T4124 3177, is a modern, classy restaurant with good value Japanese dishes. Open daily for lunch and dinner. *Hoolihans Irish Pub*, 382 Esplanade, T4194 0099, has a wide range of traditional offerings with an Irish edge. Servings are generous and it's pricey, but then there is always the quality beer! Open daily from 1100. **Cheap** *Dolly's* 410 Esplanade, T4125 5633, is a lively backpacker haunt offering regular all-you-can-eat deals, dancing and live music. Further east *O'Reilley's*, 446 Esplanade, T4125 3100, also offers all-you-can-eat pizza and pancakes on Tue nights and reasonable value at other times. Open daily from 1700 and for value breakfasts Sat/Sun from 0730. At the other end of town The *RSL*, 11 Torquay Rd, Pialba, T4128 1133, can always be relied on for value for money and sedate entertainment. Open daily.

Queensland

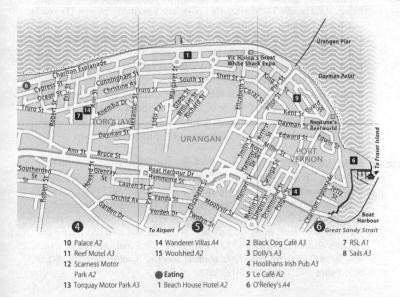

▶▶ Whale-watching in Hervey Bay

From August to November, the quiet waters of Hervey Bay echo to the haunting symphonies of migrating humpback whales. There are more than 15 whale-watch cruise operators based at the Urangan Boat Harbour, all hungry for your tourist dollar and vying to give you the opportunity to get close to the action. There are various options and a variety of boats offering half, three-quarter, full and dawn tours, ranging in price from $60 to $110. The best way to 'choose a cruise' is to head for the Whale Watch Tourist Centre at the boat harbour and take a look at the various boats, compare the tour details, or call T1800-358595. Open daily 0600-1800.

Tasman Venture II, T1800-620322, Quick Cat, T4128 9611, and Seaspray, T1800-066404, www.herveybaywhalewatch.com.au, are smaller launches offering two am/pm trips daily from $65, child $40. Blue Dolphin, T4120 3350, offer a 'whales by sail', half-day and sunset cruise option, from $75. Volante II is another smaller launch that offers three-quarter day and dawn trips from $70. Then you are moving into large catamaran territory with Whale Watch Safari (half-day, from $73), Whalesong, T4125 6222, www.whalesong.com.au, (that also do specialist year-round dolphin cruises), half-day from $70, and Spirit of Hervey Bay, T4125 5131, www.spiritofherveybay.com.au, which has the added luxury of a smooth glass bottom (half day from $110). At the top of the range is the M.V. Islander (three-quarter day, from $60) and M.V. Discovery One, (day cruise). You can also take to the air, whale-spotting with Air Fraser Island, T4125 3600, who offer 30-minutes to one-hour trips, from $50 per person, minimum of four. Hervey Bay celebrates its visiting Leviathans with an annual Whale Festival every August.

Tours & activities
For organized tours to Fraser Island see page 294

Camel Safaris *Humpbacks*, T4128 0055, offer 2 hr jaunts aboard the 'Ships of the Desert' from $39. **Diving** Diving is probably best kept for the Barrier Reef but fanatics or impatient beginners will find value for money with *Divers Mecca*, 403 Esplanade, T4125 1626. They offer good value certification courses and intro dives from $169/$80. **Fishing** *Princess II*, T4124 0400, and *The Eagle Ray*, T4125 4957, www.eaglerayfishing.com.au are the 2 main charters offering local sea, reef and night fishing. *M.V. Snapper*, T4124 3788, offers cheap family oriented trips from $33, child $18. **Horse Trekking** *The Susan River Homestead*, Maryborough-Hervey Bay Rd, T4121 6846. 2-2½ hrs, 0930/1400, from $50. **Scenic Flights** *Air Fraser Island*, T4125 3600, offer scenic flights from $165 and whale spotting, from $50. **Sea Kayaking** *Splash Safaris*, T0500-555580, offer half, full and 2-day trips exploring secluded beaches on Big Woody and Fraser Islands, from $59/$69/$165. **Sky Diving** *Skydive Hervey Bay*, T4124 9249, www.skybay.com.au offer tandems with a beach landing from 10-14,000 ft, from $219. **Water sports** *Fishing World*, 351A Esplanade, T4124 6375, and *Torquay Beach Hire*, Boat ramp, Esplanade Torquay, T4125 5528, both offer a range of hire equipment from runabouts to jet skis.

Directory

Banks *Westpac* and *National* are on the Esplanade Torquay, Commonwealth is on Bideford St, Torquay. **Camping gear** *Torquay Disposals*, 424 The Esplanade, T4125 6511. **Car hire** *Hervey Bay Economy Car Rentals*, 96 Islander Rd, T4124 6240, from $44 per day. *Nifty Rent A Car*, 463 Esplanade, T1800-627583. **Internet** The cheapest is *Bluebird Internet*, Shop 5/346 Esplanade, Scarness, T4124 2289. Other alternatives are *The Adventure Travel Centre*, 410 Esplanade, T4128 9288, and a few doors up the *Info Net Café*. All are open daily until late. **Post Office**, 428 Esplanade, Torquay. Open Mon-Fri 0830-1700, Sat 0830-1200. **Medical services** Hospital, Nissen St, T4120 6666, **Police** 142 Torquay Rd, T4128 5333.

Fraser Island

Jutting out from the eastern Australian coast like a huge trigger is the incredible 162,900 ha land mass known as Fraser Island – the biggest **sand island** in the world. Part of the **Great Sandy National Park** which extends onto the mainland south of the island, Fraser is now fully protected and was afforded World Heritage Listing in 1992. It is, without a doubt, a stunningly original place; a dynamic 800,000-year-old quirk of nature, genuinely blessed with the kind of scenery few visitors could even begin to imagine. Despite a few sand blows and seemingly endless stretches of beach, this is no desert. Blanketed in thick and variant rainforest interspersed with almost 200 freshwater lakes and numerous small streams, it will amaze even the most worldy-wise environmentalists or adventure tourists. As well as its unbelievable landscapes, its sheer scale and its rich wildlife, Fraser presents a great opportunity to try your hand at **four-wheel driving** and also plays host to one of the best **resorts** in the country. And despite the fact the island attracts over 300,000 visitors annually it is still possible to find a little peace and solitude – but only just.

Colour map 4, grid C6

If hiring a 4WD, avoid the temptation to let rip and 'see what this baby can do', as creeks and soft sand have resulted in some nasty accidents

Getting there Air There are 2 small airfields on Fraser (Toby's Gap and Orchid Beach), but most light aircraft land on East Beach at Eurong or Happy Valley. *Air Fraser Island*, T4125 3600, offer daily services from $50 return. They also offer 'Fly-Drive-Fly' ($110 one-day), 'Fly-Drive-Camp' ($190, 2-days/1 night) packages and scenic flights, from $165. *Noosa and Maroochy Flying Services*, T5450 0516, www.noosaaviation.com.au, offer shuttle from the Sunshine Coast from $99.

Ins & outs

Boat Vehicle barges *Rainbow Venture*, **Inskip Point**, Rainbow Beach, to **Hook Point** departs mainland daily from 0700-1630 (15 mins) T5486 3227 (no bookings required), from $70 return including driver, passenger-only from $12. *Fraser Dawn*, **Urangan Boat Harbour**, Hervey Bay, to **Moon Point**, departs mainland daily 0830/1530, (1 hr) returning 0930/1630, T4125444 (pre-book), from $82 return including driver, additional passengers $5.50, passenger only $16.50, one-way half price. *Fraser Ventures*, **Mary River Heads** (20 min, south of Hervey Bay), to **Wanggoolba Creek**, departs mainland Mon-Fri 0900, 1015, 1530, Sat 0700 (30 mins), returning Mon-Fri 0930/1430/1600, Sat 0730, (pre book), price as above. **Kingfisher Barge Mary River Heads** to **Kingfisher Bay** departs mainland daily 0715/1045/1400, returns 0830/1300/1530, T1800-072555 (pre-book), price as above. Note the Hook Point and Wanggoolba Creek landings require prior 4WD experience. Moon Point landing is recommended. **Passenger-only ferry** *Kingfisher Fast Cat*, Urangan Boat Harbour, Hervey Bay to Kingfisher Bay Resort, departs mainland daily 0845/1200/1600, Sun-Thu also 1830, Fri/Sat also 1900/2230, returns daily 0740/1030/1400/1700/2000, Sat/Sun extra at 2330, T4125 5511 (bookings preferable), from $35, child $17.

Getting around One of Fraser Island's greatest assets is that it has virtually no sealed roads and its single lane tracks are all **4WD** only. By far the best way to experience the island is to stay for at least 3 days and to hire your own 4WD. As you might expect, there are plenty of operators hiring 4WD and plenty of options, but generally speaking hire does not include fuel, ferry, food or accommodation/camping permits, nor does it include the cost of camping gear, which is also an additional extra. Conditions include a minimum age of 21, current drivers licence, at least a $500 bond or credit card imprint and a permit (see below). The more professional companies will also give you a thorough briefing and maps. Several of the larger **backpackers** including *Koala*, T1800-466444, www.koala-backpackers.com.au and *Palace*, T1800-063168, offer their own vehicles, guides and package deals, but if you want to get a group together and go independently several Hervey Bay based companies can oblige. *Safari 4WD*,

Walking is also a great to see the island. Hitching is also pretty easy in the busier parts of the island, but don't rely on it. There is a spartan taxi service, but thanks to the terrain and demand it is unreliable to say the least, T4127 9188. Book well in advance

Queensland

102 Boat Harbour Rd, T4124 4244, www.safari4wdhire.com.au, are one of the most professional offering a range of models from $90-$130 a day, camping kits from $16 per day and hire/accommodation packages from $573. Other reputable companies offering similar deals include *Fraser Island 4x4*, 10 Fraser St, Torquay, T4125 6355, *Bay 4WD Centre*, 54 Boat Harbour Dr, T4128 2981, and *Aussie Trax*, 56 Boat harbour Dr, T4124 4433, www.aussietraxfraserisland.com.au You can also hire 4WD on the island through the **Kingfisher Bay Resort**, T4125 5511. If you are on your own or are a couple then a 4WD package with *Air Fraser Island* is recommended. They will fly you out to Eurong, where you are supplied with a small, economical 4WD (with camping gear if required, fuel not included) and you are on your way, from $90 per day. The only drawback is that the vehicles must stay on the island and be dropped of again at Eurong. This option does avoid the expensive vehicular ferry fees and is fine if you want fly back, but it can present problems if you wish to stay at the Kingfisher Bay Resort and/or get the ferry back on foot from the island's west coast.

All vehicles on the island require a **RAM 4WD permit** that must be displayed on the windscreen. RAM permits can be obtained prior to arrival for $30 from the mainland QPWS offices, The *Hervey Bay City Council*, 77 Tavistock St, T4125 0222, *The Whale Watch Tourist Centre*, Boat Harbour, Urangan, T4128 9800, or the *River Heads Kiosk-Barge Car Park*, Ariadne St, T4125 8473. On the island permits cost $40 and can be purchased from the QPWS Eurong Office. If you breakdown there are mechanical workshops at Eurong, T4127 9173, and Orchid Beach, T4127 9220. For tow truck contact, T4127 9167, and be prepared to wave the contents of your bank account goodbye!

Fraser Island is 124 km in length and 27 km at its widest point

Information and orientation The VICs and QPWS offices on the mainland can provide most of the necessary information on the island. On the island itself there are QPWS ranger stations at **Eurong**, T4127 9128, open Mon 1000-1600, Tue/Wed/Thu 0700-1600, Fri-Sun 1400-1600, Central Station, T4127 9191, Dundubara, T4127 9138, and Waddy Point, T4127 9190 (all open variable times). The resorts, especially the Kingfisher Bay Resort, are also a valuable source of information. A vital piece of kit is the very informative and detailed 1:130,000 **Fraser Island Tourist Map** ($9) supplied by the resorts. Vehicular access is from **Hervey Bay** (Urangan) to **Moon Point** and **Kingfisher Bay**, **River Head** (20 mins south of Hervey Bay) to **Kingfisher Bay** and **Wanggoolba Creek**, and from **Rainbow Beach** to **Hook Point** which is the southernmost tip of the Island. The main resorts on the island are at **Kingfisher Bay** on the west coast and **Eurong, Happy Valley** and **Cathedral Beach** on the east. Other small communities on the east coast include **Dilli Village** to the south and **Orchid Beach** to the north the west coast is inundated with small creeks and inaccessible by 4WD. On the east coast, **East Beach** acts as one long vehicular highway from Hook Point in the south, to Orchid Bay and beyond in the north. A distance of 95 km. The interior of the island is networked by 4WD only tracks connecting the various lakes, sights and resorts. **Central Station** lies in the heart of the island, halfway between Kingfisher Bay and Eurong.

An information pack containing a detailed colour guide, camping and walking track details is supplied with the permit. **QPWS** campsite fees ($3.85 per night) apply to all national park sites on the island. QPWS fees do not apply to private resorts or campsites. Food supplies, hardware, fuel, ice and public telephones are available at the Eurong Beach Resort, Fraser Island Retreat (Happy Valley), Kingfisher Bay Resort, Cathedral Beach Resort and Orchid Beach. Additional Public telephones are located at Ungowa, Central Station, Dundubara, Waddy Point and Indian Head. There are no banks or ATMs on the island but most major resorts accept EFTPOS. There are no medical facilities, doctors or pharmacies on the island. The QPWS ranger stations and major resorts all have basic first aid and can call in an air ambulance in an emergency, T000. Food on the island is expensive so if you are camping, you are advised to take all your own supplies from the mainland.

Fraser's future ◀◀

Fraser Island, named after one Eliza Fraser, an 1836 shipwreck survivor, has a fascinating history that may date back as far as 40,000 years. The Butchulla tribe were the first indigenous people to inhabit the island, which they called K'gari. For thousands of years the Butchulla lived in harmony with their environment, but all that changed with the arrival in 1842 of the first European settlers. The indigenous people were gradually pushed out of their lands, or relocated, and the natural resources plundered. By 1904 the Butchella lost their ancient foothold on Fraser, never to return, and within a decade the colonial timber industry was in full swing, continuing unabated and uncontolled until 1991. One year later the island was declared a World Heritage area. Now, although Fraser is fully protected and still offers sanctuary to many are species, its primary usage is recreational. As such, there is an increasing range conflicts of interest that need addressing – most urgently the fate of its population of dingoes which is under threat as a result of their scavenging from tourists.

The East Beach Highway (Eurong to Orchid Beach)   Fringed by pounding surf on one side and bush on the other, barrelling up and down the 92 km natural highway of East Beach is an exhilarating experience in itself. The main access point for those arriving on the west coast is Eurong, where you can fuel up and head north, literally for as far as the eye can see. There are a number of sights as you head north, the first of which is **Lake Wabby** (4 km north of Eurong). Reached, by foot (4 km return on soft sand) Lake Wabby is one island lake that is at war with an encroaching sand blow creating a bizarre scene and the potential for sand surfing and swimming. For a stunning view you can head inland (7 km), on Cornwells Road, 2 km north of the beach car park. A walking track (5 km return) connects the **lookout** car park with the lake. Next stop (dodging the odd light aircraft landing on the beach at Happy Valley) is **Eli Creek**, which offers a cool dip in crystal clear waters. Just beyond Eli Creek (3 km) the rusting hulk of the **'Maheno'** – a trans-Tasman passenger liner that came to grief in 1935 – provides an interesting stop and a welcome landmark along the seemingly endless sandy highway. A further 2 km sees you at the unusual **Pinnacles** formation, an eroded bank of sand of varying gold and orange hues that could be straight out of the latest Star Trek movie. Just south of the Pinnacles, the 43 km Northern Road circuit ventures through ancient rainforest known as **Yidney Scrub** taking in views of the huge **Knifeblade Sand Blow**, the pretty (and pretty small) **Lake Allom** and **Boomerang Lakes**, which at 130 m above sea level are the highest dune lakes in the world. Back on East Beach, the colourful sandbanks continue to the Cathedral Beach Resort and the Dundubara Camp site which offers the truly fit and adventurous walker an opportunity to explore the turtle infested **Lake Bowarrady** (16 km return). From Dundubara it is another 19 km to **Indian Head**. One of the very few genuine rocks on the island, the Head offers a fine vantage point from which to see sharks and manta rays in the azure blue waters below (which is why swimming in the sea is ill advised around Fraser). Just beyond Indian Head at the start of **Middle Head**, the track turns inland providing access to Orchid Beach and the **Champagne Pools**. Named due to their clarity and wave action, they provide a perfect pool for swimming amongst tropical fish. Beyond the settlement of **Orchid Beach** and **Waddy Point**, four-wheel driving becomes more difficult with most hire companies banning further exploration north. But if you have your own vehicle and experience, the northern peninsula can offer solitude and fine fishing spots all the way up to **Sandy Cape** (31 km).

Sights

Queensland

The Lakes There are over 40 freshwater lakes on Fraser forming part of a vast and complex natural water storage system. The most popular are scattered around the southern interior. By far the most beautiful is **Lake MacKenzie**, with its white silica sands and crystal clear azure blue waters. It can be accessed north of Central Station or via Cornwells Road and Bennet Road from East Beach. It is, quite simply, a must-see, but try to go either early in the day or late to avoid the phalanx of tour buses. Also take sunglasses, sunscreen and insect repellent: the white sand is blinding in the sun and the flies are malicious in the extreme. Further south, **Lakes Birrabeen** and **Benaroon** also offer fine swimming and are quieter than MacKenzie, but do not share quite the same awesome aesthetics. Further south still is **Lake Boomanjin** which is the largest 'perched' lake in the world (in other words, it's very brown).

Central Station For those arriving on the west coast, Central Station provides the first glimpse of just how well wooded Fraser Island really is. Shaded by towering bunya pine, satinay and thick with umbrella like palms, this green heart of Fraser boasts many of the island's 240-recorded bird species, from brightly coloured lorikeets and honeyeaters to tiny fairy wrens. On the ground echidna and dingoes roam and even beneath it there are earthworms as long as your arm! One of the most pleasant features of Central Station are the crystal clear waters and white sandy bed of **Wanggoolba Creek** which is the main feature on the 450 m boardwalk. Central station also serves as the departure point for some excellent **walking tracks** to Lake MacKenzie and the **Pile Valley** where you will find yourself gazing heavenwards wondering if the trees could possibly grow any taller.

Tours & activities As you might expect there are innumerable tours on offer, from as far away as Brisbane and Noosa. To get the most from the island you really need at least three days so a day tour should only be considered if you are hard pressed for time. Do not be fooled in to thinking you cannot go it alone or need a guide. If you really want to learn about the island you can still do so independently through the excellent **guided tours** on offer through the resorts, especially Kingfisher Bay. Their *Wilderness Adventure Tours*, of three days/two nights (from $270 quad share/ $336 twin) or two days/one night (from $198 quad/ $234 twin) are the most expensive, but for good reason, being very entertaining, professional and with an excellent standard of accommodation, T1800-072555, www.kingfisherbay.com.au Recommended. The Kingfisher resort also offer a day tour (ex Hervey Bay) from $85, child $45 which includes a full guided tour of the island by 4WD. Other reputable tour companies worth looking into include: The *Fraser Island Company*, Hervey Bay, T4125 3933, www.fraserislandtours.com.au, offering a good range of 1-3 day safaris, from $82, child $49. *Fraser Venture*, T1800-249122, offer day tours (ex Hervey Bay) from $82, child $47 and multi-day packages with accommodation at the Eurong Beach Resort. *Fraser Explorer Tours*, T5447 3845, www.fraser-is.com, are a good option if you are coming from Noosa. Their 2-3-day guided adventure tours have the added attraction of arriving on Fraser via Teewah Beach (Great Sandy National Park, Cooloola Section) and Rainbow Beach, from $170-$304. *Tasman Venture II*, Hervey Bay, T4124 3222 offer something different with a West Coast day tour which explorers the quiet and largely inaccessibly beaches of Fraser's west coast, taking in snorkelling and perhaps a bit of dolphin-watching along the way, from $60. *Koala Backpackers*, T1800-466444, www.koala-backpackers.com.au, and *Palace Backpackers*, T1800-063168, offer specialist multi-day, self-drive, budget packages (camping), from $125.

Resources The multi award-winning **LL-L** *Kingfisher Bay Resort*, on the island's west coast, T1800-072555, www.kingfisherbay.com.au, is without doubt one of the best resorts in Australia. More an eco-village than a resort, Kingfisher Bay is highly successful in combining harmonious architecture with superb facilities and a wide variety of accommodation options. Within the main lodge are 2 excellent, if pricey restaurant/bars, with a separate and more affordable bistro/pizzeria and shopping complex nearby. The resort also offers a wide range of activities and tours and hires out its own 4WD vehicles. Backpacker lodges are also available with modern facilities, including a lively bar, but this can only be accessed on their *Wilderness Adventure Tours* programme (see below). Recommended. On the east coast is the older and more traditional **LL-A** *Eurong Beach Resort*, T4127 9122, www.fraser-is.com.au It offers a range of tidy self-contained apartments, motel-style units and cabins as well as some ageing, budget A-frame houses that can accommodate up to 8. Other budget units are also available. There is a spacious, yet characterless, restaurant/bar, a pool and a range of organized tours and activities. Well-stocked shop, café and fuel on site. Though far less salubrious than Kingfisher, it is perfectly comfortable and provides easy access to East Beach. Nearby, the **LL-L** *Fraser Island Beach Houses*, T4127 9207, www.fraserislandbeachhouses.com.au, offer another alternative in Eurong with modern, well-appointed and fully self-contained houses, with pool and spa. Further north (20 km) is the **LL-L** *Fraser Island Retreat*, Happy Valley, T4127 9144, www.fraserislandtours.com.au It consists of 9 fully serviced timber lodges in a quiet bush setting, just off East Beach and near Eli Creek (6 km). Pool, BBQ, Bistro/bar and shop. Nearby, the **LL** *Sailfish Apartments*, Happy Valley, T4127 9494, www.sailfishonfraser.com.au, offers modern 2 bedroom en suites, with pool and spa. A further 13 km sees the **L-E** *Cathedral Beach Resort and Camping Park*, T4127 9177, which is the only non-camping permit park on the island. It offers tidy cabins, on-site tents and vans all with fully equipped kitchens and non-powered sites with hot showers and a shop. There are also a number of fine holiday house lets on Fraser that are ideal for groups or families. The VICs on the mainland have full listings.

QPWS Camping The QPWS have campsites at Central Station, Lake Boomanjin, Lake McKenzie, Lake Allom, Wathumba, Waddy Point and Dundubara. Facilities include toilets and cold showers. There are coin-operated hot showers ($0.50) at Central Station, Waddy Point and Dundubara. Beach camping is permitted all along the east coast and on a few selected sites on the west coast. A nightly fee of $3.85 ($15.40 per family) applies to all campsites (Dundubara and Waddy Point must be pre-booked, all others cannot be pre-booked). **Do not feed the dingoes**

Sleeping & eating

Queensland

Capricorn Coast

*North of Hervey Bay the great sand masses of the Fraser Coast give way to fields of sugar cane and, offshore, the start of the Great Barrier Reef. The first of many Queensland towns borne of the sugar cane industry, **Bundaberg** – or 'Bundy' as it is known – is home to the famous Bundaberg **Rum distillery**. On the coast near Bundy is **Mon Repos**, one of the world's most important and accessible mainland turtle rookeries. Further north is the beautiful, historic (and strangely-named) coastal **Town of 1770**, the first place the Europeans (Captain Cook) set foot in Queensland. Along with **Agnes Waters** it serves as the gateway to the stunning southern reef island of **Lady Musgrave**. Next up is the industrial coastal port of **Gladstone**, not a particularly attractive place but gateway to arguably the most beautiful and popular Barrier Reef resort islands of them all: **Heron Island**. Straddling the **Tropic of Capricorn** just to the north of Gladstone is Queensland's proud and prosperous 'beef capital', **Rockhampton**, and just offshore, **Great Keppel Island**, another of Queensland's many beautiful, tropical island resorts.*

Bundaberg and the Southern Reef Islands

Colour map 4, grid C6
Population: 41,000
368 km north
of Brisbane,
321 km south
of Rockhampton

The small and congenial city of Bundaberg is synonymous with that alcoholic beverage, so beloved of nautical types the world over. Many refer to the city as 'Bundy', though this affectionate nickname is most often used to describe its famous **rum**, distilled in Bundaberg since 1883. Tourism isn't big business here and, aside from backpackers seeking harvest work, those who do come are really only here for the wonderfully sweet smelling **distillery**, which offers daily tours. Other attractions nearby are the day cruises to the southern reef islands of **Lady Musgrave** and **Elliot** from the Bundaberg Port Marina. Also, not to be missed and not far away is the fascinating, seasonal action at the incredible **Mon Repos turtle rookery**, near the coastal resort of **Bargara**.

Ins & outs

Getting there Air The airport is 3 km south of the city centre via the Isis Highway. *Qantas (Sunstate)*, T4152 2322, fly daily to Brisbane, Rockhampton, Mackay and Townsville. The long-distance bus terminal is at 66 Targo St, between Woondooma St and Crofton St. *McCafferty's/Greyhound*, T132030, and *Premier Motor Services*, T133410, offer inter-State services north and south. *The Bundy Express*, T4152 9700, also runs between Bundaberg and Brisbane Mon/Wed/Fri from $40. The train station is right in the heart of city on the corner Bourbong St and McLean St. The *Tilt Train* is the preferred service between Brisbane and Rockhampton but other north/southbound services pass through daily, T132235. *Stewart and Sons Travel*, 66 Targo St, T4152 9700, act as booking agents for air, bus and train operators.

Getting around *Duffy's Coaches*, 28 Barolin St, T4151 4226, serve the city and the Coral Coast (Rum Distillery/Bargara/Burnett Heads/Bundaberg Port Marina) several times daily. **Taxi**, T4151 1612.

Information and orientation The city centre, with its easily negotiable grid-system of streets, nestles on the southern bank of the Burnett River. The main drag is **Bourbong St** that runs east/west and hosts most of the city's major amenities. The reef ferries depart from the **Bundaberg Port Marina**, located on the lower reaches of the Burnett River, about 19 km northeast of the city. The coastal resorts of **Bargara, Burnett Heads** and the **Mon Repos** turtle rookery are 15 km due east. There are 2 **Visitors Information Centres** in Bundaberg. The accredited regional centre is located at 271 Bourbong St, T4152 2333, www.bdtdb.com.au, open daily 0900-1700, while the City Council has its own similar centre at 186 Bourbong St, T4153 9289. Open Mon-Fri 0830-1645, Sat/Sun 1000-1300.

Sights

"Bundaberg rum, over proofed rum, will tan your stomach and grow hair on your bum"

Without doubt the biggest tourist draw in the city is the **Bundaberg Rum Distillery**, first established in 1883. Although a relatively small operation it provides a fascinating insight into the distilling process. The one-hour tour begins with a short video that celebrates the famous Bundy brand, then you are taken to view the various aspects of the manufacturing process, before being decanted into the bar to sample the various end products. Generous distillers they are too, allowing four 'shots', which is just enough to keep you below the legal driving limit. ■ *Tours run daily on the hour Mon-Fri 1000-1500, Sat/Sun 1000-1400, from $7.70, child $2.20. T4150 8684, www.bundabergrum.aust.com Avenue St (4 km east of the city centre, head for the chimney stack!)*. A more sober attraction is the **historical buildings** that dominate the city centre. The VIC has a detailed **Heritage Walk** leaflet listing over 20 other fine examples. A popular retreat is the city's **Botanical Gardens Complex**, 1 km north of the city centre. There is also a working **steam train** that clatters round the gardens on Sundays.

The Mon Repos Turtle Rookery

Supporting the largest concentration of nesting marine turtles on the eastern Australian mainland and one of the largest loggerhead turtle rookeries in the world, the Coral Coast beach, known as Mon Repos (pronounced Mon Repo and 12 km east of Bundaberg), is a place of major ecological importance. During the day Mon Repos looks just like any other idyllic Queensland beach, but at night between mid-October and May it takes on a very different aura. Hauling themselves from the waves, just beyond the tide line, with a determination only nature can display, the often quite elderly females excavate a pit in the sand, then lay over 100 eggs, before deftly filling it in and disappearing beneath the waves, as if they had never been there at all. Towards the end of the season (January-March) the hatchlings emerge from the nest and then, almost simultaneously, like clockwork toys, run headlong towards the water as if their little lives depended on it. And they do. Only 1 in 1000 of the hatchlings will survive to maturity and ever return to the same beach to breed. Of course like any wildlife-watching attraction there are no guarantees that turtles will show up on any given night, so you may need a lot of patience. But, while you wait at the Information Centre to be escorted in groups of about 20 to watch the turtles up close, you can view static displays, or better still, join in the staff's regular and fascinating question and answer sessions, which explain the turtles' natural history, and sadly, the increasing threats humans are placing upon them. The best viewing times for nesting turtles is subject to the night tides and between November-February. Turtle hatchlings are best viewed between 1900-2400, from January-March. **Mons Repos Turtle Sanctuary and Information Centre** is open for turtle viewing October-May, 1900-0600. Ranger guided tours subject to turtle activity. (Information Centre open daily 24 hours October-May, 0600-1800 June-September), $5, child $2.50. T4159 1652. Grange Road (off Bundaberg Port Road).

■ *Daily 0730-1700. Free. Corner Hinkler Av and Gin Gin Rd.* The **Hinkler House Memorial Museum** (T4152 0222) celebrates the courageous life and times of local pioneer aviator Bert Hinkler. Born in Bundaberg in 1892, Hinkler was the first person to fly solo from Australia to England in 1928. Nearby is the **Fairymead House Sugar Museum** (T4153 6786), which documents the history of the region's most important industry. ■ *Both museums are open daily from 1000-1600, $3, child $1.* Slightly further afield (3 km east) is the **Balwin Swamp Environmental Park**, which is an attractive and peaceful area of natural wetland and open parkland, rich in native birdlife. Boardwalks are provided and entry is also free.

The 3-star **A-C** *Bargara Gardens Motel*, 13 See St, Bargara, is a good option on the coast, with self-contained villas in a quiet tropical garden setting. Back in Bundaberg, the Aussie-Irish **B** *O'Ryan's B&B*, 25 Water St, T4151 1865, is one of the few B&Bs in the town and is within walking distance of the city centre. It offers very pleasant, good value studio en suite, queen and twin with shared bathroom and fine home baking. The **E** *Bundaberg Backpackers and Travellers Lodge*, opposite the bus terminal on Targo St, T4152 2080, is under new management, which should hopefully result in much needed improvements. It is a dorms only hostel, friendly and popular with backpackers seeking work. *Bundaberg Aqua Scuba*, T4153 5761, located across the road in the bus terminal complex, also offer budget accommodation from $11.

The best motor park in Bundaberg is the **B-E** *Cane Village Holiday Park*, Twyford St (2 km south of the city centre, off Takalvan St), T4155 1022. It has en suite/standard cabins, powered and non-powered sites and a good camp kitchen. If you are visiting

Sleeping
There are lots of motels along Bourbong St, Takalvan St and Quay St, but if you have your own transport you should head for the seaside resort of Bargara (12 km east), where you will find a number of pleasant low-key resorts and beachside motor parks

Queensland

Mon Repos the 3-star **B-E** *Turtle Sands Tourist Park*, Mon Repos Beach, T4159 2340, is a good option and is within walking distance of the information centre. It has beachside en suite/standard cabins, powered and non-powered sites. Nearby, and closer to Bargara's amenities, is the spacious **C-F** *Bargara Beach Caravan Park*, The Esplanade, Bargara, T4159 2228.

Eating Other than the upmarket motel restaurants there is not much to choose from. The *Numero Uno*, 167A Bourbong St, T4151 3666, is a licensed Italian restaurant offering value pastas and pizzas. Open Mon-Sat 1130-1400/1700-late, Sun from 1700. The *Grand Hotel*, corner Targo and Bourbong St, T4151 2441, has a modern, licensed restaurant offering a traditional pub grub, value breakfasts and good coffee. For a light lunch in quiet surrounds, the *Rose Garden Cafe* in the Botanical Garden, corner Gin Gin Rd and Hinkler Av, T4153 1477, is recommended. Open daily 1000-1600.

Tours & activities **Diving** The southern Barrier Reef Islands present some excellent diving opportunities. *Salty's Dive Centre*, 208 Bourbong St, T4151 6422, www.saltys.net.au, are a very professional outfit offering open water courses with 2 day's theory on the mainland, then 3 out on the reef, from $580. 3-day/3-night reef trips (departing Tue/Fri) from $495. *Bundaberg Aqua Scuba*, 66 Targo St, T4153 5761, julian@aquascuba.com.au, are a small family run dive operator offering a good value, combination accommodation ($11)/ dive course package, from $164. *Bargara Beach Dive*, Shop 4/16 See St, Bargara, T4159 2663, also offer good shore-based courses in small-personalized groups. **Fishing** *Salty's Fishing*, T7153 4747, offer fishing and island camping trips. **Tours** *Footprints Adventures*, T4152 3659, www.footprintsadventures.com.au, offer a wide range of interesting coast and hinterland eco-4WD tours, from 4 days/3 nights ($380) to day trips from $99. Guided (night) turtle watching trips cost from $33, (includes entry to Mon Repos Sanctuary).

Directory **Banks** All the major branches have ATMs and are represented on Bourbong St. **Car hire** *Thrifty* T4151 6222, *Hertz* corner Takalvan St and Twyford St, T4155 2403 **Internet** The *Cosy Corner*, Barolin St (opposite the Post Office). Open Mon-Fri 0700-1930, Sat 0700-1700, Sun 1100-1700. **Post Office** Corner Barolin St and Bourbong St, T4153 2700. Open Mon-Fri 0830-1700, Sat 0830-1200. **Medical services** *Bundaberg Base Hospital*, Bourbong St, T4152 1222. *After Hours Medical Clinic*, Mater Hospital, 313 Bourbong St, T4153 9500. Open Mon-Fri 1800-2300, Sat 1200-2300, Sun 0800-2300. **Police** 254 Bourbong St, T4153 9111.

Lady Musgrave & Lady Elliot islands
Day cruises are also available from the Town of 1770 (see page opposite)

Lady Musgrave Island, 83 km northeast of Bundaberg, is part of the Capricornia Cays National Park and the southernmost island of the Bunker Group. With a relatively small 14 ha of coral cay in comparison to a huge 1192 ha surrounding reef, it is generally considered one of the most beautiful and abundant in wildlife, both above and below the water. The cay itself offers a safe haven to thousands of breeding seabirds and also serves as an important green turtle rookery between November-March. Then, between August-October humpback whales are also commonly seen in the vicinity. With such a large expanse of reef, the island offers some excellent snorkelling and diving and being devoid of the usual holiday resort, a very pleasant escape from the mainland. There is a campsite on the island administered by the QPWS, T4971 6500. No water; fires are banned. Bookings are essential and need to be arranged well in advance. *Lady Musgrave Barrier Reef Cruises*, based at the Bundaberg Port Marina, (19 km northeast of Bundaberg) T4159 4519, www.lmcruises.com.au, offer day trips Monday-Thursday and Saturday (0745-1745), from $130, child $65. Certified diving is available, from $30, introductory dives from $70. Whale-watching trips operate between August-October. Camping transfers are equivalent to two-day cruise fares.

Lady Elliot Island sits out on its own, about 20 km south of Lady Musgrave Island, and is one of the southernmost coral cays on the Barrier Reef. Although the cay itself is larger in size than Musgrave, the surround reef is smaller, yet almost its equal in terms of wildlife diversity. The island is also a popular diving venue with numerous wrecks lying just offshore. The biggest difference between the two is the accommodation and access. The modern **LL-L** *Lady Elliot Island Reef Resort* offers affordable suites, units and tent cabins, all the usual facilities and it has its own airfield. Naturally island activities include diving, from $30. Day-trips (by air) from Bundaberg cost from $219, child $110. Flight Transfers from Bundaberg and Hervey Bay with *Whitaker Air* cost from $168, child $84. T4125 5344, www.ladyelliot.com.au

Agnes Water and Town of 1770

Both 1770 and Agnes Water are fast-developing from being fairly inaccessible, sleepy coastal neighbours, to potentially becoming the next booming tourist destination on the central-southern Queensland coast. As well as great beaches and coastal scenery, the area boasts some excellent surfing, boating, fishing, cruising and tour opportunities, centred around the most northerly surf beach in Queensland, two fine national parks, **Eurimbula** and **Deepwater**, and **Lady Musgrave Island** on the Barrier Reef.

Colour map 4, grid C6 Population: 300 55 km east of Miriam Vale, 125 km north of Bundaberg, 120 km south of Gladstone

Getting there Town of 1770 and Agnes Waters are best accessed from the Bruce Highway at **Miriam Vale** (63 km), or from the south via Bundaberg (120 km). All access roads will soon be completely sealed. **Information** The Miriam Vale 'Discovery Coast' **VIC** is on the Bruce Highway in Miriam Vale, T4974 5428, www.barrierreef.net Open Mon-Fri 0830-1700, Sat/Sun 0900-1700, and the **Discovery Centre**, Endeavour Plaza, Agnes Water, T4974 7002, open daily 0900-1700, are the 2 main sources of local information. The **QPWS** have an office on Captain Cook Dr, Town of 1770, T4974 9350. **Internet** is available at *Daniele's Copy Centre*, Shop 4B Endeavour Plaza, Agnes Waters, T4974 7460. Open Mon-Fri 0900-1700. There is a *Westpac* bank and ATM facilities in the Agnes Waters Shopping Complex.

Ins & outs

1770 and Agnes also serve as the main departure point for local national park and reef island tours. *1770 Environmental Tours*, based at the 1770 Marina, T4974 9422, larc@1770.net, offer an exciting eco/history tour/cruise on board an amphibious vehicle (The LARC) along the coast north of 1770 to **Bustard Head** and Pancake Creek. There are three tours on offer. The *Paradise Tour* (Monday/Wednesday/Saturday 0900-1600) explores the beaches, Aboriginal middens and the stunning **views** from the Bustard Head Light Station and neighbouring cemetery, with a spot of sand boarding en route from $88, child $44. The second offering is the *Sunset Cruise* (daily at 1630) which is a one-hour exploration of Round Hill Creek and the Eurimbula National Park, from $22, child $11. The *Joyride* is the same trip during daylight hours. Book ahead. *Reef Jet*, T4974 9422, is a new cruise operation (under the same Environmental Tours banner) offering exclusive day trips to **Fitzroy Reef** with snorkelling, sea mammal watching, **reef surfing** and scuba diving, from $125, child $65. Snorkelling trips to a 20 acre coral reef in **Pancake Creek** near Bustard Head are also available from $100, child $50. A two-day Reef and LARC combo costs from $190, child $98. *1770 Great Barrier Reef Cruises*, also based at the Marina, T4974 9077, spiritof1770@discoverycoast.net~Web, offer day trips and camping

Tours & activities

transfers to **Lady Musgrave Island** (51 km east of 1770), from $130, child $65 (plus $4 reef tax). The cruise, dubbed the 'See More Sea Less' allows a whole six hours on the reef, including a stop on a floating pontoon that acts as an ideal base for snorkelling, diving and coral viewing. It departs 0800 Tuesday, Thursday, Saturday and Sunday and on demand Monday, Wednesday and Friday. Lunch included and bookings essential. A Shuttle bus is available from Bundaberg. Camping transfers to the island cost $260, child $130. For more information on Lady Musgrave Island see page 298. The *M.V. James Cook*, T4974 9422, offers day **fishing** excursions from $169 per person, and *Discovery Coast Detours*, T4974 7540, offer entertaining **6x 4WD** day tours to the Discovery Coast Hinterland, Wednesday, from $75, child $60 and to Deepwater National Park on Tuesday and Thursday from $65, child $50. If you want to hire your own 4WD contact *1770 4WD hire*, 21 Bicentennial Drive, T4974 9741. *1770 Adventure Tours*, T4974 9470 offer half, full-day and overnight **canoeing** adventures and independent hire.

Deepwater & Eurimbula National Parks

Deepwater National Park, 8 km south of Agnes, presents a mosaic of coastal vegetation including paperbark, banksias and heathland fringed with dunes and a sweeping beach studded with small rocky headlands. As well as fishing and walking it presents some fine opportunities for birdwatching and is often used as a nesting site by green turtles between January-April. There is a QPWS **campsite** (self-registration) at **Wreck Rock**, 11 km south of Agnes. It has toilets, rainwater supply and a cold shower. Fires are banned. Note the roads within the park are unsealed and 4WD is recommended.

To the northwest of Agnes is the **Eurimbula National Park**. Indented by the Round Hill Inlet and Eurimbula Creek it is an area covered in thick mangrove and freshwater paperbark swamps. As such it less accessible than Deepwater and best explored by boat. Other than the interesting flora and fauna, highlights include the panoramic views of the park and coastline from the **Ganoonga Noonga Lookout**, which can be reached by vehicle 3 km from the park entrance (10 km west of Agnes Water). Note 4WD is recommended especially in the wet season. There is a QPWS **campsite** (self-registration) at Bustard Beach with bore water and toilets. Fires are banned. For more information on both parks contact the QPWS in Bundaberg, T4131 1600, or in 1770, T4974 9350. *1770 Environmental Tours* based at the 1770 Marina offer camping transfers from $55.

Sleeping

There's a good range of accommodation in both 1770 and Agnes Water, but you should book ahead around Christmas, New Year and on public holidays

Agnes Waters L *Hoban's Hideaway*, 2510 Round Hill Rd, T4974 9144, hoban@bigpond.com.au, is an award winning B&B, located just before Agnes, offering 4 spacious en suites in a lovely timber colonial style homestead amidst a quiet bush setting. The **A** *Agnes Palm Beachside Apartments*, Captain Cook Dr, T4974 7200, offers modern self-contained apartments with in-house restaurant, while the **A-B** *Mango Tree Motel*, 7 Agnes St, T4974 9132 is slightly cheaper and 150 m from the beach. The new and unusual **C-E** *1770 Backpackers Beachouse*, Captain Cook Dr, T4974 9849, offers dorms and doubles with modern facilities and is run by a caring manager who has been in the backpacking industry for many years. The 2-star **B-F** *Agnes Water Caravan Park*, Jeffery Ct, T4974 9193, is handy for the beach and shops and offers self-contained units, cabins, powered and non-powered sites, but no camp kitchen.

1770 The **L-A** *Beachshacks*, 578 Captain Cook Dr, T4974 9463, beachshack@1770.net, are characterful, spacious and modern fully self-contained bungalows complete with thatched roofs and decks overlooking the beach. **L** *Zamia Lodge*, 3 Zamia Court, T4974 1101, jeffandpatschmidt@bigpond.com.au, is a modern 2-storey house with 2 fully self-contained en suites, one and 2 bedroom with decks in a quiet location. Good weekend deals. Although there is a basic camping ground with powered and non-powered sites near the beach in 1770, T4974 9286, the **A-F** *Captain Cook Holiday Village*, 300 m further inland on Captain Cook Dr, T4974 9219, is recommended. Set in the bush it has a good range of options from self-contained en suite cabins to campsites and a good bistro/bar.

As yet the choice is not exactly vast but things are improving. The *Deck Restaurant* at the **Eating** *Captain Cook Holiday Village* (see above) offers good value, local seafood, great views and a nice atmosphere. Open Tue-Sat for lunch and dinner. In Agnes Water the *Agnes Water Tavern*, 1 Tavern Rd, T4974 9469, is a popular haunt with locals and offers good value counter meals and has a pleasant garden bar. Open daily for lunch and dinner. There is also a bakery (good coffee) and a Chinese restaurant, T4974 9062, open Tue-Sun, lunch and dinner, in the Agnes Waters shopping centre next to the post office.

Despite its increasing popularity the public transport services to Agnes Water and 1770 **Transport** are generally poor, but now that all roads are almost entirely sealed, this situation will no doubt quickly change. *McCafferty's/Greyhound*, T131499, offer part-transfers to Agnes (from the Bruce Highway) stopping at the Fingerboard Junction Service Station (about 30 km south of Agnes and 20 km east of Miriam Vale). The backpackers can pick-up from there. *Barbours Buses*, T4974 9030, offer twice weekly services from Bundaberg. Contact the VIC for latest schedules and fares. For a taxi, T4974 9000. The nearest train station is in **Miriam Vale**, T132232.

Gladstone and Heron Island

Gladstone, named after 19th century British PM, William Gladstone, has *Colour map 4, grid B5* grown dramatically in recent years, from being a sleepy coastal town to one of *Population: 26,500* the most industrialized areas in Australia. It is now home to the country's larg- *554 km north* est aluminium smelter, largest cement operation and Queensland's biggest *of Brisbane,* power station and multi cargo port. Suffice to say, then, it's not a pretty place, *104 km south of* though not completely without tourist merit. It has one of the best **botanical** *Rockhampton* **gardens** in the state, but more significantly is the main access point for **Heron Island**, one of the most beautiful of the Reef Islands.

Getting there and around Air Gladstone airport is in the suburb of Clinton, 7 km **Ins & outs** south of the city centre. *Qantas*, T131313, and *Flight West*, T132392, bookings@flightwest.com.au, offer daily services. **Bus** Gladstone is served by *McCafferty's/Greyhound*, T132030. Long-distance buses stop at the 24 hr Mobil Service Station on Dawson Rd, just off Glenlyon Rd, T4972 3888. **Buslink** (*Gladstone Bus and Coach*), T4972 1670, are the local suburban service provider. **Taxi**, T4972 1800. **Train** The station is on Toolooa St at the end of Tank St (north of the city centre), T4976 4211. Queensland Rail north and southbound services pass through daily. Bookings, T132232. *Travelworld*, 136 Goondoon St, T4972 7277, provide a comprehensive booking service for all the above.

Information and orientation From the north, the **Port Curtis Highway** links the Bruce Highway with Gladstone city centre. Goondoon St is the main drag running northwest to southeast. From Goondoon St, Tank St veers right in to Toolooa St and Benarby Rd, which in turn provides southerly access from the Bruce Highway. The **Gladstone Visitors Information Centre** is located at the modern Marina Ferry Terminal, Bryan Jordan Dr, T4972 4000, www.gladstoneregion.org.au Open Mon-Fri 0830-1700, Sat/Sun 0900-1700. Town **maps** are available on request. The **QPWS** office is on Floor 3, Centre Point Building, 136 Goondoon St, T4972 6055. It offers reef island camping permits and information.

Queensland

Sights **Toondoon Botanical Gardens** are considered one of the best in Queensland. The 55-ha site features exclusively native species, a lake full of turtles and the Mount Biondello bush walk. ■ *Daily (seasonal times) from at least 0900-1700. Free. Café on-site and guided tours are available weekdays. Glenlyon Rd, (southern outskirts of town), T4979 3326.* Gladstone also serves as an excellent and relatively cheap base for **diving**. There are many fine sites around the Capricorn and Bunker groups of reef and coral islands, with Heron Island being considered one of the best dive sites on the reef. The *Backpack and Kayak Outdoor Adventure Store*, 1/37 Goondoon Street, T4976 9283, backpackandkayak@bigpond.com.au, offer an exciting range of dive trips, courses and **sea kayaking** adventures, from $45 (kayaking) to $450 (certification course). Recommended. Other local dive companies include *Last Wave Dive Centre*, 16 Goondoon Street, T4972 9185, and *Deep Blue Adventures*, (gear hire) T4978 7069. The VIC has comprehensive listings of local boat and **fishing** charters. *Sunset Tours*, (Traveland) T4972 2288, offer a range of day or two-day (camping) eco tours around the region from $90 per day.

Sleeping & eating The **L-A** *Auckland Hill B&B*, 15 Yarroon St, T4972 4907, www.ahbb.com.au, is a conveniently located, 4-star B&B in a restored traditional Queenslander, offering 6 spacious en suites and one luxury suite with spa, pool and off street parking. Of the numerous motels in the city the 3-star **A** *Gladstone Reef Motel*, corner of Goondoon St and Yarroon St, has dorms, singles, doubles, campsites and a good kitchen. Bike hire and pick-ups available. The best motor park in town is the **B-E** *Barney Beach Seabreeze Caravan Park*, Friend St, Barney Bay (2 km east of the town centre), T4972 1366. There, enthusiastic staff will escort you to a wide range of en suite/standard cabins, powered and non-powered sites. Good camp kitchen.

Gladstone is renowned for its locally caught seafood and in particular it's Gladstone mud crabs and coral trout. Each year in Oct it celebrates this fact with a *Seafood Festival*, but you can have your own quiet celebrations at *Flinders Seafood Restaurant*, Flinders Parade Corner, Oaka La, T4972 8322, open lunch Mon-Fri from 1100,dinner daily from 1730, or *Swaggy's Australian Restaurant*, 56 Goondoon St, T4972 1653, open lunch Mon-Fri, dinner Mon-Sat. The latter also serves up roo, croc and emu steaks. More affordable meals and $6.50 evening buffet meals are offered at *Yachties* in the Gladstone Yacht Club, 1 Goondoon St, T4972 2294. Open daily from 1200-1400 and 1800-2030. *Fordy's Seafood*, 18A Tank St, T4972 1986, is popular for fish and chips. Open Tue-Sun. Other dining options include *Atrios Café*, Shop 17A Dawson Highway, T4976 9288, open daily, and *Snoops*, Shop 1/72 Goondoon St, T4972 2392, open Mon-Fri 0700-1630.

Directory **Banks** Goondoon St. **Car hire** *Avis*, T4978 2633, and *Hertz*, T4978 4411, are both based at the airport. *Thrifty*, 69 Hanson Rd, T4972 5999. **Communications** Internet *Arthur's Computer Essentials*, 1 Edward St, T4972 0666. Open Mon-Fri 0830-1800, Sat 0830-1300. *Gladstone Library*, 144 Goondoon St, T4970 1232. Open Mon/Tue/Wed/Fri 0930-1745, Thu 0930-1945, Sat 0900-1630. **Post Office** Corner of Goondoon St and Tank St. Open Mon-Fri 0830-1730. **Medical services** Hospital, Kent St, T4976 3200. **Police** 10 Yarroon St, T4971 3222.

Heron Island & the southern coral cays Sitting amongst an extensive complex of reefs, 70 km east of Gladstone, is the tiny and idyllic coral cay known as Heron Island. Made entirely of coral (therefore a cay as opposed to a true 'island') it is world renowned for its wildlife, **diving** and its upmarket (yet not exclusive) resort. Although the reef and its myriad sea creatures is spectacular enough, the island is also the breeding ground of exotic seabirds like noddy terns and a major **green turtle** rookery. Humpback whales are also a common sight from June-November. Not surprisingly, Heron was declared a national park in 1943 and is not open to day visitors. However, note that the southern reef does offer some superb **cay camping** opportunities. The QPWS have bush camps on **Masthead** (65 km) and **North West Islands** (90 km). Take your own water and gas stove. The QPWS office in Gladstone issues permits and provide full details, T4972 1933. Bookings essential.

Sleeping and eating The newly refurbished **LL** *P&O Heron Island Resort*, T132469, www.poresorts.com.au, offers all the facilities you might expect for the location, from luxury suites to beach houses, swimming pool, restaurant, bar, dive shop and a host of other activities. Although much of the focus is on diving, one of the many great attractions of the place is the ability to literally walk from the beach on to the reef. *Harvey World Travel*, 81 Goondoon St, T4972 3488, or *Travelworld*, 136 Goondoon St, T4972 7277, can make bookings and often have cheap stand-by rates in the off season.

Transport Heron is 2 hrs by launch or 30 min by helicopter. The resort launch leaves daily at 1100 from the Gladstone, Marina on Bryan Jordan Dr, Gladstone and costs from $164 return. *Marine Helicopters*, T4978 1177, www.marineheli.com.au, fly daily from Gladstone Airport from $466 return. Masthead and North West Islands must be reached by private boat charter or helicopter.

Rockhampton

Straddling both the **Tropic of Capricorn** and picturesque **Fitzroy River**, Rockhampton, or 'Rocky' as it is affectionately known, is dubbed the **'beef capital'** of Australia. Although most visitors stay only very briefly on their way to sample the coastal delights of Yeppoon and **Great Keppel Island**, 'Rocky' has a number of fine attractions including the 'must see' **Capricorn Caves** and an elegant city centre that is well worth a look. Of course, all self-respecting carnivores will want to sample its gastronomic delights, in the form of its steaks which are the size of some European countries.

Colour map 4, grid B5
Population: 58,000
630 km north of Brisbane, 348 km south of Mackay

Getting there Rockhampton **Airport** is 4 km west of the city centre. *Qantas/Sunstate*, T131313, has regular schedules to main centres north, south and west. A taxi into town costs about $10. The long-distance **bus** terminal, T4927 2844, is located on the corner of Queen Elizabeth Dr and Bridge St, about 500 m north of the Fitzroy Bridge. *McCafferty's/Greyhound*, T132030, and *Premier Motor Services*, T133410, offer north/southbound services. The **train** station is located 1 km south of the city centre at the end of Murray St (off Bruce Highway). The **Tilt Train** is the preferred daily service to Brisbane (6½ hrs), from $81. Other slower services north/southbound are the budget **Sunlander** and luxury **Queenslander**. The *Spirit of the Outback* heads west to Longreach Wed/Sat. There is a travel centre at the station, T4932 0234.

Ins & outs

Getting around *Capricorn Sunbus*, T4936 2133, are the local suburban **bus** company. *Young's Coaches*, 274 George St, T4922 3813, offers regular daily services to the train station, Yeppoon (Route 20, from $15, child $7 return), Rosslyn Bay (cruise boats), Emu Park and Mt Morgan (Route 22). The main terminal is on Bolsover St. *Rothery's Coaches*, 13 Power St, T4922 4320 (bookings T4933 6744), also offer daily services with accommodation pick-ups to Rosslyn Bay Boat Harbour, from $15.40, child $7.70 return. **Taxi** *Rocky Cabs*, T131008

Information Rockhampton Visitors Information Centre, 208 Quay St, T4922 5339, rdpda@ozemail.com.au, is housed in the grandiose 1902 Customs House overlooking the river. Open Mon-Fri 0830-1630, Sat/Sun 0900-1600. The **QPWS** office is on the corner of Yeppoon Rd and Norman Rd, North Rockhampton, T4936 0511. The VIC also stocks QPWS information.

Sights Being a settlement borne of considerable mineral and agricultural wealth, there are numerous stately, **historical buildings** dominating the city centre. These include the 1902 **Customs House** that now houses the VIC, the 1895 **Post Office** (corner East Street Mall and Denham Street), the 1890 **Criterion Hotel** (Quay Street) and the 1887 **Supreme Court** (East Lane), which has been in continuous use now for over a century. The self-guided walk or drive *Rockhampton Heritage* leaflet available from the VIC lists many others. Maintaining the historical theme is the **Rockhampton Heritage Village** which is an 'active township museum' where you can explore the sights and sounds of original buildings, homesteads and businesses of yesteryear. Guided tours available. ■ *Mon-Fri 0900-1500, Sat/Sun 1000-1600 $5.50, child $1.10, family $11, T4936 1026. Boundary Rd off the Bruce Highway (north past Yeppoon turn-off).* Train enthusiasts will also find Rockhampton's tram history revealed at the Archer Park Steam **Tram Museum**. ■ *Tue-Sun 1000-1600, $5.50, child $2.20. Tram operates Sun 1000-1300. Denison St, T4922 2774.* The **Rockhampton Art Gallery**, 62 Victoria Parade, displays a long established collection of mainly 1940s-1970s Australian works and more recent contemporary acquisitions. ■ *Tue-Fri 1000-1600, Sat/Sun 1100-1600. Free. T4936 8248.* The **Dreamtime Centre**, set in 30 acres of parkland just off the Bruce Highway (north), offers a wide range of displays and activities, from boomerang throwing to playing the 'didge'. Guided tours are available daily

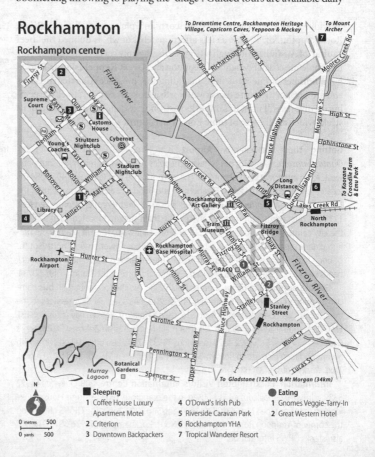

Rockhampton

Rockhampton centre

To Dreamtime Centre, Rockhampton Heritage Village, Capricorn Caves, Yeppoon & Mackay

To Mount Archer

Fitzroy River

Fitzroy St

Haynes St

Richardson St

Alexandra St

Moores Creek Rd

Main St

Musgrave St

High St

Bruce Highway

Elphinstone St

Supreme Court

Quay St

East St Mall

Customs House

Cybernet @

Strutters Nightclub

Young's Coaches

Denham St

East La

William St

Botsover La

Alma St

Stadium Nightclub

Millers La

Market St

East St

Library

Lions Creek Rd

Campbell St

Rockhampton Art Gallery

Victoria Par

North St

Tram Museum

Denison St

Rockhampton Base Hospital

Rockhampton Airport

Hunter St

Western St

Eton St

Agnes St

Canning St

Murray St

Fitzroy St

RACQ

William St

Quay St

Long Distance

Queen Elizabeth Dr

Bridge St

Lakes Creek Rd

To Koorana Crocodile Farm & Emu Park

North Rockhampton

Fitzroy Bridge

Fitzroy River

Stanley Street

Rockhampton

Caroline St

Bruce Highway

Stanley St

Wood St

Lucas St

Ann St

Pennington St

Upper Dawson Rd

Spencer St

Botanical Gardens

Murray Lagoon

To Gladstone (122km) & Mt Morgan (34km)

N

0 metres 500
0 yards 500

■ **Sleeping**
1 Coffee House Luxury Apartment Motel
2 Criterion
3 Downtown Backpackers
4 O'Dowd's Irish Pub
5 Riverside Caravan Park
6 Rockhampton YHA
7 Tropical Wanderer Resort

● **Eating**
1 Gnomes Veggie-Tarry-In
2 Great Western Hotel

Queensland

at 1030 and 1300, dance performances are usually held on Mondays, and there is the ubiquitous café and souvenir shop. ■ *Mon-Fri 1000-1530, $12, child $5.50. T4936 1655.*

On Spencer Street are the spacious **Botanical Gardens** that were first established in 1869. Amongst its leafy avenues of palms and cycads are a fernery, a Japanese garden and the peaceful garden tearooms. ■ *Open 0600-1800. Free. Guided walks Tue-Thu from 0930, $3. T4922 1654.* The **Koorana Crocodile Farm** on Coowonga Road, about 33 km east of the city on the Emu Park/Rockhampton Road, was the first private croc farm established in Queensland and is home to some mighty large specimens. Tours are at 1030-1200 and 1300-1430 and there is an interesting video presentation which informs us that crocodile dung was once used for contraception (quite how, thankfully, remains a mystery). ■ *1000-1500. $12, child $6. T4934 4749.*

The fascinating **Capricorn Caves**, 23 km north of Rockhampton, are well worth a visit. An entertaining guided tour takes you through numerous 'collapsed' caverns, beautifully lit caves and narrow tunnels, to eventually reach a natural amphitheatre where stunning acoustics are demonstrated with classical music and then, utter silence. The venue is so special it is often used for weddings and Christmas carol concerts. The cave system has been home to tens of thousands of bats and the odd harmless python for millennia, and although very few are seen, it adds that essential 'Indiana Jones' edge. The more adventurous can go on an exhilarating two- to three-hour **caving** tour and come face to face with the bats and pythons while squeezing through the infamous 'Fat Man's Misery'. There is also a café and new lodge/campsite within the grounds. Transport available from Rockhampton. ■ *Daily 0900-1600. Standard tour $13, child $6.50, 3-hr caving with own transport from $45 (1300), with transfers from Rockhampton $55 (not available Tue/Thu), half-day standard tour with transport daily from $33, full-day standard tour with transfers (Sun/Mon/Wed/Fri) from $64. Accommodation packages also available. T4934 2883, www.capricorncaves.com.au Olsen's Caves Rd.*

Sleeping There are plenty of quality places in the centre of the city including the **L** *Coffee House Luxury Apartment Motel*, corner of William St and Bolsover St, T4927 5722, the_coffeehouse@bigpond.com.au It is a very tidy, modern establishment with well appointed fully self-contained apartments, executive and standard rooms and a fine café on site. Internet. Recommended. Nearby and slightly cheaper is **B-D** *O'Dowd's Irish Pub*, 100 William St, T4927 0344, www.odowds.com.au, offering clean and good value single, twin, double and family rooms. The rather plain **B-E** *Rockhampton YHA*, is across the river on MacFarlane St, T4927 5288. It has standard doubles, some with en suite and dorms, a well-equipped kitchen, internet and tours desk. Onward trips to the coast and Great Keppel a speciality. For a traditional, historical edge overlooking the river, try the old fashioned and characterful rooms at the **C-D** *Criterion Hotel*, Quay St, T4922 1225. There are 2 main backpackers in the city. The **C-E** *Downtown Backpackers* (Oxford Hotel), corner of East St and Denham St, T4922 1837 is a clean, no frills place, right in the heart of the city, offering value small dorms, doubles, twins, singles, kitchen and TV room with internet, even a bath. There are numerous **motels** and **motor parks** scattered around the city and along the Bruce Highway. North (23 km) is the new **B-F** *Capricorn Caves Eco-Lodge and Caravan Park*, Capricorn Caves, T4934 2883, www.capricorncaves.com.au and closer to the city, the far more urban, 4-star **A-E** *Tropical Wanderer Resort*, 394 Yaamba Rd (Bruce Highway), T4926 3822. The basic 3-star **E** *Riverside Caravan Park*, next to the river just across the Fitzroy Bridge, 2 Reaney St, T4922 3779, is convenient to the city centre, but only has powered and non-powered sites with limited facilities.

Queensland

Queensland

Eating & entertainment Unless you are a vegetarian of almost religious persuasion, then you hardly need a menu in 'Rocky'. Big around here are the steaks. All the local hotels serve them though the *Criterion*, (Bush Inn) Quay St, T4922 1225, and the *Great Western*, 39 Stanley St, T4922 1862, are the best bets. Both are open daily from about 1100-late. It's not surprising to find a fine vegetarian café in the city. *Gnomes Veggie-Tarry-In*, corner Williams St and Denison La (mind the trains!), T4927 4713, is full of character. It also has live entertainment. Open Mon-Thu 0930-2200, Fri/Sat 0930-2300. For a good meat eater's breakfast and good coffee, try the *Coffee House*, corner William St and Bolsover St, T4927 5722. *O'Dowd's Irish Pub* (see above) offers traditional pub grub and live bands at weekends. The *Strutters Nightclub*, is on East St Mall. Open Wed-Sat from 2000, while sports fans can watch the big screens in the *Stadium Nightclub*, beside the Heritage Hotel on Quay St.

Tours & activities **Farmstay** There are several well renowned farm/station stays in the region, where you can go horse riding, on 4WD adventures and even learn how to milk a cow. They include The *Myella Farmstay*, 125 km southwest of the city, T4998 1290, 2 days-1-night from $143. *Kroombit Station*, T4992 2186, www.kroombit.com.au, offers an holistic outback nature experience with cattle drives, horse riding and 4WD tours (motor park on site). *Naomi Hills Cattle Station*, 160 km west of the city, T4935 9121 is a mining and aboriginal settlement with backpacker accommodation from $35. **Fishing** The **Fitzroy River** which is the largest in Queensland and the second largest in Australia offers fine fishing with barramundi, king salmon, grunter and silver dew to name but a few. *Waikari Fishing Charters*, T4928 8758, offer trips from $66. **River Cruises** *Dowies Paddleboat*, T4939 1379, plies the river from the Botanical Gardens and Murray Lagoon, 1000 and 1400, from $6, child $4. **Tours** *Get-About-Tours*, T4927 5977, offer an excellent, value range of full or half-day or evening tours to numerous locations, including the Capricorn Caves and cattle sale yards, from $30. Accommodation pick-ups. Recommended. *Capricorn Eco-Heritage Tours*, T4936 1655, offer scheduled tours to the Rockhampton Heritage Village, Dreamtime Centre and Capricorn Caves, from 0900 daily. *Little Bent-Wing Bat Tours*, T4927 2055, offer trips to see the comings and goings of tens of thousands of cave dwelling bats from Dec-Jan. Call for details. **Walking Mount Archer** (604 m), which looms large above 'Rocky's' northeastern suburbs, has a fine summit walk and lookout. Access is from the end of Moores Creek Rd, north of the Bruce Highway. Vehicular access to the summit is from Frenchville Rd (off Norman, which is off Moores Creek Rd). The *Great Western Hotels* schedule bull rides, T4922 1862, from $5.50.

Directory **Banks** All the main branches with ATMs are centred in and around the Mall on East St. The *Commonwealth Bank* offer currency exchange services, as do *Travel World* below the Leichardt Hotel on Bolsover St. **Car hire** *Avis*, T4927 3344, and *Hertz*, T4922 2500, are based at the Airport. *Red Spot*, 320 Richardson Rd, T4926 5555 offer some of the best rates in the city. **Communications** Internet *Cybernet*, 12 William St, T4927 3633, open Mon-Fri 0830-1700, or the Library, corner William and Alma St, T4936 8265. Open Mon/Tue/Fri 0915-1730, Wed 1300-2000, Thu 0915-2000, Sat 0915-1630. Book in advance. **Post Office** Corner of Denham St and The East St Mall. Open Mon-Fri 0830-1730. **Medical services** *Rockhampton Base Hospital*, Canning St, T4920 6211. **Police** Corner of Denham St and Bolsover St, T4932 1500. **Useful addresses** RACQ, 134 William St (between Kent La and Campbell St), T4927 2255

Yeppoon & around
Colour map 4, grid B5
Population: 9,000
40 km northeast of Rockhampton

Blessed by a cooling breeze and a string of pretty beaches, the small seaside settlements of Yeppoon, Rosslyn Bay and Emu Park form the main focus of the **Capricorn Coast**. Yeppoon – the largest – offers a wealth of affordable accommodation and safe swimming, while 7 km south, Rosslyn Bay provides the gateway to **Great Keppel Island**. To the north of Yeppoon, the vast coastal wilderness of the **Byfield National Park** offers sanctuary to a rich variety of water birds and is the venue for some fine four-wheel driving adventures. The Capricorn Coast **Visitors Information Centre** is located beside the Ross Creek Roundabout (Yeppoon Road), on the approach to Yeppoon, T4939 4888, www.capricorncoast.com.au ■ *Daily from 0900-1700.* Internet is available at *Dreamers Café*, 4 James Street, Yeppoon.

Getting there and around The 16 km stretch of coast between Yeppoon and Emu Park can be approached from the north (Yeppoon) via the Bruce Highway (Yaamba Rd) and Yeppoon Rd, 6 km north of the Rockhampton city centre, or from the south (Emu Park) via Lakes Creek Rd, 500 m north of the Fitzroy Bridge (Bruce Highway). *Young's Coaches*, 274 George St, T4922 3813, offers regular daily services to Yeppoon (Route 20, from $15, child $7 return), Rosslyn Bay (cruise boats), from $9.45 single, and Emu Park. *Rothery's Coaches*, 13 Power St, T4922 4320 (bookings T4933 6744), also offer daily services with accommodation pick-ups to Rosslyn Bay Boat Harbour, from $15.40, child $7.70 return.

Although most non-natives only stop briefly on their way to Great Keppel Island the surrounding coastline offers plenty to see and do. There are beaches and headlands dotted all along the 16 km stretch of road between Yeppoon and Emu Park. South of Yeppoon the small national parks of **Double Head** (above Rosslyn Harbour) and **Bluff Point**, at the southern end of **Kemp Beach**, provide short walks and viewpoints across to Great Keppel Island. South of the Bluff, Mulambin Beach stretches south to Pinnacle Point and the entrance to **Causeway Lake**, a popular spot for fishing and boating. From there the road skirts Shoal Bay and **Kinka Beach**, (considered by many as the best in the region), before arriving in Emu Park. West of Yeppoon, just of the main highway, is the distinctly knobbly volcanic peak known as **Mount Jim Crow** (221 m), which can be climbed with a bit of scrambling from the old quarry.

To the north of Yeppoon, the seemingly boundless Byfield Coastal Area is one of the largest undeveloped regions on the east coast of Australia and although the vast majority of it is taken up by the inaccessible Shoalwater Bay Military Training Area, the **Byfield National Park**, on its southern fringe, offers plenty of opportunity for nature based recreation, including camping, walking, boating, fishing, birdwatching and **four wheel driving**. The heart of the park and its bush campsites are reached via the Byfield Road and Byfield State Forest. To see the park proper and have any chance of reaching Nine Mile Beach requires 4WD, which is perhaps what makes the park so special. If such luxuries are beyond your budget then you can still get a feel for the place from the 'wetlands' west of the Rydges Resort, or the **Sandy Point** section of the park to the north. Although the road is unsealed it is easily negotiable by 2WD and offers numerous access points to **Farnborough Beach**, where you can have a stretch of lovely beach almost entirely to yourself. The **Rydges Resort** itself is also well worth a look (see below) and offers numerous activities from birdwatching to canoeing. The QPWS office in Rockhampton and the VIC (above) has detailed information on the park and its amenities. *Get-About-Tours*, T4934 8555 (see Rockhampton section), offer 4WD tours to the Byfield Forest from $30. *Central Queensland Camel Treks*, T4939 5248, offer more local and sedate camel rides from $10-$50, or, alternatively, the *Rydges Resort Horse Treks*, Farnborough Road, T4939 5111. You can also jump out of a plane, tandem, with *Capricorn Coast Skydive*, T4939 5248.

Sleeping The **LL** *Rydges Capricorn Resort*, Farnborough Rd, T4939 5111, www.capricornresort.com.au, is a hugely popular resort, set in the perfect beachside spot on the fringe of the Byfield National Park. Though expensive and designed for extended package holidays they often offer very attractive short stay deals, especially on week-days and in the low season. Bookings essential. In contrast, and surpassing even the Rydges Resort in near perfect isolation, is the **L-F** *Ferns Hideaway Resort*, located near Byfield, 50 km north of Yeppoon, T4935 1235, www.fernshideaway.com.au Set deep in the rainforest and beside a creek the colonial-style resort lodge offers log cabins with open fires and spa, basic budget rooms, campsites and a licensed bar and restaurant. The centrally located 3-star **A** *Tropical Nites* Motel, 34 Anzac Pde, T4939 1914, provides another alternative. Further afield in Kinka Beach is the excellent **A-B** *Sunlover Lodge*, 3 Camellia St,T4939 6727, www.sunlover@webcentral.com.au, that offers a fine range of quiet, modern, fully self-contained cabins and villas, some with spa and all within a short stroll to the beach. Although nothing remarkable, the friendly **C-E** *Yeppoon Backpackers*, 30 Queen St, T4939 8080, provides a popular and perfectly comfortable stopover on the way over to Great Keppel Island. It has dorms, doubles, a pool, internet, courtesy bus from Rockhampton and offers wide range of discounted day tours to Great Keppel and elsewhere. The best motor park in the area is the **A-E** *Capricorn Palms Holiday Village*, Wildin Way, Mulambin Beach (1 km south of Rosslyn Bay), T4933 6144. It has everything from deluxe villas to non-powered sites, a good camp kitchen and pool.

Eating For fine dining, or just breakfast in style, the *Rydges Capricorn Resort* is recom-mended (see above). There are 2 in-house restaurants, *The Lagoon* offering contempo-rary Australian (dinner only) and *The Tsuruya Japanese* (lunch and dinner). *The Billabong Café* serves modern Australian and is open for breakfast, lunch and dinner. For bookings, T4939 5111. In Yeppoon there are numerous small affordable eateries along the main drag, **James St**. Elsewhere, the *Keppel Bay Sailing Club*, above the beach on Anzac Pde, T4939 9500, offers value for money and a great view. Open daily for lunch and dinner. The best fish and chips in the area are to be found at the *Causeway Lake Kiosk*, beside the Causeway Bridge (between Rosslyn Bay and Kinka Beach). Daily until about 2000. The *Dreamers Café*, 4 James St, Yeppoon, has good breakfasts, coffee and internet.

Great Keppel Island

Colour map 4, grid B5
Population: nominal

Great Keppel Island (1,400 ha) is the largest of 18 islands in the Keppel group, which sit within easy reach of Rosslyn Bay. For many, Great Keppel provides their first taste of Queensland's profusion of idyllic tropical islands. Although not quite on a par with Magnetic Island off Townsville, Great Keppel still offers a fine introduction, with a wealth of beautiful sandy beaches, pleasant walks and numerous activities. It is also equally accessible and well facilitated with accommodations to suit all budgets.

Ins & outs **Getting there** *Young's Coaches*, T4922 3813, offers regular daily services from Rockhampton to Rosslyn Bay (Route 20), from $9.45 single. *Rothery's Coaches,* T4933 6744, also offer daily services from Rockhampton (*McCafferty's/Greyhound* bus termi-nal and YHA) to link with the Keppel Tourist Services departures, from $15.40, child $7.70 return. Both of the major ferry companies are based at **Rosslyn Bay** Harbour, 7 km south of Yeppoon. *Freedom Fast Cats*, T4933 6244, www.keppelbaymarina. com.au, are based at the new Keppel Bay Marina. They have a travel centre, shop, café and internet. Yacht charters are also available. The basic return fare to Great Keppel (30 mins) is $30, child $15. Ferries depart daily at 0900,1100 and 1500. Freedom also offers a range of cruise packages beyond their basic transfers to Great Keppel. These include a daily **Coral Cruise** in a glass bottom boat with fish feeding, from $49, child $27; an **Adventure Cruise** Tue/Sun with boom netting, beach games, swimming and lunch from $59, child $35; and a daily **Lunch Cruise**, from $59, child $35. Half-day/evening trips that are aimed at backpackers and including transfers to Rockhampton are also on offer weekly, from $40. Book ahead. **Keppel Tourist Services** have a ferry terminal next door to the Keppel Bay Marina, T4933 6744. They offer a very similar range of cruises and provide transfers to Great Keppel at 0730,0915,1130,1530 (and 1800 Fri only), for the same price. Note return times from Great Keppel are around 1 hr after departure from Rosslyn Bay. Secured parking is available 500 m from the Rosslyn Bay Harbour, off the main road, T4933 6670, from $8 per-day. Great Keppel has its own airfield with **Great Keppel Island Air Service**, T4939 5044, providing transfers from Rockhampton.

There are as many sublime beaches on Great Keppel as there are islands in the entire group. Despite having 17 to choose from, few get beyond **Fisherman's Beach** which fronts the main **resorts** and provides ferry access, but it's far better to be more adventurous and seek out the quieter spots. A 20-minute walk to the south is **Long Beach**, which in turn provides access to **Monkey Beach** (35 minutes) across the headland to the west. North of the resort, beyond the spit, is **Putney Beach**, which offers pleasant views across to Middle Island. There are numerous **walks** around the island with the most popular being the 45-minute trek to **Mount Wyndam**, the highest point on the island. Longer excursions will take you into the realms of solitude and the island's northeast coast beaches, including Svendsen's, **Sandhill** and Wreck Beach. Walking maps and descriptions are readily available from the ferry companies and resorts. Naturally, the main hub of activity on the island centres around the island's resorts, all of which fringe Fisherman's Beach. All the main accommodation establishments offer their own range of **activities** and tours, but day-trippers can access a wealth of water-based activities and equipment from the beach hut directly opposite the ferry drop off. There you can secure anything from parasailing ($60) to snorkel gear ($10) and even a humble beach umbrella for $6. You can also take a **camel ride** or be flung about on a large inflatable banana. The island offers some fine snorkelling and **diving**. *Keppel Reef Scuba Adventures*, have a dive shop just beyond the Spit on Putney Beach, T4939 5022, www.keppeldive.com.au Qualified dive from $77 including gear, introductory dive from $99, depart 0830 daily. They also offer island and beach drop-offs. The *Great Keppel Island Holiday Village*, T4939 8655, offer excellent **sea kayaking** trips from $35.

Beaches & activities

The LL *Great Keppel Island Resort*, T4939 5044, wwwgkeppel.com.au, is the main resort on the island located at the southern end of Fisherman's Beach. It has all the usual accommodation options from luxury villas to standard rooms, a restaurant, bar, nightclub café, pool, spas and over 40 activities. The pricey *Keppel Café*, bar and nightclub is open to non-guests. The **L-E** *YHA Great Keppel Island Backpackers Village*, T4927 5288, yhagreatkeppelisland@bigpond.com.au, is a large complex located at the northern end of Fisherman's Beach. It offers a vast range of options from group cabins sleeping up to 8 to the basic tent village. Part of the complex has just been completely renovated providing modern budget facilities. Bistro, bar and games area. The **A-E** *Great Keppel Island Holiday Village* ('Geoff and Dianna's Place'), T4939 8655, wwwgkiholidayvillage.com.au, is a laid-back place next door to the YHA complex, offering everything from a fully self-contained house to cabins, doubles/twins, dorms and custom-built tents. Fully equipped kitchen, free snorkel gear and organized kayak trips. The VIC on the mainland also has details of several self-contained holiday houses on the island. Other than the resort eateries, there is *Keppel Island Pizza* located on the waterfront. Open daily (except Mon) 1230-1400, 1800-2100. The limited groceries available at the YHA resort are pricey so you are advised to take your own food supplies.

Sleeping & eating
The island is known for offering a wide range of accommodation from luxury to budget. Before making a decision on accommodation, budget travellers should look in to the packages available from each, or from Rockhampton/ Yeppoon backpackers

Queensland

Other
Keppel Islands
Note all the
slands have a
complete fire ban

While Great Keppel Island is the main focus of activity, some of the other little islands offer more solitude, good snorkelling and camping opportunities. **Middle Island**, just north of Great Keppel, is home to an **underwater observatory** that sits above a sunken Taiwanese **wreck** teeming with monster cod and other bizarre sea creatures. The Rosslyn Bay ferry companies offer cruises daily, T4933 6744. There is a QPWS campsite on the island, but you will need to take your own water and a gas stove. Other QPWS **campsites** are located at Considine Beach on **North Keppel Island** and **Humpy Island**, which is renowned for its good snorkelling. Both sites have seasonal water supplies and toilets. For more details and permits contact the QPWS office in Rockhampton, T4936 0511 or Yeppoon, T4933 6619. **Pumpkin Island** (6 ha), just to the south of North Keppel, is a privately owned island offering five self-contained cabins sleeping five to six (from $130) and a camping area with fresh water, toilet, shower and BBQ (from $10), T4939 4413. Other than Middle Island all water transport must be arranged privately through the Keppel Bay Marina, T4933 6244, or *Keppel Reef Scuba Adventures* on Great Keppel (see above).

Central Coast

The Central Queensland Coast, between Rockhampton and Cairns is, for many, the very essence of an Australian beach holiday. Mackay, the sugar producing capital of Australia, is used as a base to explore the reef island groups of **Brampton**, **Newry** *and* **Carlisle**. *Just inland the magnificent* **Eungella National Park** *offers slopes draped in lush rainforest, wonderful waterfalls and unusual wildlife. Back on the coast and beyond the delights of the* **Cape Hillsborough National Park**, *the rush is on to reach the fast developing, coastal tourist resort of* **Airlie Beach** *– the gateway to the unimaginabley wonderful* **Whitsunday Islands**. *North of Whitsunday is Queensland's 'northern capital',* **Townsville**. *Just offshore* **Magnetic Island** *certainly lives up to its name, attracting tourists with its beautiful beaches and infectious laid-back atmosphere. Inland from Townsville, the historic and friendly gold-mining town of* **Charters Towers** *offers many their first taste of Queensland 'outback'. Between Townsville and Cairns,* **Mission Beach** *is like a mainland version of Magnetic Island and, as always, the offshore reef and tropical islands beckon.*

Mackay

Colour map 4, grid A4
Population: 75,000
340 km north
of Rockhampton,
732 km from Cairns

Driving towards Mackay at night in early summer is a surreal experience. For miles around the oceans of **sugar cane** fields are awash with the orange glow of flames that illuminate the heavens. Although the burning of harvested cane fields, in preparation for the next crop, is both a traditional and common practice, for the visitor it can look like the very world is on fire. Ever since Scots pioneer John Mackay recognized the region's agricultural potential in 1862 it has grown to become the largest sugar producing area in Australia and now hosts the biggest bulk sugar facilities in the world. Although not particularly tourist oriented, Mackay still provides a welcoming halfway stop between Brisbane and Cairns, and in itself has much to offer. As well as being the gateway to several Barrier Reef and Whitsunday Islands, Mackay is also a fine base from which to explore the superb **Eungella** and **Cape Hillsborough National Parks**. Paramount amongst the few activities on offer is diving, though simply recharging the travel batteries and soaking up the sun and the views on Mackay's excellent **Northern Beaches** may prove activity enough.

Getting there Air Mackay Airport, T4957 0255, is 2 km south of the city centre, along Sydney St and is served by *Qantas* T131313 (4 flights daily to Brisbane). *Whitsunday Island Air Taxis*, T4946 9933, www.heliaust.com.au, offer shuttle services to Proserpine and Hamilton Island from $120 one-way. Taxis meet all flights and cost about $9 into town. **Bus** Mackay is served by *McCafferty's/Greyhound*, T132030, which stop at the terminal on Milton St (between Victoria and Gordon St), T4951 3088. The **train** station is 5 km southwest of the city centre on Connor's Rd (between Archibald St and Boundary Rd of the Bruce Highway). *Queensland Rail*, T132332. Again taxis meet most trains and will cost about $10 into the city centre. Regular buses to city centre from Nebo Rd (Bruce Highway)

Getting around *Mackay Transit*, Casey Av, T4957 3330, www.mackaytransit.com.au, is the local hail 'n' ride suburban **bus** service offering services to the Northern Beaches (Mon-Fri, route 7) and Mirani (Pioneer Valley) on Thu only. A 'Day Rover' ticket costs $5.60, child $3.40. Mackay **Taxis** (24 hr), T131008.

Information The *Mackay Visitors Information Centre* is housed in a former sugar mill at 320 Nebo Rd (Bruce Highway), T4952 2677, www.mackayregion.com.au It offers full bookings services for local and Island accommodation and tours. Open Mon-Fri 0830-1700, Sat/Sun 0900-1600. The **QPWS** office is on the corner of River St and Wood St in the centre of town, T4944 7800. Offers information and permits for island and national park camping. Mon-Fri 0830-1700.

Ins & outs

Although most of the Mackay's attractions are to be found beyond the city limits, the city centre with its tropical palm-lined main street and pleasant river views is worth a look around. **Greenmount Historic Homestead** near Walkerston (15 km) is a beautifully preserved 1912 original built on the land first settled by Captain John Mackay the city's founding father. Gloria Arrow the former owner's maid is still on hand to provide a guided tour and genuine insight. ■ *Mon-Fri 0930-1230, Sun 1000-1500, $6, child $3 (includes tour), T4959 2250. Signposted from Walkerston (Peak Downs Highway).* The **Northern Beaches** of Mackay are well known for their tropical beauty and fine swimming. The best spots are at Black's Beach, Dolphin Heads (Eimeo

Sights

Queensland

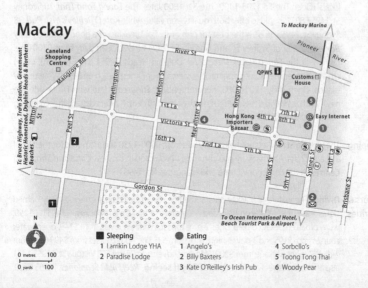

Mackay

Sleeping
1 Larrikin Lodge YHA
2 Paradise Lodge

Eating
1 Angelo's
2 Billy Baxters
3 Kate O'Reilley's Irish Pub
4 Sorbello's
5 Toong Tong Thai
6 Woody Pear

Beach) and Bocasia Beach. They are best accessed from the Mackay-Bucasia Road of the Bruce Highway. With so much sugar cane around it would be rude not to visit one of the local sugar mills. The **Fairleigh Sugar Mill** is in Fairleigh (northwest of Mackay). ■ *Mon-Fri at 1300 during the crushing season (Jun-Nov). Access and tour $14, child $7.50, T4957 4727.* To the southwest the **Polstone Sugar Cane Farm**, Masottis Road, Homebush, T4959 7298, also offer tours. ■ *Mon, Wed, Fri at 1330, Jun-Nov.*

Sleeping The **LL** *Ocean International Hotel*, 1 Bridge Rd, T4957 2044, is considered the best hotel in town, due as much to its beachside position as its level of hospitality. It offers luxury rooms with spa bath, standard rooms, a restaurant, bar, pool, sauna, and so on. Just about as classy, though slightly cheaper, is the **L** *Whitsunday Waters Resort*, on Beach Rd, Dolphin Heads, about 12 km north of the city centre, T4954 9666, www.whitsundaywaters.com.au For a **motel** look no further than Nebo Rd (Bruce Highway). Some of the better offerings in order of price are the **A** *White Lace* (73-75), T4951 4466 and the **A-B** *Rose Motel* (164). Opposite the bus terminal in Peel St is **B** *Paradise Lodge*, T4951 3644. The mainstay **backpackers** in Mackay is the *Larrikin Lodge YHA*, 32 Peel St (200 m south of the bus terminal), T4951 3728, larrikin@mackay.net.au It offers standard dorms, doubles and 1 family room with all the usual facilities in a traditional 'Queenslander'. Internet and entertaining in-house tours to Eungella National Park (Jungle Johno's). There are several good **motor parks** within the city limits. To the north (10 km) is the 3-star **B-F** *Bucasia Beachfront Caravan Park*, 2 Esplanade, Bucasia Beach, T4954 6375, which has self-contained villas, cabins, powered and non-powered sites and offers memorable views across to the Whitsunday Islands. In the south and 4 km to the city centre, is the 4-star **B-E** *Beach Tourist Park*, 8 Petrie St, Illawong Beach, T4957 4021. It offers villas, cabins, powered and non-powered sites, a good camp kitchen and internet. It is beachside but don't expect to go swimming at low tide or you'll have a 3-km walk to reach the water!

Eating *Sorbello's*, 166B Victoria St, T4957 8300 and *Angelo's*, 29 Sydney St, T4953 5111, fight it out as to who is the best Italian restaurant. Both open lunch/dinner daily from 1130. Nearby, the *Woody Pear*, 7 Wood St, T4957 4942, tries to keep the peace with a nice interior and congenial ambience. Its varied international fare is also popular with the locals. (Open Tue-Fri 1200-1400, Tue-Sat 1800-late). The *Toong Tong Thai*, 10 Sydney St, T4957 8051, is said to offer both quality and value while *Kate O'Reilley's Irish Pub*, 38 Sydney St, T4953 3522, is the best for pub grub. For breakfast or a good coffee try *Billy Baxters*, corner of Sydney St and Gordon St, T4944 0173. Open daily from 0700-late. Elsewhere the *Eimeo Hotel*, Mango Av, Dolphin Heads, T4954 6106 (12 km), offers cheap counter meals with spectacular views over Eimeo Beach and the Whitsunday Islands. Open daily 1200-2000. Recommended. *Stingrea's*, Mulherin Dr, beside the new *Mackay Marina* development north of the city centre, offers casual alfresco dining from 0700 daily, T4955 5600.

Shopping The Victoria St markets are held every Sun from 0900-1230 and are noted for their local arts and crafts. Alternatively you can shop til you drop at the new *Caneland Shopping Centre*, on the corner of Victoria and Mangrove Rd, T4951 3311.

Tours & activities **Diving** The waters of Mackay offer some fine diving including such evocatively named sights as the 'Catacombs' and 'Credlin'. *Pro Dive Mackay*, T4951 1150, www.prodivemackay.com.au, offer 2-dive trips for certified divers from $149, open water courses from $195 and 3-day/3-night trips from $355 or 5-day courses from $499 (Discount 2-dive/2-night package from $209). *Mackay Adventure Divers*, 153 Victoria St, T4953 1431 also offer courses, reef and wreck dives. **Flight seeing** *Reef Flight Seaplanes*, T4953 0220, offer a wide range of reef adventure flights and trips including the popular Bushy Reef Lagoon trip with stopover and snorkelling from $194. *Osprey Air*, T4953 3261, whitsundayheli@bigpond.com, also offer helicopter flights over Mackay and the reef.

Skydiving The folks at *Mackay Parachute Centre*, 9 Elamang St, T4957 6439, will happily strap you to their front and jump out of a plane from 10,000 ft. Prices on application.

Tours *Jungle Johno Tours*, T4951 3728, is a popular outfit, offering entertaining eco tours and camping trips to Eungella National Park and the Finch Hatton Gorge. Platypus spotting is a speciality, from $75. *Mackay Reeforest Tours*, T4953 1000, offer a wider range of day tours to Hillsborough and Eungella National Parks and the Moranbah open cast coal mine, from $85, child $53, family $255.

Banks *Commonwealth* (currency exchange), *Westpac*, *National* and *ANZ* branches are centred around the intersection of Victoria and Sydney St. **Bike hire/car hire** *Avis*, Mackay Airport, T136333, *Network Rentals*, 196 Victoria St, T4953 1022, *AAA Rentals*, 6 Endeavour St, T4957 5606. **Communications** Internet *Hong Kong Importers Bazaar*, 128 Victoria St, T4953 3188, Mon-Fri 0845-1715, Sat/Sun 0900-1400 or *Easy Internet*, 22 Sydney St, T4953 3331, Mon-Fri 0830-1730, Sat 0800-1300. **Post Office** Corner of Sydney St and Gordon St). Mon-Fri 0800-1700. **Medical services** *Mackay Base Hospital*, Bridge Rd, T4968 6000. **Police** Sydney St, T4968 3444.
Directory

Around Mackay

The islands of Brampton (464 ha) and Carlisle (518 ha) are part of the Cumberland Islands National Park that lie 32 km northeast of Mackay. Both are practically joined by a sandbank that can be walked at low tide and have a rich variety of island habitats, rising to a height of 389 m on Carlisle's Skiddaw Peak and 219 m on Brampton's eponymous peak. The waters surrounding both islands are part of the Mackay/Capricorn Section of the Great Barrier Reef Marine Park, offering some excellent dive sites. There are 11 km of **walking** tracks on Brampton giving access to Brampton Peak as well as several secluded bays and coastal habitats. In contrast walking on Carlisle Island is rough with no well-formed paths. Instead you are better to explore the beaches or take to the water with a **snorkel** and mask, especially in the channel between the two islands.
Brampton & Carlisle Islands

Sleeping Brampton is home to a mid-range family oriented **LL-L** *Brampton Resort*, T1800-737678, www.brampton.com.au, but there is no camping allowed. Carlisle Island has a basic **QPWS campsite** but all supplies must be imported. There is a seasonal water tank but a back-up supply should be taken anyway. Basic bush campsites are also available on Goldsmith, Scawfell, Cockermouth, Keswick and St Bee's Islands. Permits apply to all sites.

Transport Air *Qantas*, T131313, offer daily flights to Brampton from major Australian capital cities. Local companies also offer flights from Hamilton Island and a daily service from Mackay. A launch service for resort guests is available from Thu-Mon, at 1130 from Mackay Marina, T4951 4499. Day trips are not available and the minimum stay is 1 night. Campers can take the scheduled launch (from $50 return) and walk to the QPWS campsite or, alternatively arrange to be ferried directly to the island through the resort. For more information contact the **QPWS** office in Mackay, T4944 7800.

The Newry group consist of six national park islands situated 50 km northeast of Mackay. Like the Cumberlands, they are hilly, diverse in coastal habitat types and rich in wildlife, including sea eagles, ospreys, echidna and bandicoots.
Newry Islands

Queensland

Green sea turtles also nest between November-January on **Rabbit island**, the largest of the group. There are 2 km of walking tracks on Newry Island that lead through rainforest and open forest to elevated viewpoints. Again the waters that surround the islands are part of the Great Barrier Reef Marine Park.

Sleeping Newry Island plays host to a small, low-key **resort** with basic cabin-style accommodation, T4959 0214. The QPWS has a **campsite** with toilets and a seasonal water tank on Rabbit Island and a hut (maximum 10 at any one time) on Outer Newry Island. *Seaforth Fishing Tours*, Seaforth (23 km north of Mackay), T4959 0318, offer **transfers** for campers.

Hillsborough National Park   Although positively petite compared to most of Queensland's other mainland national parks, Hillsborough is no less impressive, boasting some superb coastal habitats, views and beaches. It is also famed for its tame, beach-loving wildlife, including grey **kangaroos**, the aptly named pretty-faced **wallabies** and the distinctly more ugly faced scrub **turkeys**. There are four **walking** tracks ranging in length from 1 to 3 km , including the 1.2 km **Juipera Plant Trail**, which highlights the food plants once utilized by the Juipera Aboriginal people. A small QPWS camp ground with limited fresh water is available at Smalley's Beach at the western end of the park, T4959 0410. Alternatively, the **B-F** *Cape Hillsborough Nature Resort*, Casuarina Bay, T4959 0262, www.capehillsboroughresort.com.au, can better accommodate you with beachfront cabins, motel units or powered and non-powered sites. There is a small store and restaurant on site.

Eungella National Park and the Pioneer Valley

The 80 km inland excursion via the Pioneer Valley from Mackay to Eungella (pronounced 'young-galah') offers an excellent diversion from the coast and access to what the aboriginal people once called 'the land of the clouds'. And whether shrouded in mist or gently baking under the midday sun, Eungella and its exquisite national park possess a rare magic.

Immediately west of Mackay, the Mackay-Eungella Road branches off the Peak Downs Highway and follows the southern bank of the Pioneer River to the small settlement of **Marian**, surrounded by a vast sea of sugar cane and home to the largest mill in the district. Just beyond **Mirani**, 10 km further west of Marian, is the **Illawong Fauna Sanctuary**, T4959 1777, which is well worth a stop. The sanctuary also has accommodation a café and its own tour company, *Gem Tours*. ■ *Daily 0900-1730, $11, child $5.50*. A further 29 km past Mirani, beyond the small hamlet of Gargett and 1 km east of Finch Hatton Township, is the turn-off to the **Finch Hatton George** section of the Eungella National Park. In the dry season the 10 km road is suitable for 2WD, but in the wet, when several creek crossings are subject to flooding, the final 6 km of gravel road often requires 4WD. At the gorge there is a private **bush camp** (see below), picnic site and access to the memorable **Wheel of Fire Falls Walk** (5 km return) and **Araluen Falls Walk** (3 km return).

Back on the main highway, the road heads towards the hills before ascending suddenly and dramatically, 800 m up to the small and pretty township of **Eungella**. At the crest of the hill is the historic **Eungella Chalet**, with its spacious lawns, swimming pool and views to blow your wig off. As well as being an ideal spot for lunch, it is also the perfect venue for hang-gliding. From the chalet the road veers 6 km south, following the crest of the hill, before arriving at **Broken River**. Here you will find a picnic area, QPWS campsite, and the associate Eungella National Park Ranger Station, where you can find information on the numerous and excellent short walks in the vicinity. ■ *Daily 0800-0900/1130-1230/1530-1630. T4958 4552.* There is also a **platypus** viewing platform nearby, but bear in mind the little characters are seen just about the same time as the average cock crows. Eungella National Park is also home to the Eungella honeyeater, the brown thornbill and the bizarre Eungella gastric brooding frog, which gets its name from the fact that it incubates its eggs in the stomach before spitting the young out of its mouth.

Finch Hatton Gorge The **C-F** *Platypus Bush Camp*, Finch Hatton Gorge Rd, T4958 3204, www.bushcamp.net.au, offers a superb and authentic bush camping experience. Created and maintained by a friendly and laid-back bushman called 'Wazza', it features basic open-air huts and campsites, set amongst the bush and beside the river. The huts range from single, through doubles to the notably more distant 'Honeymoon Hut'. Other camp features include an open-air communal kitchen, a sauna (all constructed from local cedar wood) and a fine swimming hole. Campfires are also authorized. Recommended (especially in the rain!).

Eungella As well as the magnificent views the **A-D** *Historic Eungella Chalet*, T4958 4509, has a wide range of options from self-contained cabins with open fires to motel rooms and backpacker (weekday only) beds, an à la carte restaurant, public bar and swimming pool. The **B-F** *Eungella Holiday Park*, North St, T4958 4590, www.eungella-holidaypark.com.au (take the first right beyond the chalet) has a self-contained cabin, powered and non-powered sites and the internet. The *Hideaway Café*, just beyond the chalet is well worth a stop. Take a tour of the imaginative and truly international menu while supping a coffee and soaking up the views across the valley, T4958 4533. Open daily 0800-1700.

Broken River The **L-B** *Broken River Mountain Retreat*, T4958 4528, www.brokenrivermr.com.au, has a range of studio, 1 and 2 bedroom self-contained cabins, restaurant (open to the public) and an exciting range of in-house activities from night spotting to canoeing. Across the river the **QPWS** campsite has toilets, drinking water, showers and gas BBQs. Permits available at the Ranger Station, T4958 4552. There is a small food kiosk attached to the ranger Station.

Sleeping & eating

There is no public transport to Eungella, though it is often possible to make arrangements with local tour operators, particularly *Jungle Johno Tours*, T4951 3728 (see page 313).

Transport & tours

Airlie Beach

From a sleepy coastal settlement, Airlie Beach and its neighbouring communities of **Cannonvale** and **Shute Harbour** (known collectively as **Whitsunday**) have developed into the principal gateway to the **Whitsunday Islands**, the biggest tourist attraction between Brisbane and Cairns. With over 74 of these Islands to choose from, it is no surprise that little Airlie has seen more dollars spent in the name of tourism in recent years than almost anywhere else in the State. Most people simply use Airlie as an overnight stop on the way to the island resorts or a multi-day sailing/dive cruise, but the town itself can be a great place to party and meet people, or just relax and watch the world go by.

Colour map 4, grid A4
Population: 3,000
160 km north of Mackay, 308 km south of Townsville

Getting there The long-distance **buses** stop in the car park beside the lagoon right in the heart of town or next to the Sailing Club in the Recreation reserve to the east. Either way most accommodation is within walking distance or you will be met by private shuttle. *McCafferty's/Greyhound*, T132030, offer regular daily services. *Aussie Magic Bus*, T1800-449444 offer northbound services to Cairns (via Townsville and Mission Beach) on

Ins & outs

Queensland

Sat/Mon/Thu and southbound services to Sydney (via all major coastal centres) on Mon/Wed/Sat. The nearest **train** station is in Proserpine 36 km west of Airlie (8 trains weekly, for bookings *Queensland Rail*, T132232). The train station is served by *Whitsunday Transit*, T4946 1800, that link Proserpine with Airlie Beach and Shute Harbour and meets all arrivals, from $6.50. The nearest **airports** are in Proserpine and Hamilton Island. Both are served by *Qantas*, T131313, and Flight West (from Brisbane daily), T1300-130092. *Island Air Taxis*, T4946 9933, provide local island transfers. Again, Whitsunday Transit buses meet all incoming flights in Proserpine. For **island ferry connections** see Whitsunday Islands section below.

Getting around   *Whitsunday Transit*, T4946 1800, offer regular daily **bus** services from Proserpine to Shute Harbour (through Airlie). Services between Cannonvale and Shute Harbour operate daily between 0600-1845, from $4.50 one way, with further services between Airlie Cove and Adventure Whitsunday from 1900-2230. A day pass costs $8. **Mokes** and **scooters** can be hired from *Whitsunday Moke and Scooter Hire*, 1 Laurence Cl, Cannonvale, T4948 0700. **Bikes** can be hired from some backpackers and Water's Edge Luxury Apartments, 4 Golden Orchid Dr, T4948 2655, full-day $20. For a **taxi** call *Whitsunday Taxis* T131008.

Orientation and information   Airlie Beach is situated 36 km east of Proserpine, where you will find the Whitsunday Visitors Information Centre, Bruce Highway, Proserpine, T4945 3711, www.whitsundayinformation.com.au/www.airliebeach.com.au It is the main accredited VIC for the region. The coastal settlement of Airlie Beach is the main focus for mainland accommodation and amenities. Its main drag (Shute Harbour Rd) runs south, linking it to Shute Harbour, which is the main departure point for the Whitsunday islands. The fairly non-descript settlement of Cannonvale lies just west of Airlie Beach. There are numerous independent and commission based information centres in Airlie Beach and you are advised to get the non-biased information from the

Airlie Beach

Airlie Bay

■ **Sleeping**	6 Coral Sea Resort	● **Eating**	6 Paddy Shenanigans
1 Airlie Beach	7 Koala Backpackers	1 Boltz Café & Bar	& Tricks Nightclub
2 Airlie Waterfront B&B	8 Magnums	2 Burgers in Paradise	7 Sidewalk Café
3 Beaches	Backpackers	3 Chatz Bar & Brasserie	
4 Club 13	9 Whitsunday	4 Courtyard	
5 Club Habitat	Wanderers Resort	5 KC's Bar & Grill	

0 metres 100
0 yards 100

accredited VIC before arriving. Failing that try Destination Whitsundays, upstairs corner Shute harbour Rd and The Esplanade, T1800-644563. Open daily 0800-2200. The **QPWS** office is very helpful and is located south of Airlie Beach on the corner of Mandalay St. They can supply the latest island camping information and issue the necessary permits, T4946 7022. Open Mon-Fri 0900-1700, Sat 0900-1300. There are numerous **travel centres** in Airlie including the helpful *Backpackers Travel Centre*, 257 Shute Harbour Rd, T4946 5844.

Airlie offers little in the way of 'sights', but if you have some time to spare there are a few venues worthy of investigation. Right in the heart of town, and the focus for many, is the new and glorious **lagoon** development. In the absence of a proper beach and the insidious threat of marine stingers (October-May) it has to be said that the local authorities have created a fine substitute. Elsewhere, on Waterston Road, off Shute Harbour Road, and accessed through the huge gaping jaws of a model shark is the **Vic Hislop Great White Shark Expo**, less a museum than an egocentric display of Hislop's personal vendetta against the mighty Great White. ■ *Daily 0900-1800, $16.* From one enormous and alarming set of gnashers to another, a more varied, if no less scary wildlife experience can be had at the **Barefoot Bushman's Wildlife Park** in Cannonvale. Here you can acquaint yourself with a wide array of nasty natives from the ubiquitous crocodile or taipan to the more folk-friendly and eminently more cuddly koala or roo. ■ *Daily 0900-1630, $20, child $10. Snake show 1100, croc-feeding 1200/1400. T4946 1480. 7 km west of Airlie on Shute Harbour Rd.* To spot your own wildlife take a quiet and congenial walk in a section of the **Conway National Park** between Airlie and Shute Harbour. There is a self-guided 6½ km circuit walk through mangrove forest (look out for crocs and snakes) on the way to a lookout on the slopes of **Mount Rooper**.

Sights

Despite having numerous smart resorts, apartments and a backpacker reproduction rate greater than Captain Cook's cat on shore leave, Airlie can hardly keep pace with its own popularity, so you are advised to book ahead. Many backpackers offer accommodation and activity combo deals, which are often booked from afar, but beware that, although attractive in price, they can severely limit your choice.

Sleeping

The high profile **LL** *Coral Sea Resort*, overlooking the Abel Point Marina, 25 Oceanview Dr, T4946 6458, www.coralsearesort.com.au, is Airlie's most exclusive resort satisfying all the expectations, from ocean view suites to a fine pool and à la carte restaurant. There are plenty of plush apartment complexes, including the new **LL-L** *Martinique Resort*, 18 Golden Orchid Dr, T4948 0401, www.martiniquewhitsunday.com.au, which has fully self-contained 1/2/3 bedroom apartments with fine views, a pool and a spa. The cheaper and recently renovated **LL-A** *Airlie Beach Hotel*, corner of The Esplanade and Coconut Grove, T4961 1999, www.airliebeachhotel.com.au, offers standard motel units and new, well-appointed hotel rooms in the heart of the town and has a good in-house bar/bistro (*Capers*). One of the better value, well-positioned and spacious resorts in the town is the **L** *Whitsunday Wanderers Resort*, Shute Harbour Rd, T4946 6446, which is attached to the (chain) **C-F** *Koala Backpackers*, T4946 6001, www.koala-backpackers.com.au Together they offer the full range of accommodation from a/c suites with spa to campsites with several pools and a host of activity bookings. In the heart of town the **A** *Airlie Waterfront B&B*, on the corner of Broadwater St and Mazlin St, T4946 7631, www.airliewaterfrontbnb.com.au, is one of the best B&Bs in the region and certainly the best located for all amenities.

There is no shortage of **backpackers** in Airlie. Most of these places can be put broadly into one of three categories – good value, party places and the more relaxed and peaceful. For sheer value for money the spacious and tidy **C-F** *ReefO's*, 147 Shute

Queensland

Harbour Rd, T4946 6137, www.reeforesort.com.au cannot be beaten. Dorm beds go for as little as $8 with breakfast and the en suite cabins with a/c and TV for under $50. There is a bar/restaurant and small communal kitchen on site, as well as an excellent (and honest) tour/activities desk. Its only drawback is the walk into town but regular shuttles are available. YHA members will get the usual discounts at the friendly and motel-style **C-E** *Club Habitat*, 394 Shute Harbour Rd, T4946 6312. All the major party-oriented backpackers are located right in the heart of the town. They are fiercely competitive but pretty similar, all having the full range of dorms, singles and doubles, with lively bars, nightclubs, a pool, good value eateries and internet. They can also advise on the best activities and trips but note that advice will almost certainly be biased. **C-E** *Beaches*, 362 Shute Harbour Rd, T4946 6244, **C-F** *Koala Backpackers*, (see above) and **C-E** *Magnums Backpackers*, 366 Shute Harbour Rd, T4946 6266, are the main players. For a little bit more peace and quiet there is the excellent **C-E** *Bush Village Backpackers Resort*, 2 St Martins Rd, Cannonvale, T4946 7227, which is friendly, with tidy and spacious a/c self-catering cabins, en suite doubles and dorms, a pool and a regular shuttle into town. The spacious **C-E** *Club 13*, 13 Begley St, T4946 7376, www.whitsundaybackpackers.com.au, is another quiet option, in an elevated position in the heart of Airlie. It has good a/c doubles, a pool and a fine cooked breakfast (YHA discount). At the eastern end of town is the well-facilitated **C-E** *Backpackers by the Bay*, 12 Hermitage Dr, T4946 7267, bythebay@whitsunday.net.au, which has dorms and doubles and glorious bay views

There are plenty of **motor parks** in and around town. The 4-star **B-F** *Island Getaway Caravan Resort*, a short walk east of the town centre (corner of Shute Harbour Rd and Jubilee Pocket Rd), T4946 6228, is a popular option, offering units, cabins, camp-o-tels and powered and non-powered sites. Good camp kitchen and very tame possums. Further east the low-key **B-F** *Flame Tree Tourist Village*, Shute Harbour Rd (near the airfield), T4946 9388, is in a quiet bush setting, has a characterful camp kitchen and is within easy reach of the ferry terminal. Both Koala and Magnums Backpackers in Airlie also have powered sites.

There are over 30 **QPWS campsites** throughout the Whitsunday Island group and beyond. The QPWS office on Shute Harbour Rd, T4946 7022, can provide up-to-date information, advice and issue permits. **NB** To obtain a permit you must have proof of return transportation. *Island Camping Connections*, T4946 5255, offer independent transportation by water taxis and hire out camping gear. Note the Shute Harbour scheduled ferry services stop on most major island resorts.

Eating For fine dining the award-winning *Courtyard Restaurant*, 301 Shute Harbour Rd, T4946 5700, is recommended. Open for dinner daily (except Mon). Both *Magnums* and *Beaches* Backpackers (see above) have popular bar/bistros offering a wide variety of good value dishes (including the obligatory 'roo burgers') and have a lively atmosphere. Both are open for lunch and dinner. The pseudo Irish Pub *Paddy Shenanigans*, 352 Shute Harbour Rd, T4946 5055, also offers good value bar meals and is a fine place to remain for a night out. *KC's Bar and Grill*, 382 Shute Harbour Rd, T4946 6320, is popular for seafood and meat dishes and has live entertainment daily from 2200. *Boltz Café and Bar*, 7 Beach Plaza, The Esplanade, T4946 7755, offers a varied Mediterranean lunch and dinner menu in modern surroundings and is also open for breakfast. Open daily 0700-late. *Chatz Bar and Brasserie* at the eastern end of Shute Harbour Rd, T4946 7223, also offers value lunches and dinner and is open daily until 0200. If you must *Burgers in Paradise*, 269 Shute Harbour Rd, can ease the post-party munchies and is open 24 hrs. For breakfast and good coffee try the *Sidewalk Café* on The Esplanade. Open daily from 0730. Self-caterers will find the *5-Star Supermarket*, right in the centre of town, on Shute Harbour Rd. Open daily until 2100.

The street side bars at *Magnums* and *Beaches Backpackers* are both popular and the **Entertainment** best place to meet others for the almost obligatory wild night out. At *Magnums* you don't have to stumble too far to 'shake your pants' in its own nightclub *M@ss*, that rips it up well into the wee hours (sometimes quite literally, with wet t-shirt competitions and foam parties). *Tricks* nightclub and *Paddy Shenanigan's* (see above) can also go into orbit, almost simultaneously, well beyond midnight.

With numerous dive shops, umpteen cruise operators, over 74 islands and almost as **Tours &** many vessels, the choice of water based activities and trips is mind bending. Note that **activities** the 2 big day-trip attractions are **Whitehaven Beach** and *Fantaseas* floating **'Reefworld'** pontoon. Whitehaven Beach on Whitsunday Island is world famous for its glorious white sands and crystal clear waters, while Reefworld offers the chance to dive, snorkel or view the reef from a semi-submersible or underwater observatory. Note however that both these popular options are also the most commercial and most crowded, and that the main ferry companies also offer island transfers and island 'day-tripper' specials (see page 321). Fawlty's 4WD Tropical Tours, T4948 0999 offer entertaining and value day tours to the rainforests of the Conway National Park and Cedar Creek Falls, from $42, child $25.

Cruising (Fast catamaran) The major players are *Whitsunday All Over*, 398 Shute Harbour Rd, T4946 6900, www.whitsundayallover.com.au, and *Fantasea (Blue Ferries) Cruises*, Shop 10, Whitsunday Village, T4948 2300, info@fantasea.com.au Both have offices at the Shute Harbour Ferry Terminal. Other operators include *Reefjet* (see Diving below) and *Whitehaven Express*, T4946 6922, www.whitehavenxpress.com.au All offer a wide array of day cruises to the islands or the outer reef, or indeed, both. A day cruise will cost anywhere between $60 and $150.

Diving There are numerous options with all local dive shops and most of the larger cruise companies offering day or multi-day trips and courses. You are advised to shop around, confirm exactly where you are going and how long will actually be spent on the reef. Bear in mind that generally speaking, on shorter trips, the faster the vessel the more time you will have on the reef. Remember also that the outer reef offers the clearest water and most varied fish species. *Reef Dive*, Shute Harbour Rd, T4946 6508, www.reefdive.com.au offer 3-day/3-night packages and certification from $325 *Kelly Dive and Sail*, 1 The Esplanade, T4946 4368, www.kellydive.com.au offer 3-day/3-night trip, en suite cabin, with 10 dives from $490. *Oceania Dive*, 257 Shute Harbour Rd, T4946 6032, www.oceaniadive.com.au offer 5-day open water course from $535 and 10 dive certified diver trip from $500). *Pro Dive*, 344 Shute Harbour Rd, T4948 1888, www.prodivewhitsundays.com.au, offer a 5-day Open Water Course from $499. *Reefjet*, Shop 2 Abel Point Marina, T4948 1838, www.reefjet.com.au, offer an excellent day cruise to the Bait Reef (outer reef) and Whitehaven Beach with dive and snorkelling options from $110 (snorkel only). *Tallarook*, Shop 1 Beach Plaza, T4946 4777, also offer packages but also hire dive equipment for independent divers, snorkelling gear from $4 daily and stinger suits from $6 daily.

Fishing *MV Jillian*, T4948 0999, offer entertaining half/full-day trips from the Abel Point Marina at 0830, from $99 (full day). The *MV Moruya* ,T4946 7127, is another popular option, from $97, child $48. **Flight seeing** Most of the region's flight seeing operators are based at the airfield between Airlie and Shute Harbour where there is also a good café. *HeliReef Whitsunday*, T4946 8249, www.heliaust.com.au, offer a range of flight seeing options by helicopter and are also often in evidence on the waterfront in Airlie offering short scenic flights around the bay, 10 mins from $65, 40 min Whitehaven Beach flight with 1 hr stopover from $239. *Air Whitsunday*, T4946 9111, www.airwhitsunday.com.au, and *Coral Air*, T4946 9130, greatbarrierreef@bigpond.com, both have a small fleet of seaplanes and offer both flight seeing tours and island transfers, 3 hrs from $190.

Queensland

▶▶ The sting

Although the Queensland Tourism Board are reluctant to advertise the fact, 2001/2002 saw the worst year on record for fatalities from the seasonal 'marine stingers'. Sadly, two tourists died from the horrific (but secondary) symptoms that resulted from the stings of these notorious jellyfish. The most well-known and prevalent species is the rather banal looking **Box Jellyfish** – a sort of floating custard pie with highly poisonous tentacles which trail several metres behind it. Other lesser known and poisonous species include the **Irukandji**, a particularly insidious character about the size (remarkably) of your thumbnail and another, very aptly named the 'Snotty'! All stingers pose a significant threat during the period in their life cycle (October-May) when they are in the open sea. Although there is an antivenin widely available at hospitals for the Box Jellyfish, an antivenin for the less lethal Irukandji has yet to be developed. However, rest assured that even without antivenin, provided you are quickly and liberally soaked in vinegar, are young and fit, and reach a hospital as soon as possible, you will have every chance of surviving the ordeal. Provided the following sensible precautions are taken your chances of injury are minimal: 1. Do not swim in the sea (outside the 'stinger nets' provided at most major beaches) during the 'stinger season' (October-May); 2. Do not swim alone during the stinger season; 3. Be aware of the effectiveness of vinegar for immediate treatment and call the emergency services as soon as possible; 4. Wear a wet suit; 5. Seek local knowledge as to the best locations to swim.

Island Air Taxis, T4946 9933, www.heliaust.com.au offer fixed-wing scenic flights of 30 mins-5 hrs from $79. **Horse trekking** *Morrison's Trail Rides*, T4946 5299, are based in the Conway Ranges and offer bush trekking to Cedar Creek Falls, from $66 (includes transport).

Ocean rafting *Ocean Rafting*, T4946 6848, www.oceanrafting.com.au, offer a 7-hr fast cruise around the islands and Whitehaven Beach on board their rigid inflatable. Includes snorkelling, guided rainforest and aboriginal cave walk from $70, child $42, family $203. **Parasailing** *Whitsunday Parasail*, T4948 0000, offer single (from $50) or tandem flights (from $98) and also water-ski, jet ski and wakeboard options. **Quad Biking** *Whitsunday Quad Bike Bush Adventures*, T4948 1008, www.bushadventures.com.au, are a new operation offering not only a lot of fun but great views, wildlife and history, from $110. **Sailing** Again the choices are mind-boggling. A whole host of vessels from small dinghies to world class racing yachts are available to take you at a more leisurely pace to your island and/or reef. Day, night or multi-day adventures are available. There are too many to list here. The simple advice is to shop around (see box). A day cruise will cost about $70 while a 3-day/2-night trip around $250. **Skydiving** *Skydive Oz*, Airlie Beach, T4946 9115, www.skydiveoz.com.au, offer tandem jumps from $249.

Directory **Banks** Almost all branches (with ATMs) are represented on Shute Harbour Rd in Airlie (Commonwealth/National) and Cannonvale (Westpac/National/ANZ). **Currency exchange** at *Travelex* by the Post Office. **Communications** Internet *Beaches Backpackers* (open until late) and *Destination Whitsundays*, upstairs corner Shute harbour Rd and The Esplanade, T1800-644563. Open daily 0800-2200. **Post Office** Whitehaven Village, Shute Harbour Rd (near McDonald's). Open Mon-Fri 0900-1700, Sat 0900-1100. Post Restante, T4946 6515. **Medical services** *Whitsunday Doctors Service*, Shute Harbour Rd, T494 66241. *Whitsunday Medical Centre*, 400 Shute Harbour Rd, T4946 6275 (24 hr). **Police** 8 Altmann Av, Cannonvale, T4946 6445.

Whitsunday Islands

It comes as no surprise that these sun-soaked tropical islands (all 74 plus of them), the largest offshore island chain on the east coast, are the biggest tourist draw between Brisbane and Cairns. All but seven of the islands are uninhabited and protected as national parks, making the Whitsundays one of the few places anywhere that genuinely deserve to be labelled as paradise. Blessed with perfect white beaches, tickled by crystal clear waters and smugly content in the calming embrace of the Barrier Reef, the islands would be enough of an attraction in their natural state, but they also offer everything, from an inordinate number of water based activities and cruises, to exotic resorts and isolated campsites.

Colour map 4, grid A4 Captain Cook bestowed the name Whitsunday upon the island group when he sailed past on Whit Sunday (seventh Sunday after Easter), 1770

Getting there and around Air Proserpine Airport 36 km west of Airlie Beach and Hamilton Island Airport provide air access. Both serviced by *Qantas*, T131313, and *Flight West*, T1300-130092. Lindeman is the only other island with an airfield. *Island Air Taxis*, T4946 9933, provide local island transfers by fixed wing, *HeliReef Whitsunday*, T4946 8249, www.heliaust.com.au, by helicopter and *Air Whitsunday*, T4946 9111, www.airwhitsunday.com.au, or *Coral Air*, T4946 9130, greatbarrierreef@bigpond.com, by seaplane. The fare (fixed-wing) to Hamilton costs about $60 one-way. All local fixed-wing, helicopter and seaplane companies also offer scenic flights. **Ferry Shute Harbour**, east of Airlie Beach is the main departure point for ferry services to the Whitsunday islands. *Blue Ferries (Fantasea)*, T4946 5111, www.fantasea.com.au, offer daily scheduled services to Hamilton (6 per day, from $42 return), South Molle/Daydream (6 per day, from $22 return) and Long Island (Club Croc), 3 per day, from $25 return. Their main office is located at the ferry terminal, with an additional office located at Shop 10, Whitsunday Village, Shute Harbour Rd, Airlie Beach, T4948 2300. Ferry schedules are available in all VICs and travel/tour agent offices. *Whitsunday All Over*, T1300-366494, www.whitsundayallover.com.au, is also based at the ferry terminal and offers regular services to Daydream, South Molle, Long, Lindeman, and Hamilton Island. They meet every Qantas/Flight West arrival and departure from Hamilton Island airport (book ahead). Transfer rates are priced per sector and start from $15.50. Both companies offer a range of 'Day-tripper' and adventure cruises from $40. *Whitehaven Express*, T4946 6922, www.whitehavenxpress.com.au, offers a daily trip to Whitehaven Beach (includes snorkelling) from Abel Point Marina (Cannonvale) from $80, child $40, family $230. *Mantaray*, T4946 4579, www.mantaraycharters.com.au, offer a similar day trip taking in Whitehaven Beach and snorkelling the reef at Mantaray Bay. *Island Camping Connections*, T4946 5255, are based at the ferry terminal and offer island transfers for campers by water taxi. (Book ahead). *Whitsunday Transit*, T4946 1800, offer daily bus services from Proserpine to Shute Harbour (through Airlie Beach). **Taxi** T131008. **Parking** Secured parking is available at *Whitsunday Airport*, T04-1979 0995, and the Shell Station near the Shute Harbour ferry terminal, T4946 9666, from $11 per day. There are 2 car parks at the terminal. The lower car park is paid parking and expensive. The upper car park (accessed just beyond the petrol station and from the ferry by steps) is free.

Ins & outs

Information The **Whitsunday Visitors Information Centre**, Bruce Highway, Proserpine, T4945 3711, www.whitsundayinformation.com.au, is the main accredited VIC for the islands. The **QPWS** office is very helpful and is located south of Airlie Beach on the corner of Mandalay St, T4946 7022. Open Mon-Fri 0900-1700, Sat 0900-1300. They can supply the latest information regards island camping and issue the necessary permits, from $3.50 per night. There are 33 campsites covering 18 islands.

South Molle (405 ha) is one of three little 'Molles' (South, Mid and North) that sit about 8 km from Shute Harbour. Being in such close proximity to the mainland, and therefore relatively cheap to reach, South Molle is deservedly popular

South Molle Island

Queensland

▶▶ Choose a cruise

There are numerous islands and hundreds of trips on offer. First decide, as an independent, or as a group, exactly what you would like to do – whether it be diving, snorkelling, cruising, sailing, island hopping, camping or combinations thereof. Then ask yourself what kind of vessel you would like to go on. Then ask yourself how long you want to be out there. If the trip is several days, what is the on board accommodation like? Then ask yourself where exactly you would like to go – to the outer reef, the islands or all over the place? Then there's

*the small matter of group size. Then, armed with these preferences, go shopping. For those who are short of cash, don't despair. There is of course the economical and independent option of island camping. The QPWS have numerous campsites on the islands that can be reached by scheduled ferries or by group charter boats for under $100. Do it this way, under the stars and in near solitude and you will really find out what the Whitsundays have to offer. **Island Camping Connections**, T4946 5255 offer water taxis and hire out camping gear.*

with day-trippers and offers some excellent walking and sublime views. The best of these is undoubtedly the 6 km (return) **Spion Kop** walk that climbs through forest and over open grassland to some superb viewpoints across to the outer islands. The resort on the island is both pleasant and casual, offering all the usual mod cons to in-house guests and allowing day-trippers access to the pool, bar/bistro and some activities. It is also noted for its evening entertainment. **LL** *South Molle Island Resort*, T4946 9433, www.southmolleisland.com.au There are two QPWS campsites on South Molle at **Sandy Bay** and **Paddle Bay** with toilets but no water supply. There are two other sites on small offshore islands and at Cockatoo Beach on **North Molle** but if the resort cannot offer you a lift in one of its vessels, independent access must be arranged. The Cockatoo Beach site has seasonal water supplies.

Long Island Aptly named Long Island is the closest island to the mainland running parallel with the uninhabited coastal fringes of the Conway National Park. A national park in its own right, much of its 2,000 acres of dense rainforest is inaccessible, save a loose network of tracks that connect a number of pretty beaches near the major resorts at the northern end.

Sleeping There are three established resorts on the island and 1 QPWS campsite. Offering its guests the perfect arrival point in **'Happy Bay'** is the **LL** *Club Crocodile Resort*, T4946 9400, www.clubcroc.com.au Less than 1 km south is the more eco-friendly and cheaper **LL-L** *Palm Beach Hideaway*, T4946 9233, offering peaceful beachside en suite units and cabins, surrounded by all the usual amenities. In almost perfect isolation on the island's western side is the **LL** *Whitsunday Wilderness Lodge*, T4946 9777, www.southlongisland.com.au A relaxing eco-friendly retreat with a focus on the place rather than the amenities. Accommodation is in comfortable but basic en suite beach-front units, the hosts are very professional and the lodge has its own yacht, which is part of an optional, and comprehensive daily activities schedule. Recommended. The **QPWS** campsite is situated on the western side of the island at **Sandy Bay**. It is a fine, secluded spot backed by rainforest, through which there is a track allowing you to explore and reach viewpoints overlooking the other islands. There are toilets but no water supply.

Daydream Island One of the smallest of the Whitsunday Islands (and winning the prize for the most nauseating name), Daydream is one of the closest and most accessible islands to the mainland (5 km). As such it has become a popular holiday venue. On offer for guests are a host of activities including sail boarding, jet-skiing, parasailing, reef fishing, diving and snorkelling. It's so small, the longest walk you'll have is to the bar. The **LL** *Novotel Daydream*, T4948 8488, www.daydream.net.au, resort may open its facilities to day-trippers in the near future. Call for details or ask at the VIC.

At over 100 sq km Whitsunday Island is the biggest in the group, boasting perhaps their biggest attraction – the 6 km white silica sands of **Whitehaven Beach**. Repeatedly, aerial views of this magnificent beach and the adjoining **Hill Inlet** turn up in the pages of glossy magazines and on postcards as the epitome of the words 'tropical paradise'. Though best seen from the air the beach is easily accessed by numerous day trips and island cruises, which in many ways is its downfall. Thankfully uninhabited and without a resort Whitsunday's only available accommodation comes in the form of eight **QPWS campsites** scattered around its numerous bays and inlets. The most popular of course is Whitehaven Beach, (southern end), accommodating up to 60 and has toilets, but no water supply. The only campsites with water are **Sawmill Beach** and **Dugong Beach** both of which fringe Cid Bay on the island's western side. The two campsites are connected by a 1 km walking track.

Whitsunday Island

Set right in the heart of the Whitsundays, with an unsightly group of hideous tower blocks blighting the landscape, it is seen by many as the proverbial fly in the otherwise pure ointment. But despite these drawbacks Hamilton offers something the other islands don't: it is home to the Whitsunday's main airport, a wide range of accommodation, 10 restaurants, six bars and cafés and over 85 activities. Though day-trippers are welcome, there are no campsites on Hamilton Island

Hamilton Island

Hook is the second largest island in the group and the loftiest, with **Hook Peak** (459 m) being the highest point of all the islands. Like all the others it is densely forested and inundated with picturesque bays and inlets. The most northerly of these, like **Maureen Cove** has fringing reef that offers excellent snorkelling. Picturesque **Nara Inlet** on the island's south coast has caves that support evidence of early Ngalandji Aboriginal occupation. It is also a popular anchorage for visiting yachties.

Hook Island

Sleeping and eating L-E *Hook Island Wilderness Resort*, T1800-248824, www.oz horizons.com.au, located towards the southeastern end of the island, is a low-key resort, popular with budget travellers. It offers en suite cabins, standard cabins and dorms along with numerous activities, an underwater observatory, café/bar, pool and spa. Transfers are with *Seatrek Cruises*, which depart 0830 daily from Shute Harbour, from $36 return. There are 5 **QPWS** campsites with Maureen Cove and Bloodhorn Beach (Stonehaven Bay) being the most popular. None have a water supply.

Lindeman Island (20 sq km) is one of the most southerly of the Whitsunday group and the most visited of a cluster that make up the Lindeman Island National Park. It offers all the usual natural features of picturesque inlets and bays and has over 20 km of walking tracks that take you through rainforest and grassland to spectacular views from the island's highest peak, **Mount Oldfield** (7 km return, 212 m). The island has seven beaches, with Gap Beach providing the best snorkelling. There is a *QPWS* campsite at **Boat Port**, which is the only one on the island. There are toilets but no water supply. The **LL** *Club Med Resort*, T1800-801823, is located at the northern end of the island.

Lindeman Island

Hayman Island

Hayman Island is the most northerly of the group. A fairly mountainous little jewel, clad mainly in eucalypt and close to the outer reef, it is most famous for its world class resort, the **LL** *Hayman Island Resort*, which has all you might expect for tariffs that start at $560 a double, T4940 1234, www.hayman.com.au The resort's own luxury launch 'The Sun Eagle' departs from Shute Harbour or guests are flown in by seaplane. The domain of the wealthy and costing over $300 mn to create, it is well beyond the budget of most people, but for those that can afford it, Hayman offers the epitome of a tropical island paradise.

Whitsunday to Townsville

Bowen
Colour map 4, grid A4
Population: 9,000
200 km south of
Townsville, 188 km
north of Mackay

The lazy coastal town of Bowen (named after the first Governor of Queensland) is known as the 'Salad Bowl of the North' and attracts legions of cash-strapped backpackers in search of work harvesting the mountains of tomatoes and mangoes. Other than a suntan, there is not a great deal on offer for the time pressed tourist in Bowen. However, it does boast a very relaxed charm and several superb **beaches** along its northern and eastern fringe. The best of these is **Horseshoe Bay**, but others, namely, Grays Bay, Murray Bay, Rose Bay and King's Beach are all quite magnificent. They are all quite easy to reach and the VIC can provide a map. The **VIC** is at 47 Williams Street, T4786 4494, www.bowentourism.com.au ■ *Daily 0900-1700. The free 'Bowen Holiday Guide' will provide all the local information required and has maps. The VIC also has Internet facilities.* Bowen is also well known for its **murals** that adorn numerous walls in the centre of the town and depict various historical scenes.

Sleeping and eating The **F** *Barnacles Backpackers*, 16 Gordon St, T4786 4400, **F** *Bowen Backpackers*, on the corner of Herbert St and Dalrymple St, T4786 3433, and the best placed **F** *Trinity's At The Beach*, 93 Horseshoe Bay Rd, T4786 4199, all offer basic budget accommodation and can help find work. The **A-F** *Horseshoe Bay Resort*, Horseshoe Bay, T4786 2564, is the best placed motor park in the area and offers a wide range of value accommodation from beach units and caravans to powered and unpowered sites. The *Horseshoe Bay Café*, T4786 3280, is nearby offering breakfast, lunch and dinner. Out of town the **L-E** *Bogie River Bush Lodge*, T4785 3407, www.bogiebushhouse.com.au, offers the ideal country getaway with luxury or budget accommodation in a quiet setting, friendly hosts and a wide range of activities. Book ahead.

Transport *McCafferty's/Greyhound* **buses** stop on William St near the VIC. The **train** station is located south of the town centre on Bootooloo Rd. *Bowen Travel*, 40 Williams St, T4786 2835 are booking agents for both bus and rail.

Ayr, Home Hill & The Bowling Green Bay National Park
Colour map 4, grid A3
Population: 9,000
175 km north
of Proserpine,
90 km south
of Townsville

The small sugar cane towns of Ayr and Home Hill are connected by the 1097-m **Burdekin River Road and Rail Bridge**, also known as the 'Silver Link', which for many years was the longest in Australia. On the corner of McKenzie St and Wilmington St (turn left at the police station) is the **Ayr Nature Display** with its vivid collection of over 60,000 (dead) Australian butterflies. ■ *Mon-Fri 0800-1700, Sat/Sun 0800-1200. $2.50, child $1. T4783 2189.*

Alva Beach on the fringe of the largely inaccessible and fragmented **Bowling Green Bay National Park** (Cape Bowling Green and **Mount Elliot**) 18 km north of Ayr, offers a great spot for a swim or a picnic. There are walking tracks and a QPWS campsite (the only one in the park) at **Alligator Creek**, 25 km south of Townsville, (self registration). The Burdekin **VIC** is at Plantation Park, T4783 5988. Open daily (April-September) 0900-1700, (October-March) Monday-Friday 0900-1700. **QPWS**, T4778 8203.

Townsville

Considered the capital of Queensland's north coast and the second largest city in the State, the banal-sounding Townsville took a long time to follow the example of its northerly neighbour, Cairns, and devote itself to tourism. The **waterfront** has been transformed into one of the most attractive in Australia but the rest of the city centre has some catching up to do. Despite its lack of aesthetic appeal, though, it's a friendly place with a wealth of activities now on offer and the irresistible pull of **Magnetic Island**.

Colour map 4, grid A3
Population: 130,000
1,370 km
from Brisbane,
386 km from Mackay,
345 km Cairns

Getting there **Air** Townsville is serviced from all major cities by *Qantas*, T131313, and *Virgin Blue*, T136789. *Flight West*, T4725 3855, www.flightwest.com.au, offer regular onward services throughout Queensland. *Macair*, T4035 9722, www.macair.com.au, service several locations including Cairns, Cooktown and Dunk Island. The airport, T4727 3211, is located about 5 km west of the city in the suburb of Garbutt. Airport Transfers and Tours, T4775 5544, offer regular services into town, from single/return, $7/$11. By bus Townsville is serviced by *Premier Motor Services*, T133410, and *McCafferty's/Greyhound*, T132030. Westbound destinations include Charters Towers and Mt Isa. The **Transit Centre** is located at the corner of Palmer St and Plume St, T4772 5100. Open daily 0430-2000. The railway station is on Blackwood St, just south of the Flinders Mall, next to the river. It has a travel centre, T4772 8358, (bookings T132232), www.traveltrain. qr.com.au *The Sunlander* operates 3 weekly services between Brisbane and Cairns

Ins & outs

Queensland

Townsville

	Sleeping	5	Jupiter's		**Eating**	7	Quarterdeck Bar & Bistro
1	Aquarius		Townsville	1	Covers	8	Taj Mahal & Thai International
2	Civic Guest		& Casino	2	Gauquin & Bar	9	Tim's Surf & Turf
	House	6	Rocks Guesthouse	3	Heritage Café & Bar		
3	Coral Lodge	7	Southbank Village	4	La Bamba Café		**Pubs & bars**
4	Globetrotters		Backpackers	5	La Cucina	10	Seaview Hotel
		8	Yongala Lodge	6	Molly Malone's		

(northbound Tue/Thu/Sat, southbound Mon/Thu/Sat); *The Spirit of the Tropics* operates a twice-weekly service from Brisbane to Townsville (northbound Tue/Sat, southbound Wed/Sun) and *The Inlander* operates twice-weekly services from Townsville to Mt Isa (westbound Sun/Wed, eastbound Mon/Fri). Contact the travel centre for confirmations, latest fares and departure times.

Getting around Townsville's *Sunbus*, T4725 8482, www.sunbus.com.au, offer regular daily suburban services. There is a main town centre bus terminal with posted information in the heart of the main Flinders St Mall. Fares are from $2.50, Day Pass from $10. Townsville **Taxi**, T131008 (24 hr).

Information The principal *Visitors Information Centre* is located several kilometres south of the town, on the Bruce Highway, T4778 3555. Open daily 0900-1700. If you miss that, the Information booth in the Flinders Mall, T4721 3660, can also be of assistance. Open Mon-Fri 0900-1700, Sat/Sun 0900-1300. The main website for the region is www.townsvilleonline.com.au **QPWS** information can be secured within the Reef HQ Complex, Flinders St East, T4721 2399. Open Mon-Fri 0900-1700, Sat/Sun 1000-1600.

Sights Though not on a par with Sydney Aquarium's remarkable Reef Exhibit, the long established **Reef HQ** still provides an excellent land-based introduction to the reef and its aquatic who's who. Centrepiece within the facility is a huge 750,000-litre 'Predator Exhibit', complete with genuine wave action, a part replica of the famous (local) Yongala wreck and a myriad of colourful corals, fish and, of course, the obligatory sharks. Shark feeding takes place on most days at 1500, but even more fascinating is the 'Danger Trail', which is guided presentation, daily at 1300, of some of the most deadly and dangerous creatures on the reef. ■ *Daily 0900-1700, $16, child $7, family $38, T4750 0800, www.reefHQ.org.au Flinders St East.* Within the same complex as Reef HQ is the enormous **Imax Dome Theatre**. ■ *Shows every hr from 1000-1600. $12, T4721 1481. Opening hours are reduced from Oct-May.* Next door to Reef HQ, the newly renovated **Museum of Queensland** provides an impressive insight in to the region's maritime history, with the story of **'HMS Pandora'**, the British 17th-century tall ship that ran aground on the Barrier Reef, with the loss of 31 crew, after she had been despatched by the British Admiralty in 1790 to bring the mutineers of the HMS Bounty to justice. The collection and the presentation of the Pandora story is an impressive and imaginative mix of old and new, with the stunning scale replica section of the ship. The café is also notable due to its views across the river. ■ *Museum open daily 0900-1700, $9, child $5, family $24, T4726 0606, www.mtq.qld.gov.au Flinders St East.* If you are really (really) nutty about shipwrecks and need further exposure, then the **Maritime Museum of Townsville** will oblige, with its low-key exhibits of more local wrecks, including the most famous, the 'SS Yongala'. ■ *Mon-Fri 1000-1600, Sat/Sun 1200-1600. $5, family $4. 42-68 Palmer St, South Townsville. T4721 5251.* Housed in a former bank, built in 1885, is the **Perc Tucker Gallery** on Flinders Mall, which houses an extensive collection of national and regional art. ■ *Mon/Tue/Wed/Thu 1000-1700, Sat/Sun 1000-1400. Free. T4727 9011, corner of Denham St.*

Fringing the shoreline east of the city centre is **The Strand**, decorated by a line of amazing banyan trees. Along with the Queensland Museum, it is the new 'showpiece' of the city and said by some to be the most attractive public waterfront development in Australia. Townsville's skyline is dominated by **Castle Hill**. You can climb to the summit by car or on foot and take in the memorable day or night-time views. Access by car is at the end of Burk Street (off Warburton Street, west of the town centre). The aptly named 'Goat Track' to the summit is off Stanton Street at the end Gregory Street (also off Warburton). For a more leisurely stroll, head to one or all of Townsville's **Botanical Gardens** – The shady *Palmetum* off University Road, Douglas; *Anderson Park* off Gulliver Street in Mundingburra and *Queens Gardens* off Burke Street in North Ward. The **Town Common Conservation Park** at the end Cape Pallerenda Road (west of the Strand) is another fine walking spot and a mecca for local birdwatchers, (leaflet from the QPWS in Reef HQ), T4774 1382. Some 17 km south of the city, next to the Bruce Highway, is the **Billabong Wildlife Sanctuary**, which is undoubtedly one of the best in Queensland. Fringing an authentic billabong (lake), it houses an extensive collection of natives, from the adorable wombat to the less ubiquitous crocodile and a host of poisonous snakes. ■ *Daily 0800-1700, $20, child $10, family $48, T4778 8344, www.billabongsanctuary.com.au Airport Transfers, T477 5554 offer twice daily shuttles to Billabong from $32, child $16 return (0915/1330).*

The most upmarket hotel in the city is the **LL** *Jupiter's Townsville Hotel and Casino,* **Sleeping** overlooking the new marina and Magnetic Island off Sir Leslie Theiss Dr, T4722 2333. There are plenty of modern motels on The Strand overlooking the ocean, including the **L** *Aquarius*, 75 The Strand, T4772 4255, www.aquarius-townsville.com.au Again it is something of an eyesore from the outside, but is good value and offers great views across to Magnetic Island. There are very few B&Bs and guesthouses in the city, however, both the **L** *Rocks Guesthouse*, 20 Cleveland Terr, T4771 5700, www.therocksguesthouse.com, and the **A** *Coral Lodge*, 82 Hale St, T4771 5512, urwelcome@ultra.net.au, are reputable and good value for money. Just off the Strand on Fryer St is the slightly cheaper and historic **A** *Yongala Lodge*, T4772 2477, info@historicyongala.com.au It offers a range of basic motel units from single to 2 bedroom, has a pleasant Greek/international restaurant and is a stone's throw from the waterfront.

There are plenty of **backpacker** beds in town, though most deservingly struggle to keep their guests any longer than one night in their desire to get to the much more attractive surroundings of Magnetic Island. One of the closest to the transit centre is the small but popular **C-E** *Globetrotters*, 45 Palmer St, T4771 3242, while just around the corner in McIlwarth St is the equally convenient and improved **D-E** *Southbank Village Backpackers*, T4771 5849. Although a little less convenient, the pick of the bunch has to be the tidy **C-E** *Civic Guest House*, 262 Walker St, T4771 5381, www.backpackersinn.com.au, which has a wide range of rooms (some with TV and a/c), good general facilities and regular and interesting in-house trips. For **camping** close to town, try the 3-star **B-E** *Rowes Bay Caravan Park*, west of The Strand on Heatley's Pde, T4771 3576. It has villas, cabins, powered and un-powered sites and is close to the beach, but is in severe need of a camp kitchen. Elsewhere, the 4-star **B-E** *Walkabout Palms Caravan Park*, 6 University Rd, Wulguru, T4778 2480, is well facilitated and connected to the 24-hr petrol station. Although not central to the city it is in a good position for the transitory visitor right on the main north/south highway.

Expensive As well as reputable, up-market restaurants in most of the major hotels **Eating** and motels, including *Aqua* in *Jupiter's Hotel*, and the *Zoui Alto* (superb view) on the top floor of the *Aquarius* (see above), the best bet for fine dining and dining in general, is along Flinders St East, Palmer St (east, across the river) and along the waterfront. On Flinders St East is the award winning, 2-storey, *Covers Restaurant*, 209 Flinders St, T4721 4630, offering an eclectic range of International and Australian dishes. The restaurant is upstairs with an attractive balcony, while at the street level there is a café and wine bar. Open lunch Mon-Fri, brunch Sat and Sun, dinner Mon-Sat.

Queensland

Mid-range Flinders St East offers a wide range of international, affordable options, including the popular Indian *Taj Mahal* (2/235), T4772 3422, and just above it, the *Thai International*, T4771 6242. Open daily 0530-late. A few doors down the Italian *La Cucina* (215), T4721 1500 is also good value. Open daily 1800-late. For pub grub try the tidy surroundings, menu and congenial atmosphere of *Molly Malone's* Irish Pub, corner Wickham and Flinders St East, T4771 3428. Otherwise, meat lovers will love the generous steaks at *Tim's Surf and Turf* overlooking the river on Ogden St (behind Flinders Mall), T4721 4861. Towards the water and overlooking the marina, (off Sir Leslie Theiss Dr), is the *Quarterdeck Bar and Bistro*, T4722 2261. It offers good value seafood dishes in a nice setting, with live jazz on Sun from 1600-2000. Further along the Strand is the *Gauguin Restaurant and Bar*, Gregory St Headland, T4724 5488, is another fine venue for seafood and in the perfect spot overlooking the ocean. It's open daily for lunch and dinner.

Cheap The *Heritage Café and Bar*, 137 Flinders St East, T4771 4355, has a nice atmosphere and variant, good value blackboard, while the colourful *La Bamba Café*, 3 Palmer St, T4771 6322, does cheap breakfasts. For self-caterers the Woolworths supermarket is located on Sturt St, behind the Flinders St Mall. Open weekdays till 2100.

Entertainment Flinders St East is the place to head for a steamy tropical night out. There are several pub/nightclub venues, including *The Bank*, 169 Flinders St, T4771 6148, which is open Wed-Sat till 0500. Across the road the rather unfortunately named *Mad Cow*, T4771 5727, is a little less formal and also remains open well into the wee hours. *Molly Malone's*, corner of Wickham and Flinders St East, has a happy hour daily from 1700-1800 and provides the folk or rock bands at the weekend. During the tropical afternoons and balmy evenings the Garden Bar at the *Seaview Hotel* along the Strand (corner of Gregory St) is also popular. Otherwise you might like to try your luck at the *Jupiter's Townsville Hotel and Casino* (see Sleeping), open Sun-Thu 1000-0200, Fri/Sat 1000-0400. The *Townsville Entertainment and Convention Centre* on Entertainment Dr, T4771 4222, www.tecc.net.au, is the main entertainments venue in the city and is also home to the fiercesome Townsville Crocodiles NBL team.

Tours & activities **Diving** Other than several notable reef sites, the big diving attraction in these parts is the wreck of the '**SS Yongala**', a passenger ship that sank with all 121 crew during a cyclone in 1911. Located about 17 km off Cape Bowling Green, the Yongala is often touted as one of Australia's best dives, offering diverse habitats and a huge range of species, including enormous manta rays and colourful coral gardens. Since the wreck sits at a depth 29 m and is subject to strong currents the dive presents a challenge and requires an above average level of competency. There are several companies located in Townsville or on Magnetic Island (which is often the preferred location) offering a wide variety of trips for certified divers wishing to experience the Yongala. Basic and advanced training that can culminate with the 'ultimate wreck dive' is also available. The VIC has full listings. *Diving Dreams*, 252 Walker St, T4721 2500, www.divingdreams.com.au, offer reputable 2-5 day trips from $350. Others include *Pro-Dive*, T4721 1760, www.prodive-townsville.com.au, offering a 5-day Advance Course which includes 2 dives on the Yongala from $515 and *Adrenaline Dive*, 121 Flinders St, T4724 0600, www.adrenalindive.com.au, who offer 2 dives on the wreck from $179 as well as other day trips to the reef from $130. For the Magnetic Island listings see the relevant text.

Fishing Townsville is known as a venue for sea and big game fishing. Local charters include *Gladiator*, T04-1207 3606, that offer trips around Magnetic island from $67, child $34 and family $182, the 42-ft *Fringe Benefits*, T4771 5579, offer day, half-day, overnight or extended trips with all mod cons, aboard the 75-ft Luxury yacht, *Pacific Coast*, T04-2877 8458. **Horse trekking** *Woodstock Trail Rides*, based along the Flinders Highway, T4778 8888, www.woodstocktrailrides.com.au, offer rides on a cattle station, half-day $40, full-day $90 and overnight camp $120 (includes transfers). **Skydiving** *Coral Sea Skydivers*, 14 Plume St, South Townsville, T4772 4889, www.coralseaskydivers.com.au, offer daily tandem dives onto the Strand Beach from between 8-12,000 ft, from $240. **White-water rafting** *Raging Thunder*, T4030 7990, www.ragingthunder.com.au, provide pick-ups for a range of rafting trips and packages on the Tully River, from $155.

Banks Most bank branches are represented in and around the Flinders Mall. Currency Exchange at *Wespac Bank*, 337 Flinders Mall. **Bike hire** *Townsville Car Rentals*, 12 Palmer St, South Townsville, T4772 1093, from $10 a day. **Car hire** *Hertz*, T4775 5950, *Delta*, T131390 and *Thrifty*, T4725 4600 have outlets at the airport. *Townsville Car Rentals*, have an outlet at 12 Palmer St, South Townsville, T4772 1093. **Communications** Internet *Internet Den* (opposite the VIC), 265 Flinders Mall, T4721 4500. Open 0800-2400; *Ripples Café*, in The Great Barrier Reef Wonderland, Flinders St; *Infinet*, Castletown Shopping World, Woolcock St, Kings Rd (3 km southeast of the town centre), T4772 7666. Open Mon-Fri 0900-1800, Thu 0900-2100, Sat 0900-1600. **Post Office** Sturt St. Open Mon-Fri 0830 1730, Sat 0900-1230. Post Restante open Mon-Fri 0830-1630. **Medical services** *Townsville Hospital*, 100 Agnes Smith Dr, T4781 9211. **Police** Corner of Sturt St and Stanley St, T4760 7777. **RACQ** 202 Ross River Dr, T4725 5677.

Directory

Magnetic Island

Magnetic Island or **'Maggie'** as it is affectionately known, is Townsville's biggest tourist attraction and the most easily accessible 'tropical island escape' on the reef. Lying only 8 km offshore and baking in over 320 days of sunshine a year, Maggie has always been a popular holiday spot, but the discreet permanent population makes it seem more of a desirable suburb of Townsville than a resort. There are four main villages spread along its eastern coastline which the visitor can easily navigate by both public transport, or by mini mokes (see below). With over half the island given over to **national park**, encompassing

Colour map 4, grid A3
Population: 2,250

Magnetic Island

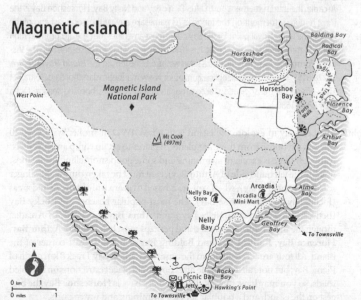

over 40 km of walking tracks, 20 picture-postcard bays and **beaches**, as well as a wealth of activities and some great budget accommodation, not to mention a resident population of **koala**, Magnestic island is well-named.

Ins & outs   **Getting there** *Sunferries Magnetic Island*, T4771 3855, www.sunferries@ultra.net.au, offer regular daily sailings from both the Flinders St Ferry Terminal and Bayswater Terminal to Picnic Bay from 0550-1855 and from $16, child $8, family $33 return. *Magnetic Island Car and Passenger Ferries*, based on Ross St, Townsville South, T4772 5422, www.riversidemarine.com.au, offer regular sailings to Geoffrey Bay (Arcadia) Mon-Fri 0600-1720, Sat 0745-1540, Sun 0745-1720, from $115 (vehicle with up to 6 passengers), $16, child $7 (passenger only), both return.

Getting around *The Magnetic Island Bus Service*, T4778 5130, runs up and down the east coast, between Picnic Bay to Horseshoe Bay every hr or so from 0620-2350. Tickets are sold on the bus from $2. One-day ($11) and 2-day ($13) unlimited passes are generally the preferred option. They also offer 3-hr guided tours from Picnic Bay at 0900 and 1300 from $30, child $15, family $75. One of the highlights of 'Maggie' is exploring the island by mini-moke, which is a small, toy-like **4WD**. *Tropical Topless Car Rentals*, Picnic St, Picnic Bay have a fleet of these and they are comfortable, good value and economical, from $60 per day, flat rate, unlimited km. Credit card deposit. Book at the Photo Shop at the end of the jetty. Recommended. Alternatively, *Moke Magnetic*, 4 The Esplanade, T4778 5377 hire mokes and vehicles seating up to 8 from $47 per day. Note however that there is a $0.44 per km charge (including petrol) on top of that. Deposit $100. *MI Wheels*, 13 Pacific Dr, Horseshoe Bay, T4778 5491 hire mokes on a sliding scale rate from $42 per day, with $0.33 per km (excludes petrol). Scooters and trail motorbikes can be hired from *Road Runner Scooter Hire*, Shop 3, Picnic Bay Mall, T4778 5222, from $28 per day. **Bikes** can be hired from some hostels and from Magnetic Island Photos, Picnic Bay Mall, T4778 5411. Note that the island speed limit is **60 kmph** and this should be adhered to at all times. For a **taxi** call T131008

Orientation and information The passenger ferries arrive at the wharf off the settlement at **Picnic Bay** on the island's southeast corner. The vehicular ferry and other passenger services arrive at the new passenger and car ferry terminal at Geoffrey Bay next to **Arcadia**, the third settlement north after Picnic Bay and **Nelly Bay**. **Horseshoe Bay** is the most remote settlement on the fringe of its namesake bay, at the northeast end of the island. The main arrival point Picnic Bay offers most amenities, but the accommodation is spread throughout the east coast. It is 10 km from Picnic Bay to Horseshoe Bay. The **Visitor Information Centre** is located a short walk from the ferry at the *Island Travel Centre*, T4778 5155, www.townsvilleonline.com.au or www.magnetic islandholidays@ultra.net They offer a full transportation, accommodation and activities booking service. Open daily 0800-1630.

Sights   The best way to explore the island is to hire a 4WD or moke. With over 20 beaches to choose from there are plenty of places to set up camp and just relax. Although there is excellent swimming and some good snorkelling spots (most notably the left hand side of Arthur Bay), care must be taken during the stinger season (October-May), when you are advised to swim only in the netted areas (Picnic Bay and Horseshoe Bay). The most popular beaches are **Rocky Bay** (between Picnic Bay and Nelly Bay,) and **Alma Bay** just north of Arcadia, though the most remote, secluded and perhaps most beautiful are **Arthur Bay**, **Florence Bay, Radical Bay** and **Balding Bay** at the northeast corner of the island. All four are accessed down the unsealed Radical Bay Track 8 km north of Picnic Bay, but note all the vehicle hire companies place restrictions on unsealed roads, so you may have to walk. Beyond these bays is **Horseshoe Bay** the biggest on the island, and a popular spot for swimming and watersports.

There are many excellent **walking tracks** on the island with the two most notable being the **Horseshoe Bay to Arthur Bay** track (3 km, two hour one-way) and in the same vicinity, the **Forts Walk** (2 km, 1½ hours return) The Horseshoe Bay to Arthur Bay track can be tackled in either direction and takes in all the secluded bays and some low-lying bush. The Forts Walk starts at the Radical Bay turn-off and follows the ridge past some old gun emplacements to the old observation tower lookout. This track is also one of the best places to observe **koalas**. Late afternoon (when they are awake and feeding) is the best time to see them. Another short walk to **Hawking's Point** lookout above Picnic Bay is also worthwhile. It starts at the end of Picnic Street (600-m, 30 minutes). To visit the more remote areas on the south and west coast requires your own 4WD, a boat or a very long trek. The unsealed track west, starts from Yule Street, Picnic Bay, beside the golf course. Sadly, the island's highest peak **Mount Cook** (497 m) is inaccessible to anything other than the local wildlife.

Picnic Bay A *Dunoon Beachfront Apartments*, The Esplanade, T4778 5161, www.dunoon.com.au, has good value 1/2 bedroom, fully self-contained apartments, surrounded by gardens with pool and spa, and is especially good for families. Right in the heart of the village is the **C-E** *Travellers Backpackers Resort*, 1 The Esplanade, T4778 5166, www.travellers-on-magnetic.com.au, en suite a/c rooms and dorms, all centred around a pool and beer garden. Internet and close to all amenities.

Nelly Bay LL-L *Magnetic International Resort*, Mandalay Av, T4778 5200, www.magnetichotel.com.au Luxury rooms, suites and family suites, licensed restaurant and pool, all set in its own 10 acre gardens. **L-C** *Magnetic Island Tropical Resort*, Yates St, T4778 5955. En suite chalet-style cabins with restaurant/bar, pool and spa, again amidst a bush setting. Recommended. Just south of Nelly Bay, sitting on its own, right on the beach is the **B-E** *Coconuts Backpackers*, 1 Nelly Bay Rd, T1800-065696, www.bakpakgroup.com.au It has an interesting range of accommodation options from dorms and 'camp-o-tels' to ocean view doubles. Limited camping facilities. In-house dive courses and a good beach party every month.

Arcadia B-F *Arcadia Hotel Resort ('Arkies')*, 7 Marine Pde, T4778 5177, is a busy, sprawling place with 30 a/c motel-style units (including dorms) close to all local amenities. Pool, spa, restaurant/bar, bistro and internet. **A** *Beaches B&B*, 39 Marine Pde, T4778 5303, is a small and pleasant beachside cottage in a quiet location, ideal for couples. **A** *Magnetic North Holiday Apartments*, 2 Endeavour Rd, T4778 5647. Standard, tidy, self-contained apartments close to Alma Bay. The eco-friendly **B-C** *Marshall's B&B*, also on Endeavour Rd, (No 3-5), T4778 5112, www.moonshine.com.au Basic but good value singles and doubles in a traditional Queenslander house surrounded by spacious gardens. No a/c and free night stand-by special (ie buy 2, get 3) from Oct-Jun.

Horseshoe Bay LL *Shaw's Apartments*, 7 Pacific Dr, T4758 1900, www.shawsontheshore.com.au New fully self-contained 2-3 bedroom, luxury apartment block, with all mod cons, right above the main grocery shop and facing the beach. Minimum 2-nights. Good for families. **A-E** *Maggie's Beach House*, 1 Pacific Dr, T4778 5144, is a modern purpose-built facility next to the beach and although the most remote and expensive of the backpackers is, deservingly, the most popular. It offers a wide range of rooms from en suites to dorms, has a pool, bar and internet café. Free, direct transfers by boat from Townsville adds to its appeal. Further from the beach is **C-F** *Geoff's Place*, 40 Horseshoe Bay Rd, T1800-285577, www.geoffsplace.com.au It is a YHA affiliate, set in spacious grounds, offering everything from basic a/c chalets to camp and powered sites. Regular, mass lorikeet feeding. Lively place with popular late night bar and bistro, pool, spa and internet

Sleeping

For budget accommodation, and during school and public holidays, you are advised to book ahead. The VIC has comprehensive listings and offers a booking service

Queensland

Eating

The restaurants and cafés on 'Maggie' tend to be very casual affairs and close early. Most of the major resorts and backpackers have cafés, bistros, or à la carte restaurants all open to the public

In the *Picnic Bay Mall*, is the *Gossip Café*, T4758 1119, that has an extensive blackboard menu and does good breakfasts and coffee. Nearby, is the *MI Chinese Restaurant*, T4778 5706. Open daily from 1100. In *Nelly Bay*, on Warboys St is *Mexican Munchies*, T4778 5658, offering vegetarian dishes. Open daily (except Wed) from 1800. Next to the supermarket is *Pizza Tonite*, T4758 1400, which offers sit down, takeaway or deliveries (closed Mon). In **Arcadia**, *Bannister's Seafood Restaurant*, 22 McCabe Cr, T4778 5700, claims to offer the best fish and chips on the island. Open daily until 2000. In **Horseshoe Bay**, *Cotters*, on the waterfront, T4778 5786, is another place offering fine seafood and overlooks the beach. Self-caterers will find grocery stores in all the main centres, that open daily until about 1900.

Entertainment

The major backpackers provide most of the island's entertainment and open late bars. The *Picnic Bay Hotel* (Thu) and backpackers (*Arkie's*/Fri, *Geoff's*/Mon) are the places to go for serious pool competitions. There are also live bands most nights at the Arkie's Resort, Arcadia.

Tours & activities

Diving Magnetic Island is a superb and relatively cheap venue to learn to dive. There are also some excellent dive sites just off the island, on the reef and, of course, over the world famous 'Yongala' wreck (see page 328). *Pleasure Divers*, 10 Marine Pde Arcadia, T4778 5788, www.pleasuredivers@austarnet.com.au, offers 3 or 4-day PADI Open Water Courses from $179, a 2-day Advanced Open Water Course (for the 'Yongala') from $279. Accommodation packages are also available. The *Magnetic Island Dive Centre*, Shop 7/4 Picnic Bay Mall, T4758 1399, www.mag.is.dive@austarnet.com.au, offer similar deals.

Horse trekking Bluey's Ranch, 38 Gifford St, Horseshoe Bay, T4778 5109, offer rides from 1-hr to half-day, from $30. **Jet skiing** If you really must create havoc then *Adrenalin Jet Ski Tours*, T4778 5533, offer a guided 85 km half-day circumnavigation of the island, from $115. Jet skis can also be hired independently from Horseshoe Bay, from $38 for 15 min, T4758 1100. **Sea kayaking** *Magnetic Island Sea Kayaks*, T4778 5424, offer half-day adventures from $45 (includes beach breakfast).

Tours The *Magnetic Island Bus Service*, T4778 5130, offer 3-hr guided tours from Picnic Bay at 0900 and 1300 from $30, child $15, family $75. *Tropicana Tours*, 2/26 Picnic St, T4758 1800, www.tropicanatours.com.au, offer an excellent and highly entertaining 8-hr "7 Days in 1' adventure around the island, from $125. Recommended. But book ahead.

Watersports *Jazza's Sailing Tours*, 90 Horseshoe Bay Rd, T4778 5530, offer a good value, 6 hr, cruise aboard the 12 m 'Jazza' from $75, child $50 (includes lunch). *Magnetic Palm Islands Rent-A-Yacht*, T4778 5644, www.miray.com.au, hire 32-ft and 43-ft yachts from $660 for 3 days/2 nights. *Ocean Runner*, T4778 5774, are a new outfit offering a range of enjoyable cruises around the island, including a sunset cruise from $90. Magnetic Island has a small 9-hole golf course in Picnic Bay, visitors welcome, $11, T4778 5188.

Directory

Banks The Post Office, Picnic Bay acts as Commonwealth Bank agents. There are ATMs at the Picnic Bay Hotel on Picnic Bay Mall, Arkie's Resort, Arcadia and the Horseshoe Bay Store. *EFTPOS* is also widely available throughout the island. **Communications Internet** The VIC at Picnic Bay, offers free internet with bookings. *Cybercafe*, Courtyard Mall (open daily 0900-1700) Picnic Bay. Most backpackers including *Arkie's* 7 Marine Pde, T4778 5176, open daily 0900-2100 and *Maggie's Beach Café*, Horseshoe Bay, open from 0900-2100). **Post Office** *Picnic Bay Mall*, Mon-Fri 0830-1700, Sat 0900-1100. **Medical services** *Medical Centre*, Sooning St, Nelly Bay, T4778 5107. **Petrol** *Arcadia Mini Mart*, 5 Bright Av, open daily 0800-1900. *Nelly Bay Store*, 36 Mandalay Av. **Police** T4778 5270.

Townsville to Mission Beach

North of Townsville, from just beyond **Ingham**, the scenery changes quite dramatically with magnificent **Hinchinbrook Island** heralding a distinctly greener and more mountainous landscape. As well as the dramatic scenery and allure of Hinchinbrook Island the coastal stretch between Townsville and Mission Beach offers a number of worthy attractions. About 65 km north of Townsville The **Paluma National Park** (west of the Bruce Highway), straddles the summit and escarpments of the Paluma Range. It supports one of the most southerly tracts of tropical rainforest, affording it World Heritage status and is host to the **Mount Spec/Crystal Creek** and **Jourama Falls**. The Mount Spec/Crystal creek Section is accessed via the small township of **Paluma** 20 km off the highway. There is a picnic site and some pleasant walking tracks near **McClelland's Lookout**. Well facilitated camping, suitable for campervans is available at **Big Crystal Creek** (6 km west of Mutarnee) at the foot of the range Advance bookings, deposit and key collection required, T4777 3112. The Jourama Falls Section is accessed 24 km south of Ingham and 6 km off the Bruce Highway. The falls, featuring a series of pink-coloured granite cascades along **Waterview Creek**, are reached with a short walk and there are two lookouts. Camping facilities are available (self-registration).

From Apr to Oct (winter) it hardly rains at all but during 'the wet' (Nov-Mar) the angry, bruised skies can unleash an aquatic onslaught of biblical proportions, turning roads into rivers

Like many sugar towns in the far north Ingham has a strong Italian connection and still celebrates the fact with the Australian-Italian Festival each May. Although a pleasant place in itself, it is most often used as a base for exploring the **Lumholtz National Park** and 305-m **Wallaman Falls** (the highest in Australia) or as the southern gateway to Hinchinbrook National Park via **Lucinda** (25 km east), home to the world's largest sugar loading jetty (5.6 km). There are guided tours of the **Victoria Sugar Mill**, the largest and oldest in the country, on Forrest Beach Road (July-November only) The Hinchinbrook **VIC** is at 21 Lannercost Street, Ingham, T4776 5211, www.acecomp.com.au/hinchinbrook ■ *Mon-Fri 0845-1700, Sat/Sun 0900-1400. The VIC can assist with accommodation and local attractions, while the QPWS office, 49 Cassidy St, T4776 1700 can provided detailed national parks information.*

Ingham
109 km Townsville

The biggest attraction of the Lumholtz National Park are the **Wallaman Falls**, which are the tallest, but not necessarily the most spectacular falls in Australia, at over 300 m. The falls, best viewed in the wet season (November-March), can be accessed by 2WD but conditions in the wet can be treacherous and you are advised to check with the QPWS before departing. From Ingham travel 8 km west to Trebonne then turn left, then right over Stone River, then left again. After a steep climb the road terminates at the QPWS **campsite** (self registration and gas BBQs). Just before the campsite there is a 2-km track to the right that takes you to the **falls lookout**. From here it is another 2 km by foot on a steep track to the base of the falls.

Lumholtz National Park

From Ingham the Bruce Highway crosses the Herbert River and climbs to reach the breathtaking **lookout** across to Hinchinbrook Island. Its mountainous outline and green cloak of rainforest seems almost connected to the mainland by the huge expanses of impenetrable mangrove swamps and islands. The beachside town of Cardwell, a further 40 km north, is fast developing into a tourist resort and provides a welcome stop on the route north as well as a base from which to explore **Hinchinbrook Island National Park**, or to sample its fishing, cruising, flightseeing or wildlife watching activities. The

Cardwell
109 km Townsville

Queensland

obvious wildlife star in these parts is the placid-looking sea cow – or **dugong** – which clings precariously to existence in local waters and is without doubt one of nature's most unusual sea creatures. The QPWS Rainforest and Reef Centre provides local tourist information, details of seasonal eco-cruises operations and issues permits for Hinchinbrook Island National Park. ■ *Daily 0830-1630. T4066 8601, hinchinbrook.camp@env.qld.gov.au 142 Victoria St, (about half way through the town by the jetty).*

Although fast developing there are as yet limited accommodation options in Cardwell

Sleeping and eating Most amenities and accommodation is on the main drag of Cardwell (Victoria St). Interstate buses stop outside the Seaview café on Victoria St south of the jetty. The YHA affiliated **A-E** *Kookaburra Holiday Park and Hinchinbrook Hostel*, 175 Victoria St (north of the jetty), T4066 8648, www.hinchin brookholiday.com.au, has everything from self-catering villas to campsites as well as dorms, doubles and twins in the well-facilitated hostel section. Pool, tours and activities bookings, internet and free bike hire for guests. For eating *Muddies Café and Bar*, 221 Victoria St, T4066 8907, can offer wholesome mains with a seafood edge as well as takeaways and sandwiches. It also shows free movies for patrons every 2nd Thu night. Open daily from 1100 till late. Happy hour daily from 1600-1800.

Tours and activities *Hinchinbrook Island Ferries*, T4066 8270, www.hinchinbrook ferries.com.au are the main operator in Cardwell and offer day cruises from $85, child $42. Fri/Sun/Wed, Nov-Jun (no sailings in Jan/Feb). *Hinchinbrook Explorer Fishing and Eco-Tours*, T4068 9716 offer full day national park or estuary fishing trips from $120 and eco-cruises from $66. For Hinchinbrook Island transportation and tours see below. *Cardwell Air Charters*, T4066 8468, www.oz-e.com.au/cardair offer a wide range of scenic flights over Hinchinbrook Island (40 mins, $80), the Reef (1 hr, $120) and 'outback' to the Undara Lava Tubes (half-day $255). They also offer a trip to see where the much-hyped TV series 'Survivor II' was filmed over the rugged Herbert River Gorge (45 mins, $95). Children half price. The more adventurous can reach the location and 280 m Blencoe Falls by road (2WD in winter only, 81 km). Details from the VIC.

Hinchinbrook Island National Park

From the moment you first see it, Hinchinbrook Island casts its irresistible spell. At almost 40,000 ha, it is the largest island national park in the world and, having changed little since white settlement in Australia, remains one of the most unspoilt. Crowned by the 1142 m peak of **Mount Bowen**, it is a wonderland of sheer cliffs, forested slopes and blinding white beaches, with some of Queensland's most weird, wonderful (and dangerous) wildlife, but presents more of a challenge than a relaxing excursion, with few designated access points and limited walking opportunities.

Getting there *Hinchinbrook Island Ferries*, T4066 8270, www.hinchin brookferries.com.au, based in Cardwell provide the northerly access to the island (including the resort) while *Hinchinbrook Wilderness Safaris*, (Bill Pearce) T4777 8307 provide southerly access from Lucinda east of Ingham. Both also offer a range of day tours and cruises. Most people doing the Thorsborne Trail attempt it from north to south using the former company for the northerly drop-off (from $60) and the latter for southerly pick up (from $45). Note sailings vary according to season. There are no sailings in Jan/Feb.

For true explorers there is only one mission – the famed **Thorsborne Trail**. This 32-km, minimum four day/three night bushwalk (also known as the East Coast Trail) is one of best in the country and takes in a wide range of habitats along the east coast from **Ramsay Bay** in the northeast, to **George Point** in the south. Only 40 walkers are allowed on the track at any one time and you must book sometimes up to a year in advance. The best time to attempt the hike is from April to September, which avoids the very wet and the very dry, though the topography of Hinchinbrook can create inclement weather at any time. The track is not graded and in some areas is rough and hard to traverse and insect repellent is an absolute must. The QPWS provide detailed information on the track and issue the relevant camping permits, T4066 8601, hinchin-brook.camp@env.qld.gov.au Their excellent broadsheet 'Thorsborne Trail' is a fine start and will soon have you applying the dubbin to your walking boots.

Most who choose to visit the island do so for a day, but you can stay longer at the **LL** *Hinchinbrook Island Resort*, T4066 8270, www.hinchinbrookresort.com.au, an excellent, if expensive, eco-friendly sanctuary with all mod cons. There are **camping** facilities (with toilets and gas fireplaces) at *Scraggy Point* (The Haven) on the Island's northwest coast and **Maucushla Bay**, near the resort. Basic bush camping sites have been established along the Thorsborne Trail with **Zoe Bay** offering toilets and water. Open fires are not allowed and you will require a gas stove and water containers. Camping permits for all sites must be obtained from the **QPWS Rainforest and Reef Centre**, 142 Victoria St, Cardwell,T4066 8601, hinchinbrook.camp@env.qld.gov.au

Mission Beach and Dunk Island

Taking its name from a former Aboriginal Mission established in the early 1900s, Mission Beach is the term given to an idyllic 14 km stretch of the Queensland Coast, from Bingil Bay to the north, to the mouth of the Hull River to the south. The area is not only the prime tourist attraction between Townsville and Cairns, but also contains ecologically important **rainforest**, being home to many unique plants and animals. This includes the almost umbrella like Licuala Palm and a rare and leggy bird called the **cassowary**.

Colour map 5, grid A6
Population: 1,000
137 km from Cairns, 250 km from Townsville

Information and orientation The Mission Beach Visitors Information Centre is at the end of the El-Arish-Mission Beach Rd, on Porter Promanade and the northern end of Mission Beach, T4068 7099, www.missionbch.com, www.mymissionbeach.com Open daily 0900-1700. It has tons of information and very helpful staff. For newcomers the area is hard to navigate, so be sure to secure the free 'Street and Business Directory'.

Ins & outs

From **Bingil Bay** in the north the community is scattered and merges through Mission Beach, and Wongaling Beach to **South Mission Beach**. The 2 main centres of activity are Mission Beach village (just south of the VIC) and **Wongaling Beach**, which is 4 km to the south on the Tully-Mission Beach Rd (Cassowary Dr), marked by a large model of the bird. The Dunk Island ferries and water taxis leave from Clump Point Jetty north of Mission Beach and from Wongaling Beach off Banfield Pde (east of Wongaling Beach on Wongaling Beach Rd). Internet is available at *Cybernet*, Campbell St, Mission Beach (open daily 0900-1800), *Zola's* across the road in the Village Green, Mission Beach, and the *Mission Beach Information Station* (tour and accommodation bookings), 4 Mission Beach Resort Shops, Wongaling Beach.

Next door to the VIC, the **Wet Tropics Environmental Centre** offers a fine introduction to the rainforest ecology and habitats of the region and if you plan on doing any rainforest walks, this is the place to get directions and avail yourself of all the detail. ■ *Daily 1000-1700*. The main tracts of accessible rainforest are to be found in the **Tam O'Shanter State Forest** that dominates the region and contains one of the largest tracts of coastal lowland rainforest in northern Queensland. There are a number of excellent **walks** on offer, including the **Licuala Walk**, a 45-minute stroll under the canopy of the rare

Sights
Between Oct-May avoid 'stingers'; play it safe and stick within the netted areas off Mission and South Mission Beaches

and beautiful Licuala Palms. There's also a good chance of seeing cassowaries. The other big attraction in these parts are the beautiful topical **beaches**, backed by the archetypal coconut palms.

Sleeping

Although there are several resorts in the area, the many excellent and characterful B&Bs and self-contained accommodations are recommended

For a spot of colour and striking architecture try the one-off **LL** *Perrier Walk Guesthouse*, Perrier Walk, Mission Beach, T4068 7141, www.perrierwalk.nq.nu It offers a choice of 3 superbly appointed en suites in a quiet garden setting with a pool and an outdoor shower, and is only a short stroll from the beach. The **L** *Licuala Lodge*, 11 Mission Circle, Mission Beach, T4068 8194, www.licualalodge.com.au, is an award winning, pole house B&B with doubles, singles, and a memorable 'jungle pool' and spa. Slightly cheaper but no less enjoyable is the **B** *Honeyeater Home stay*, 53 Reid Rd, Wongaling Beach, T4068 8741, www.uniquevillas.com.au/honeat, which offers a friendly welcome and separate accommodation in a spacious en suite. It also has a pool, guest library and offers bike hire. For an interesting eco-retreat, wildlife enthusiasts should look no further than the good value **C** *Sanctuary Retreat*, Holt Rd, Bingil Bay, T4088 6064, www.sanctuaryatmission.com, which offers secluded, minimalist forest huts in a setting designed to actively nurture and attract the local wildlife. Restaurant, internet and pick-ups. For self-contained options try the colourful comforts and boutique beach huts of **A** *Sejala*, 1 Pacific St, Mission Beach, T4068 7241, www.sejala.com.au

Backpackers From north to south there is the **C-D** *Treehouse*, Bingil Bay Rd, Bingil Bay, T4068 7137, missionbeach@yha.qld.org It is a pole house with doubles, twins and dorms, a pool and all the usual amenities. Its only drawback is its distance from the beach but shuttle buses regularly ply the route. Also in Bingil Bay is the **C-E** *Bingil Bay Backpackers*, Cutten St, T4068 7208, www.nomadsworld.com.au, that offers air-conditioned motel-style units in an elevated position with good views, a pool and lively bar/bistro. Further south in Wongaling Beach is the **C-E** *Mission Beach Backpackers Lodge*, 28 Wongaling Beach Rd, T4068 8317, www.missionbeachbackpacker.com Although nothing special, it is a popular place with a social atmosphere, offering 10/8 and 4 share dorms and separate doubles with fans or a/c, a well-equipped kitchen. It is also close to the happening bar in the Mission Beach Resort and the main shopping complex. Closer to the beach is the well established and popular **C-E** *Scotty's Beachouse Hostel*, 167 Reid Rd, T4068 8676, scottys@znet.net.au, which offers a range of unit style dorms and doubles surrounding a fine pool. It has a very relaxed atmosphere, a restaurant and reputedly the best bar in town.

There are several **motor parks** in the area with the very tidy and beachside **L-F** *Beachcomber Caravan Village*, Kennedy Esplanade, Mission Beach South, T4068 8129, being recommended.

Eating

Most of the eateries in the area are concentrated in and around the Village Green Shopping Complex, Porter Promenade, Mission Beach

For fine dining with an international menu try the award winning *Blarney's By The Beach*, 10 Wongaling Beach Rd, Wongaling Beach, T4068 8472. Open Tue-Sat for dinner and Sun for lunch. Recommended. In the far south on the shores of Lugger Bay the 'Ulysses' at the *Horizon Resort*, Explorer Dr, is also reputed to be a good restaurant and has a seafood buffet on Fri. For value *Scotty's Beachhouse Bar and Grill*, 167 Reid Rd (off Cassowary Drive) Wongaling, has a lively atmosphere and offers budget bistro meals The *Port O Call Cafe*, Shop 6, The Hub, Porter Promenade, T4068 7390, run by the Odd couple is open daily from 0800 and offers the best coffee and value breakfasts in town. There are supermarkets in the Village Green, Mission Beach and at the Wongaling Beach Shopping Complex. Open daily 0800-1900.

Tours & activities

Diving *Mission Beach Dive Charters*, Shop 8a The Reef Centre, Mission Beach, T4068 7277, offer wreck dives to the 'Lady Bowen' and general reef exploratory dives and all-day cruises from $136 (cruise only Mon/Tue/Thu/Fri/Sat from $96) as well as diver certification from $325. *Quickcat Dive*, T4068 8432, www.quickcatdive.com, offer similar trips. **Fishing** *Bounty Hunter*, T4088 6007, offer day-long sea-fishing trips from $150. In contrast *FNQ Fishing Adventures* head up the tidal river systems to catch crabbies and barramundi (amongst other things), promising a bit of crocodile spotting along the way. Half-day from $70, full-day $125. **Horse trekking** *Bush 'n' Beach*, T4068 7893, offer 1-hr rides along the beach from $50. **Sea kayaking** *Coral Sea Kayaking*, T4068 9154, www.coralseakayaking.com and *Sunbird Adventures*, T4068 8229, offer full-day voyages to Dunk Island with plenty of time to explore from $84 (half-day coastal exploration $49). **Skydiving** *Skydive Mission Beach*, based next to the Castaways Resort on Pacific Pde, T4052 1822, www.jumpthebeach.com offer tandem jumps on to Mission Beach or Dunk Island, 8000-ft from $248, 14,000 from $363 **Whitewater rafting** *RnR Rafting*, T4051 7777, www.rnrrafting.com.au, and *Raging Thunder*, T4030 7990, www.ragingthunder.com.au, provide pick-ups for a wide range of rafting trips and packages on the Tully or North Johnstone Rivers, from $135. **Wildlife night spotting** *Sunbird Adventures*, T4068 8229, offer a fascinating night walk in the Lacey's Creek Rainforest from 1900-2130 from $25. Recommended.

McCaffertys/Greyhound, Premier Motor Services and *Coral Coaches* offer regular daily **Transport** services from north and south stopping outside the Post Office on Porter Promenade in Mission Beach. Island Resort Travel, Homestead Centre, Mission Beach, T4068 7187, act as the local ticketing agents. *Mission Beach Connections*, T4059 2709, also offer daily shuttles from Cairns at 0730 and 1400, from $31 single (backpacker special $22) and Tully from $9. *Mission Beach Bus and Coach*, T4068 7400, operate daily servicing Bingil Bay to South Mission Beach single fare $1.50 day ticket $10, child $5. For a taxi call T131008 (24 hr) For Dunk Island Cruises and water taxis see Dunk Island section below.

Banks The **Post Office**, Porter Promenade acts as the Commonwealth Bank Agent. **Directory** ATMs are available in the Mission Beach Supermarket and at the Mission Beach Resort. **Car servicing and breakdowns** *Mission Beach Discount Tyres*, Stephen St (off Cassowary Dr), T4068 7013. **Medical services** Cassowary Dr, T4068 8174. **Police** Corner Cassowary Dr and Web Rd, T4068 8422.

The Aboriginal name for Dunk Island is 'Coonanglebah' meaning 'The Island **Dunk Island** of Peace and Plenty' which is far more appropriate than the name Dunk (after Lord Dunk, First Lord of the Admiralty) which was bestowed upon it by Captain James Cook in 1770. But whatever its official label this 730-ha national and marine park, lying less than 5 km off Mission Beach, is one of the most beautiful island parks and resorts north of the Whitsundays.

Getting there Dunk has its own airport and regular flights are available from major *Prices vary and are* Australian cities with *Qantas Link*, then from Cairns 4 times daily with *Macair*, T131528, *fiercely competitive,* www.macair.com.au *The Quickcat*, T4068 7289, is a water taxi which departs from *so shop around* Clump Point daily at 0730, from $29, child $14.50 return. *Dunk Island Ferry and Cruises* (MV Kavanagh), T4068 7211, also departs from Clump Point, twice daily at 0845 and 1030, from $22, child $13 return. The latter also offer Cruise options with diving, snorkelling and boom netting. As well as Dunk Island Quickcat also visit the outer reef and **Beaver Cay** which is a beautiful spot offering much better snorkelling than Dunk Island, from $140. *Dunk Island Express*, T4068 8310, departs from the beach opposite their office on Banfield Pde, Wongaling Beach, daily at 0930,1100,1230,1430,1630, from $22, child $13 return ($26 if overnight). Quickcat offers coach pick-ups from Cairns. Dunk Island Ferry and Cruises and Dunk Island Express offer local courtesy pick-ups.

Snorkelling on the island is poor compared to the reef

Sights and activities Whether staying at the resort or as day visitors the vast majority of people come to Dunk to relax big-style. But if you can drag yourself away from the beautiful stretch of palm fringed beach either side of the wharf in **Brammo Bay**, you can explore the island and its rich wildlife or sample some of the many activities on offer. The island has 13 km of **walking** tracks and the reception in the main resort building can offer free maps and information. There are plenty of options, including a complete **Island Circuit** (9.2 km, three hours) which takes in the remote **Bruce Arthur's Artists Colony/Gallery** (■ *Mon-Thu 1000-1300, $4, walking access only*). The energetic may also like to attempt the stiff climb (5.6 km, three hours, return) to the summit of **Mount Kootaloo** (271 m), the island's highest peak. *Watersports*, which is located next to the wharf, offers independent day visitors a host of equipment and water-based activities from a mask and snorkel hire ($15 a day) to windsurfing ($20 per hour), water skiing (lesson $25, 15 minutes) and even parasailing (from $55). The resort (see below) offers a **day visitor's package** that includes lunch and access to the bar, some sports facilities and the very attractive **'Butterfly Pool'** (from $28, child $17, tickets available at Watersports).

Sleeping and eating The 4-Star **LL** *Dunk Island Resort*, Brammo Bay T4068 8199, www.poresorts.com.au, offers a delightful range of units and suites, excellent amenities and a wealth of activities and sports. (Book well ahead and from Sydney office, T1800-737678). Children welcome. For the budget traveller the **QPWS** camping ground is discreetly located next to the resort. Permits can be purchased from Watersports on the island. BBQs and showers. The resort has 2 licensed **restaurants**, *EJ's on the Deck* (lunch) and the *Beachcomber Restaurant*, which offers breakfast and table d'hote dinner. BBQs are also available next to the pool. *BB's On The Beach* is a rather expensive affair, that is open to the public and located next to the wharf. Open 1100-1700.

Far North Queensland

*Without doubt, Far North Queensland offers more to see and do than any other region in Australia. The bustling, tourist-driven city of **Cairns** acts as the gateway to two of the greatest ecosystems on earth: the **Great Barrier Reef** and **Wet Tropics Rainforest**. They also offer a seemingly endless choice of activities, from world class **diving** to wilderness **outback tours**. Few venture north beyond CapeTribulation or Port Douglas to **Cooktown**, let alone **Cape York**, but for those adventurous souls that try, they will experience the very best that **4WD** has to offer, and be exposed to some of Australia's true wilderness. West of Cairns the lush, green plateau known as the **Atherton Tablelands** is a cool retreat from the coast and, beyond the Tablelands, the dusty brown horizons of the **Gulf Savannah** beckon the true adventurer. This part of Australia is real wilderness travel, where nature and the elements still rule.*

Mission Beach to Cairns

Once back on the Bruce Highway it is a short drive north to the small settlement of Silkwood and the turn-off (Old Bruce Highway) to **Mena Creek Falls** and **Paronella Park**. Built in the early 1930s by Spanish immigrant and sugar baron José Paronella, this magical estate remains a place of surreal, almost haunting beauty. Having been left to decay for many years it was saved from the jungle and restored to serve as a tourist attraction, though in recent years it has become for many the ideal place to get hitched or as a backdrop for film and television. The magnificent **castle**, which still seems to merge subtly with the environment, is the centrepiece of the 5-ha estate, along with water features, stands of bamboo and palm trees, all of which complement the romantic and historic atmosphere. Guided walks (40 minutes) are available every 30 minutes daily and are included in the admission price. There is also fish feeding and swimming is encouraged beneath the adjacent falls. A café and **camping** and caravan park are also on-site. ■ *Daily 0830-1700, $16, child $8, T4065 3225, www.paronellapark.com.au*

From Paronella, the Old Bruce Highway continues 25 km north through extensive cane fields to reach the small town of **Innisfail** on the Johnstone River. Innisfail is home to a large immigrant Italian community that found their niche in the sugar cane industry. **Mourilyan**, 10 km south of Innisfail, is home to the **Australian Sugar Industry Museum**, with its various displays extolling the region's greatest agricultural asset. ■ *Mon-Sat 0900-1700, Sun 0900-1500, $5, child $3 T4063 2656.* Just beyond Innisfail the Palmerston Highway provides the southern access route via the picturesque **Wooroonooran National Park** and Milla Milla to the Atherton Tablelands (see page 354). At **Bambina**, 28 km north of Innisfail, is the turn-off to the **Boulders** (6 km), a section of the Babinda Creek featuring huge boulders and rock platforms eroded by the waters into smooth curves and hollows. It is an area steeped in Aboriginal legend and provides an excellent spot for a picnic, bush walking or swimming. The Bruce Highway continues to Cairns, skirting the Bellenden Ker range, which includes the state's highest peak, **Mount Bartle Frere** (1,657 m). The northern terminus of the range signs itself off with an enormous 'full stop', in the form of the dramatic **Walsh's Pyramid** (922 m), reputedly the highest 'free-standing' mountain peak in the world. In its shadow is the small community of **Gordonvale**, from where the **Atherton Highway** begins its heady ascent to the Atherton Tablelands and the charming historical village of Yungaburra. Continuing north on the Bruce Highway, Walsh's Pyramid still dominates the rear view mirror as you enter the southern suburbs of Cairns.

Cairns

Wedged between rolling hills to the west, the ocean to the east and thick mangroves swamps to the north and south, Cairns is like a blossoming tourist tree that is fast outgrowing its pot. Thanks to the Great Barrier Reef on its doorstep, Cairns was always destined to become a world-class tourist destination. After Sydney it is the second most important in Australia. But the big attractions don't begin or indeed, end there. Cairns is blessed with two other world-class natural assets – its warm tropical climate and its ancient rainforest – not to mention a vast range of activities and over 600 tours on offer to take advantage of all that natural beauty.

Colour map 5, grid A6
Population: 130,000
Postcode: 4870
349 km from Townsville
740 km from Mackay
1084 km from Rockhampton
1733 km from Brisbane
2684 km from Sydney

Ins and outs

Air *Cairns International Airport* is located 6 km north of the city centre, on the Captain Cook Highway, T4052 3888, www.cairnsport.com.au International, domestic and state air carriers are all represented, including *Qantas*, T131313, *Air New Zealand*, T132476, *Cathay Pacific*, T131747, *Malaysia Airlines*, T132627, *Virgin Blue*, TT136789, *Air Niugini* (Papua New Guinea), T1300-361380, *Qantas* (Sunstate), T4086 0457 and *Flight West*, T132392. Other local charter flight companies also provide inter-island services throughout the Barrier Reef and to the Whitsunday Islands.

Getting there

Queensland

Cairns

To Cairns B&B, Trinity on the Esplanade, Airport, Flecker Botanical Gardens, Tjapukai, Mount Whitfield Environmental Park, Tanks Art Centre, Royal Flying Doctor Service Visitors Centre, Northern Beaches & Port Douglas

To Coral Cay Villa

Queensland

Trinity Bay

Cairns Base Hospital

St Monica's Cathedral

Cairns

Johno's Blues Bar

Cinema

Library

Club Five Nine

The Chapel

Cairns Central Shopping Complex

Transit Centre

Shields St

Cairns Regional Gallery

QPWS

Spence St

Casino

Interstate Terminal

Trinity Wharf

0 metres 200
0 yards 200

■ Sleeping
1 All Seasons Esplanade *F4*
2 Bel-Air *D4*
3 Bellview *F4*
4 Bohemia Resort *B2*
5 Cairns Beach House *B2*
6 Cairns City Caravan Park *A1*
7 Cairns International *H3*
8 Cairns Queenslander *B3*
9 Cairns Rainbow Inn *D2*
10 Carravella 77 *F4*
11 Carravella 149 *E4*
12 Country Comfort Outrigger *E3*
13 Dreamtime Travellers Rest *G1*
14 Fig Tree Lodge &
Willie McBride's *A2*
15 Florianna *B3*
16 Geckos *G1*
17 Global Palace *G3*
18 Hides *G3*
19 Holiday Inn *E3*
20 Inn the Tropics *E2*
21 McLeod St YHA *G2*
22 Radisson Plaza *G5*
23 Regency Palms *A2*
24 Ryan's Rest *G1*
25 Sofitel *H4*
26 Travellers Oasis *G1*

● Eating
1 Barnacle Bills *G4*
2 Breeze's *H4*
3 Café China *H3*
4 Coffee Club *G4*
5 Dundee's *H3*
6 Gypsy Dee's Café *G3*
7 International Food Court *F4*
8 La Fettucina *G2*
9 Meeting Place *F4*
10 Perrota's *G4*
11 Pesci's *G5*
12 P J O'Briens *G3*
13 Red Ochre Grill *G3*
14 Sports Bar *H3*
15 Tandoori Oven *G3*
16 Tiny's Juice Bar *H3*
17 Verdi's *G2*
18 Woolshed *G3*
19 Yamagen Japanese *H3*
20 Yanni's Taverna *F3*

● Pubs & bars
21 Courthouse Bar & Bistro *G4*
22 Frog & Firkin & Tropos *G3*
23 Pier Tavern *G5*

Harbour

Pier
Market-place
Undersea World

Marlin Marina

To Port Douglas, Green Island, Fitzroy Island & Frankland Islands

Trinity Inlet

5

Bus The interstate coach terminal is located at Trinity Wharf, Wharf St. Daily 0600-0100. *McCafferty's/Greyhound*, T132030, have offices within the terminal and operate regular daily services south to Brisbane and beyond (including onward connections to Darwin from Townsville). *Premier Motor Service*, T133410, www.premierms.com.au, also operate daily services to Brisbane and beyond. *Coral Coaches*, T4031 7577, www.coralcoaches.com.au, run regular local services to the Airport, Port Douglas, Mossman, Daintree and Cape Tribulation and long distance services to Cooktown (Wed/Fri/Sun) and Karumba/Mt Isa (Mon/Wed/Thu). They also have a booking desk within the coach terminal. *Whitecar Coaches*, T4051 9533, www.whitecarcoaches.com.au, service the Atherton Tablelands daily. **Car** In 'the wet' road conditions around Cairns and far north Queensland can be, in a word, aquatic. For up-to-date conditions and flood warnings, T131111.

Train The train station is located next to the Cairns Central Shopping Complex, Bunda St. The station Travel Centre is open Mon-Fri 0900-1700, Sat 0900 1200, T4036 9249, www.traveltrain.qr.com.au (For other long distance train/Traveltrain enquiries, T132232, 24 hrs) There are 3 coastal train services to/from Brisbane and beyond, ranging in standards of luxury and price. The *Sunlander* (departs 0835, Mon/Thu/Sat, from $162, child $82) the *Queenslander* (departs 0835, Tue First Class from $558, child $335) and the luxury, all mod cons, *Great South Pacific Express*, costs a staggering $2,830. There is one 'Outback' service, The *Savannah lander*, from Cairns to Forsayth (from $95), with connecting coach services to Chillagoe, Croydon and Normanton, (from $138). A local scenic service also operates to **Kuranda**, leaving at 0830 and 0930 Sun-Fri and 0830 Sat; from $30, child $15 ($48/$26 return). Ask about the various holiday and 'Discoverer Passes', for price reductions and packages. *Ferry Quicksilver* run a daily ferry ('Wave Piercer') service to Port Douglas from Marlin Marina, Cairns, $23 one-way, T4087 2100.

Getting around Many hotels and hostels provide shuttle services to and from the airport. *Coral Coaches*, T4031 7577, offer regular services to and from the city, from $8. The *Airport Shuttle*, T4099 5950, offers services to and from Port Douglas, Cape Tribulation and Mission Beach. A taxi will cost about $15, T131008. The main suburban bus operator is *Sunbus Marlin Coast*, T4057 7411, www.sunbus.com.au, offering regular services north, as far as Palm Cove and south as far as Gordonvale, from $1. (Day/week passes available). The bus transit centre is on Lake St (City Place) where schedules are posted. **Bike hire** is readily available in Cairns, with many of the car hire companies and hostels offering rentals from $12 a day. Companies include *MiniCar Rentals*, 47 Shield St, T4051 3030, or *Bandicoot*, 59 Sheridan St, T4051 0155.

Orientation Given its geography the centre of Cairns is compact and easily negotiable on foot. The attractive waterfront with its many hostels, hotels and restaurants fringes the ocean and **Trinity Bay** to the northeast. At the city's southern end the **Trinity Pier** complex gives way to **Trinity Inlet** and **Trinity Wharf**, where the reef ferry and interstate coach terminals are based. From there the main commercial centre runs north in a basic grid system. The **Cairns Railway Station** is located beside the new *Cairns Central Shopping Complex* just to the southwest of the town centre.

Information The number of independent 'commission based' information centres and operators in Cairns is famously out of control. For objective information and advice on accommodation and especially activities, look no further than The Tourism Tropical North Queensland accredited *Visitor Information Centre* at 5 The Esplanade, T4051 3588, F4051 0127, www.tnq.org.au Open daily 0830-1730. The **QPWS** office, 10 McLeod St, T4046 6600, www.env.qld.gov.au, has detailed information on national parks and the Barrier Reef Islands, including camping permits and bookings. Open Mon-Fri 0830-1630. Local maps are available from *Absells Map Shop* in the Andrew Jecks Arcade off Lake St.

Other useful websites include www.welcometo cairns.com.au, and www.greatbarrier reef.aus.net.au

Queensland

Sights

Most of the major sights are of course a boat trip away, but the city itself offers a number of colourful attractions. Located in the far corner of the plush Pier Shopping Complex, Pierpoint Road, is **Undersea World**, which offers a 'shallow' introduction to the living reef and its inhabitants. ■ *Daily 0800-2200, $12.50, children $7, T4041 1777.* Less scary but no less colourful is the **Cairns Regional Gallery** housed in the former 1936 Public Curators Offices on the corner of Abbott Street and Shields Street. Since 1995 the gallery has been an excellent showcase for mainly local and regional art as well as national visiting and loan exhibitions. ■ *Daily from Mon-Fri 1000-1800, Sat/Sun 1300-1800, $4, child $2, T4031 6865.* For even more colour head to **St Monica's Cathedral**, 183 Abbott Street, to see their unique stained glass windows complete with the reef. Where else in the world would you find stained glass windows depicting tropical fish? ■ *Daily. Donation only. T4051 2838.* The **Flecker Botanical Gardens** on the northwestern fringe of the city offers a small but interesting collection of tropical favourites. The gardens are set amongst fresh and saltwater habitats and intersected with boardwalks and tracks. ■ *Informative guided walks are offered at 1300 Mon-Fri. Café and shop on site. Daily 0930-1630, T4044 3398, Collins Av, Edge Hill.* A track located next to the gardens (near MacDonnell Street) takes you to the **Mount Whitfield Environmental Park** with its 7 km of walking tracks through unspoilt rainforest to take in impressive city and ocean views. Alternatively, you might like to combine your walk with a look at the **Tanks Art Centre** which is a trio of former diesel storage tanks located on the edge of the park now used as a dynamic exhibition and performance space for the local arts community. ■ *Daily 1100-1600, free. A market* *day is held on the last Sun of every month from Jun to Nov 0900-1300. 46 Collins Av, T4032 2349.* Also in Edge Hill is the **Royal Flying Doctor Service Visitors Centre,** which offers a broad introduction and history of this vital and almost iconic aspect of outback life. ■ *Mon-Sat 0900-1630, $5, child $2.50, T4053 5687, 1 Junction St.*

Next to the Skyrail terminal, in Smithfield (see page 356) is **Tjapukai** (pronounced 'Jaboguy'), an award-winning Aboriginal Cultural Park considered one of the most professional and diverse of its type in Australia. The 11-ha site offers an entertaining and educational insight into Aboriginal mythology, customs and history, and in particular, that of the Tjapukai. There is also a quality restaurant and shop on site. To make the most of the experience give yourself at least half a day. Recommended. ■ *Daily 0900-1700, $27, child $13.50, T4042 9999, www.tjapukai.com.au* North of the airport the thick mangrove swamps give way to the more alluring **northern beaches** and the expensive oceanside resorts of **Trinity Beach** and **Palm Cove.** Both offer the fine and natural sandy beaches that the waterfront in Cairns so embarrassingly lacks and therefore make an attractive base to stay outside the city. The VIC in Cairns has detailed accommodation listings. Other than Trinity Beach and Palm Cove the most northerly of the beaches, **Ellis Beach** is recommended. If you are looking for a nice spot to have lunch look no further than the new marina at **Yorkey's Knob,** Buckley Street, T4055 7711. The **Wild World Tropical Zoo** at Clifton Beach houses all the usual suspects, like crocodiles, snakes, wombats and koala, as well as a range of species unique to tropical North Queensland. Various shows are on offer throughout the day with everybody's favourite- the 'Cuddle a Koala Photo Session'- taking place daily at 1100 and 1430. The **Night Zoo** kicks off at 1900 every Monday to Thursday and Saturday and combines a sing along around a campfire with an introduction to nocturnal creatures. Includes BBQ and refreshments. Bookings essential. ■ *Daily 0830-1700, $22, child $11, T4055 3669, www.wildworld-aus.com.au   Captain Cook Highway.*

Sights around Cairns

Activities

The majority of tourist activities in Cairns are of course centred around the Great Barrier Reef. The choice is simply vast, from the most popular activities of diving and snorkelling, to cruising, sailing, kayaking and flightseeing. On land the choices are no less exciting with everything from bungee jumping to ballooning. With hundreds of operators in the city vying for your tourist dollar, you are advised to seek objective information at the official and accredited VIC. Note that many of the larger cruise and activity operators offer combination deals, which offer attractive savings. Adrenaline junkies should ask about the **Awesome Foursome** deals which can combine such adventures as an island visit, a rafting trip, a bungee jump and a skydive for around $400 (saving about $40) T4051 3588. Generally speaking younger folk should look at what is on offer with **Raging Thunder, The Adventure Company** and **Jungle Tours.**

Bungee jumping An attractive jump complex at McGregor Road in Smithfield 15 minute north of Cairns offers a 50-m jump and also the popular jungle swing, a sort of half free-fall/half swing. Bungee $109, Swing $79, T4057 7188, www.ajhackett.com.au   Open daily 0930-1730. Night jumping on request (at least then you can't see the ground!). Pick-ups available. **Fishing** Cairns has been a world-class big game fishing venue for many years and as a result there are many excellent charters with experienced guides to take you on what can be

▶▶ **Diving on the reef**

Cairns is an internationally renowned base for diving and as such is positively bursting at the seams with dive shops, operators and schools. Choosing a trip can be a real headache. Cairns is not the cheapest place to get your diving certificate but provided you have both the time and the money (from $300, basic no accommodation to $500 on board all inclusive) there is perhaps no better place to learn. And for as little as $50 on top of the price of a day cruise you can experience an **introductory dive** at one of the best sites in the world. This is generally safe, provided you are fit and healthy, choose a reputable company, with qualified instructors and then do exactly what you are told. A good tip, especially if you are going snorkelling or are a first time reef diver, is to visit **Reef Teach** (Spence Street, T4031 7794, www.reefteach.com.au), which gives you an entertaining two-hour lecture on the basics of the reef's natural history, conservation and fish/coral identification. The show starts at 1815, Monday-Saturday, and costs $13. Recommended. The best diving is to be had on the **outer reef** where the water is generally clearer and the fish species bigger. Even if you are attempting your first dive, you are advised to choose an operator that goes there, but that does not mean that the 'inner islands' and **inner reef** are any less fascinating, or indeed that the waters that surround them are at all lacking in life.

The following are just a sample of the main operators in Cairns, but there are many more on offer and prices vary. Note almost all offer competitive rates and options for certified divers and snorkellers. **ProDive**, on the corner of Abbott Street and Shields Street, T4031 5255, www.prodive-cairns.com.au, offer a range of trips including a three day/two-night certification with 11 dives from $510, one-day introductory dive from $145. **The Cairns Dive Centre**, 121 Abbott Street, T4051 7531, www.cairnsdive.com.au, offer certification from $297, and introductory dives from $120. **Reef Encounter**, 100 Abbott Street, T4050 0688, www.reeftrip.com.au, offer three-day/two-night certification, from $320. **Down Under Dive**, 287 Draper Street, T4052 8300, www.downunderdive.com.au offer three-day/two-night certification from $400. Other reputable companies include **Tusa Dive**, on the corner of Shields Street and The Esplanade, T4031 1248, www.tusadive.com.au; **Taka Dive**, 131 Lake Street, T4051 8722; **Deep Sea Divers Den**, 319 Draper Street, T4031 2223; **Mike Ball Dive Expeditions**, 28 Spence Street, T4031 5484, www.takadive.com.au; **Ocean Spirit**, 33 Lake Street, T4031 2920, www.oceanspirit.com.au; **Aquarius III**, T4051 6449, www.aquarius3.com.au; and **The Adventure Company**, 1st Floor 13 Shields Street, T4051 4777, www.adventures.com.au, who offer longer trips from six-day/five-night from $1,000.

a superb experience. Black Marlin are the biggest species, capable of reaching weights of over 1,000 pounds. Another commonly caught species is the Wahoo. For many years until his death the actor Lee Marvin came to Cairns annually to fish for Marlin. He loved the place so much that half his ashes were cast on the reef; the other half being cast back in his American home. One of the best charter companies is *Cairns Reef Charter Services*, T4031 4742, www.ausfish.com/crcs They have a fleet of ocean-going vessels and also offer an exciting range of inland trips to catch the famed barramundi. Two other reputable local companies in Cairns are *Cairns Travel and Sports fishing*, T4031 6016, and *VIP*, T4031 4355. Both offer a wide range of fishing trips. Prices start at about $75 for a half-day and $200 a day per person for big game fishing. **Golf** The Cairns region has many a good golf course with the *Paradise Palms Course*, Clifton Beach, T4059 1166, being one of Australia's best. **Hiking** *Jungle Tours*, T4032 5600, offer an excellent range of multi-day rainforest and outback-hiking adventures from $259. **Horse trekking** *Blazing Saddles*, T4059 0955, www.blazingsaddles.com.au, run a half-day trek suitable for beginners, from $85, child $65. They also offer entertaining and delightfully muddy half-day ATV safaris from $110. The *Springmount Station Stables*, T4093 4493, offer a more conventional approach with half to full day, farm stays and camp-outs, from $88, two-day $242.

Rafting Cairns is the base for some excellent rafting with a wide range of adrenaline pumping trips down the Barron, North Johnstone and Tully Rivers. The minimum age for rafting is usually 13. *Raging Thunder*, T4030 7990, www.ragingthunder.com.au, offer half, full, and multi-day trips, as well as heli-trips and many other activity combos. Half-day Barron River from $83, full-day Tully River, $145, two-day Tully River $350. *R'n'R*, Abbott Street, T4051 7777, are a similar outfit offering full-day trips down the Tully for $141, half-day on the Barron for $81. *Foaming Fury*, 19-21 Barry Street, T4031 3460, tackle the Barron, half-day $77 and also offer a full-day two-man 'sports rafting' experience on the Russell River, from $118. *Extreme Green*, Level 11, 15 Lake Street, T04-0927 3009, offer a half-day trip down the Barron for $70. *River and Sea Kayaking Raging Thunder*, T4030 7990, www.ragingthunder.com.au, offer river kayaking on the Tully from $128, full-day sea kayaking around Fitzroy island from $110, overnight from $135 and an extended 3-day/2-night adventure. *The Adventure Company*, 1st Floor, 13 Shields Street, T4051 4777, www.adventures.com.au, offer a good 3-day/2-night trip crossing King Reef and out to the North Barnard Islands from $535. **Other watersports and activities** For a good value attempt at **water-skiing** or wakeboarding try *Skii-Mee Tours*, a small and friendly family owned operation based in Brinsmead, T4031 3381, www.skiimee.com.au Scheduled day tour and instruction on Tuesday/Thursday and half/full day tours on other days by appointment, full day from $145. **Parasailing** is available with *Watersports Adventures*, T4031 7888 (10 minutes) from $72. Predictably perhaps Cairns has **jet boat** trips, T4057 5884, from $70.

Scenic flights Fixed wing flights over the reef and surrounding islands are offered by *Reefwatch Air Tours*, T4035 9808, www.reefwatch.com.au, and *Daintree Air Services*, T4034 9300, www.daintreeair.com.au 30 minutes, from $135. *Aquaflight*, T4031 4307, www.aquaflight.com.au, operate a fleet of seaplanes which have the added attraction of island and reef cay landings, from $179. Recommended. **Aerobatic** flights in a **Tiger Moth** are also on offer at the airport, T4035 9400, 20 minutes, from $110. Several companies offer **helicopter** flights, half-day trips and safaris, including *Sunlover Helicopters*, T4035 9669, www.sunloverheli.com.au, from $249. *Cairns Heli Scenic*, T4031 5999, www.cairns-heliscenic.com.au, 15 minutes from $140 and *Kestrel Aviation*, T4035 2206, www.kestrelaviation.com.au, 10 minutes from $89. For a sedate **balloon** ride with the usual bubbly breakfast try *Champagne Balloon Flights*, T4058 1688, www.champagneballoons.com.au, 30 minutes from $135. *Raging Thunder*, T4030 7911, www.ragingthunder.com.au, and *Hot Air*, T1800-800829, offer similar trips from $130. For another silent near-flight experience you might also like to try the *Flying Leap*, T4036 2127, www.flyingleap.com.au – a sort of hang-glider attached to a 300-m wire, 60 m above ground. Two flights, with pick-ups (in a van that is, not off the ground), from $50. **Skydiving** *Paul's Parachuting*, McLeod Street, T1800-225572, www.paulsparachuting.com.au, offer tandems from up to 14,000 ft, training and scenic flights from $228 (8,000-ft). Their combination skydive and certified dive package is good value at $320 *Skydive Cairns*, T4052 1822, offer similar jumps.

▶▶ Reef Island Cruises

There are a mind boggling number of reef and reef island sailing and cruise trips based in Cairns. Most give you the opportunity to dive, even for the first time, with a minimum of training, or at the very least to snorkel. The most popular day trips are to Green or Fitzroy Islands and to the outer reef. These are listed and described in the Northern Reef Islands section (see page 352). In general, for a basic inner reef island trip without extras, expect to pay anywhere between $36-55. For an Outer Reef Cruise with snorkelling, anything from $70-150. For an Outer Reef Cruise with introductory dive from $120-200 and for a luxury three-day cruise with accommodation, meals and all activities included about $1,000.

Great Adventures, T4044 9944, www.greatadventures.com.au and **Big-Cat Green Island**, T4051 0444, and **Reef Magic**, T4031 1588, www.reefmagiccruises.com.au, are the main cruise operators in Cairns and are based at Trinity Wharf. They offer a range of tour options to Green Island, and beyond that, include certified dives, introductory dives, snorkelling, sightseeing and other water based activities. Other companies that are based in Port Douglas north of Cairns also offer transfers from the city. **Great Adventures** and **Quicksilver**, T4087 2100, www.quicksilver-cruises.com.au, based in Port Douglas, both have huge **floating pontoons** moored on the outer reef where you can dive, snorkel, view the reef from a glass-bottom boat or simply sunbathe or watch the world and the fish

go by. Although this offers a fine introduction to the reef, don't expect to find any solitude. **Compass**, T4050 0666, www.reeftrip.com.au, offer an attractive alternative with a good value trip on board a modern vessel to Michaelmas and Hastings Reef (both on the outer reef). Also offered are free snorkelling, boom netting and optional dive extras, from $60. In essence it all boils down to the type of vessel, its facilities, numbers, optional extras and the actual time allowed on the reef. Generally speaking the smaller sailing companies offer the most attractive rates and perhaps more peace and quiet, but lack the speed, convenience and razzmatazz of the fast, modern catamarans. **Falla**, T4031 3488, www.fallacruises.com.au, is a charming, former Pearl Lugger that allows four hours on **Upolo Reef** 30 km from Cairns, with free snorkelling. Departs 0830, returns 1730, $60, child $35 (introductory dive only $50). **Passions of Paradise**, T4050 0676, www.passionsofparadise.com.au, is a larger, modern catamaran that also goes to Upolo Cay and Paradise Reef. From $70 (introductory dive $55). Departs daily 0800, returns 1800. **Ecstasea**, T4041 3055, www.reef-sea-charters.com.au, is a modern 60-ft luxury yacht that once again goes to Upolo Cay with free snorkelling, from $89 (Introductory dive $55). An even more luxurious trip to **Michaelmas Cay** on the outer reef is offered on the beautiful, all mod cons Ocean Spirit, T4031 2920, www.ocean spirit.com.au, though you will pay the extra at $150, (introductory dive $85).

Essentials

Sleeping
Peak season is winter and spring, not summer. Pre-booking is advised

As with everything else there is plenty of choice and something to suit all budgets. Almost all the major hotels and countless backpackers are located in the heart of the city, especially along the Esplanade, while most motels are located on the main highways in and out of town. If you are willing to splash out, want access to a proper beach, and wish to escape the heady buzz in the city proper, then ask at the VIC about the numerous apartment and resort options at Palm Beach and other **Northern Beach** resorts (located about 20 mins north of the city). Prices fluctuate according to season, with some going through the roof at peak times (May-Sep). Prices are often reduced and special deals are offered through 'the Wet' (Jan-Mar).

Hotels Almost all are multi-storey and located overlooking the ocean on The Esplanade or its neighbouring streets. The **LL** *Cairns International*, 17 Abbott St, T4031 1300, F4031 1801, www.cairnsinternational.com.au, and the **LL** *Hotel Sofitel*, 35 Wharf St, T4030 8888, (which houses the Casino) are 2 top range hotels that both enjoy a fine reputation. Elsewhere is the self-contained **LL** *Radisson Plaza* at The Pier, T4031 1411, F4031 3226, www.radissoncairns.com.au, and the slightly cheaper **LL-L** *Holiday Inn*, corner of Esplanade St and Florence St, T4050 6070, F4031 3770, www.holiday-inn.com.au For perfectly pleasant, cheaper hotel options, try the **L** *Country Comfort Outrigger*, corner of Abbott St and Florence St, T4051 6188, F4031 1806, reservations@touraust.com.au, or the **L-A** *All Seasons Esplanade*, corner of Esplanade St and Aplin St, T4031 2311, F4031 1294, www.allseasons.com.au

Motels and serviced apartments Most of the motels are located on the main drags in and out of town (Sheridan St). Some that are particularly appealing include the **L** *Regency Palms*, 219-225 McLeod St, T4031 4445, F4031 5415, www.regency palms.com.au, **L** *Cairns Queenslander*, on the corner of Digger St and Charles St, T4051 0122, F4031 1867, www.cairnsqueenslander.com.au and the **A** *Coral Cay Villa*, 267 Lake St, T4046 5100, F4031 2703, www.coralcay.com.au Of the many cheaper options, try the 'colourful' **A-B** *Cairns Rainbow Inn*, 179 Sheridan St, T4051 1022, or the historic and well placed **A** *Hides*, on the corner of Lake St and Shields St, T4051 1266. There are many other options and the VIC has full details. The **Cairns and TNQ Accommodation Centre**, 36 Aplin St, T4051 4066, Free call T1800-807730, www.accomcentre.com.au, can also be of assistance.

B&Bs and lodges Although more like a motel than a lodge the **A** *Fig Tree Lodge*, 253 Sheridan St, T4041 0000, F4041 0001, www.figtreelodge.com.au, offers fine facilities and a warm Irish welcome and a good congenial bar attached. A more traditional modern option is the **A** *Cairns B&B*, 48 Russell St, Edge Hill, T4032 4121, F4053 6557, www.cairnsbnb.com.au, (5 km from the city centre), where locals Bernie and Norah promise to impart lots of local knowledge. In Trinity Beach (Northern Beaches) the beautiful and beachside **LL** *Trinity On the Esplanade*, 21 Vasey Esplanade, Trinity Beach, T4057 6850, F4057 8099, www.trinityesplanade.com.au comes complete with four-poster beds and pool and is highly recommended. For other quality options that have single rooms, good motel style doubles and are also suited for families try the **B-E** *Inn The Tropics*, 141 Sheridan St, T4031 1088, www.cairns.net.au/~innthetropics, and the no nonsense **B-E** *Bellview*, 85-87 The Esplanade, T4031 4377.

Backpackers Again, there is plenty of choice with over 30 establishments almost all of which are within easy reach of the city centre. Most people gravitate towards the Esplanade where a string of places sit almost side by side, but you are advised to look into other options beyond that. Another small cluster of quieter hostels lies just west of the Cairns Central Shopping Plaza and railway station. All offer the usual facilities and range of dorms, twins/doubles (occasionally singles) and will attempt to lure you with attractive tour or longer stay discounts, gimmicky giveaways or simply a good sense of humour. Always look for rooms with a/c or at the very least a powerful fan and windows that open. Also check for approved fire safety regulations. Internet is readily available. On the Esplanade the **C-E** *Caravella 77*, 77 The Esplanade, T4051 2159, and *Caravella 149*, The Esplanade, T4031 5680, www.caravella.com.au, are both modern, well facilitated with good a/c doubles and free meals. Recommended. Also on the Esplanade are the **C-E** *Bel-Air*, 155-157, T4031 4790 (offers singles and girls dorm, spa), and the characterful **B-E** *Florianna*, 183, T4051 7886, flori@cairnsinfo.com.au, which are both worth looking at. Right in the city centre is the **C-D** *Global Palace*, on the corner of Lake St and Shields St, T4031 7921, www.globalpalace.com.au, which is more like a modern boutique motel than a traditional backpackers. It has great facilities including a rooftop pool and large deck from which to watch the world go by. The only criticism is that most of the a/c rooms do not have windows and may feel a bit claustrophobic.

West of the centre there are a crop of good hostels, all very similar, with a more cosy, quiet atmosphere. The **C-E** *Travellers Oasis*, 8 Scott St, T4052 1377, www.travoasis.com.au, is a large place that still maintains a nice quiet atmosphere, offering a good range of a/c rooms including value singles ($30) and a pool. The **C-E** *Dreamtime Travellers Rest*, 4 Terminus St, T4031 6753, www.dreamtime travel.com.au, is homely and friendly with a great atmosphere, well-equipped facilities and a great pool and spa, as well as proper beds, not bunks. Ask about their sister hostel in Yungaburra and the Tablelands tour package. Nearby, the well managed **C-E** *Ryan's Rest*, 18 Terminus St, T4051 4734, shares a similar quiet and homely feel. **C-E** *Geckos*, 187 Bunda St, T4031 1344, www.geckobackpackers.com.au, is new on the block. It's a rambling and spacious Queenslander with good facilities and caring staff. Rooms have fans but they are well ventilated. Good for doubles. Free meals at *The Woolshed*. The better of the 2 YHAs in the city is the **C-D** *McLeod St YHA*, 20-24 McLeod St, T4051 0772, www.yha.com.au, where the facilities are fine, but it's a bit characterless. Good tours office.

North of the centre is the popular **C-D** *Cairns Beach House*, 239 Sheridan St, T4041 4116, www.cairnsbeachhouse.com.au It has all the usual knobs and knockers and is especially noted for its pool, beer/bistro garden and party atmosphere. A little further out at 231 McLeod St is the new and excellent **B-E** *Bohemia Resort*, T4041 7290, www.bohemiaresort.com.au It is more like a tidy modern motel with great doubles and a pool and other facilities to match. Recommended. Regular shuttles into town.

Motor camps and campsites For sheer convenience there is the basic **C-E** *Cairns City Caravan Park*, on the corner of James St and Little St, T4051 1467, which is within walking distance of the town centre, but for sheer class and all mod cons look no further than the excellent **L-F** *Cairns Coconut Caravan Resort*, on the Bruce Highway (about 6 km south, corner of Anderson Rd), T4054 6644, www.coconut.com.au It is one of the best in the country.

Eating

Many of the mid-range eateries best suited for day or early evening dining are located on the Esplanade. Don't forget the options on offer in the major hotels and in the Pier Complex

Expensive The luxury hotels come complete with plush restaurants. 2 of the best are *Breeze's* in the *Hilton*, Wharf St, T4052 6786, and *Siroccos* in the *Radisson*, The Pier T4031 1411. Dinner Tue-Sat 1800-2300. Also at the *Pier* is *Pesci's*, which overlooks the Marina, T4041 1133. It is a great spot to dine on traditional and quality Aussie fare with a seafood edge. Elsewhere, the *Red Ochre Grill*, 43 Shields St, T4051 0100, is an award winning Australian restaurant, offering the best of Australian 'game' fare including kangaroo, crocodile and local seafood favourites. Open daily for lunch and dinner. For a bit of a novelty you might like to try the *$70 Dinner Cruise* on offer with *Ocean Spirit*, a large modern catamaran based at the Marlin Marina, 33 Lake St, T4031 2920, www.oceanspirit.com.au. 2½ hrs, departs 0700 Wed/Fri/Sat.

Mid range *Dundee's*, 29 Spence St, T4051 0399, is a well-established favourite, that offers good value Australian cuisine in a relaxed atmosphere. Meat lovers will love the buffalo, roo, croc and barramundi combos. The seafood platters are also excellent. *Barnacle Bills*, 65 The Esplanade, T4051 2241, is another well-established seafood favourite. For Italian *Verdi's*, corner of Shields St and Sheridan St, T4052 1010, open Mon-Fri 1200-2300, Sat/Sun 1100 and *La Fettucina*, 43 Shields St, T4031 5959, are both recommended. *Yanni's Taverna*, corner of Aplin St and Grafton St, T4041 1500, is a good Greek place offering attractive discounts between 1800 and 1900. When it comes to Asian fare *Yamagen Japanese*, corner of Grafton St and Spence St, T4052 1009, is recommended. For good Indian fare try the *Tandoori Oven*, 62B Shields St, T4031 0043, while the award winning *Café China*, is considered the best of the Chinese restaurants, corner of Spence St and Grafton St, T4041 2828. Open daily from 1030.

Cheap The *Woolshed, Sports Bar* and *P J O'Briens* (see Entertainment, below) all offer cheap backpacker meals and are open daily from about 1000. For value pub grub in a quieter Irish atmosphere try *Willie McBride's* in the Fig Tree Lodge, on the corner of

Sheridan St and Thomas St, T4041 0000. Open daily from 1800. *Gypsy Dee's Café*, 41A Shields St, T4051 5530, is a lively wee place that offers value Aussie/traditional meals but is best known for its large vegetarian selections. The *International Food court* on the *Esplanade* and the *Meeting Place* round the corner in Aplin St has a number of cheap outlets if you are looking for the old dine and dash option.

Perrota's, corner of Abbott St and Shield St, T4031 5899, located next to the art gallery **Cafés** is a fine place to watch the world go by for breakfast, lunch or dinner. Good coffee. Open from 0730. The *Coffee Club* on the Esplanade, T4041 0522, is also a popular spot and they can serve up a good breakfast for about $10. *Tiny's Juice Bar*, 45 Grafton St, T4031 4331, is a popular venue for the health conscious, with light snacks and a fine range of cool and colourful juices to cure all ills. Open daily 0730-1700.

With so many backpackers descending on the city the nightlife is very much geared to **Entertainment** the get dressed up (or down), get drunk and fall over mentality, which is fine for the majority, but finding somewhere to have a few good beers and good conversation can be difficult. With the party-set in mind Cairns now offers a great value *Ultimate Party* on Sat for $45. The 'party' sometimes of up to 200 rapacious souls tours 5 local pubs with free transport, free entry tickets, a free meal and a free drink in each pub. Sadly, free hangover cures and condoms have still to be included! Tickets are freely available or T4041 0332. If the party is heavily booked there is a re-run on Wed. While wandering around the city you will inevitably be approached by destitute and persuasive back-packers touting the various nightspots and businesses with free drink vouchers. *Barfly* is the local entertainment rag, www.barfly.com.au

Pubs There's a good range of pubs in the town from the traditional Aussie street corner hotels to sports bars and, of course, some pseudo Irish offerings. The best of the Irish pubs is the popular *PJ O'Brien's*, Shields St, T4031 5333. Open daily 1000-0300. It offers live music most nights and is not too shabby in the food depart-ment either! Along the same lines is the *Frog and Firkin*, corner of Spence St and Lake St, T4031 5305. It's nicely laid-back and also offers live music, a bistro and has a good balcony overlooking the main street. For something a little classier try the cool (as in temperature) atmosphere of the *Courthouse Bar and Bistro* located in the for-mer courthouse on Abbott St, T4031 4166. It is great during the heat of the day or for a little more decorum and offers live Jazz on Sun nights and al fresco dining. Open daily until late. For a traditional Aussie pub experience try the *Pier Tavern*, Pierpoint Rd, T4031 4677.

Clubs There are almost a dozen on 'the circuit' with the following currently enjoying the best reputation. Topping the list is the *Woolshed*, 24 Shields St, T4031 6304. It is very much backpacker oriented, offering very cheap drinks and it generally goes off well into the wee hours. *The Sports Bar*, 33 Spence St, T4041 2533. Also lures in the younger crowds with cheap drink and has live bands from Thu-Sat. *The Cha-pel*, 91 The Esplanade, T4041 4222, might offer tourist sanctuary and meals that include bread and wine during the day, but at night turns more in towards the con-fessional over cocktails and shooters. Open until 0200. *Johno's Blues Bar*, corner of Abbott St and Aplin St, T4051 8770, is a bit seedy but is a well-known live music venue. Entry is free before 2100 and on Sun there is the opportunity to show off your talents (or not) at the Talent Quest. One of the newest clubs in the city is *Club Five Nine*, on the corner of Shields St and The Esplanade, which is earning a fine reputa-tion for modern music. The well established *Tropos*, on the corner of Lake St and Spence St, T4031 2530, offers regular theme nights, while the *Playpen*, Lake St, T4051 8211, has 3 separate bars offering various levels of mayhem and a huge dance floor. *Club Trix*, 53 Spence St, T4051 8223, is essentially a gay bar, but it welcomes both straight and gay and has sexy vibes and highly entertaining drag shows.

Queensland

Cinema and casino   The *Cairns 5 Cinema* is at 108 Grafton St, T4051 1222. Cairn's fairly unremarkable *Reef Casino* is located at the bottom of the Esplanade and behind the Wharf. Open all hours.

Shopping   Cairns offers some excellent shopping. The 2 main centres are the *Cairns Central Shopping Arcade* on McLeod St, T1800-646010, and the *Pier Marketplace* beneath the Radisson Plaza Hotel on The Pier, T4051 7244. Open daily 0900-2100. There you can buy everything from opals to art works. Don't miss the *Reef Gallery* and The *Ric Steininger Photo Gallery*, www.steininger.com.au The *Cairns Night Markets* offer over 100 stalls selling a rather predictable array of arts, crafts, clothing, food and souvenirs. Open daily 1630-2300, 54-60 Abbott St, T4051 7666, More entertaining is *Rusty's Bazaar*, an eclectic conglomerate of colourful consumables located between Grafton St and Sheridan St. Open Fri evening and Sat/Sun morning. For more classy colourful panoramic photographs don't miss Peter Lik's *Wilderness Gallery*, 4 Shields St, T4031 8177, www.peterlik.com.au For Australiana and traditional attire including 'Akubra' hats try *Cairns Hatters*, 4-8 Orchid Plaza, Abbott St, T4031 6392. For books *Angus and Robertson*, Shop 141, Cairns Central Shopping Arcade, T4041 0591. **Camping** Equipment can be found in several outlets on Shields St and Grafton St, including *Adventure Equipment*, 133 Grafton, T4031 2669. For second-hand camping equipment head for *City Palace Disposals*, on the corner of Shields St and Sheridan St.

Tours   The number of operators, locations and themes are mind bending and competition is once again fierce. Most tours head north by 4WD to **Cooktown**, **Daintree** and **Cape Tribulation** via the **Mossman George**, while others turn inland to Kuranda and the **Atherton Tablelands**. Still others offer specialist wildlife tours, or safaris and then of course the Full Monty, multi-day 4WD to the 'tip' of **Cape York**. Choosing a tour is a matter of personal preference and budget, but if your are short of time or a vehicle, a tour of Daintree and Cape Tribulation is recommended since these areas are best negotiated by 4WD and you will benefit from the specialist environmental knowledge of the guides. For a more sedate tour the Atherton Tablelands and 'near' outback towns of **Chillagoe** are also recommended. Given the incredible biodiversity of the area wildlife tours are also well worthwhile. The following are just sample of the more reputable operators and more tours are mentioned in the activity sections of the relevant areas or locations. Also many of the operators listed visit other locations. For Cape York safaris see page 377.

More energetic travellers should look at what is on offer with Jungle Tours, the Adventure Company and Raging Thunder while more sedate tours are on offer with Tropic Wings and APT

Adventure tours   Choose from a leisurely paddle in a kayak with *Raging Thunder*, T4030 7911, www.ragingthunder.com.au, to a full 8-day adventure a la Survivor, the famous TV series with *The Adventure Company*, 1st Floor, 13 Shields St, T4051 4777, www.adventures.com.au Contact direct or pick up brochures from the VIC.

Atherton Tablelands   *On The Wallaby Tablelands Tours*, T4050 0650, are recommended offering tours of the Tablelands sights with excellent wildlife canoeing trips as a further option, from $60. Their 2-day/1-night accommodation/activity package based at their hostel in Yungaburra is recommended. *Northern Experience Eco Tours*, T4041 4633, offer a wildlife edge to their day tour, from $99, child $71. *Jungle Tours*, T4032 5600, also offer a good waterfalls day trip from $79.

Cairns city and local   *Cairns Discovery Tours*, T4053 5259, offer a half-day tour of city sights including the Botanical Gardens, Flying Doctor Service Visitors Centre and Northern Beaches, from $50, child $26. *The Terri-Too and Calm Water Cruises*, T4031 4007, offer a cruise exploring the harbour and mangrove, $33 and another tour option in combination with a visit to a Crocodile Farm from $49, children half fare.

Cooktown   Most of the tours on offer combine both the inland and coast roads to Cooktown. *Wilderness Challenge*, T4055 6504, www.wilderness-challenge.com.au, offer all-inclusive 1-day (fly/drive, via Daintree Coast), from $265, a 2-day from$330 and three-day from $732. *Queensland Adventure Safaris*, T4041 2418, www.qastours.

com.au, offer a 2-day 4WD trip offering a range of accommodation from $195-$310 as well as a fly/drive from$250. *APT*, T4041 9419, www.aptours.com.au and *Tropic Wings*, 278 Hartley St, T4035 3555, www.tropicwings.com.au, are 2 companies offering 'Cooktown-in-a-Day' from $124, child $62. Most of the adventure companies listed above and those that visit Daintree and The Cape also offer multi-day or overnight 4WD tours to Cooktown.

Daintree and Cape Tribulation One-day, 4WD tours generally leave Cairns about 0700 and return about 1800 and cost in the region of $115-125. *Billy Tea Bush Safaris*, T4032 0055, www.billytea.com.au, have friendly entertaining guides, day tour from $125, child $85. *Tropical Horizons*, T4055 2630, www.tropicalhorizonstours.com.au, and *Suncoast Safaris*, T4055 2999, www.suncoast-safaris.com.au, both offer very comfortable, quality, small group tours, from $119, child $73. *Trek North*, T4051 4328, www.treknorth.com.au, take small groups to Daintree and Mossman Gorge and the trip includes a cruise on the Daintree River. Good value, from $99, child $60. *Foaming Fury*, T4031 3460, www.foamingfury.com.au, and Jungle Tours, T4032 5600, www.jungletours.com.au, are mainly backpacker oriented and offer value day-trips from $89 and overnight trips from $100, staying at the Capes various backpacker establishments. *Jungle Tours*, T4032 5600, www.jungletours.com.au, also offer multi-day and more upmarket accommodation, from $180.

Kuranda *Tropic Wings*, 278 Hartley St, T4035 3555, www.tropicwings.com.au, offer an excellent tour to Kuranda that combines the Kuranda Scenic Railway and Skyline Gondola with the addition of many exciting diversions and activities, from $149, child $75. Recommended. *Value Day Tours*, T4035 5566, also offer a good range of no-nonsense options and are as the name suggests, good value.

Specialist tours Given the habitat and abundance of **wildlife** almost all tours have a heavy emphasis on the environment and wildlife, but for specialist wildlife trips in the region try *Wait-a-while Rainforest Tours*, T4098 7500, www.waitawhile.com.au, or *Wildscapes Safaris*, T4057 6272, www.wildscapes-safaris.com.au *On the Wallaby Backpackers* in Yungaburra, T4050 0650, www.dreamtimetravel.com.au offer an exciting range of tours to the Atherton Tablelands and day/night wildlife canoeing trips on Lake Tinaroo, from $70. *Wooroonooran Rainforest Safaris*, T4031 0800, www.wooroonooran-safaris.com.au, also offer sightseeing and trekking trips with a wildlife bent in the beautiful Wooroonooran National Park south of Cairns. For an interesting insight in to geology consider the *Undara Experience*, T4097 1411, www.undara.com.au In conjunction with Savannah Guides they offer day trips and excellent multi-day package deals by coach, self-drive or rail to view the 190,000 year old volcanic **Undara Lava Tubes** with additional activities and accommodation in their unique railway carriages or swag-tent village. Day-trip from $119, 2-day, from $393 and 3-day rail, from $624. Recommended.

Airline offices *Qantas*, corner of Lake St and Shields St, T4050 4000. **Banks** All the major bank branches are represented in the city centre especially at the intersection of Shields St and Abbott St. **Foreign Exchange** *Travelex* have offices at the airport and in the city at 13 Shields St, T4041 4286 and 12 Spence St, T4041 7696. *Thomas Cook*, 69 Abbott St, T4031 6860; 50 Lake St, T4051 6255, 59 The Esplanade, T4041 1000. *American Express*, Shop 29 Orchid Plaza, Abbott St, T4051 8811. Some hostels offer commission free exchange. **Car servicing** *Mac Peak Automotive*, Lot 2, Mac Peak Cr, Smithfield, T4057 7100. **Car rental** The Airport and Abbott/Lake St in the city have most outlets. *Avis*, 135 Lake St, T4051 5911, *Budget*, Airport, T4035 9500, and 153 Lake St, City, T4051 9222. *All One Rentals*, 72 Abbott St, T4031 1788. *National*, 143 Abbott St, T4051 4600. *Delta*, 403 Sheridan St, T4032 2000 and *MiniCar Rentals*, 150 Sheridan St, T4051 6818. For a standard car and 7-day hire expect to pay from $33 a day. Some of the larger companies like *Avis* also offer 4WD hire from around $146 per day Campervan rentals and

Directory

Queensland

purchase (second-hand). *Travellers Auto Barn*, 123-125 Bunda St, T4041 3722, www.travellers-autobarn.com.au Offer guaranteed buy-backs in Sydney. *Britz*, 411 Sheridan St, T4032 2611, www.britz.com.au **Chemist** *After Hours*, 29B Shields St, T4051 2466. Open 0800-2100. **Communications** Internet There are terminals every-where, including *Global Gossip*, 125 Abbott St, T4031 6411. *Backpackers World*, 12 Shields St, T4041 0999. *Travellers Contact Point*, 1st Floor, 13 Shields St, T4041 4677. *Internet Outpost* on Shields St is recommended. All are open until at least 2200. **Post office** 13 Grafton St, T4031 4382. Open Mon-Fri 0830-1700. There is a smaller post shop office in the *Orchid Shopping Plaza* (2nd Floor), Abbott St. Open as above and on Sat 0900-1500. **Library** *Cairns City Public Library*, 151 Abbott St, T4044 3720. Free internet. **Medical services** *Cairns Base Hospital*, Esplanade (north), T4050 6333. *Cairns City 24 hr Medical centre*, corner of Florence St and Grafton St, T4052 1119. **Police** Emergency T000, 5 Sheridan St, T4030 7000. **RACQ** Coral Motors, 138 McLeod St, T4051 6543. Breakdown, T131111. Radio, 103.5 HotFM (Reef report daily at 0745). **Taxi** Black and White, T4048 8333 (24 hr). **Travel Agents** Flight Centre, 24 Spence St, T4052 1077. Backpackers Travel Centre, Shields St, T4051 5100.

Northern Great Barrier Reef Islands

Cairns is the principal access point to some of the best islands of the northern Great Barrier Reef, famed for their dreamy desert island landscapes, abundant sea creatures, corals and clear waters. If **diving** is not your thing, then you must at the very least take a **day-cruise** to one of the islands and for a few hours sample the good life and, supposing you do nothing else, go **snorkelling**. There are also a number of islands that can be visited independently and where camping is permitted, but all transportation must be arranged independently. Bookings and permits are essential. For information contact the QPWS Office in Cairns

Green Island   Once you arrive in Cairns it won't take long before you see postcards of Green Island – a small outcrop of lush vegetation, fringed with white sand and sur-rounded by a huge tapestry of azure blue and green reefs. These images, almost all taken from above, look like a place that , until now, has existed only in your imagination. Green Island is a text book 'coral cay' formed by dead coral and will fulfil most of your tropical island fantasies – though you'll have to share it.

Getting there   Cruise and Tour operators   There are 2 main tour operators to Green Island. *Great Adventures*, The Wharf, Cairns, T4044 9944 (24 hrs), www.greatadven-tures.com.au, offer transfers from $46, child $23 and a wide range of tour options with activity inclusions and extras, from half-day $54, child $27/ full-day $92, child $46. Addi-tionally there is a Green Island and Outer Reef (pontoon) tour from $160, child $80. Added extras include snorkel tour from $15, intro dive from $94 and 3-4 day certification from $320. *Big Cat Green Island Reef Cruises*, The Pier Market Place, T4051 0444, www.bigcat-cruises.com.au, also offer half and full-day cruises with extras from, $52, child $29. All ferries leave from Trinity Wharf, Cairns with transfers from Port Douglas.

Being a mere 45 minutes (27 km) away by boat, it is the closest island to Cairns and at 15 ha, is one of the smallest islands on the reef. It is home to an exclusive resort but, in essence, is designed more for the day tripper in mind, with con-crete pathways leading to food outlets, bars, dive and souvenir shops, a pool and of course some well-trodden beaches. The wealth of facilities may disappoint some, but despite its size, you can still grab a snorkel and mask and find a quiet spot on the bleached white sand and from there enter that infinitely more beau-tiful and quiet world, beneath the waves. The best place to snorkel is around the pier itself, where the fish love to congregate around the pylons. If you do go snorkelling there and see what appears to be a large shark, but with a head that looks like its been put under a rolling pin, don't panic. Its a shark ray or 'bucket mouth', a totally harmless bottom feeder. Another fine set of teeth can be seen at the *Marineland Melanesia*, T4051 4032, in the heart of the island, with its small collection of aquariums and marine artefacts. ■ *Daily 0900-1600, $8.* If you are physically unable to go diving or snorkelling, you can still experience the vast array of colourful fish and corals from a glass-bottom boat or a small underwater observatory ($5) both located by the pier.

Sleeping and eating The exclusive **LL** *Green Island Resort*, T4031 3300, F4052 1511, www.greenislandresort.com.au, is the only accommodation on offer. Rooms and facilities are all mod cons and prices include many of the islands activities.

Tours and activities There are a number of tour options that give you the opportunity to combine, diving and/or snorkelling to the outer islands with a few hours exploring Green Island. Alternatively you may just want to pay the ferry fare and use the islands facilities, go snorkelling, or laze on the beach. You can also walk right round the island's 1½-km circumference in 20 mins. Snorkel, mask and fins can be hired from the Dive Shop ($12). They also offer introductory dives to non-guests (30 mins) from around $55 and full 3-4 day certification from $320. Pool access costs $5 for those with children or an inability to stray to far from the well-stocked bar.

Fitzroy Island lies 6 km off the mainland; 25 km south of Cairns and, unlike **Fitzroy Island** Green Island, is a large 339 ha continental island, formed of rock not coral and more mountainous, yet is still surrounded by coral reef. It offers more of an escape with pleasant walking tracks through dense eucalypt and tropical rainforests, rich in wildlife. One of the most popular walks is a circuit to the island's highest point (269 m), with its memorable views and 1970 lighthouse (4 km round trip). A number of quiet beaches provide good snorkelling and diving. The best beach on the island is the evocatively named **Nudey Beach** which is not, as the name suggests, a base for naturists. It can be reached in about 20 minutes from the resort. Fitzroy was used by the Gunghandji Aboriginal people as a fishing base for thousands of years and in the 1800s by itinerants harvesting sea cucumber.

Sleeping and eating The **A-D** *Fitzroy Island Resort*, T4052 1335, www.fitzroyisland resort.com.au, offers accommodation to suit all budgets from camping to hostel-style bunkhouses to beach cabins. **F Camping** requires a permit from the **QPWS** in Cairns. Check to see if the campsite is open before departure. Bookings essential. There is a kiosk on the island that offers cheap fairly unremarkable fare, while slightly pricier quality meals can be secured at the resorts *Rainforest Restaurant* (bar attached).

Tours and activities A dive shop at the resort offers introductory dive trips, for a great value $65, 3-day certification from $325 and snorkel hire from $12. Other water-sports are also available from multi day kayaking trips from $274 and day-long fishing trips from $150. These activities come as part of the resort accommodation packages, but are also offered to independent visitors. *Raging Thunder*, T4030 7990, www.ragingthunder.com.au, offer good value day, overnight and multi-day sea kayaking trips to Fitzroy the mainland.

Transport *Fitzroy Island Ferries*, T4030 7911, depart Cairns at 0830, 1030 and 1600, from $36, child$18. *Sunlover Cruises*, T4031 1055 and *Great Adventures*, T4044 9944, also service Fitzroy daily, from $80.

Queensland

Frankland Islands   A further 20 km south of Fitzroy Island are the Frankland Group, a small cluster of continental islands of which 77 ha are national park. Once again they are covered in rainforest and fringed with white sand beaches and coral reef. The islands offer a wonderfully quiet retreat in comparison to the larger, busier islands. There are QPWS **camping** areas on **Russell** and **High Islands**. Permits and bookings through the QPWS in Cairns. Access is by charter boat or with *Frankland Islands Cruise and Dive*, T4031 6300, www.franklandislands.com.au They offer camp transfers, from $146 and day tours to Normanby Island from $140, which ends with a pleasant cruise up the Mulgrave River. Also on offer is certified/introductory diving from $60 and a range of combo multi sight/tour package deals. The ferry departs daily from Cairns at 0800.

Atherton Tablelands

In the imagination, while the words 'Australia' and 'tablelands' may conjure up a dry and dusty landscape of rocky outcrops, parched eucalypts, and bounding kangaroos, when it comes to the heart of the Atherton, you are in for a big surprise. At an average height of over 800 m and subsequently the wettest region in Queensland, the Atherton Tablelands (with the exception of its westernmost settlements) are in fact most extraordinary. Here, you will find a countryside of lush fields and plump cattle, tropical forests echoing with birdsong huge brimming lakes and thunderous waterfalls. Yes, there are kangaroos, too – but these ones actually live in trees. The further west you go the drier it gets until, at the edge of the Great Divide Range, the vast and traditional 'outback' takes over. But, generally speaking, this region resembles rural Devon in England than a backdrop from 'Crocodile Dundee'. The Atherton Tablelands were once the domain of gold miners and are named after John Atherton, who in 1877 first linked the tin mines of Herberton to the then sleepy coastal port of Cairns. Today however, although some nominal mining activity remains, it is agriculture and horticulture that dominates.

Ins and outs

Getting there & around   There are 4 access roads inland from the coast. From the south the Tablelands can be reached via the Palmerston Highway (just north of Innisfail) through the scenic tropical rainforests of Wooroonooran National Park and Millaa Millaa. From Cairns you can either access the region, south, via Gordonvale and the steeply climbing Gillies Highway, or north via Smithfield, the Kuranda Range Road and Kuranda. From Port Douglas the region is best reached via the Rex Range Road and Kennedy Highway via Mareeba. If cycling, bear in mind it is an ascent of around 700 m. *Whitecar Coaches*, Trinity Wharf Terminal, Cairns, T4051 9533, www.whitecarcoaches.com.au, provide daily services to Atherton, Yungaburra, Mareeba and Kuranda. For transport to The Tablelands via Kuranda and the *Kuranda Scenic Railway* or *Skyrail Gondola*, see page 356. Note there are many day and multi-day tours to the Atherton Tablelands mainly from Cairns and if you are short for time this is, without doubt, the best way to see the region.

Orientation & information   The Atherton Tablelands (sometimes referred to as the Tropical Tablelands) extends inland roughly in a semi-circle from the Cairns coast, to the small mining settlements of Mount Molloy in the north and Chillagoe in the west, to Mount Garnet in the south. In total it is an area almost the size of Tasmania. The region's capital is the rather unremarkable town of Atherton (100 km southwest of Cairns), while the far more characterful townships of Yungaburra (83 km), Mareeba (64 km) and Kuranda (27 km) successfully satisfy the tourist and day-tripper's inquisition. You are advised to research the region from the VIC in Cairns. *The Tropical Tableland Promotion Bureau*, 42 Mabel

St, Atherton, T4091 7444, F4091 7144, www.athertontableland.com.au, is the principal accredited regional VIC. For national parks information contact the **QPWS** office in Cairns. **Cimate** Temperatures in the Tablelands are a lot cooler than the coast and in winter you'll need warm clothes (remember those).

Kuranda

The small, arty settlement of Kuranda has, thanks to its proximity to Cairns, its scenic railway and its **markets**, become the main tourist attraction of the Atherton Tablelands. Every day, especially on traditional market days (Wednesday-Sunday), the streets flood with souvenir-hunting visitors. There is no doubting the veneer of its appeal, its rustic charm or its stunning location, and there's plenty to see and do. Kuranda was first put on the map in 1891 with the completion of the railway, providing a vital link between the Hodgkinson Gold Fields and the coast. By 1920 Kuranda was already well on the way to honouring its obvious tourism appeal.

Population: 750
27 km from Cairns

Getting there The Kuranda Scenic Railway wriggles its way down the Barron George to Cairns and provides an ideal way to reach Kuranda. To add to the enjoyment you are transported in a historic loco and stop at various viewpoints, which provides some respite from the rambling commentary. It departs Kuranda 1400, 1530 Sun-Fri, 1530 Sat, $30 single, child $15. T4031 3636. For Cairns departures see page 341. There are numerous operators many of which are listed on page 351. *Coral Coaches*, T4031 7577, www.coralcoaches.com.au and *Whitecar Coaches*, Trinity Wharf Terminal, T4051 9533, www.whitecarcoaches.com.au, fight it out to service Kuranda at the most competitive price, sometimes for as little as $1. *Whitecar* are the smaller, more personable company and are therefore recommended.

Information The Kuranda Visitor Information Centre is located in Centenary Park, Therwine St, T4093 9311, F4093 7593, www.kuranda.org.au Open daily 1000-1600. It has maps and a comprehensive list of accommodation, tours and activities. Internet is available at the *Kuranda Arts Co-op*, Red House, Coondoo St (next to the Ark), T4093 9026. Open daily 1000-1600. *Kuranda Rainforest Eco-Tours* are based on the riverside of the rail bridge offering 45-min river cruises every hr from 1030-1430 from $12, child $6, family $30, T4093 7476. Canoe hire is also available, T04-0898 0016.

Ins & outs
Most visitors to Kuranda make the village part of a day-tour package from Cairns, with the highlight actually accessing it via the Barron Gorge and the Skyline Gondola, the Scenic Railway or both

The main attraction in Kuranda are its permanent **markets**. The Heritage Markets, located off Veivers Drive (across from the VIC) are open daily from 0830-1500, while the Original Markets are located nearby on Therwine Street. They are open from 0900-1500 Wednesday-Sunday, T4093 8060. The emphasis here is of course on souvenirs, with much of it being expensive and tacky, but there are some artists and craftsmen producing pieces that are both unusual and of good quality, so shop around. Although it is not actually part of the markets themselves, the **Terranova Gallery** is well worth a look as it showcases some fine work done by local artists. ■ *T4093 8814, 15 Therwine Street.* Located below the Heritage Markets is **Birdworld**, which is a free-flight complex showcasing some of Australia's most colourful (and audible) avian species. ■ *Daily 0900-1600, $11, child $4, family $28. T/F4093 9188, www.birdworldkuranda.com.au The Aviary, Zoological Gardens, 8 Thongon St also offers a similar, more low-key ornithological experience. Daily 1000-1500, T4093 7411.* Almost next door to Birdworld is the **Australian Butterfly Sanctuary**. It is reputedly the world's largest and houses hundreds of the country's most spectacular and prettiest 'Lepidoptera'. ■ *Daily 1000-1600, $12, child $6. T4093 7575, www.australianbutterflies.com.au 8 Veivers Dr.* To

Sights

Queensland

▶▶ **Skyrail rainforest cableway**

The once highly controversial Skyrail Gondola project was completed in 1995 and at 7½ km is the longest cable-gondola ride in the world. It gives visitors the opportunity to glide just metres above the rainforest canopy and through the heart of the World Heritage listed **Barron George National Park**. From the outset the mere prospect of such a project caused international uproar. Conservationists and botanists the world over were immediately up in arms and high profile local demonstrations took place. But for once, all the fears and protestations proved groundless and now Skyrail effectively combines both environmental sensitivity and education, with a generous dash of fun mixed in. The journey covers two stops, one to take in the views and guided rainforest boardwalk

from **Red Peak Station** (545 m) and another at **Barron Falls Station** where you can look at the entertaining **Rainforest Interpretive Centre**, before strolling down to the lookouts across the Barron River Gorge and **Barron Falls**. From The Barron Falls Station you then cross high above the Barron River before reaching civilization again at the pretty **Kuranda Terminal**. The Skyrail Caravonica Terminal is located 15 minutes north of Cairns on the Captain Cook Highway. Open daily 0800-1700, $30 one-way, child $15, return $45, child $22.50. Price includes Cairns transfers. T4038 1888, www.skyrail.com.au Skyrail can be combined with a return trip via the Kuranda Scenic Railway for around $59, child $30.

complete your truly comprehensive tour of all things winged and wonderful you could also consider a visit to **Batreach**, and independent wild bat rescue and rehabilitation hospital at the far end of Barang Street. ■ *Tue-Fri/Sun 1030-1430. Donations expected, T4093 8858.* There is a large local colony of flying foxes in the **Jum Rum Creek Park**, which can be accessed of Thongon Street. Other less smelly creatures of the night can be viewed at the **Djungan Nocturnal Zoo**. ■ *Daily 1000-1500, from $11, child $5. 8 Coondoo St.* The award-winning **Rainforestation Nature Park** is located a few kilometres east of Kuranda on the Kuranda Range Road. Set amidst a rainforest and orchard setting it offers the chance to experience aboriginal culture and mingle with captive native animals. There is also an exhilarating one-hour tour of the complex and rainforest in an amphibious army vehicle. ■ *Daily 0900-1600, All attractions $32.50, child $16.25, return transfers available from Kuranda ($6) and Cairns ($22). Full day tours from $55, child $27.50, T4093 9033, www.rainforest.com.au* If you did not arrive in Kuranda via the Skyrail or railway and it is the wet season then take a look at the **Barron Falls**, which can be accessed via Barron Falls Road (**Wrights Lookout**) south of the town. In 'the wet' the flood gates are opened above the falls and the results can be truly spectacular.

Sleeping

Once the last train puffs out the station and peace returns, Kurunda can be a wonderful place to stay away from the usual coastal haunts. But don't expect a wealth of options

For something completely different try the quirky **A** *Tentative Nests*, 26 Barron Falls Rd, T4093 9555, tentnest@internetnorth.com.au It is a charming, colourful and eco-friendly retreat where guests stay in self-contained 'nests' on platforms in the forests. Breakfast included, good value. Recommended. The 3-star **A-D** *Kuranda Rainforest Park*, Kuranda Heights Rd, T4093 7316, F4093 7316, www.kurandatouristpark.com.au, has cottages, cabins, powered and non powered sites. Facilities include kitchen and pool. Near the railway station, the newly renovated **C-D** *Kuranda Backpackers Hostel*, 6 Arara St, T4093 7355, www.kurandabackpackershostel.com.au, is a fine retreat with dorms, doubles and singles and good facilities. Pool, bike rental and pick-ups from Cairns. For something more luxurious you have to look further afield. The 4-star **L-A** *Cedar Park Rainforest Retreat*, Cedar Park Rd, T4093 7022, www.cedarparkresort (18 km), offers studio type apartments in a pleasant bush setting home to 2,500-year-old Acacia Cedars. Also some distance away (25 mins) but no less attractive is the **L** *Kuranda B&B*, 28 Black Mountain Rd, T4093 7151, F4093 8012, kurandabed@tpgi.com.au 4WD Tours available.

Eating

Kuranda is awash with affordable cafés and eateries so you will not be short of choice. If you can avoid the tour groups the *Rainforest View Restaurant*, 28 Coondoo St, T4093 9939, offers a wide range of fare and exactly that, while for something different and a cut of croc or roo, try the *Wangal Café*, 40 Coondoo St, T4093 9339. The *Monkeys Restaurant*, 1 Therwine St, T4093 7451, is a more traditional and cosy option. The most popular café with the locals is *Frogs*, T4093 7405 in the heart of Coondoo St, open daily 0900-1600, while the new *Oomph Restaurant*, 14 Thongon St, T4093 9144, is certainly the most friendly. Good coffee. Open 0830-until too tired!

Mareeba
Colour map 5, grid C4
Population: 7000
64 km from Cairns

Mareeba was originally used as little more than a stopping point for gold miners coming and going from the coast, until 1928 when the first tobacco plantation was established. Today the rather drab agricultural service town continues to thrive mainly on the infamous weed and more recently that other great addiction, coffee, but it does spring to life every July when it hosts the region's largest **rodeo**. There are two natural attractions around Mareeba worth looking at: The **Granite Gorge** with its inviting swimming holes is 12 km west of the town (on private land; small fee for entry). The **Mareeba Wetlands**, a 5,000-acre reserve 7 km north of Mareeba (then west on Pickford Road, from Biboohra) boasts an impressive list of species, including brolga, sea eagle, frilled lizard and the superbly named bumpy rocket frog. ■ *Visitors centre open daily 0830 1600 and guided tours are available, T4093 2304, www.mareebawetlands.com.au Recommended*. The **Mareeba Heritage Museum and VIC** is in Centenary Park, 345 Byrnes St, T/F4092 5674, www.mareebaheritagecentre.com.au They can assist with local accommodation bookings. The 3-star **C-E** *Riverside Caravan Park*, Egan Street, T4092 2309, has basic on-site vans and powered and non-powered sites.

Chillagoe
Population: 500
205 km from Cairns

Despite its proximity to Cairns, the former mining settlement of Chillagoe presents an ideal opportunity to experience the 'outback' proper, without having to embark on long and often difficult journeys from the coast by 4WD. During the dry season it is negotiable by conventional vehicles and can also be reached by train from Cairns and via Almaden, T132232. Chillagoe is a fascinating little place that combines mining history with natural **limestone caves** and **Aboriginal rock paintings**. Chillagoe was formerly a cattle station before the discovery of gold in the late 1880s dramatically transformed both the settlement and the landscape. The establishment of rail link in 1900 and a smelter a year after that, gave rise to a resident population of over 1,000 miners. For the next 40 years the area produced almost 10 tonnes of gold and 185 tonnes of silver, as well as many more tonnes of copper and lead. Though the boom days are long gone and the population has declined dramatically, it retains a hint of its former importance, in the many wind-blown, and sun-baked mining relics that remain. The **Chillagoe Heritage Museum** on Hill Street and the **Queensland Parks and Wildlife Service** office, corner of Cathedral Street and Queen Street, T4094 7163 (open daily 0830-1700) are the best sources of local information. The **QPWS** offer 1½-hour guided tours of the limestone caves at 0900 and 1500 from $6. There are more caves and old copper mines about 10 km west of the town at Mungana which is also the location of the Aboriginal **rock paintings**.

Queensland

Sleeping and eating The **A** *Chillagoe Cabins*, 22 Queen St, T4094 7206, chillcab@fastinternet.net.au, offer the best self-contained options while the **C-D** *Chillagoe Caves Lodge*, 7 King St, T4094 7106 is the best budget option, also offering powered and non-powered sites and a restaurant. There are 2 hotel/pubs the *Post Office Hotel*, 37 Queen St, T4094 7119 and the *Chillagoe Hotel*, Tower St, T4094 7168.

Lake Tinaroo & Danbulla Forest

The Barron River **Tinaroo Dam** was completed in 1958 creating a vast series of flooded valleys that now make up **Lake Tinaroo** and provide the region with essential irrigation. The lake itself has an astonishing 200 km of shoreline and is a popular spot for watersports, and fishing for barramundi. The Dunballa Forest that fringes its northern bank, hosts an excellent 28-km unsealed **scenic road** that winds its way from the dam slipway (from Tolga) to Boar Pocket Road, northeast of Yungaburra. Other than the various campsites, viewpoints and short walks on offer, other highlights include **Lake Euramoo**, a picturesque 'double explosion' crater lake, **Mobo Creek** Crater and the unmissable **Cathedral Fig**. Signposted and reached by a five-minute walk this superb example of the strangler fig species is a sight to behold, looking not so much like a cathedral, but like some huge altar stand from which 1,000 giant candles have slowly melted. The tree (though it is hard to see it as such) is 500-years-old, over 50 m tall and 40 m around the base and is especially worth visiting at dawn to hear the birdsong. Several types of nocturnal possum also inhabit the tree and are best seen with a torch after dark. From the Cathedral Fig you emerge from the forest onto Boar Pocket Road. The short diversion to the **Haynes Lookout** (left on Boar Pocket Road, heading from the forest towards Gillies Highway) is worthy of investigation. The track itself passes through some beautiful woodland before emerging at the edge of the mountain and the memorable views across the Mulgrave River valley and Bellenden Ker Range. When the winds are right the site is often used by hang-gliders. For more information on the Danbulla Forest, scenic drive and self-registration campsites ($2) contact the **Department of Natural Resources (QPWS)**, 83 Main Street, Atherton, T4091 1844, or their Tinaroo Office, T4095 8459.

Sleeping and eating The **L** *Tinaroo Waters*, 61 Bluewater Dr, T4095 8425, F4095 8025, www.tinaroowaters.com.au, is a spacious home stay set lakeside that also offers guided fishing trips. The basic 3-star **C-D** *Tinaroo Holiday Park*, Tinaroo Falls Dam, T4095 8232, offers cabins, units powered and non-powered sites. There is a licensed **restaurant** nearby, T4095 8242.

Yungaburra and around

Population: 1,000
81 km from Cairns

While Kuranda may be the most visited and high profile town in the Atherton Tablelands, sleepy little Yungaburra is without doubt the jewel. Formerly called Allumba it has changed little for over a century and offers a wonderful combination of history and alternative lifestyle and a cool and tranquil retreat from the coast. Added to its impressive gathering of listed **historical buildings** it has a number of fine accommodations, shops and restaurants and is surrounded by some of the best scenery in the Tablelands. Lakes Tinaroo, Barrine and Eacham are all within a short drive of the village and are a focal point for a number of walks, scenic drives and water-based activities including, sailing, boating, swimming, fishing, water-skiing and windsurfing Yungaburra is also one of the best and most accessible venues in country in which to see that almost surreal quirk of nature, the duck-billed **platypus**.

Getting there A spectacular way to reach Yungaburra is via the Gillies Highway and **Ins & outs**
Mulgrave River valley just south of Cairns. From the valley floor the road climbs almost
800 m up to the top of the Gilles Range. *Whitecar Coaches*, Trinity Wharf Terminal, T4051
9533 www.whitecarcoaches.com.au, run daily services to Yungaburra from $26.

Information Although residents are busy trying to rectify the situation, there is
currently no official visitor information centre in the village. However, the locals are
always glad to help and a basic information board and map is posted on Kehoe Pl in the
centre of the village. There is also a useful website, www.yungaburra.com.au The
Local *QWPS* office is located at Lake Eacham, T4095 3786, providing information about
campsites and all things environmental. Internet is available at *Flynn's Internet Café*,
17 Eacham Rd, T4095 2235.

Most of the listed **historical buildings** are constructed from local wood and **Sights**
were built between 1910 and 1920. Two of the finest examples are St Mark's and *Look out for the*
St Patrick's churches, on Eacham road both of which were erected in 1913. *Yungaburra Heritage*
Other fine examples are evident on Cedar Street next to the Lake Eacham Hotel. *Village leaflet,*
Just a few minutes southwest of the village on Curtain Fig Tree Road is the **Cur-** *available from*
tain Fig Tree, another impressive and ancient example of the strangler species. *the VICs in Cairns*
Peterson Creek that slides gently past the village (west) is home to several pairs *and Atherton or*
of **platypus**. The best place to view them is from the bottom and north of Penda *from most*
Street (end of Cedar Street) and the best time is around dawn or sometimes at *local businesses*
dusk. Sit quietly beside the river and look for any activity in the grass that fringes
the river or on its surface. They are generally well submerged but once spotted
are fairly obvious. Provided you are quiet they will generally go about their business, since their eyesight is fairly poor. A few kilometres east of the village are
two volcanic lakes, Lake Barrine and Lake Eacham. **Lake Barrine** is the largest
and has been a tourist attraction for over 80 years. It is fringed with rainforest
and circumvented by a 6-km walking track. The long established **Lake Barrine**
Rainforest Cruise and Tea House is nestled on the northern shore and offers
40-minute trips (1015, 1130, 1330 and 1530) on the lake for $8.50, child $5.50,
T4095 3847 (just off the Gillies Highway). Just south of Lake Barrine and
accessed off the Gillies Highway (or from the Malanda Road) is **Lake Eacham**.
It is surrounded by rainforest and a 3½ km-walking track and is a favourite spot
for a picnic and a cool dip. The most southerly fingers of **Lake Tinaroo** can also
be accessed northeast of the village via Barrine Road.

Other than the Lake Barrine cruises and walks surrounding both Lake Barrine and Lake Eacham there are also a number of wildlife and canoeing tours on
offer. For a spot of night possum spotting contact *Wait-a-while Rainforest*
Tours, T4098 7500, www.waitawhile.com.au, and for backpacker-oriented
wildlife and day/night canoeing trips contact the *On the Wallaby Backpackers*
(see Sleeping below). *Wildscapes Safaris*, T4057 6272, www.wildscapes-safa-
ris.com.au also offer wildlife tours and specialize in platypus spotting.

The new **LL** *Allumbah Pocket Cottages*, 24-26 Gillies Highway, T4095 3023, F4095 **Sleeping**
3300, www.allumbahpocketcottages.com au, are a cluster of spacious and well
appointed, 1-bedroom and fully self-contained cottages complete with spa. The
friendly and welcoming owners also offer 2 other exceptional 2-bedroom cottages, at
7/9 Pine St. Next door is the **A** *Curtain Fig Motel*, 16 Gillies Highway, T4095 3168, F4095
2099, www.curtainfig.com.au, which is a slightly cheaper option offering good value
spacious self-contained units and 1 large fully self-contained apartment. The historic
LL-L *Eden House Garden Cottages*, 20 Gillies Highway, T4095 3355, F4095 3377,
www.edenhouse.com.au, are also excellent, offering either deluxe spa cottages or
standard cottages which are equally spacious and classy in a quiet garden setting. Fine

Queensland

restaurant and bar on site. In the wooded surrounds of Lake Eacham you will find the luxurious and cosy **LL** *Crater Lakes Rainforest Cottages*, Lot 1, Eacham Close (off Lakes Drive), T4095 2322, www.craterlakes.com.au Back in Yungaburra the best budget option is the **C-E** *On the Wallaby Backpackers*, 34 Eacham St, T4050 0650, www.dreamtimetravel.com.au It is an excellent little backpackers offering dorms, doubles and camping for $10 (pair $15). Plenty of activities are on offer including an exciting range of wildlife and day/night canoeing tours on Lake Tinaroo from $25. Mountain bikes for hire. Pick-ups from Cairns daily. An even cheaper option is the historic and congenial **C-E** *Peeramon Hotel*, located south of Yungaburra on the Gillies Highway, Malanda Rd, T4096 5873. They have perfectly comfortable if basic doubles and singles plus units out the back for only $15 a night. The nearest motor park to Yungaburra is the basic but value **C-E** *Lake Eacham Caravan Park*, Lakes Drive, (1 km south of Lake Eacham, T4095 3730. It has cabins, powered and non-powered sites.

Eating The best place in town is the colonial-style *Eden Garden Cottage Restaurant*, 20 Gillies Highway, T4095 3377. Here you can tuck into such local delights as blue gum steak in a rustic interior or pleasant garden surroundings. *Nick's Swiss-Italian Restaurant*, also on Gillies Highway, T4095 3330, www.nicksrestaurant.com.au, is another more stylish alternative with live music at the weekends. Open daily (except Wed) for lunch and dinner 1100-2300. For a cheap steak head for the *Peeramon Hotel* (see Sleeping above), while for good coffee, a value breakfast and a warm Irish welcome try *Flynn's Internet Café*, beside the food market on Eacham Rd, T4095 2235. Open 0700-1700.

Malanda & Millaa Millaa About 18 km south of Yungaburra is the small village of Malanda at the start of the famous Tablelands waterfalls region. Malanda has its own set of falls but they are actually amongst the least impressive in the group and the village is more famous for its milk production. The main attraction in Malanda other than a cool dip in the swimming hole below the falls is the neighbouring **Malanda Environmental Centre** which has some interesting displays on the geology, climate and natural history of the Tablelands. ■ *$1, child free*. A further 24 km south of Malanda is the agricultural town of Millaa Millaa, which has its own waterfalls. The **Millaa Millaa Falls** are the first of a trio – the others being the **Zillie Falls** and **Ellinjaa Falls** – which can be explored on a 16-km circuit accessed (and signposted) just east of the town on the Palmerston Highway.

Sleeping Between Malanda and Millaa Millaa (2½ km on Hogan Rd east of Tarzali) are the delightful **LL** *Fur 'n' Feathers Rainforest Tree Houses*, T4096 5364, rainforest@north.net.au They are a trio of charming fully self-contained pole houses set in the bush offering real peace and quiet and all mod cons including a spa. There is also a separate fully self-contained, semi-detached cottage. In Millaa Millaa itself is the cheap and cheery **B** *Millaa Millaa Hotel*, Main St, T4097 2212, that has basic motel-style units. Home cooked dinner and light breakfast included. The 2-star **C-E** *Falls Holiday Park*, Malanda Rd, T4097 2290, has basic cabins, powered and non-powered sites and a café.

Mount Hypipamee National Park Located 24 km south of Atherton the Mount Hypipamee National Park is a small pocket of dense rainforest with a volcanic crater lake, waterfalls and some very special wildlife. During the day the dense forest is abuzz with many exotic birds, like the tame Lewin's honeyeaters, but it is at night that it really comes alive. Armed with a torch and a little patience (preferably after midnight) you can see several of the 13 species of **possum** that inhabit the forest, including the coppery brush tail, the green ringtail, and the squirrel glider. If you are really lucky you may also encounter the park's most famous resident the **Lumholtz's tree kangaroo** one of only two species of kangaroo that live in trees. The

The best view in northern Queensland

*The Millaa Millaa Lookout, just to the west of Millaa Millaa on the recently upgraded East Evelyn Road is said to offer the best view in North Queensland. On a clear day it is indeed memorable and encompasses a vast 180° vista from the Tablelands to the coast, interrupted only by the Bellenden Ker Range and the two highest peaks in Queensland **Mount Bartle Frere** (1622 m) and **Mount Bellenden Ker** (1591 m). At a height of 850 m the viewpoint itself offers the best insight as to why the Tablelands are so lush and cool in comparison to the coast.*

95,000-year-old **Crater Lake** is a short 10-minute walk from the car park. With its unimaginable depths, algae covered surface and eerie echoes it is quite an unnerving spectacle, and seems almost like some horrific natural dungeon. The park has picnic facilities but no camping.

Herberton
Population: 1,500
122 km from Cairns

Like so many other settlements in the region Herberton owes its existence to mining with the discovery of tin in 1880. For a few decades Herberton was the largest community in the Tablelands with a population of over 8,000, before the resource inevitably was exhausted and the towns of Atherton, Malanda, Mareeba and Millaa Millaa succeeded on the back of agriculture and timber. Although the main street itself could hardly be more timeless or Australian, the town boasts an interesting **Historical Village and Museum**, which has over 20 listed buildings, including a single composite of the original 17 pubs. ■ *From $10. T4096 2271. Broadway St.* The copious purple flowering **jacaranda trees** (September/October) are perhaps Herberton's major draw card. The Atherton to Herberton **Historic Steam Railway** provides an attractive alternative to arriving by road, with return trips from Atherton on lovingly restored loco. ■ *Wed/Sun, at 1030 (returns 1500), from $25, T4091 4871.*

Ravenshoe & around
Population: 850
147 km from Cairns

At over 900 m Ravenshoe is the highest settlement in Queenstown. Although once a bustling and at times controversial timber town, it is now a fairly sleepy little place used as a base to explore the surrounding waterfalls and rainforest. The **Millstream Falls** located 5 km west of Ravenshoe on the Kennedy Highway (on the right) are the widest in Australia, while further west still the steamy **Innot Hot Springs**; natural mineral springs that offer ideal therapy for the weary driver. *Railco* operate a lovingly restored 1920's steam loco called the **Millstream Express** from Grigg Street, Ravenshoe, north to Tumoulin (7 km), at weekends (April-January; from $25). Although not meant as a tourist attraction, the recently developed **wind farm** close to town on Windy Hill, is proving popular. The Ravenshoe Koombooloomba **VIC** has details and is located on Moore Street, T4097 7700, toptown@ledanet.com.au The VIC also houses an interesting cultural and interpretative centre. The **D-F** *Millstream Caravan Park*, Ascham Street, T4097 6491, has basic on-site vans, powered and non-powered sites. From Ravenshoe the Kennedy Highway leaves the Atherton Tablelands behind and turns its attentions west into classic outback country and the endless horizons of the **Gulf Savannah**. The **Undara Lava Tubes** on the edge of the **Undara Volcanic National Park**, 150 km south of Ravenshoe are an amazing 190,000-year-old volcanic feature that is well worth the journey. There are regular guided **tours** available (also available from Cairns) as well as a licensed restaurant, pool and five standards of accommodation (**A-F**) from charming train carriages to a swag tent village and powered sites, T4097 1411, www.undara.com.au

Queensland

Port Douglas

Colour map 5, grid A6
Population: 3,600
Post Code: 4871
61 km from Cairns,
1794 km from Brisbane

Almost since their inception the coastal ports of Cairns and Port Douglas have slugged it out as to who is the most important. But though Cairns has gone on to become a world famous heavyweight tourist resort compared to the lesser known, lightweight, Port Douglas, the latter has always put up a good fight thanks to its equal proximity to the Barrier Reef, its own swathe of golden sand and not forgetting Mossman Gorge, Daintree and Cape Tribulation. Many in the know also say that little Port Douglas has more class than its rival, however the town has lost much of its youthful charm with the massive developments multi-million dollar resorts.

Ins & outs   **Getting there and around   Air**   Port Douglas is accessed from *Cairns International Airport*. The *Airport Shuttle*, T4099 5950, offers services at least every hour daily from 0630-1630, $22, child $11. *Coral Coaches*, (Port Douglas Local Shuttle) T4099 5351, www.coralcoaches.com.au, run regular local bus services to the Cairns City, Cairns Airport, Mossman, Daintree and Cape Tribulation and also long distance services to Cooktown (Wed/Fri/Sun). *Express Chauffeured Coaches*, 5 Opal St, T4098 5473, also offer transits to/from Cairns. The main bus stops are on Grant St and at the Marina Mirage (Wharf) Complex. *Quicksilver*, T4087 2100 run a daily ferry (*Wave Pierce*) service from Marina Mirage, Wharf St, Port Douglas to Marlin Marina, Cairns, $23 one-way. The quaint *Bally Hooley Train* runs regularly from the Mirage Marina Complex to The Rainforest Habitat Wildlife Sanctuary, from $4 return. If you have your own vehicle and are visiting Port Douglas during the wet season (Nov-Mar) note that road conditions in the region can be treacherous. For up-to-date conditions and flood warnings T4051 6711. **Taxi**   *Port Douglas Taxis*, 45 Warner St, T4099 5345, (24 hrs).

Information   *Port Douglas Tourist Information Centre*, 23 Macrossan St, T4099 5599, F4099 5070, is an independent and can therefore, sometimes, be biased. Open daily 0800-1800. The *Port Douglas and Daintree Tourism* official website is www.pddt.com.au   The nearest **QPWS** office is in Mossman, 1 Front St, T4098 2188.

History   Surprisingly perhaps, Port Douglas was at one time the largest port in far North Queensland and more important than Cairns. This was thanks to one Christie Palmerston, whom in 1877 cut a vital link through the rainforests to the newly discovered Hodgkinson River goldfields on the northern fringe of the Atherton Tablelands. Almost before the last tree was felled, hordes of itinerant hopefuls descended on the new port and within a single decade the population reached over 8,000 (over twice that of today). But history also tells us that the new settlement was a very disorganized and transitory place, with little in the way of civil authority. Nowhere, was this more evident than in the inability to settle on a name. For many years it enjoyed a level of anonymity through various names including Island Point, Terrigal, Port Owen and Salisbury, before a posse of government officials arrived to christen it Port Douglas in honour of John Douglas, the then Governor of Queensland.

Sights   Like Cairns, Port Douglas places great emphasis on reef and rainforest tours with only a few local attractions pulling in the crowds. **Rainforest Habitat**, located at the southern entrance to the town is well worth a visit, offering a fine introduction to the region's rich biodiversity and natural habitats. There are over 180 species housed in three main habitat enclosures – 'wetlands', 'rainforest' and 'grassland' – with many of the tenants being tame and easily approachable. 'Breakfast with the Birds' presents a unique way to start the day and is available daily at 0800-1100, $34, child $17. ■ *Daily 0800-1730, $20,*

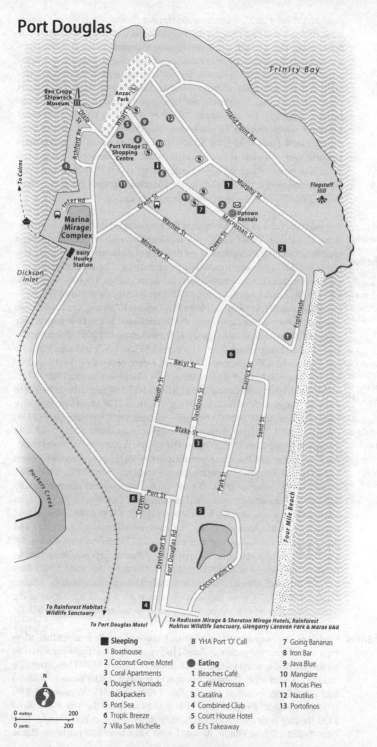

Port Douglas

◼ Sleeping	8 YHA Port 'O' Call	7 Going Bananas
1 Boathouse	**● Eating**	8 Iron Bar
2 Coconut Grove Motel	1 Beaches Café	9 Java Blue
3 Coral Apartments	2 Café Macrossan	10 Mangiare
4 Dougie's Nomads	3 Catalina	11 Mocas Pies
Backpackers	4 Combined Club	12 Nautilus
5 Port Sea	5 Court House Hotel	13 Portofinos
6 Tropic Breeze	6 EJ's Takeaway	
7 Villa San Michelle		

Queensland

child $10, T4099 3235, www.rainforesthabitat.com.au Junction of Captain Cook Highway and Port Douglas Rd. Port Douglas is rather proud of its **Four Mile Beach**, which is both scenic and inviting to cosmopolitan crowds of top-less backpackers and the more conservative resort clients. Many water-based activities are on offer for those not satisfied with merely sunbathing or swimming. A net is placed just offshore to ward off box jellyfish and other stingers (October-May) and lifeguards are usually in attendance (always swim between the flags). On the Anzac Park Pier is the **Ben Cropp Shipwreck Museum**, which displays an interesting collection of material about local shipwrecks. ■ *Daily 0900-1700, $5.50.* Anzac park also hosts the weekly **market** held every Sunday. It is a colourful affair that offers everything from sarongs to freshly squeezed orange juice. More expensive permanent boutiques are housed in the delightfully cool **Marina Mirage Complex**, Wharf Street, T4099 5775, www.marinamiragepd.com.au

Reef trips, cruising, diving & snorkelling

All the major reef operators are based at the Marina Mirage Wharf, Wharf St. Almost all of the Cairns based companies listed in the Cairns section also provide transfers from Port Douglas. The vast majority combine cruising with snorkelling and/or diving with others being dive specialists

The main operator in Port Douglas is the long established and highly professional *Quicksilver*, T4087 2100, www.quicksilver-cruises.com.au, that shuttle tourists out to their own pontoon on the edge of **Agincourt Reef**, where you can spend the day diving, snorkelling or sunbathing. There are also trips in a glass-bottom boat for those not wishing to take the plunge. The basic day-cruise with a buffet lunch costs $161, child $83. Introductory dives from $113, certified dives from $71, scenic flights from $98. Departs 1000 daily. Quicksilver also operate a luxury sailing catamaran, the '*Wavedancer*' to the **Low Isles** on the inner reef where independent (or guided) snorkelling and guided beach walks are available. Day package from $110, child $57.50 lunch included (transfer only $65, child $35). Departs 1000 daily. Other options on board slightly smaller vessels include: *Poseidon*, Shop 2, 34 Macrossan Street, T4099 4772, www.poseidon-cruises.com.au, from $130, child $95 (departs daily 0830); *Aristocat*, T4099 4727, www.aristocat.com.au, from $129, child $89, intro dive from $175, certified from $169, two one-day cruises with four dives from $339; *Calypso*, T4099 3377, www.calypsocharters.com.au, from $125, child $90, introductory dive from $175, certified from $165 (departs 0845, returns 1645). Another option are the more personable cruises on board smaller vessels including *Wavelength* (30 passengers maximum), from $130, child $90, departs 0830, returns 1630, T4099 5031, www.wavelength-reef.com.au *Sailaway* (27 passengers max, sail catamaran), four hours to Low Isles (equipped for boom-netting) from $99, child $59, T4099 5599, www.reefand rainforest.com.au *Personal Touch* (16 passengers maximum), snorkel and dive specialists (including night dives), from $125, child $85, T4099 4158, www.divingportdouglas.com *Animal Farm* (12 passengers maximum) use an ocean racing yacht, half-day $60, child $42, full-day $115, child $84, T4099 6277, www.pdsail.com.au *Haba Dive*, Bally Hooley Train Station, Marina Mirage, T4099 5254, www.habadive.com.au, enjoy a good reputation in the region. Intro dive from $190, certified from $170 and snorkelling from $130.

Other activities **Cruising** The *Lady Douglas* is a lovingly restored paddle steamer that offers trips in combination with the Bally Hooley steam train, from the wharf to explore the harbour and inland creeks, one to two hours, 1330/1145, from $23, child $12, T4099 6860. **Fishing** There are a posse of charter boats available to take you fishing, including *Hooker Too*, T4099 5136, *MV Norseman*, T4099 5031 and compact *Dragon Lady*, T04-1829 8412. A full day will cost around $130. To hire your own pontoon boat or dinghy contact *Port Douglas Boat Hire*, T4099 6277, or *Out 'n' About*, T4098 5204, from $20 per hour. **Horse**

trekking *Wonga Beach Equestrian Centre*, T4098 7583, offer entertaining rides along Wonga Beach (20 km north), including Port Douglas transfers from $75, three hours. For inland adventures including the early pioneer 'Bump Track', contact *Mowbray Valley Trail Rides*, T4099 3268, half-day from $88, child $77, full day from $125, child $110. Suitable for beginners. **Sea Kayaking** *TK Paddling*, T04-1939 1659, offer half-day trips morning or afternoon from $70. **Water sports** *Extra Action Water Sports*, based on the first jetty north of the Marina Mirage Complex, T4099 3175, offer 'fast' six-hour trips to the Low Isles and the wonderfully quiet Snapper Island from $130, parasailing from $70, and jet bike hire from $70 (30 minutes). Combination packages are also available. For a similar range and a spot of 'bumpa tubing' contact *Get High Parafly*, Mirage Marina, from $30, T4099 6366.

Almost all the tour companies mentioned in the Cairns section offer pick-ups in Port Douglas. Port Douglas based companies include *BTS Tours*, 49 Macrossan Street, T4099 5665, www.btstours.com.au, that offer full day trips to Kuranda (from $90), Daintree/Cape Tribulation (from $122) and two-day 4WD Cooktown trips from $210. *Reef and Rainforest Connections*, 8/40 Macrossan Street, T4099 5599, www.reefandrainforest.com.au, offer a wider range of trips at a similar price. *Daintree Adventures*, T4098 2808, offer a range of 'wildlife attraction' packages from $35. For a personalized, authentic and informative look at the Mossman Gorge through aboriginal eyes, contact Hazel, *Native Guide Safari Tours*, T4098 2206, www.nativeguidesafaritours.com.au, full-day from $120, child $80 ($130 includes ferry transfer from Cairns). For local mountain bike tours contact *Bike 'n' Hike*, T4099 4000.

Land based tours

As you might expect there is plenty of choice in Port Douglas with the emphasis placed heavily on a mind-boggling choice of very similar 4-star resorts and apartments. Budget travellers are also well catered for with a selection of good backpackers, cheap motels and motor parks. Rates are naturally competitive and more expensive in the high season but at any time you are advised to shop around for special rates, especially in the 'wet' (Dec-Mar).

Sleeping

The jewel in the crown of resorts and the one that really started it all in the mid 1980s is the sumptuous **LL** *Sheraton Mirage*, that takes up a large portion of the eastern side of the peninsula, T4099 5888, F4099 4424, www.sheraton.com.au/mirageportdouglas It offers just about all a body could want, all within yards of Four Mile Beach, including top class restaurants, a golf course and a pool that just has to be seen to be believed. **LL** *Port Sea*, 76 Davidson St, T4087 2000, F4087 2001, www.theportsea.com.au, is very pleasant. In the centre of town there are a number of well-appointed, self-contained, boutique apartment blocks with the **LL** *Boathouse*, 41-43 Murphy St, T4099 8800, F4099 8855, www.boathouse.com.au and the **LL** *Villa San Michele*, 39-41 Macrossan St, T4099 4088, F4099 4975, www.villasanmichele.com.au, both recommended. For a cheaper fully self-contained apartment option try the excellent **L** *Coral Apartments*, corner of Blake St and Davidson St, T4099 6166, F4099 6177, wwwportdouglas coralapartments.com.au The place is great value, has a nice quiet atmosphere, attractive pool and very friendly, helpful hosts.

For a mid-range well-positioned motel try the **A** *Port Douglas Motel*, 9 Davidson St, T4099 5248, and for budget the 2-star **A** *Coconut Grove Motel*, 58 Macrossan St, T4098 5124. For a B&B providing ideal sanctuary, yet still within reach of Port Douglas, try the beautiful **L** *Marae B&B*, Lot 1, Ponzo Rd, Shannonvale, T4098 4900, F4098 4099, www.internetnorth.com.au/marae, offering 3 very comfortable en suite rooms, 2 king and 1 double. There are 2 good **backpackers** in the town, almost within a stone's throw of one another, just off Davidson St. The **A-E** *YHA Port 'O' Call*, Port St, T4099 5422, F4099

5495, www.portcall.com.au, has excellent motel-style doubles, budget dorms and a fine restaurant/bar, internet. **C-F** *Dougie's Nomads Backpackers*, 111 Davidson St, T4099 6200, www.dougies.com.au, has a/c doubles/twins, dorms and van/campsites, bar, bike hire, internet. Both hostels provide free pick-ups from Cairns. Other than Dougie's there are several choices for powered/ non-powered sites and motor parks. Just short of port Douglas off the captain Cook Highway is the 'Big 4', **B-F** *Glengarry Caravan Park*, Mowbray River Rd, T4098 5922, Glengarry@internetnorth.com.au It has fully self-contained en suite cabins, powered/ non-powered sites, with a good camp kitchen and a pool. Closer to the centre of town, and only a short stroll from Four Mile Beach, is the 3-star, **C-E** *Tropic Breeze Van Village*, 24 Davidson St, T4099 5299. It offers cabins, powered/non-powered sites and a camp kitchen.

Eating
Again there are plenty of options, mostly centred along Macrossan St at the Marina Mirage Complex on Wharf St

Expensive *Nautilus Restaurant*, 17 Murphy St, T4099 5330. Here you can dine on exquisite dishes with an emphasis on local seafood, under the stars and a canopy of palms, before collapsing at the prospect of paying for it all. Open daily from 1830.

Mid-range Far more informal and infamous is the highly entertaining and aptly named *Going Bananas*, 87 Davidson St, T4099 5400. The owner is a true eccentric and it will almost certainly prove to be a memorable experience. Open daily from 1800. Other more centrally located options worth considering are *Portofinos*, 31 Macrossan St, T4099 5458 (daily from 1800), with its traditional dishes of seafood and excellent curries; *Mangiare*, 18 Macrossan St, T4099 4054, an Italian with a good reputation, and the long-established *Catalina*, 22 Wharf St, T4099 5287 (Tue-Sun from 1800), that offers a varied and imaginative menu.

Cheap Down on the wharf nothing beats the waterfront view and the value at The *Combined Club*, Wharf St, T4099 5553. The *Port' O Call* at the YHA is also excellent value and has a nice laid back atmosphere. For pub food the *Court House Hotel*, corner Macrossan and Wharf St, T4099 5181, is popular while the *Iron Bar*, 5 Macrossan St, T4099 4776, is well known for its imaginatively named and generous Australian dishes. For a value breakfast and lots of tropical atmosphere look no further than the *Beaches Café*, on The Esplanade, overlooking Four Mile Beach, T4099 4998 (daily from 0700). Good coffee is generally readily available in the town, though the *Java Blue*, Shop 3, 2 Macrossan St, T0499 5814 and *Café Macrossan* at 42 Macrossan St, T4099 4372, currently have the edge. **Seriously cheap** For the post-pub munchies try the no nonsense *EJ's Takeaway* next to the VIC on Macrossan St and whatever you do don't leave Port Douglas without trying the famous and delicious *Mocas Pies*, Warner St (behind Coles Supermarket).

Entertainment
Although rumour has it that major renovations are afoot, as it stands, the 1878 *Court House Hotel*, on the corner of Macrossan St and Wharf St, T4099 5181, www.courthousehotel.com.au, is a fine place to enjoy a cool 'stubbie' (beer) or lunch/dinner in the beer garden, listening to the dulcet tones of local musos singin' the blues (Mon evenings). Wed-Sun sees the more traditional contemporary bands (with an Aussie slant). Open daily 1000-2400. Almost next-door is the highly characterful and aptly named *Iron Bar*, 5 Macrossan St, T4099 4776. On top of its regular live musical offerings it demonstrates the rather dubious art of Cane Toad Racing, Tue/Thu at 2100 $3 (daily 1000-0200). There are 2 restaurant/clubs in the Mirage Marina Complex that will keep you 'boppin' well in to the wee hours – *The Vue* (*Maximus Café*), T4099 5323, open until 0200 and *Nicky G's Sports Saloon*, which closes at 0500. For wildlife of a different nature why not consider dinner at the *Rainforest Habitat Wildlife Sanctuary*. They offer an entertaining 'Habitat after Dark' dining experience under the gaze of various cute and acuitic creatures of the night, from $39, child $19.50, T4099 3235. Bookings essential.

Banks Macrossan St or in the *Port Village Centre*. Currency exchange is available at most banks and *Interforex* in the Marina Mirage Centre. **Bike hire** *Port Douglas Bike Hire*, 40 Macrossan St, T4099 5799. Half-day from $10, full-day from $14, week from $59. *Bike'n' Hike* (specialist mountain bikes), T4099 4000. Full-day from $16.50. **Car hire** *Port Douglas Car Rental*, 2/79 Davidson St, T4099 4988, from $64 per day, 4WD from $99. *Crocodile Car Rentals*, 2/50 Macrossan St, T4099 5555. *Holiday Car Hire*, 54 Macrossan St, have 4WDs from $72 per day and mokes from $50. **Car servicing and breakdown** *RACQ*, T131111, *Mossman Towing*, 23 Mill St Mossman, T4098 2848. **Communications** Internet *Uptown Rentals*, Macrossan St, T4099 5568. Open daily 0900-2200. *Cyberworld Internet Café*, 38 Macrossan St, T4099 5661. **Post office** 5 Owen St, T4099 5210. Open Mon-Fri 0900-1700, Sat 0900-1200 **Medical services** *Port Village Medical Centre*, Shop 17, Port Village Shopping Centre, Macrossan St, T4099 5043 (24 hrs). Open Mon-Fri 0800-1800, Sat/Sun 0900-1200. *Mossman District Hospital*, Mossman, T4098 2444. **Police** Wharf St, T4099 5220.

Directory

Built on the back of the sugar cane industry in the 1880s Mossman sits on the banks of the Mossman River and has one of the world's most exotic tropical gardens on its back door in the form of the Daintree Wilderness National Park. For Daintree National Park and local walks information contact the *QPWS* office in Cairns, T4046 6600.

Mossman
*Population: 1770
21 km from Port Douglas, 75 km from Cairns*

Getting there *Coral Coaches*, 37 Front St, T4099 5351, offer regular services from Cairns and Port Douglas.

The **Mossman Gorge**, 5 km west of the town, is the greatest attraction. Here, the Mossman River falls towards the town fringed with rainforest and networked with a series of short **walks**. Many combine a walk with another big attraction – its cool **swimming holes**. Although the walks are excellent, if you are fit and careful, try following the river upstream for about 2 km. This will give you an ideal opportunity to see perhaps the forest and the region's most famous resident, the huge **Ulysses blue butterfly**. Just short of the gorge car park is the base of the **Kuku-Yalanji Dreamtime Tours**. They offer excellent Aboriginal cultural awareness walks that will enlighten you on the use of certain plants for medicinal purposes. ■*Walks depart at 1000/1200/1400, 2 hrs. From $16.50,child $8.25. There is also a shop, gallery open daily 0900-1600. Pick-ups from Port Douglas 0930, from $40.70, includes walk and refreshments. T4098 2595, www.internetnorth.com.au/yalanji*

Sleeping and eating The most upmarket accommodation in the immediate area is the excellent **LL** *Silky Oaks Lodge*, located just north of the town, T4098 1666, F4098 1983, www.poresorts.com.au It offers 60 freestanding en suite chalets, doubles, (some with spa) and a fine restaurant. Complimentary activities and pick-ups are also available. Situated a short stroll from **Wonga Beach** north of the town is the little known **A-E** *Red Backs Resort*, 17 Oasis Dr, Wonga Beach, T4098 7871, F4098 7520, www.redbacks.com.au, an excellent budget resort with modern, spotless and great value suites, en suite doubles and dorm rooms, with excellent facilities. Pool, café, internet. Tour bookings and pick-ups are available. There is no campsite at Mossman Gorge. *O'Malley's Irish Pub and Hotel*, 2 Front St, Mossman, T4098 1410, is something of a local institution, serving good value pub meals.

Queensland

Daintree

Colour map 5, grid A6
Population: 100
111 km north of Cairns

The tiny, former timber town (now village) of Daintree sits at the end of the Mossman-Daintree Road, sandwiched between the western and eastern blocks of the **Daintree National Park**. At the edge of the village lies its biggest local attraction, the croc-infested **Daintree River**. The village itself exudes a quaint and original charm, quite unlike the tourist metropolis to the south. Centred round Stewart Street (and an enormous model **barramundi fish**) is a general store, Bushman's Lodge, a **small timber museum** (open daily 1000-1630, free, T4098 6166), a couple of restaurants, a school and a caravan park.

Ins & outs

Getting there *Coral Coaches*, 37 Front St, Mossman, T4099 5351, offer regular bus services from Cairns and Port Douglas to Daintree, and like most other tour companies include Daintree and its various river cruise options on most of their northbound tours. Note that road conditions around Daintree can be treacherous in the wet season (Dec-Mar). For road information, T4051 6711.

There are 2 sources of **information** in Daintree, both independent and both on Stewart St. The Daintree VIC (Daintree Connection), 5 Stewart St, T4098 6120, daintree@cyberworld.net.au, www.daintreevillage.asn.au Open daily 0900-1600. And the older *General Store Information Office*, 1 Stewart St, T4098 6146, www.daintree store.com.au Open daily 0700-2100.

Sights & activities

Most visitors come to Daintree as part of a tour package, or independently, to take a leisurely cruise on the river in search of 'Salties' – huge estuarine **crocodiles** . There are now nearly 10 **cruise** options/operators available, all of which ply the river from Daintree village to the coast, several times a day. You can either pick up the cruise near the village itself or at various points south to the Daintree/Cape Tribulation ferry crossing, but most people arrive on organized tours. For independent choice and bookings call in at the General Store.

The largest and longest serving operator is *Daintree Connection*, T4098 6120, who offer two cruises. The most popular is their 1½ hours River Cruise that departs from the village (Daintree Originals) on the hour from 1030-1600, from $20, child $7. The second is a 2½ hours Estuary Cruise that explores the lower reaches and the mouth of the river. It departs from the Ferry Crossing at 1330 daily, from $28, child $13. *Daintree Wildlife Safari*, based at the General Store, 1 Stewart Street, T4098 6125, dwsafari@internetnorth.com.au, offer 1½ hours 'Croc Spot' cruises on the hour from 0930-1530, from $20, child $7 and one-hour cruises on the hour from 1000-1600, from $17, child $6. Cruise and walk options cost 0800-1000, or 1600-1800, from $30, child $20. *Daintree Rainforest River Trains*, T4090 7676, dntrain@ozemail.com.au, operate a sort of multiple carriage affair from the Ferry Crossing on a two-hour cruise at 1030 and 1330, from $28, child $14. Pick-ups and day tours from Cairns or port Douglas are available. Smaller operators include *Daintree Lady*, T4098 6138, www.daintreerivercruises.com.au, which is a modern two-storied vessel offering more elevated views. It departs from Daintree Village, seven times a day on either a one-hour or 1½-hour tour, from $16.50 ($22), child $7 ($10). Lunch cruises are also available daily at 1245, from $32. *Chris Dahlberg's River Tours*, T4098 7997, chris@internetnorth.com.au, offer an excellent dawn cruise (departs 0600 November-March and 0630 April-October), with an emphasis on bird spotting, from $35. Recommended. *Nice 'n' Easy Cruises*, T4098 7456, also offer 1½ hour cruises from $22, or a Sunset Dinner Cruise with BBQ barramundi from $60. *Daintree River Fishing and Photography Tours*, T4090 7776, are a Mossman based company offering half or full day/night tours/cruises (including crocodile night spotting) from $65, coastal fishing from $120. Daintree born and bred *Jamie Beitzel*, T4090 7638, offers fishing and sightseeing trips, from four to eight hours ($65-120).

At the top end is the **LL** *Daintree Eco Lodge and Spa*, 20 Daintree Rd (3 km south of the village), T4098 6100, F4098 6200, www.daintree-ecolodge.com.au It enjoys a good reputation and has 15 luxury, serviced villas set in the rainforest, a specialist spa and a top class restaurant. There are a few good B&Bs in and around the village. Right in the heart is the very pleasant and friendly **A** *Red Mill House*, T/F4098 6233, redmill@internetnorth.com.au They offer various well-appointed rooms, some with shared facilities and some with en suites (separate from the main house). Overall the place has a wonderfully peaceful atmosphere with lovely gardens and plenty of wildlife that you can watch from the deck. Good value. **A** *Kenadon Homstead Cabins*, Dagmar St, T/F4098 6142, kenadon@internetnorth.com.au, has neat, double and single self-contained cabins. Breakfast included. Just 5 km to the west of the village is the **L** *River Home Cottages*, Upper Daintree Rd, T4098 6225, www.riverhomecottages.com.au 3 good fully self-contained cottages on a working farm in very quiet surroundings, spa. The **D-F** *Daintree Riverview Caravan Park*, 2 Stewart St, T4098 6119, is ageing a little but has on-site vans, powered and non-powered sites right in the heart of the village.

The most expensive option is the **Baaru Restaurant** in the eco Lodge Resort, T4098 6100, which offers good contemporary Australian cuisine. More affordable and convenient to the village is the *Big Barramundi* BBQ Garden, 12 Stewart St, T4098 6186, or the *Jacana's Restaurant*, across the road, T4098 6146, both offer fine barramundi dishes and the latter fine bottomless cups of local Daintree tea. The long-established *Daintree Tea House*, near Barrats Creek Bridge, Daintree Rd, T4098 6161, is something of a local institution, while the *Daintree Coffee Shop*, Stewart St, is located next door to the booking and information offices in the village.

Cape Tribulation

Although Cape Tribulation is the name attributed to a small settlement and headland that forms the main tourist focus of the region, the term itself is loosely used to describe a 40-km stretch of coastline within the World Heritage **Daintree National Park**, between the Daintree River mouth and the start of the controversial blot on the landscape, known as the **Bloomfield Track** (to Cooktown). Captain James Cook named it 'Tribulation' just before his ship the 'Endeavour' ran aground offshore in 1770. This is a place of wild, elemental and, at times, inhospitable beauty. It is also home to a wide variety of wildlife, including the cassowary, the crocodile, or the evocatively named wompoo pigeon. There's also the spine-tingling, uneasy feeling that if you stray too far off the road you would never be seen again. The area is generally well served with a wide range of accommodation to suit all budgets and certainly overloaded with a plethora of mainly Cairns and Port Douglas based tour operators. Note that some do not operate in the wet season (December-March) when access can be severely affected.

Colour map 5, grid A6
Population: 600
140 km from Cairns

Getting there The *Daintree River Ferry*, located 15 km southeast of Daintree village, operates daily from 0600-2400, pedestrian $2 return, vehicle $16 return. Self-drive is recommended but note all roads in the area can be treacherous in the wet season (Dec-Mar). For road information, T4051 6711. Beyond Cape Tribulation (36 km), the road degenerates into the strictly 4WD Bloomfield Track that winds its precarious 120-km way to Cooktown. Fuel is available 4 km east of Cow Bay village and 6 km north at the

Ins & outs
In the event of breakdown contact the RACQ (Cow Bay), T4098 2848

Rainforest Village Store. *Coral Coaches* (see above) offer daily scheduled services and tour packages from Cairns and Port Douglas, from $32, one-way (Cairns), tours from $52. The *Freedom Bus Company* also offer transfers from Port Douglas, T05-5504044. For tour options see Cairns (page 350) and Port Douglas (page 365).

Information Detailed information can be obtained from the VICs in Port Douglas or Cairns. Local information is available from the *Daintree Rainforest Environmental Centre* or *Bat House* (see below). For environmental and walks information contact the QPWS office in Cairns, T4046 6600. The *Australian Rainforest Foundation* website, www.wettropics.com.au, is also useful.

Sights   Five kilometres beyond the ferry crossing, the Cape Tribulation Road climbs steadily over the densely forested Waluwurriga Range to reach the **Mount Alexandra Lookout** which offers the first glimpse of the coast and the Daintree River mouth. Turning back inland and 2 km past the lookout, is the

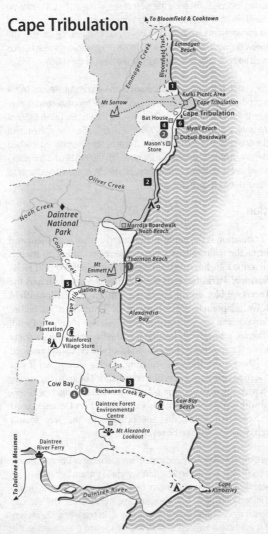

Cape Tribulation

To Bloomfield & Cooktown

Emmagen Creek

Bloomfield Track

Emmagen Beach

Mt Sorrow

Kulki Picnic Area
Cape Tribulation
Cape Tribulation

Bat House
Myall Beach
Mason's Store
Dubuji Boardwalk

Oliver Creek

Noah Creek
Daintree National Park

Marrdja Boardwalk
Noah Beach

Cooper Creek

Mt Emmett

Thornton Beach

Alexandra Bay

Cape Tribulation Rd

Tea Plantation
Rainforest Village Store

Cow Bay
Buchanan Creek Rd

Daintree Forest Environmental Centre

Cow Bay Beach

Mt Alexandra Lookout

Daintree River Ferry

To Daintree & Mossman

Daintree River

Cape Kimberley

Cape Kimberley

N

0 km   2
0 miles   2

Sleeping
1 Cape Trib Beach House
2 Coconut Beach Rainforest Resort
3 Crocodylus Village
4 Ferntree Rainforest Resort
5 Heritage Lodge
6 PK's Jungle Village

Camping
7 Club Daintree
8 Lync Haven
9 Noah Beach QPWS

Eating
1 Café by the Sea
2 Dragonfly Gallery & Café
3 Floraville Tea Garden
4 Latitude 16 Point 12 Degrees

Queensland

turn-off (east) to the **Daintree Forest Environmental Centre**, featuring excellent displays on the local flora and fauna, with the added attraction of a 400-m boardwalk (guided walks available) and a 25-m tower set amidst the forest, offering a bird's-eye view of the forest canopy. There is also a good café on site (free from the admission charge) from which to experience the forest wildlife. ■ *Daily 0830-1700, $15, child $7.50. T4098 9171.* Back on Cape Tribulation Road and just beyond the Environmental Centre, is the small settlement of **Cow Bay** with its attractive, namesake bay and **beach** that can be reached by road 6 km to the east on Buchanan Creek Road. Continuing north you are then given another interesting reminder of being in the tropics by passing a well-manicured **tea plantation** before crossing Cooper Creek and hitting the coast below Mount Emmett. Oliver Creek then sees the first of a duo of excellent boardwalks, which provides insight into the botanical delights of the forest and mangrove swamps. The '**Marrdja**' boardwalk takes about 45 minutes and is well worth a look. From here it is about 9 km before you reach the settlement of Cape Tribulation. Here, the second, equally interesting boardwalk '**Dubuji**' (also taking 45 minutes). The headland at Cape Tribulation is also well worthy of investigation, as are its two beautiful beaches – Emmagen and Myall – which sit either side like two golden bookends. The Kulki picnic area and lookout is located at the southern end of Emmagen Beach and is signposted just beyond the village. Just beyond that the Kulki turn-off (150 m) heralds the start of the **Mount Sorrow** track, a challenging 3½ km ascent rewarded with spectacular views from the 650-m summit.

While in Cape Tribulation be sure to visit the **Bat House**, opposite *PK's Backpackers*, where you'll find loving volunteers tending to the needs of injured bats. To watch these enchanting creatures suckling on a pipette goes beyond cute. Local information and a range of interesting wildlife displays are also to hand. ■ *Daily, except Mon, from 1030-1530, at least $2 donation, T4098 0063.* Beyond Cape Tribulation the road gradually degenerates to form the notorious **Bloomfield Track**. From here you are entering real 'Tiger Country' and 4WD is essential. A 2WD will only get you as far as **Emmagen Creek** which offers a limited incursion into the fringes of the dense rainforest and some good, croc-free, swimming holes. There are many environmental based activities on offer in the region, including crocodile spotting (from $17); sea kayaking (from $34); horse riding (from $55) and even candlelit diners deep in the rainforest (from $90). Most activities are best arranged through any of the main backpackers including the helpful and informative Beach House (see below). The guided rainforest walks with *Jungle Adventures*, T4098 0090, or *Mason's Tours*, T4098 0070, www.masonstours.com.au, are recommended. Their **night walks** 'spotting' the 'doe-eyed' possums of the night is a Cape Trib 'must-do' (from $28). For more adventurous day-trips consult the VICs in Cairns or Port Douglas. A 4WD day trip exploring the Bloomfield Track with *Mason's Tours* costs from $115.

Sleeping

There's a wide range of accommodation in the Cape, though most places are relatively expensive

At the upper end there is the **LL-L** *Heritage Lodge*, Turpentine Rd (near Coopers Creek), T4098 9138, www.home.aone.net.au/heritagelodge, offering, spacious, tidy en suite cabins, a pool and an a la carte restaurant on site. Further up towards Cape Tribulation itself, is the classy, yet expensive **LL** *Coconut Beach Rainforest Resort*, Cape Tribulation Rd, T4098 0033, www.coconutbeach.com.au It offers an attractive range of en suite villas and units in a quiet bush setting with a pool. Just to the south of Cape Tribulation is the **LL-D** *Ferntree Rainforest Resort*, Camelot Close, T4098 0000, www.ferntreeresort.com.au, a large 3-star complex, with fine facilities and, for a resort, a pleasantly quiet and intimate feel. The wide range of rooms, villas and suites are well appointed, the restaurant and bar is a fine place to relax and the pool is truly memorable. Occasional good deals on offer and budget accommodation with full access to facilities from $33.

There are 3 main **backpackers** in the region, all being significantly different. In the south, near Cow Bay Village (along Buchanan Creek Rd and the beach), is the YHA affiliated **B-E** *Crocodylus Village*. By far the most ecologically 'in tune', it is essentially a glorified bush camp, with an interesting array of huts (some en suite) centred around a large communal area and a landscaped pool. Its only drawback perhaps is the 3-km distance from the beach. Regular shuttle buses are however offered, as are regular daily Cairns and Port Douglas transfers, tours and activities T4098 9166, www.crocodylus@austarnet.com.au   In Cape Tribulation itself is **B-D** *PK's Jungle Village*, Cape Tribulation Rd, T4098 0040, www.pksjunglevillage.com.au, a well-established, mainstream hostel, popular with the social and party set. It offers all the usual facilities including a lively bar, restaurant, pool and a host of activities. At the top end of Cape Tribulation just before the tyres fall off a 2WD is the new and very congenial **L-D** *Cape Trib Beach House*, Cape Tribulation Rd, T4098 0030, www.capetribbeach.com.au   It offers a range of modern cabins (some en suite) from dorm to 'beachside'. The most attractive aspects are the bush setting, its quiet atmosphere, the communal bar and bistro (with internet) allocated right next to the beach. A wide range of activities and tours are also available. The only drawback is the inability to park your vehicle near the cabins. The Beach House is definitely the best budget option for couples.

Camping and powered sites are available at the **A-F** *Club Daintree*, T4090 7500, off Cape Tribulation Rd on Cape Kimberly, which may be too far south for most. Alternatively, the **A-F** *Lync Haven*, T4098 9155, www.lynchaven.com.au, is about 4 km north of Cow Bay Village. It is very eco-friendly and also has a reputable restaurant. *PK's Jungle Village* (see above) is the only option in Cape Tribulation. The **QPWS** has a basic campsite at Noah Beach, 8 km south of Cape Tribulation, but bear in mind it is closed during the wet season.

Eating   Almost all the resorts and backpackers listed above have their own restaurants or bistros, most of which are open for breakfast lunch and dinner. The most upmarket is the à la carte restaurant in the *Long House, Coconut Beach Resort* (see above, bookings essential). Alternatively you can also enjoy a more intimate al fresco dining experience at the *Ferntree Resort* (see above). There are also basic, but perfectly acceptable, offerings at the *Daintree Forest Environmental Centre* (see above), the *Floraville Tea Garden*, Cape Tribulation Rd, T4098 9100, *Latitude 16 Point 12 Degrees*, T4098 9133, Bailey's Creek Rd, both in Cow Bay, or the *Café by the Sea*, T4098 9118, 4 km south of Noah Creek on Thornton Beach. The *Drangonfly Gallery and Café*, T4098 0121, across the road from the Ferntree Resort, in Cape Tribulation, offers tasty lunches and dinners with the added attraction of local artworks and an internet loft. The basic and expensive *Mason's Store*, T4098 0072, is 2 km south of Cape Tribulation (open daily 0830-1700).

North to Cooktown   There are two routes to Cooktown, the inland route via Mount Molloy and the **Peninsula Development Road** and the coastal route via Cape Tribulation and the **Bloomfield Track**. At 334 km, compared to 248 km (both from Cairns) the inland route is the longer, but the most negotiable. The inland route is suitable for 2WD outside the wet season and the coastal route is 4WD only. Both roads are said to offer a 'challenging' drive. The really adventurous of course take their own 4WD but given that option is beyond the resources of most visitors, many settle for one of several organized **tours**, the best of which take in both routes. A combination of self-drive and tour is of course another option but if you have time a round trip going to Cooktown via the inland route and back via the coast is recommended. For tour operator listings under Cairns (page 350) and Port Douglas (page 365) or consult the major VICs. Companies regularly plying the route include *Coral Coaches*, *Wilderness Challenge* and *Adventure Safaris*.

The coastal route The infamous, notorious and controversial Bloomfield Track is said to be one of Australia's most challenging 'principal' 4WD tracks. Its creation in the mid 1980s caused considerable protest with environmentalists who were deeply concerned about the impact on the rainforest. Now established, to journey upon the Bloomfield is to subject your internal organs to the kind of treatment normally only reserved for your heavily soiled laundry in the washing machine. Just beyond the Emmagen Creek, 6 km north of Cape Tribulation, the track starts, quite innocently at first, before taking on its true character over the **Donovan Range** with its steep inclines, curves, ruts and creek crossings. And that's in the dry season. In the wet you forget it, unless you like getting out every few minutes to try and lever your vehicle out of the mud. If you are lucky, you are afforded the odd glimpse of the coast and local flora and fauna, before the track arrives almost at its halfway mark (31 km from Cape Tribulation, 45 km to Helenvale) and the remote **Bloomfield River** and **Wujai Wujai Aboriginal** community. The occasionally spectacular **Bloomfield Falls** are also nearby (1.3 km) and accessed with a 500-m walk. From the Bloomfield River the track is in better condition before eventually joining the Cooktown Road at **Helenvale** (28 km south of Cooktown).

Sleeping There are limited amenities and accommodation north of the Bloomfield River. Petrol and a basic store are available at Wujai Wujai and 4 km further north at the Bloomfield River Inn. A further 5 km will see you at the **LL** *Bloomfield Rainforest Lodge*, 14035 9166, www.bloomfieldlodge.com.au, a luxurious oasis of humanity in the coastal wilderness, offering all mod cons and numerous activity options. A cheaper luxury option are the charming bungalows at the **LL** *Mungumby Lodge*, T4060 3158, www.mungumby.com.au, near Helenvale. Again, activities and tours can be arranged and there are some fine local walking trails. The *Lions Den Pub* in Helenvale, T4060 3911, is well known for its unusual decor and as a popular stop for lunch or a welcome pint. It also has camping facilities. More remote camping is available at the **B-F** *Bloomfield Beach Camp*, T4060 8207, www.bloomfieldcabins.com 2 km north of the Bloomfield Rainforest Lodge. It also has affordable cabins and a restaurant.

The inland route Although not nearly as wild or challenging as the Bloomfield Track, the inland route to Cooktown offers some interesting scenery, historical aspects and mainly basic accommodation. Note that the most challenging part is the 54-km unsealed section between Lakeland and Helenvale. Even in the dry this can be badly rutted and in the wet season almost impassable. The now sleepy villages of **Mount Molloy** and **Mount Carbine** offer an insight into the once-thriving copper and wolfram mining industries, while the Palmer River basin, between Mount Carbine and Lakeland was once the most famous goldfield in the far north. It was these lucrative fields that essentially put Port Douglas and Cairns on the map. Also of note along the way are the spectacular views on offer from **Bob's Lookout** at the top of the Desailly Range 30 km north of Mount Carbine, the **Annan Gorge** near Helenvale and the mysterious granite formations of **Black Mountain** about 25 km south of Cooktown. The Black Mountains are home to a variety of plants and animals including the rare Godman's Rock Wallaby and the Black Mountain Frog that is found nowhere else in the world.

Queensland

Sleeping   There is basic roadside accommodation, fuel and eateries in Mt Molloy, Mt Carbine and Lakeland. The **E-F** *Mt Carbine Village and Caravan Park*, T4094 3160 has units, powered and un-powered sites. The *Palmer River Roadhouse*, 80 km north of Mt Carbine offers a welcome lunch and refreshment stop and houses a small mining museum. *RACQ* assistance is available in Mt Molloy, T4094 1260.

Cooktown

Colour map 5, grid A6
Population: 1,500
334 km from Cairns

No prizes for guessing who put this place on the map! After coming to grief on the Barrier Reef just off Cape Tribulation on his 1770 voyage of discovery, Captain Cook grounded his ship 'The Endeavour' near what is now the Endeavour River (the banks of which would later form Cooktown). For almost two months he tried to make good his misfortune and in so doing he and his crew essentially created the first 'white' settlement in Australia – something the modern day town is clearly proud of, with no fewer than six monuments dedicated to the man. It was here also, reputedly, that the Kangaroo was first described to 'civilization' along with many other unique Australian plants and animals. But though many boast about Cook's arrival in this quiet part of the far north, subsequent events have shown that his arrival was to herald the single most catastrophic event in the natural evolution of the continent – human or otherwise. Once Cook resumed his voyage the site lay dormant until the gold rush of the Palmer River basin in the 1870s. In a matter of months the cosmopolitan population grew to a staggering 30,000 plus. The boom naturally did not last and with two devastating cyclones (the worst in 1907) to make matters worse, the future of Cooktown looked bleak. But like its big cousins Cairns and Port Douglas the town has grown in stature as an attractive lifestyle proposition and a popular tourist destination. There is plenty to see and do in and around Cooktown, with the James Cook Museum the undeniable highlight.

Ins & outs   **Air** *Skytrans Airlines*, T4069 5446, www.skytrans.com.au, are one of a number of companies offering regular transfers to Cairns from $82 one-way (with 3-day advance purchase). **Bus** *Coral Coaches*, T4098 2600, ply the inland route from Cairns to Cooktown on Wed, Fri and Sun and the coastal route Tue, Sat (all year) and Thu (Jun-Oct), from $115, child $57.50 round trip. Note many tour operators in Cairns and Port Douglas offer day or multi-day trips to Cooktown, some combining road travel with a scenic return flight (see pages 350 and 365) *Cooktown Tourism*, T4069 6100, and the *Cooktown Travel Centre* T4069 5446, cooktowntravel@bigpond.com, looks after local visitor information services and can provide town maps. Both are located in the heart of the town on Charlotte St.

Sights   A good place to start is from the **Grassy Hill Lighthouse**, which is reached after a short climb at the end of Hope Street, north of the town centre. Here you can take in the views of the coast and town from the same spot Captain Cook reputedly worked out his safe passage back through the reef to the open sea. The old corrugated iron lighthouse that dominates the hill was built in England and shipped to Cooktown in 1885. For decades it served local and international shipping before being automated in 1927 and becoming obsolete in the 1980s. From Hope Street it is then a short walk south to the **James Cook Museum**. Housed in a former convent built in 1889 (just one of many historical buildings in the town), the museum is one of the most significant in Australia and features some striking exhibits, including the *HMS Endeavour*'s anchor and one of her cannons, supplemented with references to Cook's journals and oral tales from the local aboriginals. There are also interesting displays on the town's colourful and cosmopolitan history, such as the significance and influence of the Palmer River gold rush and the Chinese community, and in more recent times, the devastating cyclones that the town has endured. ■ *Daily Apr-Jan 0930-1600 (reduced hours Feb-Mar –phone first), $5.50, child $2. T4069 5386, corner of Furneaux and Helen St.*

The waterfront (Webber Esplanade) also hosts a number of interesting historical sites and plenty of reminders. The site of Cook's landing, at what is now **Bicentennial Park**, is marked with a small cairn and commemorative bronze statue of the man himself. Other sites of historical interest include the **Cooktown Cemetery**, which is at the southern edge of town along Endeavour Valley Road. There you will notice the huge contrast in nationalities and the young age at which many former pioneers died. Although a **Chinese** shrine is now a dominant feature in the cemetery, the absence of marked graves of both Chinese and the local Aboriginals is a sad indication of their perceived social standing in the community at the time. If ecological insight is more appealing than the historic, call in at **Nature's Powerhouse** in the **Botanical Gardens** which houses an excellent display about the region's reptiles and an art gallery. ■ *Daily. $2. T4069 6004. Walker St (East of the town centre).* If you are in Cooktown in mid-June, your visit may coincide with the colourful Cooktown **Discovery Festival**, when Cook's landing is commemorated with a re-enactment and a host of other events and celebrations. As well as the obvious historical attraction Cooktown offers a number of activities from self-guided local walks and historic town tours to reef fishing, cruising and snorkelling. If you can possibly afford it, a trip to **Lizard Island** (see below) by sea or air is recommended. The information centres have details and can arrange bookings. *Cooktown Cruises*, T4069 5712, offer a sedate two-hour historical and eco-cruise on the Endeavour River from $25, child $12.

The 4-star colonial-style **L-A** *Sovereign Resort Hotel*, on the corner of Charlotte St and Green St, T4069 5400, sovereign_resort@cooktown.tnq.com.au, is the most upmarket place in town offering modern 2-bedroom apartments, deluxe and standard units. It also has a reputable à la carte restaurant and a fine pool. At the southern edge of town is the **L-A** *Milkwood Lodge Rainforest Cabins*, Annan Rd, T4069 5007, www.milkwood-lodge.com, offering 6 excellent, luxury self-contained cabins in an elevated position with fine views. One of the best motel options in the heart of town is the value **A** *River of Gold Motel*, corner of Hope St and Walker St, T4069 5222, while the **C-E** *Pam's Place*, corner of Charlotte St and Boundary St, T4069 5166, pamplace@tpg.com.au is the principal backpackers in town. It offers dorms, singles and doubles and has all the usual facilities including a pool, tour desk and bike hire. There are several 3-star motor parks around town with the **A-E** *Tropical Breeze*, corner of Charlotte St and McIvor Rd, T4069 5417, being recommended and well placed. Further afield the **B-E** *Peninsula Caravan Park*, Howard St, T4069 5107, offers on-site vans, powered and un-powered sites in a quiet bush setting next to the Mt Sorrow National Park.

For fine dining the *Sovereign Resort* is perhaps your best bet along with the *Seagrens Inn* on Charlotte St, T4069 5357, both of which specialize in local seafood and Australian fare. The usual standard, value bistro meals can be found at the local *Cooktown Bowls Club*, Charlotte St, T4069 6137, and pub fare at the locally popular *Top Pub* (Cooktown Hotel), corner of Charlotte St and Walker St, T4069 5308. For coffee and breakfast try the congenial, waterfront *Cooks Landing Kiosk*, T4069 5101, on the Webber Esplanade. There is a supermarket located in the Helen Street Shopping Centre (open Mon-Sat 0800-1800, Thu 0800-1900, Sun 1000-1500).

Sleeping & eating

Queensland

Queensland

▶▶ The Cooktown Olympics

They say that Queenslanders are as 'mad as cut snakes', or as one former Australian Prime Minister put it. 'Queensland, it's not a State – it's a condition'! Whether you find this to be true will depend on your viewpoint and your experiences. However, one true story does demonstrate not so much a tendency towards mild insanity, as devilish individualism, admirable initiative and considerable character. In 2000, during the lead up to the Sydney Olympic Games, SOCOG (Sydney Organising Committee for the Olympic Games) left Far North Queensland and the proud outpost community of Cooktown off the route of the much hyped national Torch Relay Run. This was of course met with much derision and outrage. But instead of lobbying the 'southern powers that be' the good and imaginative people of Cooktown decided instead to organize their own torch relay and without delay created NOCOG (The Not the Organising Committee for the Olympic Games). In due course a substitute torch was made and the race duly run from the tip of Cape York to Cooktown. But the high jinx didn't end there. NOCOG also decided to organize their own Olympic Games – The **Relaxation Games**, which in true Queensland style and character included events like 'Armchair Sleeping' and 'Watching the Grass Grow'. Both the Torch Relay Run and the games were such a success that it attracted international media attention promoting Australia and Queensland in a way only the SOCOG, New South Wales and the Australian Capital Territory could dream of! What is even better is that no public funds were spent whatsoever and it was all done for charity, raising over $40,000 for the Flying Doctors Service. At the highly colourful closing ceremony even the torch was auctioned for $2,500 to a group of fishermen from Sydney, who promised to return it for permanent display in Cooktown after carrying it with pride, most probably all the way to the steps of the SOCOG. So are Queenslanders as 'mad as cut snakes'?
Most certainly not. 'She'll be right mate'

Directory **Banks** *Wespac*, Charlotte St, T4069 5477. **Car/4WD hire** *Cooktown Car Hire*, 1 Charlotte St, T4069 5694. **Communications** Internet *Computer Stuff*, Charlotte St, T4069 6010. **Post Office** Charlotte St. **Medical services** Hospital, Hope St, T4069 5433. **Police** 170 Charlotte St, T4069 5320. **RACQ** Cape York Tyres, corner of Charlotte St and Furneaux St, T4069 5274 **Taxis** T4069 5387.

Lizard Island Lizard Island hosts Australia's most northerly reef island resort, one of the best and inevitably perhaps one of the most exclusive. The island itself lies 270 km north of Cairns, 27 km off Cooktown. and is almost 1,000 ha, the vast majority of which is national park. All the delights of the other popular islands are on offer, with the welcome absence of over-commercialism and hordes of other tourists. There are over 24 tranquil beaches, backed by lush forests, mangroves and bush, all abounding in wildlife, while just offshore, immaculate, clear water reefs offer superb diving and snorkelling. The famous **Cod Hole** is considered one of the best dive sites on the reef and the island is also a popular base for big game fishermen in search of the elusive Black Marlin. A delightful walking track leads to **Cook's Look**, which at 359 m is the highest point on the island.

Sleeping and eating The **LL** *Lizard Island Resort*, T1800-737678, www.poresorts. com, is pretty spectacular and offers lodges and chalets with all mod cons, fine resort facilities and a 5-star restaurant. The resort offers an exciting range of guest complimentary activities from windsurfing to guided nature walks. **Camping** is available on the island, though facilities are basic and you must of course get there. Permits and bookings essential. Contact the QPWS in Cairns.

Transport Various regional air operators and vessel charter companies service Lizard Islands but prices and times vary. The **VIC** in Cooktown is the best place to enquire for the most up-to-date options. *Daintree Air Services*, T4034 9300, www.daintreeair.com.au, offer a day-trip package from $390, ex Cairns. *Skytrans Airlines*, T4069 5446, www.skytrans.com.au, also offer air charters from Cairns or Cooktown.

Cape York

Beyond Cooktown the great wilderness of Cape York beckons. For most it is enough to hear about it and to imagine its conquest. But for others the challenge is simply too great. There are essentially two ways to meet that challenge and to reach the most northerly tip of Australia. The first and by far the most sensible for those inexperienced with 4WD, is to join a professional 4WD tour operator, while the second is, of course, to go independently with an experienced group. Either way, it is not a trip for the faint hearted and is one requiring detailed planning, a reliable vehicle, proper equipment and not least of all, a dogged sense of adventure. The trip that is almost 1000 km of unsealed road, taking 10-14 days return, must also be made in the dry season (April-October) when the numerous riverbed crossings are negotiable. For those brave (or foolish) souls who do go it alone, it most certainly requires research and information well beyond the scope of this handbook. But whichever way you go, you are guaranteed a true Aussie wilderness adventure and enough memories to last a lifetime. There will also be rewarded with a lot of aches and pains and a walk like John Wayne every time you emerge from the 4WD.

Colour map 5, grid A6

Queensland

Information & tour operators

The **VIC** in Cairns can supply up to date information about the Cape and can also provide a few pointers long before departure. There are several good books about Cape York including the excellent *Cape York – An Adventurers Guide* by Ron and Viv Moon. The *Hema Regional Map of North Queensland* is a good general map. There are no specific websites on the Cape but a general search will reveal plenty of information. Beyond Cooktown there is obviously a dearth of amenities and when it comes to accommodation there is little choice beyond basic roadhouses, hotel pubs and basic campsites. The **QPWS** in Cairns can supply detailed national parks and camping information. Cairns based tour operators offering reputable trips to the Cape include *Oz Tour Safaris*, T4055 9535, info@oztours.com.au, 7-day tour from $1495 (twin share). *Billy Tea Bush Safaris*, T07-4032 0077, www.billytea.com.au, also offer attractive options. Another fascinating alternative are the air tours and mail run available with *Cape York Air*, T4035 9399, www.capeyorkair.com.au, from $297-$471.

Sights

The first significant settlement along the Peninsula Developmental Road is **Laura** where you will find basic hotel and caravan park accommodation, fuel and a café. Laura provides the base for the investigation of the beautifully preserved Split Rock Aboriginal rock paintings located 13 km to the south. Tours are available with the **Ang-gnarra Aboriginal Corporation**, T4060 3200. An undoubted highlight of the Cape York is the Lakefield National Park. Queensland's second largest, it offers a remote wonderland of diverse landscapes from grass savannah to quiet billabongs and a very impressive range of avian residents. Another highlight of the park is the Old Laura Homestead built in the 1880s during the Palmer River Gold rush. Access to the park is north of Laura and the Musgrave Roadhouse. For park information contact the local ranger, T4060 3271. The **LL** *Lotus Bird Lodge*, located between Musgrave and the western fringes of the park, T4095 0773, www.cairns.aust.com/lotusbird, offers fine, modern lodge-style accommodation with pool, restaurant, bar and organized national park tours. Beyond Musgrave, the tiny settlement of **Coen** provides the next base for accommodation and supplies and 65 km beyond that is the Archer River where you will find a roadhouse with a café and campsite. The fairly unremarkable mining town of Weipa on the shores of the Gulf of Carpentaria then marks the end of the Peninsula Developmental Road. But those heading for the tip leave the Peninsula Developmental Road well to the east and continue north on the most challenging section of the journey to reach (eventually) the most northerly settlement in Queensland–Bamaga and the Jardine National Park – before popping the cork overlooking The Endeavour Strait and Thursday Island. Before heading north to Bamaga it is well worth taking the diversion east to the remote and beautiful Iron Range National Park.

Outback Queensland

*There is no doubt that Queensland's outback has a great deal to offer. Like New South Wales, there is plenty of history relating to mining and **gem fields**, where amateur **fossicking** can still reveal lucrative finds. Fishermen too rave about their own form of hunting, with the quest for the mighty **barramundi**. But some of the more general sights and activities you will encounter in Queensland's outback you can experience nowhere else in the world, including **fossilised footprints** from a Dinosaur stampede, forever preserved in stone, or the wild annual horse races in **Birdsville** (one of Australia's most remote settlements) when the population swells from one hundred to five thousand, all most definitely as 'mad as cut snakes' and determined to have a good time. Then there is the omnipresent beauty of the environment, the rich and diverse wildlife and even a bit of mystery and intrigue, with strange light and weather phenomena. In summary, when it comes to Queensland's own huge contribution to the vast outback of this great nation, the same adjectives apply: beautiful, mysterious and brain-numbingly vast.*

*Queensland's outback does not lack for variety of sights and things to do, but the sheer difference between its main centres do present a problem for visitors. Although **Longreach** with its famous **Stoc kman's Hall of Fame** and **Qantas Museum** is arguably worth the trip in itself, **Mount Isa**, on the way to the Northern Territory, is a disappointment and in no way as interesting or well facilitated as Broken Hill. This lack of incentive often discourages travellers to venture far inland from the coast unless they are en route to the Northern Territory. However, having said that, the former gold-mining settlement of **Ravenswood** and historic town of **Charters Towers**, both only two hours from Townsville, offer a fine outback experience and one that is fairly unique to Queensland.*

Ins & outs   **Getting there and around**   From east to west, several main highways act as lifelines across the mighty Queensland outback: The **Warrego Highway** between Brisbane and Windorah; the **Capricorn and Landsborough Highways** between Rockhampton and Cloncurry and the **Flinders and Barkly Highways** (Overlander's Highway) between Townsville and Tennent's Creek. Other highways bisect these, offering routes north and south or alternative routes west to the Northern Territory, including the **Matilda Highway** from Bourke to Karumba, and the **Savannah Way**, between Cairns and the evocative **Hell's Gate**. Most of these roads are completely sealed. Outback Queensland is far better served by rail than the outback of New South Wales, yet there are no interstate services between Queensland and Northern Territory. In the south 'The Westlander' ventures from Brisbane to Charleville; through the heartlands the 'Spirit of the Outback' runs between Brisbane and Longreach, then there is the 'Inlander' between Townsville and Mount Isa. Elsewhere, covering shorter distances within the

Gulf Savannah, the 'Savannahlander' operates between Cairns and Forsayth and 'The Gulflander' between Normanton and Croydon. The latter are both old services that add a historical edge to the entire experience.

The Warrego Highway and Birdsville

From the high elevations and green rural landscapes of the Darling Downs, the Warrego Highway heads interminably west, through the small towns of **Dalby**, **Chinchilla**, **Miles** and **Roma**, before momentarily meeting the Mitchell Highway (Matilda Highway) at **Charleville** and then continuing to Windorah. From Windorah the truly brave, patient and indefatigable can then venture to the very edge of Queensland and the settlement of **Birdsville**, a place synonymous with the very word 'outback'.

1200 km from Brisbane to Windorah

The historic town of Charleville is located on the banks of the **Warrego River** and has, since the very first days of European exploration, provided an oasis in Queensland's vast outback. At the junction of the Mitchell Highway (Matilda Highway) and the Warrego Highway, it now provides a convenient overnight stopover on the way north to Longreach, or west to Windorah and, eventually, Birdsville. Other than the obvious attractions of a bed and a cool beer, the town provides a few sights worthy of investigation. The **Historic House Museum**, in the former 1881 Queensland National Bank building, provides an interesting insight in to the town's folk history and boasts various relics that once provided the vital links with the outside world including an original Cobb and Co Coach. ■ *Daily 0800-1600. $3. T4654 3349. 87 Alfred St*. The **Corones Hotel** on Wills Street is also an important historical building and was for many years the focal point of the community. It still retains much of its original charm and décor. ■ *2-hr 'Scones and Stories' tours are available, T4654 1022. $5, child $3*. The bizarre **Steiger Vortex Gun**, on the edge of the town and Graham Edwards Park (Mitchell Highway) was the brainchild of Meteorologist and inventor Clement Wragge. As a vain attempt to ease the relentless droughts experienced at the turn of the century, they fired blasts of air in to the heavens to create clouds and hopefully, rain. Sadly, all they succeeded in doing was creating lots of noise and even more despair for the community. Like many outback towns Charleville also hosts a **School of the Air**, a **Royal Flying Doctor Base** and an **observatory**, all of which are open to the public. The VIC has details. *Outback Airtours*, based at Charleville Airport, T4654 3033, www.outbackairtours.com.au, offer a range of flight seeing and outback air tours from 20 minutes to four days, $33-1,600. The **Charleville Visitors Information Centre** is on Cunnamulla Road, T4654 3057. ■ *Daily 0900-1700*. The **QPWS** have an office on Park Road, T4654 1255. ■ *Mon-Fri 0830-1630*.

Charleville
Colour map 4, grid C2
Population: 4,000
744 km west of Brisbane,
842 km from east of Birdsville

Sleeping and eating The historic **B-E** *Corones Hotel/Motel*, 33 Wills St, T4654 1022, offers tidy singles, doubles and shared backpacker rooms, some with en suite and all with a/c, as well as a good value restaurant and café. The **B-E** *Bailey Bar Caravan Park*, 196 King St, T1800-065 311, offers deluxe units with spa, standard cabins, powered and non-powered sites, BBQs and kiosk.

Transport Charleville **train** station is located on King St. *Queensland Rail*, T132232, offer a twice weekly (Wed/Fri) 'Westlander' service to Brisbane. *McCafferty's/Greyhound*, T131499, offer daily **bus** services to Brisbane and Mount Isa. *Macair*, T131313, **flights** stop en route between Brisbane and Mount Isa.

Birdsville
Colour map 5, grid B5
Population: 100
1588 km west of
Brisbane, 653 km
south of Mount Isa

As one of the most 'outback' of outback settlements in the whole of Australia, Birdsville is best known simply for its location and – believe it or not – its social life. For much of the year the historic **Birdsville Hotel**, built in 1884, provides the hub of activity and a meeting place for both locals and a cosmopolitan mix of hardy travellers and 4WD enthusiasts. But it is the **Birdsville Races**, held every September, for which the town is most famous, when the surrounding desert becomes like a light aircraft parking lot and the population swells to five thousand revellers, all determined to have a mighty good time. The township marks the start of the 519 km **Birdsville Track** that heads south, through the **Sturt Stony Desert**, to Maree in South Australia. Although one of the most remote 4WD tracks in the country it is generally considered manageable, but of course requires all the usual careful preparations, equipment and planning. Locally, a big attraction for 4WD enthusiasts and sightseers generally is the '**Big Red**', a 90-m sand dune located just 41 km west of the town. Just over 20 km west of that is the **Simpson Desert National Park**, the biggest and no doubt the most arid national park in Queensland.

Birdsville was founded in 1881 and named in 1885 after the rich variety and profusion of bird life that is attracted to local billabongs (waterholes). The **Wirrarri Centre** on Billabong Boulevard, T4656 3300, wirrarri@hotmail.com, acts as the local visitors information centre. The **QPWS** also have an office on Billabong Boulevard, T4656 3272, and can provide up to date information about the Birdsville Track and regional national parks.

Sleeping, eating and transport Stay in the standard a/c, en suite units on offer at the historic **A** *Birdsville Hotel*, 1 Adelaide St, T4656 3244, birdsvillehotel@bigpond.com.au The hotel has plenty of atmosphere and a good restaurant. Cheaper accommodation is available at the **B-E** *Birdsville Caravan Park*, Florence St, T4656 3214. *Macair*, T131313, fly to Birdsville from Brisbane and Mount Isa.

The Capricorn and Landsborough Highways

Colour map 4, grid B2
1204 km between
Rockhampton
and Cloncurry

From Rockhampton, the Capricorn Highway (Route 66) heads west, through the gem fields region and town of **Emerald**, before becoming the Landsborough Highway (section of the Matilda Highway) at **Barcaldine**. From Barcaldine the Landsborough Highway then continues west to **Longreach**, then north through **Winton** to Cloncurry, where it joins the Flinders Highway to Mount Isa. The Matilda Highway continues north from Cloncurry to terminate at Karumba on the Gulf of Carpentaria.

Carnarvon Gorge and the Gem fields
Colour map 4, grid C3

The **Carnarvon Gorge National Park** and the **Gem fields** of the Capricorn Region are easily accessible from Rockhampton and both provide an excellent diversion from the coastal route north, or outback route to Mount Isa and the Northern Territory. There are plenty of opportunities for walking, camping and gem fossicking, with the latter occasionally proving more lucrative than you might expect. Occasionally, sapphires and other gems worth many thousands of dollars are unearthed. *Gemfield Explorer*, T49275977, based in Rockhampton offer an all inclusive three-day/two-night trips (departing Mondays) taking in a mine tour and professionally guided fossicking from $266 or $240 per person for two. The VIC in Rockhampton, Emerald (T4982 4142), or Anaki (T4985 4525) can all assist with local accommodation and other specialist gem fossicking tours information. The **QPWS** in Rockhampton, T49360511, or Carnarvon, T4984 4505, can assist with all national parks walks and camping information.

The gracious outback town of Barcaldine, dubbed the 'Garden City of the West', is most famous not for its well tuned lawn mowers but its savvy sheep shearers, who laid down their blades during the 105-day **Great Shearer's Strike** of 1891. Their defiant action resulted in the formation of the Australian Labor Party, something the town is clearly very proud of. The main tourist attractions in the town all revolve around the shearers and general tributes to the working classes of Australia, including the **Tree of Knowledge**, a ghost gum (now monument) beside the railway station on Oak Street and the excellent **Australian Workers Heritage Centre** on Ash Street. ■ *Mon-Sat 0900-1700, Sun 1000-1700. $10, child $5.50. T4651 2422.* The Barcaldine Visitors Information Centre is on Oak Street, T4651 1742, tourinfo@tpg.com.au Open daily 0830-1630.

Barcaldine
Colour map 4, grid B2
Population: 1,600
577 km west of
Rockhampton,
627 km southeast
of Cloncurry

Sleeping and eating There are several standard motels in the town including the **A** *Ironbark Inn Motel*, Landsborough Highway, T4651 2311, offering units and suites, a restaurant and pool. The basic **B-E** *Homestead Caravan Park*, Blackall Rd, T4651 1308, offers standard cabins, powered and non-powered sites.

Transport Bus The city is served by *McCafferty's/Greyhound* daily. **Train** 'The Spirit of the Outback' (*Queensland Rail*, T132232) operates twice weekly services from Brisbane to Longreach (westbound from Brisbane Tue/Fri, eastbound from Longreach Thu/Sun).

Set in the very heart of Queensland's vast outback, the prosperous (and perhaps aptly named) town of Longreach, has, since its creation in 1847, provided the epitome of life in the Australian outback. It is here that the images of rugged sheep and cattle farmers have been perpetuated and are now beautifully celebrated, and where the difficulties of travel and communications over vast distances were in part alleviated with the founding of the nation's most famous airline, *Qantas*, in 1921.

Longreach
Colour map 4, grid B1
Population: 4,500
667 km west of
Rockhampton,
520 km southeast
of Cloncurry

Longreach hosts two of the outback's best known and most remarkable tourist attractions. One of these is the impressive **Australian Stockman's Hall of Fame and Outback Heritage Centre**, opened in 1988 and as much a monument as a museum, paying tribute to the settlers and pioneers of the Australian outback. A fine marriage of architecture, artefacts and state of the art displays explore almost every aspect of outback life from its Aboriginal beginnings over 40,000 years ago to modern times, and incorporate a wealth of topics from sheep shearing and natural disasters to bush sports and satellite communications. It is well worth a visit even if you are contemplating an inevitably long journey to see it. ■ *Open daily 0900-1700, $19, child $9, T4658 2166, www.outbackheritage.com.au East of the town centre on the Landsborough Highway.* The other is the **Qantas Founders Outback Museum**, established in 1988 to honour the formation of one of the world's best-loved airlines. At the moment the museum is a relatively small affair sited in the original *Qantas* hangar at Longreach Airport (3 km east of the town centre), but plans are afoot for a major $10 million revamp, with the main feature being the yet to be located, original Avro 504K that made the first commercial flight in 1921. ■ *Open daily 0900-1700. $15, child $8. T4658 3737, www.qfm.org.au* Both *Outback Aussie Tours*, T4658 3000, info@outbackaussietours.com.au, and *Longreach Outback Travel Centre*, 115A Eagle Street, T4658 1776, offer a whole host of local tours daily, from the Stockman's Hall of Fame to river cruises. From three to 11 hours and $25 -$95. Extended multi-day tours of the region are also available, from $470. The Longreach Visitors

Queensland

▶▶ **So who was the 'Jolly Swagman'**

*The famous song 'Waltzing Matilda',
written by Banjo Patterson in 1895, is said
to be an allegory based on the Great
Shearer's Strike of 1894. It specifically
highlights the death of a shearer named
Hoffmeister, one of 16 striking shearers,*

*who apparently committed suicide by
jumping in a billabong, after an armed
battle between his crew station owners
and police on the Dagworth Station near
Winton in 1894. Clearly, at the time he was
not particularly 'jolly'.*

Information Centre (a replica of the original Qantas Booking Office) is located on Eagle Street, opposite the post office, T4658 3555. ■ *Mon-Fri 0900-1700, Sat/Sun 0900-1300.* **Internet** is available at *Outback Queensland Internet*, 25 Swan Street, T4658 3937.

Sleeping and eating The **A** *Albert Park Motor Inn*, just west of the Stoc kman's Hall of Fame, Sir Hudson Fysh Dr, T4658 2411, is one of the best motels around town offering tidy single and double en suites, spa, pool and a licensed restaurant. The **B-E** *Gunnadoo Caravan Park*, Thrush Rd, T4658 1781, is the best facilitated motor park in town offering standard cabins, powered and non-powered sites, restaurant, pool and kiosk. Cheap counter meals are available daily at the *Longreach RSL Club*, 34 Duck St, T4658 1092, or the *Starlight Tavern* Eagle St, T4658 1925.

Transport   Air Longreach is served daily by *QantasLink*, T131313. **Bus** The town is served by *McCafferty's/Greyhound*, T131499, daily from Brisbane, Mount Isa and Rockhampton. **Train** *'The Spirit of the Outback'* (*Queensland Rail*, T132232) operates twice weekly services from Brisbane to Longreach (westbound from Brisbane Tue/Fri, eastbound from Longreach Thu/Sun). The *Longreach Outback Travel Centre*, 115A Eagle St, T4658 1776, act as air, coach and rail booking agents.

Winton
Colour map 4, grid B1
Population: 1,200
864 km west of
Rockhampton, 341 km
southeast of Cloncurry

Australia's most famous song and unofficial national anthem, '*Waltzing Matilda*', was written by Banjo Patterson in Winton, in 1895. The **Waltzing Matilda Centre** completed in 1998 is a tribute to the song, the songwriter and the story and incorporates a sound and light show together with various interactive displays. It also houses the **Outback Regional Art Gallery**. ■ *Daily 0830-1700. $14, child $12.* T4657 1466, *Elderslie St*. The Winton **VIC** is also in the Waltzing Matilda Centre, T4657 1466, matilda@thehub.com.au (open daily 0830-1700). Nearby The **Royal Theatre** built in 1918 is one of only two open-air theatres still functional in Australia and comes complete with canvas seating and the original projection equipment. You may however find yourself doing more stargazing than film watching. ■ *Open Wed nights, Apr-Nov. $6.50, child $4.50.* T4657 1296, **Arno's Wall** on Vindex Street is also worth a look and can only be described as a 'less than ideal Ideal Homes exhibition' set in concrete, complete with a kitchen sink and motorbike.

Sleeping and eating The historic. **C** *North Gregory Hotel*, 67 Elderslie St, T4657 1375, offers good traditional hotel-pub accommodation with single and double en suites (some with a bath) and a restaurant. The **B-E** *Matilda Country Tourist Park*, 43 Chirnside St, T4657 1607, is the best facilitated in town and offers standard cabins, powered and non-powered sites, pool and kiosk, but no camp kitchen.

Transport Bus The town is served by *McCafferty's* T131499 daily from Brisbane, Mount Isa and Rockhampton. **Train** *'The Spirit of the Outback'* (*Queensland Rail*, T132232) operates twice weekly services from Brisbane to Longreach (westbound from Brisbane Tue/Fri, eastbound from Longreach Thu/Sun) with coach services to Winton.

The **Lark Quarry Environmental Park**, 111 km south of Winton, is famous for its **Dinosaur footprints** beautifully preserved in rock that was once a muddy lake bed millions of years ago. Three species of dinosaur made over one thousand tracks during what was clearly a chaotic stampede. The VIC can provide details and directions to the site. If you do not have time to stray so far from Winton, look out for a part replica of the site in the Queensland Museum in Brisbane. While in the vicinity it is also worth checking out the remnants of the **Opalton** opal fields (123 km) and the **Carisbrooke Station Wildlife Sanctuary**, (83 km) with its Aboriginal rock paintings. Again the VIC can provide directions and details. Fossicking is permitted in designated areas in Opalton. *Carisbrooke Tours*, T4657 3984, run tours to both Lark Quarry and Carisbrooke.

Around Winton
Colour map 4, grid B1

The Flinders Highway

The Flinders Highway (sometimes referred to as the Overlander's Highway) from Townsville to Mount Isa and beyond provides the most direct route from the Queensland coast to the Northern Territory. It is an interesting option and has the added attraction of Ravenswood and Charters Towers, two historic settlements that can be easily visited on a day trip from Townsville. If you are short of time they can both provide an authentic outback experience.

889 km from Townsville to Mount Isa

Located 34 km off the Flinders Highway on the way to Charters Towers is the former gold-mining town of Ravenswood. Gold was discovered here quite by chance in 1868 and by 1869 it was in full production, two years ahead of Charters Towers. There is little left of this once thriving, cosmopolitan community, but the overgrown slag heaps dotted with old machinery and crooked old chimneys offer an interesting, if bleak reminder of more prosperous times. The mines had evocative names such as the 'General Grant', 'The Deep', 'Eureka' and 'The Sunset', the latter alone produced over 6.6 tonnes of gold. Of the 48 hotels and pubs that once dominated the town, only two still remain – the *Imperial Hotel* and *Railway Hotel*. As if stuck in a time warp, they have changed little and still offer accommodation, meals and a welcome 'coldie' away from the blazing sun. The former 1837 **Courthouse** has been fully restored and now houses a local museum. ■ *Daily (except Tue) 1000-1500, $2.* The *Ravenswood Post Office*, T4770 2136, on Macrossan Street is open daily and is a good source of information, as well as supplies and fuel.

One of the areas most unusual natural landscape features is the **'White Blow'**, a large quartz outcrop located 2 km east via Deighton Street. Some 80 km south of Ravenswood is the **Burdekin Falls Dam**, which holds back an area of water larger than Sydney Harbour. It can provide an impressive sight during floods, floods the scale of which can scarcely be imagined when you look at the **flood marker** on the west side of the bridge across the **Burdekin River**, back on the Flinders Highway.

Ravenswood
Population: 100
122 km southwest of Townsville,
84 km southeast of Charters Towers

Queensland

Charters Towers

Colour map 4, grid A3
Population: 27,000
132 km west
Townsville, 770 km
east of Mount Isa

When a young aboriginal boy discovered gold in the hills of the newly christened Burdekin River Valley in 1871, little did he know that his find would lead, almost overnight, to the creation of Queensland's second largest city and a place once called 'The World'. It is now hard to imagine Charters Towers buzzing with the activity of over 30,000 hopeful souls. In its heyday Charters Towers (which was named after mining warden W.E.S.M Charters and the hills that surround it) produced over 6 mn oz ($25 mn) of the precious metal, and although it is now better known for its beef production than its mineral resources, it remains proud of its golden heritage and is a fascinating example of a quintessential outback town. Given the depth of its history, as well as its sheer friendliness, by far the best way to experience Charters Towers is to join a guided tour of the city (see below). The **Visitors Information Centre** is housed in the former band hall building between the former Stock Exchange and City Hall, 74 Mosman Street, T4752 0314, www.charterstowers.qld.gov.au Open daily 0900-1700.

Sights   Charters Towers is rightfully proud of its gold-mining heritage and with the help of the National Trust has made some sterling efforts in the restoration and conservation of its heritage buildings and mining relics. In the centre of the city, on Mosman Street, almost next door to the VIC, is the former 1888 **Stock Exchange Building**. Built originally as a shopping arcade it was converted in to a stock exchange in 1890 and then, after the decline of mining activities, fell in to disrepair. In 1970 it was restored back to its original purpose and now hosts a number of small businesses, a gallery, café and an assay room filled with mining memorabilia, including a fascinating working model of a stamping battery. ■ *Mon-Fri 0830-1300/1400-1630, Sat/Sun 0900-1500. $2.20, $1.* Next door is the magnificent 19th century **Australian Bank of Commerce** building. For many years after its original purpose it served as a private residence before being purchased by the local council in 1992 and restored and cleverly incorporated in to the $8 mn **World Theatre** Complex. Even without a performance it is well worth a look inside. ■ *Open Mon-Fri 1000-1330, Sat 1000-1200. Guided tours daily from $6.60, child $4.40, T4787 4337.* The **Zara Clark Museum**, just north of the VIC, houses an array of historical artefacts and collections donated by local residents. ■ *Daily 1000-1500, T4787 4161. $5, child $2.20.* The **Miners Cottage**, 26 Deane Street, is an 1890 original that now houses antiques, arts and crafts and jewellery. ■ *Open Wed-Fri 1000-1630. Free. Gold panning $5.50, child $3.30 T4787 4857.* Other heritage buildings and points of interest in the city include the 1892 Post Office and 1910 Police Station on Gill Street, 1882 Pfeiffer House on Paul Street and the interior of the 1886 Civic Club on Ryan Street, which was once the haunt of 'the world's male elite', T4787 1096. Nearby, don't miss the **Relic Shop** on Ryan Street, which although hardly historical is now a very quirky second-hand mart.

On the outskirts of the city (east via Gill Street and Millchester Road) are the remains of the **Venus Battery Mill**. This is perhaps the best of all the former mining relics because it remains almost untouched in its gradual decay. As you wander around its eight huge stampers and former cyanide ponds it certainly stirs the imagination, back to the days when it was in full production. ■ *Daily 0900-1500. Fairly half-hearted guided tours are available at 1000 and 1400. $5, child $2. T4787 2222.* Just south of the city on the Flinders Highway there are two modern day features worth seeing. The **Dalrymple Sale Yards,** which is regularly in action with countless head of beef cattle, and surrounding it the regular sight of the monstrous **'road trains'** – a true indication that you are now in outback country. Nearby, **Towers Hill** provides excellent views across the city and beyond, especially at sunrise or sunset. It is also home to numerous rock wallabies. Access is south end of Mosman Street, off Black Jack Road. Gates close after sunset.

The **A-B** *Heritage Lodge Motel*, 79-97 Flinders Highway, T4787 4088, www.heritagelodge.com.au, is the most upmarket place in town offering modern self-contained units in a park setting. Alternatively, the **A** *Cattleman's Rest Motel*, corner Bridge St and Plant St, T4787 3555, comes recommended by transitory 'truckies' and business people, and is a good place to get away from tourist hype. Some units have baths and there is a good in-house restaurant. The **A-D** *York St B&B*, 58 York St, T4787 1028, yorkstreetbb@httech.com.au, is an old, spacious Queenslander with welcoming hosts, offering doubles, singles and backpacker units and a pool. Recommended. The 3-star **C-F** *Mexican Tourist Park*, corner of Church St and Tower St, T4787 1161, is the closest motor park to town and offers self-contained, a/c cabins, standard a/c cabins, powered and non-powered sites.

For eating, *Lawson's Bar and Restaurant* in the World Theatre Complex, T4787 4333, open Wed-Sun 1130-1430 and from 1800, is recommended along with the value *Gold City Chinese*, 118 Gill St, T4787 2414, open daily (except Mon) from 1130. For a coffee and light snacks in historical surroundings, try the *Stock Exchange Café*, 76 Mosman St, T4787 7954. Open Mon-Thu 0830-1700, Fri/Sat 0830-2100, Sun 0830-1600.

Sleeping & eating
In its heyday there used to be almost 100 hotels in Charters Towers, but now although traditional hotel beds are still offered most visitors stick to the motels, guesthouses or caravan parks

Charters Towers hosts 2 notable annual events, the *Charters Towers Country Music Festival* every **May Day** weekend (T4787 4500), where you can go line-dancing Matilda and the *Outback Ashes Cricket Carnival* every **Australia Day Weekend**, when more than 100 teams bat it out for glory.

Events

Long term local *Geoff Philips* provides an excellent insight in to Charters Towers old and new through **Gold City Bush Safari Tours**, T4787 2118, from $16. Recommended. Multi-day trips and adventures in remote outback areas are also a speciality. The currently active **Mount Leyshon Mine** south of the city also offer guided tours every week morning. Book through the VIC.

Tours

Bus The city is served by *McCafferty's/Greyhound* T131499, daily on the Townsville/ Mount Isa run. Likewise, by **rail**, *'The Inlander'* operates twice weekly services from Townsville to Mount Isa (westbound Sun/Wed, eastbound Mon/Fri). The train station is on the corner of Gill St and Enterprise Rd, T132232, www.traveltrain.qr.com.au *Traveland*, 13 Gill St, T4787 2622, act as bus and rail booking agents.

Transport

Banks Most branches have ATMs and are situated on Mosman St or Gill St. **Medical services** Hospital,145 Gill St, T4787 1099. **Communications** Internet VIC, or the painfully slow. **Post Office** Gill St, T4787 1047. Open Mon-Fri 0900-1700. Postcode 4820. *Charters Towers Computers*, 59 Gill St. Open Mon-Fri 0900-1700. **Police** 49 Gill St, T4787 1333. **RACQ** *Gold City Wreckers*, 21 Dundee La, T4787 2000.

Directory

Hughenden is famous for its **dinosaurs** but is also used as a base to explore the **Porcupine Gorge National Park** and is a good venue for **gem fossicking**. The Hughenden Visitors Information Centre combines with the **Dinosaur Display** ($2) on Gray Street, T4741 1021, fscinfo@tpg.com.au ■ *Daily 0900-1700*. The town's resident **Muttaburrasaurus** – or 'Mutt' as he is affectionately called – looks decidedly dense, yet strangely charming and is located

Hughenden
Colour map 4, grid A1
Population: 1,500
377 km west of Charters Towers,
512 km east of Mount Isa

Queensland

Queensland

▶▶ Station to station

Charters Towers is the stepping-stone to two popular outback stations that offer comfortable accommodation mixed with the quintessential outback experience. A-D Bluff Downs is a historic 40,000 ha working cattle station, set around the spectacular deep water lagoons of the Basalt River, 80 km north of the city. It offers a range of activities from mustering to fossil hunting and accommodation ranging from a/c backpackers quarters to homestead rooms and a self-contained cottage, T4770 4080, Bluff_Downs@hotmail.com The A-E Plain Creek Station, located to the south, half way between Charters Towers and Clermont (5 km off the Great Inland Way), T4983 5228, plaincrk@ cqhinet.net.au, and L-A Redlands Station Country Guesthouse, 50 km west off the Flinders Highway, T478 76617, offer similar outback experiences and farmstays. The Charters Towers VIC has full details. Book ahead.

near the hotel in Stansfield Street. 'Hughie' his best mate (who took dieting to alarmingly new levels) lives at the VIC. The dramatic landscapes of the **Porcupine Gorge National Park** are only 60 km north of the town (a mere 'just popping out for a pint of milk dear' in these parts) so is a good day trip. The 27 km long gorge sinks to depths of over 100 m in places and is home to a rich array of wildlife. As well as offering some good walks, the views are spectacular and you can take a dip in the various swimming holes. Access in to the gorge and basic **camping** is available at the **Pyramid Lookout**, T4741 1021. The VIC can provide directions and can advise on current road conditions (unsealed). *Adventure Wildlife and Bush Treks, T4741 1190, offer eight-hour to three-day tours to* the Porcupine National Park, White Mountains and Mount Emu.

Sleeping and eating B *Royal Hotel*, 21 Moran St, T4741 1138, royal100@ tpg.com.au, offers standard units (some en suite) and has a bistro, bar and pool. The **B-E** *Allan Terry Caravan Park*, Resolution St, T4741 1190, offers basic and Self-contained cabins, powered and non-powered sites, BBQs but no camp kitchen.

Richmond
Colour map 4, grid A1
Population: 750
489 km west of Townsville, 400 km east of Mount Isa

Richmond is roughly halfway between Townsville and Mount Isa so is often used for an overnight stay. A proud and tidy pastoral centre located on the banks of the state's longest river, the Flinders, its major attraction is dinosaurs, in particular an industrial sized crocodile called the **Kronosaurus**. The Richmond Visitors Information Centre combines with the **Richmond Fossil Centre** on the Flinders Highway, T4741 3429. ■ *Open daily 0830-1645.* The **Kronosaurus Korner Fossil Centre** in the VIC is considered one of the country's best and houses over 200 exhibits, some of which are very significant finds, including the 'Minmi' which is considered to be the nation's best preserved dinosaur skeleton, and the Richmond Pliosaur fossil, a strange marine reptile that roamed the continent 110 mn years ago when the outback was, remarkably, an inland sea. ■ *Open daily 0830-1645. $8, child $3. T4741 3429.* The local area is also good for gem fossicking. The VIC has details. *Past and Present Tours, T4741 3429,* offer three- and four-day fossil fossicking trips from $80. The. **E** *Richmond Caravan Park*, Flinders Highway, T4741 3772, has bunkhouse accommodation, powered and non-powered sites, BBQs and a pool opposite.

The copper mining town of Cloncurry (or 'The Curry' as it is known) was once the most prosperous town in north western Queensland. The VIC is located in the **Mary Kathleen Park**, Flinders Highway, T4742 1361. ■ *Mon-Fri 0800-1630, Sat/Sun 0900-1500*. The **Mary Kathleen Memorial Park** contains three buildings moved from the abandoned uranium-mining town of Mary Kathleen that once operated in the outback between Cloncurry and Mount Isa, from 1956 to 1983. As well as containing various items of historical significance (including Burke's water bottle) there is a colourful collection of ores, minerals and rocks. **The John Flynn Place** building on Daintree Street is a tribute to the founder of the Royal Flying Doctor Service and houses a small museum that celebrates the man and the concept as well as a cultural centre, outdoor theatre and the Fred McKay Art Gallery. ■ *Mon-Fri 0800-1630, Sat/Sun 0900-1500. T4742 4125*. Also worth checking out are the **sale yards** on Sir Hudson Fysh Drive, which are reputedly the largest in north west Queensland. If you are lucky there will be stock passing through and some of the monstrous road trains.

Cloncurry
Colour map 5, grid B5
Population: 2,500
119 km east of Mount Isa, 770 km west of Townsville

Sleeping and eating **B-E** *Gilbert Park Tourist Village*, McIlwraith St, T4742 1313, is well facilitated with tidy cabins, powered and non-powered sites, pool, spa and camp kitchen. **A** *Rosegreen Station*, 104 km north of Cloncurry, T4742 5995, rosegreen@bigpond.com.au, offers an outback station experience with activities including, fossil hunting, wildlife spotting, or alternatively the opportunity to just kick-back and do nothing at all.

They say 'You're not a real Aussie until you've been to the Isa', but exactly why is a bit of mystery. Without putting too fine a point on it, the places is a dump, and smelly to boot. Yet, given its position between the coast of Queensland, Darwin and Alice Springs, no one can deny its strategic importance. For many a 'truckie' and exhausted tourist the lights of Isa are like opals in a veritable ocean of emptiness and a welcoming oasis of cold drinks, a bed and communications with the outside world. The Isa owes its existence to mining and the extraction of silver, lead, copper and zinc-and not on a small scale. From its humble beginnings in the 1920s it now boasts one of the largest silver and lead mines in the world, which along with its geographical position has made it the largest and most significant town in northwest Queensland.

Mount Isa
Colour map 5, grid B5
Population: 22,000
889 km from Townsville, 634 km east of Tennant Creek

The Mount Isa **Visitors Information Centre** is located within the *Riversleigh Fossils Centre*, 19 Marian St (eastern approach to town), T4749 1555, www.riverslelgh.qld.gov.au Mon-Fri 0830 1630, Sat/Sun 0930-1430. The friendly staff can offer assistance with accommodation and mine tour bookings. For national parks and camping information contact the **QPWS**, T4743 2055. Internet is available at the Mount Isa Library, 23 West St, T4744 4267. Open Mon-Thu 1000-1800, Fri 1000-1700, Sat 0900-1200.

First stop is generally the **Riversleigh Fossil Centre** (VIC) which offers an excellent insight into the highly significant and ancient fossils found at the World Heritage listed **Riversleigh Fossil Fields** (250 km northwest of the Mount Isa). Well-presented dioramas recreate the form and habitat of some of the weird and wonderful creatures that used to inhabit the outback over 25 mn years ago, including the magnificent Tylacaleo. ■ *Mon-Fri 0830-1630, Sat/Sun 0930-1430. $9, child $5. T4749 1555. 19 Marion Street*. The **Frank Aston Underground Museum** covers far less ancient topics in

Queensland

▶▶ **Mount Isa tours**

Mount Isa's mine operations are pretty mind-bending. There are shafts stretching 1½ km below the surface and a staggering 975 km of openings. There are both surface and underground tours on offer. The four-hour underground tour costs from $60 (Monday-Friday 0730 and 1030) and can be booked at the VIC. Campbell's (see below) organize

*surface tours which vary according to the day's activities, from $18. They also offer town tours from $20, child $10, and trips further afield to Lawn Hill and the Fossil Fields (three day/ two night, safari from $495). **West Wing Aviation**, T4743 2144, offer half- or full-day scenic flights on their outback mail run.*

the form of mining, pioneer and Aboriginal displays. ■*Daily 0900-1600, $5, child $3, T4743 0610.* Mount Isa also plays host to the Flying Doctor and School of the Air services. Both offer an interesting insight in to the everyday management and attitudes to outback life. The **Flying Doctor Service** has a small visitors centre with a short video. ■ *Mon-Fri 0900-1700. $2.50. T4743 2800, 11 Barkly Highway.* The **School of the Air** offers tours daily during term time at 0900 and 1000. ■ *$2, T4744 9100. Abel Smith Par (next to Kalkadoon State High School).* Out of town the main attractions are the beautiful and remote **Lawn Hill National Park** (site of the Riversleigh Fossil Fields and **Lawn Hill Gorge**) and **Lake Moondarra**, a popular spot for boating and barramundi fishing, 15 km north of the city. The VIC has details. For an 'interesting' view of the whole town head for the **City Lookout** on Hilary Street (good at sunrise or sunset).

The VIC can assist with accommodation bookings

Sleeping and eating   L *Mercure Hotel*, on the corner of Camooweal St and Marion St, T4743 3024, is the most upmarket hotel with tidy units, restaurant and pool. There are plenty of standard **motels** including the mid-range. A-B *Copper Gate Motel*, 105 Butler St (1 km east of the town centre), T4743 3233, offering single, double and family units. The. B-E *Travellers Haven*, corner of Spence St and Pamela St, T4743 0313, is the main **backpackers** offering singles, dorms and doubles. The best-facilitated **motor park** in town is the B-E *Sunset Caravan Park*, 14 Sunset Dr (2 km north of the city centre), T4743 7668. It has standard cabins, on-site vans, powered and non-powered sites, pool and a camp kitchen. The local hotels and clubs are the best bet for value meals with the *Buffalo Buffs' Club* (corner of Grace and Simpson St, T4743 2365) and the *Irish Club* (Nineteenth Av, T4743 2577), being two of the most popular and entertaining.

Transport   Mount Isa Airport is about 6 km north west of the town off the Barkly Highway. **Taxis**, T131008, meet all inbound flights. *Macair Airlines*, T4729 4444, and *QantasLink*, T131313, both offer regular services from Brisbane and Townsville. The **train** station is at the western end of town at the end of Isa St. *Queensland Rail's 'Inlander'* service, T132232, www.traveltrain.qr.com.au, operates twice weekly services from Townsville to Mount Isa (westbound Sun/Wed, eastbound Mon/Fri). Long distance **coaches** stop outside Campbell's (see below). *McCafferty's/Greyhound*, T131499, stop daily on the Townsville/Mount Isa run. *Campbell's Tours and Travel Centre*, 27-29 Barkly Highway, T4743 2006, info@campbelllstravel.com.au, can assist with general travel bookings. For **4WD hire** T1800-077353, from $116 per day.

The Gulf Savannah

Often called the 'Outback By the Sea', the Gulf Savannah region of far north Queensland is a place of flat, forbidding emptiness, infinite horizons, vast swathes of grasslands and mile upon mile of coastline cut deep by few rivers. Most travellers will simply look at the map, with its lack of place names and infrastructure, and choose to leave the empty grids to the imagination, while others are only drawn by its mystery. To make a recommendation to investigate the Gulf Savannah, or not, and whether to choose an alternative route to the Northern Territory, would be unwise, since a trip to the real Australian outback is all about personal perceptions, expectations and personality. Having said that most of the Gulf's major sights (other than the actual Gulf itself) are located around its fringes and are quite easily accessed from Cairns or Mount Isa. These include: the remarkable **Undara Lava Tubes** and the **Undara Volcanic National Park**, south of Mount Surprise; the old mining town of **Chillagoe**; the **Cobbold Gorge** south of Forsayth and the **fossil fields** of the **Lawn Hill National Park**, north of Mount Isa. Barramundi **fishing** is also a popular activity. But whether you choose to explore the mighty Savannah thoroughly, or merely touch its fringes or its billabongs, one thing is for sure; there are no gimmicks. What you see is most definitely what you get.

Information & orientation

For up-to-date road conditions, T4031 1631

The route from Cairns to Darwin is often referred to as the **Savannah Way** and provides an alternative to the Flinders Highway between Townsville and Tennent's Creek. With a conventional vehicle the Savannah Way should only be considered in the Dry (Apr-Oct). At other times 4WD is recommended. From the east it begins in Ravenshoe in the Atherton Tablelands (Kennedy Highway) and then follows the Gulf Developmental Road, through Mount Surprise, Georgetown and Croydon, before reaching Normanton, just south of Kurumba on the Gulf of Carpentaria – a distance of 450 km, with all roads sealed. From Normanton it is then a 467 km (22 km sealed, 445 km unsealed) via Wernadinga, Burketown, Doomadgee and Hell's Gate to the QLD/NT border. Back east the small towns of Einsleigh and Forsayth are 2 of the main stops on the **Savannahlander** rail link, a popular and alternative mode of transport that many use to get a taste of the Gulf Savannah from Cairns. Another service, the **Gulflander**, shuttles between Croydon and Normanton. Information surrounding the Gulf is readily available from the main VIC in Cairns. Ask for a copy of the *'Gulf Savannah Travel Guide'*. 2 very useful websites are www.gulf-savannah.com.au and www.savannah-guides.com.au There are accredited information centres in **Georgetown** (St George St, T4062 1233, open Mon-Fri 0830-1630), **Croydon** (Samwell St, T4745 6147, open daily 0800-1700), **Normanton** (corner of Landsborough St and Haig St, T4745 1268, open Mon-Fri 0830-1700) and **Burketown** (Musgrave St, T4745 5111, open Mon-Fri 0830-1600). All can supply full, local accommodation listings and all the settlements above can provide basic supplies and amenities.

Transport & tours

Train The *Savannahlander*, T4036 9249, departs Cairns 0630 Wed arriving in Almaden at 1300; departs Almaden 0800 Thu arriving in Forsayth at 1745; departs Forsayth 0745 Fri arriving Mount Surprise at 1300; then departs Mount Surprise 0815 Sat arriving in Cairns at 1840. Savannalander Connections to Undara are available, T4062 3143. The *Gulflander*, T4745 1391, departs Normanton 0830 Wed, arriving in Croydon at 1230. It then departs Croydon 0830 Thu arriving back in Normanton at 1230. **Road transfers** are available between Georgetown and Forsayth (Mon/Thu) and Georgetown or Forsayth to Cobbald Gorge (Tue/Fri), T4062

Queensland

▶▶ **What's the story 'Morning Glory'**

The 'Morning Glory' is a bizarre weather phenomenon described as a 'spectacular propagating roll cloud' that frequents the southern margins of the Gulf of Carpentaria. Observed mainly at dawn between August and November they appear in the form of one or more rapidly advancing formations of rolling clouds that extend from horizon to horizon for up to 1000 km and at speeds of up to 60 km per hour. Rarely do the clouds build enough to create rain but they are always accompanied by short-lived, intensive wind squalls on the ground. To witness the phenomenon is often the highlight of any visit to the Gulf Savannah.

5386. *Coral Coaches* T4743 2006, offer a service between Mount Isa and Karumba via Cloncurry and Normanton, departing Mount Isa Tue/Fri and Karumba Mon/Thu. *Savannah Guides*, T4055 6504, www.savannah-guides.com.au offer a network of excellent guides that cover a whole host of destinations throughout the Gulf. *Undara Experience*, T4097 1411, www.undara.com.au offer excellent tour packages to the Undara Lava Tubes in conjunction with Snnah Gavauides.

Victoria

Victoria is the smallest and most populous mainland state and travelling around is almost akin to European travel, with towns and cities only short distances from each other. The state revolves around **Melbourne**, Australia's second largest city. Within an hour or two of the city you can swim with dolphins, or try local wines in the **Yarra Valley**. To the west are the popular coastal towns of the **Great Ocean Road**. Inland, is one of the state's best national parks, the magnificent **Grampians**, where craggy sandstone rock faces tower above swathes of forest. Towards the coast the foothills run down to the moist green fields of **Gippsland** and come to an end in the perfect sandy coves of **Wilson's Promontory** and the series of tranquil lakes, lagoons and inlets further east.Victoria is also the home territory of Australia's most famous folk hero, the bushranger, Ned Kelly, and the legendary gold diggers of the Eureka stockade, who did more than anyone else to personify the Aussie ideal of a 'fair go'.

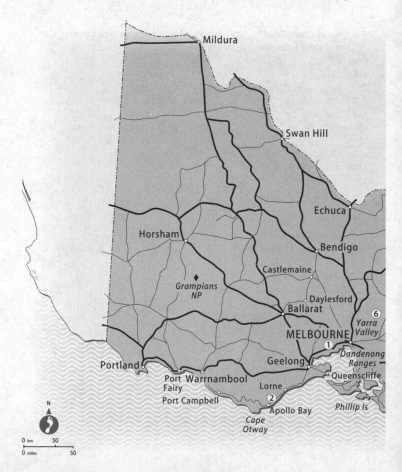

Things to do in Victoria

1 Take a stroll around the centre of **Melbourne**, allowing plenty of time to check out the excellent museum, then catch a tram to St Kilda for a sunset dinner.

2 Paddle silently in the early morning around **Lake Elizabeth** near Apollo Bay, looking out for its duckbilled residents.

3 Hike the **Mount Feathertop Loop Walk** from Harrietville or Mount Hotham, absorbing the glorious views from the Razorback Track.

4 Ride a horse up to the **Bluff**, near Mount Buller, and get a glimpse of the lives of the local cattlemen and their families.

5 Explore the broad bays, white sandy beaches and hills of **Wilsons Promontory**, keeping an eye out for wombats in the evenings.

6 Head up to **Healesville Sanctuary** and **Yarra Valley**, for a day's wildlife-spotting and wine tasting.

7 Spend some time in **Croajingalong National Park**, overnighting in lighthouse accommodation while you're there.

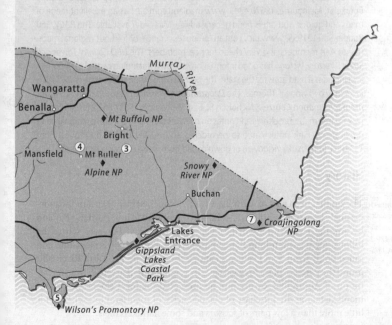

Ins and outs

Getting around
*The website
www.victrip.gov.au
is a quick method
of finding out
the easiest way of
getting from A to B*

Air As one of the smallest states, there is little demand for air travel within Victoria. *Kendell*, T131300, www.kendell.com.au, and *Qantas*, T131313, www.qantas.com.au, do however run services between Melbourne and Mildura.

Bus and train *V~Line*, T136196, www.vlinepassenger.com.au, run or act as agents for most of the internal state services. Their buses and trains leave for most Victorian country towns from Melbourne's Spencer Street Station. A variety of tickets are available, including standard economy, 1st class (about 40% more), and off-peak (about 40% less). Off-peak services to destinations within about 100 km of Melbourne leave before 1600 and after 1800, and all day at weekends. Outside this area, destinations are off-peak from Tue-Thu, and some also at weekends. Metropolitan bus and train services extend out approximately 40 km from the city centre. No backpacker buses have 'around the state services', but see regional sections for details of buses operating around the **Melbourne**, **Great Ocean Road**, **Grampians** and **Gippsland** regions. Victoria is setting up a state-wide network of cycling trails on disused railway lines. For more information contact *Rail Trail*, T5751 1283, www.railtrail.com.au Another helpful cycling organization is *Bicycle Victoria*, T9328 3000, www.bv.com.au

Information
*Tourism Victoria in
Adelaide: Lwr Grd Fl,
18-20 Grenfell St,
T08 8231 4362.
Sydney: 403 George St,
T02 9299 2288.*

Tourism Victoria, T132 842, produce an excellent series of colour brochures on each region of Victoria and will send 1 or 2 regional guides to you by post free of charge. Also see their detailed and useful website, www.visitvictoria.com The state government's main site, www.vic.gov.au, is even more comprehensive. *Parks Victoria*, T131963, www.parkweb.vic.gov.au, can give further information on national parks, and detailed notes and maps on individual parks can be downloaded from the site or ordered by phone and mailed (within Australia).

**Publications
& maps**

Information Victoria, 356 Collins St, Melbourne, T1300 366356, www.information.vic.gov.au, is a state government information service and shop selling reports, Victorian history titles and a huge range of topographic maps. *Map Land*, 372 Little Bourke St, Melbourne, T9670 4383, www.mapland.com.au, has an excellent range of maps and guides, and offers good general advice. Mail order available. The *RACV*, 360 Bourke St, T131955, www.racv.com.au, produces a range of fold-out regional maps, free to *AAA* members and very cheap for non-members. The *UBD Country Towns and Street Directory: Victoria* has good information on towns (including central Melbourne), and includes a road atlas for the state. The best walking guide to the state is *100 Walks in Victoria* by Tyrone T Thomas. The **Department of National Resources and Environment Information Centre**, 8 Nicholson St, East Melbourne, T9637 8325, is the place to pick up free maps, brochures and notes on national parks and purchase national parks publications. Park notes can also be ordered and mailed to you on request from T131963, info@parks.vic.gov.au or downloaded from www.parkweb.vic.gov.au

History

*"I never saw anything
equal to the land;
I never was so
astonished in my life."
John Batman, 1835*

The southeastern part of Australia was left untouched by Europeans for a surprisingly long time, until in 1834, Edward Henty sailed into Portland Bay and became the first pastoralist in the region. The real 'party', however, started the following year, when John Batman formed the Port Phillip Association and sailed boldy from Van Diemen's Land, a short way up the Yarra River, and found the perfect "place for a village". In a significant, if greed-driven, recognition of Aboriginal 'ownership' he presented the local elders with documents detailing the purchase of 600,000 acres of their land in exchange for little more than a few pairs of scissors and some handkerchiefs.

After robbin' the natives, Batman returned to Launceston to report to his associates, but in the meantime fellow Van Diemonian, John Pascoe Fawkner, sailed up the river and pitched up next door. The future site of Melbourne had been decided. Word spread quickly and within months newcomers were flooding into the bay, happily ignoring the government edict that this was trespass on their crown territory and all would be evicted. Within a year, however, Sydney had given up on that tactic and despatched a Superintendent to watch over the fledgling settlement.

The Aborigines, inevitably, suffered and full-scale massacres were taking place within a few years, alienating tribes that had already suffered terribly from the unwitting introduction by the Europeans of smallpox. Even worse was one of the fastest transformations from bush to agricultural land the world has ever seen. The Aborigines' traditional modes of living were simply cut from under them in as little as 15 years.

Almost from the day John Batman stepped ashore there were murmurs that the Port Phillip District shouldn't be part of New South Wales at all, but a new autonomous colony. Within five years the settlement had turned a considerable profit for the Sydney government, mostly from land sales, and this simply fuelled resentment. London was heavily petitioned and New South Wales had to give up its hold on the territory. Victorians celebrated their new colony, and name, on the 1 July 1851.

The recent discovery of gold in New South Wales, however, had the civic leaders worried. People were leaving in their hundreds for the goldfields and a serious economic collapse threatened. But they needn't have worried. After a few small-scale finds Bob and Jack Cavenagh walked into Geelong in mid-September with 60 lbs of gold. The tide turned and gold-diggers poured into Victoria, amongst them, to the considerable consternation of the ruling class, a good many ex-cons. Melbourne had suddenly become a boom town.

Part of the essential psyche of the modern Australian was born in the early Victorian goldfields. From the first the 'diggers' were classless, with aristocratic second-sons swinging picks alongside the poor that Britain had succeeding in evicting. Conditions could be grim, but at least they were their own masters. Then came Eureka, which became became a celebrated event (see page 497). The concept of a 'fair go' had been born as well as a flag, but it was selectively applied. The large number of Chinese immigrants were officially discriminated against, and often vilified, the poor began to be despised once more, as Ned Kelly was soon to find, and the Aborigines continued to suffer. Another new concept also crept into some minds, that of a 'White Australia'.

For many, however, the period from 1851-1890 was a boom time, the new colony boasting at various times the largest Australian population, greatest city, most sheep, and most grain. Though returns dwindled, the gold fuelled many of these explosive increases as well impressive civic works, free education, and new progressive, democratic legislation.

But it couldn't last, and by 1891 the banks had collapsed and economic depression settled in for a long haul. Over the next 20 years the colony had a net emigration figure of over 160,000. Recovery began with the new century and the march of Victorian industrialisation, and prosperity has largely continued apace. Between 1947 and 1954 the state's population rose 19%, most of the newcomers coming from Britain or southern Europe. With the formal abandonment of White Australia policy large numbers of Asian immigrants joined the throng in the 1970s, mostly settling in the metropolitan areas.

Melbourne

Colour map 2, grid C3
Population: 3,200,000
730 km from Adelaide,
875 km from Sydney,
830 km from
Broken Hill
www.melbourne.
vic.gov.au

Melbourne has always been 'marvellous', right from its earliest days when it was the largest, wealthiest and most refined city in the country. This former wealth, reflected in the ornate 19th century architecture and spacious public gardens, has also bred an innate confidence and serious sophisitication that gets right up the noses of Sydneysiders. By the same token, Melbournians see their New South Wales cousins as insufferably brash and hedonistic. The Victorian capital is the most European of Australian cities. Its theatres, bookshops and galleries are thronged with urban sophisticates, and its famously damp, grey weather lends the city an inward-looking focus unlike that of any other state capital. Waves of southern European migrants in the 1950s and Asian migrants in the 1970s added immeasurable colour, richness and variety to what was a conservative, anglophile society and the city now delights in its ethnic differences.

Ins and outs

Getting there
*For more details,
see Transport
on page 424*

Air Melbourne's Tullamarine airport is 20 km northwest of the city and services both domestic and international flights. Current flight information is available at www.melair.com.au or by ringing the relevant airline. Terminal facilities include car hire, bank ATMs, currency exchange and a Travellers Information Desk, T9297 1805, which provides accommodation and tour bookings as well as general information. The desk is located on the ground floor of the International terminal and stays open almost 24 hrs to service every incoming flight. **Public transport** is limited to the 478/479 services run by *Tullamarine Bus Lines*, T9338 6466, www.tullamarinebus.com.au Buses leave from the International terminal for **Moonee Ponds** approximately hourly from 0630-1915 Mon-Fri, 0845-1700 Sat, 0955-1800 Sun (20-30 mins, $4.40, concession $2.25). From **Moonee Ponds** you'll need to catch the 59 tram to Elizabeth St in the city centre (30 mins, $2.60, concessions $1.45). **Express buses** The *Skybus*, T9335 3066, runs every 30 mins, 0600-2400 (hourly 2400-0600) between the International terminal and the Spencer St Coach Station ($12) in the city centre, also stopping near the *YHAs* in Abbotsford St, North Melbourne and Courtney St, Carlton. Tickets can be purchased on board or from the information desk. A little more expensive, the *Southern Suburbs Airport Bus*, T9783 1199, has daily services every 1-2 hrs between the airport, **St Kilda** and several stops down the Mornington Peninsula as far as **Rosebud**. Bookings required. A taxi between the airport and the city will cost $35-40.

Bus The *Transit Centre*, Franklin St, is the terminal and ticket office for interstate operators *Travel Coach* (*Greyhound* and *McCafferty* as was), T132030. The **Spencer St Coach Station** is the terminus for all *V~Line* services, T136196, and the *Firefly Express Coaches* service, T9670 7500 from **Adelaide** and **Sydney**.

Train Flinders St Station is the main terminus for metropolitan *Connex* and *M-Train* services, but is also the station for *V~Line* Gippsland services. **Spencer St Station** is the main terminus for all other state *V~Line* services. All interstate trains, the *Overland*, *Ghan* and *XPT* also operate from Spencer St.

Getting around
*See also Tours,
Transport and
Directory sections
for hire information*

All metropolitan services are operated by the *Met* and if intending to use public transport it's a good idea to head for the *Met Shop*, 103 Elizabeth St. Open 0830-1655 Mon-Fri, 0900-1300 Sat. The shop has useful maps of tram, bus and train routes and timetables. For all train, bus and tram information T131638 or www.victrip.com.au A single *Metcard* fare system covers trains, trams and buses. 3 zones cover greater Melbourne, but you will rarely need anything other than a Zone 1 ticket as this covers everything within about 10 km of the city centre. A standard 'Short Trip' ticket is valid for a single journey ($1.70,

Victoria

concession $0.90). An alternative is the 2-hr ticket ($2.60, concessions $1.45). Daily ($5, concessions $2.60) and weekly ($21.70, concessions $10.80) tickets are also available. Daily cards are great value and ideal for sightseeing as they allow you to hop on and off trams, buses and trains all day within the zone purchased for not much more than the price of one return journey. Daily and weekly cards can be purchased in advance from newsagents displaying a *Metcard* logo. Also consider a 'Short Trip 10' if you'll only be using the trams to travel in and out (10 single trips for $14.20, concessions $7.15). Most services operate every day, from early morning to around midnight.

Bicycle There are plenty of hire outlets but if you want to buy check the classifieds in Sat newspapers or try *Cash is Yours*, 61 Fitzroy St, St Kilda, a pawn shop with good selection of second-hand bikes from $20-400.

Bus There is a bus for almost anywhere you could wish to go within Greater Melbourne, but the further out they travel the less frequently they go. Short Trip, 2-hr and daily tickets can be bought on board and notes are accepted.

Car Driving is not easy for visitors although distances are short and if you know your way around you can travel much more quickly than on public transport. The other main problems are the infamous 'hook turns'. These require you to get into the left-hand lane in order to execute a right hand turn, and wait for the amber light before turning. This only applies at some main intersections in the city centre and signs will indicate when the rule applies. The city has two central **CityLink road tollways** which electronically read 'e-tags' in vehicles: great for residents, a real pain for visitors. passes can be purchased, in advance or until midnight the day after you travel (the fine for travelling without a pass is about $100), from post offices and the *CityLink Customer Centre*, 67 Lorimer St, just off the Westgate Freeway. With a credit card passes can be bought (single use up to $2, 24 hr or weekend $8.50) over the phone, 0800-2000, T132629. To avoid the tolls when entering the city from the Westgate Freeway (Geelong, Highway 1) take the Kings Way exit for Richmond, Prahan and St Kilda, and the Power St exit for the city, Carlton and Fitzroy. From the South Eastern Freeway (the east, Highway 1) take the Toorak Rd exit and turn left for the city centre and suburbs. From the Calder/Tullamarine Freeways (the north west and the airport) take the first exit after the junction of the two freeways. This drops onto Bulla Rd which eventually becomes Elizabeth St in the city centre.

Train Used mostly to service to the outer suburbs. Various networks extend regular services to destinations including **Belgrave** (the **Dandenongs**), **Frankston** (connections to the **Mornington Peninsula**), **Lilydale** (connections to the **Yarra Valley** and beyond), **Stony Point** (ferry connections to **French** and **Phillip Islands**), **Werribee** and **Williamstown**. Tickets must be bought at departure stations.

Tram The trams are the main way to get about within the city centre and inner suburbs. They operate more like a bus than a train so you'll need to hail one if you want to get on and push the buzzer to indicate to the driver that you want to get off. The network of trams mostly radiate out from the city centre to the inner suburbs (see city maps) but some routes travel from suburb to suburb through the centre. Short Trip and 2-hr tickets can be bought on board, but the dispensers take coins only. Daily tickets must be purchased in advance from a newsagent displaying the *Metcard* logo.

Most of the major sights can be reached on foot and using the free City Circle tram, which travels along Flinders St, up Springs St, along La Trobe St and down Spencer St

The Melbourne Visitors Centre is in the northwest of Federation Sq (corner of Flinders St and St Kilda Rd) and offers information, brochures and bookings for Melbourne and the rest of the state. Also event ticketing, multi-lingual information and an ATM. Open daily 0900-1800. T9658 9658, tourism@melbourne.vic.gov.au The VIC runs one of the world's few **Greeter Services**, where local volunteers take visitors on a free sightseeing walk of the city centre. Greeters and visitors are matched by interests and language (over 30 languages spoken). Three days notice is required. Daily as arranged. T9658 9658, F9650 6168, greeter@melbourne.vic.gov.au There are also information booths in the Bourke St Mall and Flinders St Station.

Information
To be sent brochures in advance, write to: PO Box 2219T, VIC 3001. See also www.melbourne. vic.gov.au and www.thats melbourne.com.au

Victoria

The Travellers Aid Society has an office in Centre Point Mall, corner of Bourke St and Swanston St. They offer general advice as well as providing a rest area, lockers, showers, toilets and a cheap café. Mon-Fri 0900-1630, Sat-Sun 1100-1600. T9654 7690. They also run a **Disability Access Service**, www.vicnet.net.au/~tadas, offering advice and help, wheelchair repair and hire facilties in addition to the services mentioned before. The Travellers Aid Society also has a smaller centre with lockers and showers on the lower ground floor of Spencer St Station. Mon-Fri 0730-1930, Sat-Sun 0730-1130. Melbourne has a useful telephone interpreting service, offering assistance in communication in over 100 languages, T131 450 (24 hrs). The **Gay and Lesbian Switchboard**, T9510 5488, offers free information and advice. The radio station, Joy FM (90.7) is also a good source of information for the gay community.

Free **newspapers**, mostly catering for the clubbing and music scenes, come and go but currently include *Beat* and *Inpress*. *Bnews* and *MCV* cover the gay and lesbian scene. All are widely available in cafés and music shops. There are general listings and entertainment guides in the Thu *Herald Sun* and Fri *Age* newspapers. For more detail visit the VIC to pick up a free copy of the *Official Visitor's Guide*, a useful rundown of highlights, and *Melbourne Events*, an excellent monthly publication that has details of every event and attraction in the city and a useful map of the city centre.

History

It was decided, in 1837, that Port Phillip District's premier town would be called Williamstown, after the King, and the secondary town would be named for the British Prime Minister. As the 'inferior' settlement there was also debate about even this name, and sadly one of the rejected alternatives was the glorious Batmania. Within just two years the settlement could boast banks, a post office, dozens of pubs, a cricket club, a gentleman's club and some 28,000 residents, but its fortunes were really transformed by the goldrushes of the 1850s. The explosions in population and money fuelled almost unbelievably fast growth. By 1861 the town had founded a university, built splendid municipal buildings including a public library and Museum of Art, and installed street lighting, clean water and gas supplies. Melbournians were also already playing their own particular style of football, codified in 1866, and in 1862 hosted the first international cricket match against England.

In the 1860s and 1870s the gold was harder won and the state government introduced protectionist policies to encourage local industry and diversify the job market. The success of the new state and its fledgling city meant it became a favourite of British emigrants and speculators alike. Between 1880 and 1890 Melbourne's population jumped from 290,000 to around 440,000. But the bubble burst suddenly and the spirit of 'Marvellous Melbourne' evaporated at the turn of the decade. Banks collapsed like cards, building ground to a halt and unemployment soared. Nearly a quarter of all Melbournians were forced to leave the city between 1891 and 1900.

The resurgence of Melbourne had to wait until 1956. It was in this year that the city hosted the Olympic games, the task that finally caused it to emerge from over half a century of relative inactivity. The next couple of decades were ones of consolidation rather than flair, while by contrast its northern rival was building its famous opera house. In the 1980s Melbourne realised it was rich once more, both in finances and its diverse multicultural bedrock. The vibrant culture of today began to take shape and the city experienced ambition not seen for a century. As well as attaining the title of Australia's cultural capital, aggressive state governments set out to cement its reputation as the country's sporting centre, despite Sydney landing the 2000 Olympics.

24 hours in the city

The best way to get the feel for this sociable city in a short time is to try to catch a festival, sporting match or arts performance. If that's not possible the following suggested itinerary will give a taste of the city, its villages and progressive spirit. Head to Smith Street in Collingwood for breakfast at **Gluttony It's a Sin**, then walk down Victoria Parade to Carlton Gardens and visit the **Melbourne Museum**. Catch the City Circle tram from the bottom of the Gardens to the corner of Swanston Street and La Trobe Street. Walk north up Swanston Street to the **RMIT**. Have a look at the startling architecture and then pop into **Caffeine** in the basement for a morning shot. Head south and do a spot of shopping in the malls and arcades of the CBD. Find some lunch in a shoebox at **Centre Lane**, then walk west down Collins Street to **Rialto Towers**. Travel skyward for the views from Australia's highest building, before heading south for **South Bank**. Promenade east along the river bank and cross the river at Princes Bridge to have a look at **Federation Square**. Hire a bike in Alexandra Gardens and cycle alongside the **Yarra River** or take a river cruise from Southgate if your legs are protesting. Return to Princes Bridge and catch a tram to **St Kilda Pier**. Have dinner overlooking Port Phillip Bay at **Stokehouse**. Finally, walk or tram it up to the top of Fitzroy Street for a nightcap at **gpb**.

City centre

Melbourne has some of the best museums, galleries, gardens and architecture in the country and recent developments will ensure that Melbourne continues to possess the most impressive spread of cultural and sporting facilities in Australia. The new Melbourne Museum, the development of Federation Square and the redevelopment of the National Gallery of Victoria are all visionary projects that highlight the importance of arts to this city.

See map, next page

Opened in October 2000, this vast and striking modern museum uses the most advanced display techniques to make the museum experience lively and interesting. The *Bunjilaka Aboriginal Centre* looks at the history of Aboriginal people since white invasion and the politics of displaying their possessions and artefacts. *Koori Voices*, a photo gallery of Victorian Aboriginal people, is particularly fascinating for its contemporary recording of individual life stories. The *Mind and Body Gallery* examines humans in exhaustive detail, perhaps more than is palatable for the squeamish. Other highlights include part of the *Neighbours* set in the *Australia Gallery*, and the *Children's Museum*, where the little darlings can can check out their weight and height in 'wombats'. The museum also has an excellent shop and lots of eating choices. ■ *Daily 1000-1800. $15, children $8, concessions $11. Carlton Gdns, T131102, www.melbourne.museum.vic.gov.au Take a tram to get there.*

Melbourne Museum
Walk right around the museum to really appreciate its architecture – pop in to the Kurnie café on Nicholson St on the way

In striking architectural contrast to the Melbourne Museum, this Victorian confection was built for the International Exhibition of 1880. At the time it was Australia's largest building and grand enough to be used for the opening of the first Federal Parliament. The Victorian parliament sat here for 26 years until it was able to move back into the Victorian Parliament House (see below). The building is still run as an exhibition centre, and the museum occasionally runs tours. ■ *Carlton Gdns, T131102 to enquire.*

Royal Exhibition Building

Old Melbourne Gaol The gaol was built in the 1850s when Victoria was in the grip of a gold rush. Like Tasmania's Port Arthur, the design was based on the Model Prison at Pentonville, a system of correction that was based on isolation and silence. The three levels of cells now contain stories and death masks of female prisoners, hangmen, and of some of the 135 people hanged here. Visitors can also see the scaffold on which bushranger. Ned Kelly was hanged in 1880, as well as his death mask and a set of Kelly Gang armour. The gaol comes alive on night tours when a tour guide acts as a prisoner from 1901 to explain the history of the gaol. ■ *Daily 0930-1630. $9.90, children $6.60, concessions $7.10. Night tours Wed, Fri, Sat-Sun. $19, children $11.50, 1½ hrs. Tour bookings essential. Russell St, T9663 7228, www.nattrust.com.au*

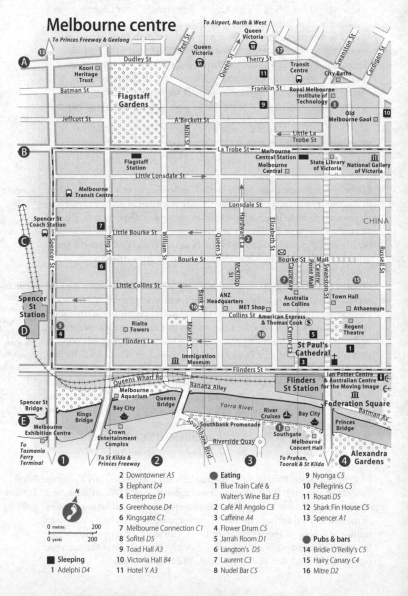

2 Downtowner *A5*	● Eating	9 Nyonga *C5*
3 Elephant *D4*	1 Blue Train Café &	10 Pellegrinis *C5*
4 Enterprize *D1*	Walter's Wine Bar *E3*	11 Rosati *D5*
5 Greenhouse *D4*	2 Café All Angolo *C3*	12 Shark Fin House *C5*
6 Kingsgate *C1*	3 Caffeine *A4*	13 Spencer *A1*
7 Melbourne Connection *C1*	4 Flower Drum *C5*	
8 Sofitel *D5*	5 Jarrah Room *D1*	● Pubs & bars
9 Toad Hall *A3*	6 Langton's *D5*	14 Bridie O'Reilly's *C5*
10 Victoria Hall *B4*	7 Laurent *C3*	15 Hairy Canary *C4*
11 Hotel Y *A3*	8 Nudel Bar *C5*	16 Mitre *D2*

■ Sleeping
1 Adelphi *D4*

Melbourne has traditionally been the wealthiest of Australian cities and this is reflected in the richness of the collection of the National Gallery of Victoria, especially the 19th century European art purchased during Melbourne's boom period. The **Ian Potter Centre: NGV Australia**, at Federation Square, will house the gallery's Australian collection from October 2002. The international collections will be displayed across the river in the revamped 1960s **NGV International**, next to the Victorian Arts Centre on St Kilda Road, due to open October 2003. ■ *Contact NGV, T9208 0222, www.ngv.vic.gov.au for charges and admission times.*

National Gallery of Victoria

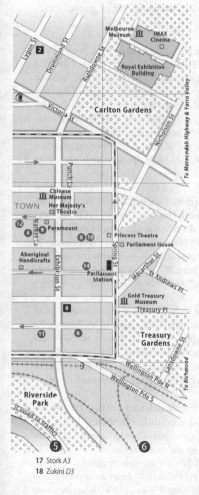

17 Stork *A3*
18 Zukini *D3*

━ City Circle Tram

Designed by Joseph Reed, who also designed the Town Hall and Exhibition Building, the doors behind the grand classical portico opened in 1856 with 3,800 books personally chosen by the philanthropist Sir Redmond Barry. In 1913 a domed reading room was added, modelled on London's British Museum Library and the Library of Congress in Washington. The library is undergoing extensive renovation and many parts of this beautiful building are closed. Redevelopment should be complete by 2004 and the library will exhibit some treasures of its collection, such as Ned Kelly's armour (see box on page 484). ■ *Mon-Thu 1000-2100, Fri-Sun 1000-1800. 328 Swanston St, corner of La Trobe St, T8664 7000, www.slv.vic.gov.au*

State Library of Victoria
The grassy forecourt is a popular meeting place and sculpture garden

In the heart of Chinatown, this museum aims to display the history and culture of Australians of Chinese descent since the mid-19th century. The Dragon Gallery houses Dai Loong, who parades annually at Chinese New Year. The gallery of Chinese Australian history examines traditional clothing, furniture and tools, then progresses to how the Chinese found prosperity and formed community ties in Australia. In the basement, an exhibition recreates the journey many Chinese took from Canton to the Victorian goldfields. The museum displays don't do justice to the fascinating history and culture of the Chinese and you'll get more out of the heritage

Chinese Museum
For those wishing to explore further we recommend a visit to the superb Chinese Museum in Bendigo or the Gum San Chinese Heritage Centre in Ararat

Victoria

walks the museum offers which include a guided tour of the museum and a walking tour of Chinatown. A Chinese banquet lunch can be added to complete the experience. ■ *Daily 1000-1630. $6.50, concessions $4.50. Tours run on demand, bookings required. $15, children $8, concessions $12, 2 hrs. Banquet lunch about $15. 22 Cohen Pl, off Little Bourke St, Chinatown, T9662 2888.*

Parliament House
When parliament is sitting visitors can watch from the Public Gallery

The extravagant colonnaded Parliament House stands at the head of a group of government buildings, churches and the serene manicured parkland of the Treasury and Fitzroy Gardens. It was built at the height of the gold rush in 1856 and this is reflected in its grandeur and interiors lavished with gold. Victoria's Parliament House was also the first home of the Australian Parliament after Federation in 1901. ■ *Tours Mon-Fri 1000, 1100, 1200, 1400, 1500, 1545 (40 mins, free). Spring St, T9651 8568. See www.parliament.vic.gov.au for sitting dates and times.*

Gold Treasury Museum

With its Renaissance-revival style, this is considered one of the finest public buildings in Australia. Built in 1858 with the optimism and profits of the gold rush, it provided offices for the governor, premier and treasurer and vaults to house the gold. By the time it was completed, however, the height of the rush was over so it has never held a great deal of gold. The museum has exhibitions on the growth of the city and life during the gold rush. The Nettleton Panorama is particularly interesting, a 360° photograph of Melbourne taken in 1862 from the top of Parliament House. ■ *Mon-Fri 0900-1700, Sat-Sun 1000-1600. $7.70, children $3.80, concessions $3.80. Spring St, opposite Collins St, T9651 2233, www.oldtreasurymuseum.org.au*

Fitzroy & Treasury Gardens

Some Melbournians consider these gardens the best in the city for their small scale, symmetry and avenues of European Elm trees. Nearby is Cook's Cottage, a tiny stone house that used to belong to Captain James Cook's family and was transported from England in 1934 to commemorate the centenary of the state of Victoria. After sunset many possums come out of the trees in Treasury Gardens and are often fed by visitors. ■ *Cook's Cottage $3.30, children $$1.65, concessions $2.20. Daily 0900-1700. T9414 4677.*

Federation Square
Sights and tourist office due to open from Oct 2002

Encompassing an entire city block next to the city, Federation Square is set to become another major arts and tourism venue in the heart of Melbourne. As well as the city's new tourist office, the square will be also home to the NGV gallery of Australian Art (see page 401) and the Australian Centre for the Moving Image, devoted to every aspect of film. The central plaza contains space for 10,000 people, and there are to be yet more restaurants, galleries and shops.

Koori Heritage Trust
Koori is the collective name given to the Aboriginal people of southeastern Australia

The trust preserves and celebrates the history and culture of the Koori people of Victoria from their own viewpoint. The centre has some hard-hitting history displays on the shocking results of the arrival of Europeans in 1835. There are also exhibitions of contemporary art and crafts by local Koori people, an extensive reference library and a small shop selling some original and reproduction art. ■ *Mon 1000-1430, Tue-Fri 0930-1630. Entry by donation. 234 Flinders La, though due to relocate to 435 King St in winter 2002 when they hope to open at weekends. T9639 6862, khtstaff@vicnet.net.au*

Immigration Museum

This former Customs House, designed in 1873 . It is an appropriate spot for an immigration museum because this part of the riverbank was known as Queens Wharf and was where the early immigrants stepped off their ships.

Melbourne's culture has been heavily influenced by immigration but this museum focuses on the how the experience affected the migrants. Personal stories are told using photographs, recordings and letters and there is even a mock ship to illustrate voyage conditions. Regular travelling exhibitions also explore the history and culture of migrants. ■ *Daily 1000-1700. $7.00, children $3.50, concessions $5.50. Corner of William St and Flinders St, T9927 2700, www.immigration.museum.vic.gov.au*

The Aquarium features the creatures of the Southern Ocean and offers the chance to get as close to those creatures as most people would wish to. By entering a glass tunnel, visitors step into the Oceanarium, a large circular room with thick perspex walls. Sharks, stingrays, turtles and fish swim around and above you, so close that you can count the rows of teeth in the mouth of a 3 m long shark. Several times a day divers get into the tank and feed the fish and visitors can do the same (the sharks are kept well fed so they don't eat their tank mates). The Aquarium also has a simulated rollercoaster ride, café and shop. ■ *Daily 0930-1800. $22, children $12, concessions $14. Tank dives – certified divers $126.50 (equipment supplied), non divers $192.50 (must complete a 2-day resort dive course). Bookings essential T9510 9081. Aquarium information T9620 0999, www.melbourneaquarium.com.au Yarra riverbank, opposite Crown Casino.*

Melbourne Aquarium

Melbourne's Southbank is the heart of the cultural and entertainment precinct. At the western end the vast, shiny **Crown Entertainment Complex**, more commonly known just as 'the casino', includes an enormous casino, hotel, cinema, over 35 restaurants, around 20 bars and nightclubs, and boutiques. To the west, beyond the Spencer Street bridge, is the **Melbourne Exhibition Centre**, and the *Polly Woodside*, an 1885 Belfast-built iron barque sitting in a rare wooden-walled dry dock and the star attraction of the **Melbourne Maritime Museum**. ■ *Daily 1000-1600. $9.90, children $6.60, concessions $7.70. T9699 9760, www.nattrust.com.au*

Southbank

At the eastern end of Southbank, by Princes Bridge, is the **Victorian Arts Centre** comprising of the circular Concert Hall and the Theatres Building crowned by a steel net and spire. The arts centre also has free galleries, a café, quality arts shop and it is possible to tour the complex. ■ *Mon-Fri 0700-late, Sat 0900-late, Sun 1000-last show. T9281 8000, www.vicartscentre.com.au* The city's best art and craft market is held here on Sundays. One of the most pleasant ways to see Southbank and the impressive border of the CBD is from the river. There are many operators offering **river cruises** in front of Southgate, the cruises depart regularly and generally last about an hour (costing about $15).

For some sports fans the MCG, as the ground is universally known, approaches the status of a temple. Built in 1853 the ground became the home of the Melbourne Cricket Club and has hosted countless historic cricket matches and Aussie Rules (Australian football) games as well as the 1956 Olympics, rock concerts and lectures. Tours of the MCG are one of Melbourne's most popular attractions and include walking into a players changing room, stepping on to the 'hallowed turf' and visiting the members' swanky Long Room. The tour also includes entry to the Australian Gallery of Sport, the Olympic Museum, the Australian Cricket Hall of Fame, and exhibitions on Aussie Rules and extreme sports. The interesting highlights include Don Bradman's cricket bat, Ian Thorpe's swimming costume, Cathy Freeman's running outfit, lots of Olympic medals and memorabilia, and the original handwritten rules, drafted in 1859, of the Aussie Rules game.

Melbourne Cricket Ground

In 2006 the MCG will house the Commonwealth Games and the ground is to be extensively renovated by then. Over $400 mn will be spent to demolish three stands, and build one new stand, new museum and entertainment facilities

Victoria

▶▶ **Getting high in Melbourne**

At 253 m, *Rialto Towers* is Australia's tallest building and the public have access to an observation deck 236 m up on the 55th floor, with as good a view as you would expect. There's also a small café up there. Sun-Thu 1000-2200, Fri-Sat 1000-2300. $10.50, children $6, concessions $8. Flinders Lane. There are also great views from the **LL-L Sofitel** hotel which takes up floors 35 to 50 of 25 Collins St, T9653 0000,

www.sofitelmelbourne.com.au *The rooms are suitably impressive, but there is also an excellent, if expensive, café and restaurant up on the 50th. If the budget doesn't allow for a sky-high meal then catch the lift up anyway for a brief glimpse, and make sure you pop to the toilet when you do. The bar at the* **Adelphi**, *187 Flinders Lane, at 10 storeys is not as high but is a subdued and sophisticated place with superb views of the southern city skyline.*

■ *Daily 0930-1630. $16, children and concessions $10. Tours run regularly from 1000-1500 on days without events, museums remain open on event days. T9657 8879, www.mcg.org.au Entrance from Jolimont St. Tram 70, Jolimont or Richmond train stations.*

Shrine of Remembrance
See Inner suburbs map, page 406

Close to Observatory Gate in the Kings Domain is the memorial to those Victorians who served or were killed during the First World War. The shrine was built in the early 1930s and provided welcome employment during the Great Depression. It is an imposing and sombre stone building with columned porticoes at each end, topped by a pyramid and surrounded by fine, narrow steps. It is a place of great dignity and solemnity. There are also good views of the city from the open balcony. ■ *Daily 1000-1700. Free. St Kilda Rd, T9654 8415, www.shrine.org.au Tram stop 19.*

Botanic Gardens

The gardens are a large oasis just to the south of the CBD. Bordered by very busy roads with the city's skyscrapers looming above it's not easy to forget that you are in a city, but the emerald lawns, ornamental lakes and wide curving paths provide a soothing respite from crowds and concrete. The main entrance is at Observatory Gate, where there's a visitor centre and the *Observatory Café* (open daily 0700-1700). There is also a quieter tea room, *The Terrace,* by the lake. Check at the Visitor Centre for daily events, there are often theatre and cinema shows outdoors in summer. There are several walking tours, including one looking at the highlights and history of these gardens. Another explores the heritage of the local Aboriginal people and examines the traditional uses for plants with an Aboriginal guide. ■ *Gardens daily 0730-1730 (Apr-Oct), 0730-2030 (Nov-Mar). Visitor Centre Mon-Sat 0900-1700, Sat-Sun 0930-1730. Free. Highlights tour Sun-Fri 1100, 1400. $4.50, concessions $3.50. Aboriginal Heritage tours Thu and Fri 1100 and alternate Suns at 1030 (bookings essential). T9252 2429. $15.40, children $6.60, concessions $11. Birdwood Av, South Yarra.*

The inner suburbs

See map on page 406

The city centre has traditionally been thought of by visitors as the area enclosed by the circle tram, but it is far better to think of Melbourne city as a collection of inner-city villages. Just to the north are Carlton, Fitzroy and Collingwood. Their proximity to the city meant that these were among the first areas to be developed as the city expanded rapidly during the gold rush.

Carlton has many fine terraces built in the 1860s but is best known for being an area where Italian immigrants settled. It's now a middle-class area where yuppies enjoy the Italian food and cafes of Lygon Street. Neighbouring **Fitzroy** also has some fine boom-time domestic architecture but had become a slum by the 1930s. Cheap rents attracted immigrants, students and artists and the area gradually gained a reputation for bohemianism. Brunswick Street is still lively and alternative although increasingly gentrified. The alternative set now claim Smith Street in **Collingwood**, just a few blocks to the east, as their own. Johnston Street, crossing Brunswick, is the centre of Melbourne's Spanish community. These areas are the liveliest of Melbourne villages and have some of the city's best cheap eating, edgy shopping, colourful street art and raw live music venues.

Just to the west of the CBD is a vast area known as **Docklands**, as big as the CBD itself. This was the city's major port until the 1960s when containers began to be used in world shipping and acres of holding sheds were no longer needed. The area is to undergo massive redevelopment over the next 15 years to turn it into a waterfront precinct for inner city apartments, offices, restaurants, shops and entertainment. The flagship of the development is the Telstra Dome, a major venue for Aussie Rules football matches and rugby league games.

Southeast of the centre, **East Melbourne** and **Richmond** hug the city's principal sporting venues, deliver a whole street of Vietnamese cuisine on Victoria Street, and offer the inner city's best range of factory outlet shopping on Bridge Road and Swan Street. Greeks populated the suburb before the Vietnamese and the community is still represented in the restaurants of Swan Street. South of the river, **Toorak** and **South Yarra** have long been the most exclusive residential suburbs, and this is mirrored in the quality of the shops and cafés at the northern end of Chapel Street. The southern end becomes funkier and less posh as it hits **Prahan**, where Greville Street is full of second-hand clothes shops, bookshops and cafés, and Commerical Street is the centre of the city's gay community. These suburbs are among the most fashionable and stylish, and unsurprisingly Chapel Street is a wonderful destination for clothes shopping. Down by the bay **St Kilda** has a charm all of its own. An early seaside resort that became seedy and run down, it's now a cosmopolitan and lively suburb but still has an edge. Only the well-heeled can afford to buy here now and some of them aren't too keen on living next to the junkies and prostitutes still seen on Grey Street. The picturesque foreshore makes this the most relaxed of the inner suburbs, and it's the best spot to spend a visit of a few days duration.

Yarra Bend Park

See Directory for bike hire

East of the Botanic Gardens the Yarra River winds in a loop up to Yarra Bend Park, about 4 km from the city centre. This is the largest and wildest of Melbourne's green spaces. Its an area of natural bushland including river cliffs, tree-lined river banks, wetland and woodland. The public heart of the park is the old wooden Studley Park Boathouse on the river. Here you can hire canoes and row boats or have lunch in the café. The Main Yarra Trail is a 30 km path running from Southbank to Templestowe and passes through the Yarra Bend Park. It is an excellent cycle trip from the city to the Studley Park Boathouse (15 km). At the northern tip of the park the trail passes the Fairfield Park Boathouse and Tea Gardens. ■ *Studley Park Boathouse, daily 0930-sunset, T9853 1972. Fairfield Park Boathouse, Sat-Sun 0830-1730 (daily Oct-Mar). Fairfield Park Dr, T9486 1501. Park office Yarra Bend Rd, Fairfield, T131963. Buses 201 and 203 from Flinders St Station stop on Studley Park Rd close to the boathouse.*

Victoria

Inner suburbs

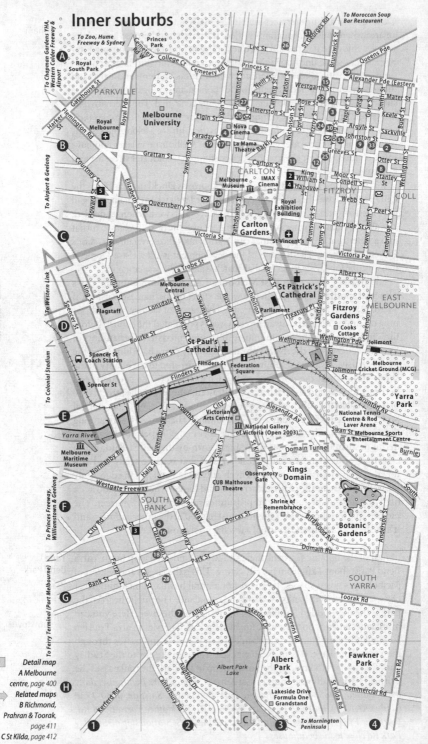

Victoria

To Zoo, Hume
Freeway & Sydney

To Chapman Gardens YHA,
Western Calder Freeway &
Airport

To Moroccan Soup
Bar Restaurant

Princes
Park

Royal
South Park

PARKVILLE

Melbourne
University

Royal
Melbourne

To Airport & Geelong

CARLTON

Melbourne
Museum

IMAX
Cinema

Nova
Cinema

La Mama
Theatre

FITZROY

COLL

Royal
Exhibition
Building

Carlton
Gardens

St Vincent's

To Western Link

La Trobe St

Melbourne
Central

Flagstaff

Spencer St
Coach Station

To Colonial Stadium

Spencer St

St Patrick's
Cathedral

Fitzroy
Gardens

EAST
MELBOURNE

Parliament

St Paul's
Cathedral

Federation
Square

Cooks
Cottage

Jolimont

Melbourne
Cricket Ground (MCG)

Yarra
Park

Victorian
Arts Centre

National Gallery
of Victoria (Open 2003)

Yarra River

Melbourne
Maritime
Museum

To Princes Freeway,
Williamstown & Geelong

To Ferry Terminal (Port Melbourne)

SOUTH
BANK

Westgate Freeway

CUB Malthouse
Theatre

Observatory
Gate

Shrine of
Remembrance

Kings
Domain

National Tennis
Centre & Rod
Laver Arena

Melbourne Sports
& Entertainment Centre

Domain Tunnel

Botanic
Gardens

SOUTH
YARRA

Fawkner
Park

Albert
Park

Albert Park
Lake

Lakeside Drive
Formula One
Grandstand

To Mornington
Peninsula

Detail map
A Melbourne
centre, page 400

Related maps
B Richmond,
Prahran & Toorak,
page 411
C St Kilda, page 412

Sleeping
1 City Scene *C1*
2 King *B3*
3 Market Inn *F1*
4 Nunnery *B3*
5 Queensberry Hill YHA *C1*

Eating
1 Ablas's *B3*
2 Aussie Indian Trendy Cuisine *B4*
3 Babka *B4*
4 Brunetti *B2*
5 Clarendon Fish & Chippers *F2*
6 EQ *E3*
7 Est Est Est *G2*
8 Gluttony It's a Sin *B4*
9 Guru da Dhaba *B4*
10 Jamaica House *C2*
11 Karnie's *B3*
12 Kazen *B3*
13 Lemongrass *C2*
14 Notturno *B2*
15 Retro *A4*
16 Sakura Teppanyaki *F2*
17 Shakahari *B2*
18 Spring *G2*
19 Threshermans Bakehouse *B2*
20 Toofeys *B3*
21 Vegie Bar *A4*
22 Viet Rose *A3*

Pubs & bars
23 Art House *C2*
24 Bar Open *B3*
25 Black Cat *B3*
26 Brandon *A3*
27 Clare Castle *B3*
28 Limerick Arms *G2*
29 Maori Chief *F2*
30 Night Cat *B4*
31 North Fitzroy Star *A3*
32 Purple Turtle *B4*
33 Tote *B4*

The rural area northeast of Melbourne is promoted as a **Valley of the Arts** for its past and present links with artists' communities. A path winds along the Yarra River from the city centre to Eltham (25 km) so hiring a bicycle is a good way to explore these leafy and tranquil areas beyond the city. An important stop along the way is the **Heide Museum of Modern Art**, the former home of art patrons John and Sunday Reed during the 1930s and 1940s. The Reeds nurtured modernism in Australia and formed close relationships with artists, particularly Sidney Nolan, painter of the famous Ned Kelly series. Artists Arthur Boyd, Joy Hester and Albert Tucker also spent much time here. The museum is set in beautiful bushland by the river and includes a sculpture garden with works by Anish Kapoor and Anthony Caro. The gallery has an exceptional collection of modern Australian art and hosts temporary exhibitions of contemporary art. ■ *$6.50, children $3.30, concessions $5.50. Tue-Fri 1000-1700, Sat-Sun 1200-1700. 7 Templestowe Rd, Bulleen (signposted from Eastern Freeway), T9850 1500, www.heide.com.au* To the northeast, in the suburb of Eltham, is **Montsalvat**, an artists' colony founded in 1934 and still home to a community of artists and craftspeople. The founder, architect and painter Justus Jörgenson, built a retreat in the style of a mediaeval French village among extensive gardens. Exhibitions are held in the Barn Gallery. ■ *$6.50, children $3.30, concessions $5.00. Daily 0900-1700. 7 Hillcrest Av, Eltham. T9439 7712.*

Now swallowed up as a Melbourne suburb, Williamstown's position across the Yarra River and out on Point Gellibrand, plus its long history as a port, give it far more of a coherent feel than most suburbs. This site was one of the first two settlements in Port Phillip Bay and was considered the most likely to survive

Bulleen & Eltham
For information on Heidelberg Artists Trail, contact Parks Victoria, T131963

Williamstown

Victoria

to become the capital. Much of the northeastern shore is home to several large commercial wharfs with a smaller marina and the public **Gem Pier** tucked in at their western end. Moored up alongside the pier is **HMAS Williamstown**, a 1942 navy corvette now mothballed as a maritime museum. Visitors have access to most parts of the ship and for the low entry fee it's well worth a visit. ■ *Sat-Sun 0900-1500. $5, children $3. T9397 2363.* Nelson Place faces the marina and pier and along with the main Ferguson Street, has the majority of the town's substantial number of cafés, ice cream parlours and restaurants. The southern side of the small peninsula is relatively undeveloped and the foreshore mostly consists of lawned reserves, with a few BBQ and picnic spots. Here too is **Williamstown Beach**, a 500-m-long stretch of golden sand with views down to Portt Cook and the Bellarine. The small **VIC** is by Gem Pier; open daily 0900-1700. *T9397 3791, www.williamstowninfo.com.au*

■ *Bayside Trains, part of the Melbourne metropolitan system, operate buses to Melbourne's City Circle railway stations (40 mins, $2.60, concessions $1.45). Departures daily every 20-30 mins from 0740 or earlier until around 2330. Sometimes a change is required at Newport. All of Williamstown's 3 stations are about a 15-20 min walk from the town centre. Bay City ferries, T9506 4144, depart Gem Pier for Melbourne (Southgate on Southbank) every ½ hr from 1030-1800 ($10, not 1100, 1500 or 1700 Mon-Sat). Also ferries to St Kilda on the hr 1100-1700 Sat-Sun ($6).*

Essentials

Sleeping
Also see Pubs and bars

Melbourne has a huge amount and range of accommodation. The city centre is first choice for most visitors, put off by the term 'suburbs', but those suburbs are as little as a 10 min walk away and they have easily as rich a café society and nightlife as the centre itself. They also offer better value and, in peak times, often more choice. Most of the accommodation is priced at a year-round rate, though some hostels will be cheaper in winter. Almost everyone will hike their prices up, some considerably, for the big 4 events, the *Melbourne Cup, Australian Open, Grand Prix* and the *AFL Grand Final*.

■ *on map, page 400*

City centre LL-L *Adelphi*, 187 Flinders La, T9650 7555, www.adelphi.com.au Small, modern, boutique hotel with a vibrant modern design you'll either love or hate. Best known for its glass-bottomed pool hanging 8 stories over the street, and its classy bar with a view. **LL-L** *Grand*, 33 Spencer St, T9611 4567, granderes@iaccess.com.au One corner of this ornate building is now a surprisingly contemporary luxury hotel. Parking plus breakfast around $30 extra. **LL-L** *Windsor*, 103 Spring St, T9633 6000, www.thewindsor.com.au Overlooking Parliament House, this is Melbourne's grandest hotel, an exclamation of wealth built in 1883. Total renovation saved the building in the 1980s and the result is impressive, particularly the ballroom.

A-C *Hotel Y*, 489 Elizabeth St, T9329 5188, hotely@ywca.net Very slick. Singles, doubles and some self-contained apartments.

There are several chain hotels along the bottom end of Spencer St, and tucked in amongst them is the **C** *Enterprize*, 44 Spencer St, T9629 6991, entrpriz@ozemail.com.au, a modest contemporary hotel with good value en suite doubles. **C-D** *Toad Hall*, 441 Elizabeth St, T9600 9010, www.toadhall-hotel.com.au 140-bed hotel with very comfortable doubles, some en suite. Backpacker dorms, some all-female en suite. Excellent communal facilities, parking $6. Not the cheapest hostel beds, and not really party-party, but worth every extra cent. Recommended.

D *Greenhouse*, 228 Flinders Ln, T1800 249207 or 9639 6400, greenhouse@friendlygroup.com.au **D-E** *Elephant*, 250 Flinders St, T9654 2616, Each with around 200 beds and a distinctly corporate feel, these backpacker hostels are not home-from-home, but both are modern, clean with good facilities and lots of organized events. Some doubles. Linen, pick-ups, internet included at *Greenhouse,* while the *Elephant* is cheaper, still with linen. **D-E** *Melbourne Connection*, 205 King St, T9642 4464, www.melbourneconnection.com.au One of the smaller city centre hostels with 80 beds, including 5 simple but pleasant doubles, stripped wood floors and comfortable communal facilities (though the kitchen could be bigger). Friendly and helpful owners give the place a good atmosphere. Recommended.

Carlton and Fitzroy L-A *Downtowner*, 66 Lygon St, T9663 5555, www.down towner.com.au Refurbished motel with surprisingly stylish, large rooms and excellent facilities. Free parking and entry to City Baths. **A-B** *King*, 122 Nicholson St, T9417 1113, www.kingaccomm.com.au Contemporarily furnished B&B in an 1867 end-of-terrace home. This place is truly exquisite, light and white with stripped wood floors and balconies overlooking Carlton Gardens. The largest of the 3 rooms is one of the most desirable in the city. Cooked breakfast, licensed. Rates *do not* vary. Recommended. **C-E** *Nunnery*, 116 Nicholson St, T1800 032635 or 9419 8637, infonunnery@ bakpakgroup.com Friendly, funky backpacker hostel in a rambling Victorian terraced house with a seriously comfortable front lounge. Free linen, breakfast, and lots of laid-on activities. Range of doubles, twins and 3-bed to the cheaper 12-bed dorms.

■ *on map, page 406*

North Melbourne C-E *Queensberry Hill YHA*, 78 Howard St, T9329 8427, queensberryhill@yhavic.org.au Massive purpose-built, 350-bed hostel with mostly 4-bed dorms, doubles and twins, some en suite. Wide range of facilities include free use of bikes and car parking. Recommended. Further north is the smaller and more homely, **D-E** *Chapman Gardens YHA*, 76 Chapman St, T9328 3595, chapman@yhavic.org.au Also with 120-beds, but again all in 4-bed dorms or smaller, and good value doubles. Modern and comfortable with a lovely gazebo and garden, free bike hire and car parking. **D-E** *City Scene*, 361 Queensberry St, T9348 9525, Small friendly hostel, within easy walking distance of the city centre.

■ *on map, page 406*

South Melbourne C-E *Market Inn*, corner of York St and Cecil St, T9690 2220, www.marketinn.com.au At the time of writing this was a tired, scruffy but comfortable former pub, it is now a NOMADS hostel with 65 beds, including 10 doubles. Free bike hire, breakfast and linen. There are plans, however, for a major extension and refurbishment in early 2002. There will then be 110 beds including en suite doubles and mini-theatrette.

■ *on map, Inner suburbs, page 406*

East Melbourne and Richmond A *Villa Donati*, 377 Church Rd, T9428 8104, www.villadonati.com Architecturally splendid 1880s town house built for the then Mayor of Richmond. Now a spacious, gracious B&B with 3 en suite rooms. Contemporary, light feel but with well chosen Italian and Asian antiques. Recommended.

■ *on map, page 411*

Victoria

B-C *Georgian Court*, 21 George St, T9419 6353, www.georgiancourt.aunz.com Large, friendly and comfortable guest house with 17 en suite and another 8 rooms with a separate bathroom each. Mostly twins and doubles, but quads possible. Substantial continental breakfast included. Off-street parking. **B-D** *Richmond Hill*, 353 Church St, T9428 6501, www.richmondhillhotel.com.au Federation terrace house, converted into a stylish, modern corporate hotel. Mostly well-equipped en suite with buffet continental breakfast. Some simpler budget rooms. Good value. There are few other small cheap hostels, though none particularly stand out.

E *Central*, 21 Bromham Pl, T9427 9826, 30-beds including a few cheap doubles on a quiet side-street. **E** *Packers Palace*, 153 Hoddle St, T9428 5932, is a scruffy and tired, but clean 32-bed hostel mostly set-up for working backpackers. Singles, twins, doubles and some quads, all with sinks and TVs. Linen included.

■ *on map, page 411* **South Yarra, Prahan and Toorak L** *Hotel Como*, 630 Chapel St, South Yarra, T9825 2222, www.hotelcomo.com.au One of Melbourne's most fashionable hotels, the Como's 107 contemporary suites are decorated with tactile fabrics and carpets. Elegant bar, sauna, spa, rooftop pool, gym, 24-hr room service. **B** *Saville*, 5 Commercial Rd, T9867 2755, www.saville.com.au Recently refurbished unsightly motel tower block. Inside there is a small slick bar and café and the 35 rooms are all en suite with good facilities including balcony. Free parking. **C** *Claremont Hotel*, 189 Toorak Rd, T1800 818851 or 9826 8000, www.hotelclaremont.com (verges on **D**). The 80 clean, bright but sparse rooms are good value. Mostly singles, doubles and twins. Linen, substantial continental breakfast, use of small kitchenette. **D-E** *Chapel St Backpackers*, T9533 6855, www.csbackpackers.com.au Right at the bottom of Chapel St, at No 22, is this friendly, family owned and run hostel with 48 beds. Mostly doubles, twins and 4-bed dorms, some all-female. Almost all are en suite with a/c, modest facilities. Linen and breakfast included. Recommended.

■ *on map, page 412*
St Kilda is a backpacking stronghold but the quality varies considerably
St Kilda LL-L *The Prince*, 2 Acland St, T9536 1111, www.theprince.com.au Sleek boutique hotel, the height of hushed minimalist luxury. The 40 en suite rooms are seriously stylish and the pool and deck one of Melbourne's finest posing spots. The smart fine dining restaurant, *Circa*, offers a business lunch for $25. The basement *Mink* bar plays the tune to an Eastern bloc theme with deep leather couches and more varieties of vodka than a Russian distiller on speed. Recommended.

A *Keslan Hall*, 57 Blessington St, T9593 9198, keslan_hall@hotmail.com Very elegant Edwardian property in a quiet street run as a premium B&B. **A-C** *Torlano*, 42 Fitzroy St, T9537 0200, www.hoteltorlano.com.au Colourful hotel with 43 comfortable, en suite rooms, some with kitchen facilities and balconies. Courtyard with guest BBQ. Small cosy bar and restaurant.

B *Barkly Quest*, 180 Barkly St, T9525 5000, www.questapartments.com.au One-bedroom, well-equipped and comfortable self-contained units. Some parking. **B-D** *Warwick Beachside*, 363 Beaconsfield Pde, T9525 4800, www.warwickbeachside.com.au Older self-contained apartments, from studios to 2-bedroom. All clean and well-equipped, however, and very good value. Secure off-street parking. Recommended.

C-D *Olembia*, 96 Barkly St, T9537 1412, www.olembia.com.au Comparable with *Toad Hall*, a very comfortable hostel that a lot of thought has gone into. 50 beds, including a dozen doubles and twins. Very competent, friendly and knowledgeable management. Bike hire $12 a day. Free off-street parking and secure bike shed. Recommended.

D-E *Enfield House*, Enfield St, T1800 302121 or 9525 4433, www.bakpakgroup.com Over 90 beds, including 4 doubles, but lively and friendly with heaps of freebies, including breakfast, and good advice on trips and employment. Kitchen facilities a bit inadequate. **D-E** *Jacksons Manor*, 53 Jackson St, T9534 1877, www.jacksonsmanor.com.au Large, rambling 1845 building with 80 beds. Doubles to 8-bed dorms.

Richmond, Prahran & Toorak

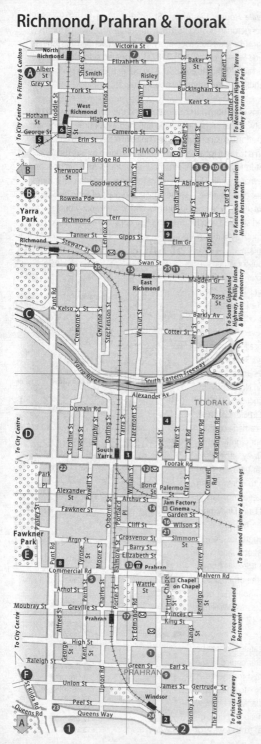

Victoria

0 metres 300
0 yards 300

■ Sleeping

1 Central *A2*
2 Chapel St Backpackers *F2*
3 Claremont *D2*
4 Como *D2*
5 Georgian Court *B1*
6 Packers Palace *A1*
7 Richmond Hill *B2*
8 Saville *F1*
9 Villa Donati *B2*

● Eating

1 Borsch *F2*
2 Brazilian *B2*
3 Djakarta *B2*
4 E Lounge *A2*
5 Flavours of India *E1*
6 Mexicali Rose *C1*
7 Minh Tan II *A2*
8 Momotaro Rahmen *B2*
9 Orange *F2*
10 Raw *B2*
11 Salona *C2*
12 Seng Hing *D2*
13 Spargos *E2*
14 Tandoor Indian *E2*
15 Torch *C2*

● Pubs & bars

16 Bridie O' Reilly's *E2*
17 Candy Bar *F1*
18 Corner *B1*
19 Depot *C1*
20 Dizzy's Jazz Bar *C1*
21 Frost Bite *E2*
22 Pigs R's *D1*
23 Pint on Punt *F1*
24 Railway *F2*
25 Swan *C2*

Related maps
A St Kilda, page 412
B Inner suburbs,
page 406

Williamstown has a majority of heritage-style B&Bs, cheaper than their city equivalents, plus a few holiday apartments

Williamstown B *Heathville House*, 171 Aitken St, off Ferguson St, T9397 5959, heath@jeack.com.au Late-Victorian hosted B&B on a quiet side street with 4 rooms (1 en suite), guest lounge and breakfast conservatory. Mostly Edwardian furnishings. **C** *Brief Encounter*, 27 Laurie St, Newport, T9391 2187. Just one en suite double room with private sitting room in a 1920s home and B&B. A bit out of the way, 3 km from the town centre, but very friendly and exceptionally good value.

Eating

● *on maps Melbourne is the Australian city most closely associated with food. It boasts incredible variety at inexpensive prices*

A quarter of all Melbournians were born outside Australia and there are roughly 110 ethnic groups living in the city. These immigrants have enriched Melbourne cuisine and sociable Melbournians can afford to eat out often. The choice of restaurants is often overwhelming. The best option is to head for an 'eat street' or area known for a particular cuisine, such as Brunswick St in Fitzroy or the Vietnamese restaurants of Richmond, and stroll up and down to see what appeals. During the day look out for the Mon-Fri business lunches at some of the fancier restaurants – starter, main and glass of wine for $20-30. Despite the vast number of seats, try to book in summer and at weekends. Foodies staying for an extended period should consider investing in a copy of *The Age Good Food Guide* (covering Victoria), both available in bookshops and newsagents.

There are several options for expensive food 'on the go' in Melbourne. The *Colonial Tramcar Restaurant*, T9696 4000, www.tramrestaurant.com.au, is actually a fleet of ornately decked out trams that shuttle around the city every lunchtime and evening. They go in for all-inclusive set menus, starting at $66 for a 3-course early dinner (1745-1915). The trams depart from the 125 tram stop on Normanby Rd, near the casino and the junction with Clarendon St South. The *Classic Carriage*, T9563 1270, www.classic-carriage.com.au, is an equally upmarket, but slightly roomier affair, this time on railway rather than tram tracks. The restaurant travels from Spencer St Station down to Geelong and back every Fri and Sat evening, taking about 3½ hrs. The *Rivers Lady Lindeman*, T9686 8668, www.rivers.net.au, is a cruise-boat restaurant, slightly less formal then the carriage operations, and with arguably the best views. It leaves from 8 Harbour Esplanade (just the other side of the Colonial Stadium), is also Fri-Sat only, heading through the docks for Williamstown, again taking about 3½ hrs.

● *On map, page 400 See also Cafés, and Pubs & bars*

Related maps A St Kilda, page 412 B Inner suburbs, page 406

City centre City centre eating tends to be daytime eating. For greater choice in the evening most people head for the inner suburbs although Chinatown (Little Bourke St) and the Southbank remain busy dinner spots. There are cheaper options on Russell St. **Hardware La**, to the west of

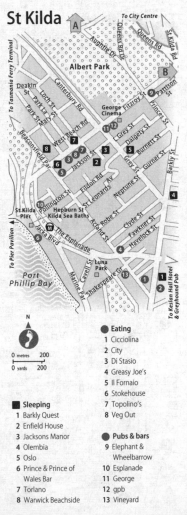

St Kilda

To City Centre

Albert Park

To Tasmania Ferry Terminal

To Pier Pavilion

St Kilda Pier

Port Phillip Bay

To Keslan Hall Hotel & Greyhound Pub

N

0 metres 200
0 yards 200

■ **Sleeping**
1 Barkly Quest
2 Enfield House
3 Jacksons Manor
4 Olembia
5 Oslo
6 Prince & Prince of Wales Bar
7 Torlano
8 Warwick Beachside

● **Eating**
1 Cicciolina
2 City
3 Di Stasio
4 Greasy Joe's
5 Il Fornaio
6 Stokehouse
7 Topolino's
8 Veg Out

● **Pubs & bars**
9 Elephant & Wheelbarrow
10 Esplanade
11 George
12 gpb
13 Vineyard

Elizabeth St, has a strip of restaurants and cafés that buzz at lunchtimes. **Centre La**, off Collins St, at first glance looks like a grimy dark alley but is one of the best places in the city centre for a cheap lunch.

Expensive *Flower Drum*, 17 Market La, T9662 3655. Mon-Sat 1200-1500, 1800-2300, Sun 1800-2230. Considered by many to be the best Chinese restaurant in Australia and well worth the painful hit to the wallet. The finest Cantonese cuisine in a light, elegant dining room, impeccable service and an excellent wine list. The Peking Duck must be tried. Expect to spend about $130 for 2 without wine. Recommended. *Langton's*, 61 Flinders La, T9663 0222. Tue-Fri 0800-2230. A basement restaurant with a hip wine bar at one end, *Langton's* consistently wins praise for its very fine French-influenced food and excellent wine list. The menu of the day is great value for lunch or early dinner. *Shark Fin House*, 131 Little Bourke St, T9663 1555. Open daily 1130-1500, 1730-2300. Does excellent Chinese food, including a monumental range of dim sum, and is usually packed at lunchtimes. Recommended.

Mid-range *Jarrah Room*, 44 Spencer St, T9629 5255. Smart, warm and earthy restaurant. Modern Australian meals with a nod to indigenous foods, including wallaby, roo and croc. *Rosati*, 95 Flinders La, T9654 7772. Open Mon-Fri 0730-2200, Sat 1800-2200. Large, light Italian café-bar in an old glass-ceilinged warehouse which the owners have succeeded in giving a welcoming, classical feel. Recommended.

Cheap *Café All Angolo*, corner of Hardware Lane and Little Bourke St, is ideal for a fast and reliable bowl of pasta in simple and unpretentious surrounds, very popular with nearby office workers. *Nudel Bar*, 76 Bourke St, T9662 9100. Small and spartan, serving excellent noodle dishes and some pasta. *Nyonqa*, 14 Market Lane, T9663 2611. Small, friendly Malaysian restaurant with a wide-ranging menu including several good value set meals. Open daily 1200-1415, 1730-2200. *Spencer*, 475 Spencer St, T9329 5111. Meals 1200-1500 Mon-Fri, 1830-2100 Mon-Sat. Victorian pub, now with a seriously smart, highly-regarded and usually lively restaurant in the lounge area. The quality rubs off on the cheap counter meals, which are well worth the stroll out from the city. Budget accommodation upstairs (**D-E**). The city abounds in tiny 'eat-in or takeaway' outlets catering for virtually any taste. There are concentrations of them at the top of Swanston St, Hardware La and many of the city's laneways, including the wonderful Centre Pl.

Southbank Expensive *Walter's Wine Bar*, Upper level Southgate, T9690 9211. Daily 1200-late. This place is one of the most treasured on Southbank, both hip and relaxed. Also fantastic views of the river, the 'best wine list in the land', and wicked deserts. **Mid-range** *EQ*, Victorian Arts Centre, T9645 0644. Daily 1100-late. Good casual Mediterranean food in a combined bar and café. Noisy but lively contemporary space. **Cheap** *Blue Train Café*, mid-level Southgate, T9696 0111. Daily 0700-2400. Fashionable and casual spot for drinks, snacks, pasta or wood-fired pizza. The cheapest places to eat on Southbank are the busy food courts at Southgate and at the casino.

There are many cafés and restaurants in the Southgate and Crown Casino complexes, many of them upmarket but it's a pleasant place to dine while gazing across to the city skyline

Carlton and Fitzroy Expensive *Lemongrass*, 176 Lygon St, T9662 2244. Open 1200-1430 Mon-Fri, daily 1730-2200. Modern, stylish Thai with friendly menus and service and extensive choices including vegetarian and interesting house specials. Lunchtime 'eat-all-you-can' buffet is excellent value. Recommended. *Toofeys*, corner of Elgin St and Drummond St, T9347 9838. Open Tue-Fri 1200-1500, Tue-Sun 1800-2200. A simple, white, contemporary dining room is the setting for simply exquisite seafood, generally regarded as the best in Melbourne. Recommended.

Mid-range *Abla's*, 109 Elgin St, T9347 0006. This small olive-green formal dining room consistently serves the best Lebanese food in town. *Gluttony It's a Sin*, 278 Smith St. Open Tue-Sat 0830-2300, Sun 1000-2100. Rich food in a café atmosphere. Everything is oversized and over-indulgent, but exceptional quality is always maintained. *Jamaica House*, 106 Lygon St, T9663 5715. Open 1200-1500 Wed-Fri, 1800-2100

● *On map, page 406 Carlton's Lygon St is sometimes called 'Little Italy' for its string of Italian restaurants. Brunswick St in Fitzroy is probably the most diverse eating street in Melbourne.*

Victoria

Mon-Sat. Bright and colourful with generous portions of spicy West Indian food, including hot curries and a beautiful peppered steak. Some cheap lunches. *Shakahari*, 201 Farady St, T9347 3848. Long-standing vegetarian restaurant with a warm, earthy but stylish interior. The limited but very fine menu will not disappoint.

Cheap *Guru da Dhaba*, 240 Johnston St, T9486 9155. Very cheap but filling northern Indian dishes in a warm and noisy dining room with terracotta walls and simple black tables. BYO. *Kazen*, 201 Brunswick St, T9417 3270. Open 1200-1500 Tue-Sat, 1800-2230 Tue-Sun. Small, Italian-influenced Japanese with dark, blue-stone walls but a much lighter atmosphere. Excellent and interesting food, licensed but cheap corkage for BYO. Recommended. *Moroccan Soup Bar*, 183 St Georges Rd, North Fitzroy. Huge vegetarian meals of superbly authentic Moroccan flavour. Of the many Italian cafés and restaurants in Lygon St, the large *Notturno*, at No 179, is one of the least expensive, and is virtually always open. Good breakfasts, pasta, pizzas, cakes and coffee. Open daily 0600-0200 or later. *Vegie Bar*, 380 Brunswick St. Open daily 1100-2200. A relaxed, friendly vegetarian café-bar in a large old bare-brick warehouse. Great menu includes wood-fired pizzas, wraps, burgers and salads. Recommended.

Seriously cheap *Aussie Indian Trendy Cuisine*, 25 Johnston St, T9419 2118. Open daily 1730-2330. The name alone merits a visit, but with good food at laughingly cheap prices, BYO and friendly service you can't really go wrong. The banquet for 2 is $25. Also takeaway. Recommended. *Viet Rose*, 363 Brunswick St. Generous quantities of laksa, vegetarian rolls and rice will defeat your stomach before your wallet.

● on map, page 406 **South Melbourne Expensive** *Est Est Est*, 440 Clarendon St, T9682 5688. Open Thu-Fri 1200-1500, Tue-Sat 1800-2200. Regarded by many reviewers as serving the best modern Australian cuisine in Melbourne. The simple, plain dining room, with red velour seats adding a rare touch of colour, also has a small trellised courtyard adjoining.

Mid-range *Sakura Teppanyaki*, 331 Clarendon St, T9699 4150. Open Mon-Fri 1100-1500, daily 1700-2300, later Fri-Sat. The chefs throw all their lively personality into their cooking, and things can get pretty boisterous here. Good fun.

Seriously cheap *Clarendon Fish and Chippers*, 293 Clarendon St. Open daily by 1130, until at least 2100. Healthy fast food, one of the very best in Melbourne, with fresh fish and great chips. *Spring*, 316 Clarendon St. Open 0800-2000 Mon-Fri, 1030-1600 Sat. A healthy fast-food joint serving 98% fat-free breakfasts, burgers and curries as well as salads and smoothies.

● on map, page 411
Richmond is one of the most international of the foodie suburbs. Most eateries are on Bridge Rd, but just to the north is Melbourne's 'Little Saigon', Victoria St, where around 50 Vietnamese restaurants jostle for attention. Greek food can be found on Swan St in Richmond between Church St and Hoddle St **East Melbourne and Richmond Expensive** *Richmond Hill Café and Larder*, 48 Bridge Rd, 9421 2808, thecafe@rhcl.com.au Mon-Fri 0900-2100, Sat 0800-2100, Sun 0900-1600. Hugely indulgent café and restaurant with wonderful cheese shop attached. Lunch includes the cheese platter and dinners are a culinary event.

Mid-range *The Brazilian*, 368 Bridge Rd, T9429 5000. Daily 0800-2200. Large, casual but sophisticated café bar with seriously inventive breakfasts and modern Australian cuisine. Ambient live music Sat 2200, Sun 1400. Recommended. *Kanzaman*, 488 Bridge Rd, T9429 3402. Open daily 1200-1530, 1800-2400. Excellent Lebanese with an exotic, richly decorated interior. *Mexicali Rose*, 103 Swan St, T9429 5550. Open Fri 1130-1430, daily 1800-2100. Friendly, earthy Mexican with generous servings of all the classics, plus a few interesting variations. *Minh Tan II*, 192 Victoria St, T9427 7131. Open daily 1000-2200. One of the busiest and most respected Vietnamese restaurants, with a huge menu including fantastic mud crabs.

Cheap *Djakarta*, 338 Bridge Rd, T9428 7086. Open daily 1800-2100. Characterful, bold and very purple Indonesian restaurant. BYO and takeaway. *E Lounge*, 409 Victoria St, T9429 6060, elounge@tpg.com.au *Not* an internet café, but some of the best thin and crispy wood-fired pizzas in the city. Very friendly, very orange. Also takeaway. Recommended. *Momotaro Rahmen*, 392 Bridge Rd, T9421 1661. Open Tue-Sat 1130-1430,

Tue-Sun 1800-2100. Small restaurant much loved for its home-made, fresh rahmen noodles and uncompromising flavours. *Salona*, 260 Swan St, T9429 1460. Open 1100-2200 Mon-Fri, 1100-2300 Sat-Sun. The best of a small cluster of traditional Greek restaurants. *Vegetarian Nirvana*, 486 Bridge Rd, T9428 1408. Open Thu-Sun 1200-1500, daily 1730-2230. Small Indian vegetarian. BYO and takeaway.

Prahan and Toorak Expensive *Jacques Reymond*, 78 Williams Rd, Prahan, T9525 2178. Tue-Fri 1200-1400, Tue-Sat 1830-2100. Considered by many to be the finest restaurant in the city, housed in an opulent Victorian mansion. The food is a brilliant blend of Asian flavours, classical techniques and seasonal produce. Very expensive but the lunchtime *menu rapide* is only $30 for a main, glass of wine and coffee.

● on map, page 411

There is no particular foodie area, the cafés and restaurants here dotted amongst the shops on Chapel St and Toorak Rd, but the choice is phenomenal. Choose your style and there's a good bet you'll be able to find it. Prahan's Commercial Rd is less expensive

Mid-range *Borsch*, 173 Chapel St, T9530 2694. Breakfasts and meals daily 1000-2130. Vibrant, friendly eastern European restaurant specializing in Polish broth and vodka. Live, gypsy-style music Mon, Wed, Sun. Evening bookings essential on music nights and weekends. Recommended.

Cheap *Flavours of India*, 68 Commercial Rd. Small, smart curry bar, popular with locals for food of exceptional quality. Also takeaway. *Seng Hing*, 242 Toorak Rd, T9827 0368. Open Mon-Fri 1200-1330, Sat-Sun 1200-1400, daily 1700-2030. Tiny, busy Chinese with some seriously cheap specials, BYO only. Also takeaway. *Tandoor Indian*, 517 Chapel St, T9827 8247. Nothing fancy about the décor here but with 20 years in business the food is excellent.

St Kilda The eating in St Kilda has been traditionally clustered along Acland St and Fitzroy St, though since the on-going renovation of St Kilda Baths, the choice on the foreshore has tripled. Italian predominates, but there are several cheap takeaway noodle and curry bars and the Jewish cake shops in Acland St melt the resolve of many a dieter. Almost everyone has pavement tables.

● on map, page 412

Expensive *Di Stasio*, 31 Fitzroy St, T9525 3999. Meals daily 1200-1500, 1800-2300. Serves some of the best Italian food in the city in soothingly tasteful surroundings. Desserts include their wonderful home-made ice-creams. Consistently full so always book ahead. Recommended.

Mid-range *Stokehouse*, 30 Jacka Bvd, T9525 5555. Meals Mon-Fri 1200-2200, Sat 1100-2400, Sun 1000-2200. Dining room daily 1200-1500, 1900-2200. With the best spot on the foreshore this award-winning bar-bistro is packed out year round. Simple ground floor bar and beach-facing terrace. Bookings not taken so arrive early for a good spot. Upstairs is an expensive, airy formal dining room, focusing on modern Australian seafood, which has the best balcony tables in Melbourne (bookings taken). Recommended. Of the cheaper traditional Italian options try either *Cicciolina*, 130 Acland St, T9525 3333, or *Topolino's*, 87 Fitzroy St, T9534 4856. Open daily 1200-0400. Both large and busy with mid-range mains, cheap pasta, pizzas and salads.

Cheap *Greasy Joe's*, 68 Acland St. Open daily 0700-2400. American retro bar and grill with excellent burgers, breakfasts and lots of pavement tables. *Veg Out*, 63 Fitzroy. Tiny vegetarian using very healthy cooking methods to produce a great variety of dishes, including curries and stir-fries. Also takeaway.

Williamstown The 1854 *Stag's Head*, corner of Ann St and Cecil St, T9397 8337, is well worth tracking down. The small, traditional front bar oozes a century or more of character and is one of the best in Melbourne, while the mid-range dining room is surprisingly formal and the food several notches above usual pub fare. A sunny, trellised courtyard completes the picture. Recommended. *Top of the Bay*, 1 The Strand, is one of Melbourne's best fish and chip shops. Open daily 1100-1900, later Sat, earlier Sun.

Victoria

Cafés

On map, page 400
These are all great
places for sipping a
coffee and watching
the world go by,
though many will also
happily supply a beer
or serve you dinner

City centre There are some clusters of cafés, such as in De Graves and the Causeway, but there are good cafés around almost every corner. *Caffeine*, Swanston St, north of La Trobe. Mon-Fri 0700-1930. This dark and groovy café is next to the *RMIT* so it is full of students and has good quality baguettes, sushi, cakes and muffins at student prices. Great value. *Laurent*, the Causeway. Open Mon-Sat 0800-1800, Sun 0900-1700. An elegant Parisienne-style patisserie that is begging for *haute couture*, but instead serves baguettes, coffee and exquisite pastries. Licensed. *Pellegrinis*, 66 Bourke St. Open Mon-Sat 0800-2330, Sun 1200-2000. This is Melbourne's original Italian café (it opened in 1954). It hasn't really changed much since then, and it still remains as a vibrant, crowded small space serving wonderful coffee and cheap pasta dishes. Recommended.

On map, page 406
This area can
confidently lay claim
to the highest density
of quality cafés in
Melbourne, coming in
all shapes and sizes

Carlton and Fitzroy *Babka*, 358 Brunswick St. Friendly, unassuming and unpretentious bakery that simply nears perfection in everything it does. Cheap lunches, licensed. Open Tue-Sun 0700-1900. Closed most of Jan. Recommended. *Karnie's*, 142 Nicholson St. Open Wed-Sat 1000-2200, Sun 0900-1630. Small, relaxed wood-panelled café with a few outside tables overlooking Carlton Gardens and the museum. Cheap, mostly Italian menu. *Retro*, 413 Brunswick St. Open daily 0700-2400. Cavernous bare-brick café with distressed wood floor and lots of formica tables. This is a grazers' paradise with loads of nibbles, plates and dips on the extensive cheap menu. Also good all-day breakfast and veggie options, licensed. Recommended. *Threshermans Bakehouse*, 221 Faraday St. Open daily 0630-2400. Spacious and relaxed café in an old car-repair shop. Great fresh juices, soups and cafeteria meals as well as the usual range of cakes and sandwiches. Recommended.

On map, page 411
Bridge Rd has a café
for almost every shop,
and they come and
go with regularity

Richmond and Prahan *Raw*, 382 Bridge Rd. Open 0700-1700. Does all-day breakfast, great coffee, cheap specials and has loads of magazines. The small and welcoming *Torch* is one of a few excellent cafés on Swan St. Open daily 0830-1800. Busy but relaxed with cheap light lunches and all-day breakfasts. Good value. Recommended. *Orange*, 126 Chapel St. Daily 0800-1800, bar 1800-0200 Thu-Sun. Tiny, dark and moody with excellent cheap food. *Spargos*, 169 Commercial Rd. Large earthy, friendly café bar with a huge cheap menu. Wonderful range of breakfasts daily 0700-1200, and wood-fired pizzas, pasta, snacks, soups and salads, daily 1200-2200, to 2300 Wed-Sat.

On map, page 412

St Kilda *City*, 192 Barkly St. Food 0900-2230. Lived-in and friendly with second-hand books and candles in bottles. Good breakfasts, cheap lunches and dinners. Recommended. *il Fornaio*, 2 Acland St. Open 0700-2200. Small, but warehousey with lots of cheap eats and pavement tables, great for breakfast. French/Italian bakery. *Pier Pavilion*, perched right at the end of St Kilda pier. Open 1000-sunset, 1000-2300 peak summer. Great spot for breakfast or simply one of the excellent coffees with a substantial slice of cake. Also cheap lunches. Recommended.

Pubs & bars

Many pubs and bars
also serve good
food at reasonable
prices and liberal
licensing laws mean
it is possible to get
a drink well into
the small hours

The city is bursting with watering holes from the sleekest cocktail bar to the grungiest of rambling Victorian-era pubs with sticky carpets. The city centre bars tend to be the most sophisticated with many wine bars and cocktail bars crossing the line into club territory and a sprinkling of traditional pubs frequented by office workers during the week. The large student population to the north of the city means that Carlton, Fitzroy and Collingwood have the heaviest concentration of live band venues and alternative pubs and bars. The inner suburbs south of the Yarra have some of the most fashionable bars and respected live music venues.

City centre *Bridie O'Reilly's*, 62 Little Collins St. Out-of-the-way Irish theme bar with 20-odd beers on tap. Pub grub 1200-1430, 1800-2100 and mainly Irish acoustic live music Tue-Thu, cover bands Fri-Sat. *Hairy Canary*, 212 Little Collins St. Open Mon-Fri 0730-0300, Sat 1000-0300, Sun 1000-0100. A smart, trendy bar and café, serving food all day, that rocks into the early hours. *Stork*, 504 Elizabeth St, T9663 6237. Welcoming, relaxed front bar with pool table and open fire. Independent bands daily with a wide mix of styles. Seriously cheap, good quality bar food and cheap, surprisingly sophisticated bistro. Also pleasant, good value double and twin rooms with kitchen and lounge facilities (**D**). Recommended. *Zukini*, 310 Flinders La. Open Mon-Fri 0730-2400, 1800-0300 Sat. Earthy, but sophisticated ground-floor bistro and basement cocktail bar with curved wood-slatted walls. Tapas and nibbles available all day. The excellent, organic mid-range a là carte is Japanese-influenced modern Australian. *The Mitre*, 2 Bank Pa, is a traditional British-style pub, now hemmed in by the high-rises, which has been quietly pulling pints since the 1860s..

● *On map, page 400 Melbourne is the headquarters of Carlton and United Brewery, who produce the hugely successful export brand Fosters*

Carlton and Fitzroy *Bar Open*, 317 Brunswick St. Small, grungy bar with an open fire, armchairs and live music Wed-Sun. *Black Cat*, 252 Brunswick St. Open Wed 1800-2300, Thu-Fri 1800-0100, Sat-Sun 1400-0100. Slick, seductive cabaret bar with live blues and jazz Thu-Sun. *The Brandon*, corner of Station St and Lee St, goes out of its way to source real ales, both keg and bottled. Simple friendly front bar and large retro lounge. Equally simple pub grub, but with interesting touches. *Clare Castle*, 421 Rathdowne St, T9347 8171, has an unremarkable public bar but a deep blue dining room serving up some of the best Italian home cooking in the area. Meals 1200-1500 Mon-Sat, 1830-2130 Tue-Sat. *Night Cat*, 141 Johnston St, Fitzroy, T9417 0090. Lush and stylish bar with roomy couches and swing and salsa bands, Thu-Sun. *North Fitzroy Star*, 32 St Georges Rd, T9482 6484. Contemporary, often exuberant styling in this traditional Victorian pub. Welcoming, with lots of nooks and crannies and open fires, the food is also well worth the trip. Cheap, inventive light lunches and bar nibbles, and a set mid-range menu later on. Food daily 1100-2300. Recommended. *Purple Turtle*, 166 Johnston St, T9416 5055. Chic, contemporary bar-restaurant in an old Victorian pub with live blues, funk and jazz Fri-Sat and Sun afternoons. The cheap interesting menu still gives a nod to a few pub favourites, and can be served in the formal dining room with its open fire. Food daily 1200-2200, but 1200-1600 Mon-Wed in winter. *The Tote*, 71 Johnston St, isn't a gambling den, but is dark and smoky all the same with a crowd of students, crusties and band types here for the alternative live music Tue-Sat. Features 'tight-arse Tuesdays' when pots are $1.10 and there's cheap entry to 3 bands.

● *On map, page 406 Carlton and Fitzroy have lots of decent pubs and bars*

Richmond and Prahan *Dizzy's Jazz Bar*, 92 Swan St, hosts live jazz Thu-Sat, while the nearby pubs, the *Corner* and *Depot* have original live bands nightly. On the junction with Church St is the traditional *Swan*, a pleasant drinkers' bar with live cover bands Wed-Sun. Also cheap counter meals daily 1200-1400, 1800-2130. There's a large *Bridie O'Reilly's* at 462 Chapel St, with live music daily. The groovy *Candy Bar*, 162 Greville St, is a laidback and friendly bar and café with sculpted fireplaces of antiqued Hebel blocks and retro furniture. DJs Thu-Sun play progressive house and there's celebrity bingo on Mon. A range of grazing options including cheap platters and dips, available daily 1200-2400. Late licence Fri-Sat. Recommended. The bar to be seen at is *Frost Bite*, corner of Chapel St and Simmons St. The cool warehouse look is complemented by industrial quantities of slush cocktails waiting on tap. Very cheap café meals, and live music Wed-Thu and Sun. Late license most nights. *The Pigs R's*, 28 Toorak Rd, is split between the large, dark, modern eating area, and the equally dark rear bar and pool room. Decent cheap grub, including breakfasts, daily 0800-2200. Live music Tue, Thur-Sun with a late licence Fri-Sat. For a friendly traditional local head for the *Railway*, 19 Chapel St, opposite Backpackers hostel.

● *On map, page 411 South Richmond has a cluster of good live music bars*

Victoria

St Kilda *The Elephant and Wheelbarrow*, Fitzroy St, is a London-style pub with over 20 beers on tap, most British or Irish. Live music Wed-Sun and a 'meet-the-*Neighbours*' session (really) on Mon. Cheap, feel-good meals, including breakfast, daily 1100-1430, 1700-2100. *The Esplanade*, Esplanade, is something of a Melbourne institution for live music, cheap food and a raucous atmosphere. *George*, corner of Fitzroy St and Grey St. Slick wine bar, in sharp contrast to the lively and grungy *gpb* beneath. The latter serves cheap pub grub daily 1200-0100, and there's interesting live music 1600-1900 Sat and 1800-2100 Sun. *Greyhound*, 1 Brighton Rd, T9534 4189, is a relaxed comfortable pub and a good live venue for everything from roots to rock and Sun night karaoke. The *Pint on Punt*, Punt St, 9510 4273, is one of Melbourne's best drinking holes. A simple, warm country-Irish-style pub with open brick fires and bare wood floors. Recommended. They also have good *Nomads* hostel accommodation upstairs (**D-E**). The *Prince of Wales* public bar, Fitzroy St, is a magnet for all types from the divine to the desperate and consequently has an unpredictable energy. Lots of pool tables, $1 pots on Mon and a busy live venue next door. The seriously laidback and cool frequent the *Vineyard*, 71 Acland St. Open daily 1000-0300. A long, casual space that can be opened onto the side street on a sunny day. Also great café food.

● On map, page 406 **South Melbourne** *The Limerick Arms*, corner of Clarendon St and Park St, had a revamp a few years ago to more reflect its name and cash-in on the rise of Irish theme bars. This isn't too forced, however, and the result is a pleasant, traditional Aussie drinking bar with an Irish flavour. DJs Fri-Sat, cheap counter meals daily 1200-1430, 1800-2100. *The Maori Chief*, corner of Moray St and York St, T9696 5363, combines a groovily shabby bar, dimly lit and furnished with retro couches, with good cheap casual food. Meals 1200-1400 Mon-Fri, 1800-2130 Mon-Sat. Recommended.

Clubs & Melbourne has a huge nightlife scene. There are countless clubs, bars, lounges and live
live music music venues. Many club nights move regularly and the clubs themselves open and
For the most close frequently. Entry is usually about $10-15. King St has a lot of clubs but is known
up-to-date for being slightly seedy. Most of the clubs listed are city based but Chapel St in South
information on Yarra is also a hot-spot.
clubbing and live
music see free street   *Heat*, at the casino, is a glitzy, large and popular venue with mainstream dance,
papers such as Beat karaoke and a cocktail bar. *Metro*, 20 Bourke St, is Australia's biggest club with regular
and Impress or international acts and mainstream dance, alternative and pop nights. *44*, 44 Lonsdale
www.melbourne.citys St, and *Lounge*, 243 Swanston St, are both good techno clubs with lots of space and
earch.com.au variety, pool tables, pinball and outdoor space. *Club 383*, 383 Lonsdale St, attracts a student crowd with cheap drinks and entry, and indie, retro pop and alternative tunes. *CBD*, 12 McKillop St, is a Fri-night only venue for hardcore house and techno. *Up-top Bar*, Level 1, 163 Russell St. Relaxed and slightly kitsch bar with DJs playing disco, house and rare groove classics, Wed-Sat. *Honkytonks*, Duckboard Pl, is a challenge to get into unless you are young, beautiful and creative but it is worth trying for the unusual décor, people-watching and the best of underground house. *Revolver*, 229 Chapel St, Prahan. A happening venue playing techno during the week with bands at weekends. Lots of space, a restaurant and relaxed vibe make this place popular with a mature and stylish crowd. *Tony Starr's Kitten Club*, 267 Little Collins St. Smooth and dim 60s club good for lounging on couches with one of their superb cocktails in hand.

    Melbourne's best **jazz clubs**, dim but no longer smoky, are *Bennets Lane*, 25 Bennets La, T9663 2856, for serious players 7 nights a week and *Dizzy's Jazz Bar*, 90 Swan St, Richmond, T9428 1233, in a former post office. Intimate and more casual, Wed-Sat, with Fri night jam sessions. Major acts play at the *Rod Laver Arena*, the *Melbourne Concert Hall* and the *MCG* and tickets for these type of events are usually sold through ticketing agencies. *Melbourne Concert Hall*, part of Victorian Arts Centre and home of Melbourne Symphony Orchestra.

Love thy Neighbours

Melbourne's most famous landmark is entirely fictitious. Ramsay Street, in the equally fictitious suburb of Erinsborough, is known in student residences the length and breadth of the UK as home to everyone's favourite neighbours. Curiously, Australians themselves are not interested in Neighbours. It gets no more attention than any other soap, although of course it is well known because of Kylie Minogue and all the other pop tarts who have tried to make musicians out of themselves. There are various tours and pub nights, solely aimed at British backpackers. **Backpacker King**, T9527 4407, have the neighbourhood covered. Tours to 'Ramsay St' run Monday-Friday (2-3 hours, $18) and include lots of soap gossip, photo stops in front of the houses, Erinsborough High School and the possibility of seeing some filming on set. 'Ramsay' Street is an ordinary residential street in the outer suburbs of Melbourne so only the outdoor filming is done here. Even more exciting for the soapoholic is the chance the press some Neighbours flesh at 'Meet the Neighbours'. Several cast members come along to the **Elephant and Wheelbarrow**, 169 Fitzroy Street, St Kilda, every Monday night for a raucous trivia night ($30). Bookings essential for tours and trivia night.

Art galleries Flinders La, has a fantastic collection of private art galleries, all free but dress up. *Anna Schwartz Gallery*, at No 185, for art, design and sculpture, *Tolarno* at No289 (Level 4) for innovation, and *Gabrielle Pizzi*, at No141, for superb Aboriginal art. For details of all current exhibtions check *Art Almanac*, a listings magazine published monthly, available in bookshops and newsagents ($2.50). **Cinema** *Astor*, 1 Chapel St, border of Prahan and St Kilda, T9510 1414. A different contemporary or classic movie every day, with lots of double bills. *George*, 135 Fitzroy St, St Kilda, T9534 6922. Mainstream movies, cheap tickets for guests at some local hostels, including *Olembia*. *Hoyts*, 140 Bourke St, T9663 3303, is one of the larger city centre theatres. *IMAX* can be found at the *Melbourne Museum* compex, Carlton Gdns, T9663 5454. *Nova*, 380 Lygon St, Carlton, T9347 5331. Mostly mainstream, but does cast its net a bit wider than most. Cheap on Mon. There is a *Village* cinema at the *Jam Factory*, 500 Chapel St, Prahan, T9827 2424, and others at 206 Bourke St, T9667 6565, and the *Crown* complex, T9278 6666. **Comedy venues** The main venues are the *Comedy Club*, 380 Lygon St, T9348 1622, for mainstream national and international acts, and *Prince Patrick Hotel*, 135 Victoria Pde, T9419 4197, for more off-the-wall fare. During the International Comedy Festival in Apr there are venues all over town. **Fairground** *Luna Park*, Cavell St. Open in summer for several rides including the impressive roller-coaster. **Theatres** The city's major theatre venue is the *Victorian Arts Centre*, 100 St Kilda Rd, T9281 8000, www.vicartscentre.com.au, with a varied programme including Melbourne's and the world's best companies. Venues include the *State Theatre*, *Playhouse* and *George Fairfax Studio*. There is also the **Chapel on Chapel**, 12 Little Chapel St, Prahan, T9522 3390. Innovative small venue with everything from comedy to dance and music to film. *La Mama*, 205 Faraday St, Carlton, T9347 6142. Legendary home of innovative theatre, established in the 70s. Reliably interesting productions and cheap tickets. *Her Majesty's Theatre*, 219 Exhibition St, T9663 3211. An ornate old lady, built in 1886, showing popular musicals. *Princess*, 163 Spring St, T9299 9800. Victorian opulence at this tiny jewel of a venue, showing musicals and mainstream theatre. *Regent*, 191 Collins St, T9299 9500. Carefully restored Spanish opulence, a venue for popular big-budget theatre, bands and film. *CUB Malthouse*, 113 Sturt St, Southbank, T9685 5111. Stylish complex with several theatres in a restored former brewery. Home to the Playbox company, who perform contemporary Australian work.

Entertainment

Victoria

Ticket agencies The main agencies are *Ticketek*, T132849, www.ticketek.com, and *Ticketmaster*, T136100, www.ticketmaster7.com.au There is a half-price ticket booth in Bourke St Mall, opposite *Myer* for same-day performances only. No telephone number – you have to go in person. Open 1000-1400 Mon, Sat, 1100-1800 Tue-Thu, 1100-1830 Fri.

Festivals
Sports fans should also watch out for the Australian Open in January, F1 Grand Prix in March and the Australian Football League Grand Final in September

Melbourne puts on an extraordinary spread of festivals throughout the year. Many of these attract the best talent in the country and bring over prestigious international artists. To see what's on and how to buy tickets pick up a copy of the free monthly *Melbourne Events* from the VIC. For forward planning see www.melbourne.vic.gov.au/festlist All of the festivals listed below are annual.

Midsumma Gay and lesbian celebration of pride, presence and profile. 3 summer weeks of street parties, events, and the Midsumma Carnival. T9415 9819, www.midsumma.org.au Held during **Jan and Feb**. *Moomba* A huge outdoor family festival centred on the Yarra, Alexandra Gdns and city centre. Sporting and cultural events inlcude dragon boat races, waterskiing, street parades and performers. T9699 4022, www.melbournemoombafestival.com.au Held over the Labour Day weekend in **Mar**. *Melbourne Food and Wine Festival* A prestigious gastonomic celebration that showcases talent and produce of the city and region. Events include master classes, food writers' forum, tasting tours and the 'world's longest lunch'. T9823 6100, www.melbfoodwinefest.com.au Held over **3 weeks in Mar**. *Melbourne International Comedy Festival* One of the world's largest laugh-fests. A month of comedy in every guise from more than a thousand Australian and international performers. Details at www.comedyfestival.com.au Held in **Apr**. *Melbourne International Film Festival* Showcases about 350 of the best films from Australia and around the world. The 2-week festival includes features, documentaries, shorts and discussion sessions with film makers in 4 main theatre venues. T9417 2011, www.melbournefilmfestival.com.au Held in **Jul**. *Melbourne Writers' Festival* This and Sydney's Writers' Festival are the literary events of the year. In previous years writers such as Bill Bryson and VS Naipaul have taken part as well as the best Australian authors. Events usually include readings, discussion panels, luncheons and lectures. T9645 9244, www.mwf.com.au 10 days in **Aug**. *Melbourne Fringe Festival* An off-shoot of the main Melbourne Festival with a more anarchic spirit. Showcases new and innovative art in all fields and has lots of free events, parties and a legendary parade down Brunswick St, Fitzroy. T9482 7545, www.melbournefringe.com.au Takes place over 3 weeks during **Sep and Oct**. *Melbourne Festival* The city's major arts festival showing the cream of local and overseas talent in theatre, dance, opera, music and the visual arts in indoor and outdoor venues all over Melbourne. T9662 4242, www.melbournefestival.com.au **Late Oct**. *Spring Racing Carnival* A horse-racing festival linked to several major races but the highlight is 'the race the nation stops for', the Melbourne Cup (a public holiday in Melbourne) held at Flemington Racecourse. Traditionally celebrated with champagne, fancy frocks, oversized hats and a bet. www.racingvictoria.net.au **First Tue in Nov**. Entry about $30 from Ticketmaster7, T136 122, or at the turnstiles on the day.

Shopping
Melbourne is famous for its wonderful clothes shopping. People fly from all over Australia just to have a shopping weekend in Melbourne (see page 424)

In the city there are 2 major department stores, the classy *David Jones* and mainstream *Myer*, both on the Bourke St Mall. The Mall is at the centre of city shopping but there are also several major indoor malls. *Melbourne Central*, corner of Swanston St and La Trobe St, encloses an old shot-tower in a glass atrium and has over 200 shops, and lockers if the shopping gets too heavy. *Australia on Collins* and *Collins 234*, both on Collins St, Melbourne's main shopping street, are large stylish complexes devoted to fashion, particularly the latter. The city is also known for its arcades, hiding small boutique shops and delicate Victorian architecture. *The Block*, on Collins St, and *The Royal Arcades*, nearby on Little Collins St, are two of the best. Shops are generally open

Mon-Fri 0900-1730 and Sat 1000-1700. Many large shops will also open on Thu and Fri nights until 2100 and Sun 1000-1700. There are also lots of produce, clothing and craft markets, usually at weekends.

Aboriginal art and crafts There are a couple of upmarket shops on Bourke St, such as *Aboriginal Creations*, at No 50, but there are also other options. The *Koori Heritage Trust* (see page 402) is one. Another is the *Aboriginal Handicrafts Shop*, the mezzanine part of the *Uniting Church Shop* at 130 Little Collins St. It may be small, but they have an excellent range of affordable pieces, from bark and paper art to didjeridus, carved wood and woven baskets. All profits go directly back to the originating communities. Open Mon-Fri 1000-1630.

There are some fine Aboriginal art galleries at the eastern end of Flinders La

Books City centre *Foreign Language Bookshop*, 259 Collins St (basement of Centreway Arcade), boasts titles in dozens of languages. *Hill of Content*, 86 Bourke St, is a small classy shop with a discerning collection of general fiction and non-fiction. A couple of doors up, at No 60, is the equally well-stocked *Paperback*. *Readers Feast*, corner of Bourke St and Swanston St, is one of the largest central bookshops. There are also a couple of large branches of *Dymocks*.

Melbourne has several superb independent booksellers offering a diverse range of books

   Suburbs *Black Mask Books*, 78 Toorak Rd, is a small independent, good on interesting contemporary fiction. *Brunswick Street Bookstore*, 305 Brunswick, Fitzroy, is a large independent with a well-chosen range and generous opening hrs, daily 1000-2300. *Hares and Hyenas*, 135 Commercial Rd, South Yarra, is the city's best gay bookshhop. There are two general independent bookshops in St Kilda on Acland St and Fitzroy St, and also *Metropolis*, 160 Acland St, specializing in art, design, film, photography and travel, including guides. *Readings*, 309 Lygon St, Carlton, is one of the largest independents with an excellent range, including music CDs, and knowledgable staff.

   Second-hand *Bookhouse*, 137 Fitzroy St, St Kilda. Loads of contemporary fiction and non-fiction. Open daily. *Booktalk*, 93 Swan St, Richmond, is also a café with good value breakfasts. Open 0830-1730 Mon-Sat, 0900-1600 Sun. *Flinders*, 256 Flinders St, has a good range of paperbacks, classic and contemporary. Open daily. *Grants*, 2 Carlton St, Prahan. Large antiquarian with lots of Australiana and hardback fiction. Open daily. *Grub Street*, 379 Brunswick St, Fitzroy. Great collection, covering a wide range of contemporary issues, non-fiction and fiction. Open daily. *Sybers*, 19 Carlisle St, St Kilda. Huge range of paperback fiction, especially sci-fi. Open Thu-Tue.

Clothes The *Crown* casino complex has some of the city's most exclusive boutiques, such as *Armani* and *Versace*. Equally swanky shopping can be found on Collins St, Toorak Rd and the city end of Chapel St, which is lined with designer label shops and chain stores, becoming steadily cheaper as you head south. In the city centre the eastern end of Collins St has expensive designer boutiques. More funky independent designers populate Little Collins St and Flinders La such as the fascinating and colourful *Christine*, 177 Flinders La, and *Alice Euphemia*, 241 Flinders La, supporting Australasian design talent.

   Factory outlets The western end of Bridge St in Richmond is the place to go for quality seconds and end-of-line goods. Brands available include *Country Road*, *Esprit*, and *Timberland*. Swan St is less label conscious and amongst the many smaller outlets, including *Body Shop*, is the enormous *Dimmey's*, a discount department store.

   Second-hand Brunswick St, Fitzroy, is still a good spot for finding choice 'pre-loved' articles, and it gets positively bargain-basement over in neighbouring Smith St. South of Commercial Rd on Chapel St, Prahan, and on the side-road Greville St, are a couple of dozen small and chic shops, including the wildly exuberant *Shag*, 130 Chapel, which is difficult to leave without having been tempted into buying something that'll turn heads. Open daily 1200-1800. There are a couple of interesting shops on Barkly St, St Kilda, near the junction with Acland St, and on Acland by the junction with Albert St.

Victoria

See also
Markets below

Food and drink City centre *3T*, 532 Elizabeth St. Lovely, calm Taiwanese tea-house, selling over 30 different leaf teas and exquisite ceramic tea-services. Tastings are encouraged. *Charmaine's* at *Southgate*, serves up consistently wonderful ice-creams, made to their own recipes. *Queen Victoria Market*, 513 Elizabeth St is the city's best destination for fresh food shopping. Mouthwatering bread, cheese and deli food, plus fruit, veg, raw seafood and meat. **Carlton** *Australian Cheese Shop*, 655 Nicholson St, North Carlton. Huge variety of Aus cheese and Milawa regional foods. *King and Godfree*, 293 Lygon St, an exceptional deli for Italian bread, pasta, small goods and imported wine, beer and spirits. **Fitzroy** has a sister branch of *Charmaine's* at 370 Brunswick St. **Prahan** *Rocky's Fruit & Veg*, 485 Chapel St. Eclectic grocer's fantastically hung with thousands of chillies, onions and artichokes. There is a 24-hr *Coles* in Chapel St. **St Kilda** *Edelweiss*, 143 Acland St, is a fine delicatessen with bakery and grocery. Open daily. Next door is *Clamms*, serving excellent fish and seafood, fresh or with chips. Also sushi. Open daily 0900-2100. There is also a 24-hr *Coles* in Barkly St.

Jewellery *Gemtec*, 245 Collins St, is one of dozens of Opal specialists in the city centre. They have a very good range of stones, settings and prices and are a 'mine-to-shop' operation. Open daily. *Gazelle*, in Centre Pl, have an interesting range, including some antiques and lots of amber. *Makers Mark Gallery*, 101 Collins St, stocks gorgeous pieces made by Australia's finest jewellers. Naturally it is expensive but if you want to see the best, it's here. *Desire*, 362 Brunswick St, Fitzroy. An extensive range of affordable jewellery from around the world, including some locally made.

See also Publications
and Maps
on page 394

Maps and guides *Information Victoria*, 356 Collins St, T1300 366 356, is a state government information service. The ground floor shop has an extensive range of maps, and books on all Australian states, specializing in Victorian local history titles. Maps and books can also be ordered online at www.information.vic.gov.au *Map Land*, 372 Little Bourke St, T9670 4383, www.mapland.com.au, has an excellent selection of Australian and international maps and guide books. Mail order available.

In 1915 a Royal Commission was held to decide whether Queen Victoria market should expand on top of a cemetery. Following approval the human remains had to be exhumed to find rest elsewhere

Markets *Gleadell St Market*, Richmond. Sat 0700-1300. A cheap, old-fashioned street market where few stallholders speak much English. Fruit, veg, bread, flowers and fish. *Prahan Market,* Commercial Rd. Open dawn-1700 Tue, Sat, dawn-1800 Thu-Fri. Fabulous and fancy fresh-food market. Fruit, veg, meat and deli food. *Queen Victoria Market* corner Elizabeth St and Victoria St. Open Tue, Thu 0600-1400, Fri 0600-1800, Sat 0600-1500, Sun 0900-1600. The market has expanded and evolved since the 1870s, and now consists of a substantial brick building housing the meat and dairy sections and a vast area of open-air sheds, selling fruit and vegetables, clothing and souvenirs. The meat hall has fresh meat, fish and seafood and the dairy hall includes nearly 40 delicatessen stalls selling bread, cheese, sliced meats, pickles, dips and sauces. The sheds can be a good place to find cheap leather goods but generally hold a lot of low-quality, mass-market junk but the food sections are well worth a wander for the friendly banter of the stall holders and extremely tempting sights and smells. There is a food court and there are places in the dairy hall to grab a bite and sit down. Visit the market as part of the *Heritage Tour*, Tue, Thu-Sat 1030, $16.50 including morning tea. There are also entertaining tours focusing on either history or tastes, such as the *Foodies Dream Tour*, Tue, Thu-Sat 1000, $22 including samples along the way. Bookings essential T9320 5835. *St Kilda Market* takes place every Sun along the curve of the Esplanade. The string of stalls offer mostly craft and gifts with a few clothes stalls. *Victorian Arts Centre Market at Southbank has high-quality art and craft stalls, Sun 1000-1800.*

Music City centre *Basement Disks*, Block Arcade. The most comfortable place to buy jazz and blues music, among flowers, couches and lollies. *Discurio*, 105 Elizabeth

St. Knowledgeable staff and a strong back catalogue of world music and jazz. *JB Hi-Fi*, 289 Elizabeth St. City chain with cheap new CDs. **Suburbs** *Melbourne Music Exchange*, 69 Swan St, Richmond. Small, but varied range of second-hand CDs. *Raoul*, 221 Barkly St, St Kilda. Small laid-back store with new and second-hand CDs. *Reload*, 326 Bridge St, Richmond. Good range of second-hand CDs. *Sister Ray*, 260 Brunswick St, Fitzroy. Well-stocked independent with large world, dance and jazz sections.

Outdoor City centre All the major outdoor and adventure shops can be found in and around Hardware La. Retailers on Little Bourke St include *Patagonia*, *Mountain Designs* and *Paddy Pallin*, at No 360, T9670 4845, which also has a range of gear for hire. The area has several travel agents and the *YHA* head office. *Snowgum* and *Trailfinders* can be found on Lonsdale St, opposite Hardware La. **Suburbs** There are a few stores on Smith St, Fitzroy, including *Mitchells* at No 172, which has a good range of gear including army surplus, end of range and seconds at bargain prices. *Pells*, Chapel St, Prahan, T9510 4099. Army surplus and camping gear. Also some for hire.

Gym and classes *Melbourne City Baths*, 420 Swanston St, city centre, T9663 5888. **Sport** **Inline skating** Skates for hire from a couple of St Kilda outlets including *Rock n Skate*, 22 Fitzroy St. $8 first hr, open daily 1000-1800, 2000 in summer. **Spa** The *Aurora*, part of the *Prince of Wales*, 2 Acland St, St Kilda, T9536 1130, is one of the largest and most decadent spa and treatment centres in the country. The *Melbourne City Baths* have much cheaper public facilities. **Swimming** *Melbourne City Baths*, heritage icon and large complex with 30 m heated indoor pool, saunas, and spas. *Hepburn St Kilda Sea Baths*, 16-18 Jacka Bvd, T9593 8182. The 150-year-old complex has been recently renovated and the 25 m heated pool is the only saltwater pool in Melbourne.

Spectator sport Aussie Rules The games of the Australian Football League (AFL) are played at the MCG and the Telstra Dome in winter. The grand final is held at the MCG on the last Sat of Sep. Fixtures listed at www.afl.com.au. tickets from *Ticketmaster7*, T136100. **Cricket** The annual highlight is the Melbourne Boxing Day Test Match (Dec 26). International test matches are played regularly in summer at the MCG, T136122, www.mcg.org.au Tickets from *Ticketmaster7*. **Motor Racing** The first Grand Prix of the F1 season is held at Albert Park in early Mar. Tickets cost about $90 for day entry, $150 for 4-day entry and from $330 for a 4-day reserved grandstand ticket. More details at www.grandprix.com.au Tickets from *Ticketmaster7*. **Horse racing** The Spring Carnival's **Melbourne Cup** is one of the country's major events, held on the first Tue in Nov at Flemington Racecourse. Grandstand tickets aren't cheap but ground entry is more reasonable (from $40). Tickets from *Ticketmaster7*. For more information T1800 352 229, www.racingvictoria.net.au **Tennis** The Australian Open, one of the 4 'grand slams', is held in Jan at the Rod Laver Arena of Melbourne Park, for more details see www.ausopen.org Tickets from *Ticketek*, T132 849.

There are dozens of ways to be shown around Melbourne, the *Melbourne Explorer*, **Tours around** T9650 7000, being one of the more conventional. This jump-on, jump-off London bus **Melbourne** drives around 2 ½-hr circuits designed to take in a good many of the city's major attractions, with about 30 stops along the way. The bus can be boarded at any point and stops include the Town Hall, the Aquarium, Flinders St Station, St Patrick's Cathedral, Melbourne Museum, Melbourne Zoo, and Bourke St Mall (Swanston St end). The Southbank and Parliament ('downtown') circuit leaves the Town Hall on the hr 1000-1200 and 1400. The longer Museum, Zoo and Swanston St ('uptown') circuit leaves the Town Hall on the ½ hr 0930-1430. Operates daily except major event days and public holidays (1 day $30, children $15, concessions $25; 2 days $50, children $25, concessions $45).

There are, however, a range of less conventional tours: **Air** *Melbourne Seaplanes*, Williamstown's Gem Pier, T9547 4454, www.seaplane.com.au, specialize in 3 main flights: a short 20-min loop around the city from $65; a 40-min loop around Brighton and

Victoria

the Dandenongs for $130; and an hour-long flight right around Port Phillip Bay for $165 which, at an extra cost, can be broken by a stop in Sorrento for lunch. Min 2 people. **Balloon** Strange as it may seem it is possible to balloon more or less right over the Melbourne skyline. Contact the very experienced *Balloon Sunrise*, T9427 7596, www.ballonsunrise.com.au ($245-325). Departures from Richmond. **Penguins** *Penguin Waters*, T9645 0533, www.penguinwaters.com.au, have sunset Fairy Penguin-watching tours departing from Southgate (berth 7, 2 hrs, $45) and St Kilda Pier (1 hr, $35). BBQ and refreshments included. **Sailing ships** 2 3-masted ships sail from Gem pier most weekends and some public holidays. They both also venture out on sunset trips in peak summer, and some longer cruises throughout the year. The older *Alma Doepel*, T9646 5211 or 018 364307, is a schooner and sail training ship which does a regular 2-hr cruise for $25, while the *Enterprise*, T9397 3477, is a modern replica of John Fawkner's vessel that keeps trips down to an hr for a little less. **Shopping** If you fancy being whisked around in a big pink bus to various shops, then *Shopping Spree Tours*, T9596 6600, www.shoppingspree.com.au, are for you (Mon-Sat, pick-ups from 0830. $60, lunch and a trip up to the Melbourne Rialto Tower included.

Bicycle A great way to see some of the sights and parks of the city and inner suburbs is to cycle around them. *City Cycle Tours*, T9585 5343, www.quantum.net.au/cct, provide the bike, refreshments and a guide for a variety of tours. Price around $10 per hr. Departure from the Treasury Gardens. **Walking** For details of Melbourne's excellent free guided walks courtesy of the *Greeter Service*, see page 397. The VIC has free brochures and maps for a variety of self-guided walks such as art walks along Swanston St and the Yarra River and heritage walks. The Golden Mile walk is a 4-km route through the city past the most significant architectural and historical features. It can be done as a self-guided walk ($4) or guided ($20, 2 hrs) on Wed, Fri, Sat at 1030 and 1330. Bookings essential, T1300 130 152. Contact *Creatours*, T9822 0556, for an interesting range of guided cultural walks that visit the studios and galleries of artists and designers. *Talkabout Tours*, T9815 1228, www.chocoholictours.com.au, offer a variety of city centre walking tours, many unashamedly focusing on an indulgent mix of chocolate, coffee and cake (generally 2 hrs, $24, goodies included).

Tours further afield

See other regional centres for more details

Two operators are particularly recommended for their smaller coach sizes and upbeat service and excursions. *Autopia Tours*, T1800 000507, www.autopiatours.com.au, have day-trips to **Phillip Island** ($60, daily), **Great Ocean Road** ($54, daily), and the **Grampians** ($50 return, $30 one-way, Sun, Tue and Fri). *Wild-Life Tours*, T9534 8868, www.wildlifetours.com.au, have similar options, though their Great Ocean Rd trip is shorter and only $41, plus a trip to **Ballarat** (also $41), and another to the **Dandenongs** ($66). Both companies offer a 3-day tour of the Great Ocean Rd plus the Grampians for $135-140, and have backpacker bus routes to **Adelaide** and **Sydney**. Larger coach companies (with larger coaches and slightly larger fares) such as *APT*, T1300 655965, www.aptours.com.au, *AAT Kings*, T1800 334009, www.aatkings.com.au, and *Gray Line*, T1300 858687, www.grayline.com, offer a wider range of day tours as far as **Ballarat**, **Echuca**, **Mt Buller** and the **Yarra Valley**.

Transport **Air** *Kendell*, T131300, www.kendell.com.au, have daily flights to Mildura King Island and the northern Tasmanian airports, also a Sun-Fri service to Mt Gambier. *Qantas* are the principal supplier of interstate flights with direct daily services to all state capitals plus Alice Springs, Tasmania and, from Thu-Sun, Cairns. *Virgin Blue* fly to all capitals except Darwin and Hobart, though they do fly daily to Cairns and Launceston.

Bus *Firefly* have good value daily buses to **Adelaide** (11 hrs, $45) and **Sydney** (11 hrs, $50). *McCafferty/Greyhound's* services include **Alice Springs**, **Melbourne**, **Perth**, and **Sydney**. *V~Line* have a daily bus/train service to **Adelaide**, and another to **Canberra**. Services from Spencer St Station. *V~Line* also operate most state services to

Victorian country towns from Spencer St Station, with a few Gippsland services from Flinders St Station. **Backpacker buses** *Groovy Grape*, T1800 661177, www.groovygrape.com.au, run trips to **Adelaide** (3 days, $425) and on to **Alice Springs**. *Wayward* run similar routes. *Autopia*, T1800 000507, www.autopiatours.com.au, have non inclusive trips to **Adelaide** (3 days, $150) and **Sydney** (3½ days, $170), as do *Wild-Life Tours*, T9534 8868, www.wildlifetours.com.au (Adelaide: 2-4 days, $129-199; Sydney: 2½-3½ days, $150-190).

Ferry *Bay City* ferries, T9506 4144, leave from Bay 7, **Southbank** (by St Kilda Rd) and 10 mins later from the Casino for **Williamstown** every ½ hr, daily from 1030-1700 (not 1400 or 1600 Mon-Sat). Connections to **St Kilda** hourly from 1100-1700, Sat-Sun only. **Interstate ferry** *TT-Line*, T132010, www.tt-line.com.au, operate overnight ferries from **Port Melbourne** to **Devonport** (13 hrs, prices vary) on Mon, Wed and Fri.

Train The overnight *Overland* heads to **Adelaide** (10 hrs, from $57) on Sun-Mon, Thu-Fri. The *Ghan* leaves for **Alice Springs** (2 nights, from $292) every Wed. The *XPT* is operated twice daily (one overnight) by NSW's *Countrylink* to **Sydney** (11 hrs, from $55 to $231 for a sleeper). Adult fares get considerably cheaper if booked in advance. Services from Spencer St Station.

Airline offices *Air New Zealand*, 200 Queen St, T9602 5900. *Garuda Indonesia*, Lvl 1, 30 Collins St, T9654 2522. *Japan Airlines*, Lvl 6, 250 Collins St, T9654 2733. *Kendell Airlines*, Lvl 4, 118 Queen St, T9642 8636. *KLM-Alitalia*, Lvl 5, 80 Collins St, T1300 303 747. *Korean Air*, 310 King St, T9920 3853. *Malaysia Airlines*, 80 Collins St, T9279 9997. *Qantas*, 233 Collins St, T9285 3000. *Singapore Airlines*, 416 Collins St, T9254 0370. *Swissair*, 343 Little Collins St, T9670 2191. *Thai Airways*, 250 Collins St, T1300 651 690. *United Airlines*, 30 Collins St, T9654 4488. *Virgin Atlantic*, 310 King St, T9920 3887.

Directory

Victoria

Banks and exchange ATMs are on all the major shopping and eating streets. *American Express*, 233 Collins St. Open Mon-Fri 0900-1700, Sat 0900-1200. *Thomas Cook*, 257 Collins St. Open 0900-1700 Mon-Fri, 1000-1400 Sat. Also 261 Bourke St, near Swanston St. Open Mon-Sat 0900-1700, Sun 1100-1500. *Travelex*, 231 Collins St. Open 0800-1830 Mon-Fri, 0800-1730 Sat, 1000-1630 Sun. **Bike hire** Around $10 for 2 hrs, $20 per day. *Borsari Cycles*, 193 Lygon St, Carlton, T9347 4100. *Freedom Machine*, 401 Chapel St, Prahan, T9827 5014. *Hire A Bicycle*, Southbank by Princes Bridge, T04 1261 6633. *St Kilda Cycles*, 11 Carlisle St, T9534 3074.

Car hire A cheap option is *Rent-a-Bomb*, T131553, www.rentabomb.com.au, who hire out cars for $85 per week for use within 50 km of the city centre. **Car parking** Beware of metered parking in the city centre, it extends as late as 2400. **Car servicing** *Brunton Motors*, corner Rathdowne St and Palmerston St, Carlton, T9347 5105. *J&S Motors*, corner of Highett St and Church St, Richmond, T9428 7597. **Chemist** *Hunter Naughton*, 470 Collins St, T9629 1147. Daily 0700-1900. *Sally Lew*, 41 Fitzroy St, St Kilda, T9534 8085. Open daily 0900-2100. Cheap film processing. **Communications** Internet at *Global Gossip*, 440 Elizabeth St, city centre. $2.50 for 20 mins, $3.95 an hr. Open daily 0900-2400. *Net City*, 65 Fitzroy St, St Kilda. $2.20 for 20 mins. Open daily 0930-2300. **Main Post Office**, Elizabeth St, open Mon-Fri 0815-1730, Sat 0900-1600. *Poste Restante* (take photo ID to collect mail) Mon-Fri 0900-1730, Sat 0900-1200.

Hairdressing Try *Pivot Point*, the public salon of the Hair Design College, 382 Lonsdale St, T9670 1011. Good cuts at a fraction of the usual cost. *Dimmey's*, Swan St, Richmond, has a discount barbers at the back.

Laundry *My Beautiful Laundrette*, 153 Brunswick St, Fitzroy. Lots of couches, internet access, and it's cheap. **Library** *State Library*, 328 Swanston St, T8664 7000, www.slv.vic.gov.au Also holds recent international newspapers. Open 1000-2100 Mon-Thu, 1000-1800 Fri-Sun. **Luggage store** Downstairs at Spencer St Station.

Medical services *Travellers Medical and Vaccination Centre*, Level 3, 393 Little Bourke St, T9602 5788. *City Health Care*, 255 Bourke St, T9650 1711. Open 0900-1800

Mon-Fri, 1000-1700 Sat. *Acland St Medical Centre*, 171 Acland St, St Kilda, T9534 0635. Open 0900-1900 Mon-Thu, 0900-1800 Fri, 0900-1200 Sat. The latter 2 clinics are visitor-friendly and bulk bill. **Medicare** Centre Point Mall, corner of Bourke St and Swanston St. Open 0900-1645 Mon-Fri. **Hospital** *Royal Melbourne*, Grattan St, Parkville, T9342 7000. *St Vincent's*, 41 Victoria Pde, Fitzroy, T9288 2211.

Radio *5UV*, 101.5 FM. Community radio operated by Adelaide Uni. *Fresh*, 92.7 FM. Dance grooves. *5MBS*, 101.5. Classical and jazz. *MMM*, 98.3 and 104.7 FM, mainstream and retro hits. *JJJ*, 95.9 and 105.5 FM. National youth network, alternative music.

Useful numbers Police 637 Flinders St, T9247 5347. **Taxi** *Arrow*, T132211, *Black Cabs*, T132227, *Silver Top*, T131008.

Work Try *Pinnacle*, T9620 9666, or *Geoffrey Nathan Consulting*, T9614 8588.

Around Melbourne

There is great variety of scenery and many activities around Melbourne so even if you are short of time you can still see something of the state's attractions within a day. The **Yarra Valley** *is a beautiful wine region with some of the most sophisticated cellar doors and accompanying restaurants in Australia. Nearby,* **Healesville** *has a wonderful wildlife sanctuary and just beyond there is a very scenic winding drive through forest and ferns on the way to Marysville. Heading south, the* **Dandenongs** *is a fine area in which to walk or drive through towering Mountain Ash forests, and if you're lucky you might just see an elusive lyrebird. The* **Mornington Peninsula**, *often just called 'the bay', has some great beaches as well as diving or swimming-with-dolphin trips, and the penguins of* **Phillip Island** *are among the region's most popular attractions.*

Mornington Peninsula

This is Melbourne's beach playground, where you can swim with dolphins, dive and sail, or take a trip to **French** and **Phillip Islands**. The peninsula's popularity and its proximity to Melbourne has resulted in ugly suburban sprawl creeping down as far as Rye and the west coast becomes overrun in summer with bodies seeking a swim. The best bits are at the bottom of the peninsula; the wine region of Red Hill, the south coast protected by the Mornington Peninsula National park and the beaches and cafés of Sorrento and Portsea near the tip. The main **VIC** for the whole peninsula is at Dromana, at the base of Arthur's Seat. ■ *Daily 0900-1700. Point Nepean Rd, T5987 3078, www.melbournesbays.org*

Ins & outs **Bus** From Frankston the *Portsea Passenger Bus Service*, T5986 5666, operates services down the Port Phillip Bay coast, with stops including **Dromana**, **Rosebud**, **Rye**, **Blairgowrie**, **Sorrento** (stop 18, corner of Melbourne Rd and Ocean Beach Rd) and **Portsea** (stop 1, National Park entrance). Full-run 1½ hrs. Mon-Fri services every 1-2 hrs, 0700-1900 (plus 2040 Fri); every 2 hrs Sat from 1000-2000; and 1045 and every 2 hrs from 1315-1915 Sun. Last buses back from Portsea at 1915 Mon-Fri, 1800 Sat and 1735 Sun. **Backpacker bus** *Van Go*, T5984 4323, sorrento@yhavic.org.au, operate an ad-hoc service from Melbourne to the *YHA* in Sorrento, taking a day to see the most interesting bits of the peninsula along the way. Ferry connections at Stony Point are also possible. **Ferry** Vehicle and passenger ferries operate between **Sorrento**, **Portsea** and **Queenscliff** on the Bellarine Peninsula. **Train** There are daily metropolitan services from **Melbourne** City Circle stations to **Frankston**, leaving every 15-20 mins from before 0800 to after midnight (1 hr, $6, concessions $3.05).

Just east of Dromana, 65 km from Melbourne, is **Arthur's Seat**, a 300-m-high hill in Arthur's Seat State Park with striking views over Port Phillip Bay. At the top there are some pleasant, easy walks in the state park, as well as the Seawinds botanic gardens and a maze. The scenic chairlift is a great way to ascend from the highway, even if you have your own transport. ■ *Daily 1100-1700. $8.50, children $6.* The region grows cool-climate chardonnays, pinot gris and pinot noir and has about 40 cellar doors, many with good views or restaurants. Most cellar doors charge a $2 tasting fee, refundable if wine is purchased. A detailed wine touring map is available from the VIC, as is a gallery touring map, illustrating the locations of many excellent galleries in the wine region.

Around Dromana & Red Hill

Near the tip of Mornington's curving arm is **Sorrento**, its shore lined with jetties, boats and brightly coloured bathing boxes. The town has been popular for seaside holidays since the 1880s and consequently has many fine old limestone buildings along the main street, Ocean Beach Road. A few kilometres further on is **Portsea**, a small suburb frequented by wealthy Melbournians and boasting the stunning Portsea Back Beach. Point Nepean is the long, thin tip of the Mornington peninsula, where it's possible to explore the gun emplacements, tunnels and bunkers of **Fort Nepean**. From the Visitor Centre there is a short drive to Gunners car park; from here you can walk to the Fort (3½ km one-way), with magnificent views over Bass Strait and the Bay, or you can take the visitors' bus. ■ *Daily 0900-1700. $8.50, children $4.50 (includes bus transport). Visitor numbers are limited by the site so booking is essential; T5984 4276.*

Sorrento & Portsea
*Colour map 2, grid C3
Sorrento is 85 km from Melbourne, 4 km from Portsea*

Both Sorrento and Portsea are full of stylish cafés, pubs and shops

Sleeping **A-B** *Hotel Sorrento*, 5 Hotham Rd, T5984 2206, www.hotelsorrento.com.au Modern rooms in an old limestone pub, some with superb bay views. This stylish pub also has excellent cheap meals and an enclosed sun terrace ideal for a beer at sunset. Live music Sat nights. Meals daily 1200-1400, 1800-2030. **A** *Eastcliff Cottage*, 881 Melbourne Rd, T5984 0668, www.babs.com.au/eastcliff 4 private traditional suites in an 1870s limestone house, each has en suite, fireplace and sitting room. **B** *Portsea Hotel*, Point Nepean Rd, T5984 2213, www.portseahotel.com.au An enormous and sophisticated pub overlooking the bay with comfortable rooms. Also expensive and mid-range contemporary meals. A perfect spot for a drink on a sunny day but very busy in summer. **C** *Oceanic Whitehall*, 231 Ocean Beach Rd, T5984 4166, F5984 3369. A grand old limestone guesthouse, traditional rooms with shared facilities, also some motel rooms with en suite. **D** *Sorrento YHA*, 3 Miranda St, T5984 4323, sorrento@yhavic.org.au Small, clean and very friendly hostel, owners will help with arranging work (Apr-Jul) in nearby wineries, and with tours and transport. There is also a good hostel at nearby Blairgowrie run by dive operators, **D-E** *Bayplay* (see tours below), with 2-6 bed dorms, pool and café.

Eating The *Continental* is more funky than the *Sorrento* with meals, including breakfast, served in a large room hung with modern art, a nightclub operates upstairs on Sat. *Skinners* is a low-key locals, spot for good coffee, and *Just Fine Food* a gourmet deli and café with busy pavement tables. For sea views there are 2 fine options, *The Baths*, T5984 1500, is on Sorrento foreshore overlooking a long skinny jetty, expensive classy dining daily 0800-2100. *Coppins*, T5984 5551, sits above Sorrento Back Beach and is a wonderful place for a casual lunch or tea and scones on a sunny afternoon. Daily 1000-1630.

There are many cafés and restaurants along Ocean Beach Rd although the 2 pubs offer the best meals and value for money

Victoria

Tours and activities Bottlenose dolphins live in Port Phillip Bay and swimming with them is becoming increasingly popular. Several operators run twice-daily swim cruises from Oct to Apr. *Polperro*, T5988 8437, www.polperro.com.au, take care to protect the dolphins and take small groups. Departing from Sorrento Pier 0830, 1330, $75 ($40 observers), bookings essential. There are many other activities on the water. the diving is superb with many shipwrecks and j-class submarines to explore as well as sheer-wall and fast-drift dives. The Bay also has leafy sea dragons and stingrays. Contact *Dive Victoria*, 3752 Point Nepean Rd, Portsea, T5984 3155 or *Bayplay Lodge*, 46 Canterbury Jetty Rd, Blairgowrie, T5988 0188, www.bayplay.com.au Surfing lessons are available from *Sorrento Surf School*, T5988 6143, ($30, 2 hrs) and day and overnight sailing trips with *Ocean Yachtmaster*, T5983 9988, www.oceanyachtmaster.com.au

Transport Bus Last buses from Portsea to the connecting train at **Frankston** are at 1915 Mon-Fri, 1800 Sat and 1735 Sun. **Ferry** Two ferries operate from Sorrento over to **Queenscliff** on the Bellarine Peninsula. The passenger-only ferry, T5984 1602, also stops at **Portsea**, daily Boxing Day to Easter. Ferries from 1030-1700 (50 mins, $7, children $5, concession $6). The larger, vehicle ferry, T5258 3244, www.searoad.com.au, crosses daily, year-round, on the hour 0700-1800. Same pedestrian prices, cars under 5½ m $38 plus passengers.

Mornington Peninsula National Park

Colour map 2, grid C3

Gunnamatta Trail Rides, T5988 6755, www.gunnamatta.com.au, offer both short and overnight horse rides through Greens Bush as well as winery rides and beach gallops

This long, straight strip of national park stretches from Portsea down to Cape Schank, protecting the last bit of coastal tea-tree on the peninsula and the spectacular sea cliffs from the golden limestone at Portsea to the brooding black basalt around **Cape Schank**. There are picnic areas and a lighthouse at the cape and some good walks. There are also regular tours of the lightstation and the lighthouse keepers' cottages have been renovated for holiday letting (**C**), which can be booked by the room or as a whole. ■ *Tours daily 1000-1700. $8, children $6, T5988 6184, lamp@AustPacInns.com.au* There is a short walk with excellent views from the Cape Schank car park out to the end of the cape. For a longer walk, **Bushrangers Bay Track** is a great coastal walk along the cliffs to Bushranger Bay, ending at Main Creek (45 minutes one-way).

French Island

Colour map 2, grid C3

Population: 50

French Island sits in Western Point Bay like an undersized plug. Much of this low island has been designated a national park, largely because of the diverse vegetation, running from mangroves and saltmarsh to heaths and open woodland. Koalas were introduced in 1923 and are thriving, as are the long-nosed potaroos. Bird life is also prolific, with 230 recorded species. Considering its proximity to Melbourne the island is usually surprisingly quiet. **Tankerton** is the main small settlement with a general store and post office, and there is a park camping area at nearby Fairhaven. There is a friendly guesthouse and café in Tankerton, the **B** *Tortoise Head*, T5980 1234, tortoise@pen.hotkey.net.au Budget accommodation at *Mcleod Eco Farm*, T5678 0155. WOOFAs welcome. Tours are available with *French Island Eco Tours*, T5980 1210, www.frenchisland ecotours.com.au Otherwise a bicycle is essential for exploring properly, and they can be hired for $10 a day from the kiosk at the end of the main Tankerton jetty. Ask at the general store for weekday hire. For more information contact the **Parks Office**, T5980 1294.

■ Inter Island Ferries, *T9585 5730, www.interislandferries.com.au, operate daily passenger services from Stony Point to French Island and on to Cowes on Phillip Island (both $8.50, 10-30 mins). They also run Seal Rock and Penguin Parade excursions. There are daily train services from Melbourne City Circle stations to Frankston, with connections from there to Stony Point (full trip 2 hrs, $6,* *concessions $3.05). Connecting services every few hours from 0542-2015 Mon-Fri, 0800-1800 Sat and 0757-1800 Sun.* Bay Connections, *T5678 5642 run tours to French Island and Phillip Island as well as dolphin and seal tours from Stony Point twice a week. Van Go, T5984 4323, sorrento@yhavic.org.au run regular tours around the peninsula from Melbourne to the Sorrento YHA, and sometimes drop-off or pick-up from Stony Point.*

Phillip Island

Phillip Island is one of Victoria's biggest attractions, with 3½ million visitors a year. Connected to the mainland by a bridge, the island is 26-km long and 9-km wide. It certainly has its natural attractions, such as the rocky coves and headlands in the south and sunny north-facing **beaches** around Cowes, but the island has long since been tamed. Some **wildlife** continues to thrive, however, and this has been the lynchpin of the island's tourism success, particularly the rather overrated **Penguin Parade**. Other visitors come for the superb **surfing** breaks along the dangerous south coast, and the safe swimming beaches on the sandy northern shores. There are some pleasant **walking** tracks throughout the island, particularly on Cape Woolamai. Newhaven, by the bridge, and Cowes are the main towns, while Rhyll has a quiet charm away from the crowds. San Remo is the 'gateway' town, a disappointing place, though accommodation is a shade cheaper than on the island itself. The **VIC** is 1 km past the bridge on Phillip Island Tourist Road, and has a great range of local information. ■ *Daily 0900-1700, T5956 7447.*

In October the island hosts the **Australian Motorcycle Grand Prix**. The event lasts for three days, see www.grandprix.com.au Tickets from *Ticketmaster7*, T136100 (three-day general entry $100, race day-entry only $60). The circuit **Visitor Centre**, with motorsport memorabilia, is open all year. ■ *Daily 1000-1700. $11, children $5.50. T5952 9400, Back Beach Rd.*

Colour map 2, grid C3
Population: 5,500
www.phillip
Island.com.au
Cowes 145 km from
Melbourne, 160 km
from Wilson's
Promontory

Train/bus *V~Line* services leave from Spencer St, **Melbourne** at 1550 Mon-Fri, 1810 Fri, 0940, 1740 Sat and 0906, 1720 Sun. **Train/ferry** There are services from **Melbourne** City Circle stations to **Frankston**, and from there to **Stony Point** (full trip 2 hrs, $6, concessions $3.05). Connecting services roughly every 2 hrs from 0542-2015 Mon-Fri, 0800-1800 Sat, and 0757-1800 Sun. *Inter Island Ferries*, T9585 5730, www.interislandferries.com.au, have daily passenger services from **Stony Point** to **Cowes** ($7.50, 30 mins). They also run Seal Rock and Penguin Parade excursions. **Tours from Melbourne** Afternoon or evening tours are offered by all the major operators. One of the best, and best value is run by *Autopia*, T1800 000507 or 9326 5536, www.autopiatours.com.au.

Ins & outs

At the far end of the island are the **Nobbies**, a series of rocky islands joined to the coast at low tide, and beyond them **Seal Rocks**, home to Australia's largest fur seal colony. A series of boardwalks weave their way down past the now defunct Seal Rocks visitor centre through penguin habitats to the rock shelf below. The seals can only be seen with powerful binoculars, but fairy penguins and gulls can often be seen sheltering under the boardwalks. The road out there is closed at dusk, when the **Penguin Parade** gets into gear. Fairy penguins burrow in their thousands in the dunes along this stretch of coast, coming ashore in the darkness after a hard day at sea. Huge grandstands and powerful lights have been erected to allow thousands of visitors to view the tired birds struggle out of the water and up the beach. Far better to dig deep and join the excellent dawn guided walk when the penguins are

Phillip Island Nature Park
Most of the wildlife attractions are managed by Phillip Island Nature Park, T1300-366422, www.penguins.org.au and saver tickets (the Nature Park Pass) can be bought at the VIC

Victoria

Around Melbourne

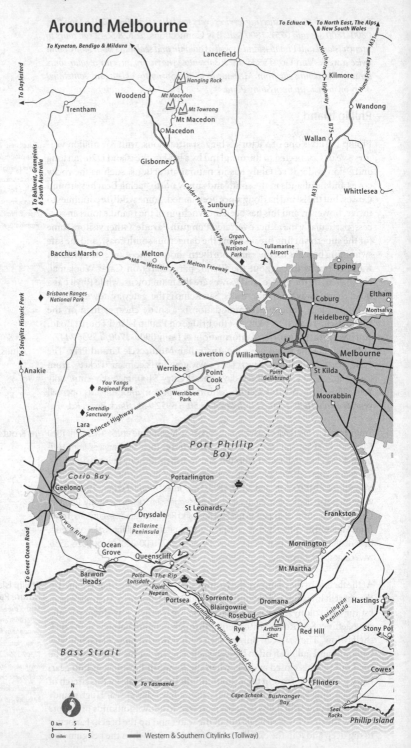

To Kyneton, Bendigo & Mildura

To Echuca   To North East, The Alps & New South Wales

To Daylesford

Lancefield

Kilmore

Hanging Rock

Mt Macedon

Woodend

Mt Towrong

Mt Macedon

Macedon

Wandong

Wallan

Trentham

Gisborne

Whittlesea

To Ballarat, Grampians & South Australia

Calder Freeway

Sunbury

Organ Pipes National Park

Tullamarine Airport

Bacchus Marsh

Melton

Melton Freeway

Epping

Western Freeway

Eltham

Brisbane Ranges National Park

Coburg

Montsalva

Heidelberg

To Steiglitz Historic Park

Melbourne

Laverton

Williamstown

Anakie

St Kilda

Werribee

Point Cook

Point Gellibrand

You Yangs Regional Park

Werribee Park

Moorabbin

Serendip Sanctuary

Princes Highway

Lara

Port Phillip Bay

Corio Bay

Portarlington

Geelong

St Leonards

Frankston

To Great Ocean Road

Drysdale

Bellarine Peninsula

Barwon River

Mornington

Ocean Grove

Queenscliff

Mt Martha

Barwon Heads

Point Lonsdale

The Rip

Point Nepean

Portsea

Sorrento

Dromana

Hastings

Blairgowrie

Rosebud

Mornington Peninsula National Park

Rye

Arthurs Seat

Red Hill

Stony Poi

Bass Strait

Mornington Peninsula

Cowes

To Tasmania

Cape Schank

Bushranger Bay

Flinders

Seal Rocks

Phillip Island

N

0 km   5

0 miles   5

Western & Southern Citylinks (Tollway)

heading out for the day. Restricted to 30 people, and no under-12s, so book ahead. Includes a buffet brekky. ■ *Visitor centre open daily from 1000, parade from dusk. $14, children $7, concessions $9.20. Dawn walks $47, concessions and children over 12 $35*. Koalas are best seen at the **Koala Conservation Centre** via an excellent series of elevated boardwalks through stands of gum trees. ■ *Daily 1000-1700. $5.60, children $2.60, concessions $3.60. Phillip Island Rd*. The Nature Park also comprises **Swan Lake**, the island's only freshwater lake near Penguin Parade, **Cape Woolamai**, with its popular and pleasant walking tracks, and **Rhyll Inlet**, a wetland habitat favoured by migratory wading birds. Swan Lake and Rhyll both have boardwalks and bird hides.

Tours & activities

The only way to get close to the **seals** is to take one of a range of excellent **boat trips** with *Bay Connections*, T5678 5642, www.bayconnections.com.au, who operate out of Cowes ($45, two hours). They also run cruises out to French Island (see page 428), Wilson's Promontory (see page 460), and **whale watching** in Winter. *Duck Truck*, T5952 2548, amaroo@waterfront.net.au, offer a variety of very good value tours from Cowes or Melbourne, around the island and out to Wilson's Promontory (whole day, $55). Their three-night package from Melbourne to the island includes some meals, transfers, some entry fees and accommodation for $120. Would-be **surfers** can take a lesson with *Out There*, T5956 6450, or *Island*, T5952 3443, who also have three shops around the island. They also hire out equipment and wetsuits. There are a wide range of **guided walks** conducted by *Surefoot Explorations*, T5952 1533, www.surefoot.com.au, who will provide transport, packed lunches and some equipment.

Victoria

Sleeping

Most of the accommodation for casual visitors is in Cowes, though there are a few options elsewhere the island. Most gets booked out for long weekends and school holidays

There are several good hosted B&Bs in **Cowes**, amongst them the outstanding **A** *Holmwood*, 37 Chapel St, Cowes, T5952 3082, www.holmwoodguesthouse.com.au 3 en suite rooms of great character, garden verandas, cosy guest lounge and 2 self-contained open-plan cottages, complemented by very friendly and knowledgable hosts. Superb licensed evening dining for residents, $50 a head. Recommended. **B** *Otira*, Ventnor Beach Rd, T5956 8294, www.otira.com.au Very comfortable rooms in traditional inland farmhouse, including an excellent family suite. Also 2 large self-contained cottages, sleeping 4 and 7. Farm 'participation' encouraged. Recommended. There are heaps of motels and apartments, mostly pretty pricey. **C** *Glen Isla*, 234 Church St, T/F5952 2822, has basic but comfortable self-contained units, 2 km from central Cowes. Other budget options are limited to the dozen or so caravan parks, including **C-D** *Beach Park*, McKenzie Rd, T5952 2113, with a wide range of sites, cabins and units, and 2 very good and friendly backpacker hostels, of which: **D-E** *Amaroo Park*, 97 Church St, T5952 2548, phillipisland@yhavic.org.au, is by far the larger, with more facilities, very cheap breakfasts and dinners (available to non-residents), a bar and pool. They also operate the *Duck Truck* and offer free transportation from Melbourne. **E** *Jock's Place*, 33 Chapel St, T5952 1655, jocksplace@waterfront.net.au, is a much smaller, cosier and quieter place to stay. **In Rhyll**, **D** *Corrigan's*, Beach Rd, T5956 9263, have 2 self-contained units with sunrise views over the bay.

Eating

Rhyll 8 km from Cowes

In Cowes *Carmichaels*, 2nd floor, the Esplanade, T5952 1300. The quality of the expensive Modern Australian cuisine can vary but the outdoor terrace facing the sea is Cowes' most atmospheric place to dine, particularly for breakfast, Sat-Sun only from 0700, Mon-Sun 1100-2100. *Jetty*, on the Esplanade also faces the water and is a large, lively and cheap place, particularly good for seafood. Attracts busloads of tour groups in summer. *Terrazo* on Thompson St, T5952 3773, is a good cheap place for Italian. Wed-Sun 1700-2030. The best café is the classy modern *Madcowes*, the Esplanade, T5952 2560, although *Euphoria* on Thompson St is also a nice casual place for lunch. Try the tiny *Island Food Store* for high-quality cake and coffee or a salad, set back from Chapel St past the supermarket. **In Rhyll**, facing the sea, is the locals' favourite spot for fish and chips, *Foreshore Bar Café*, 11 Beach Rd, T5956 9520. It also has a funky bar serving platters and nibbles. Thu-Mon 1000-2000.

Transport

Bus *V~Line* buses leave from the Esplanade, opposite the pier, Cowes, for **San Remo**, **Anderson** and **Melbourne** (3 hrs 20 mins) at 0600, 0850 Mon-Fri, 0740 and (in summer only) 1615 Sat, 1740 (summer only) and 1540 Sun. From Anderson there are several connecting buses daily Mon-Fri through **Kilcunda**, and **Wonthaggi** to **Inverloch**, also at 1210 and 2050 on Sat, and 2030 on Sun. **Ferry** *Inter Island Ferries*, T9585 5730, www.interislandferries.com.au, have daily passenger services from Cowes to **French Island** and **Stony Point** on the Mornington Peninsula (all $7.50, 10-30 mins), where there are connecting services to **Melbourne**. They also run **Seal Rock** cruises ($25, 3 hrs).

Directory

Banks Most major banks have ATMs on Thompson St, Cowes. **Bike hire** Backpacker hostels or *Ride On*, Boys Home Rd, Newhaven, T5956 7740. **Communications** **Internet** Library on Thompson Av, T5952 2842, or *Waterfront Computers*, 130 Thompson St (next to Mobil), T5952 3312. Open Mon-Fri 0900-1700, Sat 1000-1300. **Post Office**, Thompson St.

The Dandenong Ranges

Also referred to as the 'Dandenongs' or simply 'the mountain', these ranges comprise a hilly forested massif just to the east of Melbourne. Several loosely connected chunks have been designated the **Dandenong Ranges National Park** and are criss-crossed with some wonderful **walking tracks**. Great views can be had from several points, the best over Melbourne being from the summit of Mount Dandenong itself ($2.20 per car, entry before 1600). At the base of the mountain are the service towns of Fern Tree Gully and Belgrave. At the latter is the station for Puffing Billy, the popular picturesque steam train that has services winding through scenic hilly country east to Gembrook, 24 km away. ■ *Daily from 1030. Fares from $22, children $6. T1900 937069, www.puffing billy.com.au* On the mountain itself **Sassafras** is the largest and most popular town, with a good range of facilities. The main **VIC** for the Dandenongs is at Upper Fern Tree Gully. They sell the Parks Victoria walking map for $2. ■ *Daily 0900-1700. T9758 7522, www.yarrarangestourism.com, Burwood Highway.*

There are hundreds of interconnecting **walking** trails, and it is possible to organize circular walks from 10 minutes to three days in length, though longer walks may require short stretches on vehicular roads, and there is no camping on the mountain. Grants Picnic Grounds, just south of Kallista, is the start of several good loop tracks which pass through spectacular Mountain Ash forests and fern gullies. Lyrebirds live in these forests but are shy and difficult to spot. For an excellent circular walk through their territory, park at Cook's Corner and head down the Lyrebird Walk (7 km, two hours).

There are lots of gardens and arboretums, most run by Parks Victoria. For many the highlight of these are the **Alfred Nicholas Gardens**. ■ *Daily 1000-1630. $5.60, children $2.20, concessions $4.50.* A short way down unsealed Woolrich Road is the Woolrich Lookout picnic ground, the main entrance to the free **R J Hamer Forest Arboretum**. The planting is very young but this is the best picnic spot on the mountain. Close by on the main road is **Cloudehill**, a private nursery with a wonderful area of formal gardens. At the bottom of the main gardens is the gateway to the wild **Kejomah Gardens**, a series of paths carved through an old nursery, now spectacularly wild. ■ *Daily 1000-1700. Closed Tue-Wed, Jun-Aug. $5.* Around the corner are the **National Rhododendron Gardens**. ■ *Daily 1000-1700. $7.30, children $2.20, concessions $5.* Back on the main tourist road, to the south of Kalorama, is the **William Ricketts Sanctuary**, a small area of forest displaying the powerful spiritual sculptures of William Ricketts. ■ *Daily 1000-1630. $5.60, children $2.20, concessions $5.*

Oozing character is **L** *Glen Harrow*, Old Monbulk Rd, Belgrave, T9754 3232, www.glenharrow.com.au 4 exquisite old gardeners' cottages, set in 20 acres of wild, bushy gardens. Completely self-contained, furnished mostly with antiques. Recommended. Just past Mount Dandenong is possibly the best hosted B&B on the mountain, **L-A** *Attic House*, 1438 Mount Dandenong Tourist Rd, T9751 1397, www.attic house.com.au 3 very comfortable rooms in a large modern house complement exceptional hospitality. The breakfast is perfect, though cooked at weekends only. Recommended. Most places have cheaper weekday rates though none better value than the 4-day special (**C**) at **A** *Winter Rose*, 213 Mount Dandenong Tourist Rd, Ferny Creek, T9755 1269, winter_rose@bigpond.com small but charming self-contained 1890s cottage. **L-C** *Poet's Lane*, Sherbrooke Rd, T9755 2044, poets@internex.net.au, has 3 modern cottages and 17 standard motel rooms. Geared towards weddings they also have a midweek 3-night special (**D**).

Colour map 2, grid C3
Sassafras 35 km from Melbourne

The Dandenongs are a very popular destination for day-trippers, and some parts are swamped with them at weekends and school holidays

Victoria

Sleeping
There are over a hundred B&Bs on the mountain, but no hostels or caravan parks and no camping facilities, though there are a couple of cheaper motels along the Burwood Highway

Eating

Olinda is a good place to pick up picnic ingredients, and a visit to Ripe, on the main street, is a must for any visitor

As you would expect there are dozens of restaurants, cafés and bistros on the mountain. A couple of the best are almost opposite each other on the main road through Olinda. The larger, *Ranges*, T9751 2133, is bright, cheerful and popular, particularly as it is open all day from 0900 for a succession of good value breakfasts, light lunches and from Tue-Sat, and mid-range asian influenced dinners. *Credo* is more intimate with an al fresco terrace. Cheap gourmet pizza and pasta. Open every evening and from 1200 Sat-Sun. *Cook's Corner Café*, Kallista-Emerald Rd, is off the beaten track, with a cosy, relaxed interior and a few tables in the pleasant ramshackle gardens. Open every day. At the other end of the mountain the *Rendezvous Café* is also open daily 0700-1900, with wonderful views and divine breakfasts, baguettes, cakes and coffee. Recommended.

Transport

There are no local bus services on Sun

Bus/Train There are metropolitan train services daily between **Melbourne** City Circle stations, **Upper Fern Tree Gully** (1 hr, $6, concessions $3.05) and **Belgrave**, running every 20-30 mins. *U S Bus Lines*, T9754 8111, run services between **Belgrave** station and **Olinda** (the 694), stopping at **Sherbrook** and **Sassafras**. Services at 0620, 0700 and 5 past the hr from 1000-1500 Mon-Fri, and every 1-2 hrs 0820-1620 Sat. They also have a service between **Upper Fern Tree Gully** and Olinda (the 698), following the commuter hrs of 0730 and 0830, and 1610-1940 Mon-Fri only. Metropolitan fares apply, so get a day ticket in Melbourne ($10.80, concessions $4.65). A couple of operators offer half-day tours to the Dandenongs from Melbourne, while most include a brief whistle through while taking you out to *Puffing Billy* and the Yarra Valley on a day-trip. *AAT Kings*, T9663 3377, www.aatkings.com, have a daily morning tour ($43), while *Backpacka*, T9277 8577, will take you in the afternoon ($42).

The Yarra Valley

Colour map 2, grid C3 Lilydale 39 km from Melbourne www.yarravalley tourism.asn.au

The Yarra Valley is one of Victoria's best known and most visited wine districts, but not content with creating great wine some of the wineries here have restaurants of the highest standard, and dining rooms and terraces that rank amongst the most striking and scenic in the country. In summer the valley gets very busy, particularly at weekends, and for two days every March it is besieged by Melbournians attending the annual **Grape Grazing Festival**, a hugely popular, indulgent offering of food, wine and music. For details, T5962 2600.

Ins & outs

McKenzie, T5962 5088, www.mc kenzies.com.au

Getting there and around There are metropolitan **train** services daily between **Melbourne** City Circle stations and **Lilydale** (40 mins, $6, concessions $3.05), running every 20-30 mins. *McKenzie* run less frequent daily **bus** services between **Lilydale**, **Yarra Glen**, **Healesville** and **Marysville**. Several companies run day-trips from Melbourne. *All Trails*, Lilydale, T9735 5592, www.alltrails.com.au, offer guided day and weekend cycling tours, and bike hire. **Balloon flights** There are 3 operators: *Global*, T1800 627661, *Go Wild*, T9890 0339, www.gowildballooning.com, and *Peregrine*, T9662 2800, www.hotair ballooning.com.au Tasting Tours *Backpacker Winery Tours*, www.backpacker winerytours.com.au, take medium-sized groups out to 4 wineries including *Domaine Chandon*. $75, includes lunch, wine and afternoon tea. Pick-ups from Melbourne (Flinders St Station, Queensbury Hill and St Kilda). *Yarra Valley Winery Tours*, Healesville, T5962 3870, www.yarravalleywinerytours.com.au, also have Melbourne pick-ups, but run more personalized tours in smaller vehicles.

Wineries

There are over 30 wineries in the valley, most of which offer food

Eyton, Maroondah Highway, T5962 2119. Wines $20-50. Cellar door daily 1000-1700, lunches 1200-1500. Striking modern architecture with a dining room overlooking a lake. Excellent Merlot and the expensive modern Australian cuisine is regarded by many as the best in the valley. Outdoor classical concerts in summer. *Yering Station*, Melba Highway, T9730 1107. Wines

$15-50. Cellar door 1000-1700, lunches daily. Tastings and Yarra Valley produce in an old farm building, but don't miss a stroll around the new restaurant and cellars. This graceful sweep of stone and glass has the feel of a Bond movie, and the massive terrace has huge views. *McWilliam's Lilydale*, Davross Court, T5964 2016. Wines $20-25. Cellar door daily 1100-1700, flexible lunch hours. Small and very friendly winery with an octagonal conservatory dining room and vine-hung garden gazebo, both looking out over vines and gum woods. Simple cheap platters and cook-it-yourself BBQ meals. Salad bar is balanced by the scrumptious cakey puddings. *Domaine Chandon*, Maroondah Highway, T9739 1110. Wines $25-50. Cellar door daily 1030-1630. Part of the Möet group. Stylish but relaxed tasting room with a high arched window looking out over the valley. A small savoury platter is served with each $5-10 glass of bubbly. A couple are good for a snack lunch. No free tastings. *Long Gully*, Long Gully Road, T9510 5798. Wines $15-30. Cellar door daily 1100-1700. Small easy-going winery, with a very picturesque setting in its own mini-valley. Excellent and good value wines. Picnickers welcome on to the cellar door balcony.

L-A *Mt Rael*, Bridges Rd, T5962 4107, www.babs.com.au/mtrael 3 very comfortable en suite rooms, all with direct access to the balcony which has outstanding views over Healesville to the Yarra ranges. Licensed, dinners by arrangement for 6 only. Cooked breakfast. **B** *Art at Linden Gate*, Healesville Yarra Glen Rd, T9730 1861, erfrics@netstra.com.au Single self-contained B&B apartment, with limited kitchen facilities, in the mud-brick house of a local sculptor. Isolated grounds encompass a hobby vineyard and a tiny wine cellar. The upstairs gallery has a range of contemporary work. Slightly cheaper is **B** *Brentwood*, Myers Creek Rd, T5962 5028, F5962 4749. Another secluded hosted B&B in its own wooded clearing adjacent to the state forest. Lots of wildlife and walking tracks from the back door. Very friendly, 3 en suite rooms in this 100-year-old home. As an alternative to a winery lunch try the licensed *Yarra Valley Dairy*, just south of Yarra Glen on McMeikans Rd, T9739 0023. Full working dairy with a lively and relaxed café and appropriate views over cow-filled fields. Mid-range platters and light lunches, book ahead at weekends. Cheese tastings daily 1030-1700, café closes a little before.

Sleeping & eating
The valley is awash with boutique hotel and B&B accommodation, but budget options are very thin on the ground, though there are a couple in Healesville

Victoria

Healesville Sanctuary, 4 km from the little town of **Healesville**, on Badger Creek Road, is the best native wildlife park of its kind in Australia. The sanctuary has 30 ha of bushland with Badger Creek running through its centre. Visitors walk along a wide circular path (1½ km), taking side loops to see the creatures that interest them. The **VIC** in Healesville is in the old courthouse on Harker Street. ■ *Open daily 0900-1700. T59622600, info@yarravalley tourism.asn.au*

Healesville is devoted to the conservation, breeding and research of Australian wildlife and the appeal of this place is seeing animals being so well cared for, including species that are almost impossible to see in the wild, including Tasmanian devils, the endangered orange-bellied parrot, the lyrebird and leadbeater's possum. Highlights are the Animal Close-Up sessions, held several times a day, when visitors can get as close as is legally allowed to wombats and koalas. The star exhibit is the World of the Platypus, a nocturnal tunnel with glass windows so you can watch the little fellas swimming and hunting. ■ *Daily 0900-1700. $15.80, children $7.80, concessions $11.70. T5957 2800, www.zoo.org.au/hs A few buses daily from corner of Green St and Maroondah Highway, Healesville, from 0925 Mon-Fri, 0858 Sat, 1133 Sun.* **Galeena Beek**, opposite the sanctuary, is a cultural centre of the Coranderrk Koori people

Healesville Sanctuary
Colour map 2, grid C3 Healesville 60 km from Melbourne, 35 km from Marysville

which documents the 60-year tenure of the Coranderrk Aboriginal Station and the culture and history of the people. ■ *Daily 1000-1700. $6.50, children $3.50, concessions $4.50. T5962 1119.*

Sleeping and eating in Healesville C-D *Healesville*, 256 Maroondah Highway, T5962 4002. This pub has 7 funky, spacious and brightly coloured rooms upstairs with shared facilities and a good bistro with great country cooking (mid-range). Meals 1200-1430 Thu-Mon, 1800-2030 daily. Book ahead for rooms at weekends. A few doors down, the **D** *Grand*, 270 Maroondah Highway, T5962 4003, has more basic but roomy pub rooms. There are 2 great little cafés at the east end of town. *Bohdi Tree*, 317 Maroondah Highway, is a rustic, laid-back café with wholesome food and an assortment of tables in the large outdoor area, live acoustic music Fri nights. Open Wed 1200-1700, Thu-Sun 1200-2100. Daily in summer. Next door the *Pasta Shop*, is a cheery 2-room cottage café that does Healesville's best breakfast, tasty lunches and sells fresh handmade pasta and gourmet foods. Tue-Fri 0900-1730, Sat-Sun 0830-1700, restricted hrs in winter.

Transport *McKenzies* buses leave from the corner of Green St and Maroondah Highway for **Lilydale** and **Melbourne** 0730 and 1040 Mon-Fri, 1000 Sat, 1600 Sun. There are services via **Marysville** and **Taggerty** to **Alexandra** 1635 Mon-Fri, 1320 Sat, 1110 Sun.

Marysville & around
Colour map 2 grid C3
Altitude: 800 m
Marysville 34 km from Healesville, 110 km from Mansfield
www.lakemountain resort.com

On the far side of the ranges from Healesville is Marysville, an attractive, leafy village best known as the winter base for those wanting to enjoy the snows on nearby Lake Mountain. The **VIC** in Murchison Street has a lot of free brochures on the walks and drives in the area. ■ *Daily 0900-1700. T5963 4567, www.marysvilletourism.com* Some 18 km from Marysville, **Lake Mountain** is not a downhill ski centre, but there are some excellent cross-country trails and toboggan runs. When there's no snow this is still a popular destination for walkers, with a variety of short walks around and to the summit. There are many fine forest walks directly from the town itself, particularly into **Marysville State Park**. The most popular is to **Steavensons Falls**. Woods Point Road heads right through the **Yarra Ranges National Park**, with various stops including a stand of particularly lofty Mountain Ash at Tommy's Bend and the **Cumberland Memorial Scenic Reserve** at Camberville, which has several forest and falls walks and a picnic area.

Although Marysville is a small town there are over 30 accommodation options of all types, and even these can get almost fully booked out on winter weekends

Sleeping and eating   A-B *Kerami*, Kerami Cres, T5963 3260, keramihouse@mail.com One of several B&Bs, this is a 1920s wood-panelled and beamed retreat with 6 en suite rooms, cooked breakfasts, and a veranda overlooking a bush garden full of birds. **C** *Keppels*, Murchison St, T5963 3207, is a modern, colourful pub with pleasant lounge areas, mid-range meals daily and a range of hotel and motel rooms. **C** *Nanda Binya*, 29 Woods Point Rd, T5963 3433, nandabinya@virtual.net.au Built as a ski lodge this modern building has 6 spacious, simple en suite rooms, some sleeping up to 5. Optional cooked breakfast $6 extra, dinners $25. Continental breakfast included, bikes for guest use, piano, sauna and outdoor jacuzzi. Recommended. The large *Country Bakery* café has a number of tables on the well-placed verandah and is open daily 0700-1800.

Transport *McKenzies* buses (T5962 5088, www.mckenzies.com.au) leave from the newsagents on Murchison St for **Healesville** and **Melbourne** 0930 Mon-Fri, 0900 Sat, 1500 Sun. A northbound service leaves 1720 Mon, Wed, Fri, 2045 Tue, Thu, 1205 Sun, stopping at the *Taggerty Pioneer Bush Settlement* on request.

This relatively small, saw-tooth ridge of forested hills rises dramatically along-side the highway. All roads within the park are unsealed, but a visit is well worth-while, particularly for walkers. One trail, steep and challenging in places, follows almost the entire ridge from **Sugarloaf Saddle** in the south to **Little Cathedral** in the north. It hits a couple of summits and is accessible from the northern and southern entrance car parks as well as Cooks Mill. The central **Jawbone** peaks can be reached in a two-hour return walk from the Jawbone car park, and the ridge can be followed north or south from there. A full circuit will take around 6-8 hours. There is an easier 1½ hour return trail from the northern Neds Gully camp ground along the Little River to Cooks Mill camp ground. *Cooks Mill* is the best, but most popular campground. It has gas BBQs, toilets and picnic areas. Camping fees apply. BYO water. Several property-based B&Bs are in the lee of the ranges. A *Cathedral View*, at the end of South Cathedral Lane, T/F5774 7545, cathedralview@mmtourism.com.au, does indeed have one of the best of these views. This isolated mud-brick homestead hosts one couple at a time in an en suite double. Just past the lane turn-off is the **D-E** *Taggerty Pioneer Bush Settlement*, T5774 7378, bushlife@virtual.net.au A rough, rustic and very friendly property with a warmer and holistic feel. The property operates as a farm and wildlife rescue centre, participation is welcome, as are WWOOFAs. Accommodation in a variety of cottages and outbuildings. The *McKenzie* bus drops off at the gate. Recommended.

Cathedral Range State Park
20 km from Marysville For information and park notes contact parks office in Marysville, T5963 3310, or www.park web.vic.gov.au

Northwest of Melbourne

The Calder Freeway heads toward Mount Macedon and the northern **Gold-fields**. On the way it passes the small **Organ Pipes National Park**. The Organ Pipes are a series of 400 million-year-old basalt columns forming parts of the walls of a deep gorge. Further to the north and also just off the freeway is **Sunbury**, known to cricketing fans the world over as the (possible) birthplace of the **Ashes** at Rupertswood Mansion. The **VIC** is in the Old Courthouse in Macedon Street. ■ *Open daily 0900-1700. T9744 2291.*

Colour map 2, grid C3 Sunbury 40 km from Melbourne

Mount Macedon is a largely forested massif, much of which is encompassed by the **Macedon Regional Park**. **Macedon** village is at the southern base of the mountain while the much prettier Mount Macedon village is further up the southern slopes. Neither are very large and have limited facilities. To the north of the mountain is **Hanging Rock**, a rugged volcanic outcrop a couple of hundred metres high with a cascading, almost sheer northwest face that is spectacular when lit up by the early morning sun, and paths that thread maze-like through the summit boulders. The rock, made famous by the classic novel and subsequent film, *Picnic at Hanging Rock*, attracts large numbers of visitors and there's now an interpretative centre, café, picnic grounds and concreted pathways, all of which has robbed the rock of any mystery it may once have had. ■ *Daily 0800-1800. $8 per car, or $4 per person. T0418-373032.* The **Camel's Hump**, at the top of Mount Macedon, is a rocky volcanic outcrop similar to Hanging Rock. It is unburdened by the latter's fame, however, and hence free from both cost and quite often, people.

Mount Macedon & around
Colour map 2, grid C3 Woodend 70 km from Melbourne www.macedon-ranges.vic.gov.au

Trentham is the prettiest village in the district with a fine colonial high street, and Trentham Falls, the longest single-drop waterfall in the state, is 2 km north. Several state forests and parks lie to the south, including Wombat Forest, a large area of eucalypt woodland. The main VIC for the region is at the northern end of High Street in Woodend (open daily 0900-1700. T5427 2033, vic@macedon-ranges.vic.gov.au).

Victoria

Sleeping and eating In Mount Macedon B-C *Mountain Inn*, 694 Mt Macedon Rd, T5426 1755, is the best pub on the mountain itself and also a good bet for food and accommodation. 6 doubles, 3 en suite, include a full cooked breakfast. The mid-range bistro serves up big helpings of rich country food, and is mostly cheap at lunchtime. Meals daily 1200-1430, 1800-2030. **In Trentham B-C** *Fir Tree*, High St, T5424 1549. 6 rooms, some en suite, in a large Victorian former pub with very comfortable guest lounges. The place also does a mean Sun brunch, open to non-residents. *Thai Issan*, High St, T5424 8444, is an unexpected oriental gem with an elegant, contemporary dining room. Superb mid-range Thai cuisine that even has Melbournians coming to see what all the fuss is about. Open 1230-1500 Sun, 1830-2130 Fri-Sun. Recommended. The *Cosmopolitan*, corner of High St and Cosmo Rd, T5424 1616, is one of the best country pubs around Melbourne. The tiny, wood-panelled front bar is a true relic and the cheap to mid-range bistro meals a worthy alternative to *Thai Issan*. Meals 1200-1500 Sat-Sun, 1800-2000 Thu-Sat. Recommended.

Transport The *V~Line* Melbourne to Bendigo rail line passes through both **Macedon** and **Woodend** (60-70 mins, $19), continuing on through to **Kyneton**, with connections to **Bendigo** and beyond to the Murray towns. Trains to Woodend daily every hr or so, stopping less frequently at Macedon. A *V~Line* bus service connects Woodend with **Daylesford** (45 mins), stopping in Market St, **Trentham**. Departs from the station, Woodend 0940, 1745 and 1850 Mon-Fri, 1120 and 1855 Sat, 1840 Sun, and from Littles Garage, Vincent St, Daylesford 0750 and 1625 Mon-Fri, 1010 and 1630 Sat, 1630 Sun.

Kyneton

Colour map 2, grid C3
Population: 3,800
15 km from Woodend,
34 km from
Castlemaine

On the main route north to Bendigo, Kyneton prospered during the goldrush years. Today it's a service centre for surrounding agricultural districts and still acts as a useful stopping point for the goldfields or a base for the Macedon ranges. Piper Street has many historic buildings, including Kyneton Museum, which has some interesting, well-curated displays of local history and a wide range of domestic items from the 1800s. ■ *Fri-Sun 1100-1600. $3, children $1.50. T5422 1228.* The **VIC** is on High Street, at the eastern edge of town. ■ *Daily 0900-1700. T5422 6110, vic@macedon-ranges.vic.gov.au* You may see a platypus at dawn or dusk during a pleasant stroll along the Campaspe River.

Sleeping and eating B *Moorville*, 1 Powlett St, T5422 6466, moorville@iaccess. com.au Edwardian mansion by the Campaspe River with 3 en suite rooms, wide verandah, large sitting room and lovely gardens. Warm and vivacious hosts serve a great cooked breakfast and are very knowledgeable about the region. Recommended. The **D** *Central Highlands Motor Inn*, 104 High St, T5422 2011, has 10 simple motel units. There is also a small caravan park in Clowes St, T5422 1612, by the river, with on-site vans. *Gonnella's*, 72 Piper St, T5422 2022. Authentic Tuscan cuisine in a warm timber-lined room. Wed-Mon 1830-2030, Fri-Sun 1200-1400. The town's best pub is the *Club*, 41 Mollison St, a welcoming, comfortable place with open fires, exposed brick walls and good meals. Daily 1200-1400, Mon-Sat 1800-2030. *Kyneton Provender*, 30 Piper St, has lovely coffee, cakes and light lunches, and is also an excellent second-hand bookshop. Also bike hire. Daily 1000-1800. Recommended.

Transport *V~Line* train services every 1-2 hrs direct to **Melbourne** (around 70 mins, $24.60) from 0522-1901 Mon-Fri, 0650-1935 Sat, 0802-1935 Sun, also stopping at **Woodend** and **Macedon**. Services north to **Castlemaine** and **Bendigo**, sometimes stopping at **Malmsbury**, from 0859-2254 Mon-Fri, 0907-2227 Sat, 1050-2033 Sun. Connections at Bendigo for **Swan Hill**, **Mildura** and **Echuca**.

Geelong and the Bellarine Peninsula

Port Phillip Bay is denied near-circular perfection by the nub of the Bellarine Peninsula and Corio Bay. At the head of Corio is the port of Geelong, a large industrial city now making the best of a picturesque foreshore. The area is becoming sought after by Melbournians following the trend for seaside living as an affordable alternative to the fashionable Mornington Peninsula. A romantic television series set at Barwon Heads, Sea Change, has also given the Bellarine the social cachet it was lacking. Among the expanding building sites there are still some wonderful beaches and the historic town of Queenscliff, an absolute gem, on the southeastern corner.

There is little to recommend the direct drive along the Princes Highway to Geelong, but there are a couple of diversions off the road well worth taking. The **RAAF Museum** at Point Cook, part of an operational base, has displays of artefacts and memorabilia, interactive exhibits and hangers full of cool military aircraft. ■ *Tue-Fri 1000-1500. Free. T9256 1236, Point Cook Rd, 28 km from Melbourne.* From here the road west back to the highway passes Werribee and the richly ornate **Mansion at Werribee Park**, a huge Italianate mansion and the largest private residence in the state. ■ *Daily 1000-1645. $10.30, children $5.20, concessions $6.20. T9741 2444. K Road, 30 km from Melbourne. Buses from Flinders St Station, Melbourne to Werribee daily every 20-30 mins. Buses from Werribee to main entrance every 2-2½ hrs, Mon-Sat, including 0900 and 1100 (plus extra walking required). Last bus departs 1825 Mon-Fri, 1720 Sat.* The **Open Range Zoo** is a safari-style park with predominantly African grassland animals, but also plains animals from Australia, Asia and North America. Tours around the park are in custom-made coaches, and there are a couple of 30-min walks. ■ *Daily 0900-1700. $15.30, children $4.60, concessions $11.40. Tours from 1030, on the ½ hr weekdays, every 20-30 mins Sat-Sun. Last tour 1530. T9731 9600.*

A few kilometres north of the freeway is the entrance to the **You-Yangs Regional Park**, a forested rectangular block surrounding the small but prominent outcrop of the You Yangs hill range. There are several bushwalks, including those to the highest point of Flinders Peak (348 m, 450 steps), and to Big Rock, a single massive boulder with a shallow rainwater basin on the top. There are good views to Geelong and Port Phillip Bay from both. ■ *0800-1630 (1800 in summer). $3 per vehicle. T5282 3356. Visitor centre, picnic areas.* Adjacent to the park is the **Serendip Sanctuary**, an extensive wildlife park and breeding facility devoted mostly to wetland birds. Visitors can expect, with diligence, to see around 60 bird species including Bustards, Brolgas and Cape Barren geese, plus Eastern Grey kangaroos and koalas from the many walking trails. ■ *Daily 1000-1600. $5.50, children, concessions $2.75. T5282 1584. Windermere Rd.* Another 20 km west, near Anakie, is **Brisbane Ranges National Park**, best known for the large numbers of koalas in Anakie Gorge.

Melbourne to Geelong

See Around Melbourne map, page 430

Victoria

Geelong

The second largest city in Victoria, Geelong started out as the major storage and brokering point for the thriving Victorian wool industry, and there are still several huge edifices bearing the legend 'Wool Brokers' in stone or brick along their high lintels. There are some interesting back streets around James Street and Little Malop Street with a few vibrant, quirky cafés, shops and galleries. The shore area, from Cunningham Pier to Eastern Beach, has been redeveloped to

Colour map 2, grid C3
Population: 126,000
73 km from Melbourne, 89 km from Ballarat, 186 km from Warrnambool

great effect in recent years and is a popular place in which to while away a day or two, with its beach, public bathing areas, gardens and parks.

Ins & outs The main **VIC** is in the foyer of the Wool Museum. Open daily 0900-1700. T5222 2900, www.melbournesbays.org The exuberent *Geelong Walking Tours*, T5243 9391, conduct a variety of entertaining strolls, each centred on a different theme. *Map it Out*, 135 Malop St, is a map shop and a good spot to plan ahead.

Sights The **Geelong Art Gallery's** best known work is Frederick McCubbin's poignant *A Bush Burial* (1890), purchased in 1900, but it also has an unusually strong collection of contemporary paintings and works on paper. ■ *Mon-Fri 1000-1700, Sat-Sun 1300-1700. $4, concessions $2, free on Mon. Little Malop St, T5229 3645.* Opposite is the **Performing Arts Centre**, T5225 1200, staging contemporary theatre, dance and classical music. In the centre of town, on the corner of Moorabool Street and Brougham Street, is the **National Wool Museum**. Two large dedicated floors, in an original bluestone woolstore and auction room, chart the full story of the Australian food industry in both

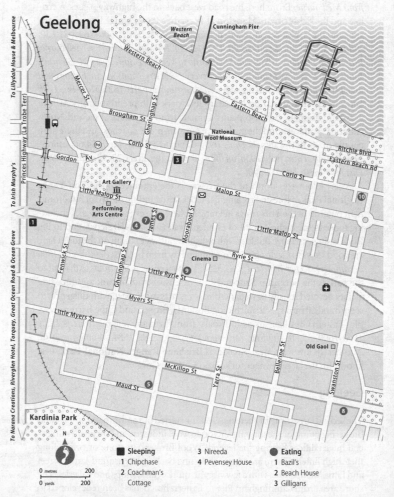

Geelong

(map labels) Western Beach · Cunningham Pier · Eastern Beach · Western Beach · Mercer St · Brougham St · Gheringhap St · Corio St · National Wool Museum · Ritchie Blvd · Eastern Beach Rd · Gordon Av · Corio St · Art Gallery · Little Malop St · Malop St · Performing Arts Centre · James St · Moorabool St · Little Malop St · Fenwick St · Gheringhap St · Cinema · Ryrie St · Little Ryrie St · Myers St · Little Myers St · McKillop St · Yarra St · Bellerine St · Old Gaol · Swanston St · Maud St · Kardinia Park

(left margin) To Lillydale House & Melbourne · Princes Highway (La Trobe Terr) · To Irish Murphy's · To Narana Creations, Riverglen Hotel, Torquay, Great Ocean Road & Ocean Grove

Victoria

0 metres 200
0 yards 200

■ **Sleeping**
1 Chipchase
2 Coachman's Cottage
3 Nireeda
4 Pevensey House

● **Eating**
1 Bazil's
2 Beach House
3 Gilligans

history and process. The on-site *Black Sheep Café* serves good value light meals daily 1000-1500. ■ *Daily 0930-1700. $7.30, children $3.65, concessions $5.90. T5227 0701.* The imposing red-brick **Old Gaol** saw service for nearly 138 years until 1991 when it finally closed as a high-security prison. It is still very much as it was then, and there are also some chilling reconstructions of prison life through the intervening decades. ■ *Sat-Sun 1300-1600. $6, children $3.50, concessions $4. McKillop St, T5221 8292.*

The east end of the city is bordered by Eastern Park. The extensive, well-managed and peaceful **Botanic Gardens** can be found here. ■ *Daily 0730-1700, to 2000 in summer. Guided walks Wed 1030, also Sun 1430 in summer if booked, $2. T5227 0387.* **Narana Creations** is an Aboriginal cultural centre incorporating a bush tucker café and indigenous art and craft gallery. Also didjeridu and boomerang demonstrations. ■ *Mon-Fri 0900-1700, Sat 1000-1600. Cultural sessions from around $60 per party. Grovedale, 10 km south on the Torquay road. T5241 5700, www.narana.com.au Buses 70-71 from Moorabool St.*

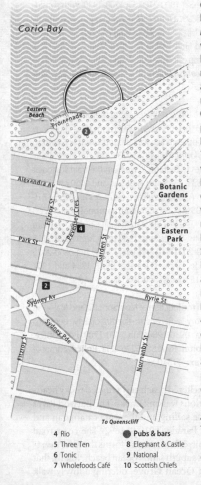

Corio Bay

Eastern Beach

Promenade

Alexandra Av

Fitzroy St

Pevensey Cres

Park St

Garden St

Sydney Av

Sydney Pde

Fitzroy St

Ryrie St

Normanby St

Botanic Gardens

Eastern Park

To Queenscliff

4 Rio
5 Three Ten
6 Tonic
7 Wholefoods Café

● Pubs & bars
8 Elephant & Castle
9 National
10 Scottish Chiefs

Sleeping

Just to north of the city centre are a cluster of motels, but there are also some superb heritage B&Bs, including **L-B** *Pevensey House*, Pevensey Cr, T5224 2810, www.pevensey-house.com.au Marvellously indulgent 1892 manor house, furnished almost entirely with 1850-90 antiques and Middle Eastern mats and rugs. 7 doubles and 5 separate bathrooms. Cooked silver-service breakfast and complementary alcohol. Recommended. **B** *Chipchase*, Ryrie St, T5229 1846, F5222 7536. Equally comfortable 1930s, wood-panelled B&B with 3 en suite doubles. Cooked breakfast. **B** *Coachman's Cottage*, Ryrie St, T5229 0264. 1872 weatherboard self-contained cottage, furnished beautifully in period style. **B-C** *Nireeda*, corner of Clare St and Corio St, T5221 0566, nireeda@bigpond.com Newly converted, contemporary studio and 2-to 3-bedroom self-contained apartments in an 1851 former hardware store. **E** *Irish Murphy's*, Aberdeen St, T5221 4335, geelong@irishmurphys.com.au One of 2 pub-based backpackers with 1 double, 3 twins and a couple of dorms. Kitchen and lounge area. This welcoming theme pub has cheap counter and Irish meals daily 1200-1430, 1800-2030, and live music Wed-Sun, $3.50 cover Fri-Sat. **E** *St Albans*, 6 Homestead Dr off Wilsons Rd, T5248 1229. Unusual backpacker accommodation in the former coach house of one of Australia's most successful horse studs (they boast 9 Melbourne Cup

Victoria

winners). 3 5-to 6-bunk dorms, open games and lounge area, small kitchen. They'll pick up if they can, otherwise buses 60, 61, 64, 65 or 67 from Moorabool St. Recommended. To the south, opposite peaceful Barwon Park in Belmont are a couple of caravan parks, including the friendly and accommodating *Riverglen*, T5243 5505. There is an indulgent country house option in **Batesford**, 11 km to the north. **A** *Lillydale House*, Dog Rocks Rd, T5276 1302, belcher@bigpond.com, has 3 beautiful en suite B&B rooms in an historic house set in 80 ha of grounds.

Eating

As part of its renaissance the city has seen a blossoming of excellent restaurants and interesting cafés

Beach House at the far end of Eastern Beach, T5221 8322. A great spot amid the foreshore gardens opposite the promenade, with a ground floor and terrace café, serving cheap meals daily 1000-dusk, and expensive modern Australian restaurant upstairs with an intimate balcony, open Wed-Sun 1800-2200, Fri-Sun 1200-1400, daily in peak summer. Nearer to the centre, *Bazil's*, Western Beach Rd, T5229 8965, is an intimate little café with a Mediterranean feel. Beautiful breakfasts, interesting lunches and mid-range dinners. Open Tue-Sun 0930-1600, Thu-Sat 1800-2000. There is also great eating away from the water with a couple of choice restaurants around the Moorabool and McKillop junction, including the sombre-looking bluestone *Three Ten*, 310 Moorabool St, T5221 1375. Inside is a smart but laid-back wine bar and mid-range bistro serving mostly modern Australian grills and cheap pasta. Open Tue-Sat 1800-2100, Fri 1200-1430. With considerably more edge is *Tonic*, James St, T522 8899, a retro café bar with mid-range, mostly southeast Asian food. Meals Tue-Sat 1100-1500, 1730-2100. *Wholefoods Café* is one of several healthy cafés around James St and Little Malop St. Open Mon-Fri 1000-1700. *Gilligans* is a very colourful fish and chip shop opposite Cunningham Pier. In addition to *Irish Murphy's* other good pubs include *Scottish Chiefs* on Corio St, and the *Elephant and Castle* out on McKillop St, T5221 3707.

Transport

V~Line buses along the Great Ocean Rd terminate at Apollo Bay, except on Fri

Bus *Gull*, 45 McKillop St, T5222 4966 run a direct daily service to **Melbourne Airport** from **Geelong** station, approx every 1½ hrs between 0600 and 1930. Bookings required. *Benders Busways*, T5278 5955, operate services around **Greater Geelong** with most leaving from Moorabool St. *Bellarine Transit*, T5223 2111, run limited services around the peninsula. *V~Line* services to **Ballarat** leave from the train station at 0820, 1235 and 1745 Mon-Fri, 2200 Fri, 0835, 1315 and 1805 Sat, and 1050 and 2000 Sun. Services along the Great Ocean Rd to **Apollo Bay** leave every 2-3 hrs 0955-1810 Mon-Fri, 0955 and 1910 Sat, 1055 and 2005 Sun. en suite **Warrnambool** operates on Fri only, leaving Apollo Bay at 1340. **Train** The *V~Line* station is off Gordon Av. There are *V~Line* services to **Melbourne** (50 mins, $19) every 10-30 mins from 0528-2115 Mon-Fri, approximately hourly from 0530-2025 Sat, and every 1-1½ hrs 0800-2025 Sun. Services direct to **Warrnambool** (2 hrs 20 mins) leave at 0947, 1334 and 1907 Mon-Fri, 0947 and 1936 Sat, and 1055, 1715 (buses) and 1953 Sun.

Directory

Banks and exchange There are ATMs on the junction of Moorabool St and Malop St. **Communications** Internet at *City Library*, adjacent to the *Art Gallery*, bookings T5222 1212. Open Mon-Fri 1000-2000, Sat 0930-1200, Sun 1400-1700. **Post Office**, corner of Moorabool St and Malop St. **Hospital** Ryrie St, T5226 7111. **Police** corner of Railway Terr and Mercer St, T5225 3100. **Taxi** T131008.

Ocean Grove & Barwon Heads

Population: 11,300 Ocean Grove is 26 km from Geelong

Barwon Heads has a small stretch of sheltered beach and a rugged rocky headland called the **Bluff**, encircled by various walking tracks. The Barwon River mouth is a good place for some gentle **sailing** and there are catamaran and skiffs for hire from *Go Sail*, Flinders Parade, T019 951892. The coast road crosses a bridge over the river to the thin 3-km-spit that forms the river's eastern bank. The bush-covered spit has a superb sandy ocean beach, Raaf's, that extends around to the beachfront of **Ocean Grove**, offering a lovely walk between the two towns. The surf here is great for beginners and there are surf-boards for hire ($8 per hour, $40 per day) at *Murf's* (no relation – ed), Hodgson Street, T5255 5525. Also boogie boards and surf advice (open daily 1000-1700, from 1100 May-October and closed Wednesday).

Point Lonsdale, just 3 km from Point Nepean, is the western guardian of the treacherous narrow channel called the Rip that separates Port Phillip Bay from the open ocean. Although not as pristine as Point Nepean, Lonsdale is still very picturesque with rocky platforms under a low cliff interspersed with small sandy beaches. A wooden jetty points out toward the Rip and from here a grassy foreshore stretches north and right around the long bay to Queens-cliff, offering a fine stroll. Just south of the jetty is the lighthouse. There are tours but they need to be booked ahead. ■ *Tours every Sun, every 30 mins 0930 1200. $5, children $3, concessions $4. T0419 513007.*

Point Lonsdale
Colour map 2, grid C3
There is some spectacular diving around here, and just off the beach is Lonsdale Wall, a 75-m vertical reef covered with sponges and corals

Queenscliff

Queenscliff began life in 1838 as a station for the pilots who still have to guide ships through the treacherous narrows. By the 1880s it had grown into a thriv-ing resort, with dozens of grand hotels catering to well-heeled Melbournians. Perhaps because of its position on a small peninsula, the town is little changed since Edwardian times and an air of graceful gentility pervades, with back streets off the main Hesse Street lined with picturesque cottages. The **VIC** is at 55 Hesse Street. ■ *Daily, times vary. T5258 4843, www.queenscliffe.vic.gov.au*

Colour map 2, grid C3
30 km from Geelong
Two spellings: Queenscliff town is part of Queenscliffe borough, which includes Point Lonsdale

Hesse Street runs parallel to Gellibrand Street which has several grand hotels facing the lawned foreshore and ends at **Shortlands Bluff**. There are views over the bay from here to Sorrento and as far as Arthurs' Seat. From the bluff, a beach and foreshore walk leads to Point Lonsdale (4½ km, two hours). The need to defend the bay grew in the minds of the authorities and led to construction of the impressive complex of **Fort Queenscliff** , which was completed in 1882. Public access is by tours only. These include entry to a small museum at week ends and during school holidays. ■ *Tours daily 1300, also 1500 at weekends. $5, children/concessions $3. T5258 1488. Corner of King St and Gellibrand St.* The far end of Gellibrand Street ends at Wharf Street and around here are the **Maritime Museum** and the old **Railway Station**. The museum displays memorabilia, including a full-size lifeboat, and displays relating to the pilots, wrecks and boats of Queenscliff history. ■ *Mon-Fri 1030-1630, Sat-Sun 1330-1630. $5, children $2, concessions $4. Weeroona Pde, T5258 3440.* The station has a collection of old steam engines, some of which are pressed into service for the scenic run to Drysdale. ■ *Sun 1115, 1330, 1430, also Tue and Thu during school holidays. 1¾ hr return. $14 return, children $8. Bikes carried, $3 one way. T5258 2069, www.bpr.org.au Symonds St.*

Sights

Much of the accommodation is still provided by the grand old hotels. The most extraordinary of these, and a real window into Edwardian decadence, is the beautifully restored **L** *Queenscliff Hotel*, 16 Gellibrand St, T5258 1066, F5258 1899. Bed and dinner packages only in summer, B&B available off-season (**B**). Lunches in the shop café 1000-1600, bar meals 1830-2030, bistro 1200-1400, 1900-2100, dining room Wed-Sat 1900-2100. Recommended. **A-B** *Pilots House*, 50 Gellibrand St, T5258 4171. 3 hosted B&B rooms in a beautiful 1876 house. **C-E** *Queenscliff Inn*, 59 Hesse St, T5258 4600, ggbrooks@primus.com.au Large and elegant Edwardian B&B with high, grand ceil-ings, comfortable drawing room, breakfast room and guest kitchen. A few budget

Sleeping & eating

dorm rooms make this one of the best YHA hostels in the country. Recommended. **C** *Royal*, 34 King St, T5258 1669. The oldest pub in town, has extensive, cheap dining areas serving sizeable portions, a pleasant rear courtyard, a comfy front bar with sofas round an open fire and 11 garish double rooms, 1 en suite. Meals daily 1200-1430, 1800-2100. There are several caravan parks, some with cabins and on-site vans (**C-D**) and all managed by *Queenscliff Tourist Parks*, T5258 1765, F5258 1750.

Tours & activities
Boats, fishing gear and licences, and sea-kayaks are for hire from *Queenscliff Marina*, Larkin Par, T5258 2166. Open daily. **Fishing** charters T5258 2802, www.gamerec.com **Motorized bicycle** hire, T5258 4796. No licence required. *See-All Charters*, T5258 3889, www.pipeline.com.au/users/bay, operate swim-with-dolphin and seal-spotting trips from the wharf.

Transport
A **horse-drawn bus** meets some of the ferries in summer and transfers passengers in a leisurely manner to the town centre, $3. **Ferry** 2 ferries operate from the wharf, 800 m from the town centre, over to **Sorrento**. The passenger-only ferry, T5984 1602, also stops at **Portsea**, daily Boxing Day to Easter. First ferry 1000, last 1740 (50 mins, $7, child $5, concession $6). The larger, vehicle ferry, T5258 3244, www.searoad.com.au, crosses daily, year-round, on the hr 0700-1800. Same passenger prices, cars under 5½ m $38 plus passengers.

Great Ocean Road and the Southwest

In some circles the natural attractions of Australia are summed up as 'the road, the rock and the reef'. The 'road' is the Great Ocean Road and images of the golden rock stacks of Port Campbell National Park are seared into the minds of most travellers long before they ever see them in the flesh. Even so, it still comes as a surprise that there is so much variety on this road, and to attempt it in a day, as many do, is sheer madness. The bays on the eastern side of Cape Otway harbour the stylish and arty villages of Lorne and Apollo Bay, and the lush hinterland of forest shelters waterfalls, glow worms and platypuses in the Angahook-Lorne State Park and Otway National Park. West of the cape the landscape dries out and straightens into the bare cliffs of Port Campbell. Further to the west, Warnambool and Portland are both large industrious cities separated by the fishing village of Port Fairy with its faint echo of Georgian Ireland. From Portland to the South Australian border is a long, wild coastline of capes and bays as far as Nelson where the broad Glenelg River flows through the dense bush of the Lower Glenelg National Park to Discovery Bay.

Ins and outs

Getting there & around
V~Line buses along the Great Ocean Rd terminate at Apollo Bay, except on Friday

The road has one of the worst accident rates in Victoria, particularly for motorbikes, so take great care. It is also very congested year-round, but particularly in summer, when it becomes a procession of large, slow coaches, sometimes even stopping dead on the highway to point out a sight or koala. If you can, plan a route from west to east to avoid all this! Most traffic and tours travel west from Melbourne along the Great Ocean Rd, then return eastwards to the city along the faster inland route, the Princes Highway.

Bus *V~Line* services along the Great Ocean Rd to **Apollo Bay** leave **Geelong** 0955 and 1510 Mon-Fri, 1810 Mon-Thu, 1915 Fri, 0955 and 1910 Sat, 1055 and 2005 Sun (2½ hrs). They stop regularly along the way, including at places such as **Aireys Inlet** and the **Wye River**. A connecting service to **Warrnambool** operates on Fri only (plus Mon, Dec-Jan), leaving Apollo Bay at 1340 (3½ hrs). This service also stops at many of the major sights along the way (but only for about 5 mins each). There are also buses between **Ballarat** and Warrnambool, and **Mount Gambier** (SA) and Warrnambool, calling at **Portland** and **Port Fairy**. **Backpacker buses** Any backpacker bus operating in Victoria will have a Great Ocean Rd run from **Melbourne**, some have several. Some come from, or continue on to **Adelaide**, others head up through the Grampians before heading back to the city. Local specialists include *Let's Go Bush*, T9662 3969, who run a 2-day-trip ($99, including accommodation, BBQ dinner and breakfast), and *Otway Discovery*, T1800 444432 or 9654 5432, who operate a useful jump-on, jump-off service ($50). They are also happy, if they have space, to take you from **Apollo Bay** to **Warrnambool**, filling in the huge gap left by *V~Line*. **Train** *V~Line* direct services from **Geelong** to **Warrnambool** (2 hrs 20 mins) leave at 0947, 1334 and 1907 Mon-Fri, 0947 and 1936 Sat, and 1055, 1715 (buses) and 1953 Sun.

One of the best day tours is run by *Go West*, T9828 2008, gowest@unite.com.au, ($54), who pick up from about a dozen **Melbourne** backpacker hostels between 0715 and 0820 every day, returning about 2130. The main **VIC** for the whole region from Geelong to Port Fairy is on the M1 north of Geelong. Daily 0900-1700. T1800 620888, www.greatoceanrd.org.au Also see www.greatoutdoors.vic.gov.au

Tours & information
Most operators do a Great Ocean Road tour

Torquay has long been known for good surfing and is the birthplace of famous surfwear labels, *Ripcurl* and *Quiksilver*. This heritage is celebrated in the **Surfworld Museum**, a lively and fascinating display on surfing culture and history. ■ *Daily 1000-1700. $6.50, children and concessions $4.50. Surf City Plaza,T5261 4606, www.surfworld.org.au* Many of the surfwear companies have huge manufacturing and retail warehouses based around **Surf City Plaza**, on the highway, where there are also seconds shops and factory outlets. Torquay sprawls along the coast but the seaward-facing Esplanade is undeveloped. The main shopping and eating streets, Gilbert Street and Bell Street, run from the highway to the Esplanade. There is a beautiful mosaic Analemmatic Sundial by **Fishermans Beach** at the northern end, pleasant BBQ and picnic areas along the grassy foreshore and walks above the golden beaches to **Point Danger**. To get on a board yourself contact *Go Ride A Wave* on Bell Street, T5263 2111, for hire and lessons. The **VIC** is at the entrance to the surf museum in *Surf City Plaza*. ■ *Daily 0900-1700, T5261 4219, www.greatceanrd.org.au Internet access, $2 for 10 mins.*

A short drive from Torquay is **Bells Beach**, one of the world's great surfing sites and a major professional competition venue. The **Ripcurl Pro Surf Classic** is held here every Easter. Standing at the top of the cliffs watching the continuous succession of long, evenly breaking waves it is easy to see why.

Torquay
Colour map 2, grid C2
Population: 6,000
23 km from Geelong, 6 km fom Bells Beach

Sleeping and eating C *Potters Inn*, 40 Bristol Rd, T5261 4131; pottersinn@bigpond.com Small friendly modern B&B, 2 en suite rooms furnished with some ceramic flourishes. Good value. Recommended. **D-E** *Bells Beach Backpackers*, 53 Highway, T5261 7070, www.bellsbeachbackpackers.com.au Fun and friendly hostel with 40 beds in 6-and 8-bunk dorms and 2 doubles. Book the latter. Car, bike and board hire, internet access $6 an hr. There is also a large caravan and camping ground backing onto Surf Beach, entrance on Bell St, T5261 2496. Bell St has most of the restaurants, takeaways and the best pub. *Nocturnal Donkey*, T5261 9575, at No 15, is a bright and breezy restaurant serving Mediterranean-style food with lots of seafood and an unusually strong vegetarian menu. *Surfrider*, almost opposite, is a sleek establishment full of surfing paraphernalia, with a cheap modern Australian lunches and mid-range dinners. *Spooners* on the highway, just south of the plaza, is a great laidback café, and *Flippin' Fresh*, a little further south on the highway, is good for fish and chips.

Victoria

Transport *V~Line* bus services along the Great Ocean Rd to **Apollo Bay** leave from the corner of Geelong Rd and Grossman's Rd at 1020 and 1535 Mon-Fri, 1835 Mon-Thu, 1940 Fri, 1020 and 1935 Sat, 1120 and 2030 Sun (2 hrs). Services to **Geelong** leave at 0815, 1145, 1450 and 1608 Mon-Fri, 0815 and 1645 Sat, 0947 and 1830 Sun.

Anglesea & Aireys Inlet

The main highway continues another 10 km past flowering heathlands to the sprawling holiday towns of Anglesea and Aireys Inlet, and in effect the start of the Great Ocean Road. Aireys Inlet has an excellent gallery featuring local artists, *Eagles Nest*, 48 Great Ocean Road, and a traditional tall white lighthouse. There is no access to the Split Point Lighthouse, affectionately known as the White Queen, but there is a short walk around the point, a tea-room and it is possible to stay in the old Lighthouse Keepers' Cottages, T5289 6306, www.aireys.com.au Just 3 km south of Aireys Inlet is a small, cosy hostel, **E** *Surfcoast Backpacker*s, 5 Cowan Avenue, Fairhaven, T5289 6886. Across the road from a wide sandy beach.

Tours and activities *GORATS*, T/F5289 6841, www.gorats.com.au, run a variety of mountain-biking, canoeing and walking tours, from $35. Also bike hire. *Tiger Moth World*, 325 Blackgate Rd, T5261 5100, www.tigermothworld.com, offers the rare chance of a flight, or even aerobatics in genuine Tiger Moth biplanes. Also tandem skydives. **Horse riding** *Blazing Saddles*, Aireys Inlet, T5289 7149. Bush and beach rides from $38 for 2 hrs. *Sea Mist*, Wensleydale Station, just inland from Aireys Inlet, T5288 7255. Trail-riding lessons and hostel-style log cabin accommodation. **Kayaking and surfing** *Go Paddling* and *Go Ride A Wave*, T5263 2111, www.graw.com.au, offer daily surf lessons in summer, and kayak lessons and trips.

Lorne

Colour map 2, grid C2
Population: 1,100
41 km from Torquay,
16 km fom Wye River

Lorne sits almost hidden by bush in the hills above the wide sandy beach of Loutit Bay, surrounded by the Angahook-Lorne State Park, an area of thick forest, rivers and many waterfalls. It is the most glamorous of the coastal towns, with classy boutiques, galleries, and fine restaurants. In January look out for the Pier to Pub swimming race. The **VIC** is at 144 Mountjoy Parade and has free town and district maps. ■ *Daily 0900-1700.* T5289 1152, lornevic@iprimus. com.au The Parks Office is at 84 Polworth Road, T5289 1732.

Sleeping
There are a large number of holiday homes for rent: contact Lorne Real Estate, T5289 1800, www.lorne realestate.com.au

L-A *Ravenswood*, corner of Smith St and Bay St, T5289 2655, ravenswood@ iprimus.com.au Friendly Edwardian B&B, beautifully decorated and furnished, 2 en suite rooms. Private balconies, cooked breakfast. Recommended. **L-B** *Erskine Falls Café and Cottages*, off Erskine Falls Rd, T5289 2666, F5289 2247. A cluster of 12 modern, self-contained, apartments, all on stilts looking out across the forest canopy toward the sea, sleeping 2-8. The small, homely café serves seriously cheap breakfasts, light meals and cream teas, daily 0830-1800 Dec-Apr, otherwise Thu-Mon 0900-1600. **B-D** *Great Ocean Rd Backpackers and Cottages*, Erskine Av, T5289 1070. Expensive hostel with large but dark dorms and a tiny kitchen, dining and common area. Also large self-contained wooden cabins in a forest setting. **C** *Qdos*, Allenvale Rd, 3 km from town centre, T5289 1989, www.qdosarts.com Strikingly designed building amongst bush and a sculpture garden. 7 double ryokan-style cabins, and a smart café with a small (mostly cheap) all-day menu. WWOOFAs welcome. Also boasts one of Victoria's best private contemporary art galleries. Recommended. **D-E** *Erskine Backpackers*, 6 Mountjoy Par, T5289 1496. Luxurious hostel surrounded by a wide veranda, 3-to 6-bunk dorms and several pleasant doubles, some in romantic garden annexes. Great kitchen facilities and games room. Unfortunately often closed during winter, but still recommended. One organization manages all the caravan parks and campsites, T5289 1382. 1 km to the west is a small outpost of accommodation and eating. The **L-D** *Grand Pacific*, T5289 1609, has smart modern bars and bistro. Cheap and mid-range lunches and dinners daily. The warren-like upper floors contain an extensive array of good value hotel and motel rooms for most budgets. Also more expensive apartments. Around the corner, **B-C** *Grazi's*, T/F5289 2422, www.grazis.com, is a bright cheerful café and B&B with 5 rooms, open daily 0830-1600. Free internet use and good room discounts in winter.

Eating

The best fish and chip shop is adjacent to the Anchorage Motel

Damo's, William St, T5289 2718. Small enclosed dining room and wonderful sail-covered terracotta terrace overlooking the foreshore. Mediterranean influence is carried over to the cheerful service and excellent food, with a range of breakfasts and cheap light lunches. Mid-range evening dining. Open daily 0900-1430, 1800-2100. Recommended. *Reifs*, 84 Mountjoy Par, T5289 2366. Slick, modern establishment with front decking overlooking the foreshore. Informal and friend. Good range of pricey breakfasts and interesting Asian and North African-influenced meals. Open Sat-Sun 1030-1430, Tue-Wed, Fri-Sat 1800-2000. Daily Nov-Apr. *Tirami-Su*, Grove Rd, T5289 1004. Lively mid-range Italian restaurant with a marvellous singing chef. Go for a later sitting and book at weekends. Open daily 1200-1500, 1800-2100. *Kafé Kaos*, 52 Mountjoy Pde. Funky and friendly café with seriously good and large gourmet wraps, burgers and interesting veggie options. Also breakfasts. Opposite the *Grand Pacific Hotel* is the *Pier Restaurant*, T5289 1119, the only one in town right on the water. Mid-range seafood and steaks, cheap pasta.

Go Paddling and *Go Ride A Wave*, T5263 2111, www.graw.com.au, offer daily surfing lessons in summer, and kayak lessons and trips. Also hire. Based at Foreshore Swimming Pool. Also shops in Torquay and Anglesea. Specialist canoe tours to a platypus colony near Forrest, details listed under Apollo Bay.

Tours & activities

V~Line bus services through to **Apollo Bay** leave from the main bus stop, outside the *Commonwealth Bank*, at 1120 and 1635 Mon-Fri, 1935 Mon-Thu, 2040 Fri, 1120 and 2035 Sat, 1225 and 2130 Sun (1 hr). Services through to **Geelong** leave at 0715, 1045, 1350 and 1515 Mon-Fri, 0715 and 1545 Sat, 0830 and 1722 Sun (1½ hrs).

Transport

Banks ATMs on Mountjoy Par. **Bike hire** *GORATS* at Aireys Inlet, T5289 6841. **Chemist** 144 Mountjoy Pde, T5289 1580. Open daily. **Communications** Internet *Lorne Online*, 150 Mountjoy Par, T5289 2080. **Post Office**, Mountjoy Par.

Directory

Comprising a narrow strip of bushland from Anglesea to the Kennet River, this small pocket of beautiful mountain ash and blue gum trees is a rare area of 'wilderness' on the Great Ocean Road, and is home to swamp wallabies, possums and kangaroos. In the heart of the park, inland from Lorne, is a cooler, wetter area of forested ridges, deep valleys and damp mossy fern gullies. This is fine bushwalking country, with forest trails leading to waterfalls and lookouts. **Erskine Falls** and **Phantom Falls** are two of the best and both are very close to Lorne. The Erskine Falls are about 8 km inland by car. The best viewing spot is at the base, over 100 steps down. The Erskine River can be followed on foot all the way to the falls from Lorne (from the Erskine River Caravan Park, to be exact). It's a pretty tortuous affair (3-4 hours one-way), and cannot be done if the river is high, but is well worth the effort if you have a day to spare.

Angahook-Lorne State Park

For more information contact Lorne Parks Office (see page 446), or www.parkweb.vic.gov.au

This winding stretch is the classic coastal highway so often pictured as representative of the Great Ocean Road. Here the Otway Ranges slope into the ocean, creating steep forested inclines, bisected by many rivers. These streams create waterfalls and sandy inlets, and many picturesque gorges and falls are

Lorne to Wye River

accessible by short walks off the road. From Lorne the road follows a headland or two, past a short walk to **Sheoak Falls** and around to the mouth of the Cumberland River. There is a deep rocky gorge here leading to falls and a lovely grassy campsite by the river. About 5 km from here, and just past Jamieson River, is a small car park. A sign here should say **Artillery Rocks**, but is frequently missing. The rocks themselves, down on the beach, are clusters of carbonate nodules that look like cannonballs amongst the weirdly beautiful eroded sandstone. **Wye River** is a tiny settlement in the steep bush above the rivermouth and sandy beach.

Sleeping and eating The wonderful pub here, the **C-F** *Wye River Hotel*, T5289 0240, has acres of sail-covered decking and cheap but adventurous food daily 1200-1400, 1800-2000. Accommodation in either motel rooms, the price of which halve in winter, or small cabins fitted out with backpacker bunks. No heating or kitchen facilities. A kilometre up the hill is **L** *Wye in the Sky*, T/F5289 0234, wits@ne.com.au Modern self-contained apartment with mesmerising views over the ocean from the balcony and floor-to-ceiling windows. Warm, friendly hosts live upstairs. Both recommended.

Wye River to Apollo Bay
Distance 30 km

The next settlement is **Kennet River**, 5 km further on, where there is a fantastic place to see **koalas**. Turn off toward the cabin park (T5289 0272) and then take the first left up the unsealed Grey River Road. Walk slowly along this road to spot many grey furry bundles in the trees. Some 6 km further up Grey River Road is a BBQ and picnic spot, with a couple of otherworldly rainforest walks leading from it. Just before the wooden bridge here the banks sparkle with **glow worms** at night, particularly on the right-hand side. To get off the beaten track, a short circuit into the forest is recommended, taking Grey River Road inland and returning to the coast road via Skenes Creek Road or Wild Dog Road just east of Apollo Bay (if you have a good map and don't mind unsealed roads). The Great Ocean Road leaves the forest and continues around Cape Patton, past a picnic area and walk, up to **Carisbrook Falls** and on to **Skenes Creek** and **Apollo Bay**.

Sleeping and eating A little way up Skenes Creek Road is **L** *Chris's at Beacon Point*, T5237 6411, chrisbeaconpoint@bigpond.com The restaurant and self-contained accommodation units hang high above the ocean and are something of a local treasure and booked out quickly. Open daily 1200-1500, 1800-2000 (till 2200 Oct-Apr).

Apollo Bay

Colour map 2, grid C2
Population: 1,200
45 km from Lorne,
49 km from Melba Gully
The town hosts a good
music festival around
the foreshore in March

At Apollo Bay the grassy bare foothills of the Otways slope down to the sea and a long sandy beach lined with cypress trees. This relaxed and friendly town offers plenty of tours and activities, excellent accommodation and restaurants and makes a good base to explore the **Otway National Park**, just to the west. Apollo Bay's fishing fleet is moored within a protected breakwater at the western end of the bay and a stroll along the pier provides lovely views of the bay. Abalone and crayfish are the main catches but a range of fresh fish can be bought from the **Fishermans Co-op** at the pier. There are amazing views of the whole eastern coast from **Marriners Lookout**, follow the alarmingly steep Marriners Lookout Road east of town. The **VIC** is well organized with helpful information sheets on walks, camping and activities. It is on the foreshore in the centre of town, next to the cypress poles where markets are held every Saturday morning. ■ *Daily 0900-1700, T5237 6529, www.greatoceanrd.org.au*

Victoria

A-B *Rayville Boat Houses*, 9 Noel St, T5237 6381, www.rayville.com.au 10 luxurious, modern weatherboard houses close to the sea, decorated in blue and yellow. **B-C** *Garden Cottage*, 7 Diana St, T5237 6034. Self-contained colonial cottage, tiny and impossibly charming with brass bed and open fire. **C** *Marriners Lookout*, end of Marriners Lookout Rd, T5237 6450. Small comfortable cottage in a lovely garden high above the sea with amazing views. Breakfast provisions. **C** *Smith's Farmhouse*, 355 Barham Valley Rd, T5237 6582. Gracious and hospitable B&B with 2 rooms in a 1920s farmhouse with picturesque valley views, beautiful timber dining and living rooms. Also a simple self-contained farmer's cottage, sleeps 8. **C-D** *Angela's Guesthouse*, 7 Campbell Court, T5237 7085, www.angelas.tourvic.com.au Spacious rooms with cheerful linen, spotless bathrooms and balconies. Angela provides the warmest hospitality imaginable and the rooms are unbelievably good value. Recommended. **E** *Surfside Backpackers*, corner of Great Ocean Rd and Gambier St, T5237 7263. Homely, welcoming hostel in a beach house by the sea, lots of doubles and a living room. All beds have electric blankets. There are also several caravan parks with cabins, try *Kooringal*, 27 Cawood St, T5237 7111.

Sleeping
Accommodation along the Great Ocean Rd is very expensive in the high season but Apollo Bay has a couple of good value gems, among the best on the road. Book ahead

Buffs, No 51, T5237 6403. Has fairly traditional and hearty food and a rustic timber dining room. *La Bimba*, upstairs at No 125, T5237 7411. Daily 0800-2030. Smart bistro, with good breakfasts and sophisticated café-style food. *Café One Five Three*, opposite the cypress poles, is large and light-filled with plenty of pavement tables and delicious foccacia, sandwiches and cakes. Daily 0900-1700. *Bay Leaf Gourmet Deli*, No 131. Daily 0800-1500. Does breakfast, cakes, and lunches with an inventive Mediterranean and Middle Eastern flair. Also open for dinner in summer. *Sandy Feet Café*, No 139. Daily 0830-1530. Perfect for veggies. There is also an attached health food shop. *Nautigals*, No 58, is an extremely laid-back internet café, also has second-hand books.

Eating
All of the cafes and restaurants can be found along the Great Ocean Rd, opposite the beach

Air *Cape Otway Aviation*, 3 Telford St, T0500-522244, scenic flights in a *Cessna* over 12 Apostles ($70) and Cape Otway ($45). Also all inclusive overnight flights to King Island ($228, minimum 4-5 people). **Cycling** *Otway Expeditions*, T5237 6341, offer a variety of mountain bike tours (from $30), including a glow-worm night ride. **Fishing** *Apollo Bay Surf and Fish*, T5237 6127, introductory rock and river fishing trips, all equipment supplied ($35, 4 hrs). Also *Apollo Bay Boat Charter*, T5237 6214, for fishing and scenic cruises. Tackle and bait shop at 39 Great Ocean Rd. **Horseriding** *Wild Dog Trails*, T5237 6441. Beach, bush and sunset rides from 2hrs to full day. **Surfing** *Hodgy's*, 143 Great Ocean Rd, T5237 7883, hires out surfboards, boogie boards and wetsuits (surf $25 ½ day, boogie $15 ½ day), also can advise on where the good waves are. **Walking** *Otway Eco Guides*, T5237 7240, www.otwayeco-guides.com.au, offer a range of interesting walks focusing on bush foods and medicine plants, koalas and Koori culture and history (approx $30, 2 hrs). Also glow-worm night walks ($16.50, 1 hr). **Wildlife** *Otwild Adventures*, T5236 2119, platycat@bigpond.com, run exceptional early morning tours to see platypus on Lake Elizabeth ($75, 4-5 hrs). Departs Forrest. Recommended.

Tours & activities

The *V~Line* bus service through to **Warrnambool** leaves the VIC on Fri at 1340 (3½ hrs), also Mon during Dec-Jan. If stuck, try *Otway Discovery*, T1800-444432 or 9654 5432, who may be able to fit you on board their tour minibus. Services through to **Lorne** and **Geelong** leave at 0655, 0940 and 1410 Mon-Fri, 0615 and 1445 Sat, 0730 and 1615 Sun (2½ hrs).

Transport

Apollo Bay marks the end of the first of the two stretches of the true Great Ocean Road. From here the route winds up into the forest-covered hills of the **Otway National Park** (see page 451). After 20 km an unsealed left turn leads 12 km to **Cape Otway** where there is a lighthouse and complex of 19th-century telegraph buildings. There are good coastal views from the balcony of the

Apollo Bay to Cape Otway
Distance 30 km

Victoria

Cape Otway Lighthouse. ■ *Daily 0900-1700. Entry $8, children $4, concessions $7. Guided tours 1100, 1400, 1500. Also self-guided tours. Tours including entry $11, $4 and $5. T5237 9240, www.lightstation.com*

Sleeping There is accommodation here in the old keeper's cottage (**B-C**). This large residence has 4 comfortable bedrooms, and lounges with sofas and open fire, as well as the incredible position. Also 2 studio rooms for couples. Recommended. 3 km from the cape is **C-E** *Bimbi Lodge*, T5237 9246, a holiday park with cabins, on-site vans and primitive backpacker accommodation. On the same road are some comfortable cabins, **A** *Cape Otway Log Cabins*, T5237 9290, otway.cabins@bigpond.com Self-contained and private, many with sea views. Back on the main road the route heads down to the picturesque Aire valley. **A** *Aire Valley Guest House*, T5237 9223, www.airevalleyguesthouse.com.au, is a luxurious old house high above the valley and has a pretty sitting room and verandas to gaze at the ocean from. Evening meals for guests on request ($25-43). Recommended.

Cape Otway to Port Campbell
Distance 90 km

The road meets the coast again at Glenaire and climbs inland once more to the pub, petrol station and tea rooms of **Lavers Hill**. This also marks the start of an inland **Forest Drive** that makes a convenient circuit back to Lorne and passes many waterfalls and walking tracks, such as Triplet Falls and Beauchamp Falls. **Melba Gully State Park** is 3 km beyond the Lavers Hill junction. Just before the park entrance is **B-C** *Cottage Flower Farm*, T5237 3208, a people- and eco-friendly hosted B&B with two en suite rooms. The road continues over Wattle Hill and **Moonlight Head**. An unsealed left turn here leads to a couple of walks well worth taking the trouble for. The **Gables**, reached in an easy 10 minute walk, is a high lookout point with extensive views over the head. The other walk descends over 300 steps to **Wreck Beach** where the anchors from two ships dashed to pieces on the rocks offshore can still be seen, embedded in the beach. Often deserted and accessible at low tide only, these sandy beaches are strewn with multi-coloured pebbles, and backed by soaring cliffs, have a wild and timeless feel about them.

Port Campbell National Park

Among the most recognisable of Australian landscapes, the striking coastline of this national park is what most people travel the Great Ocean Road to see. The landscape changes markedly from the steep forested curves of the eastern section of the road. A vast flat plain, long ago cleared for grazing, drops away abruptly to sheer limestone cliffs. As the sea has bitten deeply into the coastline some chunks of rock have been left behind. Over time these rock stacks themselves have been eroded and sculpted into arches, caves and tapering sails. The rock group known as the Twelve Apostles is the most famous but the whole coastline from Princetown almost as far as Warrnambool is scattered with beautiful rock stacks and islands.

There are parking bays and lookouts all along this stretch of road. The first is **Gibson Steps**, which is one of the few places offering access to the beach and lets you feel and see the scale of the cliffs. The next and busiest stop is for the **Twelve Apostles**, where there are several lookouts. Near by the visitor centre is a helipad and scenic flights run on demand most days; *PremiAir*, T5598 8266, offer short flights for about $70. From the air the coastline looks just like an unfinished jigsaw and a flight is well worth taking if possible.

The most fascinating area in the park is **Loch Ard Gorge** further west, a group of islands, caves, gorges and blowholes. The beautiful deep gorge is named after a Glaswegian ship that was smashed on Mutton Bird Island in 1878. Tragically, 52 people drowned, but two people survived and were

Otway National Park and Melba Gully State Park

Amongst the highlights of Otway National Park is **Maits Rest Rainforest Walk**, signposted from the Great Ocean Road. The circuit walk (30 minutes) heads into a deep gully filled with huge ancient ferns and myrtle beech. The towering mountain Ash surrounding the upper edges of the gully are also impressive (look for pale trunks as straight and smooth as a telegraph pole). Koala, swamp wallabies and yellow-bellied gliders live in the park and the spot-tailed quoll, a kind of native cat now so rare in this area that park staff request that any sightings are reported. There are many walking tracks in the forest east of Cape Otway Lighthouse Road and campsites by the beach at **Blanket Bay**. On the western side of Cape Otway there are lovely campsites on both sides of the **Aire River**, accessible from Hordern Vale Road or Sand Road near Glenaire. From Aire River there is a walk to the coast and along it to Cape Otway (22 km, eight hours return). The park extends along the coastline just past Moonlight Head. There are more campsites behind the dunes at the popular surf beach, **Johanna Beach**. Beyond the Otway National Park is a tiny remnant of similar country, preserved in **Melba Gully State Park**. Madsen's Track Nature Walk wanders through rainforest of mossy myrtle beech, blackwood and tree ferns to a big tree, a 200-year-old messmate. The park is best known for the glow worms that line the soil banks. The creatures are at their best here in winter, and begin in earnest after the third bridge on the 30-minute return walk. Take a raincoat as the park is the probably the wettest spot in Victoria. Campsite bookings at **Parks Victoria** office, Apollo Bay, T5237 6889. Detailed park notes are available at the Apollo Bay tourist office or at www.parkweb.vic.gov.au

washed into the gorge. There is a walk mapping the story of the *Loch Ard*, leading from a lookout over the wreck site, to the gorge and beach and then to the cemetery. There are also several other good short walks in the area from which to explore the features of this coastline. The Blowhole and Thunder Cave are impressive and Muttonbird Island Lookout has interesting views. Muttonbirds can be seen returning to their nests on the island at dusk from January-February. Beyond Port Campbell are more rock features, The Arch, London Bridge and The Grotto. The latter is probably the most interesting but **London Bridge** is famous for losing the arch connecting it to the mainland in 1990 and leaving some astonished tourists stranded on the far side. Adjoining this national park beyond the tiny settlement of **Peterborough** is the **Bay of Islands Coastal Park**. The Bay of Islands and Bay of Martyrs are both striking areas of countless rock stacks. There are several lookouts and accessible sandy beaches such as Boat Bay and Childers Cove.

Port Campbell

Port Campbell has a small, deep harbour looking like a neat rectangular notch cut into the cliffs, that is the only safe refuge along this shipwreck coast. The main street is Lord Street and the **VIC** is on Morris Street which intersects Lord at the roundabout, T5598 6089, portcampbellvisitor@corangamite.vic.gov.au (open daily 0900-1700). If the sea is calm *Port Campbell Boat Charters*, 32 Lord Street, T0500-556588, run scenic trips around the Twelve Apostles daily ($40). They also offer sunset cruises, diving, snorkelling and fishing trips. Swimming is safe in the bay and there is a short cliff-walk from the beach or the lookout car park above, the **Port Campbell Discovery Walk** (5-km return).

Colour map 2, grid C2
Population: 500
96 km from Apollo Bay, 65 km fom Warrnmbool

Victoria

Sleeping

A popular mid-way stop-over, Port Campbell mostly exists to service Great Ocean Rd tourists, so eating and sleeping here can be expensive

A-B *Shearwater Haven*, 12 Pleasant Dr, T5598 6532, F5598 6302. Hosted B&B in a modern house perched above Port Cambell with 2 rooms and valley views from the breakfast conservatory. **A-B** *Southern Ocean Motor Inn*, 1 Lord St, T1800-035093. Motel doubles, family units sleep 6. The smart mid-range restaurant, *Napiers*, focuses on seafood with Asian influences. T5598 6111. **B** *Daysy Hill Country Cottages*, T5598 6226, www.greatoceanrd.org.au 5 self-contained cedar cottages with spas and woodfires. **C** *Cairns Cottage*, 20 Cairns St, T5598 3450. Tired but spacious self-contained chalet, good for groups or families. **D** *Port Campbell*, T5598 6320. Friendly pub with 5 basic but comfortable doubles, Oct-Apr only. Cheap bistro and counter meals, available daily 1230-1430, 1800-2030. The rambling **D-E** *YHA*, Morris St, T5598 6305, portcampbell@yhavic.org.au, has 60-odd beds spread between dorms, several doubles and a couple of good value cabins. Good facilities include BBQ and internet access. The associated *Mathieson* building has comfier beds and smaller dorms. The caravan park has expensive cabins (**C-D**) and campsites, T5598 6492. There are very cheap, basic on-site vans at Peterborough in the **E** *Coastal Caravan Park*, T5598 5294.

Eating

All the eating is on Lord St, where there is also a small supermarket and some takeaways

20ate, 28 Lord St, T5598 6141. Café with a small, cosy room and an outdoor terrace where one can see and be seen. Mid-range mains, noodle dishes and noodle bar takeaway ($13), breakfasts and cakes. Daily 0800-2300, shorter hrs in winter. *Seafoam*, on Lord St opposite the beach, has the best position and makes the most of it with a huge deck. Good cheap and casual place for lunch or a snack. Also an internet kiosk. *Waves*, 29 Lord St, T5598 6111, waves@standard.net.au Contemporary and curvaceous mid-range restaurant. A large Modern Australian menu with lots of seafood and daily specials. Daily 0800-2100. Also stylish luxury suites (**L**).

Transport

The *V~Line* bus service through to **Warrnambool** leaves Cairns St on Fri at 1540 (1½ hrs), also Mon during Dec-Jan. The service through to **Apollo Bay** and **Geelong** leaves at 1045 Fri, also Mon during Dec-Jan (8 hrs). If stuck, try *Otway Discovery*, T1800 444432 or 9654 5432, who may be able to fit you on board their tour minibus.

Warrnambool

Colour map 2, grid C2
Population: 26,000
186 km from Geelong via Princes Highway,
28 km fom Port Fairy
For latest whale news,
T1800-637725

The Princes Highway flashes through Warrnambool along Raglan Parade, pausing only for traffic lights. This gives the passing visitor the impression of a very ordinary place with few redeeming features, which is a pity as it is only a stone's throw from long, curving **Lady Bay**, with some of the coast's best swimming and boogie-boarding beaches, and the rugged low headlands and tiny bays that stretch away from the breakwater at its western end. The **Thunder Point Coastal Walk** runs along the top of these cliffs, and at low tide offers the opportunity to wade out to **Middle Island**, with its rocky outcrops, caves and small fairy-penguin rookery. Just to the east of the city, across Hopkins River, there is a very good opportunity for seeing **southern right whales** from the free viewing platforms at **Logans Beach**, also a favoured surfing spot. Whales can be seen between mid-July and mid-September and are usually visible about 80% of the time. A kiosk hiring binoculars by the quarter hour often operates from the carpark. About 4 km to the east is the studio of one of Australia's best wildlife artists, **Robert Ulman**, at 440 Hopkins Point Road, T5565 1444. Robert welcomes visitors and original work, prints and stationery are available to buy. An impressive regional art collection is also on display at the **Warrnambool Art Gallery**. ■ *Mon-Fri 1000-1700, Sat-Sun 1200-1700. $4, children free, concessions $2. T5564 7832. 165 Timor St.* The **Customs House Gallery** on Gilles Street is a good private gallery. Warrnambool has a rich maritime history, and this is actively portrayed in the reconstructed wharf and dock-side buildings at the **Flagstaff Hill Maritime Museum**, as are the grisly fates of some of over 160 wrecks believed to be in the area. ■ *Daily 0900-1700. $12, children $5, concessions $9. T5564 7841.* The **VIC** is on the main through-road at 600 Raglan Parade. ■ *Daily 0900-1700, T5564 7837, www.warrnamboolinfo.com.au*

Of a handful of B&Bs one of the closest and best is the **A-B** *Walsingham*, 12 Henna St, T5561 7978, www.warrnambool.com/walsingham This friendly, hosted heritage B&B is a 10-min walk from the centre. 2 en suite and one 3-room suite, also 2 self-contained cottages. Recommended. **D-E** *Warrnambool Beach Backpackers*, 17 Stanley St near the shore, T5562 4874, johnpearson@hotmail.com Best of the city's 3 hostels by a wide margin and custom-built, though a good 20-min walk to the centre. Over 40 beds, mostly in large bunk dorms but with 2 doubles. Free bikes and fishing gear, bar, spacious common area and decent kitchen, some disabled facilities. Clean and friendly..

Sleeping
Warrnambool has plentiful motel and holiday park accommodation

There is a cluster of cafés, pubs and restaurants at the bottom of Liebig St. *Beach Babylon*, T5562 3714, daily 1800-2100, book Sat, is a dark and rustic place with mid-range modern Australian fare with a strong Italian influence. Platters and cheap gourmet pizzas. *Fish Tales*, opposite, daily 0800-2100, is a bright, cheerful and generally busy licensed café with a sunny courtyard. Breakfasts, foccaccias and good coffee. The Irish theme pub *Seanchai* is open daily from 1400. The cheapest feed is at *China City*, 132 Koroit St, a basic but clean and bright Chinese cafeteria with a seriously cheap all-you-can-eat buffet. The best of the pubs is the *Warrnambool*, corner of Koroit St and Kepler St, T5562 2377. Open daily 1130-1500, 1700-2000. Huge grungy front bar full of sofas and atmosphere. Separate cheap bistro and lounge bar. Live jazz every other Sun and Thu. At the far east end of the city, on the mouth of the Hopkins River is *Proudfoots*, T5561 5055. Open 0930-1700. Known as the 'Boathouse', this beautiful late-Victorian 'floating' weatherboard building has a shabby tea-room on the ground floor, but the best part is the small upstairs bar. The adjacent restaurant serves mid-range meals.

Eating

Boat hire from 430 Raglan Pde, T5560 5270. Tin motor boats for use on the Hopkins River. **Diving** *Shipwreck Coast Diving & Fishing*, 453 Raglan Pde, T5561 6108, run *PADI* courses, have gear for hire and offer boat dives. Try *Great Ocean Rd Trail Rides*, T5562 8088, for beach **horse-riding** (from $44 for 2 hrs).

Tours & activities

Bus The *V~Line* service along the Great Ocean Rd through to **Geelong** leaves the railway station at 0920 every Fri (9 hrs), also Mon during Dec-Jan. Services to **Port Fairy** leave at 1215 and 1620 Mon-Fri, 2135 Mon-Thu, 2140 Fri, 1220 and 2155 Sat, 2220 Sun (25 mins). The first service each day continues on to **Portland** and **Mount Gambier** in SA (2½ hrs). Services to **Ballarat** leave at 0655 Mon-Fri (3 hrs). **Train** *V~Line* direct services to **Geelong** (2 hrs) and **Melbourne** (3 hrs 20 mins) leave at 0638, 1225 and 1645 Mon-Fri, 0705, 1305 and 1705 Sat; 0700, 1250 and 1705 Sun.

Transport

Banks ATMs on Liebig St. **Chemist** *Lindsays*, 119 Liebig St, T5561 4310. Open Mon-Fri 0900-1800, Sat 0900-1500. **Communications** Internet at the library, Liebig St, or *Hot Spot*, 200 Timor St. $3 for 15 mins, open Mon-Fri 0900-1700, Sat 1000-1600. **Post Office**, corner of Timor St and Gilles St. **Hospital** *Base Hospital*, Ryot St, T5563 1666. **Police** 214 Koroit St, T5560 1333. **Taxi** T5561 1114.

Directory

Between Warrnambool and Port Fairy, the **Tower Hill Game Reserve** sits in a large volcanic crater, now filled with water. By the 1950s the reserve was completely stripped of its vegetation by farmers and little wildlife remained. However, in the last 50 years attempts have been made to replant the area

Tower Hill Game Reserve
12 km from Warrnambool

based on plant species detected in a detailed painting by Eugene von
Guérard of Tower Hill in 1855. It is now a refuge for emus, koalas, kangaroos and waterbirds, which are fairly easy to spot on one of several short walks
in the bush and there are pleasant picnic areas. More information is available
from the **Visitor Centre** inside the park. ■ *Daily 0900-1630, T5565 9202.*

Port Fairy

Colour map 2, grid C2
Population: 2,600
84 km from Hamilton,
67 km fom Portland

This small fishing village is one the oldest and most charming on the Great
Ocean Road. It developed, like so many Australian coastal towns, thanks to
sealers and whalers who settled here in the 1820s and 1830s but had wiped out
their catch within about 20 years. The Moyne River runs parallel to the sea
forming a safe, if narrow, harbour for the fishing fleet who unload catches of
squid, crayfish and abalone on the wharf. The town hosts the **Port Fairy Folk
Festival**, a huge annual music festival held over four days in early March (for
details see www.portfairyfolkfestival.com, but note that tickets can be sold out
months in advance). The **VIC** is on Bank St, close to the river. ■ *Daily
0900-1700, T5568 2682, www.port-fairy.com*

Sights
Port Fairy has many lovely Georgian buildings from the days when it was a
busy port and the merchant's houses, warehouses and pubs have been developed into elegant B&Bs, restaurants and galleries. The VIC has maps of walking tours around the historic buildings but the natural attractions are equally
interesting. At the end of Gipps Street there is a footbridge over to Griffith
Island which lies at the rivermouth. The **Griffith Island Circuit** traverses low
grass-covered dunes, past a shearwater (or muttonbird) colony, on the way to
the lighthouse and provides great views of the bay and coastline (1½ hours).
There is also a long coastal walk, the **Mahogany Walking Track** following the
coast from Port Fairy to Warrnambool, (22 km, six hours). Less strenuous
sightseeing can be done on a **boat cruise**, several leave from the wharf. *Port
Fairy Boat Charter*, T5568 1480, run ½-hour bay cruises ($11), whale watch-
ing ($25), and fishing and dive charters (from $55). They also run cruises to
Lady Julia Percy Island, to see a seal colony ($55). The island can be seen from
the shore at the **Crags**, a striking limestone outcrop, 12 km west.

Sleeping
*Port Fairy is
overflowing with
beautiful, expensive
B&B, cottage
and apartment
accomodation but the
budget choices are
very limited. Note that
it is almost impossible
to find a place to stay
during the folk festival*

*December-April is the
high season but
weekends can be
busy all year round*

L *Oscars Waterfront*, 41b Gipps St, T5568 3022, www.oscarswaterfront.com 5 sumptuous and elegant suites in a large house facing the river, gourmet breakfast on the balcony. **A-C** *Merrijig Inn*, 1 Campbell St, T5568 2324, www.merrijiginn.com A unique
Georgian corner inn, now with 8 individual and comfortable rooms (the attic rooms are
tiny but charming and good value), cosy sitting rooms, an old-fashioned bar and a fine
formal restaurant. Recommended. **B** *Colonial Cottages*, 27 and 49 Regent St, T5568
1234, www.ansonic.com.au/cottages 19th-century self-contained cottages decorated with antiques, fine linen, fresh flowers and open fires. Recommended. **B-C** *Skye
Beachfront Retreat*, 72 Griffith St, T5568 1181, www.skye-retreat.com.au 3 comfortable self-contained apartments on the beachfront in a large modern house, each
sleeps 4-8 and are good value for 2 couples (price covers 4 adults). **C** *Boathouse on
Moyne*, 19 Gipps St, T5568 2606, F5568 2740. 2 modern en suite rooms with a large
homely living room overlooking the river, homemade continental breakfasts. **E** *Port
Fairy YHA*, 8 Cox St, T5568 2468. Slightly tired National Trust house with 11 dorms, but
friendly and spacious and in the town centre. There are also several caravan parks,
including the excellent, *Belfast Cove*, 139 Princes Highway, T5568 1816, with good
value timber cabins and bunkhouses and private grassy sites.

Dublin House Inn, 57 Bank St, T5568 2022. Daily 1830-2130. Highly regarded for inventive modern cooking and has elegant and intimate traditional dining rooms. Also 3 comfortable double rooms (**C**) and a self-contained studio. *The Victoria*, 42 Bank St, T5568 2891. This pub has been revamped into a seriously stylish restaurant, and café and bar. Expensive fine dining in a subdued and elegant room and a large sixties retro café and outdoor courtyard. Daily lunch and dinner. There are 2 very good Italian restuarants, *Portofino*, 28 Bank St, T5568 1047, is intimate and formal with mid-range authentic cuisine and *Madagalli on Bank*, 24 Bank St, T5568 1829, Wed-Sun 1700-2030, is cheap and casual, serving pizza and pasta in a light-filled room and small courtyard. Also takeaway. *Sackville St Deli*, has tasty gourmet sandwiches, and couches. *Rebecca's*, 70 Sackville St, daily 0700-1800, is a lively and popular café, good for breakfast, also the freshest of cakes and light Mediterranean meals. For fresh fish and takeaways try *Wisharts at the Wharf*, daily 1000-1900.

Bus *V~Line* services to **Warrnambool** (30 mins) leave from the VIC on Bank St, 0555, 1125 and 1705 Mon-Fri, 0627 and 1105 Sat, 1622 Sun. Services to **Portland** leave at 1243 Mon-Fri, 2200 Mon-Thu, 2205 Fri, 1250 and 2218 Sat, 2240 Sun (50 mins). The first service each day, plus the 2205 on Fri, continues on to **Mount Gambier**.

Portland

This town was Victoria's earliest settlement, founded in 1834 by the Henty brothers who tired of waiting for official approval to settle in the area. There are fine 19th-century buildings around the port, it has expanded into a busy industrial centre. At the docks ships from all over the world shift cargos of grain, alumina, fertilizer and woodchips. On the western edge the city is dominated by a large and controversial aluminium plant, which was built on a sacred Aboriginal site. The company, Alcoa, eventually had to pay compensation. The **Portland Maritime Discovery Centre** is an interesting modern museum of the sea focusing on shipwrecks, rescue and exploration with a good café overlooking the bay. The **VIC** is in the same complex and has maps for a self-guided historic walking tour and internet access. ■ *Daily 0900-1700. Museum entry $7.70, children $3.30, concessions $5.50. T5523 2671, www.maritimediscovery.com Foreshore (Lee Breakwater Rd).*

Colour map 2, grid C1
Population: 10,000
83 km from Hamilton, 70 km fom Nelson

Victoria

B *Victoria House*, 5-7 Tyers St, T5521 7577, is a gracious 1850s house with comfortable and traditional rooms, open fires and serves a fine breakfast. The most novel self-contained place in town is **C** *Mystique*, T5523 3920, www.portlandnow.org/mystique A former crayfish boat moored alongside the fishing fleet, fitted out with double bed, kitchen, TV, stereo and marine radio. Secure parking nearby. **C** *Whaler's Cottage*, 12 Whalers Court, T5521 7522, www.portlandnow.com.au/whalerscottage Another good B&B, in the former lighthouse keeper's bluestone house on the cliff. **D** *Claremont Holiday Village*, T5521 7567, has lots of neat cabins although *Centenary* caravan park, T5523 1487, on the waterfront has cheaper options. There is also a central hostel, **E** *Portland Backpackers*, 14 Gawler St, T5523 5100, backpackers@iconnect.net.au

Most of the restaurants, takeaways and pubs can be found on Bentinck St, opposite the foreshore, and the block behind. *Edwards Waterfront*, in *Macs Hotel* 101 Bentinck St, T5523 1032. Daily 0700-2030. Has Portland's best food in a fine old corner pub, serving bistro-style Mediterranean meals of seafood, pasta, and salads. *Bay Provender*, 21 Julia St. Mon-Sat 0800-1600, Fri-Sat night in summer. Good for lunch with foccacia, cakes and an extensive choice of tea and coffee blends. *Sunstream Heathfoods*, 49 Julia St, has healthy takeaways, juices and smoothies.

▶▶ **Great South West Walk**

*A spectacular 250-km circuit, the Great South West Walk heads inland from Portland through the Cobboboonee Forest to the deep river gorge of the Lower Glenelg National Park to Nelson. From the mouth of the Glenelg River the track returns along the seemingly endless beaches and sand dunes of Discovery Bay to the high sea cliffs at Cape Bridgewater and Cape Nelson. Largely built and maintained by local volunteers, the route generally takes about 10-12 days and can also be done in day-long sections or as a forest, river, beach or cliff section. There are 16 campsites and it is also possible to stay in B&Bs or caravan parks in Cape Bridgewater and Nelson. Local volunteers may be able to provide transport to start and finish points and make food drops (petrol charge). Contact **Friends of the GSWW**, T5523 5262, gwenbennett@ yahoo.com Information, maps and detailed notes are available from the Portland and Nelson information centres and **Parks Victoria**. There is also an operator running guided walks, **South West Adventures**, T5523 3175, ftedge@ansonic.com.au Nearest **Parks Victoria** office is in Portland, 8 Julia St, T5523 3232.*

Transport **Bus** *V~Line* services to **Port Fairy** and **Warrnambool** (1½ hrs) leave from Henty Plaza at 0500 and 1030 Mon-Fri, 1620 Fri, 0530 and 1005 Sat, 1525 Sun. Services to **Mount Gambier** in SA leave at 1343 Mon-Fri, 2300 Fri, 1350 Sat, 2340 Sun (1 hr).

Around Portland **Cape Nelson** is the most southerly part of the coastline around Portland so it is topped by a tall lighthouse. The *Great South West Walk* traverses the edge of the cape's rugged cliffs and a short section can be walked for great views. There are tours of the lighthouse daily, a café, and a range of accommodation in former lighthouse keepers' cottages. Contact Cape Nelson Lightstation, T5523 5100, enquiries@lightstation.com.au for details. The next cape west is **Cape Bridgewater**, standing above the magnificent long sandy crescent of Bridgewater Bay. There are a few holiday homes here, a beach kiosk and little else but it is a fine place for a beach or cliff walk. The Great South West Walk track and a road lead right to the top of the cape where there are blowholes and a Petrified Forest. A seal colony lives at the base of these cliffs and can be seen from a lookout at the cape. *Seals by Sea* run boat trips out to the colony and into a huge sea cave. ($20, 45 minutes), T5526 7247 or enquire at the kiosk. The walking track from the kiosk to the seal viewing platform is about 5 km there and back. **C** *Sea View Lodge*, T5526 7276, is a good B&B opposite the beach, contact the VIC in Portland to book self-contained accommodation. Limited tourist information is available at the kiosk. **Mount Richmond National Park**, just inland from Cape Bridgewater and about 20 minutes drive from Portland, is known for spectacular displays of wildflowers in spring and coastal views.

Nelson A tiny settlement on the banks of the Glenelg River, Nelson is a peaceful place
Phone code: 08 from which to walk along the 50-km-long ocean beach of **Discovery Bay**
Colour map 2, grid C1 **Coastal Park** or to explore the beautiful cliffs and bush of the river gorge in
28 km from **Lower Glenelg National Park**. Canoeing and camping along the river is one
Mount Gambier of the best ways to see the gorge but there are also boat cruises up to the **Prin-**
Note that Nelson and **cess Margaret Rose Cave**. This is a highly decorated stream-cave full of sta-
the caves have the lactites, stalagmites and helictites. From Nelson it can be reached by boat or by
phone code 08 road (17 km west). There are also short walks to the river gorge, picnic areas as well as cabins and campsites. ■ *Daily 1000-1700. $6.20, children $3, concessions $5. Tours (40 mins) every hr 1000-1530. T8738 4171.* To canoe the 75 km

from Dartmoor takes about four days and there are 11 canoe camps along the way. Camping permits must be obtained from the Nelson **VIC**, combined with a parks office, on the riverfront opposite the pub. Daily 0900-1700, T8738 4051, nelsonvic@hotkey.com.au

Sleeping and eating C *Simsons Landing*, T/F8738 4232, off Simsons Landing Rd. B&B surrounded by bush and close to the river with 2 timber rooms and 2-way bathroom. **D** *Tigh na Brae*, Beach Rd, T8738 4241. A self-contained flat on the ground floor of a modern 2-storey house. Peaceful, isolated spot. Follow the signs for Town Beach. **D** *Casuarina Cabins*, North Nelson Rd, T8738 4105. 7 self-contained en suite cabins surrounded by trees and close to the National Park. *Kywong Caravan Park*, T8738 4174, has cabins (**D-E**) and is in the bush opposite *Casuarina Cabins*. The only places to eat in Nelson are the pub and the *Black Wattle Motel*, T8738 4008.

The town has a very limited selection of groceries so self-caterers should stock up in Portland or Mount Gambier

Tour operators *Glenelg River Cruises*, T8738 4191, run trips timed to include a cave tour ($20, 3½ hrs), and can also pick up walkers on the *Great South West Walk*. *Nelson Boat Hire*, T8738 4048, nelson@dove.net.au, have canoes and kayaks and can organize upriver canoe deliveries and pickups. Similarly *South West Canoe Service*, T8725 6844.

Gippsland

*Lying east of Melbourne and extending from the mountains to the coast, Gippsland is the rural heartland of Victoria, a rich landscape of rolling green dairy pasture. In the far south is the main attraction, **Wilson's Promontory**, a low range of forest-covered granite mountains, marked only by the occasional walking track, edged with isolated sandy bays and golden river inlets. Carefully maintained as a wilderness the 'Prom' offers intimate encounters with wildlife and is a stunning place to walk, swim, camp or simply laze about.*

In the centre of the region, the Gippsland Lakes system forms the largest inland waterway in Australia. Here, every small town has jetties festooned with yachts and fishing boats, particularly the villages of Paynesville and Metung. Even though the fishing and boating attracts thousands of Victorians in summer, as attested by the touristy commerce of Lakes Entrance, there are innumerable isolated spots for walking, swimming and birdwatching. Heading inland from the fertile river flats around Orbost the landscape rises to the limestone caves of Buchan and the rugged forest and gorges of the Snowy River National Park. In the east the region returns to wilderness where rivers flow through dense bush to the sea in the Croajingolong National Park, forming tranquil inlets. The largest inlet is overlooked by one of Victoria's loveliest small towns, Mallacoota, an isolated and peaceful haven for birds and other two-legged creatures.

Ins and outs

Bus The main *V~Line* train line heads out from **Melbourne** through **Dandenong** and **Warragul** to **Sale**. From Dandenong there are connecting bus services to **Bass** then **Newhaven** and **Cowes** on Phillip Island; to **Wonthaggi** and **Inverloch**; and to **Yarram** via **Leongatha**, **Fish Creek**, and **Foster**. From Sale change to buses for **Bairnsdale**, **Lakes Entrance** and other stops to the NSW border. There are also **ferries** to **Cowes** from **Stony Point** on the Mornington Peninsula. **Train** A *V~Line* railway line heads out from **Melbourne** to **Sale**. From here buses take over. The route heads east via **Bairnsdale**, **Lakes Entrance**, **Orbost**, **Cann River** and **Genoa** to the NSW border. From Cann River there is a set-down-only service to **Canberra** and another up the coast to **Batemans Bay**.

Getting there & around

Tours *Bunyip Tours*, T9600 9207, are an eco-friendly bunch who take small groups out to **Wilson's Promontary**. They offer 2 and 4-day guided treks, camping along the way (2 days $185, 4 days around $300). Equipment, except for sleeping bags and a backpack, and food included.

Information

The general tourism website is www.phillipislandand gippsland.com.au

If heading east out of Melbourne along the Princes Highway the *Gippsland Regional Tourist Information Centre* at Tynong North can provide information and bookings for the whole Gippsland region. Daily 0900-1700. T5629 2385, tourinfo@nex.net.au If travelling south out of Melbourne towards Wilson's Promontory, along the South Gippsland Highway, head for the *Prom Country Information Centre* on the highway in Korumbarra. Daily 0900-1700. T5655 2233, infocentre@sgsc.vic.gov.au

Wildlife Wonderland

Bass Highway, north of San Remo. See Around Melbourne map, page 430

Known locally as 'The Big Worm', this fascinating, eclectic set-up is worth a detour for three reasons: a chance to see the Giant Gippsland Worms, the opportunity to cuddle orphaned wombats, and the choice of seeing a preserved Great White Shark floating in a tank The worms can reach 3 m in length, though only 2 cm in diameter. Tragically these wonderful creatures are under siege from introduced worms. ■ *Daily 1000-1700. $11.90, children $6.90. T5678 2222.*

Wonthaggi

Colour map 2, grid C3
Population: 5,100
42 km from Cowes,
65 km from Foster

Wonthaggi is the largest town on the southwest Gippsland coast, worth a visit for the **Wonthaggi State Coal Mine**. This may not exactly get the pulse racing but a guided tour of the mine and accompanying museum is sobering and fascinating. ■ *Daily 1000-1630. $6.50, children $4. Tours frequently, included in entry price. T5672 3053, 3 km from town toward Cape Paterson.* The Wonthaggi **VIC** is on Watt Street, parallel to the main shopping area Graham Street. ■ *Daily 0900-1700, T5671 2444, woninfo@compac.net.au*

Sleeping A couple of kilometres further south, just north of Cape Paterson, is a gem of a B&B, the **C** *Ibis Inn*, T5672 2555. Two cheery split-level self-contained cottages, each with a double-bed mezzanine. Very comfortable, fantastic value if you take one for a week (**E**) out of peak long weekends, and this wouldn't be a bad base for exploring the area and Phillip Island. Very friendly hosts. Recommended.

Transport Bus *V~Line* buses to **Inverloch** leave from the corner of McBride Av and Watt St, 4 times a day Mon-Fri, at 1217, 2057 Sat, and 2037 Sun. Buses to **Kilcunda**, **Anderson** and **Melbourne** leave 4 times a day Mon-Fri, 0650, 1548 Sat and 1605 Sun. The 0732 Mon-Fri and first Sat and Sun services go via **Cape Paterson**.

Wonthaggi to Inverloch

Distance via coast 20 km

There are two roads east from Wonthaggi to Inverloch. The boring straight road and the **Bunurong Coastal Drive** via Cape Paterson. The latter hugs a series of craggy low cliffs above rocky shelves, exposed at low tide, interspersed by sandy coves. **Eagles Nest** is the best viewpoint, though it is worth stopping at **The Caves** in February-March as the dinosaur dig there may be in full swing. There is a dinosaur interpretation area at the **Bunurong Environment Centre and Shop** which also runs various educational programmes. ■ *Thu-Sun 1000-1600. T5674 3738, Ramsay Blvd, Inverloch..* This stretch of coast is also popular with surfers, with 'Suicide' being one of the favoured spots. The *Offshore Surf School*, T5674 3374, won't take you straight out there, but do have a range of courses available. **Inverloch** itself is a rapidly developing holiday town neatly situated at the mouth of **Anderson Inlet**. The friendly **VIC** is on Williams Street, close to the junction with A'Beckett, the main shopping street. ■ *Tue-Sun 0930-1700. T5674 3510.*

Sleeping and eating   The best 2 B&Bs are **B** *Hill Top House*, Lower Tarwin Rd, T/F5674 3514, and **B** *The Eyrie by the Inlet*, Townsend Bluff Rd, T5674 2001, eyrie@unite.com.au   *Tsunami*, Williams St, T5674 2129, is a funky bar restaurant, open for lunch and dinner until at least 2200 daily. Wide selection of mid-range Asian, Australian and cheap pasta dishes (pasta half price Tue nights). There are several takeaways and fish and chip outlets, including the highly regarded *Sea Bees* on the Boulevard.

Transport   Bus *V~Line* buses from the service station on the Esplanade to **Kilcunda**, **Anderson** and **Melbourne** 4 times a day Mon-Fri, 0620, 1530 Sat and 1635 Sun. The 0715 Mon-Fri and first Sat and Sun services go via **Cape Paterson**.

This tiny settlement, amidst lush cow-covered hills, is a worthy distraction for those with the Prom set firmly in their sights thanks to the *Koonwarra Store*, T5664 2285, a mid-range café/restaurant serving country breakfasts, lunches and dinners of the highest quality, and a takeaway. Book for meals at weekends. Recommended. Open daily 0800-1700, wine bar and diner Friday-Saturday 1830-2130.

Koonwarra
140 km Melbourne, 80 km from Wilson's Promontory

The tiny and charming settlement Fish Creek is distinguished by the enormous shiny fish that flops on the roof of the pub and the flying Friesian atop the main café, on a street of weatherboard cottages parallel to the highway. On this street there is a good second-hand bookshop, as well as a general store, post office and galleries.

Fish Creek
Colour map 2, grid C3
Population: 200
15 km from Foster, 56 km from Tidal River

Sleeping and eating   The *Flying Cow*, is a warm and friendly place for wholesome lunches (mostly vegetarian), cakes and decent coffee. Wed-Sun 1000-1700. Also casual country dinners on Sat nights Jan-Apr. *Fishy Pub*, on the highway, also has a reputation for excellent mid-range food, daily 1200-1400, 1800-2000. They have live music most weekends and basic pub rooms (**E**) or en suite motel rooms (**C**), though the former are only available weekends. A few kilometres further on is **B** *Milkwood*, 660 Harding Lawson Rd, T5683 2449, www.promaccom.com.au/milkwood.

Transport   *V~Line* buses leave from the BP service station for **Dandenong** and **Melbourne** (3 hrs) at 0800 Mon-Sat and 1537 Sun. Services east to **Foster** and **Yarram** leave at 1927 Mon-Fri, 2132 Fri, 2130 Sat and 2040 Sun.

Foster is the closest major town to Wilson's Promontory and is well supplied with supermarkets and bakeries to fuel camping expeditions. In front of the roundabout on Main Street there is a building that houses a **Parks Victoria** office, the library and Stockyard Gallery. **Tourist information** is available from the foyer and help from the gallery staff if open. The gallery stocks local pottery and paintings. ■ *Thu-Sun 1000-1600, T5682 1125.* The parks office has some information on the Prom but is not responsible for the park. The Prom office is in Tidal River.

Foster
Colour map 2, grid C3
Population: 1,000
30 km from Koonwara, 60 km from Tidal River

Sleeping and eating   B *Hillcrest Farmhouse*, 175 Ameys Track, T5682 2769, hillcrest@c031.aone.net.au   2 en suite rooms in an 1880s farmhouse, peaceful with good views. **B** *Larkrise*, Foster-Fish Creek Rd, T/F5682 2953, www.larkrise.com.au   2 comfortable modern B&B rooms with wonderful views of the Prom from the guest sitting room. Disabled access. **C** *Stockyard Creek Cottages*, McGleads Rd (signposted from roundabout), T5682 2493, www.promaccom.com.au/sycc   2 self-contained log cabins with views of the valley. **D-E** *Foster Backpackers*, office at 17 Pioneer St (turn off Main St at the post office, then turn right at T-junction), T5682 2614. 2 4-bed dorms in a

Victoria

small, quiet and clean hostel, linen included. Also 2 self-contained units. The hard-working owner farms during the day so call in advance. The caravan park is on Nelson St, turn at the Mobil service station, T5682 2440. Foster does not have many places to eat but there is an excellent café, *Rhythm*, on Bridge St, T5682 1612. Thu-Tue 0900-1700, daily 1800-2100 in peak summer. Scrumptious breakfasts, casual lunches and cakes in a small, bright jazzy room. The pub, the *Exchange*, T5682 2377, 1200-1400, 1800-2000 daily, has reasonable meals (cheap to mid-range).

Transport *V~Line* buses leave from Pulham's Store, Main St, for **Fish Creek Dandenong** and **Melbourne** (3 hrs) at 0749 Mon-Sat and 1525 Sun. Services east to **Yarram** leave at 1915 Mon-Fri, 2120 Fri, 2141 Sat and 2051 Sun.

Wilson's Promontory National Park

Colour map 2, grid C3
Tidal River 147 km
from Cowes, 229 km
from Melbourne
There are almost 500
unpowered campsites
at Tidal River so it is
teeming in busy
summer periods

'The Prom', as it is known by Victorians, is one of Victoria's top attractions, with granite-capped mountains covered in forest sloping down to the purest of white sand beaches and tannin-stained rivers meandering down to the sea. The northeastern region is a wilderness area only accessible to bushwalkers and boats. The park's most accessible beaches and bushwalks are on the western coast near **Tidal River**, the only 'settlement', where parrots, wombats and kangaroos roam around freely. Walkers can camp overnight in remote sites with basic facilities but must obtain a permit from the parks office at Tidal River. The office also has detailed notes on day and overnight walks and can offer advice on activities in the park. ■ *Daily 0900-1700, T5680 9555, www.parkweb.vic.gov.au Park entry at the gate $9 car per day.*

Ins & outs
Note that wombats
are attracted to body
heat and may curl
up beside you in
your tent if you
leave the flap open

Foster Backpackers, T5682 2614, runs a minibus to Tidal River from **Foster** on demand for a minimum of 2, ($30pp return, 50 mins). *Bay Connections*, T5678 5642, www.bayconnections.com.au, run occasional day cruises from *Port Welshpool* or *San Remo* that include stops at Waterloo Bay, Refuge Cove and cruising around the lighthouse, skull rock and a seal colony (Pt Welshpool $88, 9 hrs, San Remo $175, 15 hrs). **Guided walks** *Surefoot Explorations*, Cowes, T5952 1533, offer a day-trip with short walks (suitable for disabled) and can provide transport, packed lunches and equipment such as binoculars.

Walking
The parks office has
free detailed park
notes on most walks

The park offers dozens of trail options. **Squeaky Beach**, **Picnic Bay** and **Whisky Bay** can be reached by very short walks from car parks but the best short walk is to walk to of all these beaches from Tidal River along the coast and return (9 km return). The best views of the Prom are from the top of **Mount Oberon**. The walk up from Telegraph Saddle carpark, 3½ km from Tidal River, is wide and easy with a few rock-cut steps at the top (7 km, two hours return). Sunrise, not sunset, is the best time for photographs of Norman Bay below. (A good spot for sunset is Whisky Bay). A very popular day walk from the same car park is the track to **Sealers's Cove** (9½ km, 2½ hours one-way) passing through thick rainforest to the eastern side of the Prom. The cove has a long arc of golden sand, tightly fringed by bush. There is a basic campsite at Sealers Creek. The cove is beautiful but the walk has little variety and the return leg can feel like a bit of a slog. A more interesting day-walk is the **Oberon Bay** loop that also starts from Telegraph Saddle (19km, six hours).

There is also an extended walk (38 km, two to three days) to the lighthouse that sits on a great dome of granite on the southern tip of the promontory. The **Lighthouse Trek** can be done independently or from October-May with a ranger guide ($295-435 including accommodation and meals). Accommodation is in cottages at the lighthouse that are equipped with bunks, kitchen and bathroom. The cottages can be booked by the bed or exclusively for groups (**C-D**).

The best place to stay is undoubtedly within the park itself. There is a good range of accomodation in cabins, units and huts (**B-D**). For cabin or campsite bookings, T5680 9555, wprom@parks.vic.gov.au There is an (unbookable) international campers, area available for 1-2 nights, and if this is full there are other sleeping options within a 30-minute drive of the park. Check www.promaccom.com.au **L** *Singapore Deep*, Foley Rd, Yanakie, T/F5687 1208, stay@singaporedeep.com.au An architect-designed self-contained pavilion with walls of glass overlooking the veranda and water views. **B** *Tingara View*, 10 Tingara Close, Yanakie, T/F5687 1488, www.promaccom.com.au/tingaraview 3 pretty colonial-style one-room cottages with lovely views, cooked breakfast served in main house, dinner also offered. **C** *Coastal View*, Foley Rd, Yanakie, T5687 1248. 3 self-contained wooden cabins with spa bath and the eponymous view. Places to eat are limited to lacklustre fast food from the café at Tidal River or *Yanakie's Roadhouse*, the closest decent food is in Fish Creek or Foster. There is also a shop at Tidal River stocking a limited range of groceries and petrol.

Sleeping & eating

The Prom is so popular that accommodation is allocated by ballot for December-January (including campsites). Even at other times, weekends may have to be booked a year in advance

Running between the south Gippsland coast and the industrial valleys to the north the Strzelecki Ranges are a series of curvaceous green hills mostly devoted to commercial logging, with dairy farming on some of the lower slopes. From Leongatha a short drive to Mirboo North gets you onto the main unsealed section of the **Grand Ridge Road**, a rough logging track which stretches through some beautiful forest and affords occasional views over the ranges. However, the way can be tortuous, treacherous and is frustratingly badly signposted at present. At its eastern end it passes alongside the Tarra-Bulga National Park, which preserves a lush remnant of what was the 'Great Forest of Gippsland'. Tall and poker-straight Mountain Ash grows on the steep slopes and myrtle beech, sassafras and many species of ferns live in patches of temperate rainforest in the gullies. Parks Victoria has a **Visitor Centre** on the Grand Ridge Road in Balook with information on walking tracks, but is rarely open. ■ *Weekends and public holidays only, 1000-1600, T5196 6166*. A few short walks are signposted from the Visitor Centre car park. There are more short walks from the Bulga Picnic Area (turn right out of the Visitor Centre and take the first left), where there is a good chance of seeing a lyrebird.

Tarra-Bulga National Park

Colour map 2, grid C4
60 km from Mirboo North, 25 km from Yarram. Grand Ridge Rd generally ok for 2WD, allow 2 hrs

Victoria

Sleeping and eating Accommodation around the park is limited to a couple of caravan parks in the nearby Tarra Valley, and the **B** *Tarra-Bulga Guest House and Tea Rooms*, Balook, T5196 6141. This is an old-fashioned guesthouse (no en suite), with comfortable rooms. Price includes hearty country dinner and breakfast from the same kitchen that produces the excellent daytime light lunches. Petrol also available, though it is cheaper 25 km away in Yarram.

Gippsland Lakes

The break between central and eastern Gippsland is marked by a series of connected lakes, separated from the sea only by the long thin dune system of the eastern end of **Ninety Mile Beach**. This strip of sand, designated the **Gippsland Lakes Coastal Park**, is accessible only by boat and is realtively unspoiled, even in peak season. The main service town in the area is **Bairnsdale**, but there are some pretty settlements dotted around the margins of the lakes, and **Metung** is particularly picturesque. Soon after Yarram is the

Colour map 2, grid C4
www.lakesand wilderness.com.au

turn to Woodside Beach, which markes the start of **Ninety Mile Beach**, the long golden stretch of sand that curves all the way to Lakes Entrance. **Sale**, the administration centre for Gippsland, has all the usual services but few attractions for visitors. The **VIC** is on the Princes Highway, just west of the town centre. ■ *Daily 0900-1700. T5144 1108, www.gippslandinfo.com.au*

Tours & activities

Virtually all activity revolves around the water, with several ways of getting out onto the hundreds of square kilometres of lakes. For hourly or daily hire, *Lakes Entrance Paddle Boats*, over the footbridge in Lakeside to the spit, can provide almost anything from a body board to a small catamaran, T0419 552753. Motor boats can be hired from *Lakes Hire Boats*, Marine Parade, T5155 3113. *Riviera Nautic*, in Metung, T5156 2243, www.rivnautic.com.au, is one of the most highly regarded tourist operators in Australia, offering superb service. They have various overnight motor-cruisers and sailboats for hire, from around $250 a day (minimum two days), which is the best way to experience the lakes. *The Spray* is a 14-m-long historic ketch sailing out of Metung when there are sufficient numbers. T5156 2201, www.metung.com/spraycruises *The Lorraine* is a 1947 racing yacht offering evening 'wine and dine' cruises from Paynesville for only $30, numbers permitting. Charter available. T04-0704 9675. Also based in Paynesville, *Clint's Ski School*, T5156 6518, offers good value private lessons ($30 for 40 mins), multiple runs for the more experienced and ski-tube runs. Equipment supplied.

Bairnsdale
Colour map 2, grid C4
Population: 11,000
35 km from Lakes Entrance, 280 km from Melbourne

This, the largest town in the Lakes area, isn't actually on a lake shore itself. It is worth stopping here to see the Aboriginal **Krowathunkalong Keeping Place** which features chillingly frank descriptions of the brutal Gunnai massacres that took place in Gippsland during the 1830s-50s. ■ *Mon Fri 0900-1200, 1300-1700. $3.50, children $2.50, concessions $1.50. T5152 1891, Dalmahoy St*. For a deeper insight into the local Gunnai people, contact *Boran Glaat Cultural Tours*, T/F5152 2585. The excellent **VIC** will help with information and bookings for the whole Lakes region as well as Bairnsdale itself. ■ *Daily 0900-1700. T5152 3444, bairnsdale@lakesandwilderness.com.au*

Sleeping There are a couple of caravan parks, and several motels and B&Bs, including **B** *Tara House*, 37 Day St, T5153 2253, tarahouse@tech-net.com.au Hosted B&B with 3 en suite rooms in one of Bairnsdale's oldest residences.

Transport There are *V~Line* bus services to **Sale** and **Melbourne** from the railway station at 0600, 1225, 1535 Mon-Fri, 1250 Sat and 1401 Sun. Buses leave from the corner of Main St and Bailey St for **Lakes Entrance** 4-5 times a day Mon-Fri, 1246 Sat, and from the railway station at 1345 Sun. Further services from the station via Lakes Entrance (pick-ups only) to **Orbost**, **Cann River**, **Genoa** and NSW stops to **Narooma** or **Batemans Bay** leave at 1146 Mon-Fri, 1241 Sat and 1345 Sun. The **Canberra** buses leave the station at 1145 Mon, Thu and 1240 Sat, also stopping at Orbost and Cann River. *Omeo Bus Lines*, T5159 4231, run an occasional bus up to **Omeo**.

Paynesville
Population: 3,200
13 km from Bairnsdale, on the western shore of Lake King

Bigger than Metung, but less tacky than Lakes Entrance, Paynesville hugs a stretch of lake shore that faces **Raymond Island**. The island is a small haven for wildlife, especially koalas, with one of the country's most concentrated wild populations. It's not a park, however, and the Paynesville township effectively extends across the car ferry (every half an hour, $3.30 return, pedestrians free) to claim a portion of the island as a suburb. Further offshore, **Rotamah Island** is home to a *Bird Observatory*, T/F5156 6398, rotamah@i-o.net.au A wonderful retreat, this homestead has five rooms sleeping 19 people on a fully catered basis (around $75 a night). Own linen required. The island is teeming with wildlife, not just birds, and the owners can arrange boat transport from Paynesville.

Sleeping and eating A pleasant 30-min lakeside stroll, or 1-km drive, from Panesville town centre is **A** *Lake Gallery*, Backwater Ct, T5156 0448, www.lakegallery bedandbreakfast.com Modern designer house with 2 en suite, seriously stylish, hosted B&B rooms. The balcony overlooks the lawns running down to the lake's edge. And yes, they also run a small fine-art gallery. Recommended. **B** *Emily's House*, 65A Western Blvd, T5156 0884, emilysbb@satlink.com.au Traditional self-contained cottage with veranda and a pretty cottage garden. **C** *Espas*, Raymond Island, T/F5156 7275, www.espas.com.au Very simple but stylish en suite cabins, one with full disabled access, homely shared kitchen and living area. Also excellent modern food in the striking mid-range cafe with an outdoor deck facing Paynesville across the water. Open Fri-Sat 1000-2030, Sun 1000-1700. **D** *Old Hotel*, Esplanade, T5156 6442. 5 pub rooms, unusually all en suite, freshly decorated and furnished, continental breakfast, pleasant veranda. Also bistro with cheap menu and superb salad and veggie bar. *Fisherman's Wharf Pavilion*, T5156 0366, is right on the water and a wonderful spot either summer or winter. A café by day with breakfasts and interesting light lunches, mid-range restaurant Thu-Sat to 2000.

Metung
Colour map 2, grid C4
Between Bairnsdale and Lake Entrance

Metung is on a small spit only a few hundred metres wide, giving it the feel of a village surrounded by water. Most of the homes spreading up the low wooded hill to the rear overlook Bancroft Bay, lined with yachts and jetties. The well-heeled visitor is well catered for here, with a couple of good restaurants, wonderful day and sailing options and some luxurious accommodation.

Sleeping and eating **A** *Clovelly*, Essington Close, T5156 2428, www.babs.com.au/ clovelly Very comfortable hosted B&B, extensive verandas and gardens with good views, and each en suite has its own fern-atrium! Licensed. **B** *Anchorage*, at The Anchorage, T5156 2569, www.metung.org/anchorage Comfortable B&B with particularly wonderful wooden breakfast atrium. There are various self-contained options, including the spacious and well-furnished **C** *Arendell* cabins, set in fine lawned gardens. T/F 5156 2507, arendell@l-o.net.au *Little Mariner's*, Metung Rd, T5156 2077. Tue 1800-2030, Wed-Thu 1200-2030, Fri-Sat 0830-2030, Sun 0830-1700. Also has great seafood, but a slightly more casual feel in 2 stylish rooms. Lots of fish and variety from a long specials menu. Breakfasts at weekends. The *Allambie*, T5156 2202, is a fine if pricey breakfast restaurant in a beautiful colonial house with wide verandahs, brick terrace and garden tables. Book for summer weekends, daily 0800-1200.

Lakes Entrance
Colour map 2, grid C4
Population: 5,250
35 km from Bairnsdale,
58 km from Orbost

Standing at the only break in the long stretch of dunes that separate the Gippsland Lakes from the sea, Lakes Entrance, once a small fishing village, is dominated by dozens of motels and caravan parks slung out in two long rows along the lake side, 2 km from end to end. Over the footbridge is the **Entrance Walking Track**, a leisurely and rewarding two-hour return stroll through dunes and bush to **Ninety Mile Beach** and Flagstaff Lookout. The **Wyanga Park Winery** (see eating below) runs popular day and evening cruises from the town's Club Jetty on their launch, the *Corque*. T5155 1508. The **VIC** is at the very western end of town, on the highway. ■ *Daily 0900-1700. T5155 1966, lakes@lakesandwilderness.com.au*

Accommodation may be plentiful, but there's not a room or patch of earth to be had in the summer school holidays as hordes descend from Melbourne

Sleeping Squeezed in among the motels and caravan parks are a handful of options offering something a bit different. **L-B** *Deja Vu* is actually just to the north of town over the lake on Clara St, T5155 4330, www.dejavu.com.au This modern, glass-filled, hosted B&B, set in 7 acres of wild lakeside country, has rooms with private lake-view balconies and the first-class service is friendly and attentive, with some unexpected and unusual flourishes. Book well in advance. Recommended. **A-B** *BelleVue*, Esplanade, T5155 3055, www.bellvuelakes.com A cracking little day-time café and decent mid-range seafood restaurant help make this very comfortably furnished, family-run motel stand out from the crowd. **C** *Lazy Acre*, Roadnight St, T5155 1212, lazyacre@net-tech.com.au Several well-maintained and self-contained log cabins, one specifically designed for the disabled, each sleeping up to 6. **C** *Bellbrae*, 4 km out on Ostlers Rd, T5155 2319, bellbrae_2000@yahoo.com Very similar cabins, but cheaper and better spaced out in a forest setting, although slightly less well furnished. **E** *Riviera Backpackers*, Clarkes Rd, T5155 2444, riviera@net-tech.com.au Very well run and equipped *YHA* hostel with a good range of rooms, including several doubles, all at a good value per-head price. Cheap bike hire, pool. Friendly and knowledgeable owners. Recommended.

Eating Mid-range *Miriam's*, the Esplanade, T5155 3999. Open daily 1800-2130. First-floor restaurant with funky feel, great balcony tables in summer, and abundant candles and candelabras in the darker months. Good seafood. *Nautilus* floats on the harbour toward the western end of town, T5155 1400. Open daily 1800-2030. The owners have managed to give this floating cabin a surprising amount of character and both seafood and service are superb. Book for Sat. *Wyanga Park Winery*, 10 km north of town on Baades Rd, has tastings and a colourful, characterful café open daily 1000-1700, doubling as a restaurant, Thu-Sat 1800-2000. **Cheap** The *Central* pub has a large bistro area. Surprisingly good meals, with a self-serve salad and veggie bar. Open daily 1200-1400, 1800-2000. There are a number of cafés and takeaways along the Esplanade, including *Shell's Harbour*, with good beakfasts, light lunches and internet access, and *Fish-a-Fare* which serves up a terrific portion of fish and chips. *L'Ocean* on Myer St does the same with wheat and gluten free batter.

Transport There are *V~Line* bus services to **Bairnsdale** and **Melbourne** (4-5 hrs) from the Post Office at 0515, 1140, 1455 Mon-Fri, 1205 Sat and 1320 Sun. An additional Bairnsdale-only service departs 1830 Mon-Fri. Buses leave for **Orbost**, **Cann River**, **Genoa** and NSW stops to **Narooma** or **Batemans Bay** at 1216 Mon-Fri, 1311 Sat and 1415 Sun. The **Canberra** buses leave at 1215 Mon, Thu and 1310 Sat, also stopping at Orbost and Cann River.

Buchan and Snowy River National Park

Colour map 2, grid C5
Population: 400
55 km from Lakes Entrance, 56 km from Orbost
Limited tourist info is available from the post office or general store

Buchan is best known for its limestone caves but it is also just south of the **Snowy River National Park**. Consequently it is a good area for walking, canoeing and rafting as well as caving. There are over 300 caves in the region, the best of which are contained in the **Buchan Caves Reserve** which has two well-lit show caves with spectacular golden cave decorations. **Fairy Cave** and **Royal Cave** are famous for their pillars, stalactites, stalagmites, flowstone and calcite pools. There are 'adventure' caving tours available during Easter and Christmas holidays or when numbers permit ($16.50, two hours), and some good short walks in the reserve. The 3-km **Spring Creek Walk** is a loop that heads uphill to Spring Creek Falls and passes through remnant rainforest, mossy rocks and ferns. Lyrebirds, kookaburras and parrots may be seen (or heard) on this track. Detailed walking notes and bookings for cave tours are available from the **Parks**

Victoria office in the reserve. ■ *Daily Oct-Mar 1000, 1115, 1300, 1415, 1530, Apr-Sep 1100, 1300, 1500. $11, children $5.50, concessions $9. T5155 9264, entrance to the reserve is just north of town, before the bridge.*

B *Snowy River Wildernest*, T5154 1923. An isolated 150-ha deer farm, 30 km towards Orbost, snuggled in a wooded valley on a beautiful stretch of the Snowy River, with 2 spacious but basic self-contained houses, sleeping 11 and 10. The cheap 'restaurant' is in a rustic terrace by the main homestead. Friendly and cosy. Recommended. **C** *Buchan Valley Log Cabins*, Gelantipy Rd (just over the bridge), T/F5155 9494, www.buchanlogcabins.com.au Self-contained, 2-bedroom cabins, set on a hillside overlooking the valley. Servicable furnishings, large deck. **E** *Buchan Lodge*, Saleyard Rd (heading north, take first left after the bridge), T5155 9421. Excellent pine-log backpackers' hostel with warm, homely open kitchen and dining hall. Peaceful, rural location. Recommended. There is a camping ground in the Buchan Caves Reserve with cabins (**D**), bookings at the Parks Office, T5155 9264. At **Gelantipy**, 38 km north of Buchan, *Karoonda Park*, T5155 0220, gelantipy@yhavic.org.au, is a large, modern hostel with pool, climbing wall and tennis court that makes a good base for exploring the Snowy River National Park. A good place to eat is the *Willow Café*, T5155 9387. No fixed hours but generally open daily for breakfast, lunch and cheap dinner.

Sleeping & eating

Wild Won, T/F5155 7423, wildwonadventures@hotmail.com Adventure caving trips to Wilson's Cave, a horizontal cave suitable for beginners ($60, 2 hrs), and Honeycomb Cave, a vertical cave for experienced and fit cavers ($100, 3 hrs).

Tour operators

Wild-Life Tours buses leave from *Buchan Lodge*, 1000 Thu, Sun for **Melbourne**, via **Lakes Entrance**, **Bairnsdale**, **Phillip Island** ($65, 5 hrs), contact *Buchan Lodge* or T1300 650 288.

Transport

This beautiful hilly park of almost 100,000 ha protects deep river gorges, native pine woodlands and old-growth gum forests in the the southern stretch of the Snowy River. Much of it is virtually inaccessible, crossed only by a handful of 4WD tracks (most of which are closed in winter), but the park can be circumnavigated and certain points accessed by standard vehicles. The trip makes for a long, hard day (much of the route is on winding, unsealed roads) of around 200 km, and is best done in two with an overnight camping stop at **MacKillop Bridge**. An added third day allows time to do the excellent 15 km **Silver Mine Walking Track** from the bridge. The usual loop drive starts in Buchan, heads up Tulloch Ard Road (off Basin Road), joining the Buchan-Jindabyne Highway at Gelantipy. The route leaves the highway after another 12 km with a right turn onto the Bonang-Gelantipy Road. This is a magnificently scenic drive descending into the Snowy River Valley. Stop at **Little River Falls** and **Little River Gorge** for short walks to good lookouts. The unsealed road continues past MacKillop Bridge, where the campsite has some facilities including fireplaces and basic toilets, and leads on to **Bonang**, which has petrol, a phone and a few basic supplies. The sealed highway to the south can only be enjoyed for a couple of kilometres before the route turns right again onto the Yalmy Road and you're faced with a long, rough unsealed section, with a number of options for walking and camping along the way, including an excursion to the spectacular **Raymond Creek Falls**. ■ *All campsites are basic bush-camping areas. For more information contact the parks office in Orbost, 117 Nicholson St, T5161 1222 or www.parkweb.vic.gov.au Adventurama, T9819 1300, www.adventur ama.com.au, amongst many other challenging activities, runs a 5-day 'self-sufficient' rafting trip down the Snowy River for around $1,000. For information on canoeing trips and hire contact the Victorian Canoe Association, T9459 4251.*

Snowy River National Park
Colour map 2, grid C5
Talk to a Parks Victoria office first if considering any major treks in the park

Victoria

Errinundra National Park
Colour map 2, grid C5
70 km from Orbost

Just to the east of the Snowy River National Park, this park contains a variety of forest including Victoria's largest stand of ancient cool temperate rainforest, dominated by southern sassafras and black olive berry. Access to the park is principally from the west via the Bonang Road from Orbost, and then the unsealed Errinundra Road. On this road at **Errinundra Saddle** there is a short boardwalk through rainforest. There is a single designated camping ground, with basic toilet facilities, deep into the park at Frosty Hollow. Access from the south is via Errinundra Road. On either route, returning south along Big River Road provides access to a short walk to **Mount Ellery**, one of the three granite tors. Road conditions can deteriorate at any time of year and roads may be permanently closed in winter. Talk to Parks Victoria before considering a trip into Errinunda. ■ *For more information contact the parks office in Orbost, 117 Nicholson St, T5161 1222 or www.parkweb.vic.gov.au*

Orbost
Colour map 2, grid C5
Population: 2,100
75 km from Cann River

The Yalmy Road continues down to Orbost, sitting at the point at which the Snowy River meets the Princes Highway. Though well placed to capitalize on the considerable tourist traffic, the town offers little to the traveller except the cheapest petrol and last decent supermarkets until well into New South Wales, and a helpful **VIC**. ■ *Daily 0900-1700, T5154 2424, orbost@lakesandwilderness.com.au 13 Lochiel St.*

Sleeping and eating For anyone using the town as a base for exploring the local national parks, the most interesting place to stay is out on the Buchan Road. **C** *Kuna Kuna*, 8 km from Orbost, T5154 1825. Working dairy farm and B&B with a real family atmosphere. Two twin rooms and a hearty breakfast. Of the various uninspiring options in town, the **E** *Orbost Club*, Nicholson St, T5154 1003, offers the cheapest rooms, and also vies with the other pub for the cheapest meals, including Chinese.

Tours A couple of Orbost operators run half- to 2-day-trips up into the Snowy, Errinunda and Croajingolong parks in Landcruiser-size vehicles. Expect to pay around $125 a day. *Eastour*, T5154 2969, are enthusiastic and knowledgeable. *Waratah*, T5154 2916, is another local 4WD operator and also offers pretty cool hovercraft trips up the Snowy from $25.

Transport There are *V~Line* bus services to **Lakes Entrance**, **Bairnsdale** and **Melbourne** (6-7 hrs) from the Post Office at 1100 Mon-Fri, 1120 Sat and 1225 Sun. Buses leave for **Cann River**, **Genoa** and NSW stops to **Narooma** or **Batemans Bay** at 1300 Mon-Fri, 1355 Sat and 1500 Sun. The **Canberra** buses leave at 1300 Mon, Thu and 1355 Sat, also stopping at Cann River.

Marlo & Cape Conran
Marlo: Colour map 2, grid C5
14 km from Orbost,
18 km from Cape Conran

The tiny fishing community of Marlo at the mouth of the Snowy River is a popular long-weekend destination for Victorians, and there is a variety of caravan and cabin accommodation available. There are few facilities, however, aside from a couple of small grocery shops, one doing takeaways, and the **B-C** *Marlo*, T5154 8201, T5154 8493, an impressive pub and guesthouse. An 11,000-ha, relatively undisturbed park extends from **Cape Conran** up to the Croajingolong. There are several good marked walking trails around the cape, where there are two beautiful sandy beaches which are generally fine for swimming. Parks Victoria manages cabins (**C**) at the cape, sleeping up to six people, and a camping ground (**F**) with fire places, toilets and bush showers. At peak times cabins are allocated by lottery, and campsites are booked months in advance (T5154 8438, www.parksvic.gov.au).

Victoria

Croajingolong National Park

This wonderful park, a narrow strip south of the Princes Highway that runs for 100 km west of the state border, is best known for its long stretch of wild coastline but also encompasses eucalypt forests, rainforests, granite peaks, estuaries and heathland. The remoteness of much of the park has led to diverse flora and fauna, with over 1000 native plants and more than 300 bird species.

Croajingolong has been recognized as a World Biosphere Reserve

Getting there The only way into the park is to turn south from the highway down one of the unsealed roads leading to the coast. These are fairly bumpy tracks that are fine for 2WD in dry conditions but can be impassable when wet. **Cann River** is the principal turning off point and is basically a glorified roadhouse settlement but is home to excellent Parks Victoria office, which has a board outside indicating road and track accessibility in the Croajingolong (Mon-Fri 0800-1700, T5158 6351).The office also has free leaflets detailing many short walks in the park and can advise on road conditions. Tony Gray's *Backpacker's Shuttle*, T5158 1472, runs drop-off and pick-up services for walkers.

Ins & outs

    Getting around There is a good range of tours ($100 a day) in the national park offered by *Natural Adventures Mallacoota*, T5158 0166, Unit 3 57/59 Bastion Point Rd, Mallacoota. River and sea kayak tours get close to birds, water lizards or seals, or there are 4WD and mountain bike tours. Also bike and kayak hire (bike $25 day, kayak $45 day).

Point Hicks was the first land in Australia to be sighted by the crew of Captain's Cook's *Endeavour* in 1770 and mainland Australia's tallest lighthouse was built here in 1890. The track to Point Hicks (2¼ km) starts at the end of the road past Thurra River campsite, and passes Honeymoon Bay. There are fantastic views from the top of the lighthouse, and southern right whales are often seen just off shore in winter. ■ *Tours 1300 Fri-Mon, $5, children $3. Bookings for cottages and Thurra River campsites T5158 4268, pointhicks@bigpond.com* It is possible to walk the coast from **Bemm River** right over the NSW border into the **Nadgee Nature Reserve**. Trekking on the wild beaches makes up the bulk of the experience, but walkers will also encounter a range of spectacular coastal scenery. There are a number of campsites with facilities along the route, though water can get scarce and walkers need to carry a couple of days' supply. Numbers are restricted on all stretches of the trek, and permits are required. Contact the Cann River or Mallacoota Parks Victoria office.

Around the park

Accommodation is available in very comfortable *Point Hicks Lighthouse Keepers' Cottages* (**L**), with verandas overlooking the sea, sleep 8. Heavily booked at peak times but if free the managers will offer a rock-up rate of $100 double or offer accomodation to backpackers in a simple bungalow. Call in advance to arrange an unlocked gate. The main camping areas are all situated where rivers and creeks meet the coast, **Thurra River** (46 sites) and **Wingan Inlet** (24 sites) both have stunning locations but the sites are close together and do get very busy in peak summer and holiday periods, although it is still sleepy in comparison to the Prom.

Sleeping
Campsites must be booked at the parks office

Book well in advance for Dec-Jan and Easter

Perched on the edge of the Mallacoota Inlet and the sea, Mallacoota is a beguiling and peaceful place. Surrounded by the Croajingolong National Park and a long way from any large cities, it's a haven for wildlife, particularly birdlife. The quiet meandering waters of the inlet are surrounded by densely forested hills. To the south are several beautiful coastal beaches, like Betka Beach, a popular local swimming beach. Spectacular layered and folded rocks can be seen at Bastion Point and Quarry Beach. There are almost unlimited opportunities for coastal walks, bushwalking, fishing and boating. Once a

Mallacoota
Colour map 2, grid C5
145 km from Orbost, 85 km from Eden (NSW) Lakes Entrance VIC will help with info and bookings (T5155 1966, www.lakesand wilderness.com.au)

Victoria

year in April there is an explosion of creativity at the **Carnival in Coota** – a week-long festival of theatre, visual arts, music and literature.

The **Mallacoota Walking Track** is a 7-km loop, signposted from the main roundabout, that goes through casuarina forest and heathland, along the beach to Bastion Point and back towards town past the entrance. To explore the inlet by water there are several options. Motor boats, canoes and kayaks can be hired from the caravan near the wharf, T0438-447 558. Several cruising boats are also based at the wharf, visit their kiosks for bookings. The *MV Surveyor* will take 2-10 people to areas of their choice, T5158 0392. *MV Lochard* is an old ferryboat taking larger groups on two- to three-hour cruises around the inlet ($23, three hours), T0409-588 291 and *MV Discovery* is a modern 50 seat boat that takes longer day-trips through the inlet, the Genoa River and the isolated Wallagaraugh River, T5158 0555. There are magnificent views of the area from **Genoa Peak**, the access road is signposted from the Princes Highway, 2 km west of Genoa. From the picnic and parking area there is a 1½-km walking track to the summit, steep for the last 100 m. For trips further afield, including **Gabo Island**, contact *Wilderness Coast Ocean Charters*, T5158 0701 or T0418 553809. Tiny Gabo island is home to one of the largest fairy penguin colonies in the country, plus one of the highest lighthouses. It is possible to stay in the old lighthouse keepers' cottages on the island (**L**), but expensive for a couple. For details T5158 0219.

Most of the accomodation is in self-contained holiday flats or caravan parks

Book ahead for December-January and during the Carnival

Sleeping and eating **B** *Gypsy Point Lodge*, signposted on the road to Mallacoota, T5158 8205, www.gipsypoint.com A friendly, homely guesthouse with great views of the Genoa River. Particularly popular with birdwatchers. Price includes dinner. Also 3 self-contained cottages (**C**). **B-C** *Karbeethong Lodge*, Schnapper Point Dr, T5158 0411, www.users.bigpond.com/karbeethong Comfortable old guesthouse, 4 km north of the town centre, with wide verandas overlooking the inlet, 12 rooms, some with en suite, communal kitchen facility. Not suitable for kids. **C-D** *Adobe Mudbrick Flats*, 14 Karbeethong Hill Av, just north of the *Lodge*, T5158 0329, www.mallacoota.net/adobe 10 original and delightful hand-built self-contained flats with superb views of the inlet. This 70-acre property is shared by countless birds, possums, and even koalas. The very welcoming, knowledgable hosts help make a stay here a real experience. Recommended. **D-E** *Mallacoota*, Maurice Av, T5158 0455, F5158 0453. Lively pub, particularly on a Fri, serves cheap light lunches and mid-range dinners, including a good range of vegetarian options. They have 20 motel rooms and also a few rooms designated as a *YHA*, including an en suite double, with a small but clean kitchen. Food daily 1200-1345, 1800-2000. There are also 4 caravan parks, the most central is *Foreshore Camp Park*, T5158 0300.

Despite its size and isolation Mallacoota has a few excellent places to eat. The smartest restaurant, with a lovely wooden deck facing the water, is *The Tide* at the end of Maurice Av, T5158 0100. Daily 1130-1345, 1700-2100. Mid-range seafood, fish and steak dishes, also good casual lunches. Also good is the small, cheery and informal *Café 54*, Maurice Av, T5158 0646, Mon-Sat 0730-2030, Sun 1830-2030. There is also a fantastic funky café for vegetarians and health food lovers, *Strange Fruit*, opposite the foreshore on Allan Dr, next to the newsagent and bakery, Daily 0830-1630.

Transport There are *V~Line* bus services to **Orbost**, **Lakes Entrance** and **Melbourne** (8-9 hrs) from the *Genoa* general store, at 0900 Mon-Fri, 0920 Sat and 1025 Sun.

The High Country

The Victorian Alps, or High Country, is one of the few parts of Victoria that changes dramatically from summer to winter but it is a place that has soul at any time of year. Mysterious silent folds of forest and mountains, and mist among golden autumn trees and the vivid stripes of a snow gumtree after rain are typical elements of this compellingly beautiful region. The mountains are relatively low but receive a decent covering of snow for about three months in winter and are transformed into fashionable ski resorts, such as those at Mount Buller, Mount Hotham and Falls Creek. The High Country is also a wonderful destination in summer. Some of the state's best walking can be had in the crisp fresh air, along trails providing clear views over rows of velvety blue ridges to the baking plains below. Mount Buffalo's high plateau is scattered with granite boulders to climb and you can walk along the spine of the Alps along the Razorback ridge near Mount Hotham. Horse riding, abseiling, paragliding and mountain bike riding are also popular summer activities and there are magnificent scenic drives throughout the region.

www.alpine link.com.au To check snow, VicSnow info-line T1800 067600 or www.vicsnow report.com.au

Ins and outs

Air Mount Hotham has recently built itself an airport and *Qantas* are currently flying in package tourists in the ski season. **Bus** This huge area is not well served by bus. *V~Line* have a daily service from **Melbourne** to **Mansfield** and, in ski season, **Mount Buller**. They also run a route through **Wangaratta** and **Beechworth** to **Myrtleford**, **Porepunkah**, **Bright** and **Mount Beauty**. *APT*, the tour company, offer a ski-season day return to Mount Buller for $53. *Omeo Bus Lines*, T5159 4231, have a few services from **Bairnsdale** to **Omeo**. Other local operators run ski season

Getting there

Victoria

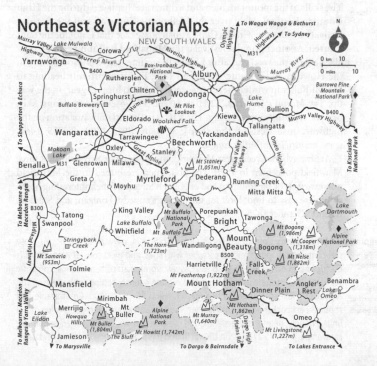

Northeast & Victorian Alps

services through **Mount Beauty** to **Falls Creek**, and from **Omeo** and **Bright** up to **Mount Hotham**. Most offer through services to and from **Melbourne**. **Car** Out of the snow season roads are usually fine, though it pays to call one of the VICs in spring and autumn to check. In winter, generally between Jun and Oct, the Bogong High Plains Rd between **Falls Creek** and the Omeo Highway, and Dargo High Plains Rd are permanently closed, as are most of the 4WD tracks. Many of the higher sealed roads, such as those up to **Mount Buffalo** and the ski resorts, are snowbound and snow chains are necessary if not mandatory. Even with these the drive up to the resorts can be tortuous, particularly from **Harrietville** up to **Mount Hotham**, with drivers having to wait for snow-plough convoys. For day skiers, the consistently safest and quickest road up to a resort is from **Omeo** to **Mount Hotham**.

Getting around   The Alps are traversed by 3 long-distance tracks: the **Alpine Walking Track** (T5755 1577, www.australianalps.ea.gov.au); the 'Murray to the Mountains' **Rail Trail** (T5751 1283, www.railtrail.com.au) for cyclists; and the equestrian **Bicentennial National Trail** (T1300-138724, www.vicnet.net.au/~bnt). The *Bogong Alpine Area* Outdoor Leisure Map is widely available for about $10, and covers the area from **Tawonga** to **Mount Hotham**, and **Harrietville** to the Omeo Highway. A good buy if you plan to spend much time in the area. All the major coach tour operators have pass-inclusive day and overnight trips to **Mount Buller** from **Melbourne**, usually for around $175-250. Non-skiing, sightseeing trips are around $100.

Mansfield and around

Colour map 2, grid C4
Population: 2,500
199 km
from Melbourne,
77 km from Benalla

A friendly country town on the southeastern border of the Alps, Mansfield acts as a base for Mount Buller and also has a long heritage of mountain cattlemen so has developed into a centre for High Country horse-riding. The skills of the mountain men and women are displayed during the **High Country Festival**. Held over the Melbourne Cup weekend the five-day festival includes the 'Cracks Cup', a bush horse race that is not for the faint hearted. Another popular festival is the **Mansfield Balloon Festival**, usually held on the weekend after Easter. In summer there is good fishing in the Howqua and Delatite rivers and Lake Eildon nearby. If heading to Mount Buller in winter there are several places to hire ski gear on the way up. Try *Manni's Ski Hire*, 32 High Street, T5775 2095, for chains, skis, boards, clothing and servicing. The **VIC** is in the old railway station on the highway, just west of the shops. ■ *Daily 0930-1700. T5775 1464, www.mansfield-mtbuller.com.au*

At Stringybark Creek, near Mansfield, the bushranger Ned Kelly shot three Mansfield policemen in 1878. The policemen are buried in the **Mansfield graveyard** at the far southern end of Highett Street and their interesting headstones are easy to find: look for the names Kennedy, Lonigan, and Scanlon, dated 27 October 1878.

Sleeping
The VIC can help with bookings. Winter is the high season but Jan-Feb is also busy. Book ahead for festival periods

B *Alpine Country Cottages*, 5 The Parade, T5775 1694, www.alpinecc.com.au Cosy self-contained wooden miners cottages with spas, and mod cons. **B** *Wombat Hills Cottages*, 55 Lochiel Rd, T/F5776 9507, www.wombat.au.com, are similar romantic self-contained stone cottages in a more remote country setting with views of the Alps over a lake. **C-E** *Travellers Lodge*, 112 High St, T57751800. Comfortable and spotless backpacker dorms with kitchen, laundry and lounge and good value motel units. Friendly, helpful owners and good location in town centre. The *High Country* caravan park, T5775 2705, is on Ultimo St and has a good range of cabins and vans.

Traditional steak and seafood can be had in the rustic surrounds of *Mingo's Bar and Grill*, 101 High St, T5775 1766. Daily 1800-2030. *Black Pepper*, 28 Highett St, T5779 1600. A huge, stylish space in the old fire station with a good Modern Australian menu (mid-range). The *Mansfield* pub on High St has a smart bistro and cheap wood-fired pizzas. Daily 1200-1400, 1800-2030. *Collopy Street Café*, corner of High St and Collopy St, is a large airy café with lots of pavement tables and café standards. Daily 0830-1700. *Sweet Potato*, 50 High St, is great for breakfast and also has good vegetarian choices including vegan, also Asian and Mediterranean dishes. Thu-Mon 1000-2030. *Café Connect* on High St is a takeaway joint with internet facilities. On the road west at Maindample, 12 km from Mansfield, is the *Bridge Inn*, T5778 7281, known locally as the 'Maindample'. This is a wonderful country pub with a small cosy front bar and excellent food. The Thu and Fri seafood nights are very popular indeed and should ideally be booked ahead. Daily 1200-1400, 1800-2000. Recommended.

Eating

Mountain biking *Mansfield Mountain Bike Tours*, T5775 2380, www.pullins.com.au, offer guided bush rides in summer, bike included from $30 per person (minimum 4 people). **Ballooning** *Global Ballooning*, T1800 627 661, www.globalballooning.com.au, offer morning champagne-breakfast flights for $240.

Tours & activities
See Mount Buller for more options

V~Line buses leave Perk's Depot for **Melbourne** at 1330 Mon-Sat, 1945 Fri, 1800 Sun. To Mount Buller in the ski season *Mansfield-Mount Buller Buslines*, T5777 2606, run 6-8 buses a day from 0700-1900 Mon-Sat, 1630 Sun, stopping at **Mirimbah** en route. *V~Line* also have a winter service, leaving at 1200 Mon-Sat, 1930, 2130 Fri, 2100 Mon-Thu, Sat, 1330 and 1630 Sun.

Transport

On the flat grazing plains between Mansfield and the Alpine foothills, **Merrijig** is little more than a road junction with a pub. The unpretentious **E** *Hunt Club*, T5777 5508, known simply as the 'Merrijig', has cheap but imaginative counter meals daily 1200-1400, 1800-2030, basic bunk-rooms and live music every Friday when opening is extended to 0130. The accommodation over the road at **D** *Merrijig Lodge*, T/F5777 5590, is amongst the best hostel accommodation in Victoria. Excellent rooms and communal facilities, double rooms, cooked breakfast $10 extra. Recommended. They are principally set up for **horse trail rides**, and are one of the most respected operators in the area.

Merrijig
Merrijig 19 km from Mansfield

Soon after Merrijig is an unsealed right hand turn onto the Howqua Track, one of the few western access points to the **Alpine National Park**. It runs first into the Howqua Hills Historic Area, once important as an Aboriginal quarrying and trade area, and later for a gold rush. The historical remains are surrounded by the foothills of the western Alps. There are several campgrounds along the road, Sheepyard Flat having the best facilities (picnic areas, toilets, walking trails). From here the unsealed Brocks Road heads into the national park proper, paralleling the walking track that leads to The Bluff, the area's most impressive outcrop. The walk to the bluff from Sheepyard Flat is 14 km, a two-day return walk, camping at Bluff Hut which is a further 3 km (Bluff Hut can also be reached via 4WD). Excellent, shorter day walks include from the flat to Frys Hut, and from Eight Mile Gap at the end of Brooks Road to Eagle Peaks.

Howqua Hills Historic Area

Victoria

Mount Buller

Colour map 2, grid C4
Altitude: 1,600 m
48 km from Mansfield
www.mtbuller.com.au

The closest of the three major ski resorts to Melbourne, Mount Buller is the only one accessible as a day-trip, making it particularly busy at weekends. Try *Snowcapers*, T1800-033123, www.alzburg.com.au, or the *Buller Bullet*, T1800-355565. Some of the 27 lifts head nearly to the top of the mountain (1,804 m), so there are dozens of runs for all abilities and many are as good for snowboarding. Whatever you do, make time to try out the 'tubing' run – basically hurtling downhill on a pumped up truck inner-tube and great fun. Travel and pass day-trip packages from Melbourne are around $120 per person. As with the other major resorts, the most economic way of getting onto the snow is with a three- or five-night mid-week 'accommodation and pass' package. Expect to pay at least $100 a day, with particularly good Jun and Sep deals at the *Abom* and *Mount Buller Chalet*. Resort entry is $13 per car in the ski season. Snow chains may be necessary to get to the car parks (hire at Mirimbah), and there is a $10 per adult taxi service between the main car park and the resort. Lift-passes are $60-70 per day. There are half a dozen hire shops in the village, including a snowboard specialist, *ABOM Boards*, T5777 6091. In winter there is a supermarket and ATM in the *Cow Camp*. The **VIC** is on the main road into the village. ■ *Mon-Fri 0830-1700, Sat-Sun 1000-1600. T5777 6077.*

Sleeping & eating
Central reservations: T1800-039049

The most luxurious place to stay is **LL-A** *Mount Buller Chalet*, T1800 810200 or 5777 6566, www.mtbullerchalet.com.au The extensive range of facilities include a heated indoor pool. Buffet breakfast included. Open year-round, as is the **L-A** *Arlberg*, T1800 032380 or 5777 6260, www.arlberg.com.au Quite unpretentious, with a range of motel-style rooms and some expensive but well-equipped self-contained apartments. Off-season the rooms can be very good value (from **C**) with some backpacker dorm beds available (**D**). There are 3 restaurants and a café, catering for most tastes and budgets, also ski hire and a small store. The **L-B** *Duck Inn*, T5777 6326, www.duckinnmtbuller, is a cosy, friendly lodge-style B&B with en suite doubles and some 3- to 5-bed-share rooms. Good facilities, cooked breakfast and an excellent mid-range restaurant. Open year-round (**C**). Recommended. There are a few budget lodges including the **C** *YHA*, T5777 6181, mountbuller@yhavic.org.au, in the centre of the village, open in ski season only, and the very small, friendly **C** *Telemark*, T9570 7220, which sleeps just 14. The large, busy *Abom*, T5777 6091, abom@skibuller.com.au, has the best range of indoor and terrace bars and a cheap cafeteria open daily during ski season 0800-2030. They also have 10 rooms, doubles to quads, that vary wildly in price (from **LL** to **C**) depending on which month of the ski season. **Bushcamping** is allowed throughout the park, though there are several designated areas with fireplaces and toilets. Self-sufficiency is paramount. Most mountain huts can be slept in, but they are technically reserved for emergency use.

Transport

In the ski season *V~Line* operate a daily service from **Melbourne** via **Mansfield** to **Mount Buller**, departing 0830 and 1800, Mon-Sat, 1030 and 1300 Sun, and returning 1200 Mon-Sat, 1815 Fri and 1630 Sun. Also in season *Mansfield-Mount Buller Buslines*, T5777 6070, run 6-8 buses a day from 1030-1900 (2230 Fri).

Around Mount Buller
If exploring, get hold of the 1:50,000 VicMaps for the area (Buller-Stirling, Tamboritha-Moroka and Howitt-Selwyn)

Mount Buller is the closest sealed point of access to several hundred square kilometres of this western end of the **Alpine National Park**, though all onward routes from here or Mirimbah are unsealed. The mountainous park is criss-crossed by walking and horse-riding trails and 4WD tracks. The easiest access for two-wheel vehicles is actually via the Howqua Track, and the most accessible shorter walks from the end of the track at Sheepyard Flat. From Mirimbah the rough unsealed Circuit Road loops around the cross-country

Victoria

skiing area of **Mount Stirling** and close to **Craigs Hut**, built for the film *The Man from Snowy River*.

Tours and activities This is one of the state's most popular **horse trailriding** areas. There are several operators, mostly based around Mansfield, including *Merrijig Lodge* and *Stoneys*, T5775 2212, www.stoneys.com.au For overnight rides expect to pay around $170 per day, all inclusive. *La Trobe University*, T5733 7000, has a campus at Mount Buller and to help generate extra income some of their tutors and equipment are available for hire. They offer a variety of activities including **mountain biking** (hire $40 a half day), **rock climbing and abseiling** (3-hr indoor sessions around $200 per group) and **4WD** tours (min 4 people, $50 each per half day). They will also guide parties of **walkers** out to one of the Alpine huts – with instructions on how to get back. *Stirling Experience*, T5777 3541, www.stirling.au.com, also run **4WD** tours in a larger vehicle which helps them keep prices extremely reasonable (full-day $85, inc food and drink). **Scenic flights** *Helicopter Pilot College*, corner of Mount Buller Rd and Jamieson Rd, Mansfield, T5775 3100.

The little town of Myrtleford sits in the lee of the massive granite mound of **Mount Buffalo** and the nearer Reform Hill and is a good place to stop off for supplies. *Ray's Ski Hire*, T5752 1306, is one of the most economical places to hire gear in the region, open daily from April to the first weekend in June 0900-1700, and daily 0630-2400 from then to mid-October.

Myrtleford
Colour map 2, grid B4
28 km from Beechworth, 30 km from Bright

Sleeping There are a couple of motels and caravan parks near the town centre, and a friendly B&B pub, the **C** *Happy Valley*, 5 km south at Ovens. Another 5 km from Ovens is **A** *Rosewhite House*, T1800 675300, www.rosewhitehouse.com.au This modern B&B has 3 rooms with great views over Happy Valley and friendly service. Recommended.

Tour operators *Adventure Guides Australia*, have climbing, abseiling and caving courses, and trips around the region, generally ranging from about $50 for half a day. T5728 1804, agati@netc.net.au *Getaway*, have trail bikes for hire and run 1- to 3-day dirt road tours to some pretty remote areas. Hire from $175 a day, tours extra. T5752 2336, getaway@alpine.albury.net.au

Transport *V~Line* buses leave from outside the *Murrayville Hotel* at 0610 Wed and Fri, 1150 Mon-Tue, Thu-Fri, 1550 Sat, and 1615 Sun for stops to **Melbourne** (4 hrs). Additional services at 1710 Wed and 1840 Fri terminate at **Wangaratta**. The service to **Bright** leaves at 0910 Mon, 1600 Mon-Tue, Thu-Fri, 2055 Wed, Fri, 1135 Sat and 1305 Sun, with the 1600 Mon and Fri service continuing on to **Mount Beauty**. In the **ski season** *Trekset*, T1800 659009, www.buslines.com.au/trekset, buses leave the *Alpine Country Kitchen* for **Bright**, **Harrietville** and **Mount Hotham** twice a day Sun-Fri and 3 times on Sat. The return service leaves for **Wangaratta**, **Melbourne Airport** and **Melbourne** up to twice a day.

Mount Buffalo National Park

A massive granite outcrop, worn down to an oval plateau, Mount Buffalo harbours extensive snow gum woodlands, grassy plains, and wildlife such as wombats and lyrebirds. Much of the park, and lookouts, can only be reached on foot, bike, horse, or cross-country ski. The highest points, such as **The Horn**, offer wonderful views, both over the plateau itself and the seemingly infinite ranks of the alpine ridges beyond.

Colour map 2, grid B4
15 km from Bright

Victoria

Victoria

Ins & outs
Contact the Parks Victoria office, T5755 1466, www.parkweb vic.gov.au

The entry gate is a few kilometres from **Porepunkah**, the nearest small service town. Roads can be snowbound or icy in winter when snowchains (for hire from ski-hire shops, such as *Rio's*, T5756 2208, at Porepunkah) are mandatory. There is currently no public transport from Porepunkah, though if staying overnight *Chalet* or *Lodge* staff may be able to arrange a lift. Entry to the park is $9 per vehicle, which includes a map and information, payable at the gates.

Activities
Contact the lodge ski school for details of winter activities, T5750 1192

Mount Buffalo is walkers' heaven, with over 100 km of tracks of varying distance and difficulty, the Gorge Walk being the best short trail. The plateau's highest points, **The Horn** (1,723 m) and **The Hump** (1,695 m), offer differing approaches. The Horn, though effectively inaccessible in winter, has handrails up the last stages and steps cut every inch of the way, making it very accessible but often crowded. The Hump on the other hand, is a more satisfying and quieter climb, and allows more exploration at the top. Other spring-autumn activities include superb **caving**, **horse riding**, **mountain biking**, **rock climbing** and **abseiling**, and **hangliding** (experienced or tandem flyers only). All can be booked via the *Mount Buffalo Chalet Adventure Office*, T5755 2275, or the VIC at Bright. Caving, climbing and abseiling are actually run by *Adventure Guides Australia*, T5728 1804, agati@netc.net.au In **Winter** snow blankets the plateau, though for a shorter period than the nearby ski resorts. There are a number of ski runs with chair lifts, and comprehensive hire facilities at the Lodge. The runs are very short, really only suitable for absolute beginners or small children.

Sleeping & eating

There are 2 non-camping options on Mount Buffalo. The **LL-A** *Chalet*, T5755 1500, www.mtbuffalochalet.com.au, is a large guesthouse-style hotel built in 1910 and still with most of the original fixtures, fittings and possibly furniture. Friendly service and a cosy old-fashioned charm. Prices reflect the location rather than luxury but it is a great place to stay. Superb, 3-course dinners are included in the price ($40 for non-residents). The cheaper options are at the **A-D** *Lodge*, T5755 1988. This modern facility, right by the main ski runs, has motel, lodge and backpacker accommodation. For most of the year the prices are in the **C-D** range, only rising during the end-Jun to end-Sep ski season when dinners are included in the motel and lodge prices. There are also cafés at the Chalet and Lodge, though the Lodge café opens only from Apr to Oct. From spring to autumn camping is allowed at 3 sites on the plateau. There are fireplaces, though firewood or gas stoves must be brought in, and basic toilets. Book in advance and pay at the park entry station, T5756 2328.

Transport

V~Line buses leave from outside the General Store, **Porepunkah**, at 0550 Wed and Fri, 1130 Mon-Tue, Thu-Fri, 1525 Sat, and 1550 Sun for stops to **Melbourne** (4 hrs). Additional services at 1650 Wed and 1820 Fri terminate at **Wangaratta**. The service to **Bright** leaves at 0930 Mon, 1625 Mon-Tue, Thu-Fri, 2120 Wed, Fri, 1200 Sat and 1330 Sun, with the 1625 Mon and Fri service continuing on to **Mount Beauty**.

Bright and around

Colour map 2, grid B4
Population: 2,600
Altitude: 340 m
30 km from Myrtleford, 55 km from Mount Hotham

Bright is the busiest town in the region, but despite large numbers of visitors, it retains an attractive small town feel and has the compensations of good restaurants and plenty of accommodation. It is also one of the world's great paragliding spots as well as being an ideal base for mountain bikers, hillwalkers, skiers and many other sports. The town makes a good base as it is close to Mount Buffalo, Mount Hotham, Beechworth and Milawa and is also famous for its avenues of poplars, maples, oaks and elms, which attract busloads of tourists in the autumn. Bright's glorious colours are celebrated during the **Autumn Festival** (late April to early May) which includes an excellent art exhibition and a street parade. The **VIC**, Bright Visitors Centre, on Gavan St, faces the river and a leafy picnic and playground area. ■ *Daily 0830 1700, T5755 2275, F5750 1655, brightvc@netc.net.au*

Sleeping

B *Holyrood*, 21 Bakers Gully Rd, 5750 1283, davideallen@bigpond.com Welcoming B&B in a large English garden with one room. Private lounge and balcony, breakfast provisions supplied. **C** *The Alpine*, 7 Anderson St, T5755 1366, starhotel@netc.net.au A large pleasant pub in the centre of town with 24 comfortable motel rooms. **E** *Bright Hikers Backpackers*, 4 Ireland, T5750 1244, www.netc.net.au/backpackers Small, friendly and comfotable hostel in the centre of Bright, owned by a hanglider and paraglider who can help with advice and bookings. **F** *Bright and Alpine Backpackers*, 106 Coronation Av, T5755 1154. Camp kitchen, lounge, BBQs, laundry and $6 cooked breakfasts. Lovely tree-covered campsite with basic two person cabins and also a self-contained house (**E**), 2 km from town centre. *Bright Caravan Park* is one of the best parks, close to town, T5755 1141.

The VIC can help with bookings for accommodation and activities. Oct-May is the busiest period as most skiers stay on the mountains in winter

Eating

Liquid Am-Bar, 8 Anderson St, T5755 2318. Casual, fun and very popular bar and restaurant with cocktails, light snacks and mid-range mains. *Simone's*, Ovens Valley Motor Inn, Corner Great Alpine Rd and Ashwood Av, T5755 2022. Mid-range. Daily 1830-2100. This authentic Italian restaurant is one of the best in the region with handmade pasta, richly flavoured meat dishes and Italian wines. *The Alpine*, 7 Anderson St, T5755 1366. This large, attractive pub has a good cheap bistro menu and choice of local wines. *Caffé Bacco*, 2d Anderson St, T5750 1711. Sat-Sun 1200-1500, Wed-Sun 1800-2100. A simple, mid-range, Mediterranean-style café with fabulous pasta and pizzas as well as a few Asian and Australian dishes, including a fine selection for vegetarians. *Café Chiaro*, 8 Barnard St, T5750 1999. Wed-Sun 1700-2100. Small and cosy place with a fire for excellent pizzas. BYO only. *Jackie's Tearooms*, 4 Ireland St, T5750 1303. Daily 0800-1630. The best daytime café in Bright with a good value breakfast and interesting foccacia, sandwiches and ploughmans.

Tours & activities

Climbing *Adventure Guides Australia*, T5728 1804, agati@netc.net.au A huge range of reasonably priced activities close to Bright at Mount Buffalo and Beechworth, Mount Hotham and Falls Creek. **Hang Gliding** *Eagle School of Microlighting and Hang Gliding*, T5750 1174. Very experienced and friendly operators who offer breathtaking tandem flights over Mount Buffalo gorge (microlight $125, 20 mins, hang glider $250, 2 hrs). **Horse riding** *Mountain Creek Trail Rides*, T5754 1924, Mountain Creek Rd, Tawonga. Horse riding in the Alpine National Park ($60 ½ day, $120 day). *Freeburgh*, offer rides from 1 hr to 3 days ($30-500). T5755 1370. **Mountain biking** *CyclePath*, Gavan St, T5750 1442, cyclepat@bright.albury.net.au A range of cycle tours from Alpine wilderness rides (sleeping in tents) to gourmet tours with B&B accommodation. Also bike hire (mountain bike $35 day, town bike $22 day). **Paragliding** *Alpine Paragliding*, Ireland St, T5755 1753. Training courses and tandem flights. **Ski hire** *JD's for Skis*, corner of Burke St and Anderson St, T5755 1557. Ski hire ($35 day), snowboards ($50 day) clothing and chain hire ($22 day). Jun-Oct, Thu-Sat 0700-1900. **Walking** Details from the Parks Office or VIC. *Bright Outdoor Centre* on Ireland St has a range of maps and gear.

Transport

V~Line buses leave from outside the Post Office at 0545 Wed and Fri, 1125 Mon-Tue, Thu-Fri, 1520 Sat, and 1545 Sun for stops to **Melbourne** (4½ hrs). Additional services at 1645 Wed and 1815 Fri terminate at **Wangaratta**. The service to **Mount Beauty**, leaves at 1635 Mon and Fri. *Trekset*, T1800 659009, www.buslines.com.au/trekset, runs a twice-daily **ski season** service to **Mount Hotham** (1½ hrs, $30 return).

Victoria

▶▶ ## Mount Feathertop Loop Walk

One of the most stunning walks in Australia, and a must for lovers of hillwalking, the loop walk from Harrietville to Hotham and back takes in striking 1,922 m Mount Feathertop. The walk is very strenuous in places, you should be fit and well prepared and only undertake the walk in good weather. It is best to allow two days, overnighting in Mount Hotham. The initial 12 km Bon Accord track is the original horse track up to Mount Hotham. It cuts over to the Razorback before it reaches the resort, so overnighting adds about 8 km to the round trip. The 11 km Razorback track to Mount Feathertop is the highlight of the walk. After the steep final ascent, double-back 1½ km to the 10 km Bungalow Spur track back down to Harrietville. As with all major walks, ensure someone knows where you're going and when you expect to be back.

Wandiligong
Population: 200
Altitude: 350 m
5 km from Bright

Wandiligong is a tiny settlement deep in a small valley, tightly enclosed by hills. This picturesque rural area was once a goldmining site with a population of 3,000 but is now a peaceful place to escape the hordes of Bright, with a friendly country pub. *The Mountain View Hotel*, T5755 1311, known locally as the 'Wandi Pub', has a great repuation for live music and also has cheap meals (weekends only) and accommodation (**C, E**). Recommended. Ask about free camping next door. On the hillside nearby are a couple of good B&Bs, **B** *Knox Farm*, School Road, T0417-367494, knoxfarm@netc.net.au and **B** *Twisted Peppermint*, T0409 552356, Higgs Lane.

Harrietville
Colour map 2, grid C4
Altitude: 500 m
25 km from Bright,
30 km from
Mount Hotham

South of Bright, on the Great Alpine Road, tiny Harrietville is at the bottom of the main spur that leads up to Mount Hotham. Mostly spread a short way along the highway that threads down the pretty valley, there isn't much here but what is here is very likeable. The highway continues up to Mount Hotham. On the way is the right hand turn to the unsealed **Dargo High Plains Road**. The stretch of highway between this junction and the resort is one of the most scenic in the Alps.

Sleeping and eating **B** *Pick & Shovel*, T/F5759 2627, www.pickandshovel.com.au, a small, new cottage meticulously re-creating colonial style at the very southern end of the village. The kind of place that has honeymooners queueing up. Breakfast provisions included. Recommended. There are a few lodge- and motel-style options. **B** *Feathertop Chalet*, T5759 2688, feather@netc.net.au, has a wide range of family-friendly facilities and the package includes a basic 3-course dinner and breakfast. **C-D** *Mountain View*, T5759 2530, www.mountainviewretreat.com.au, has hostel-style accommodation but with en suite rooms, free use of mountain bikes and a licensed dining room serving a limited choice 2-course dinner for $15, full brekkie for $10. The friendly, leafy **D-E** *Caravan Park*, T/F5759 2523, hville_cpark@netc.net.au, has well-maintained, very good value cabins and caravans. Some of the latter face onto the creek and have their own little verandas and fireplace-BBQs which can turn an overnight stop into a magical stay.

Avalon House is a contemporary gallery, second-hand bookshop, wine merchant and a great café that converts to an even better cheap BYO restaurant Fri-Sat evenings in summer, Sat in winter. Open daily 1000-1700 (1600 winter, closed Tue), restaurant evenings 1830-2100. Recommended. The main pub, *The Snowline*, has cheap meals daily all year round, 1200-1400, 1800-2030.

Transport *Trekset*, T1800-659009, www.buslines.com.au/trekset, run a twice-daily **ski season** service to and from **Mount Hotham**.

Mount Hotham and around

Though not as aprés-orientated as neighbouring Falls Creek, the Mount Hotham resort has the better skiing, particularly for advanced skiers and snowboarders, and looks set to become Victoria's premier winter playground. A couple of the lifts get close to the top of Mount Hotham (1,860 m), providing the longest runs in the state. Lift and hire prices are pretty much as for Falls Creek and a pass covers lifts in both resorts ($60 return helicopter ride). A $6 park entry fee is payable in the winter season.

Colour map 2, grid C4
Altitude: 1,700 m
55 km from Bright, 44 km from Omeo

There is plenty of accommodation in privately run 'club' lodges that tend toward the budget end – but they have to booked *well* ahead. *Mount Hotham Reservation Centre*, T1800-354555, www.hotham.net.au, organizes bookings for most of the more expensive lodges and apartments in the resort. Expect a 5-night mid-week package (including passes and lessons) to cost from around $110 a night in low ski season, to $200 a night peak. The club lodges are all clustered at the southern end of the resort and include the hostel-style **C** *Bundarra*, T9419 0965, and the excellent **C** *Trapdoor*, T9859 6522, www.trapdoor.mainpage.net The latter is open year-round. Ask about package deals. Also keeping it's doors open all year is the *General Store*, T5759 3523, thegeneralstore@optusnet.com, located approximately mid-resort. Great **cheap** food, including their very popular pizzas, served 1200-1400, 1800-2100. The team here are very friendly, offer sound advice and operate an informal budget-accommodation booking service.

Sleeping & eating

Air *Qantas* have got together with *Mount Hotham Reservations* to offer good value ski packages from **Melbourne**, **Sydney**, **Newcastle**, and **Brisbane**. T1800-344555, www.hotham.net.au **Bus** *Trekset*, T1800-659009, www.buslines.com.au/trekset, run a winter-only service to and from **Melbourne** (6 hrs, $80), stopping at **Harrietville**, **Bright** (1½ hrs, $30 return or $120 for season ticket), **Myrtleford** and **Wangaratta**. *O'Connell's*, T5159 1377, runs a slightly cheaper ski service, weekends only, from **Omeo** (40 mins, $25 return).

Transport
For winter road conditions call
T5759 3531
www.mthot ham.com.au

Dinner Plain

Perched on a flat shoulder of Mount Higginbotham, just below Mount Hotham, Dinner Plain is essentially a satellite village to the larger resort. *Molony's*, T5159 6450, is the local ski hire shop. During summer and deep into winter (until the snow is too deep) *Dinner Plain Trail Rides*, T5159 6445, have horse-riding trips.

11 km from Mount Hotham

Sleeping and eating There are a number of small, privately owned lodges available through the two booking agencies, sleeping from 2 to 20. Contact *Central Reservations*, T1800 670019, www.dinnerplain.com, or the **L** *High Plains Lodge*, T5159 6455, F5159 6405, for a range of options. The latter is also one of two hotels in the village. The budget option is restricted to the **B** *Currawong*, T1800 635589, www.currawonglodge.com.au, a very comfortable hostel-style lodge. The two hotels cater for the **expensive** end of the dining market, while the huge *Dinner Plains Hotel* provides **mid-range** meals including steaks, pizzas and pastas. The pub is party central for Dinner Plains and even draws custom down from Mount Hotham. Food daily, year round, 1200-1400, 1800-2030, live music or DJs winter and long weekends. Closes most of Oct. The *Brandy Creek* café is also open year-round. Breakfasts, light lunches, licensed. 0900-1700 in Summer, 0700-2300 Winter.

All the accommodation in the village gets booked out in Winter and the school holidays, so forward planning is required for peak times

Victoria

Mount Beauty and around

Colour map 2, grid C4
Population: 2,100
Altitude: 340 m
28 km from Bright, 32
km from Falls Creek

The highway from Bright twists and turns over the 900 m Tawonga Gap and down again into the deep broad Kiewa Valley. Here, in the shadow of Victoria's highest mountain, **Mount Bogong**, Mount Beauty's position certainly lives up to its name even if the town fails to, strung out for 5 km north, taking in **Tawonga South** and **Tawonga**. The **VIC** is on the Kiewa Valley Highway 500 m north of the centre. ■ *Daily 0900-1700, T5754 1962, www.mtbeauty.com* The town has several ski-hire outlets, but is better for mountain bikers and anglers. Cyclists and skiers are ably catered for by *Rocky Valley*, Kiewa Valley Highway, T5754 1118. Not just hire, but also maps and guidebooks. Overnight horse rides arranged by *Belle Marguerita*, Chalet Road, T5754 4348.

The walk to the summit of Mount Bogong and back can be done in a day, if walkers are fit and well prepared. Take track and weather advice from the tourist office first and ensure that they or the police know where you are going. Maps are available from *Rocky Valley*. The recommended route up to the summit starts from the Mountain Creek picnic ground, 10 km from the Bogong Hotel on the Mountain Creek Road, and follows the well-used Staircase Spur walking track. The summit is gained in 4 hours, and walkers can either retrace their steps or descend via the steep Eskdale Spur, looping back to the picnic area.

Sleeping
& eating
Accommodation
mostly consists of
apartments and
motels, with a couple
of B&Bs and caravan
parks. None are cheap,
though prices
fluctuate enormously,
and can be
substantially cheaper
than indicated here

A *Clover Gully Cottage*, Ranch Rd, Tawonga South, T/F5754 1257, www.mtbeauty.com/ clover 2-storey, self-contained chalet with provisions. Recommended. **B** *Carver's Log Cabins*, Buckland St, Tawonga South, T/F5754 4863. 8 self-contained cabins, well away from the highway, sleeping up to 6 in various combinations. Particularly good value for groups or families. **B-D** *Mount Beauty Holiday Centre*, next to *Dreamers*, 10 mins walk from the town centre, T5754 4396, F5754 4877. Well-maintained caravan park with a range of sites, on-site vans, yurts and cabins.

The best eating around here is the café bar *Bogong Jack's*, 17 km away in tiny Bogong. Open daily, 0900-1700, as a café and Fri-Sat evenings (more nights in winter as demand increases) as a lively mid-range restaurant specializing in Egyptian cuisine. *Roi's*, Tawonga, T5754 4495, is a less formal mid-range, Italian, restaurant with good menu and service. There are also a couple of cheaper Italian takeaways/cafés. Next door to *Roi's*, the *Bogong* has a lively public bar and small but comfortable lounge bar adjoining a plain bistro area. Food Thu-Sun, 1200-1400, 1800-2030. The stylish *Mount Beauty Bakery*, on Kiewa Cres, has a relaxed feel and courtyard tables. Breakfasts, cakes, pies and coffees daily 0630-1830. A great cream tea can be had at the *Sandstone Galleries*, in Tawonga.

Transport

V~Line **buses** leave for stops to **Wangaratta** and **Melbourne** at 1025 Mon and Fri. *Pyle's* coach company, Caltex Service Station, T5754 4024, www.buslines.com.au/ pyles, run a regular bus service up to **Fall's Creek** throughout the year, as well as services to **Melbourne** and **Albury**. **Taxi** T0409 573909.

Falls Creek
& around
Colour map 2, grid C4
Altitude: 1,550 m, 30
km from Mount Beauly,
65 km unsealed from
Omeo. For bookings try
Go Snow
T1800-253545,
www.fallscreek.albury.
net.au/~gosnow

The most picturesque of the three major Victorian ski resorts, Falls Creek has the look of a traditional alpine village. The approach from Mount Beauty is on a winding sealed road, through the park entry point ($20 per car in winter), opening out into a huge carpark just below the resort. The resort chairlifts climb up above the lodges to the edge of Bogong High Plains (around 1,800 m) and the Rocky Valley reservoir, with Mounts McKay and Feathertop providing the backdrop. In the June to September season snow-making facilities guarantee some decent runs. Lift passes are from $75 for a day. There are half a dozen ski hire places. *Halley's* have some reasonable deals and useful extras. Expect to pay about $25 per day for skis, boots and poles, about the same for parka and ski pants. All-in packages are usually the cheapest way to ski. No petrol available or ATMs, but there is a small supermarket, open daily all year round, and post office. The **VIC** is on the High Plains Road by the main car park. ■ *Open daily 0900-1700, T5758 3733, www.skifallscreek.com.au, www.fallscreek.com.au. Central reservations T1800-033079*

The unsealed **Bogong High Plains Road** over the plateau to the Omeo Highway is a great drive in summer, camping places along the way and some superb walking tracks taking in snow gum woodland, heath and old cattlemen's mountain huts. One of the best is a circular 2 hr walk starting at the parking area for the **Cope Hut Track**. Follow the track past the hut, continuing past some beautiful snow gums until the track splits. Take the left fork, pass a scout hut and head alongside a small creek. A short way after, by a good viewing spot, a small trail leads away to the left over a tiny bridge, signposted to **Wallace's Hut**. This hut is the oldest still existing in the Alps. There is a picnic and fireplace area here. About 50 m on an even thinner track leads off to the left, following a line of poles, indicating the **Alpine Walking Track**. This section climbs gradually up through open heath, with views from the top. The track merges into the road soon after, turn left over the brow of the hill for the parking area.

Sleeping & eating

All accommodation should be booked well ahead in the winter season. Contact Mountain Multiservice, T5758 3499, www.mountain multiservice.com.au, for information on renting private apartments

There are a couple of 'budget' options for singles and couples. **B** *Alpha*, Parallel St, T5758 3488, www.alphaskilodge.com.au Friendly hostel-style lodge with mostly doubles, twin and 4-share rooms. Price drops to **C** during the low season, and even lower from mid-Oct to May. Recommended. **B** *Four Seasons*, Falls Creek Rd, T5757 3254. Also hostel-style, mostly 4-bed dorms, slightly cheaper than *Alpha* during the peak season. *Snowgums*, Snowgums La, T5758 3601, donfell@bigpond.com, has one of the best off-season deals with dinner, bed & breakfast and en suite rooms from $50 a night. There are several dining options around the resort from the very groovy *Milch*, T5758 3770, with its Middle Eastern mezze menu, to the cheap, cheerful and lively *Man* pub, with cheap hearty bar meals. The latter is open daily in winter, serving food 1800-2200, and also has live or dance music most nights. The pub closes in Oct and on Sun-Mon from Nov-May. The warm and friendly *Wombat Café* is open daily all year, 0830-1730 in winter with hours contracting toward midday as the weather warms up.

Transport *Pyle's*, T5754 4024, www.buslines.com.au/pyles, operate a daily bus service between **Falls Creek** and **Mount Beauty**, running several times a day during the ski season. The service continues on to **Melbourne** at least once a day.

Angler's Rest

Colour map 2, grid C4 18 km from Omeo, 47 km from Falls Creek

Nestling by an idyllic valley-bottom creek on the Omeo Highway, Angler's Rest is beloved of anglers and drinkers alike as there is little here but exceptional fishing and one of Victoria's best pubs, the **D** *Blue Duck*, T5159 7220, F5159 7212. This pretty, rustic bar has a sunny veranda overlooking the extensive lawns that run down to the creek, and serves excellent cheap bar meals daily 1200-1430, 1800-2100. A dirt road turning off the highway a couple of hundred metres from the pub leads into the beautiful Bundarra River Valley, where you'll find **B-C** *Willows*, T/F5159 7241, a farm with two self-contained options; a very comfortable mud-brick house sleeping about eight, and a smaller, 100-year-old cattleman's hut, still without electricity but with a stone bathroom and gas stove. They also offer horseriding.

Victoria

**Omeo &
around**
Colour map 2, grid C4
Population: 550
120 km from
Bairnsdale
In summer, the area is
ideal for walking,
fishing and
whitewater rafting .
Walkers can get more
information from the
Omeo Parks office in
the centre of town,
T5159 1660

Omeo, once known as Victoria's most lawless goldfield, is in a long valley surrounded by soft domed hills. The town spills down the Great Alpine Road from the *Hilltop* pub to the VIC a kilometre further down. Omeo is right in the middle of the high plains grazing areas and it's the sense of a strong rural community and the beautiful valley that make the town so appealing. The **VIC** is, combined with a cuckoo clock shop. ■ *Daily 0900-1700, T5159 1552. Great Alpine Rd.* Two kilometres from Omeo on the road to Mount Hotham are the **Oriental Claims**, an alluvial gold-mining area which produced $21,000,000 worth of gold in today's money. There are 200-ft-cliffs where tonnes of earth were blasted by hoses and washed all the way down the creek. It is a remarkable testament to ingenuity, persistence and, sheer greed! **Ah Fongs Loop** is a suitably pleasant 45-minute stroll from the carpark through regenerated bush with markers pointing to the interesting relics of mining. The walking trail from Omeo starts at the swimming pool on Creek Street.

Accommodation in
Omeo is reasonably
priced so it makes a
good base for skiers.
There are no ATMs

Sleeping and eating   **C-D** *Golden Age*, Great Alpine Rd, T5159 1344. A comfortable hotel in the town centre with 15 spacious en suite rooms opening onto the 2nd floor veranda, also 5 small, fresh, budget rooms with shared facilities. Bistro-style meals in the restaurant, daily 1830-2030. **C** *The Manse*, corner of Great Alpine Rd and Day Av, T5159 1441, www.omeo.net/themanse Old-fashioned hosted B&B with wide verandas overlooking the valley. Warm hospitality and extensive continental breakfast. **F** *Omeo Alpine Camp*, Great Alpine Rd, T5159 1228. This large hall next to the church is perfect for budget travellers or groups, with big dorms, well-equipped kitchen, laundry and living room with fireplace. No one on site, ring the owners to let you in. There is also a caravan park in a pretty spot by Livingstone Creek (good trout fishing), T5159 1351, bike hire and gold-panning gear available. The *Hilltop*, T5159 1544. Omeo's only pub has cheap Chinese and standard meals daily 1200-1400, 1800-2000, and some very basic rooms (**D**).

Transport *Omeo Bus Lines*, T5159 4231, run between **Bairnsdale** and **Omeo**. *O'Connell's*, T5159 1377, run a **ski service** at weekends up to **Mount Hotham**, (40 mins, $25 return).

The Northeast

The names of the small towns in this compact, fertile region, bordered by the Murray River in the north and the High Country to the south, are the most evocative in Australian folklore, thanks to legendary bushranger Ned Kelly. Some, such as Beechworth, are also amongst the state's most appealing towns, thanks to the architectural magnificence of the goldrush era. More recently the appeal of the area has grown because of its excellent produce in the wine region of Rutherglen and the gourmet areas nearby.

Ins & outs   **Getting there and around** **Bus** *V~Line* have a few routes through the northeast from **Melbourne**. Main-line trains head through **Seymour**, **Benalla** and **Wangaratta** on to **Wodonga/Albury**, and buses from there to **Canberra** and **Sydney**. From Seymour a branch line takes trains to **Shepparton** from where buses head for **Echuca** and **Benalla**. From Wangaratta buses run down the Great Alpine Rd as far as **Mount Beauty**, and north to **Rutherglen**. There is also a bus route between Albury and Rutherglen, continuing on to **Swan Hill** and **Mildura**. An alternative bus route from Benalla to Wangaratta stops at **Glenrowan**, but only once a week.

Victoria

Benalla straddles the Broken River, and the wide stretch of water makes for a very picturesque setting. The **VIC**, near the main bridge, is combined with a **costume museum** also displaying a cell on which held Ned Kelly on a couple of occasions, plus his beloved green sash. ■ *Daily 0900-1700. $3, children $0.50, concessions $2. T/F 5762 1749, benallvic@origin.net.au* A few metres away is the town's unique, organic and tactile **ceramic mural**. Nationally renowned artists have contributed to this project since 1985 and the installation will continue to grow for many years to come. Get your thongs off and get down on the thongaphones. Over the river are the beautiful **botanic and rose gardens** and the **Art Gallery** within them. The latter has a small but significant collection of Australian art. ■ *Open daily 1000-1700. Free.* Just 2 km from the town centre is the largest **gliding club** in Australia (T5762 1058). Air experience flights are available from $80-140, depending on the tow height, and generally last 15 to 45 minutes. They also have a keenly priced 7-day course that sees a good proportion of people going solo. Bibliophiles can lose themselves for hours in *Good Reading*, one of the most comprehensive and good value secondhand bookshops in Victoria. **Stringybark Creek**, 55 km south, is the site of the fateful shootout between Kelly gang and the four policemen sent to sniff them out.

Benalla & around
Colour map 2, grid B3
Population: 11,000
132 km from Echuca,
115 km from Albury

Sleeping and eating There is virtually no accommodation in the town centre itself, but amongst the options fringing the centre is one of the region's best backpacker hostels. **B** *Belmont*, 80 Arundel St, T5762 6575, belmont@hdc.com.au This very comfortable, hosted 1920s B&B may be a little over-fussy for some tastes, but is easily the best in town. **D-E** *Trekkers Rest*, Kilfeera Rd on from Coster St, T5762 3535, www.trekkersrest.com.au Very spacious ex-roadbuilders' quarters now run as clean and cheerful budget accommodation, 2 km from town. Very friendly owners, new comfy mattresses, great showers. Recommended. *Café Raffety's*, Nunn St, T5762 4066, has a small mid-range menu of restrained modern Australian fare incorporating the best of local produce. Open Thu-Fri 1200-1430, Tue-Sat 1800-2100. *Georgina's*, Bridge St, T5762 1334, has less charm but more character and has been going strong since 1958. Cheap pasta with a strong vegetarian range and good enough to remain open every night of the week, 1800-2200.

Transport *V~Line* buses and trains leave from the railway station on Railway Place, for **Melbourne** (2 hrs) 5 times a day Mon-Sun, mostly early morning and mid to late afternoon. Services north to **Wangaratta** and **Wodonga/Albury** (1 hr) go equally as often. Buses to **Shepparton** (1 hr) and **Bendigo** (2½ hrs) leave at 0805 Mon, Wed and Fri. There is a weekly bus to **Glenrowan** leaving at 1655 on Fri.

The only town that really tries to capitalize on its chapter in the Kelly story is Glenrowan, a tacky tourist trap that witnessed one of the most extraordinary events in recent Australian history. Situated in a wide valley between two low hill ranges, Glenrowan was the scene of the 'siege' in 1880 that led to the capture of Ned Kelly and the deaths of his three comrades and two hostages. Although **Anne Jones' Inn** was incinerated during the siege the general layout of the battleground is pretty well preserved and easily observed from the top of the modern railway bridge. Virtually every local business has jumped on the Kelly bandwagon. There are currently two museum gift shops, two tearooms, a pub, a giant Ned, and the incomparable **Ned Kelly's Last Stand**, a series of intricate animated tableaux that spiritedly recall the whole story. While perhaps light on historical detail it is surprisingly evocative and good fun. ■ *Every half hour 0930-1630, 1930-2000 daily. $16, children $10, concessions $14. T5766 2367.*

Glenrowan & around
Colour map 2, grid B4
Population: 200
28 km from Benalla,
16 km from
the Wangaratta

Victoria

Ned's celebrated **Jerilderie Letter** is now available both in book form and online at www.slv.vic.gov.au/slv/exhibitions/treasures

Transport A *V~Line* bus heads off from the general store for **Wangaratta** and **Wodonga/Albury** at 1710 every Fri.

Wangaratta
Colour map 2, grid B4
Population: 22,000
44 km from Benalla,
72 km from Albury

Wangaratta has some pleasant parks, particularly on the riverbanks, and makes an ideal quick replenishment stop. South of Wangaratta, 7 km out on the Greta Road, is **Air World**, one of the largest collections of vintage and modern aircraft in the country. ■ *Daily 1000-1700. $6.60, children/concessions $4.40*. In the opposite direction, 15 km north on the Back Estcourt Road, the *Boorhaman Hotel* can make a legitimate change from wine-tasting as they brew their own **Buffalo Beer**. The town packs out during the weekend prior to the Melbourne Cup in November for the huge **Wangaratta Jazz Festival** (T5722 1666, www.wangaratta-jazz.org.au). The **VIC** has lots of information on the surrounding region. ■ *Daily 0900-1700, T5721 5711, F5721 9867. 1 km from the town centre on Tone Rd.*

Transport *V~Line* train and bus services leave from the railway station for **Benalla** and **Melbourne** (2½-3½ hrs) 4-5 times daily, and there are a similar number of services north to **Wodonga/Albury** (2 hrs 20 mins), with the daily 2115 service continuing on to **Sydney**. The service through **Beechworth** (45 mins) to **Bright** (1½ hrs) leaves at 0840 Mon, 1500 Mon-Tue, Thu-Fri, 2005 Wed, Fri, 1035 Sat and 1215 Sun, with the 1500 Mon and Fri service continuing on to **Mount Beauty**. An additional service terminating in Beechworth departs 1035 Mon-Fri. There are also buses to **Rutherglen** departing 1500 Mon-Fri, 2005 Wed, Fri and 2040 Sun. The *Speedlink* service to **Echuca** and **Adelaide** leaves daily at 0525. During the **ski season**, *Trekset*, T1800 659009, www.buslines.com.au/trekset, buses leave the *APCO* service station for **Bright**, **Harrietville** and **Mount Hotham** twice a day Sun-Fri and 3 times on Sat. The return service leaves for **Melbourne Airport** and **Melbourne** once a day Sat-Thu and twice a day Fri.

Rutherglen
Colour map 2, grid B4
Population: 1,900
Phone code: 02
38 km from
Wangaratta, 52 km
from Albury

This is the oldest wine region in Victoria and many of the 17 wineries are still owned by the families who started them four or five generations ago. The region, which is flat as a pancake, is best known for its fortified wines, Muscat, Tokay and Port, and full-bodied reds. The best time to visit is during the **Rutherglen Winery Walkabout** on the Queen's Birthday weekend in early June. This is a food and wine festival with lots of tastings, BBQs, seminars, stalls and music. For more information, T1800-622871, or www.winery walkabout.com The **VIC** has maps of the Muscat Trail, a 35-km cycle route through wineries and historic sites, and mountain bikes for hire ($22 day). ■ *Daily 1000-1700, T02-6032 9166, ruthindi@albury.net.au 13-27 Drummond St, at the western edge of town.*

A handful of B&Bs
complement the
town's motels, but
budget options are
limited to the
caravan park and
one of the pubs

Sleeping and eating **B** *Holroyd*, 28 Church St, T/F6032 8218, www.holroyd.visit rutherglen.com.au A couple of mins walk from the town centre, very comfortable hosted B&B in renovated 1928 house, with friendly, attentive owners. Splendid breakfast and expensive dinners also available. **B** *Syrah Cottage*, 1a Murphy St, T6032 8655. Self-contained period property, sleeps 4. **D** *Victoria*, Main St, T6032 8610. One of 3 basic pubs, this large building has 18 rooms, many dorm-style sleeping up to 8. *Tuileries*, next to the VIC, T6032 9033, has mid-range Modern Australian cuisine in elegant and formal surrounds. *The Gilded Grape*, at the roundabout on Main St, T6032 8077, is the best café, with fine platters, salads and sandwiches. Tables among paintings and antiques or in a pretty enclosed brick courtyard. Cheap-mid-range. Also interesting breakfasts at weekends from 0900. Thu-Sun 1000-1700, Fri-Sun 1800-2100. *Shamrock* in Main Street is a good place to eat hearty local produce (mid-range), bookings essential. The owner also runs the excellent **B** *The House at Mount Prior*, B&B, Howlong Rd, adjacent to Mount Prior Winery 15 km from Rutherglen, T02 6026 5256.

Transport *V~Line* buses leave for **Wangaratta** at 0635 Mon, Wed, Fri, 0755 Mon-Fri and 1645 Sun.

These two small communities have become known as something of a small gourmet region. There are several wineries, and producers selling mustards, honey, berries, cheese and preserves. The principal winery, *Brown Brothers*, T5720 5547, is signposted at main crossroads, Milawa. Wines $12-45, open daily 0900-1700. It harvests many varieties from all over Australia and offers an incredible tasting list of over 50 wines. Its *Epicurean Centre* is an expensive restaurant that matches food to wine so that each dish is served with the ideal drop. Daily 1100-1500. Picnic platters can also be taken into the lovely gardens. *King River Café*, Snow Road, T5727 3461. Monday 1000-1500, Wednesday-Sunday 1000-2100. Excellent cooking making the most of local produce in a stylish light-filled room with exposed brick and polished floors. Next door is the *King Valley Cellar*, T5727 3777, a showcase for wines from the nearby King Valley. Tastings and sales Thursday-Sunday 1100-1700. Fortunately the fantastic *Milawa Cheese Factory*, Factory Road, T5727 3588, is clearly signposted off the highway so you can't miss the superb cheeses, bakery and café. The café does light Italian-style lunches, 1100-1500 and becomes a restaurant Thursday-Sunday 1800-2000 for mid-range Modern Australian food with a mezes/tapas philosophy. *Milawa Royal General Store*, at the main crossroads, has a great range of gourmet products and is also a good place for a coffee. There is a pub, motel, shop and petrol at Milawa. Also a cheap though decrepit caravan park.

Milawa & Oxley
Population: 300
20 km from
Wangaratta

In the midst of the **Box-Ironbark National Park**, Chiltern is one of a small local cluster of old gold towns that have remained architecturally undisturbed since gold-rush fever abated around the turn of the century. Just a minute off the Hume Highway, the town is definitely worth a detour, especially if Beechworth is not on the itinerary. The **B** *Mulberry Tree Tea Rooms*, 28 Conness Street, T5726 1277, serves light lunches and cream teas every day and also has a couple of B&B rooms. Chiltern is on the main Wangaratta to Wodonga line and trains stop twice a day in each direction.

Chiltern
35 km from
Wangaratta, 35 km
from Myrtleford

Set in a shallow valley, surrounded by granite hills and forests of silver stringybark, Beechworth is the largest and loveliest of several well-preserved gold-rush towns in the Northeast. Beechworth was the most important administrative town in the northeast, which is why many notorious criminals were brought here, like Ned Kelly whose name in turn attracts thousands of tourists. The very helpful **VIC** is on Ford Street. ■ *Daily 0900-1700. T1300-366321, F5728 3233, www.beechworth.com*

The **Court House**, at 94 Ford Street, is where Ned Kelly was tried, along with the rest of his gang and his mother, Ellen Kelly. It has barely changed since the 1850s and now operates as a museum. ■ *Daily 1000-1600, $2, concessions $1. T5728 2721.* Opposite, the **Burke Museum**, named after explorer Robert O'Hara Burke who was superintendent of police in Beechworth from 1854 to 1858, has fascinating collections of gold-mining artifacts and an exhibition on

Beechworth
Colour map 2, grid B4
Population: 3,100
Altitude: 550 m

Victoria

▶▶ Kelly's heroes

Ned Kelly, Australian born to poor Irish immigrants in 1854, is Australia's only mythological folk hero. Often portrayed in art, literature, poetry and film as a latter-day Robin Hood, Ned was no born reformer and his career as small-time thief, occasional labourer and local tough would have remained unremarkable had not one particular brush with the law been blown out of all proportion.

A local constable, Alexander Fitzpatrick, went to the Kelly house, patently drunk, in April 1878 to arrest Ned's brother Dan on an unwarranted charge. A brief scuffle ensued, leaving Fitzpatrick with a cut wrist. He later claimed he had been shot and the whole family had tried to kill him. Ned claimed he was in NSW at the time. Arrest warrants were promptly issued and the boys fled with two friends. Their mother, with a new baby, was convicted of aiding attempted murder and sent down for three years hard labour.

Unsurprisingly, given their relationship over the years, Ned Kelly had no fondness for Victorian policemen whom he later described as 'big ugly, fat-necked, wombat-headed, big-bellied, magpie-legged, narrow-hipped, splaw-footed sons of Irish bailiffs or English landlords'. Now, though, the police had an excuse to finish the Kellys once and for all. Their search parties went out heavily-armed and equipped to bring in corpses, which the Kelly's soon learned. In October a four-man search party came fatefully close to the Kelly bush camp near Stringybark Creek. The boys decided they would have to capture the policemen in order to escape, but the plan went awry. The police, led to expect

no mercy, fought for their lives and three of them were shot dead by Ned, by his account in self defence. The other escaped.

Now the gang had become true bushrangers, beyond the law and to be hunted down with no mercy. Ned felt they may as well fulfil their role and the gang took to robbing banks, redistributing funds to their families and friends who helped them. However, he was careful of public opinion. No bystanders were killed, virtually no one hurt, and occasionally Ned justified his actions to his captives. He wrote to the authorities and press stating his case but no one would publish the letters. He intended to force a printer in Jerilderie to print one epistle but the man escaped. The document, now known as the Jerilderie Letter came to light years later.

It was the Kelly Gang who forced the final showdown, constructing four sets of distinctive home-made armour and heading for Glenrowan in June 1880. Here they took over a pub and let it be known they were there. They knew large numbers of policemen would come up on the train and planned to derail the engine just outside of town. The authorities were tipped off, however, and a siege ensued. It ended dramatically after several hours with the pub in flames and Ned Kelly walking out in his armour for a final last stand.

Dan and the two other gang members were killed, but Ned survived, wounded, and was taken to Melbourne. Despite considerable public sympathy he was swiftly tried for the Stringybark 'murders' and hanged in Melbourne Gaol in November 1880. His last words were 'Such is life'.

Ned Kelly that includes his death mask. ■ *Daily 1030-1530. $5, concessions $3. T5728 1420. Loch St.* Almost opposite the cemetery is the start of the **Gorge Scenic Drive**, a short excursion that demonstrates how well the landscape has recovered from the disturbance caused by mining.

Midway between the northern plains and the Alps, Beechworth sits amidst the beautiful **Beechworth Historic Park**. Much of it is criss-crossed by walking and bike tracks. From **Mount Pilot Lookout**, midway between Beechworth and Chiltern, there are amazing views to the north. It is reached by a steep but short walk from the carpark to the top. Nearby is an Aboriginal art site with a Tasmanian tiger among the faint images. Five km from town on the Chiltern road, the extensive **Woolshed Falls** cascade over granite outcrops amidst a low wooded gorge. In the other direction, 8 km along a picturesque road lined with chestnut and apple orchards, is the tiny town of **Stanley**. The road south from Stanley becomes unsealed, treacherous but very picturesque for the stretch up through some logging ranges, and then comes out on the Myrtleford-Yackandandah road and the idyllic **Happy Valley**.

Sleeping A *Country Charm Swiss Cottages*, 22 Malakoff Rd, T5728 2435, www.swisscottages.com.au Luxurious, self-contained, wooden cottages in a peaceful spot above the town. **A** *Kinross*, 34 Loch St, T5728 2351, www.babs.com.au/kinross Hosted B&B in an 1850s stone house almost hidden by white roses. 5 en suite rooms with fireplaces, warm hospitality and excellent cooking. Also dinners by arrangement ($33-50). A cheaper B&B option is **C** *Alba Country Rose*, 30 Malakoff Rd, T5728 1107. **C** *Laidlaw Cottage*, 12 Finch St, T5728 1719. owen@netc.net.au, is one of the cheaper self-contained colonial houses in the town. **D** *Wardens Hostel*, Ford St, T5728 1061. Backpacker-style budget accommodation with a majority of twin rooms. Very restricted kitchen facilities, but otherwise cheerful and comfortable. **E** *Empire*, Camp St, T5728 1030. Cheap but very basic pub rooms. 4 km out on the Wangaratta Road, is **B** *Black Springs Bakery*, T/F5728 2565. This ex-bakery now houses a garden and homewares shop to tickle the fancy of every francophile, a small café and interesting and extensive gardens ($3 entry). The small renovated stone barn is like a piece of Provence for 2, book well ahead. Recommended. **C** *Woolshed Cabins*, McFeeters Rd, T5728 1035. 4 simple, wooden self-contained cabins, surrounded by trees, 1 km from the falls. Shop, café and gardens Sep-Jun, Fri Mon 1000 1730.

Beechworth's popularity means that there are many excellent B&Bs and some very good restaurants, but also means there is very little budget accommodation

Eating *Bank Restaurant and Mews*, 86 Ford St, T5728 2223. Expensive and modern international restaurant, also serving mid-range lunches. Fri-Sun 1130-1430, daily 1830-2100. *Deja Food*, 32 Ford St, T5728 2352. Quirky and fun, small establishment with a very imaginative menu. Wed-Sun 1100-1500, 1830-2100. Recommended. *Gigi's*, 69 Ford St, T5728 2575, is a small and casual continental restaurant with friendly service. Cheap to mid-range. Daily 1200-1500, Thu-Sun 1830-2100. *The Green Shed*, 37 Camp St, T5728 2360, is a smart, mid-range, modern Australian in a small cottage with contemporary art on exposed brick walls. Open Thu-Sun 1200-1500, Wed-Sun 1830-2100. *Indigo Inn,* Stanley, T/F5728 6502, indigoinn@chl.com.au, is one of the oldest continuously licensed pubs in Victoria. The bar has been smartened up recently and a cheap bistro, with excellent wood-fired pizzas have been added on. The two B&B rooms (**A**) are exceptional, and the one with the walk-around fireplace is particularly exquisite. Highly recommended. Bistro Thu-Sun, 1200-2000, bookings required.

Transport *V~Line* buses leave from the corner of Camp St and Ford St at 0635 Wed and Fri, 0920 Fri, 1215 Mon-Tue, Thu-Fri, 1500 Mon-Fri, 1620 Sat, and 1645 Sun for **Wangaratta** (45 mins) and **Melbourne** (3-4 hrs). Additional services at 0700 Mon-Fri and 0920 Mon, Wed terminate at Wangaratta. The service for stops to **Bright** (1 hr) leaves at 1535 Mon-Tue, Thu-Fri, 2035 Wed, Fri, 1110 Sat and 1245 Sun, with the 1535 Mon and Fri service continuing on to **Mount Beauty**.

Victoria

Murray River

The Murray flows down from the highlands of the Great Dividing Range and forms the border between Victoria and New South Wales. Sharing the resources of the river has been a source of interstate bickering since the borders were defined and has also led to the development of twin towns, Echuca and Moama, on either side of the river. Of the two, Echuca is the most appealing. It's a picturesque town with some interesting sights and good restaurants, and preserves a feel of the river's past with its fleet of restored paddlesteamers chugging along the wide brown river and moored at the high 1850s wharf. Downriver is modern and prosperous Mildura, whose sunny climate allows fruit crops to flourish. But the corridor of fertility along the Murray is very narrow and beyond it are some of the driest areas of southeastern Australia.

Ins and outs

Getting there & around

Bus/train There are regular *V~Line* train services between **Melbourne**, **Bendigo** and **Echuca**, train and bus services between Bendigo and **Swan Hill**, and connecting bus services from Swan Hill up to **Mildura**. A limited service runs from **Rochester** (on the Bendigo-Echuca line) to **Barham** via **Cohuna**. There are also bus services between Mildura and **Ballarat** via **Maryborough**; Mildura and Echuca via Swan Hill; Echuca and **Albury** (NSW), with connections to **Sydney**; and Swan Hill and **Adelaide** (SA). **Tours** Operators offering day-trips to **Echuca** from **Melbourne**, include *Gray Line*, T9663 4455 ($99) and *Backpacka*, T9277 8577 ($93). Both include paddlesteamer cuises.

Boat There are hundreds of **houseboats** available for hire on this long stretch of the Murray, and getting out on one for a few days is the best way to appreciate the river. The best deals will be found in Mildura and Echuca. In general large groups will always find better deals than small. An over-18 'captain' with a driver's or boat licence is required, plus a large deposit and bond. Boats travel at an average of 7 kph, so do not reckon to travel far from your original mooring.

Echuca

Colour map 2, grid B3
Population: 13,900
253 km from Albury,
88 km from Bendigo,
145 km from Swan Hill

Echuca has the best of the river-trade heritage and is definitely the most rewarding of the Murray towns to visit. It knows it too, but the community has largely resisted the opportunity to descend into sheer kitsch. The largest paddlesteamer fleet in the world lines up next to the wharf and the view could almost be that of a quiet Sunday in the 1870s (if no modern houseboats are going by). February is a good time to be around Echuca when the **Southern 80 Power Boat Race** thrills tens of thousands of spectators, and the lively **Riverboat Food, Jazz and Wine Festival** sozzles nearly as many. **Moama**, just over the bridge, is Echuca's poor NSW relation, but does have a slightly cheaper range of accommodation.

Ins & outs

The bus terminal is on Hogarth St. For transport details, see page 489. The **VIC** is at 2 Heygarth St, next to the bridge to Moama. It has an accommodation booking service and shares the space with the **V~Line** booking office. Open daily 0900-1700. T5480 7555, F5482 6413, www.echucamoama.com

Sights

The port area of Echuca is owned by the local council and has been restored as a 'working' port, with shipwrights and steam engineers still working on paddlesteamers although the blacksmiths and carpenters mostly make

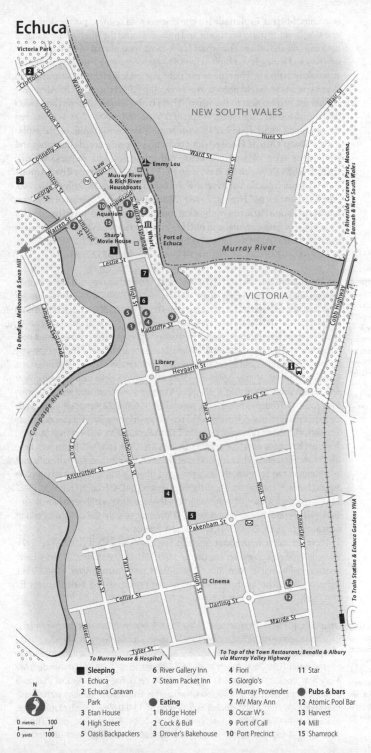

Echuca

New South Wales

Victoria

Sleeping		
1	Echuca	
2	Echuca Caravan Park	
3	Etan House	
4	High Street	
5	Oasis Backpackers	
6	River Gallery Inn	
7	Steam Packet Inn	

Eating		
1	Bridge Hotel	
2	Cock & Bull	
3	Drover's Bakehouse	
4	Fiori	
5	Giorgio's	
6	Murray Provender	
7	MV Mary Ann	
8	Oscar W's	
9	Port of Call	
10	Port Precinct	
11	Star	

Pubs & bars		
12	Atomic Pool Bar	
13	Harvest	
14	Mill	
15	Shamrock	

souvenirs. **Murray Esplanade** is a gravel street with restored port buildings on one side, housing pubs, tea rooms and museums, and the wharf and associated buildings on the other. The wharf is the most magnificent of all the Murray wharves and jetties. It was built in the 1850-60s of red gum, two storeys high to remain dry in floods. The railway ran right alongside and the tracks and an old steam engine can be clambered over as can the *PS Pevensey* and *PS Alexander Arbuthnot*, tied up next to the wharf. There is also a small museum and video display in a former cargo shed. ■ *Port of Echuca, daily 0900-1700. $10, children $6, concession $8.50. T5482 4248. www.portofechuca.org.au* Also on the esplanade is **Sharp's Movie House**, with a collection of penny arcade machines and continuous reels of wartime news, old comedies and movies. ■ *Daily 0900-1700. $11, children $7, concession $9. T5482 2361*. **Murray River Aquarium** is a small collection of Murray River fish and reptiles. ■ *Daily 0900-1700. $5.50, children $3. 640 High St, T5480 7388*. Some 35 km southeast of Echuca is **Kyabram Fauna Park**, run by the local community on a non-profit basis with a wide range of native animal and bird life in large enclosures and walk-through aviaries. Many waterfowl have also been attracted to the 32 ha wetland area. ■ *Daily 0930-1730. $8.50, children $4, concession $6. T5852 2883*.

Sleeping

Echuca and Moama are awash with motels, and it should be possible to find a room in one even in busy periods. For somehing different, be sure to book well ahead for the summer season (Dec-Apr here) and public holidays

L-A *River Gallery Inn*, 578 High St, T/F5480 6902, www.echuca.net.au/~inn 8 en suite rooms. Central location. **A** *Etan House*, 11 Connelly St, T5480 7477, www.qai.com.au/mbs/etan 4 en suite rooms, kitchen, pool, tennis court. Hosted B&B in a gracious colonial house close to the Esplanade. **A-C** *Murray House*, 55 Francis St, T5482 4944, www.innhouse.com.au/ murrayhouse 5 en suite rooms and a very good value self-contained cottage. The warmest hospitality and a sense of fun from the hosts of this very comfortable B&B in a quiet street 10 mins walk from the town centre. Recommended. **C** *Steam Packet Inn*, Murray Esplanade, T5482 3411. Simple, clean rooms. Room only or B&B. **D** *High Street*, 439 High St, T5482 1013. A budget motel chain with simple, clean en suite rooms. **E** *Echuca Gardens YHA*, Mitchell St, T5480 6522, echuca@yhavic.org.au Clean but cramped hostel 10 mins walk from the town centre. Some of the 'rooms' are actually under canvas or in small caravans. **E** *Oasis Backpackers*, 410-424 High St, T5480 7866, www.nomads world.com Bright, spacious and clean NOMADS hostel with large handmade bunks and bathrooms Picking work can be arranged Sep-Apr by friendly staff, and transport can be provided. Recommended. There are quite a few caravan parks around, but most are a fair drive from the town centre. The **C-D** *Echuca*, Crofton St, T5482 2157, is the nearest, barely a 5-min walk from the Esplanade, and they do have on-site vans, even though they are a bit pricey. **C-D** *Riverside*, over the Cobb Highway bridge, right and right again, T5482 3241, is the closest alternative.

There are many **houseboat** hirers in Echuca-Moama. *Dinky-Di*, T5482 5223, www.dinkydihouseboats.com.au, charge $880-1420 for the smallest 2- and 4-berth boats, larger available. *Rich River*, T5480 2444, and *Murray River*, T5480 2343, mrhboats@origin.net.au, have pick-ups by the Esplanade and 6-berth boats for $870-1500.

Eating

Echuca has many excellent restaurants and cafés, which get booked up in holiday seasons and most weekends. Fine dining here requires fine planning

Oscar W's, 101 Murray Esplanade, T5482 5133. A wonderful location on the wharf is matched by some of the finest of Victorian cuisine, a focus on regional produce and a comprehensive wine list. Unsurprisingly expensive, but there is a light mid-range all-day menu 1000-1600, lunch 1130-1430, dinner 1830-2100. Recommended. *MV Mary Ann*, booking office at 562 High St, T5480 2200. The only riverboat that does dinner cruises, this diesel-powered catamaran is an Italian restaurant with simple pub-style food ($55, 4 hrs). *Cock & Bull*, Warren St, T5480 6988. Excellent mid-range modern Australian meals in renovated bare-brick 130-year-old pub. Tue-Sat 1800-2100. Also a comfy self-contained 2-bedroom B&B apartment (**B**) upstairs.

Fiori, 554 High St, T5482 6688. Superb Italian pasta, salads and mid-range mains in a casual café-style interior with a glassed-in courtyard. Book in advance for weekends. Wed-Sun 1200-1400, daily 1800-2100. Recommended. *Morrisons Riverview Estate*, Merool La, Moama. T5480 0126. Welcoming cellar door and restaurant on the banks of the Murray. While gazing at the river gums and vines, drinking wine and eating excellent Italian influenced food, breakfast turns into lunch and lunch turns into afternoon tea. Daily 1000-1700. Recommended. *Star*, Murray Esplanade. T5480 1181. Modern-feel wine bar and café in wharf-side building. Good range of breakfasts, light lunches daily 0900-1600. Open till 2100 or 2200 every night, tapas Mon-Thu, à la carte modern Australian Fri-Sat. *Drover's Bakehouse*, 513 High St, T5480 1057. A large gourmet bakery that also has good salads and sandwiches, tables out the back overlook the river. Will make picnic hampers given a day's notice. *Murray Provender*, 568 High St, T5482 5295. The best place for coffee in town or a gourmet baguette or platter, picnic hampers also available. Tue-Sun 1000-1630. *Port of Call*, corner of Radcliffe St and Murray Esplanade. Large open-plan bar and 'cellar door'. About 10 wines a day available for free tastings and substantial lunch platters, easily enough for 2, good value at $15. Open Mon-Thu 1100-1900, Fri-Sun 1000-2000. *Port Precinct*, 591 High St, T5480 2163. All-day breakfasts, pancakes, burgers and foccacia in this simple, friendly café, internet access $2.50 for 15 mins. Daily 0800-1900. *Top of the Town*, corner of High St and McIvor Rd, T5482 4600. Superb fish and chip shop using only the freshest fish from the Melbourne markets. Licensed. Eat-in or takeaway. Open daily 0800-2000 (2100 in summer).

Atomic Pool Bar, 207 Darling St, Mon-Fri from 1700, Sat-Sun from 1200. Large and **Bars & clubs** groovy pool bar, gets packed with drinkers at weekends. *The Mill*, corner of Nish St and Darling St. Spacious nightclub with modern dance and retro bars, open Fri-Sat (and Thu in summer) 2130-0400. $5 entry. *Harvest*, Hare St. Airy front bar and separate bistro area. Live music every Sat night when it gets very busy and stays open till 0400. *Shamrock*, High St. Irish theme bar with more character than most, very popular Fri-Sat when local bands take to the small stage. Open to 0200 Fri-Sat.

There are various **river trips**, from 1 hr to overnight trips or a full-day cruise to wineries. **Tours &** The Port of Echuca owns 3 paddle steamers that make 1-hr cruises several times a day **activities** ($15.50), but the best option if you have time is to take one of their cruises to Morrisons Riverview Estate, only $2 more but run from 1130 to 1515 with a 2-hr stop for lunch, tastings or a walk at the winery. The *PS Emmylou* is the loveliest of the boats, although only 20 years old, and is worth the slightly higher charge. 5 cruises a day, 1½ hrs, $18, children $9. Wine tours $48, children $30. T5480 2237. Tickets from 57 Murray Esplanade. She can also be booked for meal-inclusive overnight trips ($200 per person). There are also 4-hr wine tours which include a walk through the port, a trip on the *PV Pride of the Murray* to Morrison's, then a trip by coach to two cellar doors and a cooperage, ending back in Echuca at the *Port of Call*. *Dawn Drifters*, T5483 5363, morning balloon flights over the Murray Valley and champagne breakfast ($200, 50 min flight, allow 4 hrs). *Echuca Boat and Canoe Hire*, T5480 6208, www.echucaboatcanoe hire.com This company will deliver canoeists upstream as far as Albury for a one-way paddle back, from 2-hr hire ($40) up to one week. Also motor boats $27 hr, canoes $16 hr, BBQ boat $65 for 2 hrs. On the riverbank about 500 m into Victoria Park. Another great overnight option, for equestrians, is offered by *Billabong Trail Rides* alongside their shorter rides (from $16 for ½ hr). T0428 507828.

Bus *V~Line* bus services to **Bendigo** (1 hr 20 mins) leave from the terminal at 0910, **Transport** 1400, 1640 Mon-Fri, 0905 Sat, 0810 and 1310 Sun. All these connect with **Melbourne** trains, and there are services to Melbourne at 0605, 0830 Mon-Fri, 1745 Fri-Sat, 0725,

0830 Sat, and 1505 Sun (around 4 hrs). Buses to **Rutherglen** (3½ hrs) and **Albury** (NSW, 4¼ hrs) leave at 1255 Tue, Fri, Sun and 1535 Wed. Services to **Mildura** (6½ hrs), via **Cohuna, Lake Boga** and **Swan Hill** (3 hrs) leave at 1130 Mon, Thu, Sat and 1020 Wed.

Directory **Banks** Major bank ATMs on Hare St. **Car hire** *Budget*, 249 Ogilvie Av, T5482 5233. **Car Servicing** *Wharfside Motors*, Warren St by the bridge, T5482 3281. **Communications** Internet free at the Public Library, corner of High St and Heygarth St, T5482 1997. Open Mon-Tue, Thu-Fri 1000-1730, Wed 1300-2100, Sat 1000-1300, Sun 1400-1600. **Post Office**, Pakenham St.

Around Echuca Just north of Echuca, **Barmah State Forest** is the largest red gum forest in Australia with a series of wetland lakes and lagoons. The area is a natural habitat for a wide variety of wildlife, and over 200 species of birds have been recorded. *Kingfisher*, T5480 1839, kingfisher@emmylou.com.au, run two-hour wetland cruises through the Barmah, and *Gondwana*, T5869 3347, have canoe hire from $35 for ½ day, which includes transportation from their base on the Moira Lakes Road. The **Dharnya Culture Centre**, 11 km north of Barmah on the Moira Lakes Road, T5869 3247, provides information on camping, the many driving tracks and some fine, marked walking trails. It also doubles as an Aboriginal heritage centre, with interesting information on the local Yorta Yorta people, both their historical and current struggles.

The **Kerang Wetlands**, 35 km from Echuca, are a series of over 50 lakes and lagoons and one of Australia's largest and most important wetland areas. Over 190 species are known to live or visit the wetlands including many ducks, ibis, herons, kites, pelicans and spoonbills. The best place to view this huge gathering of birdlife, particularly on Spring evenings, is the Ibis Rookery Bird Hide, signposted 10 km north of the service town of Kerang. The sight (and sound) of thousands of birds congregating, feeding and wheeling above is quite mesmerising - whether you're a bird-lover or not.

Swan Hill

Colour map 2, grid B2
Population: 9,300
145 km from Echuca,
221 km from Mildura

Laid out in a grid paralleling the Murray River, Swan Hill derives almost all its prosperity from agriculture and engineering. The signposted 4½-km walk along the river is frequently interspersed with interesting interpretive signs commenting on the rich Aboriginal heritage and European settlement. Ask for a map and guide at the VIC, which is, like almost everything else, on Campbell Street. ■ *Daily 0900-1700. T5032 3033, F5032 3032, www.swanhill.vic.gov.au* The town's chief attraction is the **Pioneer Settlement**, at Horseshoe Bend, 1 km south of the city centre, which manages to spice up the 'olde worlde' buildings formula with some inventive tours and sideshows including an optional trip on their riverboat, the *PS Pyap*. ■ *Daily 0900-1700. $16, children $8.50, concessions $11. Cruises on the PS Pyap daily 1420, $10, children $6, concessions $8. A luncheon river cruise is also available on the MV Kookaburra, book at the VIC. The sound and light tours daily at dusk are surprisingly good. T5032 1093.*

Sleeping
There are very few options other than a motel or caravan park

There is currently one **B&B**, actually a comfortable self-contained house in immaculate gardens just set back from the river and close to the Pioneer Settlement, **B** *Swanage*, 5 Mitchell St, T5032 0087. **C** *Jane Eliza*, 263 Campbell St, T5032 4411, jeliza@swanhill.net.au, is one of the most central motels and good value. Of the several caravan parks, **D-E** *Pioneer City*, T5032 4372, 2 km north of town on the Murray Valley Highway, is friendly, clean, well-maintained and even better value. Recommended.

There are just a handful of **houseboats**, unfortunately pretty expensive, based in Swan Hill but, as it's several hundred kilometres from either Echuca or Mildura, the river is comparatively quiet along this stretch. *Kookaburra*, T5032 0003, www.murray-river.net/houseboats/kookaburra, have 2 boats. Also B&B (**B**). *Murray Downs*, T/F5032 2160, has one 6-berth boat for $1150-2200.

Tellers at 223 Campbell St, T5033 1383. A great range of reasonable mid-range meals is available in this large open café bar, 1130-1430, 1800-2200. *Paddy Curran's*, 188 Campbell St. Small Irish theme pub with cheap meals. *202*, 202 Beveridge St. Popular local café with decent coffee. Open daily 0900-1800. The best breakfasts and healthy options can be found at *Café Allure*, 147 Campbell St. Inventive juices, smoothies, salads and crêpes. Open 0800-1630 Mon, 0800-1730 Tue-Fri, 0930-1430 Sat. **Eating**

V~Line **buses** leave from the Railway Station on Curlewis St for **Bendigo** and **Melbourne** 0715 Wed, 0800, 1245 Mon-Fri, 1525 Fri, 1340 Sat-Sun (5-6 hrs). Some services also stop at **Lake Boga**. There are faster **train** services (4 hrs) at 0730 Mon-Sat and 1640 Sun. Bus services head for **Mildura** (2½ hrs) at 1345 Mon-Sat, 1440 Mon, Thu, Sat, 1815 Thu, 2100 Fri, 2205 Mon-Thu, Sat and 1455, 2150 Sun. The service to **Echuca** (1½ hrs) and **Albury** (NSW, 7 hrs) leaves at 1025 Tue, Fri, Sun and 1245 Wed. Services to **Ballarat** go at 1525 Fri and 1640 Sun. **Transport**

Mildura

Mildura is a large and sprawling rural town on the Murray, surrounded by vast acres of vineyards and fruit trees. Beyond these are the mallee plains and semi-arid deserts of the outback. Like most of the other Murray towns it is popular for river sports and there's also good shopping and eating. The **VIC** forms part of the *Alfred Deakin Centre*, 180 Deakin Avenue. ■ *Mon-Fri 0900-1730, Sat-Sun 0900-1700. T5021 4424, F5021 1836, www.murrayoutback.org.au* **Mildura Arts Centre**, 199 Cureton Avenue, opposite the river, consists of an art gallery, theatre and Rio Vista, historic home of the influential Chaffey family. ■ *Daily 1000-1700. $3, children free, concession $2. T5023 3733, www.miduraarts.net.au* The paddlesteamer *PS Melbourne* is still steam-driven and goes on daily cruises down the Murray, travelling through a lock on the way, and the paddleboat *PV Rothbury* runs day cruises to Trenthams for a wine tour and tastings. ■ *PS Melbourne cruises daily 1050, 1350, 2 hrs. $18.50, children $7.50, concession $16.50. PV Rothbury winery cruises Thu 1030, 5 hrs. $42, children $20, concession $40. T5023 2200. Buy tickets on board at the Mildura Wharf.*

Colour map 2, grid A2 Population: 24,000 220 km from Swan Hill, 135 km from Renmark (SA) Many travellers come to Mildura to take advantage of plentiful fruit-picking work in the summer. It also has by far the easiest access to the magnificent Mungo National Park

L-B *Grand*, Seventh St, T5023 0511, www.milduragrand.com Over 100 rooms, room service, 3 restaurants, pool, breakfast included. Elegant hotel opened as a coffee palace in 1890, now modern with a faintly colonial feel. **C** *Elizabeth Leighton*, 116 Sturt Highway, 4 km over the bridge, T/F5021 2033, el_b+b@mildura.net.au Hosted B&B with 2 comfortable double rooms in a new large brick home overlooking the river. **C** *Riverview*, 115 Seventh St, T5023 8975, victorm@madec.edu.au. Hosted B&B in 1950s-style house close to town centre. Cooked breakfasts and en suite. **E** *International Backpackers*, 5 Cedar Av, T5021 0133, mildrapb@vic.ozland.net.au Tired and scruffy hostel catering predominantly for workers. Can organize work and transport. **E** *Treetops*, over the bridge, first left, T5023 5874. Just opening at time of writing, 5 doubles and twins with shared facilities in a basic apartment by the river. The same company hires out boats and canoes. **E** *Zippy Koala*, 206 Eighth St, T5021 5793. Small, clean and quiet backpacker option, 15 mins walk from town, limited facilities, will organize work and transport. **Houseboats** *Adventure* **Sleeping**

There are plenty of motels, motor inns and caravan parks, mostly along Fifteenth St and Deakin Av

Other types of accommodation are thinner on the ground

Houseboats, moorings 16 Sturt Highway, just over the bridge, T5023 4787, www.adventure.ozland.net.au Well-maintained boats from 2-3 bedroom with additional fold-out beds. 2-6 berth $590-$11,560, 8 berth $865-$2,430, 10 berth $1,210-$2,590. The boats also double as static **B&B** when available (**C**). For details of other houseboat companies contact the VIC.

Eating

The best places to eat are centred on Langtree Av and make the most of regional produce

Stefano's, *Grand Hotel*, T5023 0511. Mon-Sat from 1900. One of Victoria's finest restaurants, chef Stefano de Pieri offers a set-price banquet ($60) combining Northern Italian country cooking with local produce and an exhaustive wine list (800 labels!). Booked out up to 2 months in advance at weekends, but it's still worth trying in case of cancellations. ***Rendezvous***, 34 Langtree Av, T5023 1571. Long-serving Mildura institution combines a mid-range restaurant, bar and cheap bistro. The bistro has the best area, warm exposed brick and lovely courtyard with very traditional pasta, salads and steaks. ***White Monkey***, 26 Langtree St, T5022 2900. Tue-Sat 1630-2200, Sun 1100-1700. Mid-range Modern Australian food with a provincial Italian slant in a funky modern room recently built by the owner chef. Great all-day breakfasts on Sun. *O'Malleys*, corner of Deakin Av and Tenth St, T5021 4236. Large, open Irish pub with couches by the fire and snugs. Also mid-range bistro meals 1200-1400, 1830-2100 and live music Wed-Sat. Recommended. *Sandbar*, 45 Langtree Av, T5021 2181. Lively modern pub with very cheap café-style meals and a great beer garden. Live music Wed-Sat from 2230. *27 Deakin*, T5021 3627. Mon, Wed-Fri 1000-1800, Sat-Sun 1000-1500. Hip gourmet café and shop that also does picnic hampers and take-home meals. Fine coffee, lunches and all-day weekend breakfasts. *Pizza Café*, *Grand Hotel*. Daily 1200-1430, 1800-2100. Casual, rustic style with wood-fired pizzas and light Italian dishes, cheap prices and good atmosphere at weekends. Recommended. *Ziggy's*, 145 Eighth St, T5023 2626. Tue-Fri 0730-1700, Sat 0800-1400, Sun 0900-1400. Relaxed, stylish café does all-day breakfasts, including vegetarian choices, and simple Mediterranean lunches. *Trentham Estate*, 16 km from Mildura,

Mildura

Sleeping ■	4 Zippy Koala	3 Outlaws	Pubs & bars ●
1 Grand		4 Rendezvous	8 Level 1
2 International	Eating ●	5 Taco Bills	9 O'Malleys
Backpackers	1 27 Deakin	6 White Monkey	10 Sandbar
3 Riverview	2 Hudaks	7 Ziggy's	11 Setts

0 metres 300
0 yards 300

T5024 8747, has a good range of great wines for around $10-25, cellar door Mon-Fri 0900-1700, Sat-Sun 0930-1700. The stylish modern cellar door also houses a highly respected and respectable mid-range restaurant, serving mostly modern Australian fowl and fish. Tue-Sun 1130-1500.

Cameron Balloons, T5021 2876, www.cameronsmildura.com.au, fly at dawn with an enthusiastic pilot. The paddleboat *Coonawarra*, T1800 034424, has all-inclusive 4- and 5-night cruises from $440 to $880 per person. There are several **national parks** around Mildura, all of which offer great walking and camping. For further information on **Mungo National Park** contact the NSW National Parks and Wildlife Service in Buronga, corner of Sturt Highway and Malaleuca St, T5021 8900, www.npws.nsw.gov.au Small groups should consider a tour, and the best of these are run by the Aboriginal-owned company, *Harry Nanya*, T1800 630864, www.harrynanyatours.com.au Day tours available all year round, sunset tours during summer, both good value at $55. *Mallee Outback Experiences*, T5024 6007, runs day tours ($55) to **Hattah-Kulkyne National Park**, an area of lakes (periodically dry), birdlife, woodlands and mallee dunes. The owners of *Treetops* hire out boats and canoes.

Tours & activities
A visit to Mungo requires a mostly unsealed trip of over 200 km

Air The airport is 7 km out on the Sturt Highway toward Adelaide. The *Airport Bus Service*, T5022 1309 or 0428 507351, meets all flights, and picks up around the city for departures. *Kendell* fly several times a day to **Melbourne**, as do *Southern*, T5022 2444, who also fly via 'seamless' connections to the major cities in NSW, South Australia and Tasmania. **Bus/Train** *Sunraysia Bus Lines* local services leave outside the Mall for **Centre Plaza** on 15th St, roughly 1½ hourly 0745-1745, at 0945 and 1200 Sat, 1045 Sun. There are also fairly frequent buses daily to **Merbein** and **Red Cliffs**. *V~Line* buses leave for stops to **Melbourne** (7-9 hrs) from the depot in Seventh St, 0440 Mon-Sat, 0830 Mon, 0900 Tue-Fri, 1220 Fri, 1010 Sat-Sun, 1345 Sun. Services change to train at either **Swan Hill** or **Bendigo**. Services to **Ballarat** (7 hrs), via Swan Hill, leave at 1220 Fri and 1345 Sun, and via **Clunes** at 2145 Sun-Fri. Buses to **Echuca** (5-6 hrs) and **Albury** (NSW, 12-13 hrs) leave at 0720 Tue, Fri, Sun, and 0900 Wed. **Interstate** *McCafferty's/Greyhound* buses leave for **Sydney** (16½ hrs) daily at 0305. **Adelaide** buses leave daily at 0230 (5 hrs), and the **Broken Hill** service goes at 0900 (3 hrs).

Transport

Banks Major bank ATMs on Deakin Av and Eighth St. **Car Servicing** *Phil Smith Automotive*, 35 Tenth St, T5021 2358. **Communications** Internet free at the library in the Alfred Deakin Centre, T5023 5011. Open Sun-Mon 1300-1700, Tue-Fri 1000-1900, Sat 1000-1400. **Post Office**, corner of Orange Av and Eighth St. **Hospital** Thirteenth St, T5022 3333. **Parks Office** Langtree Mall (upstairs), T5022 4300. **Police** 67 Madden Av, T5023 9555. **Taxi** T5023 0033. **Working** *Madec*, T5022 1797, www.madec.edu.au/harvest, coordinates agricultural work.

Directory

Goldfields and Spa country

To many travellers the history of Victorian gold finds that are preserved and celebrated in the Goldfields area will seem unimpressively recent. The major finds were only 150 years ago but were among the largest in the world and had a profound effect on the development of the country. Ballarat and Bendigo were the richest sites and this can be seen in the extravagant public architecture of these towns. Between the two main towns lie the smaller settlements of Castlemaine and Maldon, surrounded by country that is still recovering from the ravages of mining. The spa country around Daylesford was also gold-bearing but the natural mineral springs there have proved a more enduring source of wealth for the locals.

www.goldfields.org.au

Ballarat

Population: 81,000
114 km from
Melbourne, 124 km
from Bendigo, 142 km
from Halls Gap

Ballarat began life in the 1850s as a dusty tent city, home to thousands of gold diggers. However, deeper diggings struck extensive gold-filled reefs, fuelling the city's rapid expansion and the impressive Victorian architecture that survives today, mostly along **Lydiard Street**. The gold in Ballarat was also at the root of one of Australia's most historically significant incidents: the setting up of a miner's stockade at **Eureka** in 1854, and the storming of it by British troops a few days later. Today Ballarat is the state's third largest city and sprawls for several kilometres in each direction.

Ins & outs
See also Transport, page 498

Getting around The main state **coach and train station** is on Lydiard St North. *Ballarat Transit*, T5331 7777, run local buses throughout the city, and a $1.55 single fare is valid for 2 hrs. Most routes run approximately every 30 mins, Mon-Sat from around 0700-1800. There are a few evening services Fri. City centre bus stops are north and south of the Mall on Curtis St and Litte Bridge St. Detailed timetables are available from the train station. Only the central shopping area is easily walked around.

The **VIC** is at 39 Sturt St, near the Mall, T1800 446633, www.ballarat.com Open daily 0900-1700. The **Welcome Pass** is a 2-day ticket to Sovereign Hill, the Gold Museum, Eureka Stockade and the Fine Art Gallery: $31.50, children $14.50, concessions $22. Available from any participating attraction or the VIC.

Ballarat

To Daylesford & Bendigo

To Clunes, Mildura, Pyrenees, Grampians & Adelaide

To Grampians & Adelaide

To Geelong & Port Fairy

Detail map
A Ballarat centre,
page 496

0 metres 500
0 yards 500

Sleeping
1 Ballarat Central B&B
2 Bodlyn

3 Eureka Stockade
Caravan Park
4 Mulberry Cottage

5 Rakiura
6 Sovereign Hill
Lodge

Eating
1 Boatshed
2 Chicken & Seafood King

The **Ballarat Fine Art Gallery**'s most important and celebrated possession is not a piece of art at all, but a flag. The original Eureka flag that flew over the miner's stockade in 1854 was offered to the gallery in the 1880s by the family of Trooper King, who had cut it down and kept it as a souvenir. Although fragile and missing a few pieces, the flag is a powerful and tangible link to one of the most important episodes of Australian history. The gallery also holds important collections of colonial and Heidelberg artists and is particularly strong on contemporary Australian art. ■ *Daily 1030-1700. Guided tours Mon-Fri 1400, Sat/Sun 1430. $4, children $2, concessions $3. T5331 5622, www.balgal.com 40 Lydiard St.* The **Mining Exchange Gold Shop**, 8a Lydiard St Northth, T/F5333 4242, www.thegoldshop.com.au Nuggets big and small, naked and set in jewellery. Entertaining tales, gold licences and detector hire ($75 a day). And guarded advice.

Montrose Cottage and the Eureka Museum, at 111 Eureka Street, may not be the biggest attraction in Ballarat, but is one of the best thought out and the best at giving an insight into the people who worked on the goldfields and became involved in the Eureka tragedy. The cottage was the first miner's bluestone residence on the fields, and is now the last remaining. ■ *Daily 0900-1700. $6.60, children $3. T5332 2554, www.eurekamuseum.com.au* Further up the hill is the **Eureka Stockade**, a Ballarat landmark with its enormous replica of the Eureka flag. The museum describes the general events of the stockade, day by day as the tension built, and includes two excellent short films explaining the history of the flag and the background to the stockade. ■ *Daily 0900-1700. $8, children $4, concessions $6. T5333 1854, www.sovereignhill.com.au/eureka*

On the eastern edge of town, on top of a former goldfield, is **Sovereign Hill**, an outdoor museum that aims to faithfully recreate the goldrush period of the 1850s in Ballarat. Of many similar 'pioneer villages' in Australia, Sovereign Hill is undoubtedly the best and it is certainly impressive for its scale alone, covering 30 ha. There are several bars, cafés, and a bakery and kiosk on site. ■ *Daily 1000-1700. Gold Pass $25, children $12, concessions $18 (includes entry to gold museum and mine tour). T5331 1944, www.sovereignhill.com.au Bradshaw St. There is one bus service on Sun, departing from the station then the city centre 1100, leaving Sovereign Hill 1635.* Sovereign Hill also includes a sound and light show, **Blood on the Southern Cross**, which tells the story of the Eureka Stockade. The show can be combined with an excellent buffet meal in one of Sovereign Hill's

Sights
Most of Ballarat's sights are strung out over a wide area and either independent transport or extensive use of the buses is required to get around them

Victoria

3 Lake Pavilion   ● Pubs & bars
4 Olive Grove   5 Views

pubs. ■ *Mon-Sat, 2 shows after dark, times vary. Show $30, children $16, concessions $24. Dinner and show $52.50, children $32, concessions $46. Bookings essential T5333 5777. There are also accommodation packages available and discounts for combined day entry and show.*

Across the road from Sovereign Hill is the **Gold Museum**, which has displays of gold coins and nuggets. An extensive collection of nuggets and specks found by just one man are grouped according to the creek beds around Ballarat where they were found, giving a fascinating insight into the process. ■ *Daily 0930-1720. Entry free with Sovereign Hill entry, otherwise $6.30, children $3.10, concessions $3.90. T5331 1944.*

Huge **Lake Wendouree** dominates the northwest of the city and on the lakeside are the **Botanic Gardens**, as fascinating for their statuary as for their plants. **Ballarat Wildlife Park,** at the corner of Fussell Street and York Street, has the usual suspects, plus a few unusual additions such as giant tortoises. ■ *Daily 0900-1700. Guided tour 1100. $13.50, children $7.50, concessions $11.50. T5333 5933.*

Sleeping

Much of the town's extensive range of accommodation can be seen on www.ballarat.com, and booked via the VIC. See also under Pubs & bars

LL-D *Craigs Royal Hotel*, 10 Lydiard St South, T1800 648051, craigs@acc.net.au Rambling, traditional Victorian hotel with over 40 rooms covering an extensive range of options. The characterful budget rooms are particularly good value and the spa suites suitably impressive. Buffet breakfast included. **L-B** *Ansonia*, 32 Lydiard St, T5332 4678, ansonia@ansonia.ballarat.net.au Very contemporary boutique hotel with 20 stylish en suite suites, rooms and studios and wonderful guest and dining areas. **A-D** *Sovereign Hill Lodge*, Magpie St, T5333 3409, www.sovereignhill.com.au Comfortable, modern motel-style rooms and a dedicated *YHA* hostel block with kitchen and common-room facilities. On-site Chinese restaurant. **B** *Bodlyn*, 9 Errard St, T5332 1318, kittelty@ netconnect.com.au Gracious, spacious heritage B&B, built in 1910. 3 en suite doubles, 2 guest lounges and excellent gourmet breakfast. **B** *Mulberry Cottage*, Barkly St, T5330 1964, mulberry@giant.net.au Beautifully furnished 19th-century miner's cottage. 2 bedrooms, extensive gardens and breakfast hamper. Details of other cottages from the VIC. **C** *Rakiura*, 1306 Gregory St, T5339 2343, rakiura80@hotmail.com Characterful Federation B&B. Very homely, afternoon tea and cooked breakfast. The casual single rate is half the double, making it excellent value. Recommended, though a stiff walk or bus journey

Ballarat centre

```
        N                 ■ Sleeping        2 Dyer's Steak Stable      ● Pubs & bars
                          1 Ansonia         3 Gamekeeper's Secret      8 Bakery Hill Tavern
                          2 Craigs Royal    4 Gee Cees                 9 George
                                            5 L'Espresso              10 Irish Murphy's
                          ● Eating          6 Pazani                  11 Sturt St Blues
0 metres       200        1 Bibo            7 Ruby's
0 yards        200
```

Eureka!

Many Australian historians consider the Eureka Stockade to be a seminal moment in the country's history because it was the first time that Australians had stood together and fought and died under their own flag.

The enormous influx of people during the 1850s goldrushes was ruinously expensive for the young government. Infrastructure such as roads had to be built in a hurry and the money borrowed from England. To recoup some of their expenses the government levied a heavy tax on gold-diggers, requiring them to purchase a monthly licence to permit mining in a small area of land.

Many of the diggers revelled in the freedom of being their own masters. The only time they were called to account anyone was during the regular police checks on licences and they came to fiercely resent the condescending attitude of the police. Furthermore, government officials on the goldfields were blatantly corrupt and diggers had no representation in Parliament as they were not allowed to vote.

It is possible that there may not have been so much discontent if the miners had been finding gold. The tax seemed particularly irksome when it had to be paid each month whether gold was found or not, and miners had started to work in deep shafts where they often had to dig for months just to reach the gold-bearing vein.

These concerns were felt on all the Victorian goldfields but came to a head in Ballarat in 1854. During November several

incidents caused great anger among the diggers and they began to hold protest meetings. They burned their licences in defiance of the law and raised a flag depicting the stars of the Southern Cross. The goldfields officials feared they would be attacked and called for reinforcements of British soldiers from Melbourne. The diggers anticipated a clash and built a flimsy stockade, a low fence of sharpened pickets, at the Eureka Lead which was a deep gold seam being mined by Irish diggers. Their leader, Peter Lalor, asked his fellow diggers to 'swear by the Southern Cross to stand by each other and fight to defend our rights and liberties'.

As battles go, this wasn't one of the greats – it only lasted about 15 minutes. At dawn, on Sunday 3 December, the troopers surprised the diggers, who were unprepared because they had not expected an attack on their day of rest. There were 294 armed soldiers against 120 sleepy diggers armed with homemade pikes. The diggers were quickly defeated and there were reports of soldiers shooting and bayoneting unarmed men. The Victorian public was shocked and outraged by this harsh treatment. Many men were arrested and 13 were tried for treason the following year. Their defeat became a triumph, however, when all were acquitted. Within six months of the battle the Victorian parliament passed legislation abolishing the gold licence and giving diggers the vote. Peter Lalor, who lost an arm in the battle, later became a member of Parliament.

---

from town (bus route 1, Howitt St). **D-E** *Ballarat Central B&B*, corner of Dawson St and Eyre St, T5333 7046. Huge old townhouse with over 20 rooms, mostly doubles and some good value singles. Large 1st- and 2nd-floor terraces make great BBQ and sunning spots. Continental breakfast. Kitchen as well as lounge and dining room. The *Eureka Stockade*, Stawell St, T5331 2281, is the best caravan park option for the budget-conscious.

Expensive *Dyer's Steak Stable*, Little Bridge St, T5331 2850. Consistently excellent steak house, bookings essential Fri-Sat. Open 1200-1400 Mon-Fri, 1830-2030 Mon-Sat. *Tiggie's*, 315 Learmonth Rd, Buningyong, about 10 km southeast of Ballarat on the A300, T5341 2999. Friendly, simple bare-brick restaurant becoming well-known for its melt-in-the-mouth plum puddings. Dinners Wed-Sat 1800-2200, breakfast and lunch Sun 0900-1800. Recommended. **Mid-range** *Boatshed Restaurant*, Wendouree Pde,

Eating
There are plenty of good cafés, bars and restaurants, many of which are licensed, with good ranges of wine by the glass

T5333 5533. Food daily 0700-2030. Also known as 'Gill's' café, this is a light, airy restaurant with a deck area hanging over the lake and armchairs around a fire. The breakfasts are pricey, the lunches are inventive with lots of grazing and veggie options, and the dinners are dependably good. *Gamekeeper's Secret*, corner of Mair St and Humffray St North, T5332 6000. Food daily 1100-2200. Former pub, now a bistro and bar with a friendly, warm atmosphere. The $10 lunch specials are particularly good value. *Gee Cees*, 427 Sturt St, T5331 6211. Chic café-bar and wood-fired pizzeria with a wide-ranging menu. Meals daily 0800-2100. 2 good value en suite doubles upstairs (**D**). *Pazani*, corner of Sturt St and Camp St, T5331 7100. Open 1000-2200 Tue-Sat, Sun 1000-1600. Friendly, contemporary Italian with interesting Asian flourishes. Cheap lunches include wood-fired pizzas. Live mellow music Sun. Recommended. *Rubys*, 423 Sturt St, T5333 3386. Open Sun-Tue 0700-1800, Wed-Sat 0700-2100. Stark, contemporary café-bar. Excellent, inventive modern Australian food with lots of seafood options. Recommended. **Cheap** *Bibo*, 205 Sturt St. Open daily 0800-1800. Retro café and bar with all-day breakfasts, baguettes and foccaccias, pasta noodles and wok meals. *L'Espresso*, 417 Sturt St. Open 0700-1800 Sun-Thu, 0700-2100 Fri-Sat. Dark, friendly, Italian-style café beloved by locals, attracting an eclectic crowd. Excellent coffee, antipasto and lunches which include the odd curry or souvlaki. Pavement tables. Recommended. *Olive Grove*, on the corner of Ripon St and Sturt St, is a magnificent deli and café with all-day breakfasts and cheap light lunches. Open daily 0830-1830.

Pubs & bars *Bakery Hill Tavern*, corner of Little Bridge St and Humffray St South, is one of the few traditional city centre pubs that has resisted the transformation into either theme-bar or gambling emporium. *George*, Lydiard St North, T5333 4866, george2000@giant.net.au Huge hotel with an unusual double balcony. The Main lounge bar is almost stately with many armchairs and leather sofas, but it livens up most evenings. Also an atrium café and nightclub with live music Fri-Sat. Over 20 rooms, including good value en suite doubles (**C-D**). *Irish Murphy's*, 38 Sturt St, T5331 4091, ballarat@irishmurphys.com.au The definitive Irish theme pub with lots of draught beers, cheap hearty meals daily 1200-1400, 1800-2030, and live cover bands Thu-Sun ($4 cover charge Fri-Sat). Just 4 rooms upstairs, each with twin bunks (**E**). *Sturt St Blues*, 404 Sturt St. Live blues bar, open Thu-Sat evenings. Jam sessions Sun afternoons. *Views*, 22 Wendouree Pde, T5331 4592, theviews_barcafe@hotmail.com Hip bar and bistro, with corrugated steel and polished wood fittings and almost nightly special offers to encourage eager young drinkers. Good range of food, much of it cheap, available daily 0700-2300. Accommodation (**C**) in adjacent motel-style en suite rooms.

Entertainment **Cinema** *Regent*, 49 Lydiard St North, T5331 1556. **Theatre** *Her Majesty's*, Lydiard St South. Classical and contemporary music, dance and theatre. Tickets via *Majestix*, T5333 5888. **Music** Pick up a free copy of *Forte* newspaper from record shops for a gig guide.

Transport There are *V~Line* **train** services from the railway station to **Melbourne** (1½ hrs), every hr or so from 0600-1920 Mon-Fri, 0655-1805 Sat, and about every 2 hrs from 0800-1935 Sun. There are 2 other services south. **Buses** to **Geelong** (1½ hrs) leave at 0630, 0947, 1555 Mon-Fri, 1930 Fri, 0645, 1030, 1635 Sat, and 0900, 1745 Sun. Those to **Warrnambool** leave at 1420 Mon-Fri (3 hrs). The service west to **Stawell** (1½ hrs) leaves 6 times a day Mon-Fri from 1010-1930, and 1025, 1310, 1935 Sat, 1125, 1720, 1930 Sun. The earliest of these each day continues on to **Adelaide** (9 hrs). Within the Goldfields there are 2 further routes. Buses to **Bendigo** (1¾ hrs) via **Maldon** leave at 1000 Mon-Tue, Thu-Fri and 1020 Wed, and via **Daylesford** and **Castlemaine** at 1415 Mon-Fri, 1635 Fri and 1730 Sun. Services to **Maryborough** (1 hr) via **Clunes** and **Talbot** depart 1420 Mon, Tue and Thu, 1755 Fri and 1035 Sat. Further services head via Maryborough to **Mildura** (7 hrs). These leave at 0005 Mon-Sat.

Banks The major banks have ATMs on all the major shopping and eating streets. **Car parking** The closest unrestricted parking is opposite the coach station or on Eyre St. **Car servicing** *Alien*, corner of Peel St and Grant St, T5332 7647. **Communications** Internet at *Pubic Library*, Doveton St North, T5331 1211. ID required for temporary membership. Book for up to 1 hr free per day. Open 0930-1800 Tue-Fri, 1000-1300 Sat, 1315-1600 Sun. Main **Post Office**, Armstrong St South.

Around Ballarat
Clunes: Colour map 2, grid C2,
30 km from Ballarat,
30 km from Maryborough

Along the highway that threads through the pockmarked landscape from Ballarat to Maryborough is **Clunes**. Often wrongly referred to as a ghost town, Clunes is a still busy community, but one that has neither the population nor the money to make use of many of the fine Victorian community and commercial buildings that commemorate its early optimism. Fraser Street, devoid of roadmarkings and, frequently, cars, is one of the most evocative in the state. The **Clunes Museum** illustrates the town's decline. ■ *Sat 1000-1630, Sun 1100-1630, other times by arrangement. $2.50, children $0.50. T5345 3592.*

Further up the road, **Talbot** is smaller, but has shrunk further, with very few businesses still operating. Rows of empty shop-fronts and ruminative old men sit quietly in the sun. One business that is thriving is the friendly *Bull and Mouth* pub, T5463 2325, well known in nearby **Maryborough** for its excellent flavoursome, hearty cooking. Dinner 1800-2000 Thursday-Sunday, lunch 1200-1500 Sunday. Accommodation in separate cottages. Maryborough was also a major gold town, but has survived as a large country service town. It is best known for its massive Victorian railway station.

Daylesford and Hepburn Springs

Daylesford was also caught up in the goldrush, but the numerous diggings revealed another source of wealth – mineral springs. Spa towns were still very popular in England and the discovery of natural springs in the area was quickly exploited by the locals. Most of the springs are clustered around Hepburn, though Daylesford, 4 km south, has developed as the major of the

Colour map 2, grid C3
Population: 3,300
Altitude: 700 m
45 km from Ballarat,
40 km from Kyneton

Victoria

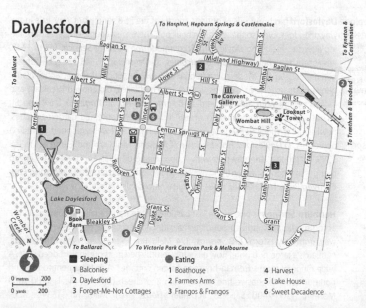

Daylesford

0 metres 200
0 yards 200

■ **Sleeping**
1 Balconies
2 Daylesford
3 Forget-Me-Not Cottages

● **Eating**
1 Boathouse
2 Farmers Arms
3 Frangos & Frangos
4 Harvest
5 Lake House
6 Sweet Decadence

two towns. Public hand pumps are dotted around both and visitors can go on tasting pump-crawls during the day. The health aspect of the towns has been taken up by various new age therapists and operators, with the happy consequence of some superb organic bakeries and cafés. Daylesford is also known as the 'gay and lesbian country capital of Australia'. It hosts *Chill Out*, Australia's only gay and lesbian country festival day, with food and wine stalls, music, arts and crafts. The event takes place in early March during the Labour Day weekend. Maps are available from the **VIC** in Daylesford, at 98 Vincent Street, T5348 1339, visitorinfo@hepburn.vic.gov.au Open daily 0900-1700.

Sights The **Convent Gallery** in Daylesford is a converted nunnery with a wonderful range of contemporary and antique jewellery, ceramics and fine art. The gardens and top gallery are worth the visit alone, and the food in the striking atrium café is also recommended. ■ *Daily 1000-1800. Gallery $3.50. Corner of Hill St and Daly St, T5348 3211.*

Both towns are in the midst of the extensive **Hepburn Regional Park**, full of natural springs, dry eucalypt woodland and relics of the goldrush era. The park is riddled with walking and multi-purpose tracks, including an easy 5-hour, 17-km roundabout set that connects Daylesford with Hepburn Springs. Free park notes and map are available from the VIC. The old volcanic cone of **Mount Franklin**, 4 km north of Hepburn, just off the main Castlemaine road, has good views of the surrounding area, picnic and BBQ spots, and a camping ground. The **Hepburn Spa Resort**, T5348 2034, www.hepburnspa.com.au, dates back to the 1890s and is still the major attraction. ■ *Open daily, 1000-2000 or later. Booked well ahead – 6 weeks is recommended, especially in the peak winter period. Also public heated mineral pools, spas and saunas with single visits from $8.80.* There are several smaller alternatives to the resort. **Acqua Viva**, 11th Street, T5348 2111, www.dayspa.com.au, is a small, calm and highly professional outfit. Bookings essential, but considerably less notice is required than at the resort.

Sleeping
Much of the accommodation operates on a two-night package only at weekends, and many of these are dinner and B&B

Daylesford has hundreds of options, mostly of the B&B variety but very little in the way of budget. Even so the town can book out. There are a couple of specialist booking agencies including *Daylesford Accommodation Booking Service*, T5348 1448, www.dabs.spa-country.net.au **B** *Balconies*, 35 Perrins St, T5348 1322, balconys@netconnect.com.au Modern, traditional B&B with a touch of the eclectic. Warm, genial hosts, extensive gardens with ornamental lakes, big cooked breakfast and indoor heated pool. Recommended. **B** *Forget-me-Not Cottages*, 9 Stanhope St, T5348 3507, www.netconnect.com.au/~forget 2 self-contained garden cottages, newly-built in mock heritage style. Very comfortable and well-equipped, including open fires. **D** *Daylesford Hotel*, corner of Midland Highway and Camp St, T5348 2335. Traditional, friendly pub with 7 good value doubles and twins. The cheap menu is of a good standard, and available daily, lunch and dinner. The *Victoria Park Caravan Park*, T/F5348 3821, has a range of affordable cabins.

Hepburn Springs is one of the last bastions of the traditional guesthouse. All the accommodation huddles around the main junction except for the *YHA* which is half-way from Daylesford. **L-B** *Springs*, 124 Main Rd, T5348 2202, www.thesprings.com.au is a large pub hotel now elegantly refurbished in its original art deco style. A wide range of rooms from in-house to garden cottages. Also treatment rooms and flotation tank, expensive fine dining room and cheap café-bar. Meals 1700-2400 Mon-Fri, 1200-2400 Sat-Sun. **A** *Dudley House*, 101 Main Rd, T5348 3033, dudley@netconnect.com.au Edwardian guesthouse that seems to have steadily increased in quality while gradually shedding rooms. There are just 4 exquisite heritage-style doubles remaining and the excellent breakfasts include the option of proper kippers. Recommended. **C** *Mooltan*, 129 Main Rd, T1800 353354, www.mooltan.com.au Rambling Federation house, purpose built as a guesthouse and still traditionally run as a B&B. The 11 rooms include 3 en suite. **D** *Wildwood YHA*, Main Rd, T5348 4435, daylesford@yhavic.org.au Simple, comfortable hostel, formerly a 1920s guesthouse, with some good value en suite doubles.

Daylesford *Lake House*, King St, T5348 3329, www.lakehouse.com.au, is at the forefront of this gastronomic effort. The expensive restaurant of this modern luxury hotel (**LL-L**) wins a continuous stream of awards for its cutting-edge modern Australian cuisine that makes every possible use of local produce. Book well ahead. *Frangos & Frangos*, Vincent St, T5348 2363. At one end large informal wooden tables cluster around the open fire, while perfectly set out fine dining tables dominate the other. The high ceilings and easy-going, friendly service generate a very southern European feel. Open all day for coffee and light snacks. Breakfast 0800-1200, lunch 1200-1500, dinner 1800-2130. Recommended. *Boathouse*, Bleakley St, T5348 1387, has veranda tables overlooking the lake and is a good spot for grazing their several snacks, dips and platters. Open daily 0900-1700, and until 2000 Sat. *Harvest*, Albert St, T5348 3994. New age meets the 1950s in this excellent seafood and vegetarian restaurant. Great breakfasts, cheap lunches and mid-range dinners. Mon night is Indian. Open daily 0900-2200. Restricted hrs in winter. *Farmers Arms*, East St, T5348 2091. Welcoming front bar and laid-back retro lounge room with lots of sofas and an open fire. The modern dining room is a bit stark, but the rich, gourmet food more than makes up for this, particularly at the cheap prices. Open daily, but meals Wed-Sun 1800-2100 only. Recommended. Of many wonderful cafés *Sweet Decadence*, Vincent St, has the edge because of the terrific breakfasts, cream teas and love of chocolate. Open daily 0930-1700.

Eating

Daylesford is well known for 2 second-hand book dealers. *Avant-garden*, Vincent St, is a huge, cavernous establishment, also with comic, magazine and CD sections. Down by the lake is the *Book Barn*, smaller but worth the visit. Both open daily.

Shopping

V~Line **bus** services leave Littles Garage, Vincent St, for **Trentham**, **Woodend** and **Melbourne** (2 hrs) at 0750, 1625 Mon-Fri, 1010 Sat and 1630 Sat-Sun. A faster service to Melbourne departs 1500 Mon-Fri. Buses to **Ballarat** (50 mins) leave at 0850 Mon-Fri, 1922 Fri and 1957 Sun. The services to **Castlemaine** (15 mins) and **Bendigo** (1 hr) leave at 1500 Mon-Fri, 1720 Fri and 1815 Sun.

Transport

Castlemaine

Castlemaine, at the centre of the **Mount Alexander** district, the richest alluvial goldfield in the world, is one of the most attractive towns in the goldfields and a place that Australians certainly could give a XXXX for. Fine 19th-century buildings, a thriving arts community and café society make it an enjoyable place to spend a few days. The arts are celebrated during the **Castlemaine State Festival**, a biennial festival of theatre, opera, dance, music and comedy, held in April, on every odd year. The **VIC** in Mostyn Street is housed in the town's most striking building, the former market hall. The hall has a good free exhibition on the history of the Mount Alexander diggings. ■ *Daily 0900-1700. T5470 6200, www.mountalexander.vic.gov.au/tourism*

Colour map 2, grid C3
Population: 6,700
119 km from Melbourne,
39 km from Bendigo,
20 km from Maldon

Victoria

Sights

Those interested in architecture will enjoy a short walking tour of the town centre. Historic walk maps are available from the VIC

The **Art Gallery and Historical Museum**, one of Victoria's finest regional galleries, is housed in an unusual art deco building and has a superb collection of Australian art, particularly colonial works. The Museum in the basement looks at how Castlemaine evolved from a camp to a city and has many interesting historical photographs, clothes and furnishings. ■ *Daily 1000-1700. $4, children free, concessions $2.* **Buda Historic Home and Gardens** was the home of a talented silversmith during the 1860s and still contains its original furnishings as well as his family's collection of arts and crafts. ■ *Wed-Sun 1200-1700. $7, children $3, concessions $5. 42 Hunter St.T5472 1032.* There are good views of the town from the **Old Castlemaine Gaol**, which operated as recently as 1990 and is now refurbished to provide unusual accommodation (see below). Exhibitions in the cells focus on conditions suffered by prisoners. ■ *Daily 1000-1500 but closed if booked for a group or function, check with the VIC. $5, children $2.50. Bowden St, T5470 5311, www.gaol.castlemaine.net.au*There are many walks in the **Mount Alexander Diggings** area surrounding the town and the VIC can provide free trail maps. There are also lively guided tours of **Herons Reef**, this goldfield is on private property and can only be visited on a tour. ■ *Mon-Fri, Oct-Jun only. Bookings at VIC or T5473 4387.*

Sleeping

There are very good value B&Bs but no backpacker hostels at present. Book well in advance for the period of the State festival

A *Castlemaine Cottages*, T5470 6485, www.castlemainecottages.com Several luxurious but homely period cottages, all self-contained with breakfast provisions supplied. **B** *Airdrie Cottage*, 34 Berkeley St, T/F5472 1979, www.airdriecottage.castlemaine.net A B&B with 2 contemporary rooms and a self-contained studio. The cottage is owned by a potter who lovingly decorates it with his favourite works of local potters and artists, and it also has a garden full of roses and lavender. **B** *Castlemaine Gaol* (see above), good fun for the novelty but unsurprisingly the cells themselves are pretty small and dark with room for just a single bunk bed and shared facilities down the hall. There are also a few larger double rooms. Pleasant common areas and a bar in the dungeon. **B** *Coach & Rose*, 68 Mostyn St, T5472 4850. 4 Victorian-style en suite rooms in a B&B in the heart of the town, large living room, games room and breakfast conservatory. **B** *Yellow House*, 95 Lyttleton St, T/F5472 3368. This elegant B&B sits on a hill high above Castlemaine, and combines furnishings and gardens inspired by Provence with a contemporary art gallery.

Eating

Caponi's, 50 Hargreaves St, T5470 5705. Daily 1700-2000. A cosy, simple place for cheap pizza. *Fuel*, 113 Mostyn St East, T5470 5000. Wed-Sat 1700-2030. Lunch at weekends. Slick automotive-inspired décor and good value modern food from laksa and curries to steak with mash. *Globe*, 81 Forest St, T5470 5055. Restaurant Wed-Sun 1830-2030, bistro and takeaway daily 1800-2030. The best fine-dining restaurant overlooking a pretty garden courtyard. This place also offers a more casual menu in the bistro and a pasta-pizza takeaway bar. *Saff's*, 64 Mostyn St East, T5470 6722. Daily 0800-1700, dinner Thu-Sat. Friendly and funky licensed café with superb fresh and tasty food such as soup, burgers, salads or foccacia. Also all-day breakfasts and more formal mains. Recommended. *Screaming Carrot*, 16 Lyttleton St, T5470 6555. Wed-Sun, hrs vary but core hrs 1000-1700, later on Fri. If the name alone doesn't make you want to investigate this vegetarian café next to the art gallery, the excellent organic, seasonal food and sour-dough bakery will. *Togs*, 58 Lyttleton St, T5470 5090. Daily 0900-1700, Fri-Sat 1800-2030. Lively and popular café and gallery in a homely cottage. The menu offers casual lunches and cakes, changing to more substantial menu of casseroles and curries in the evening. The gallery shows high quality art and craft from the local region.

V~Line **train** services leave the railway station for **Kyneton, Woodend** and **Melbourne** (1½ hrs) every 1-2 hrs from 0628-1838 Mon-Fri, 0749-1913 Sat and every 2-3 hrs from 0739-1913 Sun. There are also trains every hr or so to **Bendigo** from 1007-2140 Mon-Fri, 1009-2246 Sat and every 2-4 hrs 1112-2055 Sun. *V~Line* **bus** services to **Daylesford** and **Ballarat** (1 hr 20 mins) leave at 0815 Mon-Fri, 1845 Fri and 1920 Sun. Buses to **Maryborough** (1 hr) leave at 0745, 1150 Mon-Fri, 1920 Mon-Thu, Sat-Sun, 2010 Fri and 1015 Sat.

Transport

Maldon

A quaint, pretty village of 19th-century shopfronts and miners' cottages, Maldon is considered the best-preserved gold town in the state. Revived by tourism and carefully tended, the town is devoted to nostalgia. The miners' shops and cottages are occupied by antique shops, tea rooms, and B&Bs, and the main activities are walks around mine sites and rides on a steam train. The **VIC**, at Shire Gardens in the high street, has extensive information on self-guided tours but also offers personal tour guides for $33 an hour. ■ *Open daily 0900-1700. T5475 2569, www.maldon.org.au*

Population: 1,500 Maldon is busy at weekends but is most lively during its Folk Festival in early November

The junction of Main Street and High Street is the main heritage area, although a stroll around the surrounding streets will also reveal much early domestic architecture. The tall brick **Beehive Chimney** that rises above Maldon marks the closest mining site. The **Maldon Historic Reserve** preserves the relics of the mining era. Although much of the land is now covered by box-ironbark forest it is easy to see the old scars of tunnels, dams, mullock heaps and holes. The VIC has detailed notes on the features of the Parkins Reef Walking Track, a one-hour loop walk within the reserve. Nearby is **Carman's Tunnel**, a 570-m-tunnel chipped through solid rock in the 1880s. It has been left exactly as it was when abandoned in 1884 and tours by candlelight examine the techniques and equipment used at the time. ■ *$5, children $3, 25 mins. Sat-Sun, half-hourly from 1330-1600. T5475 2667. Turnoff from Parkins Reef Rd, 2 km south of town.* Trainspotters will love the **Victorian Goldfields Railway**, a steam train that runs from Maldon to Muckleford and back (it may be extended to Castlemaine in the future). ■ *$13, children $7, concessions $11. Sun 1130, 1300, 1430. Wed 1130, 1300. Driving lesson $895 including one night's accommodation. T5470 6658, www.vgr.com.au Station in Hornsby St, follow signs for Bendigo.*

There are fine views of the surrounding country from Mount Tarrengower (571 m)

Sleeping and eating For self-contained accommodation try **A-B** *Heritage Cottages*, 60 Main St, T5475 1094, heritage@netcon.net.au Lots of luxurious restored miners' cottages and Victorian houses, all with linen and firewood. **B** *Calder House*, 44 High St, T5475 2912. B&B in a magnificent 1860s mansion, superbly furnished with antiques, leather couches and open fires. The hosts offer very good value packages including meals at their restaurant, *Ruby's*. The only budget accommodation is **D** *Central Service Centre*, 1 Main St, T5475 2216. 3 basic en suite doubles and cheap singles with TV and kettle. The caravan park in Hospital St, T5475 2344, has cabins and vans. There is also a campsite at Butts Reserve, at the base of Mt Tarrengower. *Ruby's*, at *Calder House*, offers creative and generous country cooking (mid-range) in an elegant formal dining room. Fri-Sat 1830-2030. *Royal Wine Bar & Bistro*, 18 High St, T5475 1223, is a good for cheap pizza and pasta. Thu-Mon 1730-2100. During the day the best of the street is *Maldon Café*, a cheerful place offering breakfast, gourmet pies and sandwiches. Mon-Fri 1000-1700, Sat-Sun 0900-1700.

Transport *V~Line* bus services leave the Post Office for **Bendigo** (40 mins) at 1105 Mon-Tue, Thu-Fri and 1125 Wed. Buses to **Ballarat** (1 hr 10 mins) depart 1250 Mon-Fri.

Victoria

Bendigo

Colour map 2, grid B3
Population: 60,000
89 km from Echuca,
400 km from Mildura

Gold was found in Bendigo in 1851 and the city goldfields proved to be among the world's richest. From the 1860s-70s Bendigo's rich reefs paid for a flamboyant, opulent style of architecture that is one of the city's chief assets today. The neoclassical 'boom style' can best be seen in the Law Courts, Post Office and Shamrock Hotel on Pall Mall in the heart of the city, and View Street also has some fine examples. The liveliest time to be in Bendigo is during the **Easter Fair**, six days of street parades, fireworks, and street performers. The **VIC** is housed inside the magnificent former post office and includes an interpretative centre on the history of Bendigo. T5444 4445, www.bendigotourism.com It can also provide a map for a heritage walk and has a brochure detailing art studios and galleries in the region. ■ *Open daily 0900-1700.*

Ins & outs   **Getting around**   The **Talking Tram** and **Café Tram** depart from the Central Deborah Mine and the fountain. The former tours the city centre for an hour with a recorded commentary on Bendigo's sights; daily, hourly 1000-1600. $12.90, children $7.50,

Bendigo

Sleeping ■	Eating ●	Pubs & bars ●
1 Antoinettes	1 Bazzani & Icon Bar	8 Brian Boru
2 Buzza's Backpackers	2 Green Olive	9 Darby O'Gill's
3 Goldcreek Cottage	3 Grinders	10 Queens Arms
4 Greystanes	4 Jojoes	11 Rifle Brigade
5 Landonia	5 Malayan Orchid	12 Tonic
6 Marlborough House	6 Match Bar & Bakehouse	
7 Shamrock	7 Mully's	

concessions $11.50. T5443 8322. The expensive Café Tram shuttles up and down the short stretch of tram line in the city centre while simultaneously serving up a fine-dining experience. Daily, evenings, T5443 8255.

Sights
The central shopping area is reasonably compact and the Art Gallery, Central Deborah Gold Mine and Chinese Museum can all be reached on foot

One of Victoria's most successful deep-mine operations, and at over 400 m one of the deepest, the **Central Deborah Gold Mine** is no longer an active mine, but it is still one of the most rewarding to visit. All tours include a self-guided walk among the above-ground sheds and workings – many in their original working condition – and the small gold museum, as well as offering the opportunity to do a bit of gold panning. The standard tour goes down just a few storeys, but includes equipment demonstrations. The adventure tour descends 20 storeys for a more in-depth look. It is also possible to dine in the mine. ■ *Daily 0930-1700. 1-hr underground tour $16.50, children $9, concessions $14.50. 2-hr adventure tour $49, children $26. T5443 8322, www.central-deborah.com*

A wonderful Victorian public gallery, **Bendigo Art Gallery** is a must for anyone interested in Australian art, with paintings by John Glover, Eugene Von Guerard and Arthur Streeton. The gallery also has a good collection of contemporary art. There's also a good café and an art shop. ■ *Daily 1000-1700. Free. 42 View St, T5443 4991.* Just a few doors down is **Penfolds Fine Art Gallery**, a private gallery with changing exhibitions of contemporary and traditional art. ■ *Daily 1000-1700. Free. T5444 0007. 32 View St.*

The **Golden Dragon Museum** is a museum of Chinese-Australian history housed in a spacious circular building specifically designed to accomodate its unique dragons. Among them is Loong, the oldest imperial dragon in the world, which paraded in Melbourne at the Federation celebrations of 1901. Although a little faded and fragile, the dragon reappeared in Melbourne in 2001 at the centenary of the Federation celebrations. Sun Loong is younger but is claimed to be the world's longest imperial dragon. The full collection includes exquisite 19th-century Chinese clothing, furniture and other items of daily life. Located on Bridge Street, the former centre of the Chinese community in Bendigo, the complex also includes classical Chinese gardens and temple. ■ *Daily 0930-1700. $7, children $4, concessions $5. 5 Bridge St, T5441 5044.* There is also an impressive red temple or **Joss House** at Emu Point, built in the 1860s to worship the warrior god Kuan Kung. ■ *Daily 1000-1600. $3, children $1. T5442 1685. Follow the tram tracks from Pall Mall towards the lake to the terminus. The Joss House is just beyond the railway crossing.*

The **Bendigo Bushland Trail** is a 65-km loop walk around Bendigo through parks, state forests and reserves. The bushland is dominated by box-ironbark and whipstick mallee trees and home to kangaroos, echidnas, and possums, all regularly seen on this trail. There are also plenty of birds attracted by the wildflowers. The **O'Keefe Rail Trail** is a 19-km path along a disused railway line to Axedale. The trail passes through bushland and wildflowers and takes about three hours one-way for cyclists and six hours for walkers. Visit the VIC for detailed brochures or a booklet on many other cycle routes in the area. *Moroni's Bike Shop, 104 Mitchell Street, T5443 9644,* is not a dedicated hire outlet but can often arrange bike hire on request.

Victoria

Sleeping

A *Goldcreek Cottage*, Forest La, T5442 2183, landonia@impulse.net.au Exquisite, restored and extended self-contained miner's cottage. 3 bedrooms, particularly good wheelchair access. Recommended. **A-B** *Greystanes*, Queen St, T5442 2466, www.greystanesmanor.com 7 en suite rooms in a grand Victorian town house, now a boutique hotel. Open fires, private car park. Optional breakfast $10. **A-C** *Shamrock*, corner of Pall Mall and Williamson St, T5443 0333, www.flag.com.au A city landmark,

Victoria

this hotel was once Bendigo's finest. Now owned by *Flag Inns* it is perfectly comfortable but not kept in the grandeur to which it was once accustomed. However, the rooms are spacious and the hotel has an enjoyable ambience of faded glory. **B** *Marlborough House*, Wattle St, T5441 4142, F5441 1473. Huge, rambling and historic late-Victorian house, now a characterful eclectic B&B with 6 en suite rooms. Very friendly family hosts and lots of places to hide away in, such as the conservatory and tiny library. Recommended. **C** *Antoinettes*, Wattle St, T5442 3609, tulip@netcon.net.au 3 rooms, 1 en suite and all with beautiful antique beds, in a late Victorian B&B. **C** *Landonia*, Mollison St, T5442 2183, landonia@impulse.net.au Single suite of rooms in a beautifully refurbished and furnished Edwardian cottage. Cooked breakfast. Very good value and recommended. **D-E** *Buzza's Backpackers* (YHA), Creek St South, T5443 7680, bendigo@yhavic.org.au. Small, homely hostel with 3, 5- or 7-bed dorms and a couple of doubles. Linen included. **Caravan park C-D** *City Central*, 362 High St, T5443 6937, has cabins, on-site vans and some scruffy 4-bed dorms.

Eating   **Expensive** *Bazzani*, Howard Pl, T5441 3777. Daily 1200-1500, 1800-2030. Full-flavoured Mediterranean dishes in a warm, subdued dining room with white linen and cane chairs. **Mid-range** *Boardwalk*, Nolan St, T5443 9855. Open 0700-2100 daily, later in summer. Smart, modern lake-side café and bistro 1 km out along Pall Mall. Always popular and a particularly pleasant spot for breakfast on a sunny day, though the pressure for boardwalk tables makes a long stay uncomfortable. *Jojoes*, 4 High St, T5441 4471. Daily 1700-2100. Zesty, modern and friendly eatery with grills, pasta, salads and pizzas, open to the street with some rather noisy pavement tables. Also offers gourmet takeaway and free delivery. *Malayan Orchid*, View St, T5442 4411. Open 1200-1400 Mon-Fri, 1700-2200 daily. Large Malay, Thai and Cantonese restaurant with some pleasant atrium tables and consistently good food. **Cheap** *Mully's*, 32 Pall Mall. Daily 1000-1700. Café and gallery within the formal Victorian grandeur of the Colonial Bank building. Traditional tea and cakes as well as more substantial hot lunches and snacks. *Green Olive*, 11 Bath La. Mon-Sat 0900-1700. Fantastic café and delicatessen, extremely popular with locals for delicious Mediterranean food. Good place to pick up picnic supplies. *Match Bar and Bakehouse*, 58 Bull St, T5441 4403. A lively casual restaurant with lots of glossy wood fittings and a good value menu of wood-fired breads, pizza, pasta, risotto and noodles. *Grinders*, 361 Hargreaves St, T5442 4862. A groovy café and noodle bar with lots of fresh, tasty noodle and laksa dishes under $10.

Pubs & bars   *Brian Boru*, Chapel St, T5443 5258. A great pub that evokes a warm Irish atmosphere
Pick up a free copy   without straining to do so. Live Irish music every Fri-Sat when it's necessary to book a
of Forte newspaper   table for a meal. The food is a heart-warming mix of Irish, British and Aussie, cheap in
from record shops   the evening, seriously so at lunchtime. Recommended. *Queens Arms*, Russell St, T5443
for a gig guide   2122. Large family-orientated public and lounge bistro areas, very popular for Sat eve and Sun lunch. Cheap and mid-range menus feature a large range of interesting entrees, mains and pasta. *Rifle Brigade*, View St. Comfortable, modern bars in a refurbished Victorian pub with 3 own-brewed bitters and dark ales. A band plays 70s covers on Sat and there's karaoke on Fri. Cheap to mid-range meals include good veggie options. *Tonic*, corner of Bull St and Hargreaves St, T5441 2366, is a popular bar and club that aims for the seedily glamourous look, Thu-Sat from 1700. *The Icon* is a very stylish bar open Thu-Sun 1600-0300, next to *Bazzani*, opposite the gardens.

Entertainment   **Cinema** Mainstream at 107 Queen St, T5442 1666, arthouse at *Star*, Eaglehawk Town Hall, T5496 2231.

Transport   *V~Line* trains leave the railway station for **Melbourne** (2 hrs) every 1 hr or so from 0605-1815 Mon-Fri, 0725-1850 Sat and every 2-3 hrs on Sun from 0715-1850. Most services stop at **Castlemaine** and the Macedon area stations. Services to **Ballarat** (2 hrs) via **Castlemaine** and **Daylesford** depart at 0735 Mon-Fri, 1815 Fri and 1850 Sun. **Ballarat** via **Maldon** buses go at 1215 Mon-Fri. The *Daylink* bus to **Adelaide** (8 hrs 20 mins) via **Bordertown** leaves at 1055 Mon-Sat and 1200 Sun, while services to **Swan Hill** and **Mildura** leave at 1840 Fri and 1930 Sun. Trains to **Echuca** (1 hr 20 mins) leave at 2031 Fri and 1420 Sun, with bus services departing 1110 Mon-Fri, 1630 Mon, Fri, 1815 Tue-Thu, 1105 Sat and 1150, 1935 Sun. The **Albury** (4 hrs) service via **Shepparton**, **Benalla**, **Wangaratta** and **Wodonga** leaves at 1130 Mon, Wed and 1630 Fri.

Directory

Banks The major banks have ATMs on all the major shopping and eating streets. **Bookshop** There is a large *Dymocks* on Mitchell St, close to Pall Mall. *Book Now*, 1 Farmers Lane, suberb second-hand bookshop; delightfully old-fashioned, well organized and helpful. **Car hire** *Hertz*, Corner of High St and Thistle St, T5443 5088. **Car servicing** *Beaurepaires*, 382 Hargreaves St, T5443 9966. **Communications** Internet at *Central Library*, 253 Hargreaves St, T5443 5100. Mon-Fri 1000-1900, Sat 1000-1300. **Post Office**, corner of Williamson St and Hargreaves St. **Hospital** *Bendigo Health Care Group*, Lucan St, T5441 0222. **Parks Office** Info centre at corner of View St and Mackenzie St, T136186. **Police** Bull St, T5440 2510. **Taxi** T131008.

The Grampians and the west

In the middle of western Victoria's farming district lie the mountains of the Grampians National Park, the third largest park in Victoria. From a distance the ranges rise like a series of petrified waves, the grey sedimentary rock appearing as a crest at the tip of forested slopes. At closer range a warm gold is revealed beneath the grey in dramatic overhangs and outcrops. The natural beauty of the Grampians is enhanced by the richest concentration of wild flowers and ancient Aboriginal art sites in the state. There is a great variety of walking from easy circular walks and steep waterfall trails to remote scrambles and breathtaking climbing walls. To the west, outside the park, is the outcrop of Mount Arapiles, a famous climbing spot with wonderful views of the surrounding plains.

Victoria

Ins and outs

Bus The regular *V~Line* service from **Melbourne** and **Ballarat** to **Adelaide** stops at **Ararat**, **Stawell** and **Horsham**, and there is a useful daily run between Stawell and **Halls Gap**. A separate service between Ballarat and **Mt Gambier** stops at **Dunkeld**. There is no public transport between Halls Gap and Dunkeld, or around the National Park. **Backpacker buses** A few stopover at Halls Gap on their runs between Melbourne and Adelaide, including *Autopia*, *Oz Experience* and *Wild-Life Tours*. **Tours** Several operators run day tours from **Melbourne**, including *Wild-Life Tours*, T9534 8868, www.wildlife tours.com.au *Touring Downunder*, T5356 4251, run a daily tour around Wonderland and the nearer lookouts from Halls Gap. **Walking** The farming communities of Stawell and Horsham can be used as a base for exploring the park but the main base is at Halls Gap.

Getting there & around
The ranges are crossed by only a handful of sealed roads. These do, however, gain access to many areas of the park

For bike hire, see page 511

Ararat began as a goldfields town but is unusual for being the only town founded by Chinese diggers. It is now a small rural service-town that has some interesting museums and galleries and is close to the wine regions of the Grampians and Pyrenees. The **Gum San Chinese Heritage Centre** is a suberb new museum in a Chinese pagoda designed in the traditional style of Southern China. It represents the journey of Chinese gold diggers from Southern China to Ararat, many travelling overland from Robe in South Australia

Ararat
Colour map 2, grid C2
Population: 7,200
90 km from Ballarat,
33 km from Stawell

The Grampians

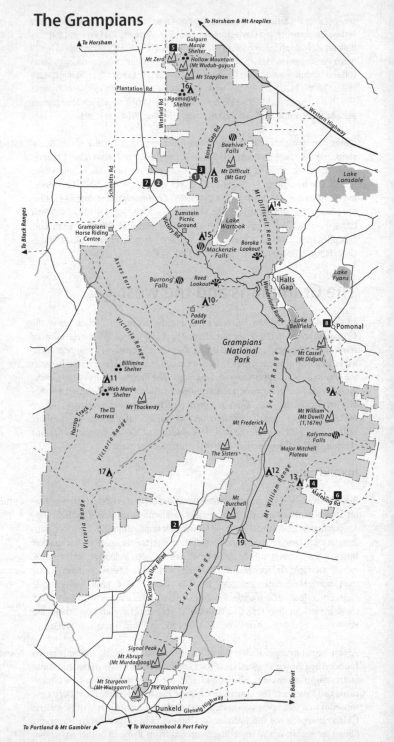

Victoria

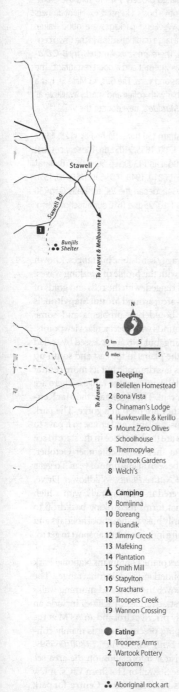

Sleeping
1 Bellellen Homestead
2 Bona Vista
3 Chinaman's Lodge
4 Hawkesville & Kerillo
5 Mount Zero Olives
  Schoolhouse
6 Thermopylae
7 Wartook Gardens
8 Welch's

⚑ Camping
9 Bomjinna
10 Boreang
11 Buandik
12 Jimmy Creek
13 Mafeking
14 Plantation
15 Smith Mill
16 Stapylton
17 Strachans
18 Troopers Creek
19 Wannon Crossing

● Eating
1 Troopers Arms
2 Wartook Pottery
  Tearooms

⁂ Aboriginal rock art

■ *Daily 1000-1630. $8, children $4, concessions $6. Western Highway, T5352 1078, www.gumsan.com.au*
The **Ararat Gallery**, in the town hall on Vincent Street, has a large collection of contemporary textiles. The **VIC** is on the highway, just to the east of the shopping area, and has a booking service for local accommodation. ■ *Daily 0900-1700. T5355 0281, www.ararat.asn.au*

Transport *V~Line* bus services to **Stawell** (25 mins) and **Horsham** (1¼-2 hrs) leave from the VIC at 1100, 2000 and 2040 Mon-Fri, with an additional service to Stawell only at 1530. Sat services go at 1135, 1420, 2045 and Sun at 1235, 1830 and 2040. Services to **Ballarat** and **Melbourne** leave at least 5 times a day Mon-Fri, 0835, 1005, 1630 Sat and 0935, 1535 and 1740 Sun.

The small town of Great Western, between Stawell and Ararat, is at the centre of a small wine region, known for producing excellent sparkling wines, fruity whites and rich reds. *Seppelts* vineyard has an extraordinary cellar, 3 km of tunnels dug by unemployed gold miners in the 1860s. There are guided tours of these tunnels, called 'the Drives', that store thousands of neatly stacked bottles. The winery also has lovely grounds to picnic in and provides BBQs. ■ *Daily 1000-1700. T5361 2239, www.seppelt.com.au Tours Mon-Sat 1030, 1330, 1500.*

The closest town to the Grampians, Stawell owes its origins to gold but is best known for the **Stawell Easter Gift**, a 120-m sprint that has been run at Easter since 1878 and offering over $100,000 in prize money. It even has its own **Hall of Fame**, holding memorabilia and photographs of winners. ■ *$3, Mon-Fri 0900-1100, longer hrs Mar-May, T5358 1326. Main St by Central Park.* The **VIC** is on the main highway.■ *Daily 0900-1700. T5358 2314, stinfo@netconnect.com.au*

Stawell & Great Western
Colour map 2, grid C2
Population: 7,000
20 km from Halls Gap

Victoria

Sleeping & eating

Both are fairly limited in Stawell, with most of the Grampians accommodation in or around Halls Gap. All accommodation is booked out well ahead at Easter

Stawell A-B *Bellellen Homestead*, Stawell-Jallukar Rd, T5358 4800, www.bellellen homestead.com.au Large, modern B&B on an isolated propery 9 km toward the Grampians. 4 very comfortable en suite rooms and attentive hosts. Licensed, excellent dinners $40, BBQs in summer, winery tours available. Weekend packages are good value. **B-C** *Walmsley House*, 19 Seaby St, T5358 3164, is a large traditional B&B in the town centre with 5 period-style rooms and wide verandas. There are several motels, try **B-C** *Diamond House*, 24 Seaby St, T5358 3366, which has internet and a good restaurant. The *Stawell Park* caravan park, T5358 2709, has cabins and vans. *The Gift*, 13 Main St, has a bistro serving lunch and dinner daily and a café bar with coffee and snacks available all day, also live music at weekends. There is a café, *Matilda's*, next door to the VIC.

Transport

V~Line bus services leave from the VIC for **Horsham** (50 mins-1½ hrs) at 1125, 1145, 2025 and 2105 Mon-Fri, 1200, 1445, 2110 Sat and 1300, 1855, 2105 Sun. The services that go on to **Adelaide** (7½ hrs) are 1145 Mon-Fri, 1200 Sat and 1300 Sun. Services to **Ballarat** and **Melbourne** leave at least 5 times a day Mon-Fri, 0810, 1940, 1605 Sat and 0910, 1510 and 1715 Sun. *Sandlants Coach Tours*, T5356 9342, depart the VIC for **Halls Gap** (30 mins) Mon-Fri 1155, Sat 1200, Sun 1300. Also Mon-Fri 0725 and 1610 during school term.

The Grampians National Park

www.visit grampians.com.au Walking maps available from the Halls Gap parks office

There are no entry fees to the National Park

The Grampians are a series of of forested, craggy sandstone hill ranges, known to the local aboriginal people as **Gariwerd**, with the profile of breaking waves. The very northern is much dryer, open and rugged, with the reds and golds of the rock showing much more strongly. This area, around **Mount Stapylton**, is beloved of rock-climbers with countless bouldering problems and some incredible over-hanging faces. The park abounds with spectacular viewpoints. Most can only be gained by strenuous walking, but two are accessed by sealed roads. The **Boroka Lookout** has views to the plains in the east and south up Fyans Valley to Halls Gap. **Reed Lookout** is less dramatic but its more central position gives 360° views and a better mental picture of the ranges. There are waterfalls dotted all over, best of course after rain. The biggest are the **MacKenzie Falls**. Thunderous when flowing well, they are deep in a gorge. The park abounds with wildlife, particularly kangaroos, wallabies and emus, so it pays to watch your speed if driving. The Grampians are the best place in the state to see the state's widest variety of **wildflowers**, at their best September-October, though some, including many orchids, can be seen at any time of year. To get a better look at the flora head for *Mt Cassel Native Plants*, Wildflower Drive, Pomonal, T5356 6351. The ranges are covered in walking trails, with a high concentration in the Wonderland range that forms the striking backdrop to Halls Gap, though these can get extraordinarily busy in the school holidays and long weekends. Other walks in the park require independent transport to get to.

Halls Gap

Colour map 2, grid C2 Population: 300 The town is busy in summer and during school holidays

Halls Gap is the only town within the borders of the Grampians National Park and sits in a tight valley enclosed by the Wonderland and Boronia ranges. The Wonderland bluffs and crags almost hang over the town and morning walks show off the warm golden-red rock to best advantage. Facilities include an expensive food-store, post office, reasonably priced petrol and an ATM at the petrol station. There is a **VIC** in the shopping precinct but it is mainly concerned with booking accommodation. ■ *Daily 0900-1700. T1800 065599, tourinfo@netconnect.com.au* For general visitor information on the area see www.grampians.org.au or talk to staff at the Stawell or Horsham VICs. A few kilometres deeper into the valley is the **Parks Victoria Visitor Centre**, for park information, interpretative displays and the best range of maps and walking

Victoria

advice. They sell three general maps on walks in Wonderland, and the Northern and Southern regions ($3.30 each) but serious walkers will need the more detailed topographic maps, also available at the parks office. ■ *Daily 0900-1700. T5356 4381, www.parkweb.vic.gov.au* Just behind is the distinctive red roof of **Brambuk Aboriginal Cultural Centre,** built in the shape of a cockatoo and representing symbolic features of the five Koori communities involved in running the centre. Brambuk shows an excellent short film on the creation of Gariwerd but the focus is on active participation so there are few museum-style displays. A chat to staff, a walk to see bush tucker plants in the garden or a tour of rock-art sites are the kind of activities available. There is also a café upstairs with some traditional bush tucker and a souvenir shop. ■ *Daily 1000-1700. Entrance free, film $4.40, children $2.40, concessions $3.40. Rock-art tours approx $70 day. Activities need to be booked in advance. T5356 4452.*

Bike Hire *GAP,* Silver Creek shopping alley, though frequently closed. **Communications** Internet at *Tim's Place,* $6 per hr for non-residents. **Post Office** in the main shopping area.

Several days could be spent hiking in **Wonderland** alone, making this area one of the best walking areas in the state for those without their own transport. Another excellent aspect of the range is the number of circular routes that can be tackled. The best, and most popular loop is the four-hour circuit from Halls Gap that heads up past **Splitters Falls**, accessible via a short fern gully, through stands of native pines to **Wonderland** car park, through the rocky gorges of the **Grand Canyon** and **Silent Street**, and up to superb **Pinnacle Lookout**. The return path is more direct, descending gradually through stringybark forest and heath back to the central caravan park.

There are several short walks off Mount Victory Road in the **northern Grampians**. From Reed Lookout it is a short stroll to the **Balconies**, a set of horizontally jutting rock ledges with impressive views to the south-west. Although accessible only by unsealed Winfield Road, the low northern peaks of **Mount Zero**, **Hollow Mountain** and **Mount Stapylton**, make fantastic short walks. The first two involve a little scrambling but are well marked and can be done in a little over an hour each, though Hollow Mountain particularly will beg a longer stay. The approach to Mount Stapylton is more challenging (two hours). Most challenging of all are the walks involving the climb up **Mount Difficult** (five hours return). The easiest approach is from Troopers Creek campground. Also accessible from the sealed Roses Gap Road are **Beehive Falls**, the longest single drop in the ranges. The walk from Mount Zero to Halls Gap, along the Mount Difficult range, takes in much of the most striking scenery in the Grampians and can be done in four days. There are four principal walking areas in the **southern Grampians**. The most varied, but still accessible via sealed roads, is **Mount William** and, just to the south of it, the **Major Mitchell Plateau** which has a bush campsite. A sealed road heads to the top of Mount William, but the last 2 km are for walkers only. Allow an hour return. From here a track winds across the plateau and down to Jimmy Creek campground. This can be done in a very full day, though an overnight option makes it more rewarding. Accessible only by unsealed roads is the three-day loop from the Buandik campground around the impressive buttress of the **Fortress** and **Mount Thackeray**, which each have a bush campsite. In the maze of unsealed roads just west of Halls Gap is **Paddy Castle**. This low outcrop offers a real feeling of being out in the untamed wilderness, though only a 10-minute walk from the car park. There is a variety of short walks around Dunkeld. Both **Mount Sturgeon** and **Mount Abrupt**

Walking
Rain and cold winds can come at any time of year, be well prepared on any but the shortest walks. A number of the walks in and around Wonderland have been specially constructed to allow wheelchair access. Contact the parks office for details. Tim's Place can hire out camping gear

Victoria

can be ascended in separate walks of about 2½ hours return. Close to the town is a one hour return walk up the **Piccaninny**, a good place to see wildflowers.

Tours & activities

Touring Downunder, T5356 4251, run a daily mini-bus tour around Wonderland for $35. They also offer a range of individually tailored 4WD tours. Two Halls Gap companies specialize in offering activities to independent visitors, from abseiling and climbing to canoeing and mountain biking. From about $35 for half a day. Try either *Adventure Company*, T5356 4540, www.adventure co.com.au, or *Great Grampians Activities*, T5356 4654, www.grampians tours.com The experienced *Base Camp and Beyond*, Halls Gap, T5356 4300, basecamp@grampians.net.au, offer rock-climbing and abseiling trips and courses from around $200 per day per group. *Grampians Bushwalking Club*, T5358 4719, head out on a range of walks and other activities every fortnight.

Sleeping

Most of the accommodation in Halls Gap is strung out for 4 km along Grampians Rd so those without transport should be aware of the walking distance to the main shops and walk start points

In Halls Gap A-B *Mountain Grand*, Grampians Rd, T5356 4232, www.mountaingrand.com.au Large, comfortable B&B hotel with 10 en suite rooms and 2 suites. The mid-range dining room has balcony tables and live jazz on Sat nights. Of the many holiday parks and motels along Grampians Rd, try **B** *Wonderland Cabins*, Ellis St, T5356 4264, grampians_wonderland@netconnect.com.au 6 spacious, self-contained wood cottages, each sleeping 4. All on a large forested plot that backs onto the Wonderland range. There are 3 backpacker hostels in the town, and all can be safely recommended. All are friendly, clean and well-equipped. **D-E** *Brambuk*, Grampians Rd, T5356 4250, has 50 beds in 8- to 12-bed dorms, and some doubles. All rooms are en suite, there are good kitchen facilities, and linen, light breakfast and entry to the *Dreamtime Theatre* is included. **D-E** *Tim's Place*, Grampians Rd, T/F5356 4288, tim@timsplace.net Formerly *Tim's Other Place*, this small eco-friendly weatherboard house is a home-from-home hostel with small dorms and a couple of doubles, some in exterior garden cabins, and a host of free extras. These include bikes, entry to the *Dreamtime Theatre*, late check-out, linen and breakfast. Internet $3 an hr for guests. The **D-E** *Grampians YHA Eco-Hostel*, Grampians Rd, T5356 4544, grampians@yhavic.org.au, is one of the YHA's best. This may be mud-brick and eco-friendly, but rustic it isn't. The very comfortable lounges are more reminiscent of a boutique hotel. 60 beds, including 10 doubles/twins, and excellent facilities. The *Caravan and Tourist Park*, Dunkeld Rd, T5356 4251, has a good range of cabins and on-site vans.

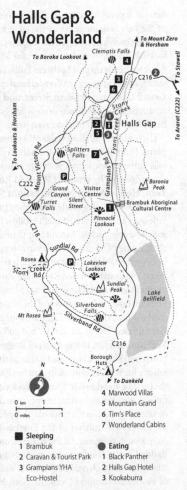

Halls Gap & Wonderland

Sleeping
1 Brambuk
2 Caravan & Tourist Park
3 Grampians YHA Eco-Hostel
4 Marwood Villas
5 Mountain Grand
6 Tim's Place
7 Wonderland Cabins

Eating
1 Black Panther
2 Halls Gap Hotel
3 Kookaburra

Rock art of Gariwerd ◀◀

The Grampians have a very rich concentration of rock art painted by the local Koori groups. Many of the paintings are thought to be at least 5,000 years old, perhaps as old as 20,000 years. Of about 60 sites, just a few are open to the public and of these the most significant is **Bunjils Shelter**, on the Stawell to Pomonal road the (C221). In the northern Grampians there are two accessible sites. **Gulgurn Manja Shelter** (pronounced Gulkurn Manya), near Hollow Mountain, was used to make stone tools and is painted with emu tracks and the handprints of children. The shelter is a ½-km walk from the Hollow Mountain campsite.

Ngamadjidj Shelter is thought to have been a favoured camping place. This shelter is a short walk from Stapylton Campground on Plantation Road. In the southern Grampians the sites are slightly more difficult to access. **Bilimina Shelter** has Gariwerd's most extensive paintings on a rock overhang. To reach the overhang take the 45-minute circuit from Buandik Picnic Area. Nearby is **Wab Manja** (pronounced Web Manya), a ½-hour uphill walk from the Harrop track car park. For more information on rock art talk to the staff at the **Brambuk Aboriginal Cultural Centre** in Halls Gap.

Victoria

Around the park A-B *Mount Zero Olives Schoolhouse*, Winfields Rd, T5383 8280, www.mountzeroolives.com. Late Victorian weatherboard schoolhouse transported to an isolated olive farm in the lee of Mt Zero. 2 light en suite doubles. Unsealed access only. **B** *Wartook Gardens*, Mt Victory Rd, T5383 6200, www.wartookgardens.com.au Simple, supremely welcoming, hosted B&B, with 3 bedrooms, private bathrooms and views across their isolated property to the Asses Ears ranges. Breakfast and family-style dinners ($30). Recommended. **B** *Welch's*, Wildflower Dr, Pomonal, T5356 6311, welchs@netconnect.com.au Unusual hexagonal family home with 3 rooms, the best being the 1st floor 'turret' room with almost 360° views. The hosts supply a great breakfast. **C** *Bona Vista*, Victoria Valley Rd, T5574 0225. Self-contained Victorian weatherboard cottage in an isolated paddock in the midst of the Victoria valley. The wood-panelled interior oozes character and charm. Sleeps 8. Recommended. **C** *Hawkesville & Kerillo*, Mafeking Rd, T/F5354 6244, is a picturesque sheep farm with views to the mountains and 2 self contained cottages. There are over a dozen **campgrounds** in the park, all with specified sites, picnic tables, fireplaces and toilets. The largest are Stapylton, Smith Mill, Borough Huts and Boreang and have more-or-less year round water. Of the remainder, with 10 sites or less, Wannon Crossing and Strachans also usually have a supply. Camping is $10 per site, payable at the campground, coving up to 6 people and 1 vehicle. Campgrounds get busy over long weekends, the Dec-Jan summer periods and Easter. The Halls Gap Parks office maintains a daily list of where there are available sites. There are also a small number of designated bush sites for overnight walkers.

Kookaburra, Main Rd, Halls Gap, T5356 4222, is the classiest place in town by a country mile, but their tight grip on the quality market means expensive prices. Open daily for coffee and cake, meals 1200-1500, 1800-2000, later in summer. Best value is the pub, the *Halls Gap Hotel*, a friendly, modern bar and bistro. Cheap, hearty counter meals daily 1200-1400, 1800-2000. *Troopers Arms*, Roses Gap Rd, T5383 6203, www.chinamanslodge.homestead.com, is a huge wooden barn that was purpose built as a pub, one of the very few in Australia within the borders of a National Park. Meals should be arranged in advance except in peak summer season when the place goes with a considerable swing. On Sat they have a spit roast on the huge open fire, making the excursion particularly worth while. Open daily from 1000 until the last customer leaves. They own the **B-C** *Chinaman's Lodge*, 4 small, rustic, self-contained cottages set on a huge property of open woodland. **Eating**

Transport   **To/from Halls Gap** *Sandlants Coach Tours*, T5356 9342, departs from opposite the post office for **Stawell** (30 mins) Mon-Fri 1330, Sat 1250, Sun 1630. Also Mon-Fri 0755, 1640 during school term only. Many of the tour buses will also ferry people out. *Autopia*, T9326 5536, leave for **Melbourne** ($30) at 1430 Sun, Tue-Wed and Fri. *Wild-life Tours*, T9747 1882, leave for **Adelaide** ($35) at the same times. They also have buses to **Warrnambool** ($25) and then the Great Ocean Rd, departing 1700 Mon, Thu and Sat.

Mount Arapiles
10 km from Natimuk

Mount Arapiles, an isolated sandstone outcrop reaching just 230 m above the wide billiard-table plains, is known to the rock-climbing community as one of the world's best, with over 2,000 recognized climbs. The service centre for Mount Arapiles is the tiny community of **Natimuk**. Life here revolves around the pub, the unpretentious **C-D** *National*, T5387 1300, which serves good cheap meals and provides clean, comfortable and extremely good value accommodation. The town also has a small park with BBQs, small store, post office, chemist, service station and petrol.Two operators in Natimuk offer a wide range of guided climbs and tuition: *Climbing Company*, T5387 1329, climbco@wimmera.com.au; and *Climbing Guides*, T/F5387 1284, climbacg@netconnect.com.au *The Mountain Shop*, T5387 1529, has an excellent range of climbing gear (basic stuff for hire), maps and guides.

Little Desert National Park
Take plenty of water and don't walk during the middle of the day. Park notes are available at the Horsham VIC. For more information contact Parks Victoria, T131963, www.parkweb vic.gov.au

Little Desert is not a spectacular park and does not receive many visitors but it offers peaceful bushland, wildlife, and the chance of seeing the rare and shy mallee fowl. The park extends from the Wimmera River, just northwest of Horsham, to the South Australian border and covers 132,000 ha. It was created to preserve the habitat of the endangered mallee fowl, a large ground bird that looks a little like a pheasant. Most tracks in the park are only suitable for 4WD vehicles. The main access points are on the eastern border of the park. **Horseshoe Bend**, near Dimboola, is a basic camping ground with picnic facilities by the River Red gums of the Wimmera River and there are two short walks. **Kiata Campground** and **Sanctuary Picnic Ground** are accessible from the Western Highway between Dimboola and Nhill for details. The towns of **Nhill** and **Dimboola** have motels and caravan parks, contact the VIC in Nhill, T5391 1811, www.hindmarsh.vic.gov.au **C** *Little Desert Log Cabins*, T5389 1122, www.littledesertlogcabins.com.au, is a good place to stay . **D-E** *Little Desert Tours & Lodge*, T5391 5232, is on the northern border south of Nhill and has simple bunkrooms and doubles. The *Lodge* also runs 4WD tours and has a mallee fowl aviary. *Oasis Desert Adventures*, T0419 394912, www.travlink. com.au/oasis, based near Dimboola, run a wide range of tours.

The Wimmera   The Wimmera is a hot, dry agricultural area, irrigated by water from the Grampains. Much of the land was granted to Australian soldiers after the World Wars in the 'soldier settlement'. On the north bank of the Wimmera River is the rural service-town of **Horsham**. The VIC is on O'Callaghan Parade, leading off Firebrace at the southern end. ■ *Daily 0900-1700. T5382 1832, tourism@hrcc.vic.gov.au* **B-C** *Horsham House*, 27 Roberts Avenue, T5382 5053, www.horshamhouse.com.au A traditional B&B in the town centre with two suites and a cottage, lovely sun room and pool. **C** *Olde Horsham Inn*, Western Highway, T5381 0033, has more character than most, English gardens, a pool, and a decent restaurant. A couple of pubs also offer accommodation. *V~Line* bus services leave from the Old Police Station, Roberts Av, for Adelaide at 1310 Monday-Friday, 1325 Saturday and 1425 Sunday. Services to Stawell and Melbourne leave at 0630, 1320 and 1550 Monday-Friday, 0713, 0850, 1440 Saturday and 0815, 1420 and 1550 Sunday.

Western Australia

▶▶   **Footprint feature**

The first thing to be said about Western Australia is that it's big – very big – covering a third of the Australian continent. This means the state contains a great diversity of landscapes, ranging from its tropical northern regions to the baking deserts of the interior, all the way down to its southern coast feeling the cold blast of Antarctica. Just ten percent of Australians inhabit all this space and three-quarters of them live in Perth. Western Australians live closer to Singapore than Sydney and their isolation, combined with the state's great mineral wealth, has fostered an independent spirit. To Western Australians the rest of Australia is just 'the eastern states'. The small population and great distance from the rest of the country also means the state is wonderfully unspoilt and has comparatively little tourism development. The wild scenery, wildlife and almost indecent amount of sunshine make Western Australia a destination you'd be unwise to miss. Most people arrive in **Perth**, a green and spacious city, and promptly head for the playground of the southwest corner, where the warm water of the Indian Ocean laps blinding, with a hinterland of caves, forest and wine regions. North of Perth the landscape becomes more arid but **Shark Bay** rears dolphins, dugongs and turtles, while further north the **Ningaloo Reef** attracts the mighty whale shark. Inland, the raw red country of the **Pilbara** gives way to the magnificent narrow gorges of **Karijini National Park**. And right at the top of the state is the **Kimberley**, with some of the most stunning yet little-visited range country in Australia, including the amazing **Bungle Bungles**.

Things to do in Western Australia

1   Carve out enough time in **Kununurra** to take a trip into the **Bungle Bungles** to canoe the **Ord River** and visit El Questro.
2   Experience 'Broometime' and take a leisurely cruise on the coastal waters around the town.
3   Explore the fantastic and tortuous gorges of the **Karijini National Park.**
4   From April-July, make the trip up to **Exmouth** to swim with the whale sharks and snorkel on the Ningaloo Reef.
5   Hike a section or two of the **Bibbulmun Track** along the south coast between Pemberton and Albany.
6   In **Fremantle** stroll the cappuccino strip, eat fish and chips on the wharf, then take the night tour of the Prison.
7   Canoe the gorges of the **Kalbarri National Park** and take a scenic flight up to **Monkey Mia** to see the dolphins.

Western Australia

Ins and outs

Getting around   **Air** As the biggest state, with an extensive mining industry, air travel is common within WA. Though not usually very cheap, a couple of flights can save days of travel if you're short of time. *Skywest*, T131300, www.skywest.com.au, is the principal state airline with flights from Perth to all the major towns and cities south of Karratha, including Monkey Mia, but excepting Kalgoorlie. *Northwest Regional Airlines*, T08 9192 1369, www.northwestregional.com.au, connect the northern towns from Exmouth to Halls Creek, while NT's *Air North*, T8920 4000, www.airnorth.com.au, have connections between Broome, Kununurra and Darwin. *Qantas*, T131313, www.qantas.com.au, provide direct flights from Perth to Kalgoorlie and the main northern towns. **Bus/train** Westrail, T131053, www.wagr.wa.gov.au, run the main services around the state though their network only extends as far as Norseman in the east and Kalbarri/Meekatharra to the north. *Integrity*, T9226 1339, www.integritycoachlines.com.au, run buses up the coast as far as Exmouth. The national carriers *McCafferty's/Greyhound* plug the gap further with services right through to Darwin in the north and Adelaide to the east. **Backpacker buses** *Australian Adventure Travel*, T9248 2355, www.safaris.net.au, have an 8-day Perth to Broome trip plus a 4-day Kimberley adventure. *Easyrider*, T9226 0307, www.easyriderbp.com.au. Several 'jump-on, jump-off' options around the southwest and north as far as Broome. *Nullarbor Traveller*, T1800 816858, info@the-traveller.com.au. Week-long trips between Perth and Adelaide. *Red Earth Safaris*, T1800 501968 or 9246 7282, www.redearthsafaris.com.au. All-inclusive trips around the south-west and up coast as far as Exmouth. *Travelabout*, T1800 621200 or 9244 1200, www.travelabout.au.com). Lots of options around the southwest and up the coast as far as Darwin. Also along the Outback Highway via Uluru to Alice Springs.

Information   The state government tourism body is the **Western Australian Tourist Commis-**
For details of the   **sion**. For brochures and information T1300-361351, or see their website,
Bibbulmun & Cape   www.westernaustralia.net The state government's own site is www.wa.gov.au and
to Cape Tracks,   this has some useful links. Backpackers will find **Traveller's Club** in Perth, T9226
see boxes on   0660, www.travellersclub.com.au, a useful source of help and information. The
pages 576 & 561   **Department of Conservation and Land Management** (CALM) T08-9334 0333, www.naturebase.net, give further information on national and conservation parks, and details of visiting and staying in them. Park entry fees are usually $9 a car but it is better value to buy a Holiday Pass ($22.50) allowing entry into all WA parks for 4 weeks. If you plan a longer stay it's worth considering the Annual Pass ($51), valid for 12 months from date of purchase. These can be bought at many parks and VICs or from the **Perth Visitor Centre** in Forrest Pl.

Maps *Map World*, 900 Hay St, Perth, T9322 5733, stock an excellent range of national, state and regional maps and guide books. They have a full range of topographic maps, as well as bike maps, Bibbulmun and Cape-to-Cape track maps. The *Streetsmart* series of regional touring maps are produced by the government and are probably the best maps available for drivers. These can be bought online at www.landonline.com.au, from some bookshops and VICs or from *The Central Map Agency*, T9273 755

5, 1 Midland Sq, Midland, www.dola.wa.gov.au The *RAC*, 228 Adelaide Terr, Perth, T9421 4400, also publish fold-out maps to most areas of the state, only $3 for members. *UBD Country Towns and Street Directory: Western Australia*, has good information on towns (excluding Perth) and includes a road atlas of the whole state.

History

The time-lag between European discovery and colonization in the eastern states was a matter of decades. In the west of Australia it took centuries. The

Portuguese sailor Dirk Hartog found the coast in 1616, and in the following 200 years the entire western, northern and southern coasts were well mapped out by Portuguese, Dutch and English sailors. The Dutch East India Company even considered establishing a colony here in 1718, but it wasn't until 1826 that the British made anl encampment at King William Sound (now Albany), mainly to counter perceived French ambitions. Three years later Captain James Stirling was sent to found the Swan River Colony. Not untypically, Stirling discounted the local Aboriginal tribes, offering no treaty and ignoring them in his planning.

The early settlements of Fremantle and Perth got off to a slow start, despite private backing from English speculators. The finding of the fertile Avon Valley in 1830 and the crushing of Aboriginal opposition at the 'battle' of Pinjarra in 1834 did lead to the establishment of a reasonable wool industry, but a generation later, in 1850, the colony could still only boast a population of 5,500 Europeans. In 1892 the colony found gold around Coolgardie and Western Australia finally made the leap forward that the other colonies had made decades earlier. The goldfields were supplied with water via an ambitious pipeline and a railway to Fremantle, thereby ensuring pre-eminence to the capital, Perth.

In 1900 the colonists voted, largely due to the insistence of the Kalgoorlie goldminers, to join the Australian Federation. By 1912 the population had increased sharply to over 300,000 whites, and an uncounted and declining number of Aboriginal people no longer seen as significant. Two world wars, during which WA lost a disproportionate number of its men, and the depression of the 1930s, slowed but could not stall the economic growth of the new state and postwar migration helped swell the population to over 700,000 by 1960. The state continued to prosper from vast quantities of grain and wool for export, gold production and cattle. Since the 1960s this wealth has increased with the discovery of massive quantities of nickel, iron-ore, bauxite and oil in the north, along with diamonds in eastern Kimberley.

The impact on the culture and environment that existed prior to 1829 cannot be understated. Entire peoples vanished over much of this vast area, and where they managed to survive their cultures were massively disrupted. Huge tracts of land were cleared of native vegetation to make way for wheat and wool, and much of this has resulted in a rising water table, bringing with it enough salt to ruin huge areas of land. The amount of species lost among both plant and animal life, will never be accurately known but was certainly substantial.

Perth

One of the most isolated cities in the world, Perth is a green, clean and spacious city on the banks of the wide, blue Swan River. Although it is about the same age as Adelaide there is little evidence of its past. It's a sparkling, modern place, reminiscent of American cities with its freeway flyovers and dependence on the car. Perth's best asset is an incredible climate. The sun simply never stops shining and each perfect sunny day is simply taken for granted. Naturally, this makes for an outdoor city where the beaches, ocean, river and parks are the favourite haunts of the friendly, informal and laid-back people of Perth. The city centre is often criticised for being soulless by day and empty by night, and it is true that it suffers from a lack of inner-city residents. The action in Perth is to be found out in the suburbs and in fun and colourful Fremantle, which contains some of the country's finest Victorian buildings.

Colour map 7, grid B5
Population: 1,300,000
2,705 km from Adelaide, 4,175 km from Darwin

Western Australia

Ins and outs

Getting there
For more details,
see Transport, page
536, and individual
suburb sections

Air There are 2 terminals, a little over 10 km east of the city centre. With no direct link between the 2, transfers are via the perimeter highways. The **domestic terminal**, Brearley Av, has as a wide range of services including ATMs, *Travelex* foreign exchange, and all the major car hire firms. Transport to Perth is via taxi (around $20-25), the *Airport Shuttle* minibus, T9225 6222, ($10, you'll need to phone and book to get out to the airport), or the *Transperth* bus (bus stop opposite *Qantas* terminal, $2.80, 35 mins) to the City Busport. Buses leave at least every 30-60 mins from 0705-2205. The **international terminal**, Horrie Miller Dr, is slightly further out. Facilities are just as comprehensive, but there is no public bus route from this terminal, so it's either the shuttle ($11) or a taxi (about $25).

The **Wellington Street Bus Station** is the main terminal for interstate coaches and some independent state services such as *Integrity. Travel Coach* run the interstate services to Adelaide, Darwin and beyond. Their ticket office, T9321 6211, is on the upper level walkway, open Mon-Tue, Thu, Sat 0600-1715, Wed, Fri-Sat 0600-1900. *Westrail*, T131053, operate most coach and train services within the state from the **East Perth Station**. The **Railway Station** on Wellington St services the 4 suburban lines, while most metropolitan buses terminate at the **City Busport**.

Getting around
See page 537,
for bike and
car hire

Bus Both Perth and Fremantle have free city centre buses known as **CATs** (Central Area Transit), T136213. There are 2 circuits in central Perth. The *Blue Cat* travels around Northbridge, though the city centre, and around Riverside Dr and Mounts Bay Rd. Buses every 8 mins from 0650-1820 Mon-Fri, and every 15 mins from 1820-0105 Fri, 0830-0100 Sat, and 1000-1700 Sun. The *Red Cat* heads to East Perth just short of the WACA, and to West Perth as far as Outram St. The service runs much of the length of Hay St in a westerly direction, and Murray St the other way. Buses every 5 mins from 0650-1820 Mon-Fri, and every 45 mins from 1000-1815 Sat-Sun. Both Red and Blue services run within 200 m or so of the Wellington St stations, the Blue Cat stops at both the City Busport and Barrack Sq (for the Barrack St Jetty). *Transperth*, T136213, www.transperth.wa.gov.au, operate the city's buses, trains and ferries and have several information centres where you can pick up timetables and ask for help. These are located in the Plaza Arcade, at City Busport, the main Railway Station and Wellington St Bus Station. **Urban bus routes** tend to radiate out from the city centre, and travelling between peripheral areas, though usually possible, can be a tortuous affair. Routes extend beyond Hillarys to the north, out to the Swan Valley and Perth Hills, and south as far as Mandurah. **Fares** are worked out according to how many zones you cross. The central suburbs are encompassed by zone 1, and zone 2 extends outwards to include Fremantle, Cottesloe, Scarborough and Midland. Tickets are valid for 2 hrs, and cost $1.80 for travel within one zone, and $2.80 for 2 zones. A multi-zone **DayRider** ticket is available for $7.10 after 0900 and is valid all day. Buying these in packs of 10 saves about 15%. The **FamilyRider** ticket allows 2 adults and up to 5 children to travel anywhere and back for $7.10. Standard tickets, DayRiders and FamilyRiders can be purchased on board buses and ferries, and at train stations. Bulk tickets (MultiRiders) have to be bought at *Transperth* info centres, or the many retail outlets that stock them.

As it's a fairly flat city Perth is ideal for **cycling**. Pick up detailed maps of cycle routes, for example the *Bikewest Perth Bike Map Series* ($6), from *Map World*. *Extreme Cycles*, corner of Wellington St and Queen St, T9481 5448, is a cycle shop that offers repairs and a useful service for cyclists. For $2 day you can store your bike safely, shower and secure your gear in a locker. The *Cycle Centre*, 282 Hay St, near *Perth Mint*, T9325 1176, sells new and 2nd-hand bikes from about $100 and offers visitors a by-back scheme. Open daily.

Western Australia

Great places to stay in WA

◀◀

100 Hubble, Fremantle (page 540)
Black Cockatoo, Nannup (page 567)
The Cove, Denmark (page 574)
Dongara Denison Backpackers
(page 594)
Ellenbrae Station, Gibb River Road
(page 634)

Rottnest Lodge, Rottnest Island
(page 543)
Lily Windmill, Stirling Range (page 581)
Marina Beach, Exmouth (page 611)
McAlpine House, Broome (page 625)
Monastery Guesthouse, New Norcia
(page 550)

Ferries *Transperth* operate ferries from Barrack St Jetty over to **South Perth**. They leave every 20-30 mins daily from 0750-1915, and until 2115 Sat-Sun during Sep-Apr. Last return ferry is at 1930 (2130 Fri-Sat during Sep-Apr).

Train There are 4 suburban lines from Perth station. All run regular services from early morning to past midnight. To the north the *Joondalup* line stops at Leederville and Stirling (with buses to Scarborough Beach) on the way, while the *Fremantle* line calls at Subiaco, Claremont and Cottesloe (with a 15-min walk to the beach). The *Midland* line has stops at East Perth (for *Westrail* services) and Guildford (the Swan Valley), and trains to *Armadale* call at Burswood. Fares are as per the bus services.

Perth covers a massive area for its relatively small number of residents. The city is approximately 3 times the size of Greater London with about an eighth of the population. The core of the city lines the banks of the Swan River from its mouth at Fremantle to the central business district, 19 km upstream, just north of an open basin known as Perth Water. Perth is contained by the coastline to the west and the low 'Perth hills' of the Darling Ranges in the east, a corridor of about 40 km, and in the last 10 years has expanded northwards to Joondalup and to the south almost as far as Rockingham. The city centre is a small grid, just north of the river, of about 2 km by 1 km. The river is bordered by a strip of green lawn throughout the entire city area threaded with walking tracks. However, although the central business district faces the river it is cut off from it by busy roads and freeways so the foreshore is not the asset it could be.

Orientation & information

For tourist information head for the *Perth Visitor Centre*, the main VIC for the state. You can pick up free maps and brochures for each state region and it acts as a travel agent and sells national park passes. Forrest Pl, T1300-361 351, www.westernaustralia.net, Mon-Thu 0800-1800, Fri 0800-1900, Sat 0830-1230. An information kiosk at the junction of Forrest Pl and the Murray St Mall can provide information and help on anything in the city. It is run by volunteers and is not aimed specifically at tourists but it's a good place to ask for directions or advice. There is also a very useful contact point for backpackers, *Traveller's Club*, 499 Wellington St, T9226 0660, www.travellersclub.com.au They have well-used travellers' noticeboards, cheap internet use and act as a tour booking centre, as well as offering help and information. Mon-Sat 0900-200, Sun 1000-2000. General entertainment listings are published daily in the state newspaper, the *West Australian*. Live music and clubbing is covered by free newspapers, *Xpress* and *Hype*, both published weekly on Thu and can be picked up in music shops. Events such as festivals and sporting matches are listed at www.events.tourism.wa.gov.au **Gay and lesbian** Information, counselling and support for gay travellers can be found from *Gay and Lesbian Community Services of WA*, 2 Delhi St, West Perth. T9420 7201, www.glcs.org.au Also look for *Shout*, a free newspaper published fortnightly covering WA gay and lesbian news, entertainment, lifestyle and listings.

Western Australia

★

24 hours in the city

Start the day at *Kings Park*. Admire the view, followed by breakfast at *Frasers* and a walk in the botanic gardens. Catch the CAT from the park to the railway station and explore the **Art Gallery** or **Museum** in the Cultural Centre, followed by a spot of shopping in the malls, arcades and in King Street. Walk down to Barrack Street jetty and have lunch at *The Lucky Shag* pub. After lunch have a look at **Swan Bells**, then catch the ferry to **South Perth**. Hire a catamaran and sail on the river for an hour or two. In the late afternoon head back to the Barrack Street Jetty and catch a ferry down-river to **Fremantle**. Stroll around the streets, then have dinner at Fishing Boat Harbour and a coffee afterwards on the cappuccino strip. If you're still up for it catch a band or DJ at *Kulcha* or the *Fly by Night Club*.

Sights

Perth is primarily an outdoor city; a place to soak up the sunny climate by going to the beach. The city does not have the population to support huge public institutions and much of its early colonial architecture has been demolished to make way for a shiny modern city. Kings Park, just west of the city centre, is the city's most popular attraction and is much used by the locals for its views, peaceful walks and picnic spots, café and outdoor cinema. The new Swan Bells tower also has good city views, and can easily be combined with a visit to Perth Zoo, an unexpected oasis of bush and jungle set back from the river bank of South Perth.

Cultural Centre The most impressive cultural sights, the **Art Gallery of Western Australia** and the **Western Australian Museum**, are gathered together in the plaza called the Cultural Centre, just north of the railway line, that connects the city and Northbridge. The art gallery houses temporary exhibitions as well as Aboriginal art and contemporary art collections. The gallery's collection of Aboriginal Art is one of the most extensive and impressive in Australia. The café opposite does good Mediterranean-style food, Monday-Friday 0800-1700, Saturday-Sunday 0900-1700. ■ *Daily 1000-1700. Free. Guided tours at 1300 Tue- Wed, Fri-Sun. T9492 6600, www.artgallery.wa.gov.au Perth Cultural Centre, Blue CAT route, stop 7. Walkway to Perth Train Station. Several car parks on Roe St.*

The museum sprawls over a large area containing many different architectural styles. The main entrance on James Street joins the Jubilee Building and Hackett Hall, the former built in 1899 in Victorian Byzantine style and housing the Mammal Gallery, the latter built in 1903 and now a backdrop to the museum's best exhibition, 'WA Land and People'. Displays on the European history of WA are shown in the Old Gaol. Beyond the gaol is the 1970s Francis Street Building, home to the fascinating **Aboriginal Gallery** – called *Katta Djinoong*, meaning 'see us and understand us' – which examines the past and present of WA's different indigenous groups, and contemporary issues such as the 'stolen generation'. There is a bookshop and a café for light snacks and drinks. ■ *Daily 0930-1700. Free. T9427 2700, www.museum.wa.gov.au Perth Cultural Centre, Blue CAT route, stop 7.*

Perth Mint
The mint is the major refiner of WA gold and buys and sells gold at market prices

Several display rooms are open to the public. Some have windows through to the production area, others contain some of WA's most historic and largest nuggets, and one contains a solid, 400-oz gold bar. There are regular guided tours and some culminate in a live 'gold pour', quite a sight. Entry to the shop is free. ■ *0900-1600 Mon-Fri, 0900-1300 Sat-Sun. Tours every 30 mins, daily*

0930-1430. 'Gold pours' on the hour, 1000-1500 Mon-Fri, 1000-1200 Sat-Sun. Entry and tours $6.60, children $3.30, concessions $5.50. T9421 7223, www.perthmint.com.au Hay St, Red CAT route, stop 10.

The centrepiece of Old Perth Port is a striking, 80-m bell tower which houses the original 18th-century bells of St Martin-in-the-Fields church in Trafalgar Square in London, given to WA to commemorate Australia's bicentenary in 1988. Visitor access reaches the sixth floor, an open-air platform with good views of both river and city. ■ *Daily 1000-1800. $6, children $3, concessions $3. The bells are rung 1230-1400 Wed-Thu and Sat-Sun, and Tue 1830-2000. T9218 8183, www.barracksquare.wa.gov.au Barrack Sq, Blue CAT route, stop 19.*

Swan Bells

Now used almost exclusively for cricket, the WACA (pronounced simply 'wacker'), parts of which are over a century old, is WA's premier sporting stadium. There are regular tours of the ground and a small but fascinating museum, mostly filled with a 100 years worth of cricketing memorabilia and including a Bradman room. ■ *Museum open daily 1000-1500 except match days. $3, children and concessions $1. Tours 1000 Tue, Thu except match days. $5, children and concessions $2, includes museum entry. T9265 7222, www.waca.com.au Nelson Cres, off Murray St, Red CAT route, stop 6.*

The WACA
Head for gate 2 for both tours and museum

This huge playground for the city and central suburbs is just about everything you could want a park to be. A large area of natural bush, threaded through with unsigned bushwalks, is bordered to the south and east by broad bands of carefully manicured lawns and gardens, these in turn encompassing the excellent **Botanic Gardens**. From many of these are tremendous views across to the city centre and Barrack Street jetty, particularly beautiful at sunset, and very popular with picnickers. The visitor centre at the end of Fraser Avenue has maps of the park ($1), self-guided walking maps, and details of the various ongoing events and activities. ■ *Daily 0930-1600. T9480 3600, www.kpbg.wa.gov.au Free guided walks from the old Karri log near the centre of the park every day at 1000 and 1400 (bookings not necessary); 1½- 2½ hours.*

Kings Park
The 33 bus from from St Georges Terr to Fraser Ave or Blue CAT bus to stop 21 and walk up Jacob's Ladder

Free unrestricted parking throughout the park

The incongruous old windmill tucked under the freeway is an unusual survivor from the early days of the Swan River Settlement in the 1830s. Although it looks quaint, it is technically an industrial site and one of the oldest in the state. An exhibition in the whitewashed miller's cottage explains the history of the Mill. ■ *Daily 1000-1600. $2, children $1. T9367 5788. South Perth, by Narrows Bridge. Catch a ferry to Mends St jetty, then walk towards the bridge (10 mins) or take bus no's 108 or 109 from the Busport.*

The Old Mill

The zoo covers just 19 ha in a block between the river and the freeway but manages to squeeze in 1,800 animals in attractive natural settings. It also participates in a native species breeding program, that aims to save the many local WA species close to extinction, releasing zoo-bred animals to the wild. ■ *Daily 0900-1700. $13, children $6.50, concessions $10. T9367 7988, www.perthzoo.wa.gov.au 20 Labouchere Rd, South Perth. Transperth ferry from Barrack St jetty to Mends St jetty, then a 5-min walk.*

Perth Zoo

Western Australia

Central suburbs

The suburbs north of the river and west of the city centre are some of the most attractive in the city, and most have small eating and shopping strips that are more lively and interesting than the city centre

Northbridge is purely a resturant, entertainment and nightlife precinct, all squeezed into an area of about 1 sq km, with plenty of variety and cheap eating to be had. **Subiaco** is increasingly taking over from Northbridge as an eating destination, although it is more expensive and too trendy for some. Subiaco has the largest and busiest suburban commercial strip and great shopping. **West Perth**, between Subiaco and the city centre, is mostly a professional suburb. **East Perth**, on the other side of the city centre, is developing into a centre for accommodation and eating but is still fairly quiet and businesslike. **Leederville**, just north of Subiaco, is an alternative and funky suburb with some great cafés, a lively pub and an art-house cinema with indoor and outdoor screens. **Claremont** has some great shopping and is the haunt of 'ladies who lunch' and their privately educated kids. **South Perth**,

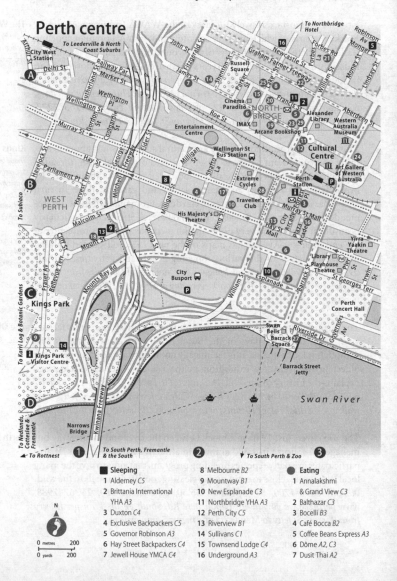

Perth centre

Sleeping
1 Alderney *C5*
2 Brittania International YHA *A3*
3 Duxton *C4*
4 Exclusive Backpackers *C5*
5 Governor Robinson *A3*
6 Hay Street Backpackers *C4*
7 Jewell House YMCA *C4*
8 Melbourne *B2*
9 Mountway *B1*
10 New Esplanade *C3*
11 Northbridge YHA *A3*
12 Perth City *C5*
13 Riverview *B1*
14 Sullivans *C1*
15 Townsend Lodge *C4*
16 Underground *A3*

Eating
1 Annalakshmi & Grand View *C3*
2 Balthazar *C3*
3 Bocelli *B3*
4 Café Bocca *B2*
5 Coffee Beans Express *A3*
6 Dôme *A2, C3*
7 Dusit Thai *A2*

just across Perth Water, is a great place for sailing or waterskiing and there are several cafés and restaurants on the river bank.

These suburbs are mostly residential but most have at least one great café or restaurant on the beach. Swimming is fine at all of the beaches, although there is often a steep shore break, so watch for rips. For the reassurance of lifeguards, swim between the flags at Cottesloe or Scarborough beaches. All west coast beaches are most pleasant in the morning before the sea breeze, known locally as the Fremantle Doctor for the relief it brings, kicks in in the afternoon. The early evening is also a lovely time, when the sun melts into the Indian ocean. There are often magnificent sunsets.

Coastal suburbs
Colour map 7, grid B5
Cottesloe 11 km from city centre, 7 km from Fremantle, 12 km from Scarborough, 20 km from Hillarys

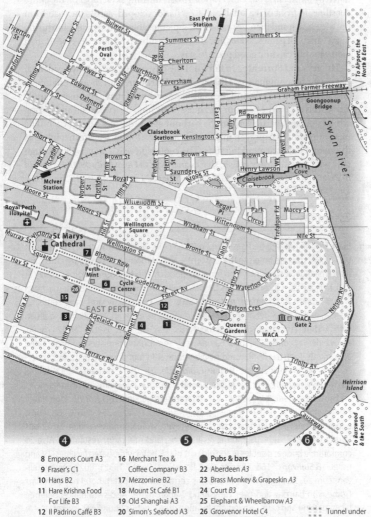

Western Australia

8 Emperors Court A3	16 Merchant Tea &
9 Fraser's C1	Coffee Company B3
10 Hans B2	17 Mezzonine B2
11 Hare Krishna Food	18 Mount St Café B1
For Life B3	19 Old Shanghai A3
12 Il Padrino Caffé B3	20 Simon's Seafood A3
13 Jaws Kaiten Sushi B3	21 Viet Hoa A3
14 Lotus Vegetarian A2	
15 Maya Masala A2	

● **Pubs & bars**
22 Aberdeen *A3*
23 Brass Monkey & Grapeskin *A3*
24 Court *B3*
25 Elephant & Wheelbarrow *A3*
26 Grosvenor Hotel C4
27 Lucky Shag C3
28 Moon & Sixpence B3
29 Universal Wine Bar A3

▦▦▦ Tunnel under
construction
-◄- Red Cat route
- ◄- Blue Cat route

Perth's most attractive and lively beach suburb, **Cottesloe** is the kind of place to make anyone envy the local lifestyle. The blindingly white beaches slope into the clear, warm water of the Indian Ocean and there is usually a bit of a swell for bodysurfing. The cafés overlooking the ocean are busy from sunrise to sunset and there's an all-pervading contented, laid-back atmosphere.

One long, sweeping beach extends all the way from Cottesloe to Scarborough and offers a quieter beach scene than those suburbs. **City Beach** has an extensive grassy foreshore hard up against a very broad section of beach. Facilities include BBQs, picnic tables and toilets and a small complex with a kiosk, café and an excellent restaurant. About 1 km north, **Floreat Beach** is more modest, but there are BBQs, picnic tables and free beach volleyball courts (ball from kiosk). **Scarborough**'s long, wide beach is dominated by the *Rendezvous Observation Tower*, the only skyscraper on the entire coastline. In front of it a small café strip has developed, across the road from the wide beach and there are a few BBQs, picnic tables and a small cabin hiring out a variety of games, skates and bikes. The suburb is more developed than Cottesloe but can be a good place to stay.

Hillarys and **Sorrento**, 25 km from the city centre, are mostly residential but have a pleasant marina, **Hillarys Boat Harbour**, with shops, restaurants and activities on and around the mall-like **Sorrento Quay**. Two major family attractions means the harbour and quay really hum on a weekend and during school holidays, particularly as the harbour also protects a sandy beach. The main attraction is **Aqwa**, an impressive showcase for the sea-life that inhabits the coastal waters around the state. The centre-piece is a large walk-through tank with a good variety of fish, sharks and rays. ■ *Open daily 0900-1700, and to 2100 Wed from Nov-Apr. $16.50, children $11, concessions $15. Southside Dr, T9447 7500, www.aqwa.com.au.*

Essentials

Sleeping
■ *On map*
See also Fremantle, page 540

LL-A *The Duxton*, 1 St Georges Terr, T1800-681118, www.duxton.com, is the closest of the big corporate hotels to the city centre and its rooms and services set the standard. The main restaurant is also seriously good. **A** *The Melbourne*, corner of Hay St and Milligan St, City, T9320 3333, www.melbournehotel.com.au Boutique hotel with 35 rooms in an ornate, restored 1890s pub building. Rooms have standard, unimaginative hotel décor, TV, en suite, minibar, some with verandah. Also a bar, café and restaurant. **B** *The Alderney*, 193 Hay St, East Perth. T92225 6600, www.alderney.com.au, has over 60 new, very comfortably furnished, self-contained apartments. Each has double and twin bedrooms. Indoor pool and gym, and undercover parking are included. **B** *New Esplanade*, 18 The Esplanade, T9325 2000, www.newesplanade.com.au Modern hotel with attractive rooms, some great views and an almost perfect location. Also underground parking. **B-D** *Northbridge Hotel*, corner of Lake St and Brisbane St, Northbridge. T9328 5254, www.hotelnorth bridge.com.au Renovated old corner hotel with wraparound verandah. Luxurious hotel rooms (50) with spa and full facilities, bar and mid-range restaurant. Also 20 comfortable budget doubles in the old part of the hotel with shared facilities, TV and fridge. **B** *Sullivans*, 166 Mounts Bay Rd, West Perth. T9321 8022, www.sullivans.com.au Just below Kings Park, this comfortable, modern hotel has 68 rooms (some with balcony and river views) and 2 apartments. Also swimming pool, free bikes, parking and café. Convenient location, free city bus (Blue CAT) at door.

C *Amber Rose*, 102 Bagot Rd, Subiaco. T9382 3669, www.amberrose.com.au 2 fresh and elegant rooms, both with en suite and tea/coffee facilties, in a large 1915 house. Shared guest sitting room and garden breakfast room. 10-min walk to heart of

Subi. Good value. **C** *Caesia House*, 32 Thomas St, Nedlands. T9389 8174, www.caesiahouse.com Comfortable modern house with 2 en suite rooms. Garden pool, excellent breakfast and very knowledgable hosts, particularly on nearby Kings Park and its flora. **C** *Perth City*, 200 Hay St, T9220 7000, www.perthcity.com.au One of Perth's newest hotels, the staff are friendly and the furnishings bright and cheerful. **C** *Riverview*, 42 Mount St, West Perth. T9321 8963, www.riverview.au.com Stylish, well-equipped studio apartments, all with balconies or patio gardens. Good quality and value for couples. **C** *Rose Moore*, 2 Winifred St, Mosman Park. T9384 8214. Pretty wooden cottage in a lovely garden. Quiet street but close to Stirling Highway and Cottesloe. Country-style en suite rooms and cooked breakfast. **C** *Sanno Perth*, Brearley Av, T9277 7777, is a well-placed if very ordinary motel by the main turn-off to the domestic airport terminal.

D *Jewell House YMCA*, 180 Goderich St, T9325 8488, www.ymcajewellhouse.com, a tower block with over 200 clean and cheerful rooms, all including linen. Most floors are single sex. There is free off-street parking and a cafeteria supplies seriously cheap breakfasts and dinners, 0700-0900 and 1730-1900, open to non-residents. **D** *Mountway*, 36 Mount St, West Perth. T9321 8307, www.mountwayunits.com.au, Considerably less glamorous than its neighbouring high-rise apartment blocks, self-contained units overlook the freeway and city. Kitchens are basic, the traffic noise can be considerable and there's no a/c, but they are fairly spacious, all have balconies and facilities include $3 per hr internet and off-street parking.

Perth orientation

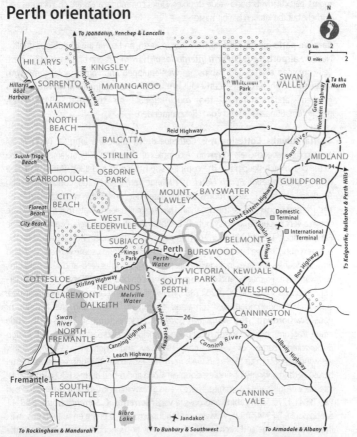

Northbridge has been troubled in the last 5 years or so by street gangs. It feels perfectly safe to visit and most of the backpacker hostels are located here so it is full of travellers but it's wise to take a few precautions Also consider staying in the excellent hostels in Fremantle or Cottesloe

Backpacker hostels **D-E** *Brittania International YHA*, 253 William St, T9328 6121, brittannia@yhawa.com.au An older crowd and families stay at this large, clean and comfortable hostel with 160 beds. Excellent kitchen and dining facilities but no parking. **D-E** *Governor Robinson*, 7 Robinson Av, T9328 3200, www.govrobinsons.com.au Boutique hostel occupies 100-year old cottages and a sympathetic extension in a very quiet street, 10 mins walk from the centre. Fresh, light rooms and linen, backpack-sized lockers, classy bathrooms. Doubles, (some en suite), are of hotel standard. No pickups, street parking. **D-E** *Hay Street Backpackers*, Hay St, T9221 9880, haystreetbackpackers@hotmail.com Relatively small, well-maintained hostel with 80 beds in dorms, singles and doubles, some en suite. Clean spacious rooms, swimming pool and a/c, also good on diving advice. **D-E** *Northbridge YHA*, 46 Francis St, T9328 7794. One of the best in central Northbridge, this 100-bed hostel is colourful and lively with a lovely spacious outdoor courtyard full of couches and tables. Regular BBQs and football games. Bike hire $15 day. Staff are willing to help you find work. **D** *Townsend Lodge*, 240 Adelaide Terr, T9325 4143, www.townsend.wa.edu.au Mostly used for student accommodation, the friendly *Townsend* has 60 single rooms on separate male and female floors. Lots of facilities include off-street parking and courtyard BBQ. Price drops by a third for stays of 3 nights or more. **D-E** *Underground*, 268 Newcastle St, T9228 3755. Excellent and central hostel with swimming pool, bar, well-equipped kitchen and spacious internet and guest area. Clean and friendly. 24 hr reception. Parking. **E** *Exclusive Backpackers*, 158 Adelaide Terr, T9221 9991, exclusiv@pielink.com, verges on a boutique hotel for the quality of its 10 rooms, particularly its good-value doubles. Quiet communal areas are characterful and homely, but the kitchen is a bit basic.

Caravan parks are few and far between in Perth, and some are of dubious quality. Near the **airport**, the **C-D** *Perth International*, however, is one of the country's best. Self-contained chalets and cabins are well-equipped and comfortable, some with spas, others with the budget-conscious in mind, the grounds immaculate, the facilities excellent, and nothing is too much trouble for the staff. T9453 6677, perthinternational@bigpond.com Recommended.

Coastal suburbs Cottesloe A-B *Cottesloe Beach Chalets*, 6 John St, T9383 5000, www.cottesloebeachchalets.com.au A complex of 30 modern, self-contained flats close to the beach each sleeping 5. The complex also has a pool and BBQs. Price covers 1-5 people. **B-C** *Cottesloe Beach Hotel*, 104 Marine Terr, T9383 1100, cbh@wasp.net.au Art-deco hotel with 13 small rooms. Slightly dated but comfortable with standard facilities. The best rooms (6) face the ocean and have a small balcony. Note that the rooms are above a very popular and noisy pub. **D-E** *Ocean Beach Backpackers*, corner of Marine Par and Eric St, T9384 5111, www.obh.com.au A stylish, modern hostel owned by the pub next door, this is a fine place to relax. Light, spacious dorms, some with sea view and en suite doubles. Facilities include in-house café, bike, scooter, jeep, and surfboard hire, daily van run to Fremantle and city, airport pickups on booking. **Hillarys A** Hillarys Harbour Resort, 68 Southside Dr, T9262 7888, www.hillarysresort.com.au, has well furnished, comfortable and modern self-contained apartments overlooking the harbour or pool. **Scarborough B-E** *Mandarin Gardens*, 20 Wheatcroft St, T9245 1838. Wide range of accommodation to suit most budgets, including backpacker dorms. **D-E** *Indigo Backpackers*, corner of West Coast Highway and Brighton St, T9245 3388, www.indigonet.com.au A 5-min walk from The Esplanade, this unpretentious hostel has 60 beds in a variety of singles, doubles, 4-bed and 6-bed dorms. BBQ garden area, internet café, bike and board hire. There is also a caravan park, **C-D** *Star Haven*, 18 Pearl Par, T9341 1770, with cabins and on-site vans. **Sorrento C** *Sorrento House B&B*, 11 Sandpiper St, T/F9447 0995, www.sorrentohouse.com.au 2 bright en suite rooms sharing a private lounge and kitchenette. Very friendly hosts, good facilities and use of the family pool. Recommended. About 4 km inland from Hillarys are 2 **caravan parks**, both close to Wanneroo Rd. *Cherokee Village*, 10 Hocking Rd, T9409 9039, has self-contained cabins, some en suite. *Kingsway Tourist Park*, corner Kingsway and Wanneroo Rd, T9409 9267, has chalets and smaller cabins.

Eating in Perth is characterized by location rather than cuisine; it is overwhelmingly an outdoor scene that makes the most of a stable, sunny climate. Many restaurants have very little indoor space and every eating area is crammed with pavement tables or open terraces. Despite the isolation, the food is fresh and varied. Seafood is very good and Asian or Italian food is very popular.

Eating
● *On map*
See also Pubs & bars,
page 531

Expensive *Altos*, 424 Hay St, Subiaco, T9382 3292. Dark, atmospheric dining room suited to the serious business of eating top-quality cuisine. The menu is tight on choice, but supported by a considerable wine list. Open 1200-2200 Mon-Fri, 1700-2230 Sat. *Balthazar*, 6 The Esplanade, T9421 1206. Indulgent wine bar and restaurant, modern metal and wood architecture. Mediterranean influenced food is matched by the music and supported by an extensive wine list. Also a cheap bar menu. Open 1130-2230 Mon-Fri, 1800-2230 Sat. Recommended. *Fraser's*, Fraser Av, T9481 7100, has for years been one of the city's best. The quality has slipped in the last few years but it's still pretty impressive. Cuisine is modern Australian, predominantly seafood, with a few grills, and it's supported by an extensive, quality wine list. Buffet breakfasts 0700-1000, 0730 Sun, lunch 1200-1500, dinner 1800-2200. *Grand View*, 3rd floor, 12 The Esplanade, T9325 2344. One of Perth's best Chinese restaurants, with great views across parkland to the Swan Bells and the river, and an extensive menu. Open 1200-1430 and 1800-2200. *Jojo's*, Broadway Jetty, Nedlands, T9386 8757. One of Perth's finest water-view restaurants, with a sophisticated dining room and a few tables on the jetty boardwalk. The menu is seafood heaven, complemented by a quality, WA-orientated wine list. Open 1200-1500 Wed-Fri, Sun and daily 1800-2200. Their adjacent café is slightly cheaper and far less formal. Open daily for breakfast and lunch, 0800-1100 and 1130-1500.

Mid-range *Buddhabar*, 88 Rokeby Rd, Subiaco, T9382 2941. Hip Indian that puts as much creativity into its music and surrounds as its curries. Relaxed and friendly, their late-night 'supper clubs' give a whole new cultured meaning to a late-night curry. Open 1200-1430 Thu-Sat, 1800-2200 Tue-Sun, 2300-1300 Fri-Sat. *Café Bocca*, Shafto Lane, T9226 4030. Stylish, contemporary Italian in a lovely shady courtyard by a tranquil fountain. Most tables outdoors. Mon-Thu 0730-1530, Fri 0730-2200. *Dusit Thai*, 249 James St, T9328 7647. Elegant and ornate Thai serving consistently fresh and creative food. Licensed and BYO. Thu-Fri 1200-1400, Tue-Sun 1800-2100. *Emperors Court*, 66 Lake St, T9328 8860. The city's best Cantonese restaurant in soothingly dim and calming rooms. Seafood and Cantonese claypots are specialities. Mon-Fri 1100-1500, Sat-Sun 1000-1500. Daily 1730-2300. *Kailis Bros Fish Café*, 101 Oxford St, Leederville, T9443 6300. An unusual but elegant seafood restaurant that shares an open space with a fresh-fish market. Greek mezze plates, dips and wonderful seafood platters. Daily 0830-2130. *Oriel*, 483 Hay St, Subiaco, T9382 1886. A quality, licensed, 24-hr eatery and a Subi institution. Breakfast is 0100-1130, and 'lunch' is served 1200-2445. A wide ranging menu that includes everything from a sandwich to scotch fillet, and the cakes are superb. *Simon's Seafood*, 73 Francis St, T9227 9055. Long-established and comfortable restaurant serving the freshest of fish and seafood in very traditional ways. Good-value set menus. Licensed and BYO. Mon-Fri 1200-1430, Mon-Sat 1800-2100.

Cheap *Annalakshmi*, 1st floor, 12 The Esplanade, T9221 3003. A friendly Indian vegetarian buffet with views over to Swan Bells and the river. All profits go to charity and, unusually, you simply pay what you feel you can afford. Open 1200-1430 Mon-Fri, 1830-2130 Mon-Sat. No alcohol allowed. *Emporium*, 114 Rokeby Rd,

Subiaco, T9388 3077. Large eat-in or take-away seafood restaurant and fish and chip shop. Some seriously cheap lunch specials, also Greek salads. Open 1100-1500 Mon-Sat, 1700-2100 daily. *Hans*, Hay St (next to *Elizabeth's* bookshop). A slightly scruffy casual spot that is always packed for its good value Thai, Japanese and Chinese dishes. *Hare Krishna Food for Life*, 200 William St. A bargain for vegetarians, the Hare Krishnas offer an all-you-can-eat buffet for $6 of curry, pasta, chutneys, desserts and drinks. Daily 1200-1430. Take-away only $2 between 1700 and 1800. *Il Padrino Caffé*, 198 William St, T9227 9065. Welcoming and casual Italian, lined with owner Nunzio's claims to fame. He was voted the world's best pizza maker in 2001 in an international contest. Also makes pretty mean pasta and traditional meat-based dishes. Good value specials every Tue. Tue-Fri 1100-1500, 1700-2100, Sat 1700-2100. *Jaws Kaiten Sushi*, Hay St Mall. A true sushi bar with seats in a horseshoe facing the dishes whizzing past on the conveyor belt. Always a busy lunch spot for office workers. Daily 1130-1800. *Kafeneon*, 31A Hampden Ave, Nedlands, T9386 6181. Charming and long-established Greek restaurant with quiet, garden tables, warm service and delicious *spanokopita*. Tue-Fri 1200-1430, Tue-Sat 1800-2100. *Lotus Vegetarian*, 220 James St, T9228 2882. A buffet with veggie versions of Chinese, Indian and Malaysian favourites. The surroundings are fairly simple but its' good value food with friendly service. Lunch $1150, dinner $14 (Fri-Sat $17). Thu-Sun 1130-1430 Tue-Sun 1800-2100. *Maya Masala*, corner of Lake St and Francis St, T9328 5655. Wonderful Indian food in quite groovy, contemporary style. Prices are almost too good to be true, especially for the thali at $12.50. Licensed and BYO. Tue-Sun 1130-1430, 1730-2100. Recommended. *Mezzonine*, 49 King St, T9481 1148. Lively and modern café and restaurant open to the street with a rooftop terrace, attracts trendy arts and fashion crowd. Casual modern Australian dishes, coffee and papers. Live jazz on Thu night. *Pronto*, 16 Bay View Terr, Claremont, T9284 6090. Always buzzing for its clever combination of effusive, charming service, colourful smart room and good value pizzas and pasta. Mon-Sat 0730-2200. *Viet Hoa*, 349 William St, T9328 2127. Vietnamese and Chinese in this large, businesslike restaurant. Always very busy and great value. Most dishes under $10. Daily 1000-2200.

There are several food courts in the city and Northbridge which are cheap but can also be dim, messy and crowded. *Old Shanghai*, on James St, has a good range of Asian stalls. Tue-Thu 1100-2200, Fri-Sun 1100-2300. There is a good one upstairs in the City Arcade with an outdoor terrace overlooking Murray St Mall.

Coastal suburbs City Beach *Oceanus*, T9385 7555, which hangs over the beach and has floor-to-ceiling windows overlooking the ocean. Daily 1200-1430 and 1800-2130. You musn't miss *Blue Duck*, 151 Marine Par, **Cottesloe**, T9385 2499. The café hangs above the beach with mesmerising views. Particularly good for breakfast, light lunches include wood-fired pizzas and inventive salads (cheap), more emphasis on fish and seafood for mid-range dinner. Daily 0630-2000. Recommended. **Floreat Beach** Relaxed beachside café, the *Costa Azzurra*, T9285 0048, serves a range of cheap, light Mediterranean meals from 0700-2200 in summer, 0900-2100 in winter. In summer their Latino dance evenings on Wed give you the chance to strut your stuff. There are nearly 20 eating options on **Hillarys** Boat Harbour Quay, from ice-cream parlours to upmarket restaurants. *Spinnakers*, 95 Northside Dr, T9203 5266, ploughs its lone furrow on the 'opposite' side of the harbour to all the rest. Its great position is enhanced by friendly service, fresh, simple meals and a bright, cheerful décor. Open 0700 and for breakfast, with lunch 1100-1500. Coffee and terrific cakes to 1730. Recommended. Good restaurants outside the **Scarborough**'s *Rendezous* complex include the expensive traditional Italian *Brighton Beach*, corner of The Esplanade and Brighton St, T9341 8699, and earthy Italian café *Villa Bianchi*, corner of The Esplanade and Scarborough Beach Rd, daily 0700-2230.

Bocelli, a large and bustling outdoor café in the heart of Forrest Pl this is a good place for a casual bite while watching the crowds. Gourmet sandwiches, cakes, drinks, also breakfasts. Daily until 1800 (2100 Fri). *Coffee Beans Express*, Francis St, next to the post office. A rare lunch bar where you can grab a basic toasted sandwich or a drink from the fridge, with sunny yellow chairs for patrons on the plaza. Mon-Fri 0600-1700. *Dôme*, 201 Trinity Arcade (corner of St Georges Terr). A successful chain that aims for a French bistro feel. All-day breakfasts, light meals, cakes and decent coffee in a long breezy room overlooking St Georges Terr. There's another branch on James St. *Merchant Tea and Coffee Company*, 183 Murray St Mall. An elegant respite from the mall, lined with dark wood and with cool, high ceilings. Sandwiches, cakes and coffee ordered at the counter. Also pavement tables. Daily 0700-1900 (0900 Sun). *Mount Street Café*, 42 Mount St, T9485 1411, has a bit of a monopoly in this part of Perth, but is by no means complacent. The front terrace is a pleasant place to hang out with a coffee and the excellent mid-range food is fresh and healthy. Open 0730-1700 daily, to 2200 Fri. *Cino to Go*, 136 Oxford St, Leederville, T9242 4688. A small and lively café with excellent coffee, cakes and pannini, daily 0700-2300. Also good is the similar *Oxford 130* next door, daily 0630-2400. *Walk Café*, 5 Forrest Walk, Subiaco. Cool, contemporary and relaxed with plenty of outside tables. Light lunches have a Greek slant and come in big helpings. Open 0730-1800.

Cafés
● On map
Many cafés stay open later on Fri night

City centre The *Grosvenor Hotel*, corner of Hay St and Hills St, T9325 3799. Old pub featuring original live music Thu-Sat evenings and acoustic Sun afternoons. The *Lucky Shag*, Barrack St Jetty, T9221 6011. Casual, contemporary bar. Laid-back cover bands Fri-Sat evenings, live jazz Sun afternoon. The very British *Moon and Sixpence*, 300 Murray St, is popular with backpackers wanting a drink in the sun. **Northbridge** *Aberdeen*, 84 Aberdeen St, T9227 9361. Serious posing joint crammed with sexy young things on Fri-Sat nights. Mon, Wed, Fri and Sat only. *Brass Monkey*, corner of William St and James St, T9227 9596. Northbridge's classiest pub and a distinctive landmark, built in 1897. Mellow old front bar, quiet courtyard seats and the Tap Room for serious beer drinkers and sports watchers. Excellent brasserie upstairs and sophisticated wine bar, *Grapeskin* next door. *Court*, 50 Beaufort St, T9328 5292. Gay venue with DJs 6 nights a week, live shows and karaoke. Also pool tables, bar snacks and a beer garden. *Elephant and Wheelbarrow*, 53 Lake St, T9228 4433. British-style pub popular with backpackers. About 15 British and Irish beers on tap, live covers and retro music Wed-Sun, cheap pub grub and a pleasant shady terrace. *Universal Wine Bar*, 221 William St, T9227 6711. Hip without being slick. Live blues and jazz every night. Mon-Fri 1130-2400, Sat 1600-0200. **Inner suburbs** *Leederville*, 742 Newcastle St, T9444 8388, is known for its heaving Sunday sessions in the beer garden with live music, podium dancing and 5 bars. *RedRock*, 1 Bay View Terr, Claremont, T9384 0977. Trendy corner pub with a large posing terrace and lots of standing space, attracts style-conscious yuppies. Live music Thu-Sun, usually funk, swing, jazz or DJ. Free pool on Sun. *Subiaco Hotel*, corner of Rokeby Rd and Hay St, T9381 3069. Large historic hotel refurbished in smart, contemporary style, and now the social hub of Subi. 3 main areas comprise: the edgy public bar, serving up seriously cheap counter meals, 1200-2300, and R'n'B cover bands Thu, Sat, DJs Fri; lounge bar littered with comfy sofas and easy chairs; and the cheery *Subiaco Café*, the hotel's upmarket, mid-range terrace restaurant. A jazz band plays in the latter on Wed and Sat nights. Café meals 0700-2345. **Cottesloe** *Cottesloe Beach Hotel*, 104 Marine Terr. The mustard-coloured, art-deco *Cott* has an ocean-facing balcony (although the view is not quite as good as the OBH) and a contemporary stylish bar. The session is most popular here and the pub has live music Wed-Sat. The pub also has an ATM and a pleasant colourful café, daily 0700-2200. *Ocean Beach Hotel*, corner of Marine Pde and Eric St. The long back bar has pool tables but the front bar is the one to head for at sunset.

Pubs & bars
● On map
Cottesloe is renowned for its 'Sunday session' in the extensive beer gardens of the 'Cott' or the 'OBH'

Western Australia

Entertainment

Also see the clubbing website, www.tekno scape.com.au

Cinema Screening details are published daily in the *West Australian* newspaper. *Ace Cinema*, 500 Hay St, Subiaco T9388 6500. *Cinema Paradiso*, 164 James St, North-bridge. T9227 1771. Art-house features. *Hoyts Cinecentre*, corner of Murray St and Bar-rack St, City centre. T9325 2844. Mainstream releases. *Imax*, 14 Lake St, Northbridge, T9328 0600. Large format IMAX films. *Luna*, 155 Oxford St, Leederville. T9444 4056, www.lunapalace.com.au Mainstream and alternative features. *Windsor Twin*, 98 Stirling Highway, Nedlands T9386 3554. Old-fashioned, small art-house cinema. One of the best things to do in Perth is to see a film at an **outdoor cinema**. Season limited to summer only. *Luna Outdoor Nextdoor* in Leederville aims to screen films that can't be seen elsewhere such as Japanese horror or cult skate flicks. *Somerville Auditorium* at UWA, T9380 1732, and *Joondalup Picture Garden*, T8400 5888, at Edith Cowan University in Joondalup both screen art-house and foreign films from the Perth Interna-tional Arts Festival (Jan-Mar). *Sunset Cinema*, Kings Park, screens popular favourites and cult classics (Jan-Mar).

Clubs *Connections*, 81 James St, T9328 1870. A Perth institution, this welcoming gay club has been running for 25 years and promises 'disco glory'. Tue-Sat 2200-late, Sun from 2100. Free entry for first hour. *Hip-E Club*, corner of Newcastle and Oxford St (rear of Leederville Village), T9227 8899, www.hipeclub.com.au '60s and '70s psychedelica and backpacker specials. Tue-Sun from 2000. *Club Red Sea*, 83 Rokeby Rd, Subiaco, T9382 2022. Laid-back music bar playing familiar dance tracks from the mid-90s to present. A safe and relaxed haunt of the 25-30 crowd, it gets very busy and often only members get in. Call ahead during the day to secure entry. Open Fri-Sat from 2100. *Metro City*, 146 Roe St, Northbridge, T9228 0500, is a huge commercial dance club with 10 bars and a 18-25 crowd. $10 entry. Try *Rise*, 139 James St, or *The Church*, 69 Lake St, for trance, techno and house.

For smaller venues see Pubs & bars on page 531

Live music The *Entertainment Centre* on Wellington St is a venue for large shows, music concerts and sporting events. Tickets from the box office or *Ticketmaster7*. *Perth Concert Hall*, 5 St Georges Terr, T9231 9900. The main venue for classical perfor-mances, particularly from the West Australian Symphony Orchestra. Check listings papers for more venues. The main ticket agent in Perth for all kinds of events and per-formances is *Ticketmaster7*, info T1900 933666, bookings T136100, www.ticket master7.com Ask for the nearest retail outlet.

Theatre *His Majesty's*, 825 Hay St, T9265 0912, is a beautiful Edwardian theatre and the state's main venue. Also home of the WA Ballet and WA Opera companies. *Playhouse*, 3 Pier St, 9325 3355. Home of the Perth Theatre Company, producing contemporary and classic works with local and national performers. *Yirra Yaakin*, 65 Murray St, T9202 1966. A Noongar company that produces Aboriginal theatre using Aboriginal writers, directors, designers and production staff. *Subiaco Theatre Cen-tre*, 180 Hammersley Rd, T9382 3385. A major venue set in lovely gardens near the top of Rokeby Rd. A 300-seat auditorium and smaller studio performance space. Theatre tickets are usually handled by *BOCS Ticketing*, T9484 1133, www.bocsticketing.com.au BOCS ticket outlets at the Perth Concert Hall, His Maj-esty's Theatre, Playhouse Theatre and Subiaco Theatre Centre.

Festivals & events

Perth has just one major festival and lacks major sporting events due to its small population. Most events are held during spring and summer

The main arts event of the year, held around **Jan-Feb**, is the *Perth International Arts Festival*, which includes the best local and international theatre, opera, dance, visual arts and music. A film festival is also part of the programme, held outdoors from **Dec-Mar** at the Somerville at UWA and Joondalup Pines at Edith Cowan University. For more deatils check out www.perthfestival.com.au A *Fringe Festival* is also held at the same time as the main arts festival, see www.wafringe.com.au The *Artrage Festival* is another good alternative arts festival. It includes theatre, dance, music, street perform-ers, comedy and visual arts, and is held in Perth and Fremantle during **Dec**. A popular sporting event, the *Hopman Cup*, is a tennis championship that attracts some big tennis names, held in **early Jan**. Later in the year, look out for the *Avon Descent*, a 133-km white-water competition on the Avon River from Northam to Perth, held in early Aug. The *Kings Park Wildflower Festival* is held over 10 days in **late Sep**.

Perth's compact shopping area consists of the parallel Hay St and Murray St malls and the arcades connecting them. The shopping also contines west along Hay St as far as King St, which is a trendy pocket of fashion and homewares shopping, galleries and cafes.The city has 2 major department stores, *Myers* in Forrest Pl, and *David Jones* occupying a block between the malls. These both sell almost everything and have excellent food halls.

Shopping
General shopping hours are Monday-Saturday 0900-1730; late-night shopping until 2100 in the city on Friday, and in the suburbs and Fremantle on Thursday

On Sunday, city hours are 1200-1800, Fremantle 1000-1600

Art and craft Craftwest Gallery, 357 Murray St, T9226 2161. A gallery and shop featuring the very best of contemporary Australian design, including ceramics, glass work, jewellery, textiles, sculpture and wood work. Recommended. Mon-Thu 0900-1730, Fri 0900-2100, Sat 0900-1700. *Creative Native*, 32 King St, T9322 3398. Large commercial Aboriginal art gallery. Also some good books on Aboriginal art.

Books and maps The main chains are *Dymocks* and *Angus and Robertson*, both have branches in the Hay St Mall and can be found in suburban shopping centres. *All Foreign Language Bookshop*, 101 William St, T9485 1246. Mon-Sat 0900-1700. A good range of guide books as well as books in over 100 languages. *Arcane Bookshop*, 212 William St, Northbridge, T9328 5073. A small jewel with literary fiction, film, drama, feminist and gay titles. *Elizabeth's Second-hand Bookshop*, 820 Hay St, T9481 8848. Perth's best second-hand range, also suburban branches. *Map World*, 900 Hay St, T9322 5733. Maps and guide books for every state and country. Full range of topographic maps, also bike maps, and Bibbulman and Cape-to-Cape track maps.

Clothes The best clothes shopping is found in the boutiques of Subiaco and Claremont. Surf and swimwear outlets are everywhere, the largest range can be found at Vidlers, 14 Station St, Cottesloe. *Elements*, 375 Hay St, has a great range of brightly coloured separates and downstairs a factory outlet with some serious bargains, particularly boardshorts and 1-piece swimsuits. *Outback Red*, Plaza Arcade, and *R.M. Williams*, upstairs in the Carillion Arcade, both sell rugged country wear such as boots, hats and moleskins.

Food and drink *Kakulas Brothers*, 183 William St, Northbridge. T9328 5744. A cornucopia of groceries and delicatessen food such as cheese, meats, nuts and dried fruit. *Lamont's*, corner of St Georges Terr and King St, T9321 9928. Gourmet food and wine products, also the best quality take-aways – Mediterranean-influenced pasta, salad, risotto, sandwiches and cakes. Picnic hampers can be ordered (before 1500) and delivered. Mon-Fri 0700-1900.

Jewellery The city centre is awash with jewellery shops. One of the best is *Rosendorf's*, 673 Hay St Mall, for Argyle diamonds, Broome pearls and Australian opal in a classy environment. For silver jewellery in the city there is none better than *Antiku*, City Arcade. For cheaper imported jewellery try the Subiaco or Fremantle markets.

Markets The king of Perth markets is actually to be found in Fremantle but the runners up would be the popular weekend markets in Subiaco. These markets are all fairly permanent well-established affairs. *Canning Vale Markets*, 280 Bannister Rd, Canning Vale, just east of Jandakot airport. Huge flea-market with 100s of stalls. Sun 0700-1400. During the week this is Perth's wholesale market for meat, fish, flowers and fruit and veg. *Pavilion Market*, 2 Rokeby Rd, Subiaco. Indoor market with about 50 stalls selling jewellery, clothing, leather, pottery. Also a good food hall. Open Thu-Fri, 1000-2100, Sat-Sun 1000-1700.

Outdoor *Kathmandu*, 884 Hay St, and *Paddy Pallins*, 895 Hay St (opposite *Map World*). For cheaper gear try *Shimensons Budget Backpacker Supplies*, 148 William St, T9321 8784, or *Midland Army Navy Disposal*, 360 Murray St. Also army surplus stores

Western Australia

on corner of Wellington St and Pier St. *Mainpeak*, 415 Hay St, Subiaco, T9388 9072, www.mainpeak.com.au Well-stocked store, strong on local knowledge. Trekking slide-shows year-round, also *hire* of almost all gear except boots. Maps for Bibbulmun and Cape to Cape tracks. They have another store at 31 Jarrad St, Cottesloe, T9385 2552, which also hires out sea-kayaks.

Sport   **Diving**   *Diving Ventures*, T9228 2630, www.dventures.com.au, run PADI courses and dive trips to Rottnest. **Golf**   Perth has many excellent courses that welcome visitors and have relatively low fees. *Burswood Park*, Burswood Casino Complex, Great Eastern Highway, T9362 7576. Great city views and central location. Green fees $13 for 9 holes, $22 for 18 holes ($5 more Sat-Sun). Also equipment hire. *Vines Resort*, Verdelho Dr, Swan Valley, T9297 0777. A 36-hole championship course along the banks of Ellen Brook, good facilities nearby at the resort. Hosts the Heineken Classic in late Jan/early Feb, Australia's richest tournament. *Wembley*, The Boulevard, Floreat, T9484 2500. A couple of 18-hole layouts, also driving range, pro shop and bar. **Fitness and swimming**   *Beatty Park*, Vincent St, North Perth, T9273 6080. Gym and 3 pools (25 m, 30 m, 50 m). *Challenge Stadium*, Stephenson Av, Mount Claremont, 9441 8222. Heated indoor 50-m swimming and diving pools. Also fitness centre, basketball court and café. **Kitesurfing**   This rapidly-growing sport of surfing harnessed to a parachute offers awesome power and speed. Lessons from *Choice Kitesurfing*, T0438 382638, choicekitesurfing@yahoo.com. Beginners $100 for 2 hrs, Int/Adv $80 hr. **Parasailing**   *South Perth Parasailing*, Mill Point Rd, T0408 382 595, skyflightparasail@hotmail.com. Daily in summer. **Sailing**   *Funcats*, Coode St Jetty, T0408 926003, www.funcats.com.au Surfcat hire for $23 hr, free tuition. Daily 0930-1830, Sep-May. **Waterskiing**   *Wake Up WA*, Narrows Bridge, South Perth, T0402 476487. Waterskiing, wakeboarding and kneeboarding is $20 for 15 mins, tuberiding $10 for 10 mins. Tue-Sun 0800 to sunset, Nov-Apr.

Spectator sport   **AFL (Australian Rules)** The *West Coast Eagles* and the *Fremantle Dockers* both play at the Subiaco Oval. Each have home games, once a fortnight on either a Sat or Sun, from the end of Mar to Aug. See www.afl.com.au for fixtures. Tickets from *Ticketmaster7*, T1300 136100. Tickets go on sale 2 weeks before a match and often sell out, so it pays to book. **Cricket**   The state side, the *Western Warriors*, play at the WACA during summer, and the ground also occasionally hosts international matches. Call T9265 7222, or see www.waca.com.au, for a programme. Contact *Ticketmaster7* for bookings.

Tours &   **Boat cruises**   Several companies operate cruises on the Swan River from the Barrack St
excursions   jetty, including *Boat Torque Cruises*, T9421 5888, www.boattorque.com.au (see also
See also Rottnest,   page 536), and *Captain Cook*, T9325 3341, www.captaincookcruises.com.au Cruises
page 543   range from short runs to Fremantle, lunch and dinner cruises (around $45-85), to gourmet wine-tasting trips upriver to Swan Valley ($100). The paddle boat *Decoy*, T9581 2383, steams out every Sun in summer, 1400-1700, for a jazz cruise. *Aqwa* at Hillarys runs summer trips to the seals and dolphins in local Marmion Marine Park (2 hrs, 0800 and 1030, Thu-Fri, Sun, $85), and day-long snorkelling expeditions to **Rottnest** (0800 Mon, Wed, Sat, $155). *Mills Charters*, T9246 5334, head out deep-sea fishing most days depending on demand at 0630 ($100), and also offer 3-hr whale-watching trips ($30, children $15). **Bus and minibus** *Planet Perth*, T9225 6622, www.planetperth.com.au, have a couple of local options, including an afternoon in Swan Valley ($40) and an evening BBQ tour to Caversham Wildlife Park ($40), as well as pre-arranged trips further afield. *Super Roo*, T9367 5465, super_roo@iprimus.com.au, head out every Mon, Wed and Fri on a backpacker- orientated whizz around Kings Park, the coastal suburbs and Swan Valley ($95). *Swan Gold*, T9451 5333, www.swangold.com, run a variety of trips including Swan Valley, the Avon Valley and a summer run to Penguin Island. **Camping** *Active Safaris* and

Aussie Outback Safaris, T9593 4464, aussie_outback_safaris@hotmail.com, offer 4-day west coast trips up as far as Monkey Mia for $385, departing Fri and Tue respectively. *All Terrain Safaris*, T9295 6680, www.allterrain.com.au, have a range of west coast tours, some one-way, starting with a 5-day trip that goes as far as Coral Bay ($695). **Cycling** *WA Cycle Tours*, T9381 3441, www.wacycletours.com.au, focus on Perth, Fremantle and the Swan Valley, with self-guided or guided options. *WA Mountain Bike Tours*, T/F9295 1716, head out into the forests of the Perth Hills for day or half-day guided trips. In Swan Valley, *Black Swan Tours*, T9296 2568, www.blackswan tours.com.au, offer a number of different options, geared toward small groups, as do *Out & About*, T9377 3376, oaat@multiline.com.au **Diving** The *Sorrento Quay Dive Shop*, Northside Dr, T9448 6343, www.sorrentoquaydive.com.au, has diving gear for hire (full kit $55 per day) and also organizes dives to both the Marmion Marine Park limestone reef (Thu-Fri, Sun, 2 hrs, $85 inc gear) and Rottnest (Sat, full day, $120). One-week PADI courses $450, snorkel hire $15 per day. At *Aqwa* you can arrange to scuba or snorkel with either the sharks or seals ($90). **Eco tours** CALM together with the UWA organize a number of research expeditions around WA each year where small numbers of the general public are invited to join them. Trips are around 6-10 days, costs are between $250-500 per day, and conditions are usually pretty basic. Locations are, however, incredible and activities usually revolve around turtle-tagging or the trapping and identification of many other marine and land-animal species. T9380 2433, www.naturebase.net **Farm stays and cabins** *Australian Adventure Travel*, T9248 2355, www.safaris.net.au, run 3- and 5-day tours up the west coast (Sat, $385 and Wed, $605). *Active Safaris*, T9450 7776, www.activesafaris.com.au, have a 2-day whizz around the southwest, staying in simple forest cabins ($242, departs Wed and, in spring, Sat). **4WD** *Explorer Tours*, T9361 0940, www.explorertours.com.au, specialize in following in the footsteps (albeit in air-conditioned 4WDs) of early WA explorers. Tours generally from 8 to 21 days, including the central desert, Mount Augustus and the Murchison, and the northwest. **Kayaking** *Kayaking Rivergods*, T9259 0749, www.rivergods.com au, head out daily Sep-Jun to Penguin Island off Rockingham to see the penguins and seals. Personalized canoeing and rafting trips also available. **Rafting** *Wildside Adventures*, T1300 886688, www.wildside.net.au, raft the local Avon, Murray (both Jun-Oct) and Collie rivers (dam-fed, so Oct-May only). Day trips $120-140, overnight adventures on the Collie $220. **Scenic flights** *Sunset Coast*, T9298 829, offer a range of flights from Jandakot Airport. 1-hr flight over Perth, Beaches and Rottnest is $110, min 2 people. **Skating** A foreshore hire-van at Scarborough hires in-line skates for $7 per hr or $18 per day, and it's the same price for bike hire. **Skydiving** *WA Skydiving Academy*, T1800 245066, www.waskydiving.com.au Tandem freefall from $190, assisted freefall with full training $425. **Surfing** *Bluewater*, 21 Scarborough Beach Rd, Scarborough, hires out bodyboards for $10 per day and sell snorkel gear and fishing tackle. *WA Surfaris*, bookings via T1800 016969, www.travellersclub.com.au, head down to the Cape-to-Cape region every Fri for a weekend of surfing, walking and sightseeing. Lessons included, $260.

There are over a dozen companies offering trips from 1 to 10 days around the WA coast and venturing inland. Most involve some degree of four-wheel driving and adventure activities. Make sure you ask around and chat to some of the operators before committing yourself. Ask about the average age and size of the tour group, the activity level, and details of the itinerary so you can be sure you will see and experience what you want to in a way that suits your ability and comfort level. *Pinnacle Tours*, T9221 5411, www.pinnacletours.com.au, are the most luxurious large operator, with several 1-day options to southwest destinations (around $130-140), 2- to 5-day tours around the southwest ($200 per day, 2-day Margaret River daily, other tours depart Sun-Tue), and 3- and 5-day trips (departing Fri and Mon) up the west coast ($150-200 per day). *Western Travel Bug*, T9204 4600, www.travelbug.com.au, make use of budget motels on their 2- to 6-day south-west tours ($120 per day). Departures 3 times a week, inc Sat.

Western Australia

Transport   **Air** *Skywest* operate direct flights daily to Albany, Esperance, Geraldton, Monkey Mia (Mon, Wed, Fri-Sat), Exmouth and Karratha (Mon-Wed, Fri). *Qantas* provide daily direct flights to Kalgoorlie, Karratha, Port Hedland and Broome. They also have daily flights to most state capitals (not Canberra or Hobart), Alice Springs and Ayers Rock. *Virgin Blue* fly daily to Adelaide and Melbourne.

Buses/trains The majority of services are run by the state-owned company *Westrail*, T131053, www.wagr.wa.gov.au, whose routes extend right around the southwest, east as far as **Norseman**, and north as far as **Geraldton** and **Meekatharra**. Their most useful rail services for the visitor are the Prospector line to **Toodyay**, **Northam** and **Kalgoorlie**, and the Australind line to **Bunbury**. There are a handful of other operators that may prove more convenient or cheaper. *South West Coachlines*, 3 Mounts Bay Rd, T9324 2333, have a couple of southern routes, including one terminating at **Dunsborough**, and another to **Manjimup**. *Perth Goldfields Express*, T9021 2954, head out to **Kalgoorlie** and then north to **Laverton**. *Integrity*, T9226 1339, www.integritycoachlines.com.au, run up the **Brand Highway** via **Geraldton** and **Coral Bay** to **Exmouth**. Given the sparsity of land transport in some parts of the state, *McCafferty's/Greyhound*, usually a considered an interstate operator only, provide a few further, very useful options. Their main GX620 northbound service leaves **Perth** at 1000, travels up the **Brand Highway** through **Geraldton**, stops at **Carnarvon** and **Port Hedland**, and continues on via **Broome** and **Kununurra** to **Katherine**. A separate service, GX683, heads up to **Exmouth** at 1830 Wed, Fri and Sun, calling at all the major coastal towns from **Cervantes** northward.

Backpacker buses   *Easyrider*, T9226 0307, www.easyriderbp.com.au, offer several 'jump-on, jump-off' options up to **Exmouth** and **Broome**, and around the southwest. *Nullarbor Traveller*, T1800 816858, info@the-traveller.com.au, run excellent 9 day adventure trips to **Adelaide** ($891), while *Remote Outback Cycle Tours*, T9279 6969, www.cycletours.com.au, offer superb 4WD and cycle combination tours to **Uluru** in NT ($900). The 6-day trip leaves about once a month May-Oct. For direct 4WD trips to **Alice Springs** contact *Travelabout*, T1800 621200, www.travelabout.au.com, who also head down to the southwest and up around the coast as far as **Darwin**. *Design a Tour*, T9841 7778, take 10 days to 4WD to Broome and includes Karijini ($1,500, departs Thu, Mar-Oct), while *West Coast Explorer*, T9418 8835, make it all the way to Darwin in18 days ($2,150, also departs Thu).

Interstate buses   *McCafferty's/Greyhound* have a daily coach to **Katherine** and **Darwin** (60 hrs) from Wellington St Bus Station at 1000. Their eastbound service to **Adelaide** (40 hrs) leaves at 1430 Mon, Wed and Fri.

Interstate train The *Indian Pacific*, T132147, www.gsr.com.au, heads out to **Adelaide** (43 hrs) and Sydney (70 hrs) at 1055 every Mon and Fri.

For maximum time at Rottnest leave early from Fremantle   **Ferry** Several companies operate ferries to Rottnest Island from the Barrack St Jetty, including *Boat Torque*, T9421 5888, www.boattorque.com.au, and *Oceanic Cruises*, T9325 1191, www.oceaniccruises.com.au Return fares around $55, children $20, with several departures a day from 0845. As well as the tourist ferries to Rottnest and up the Swan River, a regular ferry travels between Barrack St jetty and South Perth (Perth Zoo).

Directory   **Airlines** *Air New Zealand*, T132476. *British Airways*, 77 St Georges Terr, T9425 7711. *Garuda Indonesia*, 40 The Esplanade, T9481 0963. *Malaysia Airlines*, 56 William St, T9263 7007. *Qantas*, 55 William St, T9225 8282. *Royal Brunei*, 189 St Georges Terr, T9321 8757. *Singapore Airlines*, 178 St Georges Terr, T9265 0500. *Skywest*, Perth Domestic Airport, T131300. *South African Airways*, 68 St Georges Terr, T9322 7388. **Banks** The major banks have ATMs on Hay St Mall and Murray St Mall. They are also liberally located in all the central suburbs. *American Express*, Hay St Mall, T9261 2711. *Thomas Cook*, Hay St Mall, corner of Piccadilly Arcade. Mon-Fri 0845-1645, Sat 1000-1400. **Bike hire** Around

$15 a day. *About Bike Hire*, T9221 2665, www.aboutbikehire.com.au Causeway car park, Riverside Drive, East Perth. Mon-Sat 1000-1700, Sun 0900-1700. *Bike Force*, 391 Hay St, Subiaco, T9382 1663. **Car hire** *Bayswater*, T9325 1000, www.bayswatercarrental.com.au, are among the best-value operators in the city, though they do not have a depot at either airport terminal. **Communications** Internet free at *Alexander Library*, 1 hr only, bookings required T9427 3104. *Traveller's Club*, 499 Wellington St, T9226 0660. $2 per hr ($1 per hr 1700-1800). **Post Office** Forrest Pl. Mon-Fri 0800-1730, Sat 0900-1230, Sun 1200-1600. **Poste Restante** (take photo ID to collect mail) Mon-Fri 0800-1700. **Medical services** *Perth Medical Centre*, Hay St Mall, T9481 4342. Mon-Thu 0800-1800, Fri 0800-1700, Sat 0900-1500. Free with Medicare card. For specialist medical travel advice and vaccinations see the *TMVC* in Fremantle. *Royal Perth Hospital*, Wellington St, City, T9224 2244. *Sir Charles Gairdner*, Hospital Av, Nedlands, T9346 3333. **Dental** *Lifecare Dental*, Upper level, Perth train station. T9221 2777. Daily 0800-0800. *Medicare*, T132011. For claims or to register visit their city office in Wesley Arcade (upstairs) off William St or Hay St. **Police** 1 Hay St, East Perth, T9222 1048. **Taxi** *Black & White*, T131008, *Swan*, T131330.

Around Perth

Though the city of Perth itself may comes as a disappointment to some, there are some wonderful attractions close at hand. The old port of Fremantle is charm personified and Rottnest Island, once a penal settlement and now Perth's holiday playground, is just 20 km west of the city and feels a long way from the metropolitan commotion. Further afield, the region around Perth is less arresting than others in the state, although some places do stand out, such as the Pinnacles, York and New Norcia. The Swan Valley is Perth's very own wine region, less than an hour's drive from the city centre. To the east, beyond the Perth Hills, lies the fertile Avon Valley where some of the state's oldest colonial settlements can be found, including the charming town of York. Heading north into a more arid region, the sand dunes of Lancelin and the Pinnacles near Cervantes are well worth seeing at sunset and can be combined with a visit to the incongruous monastic settlement of New Norcia.

Fremantle

Founded at the same time as Perth, Fremantle – or 'Freo' as the locals call it – has kept the 19th-century buildings that the city has lost and as a result has retained its character and spirit. A strong community of immigrants and artists contribute to the port city's alternative soul and the lively atmosphere draws people from all over Perth, particularly at weekends. Many Southern Europeans have settled here and their simple Italian cafés have merged into the busy 'cappuccino strip' of the olive-tree-lined **South Terrace**. The **Fishing Boat Harbour** has become an alternative hub of eating and entertainment activity, and manages to mix some seriously good restaurants in with some of the country's biggest fish and chip shops. There are also many interesting sights here such as the Maritime Museum and the Roundhouse.

Colour map 7, grid B5 20 km from City centre, 7 km from Cottesloe

Airport The private *Airport Shuttle* runs between Perth airport and **Fremantle** approximately hourly from 0830-1715 and 2000-2330. Bookings essential, T9383 4115. Fares $15 single, groups from $9. A cheaper ($3.60, concessions $1.60) but much longer option from the domestic terminal is to take either the No 37 or 39 buses to the City Busport (see page 520) and change. A taxi will be around $40-50. **Bus** The main service between the City Busport and Fremantle is the 105 which runs every 30-60 mins, daily

Getting there
For further bus and train information see Getting around, page 520 or www.transperth. wa.gov.au, T136213

from at least 0900-2330 (45 mins). Single tickets $2.80, concession $1.30. **Train** The Fremantle Line runs between **Perth** and Fremantle via **Subiaco**, **Claremont** and **Cottesloe**. Services every 10-15 mins from 0530-1630 and every 30-60 mins from 1900-0200. Sun services at similar times from 0700-2400. The journey takes about 30 mins. Prices as per the bus.

Getting around
Nothing in Freo is more than a 15-min walk, and there are plenty of ways to get about

Bus As well as the many scheduled services, the free *Fremantle CAT* circles around the town in a figure of 8 that stretches from the railway station to the History Museum, and from **Victoria Quay** to south of the hospital. Buses leave every 10 mins or so, 0730-1830 Mon-Fri and 1000-1830 Sat-Sun. The main bus terminal is in front of the railway station. *Fremantle Tram Tours*, T9339 8719, make 3 runs a day between the **Town Hall** and **East St Jetty** (5 mins, $2.50), leaving at 1055, 1500 and 1525.

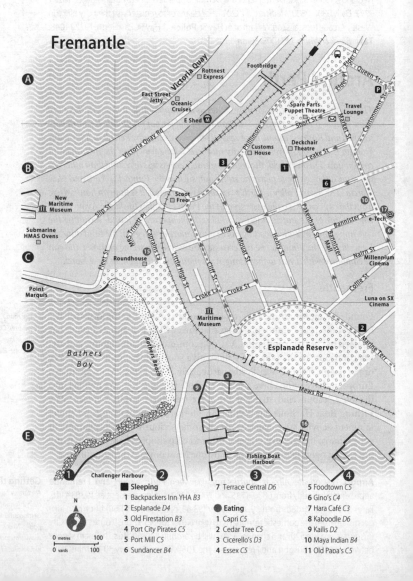

Fremantle

Sleeping ■		Eating ●	
1 Backpackers Inn YHA *B3*		1 Capri *C5*	7 Hara Café *C3*
2 Esplanade *D4*		2 Cedar Tree *C5*	8 Kaboodle *D6*
3 Old Firestation *B3*		3 Cicerello's *D3*	9 Kailis *D2*
4 Port City Pirates *C5*		4 Essex *C5*	10 Maya Indian *B4*
5 Port Mill *C5*	7 Terrace Central *D6*	5 Foodtown *C5*	11 Old Papa's *C5*
6 Sundancer *B4*		6 Gino's *C4*	

0 metres 100
0 vards 100

The *Travel Lounge*, 16 Market St, T9335 8776, www.thetravellounge.com.au, acts as a general booking agent but are also happy to provide information and advice to all travellers. Open daily 0700-2300. The **VIC** is located in the town hall in Kings Sq, T9431 7878, holzwart@wantree.com.au Open Mon-Fri 0900-1700, Sat 0900-1600, Sun 1200-1630.

Information
Also try:
www.freofocus.com.au

There are some interesting historic sights in Fremantle, listed below, but it is also well worth having a walk around the well-preserved port precinct of the 'west end'. Phillimore Street and Cliff Street and the surrounding streets contain some lovely Victorian buildings, such as the Customs House. The **Roundhouse**, Western Australia's oldest building and not actually round, was built in 1831 as a local lock-up. Too small for a penal establishment when British convicts later arrived, it finally fell into disuse around. ■ *Daily 1030-1530. Entry by gold coin donation. T9336 6897. Information room in the adjacent tea-rooms. Between High St and Bathers Bay.* The *Oberon* class submarine **HMAS Ovens**, was commissioned in 1969 and saw active service for over 25 years. Today it is in dry-dock and managed by the WA Maritime Museum. The submarine is in very much the state it was when decommissioned in 1995, giving a rare glimpse into the lives of the submariners who crewed it. ■ *Tours daily every 15-30 mins, 1100-1600 Fri-Sat, 1000-1600 Sun (1¼ hrs). Also Wed-Thu in school holidays. $8.80, children $3.30, concessions $5.50. T9430 6756, www.mm.wa.gov.au Slip St.*

Sights
Freo's sights are best reached on foot with plenty of refuelling café-stops
A huge new modern section of the Maritime Museum is due to open on Victoria Quay in 2003

Housed in a complex of old dock buildings the **Fremantle Maritime Museum** is primarily dedicated to the preservation and display of artefacts from the principal WA shipwrecks, mostly of the Dutch East India Company, and presents an interesting historical overview of European exploration of Australia's west coast. ■ *Daily 0930-1700. Free tours 1000, 1100, 1400, 1500. Entry by gold coin donation. T9431 8444, www.mm.wa.gov.au Corner Cliff St and Marine Terr.* Dating from 1852, **Fremantle Prison** was built as a replacement for the Roundhouse when it became clear that a much bigger prison would be required. Built by the first convict groups to be sent to Fremantle, it took about five years to construct. Such was the solidity of construction that the prison was still in use in 1991. Entry is by tour only,

12 Old Shanghai
Foodcourt *C5*
13 Pizza Bellaroma *C5*
14 Primavera *E5*
15 Tea at the
Roundhouse *C2*

● **Pubs & bars**
16 Little Creatures *E4*
17 Newport *B4*
18 Norfolk *C6*
19 Sail & Anchor *C5*

---- CAT Bus

Western Australia

but these are lively and informative, with a few surprises. If you have time, book onto one of the spooky night tours (usually about 1900) as these are even more entertaining. ■ *Tours daily every 30 mins 1000-1700 (1¼ hrs). $14.30, children $7.15, concessions $11. Night tours $17, children $8.80, concessions $13.20. Information room free, open 0900-1700. T9430 7177. The Terrace, behind Fremantle Oval.* **Fremantle History Museum and Arts Centre** is an impressive but imposing gothic, limestone building dating back to the 1860s. It too was built by the convicts and used to house those of their colleagues who had gone 'mad' and were deemed dangerous. The museum is dedicated to the history of Fremantle, and to the building itself, and has some excellent displays. The Arts Centre holds regular exhibitions of contemporary visual arts and crafts. ■ *Musuem open Sun-Fri 1030-1630, Sat 1300-1700 Entry by gold coin donation. T9430 7966, www.museum.wa.gov.au Arts Centre open daily 1000-1700. Free entry. T9432 9555, www.fac.org.au 1 Finnerty St.*

Sleeping
■ *On map*
See also
Pubs and bars

The **LL-L** *Esplanade*, corner of Marine Terr and Essex St, T9432 4000, www.esplanadehotelfremantle.com.au, is Freo's flagship accommodation, an elegant Federation hotel that has been the automatic choice for many visitors for over a century. Facilities include 2 courtyard pools, smorgasbord and à la carte restaurants, fitness centre and bicycle hire. **A-B** *Port Mill*, 17 Essex St, T9433 3832, portmill@bigpond.com. B&B opposite an 1863 flour mill. 3 bright, en suite rooms all have balconies, though the front 2 have much better views. **B** *100 Hubble*, 100 Hubble St, East Fremantle. T9339 8080, www.100hubble.com Charming self-contained accommodation that is utterly original and quite magical. Sleeps 6, 4 in a cosy converted railway carriage. The kitchen fits into a wooden wheelhouse, shower in a red telephone box, bathroom in the garden. Also a lawn, BBQ, sun lounges, sun deck and lots of tranquil corners for a snooze. Recommended. **B** *Fothergills*, 20 Ord St, T9335 6784, fotherg@iinet.net.au Large, stately colonial house. B&B in 2 spacious en suite rooms, subdued but luxurious, and a very pleasant upstairs balcony. Breakfast in a sunny conservatory. Some parking. **C** *Terrace Central*, 83 South Terr, T/F9335 6600, portfremantle@bigpond.com, is a bright and breezily decorated 1890s cottage with 7 spacious rooms. No en suites but plenty of bathrooms, continental breakfast. Good value. **D-E** *Backpackers Inn YHA*, 11 Packenham St, T9431 7061, www.line.com.au/freoinn, has 41 rooms and good facilities. Doubles are pricey but en suite. The **E** *Old Firestation*, 18 Phillimore St, T9430 5454, www.firestation.fdns.net, is in need of a face-lift but has a laid-back atmosphere and lots of freebies, including off-street parking. They are also good at tracking down employment and have $3 curries for residents in the downstairs *Bengal*. **E** *Port City Pirates*, 11 Essex St, T9335 6635, is one of the smallest and quietest hostels with only 50 beds, including singles and doubles. It still has a good range of facilities, however, including a courtyard BBQ, internet, and very friendly management. **E** *Sundancer*, 80 High St, T1800 061144, sundancer_resort@tpg.com.au, is the best of the big hostels and very well positioned. Rooms and generous communal facilities are bright and clean, and the sunny rear courtyard has a spa.

Eating
● *On map*
The choice in Fremantle is staggering and it's a favourite destination for those who live in Perth. Almost every restaurant and café has outdoor tables

Expensive *Essex*, 20 Essex St, T9335 5275. A bastion of good taste and fine food, the traditional *Essex* serves simply excellent seafood and collects awards like a chef collects sauce stains. Lunches Wed, Fri, Sun, dinners every day. *Red Herring*, 26 Riverside Rd, East Fremantle, T9339 1611. Considered one of the best seafood restaurants in Perth and running out of wall space for its awards, this contemporary restaurant sits on pylons over the river. Save room for the fine dessert and cheese menu. Excellent wine list and wine-matching suggestions.

Mid-range *Cedar Tree*, 36 South Terr, T9336 7669. Traditional and contemporary Lebanese food in a chic open space. Bellydancing Fri-Sat. *Primavera*, corner of Marine Terr and Arundel St, T9335 1744, is one of the town's favourite Italian venues, specializing in risotto, pasta, seafood freshly caught by the owner's brother, and home-made gelati. Licensed, with an extensive list of WA wines, but BYO corkage (bottled wine only) just $3.50. Open all day, Tue-Sun, lunch 1200-1430, dinner 1830-2130.

Cheap *Capri*, 21 South Terr, T9335 1399. Classic old-fashioned Italian cooking in a simple wood-panelled room. No fuss, no frills just wonderful flavours. Also plenty of seafood dishes. Daily 1200-1400, 1700-2200. *Hara Café*, 33 High St, T9335 6118. Small, earthy and laid-back vegetarian joint with an emphasis on Indian cuisine. Some vegan options available. Open from 1100 Mon-Fri, 1200 Sat, to 1600 Mon-Tue, 2100 Wed-Sat. *Left Bank*, 15 Riverside Rd, East Fremantle, T9319 1315. A large open pub on the river that concentrates on its food. Classy mid-range restaurant upstairs. Café daily from 0700, restaurant Mon-Sat from 1200. One of the more popular spots for the traditional Perth Sunday session. *Maya Indian*, 75 Market St, 9335 2796. There's nothing interesting about the scruffy décor but the authentic Indian food here has won many awards and it's always busy. A short, traditional menu, BYO only. Tue-Sun 1800-2200. *Pizza Bellaroma*, 14 South Terr, T9335 1554. The best pizza and chilli mussels in an unpretentious setting. BYO. Lunch and dinner Tue-Sun. For **seriously cheap** food head for the 2 food courts. *Old Shanghai Food Court*, Henderson Mall has everything from Japanese to juices and lots of pavement tables in the mall. Wed-Thu 1100-2100, Fri-Sat 1100-2130. *Foodtown*, Essex St, here fish and chips jostle with sushi, noodles, Thai, Italian and Chinese, plus there's a bar. Open 1100-2100 Tue-Sun, to 2200 Fri-Sat. For fish and chips, there are 3 choices down at the boat harbour. On the harbour itself *Cicerello's* and *Kailis* dominate. Both are massive boathouse-style buildings that serve up portions to hundreds of tourists every day around 0930-2030.

Cafés

● *On map*

The city's large Italian population have helped to build a very continental culture of coffee drinking

Gino's, 1 South Terr, T9336 1464. One of the original Italian cafés, Gino's has stuck to its simple formula of fast, honest Italian food and great coffee. Lots of space inside and out, order at the counter. Mon-Fri 0600-2200, Sat-Sun 0600-2300. *Kaboodle*, 79 South Terr, 19433 1170. Laid-back and funky with its own gallery and a covered rear courtyard. Internet free (15 mins) with coffee or $3 for 30 mins. Licensed. Acoustic and jam sessions Wed-Sat evenings. Open Wed-Sat 0800-0100, Sun-Tue 0800-1800. Recommended. *Old Papa's*, 17 South Terr, T9335 4655. Along with *Gino's*, one of Freo's old survivors but perhaps trading on its reputation. Extensive breakfast menu, cheap pasta and pizza, good gelati. Daily 0545-2130. *Tea at the Roundhouse*, Fleet St, the Roundhouse precinct, T9431 7555. Converted 1905 pilot's cottage, well away from the bustle of the harbour or South Terr, makes a delightful tearoom with cool, genteel inside rooms and a few tables on the front veranda. Open 0830-1730 . Also simple, fresh dinners Fri-Sat to 2200.

Pubs & bars

● *On map*

Clancy's Fish Pub, 51 Cantonment St, T9335 1351. A bit out of the way but one of the most relaxed pubs in Freo, *Clancy's* has a funky, alternative feel and great food available all day (1200-2100). Always packed for the Sun session. *Little Creatures*, 40 Mews Rd, T9430 5555, is a former boat shed and crocodile farm, now a cool, cavernous brewery and bar. Excellent, inventive cheap food, including wood-fired pizzas, mussels and tapas, available all day. Open from 1000 Mon-Fri, 0900 Sat-Sun, to at least 2300. *Newport*, corner of Market St and South Terr, T9335 2428. A lively, relaxed pub. Pool tables, atrium courtyard, dedicated room for pop-music bands on Fri-Sun and DJs Thu. *Norfolk*, corner Norfolk St and South Terr, T9335 5405. A really social pub with a great enclosed, stone courtyard, huge on Sun afternoons. Live jazz on Sat afternoons and evenings. Cheap bar food available daily 100-2100. The 9 rooms are some of the town's best pub options (**C**). *Sail & Anchor*, 64 South Terr, T9335 8433. The pub that started the boutique beer-and-good-food revolution in Freo around the time of the Americas Cup. Does cheap wood fired pizzas and casual light meals, while the elegant brasserie offers fine mid-range modern Australian cuisine on the balcony. Also a good bottle shop and brewery tours Mon 1700, Sat 1100, Sun 1000.

Western Australia

Entertainment **Cinema** *Luna on SX*, Essex St, T9430 5999. Fremantle's grooviest cinema, with a $10 double-feature at 1430 Sun. *Millennium*, Collie St, T9430 6988. Mainstream features. **Clubs** Although Fremantle is not the automatic choice for Perth's clubbers there are a couple of options, including *Kulcha* and *Metropolis*, both on South Terr. **Festivals** The Fremantle Festival is held annually in mid-Nov at various venues around the city. The city held its first Fremantle International Jazz Festival in Jan 2002 and plans to hold the festival annually over the Australia Day weekend. **Theatre** The *Deckchair Theatre*, 33 Packenham St, T9430 4771, put on contemporary, home-grown productions, often with a Fremantle or multicultural theme.

Shopping
There is some excellent shopping in the port city, with many quirky and interesting shops that help to give Fremantle its character

High-quality Aboriginal art at *Creative Native*, *Japinka* and *Indigenart*, all on High St. Excellent and reasonably priced craftwork (ceramics, wood, textiles, jewellery) by WA artists at *Fremantle Arts Centre*, 1 Finnerty St, T9432 9569. Book lovers should not miss the superb *New Edition*, 50 South Terr, T9335 2383. Daily 0930-2230. Fremantle shopping hours are generally 0900-1730 with the exception of late-night shopping on Thu until 2100. Most shops are also open at the weekend. The **Fremantle Markets** are the best in WA, still held in the original Victorian market hall. The markets have a fresh fruit and vegetable section and sell clothes, jewellery, art and wonderful fresh food such as bread, cheese and fish. Open Fri 0900-2100, Sat 0900-1700, Sun 1000-1700. The **E Shed Markets** are not as good but are worth a look if you're waiting for a ferry. Open 0900-1800 Fri-Sun, foodcourt and cafés open to 2000.

Tours & activities **Boat cruises** *Fremantle Harbour Tours*, T0418 924580, depart from the Fishing Boat Harbour, opposite *Joe's*, up to 5 times daily for a spin around both commercial harbours (1 hr, $18, children $10, concessions $15). *Captain Cook Cruises*, T9325 3341, www.captaincookcruises.com.au, run several cruises from East St Jetty. There are daily cruises to Perth (90 mins, $14) at 0945 and 1400, and lunch cruises (3 hrs, $45) at 1225. *Oceanic Cruises*, T9430 5127, www.oceaniccruises.com.au, also leave from East St Jetty for Perth, up to 4 times a day, and call at **Claremont**. Fares are a little cheaper and the journey is a bit quicker (1 hr, $11). They also offer a couple of excellent buffet-lunch cruises, including to Carnac Island. *Rottnest Express*, T9335 6406, www.rottnestexpress.com.au, take their boat *Sea Eagle* out to cruise past Garden Island every Sun at 1140 from Victoria Quay ($39, 4 hrs, basic BBQ included). Also whale-watching tours in season (Sep-Nov). **Bus** *Fremantle Tramswest Tours*, T9339 8719, www.tramswest.com.au Town tours on buses disguised as trams. The best quick introduction to Fremantle is their *Historical Trail* (45 mins, $8, concessions $7) which leaves at 1000, 1200, 1400 and 1600. They also have a good value 5-hr combined tram/boat tour of Fremantle and Perth (1000, 1400, $40, children $20). **Diving** *Diving Ventures*, 384 South Terr, T9430 5130, www.dventures.com.au, run PADI courses and dive trips to Rottnest and Dunsborough (sight of the sunken *HMAS Swan*). *Dolphin*, 1 Cantonment St, T9336 6286, freodive@dolphindiveshop.com, organize several boat dives, including wreck and night dives, and have hire facilities. They also run a 'snorkel with seals' on Wed. **Parasailing** *Fremantle Parasailing*, Fishing Boat Harbour, T9203 9998, offer a quick parasail for $60 and also ski-tubing (30 mins, $80). **Sailing** The *Leeuwin* is Fremantle's resident tall ship. It sails out on a variety of different trips depending on the season. In summer it is based in the port and there are lots of opportunities to get aboard for a day sail, mostly at weekends. Most last 3-5 hrs and cost $50-100. T9430 4105 or www.leeuwin.com for the current schedule. *Oceanic Cruises* head out on summer Suns for 4-5 hrs on their 30-m sailing schooner, the *MV Oceanic*. It sails down past Carnac and Garden Island, stopping briefly for a BBQ and a swim, and is great value at $50. The much smaller *Yacht Starsound*, T9335 3844, heads out on a variety of whale-watching and day-trips, including a regular sail around Carnac and Rottnest on Tue and Sun (0900-1800), and a twilight cruise (1700 Wed, 3 hrs, $45). Overnight trips also available.

Ferry *Oceanic Cruises*, T9335 2666, www.oceaniccruises.com.au, and *Rottnest Express*, T9335 6406, www.rottnestexpress.com.au, offer several services a day from Victoria Quay. *Boat Torque Cruises*, T9430 5844, leave from less accessible Rous Head Harbour. Parking will be an additional $5-8 a day.

Transport
Fremantle has the cheapest ferry options to Rottnest

Banks ATMs for the major banks on Adelaide St, between Point St and Queen St. *Interforex*, next to the VIC. Daily 0800-1930. *Thomas Cook*, High St Mall, Mon-Fri 0900-1700, Sat 0900-1500, Sun 1000-1500. **Bike hire** *Fleet Cycles*, 66 Adelaide St, T9430 5414. $20 day. Mon-Fri 0900-1730, Sat 0900-1700, Sun 1100-1700. **Car hire** *Ace*, T9221 1333, www.acerent.com.au *Perth*, T9430 4322, www.perth rentacar.com.au **Communications** Internet *Travel Lounge*, 16 Market St, daily 0700-2300. $5 hr. *e-Tech*, 41South Terr, Mon-Fri 0830-1930, Sat-Sun 1000-1800. $6 hr. **Post Office**, 13 Market St. **Medical services** *Travellers Medical and Vaccination Centre*, Unit 5, 89 South Terr, 9336 6630. *Fremantle Hospital*, corner Alma St and South Terr, T9431 3333. **Police** Henderson St, T9430 1222. **Scooter hire** *Scoot Freo*, 2 Phillimore St, T9336 5933, hire out both standard scooters ($25 for 1½ hrs to $65 per day) and 3-wheel, 2-person scootcars ($40 per hr, $100 for 4 hrs). Minimum age 21. Open Mon-Fri 1000-1600, Sat-Sun 0900-1700. Closed if wet. **Taxi** *Swan*, T9444 4444, *Black & White*, T9333 3333.

Directory

Rottnest Island

Rotto, as it's known locally, has become a favourite holiday destination for Perth families and those celebrating the end of school or university. The entire coast is one long stretch of magical sandy bays and clear aquamarine water. The off-shore reefs are full of brightly coloured fish, exotic corals and limestone caves, and are littered with wrecks. The island itself is 11 km long and 4 km wide and covered in low bushy scrub with some patches of eucalypt woodland. Much of this provides cover for the island's famous small wallaby, the **quokka**, which stands at only 30 cm high. The island's curious name derives from the Dutch word for 'rat nest'. The Dutch explorers who first landed likened the mini wallabies to rats and the island was overrun with them. There are now around 9,000 on the island and constant interaction with people has made some of them quite tame so you have a very good chance of seeing them. There are few permanent human residents as the island is carefully managed to preserve the environment and scarce water resources. The number of overnight visitors is kept to a sustainable level and cars are not allowed.

*Colour map 7, grid B5
Visitors are asked not to touch or feed the quokka*

If you're confined to the settlements you should always be able to find them hanging around the shop at Geordie Bay, alongside the Garden Lake boardwalk behind the Lodge, and at the short boardwalk opposite the turn-off to Kingston Barracks

Getting there There are 2 ways of getting to **Rotto**, by air and by ferry. **Air** *Rottnest Air Taxi*, T9292 5027, offer return trips from Jandakot airport, east of **Fremantle**. Fares from $60 per person, depending on numbers. Once on the island they also offer quick scenic flights from $20. **Ferries** run from **Barrack St Jetty** in **Perth**, and from **Fremantle** and **Hillarys**. It is usually cheapest to get public transport to Fremantle and catch the ferry from there. From Hillarys' Sorrento Quay, *Boat Torque Cruises*, T9246 1039, operate a ferry 2-4 times a day ($50 day return, children $14.50, concessions $40).

Ins & outs
See under the relevant departure point for ferry details

Bicycle Bikes can be taken on the ferries free of charge, and the ferry companies also offer slightly cheaper bike hire than that on the island. Beware, however, that the coast road around the island undulates over the dunes like a roller-coaster. The slopes may be short, but they are often quite steep and cycling is a tiring business. Also note that there is no fresh water west of either Geordie Bay or Kingston Barracks. Hire on the island is from *Rottnest Bike Hire*, T9292 5105, who have a wide range to suit all ages including some tandems and electric wheelchairs. Open 0830-1700. **Bus** A free

Getting around
Only essential service vehicles and buses are allowed on the island

Western Australia

shuttle bus operates every 30 mins between Geordie Bay, Longreach Bay, Thomson Bay Settlement, the airport and Kingston Barracks. Services operate 0800-2100. The *Bayseeker* bus travels clockwise right around the coast road, but doesn't get out to the 'West End'. It operates a 'jump-on, jump-off' system with about 20 stops on the circuit and goes about every 20-40 mins. A day fare is $5.50, children $2.20, concessions $3.30. Services from 0830-1700. **Train** The island's sole train shuttles to and fro between the southern end of the Settlement and Oliver Hill lookout. Fare includes a tour at Oliver Hill, except for the last ride of the day. 2-hr round trips hourly 1030-1430. Tickets $9.90, children $4.95, concessions $7.15, available from the VIC.

Information & services The island's **VIC** is in the centre of Thomson Bay Settlement. Open daily 0815-1700. T9372 9752, www.rottnest.wa.gov.au Also in Thomson Bay is a small shopping mall with a post office, ATM, take-away, general store, bakery and clothes/gift shop. There's also a store at Geordie Bay. Both open daily. The island has a nursing post, T9292 5030, police station, T9292 5030, and rangers office, T9372 9788.

Sights
Thomson Bay Settlement is the main settlement on the island

The entire Thomson Bay Settlement is something of an open-air museum, and the general layout is claimed to be Australia's oldest intact streetscape. Most interesting is the part of the *Rottnest Lodge* known as the **Quod**, and the heritage precinct in front of it. Once one of the most feared places on the island, it was built in 1838 to house dozens of Aboriginal 'criminals' in horrendous conditions. There were still prisoners on the island when it was converted into a tourist hostel in 1911. The **museum**, just behind the general store in the mall, is the main repository of the island's rather sorry history. ■ *Daily 1100-1600. $2.20, children 55c, concessions $1.10.* Almost in the centre of the island is **Oliver Hill**, used during the Second World War as a gun emplacement. Underground is a small maze of underground tunnels. ■ *Tours on the hour from 1000. $2.20, children $0.55, concessions $1.10 or included in cost of the train from Thomson Bay. Allow about 1 hr to walk, 30 mins to cycle.* Most visitors come simply for the **beaches**, of which there over a dozen. Reefs lie just offshore from some beaches and many are enclosed by dramatic limestone headlands. The most sheltered are along the north shore and these also get the busiest, especially the **Basin**, the most picturesque bay on the island. Other beautiful small bays a bit further from Thomson Bay include **Little Armstrong** on the north shore and **Little Salmon** on the south. The latter is also a particularly good snorkelling spot, but the water can get a bit choppy in the afternoons. **Longreach** and **Geordie** are long sweeping bays overlooked by accommodation and often crowded with private boats.

Sleeping & eating Most of the accommodation on the island is in self-contained cottages, villas or cabins (**L-D**), and this needs to be booked through the *Accommodation Office*, T9432 9111, which also hires out televisions and video recorders (videos at the *Family Fun Park*). During the Dec-Jan summer period it is virtually impossible to find a room, cabin or patch of ground on the island unless you've booked it months in advance. The best chance you will have is at the *YHA*. Even outside of this period weekends commonly see the island booked almost full, so either plan well ahead or plan for a mid-week visit.

Some of the ferry companies offer ferry/accommodation/bike packages that shave a few dollars off the usual total cost. **L-A** *Rottnest Lodge*, T9292 5161, www.rottnestlodge.com.au, is the island's premier establishment, and incorporates many of the early colonial prison buildings. Meals are open to non-residents and are surprisingly reasonably priced given its decidedly upmarket feel. Breakfast is a full buffet 0700-1000, with choice of cheap buffet (1200-1400) or a là carte (1200-1530) for lunch. The evening menu is expensive, but the food is the best on the island, served 1800-2100.

A *Rottnest Hotel*, T9292 5011, rottnesthotel@axismgt.com.au, converted from a former residence for the Western Australian Governor, has a dozen motel-style rooms which lack the ambience of the *Lodge*. It has 2 dining options and as the only pub on the island is its life and soul. *Hampton's* bar serves up cheap BBQs plus seriously cheap bar snacks. *Vlamingh's* is a large restaurant with a substantial terrace area serving mid-range seafood and grills. Meals available 1200-1400 and 1800-2100. **D-E** *Rottnest Youth Hostel* (*YHA*), T9372 9780, occupies part of the red-brick military barracks built in 1936, 1 km from Thomson Bay. Facilities are good, and the staff are friendly and helpful. The office is open daily 0800-1700. There is a small area set aside for **camping** in Thomson Bay – it is not allowed over the rest of the island. Adults $5.50 per night, children $2.75. Book at the Accommodation Office. In the centre of Thomson Bay with terrace views over the harbour is the *Dôme*, part of the gallic-style chain. Open 0700-2100. Just along from the *Dôme* are the island's *Tea rooms* whose long boardwalk also looks out over the harbour. Open 0700-2100, they are slightly cheaper and less highbrow than their neighbours, but nevertheless offer a good range of breakfasts and hot meals. All the establishments above are licensed. The *Captain's Kitchen*, Kingston Barracks, is a seriously cheap, no-frills catering outfit that produces buffet and set meals 3 times a day every day. Excellent value. Meals at 0700-0845 (0800-1000 Sun), 1200-1400, and 1800-2000. Meal tickets bought at the hostel reception are cheaper.

Astronomical *Astro Tours*, T0500 831111, take small parties and large telescopes out beyond Geordie Bay for 2 hrs of commentated star-gazing. This is one of the best tours of its kind. Nightly at 2000. Adults $25, children $15. **Boats and kayaks** The *Underwater Explorer*, T9421 5888, www.underwaterexplorer.com.au, is a large glass-bottomed boat that heads out several times a day on a variety of short cruises. *Capricorn Kayak Tours*, T9433 3902, www.capricornkayak.com.au, take small groups out sea-kayaking around some of the island's best offshore spots. Small, covered, glass-bottomed boats can be hired at Geordie Bay ($20 for ½ hr) at 0930-1730. T0407 009283. **Bus** A 2-hr bus tour sets off around the island a few times each day, with full commentary on the human and natural history of the island. The tour includes visits to Wadjemup Lighthouse and the West End. Adults $15, children $7.50, concessions $9.90. **Diving and snorkelling** is excellent off Rottnest, with a large variety of wrecks, fish, corals and limestone caves. *Malibu Diving*, T9292 5111, www.rottnestdiving.com.au, hire out full kit for $70 a day and also organize a variety of boat dives every day, for $40-60 per dive, depending on kit supplied. Open daily 0800-1800. *Diving Ventures*, T9430 5130, www.dventures.com.au, offer a good-value 2-dive day trip from Perth and Fremantle for $155 with all equipment supplied. Also introductory dives for $170 from Oct-May. Unsurprisingly snorkelling is also superb off much of the Rottnest coast, with particularly good spots off Parker Point, where there is a marked out trail, and at Little Salmon Bay, and parts of Salmon Bay and the Basin. Gear can be hired at the *Malibu Diving* for $17 a day, and the VIC sells an excellent, very detailed guide to Rottnest snorkelling for $5.50. Wind direction dictates the best spots so enquire at *Malibu Diving* before setting out.

Tours & activities

Swan Valley

The Swan Valley is really half a valley, bordered to the east by the Darling Range, but running flat to the west all the way to the northern Perth suburbs. It was settled early in Perth's history, providing better agricultural land than further down the Swan River, and vines were being grown by 1836 at what is now Houghton's, the valley's best-known winery. At the southern end of the valley is Guildford, an inland port established in 1829, but falling out of favour early in its history, a fact that has helped preserve many of its early Victorian buildings.

Ins & outs
Also see Tours and activities, p x

Guildford 20 km from Perth

Getting there and around There are frequent **train** services from **East Perth** station to **Guildford** and **Midland** and infrequent **buses** from there, but this is not the ideal way to tour the valley. Ideally you need your own transport, or to jump on a tour. **Taxi** A taxi to or from the airport will be about $25, and nearly double that from **Perth**.

Information The main **VIC** for the region is in Guildford on the south side of James St. Open daily 0900-1700. T9379 9420, www.swanvalley-holiday.com.au

Wineries
There are about 30 wineries in the region, ranging from one of the largest producers in the state to several one-person operations. Cellar door hours vary widely, but they are often closed Mon-Tue. Most wineries charge $2 for a tasting, usually refundable with a purchase, and many have restaurants with vine-covered courtyards

Sandalford, 3210 West Swan Road, T9374 9366, www.sandalford.com has an extensive range of wines here and the winery offers a full appreciation and tasting session as part of a guided tour. Expensive modern Australian cuisine with a strong Italian influence, served 1000-1700 daily and 1800-2100 Saturday and Sunday. A river cruise to the winery from Perth includes a tour and lunch. ■ *Cellar door open daily 1000-1700. Wine appreciation tour daily 1100, 1400, 1500. 75 mins, $15. Swan river cruise daily 1000, $149, bookings required.* **Sittella**, Barrett Street, T9296 2600, can claim one of the valley's best views from their large, covered wooden deck. Open for mid-range lunch and tastings 1100-1600 Wednesday to Sunday. Recommended. **Edgecombe**, Gnangara Road, T9296 4307, is one of the most laid-back and welcoming wineries in the valley. Wines $13-20, open 0900-1800 daily. **Houghton**, Dale Road, T9274 9540, is the valley's expansive elder statesman and now produces some of the most popular wines in Australia. Wines $12-40, open daily 1000-1700. **Mann**, Memorial Avenue, T9296 4348, is a one-man operation continuing three generations of expertise in producing a smooth, dry *Méthode Champenoise*. A bargain at $18, the cellar door is open Saturday, Sunday and most weekdays 1000-1700, (August to January). **Westfield**, Memorial Avenue, T9296 4356, is the real McCoy, with tastings in the cool, 1927 cellar, surrounded by dozens of aromatic barrels. New vintages are still only $15-25. Open 0900-1700 Monday to Saturday, 1100-1600 Sunday.

Sleeping
There's not as much choice as the better known wine region of Margaret River, but there are a few very pleasant options nonetheless

L-A *Hansons*, 60 Forest Rd, T9296 3366, www.hansons.com.au, is a modern boutique hotel with 10 rooms, all en suite with own balcony or courtyard, the expensive mod Australian cuisine is also hard to beat and is accompanied by the valley's best wine list. Breakfast included. Meals 0800-1030, 1900-2100. Recommended. **L-C** *Rose & Crown*, 105 Swan St, Guildford, T9279 8444, rcrown@iinet.net.au This grand old coaching inn is officially the oldest pub in WA, and does indeed ooze its early colonial character. 4 en suite rooms. Meals available 0700-0900, 1200-1500, 1800-2100 Mon-Sat. **B** *Settlers Rest*, George St, T/F9250 4540, www.settlersrest.com.au Historic, beautifully furnished, 3-bedroom weatherboard cottage in a quiet, central spot. Open fires, a/c and traditional verandahs. **C** *Susannah Brook Chalets*, Bisdee Rd, T9296 4733. 2 a/c cabins in a quiet bush setting near *Lamonts*. Bed-sit style with limited kitchenette. One of the valley's cheapest options. **C** *Tampara* Anglesea Cres, T9297 3221, tampara@optusnet.com.au, is a large modern home purpose-built in opulent colonial style as a traditional B&B with 3 rooms. Recommended. There are a handful of caravan parks in the valley, including the **Perth Big 4** at 91 Benara Rd, T1800 679992 or 9279 6700, perthholiday@bigpond.com

Eating & drinking
Aside from the wineries, there are a number of restaurants, cafés and specialist outlets dotted around the valley

Expensive *Whiteman's Abroad*, 34 Johnson St, Guildford, T9379 2990. Excellent dining either inside a beautiful colonial house or alfresco in the gardens. Lunch, cream teas and dinners available 1030-2100 Wed-Sun, and gourmet breakfasts from 0900 Sun. Recommended. **Mid-range** *Kappy's*, 120 Swan St, Guildford, T6278 2882, is a straightforward Italian with a pleasant contemporary dining room. Open 1200-1500 Mon-Fri, 1800-2130 Mon-Sat. **Cheap** *Vineyard Restaurant and Teahouse*, 55 Benara Rd, T9377 6432. Serves deceptively simple light lunches such as pies, tarts and salads, as well as cream teas. Inexpensive but very tasty. Open daily 1000-1600.

Recommended. **Cafés** *Old Cottage Café*, West Swan Rd, T9250 3638. Quaint 1915 weatherboard cottage serving light lunches, cream teas and mid-range dinners. Mostly Italian-influenced home cooking with a few good veggie options. Open 0830, to 1700 Mon, Wed, 2100 Thu-Sat and 1930 Sun. **Breweries and bars** The *Duckstein*, West Swan Rd, T9296 0620, is the valley's longest-established independent brewer, proudly Bavarian in style and content. Traditional German fare available to accompany the beer. Open Wed-Sun 1100-2200. The *Ironbark Brewery*, Benara Rd, T041 2546738, serves its own beers in a much more contemporary bar. Also brewing its own potent selection, under the label *Inchant*, is the *Rose & Crown* in Guildford. The best place to try them is in the original, very atmospheric cellar bar.

WA Cycle Tours, T9381 3441, www.wacycletours.com.au, have bikes available for a self-guided tours. *Boat Torque Cruises*, T9421 5888, head up from Barrack St Jetty in Perth for a regular day trip. *Epicurean Tours*, T9479 4130, take out small groups for knowledgable and indulgent trips around the valley. *Black Swan Tours*, T9296 2568, www.blackswantours.com.au, offer a number of different tours with pick-ups from central Perth or Midland. Airport transfers also available.

Tours & activities
Also see under Wineries on previous page

The Perth Hills

The sharp, 400-m high, western escarpment of the Darling Ranges runs parallel to the coast about 30 km inland, forming the western border to WA's huge and ancient inland plateau. Large areas of the scarp have been set aside as reserves and parks, preserving the characteristic gum woodlands and providing city-dwellers and visitors with an extensive network of bush-walking, mountain-biking and horse-riding tracks.

Getting there and around Metropolitan **buses** for **Mundaring** leave from the train station at **Midland**. The 318, 319 and 320 are principal services, leaving Midland several times a day. Buses to **Kalamunda** leave Perth City Busport several times a day.

Ins & outs

   Information The main VICs for the central Perth Hills are in Kalamunda and in highway straddling Mundaring. Kalamunda open 1000-1500 Fri-Sun. 11 Headingly Rd, T9293 0299. Mundaring open daily 1000-1600. 7225 Great Eastern Highway, T9295 0202. The **CALM** office for the hills is 1 km east of Mundaring Weir on the Mundaring Weir Rd. They hold a good stock of brochures and maps including those for the Bibbulmun Track ($6 each), and will advise on current trail accessibility. Open 1000-1630 Mon-Fri, T9295 1955.

Kalamunda has grown to be a good sized modern town, seemingly built around a central shopping centre and shoving its history to the fringes. Its main claim to fame is as the northern terminus of the **Bibbulmun Track**, but the **Kalamunda History Village** is well worth a stroll around. Although a small example of an 'assembled' village, all the dozen or so buildings and their copious contents are authentic and well laid out around the town's original railway station. A good insight into life in WA around the early 20th century. ■ *1000-1500 Mon-Thu, Sat, and 1330-1630 Sun. $4, children $1, concessions $3. T9293 1371, Railway Rd.*

Kalamunda
Colour map 7, grid B5
Kalamunda 25 km from Perth, 25 km from Mundaring

Sleeping and eating C *Lady Muck*, Mundaring Weir Rd, T9257 2475, is a small, modern home-style B&B with 3 rooms, 1 en suite, and an engaging, friendly host. Substantial continental breakfast. The 1902 **D** *Kalamunda Hotel*, 43 Railway Terr, T9257 1084, kalamunda_hotel@one.net.au, has 3 simple upstairs doubles, but all en suite with a/c. Meals daily 1200-1500, 1800-2100. *Le Paris-Brest*, Haynes St, Kalamunda, T9293 2752, is

Western Australia

something of a cultural oasis in Kalamunda, a cheerful Gallic corner providing a patisserie and café, ongoing art exhibitions, and monthly live jazz on their wraparound terrace. Open 0700-1730 Tue-Sun and public holidays, jazz on the 1st Sat of each month.

Bickley Valley
Colour map 7, grid B5
10 km from Kalamunda

One of several small valleys that have been partially cultivated for fruit and wine, Bickley is one of the most picturesque. There are a handful of small wineries dotted along and just off Aldersyde Raod and Walnut Road, but they are only open for tastings at weekends. The *Packing Shed*, T9291 8425, is the restaurant of the *Lawnbrook Estate*, now much better known for its food than its wine. The excellent mid-range food is Mediterranean in style, spiced up with the odd curry. ■ *Open for lunches and teas, 1000-1800 Sat-Sun.* At the far end of the valley is the **Perth Observatory** which regularly holds viewing nights throughout the year. Bookings are essential. ■ *Viewing nights $17, children and concessions $12. A couple of 1½ hr sessions each evening. Walnut Rd, T9293 8255, www.wa.gov.au/perthobs* If you're tempted to stay around here, try **B** *Lonsdales*, Walnut Road, Bickley Valley, T9293 8106, www.wantree. com.au/~lonsdale, a secluded modern B&B built of jarrah and recycled bricks, set amongst woodland and great for chilling out. Garden pool, lots of wildlife and full breakfast. Recommended.

Around Mundaring
Colour map 7, grid B5
Mundaring 40 km from Perth, 10 km from John Forrest National Park, 8 km from Mundarig Weir

In 1895, when the WA eastern goldfields rush was in full swing, **Mundaring Weir** was built as the reservoir and pumping station to supply the pipeline carrying water to the Coolgardie and Kalgoorlie goldfields. Today a small huddle of houses sits in the forest to the north of the main dam wall, amidst them the excellent pub built to cater for the original workers and engineers, and a *YHA* hostel. A little beyond the village the **CY O'Connor Museum** utilizes the original pump-house and carefully charts the development of the goldrushes and the building of both dam and pipeline. ■ *1030-1500 Mon, Wed-Fri, and 1200-1700 Sun. $3. National Trust operated, T9295 2455.* About 10 km from Mundaring is the **John Forrest National Park**, one of the biggest parks in the hills. It extends about 4 km along the side of the Great Eastern Highway and 5 km north, and is dedicated to preserving the original wildlife and eucalypt woodlands of the scarp. The main draw of the park is its **walking trails**, best undertaken in winter or spring when the brooks are flowing, ranging from 45 minute introductory strolls to seven hour loop walks taking in much of the scenery and some excellent viewpoints. There's a pub at the visitor area. Entry $9 per vehicle, T9298 8344

Sleeping and eating The **C** *Mundaring Weir Hotel*, Mundaring Weir, T9295 1106, www.mundaringweirhotel.com.au, is a grand old pub hotel perched on the hill above the weir pump stations, and a favourite Sun lunch destination for locals. Fresh, inventive meals, mostly cheap, available 1200-1430 daily, 1800-2000 Fri-Sat. Accommodation in 8 motel-style units by the pool. Room/dinner packages only, Fri-Sat. The **E** *Djaril Mari YHA* hostel, T9295 1809, is a small relaxed hostel with 24 beds in 4-bunk dorms and another couple of 6-bunk rooms in a separate cottage with its own facilities.

North of Perth

The coastal road north of Perth runs only as far as Lancelin at present. On the way Yanchep National Park makes a fine day-trip from Perth, with its tranquil lakes and birdlife, but it is worth continuing north for a night in Lancelin. It's windsurfing heaven but less active souls can enjoy the long expanse of silky dunes that are magical at sunset and only a short walk from the town centre.

Inland is the curious settlement of New Norcia, a small community of Benedictine monks living a contemplative life in their grand edifices as road trains thunder past on the Great Northern Highway.

Getting there and around Bus Some *Westrail* buses pass through **Gingin** on their way north, departing **East Perth** at 0830 Mon-Sat, 1730 Fri and 1630 Sun. Other services (N2) head to **Geraldton** via **New Norcia**, leaving at 0930 Tue, Thu, 1700 Fri, 1515 Sun. *Integrity*, Wellington St Bus Station, Perth, T9226 1339, www.integritycoachlines.com.au, also operate a service up the west coast, stopping at **Gingin**. Their buses leave at 1730 Mon-Fri, 0700 Tue, 1930 Thu and Sun.

Ins & outs
Also see Tours and activities, p x

Just 15 km beyond Perth's northernmost suburbs, lies one of region's best parks. Encompassing two lakes, Loch McNess and the larger North Lake, the park has a wide range of attractions for the visitor, including limestone caves, walking trails and a great deal of wildlife. As well as the wild roos and dozens of bird species, there is a large koala enclosure. The **visitor centre** is close to the park entrance, next to a kiosk and tea room. The *Yanchep Inn* pub, a couple of hundred metres north, serves food and has a few rooms (**C**). ■ *Park open daily, entry $9 per car. Per activity, $6.50, children $3.50, concessions $5. T9561 1004, yanchep@calm.wa.gov.au*

Yanchep National Park
Colour map 7, grid B5 50 km from Perth, 80 km from Lancelin

Activities The park puts on a constant programme of activities, some of which are free. **Aboriginal performances** of dancing, didjeridu playing and weapon throwing take place regularly throughout the day. There are also cultural talks and demonstrations about the area's traditional Aboriginal lifestyle. **Boating** Rowing boats on Loch McNess can be hired at the visitor centre. **Caves** There are regular tours to Crystal Cave, and the public can also book to explore Yonderup Cave. **Walking** Several short walks of around 2 km (1 hr) head around Loch McNess and the caves area, all are described on the free map you will receive on entering the park.

Contact the visitor centre for a current programme

At the end of the coastal highway, Lancelin is a small fishing town, a firm favourite of **windsurfers** and **kitesurfers** during the main October-May season. The strong, dependable offshore winds are also responsible for the naked **dunes** that run for a couple of kilometres just inland of the town. They make an excellent venue for sandboarding, and are also used by local trailbikers, four-wheel drivers and tour operators, but are at their most awesome when devoid of traffic and lit up by a good sunset when they fleetingly turn blush pink. The dunes start about 1 km north of town, and you should arrive about 25 minutes before sunset to get the full effect.

Lancelin
Colour map 7, grid B4 Population: 1,500 130 km from Perth, 75 km from Gingin.

The town has all the basic services, including ATMs

Sleeping and eating **C** *Lancelin Inn*, north end of town, T9655 1005, has motel-style en suite rooms and a mid-range dining room overlooking the shore. Meals daily 1200-1400 and 1800-2000. The friendly **D-E** *Lancelin Lodge*, south end of town on Hopkins St, T9655 2020, www.lancelinlodge.com.au, has just about everything you look for in a hostel. Great rooms and communal facilities, pool, lots of freebies including bikes, and excellent local knowledge. They will even pick up from Perth (cost involved). Recommended. There are 2 **caravan parks**, both with on-site vans and both close to the shore. The one at the north end, T9655 1115, is also close to the dunes. The mid-range *El Tropo*, in the main shopping strip, T9655 1448, is the best restaurant. Licensed, open evenings only. Equally characterful is the modern but rustic *Endeavour Tavern*, with pub garden overlooking the ocean. DJs and live music every weekend. The licensed or BYO *Crayside Café*, near the boat ramp at the south end, T9655 2828, is cheerful and unpretentious and serves lots of cheap rice dishes, seafood and pizzas. Open daily 0900-2100.

Western Australia

Surf-cam and weather
updates at
www.oceanclassic.org

Tours and activities 4WD dune tours and sandboarding *Bigfoot*, T9655 2550, www.bigfootbus.com.au, is a jacked-up yellow bus with simply enormous tyres, claiming to be the world's biggest 4WD. Tours (1¼ hrs, $30) several times a day into the dunes for a bit of a roller-coaster drive and a spot of sandboarding. *Sandcruza*, T0403 430079, will take parties of 1-5 into the dunes for photography or sandboarding for $75 per party (45 min). Sandboard hire from *Lancelin Surfsports*, T0655 1441. **Diving and snorkelling** *Lancelin Dive and Charter*, T0417 727722. **Windsurfing and surfing** *Werner's*, T04-0742 6469, windslanc@hotmail.com Board hire (from $15 per hr) and lessons.

New Norcia

Colour map 7, grid B5
Population: 50
132 km from Perth
To see more of New
Norcia you need to
take a guided tour,
which visits the
monastery, colleges
and Abbey Church.
Visitors are also
welcome to join the 16
remaining monks for
prayers or early
morning mass

New Norcia is one of the most unusual settlements in Australia. A small community of **Benedictine** monks live a traditional Benedictine life of work and prayer within an astonishingly grand setting on the hot and dry Victoria Plains. The first Abbot, Dom Rosendo Salvado, arrived in 1846 and aimed to encourage local Aboriginal people to become farmers and to educate Aboriginal children within a self-sufficient religious community. Later, New Norcia became less of a bush mission and more of a monastic community and centre for education. Today, much of the place is off-limits but there is an interesting **museum** and **art gallery** that focusing on the history of the mission and displaying some of New Norcia's rare and valuable artworks and treasures. A shop here sells high-quality pottery, souvenirs and things the monks make, including olive oil and the renowned New Norcia bread, made daily in a wood-fired oven. ■ *Museum and Art Gallery open 0930-1700 (Aug-Oct), 1000-1630 (Nov-Jul). $5, children $1, concessions $4. Tours daily 1100, 1330. $12, children $5.50 (2 hrs). T9654 8056, www.newnorcia.wa.edu.au Great Northern Highway.*

Sleeping and eating There are only 2 options for sleeping. The guesthouse, T9654 8002, has 8 comfortable en suite, twin rooms around a courtyard within the monastery. The price (**C**) includes 3 meals of the same fare as the monks. Male guests may be invited to eat with the monks. Book in advance, especially at weekends. There is also an externally impressive hotel, T9654 8034, which inside transforms into a pretty simple country pub with tired twin and single rooms (**C**). Shared facilities and no meals included. The hotel has cheap lunches daily 1200-1400 and mid-range dinners, Mon-Sat 1800-2000. There is also a roadhouse where you can get fast food and take-aways, open daily 0800-2000.

Avon Valley

To the east of the Darling Ranges lies the fertile Avon Valley, where the Avon River flows through countryside of rolling hills, pasture and woodland. Parched and hot in summer, the valley becomes green and lush with the winter rains. Some of the oldest towns in WA can be found here, full of historic buildings, most notably York.

Ins & outs
Also see Tours
and activities, p x

Getting there and around The *Westrail Prospector* train service leaves **East Perth** for **Northam** (1½ hrs) at 0715 Mon-Sat, 1430 Mon, Fri and 1410 Sun, continuing on to **Kalgoorlie**. Their E2 bus service to **Albany** calls at both **Northam** and **York** (2 hrs), departing at 0900 Mon, Fri, 1700 Tue, 0945 Wed, 1800 Fri, and 1300 Sun.

Northam

Colour map 7, grid B5
Population: 6000
95 km from Perth, 460
km from Kalgoorlie

The Avon Valley's main service town offers little for tourists, although once a year during the first weekend in August the town is packed with spectators and participants for the 133-km Avon Descent race for canoeists and power boats. The **VIC** is on Grey St, adjacent to both the river and the suspension bridge. ■ *Daily 0900-1700. T9622 2100, northam@avon.net.au*

Western Australia

Sleeping and eating The **A-B** *Shamrock Hotel*, 112 Fitzgerald St, T9622 1092, has recently been splendidly renovated in keeping with its Victorian heritage. Mid-range meals Mon-Sat 1830-2000, and café offering seriously cheap buffets 1130-1430 Tue-Fri and Wed 1800-2000. Also open for cheap lunches 1030-1500 Sat-Sun. One of the few B&Bs in town, the century-old **C** *Liddelow on Avon*, 38 Broome Terr, T/F9622 5647, is just over the river. **E** *Northam Guesthouse*, 51 Wellington St, T9622 2301, has 30 basic rooms, mostly doubles, twins and singles and use of a kitchen. A good eating alternative to the *Shamrock* is the *Fitzgerald Hotel*, 174 Fitzgerald St, T9622 5511, which does cheap lunches daily 1200-1400 and mid-range evening meals 1800-2100.

Settled in 1831 as the oldest inland town in WA, York lost out to Northam as the major rail junction to the goldfields and regional centre. This left it with a magnificent collection of 19th-century buildings and now the town is an appealing, friendly place with museums, cafés, antique and book shops along the main street that draw lots of visitors from Perth at weekends. York is also known for its festivals involving vintage cars in July and jazz at the end of September. For more information contact the friendly **VIC** in the town hall. ■ *Daily 0900-1700. 81 Avon Terr, T9641 1301, www.yorktouristbureau.com.au*

York

Colour map 7, grid B5
Population: 3,000
95 km from Perth, 35 km from Northam

The chief attraction of York is its remarkably preserved architecture, so it is well worth a stroll up and down the main street, Avon Terrace, and some of the back streets. The VIC can supply a map with the main buildings featured. The most impressive building is the **Town Hall**, a magnificently opulent Edwardian hall of red brick and yellow columns. Visitors are welcome to explore the building. Also in the main street is the **Old Gaol and Courthouse**, dating from the 1890s and now managed by the National Trust as a museum. ■ *Tue-Sun 1200-1600. $3.30, children and concessions $1.65. T9641 2072. Avon Terr.* Next door is one of York's biggest attractions, the **York Motor Musuem**, a private collection of classic cars and sports cars valued at $20 million. ■ *Daily 0930-1500. $7.50, children $5.50, concessions $6.50. T9641 1288. 116 Avon Terr.* York is also known for antique shops and galleries, including **Jah-Roc** and the **Convent Gallery**.

Sleeping One of the most authentic heritage experiences, though with many modern conveniences, is in the pretty and well-established gardens of **B** *Wansborough House*, 22 Avon Terr, T/F9641 2887. Recommended. Nearly as old is the traditional B&B next door, **B** *Langsford House*, T9641 1440, a small brick manor with a rich internal décor and full of period antiques. At peak times a bit pricey, the 4 en suite rooms can be up to half-price midweek. **B** *York Cottages*, Morris Edwards Dr, T/F9641 2125, yorkcottages@wn.com.au, are modern and fully self-contained, and so actually more luxurious than their ancient counterparts. Both have open fires and can sleep up to 6. The **C-D** *Castle*, 97 Avon Terr, T9641 1007, castlehotel@westnet.com.au, is the best of the 3 pubs. The admittedly very pleasant **C** *Kookaburra Dream Hostel*, T9641 2936, kookaburras@westnet.com.au, is only worth a look if they have seriously revised their pricing. The *Mount Bakewell Caravan Park*, 2 km north of town on Eighth Rd, T9641 1421, is shady and well-managed with well-equipped on-site vans.

Unsurprisingly there are a good number of heritage, and heritage-style B&Bs around the town, mostly in the A-B price range, though bargains can be had in the Dec-Mar off-season when Perth weekenders find it too hot

Eating *Café Bugatti*, 104 Avon Terr, T9641 1583. The town favourite with great coffee and a good range of traditional Italian dishes. Open Wed-Mon 0900-1500, Fri-Sat 1800-2000. The *Castle* pub serves up a range decent mid-range meals 1200-1430 Wed-Sun and 1800-2030 daily. *Emerald Inn*, 87 Avon Terr, T9641 2355. Charming café and bookshop offering cakes, biscuits and a few simple light meals. Recommended. Open Mon-Thu 0900-1800, Fri-Sun 0900-2200. *Jules Shoppe*, 119 Avon Terr. A good spot for a bite of wholesome lunch, with a few tables on the pavement. Open Thu-Tue

Restaurants in York are good value and there are a few excellent cafés but note that many are closed early in the week

Western Australia

0800-1700. *Yorky's Coffee Carriage*, South St. Novel café in a railway carriage parked by the river bank. Open Thu-Sun 1000-2000. If time and transport allow try to get out to *Greenhills Inn*, 8 Greenhill Rd, T9641 4095 (22 km from York along the road to Quairading). A pub with loads of character, full of antiques and an interesting mix of locals. The restaurant does excellent modern Australian meals, about $40 for a 3-couse set menu. Bed and breakfast is also available (**B**).

South of Perth

To the south of Perth stretches an almost unbroken line of coastal development, including the towns of Rockingham and Mandurah. While they can't compete with the really spectacular attractions further south both towns are worth a look for their relaxed pace, water activities and dolphins.

Ins & outs
Also see Tours and activities, p x

Getting there and around Bus *Westrail's* southwest services stop in **Mandurah**, though they are no faster or cheaper than the metropolitan services. The direct service that leaves East Perth at 1220 Sun can, however, be preferable to changing in Rockingham, as can *South West Coachline's* daily 0845 run (T9324 2333). **Metropolitan bus** There are several services a day between **Perth's** City Busport and **Rockingham** ($5.20, 50 mins, daily); **Fremantle** and Rockingham ($4.30, 45 mins, Mon-Fri); Perth and **Mandurah** ($7.60, 1¼ hrs, Mon-Fri); and between Rockingham and Mandurah ($3.60, 40 mins, daily). **Train** *Westrail's Australind* line stops at **Serpentine** and **Pinjarra** on its way to **Bunbury**. Services leave Perth daily at 0930 and 1745.

Rockingham
Colour map 7, grid B5
Population: 72,000
30 km from Fremantle, 30 km from Mandurah

Rockingham and its suburbs sit on a roughly square peninsula, with a thin line of dunes and foreshore just separating these developments from the many excellent beaches. The waters around the peninsula teem with wildlife and have been declared a marine park. Bang in the middle of it, **Penguin Island** is a must for any visitor. The island is a sanctuary for birdlife, including fairy penguins, and most of it is off limits, though you can still access many of its beaches, plus the **Island Discovery Centre**, where penguins get a modest feed at 1030, 1230 and 1430 daily (weather permitting).■ *Entry to penguin feeds $5, children $3.30, concessions $4.40. Half-price for ferry passengers. Closed Jun to mid-Sep.* A **ferry** leaves every hour, daily, from the beach opposite the island 0900-1500, last return 1600. They also operate a variety of cruises around the island to see and swim with the local sea lions. ■ *Island ferry $8.50 return, children $5.50, concessions $7.50. Island cruises $21, snorkel cruises $28-45. Summer Sunday BBQ cruises $65. T9528 2004, rst@iinet.net.au* The ferry does not operate June to mid-September when the island is closed to visitors. The VIC is on Kent Street, close to Rockingham Beach. The office acts as an agent for much of the city's considerable number of holiday homes and units. ■ *0900-1700 Mon-Fri, 0900-1600 Sat-Sun. 43 Kent St, T9592 3464, rtc@iinet.net.au*

Self-contained apartments, units and holiday homes are the big thing in Rockingham

Sleeping L-B *Beachside Apartments*, 58 Kent St, T1800 888873 or 9529 3777, beachside@iinet.net.au, is at the top end of the market with several smart modern 1- to 3-bedroom apartments overlooking the Rockingham foreshore and beach. At the budget end try **D** *CWA Apartments*, 108 Parkin St, T9527 9560, set about 200 m back from northern Palm Beach. There are a number of B&Bs in town, all priced around $80-90. **C** *Pelican's Landing*, 352 Safety Bay Rd, T/F9592 3058, www.pelicans.com.au, have the best ocean views over Safety Bay from their breakfast and lounge room. Some rooms en suite. The recently refurbished pub at the **C** *Waikiki Hotel*, 434 Safety Bay Rd, T9592 1380, is right opposite the main southern beach facilities and has 16 comfortable motel units.

Eating *Winstons*, on the main Rockingham Rd cappuccino strip, T9527 1163, is open for breakfast and mid-range meals every day 0730-2000. Snacks and coffee outside of main mealtimes. Almost next door, *Beachcombers*, T9527 7195, is a little less formal and has slightly more edge. Open daily from 0700 it stays open to 2100 for dinners Wed-Sat. At the ferry 'terminal' opposite Penguin Island *Pengos*, T9528 2004, is a simple café with a surprisingly inventive mid-range lunch and dinner menu. Open 0800-1800 Mon-Tue, 0800-2100 Wed-Sun.

Tours and activities Boat hire *Palm Beach Boat Hire*, T9330 8782, hire out surfcats, canoes, windsurfers and aqua bikes. **Cycling** The entire peninsula foreshore makes for a pleasant ride. Bikes can be hired during Dec-Apr from a van at Safety Bay Beach, T0411 299945, $16 per ½ day. **Diving** *Malibu Diving*, T9527 9211, malibu@vianet.net.au, organize boat dives out to the marine park. **Dolphin cruises** *Rockingham Dolphins*, www.dolphins.com.au, run 2 excellent tours, both operating daily between mid-Sep and May. The *Dolphin Watch* cruise (T04-0909 0011, $50, children $25) leaves the Yacht Club jetty, the Esplanade, Rockingham, at 0830, returning about 1100. The *Swim with Dolphins* cruise (T9591 1333, $145 inc snorkelling gear, wetsuits and lunch) leaves the jetty at 0740, returning around 1200-1300. There are Perth bus pick-ups for both tours from the Wellington St Bus Station. **Sailing** *Ancient Mariner Adventure Cruises*, T0427-772278, sail out from the Yacht Club jetty for 2½-hr cruises ($33, children $16.50).

There are also opportunities to watch or swim with dolphins at Mandurah and Bunbury

Straddling the Mandurah Estuary, Mandurah is dominated by water activities and waterside living in flashy canal developments. The town is closely associated with crabs, which can be picked up in the estuary and are celebrated in an annual crab festival in February. **Dolphins** are also often seen in the estuary and are the focus for regular boat cruises and swim tours. The VIC sits just behind the attractive boardwalk area at the northern end of Mandjar Bay. ■ *Mon-Fri 0900-1700, Sat-Sun 0930-1600. T9550 3999, visitor@mandurah.wa.gov.au, www.peeltour.net.au 75 Mandurah Terr.*

Mandurah
Colour map 7, grid B5
Population: 50,000
110 km from Bunbury, 20 km from Pinjarra

Sleeping L-A *Dolphin Houseboats*, T9535 9898, www.dolphinhouseboats.com Ocean Marina. Attractive and comfortable 6- or 8-berth houseboats. Most with bunks, kitchen, bathroom and eating area. Price applies to boat so good value for 4-8. Prices rise steeply for weekends and public holidays. **B-C** *Mandurah Holiday Village*, 124 Mandurah Terr, T9535 4633, www.mandurahholidayvillage.au.com Pleasant modern units, some with spa, in shady grounds with pool, tennis court, BBQ and laundry. **C** *Foreshore Motel*, 2 Gibson St. T9535 5577, mandurahforeshore@bigpond.com. Good location a few steps from the foreshore café strip, 18 standard a/c rooms. **C-D** *Mandurah Caravan Park*, 603 Pinjarra Rd, T9535 1171. Large park with chalets and cabins, pool, kiosk and playground. **D-E** *Belvedere*, 153 Mandurah Terr, T9535 1213. Small and quiet caravan park close to town centre with on-site vans and cabins.

Most accommodation in town is holiday units and houses. There are no backpacker hostels at present so caravan parks are the best option for budget travellers

Eating *Café Pronto*, corner of Mandurah Terr and Pinjarra Rd, T9535 1004. Daily 0700-2100. One of the best places to eat in town. Mid-range food is a good mix of seafood, steak and Asian dishes like curries, stir frys and warm salads. Also more snacky light meals (cheap), wood-fired pizzas and extensive all-day breakfast menu. *Stage Door*, Mandurah Performing Arts Centre, T9550 3900. Bar and brasserie with stunning views and boardwalk tables. Mid-range seafood and grills and plenty of lighter meals. Jazz on Sun from 1500. Daily 0900-2100. *Cicerellos*, Boardwalk, T9535 9777. A branch of the famous Fremantle restaurant, this place does upmarket fish and chips. Also take-away. *Penang House*, 45 Mandurah Terr, T9535 8891. One of the town's most popular restaurants. Good Chinese and Malaysian dishes under $15. BYO. Daily

There are picnic tables and free BBQs on the foreshore

Western Australia

1130-1430, 1630-2100. *Dôme*, Boardwalk, T9581 1666. One of Mandurah's most popular cafés, opening onto the boardwalk. Daily 0700-2100. *Reading Room Book Café*, 15 Mandurah Terr, T0421 300 724. Welcoming café with idiosyncratic style that stands out from the clones. Wholesome, homemade food. Daily 1000-1700.

A free Mandurah Boating Guide is available at the VIC, with a map of local waters and details of boating regulations

Tours and activities Aboriginal culture   *Kwillana Dreaming* run excellent tours that introduce travellers to the Noongar culture and history in the Mandurah region. eco-tours of flora and fauna, canoe tours on Goegrup Lake and Serpentine River, (both $95, 5 hrs) and half-day tours around the city ($45, 3 hrs). Bookings and pickups from VIC, also pickups from Perth. **Boat hire**   *Mandurah Boat Hire*, T9535 5877, have runabouts and punts for hire, bait, crab nets and tackle. Daily 0700-1900. Pontoons $35-45 hr, dinghies $30 hr. **Crabbing**   Blue manna crabs can be caught in the Peel Inlet and Mandurah Estuary in summer and autumn. The Fisheries Dept of WA sets rules on methods, size and quantity, check with the VIC. Equipment can be hired from the boat hire businesses and *Tuckey's Tackle and Dive*, 2 Mandurah Terr. **Dolphin cruises** *Dolphin Encounters*, T0407-090284, 2½-hr cruise operates Nov-Jun only in the Mandurah Estuary and it is possible to swim or watch. Swim $110, Watch $77, all snorkelling equipment provided. Bookings essential. There are also enjoyable dolphin-spotting cruises in the estuary several times a day. *Mandjar*, T9535 3324, leaves from the boardwalk jetty at 1100, 1300, 1430 ($11, 1 hr). Tickets on board or at VIC.

Dwellingup
Colour map 7, grid B5
Population: 400
50 km from Mandurah

The best time to visit the forests around Dwellingup is spring or autumn

The sleepy town of Dwellingup, in the hills surrounded by extensive jarrah forests, has a long history in the timber felling and milling industry, but there is little of this heritage left to speak of as most of the town was razed to the ground by a fierce bushfire that swept through in 1961. The focus of the town is now switching more and more to providing activities that best show off the extensive natural attractions around the town, primarily the forest and the Murray River. Facilities are modest, including a pub, store, post office and an expensive petrol station. The **VIC** is on Marrinup Street, opposite the pub, and has a good range of local maps and guides. ■ *Daily 1000-1500. T9538 1108, www.murray.wa.gov.au* The local **CALM** office is nearby on Banksiadale Road. ■ *T9538 1078, dwell.dis@calm.wa.gov.au* Just to the north of the town the is the **Forest Heritage Centre** which has several bushwalks focusing on a different aspect of the forest, a forest interpretative centre, a gallery and shop selling exquisite handmade wooden furniture and turned items. ■ *Daily 1000-1700. $5.50, children $2.20, concessions $4.40. Acacia St, signposted 1 km from the VIC. T9538 1395, fhc@iinet.net.au* South of Dwellingup, 7 km down Nanga Road, is the northern boundary of **Lane Poole Reserve**, an extensive area of very pretty jarrah and marri forest through which the Murray River runs. There are a number of bush and riverside campsites, most with fireplaces, picnic tables and toilets. The Bibbulmun Track passes right through the reserve and there are other walking and mountain-biking trails, and lots of swimming spots. Note that within the reserve all roads are unsealed. ■ *Camping $10 per night for 2 adults. Firewood available in Dwellingup for $5 per bag, but gas stoves only are allowed during Dec-Mar. T9538 1078. A detailed map and guide is available at Dwellingup Adventures for $1.*

Sleeping and eating   There are a handful of B&Bs in the forest surrounding the town, including **C** *Berryvale Lodge*, 1082 Williams Rd, T9538 1239, www.berryvale lodge.com.au, a large, rammed-earth home with a comfortable first floor dedicated to guests. The **C-D** *Dwellingup Community Hotel/Motel*, Marrinup St, T9538 1056, is a large, friendly pub with cheap meals, bands during the afternoon 'Sunday sesh', cheap hotel rooms, including singles, and a few external motel rooms. Meals 1200-1400 daily,

Western Australia

1800-2000 Mon-Sat. The *Forest Heritage Centre* has a few dorms suitable for backpackers. ***Millhouse***, McLarty St, T9538 1122, is the town's little touch of class, a chic mid-range restaurant, café and chocolate-maker that's unfortunately only open Fri-Sun, daily some school holidays. Hours vary so phone ahead.

Activities Canoeing and rafting *Dwellingup Adventures*, T9538 1127, dwgupadv@southwest.com.au, organize a variety of self-guided rafting and canoeing tours along the Murray. They range from half-day excursions (from $60 for a 2-person canoe), to overnight hike/canoe adventures, camping out in Lane Poole Reserve (from $60 to $115 for a 2-person canoe, depending on starting point from Dwellingup). Hire of camping gear available (tent and stove $22 per day). **Mountain biking** ***WA Mountain Bike Tours***, T9295 1716, www.wambtours.com.au, organize half- full- and 4-day tours around Dwellingup and beyond.

Dryandra Woodlands

Colour map 7, grid D/C5
160 km from Perth, 140 km from Dwellingup

Dryandra is a vital remnant of the kind of vegetation that used to cover the area before it was cleared for farming. The park is best known for the **numbat**, an ant- and termite-eating marsupial that feeds in daylight hours but is difficult to see because of its keen senses of hearing and smell. Other rare animals of the Dryandra are **woylie** and **tammar** wallabies. The reserve is also a haven for birds and bird-spotters have counted about 130 species here. Here you may see some of WA rarest animals if you are patient. There is comfortable self-contained accommodation within the reserve in the Dryandra settlement. Simple timber workers cottages (**E**) are equipped with a full kitchen and BBQ but you need your own linen. For bookings contact the caretaker, T9884 5231. There are also good campsites at Congelin Dam. The nearest town to pick up supplies is Narrogin, a large farming community 27 km east, and you can get CALM brochures on Dryandra from the **Narrogin VIC.** ■ *Mon-Fri 0930-1630, Sat-Sun 1000-1600. T9881 2064, Earl St.*

The Southwest

Some of the most beautiful and varied country in WA is packed into the neat rectangular notch of the capes region and the richly timbered country inland. From Cape Naturaliste to Cape Leeuwin you can go caving in limestone caves near the coast, reef and wreck diving, whale watching in winter, and swim with dolphins further north in the region's main town of Bunbury. The hinterland area known as the 'timber towns' offers magnificent walking and driving through tall karri forest and the chance to climb to dizzying heights on a few of the giant fire-spotting trees. Of course, all this natural beauty is no secret – it is Western Australian's busiest and most developed area outside Perth – but if you want to escape there are still plenty of wild and quiet places to be found.

Ins and outs

Getting there & around

To the Cape to Cape area *Westrail* buses leave the East Perth Terminal for **Bunbury** (3 hrs), **Busselton** (4 hrs), **Dunsborough** (4½ hrs), **Yallingup, Margaret River** (5½ hrs), and **Augusta** (6 hrs). Services leave at 0830 and 1220 Sun-Fri and 1700 Fri, with some continuing on to **Nannup** and **Pemberton**. Some other timber towns services stop at Donnybrook. ***South West Coachlines***, T9324 2333, buses leave from the City Bus Port, Mounts Bay Rd, daily at 0845, 1315 and 1745 for **Bunbury** (3 hrs) and **Busselton** (4 hrs), with connections for **Dunsborough**. **Train** The *Westrail* Australind line runs between Perth Railway Station and **Bunbury**. Services daily at 0930 and 1745 (2¼ hrs).

To the timber towns *Westrail* have services from the East Perth terminal to **Pemberton** (5½ hrs) via **Balingup, Greenbushes, Bridgetown**, and **Manjimup** that leave at 1220 Mon, Wed and 1530 Sun. They also have services from Bunbury VIC that call additionally at **Northcliffe** before continuing on to **Albany**. These depart at 1130 Mon-Sat, 1140 Sun and 1618 Fri. The 1130 Wed and Fri buses do not call at Pemberton or Northcliffe. **Nannup** is served by a service between **Pemberton** and **Augusta** in the Capes region. *South West Coachlines* services leave from the City Bus Port, Perth, and call at **Balingup, Greenbushes, Bridgetown** and **Manjimup**.

Bunbury

Colour map 7, grid C5
Population: 28,000
180 km from Perth,
100 km from Margaret
River, 160 km from
Pemberton

Sitting on Koombana Bay, at the northern end of the beautiful sweep of Geographe Bay, Bunbury is the major port for the southwest. The city's greatest natural attraction is its resident population of **dolphins** who live in Koombana Bay and swim in to the beach regularly. Bunbury also has a sophisticated 'cappuccino strip' along Victoria Street, good shopping and beautiful ocean beaches on Geographe Bay. It's an appealing and relaxed place with the services of a large city and the slow, sunny pace of a small seaside town. The **VIC** is housed in the former railway station in the centre of town. ■ *Daily 0900-1700. T9721 7922, www.tourismbunbury.com.au Carmody Pl.*

Ins & outs   The town centre is very compact and almost everything of interest can easily be reached on foot. Buses from the railway station into town leave every 20-40 mins, between 0730-1800 Mon-Fri, and 0740-1415 Sat. Buses leaving town depart from the bus station next to the VIC.

Sights
There are also dolphin view and swim cruises at Mandurah and Rockingham

To encounter the bottlenose dolphins that live in the bay you can simply wade in off the beach at the Dolphin Discovery Centre, take a short cruise into the bay, kayak through their territory or go on an outstanding swim tour. The **Dolphin Discovery Centre** manages dolphin beach encounters and conducts research into the Koombana Bay pods. The centre has a small museum that explains the biology and behaviour of dolphins but the main attraction is the interactive zone, an area of shallow water that has been roped off to allow encounters between dolphins and people. The crowds are usually small, especially if you arrive early (0800-0900) which is also when you have the best chance of seeing the dolphins. Cruises and swim tours leave from the beach and should be booked at the centre. Other facilites include a basic café, souvenir shop, and showers. ■ *Daily 0800-1700 Nov-Apr, 0900-01400 May-Oct. $2, children $1, concessions $1. T9791 3088, www.dolphindiscovery.com.au Koombana Dr, 1½ km from town centre.*

Mangrove Cove walk is opposite the Dolphin Discovery Centre, and just to the south of the town centre is **Big Swamp**, a wetland that attracts water birds such as herons and swans. Long-necked turtles can also be seen there. Adjacent to the Big Swamp is the **Big Swamp Wildlife Park**, whose reception doubles as a free Swamp Interpretative Area. The wildlife park has a few free-roaming kangaroos, some emus, a wombat and a large aviary, but there's nothing here to really get excited about. ■ *Daily 1000-1700. $5, children $3, concessions $4. Hayward St, T9721 8380.*

Dolphin cruises   Taking a **boat cruise** into the bay allows you to see the dolphins in their own environment and engaging in natural behaviour such as catching fish or raising calves. During the summer *Naturaliste Charters* also run swim tours. Participants don wetsuits and snorkelling gear and jump in for about 15 minutes at a time. To see the dolphins underwater, hear them clicking and whistling and have them swim around you is an unforgettable experience. ■ *Dolphin cruises daily 0930, 1100, 1400. $25, concessions $22. Swim Tour daily 0800, 1100 (Dec-Apr) $90. Bookings at the discovery centre.*

Sleeping

L-C *The Clifton*, corner of Clifton St and Molloy St, T9721 4300, www.theclifton.com.au The most expensive suites in this luxurious hotel are in its central, impeccably refurbished Victorian manor house, *Grittleton Lodge*. **B** *Ellen's Cottage*, 41 King Rd, T9721 4082, www.justsouth.com.au Historic, self-contained farmer's cottage with many period features. Modern kitchen and laundry appliances but no TV or phone. Breakfast basket supplied. **C** *Aran Brae*, 5 Sherry St, T9721 2177. B&B with an en suite garden apartment, private courtyard and BBQ, and a very warm, Irish welcome. **C-D** *Welcome Inn*, Ocean Dr, T9721 3100. Well positioned, friendly motel, overlooking the back beach and a 10-min stroll from Victoria St. There are several other motels further along the drive. **D-E** *Wander Inn*, 16 Clifton St, T9721 3242, wanderinnbp@yahoo.com Excellent friendly and clean backpackers in a great location by the cafés and the beach. Lovely, shady back garden and BBQ area, and all the usual facilities. Also bike hire. **B-D** *Koombana Bay Holiday Resort*, Koombana Dr, T9791 3900, www.kbhr.com.au Well-maintained **caravan park** opposite the Dolphin Discovery Centre with chalets and cabins. The complex has a pool, campers' kitchen, shop, café and tennis courts, and is the closest to town.

Eating

Louisa's, *The Clifton*, Clifton St, T9721 4300. Very fine heritage dining rooms complement the excellent and expensive fusion cuisine. Open 1200-1400 Tue-Fri, 1800-2100 Mon-Sat. *Jumping J's*, 62 Victoria St, T9721 6075. Popular and lively mid-range joint. Lots of grills and old favourites on offer and the food is consistently good here. Also a good breakfast menu. Daily 0800-2100. *Mojo's*, Victoria St, T9792 5900. Sleek and stylish place offering all-day breakfast and cheap café menu. In the evening meals change to modern Australian, daily 0830-2200. *Just One Thai*, 109A Victoria St, T9721 1205. BYO. Authentic cheap Thai cooking with a good range of seafood dishes. Tue-Fri 1200-1400, daily 0600-2100. Also take-away. *Benessé*, 83 Victoria St, T9791 4030. The best coffee on the strip can be found in this laid-back understated café. Daily 0700-2100. *Ex-tension*, Ocean Dr, T9791 2141. Hanging over this beach the café is a good spot to catch a sunset. Mid-range grills and seafood, other cheap options and also a kiosk. Open 0700-1500 Mon-Tue, 0700-2100 Wed-Sun.

Pubs & bars

Fitzgeralds, 22 Victoria St, T9791 2295. In a former warehouse, this is a pub that stands out from the crowd. Friendly staff and great, cheap bar meals 1800-2200. Open Thu-Sat 1800-0300, Sun 2000-2400. Recommended. The *Reef*, Victoria St, T9791 6677, is Bunbury's principal party pub. Lots goes on here, mostly Wed-Sat. *Rose*, Victoria St, T9721 4533. This 100-year-old pub with fine iron-lace verandas is an elegant and civilized place for a drink. Cheap bar meals daily 1200-1400, 1800-2000. Also 25 tired motel rooms and 10 hotel rooms with shared facilities (**C-D**).

Tours & Activities

Scenic flights *South West Microlights*, T9795 9092. Tandem flights over Koombana Bay $80. **Sea kayaking** *Decked Out Adventures*, T9791 9888 or T0428 943483, dekkedout@iprimus.com.au Enjoyable kayaking tours around Bunbury waters from $50 half day, $80 day. Also tours in the Capes region and kayak hire from $45 a day.

Transport

Bus *Westrail* bus services leave from the VIC for **Perth** at 1140 Mon, Wed, Fri, 1115 Tue, Thu, Sat, and 1740 Sun-Fri. Services to the **Capes region** depart 1526 Sun-Thu, 2008 Fri, and from the railway station at 1140 Sun-Fri. Services to **Donnybrook** and the **timber towns (Pemberton** 2½ hrs) leave the VIC at 1528 Mon, Wed and 1833 Sun.

Additional services which continue on to Northcliffe, and south coast towns to **Albany** (6½ hrs) leave at 1130 Mon-Sat and 1140 Sun (Wed and Fri services do not stop at **Pemberton** or **Northcliffe**). *South West Coachlines* services leave from Bicentennial Sq at 0845, 1400 and 1845 daily. Their **Busselton** services leave 1135 and 2020 daily, 1605 Sat-Sun and 1620 Mon-Fri. **Train** The *Australind* heads up to **Pinjarra**, **Serpentine** and **Perth** daily at 0600 and 1440.

Directory **Banks** Major banks have branches and ATMs on the southern end of Victoria St, except *Commonwealth* which is on Stephen St. **Bike hire** *Decked Out Adventures*, T9791 9888 or T0428 943483. $25 day, also general equipment hire including tents, backpacks, fishing rods and camping gear. **Car Hire** *Avis*, 55 Forrest Av, T9721 7873. *Bunbury Cheaper*, 4 Mervyn St, T9721 4822. Cheap older-model cars but no bombs. **Communications** Internet: *Internet Planet*, Victoria St. Mon-Thu 0900-1900, Fri 0900-1800, Sat 1000-1800. $6 hr. **Post Office**, corner of Victoria St and Stirling St. **Medical services** *Bunbury Regional Hospital*, Bussell Highway, corner of Robertson Dr, T9722 1000. **Police** 29 Symmons St, T9791 2422. **Taxi** T9721 2300.

Busselton

Colour map 7, grid C5
Population: 10,500
55 km from Bunbury,
45 km from
Margaret River

Originally one of the main export ports for WA's timber, Busselton is now simply a relaxed family holiday town with a large number of tourist parks and motels strung out along the Bussell Highway. The **beach** is a beauty, with lots of white sand sloping gently into the usually clear water. The **Old Courthouse Complex**, at the end of Queen Street, now houses art and craft businesses instead of criminals and Aboriginals. **Busselton Jetty**, nearly 2 km long, is a very pleasant walk and conceals beneath its timbers a riot of marine life. It takes about 25 minutes to walk to the end, but if your legs don't fancy it a small tourist train heads out there, too. During a quick snorkel you will be able to see much of the coral and fish life living on and around the piles, but to really appreciate this wonderful artificial reef a scuba dive is necessary, at night if possible. See next page for diving options. ■ *Entry to jetty $2.50, children and concessions $1.50. Trains daily unless windy, on the hr, 1000-1600. Tickets $7.50, children and concessions $5.50, divers with scuba equipment $13. Interpretative centre free, open daily 1000-1600, T9754 3689.* From 2003 the new **Under Water Observatory** should be open. For an additional $12 you will be able to walk, or catch a lift down into an underwater room located at the gap. The **VIC** is also the *Westrail* bus terminal. ■ *0830-1700 Mon-Fri, 1000-1600 Sat-Sun. 38 Peel Terr, T9752 1288, info@bsn.downsouth.com.au* Just around the corner on Albert Street is the stop for South West Coachlines.

Sleeping & eating There are 2 good B&Bs, both on West St: **C** *Jacaranda*, T9752 1246, pepper@compwest.net.au, and **C** *Geographe*, T9752 1451, geoguest@iinet.net.au All the town's many motels are strung out along the highway. The closest, and one of the cheapest is the **C-D** *Paradise*, Pries Av, T9752 1200. As well as standard motel doubles they have a 'lodge' with a few good value singles, a TV room and kitchenette. **E** *Busselton Backpackers*, 14 Peel Terr, T9754 2763, is a converted home that sleeps 17 in small dorms and doubles. There are a number of caravan parks along the highway, though some are several km from the town centre. Closest is the *Kookaburra*, Marine Terr, T9752 1516. The expensive *Goose*, 6 Prince St, T9754 7700, offers the best cuisine in town. Open 0900-2100 Tue-Sat. Recommended. *Equinox*, T9752 4641, is a large, friendly café on the foreshore near the jetty. Cheap light lunches and mid-range evening meals include snacks and platters. Open daily 0800-2100, kiosk to 1800, later in peak summer.

Diving in Geographe Bay

The Bay north of Busselton and Dunsborough is a huge sea-grass plain, known as a good place to spot the beautiful common sea dragon. As well as the amazing 'reef' under **Busselton Jetty***, there are two other artificial reefs in the bay, plus the limestone contour called* **4-Mile Reef** *that runs east to west across it. This is covered in many types of corals and sponges, attracts whales and is about 18 m*

deep. The first **Artificial Reef** *is a collection of constructions made from old car tyres, covering around 1 ha under about 21 m of water, and now harbouring a large array of marine life. Most recently, and spectacularly, the* **HMAS Swan** *is rapidly building its own collection of sealife, and is an unforgettable dive, definitely the star attraction in the bay. The warship was sunk in 1997 in 30 m of water off Eagle Bay near Dunsborough.*

Diving and snorkelling There are 2 operators in town, both offering regular boat dives to the jetty and the *Swan* (see page below), and equipment hire. Contact both to see what they're running and who's got places. Expect to pay from $135 for a 2-dive trip including gear, and $70-100 for a single jetty dive. The *Dive Shed*, 21 Queen St, T9754 1615, www.diveshed.com.au, is marginally cheaper and also offers an introductory dive at the jetty for $85. *Naturaliste Diving Academy*, 103 Queen St, T9752 2096, www.natdive.com, run regular PADI courses and have the cheapest snorkel hire.

Tours & activities

Bus *Westrail* bus services leave from the VIC for **Perth** at 1035 Mon, Wed, Fri, 1022 Tue, Thu, Sat, and 1652 Sun-Fri. Services to **Capes region** depart 1248 Sun-Fri, 1626 Sun-Thu and 2112 Fri. *South West Coachlines* northbound services leave at 0740, 1300 and 1745 daily. Their **Dunsborough** services leave at 0620 daily, 1705 Sat-Sun and 1730 Mon-Fri.

Transport

Dunsborough and around

Sharing the same long, north-facing beach as Busselton, Dunsborough is as much a holiday town as its neighbour, but more for its proximity to the Cape Naturaliste and the region's main wine area. Other than heading for the beach there is not a great deal to do in the town itself, and most visitors use it as a base to explore the northern part of the capes region, dive the **HMAS Swan** and head out on the various tours. The **VIC** is in the Dunsborough Park Shopping Centre, as are many of the town's services, and can supply details of the private holiday homes and units available for let. ■ *0900-1700 Mon-Fri, to 1600 Sat, and 1000-1600 Sun. T9755 3299, info@dboro.downsouth.com.au*

Colour map 7, grid C5
Population: 1,500
24 km from Busselton,
45 km from Margaret River

　　Cape Naturaliste is a wild triangle of hardly developed land where you can find a perfect beach and peaceful isolation less than half an hour's drive from Dunsborough and Busselton. Dunsborough sits at its eastern corner on Geographe Bay and a string of spectacular quiet, bay beaches stretch to the tip where there is a lighthouse. These beaches all have dazzling fine white sand, turquoise water and shallow safe swimming. **Meelup** is the busiest beach, with picnic tables and toilets, but the prettiest is **Bunker Bay**, near the tip of the cape. The only point to access the wilder western coast of the cape is at **Sugarloaf Rock**, an idyllic swimming spot in calm weather, 4 km past the turn-off for the holiday home settlement of Eagle Bay. The Cape Naturaliste **Lighthouse** is at the end of the main road, set back from the coast by a few kilometres, and still in use today. Self-guided tours allow access to the lens and balcony and a small museum in a lighthouse keeper's cottage. ■ *Daily 0930-1600. T9755 3955. $6.50, children $2.50.* There are several walking tracks from the cape (track access is free), pick up a walking trail map ($2.20) from the lighthouse shop.

Sleeping & eating
A *Ocean View*, Geographe Bay Rd, T9756 8934, is a complex of 4 modern, furnished houses, all facing the beach with 1st-floor balconies overlooking the ocean. Recommended. **C-E** *Dunsborough Inn*, 50 Dunn Bay Rd, T9756 7277, www.dunsboroughinn.com, is a modern brick complex, with 6 open-plan self-contained units and a separate budget section with doubles, triples, quads, and clean and comprehensive hostel-style communal facilities. The friendly owners often take guests out on snorkelling trips. **D** *Three Pines Beach YHA*, 201 Geographe Bay Rd, T9755 3107, dunsboroughyha@hotmail.com, is homely and lively with 70 beds in small dorms and a few doubles and twins. Fantastic beachside position with a huge rear garden overlooking the ocean. Bike hire and regular lifts alleviate the 40-min walk to town. Recommended. **B-D** *Dunsborough Lakes*, Caves Rd, T9756 8300, is the town's only caravan park, and a little out of town but is spacious with a good range of facilities.

The expensive *Bay Cottage*, Dunn Bay Rd, T9755 3554, is an unassuming-looking restaurant on the outskirts of town, but the modern Australian food is excellent. Open 1800-2030 Tue-Sat. Best value in town is *Artézen*, 234 Naturaliste Terr, T9755 3325. This chic but earthy café serves up an interesting range of cheap light meals. Open all day, meals, including breakfast, 0800-1500 daily and 1800-2100 Mon-Sat. *Newberry*, 6 Newberry Rd, off Naturaliste Terr, T9755 3631, pleasantly combines a bookshop, gallery and café. Open 1000-1600 Tue-Sun.

Tours & activities
Diving The main diving season is Nov-Apr, and not much happens Jul-Aug. You'll pay about $160 for a 2-dive trip to the *Swan*, including gear hire, and about $95 for a single dive. *Cape Dive*, Naturaliste Terr, T9756 8778, www.capedive.com, are the local specialists and have dozens of dive combinations, mostly focusing on the *Swan*. Their snorkel hire is $11 a day. **Sailing** The *Willie* is a sleek, twin-masted pearl lugger, based in Dunsborough during Sep-Apr. It heads out most days between Sep and Feb on whale-watching, sunset, *Swan* and 'boom-net' cruises. Trips are good value ($40-60), really great fun and last 2-3 hrs. T0428 919781, www.cannonball.com.au/willie **Whalewatching** *Naturaliste Charter* (see above) run trips daily during the Sep to mid-Dec season, usually at 1000 and 1300 (3 hrs, $45, children $25, concessions $42). **Wine tasting** *Taste the South*, T9756 7958, tastethesouth@netserv.net.au, run informative, flexible and fun mini-bus tours around the Margaret River region. $48 for a half day, $68-90 for a full day.

Transport
Bus *Westrail* northbound services leave from the VIC at 1004 Mon, Wed, Fri, 0954 Tue, Thu, Sat, and 1624 Sun-Fri. Services south depart 1316 Sun-Fri, 1656 Sun-Thu, 2140 Fri. *South West Coachlines* Busselton services leave at 0705 daily, continuing on to **Perth**, and from the Beach Shop at 1805 Mon-Fri, 1740 Sat-Sun.

Yallingup and around

Colour map 7, grid C4
Population: 100
10 km from Dunsborough,
20 km from Wilyabrup wineries.

Yallingup is a Noongar word meaning 'place of love'

The tiny beach settlement of Yallingup spreads down a hill to a long beach and reef-protected lagoon. To the north and south are isolated and pristine surfing beaches. The main attractions are swimming, surfing, and the **Ngilgi Cave** (pronounced nil-gee), a beautifully deep and decorated limestone cave, with magnificent shawls, stalagmites, stalactites and helictites. ■ *Entry to the cave is only by semi-guided tour. Daily tours every 30 mins on the half hr 0930-1530. $14, children $5 (cash only). Adventure tours $40, 3 hrs (bookings essential). T9755 2152, www.downsouth.com.au* Just past the cave, at the top of the hill, is the venerable *Caves House*, a caravan park, and shop. Follow the road downhill to reach the beach and the main area of holiday homes. By the beach there is a grassy foreshore with playground and BBQs. Also a café, gallery and *Yallingup Surf Shop*, T9755 2036, hiring out surfboards and beach umbrellas

Cape-to-Cape Walking Track

The spectacular **Cape-to-Cape Track** is a must if you are staying in the area for any length of time. This track follows the coastline from Cape Naturaliste to Cape Leeuwin (140 km) and is a superb way to see the coastal and forest scenery in the region, much of it inaccessible by car. The walk, rated as one of the best coastal walks in the country, is mostly within the **Leewin-Naturaliste National Park**, a narrow strip less than 10 km wide in places, along a limestone ridge. Unusually for a long Australian track it is accessible year-round, rarely either too hot or cold. There are regular road access points so it is easy to walk short sections or day trips. Most short or day walks will involve returning along the same path unless you can arrange a pickup. Basic campsites reserved for walkers can be used along the way. Tents, water and fuel stoves must all be carried and waste carried out. The track is administered by **CALM** who produce an excellent pack ($8) containing walk maps and notes in five sections covering the entire route. There are no charges or permits. For more information contact CALM in Busselton, T9752 1677, CALM in Margaret River, T9757 2322, or see www.naturebase.net A few companies organize guided walks along the track. **Environmental Encounters**, T9375 7885, www.environmentalencounters.com.au, periodically run 7-day fully-supported trips that cover the entire track, for around $1,000. To walk the whole track from Cape Naturaliste to Cape Leeuwin via Yallingup and Prevelly, takes about a week. Although campsites are provided where there are no commercial facilities, there may be long stretches where no water is available. For further details contact. 'Friends of the Cape-to-Cape'. capetrack@hotmail.com

(deposit and ID required), daily 0900-1700. Surfing lessons are available from *Yallingup Surf School*, T9755 2755, for $70. This heads uphill past Ngilgi Cave and a lookout and circles back to the coast. You can access the Cape to Cape track from the foreshore.

Ten kilometres south of Yallingup, is **Canal Rocks**, a bare rocky headland with a maze of fissures worn so deep and wide as to create a series of islands, separated by canal-like channels and pools. Another 10 kilometres south via Wyardup Road, but just a magnificent 2 km cliff-top walk from the rocks via the Cape-to-Cape track, are **Wyardup Rocks** and **Indijup Beach**. The rocks are similar, though not quite as broken up as Canal Rocks and are immediately adjacent to the magnificent beach.

The area between Dunsborough and Yallingup, is covered in a maze of picturesque, mostly sealed lanes, with a **gallery** or **winery** seemingly around every corner. *Happs*, Commonage Road, T9755 3479, is a welcoming, rustic winery and pottery. *Gunyulgup Galleries*, T9755 2177, Gunyulgup Valley Drive, Yallingup, is the finest gallery in the southwest. The main cluster of wineries in this northern end of the region is on, or just off, Wildwood Road. *Abbey Vale*, T9217 6700, is open 1030-1630. *Clairault*, off Pusey Road, T9755 6225, open 1000-1700, is the largest family-owned-and-run winery in the region, and has one of the most stylish tasting and dining rooms.

Aside from the caravan parks, accommodation in the area isn't cheap, and coastal prices skyrocket in the peak Dec-Jan period when even an unpowered tent site will set you back over $30. **A-C** *Caves House*, Yallingup Beach Rd, Yallingup, T9755 2131, www.caveshouse.com.au is a 1930s building with faded art-deco charm and wonderful gardens. **A** *Chandler's Villas*, Smiths Beach, T/F9755 2062. Compromises 3 widely-separated tiers of rammed earth and wood self-contained cottages, all with

Sleeping & eating

Western Australia

clear panoramic views over Smiths Beach which is a 10-min walk away. Each sleeps up to 6. Of a handful of **caravan parks**, **B-D** *Yallingup Beach* holiday park, T9755 2164, www.yallingupbeach.com.au, has superb views, cabins, on-site vans, a kiosk and grassy sites. Alternatively, *Canal Rocks Beach Resort*, Smiths Beach, T9755 2116, www.canalrocks.com.au, has a wide range of slightly pricier options. It's a short walk to the beach and facilities include a shop, open 0730-2200, take-away and the *Rocks* café. *Lamont's*, next to Gunyulgup Gallery, T9755 2434. A new venue for one of Perth's best-known chefs, the food here is some of the best in the region. Daily 1000-1800, Sat 1000-2030. Recommended. *Café Laguna*, Dawson Dr (by Yallingup beach), T9755 2133. Smart beach-style café with water views and expensive modern Australian food. Good place for breakfast. *Rocks Café*, Smiths Beach, T9755 2116, serves meals in the simple, surfie dining room or on the small outside deck. Breakfasts all day from 0730, cheap light lunches 1130-1730 and mostly expensive dinners 1800-2030.

Transport   **Bus** *Westrail* northbound services leave from the town hall at 0955 Mon, Wed, Fri, 0945 Tue, Thu, Sat, and 1615 Sun-Fri. Services south depart 1325 Sun-Fri, 1705 Sun-Thu, 2149 Fri.

Margaret River and around

Colour map 7, grid C5
Population: 3,000
100 km from Bunbury
via Bussell Highway,
55 km from Augusta
via Caves Rd

Margaret River is famous for two things: wine and surf. The region produces some of Australia's best premium wines, while at nearby Prevelly the surf is exceptional. The town of Margaret River makes a convenient base for both these attractions, and the Capes region in general. The town also acts as a focus for talented artists and craftspeople in the region and has restaurants, galleries, and accommodation that are the equal of any in the country. The **VIC** has a room showcasing the wineries of the region and can help with bookings. ■ *Daily 0900-1700. T9757 2911, amrta@netserv.net.au Bussell Highway, corner of Turnbridge St.*

Sights   Visiting **galleries** is another enjoyable aspect of the area. Many studios are in the countryside but there are a few galleries in town that showcase regional work such as *Margaret River Art Gallery*, at 83 Bussell Highway, and *Margaret River Pottery*, 91 Bussell Highway. Ask at the VIC for a list if you want to go on a gallery crawl. **Eagles Heritage Centre** on Boodijup Road is the only wildlife park of its kind in Australia, dedicated to rescuing and rehabilitating birds of prey. ■ *Daily 1000-1700, displays 1100 and 1330 (1 hr). $8, children $4, concessions $6. , T9757 2960, www.eaglesheritage.com.au* **Ellensbrook**, 13 km from Margaret River, was one of the earliest houses in the district. It has been restored by the National Trust and is a fine example of a European pioneer house. ■ *House open Thu-Sun 0945-1615 (may be open Mon-Wed). $4, children $2, concession $3. Grounds open daily, donation appreciated.*

Prevelly, 9 km from Margaret River, is the closest beach and the location for the legendary international surf competition, **Margaret River Masters**, held in April (www.salomonmasters.com). Surfers Point, at the northern edge of Prevelly, is a powerful reef break and the surfers car park there is a great place to watch the action on a big day. Here the eucalypt green of Margaret River meets the aquamarine of the Indian ocean. At the southern end is **Gnarabup Beach** where a humble but picturesque café perches above the water. Nearby, is the site of a controversial high-density modern housing development, that goes to the heart of the future of the capes region. Facilities at Prevelly and Gnarabup are limited.

Western Australia

Cape to Cape

Pierro, T9755 6220, open 1000-1700, has a rustic feel but superb quality wines. ***Vasse Felix***, T9756 5000, www.vassefelix.com.au, is still making some of the region's best wines. Everything open 1000-1700, except the expensive restaurant (1200-1500). On Metricup Rd, ***Woody Nook***, T9755 6547, 1000-1630, is laid-back and rustic. The Cabernet Sauvignon and Sauvignon Blanc are consistently good and an unpretentious café, T9755 7030, serves hearty meals. The ***Grove***, T9755 7458, www.thegrovevineyard.com.au, is a stylish fusion of tasting themes, sharing the same buildings with the objective of offering the visitor something a bit different. Tastings 0900-1600. Off Metricup Rd, on Harmons Mill Road is ***Hay Shed Hill***, T9755 6305, open 1030-1700, one of the friendliest wineries in the region. Their flagship wines are a treat, including a rich velvety Pinot Noir. Picnickers welcome. Just outside Cowaramup is small, rustic ***Treeton Estate***, Treeton Rd, T9755 5481, open daily 1000-1800. Drinkable, light summer wines plus patés and Margaret River cheeses to eat at a few outdoor tables. ***Margaret River Regional Wine Centre***, T9755 5501, www.mrwines.com, stock almost every wine made in the region. They act as an information centre, can help plan a wine-tasting itinerary based on your tastes and time, and have wine tastings. Open Mon-Sat 1000-1900, Sun 1200-1800.

South of Margaret River *Xanadu*, T9757 3066, open 1000-1700. Everything about this place is smart and savvy, but casual. The mid-range meals, available 1200-1600, are the equal of those you'll get at much pricier establishments. Recommended. The ***Minot*** 'cellar door', off Exmoor Dr (opposite the Eagles Heritage Centre), T9757 3579, is simply a modest table outside the owners' bungalow home. They produce a light, refreshing Semillon Sauvignon Blanc ($13), and a fabulously rich Cabernet ($23). 'Open' 1000-1700, but phone ahead. ***Voyager***, T9757 6354, open 1000-1700, is arguably the most

Wineries

The Wilyabrup wineries are mostly packed along Caves Rd, between Yallingup and Margaret River. The small number of wineries near Margaret River itself mostly lie along or just off Boodijup Rd

Western Australia

scenic winery in the region. Landscaped rose-gardens and white-washed walls surround a gleaming white Cape Dutch style cellar door and restaurant, lunches 1200-1430. Both it and Leeuwin are well signposted a little way past Exmoor Dr. *Leeuwin Estate*, T9757 6253, www.leeuwinestate.com.au, open 1000-1630, is the best known winery in the region, with a stylish, expensive restaurant, excellent wines and fascinating art gallery. Also host the Leeuwin Concert Series every summer, a few days of mostly classical performances that are the South West's premier event. Book well ahead for tickets ($100+) and accommodation.

Sleeping **L** *Basildene Manor*, Wallcliffe Rd, T9757 3140. The finest accommodation in the area, built in 1912, this historic stone house sits in lovely grounds. 17 splendid rooms, several guest lounges, outdoor pool and a welcoming, homely feel. Recommended. **B** *Margarets Forest*, 96 Bussell Highway, T9758 7188, www.margaretsforest.com.au A complex of stylish and contemporary self-contained studios and apartments in the centre of town. **C** *Bridgefield*, 73 Bussell Highway, T9757 3007. Lovely National Trust listed guesthouse close to the river. Warm hospitality and excellent value. The only flaw is the traffic noise. **C** *Margaret River Guesthouse*, Valley Rd, T9757 2349, www.tourist vision.com.au A former convent in a quiet side street with beautiful English garden, this B&B has 8 comfortable rooms. Huge breakfast. **D-E** *Inne Town Backpackers*, 93 Bussell Highway, T9757 3698. Small, scruffy hostel that has the major advantage of being in the centre of town. Dorms and doubles. **D-E** *Margaret River Lodge*, 220 Railway Terr, T9757 9532, www.mrlodge.com.au Backpackers in quiet bush location about 2 km from town centre. Rammed-earth buildings, pool, BBQs and bike hire. Pickups from coach stop. There are 2 **caravan parks** close to the town centre. *Margaret River Tourist Park*, 44 Station Rd, T9757 2180, has timber cottages (**D**) with kitchen and en suite, pool and good shady, grassy tent sites. **In Prevelly** the: **L-B** *Margarets Beach Resort*, Walcliffe Rd, T9757 1227, www.assuredhospitality.com.au Luxurious self-contained apartments, and **C-E** *Surf Point Lodge*, Riedle Dr, T9757 1777, www.surfpoint.com.au has luxurious but soulless backpacker accommodation.

Eating *Vat 107*, 107 Bussell Highway, T9758 8877. One of the best places to eat in the country and eating here really is worth every (expensive) cent. The food is an innovative mix of local produce and world cuisines. Open daily for breakfast 0900-1130, lunch 1130-1800, dinner 1800-2030. Recommended. Has 4 elegant contemporary spa suites (**A**). *Arc of Iris*, 151 Bussell Highway, T9757 3112. Funky little café and long-standing locals' favourite. Good value mid-range food. BYO. Thu-Sun 1200-1400, daily 1800-2030. Recommended. *Goodfellas*, 97 Bussell Highway, T9757 3184. Lively, cheap, pizza and pasta café with an upstairs balcony. BYO. Daily 1800-2030. *Urban Bean*, 157 Bussell Highway, T9757 3480. Deservedly popular café wit outdoor terrace. Daily 0700-1700. *Urchins*, Town Sq, Bussell Highway, T9757 3808. Essentially a fish and chip joint but with a twist. The menu includes Thai seafood, sushi, and chilli fish. Eat-in or take-away. Daily 1700-2000. BYO.

Pubs & bars The *Margaret River Hotel* is a classy and civilized pub with lots of outdoor terrace tables. Karaoke Thu, bands and DJs Fri-Sat. Also houses the sophisticated *D'Vine* bistro. Pleasant en suite rooms upstairs (**B-C**) but these can be noisy. *Settlers Tavern*, 114 Bussell Highway, T9757 2398. A traditional Aussie pub with beer garden on the streetfront, pool tables, TVs and TAB. Also busy live venue Wed-Sat. *Wino's*, 85 Bussell Highway, T9758 7155. A very hip, but down-to-earth wine bar. Huge range of local wines by the glass and an excellent 'grits' menu, lots of small $5 nibble dishes. Also mid-range mains in a casual fusion style. Daily 1100-late.

Canoeing *Bushtucker Tours*, T9757 1084, www.bushtuckertours.com, run one of the best tours in the southwest. The 4 hr trip ($40, children $20), which leaves daily at 1000, takes in a bit of a paddle, a short bushwalk, a cave tour and a bush-tucker picnic. A similar tour without the caving leaves at 0930 (4 hrs, $35). **Outdoor** *Outdoor Discoveries*, T0407 084945, outdoor@iinet.net.au, organize all sorts of activities for small groups, including caving, abseiling, bushwalking, canoeing and rock climbing.
Surfing 24-hr surf report T1900 922 995. *Beach Life Surf Shop*, 117 Bussell Highway, T9757 2888. Board hire from $20 half day. Also book lessons here for *Margaret River Surf School*. Group lessons at 1000 daily, $35 per person including equipment.
Wine tasting There are number of options including a personal tour in a Bentley with the *Margaret River Lady*, T9757 1212, www.thewinetourco.com.au, perfect if you're loaded or out to impress. A little less hard on the wallet are *Margaret River Tours*, T0419 917166, www.margaretrivertours.com, who use a variety of vehicles from minibuses to 4WD, and cheapest of all, *Bushtucker Tours* ($50), who inevitably include a bit of an indigenous food tasting.

**Tours &
Activities**

Bus *Westrail* northbound services leave from **Charles West Rd** at 0915 Mon, Wed, Fri, 0905 Tue, Thu, Sat, and 1535 Sun-Fri. Services south depart 1405 Sun-Fri, 1745 Sun-Thu, 2229 Fri. The 0915 buses continue on to **Nannup** and **Pemberton**.

Transport

There are 300 known caves in the region, riddling the limestone rock like holes in a cheese, but less than a dozen are open to the public. **Mammoth Cave** was a long-standing shelter for Aboriginal tribes and many species of animals. ■ *0900-1600. Self-guided, allow 45 mins. $14.50, children $6.* T9757 7514. *Weekly tickets to Mammoth, Lake and Jewel caves are $35, children $15. Some* 3 km south of Mammoth is **Cave Works** interpretation centre, which describes the geology of the region and how the caves were formed. ■ *0900-1500. Entry free with a Mammoth, Lake or Jewel cave ticket, otherwise $3, children $2.* T9757 7411. Adjacent is a welcome **café**, open 0830-1700. Cave Works is also the entry point for **Lake Cave**, a relatively small but beautiful and peaceful chamber the entire floor of which is covered by a shallow lake. ■ *Entry by tour, on the half hr, 0930-1530. Allow 1 hr. $14.50, children $6.* Conto Road becomes unsealed after Cave Works and heads 3 km down to **Conto Beach** and the bush campground of **Conto Field**, the closest such campsite to a beach in the region. It is a stunning piece of coast and you are unlikely to have to share it with anyone if you explore a bit. Back on Caves Road, 2 km south of Conto Road, is **Giants Cave**, a self-guided CALM-managed cave with a series of massive chambers. This is one of the more adventurous of the caves with several ladders and some scrambling required – so wear stout shoes. ■ *0930-1530. Allow 1 hr. $10, children $5.* T9757 7422. If you only have time to see one cave then try to get to **Jewel Cave**. It is the largest and one of the deepest caves open to the public. The decorations are fantastic, especially the helictites and straws. ■ *Entry by tour, on the half hr, 0930-1530. Allow 1 hr. $14.50, children $6.* T9758 4541. **Moondyne Cave** is an adventure cave, but a fairly mild one, that will give you an idea of what caving is about. ■ *Guided adventure tour, daily at 1400. Bookings (via Cave Works, T9757 7411, Mammoth or Lake caves). Allow 2 hrs. $27.50, children $19.*

Caves Road
*Cave Works 17 km
from Margaret River*

Western Australia

▶▶ **Whale watching off the capes**

Humpback and *southern right* whales cruise past the capes during their yearly migration north from Antarctica. They hang about Cape Leeuwin during June-August, then head up the coast, coming close to shore at Gracetown and Sugarloaf, before spending another three months or so around Cape Naturaliste. There are whale watching boat tours from Augusta (June-September) and Dunsborough (September-December) which often get very close to the whales due to their great curiosity. If you can pick your time then head south, as during this period the Humpbacks are particularly active, often breaching, spy-hopping and catching the attention of the tourists.

Augusta and Cape Leeuwin

Colour map 7, grid C5
Population: 1,100
90 km from Nannup,
125 km from Pemberton
At Turner St Jetty stingrays will sometimes come in to feed if a little bait is dropped in the water

The small, friendly town of Augusta hugs the picturesque west bank at the mouth of the **Blackwood River**, the region's largest river, and continues a little way down the eastern side of **Cape Leeuwin**. The town's interesting history is illustrated by the many exhibits and photographs in the **Augusta Historical Museum**, including a fascinating section on the mass strandings of whales that happened here in 1986-89. ■ *Daily 1000-1200 and 1400-1600. $2, children $0.50. Blackwood Av, T9758 1948.* The helpful **VIC** is at the far end of the main shopping drag. ■ *0900-1700 Mon-Fri, 0900-1300 Sat-Sun. T9758 0166, aupro@netserv.net.au.*

Sleeping & eating

B-D *Augusta Hotel/Motel* Blackwood Av, T9758 1944, www.augusta-resorts.com.au Resort-style pub hotel with motel rooms, self-contained cottages, and a backpackers lodge. Counter meals 1200-1400, 1800-2030, plus a mid-range restaurant open in summer. **C** *Juniper's East Bank Studio*, T9758 1693, www.mron line.com.au/accom/juniper Artistic, peaceful self-contained cottage for 2 in the tiny cluster of houses on the far side of the river. The owners will ferry you over, though you can make the 40-km drive if you choose. Recommended. The friendly **C-E** *Baywatch Manor YHA*, 88 Blackwood Av, T9758 1290, is a clean and modern, purpose-built hostel with 36 beds in comfortable singles, twins and doubles, some en suite. Communal facilities are excellent. Recommended. Augusta has a number of B&Bs including **C** *Warmstone*, 5 Parry Court, T9758 1036, a pretty, white, weatherboard home with 2 rooms. There are **4 caravan** parks within 1½ km of the town centre. **E** *Doonbanks*, T9758 1517, is the closest to town and has a few cabins, while **E** *Westbay Retreat*, T9758 1572, has a few very pretty on-site vans plus the most stylish toilet block you're ever likely to clap your eyes on. *Colourpatch*, Albany Terr, T9758 1295. Simple, cheerful café with cheap meals to match and a terrace overlooking the river. Meals 0800-1000, 1200-1400 and 1800-2000.

Tours & activities

Bike hire from *Leeuwin Souvenirs*, Blackwood Av, next to the post office, T9758 1695. $12 for half a day, open daily. Also second-hand books and book exchange. **Boat cruise** The *Miss Flinders*, operated by the hotel, is a covered motor-cruiser that heads up the Blackwood River, the largest and one of the most unspoiled rivers in the southwest. Enquire at a hotel or the VIC for current schedule. **Sailing** Surfcats available from the Turner Caravan Park in summer, T9758 1593. **Whalewatching** *Naturaliste Charters*, T9755 2276, www.whales-australia.com, head out 1000 daily, Jun-Sep, and see whales almost every day (3 hrs, $45, children $25, concessions $42). Do not miss this tour if there are whales around.

Transport

Bus *Westrail* northbound services leave opposite the newsagents at 0840 Mon, Wed, Fri, 0830 Tue, Thu, Sat, and 1505 Sun-Fri. Services to **Nannup** and **Pemberton** depart 1815 Tue, Thu and Sun.

Most of Cape Leeuwin, the southern end of the low coastal hill range of the capes, is part of the national park and so is free of development. The cape marks the geographical point at which the Southern Ocean and Indian Ocean meet. On the promontory at the end of the cape is the **lighthouse**, built in the 1880s. There is not a great deal to see on the lighthouse tour except the excellent views from the top, but these and the guide's lively tales make it well worth the trip. ■ *Promontory precinct open daily 0845-1700, free entry. Lighthouse tours every ¾ hr 0900-1115 and 1300-1600. $6, children $3. 8km from Augusta. May not run if very windy, T9758 1920 to check.* For an excellent view over the entire promontory take the unsealed scenic drive just before the waterwheel car park. The main lookout is about 1 km along this road on the left.

Cape Leeuwin
In 2001 Cape Leeuwin Lighthouse received the furthest ever delivered pizza – all the way from New York in 24 hrs

The timber towns

The timber towns of Nannup, Balingup, Bridgetown, Manjimup and Pemberton all sit within the region's vast expanse of forested country and sprang up when a timber industry developed in the southwest in the late 19th and early 20th century. They have suffered in the last few decades from the decline of the timber industry and are now hoping, some reluctantly, that tourism will keep them going. Nannup and Pemberton are the most attractive, full of characteristic timber-workers' cottages. Both are still small and fairly undeveloped, but with good facilities in beautiful surroundings.

A pretty and historic town by the banks of the Blackwood River, Nannup is a sleepy and peaceful place to unwind, with canoeing on the **Blackwood** or walking in the forest the main things to do. The busiest time of year is the Nannup Music Festival, held in early March. The **VIC** is located in the former police station at the northern end of town by the river bank and bridge. ■ *Daily 0900-1700. T9756 1211, nannuptb@compwest.net.au 4 Brockman St.* One of the few timber mills still operating in the region is the **Nannup Timber Processing Mill**. ■ *Free tours Mon, Wed, Fri 0930. Meet at the mill office, enclosed shoes must be worn. Free. Enquiries to the VIC. Mill located on Vasse Highway at southern edge of town.* For **Barrabup** and **Workers Pools** head north cross the river and take the first left into Mowen Road, then follow the signs (9 km). Both are tranquil emerald-green swimming holes surrounded by forest. Each has camping sites, picnic tables and BBQs. Visit the CALM office in Warren Street for walking suggestions. ■ *Mon-Fri 0900-1600.* Between Nannup and Manjimup, is Donnelly, a former timber-milling town, where you can stay in former workers' cottages (**C**). It's very peaceful and full of wildlife, much of it practically tame. For details and bookings, T9772 1244. The Bibbulmun Track (see page 576) passes close by.

Nannup
Colour map 7, grid C5
Population: 800
60 km from Busselton, 90 km from Augusta

Sleeping and eating B *Holberry House*, Grange Rd. T9756 1276, www.holberry house.com A large, stone guesthouse on a hillside above Nannup in beautiful grounds. 6 rooms, guest lounge and conservatory. For self contained accommodation try **C** *Blackwood River Cottages*, T9756 1252, River Rd, 2km southwest of Nannup on the road to Augusta. Both the above have secluded timber cabins surrounded by bush. **C-D** *Nannup Hotel*, 12 Warren Rd, T9756 1080. The town's utilitarian pub has motel units and basic hotel rooms. **D-E** *Black Cockatoo*, 27 Grange Rd, T9756 1035. This backpackers in an old timber cottage is something special. The owners have combined their interests in the environment, arts and spirituality to create a unique and welcoming place to stay. Campers can use the lawn and facilities for $11. Book ahead. Recommended. There are 2 site-only **caravan parks** by the river, run by the VIC. Campers should also consider the

Western Australia

sites at Barrabup Pool. There are 2 excellent places to **eat**, both mid-range. *Mulberry Tree*, 62 Warren Rd, T9756 3038, is more formal, while *Hamish's Cafe*, 1 Warren Rd, T9756 1287, is a lively place full of art, sculpture and recycled materials. Wed-Fri, Sun 1000-1430, Fri 1830-2030. A good place for lunch is *Blackwood Wines* on Kearney St, about 30 mins walk from the VIC along the riverbank, Thu-Tue 1200-1400.

Tours and Activities Canoeing *Blackwood River Canoeing*, T9756 1209, can take you on a half-day paddle ($25) or help you with extended trips, supplying equipment and transport so that you can canoe a section of the river for 2-5 days (from $35 a day). *Blackwood Forest Canoeing*, T9756 1252, also run half-day trips ($25).

Transport Bus *Westrail* services leave from the VIC for **Pemberton** at 1922 Tue, Thu and Sun. Their **Augusta** and **capes region** buses depart 0723 Mon, Wed and Fri.

Bridgetown

Colour map 7, grid C5
Population: 2,100
45 km from Nannup,
95 km from Bunbury

A service town for the local agricultural area, Bridgetown nestles alongside the Blackwood River, and is not without its charms. The surrounding, sharply undulating and partly forested hills, are very scenic, but the town itself struggles to offer much to the visitor except during the second week of November when there are garden and blues festivals. **Bridgedale House** encapsulates the spirit of much of Bridgetown's history and was the first house in the district. ■ *1000-1430 Sat-Sun, but possibly at other days and times subject to the availability of volunteers. $3.30, children $1.65. T9761 1508 or contact VIC.* The VIC is on Hampton Street. ■ *Daily 0900-1700. T9761 1740, tourist1@iinet.net.au*

Sleeping and eating B *Ford House*, Eedle Terr, T9761 1816, www.wn.com.au/ford.house, is a recent winner of WA's B&B of the year award. This 1896 former magistrates cottage has 2 doubles and 2 singles, sharing a bathroom. Also 2 large, significantly more luxurious, en suite rooms in another weatherboard house. **C** *Tortoiseshell Farm*, 12 km east of Bridgetown, partly via unsealed roads, T/F9761 1089, is a modern B&B farmhouse with real character, wonderful hosts and sweeping veranda views. Recommended. The **C-D** *Freemasons Arms*, Hampton St, T9761 1725, is a large traditional pub. Cheap counter meals and simple hotel double rooms or en suite motel units. The only, rather lacklustre, caravan park, T9761 1053, is on the far bank of the river, 1 km from the town centre. On-site vans and cabins. *Lucifer's*, Hampton St, T9761 2221, serves cheap to mid-range meals. BYO, open 1800-2130 Tue-Sun. The *Tongue & Groove*, Eedle Terr, serves light lunches 1000-1700 Fri-Sun. The *Cidery*, Gifford St, T9761 2204, sells their own strong-brewed ciders and beers from a large barn. Cheap lunches at weekends, otherwise bring a picnic (as long as you buy a drink or 2). Open 1100-1600 Wed-Sun.

Transport Bus *Westrail* services leave from the Boat Park for stops to **Perth** at 0940 Mon, Tue, Thu, and 1357 Sun, and for **Bunbury** at 1247 Mon-Sat (change to *Australind* train for **Perth**). **Pemberton** buses depart 1317 Mon, Tue, Thu, Sat, 1702 Mon, Wed, 1752 Fri, and 1327, 2007 Sun. Some services continue on to **Albany**, as do additional buses at 1317 Wed and Fri. *South West Coachlines* head to **Perth** at 0700 Mon-Fri, and to **Manjimup** at 1800 Mon-Fri.

Manjimup

Colour map 7, grid C5
Population: 4,400
35 km from Bridgetown
120 km from Walpole,
160 km from Mount Barker

Manjimup is the major service town for the central timber region. There's not much to interest travellers but if you have the time and inclination a visit to the **Manjimup Regional Timber Park** by the VIC can be interesting. There is an age of steam museum, timber museum, historic hamlet, lookout tower and pleasant grounds. ■ *Daily 0900-1700. T9771 1831. Entry to Timber Park by donation. corner of Rose St and Edwards St.* About 20 km west of Manjimup are the **Four Aces**, four karri giants around 67-79 m high, and a short forest walk.

One Tree Bridge is another picnic and walking site around a pioneer bridge but both of these areas are pretty out-of-the-way unless you are walking the Bibbulmun Track. There is a nice café here though, *Graphiti*, T9772 1283. ■*Wed-Sun 1000-1700*. About 9 km south of Manjimup, just off the main highway, the **Diamond Tree** is one of the original fire-spotting trees. Reaching a height of 51 metres, and several metres above the surrounding canopy, there are panoramic views from the platform at the top. It's less well known than the Gloucester Tree (see next page), so draws fewer people.

Sleeping and eating C *Lavender Cottage*, T9777 1760. Pretty, self-contained, white weatherboard cottage in the English-style garden of a larger house. Breakfast included. The **D** *Manjimup Hotel*, Giblett St, T9771 1322, johnpeos@karriweb.com.au, has a smart lounge bar and serves cheap but adventurous counter meals, and there's a salad and veggie bar. Both single and double hotel and motel rooms available. Meals daily 1200-1400, 1800-2030. There is also a site-only caravan park close to town. The most pleasant café in town is *Slice of Heaven*, Rose St, serving up foccaccias, wraps and light lunches, 0900-1700 Mon-Fri and 0900-1300 Sat.

Transport Bus *Westrail* services leave from the VIC for stops to **Perth** at 0913 Mon, Tue, Thu, and 1328 Sun, and for **Bunbury** at 1218 Mon-Sat (change to *Australind* train for **Perth**). **Pemberton** buses depart 1408 Mon, Tue, Thu, Sat, 1733 Mon, Wed, 1843 Fri, and 1418, 2038 Sun. Some services continue on to **Albany**, as do additional buses at 1408 Wed and Fri. *South West Coachlines* head to **Perth** at 0630 Mon-Fri.

Pemberton

Colour map 7, grid C5
Population: 1,000
31 km from Manjimup, 31 km from Northcliffe.

The VIC sells a good brochure on 30 walks in the area ($3.30)

Pemberton grew up around its timber mill and the town is full of identical wooden workers' cottages that lend it a quaint toytown feel. The mill still operates, although on reduced hours. It is likely to close in the next few years and the town is slowly shifting its focus to tourism and other ventures. Pemberton is the focal point for an emerging wine region, a couple of superb woodcraft galleries and wonderfully scenic bushwalking and driving country amid the soaring forests. The Bibbulmun Track passes right through the town on its way down to the coast. The **VIC**, is on the main street which becomes Brockman Street where the Vasse Highway passes through the town centre. ■ *Daily 0900-1700*. T9776 1133, www.pembertontourist.com.au

The **Gloucester Tree**, 3 km from town in the tiny Gloucester National Park, is a knee-wobbling 64-m climb and was named after the visiting Duke of Gloucester who helped drill some of the holes. There are several picnic tables and a few short walks here. ■ *Park entry $9 per car*. One of the most popular ways to see the forest is to take one of the **Pemberton Trams**, which run along lines to Warren River Bridge and Northcliffe. There are a couple of stops where you can get off and wander in the forest. ■ *Daily 1045, 1400 to Warren River ($14, 2 hrs), 1015 Tue, Thu, Sat (Sep-Apr) to Northcliffe ($34, 5½ hrs). T9776 1322, Railway Cres*. Don't miss the **Fine Woodcraft Gallery**, one of the best in the region. ■ *Daily 0900-1700. T9776 1399. Dickinson St*. Just north of town, the **Big Brook Dam**, which supplies water for the town, is a beautiful stretch of water surrounded by tall karri forest and a lovely spot for a picnic, drive or camping. There is a walking circuit of the dam (4 km), picnic tables and a free campsite in a leafy clearing, with toilets and fires only. The Bibbulmun Track passes along the dam to Pemberton and makes a very pleasant walk from town.

Wineries The Pemberton wine region lies in a cooler, wetter area than the Margaret River wineries so cool climate varieties such as Sauvignon Blanc, Semillon, Pinot and Merlot dominate. There are about 10 cellar doors, a few with good restaurants. **Gloucester Ridge**, Burma Road, T9776 1035, is open

Western Australia

▶▶ **A tree-mendous experience**

From the 1950s to the mid-1970s, when aerial observation became the preferred method of fire-spotting in the region, there were eight fire-spotting towers around Manjimup and Pemberton used by the local communities to pinpoint fires when smoke was seen. Each used a living tree as a central pillar. As well as still being a back-up to the planes, two of the original trees used are now open to the public, the 64-m Gloucester Tree, in Gloucester National Park, and the 51-m Diamond Tree. In 1988 another was 'constructed', with less damage to the tree, in Warren National Park – the Bicentennial Tree. At 75 m this is the most challenging, but also the most rewarding. All three will give most people the willies, particularly on the way down when you have to look down at your feet (and thus the ground) the whole way. Only four people are allowed at the top of each tree at one time, so try to avoid the crowds by arriving early morning or late afternoon. Climbing can be dangerous in the wet or when windy so watch your step.

daily 1100-1700, lunches 1130-1430. The Sauvignon Blanc and Cabernet Sauvignon are particularly good of the dozen or more wines available for tasting. The mid-range restaurant offers local produce like marron and trout. There's also a good-value cheese platter served with a glass of wine. **Warren**, Conte Road (unsealed), 3 km from town, T9776 1115, open daily 1100-1700 and is a small family-owned winery specializing in superb reds that are made for cellaring. **Salitage**, Vasse Highway (10 km east), T9776 1771, open daily 1000-1600, is Pemberton's grandest winery with some of the best of the region's wines. The restaurant offers mid-range modern Australian (Friday-Monday 1200-1430). There are also tours at 1100 daily.

Accommodation is mostly in self-contained cottages; the busiest period is in January and it is often very quiet in winter when you may get a good discount if you ask

Sleeping and eating L-A *Karri Valley Resort*, T9776 2020, www.karrivalleyresort.com.au Scenic resort on Lake Beedelup, 20 km west of Pemberton. Timber chalets, motel-style rooms and a restaurant. Also a wide range of activities, all open to non-residents, including horseriding, bushwalking, and canoeing. **A-B** *Pemberton Hotel*, Brockman St, T9776 1017, www.pembertonhotel.com 30 luxurious rooms, some with spa, balcony and kitchenette. **B** *Treenbrook Cottages*, Vasse Highway, 5 km northwest of town. T9776 1638, treenbrk@karriweb.com.au 4 charming, rustic cottages, 2 bedrooms, full kitchen, woodfire, BBQ, and lots of bushwalking trails in the adjoining forest. **C** *Glenhaven*, 25 Browns Rd. T9776 0028, glenhaven@wn.com.au Warm and friendly B&B with Scottish hosts. 3 comfy en suite rooms, each with private verandah, cooked breakfast and afternoon tea included. Recommended. **D-E** *Pemberton Backpackers*, 7 Brockman St. T9776 1105, pembertonbackpackers@wn.com.au Old, timber building in the main street with a large central lounge and woodfire, utilitarian kitchen and standard bunk rooms. Also bike hire and some seasonal work. **D-E** *Pemberton YHA*, Stirling Rd. T9776 1153, pembertonyha@westnest.com.au Hostel in bush near the Big Brook Dam. Beds are in 6 former timber workers' cottages, each with 2 bedrooms, own kitchen and lounge. The **caravan park**, Pump Hill Rd, T9776 1300, also has some timber cabins.

The wineries provide some of the best food in Pemberton and some may be open for evening meals at weekends. The *Pemberton Hotel*, T9776 1017, serves cheap, standard favourites served in a pretty dining room daily 1200-1400, 1800-2000, and *Café Mazz* is part of the stylish, modern wing made of rammed earth and local timber. The café food is a more modern and casual, daily 0700-2030. *Coffee Connection*, T9776 1159, at the *Fine Woodcraft Gallery*, Dickinson Rd. The best café in town by a long stretch. Daily 1000-1600. *Pembee Fish Café*, Brockman St. A bright, casual café for fish and chips or pizza to eat in the small colourful dining room or take-away. BYO.

Tours and activities 4WD *Pemberton Discovery Tours*, T9776 0484, www.wn.com.au/pdt Excellent trips into D'Entrecasteaux National Park and the Yeagarup Dunes and Warren National Park. Beaches, river, and forest with a lively and flexible guide. Also winery tours. From $40 ½ day, $80 full day. **Walking** *Pemberton Hiking Company*, T9776 1559, pemhike@wn.com.au Guided walks with a knowledgeable local and environmentalist. Also canoeing on the Warren, Yeagarup Dunes on foot, night walks and 2-5 day wilderness walks.

Transport Bus *Westrail* services leave from the VIC for stops to **Perth** at 0845 Mon, Tue, Thu, and 1254 Sun, and for **Bunbury** at 1125 Tue, Wed, Fri and Sat (change to *Australind* train for **Perth**). Buses to **Northcliffe**, **Walpole** (2 hrs), **Denmark** and **Albany** (3½ hrs) leave at 1431 Mon, Tue, Thu, Sat, 1906 Fri, and 1441 Sun. Their **Nannup** and **Capes** region buses depart 0630 Mon, Wed and Fri.

The unsealed Old Vasse Road, which runs from 12 km west of Pemberton to 8 km south, passes right through the heart of **Warren National Park**. Nearer the Northcliffe Road end is the **Bicentennial Tree**, the 75-m living lookout constructed in 1988. There are wonderful views over the surrounding canopy from the top. Also off the through road is a 9-km, one-way loop route called the **Heartbreak Trail** which runs down to the banks of the Warren River and then follows its course among the stately karri trees for about 5 km. There are several beautiful riverside camping and picnic spots along the way, and a high lookout near the end with views over the river valley. About half-way along the Old Vasse Road is the *Old Vasse*, café, open daily 1000-1600, and the associated self-contained and very smart **A-B** *Marima Cottages*, T/F9776 1211, www.marima.com.au Each of the cottages is set on the boundary between the encircling forest and the modest paddock.

Warren, D'Entrecasteaux & Shannon national parks
For all 3 parks: vehicle entry $9, camping $10

D'Entrecasteaux National Park is a large area of wilderness along the coast south of Pemberton. Stretching 130 km from Black Point south of Nannup to the border of the Walpole-Nornalup National Park in the east, most of it is inaccessible and all except one route into the park require extensive 4WD experience. However, there are good tours into the park, from operators in Pemberton and Walpole. If you can get there it is a stunning area of almost untouched beaches, cliffs, heathland and forest. Immediately south of Pemberton are the **Yeagerup Dunes**, a spectacular place where the forest abruptly meets high creamy dunes. In fact the dunes are mobile and fast swallowing the forest. The only sealed road access is south of Northcliffe, leading to **Windy Harbour** (25 km). There is a fishing shack settlement there and a campground ($5) but the real attraction is **Salmon Beach**, 3 km west by unsealed road. This is a perfect, long stretch of sand below high, rugged cliffs. Picnic tables and toilets by the car park are the only facilities. From the beach take the loop drive back to Windy Harbour via Point D'Entrecasteaux for wonderful coastal views. The best spot for supplies if you fancy camping here is **Northcliffe**.

Sitting astride the main highway south to Walpole, and named after the river that runs north to south through it, **Shannon National Park** is best known for the **Great Forest Trees Drive**, a 48-km one-way loop through varied forest country. The unsealed route crosses the highway at two points so you can just do half of it. The southern half, the first turn you see if driving south, is the best as it takes you to **Big Tree Grove** within 5 km, a small but impressive cluster of karri trees around 85 m high and over 300 years old. At the far end of this part of the drive, near the highway, is a peaceful campsite and basic 8-bed lodge, contact CALM, T9776 1207, for bookings. There are also some walking trails in the park, for which see the information board at the campsite.

Western Australia

South coast

From Walpole to Esperance, the granite of the long southern coastline is weathered into smooth rounded boulders, headlands and islands, striking bays and archipelagos, and fine, clean sand, leaving the water as clear as liquid glass. Some of the most beautiful beaches in the country are found here, especially in the Cape Le Grand National Park near Esperance, the downside being that the water is barely warmer than a polar bear's bath. This makes summers mild and winters surprisingly cold, although winter is the best time to see southern right whales near the historic town of Albany. The south coast also receives relatively high rainfall. Further inland, the low granite range of the Porongorup National Park provides gentle walks and good views of the more dramatic Stirling Ranges, rising above the state's vast wheat plains. This magnificent region of forest, mountains, beaches and wilderness offers superb walking, as well as canoeing, boat cruises and coastal drives.

Ins and outs

Getting there & around **Air** *Skywest* fly directly from Perth to both Albany and Esperance. **Bus To Albany** *Westrail* have services running on 2 routes from the **East Perth** terminal to Albany (8 hrs). The S1 services go via **Armadale** and **Mt Barker**, leaving at 0900 Mon-Sat, 1500 Sun, while the S2 services head via **Mundaring**, **Northam** and **Mt Barker**. The S3 buses head first through the timber towns before calling at **Walpole**, **Denmark** and **Albany**. Most of these services leave **Bunbury** VIC at 1130 Mon-Sat and 1140 Sun, with one leaving directly from **Perth** at 1300 Fri. At **Pemberton** there are connections to and from **Augusta**. There are twice-weekly services (E4) between **Albany** and **Esperance** (6½ hrs). **To Esperance** *Westrail* have routes from East Perth Terminal via the wheat belt and Ravensthorpe (E1, 10 hrs), leaving 0800 Mon, Wed and Fri; Midland, York, Hyden (Wave Rock) and Ravensthorpe (E2, 10 hrs), leaving 0800 Tue; Midland, York and Ravensthorpe (E2), leaving 0800 Thu and Sun; and via Kalgoorlie (E3, 11 hrs) departing 0915 Mon. Additional services from Kalgoorlie railway station leave at 1525 Tue and Fri.

Walpole and around

Colour map 7, grid C5
Population: 500
120 km from Pemberton, 65 km from Denmark

Walpole is a tiny, sparse-looking town on the northern shore of Walpole Inlet. Most travellers only come here for the **Tree Top Walk**, but the natural forest and coastal attractions are such that many who come for a night end up staying several. The inlets and the town are almost entirely enclosed by the **Walpole-Nornalup National Park**, which extends for several kilometres in each direction and encompasses one of the best-preserved coastal forest and heath areas in the state, known as the Nuyts Wilderness Area. The **Bibbulmun Track** runs right through the town, and several sections of it, some of the best on its entire course, can easily be done as day walks using the town as a base. A shorter, 2-km loop walk through karri forest runs directly from behind the VIC. There are extensive views of the entire region from **Mount Frankland** (30 km), ask at the extremely helpful **Walpole VIC** for directions, opposite the main shopping strip. ■ *Daily 0900-1700. T9840 1111, wnta@wn.com.au*

Sights On the other side of Nornalup, 12 km from Walpole, is the **Valley of the Giants**, an area of forest with a high density of good-sized karri, tingle and other trees. In 1996 CALM opened the 600-m **Tree Top Walk**, a sloping steel walkway, suspended up to 40 m above the forest floor and passing several forest giants at canopy level. Although the walkway does sway, the sense of awe most people feel is enough to make them forget their vertigo, and the clever design means no steps are involved. A separate forest-floor walk, the **Ancient Empire**, identifies several species of giant forest tree and introduces you to a few striking individuals. ■ *Walks open daily 0900-1700, last entry 1615. $6, children $2.50. T9840 8263.* On the coast, the beaches match the forest in natural beauty. **Conspicuous Cliffs** is the most beautiful in the area that can be reached by a 2WD, and is a long sweep of broad sand, backed by cliffs. The lookout here is a popular spot for whale watching (July-August and October-November). On the road to Denmark is **Parrot Jungle**, a modest-sized bird park with an excellent collection of some of the world's most brightly coloured parrots and macaws. Some of their rescued and hand-reared birds roam free about the park and visitors are invited to be perched upon, a memorable and unusual opportunity. ■ *Daily 0900-1700 Sep-Apr, otherwise 1000-1600. $7, children $3. T9840 8335.*

B *Riverside Retreat*, South Coast Highway, near Nornalup, T9840 1255, www.riversideretreat.come.au Good location with splendid views over the eastern end of Nornalup Inlet. The 6 chalets are clean, well-equipped and comfortable rather than luxurious, and sleep up to 8. **C** *Tingledale Cottage*, off Hazelvale Rd, T9840 8181, www.tingledalecottage.bizland.com Charming, isolated wooden cottage in a forest setting with outdoor spa. Semi self-contained. **D** *Tingle All Over*, Nockolds St, T9840 1041. Clean and well-presented budget accommodation, aimed at the mature market. *YHA* affiliated, share bathroom and kitchen. **D-E** *Walpole Backpackers*, Pier St, T/F9840 1244, walpolebackpackers@bigpond.com Laid-back, open-plan hostel with 23 beds, some in doubles. Excellent facilities, friendly owner-managers also run *Walpole De-tours*. Recommended. There are 4 caravan parks in the area. *Rest Point Caravan Park*, Rest Point Rd, T9840 1032, has the best location, overlooking Walpole Inlet, and is about a 2-km walk from Walpole. *Coalmine Beach*, T9840 1026, is a similar distance away and is very close to Nornalup Inlet. Of the 2 it has the better facilities. Both have cabins, neither have on-site vans, but *Valley of the Giants Eco Park*, South Coast Highway, Nornalup, T9840 1313, does.

The *Tea House*, Nornalup, 6 km from Walpole T9840 1422, is the smartest café in the area. Open at 1000, they serve light lunches and snacks daily 1200-1500, and inventive mid-range dinners 1800-2000 Wed-Sat. In Walpole the preferred choice is usually the *Top Deck*, T9840 1344, an unpretentious café that takes care to serve consistently good food. Open all day from 0830 for breakfast, lunch 1100-1430 and mid-range dinner 1800-2000. Normally closed Mon and Thu, and other days in winter. The *Walpole Hotel*, T9840 1023, serves cheap counter and mid-range brasserie meals every day, 1200-1400 and 1800-2000.

4WD and minibus tours *Walpole De-tours*, T/F9840 1244, walpolebackpackers@ excite.com.au From isolated sunset beach trips to overnight adventures, these are some of the cheapest and yet most memorable and information-packed tours in WA. Their 6-hr tour, including 4WD beach trip, Mt Frankland climb and Tree Top Walk (entry fee extra), is a bargain-tastic $35. Call ahead to ask what the current programme is. They are also happy to arrange drop-offs to various spots of the **Bibbulmun Track**, either to walk on or walk back to Walpole. **Bike hire** *Norm's Tyre & Hire*, Walpole, T9840 1297. $15-22 per day. **Boat cruises** *Wild Over Walpole*, T9840 1036, www.wowwilderness.com.au Enthusiastic, informative and entertaining cruises around the inlets (2½ hrs, $25) or, on most Sun, memorable trips up the Frankland River (3½ hrs, $30). Departures 1000 daily from the jetties near the pub. **Canoe hire** *Nornalup Riverside Café*, T9840 1157. $12.50 per hr, $30 per day. Canoe from here up the near-pristine Frankland River.

Sleeping

Eating

Tours & activities

Western Australia

Transport **Bus** *Westrail* buses leave from the post office for the **timber towns** and **Bunbury** at 0948 Tue-Wed, Fri-Sat, 1023 Mon, Thu, and 1053 Sun (Mon and Thu services do not stop at **Northcliffe** or **Pemberton**). All have immediate onward connections to **Perth**. Eastbound buses to **Denmark** and **Albany** depart 1617 Mon-Tue, Thu, Sat, 1542 Wed, Fri, 2052 Fri and 1627 Sun.

Denmark and around

Colour map 7, grid C6
Population: 2,000
55 km from Mount Barker, 55 km from Albany

This small, appealing town on the western bank of the Denmark River is close to some of the most stunning beaches and headlands on the southern coast. **William Bay National Park**, just to the west of Denmark, includes the magical Greens Pool, Elephant Rocks and Madfish Bay, scattered with leviathan granite boulders. The town is home to many **artists** and **winemakers** and their galleries and cellar doors are found along the Scotsdale and Mount Shadforth roads in the hills above town. The **VIC** is halfway along Strickland Street. ■ *Daily 0900-1700. T9848 2055, touristb@denmarkwa.net.au* The **Denmark Environment Centre** is a focus for conservationists and greenies in the area and is a good place to go to pick up publications on flora and fauna or information on any green events. ■ *Mon-Fri 1000-1600, Sat 1000-1300. T9848 1644. 25 Strickland St.*

Sleeping There is a lot of accommodation around Denmark, particularly self-contained chalets and cottages. Contact the VIC if none of these fit the bill. Several have superb views over the inlets, including **A-B** *Karma Chalets*, South Coast Highway, T9848 1568, www.karmachalets.com.au 8 luxury houses on stilts, some with spas, backing onto karri forest. **B** *Cove*, Payne Rd, T9848 1770, sits on about 20 ha of mixed forest, through which bushwalks wind directly down to the inlet. 5 hand-built wood cottages sleeping from 2 to 20, including the wonderful 'Sanctum' and 'Tingle'. The hosts are keen bushwalkers and are happy to do Bibbulmun drop-offs and pick-ups. Recommended. **C** *Bambrey Green Cottage*, T9848 1437, Bambrey St, off South Coast Highway. Charming self-contained cottage with period furnishings and polished wooden floors, by the river. There are also quite a few **B&Bs** around town, including **C** *Mount Lindesay View*, corner of Mount Shadforth Rd and McNabb Rd, T9848 1933, mtlindesayview@westnet.com.au 3 comfortable en suite rooms, good food and great views over the valleys to the north. **C-E** *Waterfront*, 63 Inlet Dr. T9848 1147, www.denmarkwaterfront.com.au A good range of accommodation in this complex among karri trees on the inlet shore 2½ km from town. Studios and motel rooms are all bright and cheery and built in a rustic timber-and-earth style. Also 4 pleasant budget dorm rooms which sleep 4 or can be had as a private double. Fairly basic shared kitchen and bathroom but a nice veranda. Free pick-ups for backpackers. **E** *Blue Wren Travellers Rest*, 17 Price St. T9848 3300, www.bluewren.batcave.net 20 beds in this new backpacker hostel, in an old timber-worker's cottage extended to accommodate modern dorms and bathrooms. A little spartan but clean and friendly, with central location. Of several **caravan parks** the closest is *Rivermouth*, T/F9848 1262, which has on-site vans.

Eating *The Observatory*, Karri Mia, Mount Shadforth Rd, T9848 2600. Stylish dining room and an outside deck, both with superb views over the inlets. Traditional but excellent expensive evening meals, and cheap light lunches. Open all day, breakfast 0800-1030 Sat-Sun, lunch and dinner 1130-1500, 1800-2100 daily. Recommended. *Waterfront*, 63 Inlet Drive, T9848 1147. Attractive rustic timber, mid-range restaurant perched on a hillside overlooking Wilson Inlet, 3 km from town. Garlic prawns and seafood are specialities, the menu also includes fairly classic meat dishes. Licensed or BYO, no corkage. Daily 1200-1400, 1830-2030. *Bandaleros*, Hollings Rd, T9848 2188, is a cheap popular Mexican restaurant opposite the river. Cosy timber décor and all the traditional Mexican dishes such as enchiladas and burritos. Open Mon-Sat 1800-2030. **Denmark Hotel**, Hollings Rd, T9848 2206. The pub has a large, modern dining room overlooking the river and does cheap(ish) pub meals. **Cafés** *Café Lushus*, 18 Hollings Rd, T9848 1299. Colourful and groovy place full of original art and laid-back locals. The blackboard menu offers lots of choice and may include dishes such as curry, noodles or turkish bread. Daily 0830-1700 and evenings over summer and major holidays.

4WD *Little River Discovery*, T9848 2604. Day tours by local naturalists to West Cape Howe National Park ($70), Valley of the Giants ($75) and short local tours (from $22) to see wildflowers, birds, beaches or wineries. **Aboriginal culture** *Chiriger Dreamtime*, T9840 9511, hvderschow@bigpond.com Sunset boat cruise to explore local indigenous history and traditions, try bush tucker, and play the didjeridu. The guide is an Aboriginal park ranger, knowledgeable and interesting. Tours 1800 Sat ($32, 2 hrs). Book at VIC. **Boat cruise** *Sandpiper*, T9848 1734. Daily cruise on Denmark River and Wilson Inlet. Morning tea provided ($16, 2 hrs). Departs town jetty at 1000 (Oct-Jun). **Boat and canoe hire** On the river by Berridge Park, Sep-Apr 0900-1600. **Canoeing** *Denmark Tours*, T9848 1055, www.denmarktours.com.au Daily canoe and kayak tours on the Denmark and Hay rivers ($29, 2½ hrs). Also walking and driving tours anywhere in the region on request. **Surfing** *Aido's Boardroom*, T9848 3305, South Coast Highway. 2-hr Lessons $33 for 3, $44 for 2. Board hire $10 hr, $25 for 3 hrs.

Tours & activities

Bus *Westrail* buses leave from the VIC for **Walpole**, the **timber towns** and **Bunbury** at 0852 Tue-Wed, Fri-Sat, 0927 Mon, Thu, and 0957 Sun (Mon and Thu services do not stop at **Northcliffe** or **Pemberton**). Eastbound buses to **Albany** depart 1713 Mon-Tue, Thu, Sat, 1638 Wed, Fri, 2148 Fri and 1723 Sun

Transport

Ocean Beach, 11 km from Denmark, is a popular spot for locals and holidaymakers alike. Where the road ends you can look directly south at **Wilson Head** where a shelf of rock, extending a 100 m or so east, creates fantastic curling waves. The view is magical enough, but gets even better if you take the trouble to scramble the 200 m down the informal path to the granite boulders below. From Denmark two roads head northwest that have been designated as tourist drives. **Mount Shadforth Road**, winds west along the range of hills culminating in Mount Shadforth (300 m) after 10 km. Beyond Mount Shadforth an unsealed section leads to McLeod Road. A right turn here heads up to the western end of the 'tourist' section of **Scotsdale Road** after passing *Somerset Hill Winery*, T9840 9388. Open daily 1100-1600, a true cellar built recently along Mediterranean lines. The 20-km drive back to Denmark heads through a mix of pastoral and forest country, and past a few more wineries and galleries. Close to the town centre is the *Howard Park* winery, T9848 2345, open daily 1000-1600, wines $14-75. These people regularly make some of the best wines in the region, including their 'drink-now' range, *Madfish*, which has received international recognition.

The granite that makes up much of the south coast takes on some of its most spectacular sculpted forms in the gentle headland at the east end of William Bay, in **William Bay National Park**. The mesmeric **Greens Pool** is a clear sandy bay, 18 km from Denmark, sheltered not by an island or reef, but by a collection of domed boulders scattered for several hundred metres about 100 m offshore. Parking in the Elephant Rocks car park, just 50 m along the unsealed section, gives just as quick walking access to the pool, as well as to **Elephant Rocks**, a cluster of gigantic boulders nuzzling the nearside of a tiny sandy inlet, more like beached whales than elephants.

Around Denmark

Western Australia

▶▶ **The Bibbulmun Track**

Starting in Kalamunda, the long-distance Bibbulmun walking trail winds its way south through North Bannister, Dwellingup, Balingup, Pemberton and Walpole before finally ending up, 963 km later, in Albany. As well as passing through these picturesque towns the track also winds through several reserves and parks, much of the southern forests and some of the spectacular south coast. There are nearly 50 bush campsites en route, each with a simple three-sided timber bunk shelter, picnic tables, water tank and pit toilets. Note that there are no cooking facilities, water needs to be boiled or treated, and there is no toilet paper. The whole walk generally takes about 6-8 weeks, but few tackle it in a single go and CALM have suggestions for various short day sections. The track is by far at its best in spring and autumn. Think twice, and then again before tackling any of it in high summer. There is a two-volume guide to the track and a series of eight maps also dedicated to it, all available at Perth's **Map World** amongst other outlets. For more information see www.bibbulmuntrack.org.au or www.calm.wa.gov.au/tourism/bibbulmun _splash.com, or contact the Friends of the Bibbulmun Track on T9481 0551.

Albany and around

Colour map 7, grid C6
Population: 20,500
385 km from
Margaret River, 410
km from Perth,
480 km from
Esperance

Despite the advanced age of Albany in Western Australian terms, the lasting impression is not of its heritage but its beautiful natural harbour. The city sits on the northern shore of **Princess Royal Harbour** and **King George Sound** and overlooks both the curving arm of the peninsula and the granite islands of the sound. Its small-scale city centre makes it a relaxed and friendly place and many people enjoy its mild climate. There are great national parks in every direction but **Torndirrup National Park** is the closest and has some impressive granite rock formations, cliffs and magical ocean beaches. The main activity in winter is whale watching. The **VIC** is housed in the former railway station on the waterfront. ■ *Mon-Fri 0830-1730, Sat-Sun 0900-1700. T9841 1088, www.albany.wa.gov.au Princess Royal Dr.*

Ins & outs   **Getting around** *Love's Bus Service*, T9841 1211, runs a handful of services around the northern city suburbs, all starting and terminating at Peels Pl. The 301 heads out along Middleton Rd to Middleton Beach and Emu Point at 0845, 1100, 1305 and 1450 Mon-Fri, and 1030, 1210 Sat. There are no public services to Torndirrup National Park.

Sights
See also Around Albany, page 579

Albany is the site of the first European settlement of Western Australia. British authorities decided to order settlement of King George Sound in 1825 to forestall the French who were reported to be continually present in the southern coastal waters that year. Settlement was established in 1826 by Major Lockyer. A replica of his ship, the **Brig Amity** has been built and stands roughly in the place that the original ship docked. Visitors can clamber all over the boat and below deck to see the cramped conditions sailors of the 19th century had to endure. ■ *Daily 0900-1700. $2.50, children $0.55. Access via the museum.* Just next door is the Residency, the original home of Government Residents. It now houses the **West Australian Museum – Albany** and displays on the region's geological, maritime and social history. ■ *Daily 1000-1700. Free. T9841 4844, www.museum.wa.gov.au Residency Rd.* Behind the museum lie the high, spiky walls of the **Old Gaol**, built in 1852 as a convict depot but converted to a gaol in 1873 and also used for police quarters. The Albany Historical Society now runs it as a museum of early European local history. Some cells have displays on the ghoulish crimes of their former inhabitants. ■ *Daily 1000-1615. $4, children $2.50 (price includes entry to Patrick Taylor Cottage). T9841 5403. Stirling Terr.*

The city sits between two hills, **Mount Melville** and **Mount Clarence**, both of which have impressive viewpoints that can be driven to (to within about a 100 m or so). Further to the east, forming the northern headland of the Ataturk Entrance, is the city's third major hill, **Mount Adelaide**. It was atop Mount Adelaide that the city's defences were chiefly constructed at the end of the 19th century. **Princess Royal Fortress** has been restored and you can visit its museums, gun emplacements, lookouts and café. ■ *Daily 0900-1700. $3, children $1, concessions $2.*

C *Discovery Inn*, 9 Middleton Rd, 200 m from Middleton beach, T9842 5535, **Sleeping** www.discoveryinn.net.au Guesthouse with 12 rooms, some en suite. Full cooked brekkie can be taken in the pleasant central courtyard. **C** *Memories*, 118 Brunswick Rd, T9842 9787, memoriesbandb@bigpond.com 3 artistic and elegant en suite rooms in an 1880s house overlooking the harbour. Warm hosts and substantial cooked breakfasts. Recommended. **C** *Quayside*, 7 Festing St, T9841 2940. Large and modern B&B with great views over the bay. Comfortable unfussy rooms and friendly hosts. **D-E** *Albany Backpackers*, corner of Stirling Terr and Spencer St, T9842 5255, www.albanybackpackers.com.au Lively hostel with lots of activities arranged, such as pasta, pool and video nights. **D-E** *Bayview YHA*, 49 Duke St, T9842 3388, www.yha.com.au Friendly, clean and quiet backpackers with lots of space, sea views

Western Australia

and good facilities. Bike, board and snorkel hire. **D** *Cruize Inn*, 122 Middleton Rd, 1 km from beach, 2½ km from city centre, T9842 9599, www.cruizeinn.com Bright and breezy guesthouse run on the laid-back lines of a backpacker hostel. 2 twins, 2 doubles, lots of facilities including open-plan kitchen and lounge room, and bike hire, plus a friendly, fun host. Pick-ups available. Recommended. **Caravan parks B-E** *Rose Gardens*, 45 Mermaid Av, Emu Point, T9844 1041, have on-site vans, and they have a store and fuel. **C-D** *Frenchman Bay*, T9844 4015. Friendly caravan park with a good spot close to the beach and a small store and café.

Eating   *Leonardo's*, 166 Stirling Terr, T9841 1732. Local, fresh produce combined with an Italian influence, intimate yet formal. Mon-Sat 1830-2030. Expensive, but BYO. *Al Fornetto's*, 132 York St, T9842 1060. A reliable favourite for excellent mid-range Italian food. Book ahead. Daily 1800-2030. *Argyles*, 42 Stirling Terr, T9842 9696. A cosy bistro serving tasty and satisfying modern Australian food. Good value and there is a set-price menu ($20) available from 1730 daily. *Curry Pot*, 38 Stirling Terr, T9842 9399. Small, pleasant and cheap Indian with an all-you-can-eat banquet for $14. Of 12 dishes, half are vegetarian. Daily 1730-2100. *Dylans*, 82 Stirling Terr, T9841 8720. Casual, unpretentious place that does breakfasts, burgers, pancakes and ice cream sundaes. BYO. Daily 0700-2030. *Harvest Moon*, 86 Stirling Terr, T9841 8833. One of Albany's best, this homely and wholesome café makes great vegetarian bakes, quiches, soups and fresh salads. Recommended. *Rookley's*, 36 Peels Pl, T9842 2236. The best position and outdoor terrace tables from which to watch the action on York St. Excellent gourmet sweet and savoury pies, fresh bread and pastries. Open Mon-Fri 0900-1730, Sat 0830-1600. *Naked Bean*, 14 Peels Pl, T9841 1815. Gourmet lunches and the best cakes in town in an attractive, contemporary space. Open Mon-Fri 0800-1700, Sat 0800-1600.

Pubs   *Albany*, 244 York St, T9842 3337. A smart and busy pub, its street terrace is one of the
& clubs   town's most popular spots on a sunny day. Restaurant meals daily 1200-1430, 1800-2100. *Earl of Spencer*, corner of Earl St and Spencer St, T9841 1322. Cosy, traditional feel, English and Irish beers, and excellent food make it about as close to a real English pub as you'll find in WA. Meals (cheap) Mon-Sat 1200-1400, daily 1800-2100. Live folk, jazz or blues every weekend. *Heaven Dance Club*, 146 Stirling Terr, T9841 7688. DJs and bands Thu-Sun. *White Star*, 72 Stirling Terr, T9841 1733. Welcoming and relaxed pub popular with visitors and locals alike, Thu is a big backpacker night. Counter meals served Mon-Sat 1200-1400, daily 0600-2100.

Tours &   **4WD and camping** *Surf-ari*, T9844 7580, take small groups out exploring the south
activities   coast with an emphasis on learning to surf. 3 days $330, 4 days $440. **Adventure activities** *Adrenalin Plus*, T9842 2127, www.adrenalinplus.iinet.net.au Abseiling, canoeing, rock-climbing and guided walks. Most take place in the regional national parks, and there are some overnight options. Costs around $40-65 half day, $75-125 per day, $220 for a weekend camping trip. There is an 11-m indoor climbing wall at the *Leisure and Aquatic Centre*, Barker Rd, T9841 2788. **Bike and board hire** *Bay View YHA* and *Cruize Inn* each have bikes plus a range of gear for their guests. **Boat cruises** The sailing yacht *MSV Big Day Out*, T0409 107180, heads out from the town jetty most days at 0930 (3 hrs) and 1300 (1½ hrs) for scenic cruises that include **whale-watching** during the May-Oct season. *Silver Star*, T0428 936711, www.whales.com.au, offer similar trips. **Diving** A number of companies offer diving trips out to the *HMAS Perth*, a navy ship sunk to create an articficial reef in 2001, and other sites, including *South Coast Diving Supplies*, T/F9841 7176, whale@divealbany.com.au, and *Albany Dive*, T0429 664874, www.albany dive.com Expect to pay around $140 for a twin-dive boat trip. **Fishing** *Spinners*, T9841 7151, spinnerscharters@bigpond.com, offer full-day ocean fishing trips for

around $140. **Mini-coach** *Albany Escape*, T9844 1945, escape@albanyis.com.au, offer a number of tours including to the Stirling Range (full day, $80), William Bay and Tree Top Walk (full day, $80 not including entry fees), and Torndirrup and Whale World (half day, $40 not including entry fees). The latter tour goes regularly at 1245 Mon, Wed, Fri and 0830 Sun. *Over the Horizon*, T9844 1123, specialize in exploring the regional national parks, including the Porongurups, Stirling Range and Fitzgerald River.

Banks Several banks and ATMs on York St. **Car hire** *Albany Car Rentals*, 386 Albany Highway, T9841 7077. *Budget Rent-a-car*, 255 Albany Highway, T9841 7799. **Communications** Post Office, corner of York St and Grey St. **Internet** at a few outlets including *Eco Tourist Centre*, corner York and Stirling Terr. $2, 15 mins. **Medical services** *Southern Regional Medical Group*, 32 Albany Highway (near York St roundabout), T9841 2733. *Albany Regional Hospital*, Warden Av, T9892 2222. **Outdoor equipment** *Albany Campers*, T9841 8601. Camper trailer, tents and equipment hire. **Police** 210 Stirling Terr, T9841 0555. **Taxi** T9841 7000. | Directory

Bus *Westrail* buses leave from the VIC for **Denmark**, **Walpole**, the **timber towns** and **Bunbury** at 0805 Tue-Wed, Fri-Sat, 0840 Mon, Thu, and 0910 Sun (Mon and Thu services do not stop at **Northcliffe** or **Pemberton**). Northbound buses to **Perth** via **Mt Barker** depart 0900 Mon-Sat, 0915 Mon, Thu, 0605 and 1730 Fri, 1100 Sat, 1315 and 1500 Sun. *Esperance* services leave at 1145 Mon and Thu. En-route connections to **Bremer Bay** must be arranged in advance, as must one to **Hopetoun** (Mon only). | Transport

Occupying the ocean-side part of the peninsula that forms the southern arm of both Princess Royal Harbour and King George Sound, **Torndirrup National Park** protects one of WA's most striking stretches of granite coast. The final 6 km of Frenchman Bay Road winds through the inland part of the park, with a series of side-roads, mostly sealed, leading to the coast's most spectacular landmarks. All the side roads are worth exploring if you have time but the main sights are the **Gap** and **Natural Bridge**. The first is a 25 m deep chasm perpendicular to the cliff edge, a real wave trap that sees the sea thumping into the rocks. Just 50 m away a similar chasm is bridged at the end by a massive natural arch. **Salmon Holes** and **Misery Beach** are both stunning beaches, the latter more protected as is **Frenchman Bay**, a lovely little beach complete with BBQs and picnic tables. | Around Albany

Whale World is a former whaling station turned museum. Most of the extensive complex comprises the old whale-processing buildings, plus one of the last hunting ships, preserved more-or-less as it was the day the station closed in 1978. Displays, films and diaramas leave little to the imagination, so may not be for the weak of stomach. It is, however, a rare glimpse into the inner life of this emotive industry, and a fascinating couple of hours can be spent here. ■ *Daily 0900-1700, tours on the hour 1000-1600 (40 mins). $12, children $4.50, concessions $9.50. Frenchman Bay Rd, 20 km from Albany, T9844 4021, www.whaleworld.org*

Just to the east of Albany, about 35 km by road, is the magical **Two Peoples Bay Nature Reserve**. The reserve has some very rare fauna, in fact two species thought to be extinct have been found here, the noisy scrub bird and Gilbert's potoroo, though you're unlikely to see either of them. The reserve also has one of the best beaches in the area, **Little Beach**, a smooth white stretch of sand, scattered with boulders. At the picnic ground by the visitor centre there is a 2-km walking circuit with several lookouts providing views over the bay and towards Mount Manypeaks. The road is not sealed but fine for 2WD. ■ *Visitor centre open 1000-1600 daily in summer, otherwise Wed, Sat-Sun. T9846 4276.*

Western Australia

Mount Barker
Colour map 7, grid C6
Population: 1,700
50 km from Albany, 80 km from Bluff Knoll, Stirling Range

The main appeal of Mount Barker, a pleasant agricultural service town, is its location just east of the **Porongorup National Park** and south of the **Stirling Range National Park**. The VIC is in the old railway station on the Albany Highway and is probably the most efficient in the state. ■ *Mon-Fri 0900-1700, Sat 0900-1500, Sun 1000-1500. T9851 1163, www.mountbarkerwa.com*

Sleeping and eating C *Abbeyholme*, Mitchell St, T9851 1101, abbeyholme@ wn.com.au B&B in a fine, stone house built in 1869. 2 elegant en suite rooms, large guest lounge, cooked breakfast. **D-E** *Chill Out Backpackers*, 79 Hassell St, T9851 2798. Modern, comfortable hostel about 1 km south of the VIC. Singles, doubles and dorms and spacious living area. There is also a **caravan park**, T9851 1691, on Albany Highway just north of town with cabins, on-site vans (**E**) and basic dongas. Fine dining is provided by *The Wright Chef's*, 34 Albany Highway, T9851 1728. Short menu of rich mid-range French cuisine. BYO. Open Wed, Sun 1130-1430, Thu-Sat 1830-2030. The *Plantagenet* pub, 9 Lowood Rd, T9851 1008, has a good reputation for its mid-range food, particularly steak. Mon-Fri 1200-1400, Mon-Sat 1800-2000.

Transport Bus *Westrail* services leave from the railway station for **Perth** at least once a day. Buses for **Albany** depart 1426 Mon-Fri, 1517 Sat, 2014 Sun.

Porongurup National Park
Porongurup 22 km from Mount Barker, 50 km from Albany
No entry charge, no camping

Porongurup is a small area of karri forest encompassing the Porongurup Range, only about 12 km long and a few kilometres wide. Walking in the hills is very enjoyable as most walks include both gentle forest trails and fantastic views of the Stirling Range and King George Sound. The **Nancy Peak** circuit (5½ km, two hours) gives a good overview but if you only have time for one walk, then head for the **Castle Rock** walk (4 km, 1½ hours return) the best short walk on this coast but you need to be agile at the top. There are two main entry points, both from the northern side. Bolganup Road leads from the main settlement area to a pleasant shady clearing where there are picnic tables and BBQs, and the start of most of the walking trails. About 6 km further east Castle Rock Road, unsealed but only 1 km long, gives access to Castle Rock and Balancing Rock trail only.

The YHA can often pick up from Mount Barker

Sleeping and eating Porongurup settlement is little more than a shop and service station with tearooms and a modest but homely **E** *YHA* (T9853 1110). Opposite is the area's upmarket option, **A-C** *Karribank*, T9853 1022, www.karribank.com.au , with some beautifully furnished century-old cottage rooms and cheaper modern chalets. Restaurant open all day, meal times 0830-0930, 1200-1430 and evenings from 1830, bookings appreciated. Next to the shop, **C** *Bolganup Homestead*, T9853 1049, has 3 large self-contained apartments, simply but comfortably furnished. Wonderful veranda. Good value for 2, a bargain for 4-6. Recommended. The **C-E** *Porongurup Range Tourist Park*, T9853 1057, has on-site vans and cabins, plus an excellent camp kitchen and common room. *Maleeya's Thai Café*, 1376 Porongurup Rd, 6 km west of Porongurup, T9853 1123, serves wonderful authentic Thai food. Only 6 tables so book ahead. BYO only. Open Thu-Sun 1800-2000. Recommended.

Stirling Range National Park
Loop drive (some unsealed) approximately 180 km from Mount Barker, 260 km from Albany

The **Stirling Range** is an island of pointy bush-covered peaks, rising sharply from an endless expanse of flat, cleared farmland. The park is particularly noted for its incredible diversity of flora – there are over 1,500 plant species within the park, an area about 65 km by 20 km. There are also many excellent peak walks giving fine views over the surrounding plains. **Bluff Knoll** – at 1,073 m the highest point in the Southwest – is the classic, but **Toolbrunup Peak** (1,054 m) is a more challenging walk with better views although only for those who are fit, agile and enjoy scrambling over large boulders. Both walks ascend about 600 m and take three to four hours. For drivers there is an unsealed scenic drive running east to west through the heart of the range (50 km). ■ *Park fees ($9 car) payable at Bluff Knoll turn-off. For further enquiries contact the park ranger, T9827 9230. Check the forecast before walking as weather can change rapidly on the high peaks and low cloud can cause wind chill and obscure the route.*

Sleeping and eating No visit to the Stirlings is complete without a trip to **B-C** *The Lily*, Chester Pass Rd, 12 km north of Bluff Knoll turn-off. T9827 9205, www.thelily.com.au This 16th-century replica Dutch windmill has elegant and homely rooms and an excellent café, open Tue-Sun 1000-1700, candlelit dinners by arrangement. Recommended. **B-E** *Stirling Range Retreat*, Chester Pass Rd, opposite Bluff Knoll turn-off. T9827 9229, www.stirlingrange.com.au Self-contained chalets, cabins, vans, campsites and swimming pool (Nov-Mar). Friendly, helpful staff can advise on walking, weather and arrange pick-ups and drop-offs for walkers. They also run good-value short guided walks, slide nights during the wild-flower season (Sep-Oct) and sell guides for extended walks in the national park. There is a park campsite ($10) at Moingup Springs, just off the Chester Pass Rd, with toilets and BBQs.

The road to Esperance is a long and mostly featureless one, but there are a few places along the way where you can break the journey and a magnificent wilderness within the **Fitzgerald River National Park**. At **Ravensthorpe**, 290 km from Albany, there's a VIC, T9838 1277 (next to the BP service station), pub and caravan park. **Hopetoun**, 50 km off the highway due south of Ravensthorpe, is a sleepy little coastal town that provides the best access to Fitzgerald River. Tourist information is available from *Barnacles Café.* **C** *Hopetoun Motel and Chalet Village*, T9838 3219, has motel rooms or self-contained units and chalets. The old pub on the foreshore, **E** *Port Hotel*, T9838 3053, has simple rooms and backpackers beds.

Albany to Esperance
Distance: 480 km There are petrol stations roughly every 100 km. Fuel in Ravensthorpe can be considerably pricier than in Albany and Esperance

The large wilderness area of **Fitzgerald River National Park** stretches between Bremer Bay and Hopetoun, and inland almost as far as the highway. It is one of the state's most important national parks, although an undeveloped and remote one, and has been registered as a UNESCO international biosphere reserve. It contains about 1,900 plant species (a fifth of the state's total number of species) in an area of almost 330,000 ha. There are two main access points to the park and both can be driven as loops off the South Coast Highway, although note that both roads are unsealed. At the western end of the park, you can drive a 100 km unsealed half-loop from the highway along Devils Creek Road (just past Gairdner wheat bin), Pabelup Drive and Quiss Road (19 km east of Jerramungup). This gives access to Mount Maxwell and West Mount Barren for great views, and to **Point Ann**, an excellent spot for whale watching (August-September) and camping. At the eastern end of the park, the main access route is West River Road from the highway (73 km east of Jerramungup, 41 km west of Ravensthorpe), which becomes Hammersley Drive and leads to Hopetoun (65 km). There are fine views and quiet camping spots by **Hamersley Inlet**. The road passes south of **East Mount Barren**, 12 km west of Hopetoun and you can climb to the top (3 km, 2½ hours) along a ridge for views along much of the park's coastline. ■ *Park fees $9 car. For more information contact the CALM ranger, T9835 5043.*

Western Australia

Esperance and around

Colour map 5, grid C2
Population: 10,000
725 km from Perth, 415
km from Kalgoorlie

Esperance is a port town overlooking the **Archipelago of the Recherche**, a beautiful wide bay full of more than a 100 granite islands. It is one of the most isolated towns in the state and a practical place with few frills. Little remains from its days as a busy port for the Coolgardie goldrush. What draws visitors today are the stunning beaches and coastal scenery both to the west and, further out, to the east of the town. The **VIC** is on Dempster Street, part of a **museum village**, a collection of restored old buildings. ■ *Daily 0900-1700. T9071 2330, www.visitesperance.com*

The coast west of Esperance is a series of white-sand bays and intermediate granite headlands. The contrast of snow-like sand and azure-blue water has captivated visitors since Captain Jean Michel Huon de Kermadec discovered this coast in 1792 sailing aboard *L'Esperance*. Beyond the beaches over a 100 domed islands compete for attention, and there are views are far as Cape Le Grand. A coast road, recently named the **Great Ocean Drive**, snakes above the beaches and over the headlands. At the start of the drive is an excellent lookout at **Wireless Hill**, followed shortly by **West Beach**, a good surfing beach, and **Blue Haven Beach**, one of the safest local swimming spots, though there is no patrol. A large headland separates these beaches from Twilight Bay, the west end of which, **Twilight Beach**, is famously picturesque.

Sleeping

Book well ahead in school and public holidays as the town fills up with visitors from Kalgoorlie

A *Esperance Seaside Apartments*, 14 The Esplanade, T9072 0044, www.eperanceseaside.com 20 modern 1 to 3 bedroom self-contained houses, well-equipped with large balconies that have oblique views over the bay. **C** *Blackforest Retreat*, Helms Dr off Pink Lake Dr, 8 km from town, T9071 5357, F9072 0846. A single self-contained mud-brick cottage on an isolated property, beautifully furnished. Very hospitable hosts, excellent value, recommended. **C** *Old Hospital Motel and B&B*, William St, T9071 3587. A rambling tin building, smartly refurbished. Range of rooms with distinctly more character than the average motel, particularly the 'VIP' room. One double B&B room with shared facilities. **D-E** *Blue Waters YHA*, 299 Goldfields Rd, 2 km from town centre, T9071 1040, yhaesperance@hotmail.com.au Large, single-storey hostel opposite the beach with lots of outside and communal space. Mostly doubles and quads, bikes available. **D-E** *Esperance Backpackers*, 14 Emily St, T9071 4724, esperancebackpackers@westnet.com.au More convenient for town, though with more modest facilities, this hostel has about 40 beds and runs tours. Both offer pickups. **Caravan parks** The closest to town is *Esperance Bay*, 162 Dempster St, T/F9071 2237, with cabins, chalets and a good range of facilities.

Eating

Gray Starling, 126 Dempster St, T9071 5880. Imaginative and good value evening meals in an elegant yet casual setting. Mid-range but some cheaper pasta and salad options. BYO. Mon-Sat 1700-2030. The best spot almost anytime of day is the *Taylor Street Tearooms*, T9071 4317, a 1930s weatherboard building with spacious verandas overlooking the town beach. Meals all day 0700-2200 include a good range of cheap light snacks and more substantial mid-range mains. Recommended. *Esperance Woodfire*, corner of Dempster St and William St makes good pizza, take-away or eat-in. Tue-Sun 1730-2300.

Tours & activities

4WD *Aussie Bight Expeditions*, T9071 7778, aussiebight@bigpond.com Wide range of tours in a purpose-built vehicle. Regular half-day ($58) and full-day ($132) tours to Cape Le Grand and Cape Arid include lunch and/or tea. *Esperance Backpackers* take parties of 6 out for day and overnight trips to the national parks, usually involving beach fishing. Good value and fun ($55 day trip, $90 per day all-inclusive for overnight). **Boat cruises** *Mackenzies*, 71 The Esplanade, T9071 5757, www.emerge.net.au/ ~macruise Excellent boat trips out around the Bay of Isles from Taylor St Jetty (daily 0900, 3½ hrs,

Western Australia

$53, children $20) on their 20-m catamaran. If you can, get onto one of their full-day eco-tours. Wed, Sun during Sep-Apr and daily in Jan ($79, children $24). **Diving** Unusually in WA, diving off Esperance is possible almost every day of the year (in a thick wetsuit!), thanks to the shelter given by the many islands. *Esperance Diving & Fishing*, 72 The Esplanade, T9071 5111, www.gei.net.au/~espdive, organize several boat dives a week. **Island camping** *Mackenzies* organize stays on Woody Island, either in safari huts or pre-erected tents (**C-E**), during Sep-Apr. **Mini-coach** *Vacation Country Tours*, T9071 2227. Trips include *Town and Coast* ($30), and *Cape Le Grand* ($50). **Scenic flights** *Esperance Air Service*, T9071 1467. Bay of Isles flights (45 min, $55) and out to the Australian Bight (1½ hrs, $165). Min 4 people. **Snorkelling** The ruined far end of the tanker jetty is covered in multi-coloured soft corals and attracts lots of fish and sea dragons. Hire snorkel gear and fins for $20 a day from *Esperance Diving & Fishing*.

Air The Aiport is 22 km from town on Norseman Rd. Car hire and taxis available. Direct **Transport** *Skywest*, T9075 4145, flights to **Perth** daily. **Bus** *Westrail* services leave Dempster St for **Albany** at 0800 Tue and Fri. Connections en route to **Bremer Bay** must be arranged in advance, as must one to **Hopetoun** (Fri only). Buses to **Perth** depart 0800 Mon-Sat, with Thu services dropping off at **Hyden** (Wave Rock). **Norseman** and **Kalgoorlie** buses leave at 0835 Tue, Fri, and 1400 Sun. The Sun service is via **Coolgardie**, the Tue and Fri ones have onward connections to Perth.

Cape Le Grand National Park, 60 km from Esperance, has beaches so perfect **Around** you may never have seen better, and this is what people come to Esperance for. **Esperance** The beaches are blindingly beautiful coves of silky white sand, rosy granite boulders, car park water deepening to sapphire blue. **Hellfire Bay** is possibly the prettiest but often the busiest. **Thistle Cove** is more tightly enclosed and a five-minute walk leads down to the beach so it tends to be quieter. Both are accessed by short unsealed roads. **Lucky Bay** is the best known but vehicle access and an overlooking campground rob it of the magical isolation of the other two. A **coastal walk** runs from Le Grand Beach to Rossiter Bay (15 km one-way). Signs at each beach give estimates of the length of each section. Another great walk is at **Frenchmans Peak** (262 m) which gives views over the whole park. Wear boots and allow 1½ hours return. Take plenty of water. There are small camping areas (no bookings taken) at Lucky Bay and Le Grand Beach ($12.50 site). ■ *Park entry fee $9 per car. CALM ranger, T9075 9022.*

Cape Arid National Park, 130 km from Esperance, is mostly a wilderness area, about eight times the size of Cape Le Grand and with similar scenery. Naturally it is a peaceful spot, the fishing and long white beaches are excellent and it is not unusual to have a campground to yourself. Only the western coastal regions are accessible to 2WD, all other tracks are challenging 4WD routes. Thomas River and Seal Creek are the main campsites on the coast, with toilets, picnic tables and limited water supplies. Thomas River also has gas BBQs and several walking trails. ■ *Park entry fee $9 car. CALM ranger T9075 0055.*

Roughly midway between Perth and Esperance is the small town of **Hyden** and its claim to fame, **Wave Rock**. This formation is part of a granite outcrop that has eroded on one edge into the shape of a breaking wave 15 m high. Entry fee is $6 per car. There is a clutch of very touristy shops near the car park, including a souvenir shop. Drinks are available from the kiosk (open daily 0830-1800) and light meals and info from the café in the *Wildflower Shoppe*, daily 0930-1730, T9880 5182. To stay overnight try the **C** *Wave Rock Motel*, T9880 5052, in Hyden next to the roadhouse or the caravan park, T9880 5022, near the rock.

Western Australia

Goldfields and the southeast

Www.kalgoorlieand
wagoldfields.com.au

The main WA gold rushes started in 1892 and within a few short years WA's population had increased tenfold to around 100,000 people, most either busily digging or supporting diggers in the region around Coolgardie, creating huge towns in the process. Most of these towns have dwindled to a fraction of their previous size, one of the few exceptions being Kalgoorlie which is still a gold-mining town, where current mining technology seems to almost belittle the backbreaking efforts of the early days preserved in the area's museums and hand-dug mines. At the eastern fringes of the goldfields begin the Great Victoria Desert and, to the south, the vast Nullarbor, the largest slab of limestone on the planet and one of the flattest, driest places in Australia.

Ins & outs

Getting there Air *Qantas* fly daily from Perth to Kalgoorlie, and from Adelaide at weekends. **Bus/train** *Westrail's Prospector* train and bus services depart East Perth Terminal at 0715 Mon-Sat, 1430 Mon, Fri and 1410 Sun (Kalgoorlie 8-9 hrs). There are also services from Dempster St, Esperance at 0835 Tue, Fri and 1400 Sun (5 hrs). The *Perth Goldfields Express*, T1800 620440, bus makes an express run along the Great Eastern Highway from East Perth, stopping at Coolgardie and Kalgoorlie (7 hrs) on its way to Menzies and, on Wed, Fri and Sun, as far as Laverton. Departs 0745 Tue-Sat, 1430 Sun. *Travel Coach's* GX607 bus service leaves Perth at 1430 Mon, Wed and Fri, stopping at Coolgardie, Kalgoorlie and Norseman on its way to Adelaide. The *Indian Pacific*, T132147, stops at Kalgoorlie on its journeys between Perth and the eastern states.

Coolgardie

Colour map 5,
grid C1
Population: 1,100
560 km from Perth,
170 km from
Norseman

The streets of Coolgardie are wide enough to turn a camel train in but the bustle of miners, cameleers and shopkeepers that would have attended such an event is long gone. It is now virtually a ghost town, the remaining businesses hanging on thanks to visitors drawn by the the magnificent golden stone buildings on **Bayley Street**. The town sprang up around the first gold find at Fly Flat in 1892 and boomed on alluvial gold for about a decade. Despite the disease and hardship caused by lack of water, searing heat and isolation, Coolgardie had a population of 16,000 at its height and was the third-largest town in Western Australia. By the time water arrived in 1902, thanks to C.Y. O'Connor's pipeline from Perth, the easy gold was gone and miners moved east to Kalgoorlie.

Sights

A series of historical markers have been placed around the town to show what once stood in the large empty lots of the present

Much of the town's goldfields heritage has gone so the appeal lies in wandering past the grand façades and humble tin miners' shacks in order to conjure up the optimism and hardship of life here. There are also a couple of interesting museums to explore. The finest building on Bayley Street is the **Warden's Court Building**, built in 1898 to house the Mines Department and Gold Warden's Court. It now houses the **VIC** (daily 0900-1700, T9026 6090) and the **Goldfields Exhibition Museum**, a massive, dated but still fascinating collection of mining memorabilia. ■ *Daily 0900-1700. $3.30, children $1.10, concessions $2.75.* Many of the town's other attractions require a vivid imagination to be of real interest, but take the time to stroll around the main **cemetery**, 2 km to the west of town. There are hundreds of graves, most marked simply by a small numbered plaque. Those with more personal headstones reveal the goldfields' tragic side, a hint of the thousands of hopeful, mostly 20 to 40 year-olds who died in mining accidents or of disease.

The **C-D** *Coolgardie Motel*, Bayley St, T9026 6080, is the most central accommodation. There are very basic budget options at the pub, the **E** *Hotel Denver City*, Bayley St, T9026 6031, or the **E** *Railway Lodge* on the opposite corner, T9026 6238. The latter has ill-kempt kitchen facilities. Of 2 caravan parks the simple but friendly **E** *Haven*, opposite the main cemetery, T9026 6123, has on-site vans, a lawned area, well-equipped camp kitchen and usually a couple of dozen rescued kangaroos roaming the grounds. Meals at the motels or at the pub (cheap) daily 1200-1400, 1900-2100.

Sleeping & eating

Westrail **bus** services leave from opposite Caltex for **Perth** at 1455 Mon and Fri, and for **Kalgoorlie** at 2140 Mon and Fri. Services to **Esperance** every Fri at 1553. The Perth Goldfields Express bus leaves **Caltex** for stops to **Perth** 0925 Mon, 1510 Tue, Thu, Fri, 2325 Wed and Fri. The northbound service leaves 2050 Sun, 1410 Tue-Sat. *Travel Coach* services to **Perth** leave at 2350 Tue, Thu and Sat, while their **Kalgoorlie**, **Port Augusta** and **Adelaide** bus goes at 2155 Mon, Wed and Fri.

Transport

Kalgoorlie-Boulder

The twin town of Kalgoorlie-Boulder prides itself on a raw, frontier town atmosphere with its 'red light' street, *skimpies* (scantily-clad barmaids), gambling amd brothels. But while it's true that the place has a certain rough edge, essentially it's a prosperous modern city where many residents enjoy the comforts of high wages. Sitting on the richest gold field in Australia, 'Kal', as it's known locally, is the great survivor of the goldfields towns. Some 35 million ounces have been extracted from the ground since lucky Irish diggers Hannan, Flanagan and Shea found some nuggets here in 1893. The alluvial gold near the surface was worked out by the early 1900s but Kalgoorlie has since been developed by large companies with the capital to mine reefs deep underground. Gold is still mined in the **Super Pit** at Boulder, using the most advanced large-scale methods of ore crushing and chemical extraction.

Colour map 5, grid C2
Population: 32,000
38 km from
Coolgardie, 195 km
from Norseman

Getting there and around Kalgoorlie-Boulder is a very spread out city, with the 2 centres some 4 km apart, and the main sights equally spaced out. **Air** The airport is 5 km south of Kalgoorlie, 4 km west of Boulder. Taxis meet all flights and cost around $10. **Bus** Local services, T9021 2655, run between the VIC, Kalgoorlie, and central Boulder approximately every 30 mins 0740-1715 Mon-Fri, and hourly 0810-1230 Sat. Fares are $1.80 per trip. *Goldrush Tours*, T1800 620440 or 9021 2954, run a quick morning trip around the main sights, but not the *Hall of Fame* (2 hrs, $25, children $5, concessions $20). Accommodation pick-ups from 0930. **Information** The main **VIC** is in central Kalgoorlie. Open 0830-1700 Mon-Fri, 0900-1700 Sat-Sun. T9021 1966, kbtc@emerge.net.au 250 Hannan St.

Ins & outs

The town's mining heritage and future is best explored at Kalgoorlie's brand-new **Mining Hall of Fame**, an impressive national museum that explores the history, achievements and techniques of all types of mining in Australia. There is also a stylish café and wonderful views of the town from the Observation Deck. The complex incorporates the site of **Hannan's North Historic Mining Reserve**, a traditional mine, now closed. It is possible to go underground and see examples of hand-cut mining shafts as well as more recent explosive and drilling methods. You can also watch a simulated gold pour, pan for gold or just wander amongst the old tin sheds and timber headframes to get a sense of what mining used to be like. ■ *Daily 0900-1630. $20, children $10. Mine tours 0930, 1100, 1230, 1400, 1500. Gold pour 1100, 1300, 1500. T9091 4074, www.mininghall.com.au Goldfields Highway, 3 km north of town.*

Sights

Western Australia

Hannan Street has many fine civic buildings, built with the money from the goldfields and the optimistic solidity inspired by the Federation in 1901. One such building is the **Town Hall**, a beautiful and elaborate Edwardian confection in pastel shades, with impressive fittings, as well as a collection of art and memorabilia. A statue of Paddy Hannan, the first man to discover gold in Kalgoorlie, stands outside. ■ *Mon-Fri 0900-1630. Free.* Further up from the museum is Hannan Street's main intersection, notable for three magnificent old pubs. Pop inside the *Palace* to see the mirror and poem attributed to former American president Herbert Hoover who is supposed to have fallen in love with a barmaid while working as a mine manager near Kalgoorlie in the late 1890s. At the top of Hannan Street a red steel headframe rises above the grand old pubs and iron-lace verandahs of the main street. This landmark is part of the **Museum of the Goldfields**, and a lift to the top provides good views of the town. The museum has wide-ranging displays on social and cultural aspects of early goldfields life, such as the harvesting of local sandalwood, extravagant trade union banners and a frightening dental surgery. Don't miss the gold nuggets in the basement and the proudly parochial gold jewellery, featuring picks, shovels and buckets, that lucky miner's wives used to be showered with. ■ *Daily 1000-1630. Entry by donation. Free guided tours at 1100, 1430. T9021 8533, mog@gold.net.au 17 Hannan St.* Serious rock hounds should head for another museum nearby, the **WA School of Mines Mineral Museum**, which has 3,000 mineral and ore specimens and replicas of huge gold nuggets like the Golden Eagle. ■ *Mon-Fri 0830-1230. Free. T9088 6001. Corner of Cassidy St and Egan St.*

Kalgoorlie

■	Sleeping	3	Golddust	●	Eating	3	Monty's
	1	Australia	4	Goldfields		1	Akudjura	4	Star & Garter
	2	Cheetham Lodge	5	Palace		2	Kalgoorlie Hotel		

0 metres   200
0 yards   200

To see a less seemly and more seamy side of the city, head for **Hay Steet**, the 'red-light' street, which has survived various incarnations from the crowded open tents of a century ago to the later tin sheds known as 'starting stalls' for their similarity to the narrow pens that confine horses at the start of a race. Changes to prostitution laws mean sex workers no longer stroll the street and the few remaining brothels have now smartened up considerably. One in particular, **Langtrees 181**, has turned itself into a place of five-star comfort where guests are welcome simply to use the pool or bar or to take one of the Australia's most unusual and fascinating tours. During the tour visitors are shown all of the brothel's themed rooms, which include a box-ing-ring bed, a room like a mine shaft and an Afghan boudoir. Except for the guide's anecdotes, the erotic art and the price list of 'services' you could be touring an upmarket hotel. ■ *Tours daily 1300, 1500, 1900. $25, 1½ hrs. Over 18s only. T9026 2181, www.langtrees.com 181 Hay St.*

The township of **Boulder** is effectively a Kalgoorlie suburb and once ser-viced a strip of traditional mines known as the 'Golden Mile'. These mines have now been swallowed up by the **Super Pit**, an open-cut gold mine owned by Kalgoorlie Consolidated Gold Mines (KCGM). The mine con-sists of a hole in the ground of staggeringly huge proportions (currently about 3 km long by 1 km wide, and 300 m deep). It can only be seen from the **Super Pit Lookout.** ■ *Daily 0600-1900. Blasts are conducted daily, usually about 1300, but check with the VIC for times. Outram St, off Goldfields High-way.* Out at the airport there is a chance to visit the working **Royal Flying Doctor Service** (RFDS) base, where you can hop aboard a plane (if they're not all in use) and see the cramped conditions the medics have to work with. Guided tours also include an introductory video and displays on the history of the service. ■ *Tours on demand Mon-Fri 1100-1500. Entry by donation. T9093 1500. Turn left at the roundabout on Hart Kerspien Dr.*

Sleeping

Much of the twin-town's accommodation, particularly at the budget end, is geared towards itinerant mine workers – 'please remove muddy boots' is a common sign

There are several historic pub hotels in Kalgoorlie city centre. Most exclusive (not even a front bar!) is the beautifully filligreed **L-C** *Australia Hotel*, corner of Hannan St and Maritana St, T9021 1320, www.oldaustraliahotel.com.au On the opposite cor ner is the **C** *Palace Hotel*, T9021 2788, www.palacehotel.com.au Their 'executive' en suite rooms are smartly furnished, motel-style, with direct balcony access, while the standard options are distinctly shabbier though not a lot cheaper. Boulder's **D** *Historic Cornwall Hotel*, corner of Hopkins St and Goldfields Highway, T9093 2510, cornwallhotel@bigpond.com, offers a simpler, more traditional B&B option, though service standards are equally high. Other budget options include the good value **D** *Cheetham Lodge*, Cheetham St, T9022 2911, a modern, clean and quiet workers' lodge with a/c and TV in every double and single room. Also en suites. The 2 backpacker hostels are almost adjacent on Hay St, right opposite *Langtree's*. Both have excellent facilities, including pools, will help find work (mostly hospitality), and there is little to choose between them. However, the spacious **D-E** *Golddust*, T9091 3737, golddust@aurum.net.au, is considered friendlier by some, is open all day, has free bikes, and its dorm beds are marginally cheaper. **E** *Goldfields*, T9091 1482, goldbpak@gold.net.au, has fewer beds per dorm and cheaper doubles. None of the 5 caravan parks are very close to Kalgoorlie town centre, but are the best bet for self-contained units. The best close option is the **C-D** *Prospector*, Great Eastern High-way, T1800 800907 or 9021 2524, which is 2½ km away.

Eating

The pubs provide the best dining in town. At the top of the tree is the expensive, almost club-like *Historic Cornwall*, with a pre-dinner bar, classy dining room and wonderful 'smokers' bar'. Excellent, creative menu and very attentive, friendly service. Meals Tue-Sat 1830-2100. Recommended. Many of the pubs down Hannan St have large and expensive first-floor verandah restaurants, usually in marked contrast to their ground-floor bars, including the *Australia*, open Mon-Sat 1830-2100, and *Palace*. These are fine places to while away an evening. The *Kalgoorlie Hotel*, commonly known as *Judd's*, corner of Wilson St, T9021 3046, offers a range of cheap, inventive wood-fired pizzas alongside the finer fare on the balcony and also down in the bar. Meals 1200-1230, 1800-2200. The *Star & Garter*, on the junction with Nethercott St, T9026 3399, doesn't have a balcony but is a another good, cheap, pub option with an excellent veg and salad bar thrown in. Meals daily 0600-0900, 1200-1400, 1800-2100. Aside from the pubs there are a couple of worthy **cafés**. The stylish and contemporary *Akudjura*, 418 Hannan St, T9091 3311, does particularly good breakfasts and offers lots of choice for a cheap lunch and mid-range dinner too. Open daily 0700-2100. Recommended. *Monty's*, corner of Hannan St and Shamrock St, T9022 8288, has an international, mostly mid-range menu with a good range of veggie options. Open 24 hrs.

Entertainment **Cinema** *Ace*, Oswald St, T9021 2199. **Pubs and clubs** The city can no longer support the 93 pubs and 8 breweries of 1902, but drinking is still a huge part of Kalgoorlie culture. Nightlife revolves around the *Exchange*, corner of Hannan and Maritana St, with live bands every night and a 0400 licence, and the *Kalgoorlie* and *Palace* hotels. The *Pulse* nightclub, 151 Hay St, has its own brewery.

Tours & **Aboriginal** *Aboriginal Bush Tours*, T9093 3745, geoffstokes@bigpond.com, is an
activities excellent one-man operation. Day trips $80, overnight bush camps $170. **Air** *Goldfields Air Services*, T9093 2116, operate from the northern tip of the airport, at the end of Burt St. Flights over the Super Pit from $35 (min 2 people). **Bus** *Goldrush Tours*, T9021 2954, run various afternoon tours around mine sites (leaving 1200 daily, 4½ hrs, $55, $children $10, concessions $50). Also occasional overnight station stays. **Gold** *Goldfields 4WD Tours*, T0419 915670, roger@matrix.net.au, have a 4WD, prospecting equipment and the crucial local knowledge, available for group charter.

Transport **Air** *Qantas* fly daily to *Perth* and to *Adelaide* at weekends. **Bus/train** The *Perth Goldfields Express*, T9021 2954, bus leaves Lane St for **Coolgardie** and **Perth** 0900 Mon, 1445 Tue, Thu, Fri, 2300 Wed and Fri. The northbound service leaves 2120 Sun, 1435 Tue-Sat. *Westrail's Prospector* services (some bus) leave the railway station for Perth at 0655 Mon-Sat, 1430 Mon, Fri and 1325 Sun. Their **Norseman** and **Esperance** services leave the station at 1735 Mon, 1525 Tue and Fri. The Fri bus stops in **Coolgardie**. *Travel Coach* services to **Perth** leave the BP Monster Roadhouse at 2315 Tue, Thu and Sat, while their **Port Augusta** and **Adelaide** (32 hrs) bus goes at 2250 Mon, Wed and Fri. The *Indian Pacific* train to **Perth** leaves at 2230 Wed and Sat (11 hrs), and the eastbound service departs 2320 Mon and Fri.

Directory **Banks** Branches and ATMs on Hannan St. **Bike hire** Backpacker hostels or
Kalgoorlie has the *Johnstons*, 78 Boulder Rd, T9021 1157. **Car hire** All the major companies are out at
cheapest fuel in the airport and in town. *Halfpenny*, T9021 1804, cars@kalgoorlie.com, is the cheap
the Goldfields local option. **Car servicing** Gull, corner of Egan St and Maritana St, T9021 2991. **Communications** Internet kiosks at hostels and some pubs, also at *NetZone*, next to the *Exchange*, $10 per hr. Open 1000-1900 Mon-Fri, 1000-1700 Sat-Sun. **Post Offices**, Hannan St, Kalgoorlie, and Burt St, Boulder. **Medical services** Hospital, Piccadilly St, T9080 5888. **Police** Brookman St, T9021 9777. Taxi T9091 5233. **Sport and swimming** *Oasis* sports centre, Johnston St, close to the airport, T9022 2922.

Western Australia

A main highway heads north from Kal to the central mining towns. At present it is sealed only as far as Wiluna, 200 km short of the Great Northern Highway at Meekatharra, though there are plans to complete the sealed connection. About 40 km from Kalgoorlie the road passes the *Broad Arrow Tavern*, T9024 2058, a raw, tin building that has been a licenced and characterful pub for over a century. Welcome cold beers and decent meals are available daily from 1100. Continuing north the highway passes through the small, stately gold-mining town of **Menzies** after a further 95 km, and then on to the towns of **Leonora** and **Gwalia**. The latter is more or less a ghost town but well worth a stop to stroll around the historical precinct. There are a few sleeping options in Leonora, including two hotel pubs, the *Central*, T9037 6042, and the *White House*, T9037 6030, and a caravan park (T9037 6568).

From Leonora the sealed 125-km road to the small mining town of **Laverton** is the first stretch of the **Outback Highway**. Laverton has the last decent supermarket and cheapest diesel before hitting the dirt, as well as a post office, car hire, the *Desert Inn* pub and motel, T9031 1188, and *Desert Pea Caravan Park*, T9031 1072. From Laverton the road becomes unsealed for the full distance across the central deserts to Kata Tjuta (the 'Olgas') in the Northern Territory. This is generally considered a 4WD only route, and even then it is recommended to travel in a well-prepared and self-sufficient convoy. From Laverton it's 315 km to the *Tjukayirla Roadhouse*. ■ *T9037 1108. Fuel and meals daily 0800-1800, plus accommodation.* From here it's a further 255 km to the small town of **Warburton**, where you'll find another roadhouse. ■ *0800-1700 Mon-Fri, 0900-1500 Sat-Sun, T8956 7656.* If you do get out this way, don't miss a visit to the **Tjulyuru Cultural Centre**, which showcases locally produced Aboriginal art, artefacts, ceremony and history. There is also a shop where you can purchase locally made art, ceramics and artefacts. ■ *Mon-Fri 0800-1700. Free. T8956 7966, www.tjulyuru.com* Further diesel and food are available at **Giles**, 230 km from Warburton, and the *Docker River* roadhouse, another 100 km further on in NT. *Warakurna Roadhouse*, ■ *0830-1800 Mon-Fri, 0900-1500 Sat-Sun, Giles, T8956 7344.* Separate permits are required for traversing Aboriginal lands in both WA and NT. Contact the Ngaanyatjarra Council, 8 Victoria Avenue, Perth, T9325 4630, for WA, and the Central Land Council, 31 Stuart Highway, Alice Springs, T8951 6320, for NT.

The **Gunbarrel Highway** is the hopelessly exaggerated name given to the poorly-maintained 4WD track that stretches across the centre of Western Australia, from **Wiluna** to **Warburton** where it meets the **Great Central Road**. This is considered one of the great Outback adventures of WA is not for the faint-hearted, even as part of an organized guided trip. Diesel and limited accommodation available at *Carnegie Homestead*, T9981 2991, 344 km from Wiluna. The hardest parts of the drive are encountered on the 450 km stretch between here and Warburton. Independent travellers should only consider this route after careful research and planning.

Located at the junction of the highways north to Kalgoorlie and Perth, south to Esperance and east to the Nullarbor, this is a friendly town that makes a good overnight stop. Perhaps the only Australian town to be founded by a horse, Norseman commemorates 'Hardy Norseman' who was tethered here in 1894 and scratched up some gold overnight (his statue is at the junction of Roberts Street and Ramsay Street). Since then the town has produced 5,000,000 oz of gold and continues to produce about 100,000 oz a year from the working mines of the Central Norseman Gold Corporation (CNGC). The

North of Kalgoorlie-Boulder

Central Standard Time applies in NT. For current road conditions T1800-013314 (WA section) and T1800-246199 (NT section)

For more information on the highway, see www.outback-Highway.gov.au and Westprint 'Gunbarrel' map Unleaded fuel is not available on these routes

Norseman

Colour map 5, grid C2 Population: 1,300 195 km from Kalgoorlie, 210 km from Esperance

VIC is the first in WA if travelling from the east so holds information on the whole state as well as local information. ■ *Daily 0900-1700. T9039 1071, nsmntour@wn.com.au 68 Roberts St.*

Sleeping and eating C *Great Western*, Prinsep St, T9039 1633, F9039 1692. A pleasant modern motel with pool and mid-range restaurant. Budget travellers should head for the excellent **D-E** *Lodge 101*, 101 Prinsep St, T9039 1541. Warm, welcoming hosts and spotlessly clean, homely doubles, twins and dorms. Also guest kitchen, laundry and free pick-up from the bus stop at the *BP* roadhouse. Next door to the motel there is a good **caravan park**, *Gateway*, T9039 1500, with a range of cabins and vans. *Topic Caterers* is a mine workers' canteen but everyone is welcome. Only $11 for a hot buffet, salads, deserts, and non-alcoholic drinks. Daily 1700-1930. Recommended. To find it head east from the Ramsay St roundabouts, over the railway line then first left. The dining room is at the top of the t-junction just past the huge tailings heap.

Fuel: cheapest until Ceduna in SA **Transport** *Westrail* buses leave the BP roadhouse for **Kalgoorlie** at 1115 Tue, Fri and 1640 Sun. Their **Esperance** service departs 2010 Mon, 1800 Tue and 1815 Fri. *McCafferty/Greyhound's* services to **Perth** leave the BP roadhouse at 2050 Tue, Thu and Sat, while their **Port Augusta** and **Adelaide** bus goes at 0120 Tue, Thu and Sat.

Directory Banks *ANZ* ATM in Roberts St. **Communications** Internet at *Norseman Telecentre*, by swimming pool on Roberts St, Mon-Fri 0900-1700. **Post Office**, corner Prinsep St and Ramsay St.

The Eyre Highway

In a country with a lot of long, straight and quiet roads, the Eyre Highway enjoys near mythical status for its association with the Nullarbor, even though the 1,225 km of bitumen that connects Norseman in Western Australia to Ceduna in South Australia passes only briefly through the true Nullarbor (the name is a corruption of the Latin for 'no tree'). Much of the drive is through a mix of timeless gum woods, low scrub and worn grazing land, and what is really striking is just how flat the entire landscape is. Fortunately there are a few interesting stops to break the journey, such as whalewatching and spectacular cliffs at the Head of Bight, caves and blowholes around Cocklebiddy and the sand dunes and beach around the telegraph station at Eucla.

Ins & outs **Getting there** The Eyre Highway can be travelled at any time of year, but it is scorching in summer and can be wet in winter. Spring is preferable to autumn as southern right whales can usually be seen at the Head of Bight until October. **Car** Fuel prices increase around Cunderdin and again after Merredin. Norseman provides the last reasonably priced fuel, food shopping and a great hostel. **Bicycle** This is a punishing bike ride that is not to be embarked upon lightly, but is certainly possible. Prepare with care and inform roadhouses along the route of your itinerary. **Adventure bus** *Nullarbor Traveller*, T1800 816858 or 8364 0407, info@the-traveller.com.au, run very enjoyable 7-day 4WD adventure trips from Perth to Adelaide ($693). 2 to 3 days are spent crossing the Nullarbor. Departures every fortnight.

Information Sleeping and eating options are almost completely limited to roadhouses. Most offer a reasonably full range from camping facilities to deluxe motel rooms, and take-aways to licensed restaurants. Beware the term 'backpacker accommodation' – this is usually a budget room or dorm that shares bathroom facilities with the camping area. Kitchens are uncommon, the best are at Balladonia, Eyre Bird

Observatory, Madura and Eucla. If you are travelling under your own steam and can camp independently then the roadside parking areas are an option. Note there are no real grocery-buying opportunities until Penong, 70 km short of Ceduna. Emergency phones are infrequent, but generally found halfway between roadhouses. Water tanks (which may be empty) are located 131 km east of Balladonia, 21 km east of Caiguna, and 48 and 114 kms east of Madura.

Norseman to Eucla

The first roadhouse, 195 km from Norseman is the **C-E***Balladonia*, T9039 3453, www.balladonia.bigpond.com It's pretty lucky to be here since NASA's **Skylab** disintegrated right overhead and locals have been tripping over chunks of it ever since. Their free and interesting **museum** displays several bits. Accommodation ranges from deluxe to backpacker and campsites. Free BBQ, licensed bar and pool tables. Good range of home-made food and coffee from the bistro. Showers available for non-residents $3.50. Petrol and food available 0600-2100 summer, 0800-2030 winter. Between Balladonia and Caiguna is the straightest bit of bitumen in the world – all 145 km of it! In Caiguna, 180 km from Balladonia, is the **C-E** *John Eyre*, T9039 3459, a bare and shadeless site with basic, clean motel units and dongas and camping but no kitchen facilities. Showers for non-residents $3.50. Roadhouse menu. Open 24 hours. The unmarked turn-off for **Cocklebiddy Cave** is at the rear of a small parking bay 54 km from Caiguna and 10 km short of Cocklebiddy. The track, rough but fine for 2WD when dry, passes a sign for Nuytsland Nature Reserve after 100 m then interweaves its way for 10 km to the cave. One of many huge Nullarbor caves, this is the most accessible and a rewarding excursion. Wear sturdy shoes for the steep and rocky climb down and take a good torch each. The large lake at the bottom makes for a cold and muddy but welcome swim. Allow 2½ hours. The **C-E** *Cocklebiddy Wedgetail Inn*, T9039 3462, 80 km from Caiguna, has a licensed restaurant and bar. Showers for non-residents $2. Roadhouse menu. Petrol 0630-1900, food 0600-2100. A 4WD track behind leads to **Twilight Cove**, a favourite local camping beach. If you've any plans to stay in the area, take the time to stay at the isolated **B** *Eyre Bird Observatory*, T9039 3450, occupying an old telegraph station 38 km off the highway and right on the coast. Staff will collect you if you are in a 2WD vehicle. Prices are all-inclusive except for linen, advance bookings essential. Recommended.

The highway drops down through the Madura Pass from the Hampton Tablelands 92 km after Cocklebiddy. The **D-E** *Madura Pass Oasis*, T9039 3464, is a large resort-style roadhouse at the base of the escarpment, with shady gum trees and a swimming pool. Pleasant mid-range licenced restaurant and small bar. Camping area with BBQs. If you want to cool off on the way through, the pool and showers are $2 and are open 0630-2000. Some 116 km further east, the **D** *Mundrabilla Roadhouse*, T9039 3465, has the cheapest petrol for several hundred kilometres in either direction, as well as good value rooms, bar, café and camping. Open 0530-2300.

Eucla, 70 km from Mundrabilla and home to one of Australia's busiest telegraph stations in the 1880s, makes a good stop just before the South Australian border. Accommodation at **C-E** *Eucla*, T9039 3468, a motel with budget rooms and camping. Restaurant, café and interesting bar. Showers $1, swimming pool, BBQs, museum, golf, 4WD day tours. Open 0600-2200. The **South Australian border** and the *Border Village* roadhouse are just 12 km further on (see page 795 for the remainder of the route to Ceduna).

The Midwest

When in the Midwest makes sure you taste fresh BBQ crayfish

The dry Midwest divides the verdant green of Perth and the Southwest from the parched desert browns further north. The region's windy coastline is a long, straight stretch of narrow beaches and high white dunes, gradually rising to the limestone cliffs of Kalbarri. At Cervantes low cliffs are peopled by fields of eerie limestone columns, called the **Pinnacles***. The major port of* **Geraldton***, one of the state's largest cities, has superb windsurfing conditions and excellent diving and snorkelling on the coral reefs of the Houtman Abrolhos islands 60 km offshore. For many, though,* **Kalbarri** *is the queen of the midwest. This small seaside town can boast a beautiful location, fine beaches, and a national park with stunning river and coastal gorges.*

Ins and outs

Getting there & around **Air** *Skywest* has daily flights from Perth to **Geraldton**. **Bus** *Westrail* buses pass through the region on 3 routes. The main (N1) services to **Geraldton** (6 hrs) leave East Perth Terminal at 0830 Mon-Sat, 1730 Fri and 1630 Sat, stops include **Gingin**, **Dongara** and **Greenough**. On Mon, Wed, Fri it continues on to **Kalbarri**. Other services head to Geraldton via **New Norcia** and **Moora** (N2), leaving 0930 Tue, Thu, 1700 Fri, 1515 Sun; and via **Northam** and **Morawa** (N3), leaving 0715 Mon and 0930 Thu. From Geraldton they have 2 services a week to **Meekatharra**, departing Mon, Wed. *Integrity*, Wellington St Bus Station, Perth, T1800 226339 or 9226 1339, www.integritycoachlines.com.au, operate a service up the Brand Highway, stopping at **Gingin**, **Dongara**, **Geraldton** (5½ hrs, $30) and **Northampton**, before continuing on to **Exmouth**. Buses leave at 0700 Tue, 1930 Thu and Sun, with a Mon-Fri service terminating at Geraldton that departs 1730. *McCafferty's/Greyhound* services are commonly used by travellers, but the timetable makes it notoriously difficult, particularly if you want to stop off at Kalbarri, Monkey Mia and Coral Bay. Their GX683 service heads up to Exmouth from Perth at 1830 Wed, Fri and Sun, calling at all the major coastal towns from **Cervantes** northward. A more direct Brand Highway service, bypassing *Cervantes* and *Kalbarri*, leaves daily at 1000. Their inland service via **Mt Magnet** and **Meekatharra** departs 1330 Fri (and Sun during school holidays).

Cervantes
Colour map 7, grid B4
Population: 500
225 km from Perth, 25 km from Jurien

This small crayfishing community has the good fortune of being the closest to **Nambung National Park** and its famous **Pinnacles**, although most people visit the park on a day trip so the town remains essentially undeveloped. The most exotic thing about Cervantes, named after a locally wrecked ship, is its Spanish street names, chosen from the Miguel de Cervantes' novel *Don Quixote*.

Sleeping and eating C *Cervantes Pinnacles Motel*, Aragon St, T9652 7145, a large modern motel with 40 standard rooms, pool, bar and restaurant. **D-E** *Pinnacles Beach Backpackers*, 91 Seville St, T9652 7377, www.wn.com.au/pbbackpackers Clean, comfortable, attractive and welcoming. Currently 40 beds, including doubles, though a new 40-bed block is under construction and will include a licensed café. Recommended. The **caravan park** on Aragon St, T9652 7060, has cheap, clean cabins and vans. There is a small shopping centre with a general store and take-away shop, by the *Ronsard Bay Tavern*, Cadiz St, T9652 7041, which has a large open-plan dining room (meals daily 1130-1400, 1830-2030) and a standard public bar.

Transport *McCafferty's/Greyhound* northbound coastal **bus** services leave the Shell garage at 2220 Wed, Fri and Sun, and from the Brand Highway intersection at 1320 daily (for Geraldton and **Broome**). Their **Perth** buses depart 1330 daily from the highway, and 0635 Tue, Fri and Sun from town. *Happy Day* buses pick up *McCafferty/Greyhound* passengers from the Cervantes turn-off on the Brand Highway, and transfer back out there. Bookings via *McCafferty/Greyhound* (T132030).

This national park protects an otherworldly forest of spiky rocks rising out of a yellow sandy desert. The Pinnacles are one of the most recognizable images of Western Australia (see the cover of this guide) and they are certainly a striking sight. Dutch sailors passing by in the 17th century marked them on their charts and likened them to the crumbling remains of an ancient city. The rock formations are surprisingly extensive, covering an area of several square kilometres, and there are thousands of them, taking varied forms, from narrow towers 5-m high to modest stubs barely half a metre high. The best time to see the park is in the soft light of early morning or at sunset, although sunset is quite busy with tour groups. The road is sandy but hard-packed and perfectly suitable for 2WD. A loop road (3½ km) traverses the main area of formations and you can stop along the way and walk among them. Of the two picnic spots by the beach on the way out, at **Kangaroo Point** and **Hangover Bay**. ■ *Park entry fee $9 car or $3.40 per person.*

Nambung National Park (the Pinnacles)
Colour map 7, grid B5
19 km from Cervantes, 6 km unsealed

Tours *Happy Day Tours* head out most days at 0800 for a thorough 3-hr tour ($25). Good value, though you'll miss the deep colours of sunrise or sunset. Book via *McCafferty/Greyhound* (T132030). *Turquoise Coast Enviro Tours*, T9652 7047, miken@wn.com.au, run personalized 4WD tours of the national parks in the area (most are only accessible by 4WD). The all-day tour starts with the Pinnacles and also takes in Lesueur and Stockyard Gully parks. Prices vary according to group size and duration.

Greenough Hamlet, a settlers' village dating back to the 1860s, is now uninhabited and maintained as a partially furnished open-air museum by the National Trust. A dozen buildings are still extant, including the gaol, two churches and a tea-room. ■ *Daily 0900-1600. $4.50, children and concessions $2.50. T9926 1084.* Further up the highway, past the wind-tortured 'leaning trees' is the **Pioneer Museum**, another of the area's pioneer homes and now a folk museum stuffed full of everyday artefacts from the late 1800s. ■ *1000-1600 Tue-Sun. $3, children $1, concessions $2. T9926 1058.*

Greenough
Colour map 7, grid A4
www.green ough.wa.gov.au
40 km from Dongara, 25 km from Geraldton

Sleeping and eating C *Rock of Ages* B&B, T/F9926 1154, is an 1857 thick-stone-walled cottage, opposite the Pioneer Museum, originally built by WA's 'convict no. 2', John Patience. It's been beautifully restored, furnished mostly in period as a B&B, and has a small garden with gazebo spa and BBQ. Three double rooms share a single bathroom. Recommended. **D** *Bentwood Hollow Farm*, T/F9926 1195, set back off the Brand Highway, has a single, self-contained rammed-earth cottage. Private garden with BBQ, access to the family swimming pool, and optional breakfast. One double, one 4-bunk room. Comfortably and cheerfully furnished, and excellent value. The **D** *Hampton Arms*, Company Rd, T9926 1057, www.wn.com.au/hampton, is one of WA's great historic pubs, the bookshop here simply adding to the feel of antiquity. There's a small, rustic bar, mid-range restaurant serving simple, quality grills, seafood and gourmet pies, 6 double rooms and a covered rear courtyard. Open 1000-2200 Wed-Sun, meals 1130-1430, 1800-2030. Recommended.

For the Hampton Arms take the road behind the 'S' bend roadhouse (it's only unsealed for 100 m)

Transport **Bus** *Westrail* buses leave the Hamlet turn-off for **Geraldton** (20 mins) at 1409 Mon-Sat, 1610 Tue, Thu, 1109 and 1130 Fri, 0945 and 1009 Sun. **Perth** services depart 0850 Mon-Fri, 0950 Tue, Thu, 1720 and 1750 Fri, 0950 Sat, 1535 and 1650 Sun.

Western Australia

Dongara
Colour map 7, grid A4
Population: 1,900
Dongara 65 km
from Geraldton

The historic town of Dongara retains many buildings over a century old and with a picturesque main street lined with huge mature Moreton Bay Fig trees. It was first settled in the 1850s as the centre of a new agricultural area. The Irwin District Museum has photographic displays and memorabilia that explore local history and shipwrecks. ■ *Open 1000-1600 Mon-Fri when volunteers are available. T9927 1323. Waldeck St, adjacent to the VIC.* The **VIC** occupies part of the old Police Station which also houses the library. ■ *Open 0900-1700 Mon-Fri, 0900-1400 Sat-Sun. T9927 1404, donlibrary@hotmail.com 9 Waldeck St.*

Dongara has a range
of good value
accommodation.
These are particularly
recommended

Sleeping and eating   The old **D** *Priory Lodge*, 11 St Dominics Rd, T/F9927 1090, has an unfussy, comfortable public bar, huge beer garden opposite the river, and 17 plain, spacious doubles and singles. Guest kitchen and lounge. Simple, cheap and wholesome meals daily 1200-1400, 1800-2000. Recommended. **E** *Dongara Port Denison Backpackers* (YHA), 32 Waldeck St, T9927 1581, dongarabackpack@westnet.com.au, is a charming, friendly, easy-going hostel in a converted weatherboard cottage and 1906 railway carriage (the 'Snorient Express'). Some doubles, pick-ups, quiet garden with BBQ and excellent local knowledge. Recommended. The BYO *Coffee Tree*, 8 Moreton Terr, T9927 1400, has a small pavement terrace under one of the larger fig trees. All-day breakfast, sandwiches and salads, coffee and cake. Open daily 0800-1600.

Tours and activities   *Icon Charters*, Port Denison, T9927 1256, organize a number of boat trips, including sea lion interaction (6 hrs, $150) and whale-watching (2½ hrs, $40). All are numbers dependent and available Jul-Oct. *Dongara Coastal*, 8 km north on the Brand Hwy, T9927 2049. 2 hr bush and beach horse rides ($40). A couple of the local cray boat captains take out temporary 'crew' for around $20 a day during the Nov-Jun season. Own provisions required, but many find this a fascinating and very enjoyable experience. Book at hostel or tourist office. *Arkell Air Charter*, T9927 1267, run a variety of scenic flights from $55. The operator also enjoys organizing excellent day trips to the **Abrolhos Islands** that can be as cheap as $100 per person.

Geraldton

Colour map 7, grid A4
Population: 20,000
425 km from Perth,
480 km from
Carnarvon

Often dismissed as a large and uninteresting port city, Geraldton does have a fantastic sunny climate and strong, reliable westerlies make it a mecca for windsurfers. It also has some interesting sights (many of which are free) and is the base for dive and snorkel tours out to the **Houtman Abrolhos islands**, a remote group of coral islands teeming with fish and only inhabited for a few months a year by local crayfishermen. All the services of a large town can be found here and if you are heading north this will be the last place you find such services for a long while. The **VIC** is located in the **Bill Sewell Complex**, along with a simple café and a backpacker hostel. ■ *Mon-Fri 0830-1700, Sat 0900-1630, Sun 0930-1630. T9921 3999, www.geraldtontourist.com.au*

Ins and outs   Geraldton is a very spread out town, some 10 km north to south, and many of the main sights are outside of the city centre. **Bike hire** is available from the VIC, and there are several local **bus services**, T9923 1100 from Anzac Terr.

Sights   Just south of the Bill Sewell tourist complex is the **Old Geraldton Gaol Craft Centre**, a whitewashed stone gaol built in 1858 and last used in 1986, and now taken over by an army of craftspeople who look after it and sell their work from the cells. ■ *Daily 1000-1600. Free. T9921 1614. Chapman Rd. Buses 201 and 601.* Almost opposite, on the other side of the railway line, is the impressive new **Western Australian Museum – Geraldton**, which

Western Australia (vertical sidebar text)

deals with all things maritime. The Shipwreck Hall is the heart of the collection. It contains relics from the wrecks of the Dutch merhcantmen *Batavia* and *Zuytdorp*, and tells the fascinating tales of those ships and others wrecked on the Batavia coast in the 18th century. ■ *Daily 1000-1600. Entry by donation. T9921 5080, www.museum.wa.gov.au 1 Museum Place.* On a small rise overlooking the city, the **HMAS Sydney Memorial** is a new and beautiful landmark. The memorial was built in 2001 to remember the victims of the *HMAS Sydney*, an Australian naval ship sunk somewhere off the coast with all 645 hands in 1941. ■ *Mt Scott. Accessible from car park on Gummer Av.* The **Geraldton Regional Art Gallery**, housed in the former Town Hall, features collections of local contemporary art as well as major touring exhibitions. ■ *Tue-Sat 1000-1700, Sun-Mon 1330-1630. Free. T9921 6811. 24 Chapman Rd.* **St Francis Xavier Cathedral** is the town's Catholic cathedral, a splendid edifice in golden stone built between 1916 and 1938, and designed by the indefatigable Monsignor John Hawes. To some the inside of the building, with its grey and orange stripes, will seem fairly psychedelic. Open to the public every day, there are guided tours at 1000 Monday and 1400 Friday. At **Fisherman's Harbour** during the crayfishing season you can tour the Live Lobster factory to find out more about this valuable industry. ■ *Mon-Fri 0930, 1030, Sat 0930, Nov-Jun. Free. Covered shoes must be worn. T9921 7084. 3 km from the town centre on West End's northern shore.*

Geraldton

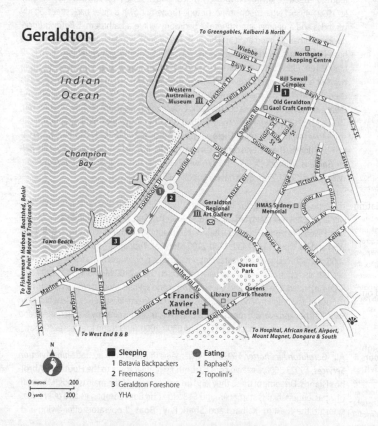

Sleeping ■
1 Batavia Backpackers
2 Freemasons
3 Geraldton Foreshore YHA

Eating ●
1 Raphael's
2 Topolini's

▶▶ **Houtman Abrolhos islands**

The Houtman Abrolhos Islands are a maze of low coral islands lying 60 km west of Geraldton. Essentially built-up reefs, they are uninhabited, except for a few crayfishermen in the short cray season (March-June). Their low-lying nature and treacherous outlying reefs mean they are very difficult to spot and they are the final resting place of at least 19 vessels, including the ill-fated Batavia. Indeed the name Abrolhos is thought to be a corruption of the Portuguese words for 'keep your eyes open'. The principal attractions for visitors however, are the crystal-clear waters and huge diversity of sea life. The islands encompass the world's most southerly coral reefs but also have a rich variety of more temperate species, a mix quite fascinating to marine biologists. They are also home to sea lions, turtles and dozens of species of sea birds. The snorkelling and diving here is outstanding for the coral gardens and many types of reef and pelagic fish. Arriving by air is the better option for a short trip as the views are wonderful and the sea crossing can be a bit rough.

Sleeping
See also under Greenough, page 593

B-C *African Reef*, corner of Willcock Dr and Broadhead Av, T9964 5566, www.africanreef.com.au, is a motel resort 3 km south, overlooking Tarcoola beach. All rooms have kitchenettes, but their all-day terrace café has one of the best locations in town, with sweeping views around the bay. **B-C** *Greengables*, Hackett Rd, T9938 2332, www.wn.com.au/greengables Large and modern family home with 4 B&B guest rooms, 2 en suite, 6 km from town. Very welcoming hosts. **C** *West End B&B*, 104 Gregory St, T9921 4956. Large, rough-stone, historic property down a quiet back street. Shady verandas and a genteel atmosphere. 2 bedrooms share a bathroom. **E** *Batavia Backpackers*, corner of Chapman St and Bayly St, T9964 3001, is a clean and friendly, 100-bed hostel with large verandahs, behind the VIC. The **E** *Freemasons Hotel* (the 'Freo'), 79 Marine Terr, T9964 3457, www.wn.com.au/freemasons, has 50 new bunkbeds, mostly in twins or quads, veranda access and a small lounge-cum-kitchenette. Live bands or DJs every Fri-Sat. The bar meals are excellent, available daily 1200-1430, 1800-2030, and there's a cook-your-own area out the back. **E** *Geraldton Foreshore YHA*, 172 Marine Terr, T9921 3275. Charming and homely 50-bed hostel in a spacious old house facing the small town swimming beach. There are sunny, enclosed verandahs, hammocks, and 3- to 4-bed dorms. There are no central **caravan parks**, but 2 of the best positioned are *Belair Gardens*, Willcock Dr, T9921 1997, which has on-site vans, and *Separation Point*, Willcock Dr, T9921 2763. Both have a good facilities and cabins.

Eating
In contrast to Geraldton's relatively cheap accommodation and many free sights, the restaurants in town are generally pretty pricey

The expensive *Boatshed*, 357 Marine Terr, T9921 5500, is the town's seafood specialist, with a pleasant rear courtyard. Open 1800-2030 Tue-Sun. Friendly *Raphael's*, 84 Marine Terr, T9965 4441, is one of several Italian restaurants, and has eat-all-you-can buffets on Wed and Fri. Open 1130-1430, 1730-2100 Mon-Sat. *Topolini's*, 158 Marine Terr, T9964 5866, is a high-ceilinged, airy restaurant serving cheap pizza and pasta for lunch and dinner, but also open all day as a laid-back café. Open 0900-2100 Mon-Sat, 0800-2000 Sun. Recommended. The cheap and cheerful *Tropicano's*, Point Moore, has views across to the ocean and resident windsurfers. Substantial, cheap breakfasts (an excellent buffet on Sun), lunches and evening meals. Loads of choice, much inspired by Mediterranean and Asian cooking. Licensed, but free BYO. Open 0800-2000 Sun-Fri and to at least 2400 Sat.

Tours & activities
www.abrolhos islands.com.au
See also Dongara, page 594

Air *Geraldton Air Charter*, T9923 3434, geroair@midwest.com.au, and *Shine Aviation Services*, T9923 3600, sas@wn.com.au, both fly regular tours to the **Houtman Abrolhos Islands**. On some of these they land on one or more of the main islands. Minimum of 2 passengers, flights start at around $130 for 1 hr. Both companies also offer excursions up the coast to **Kalbarri** and **Shark Bay**. **Boat** 2 operators offer diving and fishing trips out from Geraldton to the islands, for between 1 and 14 days. **Abrolhos Escape Charters**, T0428 382595, www.abrolhoscharters.com.au, are the cheaper (around $170 a day), though have a smaller, single-engined boat so the crossing can be a bit rougher. **Eco Abrolhos**, T9964 7887, www.wn.com.au/abrolhosbookings, have a larger, twin-engined vessel, maximum 12 passengers at around $250 per day, making the trip that bit more luxurious. Diving gear will be extra for both companies. **Diving** The clean waters off Geraldton can be excellent for diving, but winds and silt from the Chapman River often ruin visibility. The best time is mid-Feb to mid-May. Phone **Batavia Coast Dive Academy**, 153 Marine Terr, T9921 4229, ahead for current conditions. They hire out scuba gear for shore dives for $72 a day and run one morning boat dive a day, according to demand and conditions ($55 including gear, about 2½ hrs). **Surfing and windsurfing** Geraldton is Australia's 'windsurfing capital', and there are good wind and water conditions for most of the year. **Sail West**, Point Moore, T9964 1722, www.wn.com.au/sailwest, hire out windsurfers ($90 per day) and surfboards ($30 per day), from their shop next to the lighthouse. Open daily when the wind is above 20 knots. The **Batavia Coast Surf Academy**, T0418 903379, offers day courses in surfboarding for $99, including all equipment.

Transport

Air Skywest fly daily to **Perth**. **Bus** There are daily Westrail services to **Perth** from the railway station. The N1 route buses leave 0830 Mon-Fri, 1730 Fri, 0930 Sat, and 1630 Sun. N2 services depart 0930 Tue, Thu, 1700 Fri and 1515 Sun, and N3 buses head off at 1130 Tue and 1025 Fri. The **Northampton** and **Kalbarri** service leaves 1440 Mon, Wed and Fri. Buses to **Mt Magnet**, **Cue** and **Meekatharra** depart 1315 Mon and 1430 Wed. Integrity services head north from the VIC at 0110 Fri and Mon (i.e. Thu and Sun nights), and 1310 Tue. Their southbound buses depart 0050 Tue and Sat, 1300 Wed and 0700 Mon-Fri. McCafferty's/Greyhound northbound services leave the VIC at 1615 daily (**Carnarvon** and **Broome**) and 0110 Mon, Thu and Sat (coastal towns to **Exmouth**). **Perth** buses depart 1050 daily, and 0340 Tue, Fri and Sun (coastal route).

Directory

Banks All the main banks, with ATMs, have branches along Marine Terr or Chapman Rd. **Communications** Internet is free at the library, but $5.50 for 30 mins for email. Open 0930-1300 Tue-Sat, 1300 to at least 1630 Sun-Fri. Otherwise try Go Health, Marine Terr. The **Post Office** is at 50 Durlacher St. **Medical services** Geraldton Regional Hospital, Shenton St, T9956 2222. **Police** Forrest St, T9964 1511. **Taxi** T9921 7000.

Fill up with cheap fuel at the 440 Roadhouse, 10 km north of town

Northampton

Colour map 7, grid A4
Population: 800
55 km from Geraldton, 225 km from the Overlander roadhouse

This historic town, the first of Western Australia's many mining towns, still has many fine old stone buildings, though few have been put to good use. There is a fine Catholic church, **St Mary in Ara Coeli**, built in 1936 to a design by Monsignor John Hawes. Its rough-hewn stone and restrained decoration is typical of Hawes' work. The impressive two-storey building next door is the former **Sacred Heart Convent** and was also designed by Monsignor Hawes. You can stay here (**E**) but it is a bit stark and functional inside. It sleeps 40 in a variety of rooms from one double to a 10-bed dorm, and has a clean communal kitchen and lounge area. One of the best accommodation options in the region is 18 km up the road, just short of tiny Horrocks. **C** *Willow Gully*, T/F9934 3093, www.wn.com.au/nhp, was convict-built sometime before 1861. No longer an agriculturally-run property the owners have restored a fine 1-bedroom workers cottage for holiday rental. Its thick, rough stone, whitewashed walls keep out the summer heat. Very warm welcome, simple but fine furnishings, flagstone courtyard and neat kitchen garden make this a great retreat. Recommended. The **VIC** on main Hampton Road can provide brochures for a heritage walk. ■ *Mon-Fri 0900-1500, Sat 0900-1300.* T9934 1488, www.wn.com.au/northampto Old Police Station, Hampton Rd.

Transport Bus *Westrail* services leave the *Lions* bus shelter for **Geraldton** at 0825 Tue, Thu and Sat. Buses to **Kalbarri** depart 1430 Mon, Wed and Fri. *Integrity* services head north from the VIC at 0210 Fri and Mon (i.e. Thu and Sun nights), and 1340 Tue. Their southbound buses depart 2359 Mon, Fri, and 1145 Wed. *McCafferty's/Greyhound* northbound services leave the Shell garage at 1655 daily (**Carnarvon** and **Broome**) and 0150 Mon, Thu and Sat (coastal towns to **Exmouth**). **Perth** buses depart 0955 daily, and 0300 Tue, Fri and Sun (coastal route).

Kalbarri

Colour map 6, grid C2
Population: 1,800
100 km from
Northampton, 250 km
from Overlander
Roadhouse

The most picturesque coastal town in the state, Kalbarri sits at the mouth of the Murchison River where it winds through shoals of sand to the ocean. A reef protects the calm waters of the inlet, forming a safe harbour for the crayfishing fleet moored here and a tranquil place for swimming, sailing and fishing. Upriver, the Murchison meanders through deep gorges of spectacular red rock. The most striking formations and tight loops of riverbed are enclosed within the **Kalbarri National Park**. The park also extends along the coast south of town and contains high coastal cliffs, gorges and magical sheltered coves. This wealth of natural beauty is complemented by a great range of tours, activities and services. The **VIC** is opposite the foreshore, on Grey St. ■ *Daily 0900-1700. T1800 639468 or 9937 1104, www.kalbarriwa.info*

Sights

From end to end
Kalbarri is about
2 km, and the closest
coastal gorges are 5
km south, so you can
do a lot of walking
without your own
transport. See page
601 for Kalbarri
National Park

The **Kalbarri Wildflower Centre** has grown a large number of the local wildflowers in one small area that borders the national park. A 2-km trail winds through the various areas and past several hundred species, most of them bursting into flower during July-October. ■ *Daily 0900-1700 during Jul-Nov. $3.50, children free. Tours daily at 1000. Tearooms open year-round. T/F9937 1229. 1 km north of town, behind the tourist info bay.* **Kalbarri Oceanarium** is a modest-sized but well-stocked outfit with a dozen eye-level tanks featuring most of the species of fish and crustaceans that can be found in the sea off Kalbarri. ■ *Daily 1000-1600. $6, children $4. T9937 2027. North end of Grey St, by the jetty.* **Rainbow Jungle** claims to be the foremost Australian parrot breeding centre and is certainly one of the more impressive aviaries in the country. Visitors can stroll amongst the birds and are even stay for a picnic and make use of the BBQs. Worth a visit even on a hot day. ■ *Daily 0900-1700, Sun 1000-1700. $8.90, children $3.50. 3½ km south on Red Bluff Rd, T9937 1248. Opposite*

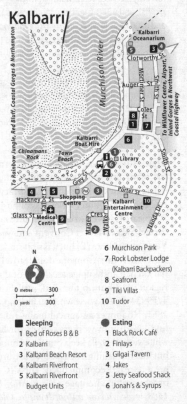

Kalbarri

6	Murchison Park
7	Rock Lobster Lodge (Kalbarri Backpackers)
8	Seafront
9	Tiki Villas
10	Tudor

■ Sleeping
1 Bed of Roses B & B
2 Kalbarri
3 Kalbarri Beach Resort
4 Kalbarri Riverfront
5 Kalbarri Riverfront
   Budget Units

● Eating
1 Black Rock Café
2 Finlays
3 Gilgai Tavern
4 Jakes
5 Jetty Seafood Shack
6 Jonah's & Syrups

Rainbow Jungle is a parking bay for an ocean **beach**, one of the most attractive around Kalbarri. Once on the sand it is about 4 km north to Chinamans Rocks and the beach at the mouth of the Murchison River, and 800 m south to **Jakes**, Kalbarri's well-known surf break. This is definitely not recommended for beginners, though the bay just beforehand is great for boogie boarding, as is **Red Bluff** beach another kilometre further south.

B-C *Bed of Roses B&B*, Grey St, T/F9937 1112, roses@westnet.com.au, can boast the **Sleeping** most attractive and luxurious room in town, with a balcony overlooking the river mouth. The 2 standard rooms are also very pretty, and all have their own lounge areas. Gourmet 5-course brekky. Recommended. Next door is **B** *Seafront*, T9937 1025, www.wn.com.au/ksfv, a simple but striking wooden foreshore B&B house with balconies overlooking the river. The owners also operate **B** *Seafront Villas*, a complex of good quality self-contained units.

The bulk of accommodation available is in complexes of **self-contained** units, all very much designed to a common plan and mostly located on the foreshore. The competition means high standards, generally well-equipped kitchens, good laundry facilities and many have on-site pools. Almost all are designed for families, with 2 or 3 bedrooms. Prices can drop considerably in low season. The complexes range in size from **B** *Kalbarri Beach Resort*, T1800 096002 or 9937 1061, www.kalbarribeachresort.com.au, with over 100 units to the **C** *Kalbarri Riverfront*, T9937 1032, www.westnet.com.au/fg with only 2 units, however they are among the best-positioned and well-furnished in town. Recommended. They also manage the only budget units on the foreshore, **C** *Kalbarri Riverfront Budget Units*, which are considerably more pleasant inside than they look from the outside. A true budget, though somewhat unsavoury, option is provided by **E** *Tiki Villas*, 35 Glass St, T9937 1877. Their dozen units sleep from 6 to 10. They're large and reasonably well-equipped but the quality is as pared down as the price. Unusually for a popular Australian holiday town, **motels** are notable for their absence with only the **C** *Kalbarri Hotel*, T9937 1000, providing a few motel rooms.

The only backpacker **hostel** is the **E** *Rock Lobster Lodge* (also known as 'Kalbarri Backpackers'), T9937 1430, kalbbacpak@wn.com.au With nearly 100 beds it isn't quite home-from-home, but facilities are reasonably comprehensive (including a pool). There are 5 **caravan parks** in and around the town, with camping sites all around $20. **C-D** *Red Bluff Caravan Park*, Red Bluff Beach Rd, 4 km south of town, T9937 1080, has sites and cabins, a camp kitchen, take-aways and fuel. Adjacent to Red Bluff car park, it's about 150 m from the beach. Of those in town the best situated is **C-D** *Murchison Park*, corner of Grey St and Wood St, T9937 1005, which has cabins, on-site vans and a good range of facilities. **D** *Tudor*, Porter St, T9937 1077, has the best value cabins.

The best spot in town is the **Black Rock Café**, T9937 1062, open daily from **Eating** 0700-2000. Dinners can verge on the expensive and breakfast and lunch are also pricey but worth it. Licensed and BYO, recommended. The *Gilgai Tavern* does great cheap to mid-range meals daily, 1200-1400 and 1800-2030. The few other eat-in establishments open in the evenings only. *Finlays*, Magee Cres, off Walker St, T9937 1260, provides a cheap BBQ feed with plenty of outdoor seating. BYO. Gets very busy with tourists in summer so arrive early, as you can't book. *Jakes*, T9937 2222, in the grounds of the *Kalbarri Beach Resort*, serves up a substantial, good value feed, daily 1730-2030. There are several takeaway options including 3 fish and chip shops, the *Syrups* healthfood outlet, pizza and pasta, and Chinese. *Jonah's*, next to the VIC, generally serves up the best (and most expensive) fish, while the *Jetty Seafood Shack* at the top end of town offers the best value portion.

Pubs & bars   Kalbarri has 2 **pubs**. The larger, the *Kalbarri Hotel*, is the social hub of the town. The *Gilgai Tavern* over the road is a smaller, quieter option. Both have occasional live music.

Tours & activities

There are dozens of river, sea and bus tours available, plus a good many adventure activities. All can be booked via the VIC. Some can be very demanding in hot weather, check what is supplied and be well prepared with drinks and for the sun

4WD *Kalbarri Safari Tours*, T9937 1011, kalsaf@wn.com.au, run a variety of very enjoyable trips, from sandboarding the coastal dunes near Lynton ($55), to 2-day driving and trekking expeditions into *Kalbarri National Park* ($138, all-inclusive). **Abseiling** *Kalbarri Abseil*, T9937 1618, head out most mornings to the **Z Bend** gorge and conduct abseils on the cliffs above the river ($60, children $50). **Bus** *Kalbarri Coach Tours*, T9937 1161, www.wn.com.au/coachtours, offer a variety of trips from a quick jaunt round town ($29, 4 hr), to tours of the national park (from $42 a half day), and day trips up to **Shark Bay** ($120). **Boat cruises** 2 licensed boats offer cruises upriver. Morning trips (3½-4 hrs) are $30, sunset cruises (2½-3 hrs) are $25. Both fishing boats also offer sunset coastal cruises ($24-44, children $15-25), and **whale-watching** trips in winter according to demand. *Kalbarri Explorer*, T9937 2027, www.kalbarriexplorer.com.au, head out Aug-Nov, and also for a popular 'cray-pot pull' and shark-feeding trip during Jan-May (both $2½ hrs, $45, children $25). **Boat hire** On the beach opposite the VIC, *Kalbarri Boat Hire*, T9937 1245, is open daily and has a wide variety of boats available, from canoes to small motor boats, windsurfers to catamarans. Prices vary from $11-30 an hour. If you've ever wanted to learn to sail, this is an excellent spot to have a go. **Camel** *Kalbarri Camel Safaris*, T9937 1211, are 3 km south on Red Bluff Rd. 45-min bush rides for $20, children $15. **Canoe** *Kalbarri Boat Hire* take groups a short way up the Murchison for a gentle paddle around the lower reaches of the river. Bush breakfast included (4 hrs, $44, children from $15). *Kalbarri Adventure Tours*, T9937 1677, www.kalbarri tours.com.au, run more adventurous day trips into the inland gorges ($60). A great way to see the national park in a day. **Dive and fishing hire** Fishing tackle ($15 per day), snorkel ($15) and scuba gear ($60) available from *Kalbarri Sports & Dive*, Kalbarri Arcade. Open Mon-Sat 0830-1730, also Sun in summer. **Fishing** The *Kalbarri Explorer*, T9937 2027, www.kalbarri explorer.com.au, and *Reefwalker*, T9937 1356, www.reefwalker.com.au, both run day sea-fishing trips for $130. **Horse riding** *Big River Ranch*, 2 km north of town, T9937 1214, www.wn.com.au/bigriverranch, have a range of bush and beach rides from 1 hr ($30) to 4 hrs ($66). **Scenic flights** *Kalbarri Air Charter*, T/F9937 1130, kalbarriair@wn.com.au, offer a range of flights from a 20-min zip along the coastal cliffs ($40, children $30) to an excellent morning excursion up to **Monkey Mia** ($195, children $120). Aircraft can also be chartered by groups for trips further afield.

Transport   **Bus** *Westrail* services leave the VIC for **Northampton**, **Geraldton** and **Perth** at 0710 Tue, Thu and Sat. *McCafferty's/Greyhound* northbound services leave at 0315 Mon, Thu and Sat (coastal towns to **Exmouth**). Their **Perth** buses depart 0150 Tue, Fri and Sun (coastal route).

Directory   **Banks** ATM in Kalbarri Arcade. **Bike hire** Bicycles from *Kalbarri Entertainment Centre*, Porter St, T9937 1105, from $7 for half a day. Scooters can be hired from *Jonah's* fish and chip shop on Grey St, $25 for an hr to $60 a day. Two-seaters also available at about double the price. **Car hire** *Rock Lobster Lodge*, corner of Woods St and Mortimer St, T9937 1430, has a 4WD available for $77 a day, local use only. Insured for unsealed roads, it's handy for getting out to the inland gorges. **Communications** Internet at several cafés and shops. All around $4-5 per half hr, though the hostel is cheaper. **Post Office**, Kalbarri Arcade. **Medical services** Medical Centre at Glass St, T9937 0100. **Police** Grey St, T9937 1006. **Taxi** T9937 1888. **Useful addresses** CALM office 1 km north of town, T9937 1140.

Western Australia

Kalbarri National Park

As the Murchison River flows down to the sea it cuts through a bed of Tumblagooda sandstone. About 50 km from the river mouth, beautiful **gorges** have formed from this unusual red and white banded rock. The national park encloses these gorges and a large area of coastal heath known for spectacular **wildflowers** in winter and spring (July-October). The coastal section of the park also includes dramatic gorges and cliffs, cut by the sea into rugged notches and rock platforms, quite different from the inland gorges. Kalbarri National Park has many excellent **lookouts** over the gorges and a few **walking tracks** aimed at reasonably agile walkers. There are also **canoeing** and **abseiling** tours in the park. ■ *For more information contact the CALM ranger, T9937 1192. Vehicle entry fee of $9 applies for the inland gorges only. No camping.*

The inland gorges can be extremely hot in summer so the park is busier in winter. If you are around in summer make sure you take plenty of water and only walk in the early morning and late afternoon

South of the river, the ocean beaches gradually rise to a long stretch of golden sandstone cliffs. This southern coastline is also part of the national park and there are a series of excellent lookouts and tracks down to the rock platforms and beaches. **Red Bluff** is the imposing knoll that can be seen from the town beaches and the first of the park lookouts (5 km from town). There is an 800-m return walk to the top of the bluff from where you can see the whole coastline and this is also a great spot in calm winter weather for whale watching. A loop walk from **Mushroom Rock** to **Rainbow Valley** takes just over an hour and allows you to explore the rock platforms and the arid hillside. **Pot Alley Gorge** is a delightful narrow gorge with interesting rocks and a beach ideal for secluded sunbathing. **Eagle Gorge** also has a good (but less protected) sandy beach reached from a track by the lookout, and extensive rock platforms to explore (8½ km from town). The last lookout (16 km from town) is over a rock stack, **Island Rock**, and high cliffs that are particularly beautiful at sunset.

There are three main access points to the **inland gorges**, all situated at scenic bends and loops in the river's course. Shortly after leaving town there is also a great lookout over Kalbarri called **Meanarra Hill**, reached by a short walk from the car park. After a further 11 km the first park turn-off is on the left. This leads to Nature's Window (26 km) and Z Bend (25 km). **Nature's Window** is a rock arch that overlooks a tight bend in the river called **The Loop**. The walk around The Loop is excellent, following the ridge at first and then dropping down to the riverbed (8 km, three hours). At **Z-bend** there is a lookout over a right angle in the gorge and with some careful rock hopping you can get down to the river and explore. Take the unmarked but well-used track to the right of the lookout. This is also a lovely place for a swim as the river doesn't flow all year round and is often a series of calm shallow pools. You need to return to the main road and travel another 24 km to get to **Hawks Head** and **Ross Graham**. These are both good lookouts and there are easier tracks down to the river. It is possible for experienced walkers to tackle the 38 km (four days) from Ross Graham Lookout to The Loop or shorter two day walks but you must notify the ranger first. There are picnic tables and toilets at all car parks. Nature's Window and Z Bend also have gas BBQs.

Alternative routes north

During July to September, it is well worth considering the route from Perth to **Moora** (preferably via **New Norcia**), and from there to **Mullewa** via **Carnamah**, **Perenjori**, and **Morawa** to **Mullewa**. The quality and richness of the wildflowers along the way varies from year to year, depending chiefly on the amount of rainfall the region receives the preceding winter, but can be quite

The Wildflower Way
Mullewa 550 km from Perth, 100 km from Geraldton

Western Australia

fantastic. The VICs at Mullewa and Morawa are happy to advise on that year's blooms and the best places to seek them out on your way through. This region is also interesting for the unusual church architecture of **Monsignor John Hawes**, for example the Church of the Holy Cross in Davis Street **Morawa**, or The Church of Our Lady of Mount Carmel in **Mullewa**, which is one of Hawes' finest works. The Priest House nearby is maintained as a museum of Hawes' life. ■ *Daily 1000-1200 (Jul-Oct only). For more information contact the VIC (July-October only) on Jose Street, T9961 1505, or the shire office on Padbury Street, T9961 1007.* Mullewa has motel and hotel rooms at the friendly **C** *Railway Hotel*, T9961 1050, and a caravan park with sites only (enquire at *Yarrumba* service station on Jose Street). From Mullewa you can choose to head out to the North West Coastal Highway at Geraldton or inland to Mount Magnet (245 km) and the Great Northern Highway. **Yalgoo**, 120 km east of Mullewa, is a charming old gold-mining town with a lovely John Hawes chapel, the Dominican Chapel of St Hyacinth. Ask at the shire office for the key and a heritage trail booklet to explore Yalgoo.

Great Northern Highway
See page 635 for the northern extension of the highway

If you're heading north toward the central Pilbara or the Kimberley then the Great Northern Highway can save a few hundred kilometres when compared to the coastal highways, but it's a monotonous journey through a flat and featureless landscape. The route splits from the Brand Highway just north of the Swan Valley and continues via New Norcia through wildflower country to the vast inland plains beyond the small town of Wubin, 270 km from Perth. From there the towns and fuel-stops become considerably more scarce, the 290 km to Mount Magnet interrupted by just one fuel-stop midway at Paynes Find.

The first stop for travellers heading north is **Mount Magnet**, of interest mainly for the number of **open-cut goldmines** that surround it. There are three pub hotels in town, the most enticing being the **C-D** *Commercial Club*, Hepburn Street, T9963 4021. Budget travellers are well catered for by the **D** *Miners Rest*, signposted off Richardson Street, T9963 4380, a five-minute walk from the main street. Book ahead as they're usually busy. Alternatively, the caravan park, T9963 4198, has an extremely cheap but perfectly respectable on-site van (**F**) as well as sites. For eating, there's a basic deli café, the *Diggers Diner* on Hepburn Street, and a miners' canteen, the *Monadelphous*, (open 0500-1700 and 1700-1930) which is a real treat for travellers at only $7.50 per sitting. It's 50 m behind the BP fuel station, just off the Sandstone Road. The all-day *Swagman* roadhouse, on the highway just north of town, is known for doing an excellent breakfast. *McCafferty's/Greyhound* northbound bus services leave the Shell roadhouse at 2125 Friday (and Sunday during school holidays). Their **Perth** buses depart 0550 Sun (and Tue during school holidays).

About 80 km further north is **Cue**, the smallest of the Midwest gold-mining towns and not without its charm. The **C** *Murchison Club Hotel*, T9963 1020, has motel-style units out the back and meals daily. There is also a B&B, the **C** *Queen of the Murchison*, T9963 1625. Another small gold-mining town, though less appealing than Cue, is **Meekatharra** which has established itself as the main service town for a large pastoral and mining district. There are two pub hotels in town. The **C** *Royal Mail*, Main Street, T9981 1148, royalmail@benet.net.au, and the more basic **D** *Commercial*, T9981 1020. The **D** *Meekatharra Caravan Park*, Main Street, T9981 1253, has pricey but well-equipped on-site vans. Next door to the *Commercial* is the *Main St Café*, which is good for cheap meals. *McCafferty's/Greyhound* northbound bus services leave the Shell roadhouse at 2355 Friday (and Sunday during school holidays). Their Perth buses depart at 0340 Sunday (and Tuesday during school holidays).

Western Australia

From Meekatharra it's 620 km of rough unsealed road through scrub country to Carnarvon, for the Gascoyne, or 430 km of enervating highway to **Newman**, for the Pilbara. On the latter route it's 255 km before the one and only fuel-stop on the way at the **D** *Kumarina Roadhouse*, T9981 2930. Newman has plenty of services, including bank ATMs, and accommodation at the **A-D** *Seasons Hotel*, Newman Drive, T9177 8666, www.seasons hotel.com.au, with upmarket and budget options, and also has the best restaurant (mid-range), open daily 1800-2030, as well as the **B** *Newman Hotel*, Newman Drive, T9175 1101, the town's main pub. *McCafferty's/Greyhound* bus to Port Hedland leaves the VIC at 0445 Saturday, while the Perth bus departs the same day at 2225.

The Gascoyne

The hot and arid Gascoyne region, from Shark Bay in the south to the North West Cape in the north, is a magnificent region for seeing marine life. Elsewhere in the country only the Great Barrier Reef can rival it. The sheltered waters of Shark Bay harbour dugongs and turtles as well as the dolphins which come in to shore to be hand fed at Monkey Mia. Further north the Ningaloo Reef shadows the coast for over 250 km. When the coral spawns in March each year it attracts the world's largest fish, the whale shark. Snorkelling alongside them as they feed is one of the most exciting wildlife experiences Australia can offer. If that isn't enough, the reef comes so close to shore at some points that you only need to walk off the beach to snorkel among coral, fish, turtles and rays, and you can watch turtles laying and hatching in summer. Inland, you can find the red dirt and open spaces of Outback country around the Kennedy Ranges or Mount Augustus.

www.gdc.wa.gov.au

Getting there and around **Air** *Skywest* fly from Perth, every Mon, Wed and Fri-Sat, to Monkey Mia. They also have daily flights to **Exmouth**, and a connection to there from Monkey Mia on Wed and Sat. *Northwest Regional Airlines*, T9192 1369, www.northwestregional.com.au, have flights between most of the northern WA towns from Exmouth to Halls Creek. **Bus** *Integrity*, Wellington St Bus Station, Perth, T9226 1339, www.integritycoachlines.com.au, operate a service up the west coast, stopping at **Geraldton**, **Carnarvon** (11½ hrs), **Coral Bay** (15½ hrs), and terminating at **Exmouth** (17 hrs). Buses leave at 1930 Thu and Sun, with a Carnarvon only service at 0700 Tue. *McCafferty's/Greyhound's* main GX620 northbound service leaves Perth at 1000, travels up the Brand Highway through Geraldton, stops at **Carnarvon** and continues on via **Broome** and to **Katherine**. A separate service, GX683, heads up to **Exmouth** at 1830 Wed, Fri and Sun, calling at the **Overlander**, **Carnarvon**, **Coral Bay** and **Learmonth**. A connection to *Shark Bay* leaves the Overlander at 0715 and 2230 Mon, Thu and Sat.

Ins & outs

The 24-hr **D-E** *Overlander roadhouse*, T9942 5916, marks the turn-off to Denham and Monkey Mia. They have an ATM, a good range of cheap meals is available 0600-2400, internet access is currently being organized, and the standard accommodation is basic but includes clean linen and a/c.

Shark Bay

Shark Bay is formed by two long peninsulas lying parallel to the coast, like the prongs of a fork. The middle prong is the Peron Peninsula, and the western prong is formed by the Zuytdorp Cliffs and Dirk Hartog Island. These are the most westerly bits of land in Australia, forming an extraordinary sheltered marine environment in its countless small bays. The waters of Shark Bay are always a startling turquoise and as clear as a swimming pool thanks to its shallowness; the average depth of the bay is 10 m and much of it is no more than 1 m deep. It is moteoroomony of dolphins, some of which come in to shore at Monkey Mia, but there are also dugongs, turtles, rays and sharks living in these waters and all are easily seen on a boat trip, or sometimes from the shore. The land is also a refuge for wildlife. Although its low arid scrub and red sand looks too harsh and barren for anything to survive, the Francois Peron National Park is the focus for a programme to save endangered native species. The small town of Denham and the tourist facilities at Monkey Mia provide comfortable lodging for visitors but most of the Shark Bay region is a wilderness, where you can see some rare or beautiful creatures at close range. Shark Bay was declared a World Heritage Area in 1991 for its rare stromatolites, extensive seagrass beds, endangered animals and natural beauty.

Western Australia

Hamelin

Colour map 6, grid C1
35 km from the Overlander, 105 km from Denham
In pre-Cambrian times stromalites were the Earth's most ubiquitous lifeform

Hamelin Pool is a wide shallow estuary on the eastern side of Shark Bay and of great scientific interest because of the resident colonies of **stromatolites**, boulder-like formations which are the direct result of sediments becoming trapped by thin organic mats of cyanobacteria over thousands of years. In the 1880s this spot was chosen as the site of one of WA's **telegraph repeater stations**. The original station is now a modest museum, devoted to an explanation of the stromatolites (including a video and a very rare aquarium colony) and the heritage of the telegraph system. ■ *0830-1730. $5.50, children and concessions $3, T9942 5905*. There's also a tearoom serving cold drinks and snack lunches, daily 0830-1730. Campers can use the lawns, and they and day customers can use the BBQ facilities. There are also caravan sites and a single cabin (**D**), sleeping up to four. From Hamelin the highway follows the centre of the promontory for about 50 km until the turn to **Shelly Beach**, where the beach underfoot is actually crushed cockle shells. Deep under the beach the shells cement together and the resulting coquina limestone has been used around Shark Bay as a building material.

Denham

Colour map 6, grid C1
Population: 1,200
375 km from Kalbarri, 330 km from Carnarvon

Denham is a small and friendly town that caters to much of the ever increasing tourist trade to **Monkey Mia**. The main industry is fishing, though recently the pearl industry has been revived and **pearl farms** have been established in the bay, producing fine black specimens. The town provides basic services such as fuel and a supermarket. The helpful **VIC** is in a small souvenir shop on the main street, Knight Terrace. ■ *Open daily 0900-1700. T9948 1253, www.sharkbay.asn.au*

There is a fair range of reasonably priced accommodation in Denham, mostly in self-contained units and caravan parks. The busiest period is the winter-spring season (Jul-Oct) but all school and public holidays and the Dec-Jan Christmas period are also usually booked out well in advance

Sleeping and eating **B** *Heritage Resort Hotel*, corner of Knight Terr and Durlacher St, T9948 1133, heritageresort@bigpond.com Large hotel with the best rooms in town, some with ocean views. Good mid-range meals 1200-1500 and 1800-2100. **B-E** *Bay Lodge* (YHA), Knight Terr, T9948 1278, has motel rooms, some facing the ocean, self-contained chalets, and several units grouped around the pool set aside as 2-6 bed backpacker dorms, with small kitchens, television area and bathroom. **C-D** *Shark Bay Holiday Cottages*, 3 Knight Terr, T9948 1206, www.sharkbaycottages.com.au Simple clean and comfortable self-contained fibro cottages opposite the beach. All a/c. Communal pool. There are three **caravan parks**, all with cabins and on-site vans. *Denham Seaside* at the northern end of Knight Terr, T9948 1242, has the best position, and good facilities. *Old Pearler* corner of Durlacher St and Knight Terr, T9948 1373, has a cosy rustic interior and disappointing mid-range to expensive seafood and steak. Good cheap meals are available at the *Bay Café*, next to the VIC. Daily 1000-1530, 1700-2100.

Tours   4WD Tours *Majestic Tours*, T9948 1627, sharkbaymajestictours@wn.com.au Tours to Shell Beach and Eagle Bluff (½ day, $45), stromatolites and telegraph station (full day $99) and Francois Peron National Park (full day $99). *Outback Coast*, T9948 1445, outbackcoast4wd@wn.com.au This company offers very similar tours at slightly lower prices but the charter is exclusive so you need to be able to get 4 people together. **Scenic flights** *Shark Bay Air Charter*, T9948 1773. Flights are an excellent way to see these meandering peninsulas, and sharks, dugongs and dolphins are clearly visible from the air ($43-100).

Transport   Air A shuttle bus, T9948 1358, meets all flights into Monkey Mia airport. *Skywest* have flights to **Perth** every Mon, Wed and Fri-Sat, and to **Exmouth** every Wed and Sat. **Bus** A different shuttle, T9948 1627, meets every *McCafferty's/Greyhound* service at the **Overlander**, continuing on to Monkey Mia. Bookings required. *Bay Lodge* run a free shuttle to Monkey Mia, departing at 0745, and returning 1630. Non-residents welcome if seats are available and they pay an $8 donation to the Silver Chain nursing organization. **Taxi** It's a $40 one-way trip to Monkey Mia, T9948 1331.

Directory   Banks *Bankwest* ATM at *Heritage Resort*. **Bike hire** from *Shell* garage. **Car hire** *Shark Bay Car Hire*, T9948 1247. 4WD hire from $90 day, which allows exploration of the national park. **Communications   Post Office**, back of newsagent on Knight Terr. **Internet** at VIC, $5 for ½ hr. **Medical services** Emergency care (24 hrs) at *Silver Chain Nursing Post*, 35 Hughes St, T9948 1213. **Snorkel hire** from VIC, $10 day.

Francois Peron National Park
Colour map 6, grid C1
See under Denham for tours into the park

This park, named after a French naturalist who explored Shark Bay as part of Baudin's expedition on the *Geographe* and *Naturaliste* in 1801 and 1803, covers the northern tip of the Peron Peninsula, from the Monkey Mia Road north to Cape Peron. A dramatic series of cliffs and bays, where red rocks merge into white sand and turquoise sea, encloses dry and arid sandy plains dotted with many salt pans (birridas). The park is home to malleefowl, bilbies, woylies, bandicoots and many other species. These mostly nocturnal species are seldom seen but thorny devils are quite common and dolphins, dugongs and turtles may be spotted from the cliffs at Cape Peron. There is a visitor centre at the old station homestead, and also an outdoor hot tub fed by an artesian bore. The homestead is usually accessible by 2WD (10 km, unscaled) but the rest of the park is for high clearance 4WD only. ■ *Park fees $9 car, camping $10 for 2. Visitor centre open daily 0800-1630. For more information contact CALM in Denham, T9948 1208. Knight Terr.*

Monkey Mia
Colour map 6, grid C1
30 km from Denham

Dolphins have lived in Shark Bay for millenia but the current encounters with humans only began in the 1960s when fishermen began to hand-feed dolphins. The dolphins were happy to accept a free and visited settlements regularly. Even though the place is incredibly remote, the pull of wild dolphins is irresistible and has made the area internationally famous. Interaction is now very carefully managed to keep the dolphins wild and minimize the impact of hundreds of visitors a day. One of the best things to do in Monkey Mia is to actually leave the beach and take a boat cruise to see the dolphins in their own environment, as well as many other incredible animals such as dugongs and turtles. The **visitor centre** has displays on the biology and behaviour of dolphins and shows regular videos on marine life. ■ *There is a fee to enter the Monkey Mia Reserve, not covered by national park passes. Day pass $6, children $2 (valid for one day and the following morning). Holiday pass $9, children $4 (valid for 4 weeks). For more information contact the CALM office, T9948 1366, calmmonkeymia@wn.com.au*

▶▶ Dolphin encounters

Free spirits wanting to commune with nature may be a little disappointed with the Monkey Mia experience. This is how it works. The dolphins swim in to a section of beach by the jetty that is closed to boats and swimmers. When (or rather if) the dolphins arrive, people, sometimes in their hundreds, line up along the beach, ankles only in the water (don't put suncreen on your legs as it irritates the dolphin's eyes). A CALM officer talks about the dolphins for about half an hour and makes sure that the dolphins are not touched or disturbed. The dolphins are often only a few feet away and nuzzle the officers' calves like dogs wanting their dinner. When the CALM officers decide to feed the dolphins everyone is asked to step out of the water and a few lucky souls are picked to come forward and give a dolphin a fish. Only a few mature female dolphins and their three daughters are fed and they get no more than a third of their daily requirements so they will not become dependent on handouts. CALM decided to begin feeding the younger dolphins in mid-2002 amid concern from the local shire that the tourism industry will collapse when the mature dolphins die within the next few years. When the feeding is finished the dolphins usually swim away, but if they don't you can step back in the water to your knees again. Even in these crowded and controlled conditions it is wonderful to be so close to these wild dolphins. To get the best out of the experience plan to spend the whole day at Monkey Mia or, better still, make it an overnight trip. The dolphins usually arrive about 0800 and after they have been fed the main crowds disappear on their tour buses. As feeding is allowed three times between 0800 and 1300, there is a good chance that the dolphins will reappear and you'll have a less crowded encounter. Take an afternoon and sunset cruise and you can't fail to have an awesome day.

Sleeping and eating All the facilities at Monkey Mia are in one complex, in front of the beach where the dolphins come in. The **A-E** *Dolphin Resort*, T9948 1320, www.monkeymia.com.au, has very comfortable beachfront villas, self-contained cabins, canvas 'condos' (all a/c), on-site vans, backpacker dongas and camping sites. Facilities include a pool, campers kitchen and BBQs. The complex also has a small expensive store with fuel pumps, open 0700-1800, a take-away café serving pizzas, burgers etc. 1000-2000 and an overpriced café bar, the *Boughshed*, which serves as the resort restaurant. The food is perfectly okay and it's undoubtedly a great place to sit and watch the beach, but you'll pay for the privilege. However, you can grab something from the take-away and eat on the grass in front of the café and enjoy the same view. Meals 0700-1400, 1830-2030.

Tours and activities **4WD Tours** *Design A Tour*, T9948 1880. Day tours to Hamelin and Shell Beach ($80) and Peron National Park ($80). **Boat cruises** 2 operators offer sailing cruises into the bay. *Shotover*, T9948 1481, is a 18-m open catamaran, with large nets slung between the hulls that you can sit in, as well as plentiful deck seating. Shade is provided by the in the water. Daily cruises: short morning cruise 0900 (1 hr, $29), wildlife spotting 1030 (2 hrs, $44), dugong spotting cruise 1300 (2½ hrs, $49), sunset cruise (1½ hrs, $39). If you don't see any sea life you can take another cruise for free. *Aristocat 2*, T9948 1446, has a large enclosed cabin, making it slower to move around, but perhaps more reassuring for those sensitive to the sun. They offer similar cruises at the same prices. Daily cruises 0900, 1100, 1330, sunset. Both operators offer a free sunset cruise if you take the afternoon cruise. *Blue Lagoon Pearl*, T9948 1325, is a small glass-bottom boat that takes visitors out to the pearl farm where you can learn about the industry and buy pearl jewellery. Daily at 1100, 1400 from the jetty (1½ hrs, $20). Buy tickets for all cruises from the booths on the boardwalk.

Boat and snorkel hire *Westcoast Watersports* offers kayak hire ($12 hr), electric glass-bottom boat hire ($30 hr) and snorkel hire ($3 hr) from the marquee at the end of the beach. **Fishing** *Sportfishing Safaris*, T9948 1846. Fishing charters for novice or experienced anglers. Half day $85, full day $130. **Walking** There is a short loop walk around Monkey Mia (2 km) that takes you past an ancient Aboriginal site and provides good views from a low ridge. Pick up a walk sheet from the visitor centre.

This monotonous stretch is broken only by the welcoming **E** *Wooramel* roadhouse, 75 km from the Overlander, T9942 5910, which pumps the cheapest fuel after Geraldton. Fantastic pastries, also breakfasts, snacks and burgers, ATM, single and double a/c dongas. Meals, fuel and pastries 0600-2100. Recommended. Just short of Carnarvon, the highway north is interrupted by a T-junction (*the* T-junction in local parlance), the focus of a cluster of 24-hr roadhouses, fruit plantations and caravan parks.

The Overlander to Carnarvon
Distance 200 km

Carnarvon is one of the few surviving ports along the west coast and has consolidated its early prosperity by making the most of the **Gascoyne River**. Most of the time the bed of this mighty river is exposed as a wide ribbon of sand but the Gascoyne flows deep underground all year round and is tapped by local fruit growers for irrigation. Consequently Carnarvon appears as something of an oasis among the dry, scrubby plains to the north and south. The town has little to detain travellers other than a couple of **banana plantations**. *Munro's*, South River Road, T9941 8104, conduct tours at 1100 ($3.30, 30 minutes, open 1000-1600 Sunday-Friday June-October, Sunday-Thursday November-May). *Westoby*, 500 Robinson Street, T9941 8003, is fairly close to the town centre and has entertaining informative tours at 1100 and 1400 ($3.50, 30 minutes, open 1000-1600 Wednesday-Monday, Friday 1800-2100). The town also makes a useful base for exploring the rugged coastline to the north. The very helpful and friendly **VIC** is on the main street, Robinson Street. ■ *Open daily 0900-1700. T9941 1146, cvontourist@ wn.com.au Corner of Camel La.*

Carnarvon
Colour map 6, grid B1
Population: 6,900
480 km from Geraldton, 370 km from Exmouth, 360 km from Nanutarra roadhouse

Sleeping and eating The only B&B in town is the **B** *Outcamp*, Olivia Terr, T9941 2421, comfortable but lacking character. Luckily this is more than made up for by the welcoming, knowledgeable hosts and excellent breakfasts. 5 rooms, no en suites. **C** *Fascine Lodge*, David Brand Dr, T9941 2411, is a comfortable upmarket motel with bar, restaurant, pool and airport pick-ups. **C** *Gascoyne*, Olivia Terr, T9941 1412, mid-range pub which has been the town's gastronomic mainstay for some years. Further along Olivia Terr the **D-E** *Carnarvon*, T9941 1181, has a glass-walled waterfront bar and alfresco beer garden, serving as both bistro and café. Both pubs have basic motel accommodation and serve meals 1200-1400 and 1800-2030. The *Carnarvon* also has basic backpacker dorms. **D-E** *Carnarvon Backpackers*, Olivia Terr, T9941 1095, carnarvon.backpacker@bigpond.com, is very much a workers' hostel. They can help find fruit-picking jobs and run a daily shuttle bus in season to the major employers. The facilities are pretty scruffy but they are the only place that will open for the 0430 bus. Of the many **caravan parks**, the closest is the *Carnarvon Tourist Centre*, Robinson St, T9941 1438, which has a good range of cabins, on-site vans and sites.

Tours 4WD *Stockman Safaris*, T9941 2421, stockmansafaris@wn.com.au, offer a range of Outback tours that include combinations of the rarely visited western escarpment of the Kennedy Ranges, authentic station homesteads and the rugged coast north of the Blowholes. Day trips from $130, 3-day excursions around $600.

Western Australia

Transport Bus *Integrity* services head for **Coral Bay** and **Exmouth** from the civic centre at 0830 Fri and Mon. Their southbound buses depart 1900 Mon, Fri, and 0700 Wed. *McCafferty's/Greyhound* northbound services leave the civic centre at 2225 daily (**Broome** and **Katherine**) and 0855 Mon, Thu and Sat (**Coral Bay** and **Exmouth**). **Perth** buses depart 0425 daily, and 2010 Mon, Thu and Sat (Midwest coastal route). A **bus**, T9941 8336, operates from Alexandra St on Mon, Wed and Fri. Services include an 0930 run to Babbage Island and the jetty, returning 1145, and a 1030 bus to *Westoby Plantation*, returning 1415. Single fares $1.05 or $5.30 for a day pass.

Directory Banks Major banks and ATMs on Robinson St. **Communications Internet** at the library, Stuart St, open 0900-1730 Mon-Wed, Fri, 1300-2000 Thu and 0900-1200 Sat. Also at the *Kodak* shop on Robinson St. Both $5 for 30 mins. **Post Office** on Camel Lane. **Medical services** *Carnarvon Regional Hospital*, Cleaver St, T9941 1555. **Outdoor** *Tel-O-Mac*, 348 Robinson St, T9941 1873. Has some snorkel gear available for hire. **Police** Robinson St, T9941 1444. **Taxi** T131008. **Work** The fruit picking and packing season extends for most of the year Apr-Jan, while the fishing season is Apr-Sep. Expect to earn upward of $10 an hr. The backpacker hostel can help find work.

The Kennedy Range and Mount Augustus

Colour map 6, grid B2
Eastern bluffs 245 km
from Carnarvon,
75 km from
Gascoyne Junction

The **Kennedy Range** forms a dramatic flame-coloured mesa, 75 km long, running north to south. The range, a long drive from anywhere on an unsealed road, nevertheless offers the chance to experience the Outback, and perhaps a local station stay. Much of it is inaccessible except on tours but on the eastern side there are three narrow gorges that can be explored and a campground right at the base of the 100-m cliffs. Each gorge is less than 1 km apart and there are short walks along the creek beds. The sheer variety of the rock shapes and colours is utterly captivating and the cliffs themselves are at their best at dawn when they can take on spectacular yellow, orange and red hues. The campground has a toilet but no other facilities. Take plenty of water. The best time to visit the park is June-September when it is relatively cool. Roads are fine for 2WD except after heavy rain, when the roads will be closed. ■ *No entry fee or camping fees. For more information contact the CALM office in Denham, T9948 1208. Road conditions T9941 0777.*

Colour map 6, grid B3
Mount Augustus 300
km from Gascoyne
Junction, 330 km
from Meekatharra

Little known and remote **Mount Augustus** (1105 m) rises abruptly 858 m from a red, arid sandplain, and is about 8 km long. The Wadjari people call the mountain Burringurrah after an ancestor figure who ran away from his initiation into manhood and was speared in the right leg. The elongated monocline represents his body as he fell. There are several bush walks starting from points on the 49 km loop around the base. The most exciting is the summit trail (12 km, 6 hours return), a long and challenging walk rewarded by extensive views. For this walk make sure you leave early, take plenty of water and tell someone when you expect to return. There are also good views from Edney's Lookout (6 km, 2½ hours), part of an easier, well-defined trail. Aboriginal rock engravings can be seen at Mundee and Ooramboo. The best time to visit this park is during the cooler months of April-October. Roads are usually fine for 2WD but remote driving rules apply. ■ *No camping in the park, see options below. Park maps and advice at Mt Augustus Tourist Resort. For more information contact CALM office in Denham T9948 1208.*

There are a few 'local' options within 70 km of the **Kennedy Ranges**. **L-A** *Bidgemia Station*, T9943 0501, bidgemia@wn.com.au, 11 km east of Gascoyne Junction on the banks of the river, has 2 sets of 5 rooms of varying standard and comfort. The tariff is pricey but includes all meals and drinks with the station owners, and use of the pool. Recommended. The **D** *Gascoyne Junction Hotel*, T9943 0504, is a classic Outback tin pub with a friendly bar. All the single and double donger rooms are a/c, and there are also camping sites. A range of cheap meals are available daily, 1200-1400 and 1800-2000 Apr-Oct. Drinks, basic supplies and fuel available 0800-2000. On the northeastern side of **Mt Augustus**, **D** *Mt Augustus Outback Tourist Resort*, T9943 0527, has simple twin rooms (shared facilities), powered sites, basic groceries and fuel. **A-B** *Mt Cobra Station*, T9943 0565, is 37 km west of Mt Augustus and has en suite motel rooms, homestead rooms with shared facilities and campsites. Fuel and meals are also available. Closed Sat.

Sleeping & eating
Gascoyne Junction 170 km from Carnarvon, 450 km from Meekatharra

140 km north of Carnarvon and 225 km south of Exmouth is the **D***Minilya Roadhouse*, T9942 5922, has above average (air-conditioned!) toilets and serves decent cheap meals and take-aways, has comfortable donga rooms, an en suite four-bed cabin, all a/c, as well as lawned caravan sites. They also sell the last relatively inexpensive fuel if you're heading north. Open 0600-2200, meals to 2100.

Carnarvon to Coral Bay
Minilya 140 km from Carnarvon

This pretty, shallow bay is just a notch in a long coastline of white sand, dunes and desert but is also one of the few accessible spots where the **Ningaloo Reef** within 50 m of the shore. The reef is full of colourful fish, clams, sea cucumbers, rays and even the occasional turtle, though the coral itself is more notable for its intricate shapes and forms than any vibrancy of colour. All you need to do is grab a snorkel, mask and fins and wade in. There are also a variety of boat trips that take you further out onto the reef to snorkel or dive with **manta rays**, **turtles** and **whale sharks**, or spot **humpback whales**, **dugongs** and **dolphins**, so it's a pretty special place for anyone who loves marine wildlife. The settlement itself is just a small, cluster of low-key resorts where you can walk barefoot from your door to the beach in two minutes. Coral Bay, though, is a community holding its breath in fear of the future. Each year there are more operators, activities and visitors, but the main concern is a proposed marina and resort development, known as Maud's Landing, that many locals are afraid will destroy the wild environment that brings people here. The Wilderness Society is running a campaign against the development, for more information see www.saveningaloo.org For information on the Coral Bay environment and wildlife, call in at the *Coastal Adventure Tours* office and internet café ($3 for 30 minutes). One of the best of the websites offering information is www.coralbay informationcentre.com.au Facilities are modest, but there is a supermarket (open daily 0730-1900), newsagent, gift shops and fuel also available.

Coral Bay
Colour map 6, grid B1
Population: 300
240 km from Carnarvon, 150 km from Exmouth

Western Australia

Sleeping and eating All establishments are on the main street, Robinson St. **L-E** *Ningaloo Reef Resort*, T9942 5934, www.coralbay.org, is the bay's only resort-style hotel, with many rooms having ocean views. Mid-range and cheap meals and snacks available throughout the day to 2000. Don't be tempted by the backpacker rooms unless it's your only option. **A-D** *Bayview Coral Bay*, TT9942 5932, www.coralbaywa.com A great range of accommodation from self-contained villas with sea views, motel-style rooms, chalets, cabins, on-site vans and a grassy caravan and camping park. All are bright, clean and a/c. The licensed *Ningaloo Reef Café* is part of the same complex. This colourful, open space has a cheap simple menu of fish, steak, pasta and pizzas. Also take-aways, open daily 1730-2130. **C** *People's Caravan Park*, T9942 5933. Mostly caravan and grassy camping sites, some with views of the bay. Currently 2 en suite, a/c cabins. The **D-E** *Ningaloo Club*, T9385 7411, www.ningalooclub.com, is a large new hostel

Coral Bay is always booked out weeks in advance for school and public holidays

arranged around a pool-filled central courtyard. The kitchen is small but well equipped. Linen included, some rooms are a/c. Cheap internet and simple brekkie. *Fins*, by the fuel station, T9942 5036, is a small terrace restaurant, verging on the expensive, but BYO and easily the best food in town. Open for breakfasts, coffee and snacks all day from 0730, evening dining 1700-2100. Bookings essential during busy periods.

All tracks up and down the coast from Coral Bay are 4WD only. There is a profusion of booking offices, and most will sell most of the tours available, making shopping around a confusing business. Mermaids Cave, T9942 5955, Coral Bay Shopping Centre, have a small information booth inside which is a good first port of call

Tours and activities 4WD *Coral Coast Tours*, T0427 180568, www.coralcoast tours.com Tours lasting 2-8 hrs in and around the coast dunes of Coral Bay, including a trip up to Cape Range ($130). **Boat hire** Glass-bottomed canoes available from the hire caravan at the far end of the main beach ($16.50 per hr). **Diving** *Ningaloo Reef Dive Centre*, Coral Bay Shopping Centre, T9942 5824. Dive trips (2-dive safaris $165) and PADI tuition (open-water courses start every Sat, $360), plus a discover scuba day, including dives at 2 bay sites ($185). Full gear hire $70 per day, open 0730-1730. Dive medicals can be arranged in Coral Bay. **Fishing** The *Mahi Mahi*, T/F9942 5874, mahimahi1@bigpond.com, offer half-day, full-day ($140) and overnight trips, also whale watching. There are other options if they're full or not operating. **Glass-bottomed boats** There are 3 boats offering cruises of 1-2 hrs over the coral, each of which stop for snorkelling sessions at some of the best offshore spots. Snorkel hire is included. *Coral Bay Charter*, T9942 5932, are very experienced and their 2-hr ($35) trips at 1015 and 1230 usually visit two snorkelling spots. **Manta rays** A couple of boats offer trips out to snorkel with these massive but gentle rays. *Coral Bay Adventures*, T9942 5955, www.coralbayadventures.com.au, are marginally the more expensive (half day, $104), but a spotter plane increases the chances of finding rays. *Ningaloo Reef Dive Centre* offer half-day trips to dive with mantas for $150. **Quad bikes** *Quad-Treks*, T9948 5190, quadtreks@bigpond.com, are one of 2 companies operating these 4-wheel motorbikes out along the dunes and beaches. Great fun. Options include 3-hr snorkelling trips to some favoured turtle spots ($65), and sunset trips which include more challenging terrain and the thrill of a return run in the dark. **Sailing cruises** The *Coral Breeze*, T9948 5190, admin@coastaladventuretours.com, is a fairly small catamaran than heads out for 4-hr wildlife spotting and snorkelling trips ($55) and 2-hr BYO sunset cruises ($38). This is one of the most peaceful and rewarding ways of seeing the bay, and the cruises are excellent value. **Scenic flights** *Coral Bay Adventures* can organize a variety of flights from a 30-min wildlife tour ($35 each for 3 people, $49 each for 2) to a 2 hr 'Ninglaoo Odyssey' ($125 each for 2, $190 each for 3) that includes a flyover of the Cape Range. **Snorkelling** Snorkel hire at the caravan at the far end of the main beach ($5.50 per half day). Unless you specifically want to see turtles, sharks or rays, then it is hard to beat simply snorkelling straight off the main beach (head out beyond the 5 knot sign just south of the main beach then drift back toward the moorings). If you want to be fairly sure of seeing turtles then head out on the appropriate boat or quad-bike trip. Most boat operators offer a half-day snorkel, including the *Ningaloo Reef Dive Centre* ($50) and *Ningaloo Experience*, T9942 5877 ($55). **Whale sharks** Although Exmouth is hailed as the world's whale shark 'capital', a couple of Coral Bay boats do offer snorkelling trips to try and find them in season (Apr-Jun). They include *Coral Bay Adventures* (full day $310). **Whale-watching** Most of the larger boat operators and *Ningaloo Reef Dive Centre* offer tours to see humpback whales in season (Jun-Nov).

Transport **Air** A shuttle bus to Coral Bay, T9942 5955, meets every *Skywest* flight into Exmouth's

Fuel is consistently cheaper in Coral Bay than in Exmouth

Learmonth Airport ($65) if booked in advance, though its about $20 cheaper to catch the shuttle to Exmouth then the scheduled buses back down. **Bus** *Integrity* services head for **Exmouth** from Bayview at 1110 Mon and Fri. Their southbound buses depart 1515 Mon and Fri. *McCafferty's/Greyhound* northbound services leave the general store for Exmouth at 1215 Mon, Thu and Sat. **Carnarvon** and **Perth** buses depart 1640 Mon, Thu and Sat (Midwest coastal route).

Western Australia

Exmouth

Sitting near the tip of the North West Cape, Exmouth faces the calm waters of the Exmouth Gulf and is separated by the low hills of Cape Range from the beaches of the Ningaloo Marine Park. Surprisingly, the town doesn't have a coastal feel. It's a practical place that was built to service the local military base. However, its proximity to the extraordinary wildlife of the **Ningaloo Reef** make it a special place for eco-tourism. It is possible to swim with **whale sharks**, watch **turtles** laying and hatching, spot migrating **humpback whales**, snorkel over coral from the beach, and dive on almost untouched sites. There are also red rocky gorges and campsites by perfect beaches in the Cape Range National Park. The only drawback is the intense heat and aridity of the cape – most people visit in winter when temperatures drop to 25-30 °C. The helpful **VIC** is on the main through road, Murat St. ■ *Daily 0900-1700. T9949 1176, www.exmouth-australia.com*

Colour map 6, grid A1
Population: 3,100
615 km from Tom Price (Karijini), 555 km from Karratha

A-E *Potshot*, Murat Rd, T9949 1200, F9949 1486. The town's largest resort complex, with different accommodation types in brick poolside units. Standard motel rooms, self-contained apartments, as well as modern, well-equipped villas across the road. Their *Excape Backpackers* has modern but characterless a/c dorms, a large industrial kitchen and use of resort facilities. **B-E** *Exmouth Cape Tourist Village (Pete's Backpackers)*, Murat Rd, T9949 1101, www.exmouthvillage.com A range of a/c, en suite cottages and cabins are available exclusively, or as mini backpacker dorms. Also caravan and camp sites. They also run the airport *McCafferty/Greyhound* shuttle and the on-site *Village Dive* centre. **B-C** *Ningaloo Lighthouse Caravan Park*, 17 km north of town on Cape Range Way, T9949 1478, www.ningaloolighthouse.com Well-run park with smart self-contained chalets, all with private verandah and BBQ. The 'Lookout' chalets perch high above the park have wonderful sea views. There's also a shop, pool, snorkel hire, cheap fuel and daytime café (Apr-Oct). **C-E** *Marina Beach*, Market St, 4 km south of town, T9949 1500, www.ningaloochase.com.au, is a surprisingly luxurious hostel complex almost completely under canvas. Large, en suite safari tents make up 6-bed dorms and premium doubles, other doubles in 2-person tents. Excellent communal facilities include open-air pool, chill out deck, café-bar and camp kitchen. Direct beach access, free pick-ups and free bikes. Recommended. **C** *Ningaloo Lodge*, Lefroy St, T1800 880949 or 9949 4949, www.ningaloolodge.com.au Well-thought-out and comfortable motel with twins and doubles, courtyard pool and communal kitchen, dining, television and games rooms.

Sleeping
Exmouth is well set-up for travellers, with a good range of accommodation, tours and activities

Whaler's, Kennedy St, T9949 2416, is the town's main upmarket joint, with plenty of tables on a covered terrace. Open 0830-1500 for breakfasts and light lunches, and 1830-2100 for mid-range meals. Licensed. The *Potshot* has 2 dining options. The shady pool-side bar serves mid-range steak and seafood meals 0700-1830 and (in peak season) 1830-2100, and a pricier bistro at the other end of the complex, open 1130-1400 and 1830-2100. Tucked behind Ampol on Maidstone Cres, the *Rock Cod Café*, T9949 1249, is a cheap BYO terrace café offering the best value seafood in town. Open 1700-2130.

Eating

As always in WA, remember that conditions for snorkelling are best in the morning before the wind arrives. If you have your own transport you can snorkel from many beaches in the **Cape Range National Park** (see p xxx) where you can expect to see a great variety of fish and coral, and perhaps turtles, rays and reef sharks (harmless!). The best site is **Turquoise Bay** but take care as there is a very strong current and a break in the reef. Check conditions at the park entry booth or Milyering before snorkelling here – high tide is the worst time. **Guided beach snorkelling** From Exmouth *Ningaloo Chase* T9949 1500, www.ningaloochase.com.au, run day trips to look for turtles ($65)

Snorkelling on the Ningaloo

Western Australia

▶▶ **Swimming with whale sharks**

Imagine swimming with a shark the size of a bus, in water 1 km deep. You stand on the back of boat all suited up in snorkel, fins and wetsuit and the divemaster shouts 'go, go, go' like Murray Walker at a grand prix. Adrenaline surges and suddenly you're looking through your mask at a mouth as big as a bath coming straight for you. Shock paralyzes you for a second as your mind screams at you to 'get out of the way'!

Swimming with whale sharks may be one of the most memorable and exciting things you do in your lifetime. They are plankton feeders, rare and gentle beasts that can reach 18 m but are more often seen at 4-12 m. Little is known about them except that they travel in a band around the equator and arrive to feed at the Ningaloo Reef after the coral spawning in March and April. The sharks swim just under the surface as sunlight sparkles on their blue-grey bodies and delicate pattern of white spots. When spotted by a boat, snorkellers jump in and accompany a shark for a while, just like

the fleet of remora fish that hang around its mouth and belly. Some sharks seem mildly curious about their new fluoro-coloured gasping, flapping friends but others seem about as bothered as an elephant by a gnat.

Fisherman had seen a few on the Ningaloo Reef over the years but it wasn't until the late 1980's that marine biologists began to realize just how unusual but regular these sightings were. During the 1990s tours were developed to take visitors out to swim with the whale sharks and it has become big business in Exmouth. CALM have developed strict guidelines for swimming and boating around them that is hoped will keep the whale sharks undisturbed. Of course these are wild creatures and sightings are not guaranteed (although some operators offer a second trip for free if you don't see any). Experiences can vary from hectic five-minute swims to magical 40-minute floats but are always extraordinary.

which also include a hike into Yardie Creek. *Ningaloo Reef Retreat*, T9949 4073, www.ningalooreefretreat.com, take people out from their secluded beach. Again, encounters with turtles are likely. Half-day, $50. **Boat trips** *Ningaloo Ecology*, T9949 2255, run 1-hr (1000 and 1400, $25) and 2-hr (1130, $35) boat trips from the Tantabiddi boat ramp. The glass-bottom boat heads out a few hundred metres to the reef and is a good way to see fish, coral and turtles even if you don't snorkel. The 2-hr trip includes about an hour of snorkelling and includes town transfers. **Kayaking** *Ningaloo Reef Retreat* take small groups to the Blue Lagoon, one of the finest snorkelling sites on the whole reef. You kayak about 1 km offshore to the lagoon where you have a very good chance of seeing turtles and huge cow-tailed stingrays. Cost $80, including lunch and town pick-up. Combine this with a beach snorkel and swag overnight for an extra $5. Recommended. *Capricorn Kayak Tours*, T9949 4431, www.capricornkayak.com.au, offer various options from a sunset paddle and BBQ at Bundegi ($49) to multi-day camping safaris (5-days for $745, minimum 4 people). April-October only. **Snorkel hire** *Exmouth Diving Centre*, *Potshot Hotel*, hire out snorkel sets for $13.20 per day, while you can pick up a set at the *Lighthouse Caravan Park* for $15 for 24 hrs.

Other tours **4WD** *Ningaloo Safari Tours*, 9949 1550, ningaloosafari@nwc.net.au Knowledgeable
& activities and enthusiastic tours into Cape Range National Park, including Shothole Canyon, Charles Knife Rd, 4WD over the top of the range to Yardie Creek and a snorkel at Turquoise Bay. Lunch and tea breaks included (full day, $145). Recommended. **Camel rides** *Camel Expeditions*, T0427 247633, www.camel-expeditions.com A range of rides from 1-hr sunset ride ($29) to overnight camps in the ranges (2 days, $180). **Camping adventures** *Ningaloo Chase* have a canvas beachside camp just south of Yardie Creek. Overnight visits are $185, 2 nights for $345, and include transfers, meals,

drinks (BYO alcohol) and activities. Also beachside, and close to a spectacular snorkelling area, *Ningaloo Reef Retreat* offer a similar, though slightly less structured experience, actually within the national park. Overnight swag stays are $135, including the brilliant kayak trip described above. **Diving** Diving on the Ningaloo can be exceptional, with hundreds of species of fish and coral. There are a number of operators in town, each with their own specialities. *Diving Ventures*, Maidstone Cres, T9949 2300, www.dventures.com.au, have a wide range of options and PADI courses, from 1-day, 2-dive trips to the reef or islands, to 5-day whale-shark and dive safaris. Recommended. *Exmouth Dive Centre*, *Potshot Hotel*, T9949 1201, www.exmouthdiving.com.au, have one of the widest ranges of single-day options. *Village Dive*, T9949 1101, www.exmouthdiving.com, specialize in the Muiron Islands, so can usually find good dive spots any time of the year, while *Coral Coast*, T9949 1044, have the sole license to dive off the nearby disused navy pier, home to around 200 fish species. **Fishing** Several boats run game fishing trips, though the choice is reduced during whale shark season. Flexible and friendly *Ocean Quest Charters*, T9949 1111, offer full- and half-day trips. **Quad-bikes** *Coastal Quad Bike Tours*, T9949 1607. Full-day, half-day ($100) and 1-3 hr (2 hrs, $50) tours on Exmouth Gulf, some combined with fishing and snorkelling. **Turtle watching** Turtles come ashore in the Cape Range National Park to breed and lay eggs and it is possible to have the rare experience of watching them doing so. Nesting turtles lumber onto the northern end of the cape (Hunters, Mauritius, Jacobsz and Jansz beaches) during Oct-Feb at night just before high tide and for two hours afterwards. Hatchlings emerge Jan-Apr between the hours 1700-2000 and scamper to the water's edge. Turtles must not be disturbed by noise, light or touching – it is very important to follow the CALM code of conduct for turtle watching (pick a copy up at their office in town) or the turtles may stop nesting here. *Ningaloo Safari Tours*, 9949 1550, run an evening turtle-watching tour ($30) in season (Nov-Mar). **Whale sharks** The sharks come in to feed off the reef from Apr-Jul, though at the fringes of the season they are generally fewer and smaller. Come during May-Jun for the best chance of seeing a real biggie (12-m sharks are not uncommon). Half a dozen boats offer day trips to snorkel with them for around $300. 2 of the best operators are the full-time dive companies *Diving Ventures* and *Exmouth Dive Centre*, who also include diving and snorkelling time. **Whale watching** Humpback whales migrate along the Ningaloo during Jul-Oct, and most of the dive and boat operators run whale-watching trips during that period.

Transport
See following section for buses to Cape Range National Park

Air The airport is 35 km south of Exmouth. A town shuttle, T9949 1101, meets each of the daily *Skywest* flights ($17), and the *Northwest Regional Airlines* flights on request. *Allen's*, *Budget* and *Avis* hire cars available. *Skywest* have daily flights to **Perth**, while *Northwest Regional Airlines* fly to **Broome** via **Karratha** and **Port Hedland** every Mon and Fri. **Bus** *Integrity* southbound services depart from the VIC at 1330 Mon and Fri. *McCafferty's/Greyhound* buses depart 1445 Mon, Thu and Sat (Midwest coastal route). If heading to **Broome** and **Katherine** you will need to catch the shuttle service, T9949 1101, that leaves daily at 2255. This connects with the eastbound GX620 service at the Giralia turn-off (1 hr wait), and also with the daily southbound GX850 service. **Backpacker Buses** *Easyrider*, T9226 0307, www.easyriderbp.com.au, have several options east to **Broome** and south to **Perth**.

Directory
Fuel at the Lighthouse Caravan Park is usually considerably cheaper than in town, but is cash only

Banks Two bank branches, plus ATMs in the two supermarkets (open daily). **CALM** 22 Nimitz St, T9949 1676. Open Mon-Fri 0800-1700. Brochures and park advice. **Car hire** *Allen's*, T9949 2403. Also at *Exmouth Cape Tourist Village*. **Car servicing** *Exmouth Automotive & Boating*, Griffiths Way, T9949 2795. **Communications** Cheapest **Internet** at *Ningaloo Blue* ($6 per hr), corner of Kennedy St and Thew St. Open daily 1000-1900. **Post Office** on Maidstone Cres. **Medical services** Hospital on Lyon St, T9949 1011. **Police** Riggs St, T9949 2444. **Taxi** T0409 994933.

Western Australia

Cape Range National Park
Colour map 6, grid A1
Milyering 50 km from Exmouth

Cape Range National Park is an unforgiving, rocky strip of land on the western side of North West Cape, adjoining the Ningaloo Marine Park. The glittering turquoise sea fringing the park just seems to emphasise its aridity and kangaroos have to seek shade under bushes only knee high. However, this is the place to access the wonderful Ningaloo Reef.

Getting there The *Ningaloo Reef Retreat*, T9949 1776, operate a bus service between Exmouth and Turquoise Bay, with stops including the Sea Breeze Resort, Lighthouse Caravan Park, Tantabiddi and Milyering. The outward service leaves the main shopping area at 0850, arriving Turquoise Bay at 1025 ($22 return). The return service leaves the bay at 1445. Services daily from Apr-Oct, otherwise Mon-Tue and Fri-Sat. Day passengers to Turquoise Bay can borrow a snorkel set for free.

The park's **Milyering Visitor Centre**, 13 km inside the northern park boundary, houses an interpretative centre and small shop with a limited range of drinks and snacks. **Turquoise Bay**, a beautiful white swimming beach, is another 10 km south. There are a few shade sails and a toilet here but no other facilities. About 15 km from Milyering is **Mandu Mandu Gorge**, where there is a 3-km (return) walk into the dry gorge. Right at the end of the sealed road is **Yardie Creek**, a short gorge with sheer red walls and a colony of black-footed rock wallabies. Yardie Creek has a picnic area, a boat cruise along the creek (Wednesday, Friday, Sunday at 1200, T9949 2659) and a short, rocky track (1½ km return) along the northern side of the gorge. There are also two gorges that can be accessed from the eastern side of the cape, **Shothole Canyon** and **Charles Knife**, with great views of the gulf, but the unsealed access roads are very rough. It is very hot outside of winter and there is no drinking water available in the park so take plenty with you. ■ *Milyering open daily 1000-1600 (closed 1230-1315), park open 24 hrs, T9949 2808. Park entry $9 per vehicle or $3.30 per person. Camping $10 for 2 people. Ranger collects camping fees.*

Sleeping A-B *Ningaloo Reef Retreat*, T9949 4073, www.ningalooreefretreat.com, is the only commercial accommodation within the park itself. They have 4 comfortable 4-bed, en suite safari tents overlooking the beach and ocean, plus a small kitchen, chill-out area and ablution block. The price includes all meals, drinks (BYO alcohol) and activities including guided kayaking and snorkelling. The budget option is in a swag. Recommended. There are lots of **campgrounds** within the park, mostly close to the beach and with bush toilets. The VIC and CALM have a comprehensive list that details the qualities of each site. Only Lakeside, near Milyering, is close to a snorkelling site. No bookings are taken so call ahead for availability during the Apr-Oct peak season.

Exmouth to Nanutarra roadhouse
Colour map 6, grid A2
Nanutarra roadhouse 280 km from Exmouth, 370 km from Carnarvon

If heading east there is a sealed short-cut connecting the Exmouth Road with the North West Coastal Highway. Halfway along this road is **L-D** *Giralia*, T9942 5937, raeblake@bigpond.com, 130 km from Exmouth, and one of the best station stays in the region. They have four en suite and fully catered doubles and twins in the main homestead, also a self-contained cottage, a pretty quadrangle of simple air-conditioned donga rooms and a bush camp. Basic kitchen facilities but the hosts also cook up a meal for budget guests every evening. After the junction with the main highway the slow greening of the landscape continues and the monotonous flat becomes punctuated with the first signs of the main Pilbara ranges. The **D** *Nanutarra Roadhouse*, T9943 0521, has a few air-conditioned donga rooms, camp sites and a licensed café. Meals 0630-2200, fuel till 2400. The roadhouse marks one of the north's major junctions, and from here it's 265 km to **Karratha** and 350 km to **Tom Price**.

The Pilbara

The Pilbara has iron in its ancient dark-red stone and in its very soul. Almost half of all Australia's mineral wealth is mined and exported from the Pilbara and almost every town has been created by mining companies in the last few decades. Most of the Pilbara's population lives on the coast in the industrial ports of Dampier and Port Hedland or residential suburbs such as Karratha, Wickham and South Hedland but the most striking and distinctive landscapes of the Pilbara are found inland. It is a region of stark beauty and grandeur where just two colours dominate – red and gold. This scenery is seen at its best in one of Australia's finest national parks, Karijini. Deep, narrow gorges have been carved into the Hamersley Range to create an oasis of rock pools and waterfalls, some reached only by nerve-jangling adventure routes. Millstream-Chichester National Park is another area of rugged landscape relieved by water and has idyllic campsites beside spring-fed pools lined with palm trees.

Try to visit in winter to avoid any cyclones and the unrelenting heat

Ins and outs

Air *Skywest* and *Qantas* both have daily flights to **Karratha**, and the latter also fly daily to Port Hedland. *Northwest Regional Airlines*, T9192 1369, www.northwestregional.com.au, have flights between most of the northern WA towns from Exmouth to Halls Creek. **Bus** *McCafferty's/Greyhound* main GX620 northbound service leaves Perth daily at 1000, travels up the coastal Brand Highway, stops at Karratha (21 hrs) and continues on via **Port Hedland** to Broome, the Kimberley and the Northern Territory. Their GX850 service traces the same route in the opposite direction, leaving Darwin at 0730. The weekly GX661 service leaves Perth every Fri at 1330, heading up via **Newman** and the *Auski Roadhouse*, terminating in Port Hedland.

Getting there and around
For road conditions T9172 1277

The industrial towns of Karratha and Dampier offer little to interest visitors but are a useful base for trips to the **Millstream-Chichester** and **Karijini** national parks inland, and the islands of the **Dampier Archipelago** just offshore. There are also ancient **aboriginal rock carvings** to see in the Karratha Hills behind the VIC and on the Burrup Peninsula, from where you can take in the mind-boggling scale of Dampier's port facilites and natural gas plant. The **VIC** in Karratha is well-organized and helpful, and can be found just off the main junction into town. ■ *Mon-Fri 0830-1700, Sat-Sun 0900-1600 (Apr-Nov), Mon-Fri 0900-1700, Sat 0900-1200 (Dec-Mar). T9144 4600, info@karratha.com*

Karratha & Dampier
Colour map 6, grid A2
Populations: Karratha 10,000, Dampier 1,400
Karratha 265 km from Nanutarra roadhouse, 245 km from Port Hedland

Sleeping and eating **B** *Karratha Apartments*, Galbraith Rd, 2 km from town, T9143 9222, karratha.apartments@kisser.net.au, have 10 fully self-contained, spacious chalets grouped around a pleasant pool and BBQ area. There are a handful of high-standard motels in both Karratha and Dampier (generally cheaper in the latter) catering for the large business market. The best balance between price and quality can be found at the **C** *Peninsula Palms*, The Esplanade, Dampier, T9183 1888. The only hostel is the **D-E** *Karratha Backpackers*, Wellard Way, T9144 4904l, a tired, brick ex-motel with 30-odd beds in 10 rooms, including 1 double. Courtyard BBQ, games room. Rooms a/c, but coin-operated ($1 per hr). Karratha boasts 3 **caravan parks**, none close to the town centre, and Dampier has a sites-only park. *Karratha Caravan Park*, near the industrial estate off Karratha Rd, T9185 1012, has the cheapest on-site vans and cabins. The area's undisputed best eating is the expensive *Etcetera*, T9185 3111, at the upmarket *Karratha International* hotel, a contemporary open space overlooking the hotel's central pool courtyard, has an extensive menu. Meals 0600-0930, 1200-1400

Western Australia

▶▶ **Dampier Archipelago**

There are 42 low rocky islands in the archipelago, about 20 km west of Karratha, and a wonderfully rich marine life. Turtles nest on the beaches and whales, dolphins and dugong inhabit island waters. Fringing coral reefs provide great diving and much of it has hardly been explored. CALM have estimated that there are 600 species of fish in the archipelago and naturally this is a popular local fishing ground. More than half of the islands are classed as reserves but industrial development has always come before environmental concerns in the area so the marine life is relatively unprotected. There are currently plans to create a marine conservation reserve for the area from the Dampier Archipelago to Cape Preston but a final decision has yet to be made.

and 1800-2100. The hotel also boasts the best of the town's watering holes, the unpretentious *Gecko's*. *Barnacle Bob's*, The Esplanade, T9183 1053, is a mid-range alfresco fish restaurant that overlooks the Dampier Yacht Club and harbour. Licensed, it's open 1200-1400 Sat-Sun and 1700-2100 Tue-Sun.

Tours and activities Diving *Adventure Dive Charters*, Sharp Av, Karratha, T9185 1957, organize dive trips to the Dampier Archipelago and the Montebello Islands. Minimum 4 people, $125 per person including all gear and 2 dives. **Fishing** *Aqualand Charters*, T9183 1885. Charters for small groups (1-4) in Dampier Archipelago and inshore waters. From $165 per person, full day. **National Parks** *Snappy Gum Safaris*, T9185 1278, www.snappygum.karratha.com.au, run a range of trips into **Karijini** and **Millstream-Chichester** during the cool season of May-Oct. Karijini lookouts and gorges 2 days $290, 3-day adventure tour $390, both national parks (staying in a Tom Price motel) 3 days $490. Day tours into Millstream run all year round, $75.

Transport Air *Karratha Airport*, roughly between the 2 towns, is one of Australia's busiest domestic airports, handling about 500 people a day, almost all workers. There is a bar and café and all the major hire car companies have manned desks. A taxi to Karratha will be about $15. *Northwest Regional Airlines* have flights to **Broome** via **Port Hedland** every Mon, Wed and Fri, and to **Exmouth** every Mon and Fri. *Qantas* and *Skywest* have daily flights to **Perth** and the latter also fly, at weekends, to **Port Hedland**. **Bus** The daily *McCafferty's/Greyhound* Perth to Darwin service leaves the Shell service station for **Port Hedland** and **Broome** (11 hrs) at 0730. The Perth-bound service departs 1950.

Karratha and Dampier have the cheapest fuel in the area **Directory Banks** All the major banks, with ATMs, on Hedland Pl, Karratha town centre. **Bike hire** *Bike Force*, Sharp Av, Karratha, T9185 4455. **Car servicing** *K-Mart Auto*, Karratha City, T9185 3656. **Communications** Internet at VIC for $6 per ½ hr or *Boomerang* café in the shopping centre. **Post Office** opposite Karratha City, off Welcome Rd. **Medical services** *Nickol Bay Hospital*, Dampier Rd, Karratha, T9144 0330. **Police** Welcome Rd, T9144 2233. **Taxi** T9185 4444.

Roebourne & around
Colour map 6, grid A3
Population: 1,000
40 km from Karratha,
205 km from
Port Hedland

The original regional capital, Roebourne has declined to a small scruffy junction town straddling the main highway. Some impressive colonial buildings survive, notably the gaol which is now a **museum** and the area's **VIC**. The gaol holds a small collection of historical photographs and prison memorabilia and sells local arts and crafts. ■ *0900-1700 Mon-Fri, 0900-1600 Sat-Sun (May-Oct), 0900-1500 Mon-Fri, 0900-1200 Sat (Nov-Apr). Museum entry by gold coin donation. T9182 1060, roebourne_tourist@kisser.net.au* A relatively cheap **caravan park**, T9182 1063, lies on the far side of the river. It has sites,

Western Australia

on-site vans and a pool. The daily *McCafferty's/Greyhound* Perth to Darwin service leaves outside the *Victoria Hotel* for Broome (10½ hours) at 0755. The Perth-bound service departs 1905.

Some 12 km from Roebourne, **Cossack** has declined dramatically since the 19th century and now only a handful of magnificent bluestone colonial government buildings remain, giving the place an air of faded dignity. These have been restored and put to use. The old courthouse is now a **museum** with an interesting collection of local memorabilia and photographs. ■ *Daily 0900-1700, gold coin donation.* The impressive bond store opens as a **café** 1000-1400, daily during May-October, otherwise at weekends, and the police quarters have been converted into the peaceful **E** *Cossack Backpackers*, T9182 1190, which has one large dorm, three doubles, and a shady verandah and garden (free pick-ups from Roebourne).

The small community of **Point Samson**, 20 km from Roebourne, is a fishing port. At low tide you can snorkel at **Honeymoon Cove** on a coral reef 20 m from shore, but Point Samson is best known for *Moby's Kitchen*, T9187 1435, a legendary spot for the freshest, tastiest fish and chips imaginable, served at outdoor wooden benches overlooking the sea. Open 1100-1400, 1700-2030 Monday-Friday, 1100-2030 Saturday-Sunday. Recommended. You can bring your own drinks or buy them upstairs at the *Trawlers Tavern*, T9187 1503, a relaxed, friendly verandah bar that appeals to both locals and visitors alike. Meals 1200-1430, 1800-2100 Monday-Friday, 1200-2100 Saturday-Sunday.

The only stop before Port Hedland (120 km) is the **C-F** *Whim Creek Hotel*, T9176 4914, an atmospheric old two storey corrugated-iron pub turned roadhouse with a warm welcome, excellent food (Tuesday-Saturday 0730-1430, 1800-2000, Sunday 0730 1500), a shady beer garden and even orphaned kangaroos wandering about. Hotel rooms have air conditioning, TV and fridge and there are also cheap backpacker rooms (without air conditioning so only bearable May-September).

As you approach this national park from the north you pass through classic Pilbara landscape and begin to see the unusual beauty of this region. Flat-topped ranges and hills of the darkest red are dotted with yellow tufts of spinifex. The flat expanse of the plains below is broken only by green ribbons of white-barked gum trees along the banks of stony creek beds.

Millstream-Chichester National Park
Colour map 6, grid A3
Python Pool 125 km from Karratha, 90 km from Roebourne

Getting around All access roads to the national park are unsealed and although rocky are generally fine for 2WD, except after heavy rain. Ask for current conditions at the Karratha VIC. If travelling from Karratha there are 2 main routes. The shortest route in from the highway is 30 km east of Roebourne and leads to Python Pool, but there is also a *Hamersley Iron Company* road that runs direct from Karratha through the western end of the park, joining the shire road midway between Python Pool and Millstream. It continues south to Tom Price (185 km). A permit must be obtained to use this road, from the Karratha VIC or the Shell garage at Tom Price. Company road conditions on T9143 6464. There is no petrol available between Karratha/Roebourne and Tom Price/Auski so plan carefully and also take plenty of water.

See Karratha for details of tours

The park itself has two distinct visitor areas. The northern end provides stunning views over the landscape from **Mount Herbert**, best at sunset. Just 5 km away, **Python Pool**, a deep swimming hole below a sheer rock wall, is wonderful at sunrise so it's a good place to spend the night although nearby Snake Creek campground is stony and shadeless. Mount Herbert is at the northern edge of a huge, fairly featureless plateau. At the southern end, 60 km away, is the freshwater oasis of **Millstream**. Here there are permanent spring-fed pools in the Fortescue River, lined with palm trees, rushes and tall gums, and idyllic swimming and camping spots. The park visitor centre, in an old farm homestead, is not staffed but has interesting displays on the history and environment of the park and a box to put your park fees in. Kangaroos often rest in the shade of the homestead grounds, where there is also a pretty picnic spot. Nearby **Deep Reach Pool** and **Crossing Pool** both have shady campsites with toilets, BBQs and ladders into the river if you feel like a swim (you will). Crossing Pool, on the northern bank, tends to be the quietest although both are busy in the winter high season. There are a few walks detailed in the free park brochure. ■ *Park fees $9 car, camping $10 for 2. For more information contact CALM, Karratha, T9143 1488. Water available but must be treated.*

Port Hedland
Colour map 5, grid B1
Population (inc South Hedland): 12,900
265 km from Auski Roadhouse (Karijini),
610 km from Broome

Port Hedland isn't a pretty town, dominated as it is by huge stockpiles of ore, heavy industry and loading facilities, and the thin film of red dust that covers everything doesn't help. It does, however, making a good base for taking a tour into the **Karijini National Park**, 250 km to the south. The helpful **VIC** is on the main Wedge Street. ■ *0830-1700 Mon-Fri. Sat: 0830-1600 (Jun-Oct), 0830-1300 (Nov-May). Sun: 1200-1600 Jun-Oct. T9173 1711, www.porthedlandtouristbureau.com* One worthwhile sight is **Cemetary Beach**, opposite the *Mercure*, scene of turtle nesting and hatching during November-March. Contact the VIC for guidance on seeing them.

Contact the VIC for additional options in South Hedland

Sleeping and eating A *Mercure*, Lukis St, T9173 1511, mercure_hedland@bigpond.com, is well maintained and has a pool and a patio dining area overlooking the sea. The mid-range meals are generally the best in town, available 0600-0900, 1200-1400 and 1800-2100. **C-E** *Esplanade Hotel*, The Esplanade, T9173 1798, is a large traditional pub with a range of simple upstairs a/c rooms plus a kitchenette, and several motel rooms. Cheap counter meals 0600-0730, 1130-1330 and 1800-2000 when the mid-range dining room is also open. **D** *Ocean Lodge*, behind *Bruno's*, Richardson St, T9173 2635, has the best value motel-style a/c en suite rooms in town. There are a number of backpacker options near the town centre. The best of these is currently **D-E** *Dingo's Oasis*, Kingsmill St, T9173 1000, dingosoasis@hotmail.com, a small modern hostel overlooking one of the more picturesque parts of the town's foreshore. It has a variety of a/c rooms, and well-equipped communal facilities. Courtesy car for free pick-ups and local trips. **D-E** *Dingo's Ironclad* is the *Oasis'* overspill hostel just around the corner, and if anything is slightly more comfortable, though without the garden and views. **D-E** *Frog's Port Hedland Backpackers*, Richardson St, T9173 3282, was being refurbished at time of writing but looked set to give *Oasis* a run for their money. The closest **caravan park** to the town centre, though still 6 km away, is at Point Cooke, T9173 1271. **Eating out** in Port Hedland, even at the *Mercure*, isn't exactly high class, but it is generally good quality. *Bruno's Pizzeria*, Richardson St, T9173 2047, is a friendly mid-range licensed Italian restaurant. Open 1730-0200, also take-aways.

Tours and activities 2 companies head into Karijini National Park, each for 3 days of adventure ($395) and these are the only companies who operate throughout the year. Both bush camp with a bonfire just outside the park and the trip involves lots of walking and swimming, including sections of the 'Miracle Mile' if you wish. Just about everything is included in the price. *Dingo's Treks*, T9173 1000, dingosoasis@hotmail.com, run by the very entertaining Chris, leave every Sat, while *Pilbara Outback Safaris*, T9172 2428, leave on Tue. *Big Blue* head out most days during the Jul-Oct season to see the humpback whales migrating (3 hrs, $75).

Transport Air *Northwest Regional Airlines* have flights to **Broome** every Mon, Wed and Fri, to **Exmouth** via Karratha every Mon and Fri, and to **Karratha** only every Wed and Sun. *Qantas* fly daily to **Perth** and, at weekends, to **Karratha**. **Bus** The daily *McCafferty's/Greyhound* Perth to Darwin GX620 service leaves the Tourist Bureau for **Broome** (7 hrs), the Kimberley and Northern Territory at 1100. The coastal Perth-bound GX680 service departs 1555, while the inland GX673 bus heads out once a week, on Fri, at the same time.

Cheapest fuel in the region generally at the Shell roadhouse on the highway opposite the airport

Directory Banks Main banks and ATMs in Wedge St. **Car servicing** *Pilbara 4X4 Recovery*, T0418 951804, are the local recovery experts and also hire out 'Pilbara Packs' consisting of all the essential extra vehicle kit you wish you had but couldn't afford. **Communications** Internet access at the VIC. **Post Office**, Wedge St.

Karijini National Park

Northern and central Australia contain so many impressive red-walled gorges that some visitors get gorge fatigue (a malady similar to cathedral fatigue in Europe) but Karijini is the dessert course you'll find you still have room for. The park contains extraordinary deep and narrow gorges full of waterfalls, idyllic swimming pools and challenging walks, yet it is hardly known, even within Australia. The park sits within the heart of one of the world's most ancient landscapes, the **Hamersley Plateau**, where creeks have carved 100-m deep chasms into layers of 2,500 million year-old sedimentary rock. Unusually, you enter the park from the plateau and descend into the gorges which means there are some excellent lookouts. The most spectacular feature of the park can be seen from **Oxers Lookout**, where four gorges meet below the golden spinifex and crooked white snappy gum trees of the plateau.

Colour map 6, grid A3 Central gorges 80 km from Tom Price, 110 km from Auski roadhouse

Getting there and around *McCafferty's/Greyhound* **bus** service from Perth to Port Hedland stops at Auski roadhouse at 0655 on Sat, in time to be picked up for a *Dingo's* 3-day tour (returning to Port Hedland). A **tour** is a good way to see Karijini, especially if you want some adventure, but choose your tour carefully, checking that the age and activity level will suit you. *Dingo's Treks* may also be able to offer a 'tag-along' option if you have your own transport (recommended if you would like to tackle the more adventurous parts of Weano and Hancock). From Tom Price there are two options. *Lestok Tours*, T9189 2032, lestok@norcom, run a regular day trip, departing at 0800 ($100, children $50). *Design A Tour*, T9188 1670, www.dat.com.au, also offer day tours ($105), from May-Oct. For details of 4WD tours from Port Hedland and Karratha, see pages 618 and 615. *Karijini Helicopters*, T9176 6900, www.karijiniheli.com, operate **scenic flights** over Karijini from the *Auski Roadhouse*, from $90 (20 mins).

Ins & outs *All access is via unsealed roads*

Although this is the state's second largest park, all of the main facilities and walks are found fairly close to each other in the northern section of the park, above Karijini Drive. Head first for the **visitor centre**. An interpretative display explains the history and geology of the park and the viewpoint of its Banyjima, Yinhawangka, and Kurrama traditional owners. Maps, drinks and souvenirs are available and there are toilets, showers and phones by the car park. The park is generally open all year round, although most pleasant during Apr-Sep. Visitor centre open daily 0900-1600 (limited hrs in summer). Park fees $9 per car, camping $10 site. T9189 8121. Roads are unsealed and rocky (2WD but punctures are common). The Nanutarra-Wittenoom Rd north of Hamersley Gorge may be impassable from Dec-Apr.

Western Australia

Exploring the gorges

Walking and swimming are the two main activities around here, but Karijini is also known for some very exciting adventure trails. Because some gorges are only as narrow as one to two metres wide, or filled with water, you cannot always walk between the gorge walls but have to clamber along steep sides on narrow ledges of dark red ironstone, swimming and climbing through difficult sections. The extremely hair-raising 'Miracle Mile' contains the most challenging terrain and some sections are considered very dangerous. The routes beyond Kermits Pool in **Hancock Gorge** and Handrail Pool in **Weano Gorge** should only be attempted with an experienced guide, but adrenaline junkies will no doubt always find this a lot of fun. There are easy walks but you will not always be able to see the best of this awesome park unless you are reasonably fit, agile and not too worried by the heights.

There are three main areas to visit in the park. **Dales Gorge** is 10 km east of the visitor centre, where you can walk up the gorge to a wide cascade, Fortescue Falls, and beyond the falls to Fern Pool which is a lovely large swimming hole (1 km). Return to the top of the gorge by the same path or alternatively you can walk down the centre of the gorge and turn left at the end to join the trail to **Circular Pool**, a lush rock bowl dripping with ferns. At the point where you turn, a steep path joins the car park to the pool (800 m) so you don't need to retrace your steps. There is also an easy rim trail overlooking Dales Gorge and Circular Pool (2 km). The most impressive area however is 30 km west of the visitor centre, at the junction of **Weano, Joffre, Hancock** and **Red gorges**. There are several lookouts here, including Oxer Lookout, and trails into Joffre (3 km), Knox (2 km), Weano (1 km to Handrail Pool) and Hancock Gorges (1½ km to Kermits Pool). These are all enjoyable and involve some scrambling but the latter two offer a taste of Karijini adventure that most people can manage without a guide. One of the prettiest gorges to visit is nearby **Kalamina Gorge**, which is also one of the easiest to explore. **Hamersley Gorge** is another delightful spot, although on the far western border 100 km from the visitor centre. This is an open gorge with dramatically folded rock walls in wonderful shades of purple, green and pink. Fortescue River flows through the gorge, creating beautiful pools and waterfalls. If you head upstream you will pass a deep 'spa' pool, scoured out by boulders, on the way to the pretty fern-lined Grotto (1 km, difficult). Finally if you want to get a birds-eye perspective on the whole landscape you can climb **Mount Bruce**, which is famous for being WA's second highest mountain at 1,235 m. This is the island peak visible from the western end of Karijini Drive and the track is a long but very rewarding slog up to the western face (9 km, 6 hrs return).

Sleeping & eating

Tom Price 115 km from Auski roadhouse, 350 km from Nanutarra

There are 3 campgrounds within the park, **Weano** and **Joffre** in the central area and **Dales** campground, 10 km east of the visitor centre. All have gas BBQs, picnic tables, bush toilets, stony ground and limited shade but only Dales campgound has caravan sites (unpowered) and allows the use of generators. Please note though that campfires are not permitted within the park area. Outside the park, the closest options are at **Tom Price**. B *Karijini Lodge Motel*, Stadium Rd, T9189 1110, easily has the most luxurious rooms in town and also the best dining facilities (mid-range). The **B** *Tom Price Hotel*, Central Rd, T9189 1101, has slightly cheaper motel-style rooms and serves both cheap counter and mid-range restaurant meals 1200-1400 and 1800-2000. The **C-E** *Tom Price* **caravan park**, 2 km from town, T9189 1515, has self-contained A-frame units, 4-bed dorms in dongas, and a campers' kitchen. The town also has an assortment of take-aways plus Thai and Chinese restaurants and a huge supermarket, open daily. **B-D** *Auski Tourist Village Munjina* (the 'Auski roadhouse'), out on the Great Northern Highway, T9176 6988. Has 20 comfortable motel rooms, budget twins without en suite, and powered and unpowered sites. There are snacks all days and meals are served 1800-2030. There is also budget accommodation at **Wittenoom** a former blue-asbestos mining town just on the northern border of Karijini, 42 km from Auski roadhouse. **C** *Wittenoom Guest House*, T9189 7060, has twin and dorm rooms with shared facilities, and camping sites. The government does not recommend visits to the town but advises visitors in Wittenoom to take the following precautions – keep to main roads, keep car windows closed, keep away from asbestos tailings and do not camp outside designated areas.

Design A Tour, T9188 1670, www.dat.com.au, also offer day tours to the national park, from both Tom Price and the Auski roadhouse ($105), May-Oct. **Tours**

McCafferty's/Greyhound's **Port Hedland** service leaves the Auski Roadhouse at 0735 Sat, while the **Perth** bus departs the same day at 1935. **Transport**

This is one of the most tedious stretches of road in WA, particularly the last 300 or so km. There are sections where the vegetation struggles to get above knee height, and the endless flat vista can lull you into a trance that is probably not the safest of driving techniques. The first roadhouse, **D** *Pardoo*, 150 km from Port Hedand, T9176 4916, has air-conditoned singles and doubles in the usual dongas, is open for fuel 0600-2200, has a licensed bar, a small range of supplies and serves meals till 2000. The main place of interest on the road is **Eighty Mile Beach**, 10 unsealed km off the highway and 105 km from Pardoo. The beach stretches, unsurprisingly, as far as the eye can see in either direction and slopes gently down to the water, a favoured fishing spot though not recommended for a swim. Adjacent to the beach is the **C** *Eighty Mile Beach Caravan Park*, T9176 5941, which has seven air-conditioned cabins and hundreds of shady camping sites. Facilities are good, including a small store and take-away. Book well ahead for the June-September peak season. The **C-E** *Sandfire* roadhouse, T9176 5944, 140 km from Pardoo, is the last before the junction with Broome Road, 290 km up the track, so make sure you have enough fuel. Accommodation in en suite, a/c motel units and much simpler dongers. Fuel and meals 0600-2200. The small bar is definitely worth a look in.

Port Hedland to Broome
Fuel is around $0.10 more expensive than Port Hedland and Broome along this stretch

About 40 km east of Port Hedland is the turning to **Marble Bar** (150 km), a tiny, Outback town with a wide main street of corrugated-iron buildings which proudly claims to be the hottest town in Australia, not exactly a strong selling point. The town is surrounded by spectacular Pilbara scenery of low spinifex-covered ranges and dark-red ironstone ridges. Just outside Marble Bar is the beautiful rock bar of jasper across the Coongan River that gives the town its name and **Chinamans Pool** nearby where you can swim. There are three places to stay in Marble Bar: the **C-D** *Ironclad* pub, T9176 1066, which has motel and budget rooms and does counter meals 1200-1330, 1800-2000; **C** *Marble Bar Travellers Stop*, a roadhouse with motel rooms and a reasonable restaurant; and a **caravan park**, T9176 1067, with sites only.

Western Australia

The Kimberley

www.kimberley tourism.com

The far north of the state is called the Kimberley, an area larger than Germany with a population of 30,000. It's a wild and rugged region of gorges and waterfalls, cattle stations and diamond mines, spectacular coastline and ancient Aboriginal art. The Kimberley is part of Australia's tropical north with a summer monsoon that throws a green cloak over the grassy plains and scrub covered ranges, and turns the rivers into powerful torrents. During the dry season the rivers shrink to a series of pools, waterfalls slow to a trickle and heat and humidity drop to a comfortable level. There are only three major roads in the Kimberley and just one of them is sealed – the Great Northern Highway from Broome to Kununurra. Broome is a sophisticated coastal resort of entirely unique character, while Kununurra, on the eastern edge of the state, is surrounded by beautiful Kimberley range country and fertile land fed by the Ord River. The Gibb River Road connects the same towns and provides access to the region's most beautiful gorges in cattle station country but this is a challenging route. Halfway along this road an even rougher track, the Kalumburu Road, heads north to the coast, with a side track to the Mitchell Plateau. There are many places so remote that you can only see them by boat, plane or 4WD, such as the western coast, Buccaneer Archipelago and the domes of the Bungle Bungle Range.

Ins & outs

Getting there and around **Air** *Qantas* have daily flights from Perth to **Broome**, and from Alice Springs and Ayers Rock every Sat-Mon and Wed. *Air North*, T8920 4000, www.airnorth.com.au, fly daily from Darwin to both Broome and **Kununurra**. *Northwest Regional Airlines*, T9192 1369, www.northwestregional.com.au, have flights between most of the northern WA towns from Exmouth to Halls Creek. **Bus** *McCaffertys/Greyhound* have daily services traversing the region between **Perth** and **Darwin** via the main highway, stopping at all towns except Wyndham. There are no scheduled services along the Gibb River Rd, which is closed for much of the wet season. The road is possible in 2WD in the dry season, but is notoriously wearing on vehicles, particularly tyres and axles. Several tour and backpacker buses do, however, ply the Gibb River Road between Broome and Kununurra, and even Darwin. See relevant town entries for details.

Broome

Colour map 5, grid A1
Population: 12,000
610 km from Port Hedland, 1,060 km from Kununurra

Turquoise water, red cliffs, white sand and green mangroves: – Broome is a town full of vivid colour and tropical lushness, together with an interesting history and a composition quite unlike any other Australian town. It was established on the shore of Roebuck Bay in the 1890s as a telegraph cable station and a base for pearl shell merchants and their divers. During the boom years before the First World War Broome supplied 80% of the world's pearl shell, mostly used for buttons. The first pearl divers were Aboriginal, then later Malaysian, Indonesian, Chinese or Japanese. Consequently the people of Broome are a unusual mix of Aboriginal, Asian and European heritage. When plastic buttons were invented in the 1950s Broome survived by learning to produce cultured pearls and has since prospered, not only on the profits from the world's largest and most lustrous pearls, but also, more recently, from tourism. Refined and expensive resorts at Cable Beach have brought the town much attention and sophistication, and although it is probably true that Broome has lost some of its unique character, it remains a fascinating oasis and a very enjoyable place to spend a few days. ■ *VIC open Mon-Fri 0800-1700, Sat-Sun 0900-1600 (Apr-Sep) Mon-Fri 0900-1700, Sat-Sun 0900-1300 (Oct-Mar). T9192 2222, tourism@broome.wt.com.au Corner of Broome Highway and Bagot St.*

Airport Less than 2 km from the town centre, a taxi to most accommodation is under $10 if no pick-up is offered. Facilities include all the major car hire companies, a café and luggage lockers. The *McCaffertys/Greyhound* **bus terminal** is at the VIC, *Integrity* leaves from Terry's Travel on Carnarvon St. **Local bus services** The *Town Bus Service*, operates its single winding route between *Broometime Lodge*, the town centre and Cable Beach, and back, daily every hour between 0720 and 1830. Some services extend to the Shell House. The last bus back from Cable Beach leaves at 1815. Single trips $2.70, day passes $8.50. *Broome Day Tours*, T1800 801068, trundle around both the town and lower peninsula, taking in Gantheaume Point, the Deep Water Jetty, Town Beach and Chinatown. Departs around 0800 every day May-Oct, Mon, Wed, Fri and Sun from Nov-Apr (4 hrs, $49).

Getting there & around
Road conditions
T9158 4333
For further details and hire, see page 627

Broome is a place to take it easy, 'slip into Broometime' as the locals say, but there are quite a few sights to explore. **Chinatown** is the oldest part of town and is still the main focus of Broome. Carnarvon Street and Dampier Terrace are lined with architecture characteristic of its history, corrugated iron and verandahs blended with Chinese flourishes such as red trims and lattice. Modern boats now use the jetty at the Deep Water Port but two historic pearl luggers survive near the old jetty and can be seen at **Pearl Luggers**. This is the best place to learn about the pearling industry of the old days as a former pearl diver tells riveting tales that leave nothing to the imagination. Every Thursday there is a special evening tour that includes the chance to taste pearl meat

Sights
www.ebroome.com
Most of the sights are linked by the town bus

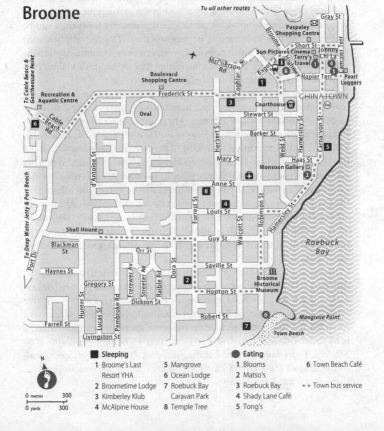

Broome

Sleeping
1 Broome's Last Resort YHA
2 Broometime Lodge
3 Kimberley Klub
4 McAlpine House
5 Mangrove
6 Ocean Lodge
7 Roebuck Bay Caravan Park
8 Temple Tree

Eating
1 Blooms
2 Matso's
3 Roebuck Bay
4 Shady Lane Café
5 Tong's
6 Town Beach Café
- - Town bus service

0 metres 300
0 yards 300

worth US$500 a kilo in Asia. ■ *Tours Mon-Fri 1100, 1400, Sat-Sun 1100.*
$18.50, children $9, concession $16.50. Bookings essential for Thu tour
(1800-2030, $48). T9192 2059. 44 Dampier Terr.

The commercial **Monsoon Gallery**, next door to *Matso's*, is housed in a
fine old pearling master's residence and is worth a visit to see an example of
early Broome architecture as well as the fine collection of art and jewellery.
■ *Daily 1000-1600. Free. Corner of Hamersley and Carnarvon St.* About 1
km south is the **Broome Historical Museum**, which has a small but well-
arranged and quite fascinating collection of artefacts, memorabilia and
photographs charting the whole history of the European and Asian colonists. ■ *Daily 1000-1300. $5, children $1, concessions $3. Hamersley St,*
T9192 2075. Not far away is the **town beach**, a small and shallow bay with
golden sand and Broome's amazing opaque turquoise water, fringed by a
low rocky headland on one side and mangroves on the other. This is the best
place to see the rare phenomenon called **staircase to the moon**, when the
moonlight shines on pools of water left behind by the tide to create the illusion. Pick up a monthly visitor guide from the VIC for 'staircase' dates and
tide times. In the **Shell House** the owners display their compact collection of
6,000 shells from hundreds of mostly local species. The main business of the
place is as a shop selling shells and mother-of-pearl jewellery so entry is free.
■ *Mon-Fri 0900-1700, Sat-Sun 0900-1300. T9192 1423. 95 Guy St.*

Gantheaume Point is a jumble of red rock stacks that make a striking contrast to the turquoise sea beyond. It is a lovely place to watch the sun set,
although the light for photography is best in the morning. It is also one of
many areas around Broome where fossilized **dinosaurs footprints** can be
seen in rock shelves. They are just at the base of the cliff but can only be seen at
very low tide (60 cm), which only occurs once or twice a month. Around the
corner, **Reddell Beach**, known for interesting rock formations and sheer pin-
dan cliffs, runs along the southern edge of the peninsula.

Cable Beach is a perfect, long, wide white-sand beach, 6 km from the
town centre. This is the perfect spot to watch the sunset, and the classic way
to do this is on the back of a **camel**. There are a couple of operators who
offer the experience, including *Ships of the Desert*, T9192 6383 (one hour,
$30, or full-day expeditions for $75). Alternatively *Cable Stables*, T0401
088473, offer beach and bush **horse-rides** for $50 for two hours. When the
tide is high it is also a relatively safe place to **swim** and there is usually a life-
guard patrol in winter. If you prefer being on the water rather than in it,
then a couple of options present themselves. A small beach shack hires out
surf and **boogie boards** (for $3-10 per hour) and is open daily 0830-1630.
They also hire out umbrellas and deckchairs. A little further down the
beach you can hire **surfcats** and slightly larger **catamarans** (both $30 per
hour, T0412 087080).

In the centre of the cluster of tourist resorts at Cable is **Broome Crocodile Park**, the public arm of a large commercial crocodile farming operation. Dozens of pens hold hundreds of crocs and alligators from five
species, but mostly the big Estuarine (or Saltwater) crocodiles of northern
Australia. The tours are fascinating and you usually get to see and touch a
baby croc. Allow 1½ hrs. ■ *Apr-Oct: 1000-1700 Mon-Fri, 1400-1700*
Sat-Sun. Tours daily 1500 and, during Jun-Oct, 1100 Mon-Fri. Spiced with
croc feeding at 1500 Wed-Sun. $15 inc tour, children $8, concessions $12.
Cable Beach Rd, T9192 1489.

LL-L *Cable Beach Club Resort*, Cable Beach Rd, Cable Beach, T9192 0400, info@cablebeachclub.com, is Broome's premier holiday accommodation, an exquisitely designed resort hotel with excellent facilities and restaurants. Recommended. **LL-L** *McAlpine House*, Herbert St, T9192 3886, reservations@mcalpinehouse.com The most exclusive B&B in town, and one of the very best examples of Broome architecture, this town house dates back to 1910 when it was built by a local pearling master. 6 exquisite and well-equipped rooms (although 3 share bathrooms). Tropical breakfast in the open-air dining room next to the courtyard pool. Recommended. The **L-A** *Mangrove*, Carnarvon St, T9192 1303, www.mangrovehotel.com, is a large resort-style hotel occupying the best shoreside location in town. The architecture is unremarkable but the food is very good and the luxury suites are quite striking. **A** *Cable Beachside Resort*, Murray Rd, Cable Beach, T9193 5545, comprises a group of fully self-contained, well-equipped units grouped around a central pool area. **C** *Broometime Lodge*, Forrest St, T1800 804322 or 9193 5067, broometimelodge@australiamail.com Simple but comfortable a/c motel rooms, many en suite, and a range of facilities including a simple kitchen area, dining room, TV room and pool. **C** *Ocean Lodge*, Cable Beach Rd, T9193 7700, oceanlodge@kimberleytravel.com Reasonably priced motel with good facilities. All rooms are en suite, a/c and have kitchenettes. **C** *Temple Tree*, 31 Anne St, T9193 5728, www.templetree.wabnbs.com, is a modest but welcoming B&B with 2 en suite rooms and a stately spreading frangipani shading the back garden. Breakfasts and optional cheap dinners are superb. Very good value. Recommended.

Backpacker hostels C-D *Kimberley Klub*, Frederick St, T9192 3233, www.kimberleyklub.com, is a superb large hostel, and very much a party destination. It centres around a large open-plan games, dining, bar and pool area. Beds in spacious 10- and 5-bed dorms, plus a few doubles. Pricey, but breakfast included. No a/c, but still recommended. **D-E** *Broome's Last Resort YHA*, Bagot St, T9193 5000. Tired, and a bit grungy, this hostel is favoured by seasonal workers as the cheapest and most convenient for town. Communal facilities are reasonably good, however, and include a pool. Rooms are non-a/c. **D** *Cable Beach Backpackers*, Sanctuary Rd, T9193 5511, meyo@tpg.com.au, is another resort-style hostel along similar lines to the *Klub*. Facilities are very good, and lots of freebies and cheap deals are thrown in, including a regular town centre shuttle. Some rooms are a/c. Of several **caravan parks**, the **D** *Roebuck Bay*, T9192 1366, has foreshore camping sites and basic a/c on-site vans.

Expensive The *Old Zoo Café*, Sanctuary Rd, Cable Beach, T9193 6200, is the most intimate of Cable's eateries. Breakfasts and light lunches by day, the expensive evening menu offers inventive takes on traditional Australian themes. Licensed, meals 0700-2200 (closed Mon, Oct-Mar). Recommended. **Mid-range** *Blooms*, Canarvon St, T9193 6366. Casual and stylish licensed café with a good range of meals available all day. Breakfast, baguettes, laksas, salads, pizza and pasta. Generous helpings and friendly service. Licensed, open daily 0700-2130. Mon-Sat 1800-2100. The licensed *Cable Beach Bar & Grill*, T9193 5090, has a prime position on the grassy foreshore overlooking the Cable Beach, with tables both on a shaded patio and in the open dining room. Both main restaurant and the adjacent take-away kiosk are open for meals 0700-2100 daily. *Matso's*, Hamersley St, T9193 5811 This restaurant has the best setting in town – a classic breezy Broome house with wraparound verandahs overlooking Roebuck Bay. Imaginative modern Australian cooking, great service and their own range of coolers and beers to taste, including a refreshing alcoholic ginger beer. Open daily 0700-2100. Recommended. *Tong's*, Napier Terr, T9192 2080. The best of the town's many Chinese restaurants though you wouldn't think so from the outside. Licensed, it's open daily 1730-2130. **Cheap** All of the following are generally cheap but can slip into mid-range territory in the evening. *Old Mac's Sunset Bar* at the Cable Beach Club Resort is the perfect spot to watch the sun sink romantically

Sleeping
Broome has easily the widest range of accommodation north of Perth, and this is simply a small selection from what is available. Contact the VIC for other options, and if you're around for a while consider a spell out on the Dampier Peninsula. Book well ahead for the peak April-September season

Eating
Evening bookings advisable at most restaurants during May-September

Western Australia

into the ocean (arrive early in peak season). Very good value. Food 1600-2100. *Roe-buck Bay*, Dampier Terr, T9192 1221. Large, lively pub with hearty meals daily 1200-1400, 1800-2000, particularly popular on Sun when they serve up a substantial tasty roast. *Shady Lane Café*, Johnny Chi Lane, between Canarvon St and Dampier Terr. Funky place popular with locals. Outdoor tables are quiet and cool under a profusion of palms. Daily 0700-1500. *Town Beach Café*, Robinson St, T9193 5585. Another local favourite, laid-back and unpretentious café, superb fish suppers. All the tables are out front, covered by sailcloth and overlooking the beach. Open from 0730-2100 Tue-Sat, 0730-1300 Sun, and 1730-2100 Mon. Recommended. *Wharf*, Port Drive, adjacent to the deep water jetty, T9192 5800. A no-frills licensed restaurant serving fresh and generous helpings of seafood, Asian dishes and salads at a price achieved with paper plates and plastic cutlery. The smart outdoor tables overlook the deep water jetty and Roebuck Bay. Daily 1100-2200.

Entertainment **Cinema** *Sun Pictures*, Carnarvon St, T9192 3738, is one of the oldest original picture houses in the world. Built in 1916 the screen is outdoors and most of the deckchair seats are out under the stars.

Shopping **Pearls and jewellery** There are half a dozen exclusive pearl boutiques on Dampier Terr (prices start at $500 and then rocket). *Linneys* sell fine traditional pearls and the business is owned by a local family. Try *Georgia Morgan* for more contemporary designs. Cheaper, casual jewellery made of pearl shell can be found at the *Shell House*, Courthouse Markets, Sat 0800-1300, and smaller Johnny Chi Lane market, Sun 0800-1230. **Outdoor** *Kimberley Camping and Outback Supplies*, 65 Frederick St, T9193 5354, kcaos@tpg.com.au, have an excellent range of gear. Much essential kit is available for hire, and they make up good value hire packs for camping and 4WD expeditions. **Books** *Kimberley Bookshop*, 6 Napier Terr, T9192 1944.

**Tours &
activities**
*Flights and tours
over and into the
Kimberley are usually
better value
from Derby*

Aboriginal culture *Mamabulanjin Aboriginal Tours*, 640 Dora St, T9192 2660, mabtours@wn.com.au Broome through Aboriginal eyes – tours can include bush tucker, weapon throwing and learning about hunting techniques. From $88 per day, $55 per ½ day. **Astronomical** *Astro Tours*, T0500 831111, mail@astrotours.net, head about 10 km out of Broome twice an evening up to 4 nights a week during Apr-Nov. Their guided tour of the night sky is both animated and fascinating, one of the country's very best, and 8 telescopes means plenty of viewing time. $50, children $25. **Boat trips** *Dampier Creek Boat Tours*, T9192 1669, head up the town creek through the mangroves, dipping in fishing lines along the way (3 hrs, $70). *Spirit of Broome*, T9193 5025. Breakfast or sunset tours by hovercraft ($88-99). **Coastal cruises** Luxury tours of the Kimberley coast from $7000 for 14 days (see box on page 631). *Great Escape*, Johnny Chi Lane, T9193 5983, www.kimberleyescape.com *North Star*, 25 Carnarvon St, T9192 1829, www.northstarcruises.com.au *Pearl Sea*, T9193 6131, www.pearlseacruises.com 126 Herbert St. **Diving** *Workline*, Short St, T9192 2233, organize local trips off Gantheaume Point, around $150 for a 2-dive trip, but only once a fortnight when the tide is very low. They also hire out gear, run PADI courses and can also advise on diving on the **Rowley Shoals**, 3 coral atolls 170 km northwest of Broome that are considered one of the very best, and most pristine diving sites in the world. The season for the shoals is very short, generally Sep-Nov. Trips out are a minimum 5 nights and cost around $500-800 per day. **Fishing** *Lucky Strike*, T9193 7375, luckystr@tpg.com.au, are one of several reef-fishing operators heading out from Broome during Apr-Dec. Prices are around $200 per day. *Ice Man*, T0408 915569, sometimes head out on half-day trips. **4WD** *Over the Top*, T9192 5211, www.4wdtourswa.com, head out on both day and overnight trips that include stops at Beagle Bay, Lombadina and Cape Leveque. Day tours every Tue and Fri,

Apr-Dec ($205), overnight trips every Mon, Apr-Nov ($310). The guides are good fun and all food and equipment included. They also offer an overnight trip every Sun and Wed from Apr-Nov ($340) that takes in Windjana, Tunnel and Geike. Their excellent 5 day west Kimberley adventure safari leaves every Mon, May-Oct ($990, swag option $830). *Kimberley Adventure Tours*, T/F9168 3368, specialize in one-way trips along the Gibb River Road to **Kununurra** and Darwin (9 days, Apr-Oct, $1,500). **History** *Broome Sightseeing Tours*, T9192 5041. Interesting look at Broome's history and main sights, max 4 ($55, 3 hrs). Mon-Fri 0815. **Sailing trips** *Oceanic Cruises*, T9193 6679, www.oceaniccruises.com.au, take out their impressive 35 m schooner every day, Sun-Fri, from May-Sep. Lunch cruises leave at 1000 (4 hrs, $69) and include a simple but good quality BBQ lunch, while the sunset cruise heads out at 1600 (2 hrs, $35). Staying aboard all day ($95) is one of WA's best value day sailing experiences. *Willie Pearl Lugger Cruises*, T0418 919781, take their original lugger out most days between Jun-Sep for sunset and afternoon 'boom net' cruises (both $60). **Scenic flights** *Broome Aviation*, T9192 1369, www.broomeaviation.com, fly around the Broome peninsula and Willie Creek (25 mins, $100). They also have a number of Kimberley options including, in the off-season, a good-value day trip to the Buccaneer Archipelago and Cape Leveque. This includes lunch and 2½ hrs flying time (0900, 6½ hrs, $350). *King Leopold Air*, T9193 7155, www.kingleopoldair.com.au, offer a variety of flights over the western Kimberley and over the Bungle Bungles via Windjana Gorge. Costs are around $150 per hr. *Windrider Safaris*, T0407 010772, take budding pilots up in their microlights for a mini-lesson and aerial sightsee. Options include going up to see the beautiful sunrise or sunset. A 30-min intro and flight is $145. **Wildlife** *Kimberley Birdwatching*, T/F9192 1246, kimbird@ tpg.com.au, offer regular and custom tours from 3 hrs to 3 weeks. The nthusiastic and deeply knowledgeable, George Swann's trips are a must for all visiting bird-watchers and well-worth considering for anyone wanting to see more of the area and its wildlife. The programmes vary.

Transport
See also Tours & activities above

Air *Northwest Regional Airlines* have flights to **Exmouth** via **Port Hedland** and **Karratha** every Mon and Fri, to Port Hedland and Karratha every Wed, and Karratha only on Sun. They also fly to **Fitzroy Crossing** and **Halls Creek** every Mon-Sat. *Qantas* have a daily service to **Perth**, and fly every Tue, Thu, Sat-Sun to **Alice Springs** and **Ayers Rock**. *Air North* fly daily to **Kununurra** and **Darwin**. **Bus** *McCafferty's/Greyhound* service to **Derby**, **Kununurra** (14 hrs) and the Northern Territory leaves the VIC daily at 1900. The Perth-bound bus departs 0830. **Backpacker buses** *Easyrider*, T9226 0307, www.easyriderbp.com.au, have several ticket options west, including **Exmouth** and **Perth**. *Travelabout*, T9244 1200, www.travelabout.au.com, run several trips, some 4WD, to **Darwin** and **Perth**.

Directory
Cheap fuel at Woody's, Dampier Terr

Banks The major bank branches, with ATMs, are in Chinatown, on Carnarvon St. **Bike hire** *Broome Cycle & Scoot*, 2 Hamersley St, T9192 1871. Bikes $15 day, also scooters and buggys. **Car hire** All the majors and several inexpensive local operators including *Broome Broome*, T0417 949727, bbcrent@wn.com.au, who have a good range from 3-door hatchbacks to Landcruisers. If you're going to do a bit of distance check out *Just Broome*, T9192 6636, who have more free km and cheaper per km excess than most. *Willie Creek*, T9192 3311, have excellent packages for small 4WDs. **Car servicing** *Minishull*, Guy St, opposite Shell House, T9192 1168. **Communications** Internet at *Broome Telecentre*, 40 Dampier Terr or *Internet Outpost*, 16 Carnarvon St. **Post Office** Carnarvon St. **Medical services** *Broome District Hospital*, Robinson St, T9192 9222. **Police** Hamersley St, T9192 1212. **Taxi** T9192 1133. **Useful addresses** CALM West Kimberley HQ, 111 Herbert St, T9192 1036.

Western Australia

Around Broome

Willie Creek, on a wide tidal inlet at the bottom of the Dampier Peninsula, is the only Broome pearl farm that receives visitors and that is because it's actually a demonstration farm, nowhere near the valuable commercial beds. A quick boat trip allows visitors to see how the oysters are suspended in water and the tour ends with a look at the finished product in the showroom. ■ *Half-day tours $59 including. 37 km transfer from Broome, or $25 if you self-drive to Willie Creek (4WD recommended). Full-day tour $120 including Pearl Luggers, brief town tour, lunch at Old Zoo Café, and Willie Creek. T9193 6000, www.williecreekpearls.com.au* On the edge of Roebuck Bay, the **Broome Bird Observatory** is one of the best places in Australia to see migratory shorebirds and it is also a peaceful place to stay. Regular half-day tours may include seeing the migrations, or exploring the mangroves or bush ($60 from Broome, self-drive $35). Accommodation includes self-contained chalets (**C**), double, single and bunk rooms (**D-E**) and bush campsites (both powered and unpowered). The observatory is 25 km from Broome, on the highway opposite the Cape Leveque turn-off. ■ *T9193 5600, bbo@tpgi.com.au Return transfers from Broome for overnight guests $30 per person. Bookings essential for tours and accommodation.*

Kimberley

Sleeping
1 Beverley Springs Homestead
2 Drysdale River Station
3 El Questro
4 Ellenbrae Station
5 Emma Gorge
6 Lake Argyle Tourist Village
7 Mount Elizabeth Station
8 Mount Hart Wilderness Lodge
9 Willare Bridge Roadhouse

Forming a large triangle north of Broome, the Dampier Peninsula is a huge area and home to several **Aboriginal communities**. Access is limited but some communities offer tours and accommodation (book ahead). The land is entirely covered in long grass and spindly trees but the coastline continues Broome's spectacular blend of red cliffs, white beaches and chalky blue sea. Just one dirt road traverses the entire peninsula from Broome to its tip at Cape Leveque (220 km) and it's a shocker. Ruts, sand, rocks and pools of water make this a road for high-clearance 4WD vehicles only. Following the Cape Leveque Road for about an hour, the first main stop is the **Beagle Bay** community, notable for its church with altar, walls and floor lined with pearl shell. ■ *Call into the office when entering the community. $5 entry fee. Fuel is sometimes available, but there's no accommodation. T9192 4913.* After leaving Beagle Bay, it is 28 km to the **Middle Lagoon** turn-off (then 33 km along the turn-off). Accommodation is available in beach shelters (**D**), self-contained cabins (**A-B**) or campsites. ■ *T/F9192 4002. No fuel or supplies except ice and drinks. Day visitors $8 car.*

Continuing north for about 50 km, you'll reach the picturesque and friendly Aboriginal community of **Lombadina**, a former mission settlement. The local Bard people, many of whom are still Catholics, offer the best range of accommodation and tours, including fishing and whale watching charters (from $275 per person per day), mud crabbing and bush walking ($33-66 half day), and four-wheel driving ($99 day). Accommodation in 4-bed backpacker dorms (**D**) and self-contained units (**B**). ■ *T9192 4936, www.ibizwa.com/lombadina Day visitors $5 car, payable at office or craft shop. Drop-offs/pickups can be arranged with Over the Top tours.*

Cape Leveque lies at the end of the road, capped by red cliffs, rocky coves and white beaches. *Kooljaman*, T9192 4970, www.kooljaman.com.au, is a popular resort at the cape, owned by the Djarindjin and One Arm Point communities but usually run by non-Aboriginal managers. Accommodation is in beach shelters (**D**), units (**C**), open paperbark cabins (**B**) and safari tents (**A**). Facilities include a kiosk, restaurant, scenic flights and boat tours but most people just come to swim, walk and fish. On the eastern side of the peninsula is the **Mudnunn** community, T9192 4121, who allow camping and sometimes run mud-crabbing tours in the mangroves for $55. The route east across the foot of the Dampier Peninsula to Derby passes through a flat country of grass and woodland. The main stop is the **D** *Willare Bridge* roadhouse, T9191 4775. ■ *Daily 0600-2200, with donga rooms, campsites and BBQ.*

Dampier Peninsula
See Broome for details of tours

Western Australia

Just short of the bridge over the Fitzroy River, are some picnic sites. After 15 km the road divides, heading east to Fitzroy Crossing (220 km) or north to Derby (42 km).

Derby
Colour map 5, grid A2
Population: 3,200
220 km from Broome,
260 km from
Fitzroy Crossing

Derby sits on a narrow spur of land surrounded by tidal mud flats, close to where the mighty Fitzroy River flows into King Sound. The entrance to the sound is a maze of a thousand islands, the **Buccaneer Archipelago**, a spectacular area to explore by boat or plane. The town was one of the earliest in the Kimberley, established in 1883 as a port for wool and pearl shell exports, but now used to ship zinc and lead from mines near Fitzroy Crossing. The unusual D-shaped jetty has been constructed to cope with one of the highest tides in the world (11.8 m). Although the town has only a few attractions for visitors, its position at the start of the Gibb River Road and close to the spectacular Kimberley coast means that tours and cruises from Derby are very good value. On the way into Derby stop and have a look at the impressive 1,500-year-old **Boab Prison Tree**, thought to have held Aboriginal prisoners captured by pearling 'blackbirders'. Derby also has a large supermarket, camping store, car rental agencies, *ANZ* ATM and fuel. The efficient **VIC** is on Clarendon Street. ■ *0830-1630 Mon-Fri, Sat-Sun 0900-1200 (longer weekend hrs Jun-Aug). T9191 1426, www.derbytourism.com*

Sleeping and eating B *Kimberley Cottages*, Windjana Rd, T9191 1114. Self-contained chalets with 2 or 3 bedrooms, about 10 mins from town. **B-C** *King Sound Resort*, Loch St, T9193 1044. Derby's best hotel, facilities include 82 a/c rooms, a good bistro, bar and pool. **C-D** *Spinifex*, Clarendon St, T9191 1233. The town's only pub has very basic, scruffy budget rooms and adequate but tired 'deluxe' rooms. The pub also does counter meals daily and has a smarter café next door. **C-D** *West Kimberley Lodge*, Sutherland St, T9191 1031. Excellent budget accommodation with spotless a/c rooms (some en suite), kitchen, pool, BBQ and shady garden areas. There is also one caravan park, *Kimberley Entrance* on Rowan St, T9193 1055 (sites only). Eating is limited to the resort, pub or the excellent *Wharf* on the jetty, T9191 1195, serving fresh fish, seafood and grilled chicken (BYO). Open Tue-Sun 1100-2100 (Jun-Aug) Wed-Sat 1800-2100 (Sep-May), take-aways Tue-Sun 1100-2100. Take-aways are also available from *Derby Take-aways*, next to the VIC, daily 1100-1400, 1700-2300. *Tides Café*, over the road.

Tours and activities 4WD *West Kimberley Tours*, T9193 1442, www.westkimberleytours.com.au run the Kimberley's best value day tour on the Gibb River Rd. Only $90 for Windjana Gorge and Tunnel Creek, tours run all year round. A 2-day tour includes Bell Gorge. *Bushtrack Safaris*, T9191 1547. Off-the-beaten track tours into the west Kimberley, including Walcott Inlet and Mitchell Falls, with knowledgeable guides of pioneering stock. Some options include air and sea travel, from 4 to 14 days. **Boat cruises** *Buccaneer Sea Safaris*, T9191 1991, www.buccaneersafaris.com Experienced operators offer coastal cruises to the Buccaneer Archipelago, Walcott Inlet, and Prince Regent River from 3 to 14 days, some combined with a flight to Cockatoo Island. *Unreel*, T9193 1999, www.unreeladventures.com specialize in sportfishing trips but sometimes offer 3-day trips around the archipelago for about $300 per day all inclusive. **Scenic flights** Two operators offer flights over the Kimberley. *Golden Eagle Airlines*, T9191 1132, www.goldeneagleairlines.com, and *King Leopold Air*, T9193 7155, www.kingleopoldair.com.au Both offer flights over Buccaneer Archipelago, Horizontal Waterfall, Cockatoo Island and Cape Leveque. From $180 for 1hr 45 mins over the archipelago. **Swimming** 25-m public pool, corner of Johnston St and Clarendon St. Open 0600-1730, Sat-Sun 1000-1730.

Western Australia

Kimberley Coast

The Kimberley coast, from King Sound near Derby to the Cambridge Gulf of Wyndham, is an extraordinarily ragged coastline with countless bays, inlets, and many thousand of islands just offshore. Very little of it is accessible by land, partly because it is private Aboriginal-owned land but also because the terrain is just so remote and rugged that there are simply no roads into the coastal regions. However, the jaw-dropping beauty of the pristine Kimberley coast can be seen by boat or on a scenic flight. The highlights include the **Buccaneer Archipelago,** *also known as the 'thousand islands', containing the unusual* **Horizontal Waterfall** *at Talbot Bay. An Inlet within the bay has a very narrow opening and when the tide drops it falls faster than the water can escape from the inlet, creating waves and whirlpools that churn like a waterfall.* **King Cascades** *is a charming stepped waterfall at the end of a narrow channel within the* **Prince Regent Nature Reserve** *and right up on the northern coastline,* **King George Falls** *is an*

appropriately majestic twin cascade of water dropping over 100-m cliffs. The boat cruises are aimed firmly at the luxury market (from $7,000 per person) with the kind of boats that have comfortable bedrooms, three levels and a helipad on deck. Cruises usually takes about two weeks from Broome to Wyndham or vice versa and include fishing, swimming, sightseeing and the chance to get on shore and see Bradshaw and Wandjina rock art. See Broome for more details. Scenic flights over the Buccaneer Archipelago operate from Broome and Derby but Derby flights are cheaper because the town is much closer. There are also slightly shorter and cheaper cruise options from Derby. The other way to experience this coastline is to stay in a remote safari camp; incredible spots but also very expensive (from $500 per day). For more information contact **Kimberley Coastal Camp,** *T0417 902 006, www.kimberleycoastalcamp.com.au and* **Faraway Bay,** *T9169 1214, www.farawaybay.com.au*

Transport Air *Northwest Regional Airlines* have flights to **Exmouth** via **Port Hedland** and **Karratha** every Mon and Fri, to Port Hedland and Karratha every Wed and Karratha only on Sun. They fly to **Fitzroy Crossing** and **Halls Creek** every Mon-Sat. **Bus** *McCafferty's/Greyhound* daily eastbound services to **Fitzroy Crossing** (3 hrs), **Halls Creek** (7 hrs), and **Kununurra** (12 hrs) leave the VIC daily at 2145. The Perth-bound bus via **Broome** (2½ hrs) departs 0500.

The Gibb River Road

This legendary road is both an experience and a challenge; 660 km of unsealed gravel and dirt created in the 1960s as a way for the cattle stations of this region to get their stock to Derby and Wyndham ports. Although now used more frequently by travellers, the alarming sight of a huge cattle road train barrelling along in clouds of dust is still common. The Gibb River Road leads from Derby and Kununurra and passes through remote range country and grass plains, threaded with creeks, gorges and waterfalls. It also provides access to the northern Kimberley along the even more rugged Kalumburu Road, including the **Mitchell Plateau** with its spectacular series of waterfalls, and countless mysterious **Aboriginal rock art** sites. Part of the Gibb River Road experience is also staying at the cattle stations along the way, meeting their owners and perhaps taking a tour or scenic flight to explore privately owned landscapes seen by few. There are also good campsites close to several beautiful gorges, where you can go for a walk or swim.

4WD is recommended – allow at least 4 days to cross. Enquire at either the Derby or Kununurra VICs before tackling this route. There are plenty of operators offering adventure tours for about $150 a day (see Broome, Derby and Kununurra for options)

Western Australia

Ins & outs

Road conditions vary along the route, during the season and from year to year so it is essential to check current conditions before setting out (Main Roads WA, T1800 013 314). www.exploroz.com has some good tips and travellers' comments

Generally the road is only passable in the dry season (May-Nov) and the eastern section from the Kalumburu Rd junction to the Pentecost River is much rougher and more corrugated than the western section. Although you can sometimes travel the road in a 2WD, the road is very rough and stony, there are many creek crossings, and many of the stations and gorges off the road are found at the end of even rougher tracks. Finally, the Pentecost River crossing is long and hazardous, and unless the river is dry or extremely low, 2WD vehicles will not have the clearance to cross it. Despite the increasing numbers of Australian travellers on the road looking for adventure, it is still a remote, wilderness route. Vehicles need to be in excellent condition and you'll need to carry extra fuel, water and spare wheels. For more information see the *Gibb River and Kalumburu Roads Travellers Guide* ($3), produced every year by the Derby Tourist Bureau. Available from Derby, Broome and Kununurra VICs, it can also be ordered by phone. If the worst happens, for road rescue from Kununurra call T9169 1556, from Derby T9193 1205.

Derby to Windjana Gorge

Windjana Gorge 145 km from Derby, 145 km from Fitzroy Crossing

The western half of the Gibb River Road (GRR) is both the easiest and the most interesting. The road starts 6 km south of Derby and is sealed for 62 km. The next 57 km to the Windjana Gorge turn-off is a wide gravel road, usually fairly smooth and fine for 2WD. The striking **Windjana Gorge National Park** is on Leopold Downs Road, 20 km south of the GRR turn-off. Dark-grey fluted stone forms impressive cliffs above the plains, broken by a narrow gap where the Lennard River has carved a gorge into the range. The broad sandy river banks are lined with trees and provide a basking spot for a large population of freshwater crocodiles. Swimming is not recommended. You can follow a sandy path up to the end of the gorge (3½ km one way) although the most pleasant area is close to the entrance, by Bandingan Rock, the large white rock in the river that the *Bunaba* linked with the spirits of babies. There is a campsite nearby with fine views of the cliff face, as well as showers (cold) and toilets. **Tunnel Creek National Park**, where the creek has carved a 750-m tunnel through the Napier Range, is 35 km further south on the same road. Check on the water level in the tunnel. During the dry season it varies between waist and knee high but it's good fun on a hot day to take a torch and wade through the cold pools in the tunnel to the far end. The rocks are sharp though so wear sandals. There is a break in the middle so the dark sections are short, look out for bats and rock art. The unsealed Leopold Downs Road that links these parks is usually fine for 2WD in the dry season but there are a couple of creek crossings that can be troublesome so check road conditions with the Derby VIC. Do not attempt to walk Tunnel Creek in the wet season as it can flood suddenly. ■ *Windjana Gorge camping $9 per person. For more information contact CALM Broome, T9192 1036.*

Windjana Gorge to the Kalumburu Road

Mount Barnett Homestead 200 km from Windjana Gorge, 110 km from Kalumburu Rd

Shortly after the Windjana turn-off the Gibb River Road road passes through the narrow Yammera Gap in the Napier Range. Continuing east through open grassland the road slowly ascends into the red-sandstone King Leopold Ranges, named after the Belgian king. Within these ranges, *Mount Hart Wilderness Lodge*, T9191 4645, www.mthart.com.au, offers comfortable homestead accommodation ($150 per person for dinner, B&B), canoeing and bushwalking. Deep and narrow **Lennard Gorge**, 7 km east then reached by a rough 8-km access road (4WD only for the last few kilometres), has waterfalls and rock pools to swim in. Another 23 km east is the turn-off for **Bell Gorge**, which many consider the most beautiful on the road. It is 29 km down a rocky road with a few creek crossings. There are lovely secluded campsites by Bell Creek but only ten of them; otherwise camp at Silent Grove (19 km from GRR) which has the advantage of showers (cold). Pick up a tag at Silent Grove for Bell Creek sites. Camping is $9 per person. A 15-minute walk leads from the gorge car park down to the wide picturesque waterfall and swimming pool below. To get to the lower pool cross the rock bar and head uphill for 50 m before dropping down to the left. Take care as the route is not well marked and is steep and slippery. Back on the main road it is only 7 km to *Imintji Store*, T9191 7471. The shop has a good range of groceries, diesel and a mechanical workshop (T9191 7887).

Leaving the ranges behind, you shortly pass the turn-off for *Old Mornington Bush Camp*, T9191 7406, oldmornington@bigpond.com This private wildlife sanctuary is owned by the Australian Wildlife Conservancy Consortium, and although 100 km off the GRR, is well worth a visit for its stunning river and gorge scenery, canoeing and wildlife tours. There are safari tents, camping ($10), meals, a bar and canoe hire. On the northern side of the GRR is *Beverley Springs Homestead*, T9191 4646, a working cattle station with more beautiful gorges, swimming spots and rock-art sites. Accommodation is in charming circular huts, homestead rooms (both $126 per person dinner, B&B), and camping ($10). **Galvans Gorge** is 35 km after the homestead turn-off. Although not signposted at the time of writing, look for a camera sign and a closed gate on the northern side of the road. Park by the gate and it's an easy 10-minute walk to an idyllic swimming hole under a small waterfall.

The next stop, 20 km east, is an essential one. *Mount Barnett Roadhouse*, T9197 7007, sells the only fuel between here and *El Questro* (324 km east). There are also plenty of groceries, showers, a phone and camping permits to nearby **Manning Gorge** for sale ($10). An hour's walk from this campsite gets you to a wide rock platform over the river and impressive falls. **Barnett River Gorge** is 22 km east of the roadhouse and provides more swimming within a shorter walk (5-20 minutes) but note that the 5 km access road is very rough. A further 10 km past the gorge turn-off, *Mount Elizabeth Station*, T9191 4644, is an interesting place to stay. A working cattle station with homestead ($130 dinner, B&B) and camping ($11) accommodation, they also offer tours of Bradshaw and Wandjina rock-art sites with an Aboriginal guide and scenic flights. Tours and flights subject to station activities – book in advance. The junction of the Gibb River Road and Kalumburu Road is another 68 km to the east.

This road runs north from the Gibb River Road to the coastline and traverses some of the most wild, remote and unpopulated country in Australia. It's a rough, narrow and winding track only accessible to well-equipped 4WD vehicles and closed during the wet season. The **C** *Drysdale River Station*, T9161 4326, www.drysdaleriver.com.au, is reached 59 km after the Gibb River Road junction. This welcoming place has a restaurant, bar, rooms and campsites. It also has fuel, groceries, phone, tyre repairs and runs scenic plane flights over Mitchell Falls and Prince Regent Nature Reserve (from $200, 2 hrs). The turn-off for the **Mitchell Plateau** and the newly created **Mitchell River National Park** is another 103 km north. CALM manage the park with the Wunambal traditional owners. It contains stands of palms, patches of rainforest, rare animals and rock art but the main attraction is the stunning **Mitchell Falls** which can be reached by a difficult 6 km return walk or a scenic flight. Helicopters are stationed by the Punamii-unpuu campground in the dry season. For most people this area is best visited on a tour (see pages 626 and 630). Continuing north on Kalumburu Road it is another 105 km to the Aboriginal community of **Kalumburu**. **D** *Kalumburu Mission*, T9161 4333, offers motel rooms, campsites, a café, general store and fuel (Monday-Friday 0715-1115, 1330-1600 only). A vehicle permit ($25) should be obtained by post from *Kalumburu Aboriginal Corporation* (PMB 10 via Wyndham, WA 6740) or on arrival from the office (Monday-Friday 0800-1200, 1400-1600).

The Kalumburu Road & Mitchell Plateau
Kalumburu 267 km from Gibb River Rd, Mitchell Falls 245 km from Gibb River Rd

Western Australia

Drysdale River National Park lies to the southeast of the community. This is a huge conservation area with no facilities, no marked trails and no roads. The park contains one of the Kimberley's richest concentrations of Bradshaw rock-art sites, gorges, waterfalls and rare flora and fauna. Visitors must register with CALM. *Willis's Walkabouts*, T8985 2134, www.bushwalkingholidays.com.au offer walking trips into this park. The large area to the south of the Mitchell Plateau called **Prince Regent Nature Reserve** is another stunning area of rocky country, falls and gorges but entry is by permit only. There are no roads so the reserve can only be accessed by sea, usually on one of the coastal cruise boats. ■ *For more information on these areas contact CALM Kununurra T9161 4405, www.naturebase.com.au*

Kalumburu Road to the Pentecost River
Pentecost River 185 km from Kalumburu Rd, 55 km from Great Northern Highway

From this point only 240 km of the Gibb River Road remains but if any stretch of road is likely to test your patience, tyres, axles (and the amalgalm in your fillings) it will be this very corrugated one. There are no places to stop or to camp except for the station stays and the scenery is less interesting until you reach the imposing bluffs of the **Cockburn Range** on the far side of the Pentecost. *Ellenbrae Station*, nearly halfway, T9161 4325, has some charming open-plan accommodation with a few quirky touches like an outdoor bath-tub ($99 dinner, B&B) is only 5 km off the main road and also offers camping ($10). Recommended. There are a few 'jump-ups' or steep hills in the next 40-50 km: make sure you keep well to the left on these hills as you can't see what is hurtling in the opposite direction. The last stop before crossing the Pentecost (9 km further east) is *Home Valley Station*, T9161 4322, with camp-sites and hot showers. Note that the Pentecost riverbed crossing can be waist-deep in water at the beginning of the season, so seek advice before attempting it. There are also plenty of salties in this river so walking across it to check the depth is not recommended!

El Questro & Emma Gorge
El Questro 40 km from Pentecost River, 100 km from Kununurra

Park and resorts open Apr-Oct

After crossing the Pentecost River, it is 25 km to the **El Questro Wilderness Park** turn-off, and a further 16 km (4WD recommended) south to *El Questro Station*, T9161 4318, (bookings 9169 1777), www.elquestro.com.au El Questro, a million-acre cattle property owned by the English Burrell family but managed by the *Accor Asia Pacific* hotel group, is a friendly, down-to-earth place run as a wilderness park (effectively a private national park complete with rangers). Deep-red gorges, natural springs, major rivers, Aboriginal rock art and loads of wildlife are all part of the El Questro experience. There are three levels of accommodation at the station: camping (either at private riverside spots or the main campground; no powered sites), stylish tropical bungalows overlooking the Pentecost River (**A**), or the incredible world-class Homestead (from $725 per person including meals, bar and activities). The station has a small shop, a steakhouse restaurant, outdoor bar and offers lots of tours and activities including helicopter flights and horse-riding. Of many beautiful walks (details on trail notes at the store) one of the most exciting is the **El Questro Gorge Walk** (four hours, 7 km return), up a narrow gorge with towering sheer walls, rock pools and lots of boulder hopping. The **Chamberlain Gorge** cruise is one of the most popular activities (daily at 1400, $40), involving a short cruise to look at Wandjina and Bradshaw rock art. You need at least two days at El Questro to have a reasonable look around but you could easily spend several more. Note that some sights are only accessible to 4WD vehicles. All visitors must buy a Wilderness Pass Permit ($12.50), valid for a week.

The last stop on the Gibb River Road, 10 km from the El Questro turn-off, is *Emma Gorge*, also part of El Questro. This small, appealing resort at the base of the Cockburn Range has 45 permanent tented cabins (**A-B**) scattered among palms trees and pandanus. The **Emma Gorge Trail** (1½ hours, 3 km return) is a fine walk between the 120-m, vividly orange gorge walls, along the creek bed to a pretty droplet waterfall and plunge pool. Getting to the waterfall requires a lot of clambering over rocks and boulders, ask resort staff if you are not sure whether to tackle it. There is also a more challenging guided walk, **Emma Dreaming**, up to the top of Cockburn Range that includes Bradshaw rock-art sites, swimming and fabulous views (10 hours, $150). The main reception building has a very good restaurant on an outdoor deck (daily 1200-1400, 1830-2030). Only 85 km from Kununurra (25 km on gravel), Emma Gorge can also make a very pleasant 2WD day trip. Day visitors need to buy a $5.50 Gorge Walk Pass. The Wilderness Pass Permit includes Emma Gorge. See Kununurra for details of a day tour to Emma Gorge and El Questro.

The Great Northern Highway

The Gibb River Road is one of Australia's great Outback drives but if time or resources compel you to take the sealed highway route this is not necessarily second-best option. The stretch between Halls Creek and Kununurra is one of the most scenic of any major highway in the country, and it also gives you a chance to see the magnificent **Purnululu National Park** (the **Bungle Bungles**).The 260-km stretch from Derby to Fitzroy Crossing holds very little of interest and there are no services until Fitzroy Crossing. If conditions allow, consider taking the **Gibb River Road** for 120 km (62 km sealed) to the Windjana Gorge turn-off. The Leopold Downs Road passes **Windjana Gorge** and **Tunnel Creek** (see page 632) before rejoining the Northern Highway just 42 km west of Fitzroy Crossing. There a couple of creek crossings, but it is usually okay for 2WD during the dry season.

On the banks of one of the Kimberley's greatest rivers, the small town of Fitzroy provides services and supplies for the mining and pastoral industries and more than 30 Aboriginal communities in the area. The main appeal for visitors is the beautiful **Geikie Gorge**, the only gorge in the Kimberley that can be reached by sealed road. There's an excellent **VIC**, just off the highway. ■ *Daily 0900-1700 (Apr-Sep), Mon-Fri 0900-1700, Sat 0900-1300 (Oct-Mar). T9191 5355, fitzroytb@bigpond.com* **A-B** *Fitzroy River Lodge*, Great Northern Highway, T9191 5141, just east of the town centre, is a quiet, pleasant place to stay with smart but very expensive rooms, overpriced safari tents and good shaded grassy camping and powered sites (no camp kitchen). Other facilities include a restaurant (expensive), counter meals available 1200-2000, a bar and swimming pool. **C** *Crossing Inn*, T9191 5080, has nine contemporary air-conditioned units with kitchenette and pleasant views over the river. Meals for house guests only. The raucous bar is half owned by local Aboriginal people and profits are used to help find solutions to alcohol abuse. There is a small supermarket and both roadhouses do take aways. *McCafferty's/Greyhound* daily east-bound services to Halls Creek (3½ hours), Warmun (6½ hours) and Kununurra (nine hours) leave the VIC daily at 0100 and *Fitzroy Lodge* at 0102. The Perth-bound bus via Derby and Broome (six hours) departs the VIC at 0145, the lodge at 0130.

Geike Gorge National Park is 20 km from Fitzroy Crossing. The 30-m cliffs of the gorge are studded with fossils and caves, and regular annual flooding scours the lower walls creating a striking line of clean white limestone below orange and grey rock. The gorge is best seen on a **boat cruise**, on which you can also see freshwater crocodiles and lots of birdlife. CALM run a

Western Australia

Fitzroy Crossing & around
Colour map 5, grid A2
Population: 1,150
395 km from Broome,
290 km from
Halls Creek
Fuel gets progressively
more expensive
at Halls Creek
and Warmun

one-hour cruise that examines geological and natural features in boats that can take up to 180 people. *Darngku Heritage Cruises*, T9191 5552, offer a more intimate look at the gorge from the perspective of the traditional owners, the Bunaba people. Their tours include **walks**, bush tucker, demonstrations of fire-lighting or spear making and other aspects of Aboriginal culture. There are also a couple of short walks along the riverbed. The river walk leads from the gazebo to the sandbar and you may see basking crocodiles and birds (20 minutes return). The Reef Walk (3 km, one hour return) heads upstream along the base of the rocks (where fossils can be seen) until you reach the dramatic West Wall. Follow the river bank back for good views of the East Wall. ■ *Park open 0630-1830 (Apr-Nov). No fees, no camping. Toilets, BBQs. Tour tickets and information at Gazebo. CALM cruise 0800, 1500 (Apr-May, Sep-Oct) 0800, 0930, 1100, 1500 (Jun-Aug) $20, no bookings necessary. Darngku tours 0815-1330 and 1400-1700 (Apr-Dec). $50, 3 hrs or $110, 5 hrs (includes lunch). Bookings at VIC. 5-hr tour must be booked in advance.*

Halls Creek & around
Colour map 5, grid A2
Population: 1,800
545 km from Derby,
165 km from Warmun

A far better stop on the highway than Fitzroy, Halls Creek has a good range of facilities (though no ATM), an **Aboriginal Arts Centre** and, buried in the caravan park, *Arteon* jewellers, T9168 6447, who make organic-looking pieces from local gold, diamonds and pearls. The **VIC** is on the main highway in the centre of town. ■ *0830-1630, daily from May-Oct, otherwise Mon-Fri. Internet access $2 for 20 mins. T9168 6262, visitors@hcshire.wa.gov.au* There are a few tour possibilities from Halls Creek. *Oasis Air*, T9168 6462, organize on-demand scenic flights over the **Bungle Bungles** (80 minutes, $250 each for two people, $170 each for three) and the Wolfe Creek Meteor Crater (70 minutes, $220 each for two, $145 for three). Some 16 km west of Halls Creek is the junction to the unsealed **Tanami Track**, which leads to the **Wolfe Creek Meteor Crater**, the second-largest of its kind in the world at over 900 m across. About 300,000 years old, it's also one of the best preserved on the planet. As a diversion off the main highway it's a big effort, and you should consider flying over it instead, but the side-trip off the Tanami involves only about 40 km of rough driving. The Tanami continues on its way to *Alice Springs*, frequently accessible by 2WD, though you should check first with the police at Halls Creek (T9168 6000), or Main Roads WA (T1800 013314). The road's chief difficulty is the scarcity of roadhouses – be prepared to go 700 km without a fill-up.

Hall Creek's 3 options supply a surprisingly wide choice of accommodation

Sleeping and eating The **A-E** *Kimberley Hotel*, Roberta St, T9168 6101, kimberleyhotel@bigpond.com, has both standard and large motel-style rooms, plus a couple of en suite, a/c 4-bunk backpacker rooms. The courtyard pool, cocktail bar and restaurant area is the most attractive between Broome and Kununurra, mid-range meals are available 0700-0830 and 1800-2030, and there is also a guest BBQ area. **C-D** *Halls Creek Motel*, main highway, T9168 0001, hallscreekmotel@westnet.com.au, has similar rooms to the Kimberley standard at a very similar price. Their budget rooms are well equipped and available as twins or good value singles. Pool, guest kitchen and mid-range restaurant, open 1830-2030. The **caravan park**, T9168 6169, has reasonably priced on-site vans and cabins. *Chok's* is a small café and take-away within the VIC, open 0700-1900 Mon-Fri, 0900-1400 and 1700-1900 Sat, and 0900-1400 Sun. Most of the town's many fuel stops also do take-aways.

Transport *McCafferty's/Greyhound* daily eastbound services to **Warmun** (2 hrs) and **Kununurra** (5 hrs) leave the Poincianna roadhouse daily at 0440. The Perth-bound bus via **Derby** and **Broome** (9½ hrs) departs at 2210.

Purnululu National Park (the Bungle Bungles)

The magnificent landscape of **Purnululu National Park**, most commonly just called the **Bungles**, is still little known and it is not easy or cheap to visit but utterly unforgettable if you do. The most striking feature of this park are the sandstone 'beehive' domes of the Bungle Bungle range, found in the southern area of the park, and part of a landscape formed 360 million years ago. The domes are striped with orange and grey bands that are astonishingly regular across the whole formation. The Piccaninny Creek bed winds through this surreal landscape of rippled rock, unlike any other in Australia. The western part of the range is a long, imposing wall of conglomerate rock up to 200 m high, eroded into deep, narrow chasms full of palm trees. Aboriginal people have lived here for at least 20,000 years and it contains many significant cultural and archaeological sites closed to the public. Until the 1980s the Bungles were known only to the Aboriginal owners and a few cattle drovers. Then in 1983 a German documentary crew filmed aerial footage of the park and when these images of the Bungles were screened in Australia the television station was deluged with callers wanting to know where this incredible place was. In 1986, the first visitors were allowed into the area and 1,800 people drove into the Bungles on a track so rough that it took 12 hours to travel the 50 km. The same track now takes around three hours but it is still a rough 4WD-only road that keeps the numbers of visitors low. In 2001 about 25,000 people visited the park but over 200,000 took scenic flights over it.

Around the time of the declaration of the national park in 1987 the government intended that the park be jointly managed by CALM and traditional owners. However management terms have still not been agreed and the process complicated by dispute between the Jaru and Kija people, both claiming ownership of certain areas of the park. Negotiations and court cases are continuing. In the meantime, the park was nominated for World Heritage Listing in 2002 and this will also influence its future development. There is a **visitor centre** close to the park entrance where you can pick up information, pay park and camping fees. ■ *Park open Apr-Dec only. Visitor centre open daily 0800-1200, 1300-1600. Public phone at visitor centre. Park fee $9 car, camping $9, children $2. For more information contact CALM Kununurra, T9168 4200.*

Colour map 5, grid A3
160 km from Halls Creek, 105 km from Warmun

It takes at least 4 hrs getting in and out of the park

Ins & outs
See also tours from Broome, Derby, Halls Creek, Warmun and Kununurra

Unless you have a sturdy 4WD and can drive yourself in you'll need to take a **tour**. As always, when choosing a tour, check the age group and activity level offered. Generally the more expensive the tour, the less physical activity will be included and you'll be paying for extra comforts and service. If you want to spend a few days in the park you'll need to take a dedicated Bungles tour from Kununurra or Halls Creek, other companies fit the Bungles in as a quick stop on a 5- to 10-day Broome-Darwin tour or Kimberley tour. Most tours allow time for a scenic helicopter flight, which leave from Bellburn airstrip within the park during Apr-Dec (30 minutes, $180). If self-driving book flights ahead on T9168 7335, or visit the airstrip office. *East Kimberley Tours*, T9168 2213, www.eastkimberleytours.com, offer a 1-day tour from Turkey Creek Roadhouse into Echidna Chasm, Cathedral Gorge and domes ($165, 0530-1900). 2-day option $375. *Bungle Bungle Adventures* offer 4WD trips from Kununurra (see page 642) but can pick up/drop off at Turkey Creek Roadhouse for the *McCafferty's/Greyhound* connection.

Exploring the Bungles

The main activity in the Bungles is walking and you do need to be fairly fit and agile to see what the park has to offer, although the beehive domes are easily seen within a short distance of the Piccaninny car park. Most trails involve walking on pebbles or over boulders so make sure you take sturdy footwear. At the northern end of the park, **Echidna Chasm Trail** (2 km return) leads up a creek bed into the high walls of the chasm, narrowing to just a few metres across. Look out for the unusual nest of the male bowerbird in this area, a ribcage of sticks with pebbles and bones at the entrance. **Froghole Trail** (1 km return) is a more open walk, past huge boulders of conglomerate and lush vegetation to a dry waterfall and semi-permanent pool. If you don't have time to do all of the walks, take the **Mini-Palms Trail** (5 km return) which offers elements of both Echidna and Froghole. This lovely walk follows a pebbly creek bed into an large oasis of palms surrounded by high domes. After climbing up past large boulders, the trail reaches a platform overlooking a narrow chasm. At the southern end of the park, the **Piccaninny Creek** area is surrounded by beehive domes. The main walk is **Cathedral Gorge Trail** (3 km return), heading between the domes into a an enormous bowl-shaped cavern and a shallow pool. The **Domes Trail** (1 km) is a loop off Cathedral Gorge Trail, just after the car park, providing more views of domes. The best walk, though, is simply to follow the dry bed of Piccaninny Creek until you have had enough and return, for this provides spectacular perspectives on the domes the whole way. If you take plenty of water, food and camera film this can easily occupy you for a whole day (14 km return to the 'elbow'). This route is also the start of the **Picaninny Gorge Trail** (30 km return) for experienced walkers. It's 7 km from the car park to the mouth of the gorge (the 'elbow'), then another 8 km along the gorge to the pools and side gorges, or 'fingers', at the end. Camping is allowed at the gorge but there are no facilities so you must carry in a fuel stove. To walk this trail, you must register and pay for your campsite ($5 per person) at the visitor centre. The main park **camping** areas, Kurrajong and Walardi, have toilets, water and firewood.

Warmun (Turkey Creek Roadhouse)

Colour map 5, grid A3
Population: 300
210 km from Wyndham, 200 km from Kununurra

Warmun is an Aboriginal community, just northwest of Purnululu National Park, which has an excellent art gallery, *Warmun Arts Centre*. The Warmun community artists produce bold, streamlined images using natural ochres and pigments in coarse form that gives their work a textured surface. Their distinctive paintings usually sell for several thousand dollars and attract much international interest. ■ *Mon-Fri 0900-1600 but may be closed for special viewings.* T9168 7496, www.warmunart.com *Visitors are asked to phone for an appointment.* Facilities for visitors are found at the B-E *Turkey Creek Roadhouse*, T9168 7882, 2 km north of the community, which has a small store, take-aways, motel rooms and dorms, open 0600-2000. Turkey Creek is also the base for scenic helicopter flights over the **Bungle Bungles** (45 minutes, $200), a good option as the helicopter heads over rows and rows of spectacular ranges and cattle-station country to reach the Bungles so you get more 'wow' for your dollar. *Slingair Heliwork*, T9168 7337, www.slingair.com.au, has an office by the roadhouse. On the way to Kununurra, after about 100 km, look out for a small 'scenic lookout' sign and turn-off. This leads after a short distance to a parking area with spectacular views over the **Ragged Range**.

Transport *McCafferty's/Greyhound* daily eastbound services to **Kununurra** (2½ hrs) leave the roadhouse daily at 0705. The Perth bus via **Derby** and **Broome** (11½ hrs) departs at 2000.

Wyndham & around

Colour map 5, grid A2
Population: 800
95 km from El Questro, 105 km from Kununurra

Sitting at the wide, flat confluence of five of WA's biggest rivers, rundown Wyndham is surrounded by some spectacular hill ranges and the most concentrated population of crocs in Australia. It is split into two centres – Wyndham Port and, 4 km inland, the main town which has most of the few facilities. A road east of the main town leads up Bastion Hill to **Five Rivers Lookout**, actually a series of lookouts all the way uphill, the best two being the first and last. The views from both are breathtaking, especially at sunrise and sunset. The excellent **Crocodile Park**, just beyond the port, has lively feeding tours daily around the extensive ponds, plus the added benefit of seeing their collection of Komodo dragons. The shop has a good range of leather goods and souvenirs. ■ *0830-1600 Apr-Nov, by appointment in the wet season. Tours 1100. $14, children $8, concessions $10. T9161 1124.* One of the few tour operators based in the town is Aboriginal-run *Ilpaya*, T/F9161 1990, who offer anything from a two-hour sunset trip around town ($25) to an in-depth look at everything the area has to offer ($210). Reached by a short road not far from the Wyndham turn-off is the **Grotto**, a deep and narrow chasm with a waterfall at one end (running in the wet season only) and a permanent waterhole at the bottom, reached via 150-odd steps. A good spot for a swim and a picnic. On the other side of the highway, closer to Wyndham, reached via 10 km of unsealed roads is the **Parrys Lagoon Nature Reserve**, a huge network of lily-covered pools on the wide flood plain that attracts dozens of species of resident and migratory birds. Boardwalks and hides make the most of a truly magical spot.

Sleeping and eating 6 km further down the rough track from Parrys Lagoon (see above) is peaceful **A-D** *Parry Creek Farm*, T9161 1139, an eco-retreat straddling a billabong with 3 over-priced self-contained cabins, 3 good value rooms, a friendly café, pool, camping grounds and camp kitchen. The kind of place you come for a night and stay for several. Café open to all, 0700-2000 (Apr-Oct). **C-D** *Wyndham Town Hotel*, Wyndham Port, T9161 1202, has standard and 'de-luxe' (read 'carpeted') rooms, all en suite and a/c. Public and lounge bars are neatly segregated and mid-range meals and cheap snacks are available in the latter 1200-1400 and 1800-2030. The **E** *Wyndham Caravan Park*, town centre, T9161 1401, has some good value a/c donga singles and doubles, and the owners also run a basic hostel-style guesthouse in the port, **B** *Gulf Breeze*, T9161 1401. Another option southwest of Wyndham for those with 4WD is **C-E** *Digger's Rest Station*, T9161 1029, www.diggers-rest.com A working cattle station with safari huts, homestead rooms, swag and camping options. Also horse riding (from 1 hr rides to 7-day treks).

Kununurra and around

Surrounded by range country and the bountiful waters of the Ord River, Kununurra has the most picturesque setting of any town in the Kimberley. Built in the 1960s as a service town for the Ord River Irrigation Scheme, the town has matured into a confident and growing community supported by agriculture, diamond mining and tourism. The river is dammed to the south of Kununurra, forming **Lake Argyle**, Australia's largest inland waterway, and holding back the wet-season water so the Ord can flow steadily all year around. The lake and river lie beneath the **Carr Boyd Ranges**, typically red-rugged, Kimberley sandstone, and are strikingly beautiful. A boat or canoe trip from Lake Argyle

Colour map 5 grid A3
Population: 5,000
910 from Derby,
510 km from Katherine (NT)

Western Australia

to Kununurra along the **Ord River**, through 55 km of ranges, gorges and lush greenery, is one of the WA's highlights and should not be missed. Comfortable accommodation, services and a wide range of tours make Kununurra an ideal base for exploring the East Kimberley. The friendly and very efficient **VIC** is on Coolibah Drive, the main loop road in the town centre. ■ *Jul-Aug: 0800-1700 daily. Sep-Jun: 0900-1600 Mon-Fri, plus (May-Jun and Sep) 0900-1200 Sat. T9168 1177, www.eastkimberley.com*

Sights On Kununurra's eastern border, the **Mirima National Park** is a delightful pocket of rich-red sandstone outcrops, with similarities to the Bungle Bungle range. If you have limited time this beautiful park (plus a cruise on the Ord River) will show you the best of Kununurra's scenery. There are two short walks in Hidden Valley, an oasis of beehive domes and ridges among boabs and ghost gums. There's a loop walk (400 m) from the car park focusing on native plants, and a lookout trail (800 m) off this loop which climbs up a ridge overlooking the valley and the town. ■ *Park entry fee $9 per car. No camping, no water. 2 km from town.* The lookout in the park is a fine place to watch sunset or sunrise, as is **Kelly's Knob**, the steep-sided hill just north of town. The lookout is at the end of Kelly Road, a short walk up from the car park. Kununurra's western border is formed by the **Diversion Dam**, a span of radial gates that hold back the Ord River and feed water to the irrigated plains around the town. About 16,000 hectares are under cultivation and the main produce is sugar cane and fruit crops such as melons, bananas, and mangoes. From the town, Ivanhoe and Weaber Plain Roads head north into the **farming** area and it is possible to visit melon and banana farms, and the wonderful *Hoochery*, T9168 2467, a cane distillery and barn bar selling a smooth Ord River Rum and a beautiful chocolate and coffee Cane Royal. ■ *Cakes and coffee, and free tours on the hour 1000-1500 (1000-1100 Sat). 0900-1600 Mon-Fri, 0900-1200 Sat.*

Below the Diversion Dam, the **Lower Ord** flows out to Cambridge Gulf, and despite damming and irrigation 80% of the Ord's flow still reaches the

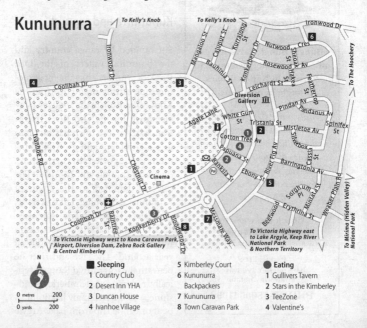

Kununurra

Sleeping
1 Country Club
2 Desert Inn YHA
3 Duncan House
4 Ivanhoe Village
5 Kimberley Court
6 Kununurra Backpackers
7 Kununurra
8 Town Caravan Park

Eating
1 Gullivers Tavern
2 Stars in the Kimberley
3 TeeZone
4 Valentine's

Western Australia

sea. Saltwater crocodiles are found in this lower part of the river as they can't get above the dam, to the waters called **Lake Kununurra**. This lake and its many lagoons are a lush series of waterways, full of birds, fish and freshwater crocodiles. Unusual striped rock found only on an island in Lake Argyle is polished and sold at the *Zebra Rock Gallery*, on the western bank of Lake Kununurra, opposite the 'sleeping buddha' hill. ■ *Daily 0800-1800. $1, children $0.50. Packsaddle Rd, 15 km from town. Zebra rock souvenirs are also available in town.* If you follow the river upstream from here for 55 km you'll reach **Lake Argyle** but by road the lake is 70 km south of town. To the south of the lake, **Argyle Diamond Mine** is the largest diamond producer in the world, producing about 30% of the global supply, and is known for its coloured diamonds. Pink, cognac and champagne Argyle diamonds can all be seen in Kununurra's jewellery shops. The vast open-cut mine, and extensive processing plant can only be visited on the in-depth and illuminating tours.

Sleeping

All accommodation, particularly the caravan parks, get very busy during Jun-Aug

The **A** *Country Club*, Coolibah Dr, T9168 1024, www.countryclubhotel.com.au, is the town's main upmarket option with large, comfortable but colourless rooms in palm-fringed garden blocks. Facilities include a large pool and good restaurants. **B** *Duncan House*, Coolibah Dr, T9168 2436, johnsonk@bigpond.com Modern B&B that provides high quality hotel-style rooms. Very comfortable and well-appointed. **B-E** *Kimberley Court*, River Fig Rd, T9168 1411, kcmotel@hotmail.com, manages to offer some good-value rooms, including a/c en suite doubles which are only as cheap as they are because you supply the linen and clean 'em up after. Swimming pool, cramped backpacker-style bunk dorms, and filthy but useable kitchen (no utensils), but do not expect a hostel atmosphere. **C** *Kununurra Hotel*, Messmate Way, T9168 1344, hotelknx@wn.com.au, has a/c and en suite rooms and offering good value for the level of quality. Both mid-range restaurant and counter meals are a cut above usual pub fare, available 1200-1400 and 1800-2100 daily. **D-F** *Desert Inn YHA*, Konkerberry Dr, T9169 1257, adventur@comswest.net.au, is a clean and colourful 50-bed hostel close to the town centre, with dorms, doubles and a pool. A/c (on timers) in some rooms. Cooks, however, will find the kitchen poorly equipped. The larger **D-E** *Kununurra Backpackers*, Nutwood Cres, T1800 641998 or 9169 1998, www.adventure.kimberley.net.au, is a longer walk to the shops, but closer to Hidden Valley and the Knob. The friendly, enthusiastic owners have created a water-garden based hostel with a good range of a/c rooms and facilities, including a pool. Their canoe and Bungles tours are second to none. Recommended. There are 5 **caravan parks** in and around town, all with shady sites and good facilities. **C** *Ivanhoe Village*, corner Coolibah Dr and Ivanhoe Rd, T9169 1995, big4kununurra@westnet.com.au, is considered the most luxurious with excellent cabin accommodation. **C** *Kona*, Lakeview Dr, T9168 1031, is one of 3 with water views and has sites, cabins and on-site vans, as does the **C** *Town Caravan Park*, Bloodwood Dr, T9168 1763, which is the closest to the town centre. At Lake Argyle accommodation is available at **C** *Lake Argyle Tourist Village*, T9168 7360, a caravan park and motel complex. Facilities include a swimming pool, and pub serving counter meals.

Eating

The expensive Chinese *Chopstick's* and *Kelly's* grill bar are both part of the *Country Club*. The latter has a large, pleasant alfresco area. Both serve meals daily 1800-2100. *Stars in the Kimberley*, Papuana St, T9168 1122. A smart, earthy BYO café, restaurant and deli. All-day breakfasts, snacks, coffee, excellent cakes and well-presented, fresh, mid-range meals available daily 0700-2130. Recommended, as is booking. The *TeeZone*, Konkerberry Dr, T9168 1837, is a licensed steak and pancake house with a mini-golf course out the back. *Gullivers Tavern*, Konkerberry Dr, T9168 1666, serve cheap counter meals from 1200-1330 Mon-Sat and 1830-2000 daily, including a good value Sunday roast. *Valentine's*, Cotton Tree Av, is a cheap BYO Mexican and pizza joint, open daily 1700-2100. Also take-away.

Western Australia

Tours & activities

Many operators combine tours, making interesting full-day options. Contact the VIC for what's possible. Own transport to the lake may be required for Lake Argyle cruises, otherwise generally $15 for transfers

Air *Alligator Airways*, T9168 1333, www.alligatorairways.com.au A range of scenic flights including Kimberley coast (from $420, 6 hrs) Lake Argyle and Bungle air/ground day trips (from $325). The Lake/Bungle/Mine flight is one of the most varied and good value trips the Kimberley has to offer. *Slingair/Heliwork*, T9169 1300, offer a similar range of flights. **Boat cruises** *Argyle Expeditions*, T9168 7040. Breakfast and sunset BBQ Lake Argyle cruises on their splendid 15-m motor cruiser, including swimming and wildlife spotting ($45, 3 hrs). Max 20 passengers. Also lake fishing ($95, 4 hrs) and magical overnight trips (min 6 people, from $900 per group). *Lake Argyle Cruises*, T9168 7361, take out a flat-bottomed launch to explain the dam construction and crocs, wallabies and birdlife. *Kununurra Cruises*, T9168 1718. Sunset BBQ cruise on Lake Kununurra. Great BBQ ($45, 2½ hrs). Also BBQ breakfast and bird-spotting cruises. *Ord Tours*, T9169 1165. Tours on the lower Ord beyond the Diversion Dam – the only cruise where you get to see saltwater crocs ($45, 2 hrs). Also full day and flight options. *Triple J*, T9168 2682. Outstanding trip down the Ord River in a zippy boat, stopping for wildlife and scenic features ($100, 5-6 hrs). **Canoeing** *Big Waters*, T1800 641998, www.adventure.kimberley.net.au Good value 3-day self-guided canoe safari from Lake Argyle to Kununurra along Ord River. Transport, equipment and permanent camps supplied, you supply food and muscle ($135). *Kimberley Canoeing*, T1800 805010, offer a similar trip but also a one-day option – canoe from Lake Argyle until 1400 pickup, then 32-km boat trip back to town ($105). **El Questro** Day tours to the Kimberley's well-known station resort include Chamberlain Gorge boat tour, Emma Gorge walk, Zebedee Springs, morning and afternoon tea. Departs 0700 most days (12 hrs, $145, children $72.50), T9169 1777. **4WD** *East Kimberley Tours*, T9168 2213, www.eastkimberleytours.com 'Fly-in-fly-out' Bungles trips, with gorge walks and accommodation in an established, serviced camp ($380 day, $690 2 days). *Bungle Bungle Adventures*, T1800 641998, www.adventure.kimberley.net.au, offer excellent Bungles trips by road. These tours are great value and show you more of the park than most other operators, particularly on the 3-day trip. Lots of walking, splendid food, swag camping and a well-informed guide. Recommended. Thu-Fri $290, Sun-Tue $430. Also pickups/drop off at Turkey Creek. *Kimberley Adventure Tours*, T9168 3368, www.kimberleyadventures.com.au, run serious adventure trips around the eastern and central Kimberley, such as a Mitchell Plateau hiking tour (5 days, $750). Also 7-day ($1,190) Gibb River Rd trips. *Kimberley Wilderness Adventures*, T9192 5741, www.kimberley wilderness.com.au, offer upmarket tours to see the Kimberley in comfort, with accommodation in homesteads or luxurious safari camps. Gibb River Rd, Kununurra to Broome (6 days, $1,995), Kimberley region (13 days, $3,000), Bungles fly-drive (2 days, $645). **Swimming** is considered safe in the upper Ord as freshies won't bite but most accommodation places have a pool. **Walking** *Willis's Walkabouts*, T8985 2135, www.bushwalkingholidays.com.au Based in Darwin, this well-established company offers many bushwalking tours in the Kimberley, including some 'light pack' options (from $115 day).

DO NOT swim in the Lower Ord, beyond Diversion Dam as saltwater crocs will bite and worse!

Transport

Air The airport is 5 km west of town, most accommodation providers offer pick-ups. Facilities include all the major car hire companies. *Air North* fly daily to **Broome** and **Darwin**. **Bus** *McCafferty's/Greyhound* daily eastbound services to **Katherine** (8 hrs) and **Darwin** (12 hrs) leave the BP roadhouse, Messmate Way, daily at 0945. The Perth bus via **Broome** (14 hrs) departs at 1745.The Great Northern Highway heads past the junction to Lake Argyle before crossing the border into the **Northern Territory** (44 km). Very shortly after this is the turn-off to **Keep River National Park**, one of NT's lesser-known parks but well worth the excursion (see page 686).

Directory

Banks *Commonwealth* with ATM on Coolibah Dr. **Car and equipment hire** *Kimberley Outback Hire*, Mango St, T9168 1657, have tough 4WDs from $105 per day; also a good range of camping gear. **Communications** Internet widely available. **Post Office**, Coolibah St. **Shopping** Boab, Coolibah St. For books and maps.

Northern Territory

The Northern Territory is a neat rectangle of land in the northern heart of Australia with a ragged coastline of mangroves, tidal flats, islands and sky-blue ocean. The state is evenly divided into two halves by climate and environment – each almost the opposite of the other. **The Centre** is classic Outback country and its stark beauty is considered as Australian as the beach. The desert sand is as paprika red and all of the ancient low hill ranges are weathered to a harmonious rust colour. Nothing breaks the horizon except spinifex, low scrub and the occasional lithe white trunk of a ghost gum. The northern part of the state, prosaically called the **Top End**, is a tropical region of wetlands, waterfalls and powerful rivers. It is a state of extraordinary landscapes, many protected within some of the country's finest national parks. In the Top End you can see some of the world's best rock art, cruise among waterlillies and crocodiles in **Kakadu National Park** or swim under the waterfalls and rock walls of **Litchfield** and **Nitmiluk** national parks. The Centre is the place to experience the space and silence of Australia while walking around majestic **Uluru** and **Kata Tjuta**, to feel small amid the immensity of the **Outback** or marvel at the night-time brilliance of the stars.

Things to do in the Northern Territory

1. As well as touring the gorges of the **West MacDonnell Ranges**, make a detour south to see Hermannsberg's **Cultural Precinct** and, if you have a 4WD, nearby **Palm Valley**.
2. While in **Alice Springs** explore the **Desert Park**, **Cultural Precinct** and **Telegraph Station**.
3. Spend a morning canoeing up **Katherine Gorge**, and the late afternoon walking to the top of **Crocodile Rock** to experience the sunset.
4. Take at least two days to see **Kakadu National Park**, making sure you see **Ubirr**, **Yellow Waters** and the **Twin Falls**.
5. Visit the **Territory Wildlife Park** for a morning, spending a leisurely lunchtime picnicking and swimming at **Berry Springs** next door.
6. Watch the sunrise at **Uluru**, take a morning walk with an Anangu guide, then walk around the rock until the sun sets.
7. While in Darwin make the effort to get out to see the **Museum and Art Gallery** and **Crocodylus**, finsihing the day with a harbour cruise.
8. Walk around the rim of **Kings Canyon**, strolling out later from the resort to watch the sun set on **Carmichael Crag**.

Above all, in a state where almost a third of the population is Aboriginal, it is a place to explore another way of thinking by meeting people who know their way around the deserts and wetlands as well as you know your way around a supermarket. Here you can not only admire the landscape but belong to it.

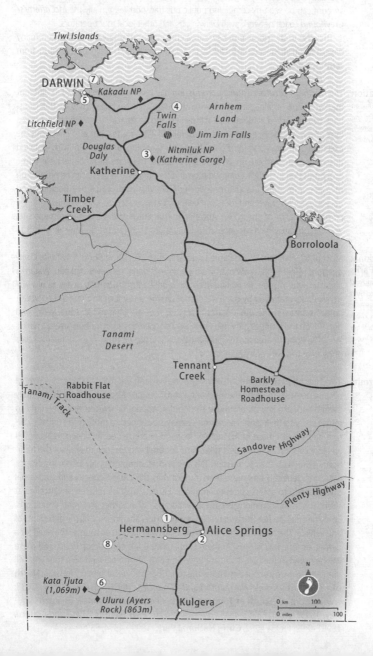

Northern Territory

Ins and outs

Getting around
If planning a trip or holiday to the Top End consider a detour to Kununurra (WA)

Air It is possible to get between the major centres by air, with *Air North*, T8920 4000, www.airnorth.com.au, shuttling between Darwin, Katherine, Tennant Creek and Alice Springs, and several smaller operators complementing these services. *Qantas*, T131313, www.qantas.com.au, also fly between Darwin and Alice Springs.

Bus The easiest way of getting around the NT is under your steam, but a surprising amount can be seen by combining public bus transport (essentially the *McCafferty's/ Greyhound* coach network) with Darwin bus and other local tour operators.

Bicycle In the popular dry season a constant northerly wind kicks in on many days, making life miserable for cyclists travelling south so try to plan your route from south to north.

Information
The state has an interpretation and translator service, T1800 676 254

The *Northern Territory Tourist Commission* has several websites aimed at different markets. The main site is www.ntholidays.com, while www.australiasout-back.com is aimed at independent travellers and backpackers. Drivers should take a look at www.ntexplore.com for brief details of 4WD routes, but also check out the excellent site www.exploroz.com guide to planning a 4WD trip with detailed descriptions and advice on 4WD Outback routes. The state produces excellent free brochures that include accommodation and tour prices and these can be ordered on the general info line, T133068, or collected from VICs when you arrive. Bookings and packages for NT travel and tours can be found at www.territorydiscoveries.com, the commercial arm of the NTTC. Another useful site is the state government site, www.nt.gov.au, which has general information on the Territory and an event listing.

National Parks
Both Kakadu and Uluru-Kata Tjuta have entrance charges, check whether these are included in any tours you book

Most of NT's National Parks come under the auspices of the *Parks & Wildlife Commission*, T8999 5511, www.nt.gov.au/ipe/paw 3 parks, however (Kakadu, Watarrka and Uluru-Kata Tjuta) are managed by the federal *Parks Australia*, www.ea.gov.au/parks Parks managed by the PWC do not charge entry fees so there are no visitor passes sold as in the other states. Camping fees are charged in some parks and depend on the facilities provided (from $4-7 per person). Information on each park is available from the websites and park notes can be picked up at VICs (for nearby parks only) or at the park entry points.

Permits
If you intend to travel through or visit Aboriginal land (off main highways) you must obtain permission from the relevant Land Council. Aboriginal land is privately owned and, like any other private landholder, Aboriginal owners have the right to refuse entry to their land. The permit system is designed to protect the privacy, culture and environment of Aboriginal people. Generally, you will need to allow 2-4 weeks to obtain a permit, as it takes time for the Land Council to contact the traditional owners for their permission. It is also important not to apply too far in advance (which is generally any more than a month) as the Land Councils and traditional owners need to assess current conditions. Permits may be refused or cancelled at short notice for ceremonial reasons or because of weather and road conditions. Some permits are free but others require a small fee, and apply to all the occupants of one vehicle. The main areas for which travellers are likely to encounter the need for a permit are the Tiwi Islands, Arnhem Land and the Mereenie Loop Road, and these will be noted in the text. If you are travelling into Aboriginal land on a tour you will not need to worry about permits as the tour operator will obtain permission. **North of Tennant Creek** *Northern Land Council*, T8920 5100, F8945 2633, www.nlc.org.au **South of Tennant Creek** *Central Land Council*, 33 Stuart Highway, T8951 6320, F8953 4343, www.clc.org.au **Tiwi Islands** *Tiwi Land Council*, T8981 4898, F8981 4282. **Gurig National Park** T8999 4814, F8999 4524

Maps NT, 1st floor, Nichols Pl, corner of Cavenagh St and Bennett St, T8999 7032, sells **Publications**
a good range of local, national and international maps from the government's Land **& maps**
Information Centre in Darwin. Topographic maps of the state are also available here.
Open Mon-Fri 0800-1600. There are also *Maps NT* offices in Alice Springs (21 Gregory
Terr, T8951 5316), Tennant Creek (Leichhardt St, T8962 4523) and Katherine
Randazzo Building, (16 Katherine Terr, T8973 8100) but their ranges of maps are
more limited. *Camping Guide to NT*, complied by Lewis and Savage of *Boiling Billy
Publications*, is a very useful rundown of sites and facilities. This is available from
bookshops and *AANT*, 79-81 Smith St, Darwin, who also sell NT maps.

History

Australia's northern lands were the last to fall under the greedy eye of the
British. A couple of attempts were made at establishing colonial settlements
on the north coast and islands between the 1820s and 1840s, but the climate,
disease and a failure to entice passing European trading vessels cut them
short. European settlement and development of the far north of the country
was finally initiated from two principal directions. In the 1850s pastoralists
in QLD and NSW began to take an interest in administering this neglected
region, but South Australia was the most persistent in its overtures to London. They petitioned for the region to be annexed as their 'Northern Territory' and received assent in 1863.

The South Australian government quickly decided to formally open up
the territory for settlement and for a while were very positive about their
northern acquisition, despite considerable setbacks and difficulties. In 1870
the state further cemented its interest by declaring itself the builder and
operator of a national Overland Telegraph link from north to south, beating
off stiff competition from Queensland. Charles Todd undertook the construction of the line from Adelaide to the fledgling northern town of
Palmerston (soon to be known as Darwin), and followed in the footsteps of
John McDouall Stuart who had pioneered the route on his third attempt at
crossing the continent a decade before. The optimism and supreme confidence of these early travellers in the Territory is revealed by Stuart's com-
ment upon planting the British flag on top of what was later to become
known as Central Mount Stuart in 1860; "may it be a sign to the natives that
the dawn of liberty, civilization, and Christianity is about to break upon
them." In building the telegraph line Todd opened up a well-surveyed track
into the territory for another wave of pastoralists and mineral prospectors,
and also unwittingly established a number of settlements on the way, one of
which he named after his wife, Alice.

Despite this initial optimisim, the Northern Territory proved a fiendishly
difficult land from which to make a living, let alone a profit. Soils were less
productive than expected, the 'wet' a serious impediment, extensive mineral wealth scarce or unprofitable, and simply the isolation a further economic millstone. In 1911 South Australia handed it over to the new
Commonwealth Government, their only major stipulation being the completion of the railway line from Alice Springs to Darwin. Unfortunately for
them they did not insist on a time frame and the line is only now being constructed for completion in 2004.

Northern Territory

▶▶ **Great places to stay in Northern Territory**

The borders of the Northern Territory were defined by default; the Territory was simply the space left when the other states had decided their own borders. In other words it was the bit of Australia that none of the founding states particularly wanted, and despite the brief vying for ownership in the early 1860s, South Australia's final rejection confirmed that status politically. There was even talk of handing the Territory back to the British. It took the Second World War to finally bring prominence and importance to this part of Australia, when it became the effective base for much of Australia's and the USA's Pacific war effort. Darwin suffered an air raid on the 19th of February 1942 by the same Japanese bombers that had attacked Pearl Harbor with similar intensity just three months earlier. This was just the first of 64 raids that virtually annihilated the town by the end of 1943.

After the war the Territory shared in some of the prosperity that was washing over the rest of the country, though much of it went into rebuilding its few towns and consolidating its hard-won agricultural and mining industries. Darwin was just about back on its feet when Cyclone Tracy struck on Christmas Eve 1974, delivering a seasonal gift of devastation almost unequalled in Australian history. The year was one of great highs and lows. Months before, Territorians finally reacquired the vote they lost in 1911 to elect their first full Legislative Assembly. The majority party, the conservative Country-Liberal Party, stayed in power for the next 27 years, though political power has now shifted to the Australian Labor Party. Although the Northern Territory is self-governing, it still does not have the full rights of a state – for example the federal government retains the power to make laws for the Territory and to override laws made by the Northern Territory Legislative Assembly, which it did in 1999 to quash new Territory laws allowing euthanasia.

In typically pugnacious Territory spirit, the rebuilding of Darwin quickly began again in after Tracy and the population of the Territory has been growing steadily since. However, it still has by far the smallest state population at 200,000 – just one percent of the Australian population. Surprisingly, 75% of Territorians live in cities and towns despite their tough bushie image, and most work in the mining or service industries. A good part of the Northern Territory's future prosperity is tied up with tourism. Ayers Rock, later reverting to its traditional name of Uluru, was the state's first major tourist destination. The 'rock' is now a travel ambition for most Australians and international visitors and is a national icon. Kakadu came to prominence in the 1960s-70s, largely because of the interest of David Attenborough, but really hit the spotlight in the late 1980s thanks to the film *Crocodile Dundee*, much of which was filmed in the park.

Darwin

In the minds of southerners Darwin will always be the last frontier – the home of nefarious characters and fugitives. But if anything has been constant in this city it is change. Bombarded by cyclones and destroyed by Japanese bombs, Darwin has had to shed its skin as regularly as a snake since 1869. The result is a modern, tropical city of spreading trees and palms, tall apartment blocks and neat suburbs. The population of Darwin has doubled in the last 20 years, making it a young and multicultural city, as befits a place closer to Singapore and Jakarta than it is to Canberra. The city centre is contained within a narrow peninsula at the eastern entrance to Darwin Harbour, a body of topaz-blue water twice the size of Sydney's harbour. North of the city centre, residential suburbs spread up the coast bordered by mangroves and yellow cliffs. The locals make the most of all this coastline, and it also provides some of the most enjoyable activities for visitors, such as the sunset markets on Mindil Beach, a cruise from Cullen Bay marina, fish and chips at Stokes Hill Wharf or outdoor cinema on the docks. Small, informal and friendly, Darwin operates at a relaxed pace and caters well for travellers. There are countless coach tours, 4WD tours and scenic flights into the incomparable Kakadu National Park, 200 km to the east, and many other areas nearby such as the Tiwi Islands and Litchfield National Park.

Colour map 5, grid A3
Population: 70,000
1,855 km from Broome (WA),
1,455 km from Alice Springs,
2,790 km from Cairns (QLD)

Ins and outs

Airport 11 km from the city centre, T8945 3747, www.darwinairport.com.au The *Airport Shuttle*, Mitchell St Tourist Precinct, T8981 5066, meets all incoming flights, and picks up from city accommodation on request for departures (20 mins, $8; $14 return). They also service local and scenic flights. A taxi costs $18-20. The airport has a couple of ATMs, foreign exchange desk, tourist information kiosk, and desks for all the major car hire companies. **Bike** Darwin is pretty flat so it is a good place for cycling. Bike hire is available from most hostels and you can pick up a free map of Darwin cycle paths (*Darwin and Palmerston Recreation and Cycle Guide*) from the VIC or the city council office on Harry Chan Av. The **Central Bus Station** (Transit Centre) is in the heart of the 'backpacker district', behind the Mitchell St Tourist Precinct, and handles all *McCafferty's/Greyhound* services, (T8941 0911). **Local bus services** are operated by *Darwinbus*, T8924 7666, and most start either in Harry Chan Av in the city centre, or at the Casuarina Interchange, north of the airport. Most routes run daily, every 30-80 mins between 0800-2100, though there are significant variations. Single fares from $2, depending on destination, all-day unlimited 'tourcard' tickets ($5, children $2.50) and 7-day passes ($25, children $12.50) are also available. Tourcards must be bought from main interchanges or at the VIC. Timetables are from the VIC and Information kiosk. **City centre minibus taxis**, T8928 1100, will take you anywhere within the CBD for $2, stopping to pick up and drop off other passengers along the way. Note that Darwin locals don't hail taxis (conventional or minibus); you either need to phone for a pick-up or wait at a taxi or minibus stand. There are stands for both types of taxi on Knuckey St, by the northern end of Darwin Mall.

Getting there & around
For more details, see also page 662

The city centre is very compact, easily covered on foot, and the wharf, Cullen Bay, the Botanic Gardens, and Mindil Beach are all within a 30-min walk

The Top End's principal VIC is on the corner of Knuckey St and Mitchell St, T8936 2499, www.tourismtopend.com.au Open 0900-1730 Mon-Fri, 0900-1245 Sat, 1000-1345 Sun. There is a smaller *Darwin City Information* kiosk in the Mall, 0900-1730 Mon-Fri, 0900-1500 Sat, 1000-1500 Sun. There is no comprehensive listings guide but the nearest thing to it is the monthly free newspaper *The Guide*, which you can pick up from where you're staying. *This Week in Darwin* (published every three months despite the

Information

Northern Territory

name) and *Darwin and the Top End Today* (published twice a year) are both free advertising booklets but full of useful info and maps, available from the VIC. *Artsmark* produce *Top End Arts*, a useful monthly listings sheet for arts and cultural events. Pick up a copy from the VIC or see www.darwinarts.com.au The daily *Northern Territory News* newspaper has a limited entertainment section on Sat. Weekly cinema timetables are available at the VIC or kiosk. The main *Parks and Wildlife Commission* office is in Palmerston, 20 km from the city, but the VIC has a parks information counter where you can pick up NT park notes and maps.

Gay & lesbian   For gay travellers the *NT Aids Council*, 6 Manton St, T8941 1711, www.ntac.org.au, is a good source of information and produces a monthly guide to gay Darwin, *Gay NT*. The council also organizes the annual city Gay Pride week. *Gay NT* can be found at their office or via *Absolutely* bookshop on Marina Boulevard, Cullen Bay.

Sights

See also pages
663 and 668 There is plenty to do in Darwin but you'll need to get about a bit as many of Darwin's best attractions are located away from the city centre, up around Fannie Bay and on the airport ring road. It is well worth having a stroll around the Esplanade and Parliament House area though, as this is the only place in Darwin where you get a real sense of its history, as well as lovely views of the harbour.

City centre &   One of the city's most popular attractions is **Aquascene** at Doctors Gully. It
Bicentennial   started 40 years ago with a local tossing scraps to fish in this pretty cove and
Park   has developed into a fish visitation of almost biblical proportions. Every day at high tide, milkfish, mullet and other species arrive to feed on bread thrown by tourists. There's not much to see other than a lot of splashing, but kids love it. ■ *Open at high tide only. Weekly feeding times advertised in the paper on Wed, Sat. $6, children $3.60. T8981 7837, www.aquascene.com.au 20 Doctors Gully Rd.* From Doctors Gully the foreshore **Bicentennial Park** runs along the west side of the city centre right around to the commercial wharves at the southern end. Popular with locals and tourists alike, there are lookouts over the harbour, war memorials and large grassy areas. There is a path through the park, close to the cliff edge, but it is worth deviating from this for a quick look at Lyons Cottage and Old Admiralty House on the Esplanade. **Lyons Cottage** was built in 1925 to house staff of the British-Australian Telegraph Compan, a stone bungalow of classic colonial design for tropical conditions, it now houses exhibitions of the early European and Larrakia history of Darwin. ■ *Daily 1000-1630. Free. Corner of the Esplanade and Knuckey St.* **Old Admiralty House** is on the opposite corner. This is not open to visitors but is of interest as it is one of very few pre-war (1937) houses that survived both bombing and cyclones and is a fine example of tropical architecture. Continuing towards the wharves, the unusual modern edifice of **Parliament House** looms up ahead. Built in 1994, it stands on the site of the former post and telegraph office destroyed by the first bombing raid on Darwin in 1942. Parliament House has a fine reception hall with an interesting display on state political history, good views of the harbour, a café and craft shop. The building also houses the **state library**, good for catching up on foreign newspapers. ■ *Reception hall open daily – enter from Smith St. Free guided tours of Parliament House run every Sat at 1000, 1200. Bookings essential, T8946 1425. Northern Territory Library open Mon-Fri 1000-1800, Sat-Sun 1300-1700. T8999 7177, www.ntlib.nt.gov.au*

24 hours in the city ★

Start the day with an early morning stroll around the foreshore **Bicentennial Park**, continuing past **Parliament Houese and Government House**, through the Mall and down **Mitchell Street**. Either make a side trip on the way to **Indo Pacific Marine**, or make the trip out to **Crocodylus** to catch their feeding tour at 1000 and see the 'croc museum'. Around midday drive or hire a bike and cycle up around Fannie Bay to **East Point**, stopping at the **Museum and Art Gallery** on the way for a look around and a spot of lunch. On the way back call in on the commercial gallery *Framed*. Jump on a twilight cruise from **Cullen Bay** marina, perhaps calling in at *Buzz Café* for a drink while waiting for your yacht. After the cruise make for the **Mindil Beach Markets** if it happens to be a Thursday, or jump in a cab and head for **Stokes Hill Wharf** for fish and chips or a cheap Thai meal. Finish the night in one of the Mitchell Street pubs or avoid the backpacker crowd at *Uncle John's Bar* at the Mississippi Queen.

Following the road around, the charming white gabled building opposite is Government House (1879). On the same side of the road, about 50 m further, is **Survivors Lookout**, where you can see historical photographs of Darwin. The elegant stone buildings nearby are the former police station and court-house buildings (1884), now used by the government Administrator, and one of a small cluster of old buildings surviving at this southern end of the city centre. Deep underneath here are five long, wide tunnels, built between 1943 and 1945 as bomb-proof storage tanks for naval and commercial shipping fuel. Although they were completed too late to be of strategic use, and never saw a drop of oil, two have been heritage listed and are open to the public as the **WWII Oil Storage Tunnels**. The largest is 171 m long, 5 m high and 4½ m wide, and has pictures of Darwin during the war set every 10 m or so along its length. ■ *Daily 0900-1700 from May-Oct; 1000-1400 Tue-Fri other months. $4.50. Accessible from both the Esplanade and Kitchener Dr.* If you walk back towards the city along Smith Street, **Christ Church Cathedral** on the corner is an example of the damage caused by Cyclone Tracy in 1974. The porch is all that remains of the original 1902 building, now joined to an incompatible modern cathedral. Further up, on the left, the **Town Hall** (1883), is another casualty of the cyclone, but **Browns Mart** (1885) opposite managed to survive and is now used as a theatre venue. On the corner of the Mall, the **Victoria Hotel** was built in 1890 with the intention of creating the grandest hotel in the Territory and is certainly still a grand place for a cold beer.

Stokes Hill Wharf

As well as a great collection of cheap eateries, there are two sea-themed visitor attractions at the point at which this wharf meets the shore. **Indo Pacific Marine** consists of about 20 water tanks of varying sizes, each containing a self-sustaining coral-based ecosystem between 17 and 27 years old. Detailed displays on marine environments, and a 40-minute video about coral evolution and behaviour, make this a fascinating visit (allow two hours). Seeing the systems at night, when the corals are at their most active, is even better, but can only be done in conjunction with a pricey wine-and-seafood buffet. ■ *Daily 1000-1700. $16, children $6, concessions $14. Evening tour and buffet at 1900 Wed-Sun, $70. T8981 1294.* Sharing the same building is the **Australian Pearling Exhibition**, a small museum with mostly static displays and memorabilia charting the development and history of the industry. A display of modern pearl jewellery makes up part of the exhibition. ■ *Daily 1000-1630. $6.60, children and concessions $3.30. T8999 6573.*

Northern Territory

Northern Territory

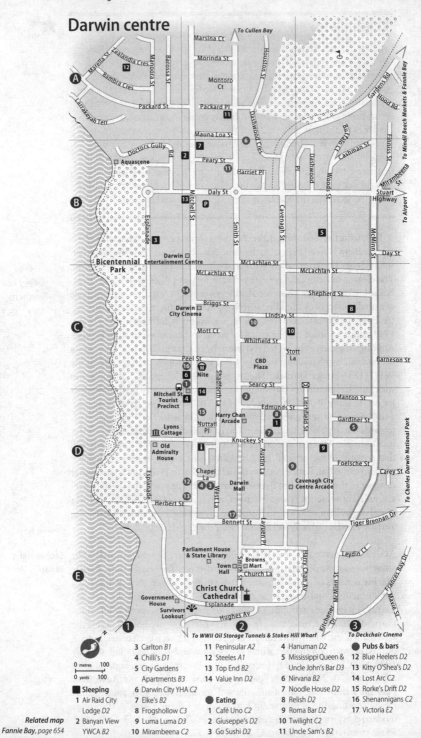

Darwin centre

Related map
Fannie Bay, page 654

■ **Sleeping**
1 Air Raid City Lodge *D2*
2 Banyan View YWCA *B2*
3 Carlton *B1*
4 Chilli's *D1*
5 City Gardens Apartments *B3*
6 Darwin City YHA *C2*
7 Elke's *B2*
8 Frogshollow *C3*
9 Luma Luma *D3*
10 Mirambeena *C2*
11 Peninsular *A2*
12 Steeles *A1*
13 Top End *B2*
14 Value Inn *D2*

● **Eating**
1 Café Uno *C2*
2 Giuseppe's *D2*
3 Go Sushi *D2*
4 Hanuman *D2*
5 Mississippi Queen & Uncle John's Bar *D3*
6 Nirvana *B2*
7 Noodle House *D2*
8 Relish *D2*
9 Roma Bar *D2*
10 Twilight *C2*
11 Uncle Sam's *B2*

● **Pubs & bars**
12 Blue Heelers *D2*
13 Kitty O'Shea's *D2*
14 Lost Arc *C2*
15 Rorke's Drift *D2*
16 Shenannigans *C2*
17 Victoria *E2*

The Botanic Gardens, established in 1886 as a botanical experiment and now **Botanic** devoted to relaxation and conservation, have suffered over the years from **Gardens** cyclones, wildfires and bombings, and look a little neglected. Managed by the NT Parks and Wildlife Commission, the gardens are about to undergo extensive redevelopment that will bring them up to the standard of other state capital botanic gardens. There are plans for a visitor centre and café overlooking a wetland lake, an orchid house and a walkway over Gilruth Avenue to link the main area of the park to sections beside Fannie Bay and the proposed Larrakia Nation Cultural Centre. At present the best area is the rainforest gully, with a waterfall, ponds and lush understorey of palms, cycads and bamboo. There are several interesting self-guided walks that illustrate Aboriginal plant use (pick up a brochure from the garden information centre) and short walks among the mangroves and coastal plants on the bay side. In the southern area of the gardens there is an excellent playground and a natural amphitheatre, often used as a venue for plays or musical performances. ■ *Information centre open daily 0830-1600. Free. T8981 1958. Gardens Rd, Fannie Bay. Bus routes 4 and 6 along Gilruth Av, then a 5-min walk to the entrance on Gardens Rd.*

This large modern museum, on the foreshore overlooking Fannie Bay, has a **Museum &** fine collection of **Aboriginal art** including bark paintings from Arnhem **Art Gallery of** Land, totems and paintings from the Tiwi Islands and contemporary acrylics. **the Northern** Although the museum also holds a Visual Arts collection of non-indigenous **Territory** artworks from 1768 to the present, little of this is on display and the focus of this institution leans more towards museum than gallery. There is an excellent imaginative display of northern-Australian geology and fauna in the Transformations Gallery, which documents the impact of **Cyclone Tracy** on the city in 1974, including a spooky room in which to listen to howling wind. The unusual **Maritime Gallery** houses a collection of boats from the Top End and Southeast Asia, including canoes, a pearl lugger, Indonesian *perahu* and other traditional fishing craft. You can also visit **Sweetheart**, the 5-m stuffed estuarine crocodile, named after Sweet billabong where he lived in the 1970s and used to attack the outboard motors of dinghies and toss fishermen out of their boats. The museum and art gallery also hosts regular touring exhibitions, check the museum programme for current details. There is also a great café here (see Eating, page 657). ■ *Mon-Fri 0900-1700, Sat-Sun 1000-1700. Free. T8999 8201, Conacher St. Bus routes 4 and 6 then a 1-km walk.*

The first gaol in Darwin was on the corner of Mitchell Street and the Esplanade **Fannie Bay** but the locals weren't fond of prisoners being quite so visible so a new gaol was **Gaol** opened in 1883 out at Fannie Bay – at that time miles away from civilization. Like most of Darwin, the gaol has been rebuilt many times folowing cyclones and bombing so the only old buildings are the original cell block and the stone Infirmary, built in 1887. Most of the buildings are corrugated iron sheds with mesh wire cells built in the 1950s and 1960s. The site is currently being restored by the Museum and Art Gallery of NT, and signs and displays are minimal. The gaol was closed in 1979 and its prisoners transferred to Darwin Prison at Berrimah. ■ *Daily 1000-1630. Free. East Point Rd, bus routes 4 and 6.*

East Point is the northern pincer of the headlands that form Fannie Bay. **East Point** This was one of Darwin's main defensive placements during the war but it is **Reserve** now a **recreation reserve**. A path follows the water's edge out to the point and a walk or cycle here is a fine place to take in wonderful views over the pale-turquoise water of the bay to the tower blocks of the city centre. There

Northern Territory

are BBQs and picnic tables on the foreshore and a swimming area in Lake Alexander. You can swim from the calm sandy beaches of the reserve but it is not advised during October-May because of box jellyfish. The gun emplacements and command post at the point have been turned into the **East Point Military Museum**, which boasts an impressive collection of weapons and a fascinating display and video on the bombing of Darwin – the city was bombed 64 times between 1942 and 1944. The museum also has an outdoor collection of anti-tank and anti-aircraft guns and military vehicles. Those

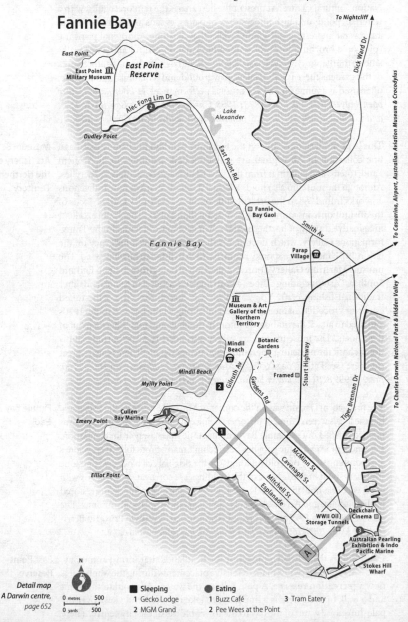

Fannie Bay

To Nightcliff

East Point

East Point Military Museum

East Point Reserve

Alec Fong Lim Dr

Dudley Point

Lake Alexander

East Point Rd

Dick Ward Dr

Fannie Bay

Fannie Bay Gaol

Smith Av

Parap Village

Museum & Art Gallery of the Northern Territory

Mindil Beach

Botanic Gardens

Mindil Beach

Myilly Point

Gilruth Av

Gardens Rd

Framed

Stuart Highway

Tiger Brennan Dr

Cullen Bay Marina

Emery Point

Elliot Point

McMinn St

Cavenagh St

Mitchell St

Esplanade

WWII Oil Storage Tunnels

Deckchair Cinema

Australian Pearling Exhibition & Indo Pacific Marine

Stokes Hill Wharf

To Casuarina, Airport, Australian Aviation Museum & Crocodylus

To Charles Darwin National Park & Hidden Valley

N

Detail map
A Darwin centre,
page 652

0 metres 500
0 yards 500

■ **Sleeping**
1 Gecko Lodge
2 MGM Grand

● **Eating**
1 Buzz Café
2 Pee Wees at the Point
3 Tram Eatery

Northern Territory

interested in tracking down Second World War historic sites throughout the Territory should pick up the Historic Trail brochures available at the museum.■ *Daily 0930-1700. $10, children $5, concessions $9. T8981 9702, www.epmm.com.au Bus routes 4 and 6 plus a 2½-km walk.*

One of the country's best aircraft museums, the AAM is in one massive hanger **Australian** built to house Darwin's very own cold-war era B-52 bomber, permanently on **Aviation** loan from the United States Air Force – only one of two of these gigantic aircraft **Museum** outside the USA. Aside from this giant, the core of the collection is connected with the Second World War and Darwin's role in the conflict, from a life-size model Spitfire to the remains of several Japanese, Australian and American planes. Knowledgeable staff are happy to conduct impromptu tours if they're not busy. ■ *Daily 0900-1700. $11, children $6, concessions $7.50. T8947 2145, www.darwinsairwar.com.au 557 Stuart Highway, bus routes 5 and 8.*

Arguably the best of the Top End crocodile parks, if only for the incredibly **Crocodylus** detailed, fascinating and graphic crocodilian museum which will tell and show you everything you ever wanted to know about crocs, and a lot more you didn't want to know. The main park comprises a series of breeding and rearing pens, two large enclosed lagoons and several other enclosures housing a variety of both indigenous and exotic wildlife. The best way to see the park is on one of the entertaining guided feeding tours. ■ *Daily 0900-1700; tours 1000, 1200 and 1400, including feeding; feeding only 1530. $22, children $11, concessions 10 15% off adult entry. T8922 4500, www.wmi.com.au Brandt Rd, east of airport, bus route 5 then 1-km walk. Croc Park shuttle bus departs city centre 0920, $14 return, T8928 1100.*

Essentials

Most of Darwin's top-flight hotels are spaced out along the Esplanade. One of the most **Sleeping** impressive, the **L** *Carlton*, T8980 0800, res@carlton-darwin.com.au, is one of the most egalitarian in not charging a surcharge for harbour views – it's simply first-come, first-served. The **L-A** *MGM Grand*, Gilruth Av, Fannie Bay, T8943 8888, www.mgmgrand.com.au, incorporates the city's main casino. Slightly less expensive than the Esplanade equivalents and without the glamour that a casino hotel may suggest to some. A few rooms overlook Mindil Beach, as do some of the tables in the expensive 3rd floor *E'voo* restaurant. **L-A** *Mirambeena*, 64 Cavenagh St, T8946 0111, info@mirambeena.com.au, is a resort-style hotel with self-contained apartments and comfortable standard rooms. Facilities include a huge pool, adjacent courtyard bar and a good standard in-house restaurant, *Treetops*, open 1800-2130.

A *City Gardens Apartments*, 93 Woods St, T8941 2888, www.citygardens apts.com.au 16 spacious and well-equipped self-contained units, with full kitchens, set on 2 storeys around a central courtyard pool. Each has double and twin bedrooms. Recommended. **A-B** *Luma Luma*, 26 Knuckey St, T8981 1899, www.luma luma.com.au 8-storey block with 74 modern, self-contained studio, 1- and 2-bedroom apartments with balconies overlooking the city. Courtyard pool.

The friendly **B** *Peninsular*, 115 Smith St, T8981 1922, peninsularapts@octa4.net.au, has similar, though more careworn options a little further out. Their large rooms can accommodate groups and families, for which they're pretty good value. **B-D** *Steeles*, 4 Zealandia Cres, T/F8941 3636, www.steeles-at-larrakeyah.com.au Very welcoming B&B with 2 pretty, external, en suite double rooms, garden pool and large covered breakfast and chill-out area. The cheaper option ien suiteky and certain touches like fresh flowers, but still a haven for couples on a budget. Recommended. The **B** *Top End*

Hotel, corner of Mitchell St and Daly St, T8981 6511, has some of the most comfortable motel-style rooms in its price-range, all grouped around a garden and pool, and situateded just far enough, but not too far, from the hotel's excellent bars.

The **C** *Air Raid City Lodge*, 35 Cavenagh St, T8981 9214, pauldich@hotmail.com, has 24 single, double and family rooms, all a/c and en suite. Guests have access to basic kitchens, but everything has a pretty tired feel about it and most rooms do not have windows. The slightly pricier **C** *Value Inn*, 50 Mitchell St, T8981 4733, reservations@valueinn.com.au, has similarly equipped but significantly smarter hotel rooms, plus a courtyard pool, but no kitchen facilities.

The eccentric **D-F** *Mississippi Queen*, 6 Gardiner St, T8981 3358, www.rail-bar.com, is several extraordinary things rolled into one unlikely but strangely cohesive whole. Accommodation in a couple of basic a/c rooms and half a dozen, mostly a/c caravans, dotted about the jungle-cum-garden, that range from the spectacularly unkempt to surprisingly quaint and romantic. No en suites, no kitchen facilities and no camping.

Backpacker hostels The *YWCA/YHA* and smaller independents are generally pretty laid-back, however, and the best choices if you're around for a while. In the wet season, take the time to look at a couple of rooms before choosing. In the busy dry season book ahead, being careful to check exactly what size room and facilities you will be getting. Most hostels offer a refund for some or all of the airport shuttle if you stay 2 or more nights, offer a free light breakfast, and have overnight a/c. The **D-E** *Banyan View YWCA*, 119 Mitchell St, T8981 8644, ywcadwn_bvl@optusnet.com.au, is one of the city's smaller and quieter options with 77 beds in twins, including one en suite, and good-value 4-bed dorms. Optional a/c. Communal facilities are a little institutional but there's a large and peaceful garden out the back with a spa. **D-E** *Chilli's*, 69 Mitchell St, T8941 9722, www.chillis.com.au Twins, doubles and pricey dorms up to 8-bed make up this lively 169-bed hostel in the heart of the backpacker area. All rooms have sinks, dorms have individual lockers, some twins have showers. Communal facilities mostly based on large alfresco balconies, including 2 spas on a rear sun-deck. **D** *Darwin City YHA*, 69 Mitchell St, T8981 3995, darwinyha@yhant.org.au, has a similar feel and design to *Chilli's*, but on a larger scale with slightly better communal facilities including a large courtyard pool. It has 324 beds in mostly 4- and 8-bed dorms, with a few excellent, if pricey, doubles. Very comfortable, clean and efficient, this is the best of the larger hostels. **D-E** *Elke's*, 112 Mitchell St, T8981 8399, www.elkes backpackers.com.au One of the city's cheaper options, this medium-sized hostel occupies 3 separate old houses arranged around a pool area. Though clean, the whole place is getting distinctly rundown, however, and some of the communal facilities, particularly the kitchens, are not really adequate. **D-E** *Frogshollow*, 27 Lindsay St, T8941 2600, www.frogshollownet.au Friendly and helpful, clean and well-maintained small hostel with most rooms off the first-floor balconies. Quiet location close to town, good dorms, a range of doubles, attractive courtyard pool area and one of Darwin's better hostel kitchens. Recommended. **D-E** *Gecko Lodge*, 146 Mitchell St, T8981 5569, www.geckolodge.com.au Laid-back, slightly scruffy hostel whose dorms might not be first choice, but which does have an adjacent 1950s house, dubbed 'Waynesworld', with just 3 large doubles, stripped with wood floors, kitchen and bathroom. They also do very cheap car hire.

There are just 2 **caravan parks** within 10 km of the city centre, most being further out along the Stuart Highway. Closest is the **C-E** *Leprechaun Motel and Caravan Park*, 378 Stuart Highway, adjacent to the Airport Gates Shell roadhouse about 6 km from the centre, T8984 3400. They have cheap motel rooms, self-contained cabins, simple backpacker accommodation, and camping sites. Facilities include pool and kitchen. Another 4 km further out is **C-D** *Shady Glen*, corner of Stuart Highway and Farrell Cres, T8984 3330, which has cabins and on-site vans.

You may hear that Darwin hostels are all run by sharks, out to flog you Kakadu tours or bust. Some, it is true, do make a significant part of their income from tour commissions and will encourage you to book with them

Northern Territory

Darwin's cuisine is influenced by the city's proximity to Asia and its large Asian population. There are countless small noodle outlets in the city and its regular markets. Fresh fish and seafood is also a feature of most menus and Darwin is a good place to try local treats such as barramundi. Although there are some excellent upmarket restaurants in the city, the population is too small to support many of them and the defining feature of Darwin eating is its excellent value for money. If you eat at the Asian food halls, markets or Stokes Hill Wharf you'll get away with change from $10. Open-air street dining is becoming more common but the city council is way behind other Australian capitals in allowing this. The humidity of the 'build up' and wet season mean that many patrons prefer to eat indoors for half the year anyway.

Expensive The richly and fascinatingly furnished formal dining rooms of the licensed *Mississippi Queen*, Gardiner St, T8981 3358, are the setting for a nightly set-priced ($40) but open-choice 3-course meal. Tables by reservation only, seating from 1930. *Pee Wees at the Point*, Alec Fong Lim Dr, T8981 6868. This sophisticated contemporary restaurant hovers above Fannie Bay at East Point, with spectacular water views. Modern Australian food with an emphasis on local seafood is served in a light and open space. Arrive early to enjoy the view before dark. Daily 1830-2030. *Twilight*, 2 Lindsay St, T8981 8631, is known for the city's best contemporary Australian cuisine, served in a classic tropical house and lush garden. Dinner served 1830-2130. Licensed but BYO wine. Recommended.

Mid-range *Café Uno*, Mitchell St Tourist Precinct, T8942 2500. Deep, rich colours and soft, covered chairs help generate a cosy feel in the large dining room of this casual Italian café and restaurant. Open 0830-2330 for snacks, coffee and cake, with pasta, pizza, grills, and salads at lunchtime and evening. Pavement tables, licensed. Verging on the expensive, *Hanuman*, 28 Mitchell St, T8941 3500, is a very classy Asian restaurant specializing in serving fine authentic Indian and Thai cuisine. Open 1200-1430 and 1830-2130 Mon-Fri, 1830-2230 Sat-Sun. Licensed, recommended. *Nirvana*, Smith St, T8981 2025. Slightly more laid-back establishment with a wide-ranging Indian, Malay and Thai menu including an excellent veggie selection. Live jazz and blues spices up proceedings in the front dining room every Tue-Sat. Open daily 1830-2200.

Cheap *Cornucopia*, at the Museum and Art Gallery of NT makes the most of its superb position overlooking the bay with a large outdoor terrace. Fine meals range from a light salad to a hearty barra fillet (mid-range). Fabulous cakes and coffee. Licensed. Open Mon-Fri 0900-1700, Sat-Sun 1000-1700. Recommended. *Go Sushi*, behind Hanuman off Mitchell St, is a busy licensed sushi bar with a 'train' operating 1100-1530 and 1730-2100. Open 1000-2100 Mon-Sat. All plates $3 from 1000-1700 Sat. The *Noodle House*, 33 Knuckey St, T8941 1742, is a popular BYO Chinese, open 1100-1400 Mon-Sat and daily 1800-2200. *Twilight* is open from 1130 Mon-Fri and 1000 Sat-Sun to give those a little less hungry, or well-heeled, a taste from their excellent kitchen. Nothing over $13, the lunch menu features grills, seafood and tapas, including a good range of vegetarian.

Seriously cheap Darwin abounds in food halls with several off the central Mall, including the large and busy *Galleria* and one in Mitchell St Tourist Precinct. Most of the food outlets in these halls serve Asian food and are generally open during most of the day Mon-Fri and Sat morning. One vegetarian outlet, *Simplys*, is in the Star Village Arcade off the Mall. The popular Indonesian *Sari Rasu* is away from these hot spots, opposite *Redback* in the Cavenagh City centre Arcade. Open 1200-1500 Mon-Fri. Also off the usual track is the *Nudel Bar*, Harry Chan Arcade, 60 Smith St, serving excellent noodles and rice dishes. Open 1130-1430 and 1730-2230 Mon-Sat. In the evenings head for Stokes Hill Wharf where a range of takeaways, from fish and chips to Asian, share a number of outside tables overlooking the outer wharf. A small offy supplies the wine and beer. *Kim's* is particularly recommended. On Thu evenings (dry season only) the Mindil Beach Market (see page 659) makes an excellent alternative. A 24-hr choice is *Uncle Sam's*, an Asian diner and takeaway on Smith St.

Eating
See also Cafés and Bars sections

All opening hours indicated are for the dry season. Some establishments will close earlier during the wet season

Northern Territory

Cafés The *Buzz Café*, at the side of the marina, Cullen Bay, T8941 1141, is the best of the city's café bars, both in terms of style and location, with tables out on the deck. Breakfasts, snacks or mid-range meals available 1130-0200 Mon-Fri, 0930-0200 Sat-Sun. Both their toilets are interesting, but the men's urinal has to be seen to be believed. Recommended. *Relish*, corner of Edmunds St and Cavenagh St, next to *Air Raid City Lodge*, specializes in mouth-watering gourmet snacks. Open 0630-1700 Mon-Sat. The *Roma Bar*, 50 Cavenagh St, an unreconstructed, earthy joint is something of a city institution, serving excellent breakfasts and a range of hot snacks, lunches and sandwiches. A good spot to chill out over a paper. Open 0700-1630 Mon-Fri, 0800-1400 Sat-Sun. The *Tram Eatery*, McMinn St, consists of 2 old Melbourne tramcars situated on the foreshore of the wharf, converted into a simple takeaway, with a few shaded tables. Open 1030-2030 Wed-Mon, also Tue during peak dry season.

Bars & The *Blue Heelers Bar*, Mitchell St, is a barn of a place, appropriately festooned with
Nightclubs rusting agricultural implements. Meals, served 1200-1400 and 1800-1930, are a flat $5 for basic Aussie tucker such as damper, roasts and stews. *Kitty O'Shea's*, Mitchell St. Irish theme bar with acoustic live music every Fri night, hot snacks all day 1200-2100 and more substantial cheap counter meals 1200-1400 and 1800-2100. The *Lost Arc*, 89 Mitchell St, T8942 3300, is a cool, contemporary bar open 1600-0400 Sun-Thu, 1200-0200 Fri and 1600-0200 Sat, offering $5.50 meals and playing retro disco most evenings. Upstairs is the Discovery nightclub, playing r'n'b and commercial modern dance, Fri and Sat 2100-0400. Entry $6-8. *Rorke's Drift*, Mitchell St, is the most upmarket of the main city pubs, and has recently built a large terrace out into the street. Karaoke assails the eardrums Mon and Wed, and there's a live cover band every Tue. Decent pubs meals served 1200-2200. The *Top End Hotel*, corner of Mitchell St and Dalt St, has a number of bars including the popular *Lizards Bar & Grill*, a shaded alfresco spot serving hearty BBQ grills 1800-2130, but open from 1500 Mon-Fri and 1200 Sat-Sun. Recommended. Mississippi Queen's *Uncle John's Bar*, Gardiner St, a converted railway carriage from the defunct NT passenger lines, creates a late-night, anything-goes atmosphere that spills out into the extensive garden area. Contemporary Australian jazz every Sun from 1800. Decent cheap counter meals available 1900-0100. The *Victoria*, in the Mall, is Darwin's 'backpacker central', serving $5.50 basic meals. Also live music most nights, cheap jugs of beer, regular party games and big screens showing English premiership soccer. Open till 0400 daily, $6 entry after 2400 Fri-Sat, meals 1200-1430, 1800-2000.

Entertainment **Cinema** Mainstream releases at *Darwin City Cinemas*, Mitchell St, info T8981 3111, and at their Casuarina complex. The licensed, outdoor *Deckchair Cinema*, Mavie St, shows art house, classic and some current films. Open most days, Wed-Sun between Apr-Nov. T8981 0700. **Theatre** *Darwin Entertainment Centre*, Mitchell St, opposite McLachlan St, T8980 3333, www.darwinentcentnet.au Touring and local theatre, dance and music. They are also the main ticket office for most Top End events and Darwin sport such as the V8 Supercars at Hidden Valley. *Browns Mart*, 12 Smith St, T8981 5522. Arts centre and performance venue in one of Darwin's few 19th-century buildings. Performances are also sometimes held in Civic Park next door and the ruins of Town Hall opposite.

Festivals Every other year in **May** Darwin hosts the *Arafura Games*, bringing together 4000 athletes and officials from 25 countries in the Asia-Pacific region. The next games will be held in 2003. A tenth of Darwin's population is of Greek descent, mostly the result of chain migration from the island of Kalymnos, so the city holds a lively *Greek Glenti* on the Esplanade in **Jun**. The *Darwin Cup Carnival* is a horse racing event that runs for four weeks in **Jul and Aug**, culminating in the Darwin Cup race on the last day (early Aug). The carnival is held at the Fannie Bay Racecourse. The *Darwin Beer Can*

Regatta is usually held within a day or two of the Darwin Cup. Competitors launch boats made of beer cans off Mindil Beach and race each other for cash prizes. The main festival of the year is the *Festival of Darwin*, held from **mid-Aug to early Sep**. This differs from other arts festivals held in state capitals as it concentrates on performers and artists from the region rather than international artists. Many northern Aboriginal communities get involved so it provides a great opportunity to see Aboriginal performances or artwork. The festival also reflects the involvement of Darwin's multicultural community. Regular events include a street parade and concert on the Esplanade. For more information pick up a programme from the VIC or contact the festival office T8981 0083, www.darwinfestival.org.au During the festival period make sure you get to the Museum and Art Gallery of NT to see the exhibition of entries for the *National Aboriginal and Torres Strait Islander Art Award*, some of the best work in the country. Just before the main festival there is also a *Fringe Festival*. For details of events pick up a programme around town or contact the Fringe hotline T8981 5734, darwinfringe@octa4.net.au

Shopping

Some of the best shopping in Darwin is to be found in the regular markets

In the city centre the **Mall** and its many arcades sport a range of unexciting clothes and tourist gift shops, with a smattering of cafés and specialist outlets. There's a huge **Woolworths** food store in the CBD Plaza between Cavenagh St and Smith St, open until 2400 Mon-Sat, and late on Sun. Darwin locals often use this supermarket as a useful landmark. 'New Woolies' is the one just mentioned, 'Old Woolies' is a smaller, scruffier version on Smith St, opposite the mall. The city's biggest modern Mall is **Casuarina Shopping Centre**, north of the airport, with nearly 200 stores of all sizes and varieties.

Markets The wonderful **Mindil Beach Markets** are held on the foreshore just behind the sandhills, every Thu evening, around 1700-2100, during the dry season. The markets also operate on Sun evenings from 1600-2100 during Jun-Sep but this is usually a much quieter affair. Dozens of craft stalls mingle with an even greater number of seriously cheap food stalls, selling everything from Filipino to fish and chips. There's pancakes and fruit salads for afters, but you'll need to BYO alcohol if you fancy a glass or bottle with your meal while sitting on the beach watching the sunset. A Darwin favourite, parking can be a hassle: walk from the city centre if you can. **Parap Market** runs on Sat mornings all year round and consist of smaller collection of Asian food stalls, fresh fruit and veg stalls and crafty things. It has a low-key, villagey atmosphere and is popular with locals. Similar markets are held on Sun from 0800-1400 in the northern suburb of Nightcliff. The **Nite Markets** in Mitchell St, close to the Tourist Precinct, are little more than a few craft and art stalls (no food), but are open daily, 1700-2300.

Art and jewellery *Framed*, corner of Geranium St and the Stuart Highway, is one of the NT's best commercial galleries, featuring some of the very best Aboriginal and European-style artworks, jewellery, sculptures and ceramics. *Indigenous Creations* in the Mall, and *Raintree*, 20 Knuckey St, have some of the best ranges of Aboriginal art and creations in the city centre. The NT *Craft Council* has a small shop in the foyer of Parliament House and this a good place to pick up reasonably priced and locally made gifts. Open Mon-Fri 0930-1530.

Books and maps New *Bookworld*, the Mall, has a wide range, particularly good on Australiana and Aboriginal culture. In Cullen Bay *Absolutely*, Marina Blvd, has an absorbing range of hand-picked 'good reads', plus good Australiana, Aboriginal and gay/lesbian sections. It's open daily 1000-2200. Local and international maps can be found at the government office, *Maps NT*, 1st floor, Nichols Pl, corner of Cavenagh St and Bennett St, T8999 7032. **Second-hand** *Dusty Jackets*, above the Roma Bar on Cavenagh St, has a huge range, specializing in literature, Australiana and antiquarian but with a lot else besides. *Readback*, Darwin Plaza, the Mall, also has a massive range, this time mostly in paperback fiction, especially sci-fi. There are smaller selections to be found at places such as the *Book X* in the Mitchell St Tourist Precinct.

Northern Territory

Outdoor gear   The *NT General Store*, 42 Cavenagh St, has a huge range and stock of gear and maps for sale, while *Gone Bush*, T04-1375 7000, gonebush@octa4.net.au , hires out camping gear, delivered to your accommodation.

**Tours in &
around Darwin**
*Also see Excursions
on next page*

Art tours to the Tiwi Islands from Darwin are an opportunity to meet the friendly Tiwi, see the islands and buy some beautiful artwork at half the prices on the mainland. *Tiwi Art Tours*, T8924 1115, www.aussieadventure.com.au, fly to Bathurst Island for one ($298) or two days ($564). The tour includes visiting 2 art centres and the Patakijiyali Museum, documenting mission days and traditional life. A display of craft work and dancing, a smoke ceremony, a look at the Catholic church and a visit to a burial site are also part of this trip. There is also a day-tour for art collectors and enthusiasts that visits 3 art centres on both islands (Mon-Fri, $380, minimum 3 people). Contact *Tiwi Art Network*, T8941 3593, www.tiwiart.com for enquiries and bookings. **Boat cruises** Several boats offer lunch and sunset harbour cruises, all departing from Cullen Bay. *Darwin Pearl Lugger Cruises*, T8942 3131, www.darwinharbour cruise.com.au, head out on a pearl lugger for lunch BBQ and swim trips ($55), evening sunset cruises either with nibbles ($46) or, on their sister sailing boat *Tumlaren*, a full evening meal ($65). The *Starchaser*, T8941 4000, www.star chaser.com.au, is a modern sailing yacht running a sunset cruise for $46. All vessels are licensed. **Bus and minibus** The *Tour Tub*, T8985 6322, trundles around a city centre and Fannie Bay circuit starting at the north end of the Mall, on the hr from 0900-1600. Drop-offs on the 'hop-on, hop-off' service include Stokes Hill Wharf, Cullen Bay, the Museum and Art Gallery and East Point. Full-day ticket $25, half-day (from 1300) $15. The *Rainbow Bus Service*, T8948 4248, runs a Stuart Highway service, leaving from the Mitchell St Tourist Precinct transit centre at 0800, Mon, Wed and Fri (other days if sufficient booked passengers). Stops include Darwin Crocodile Farm, Berry Springs and the Territory Wildlife Park. *Darwin Day Tours*, T8924 1124, www.darwindaytours.com, have a wide range of options including a daily afternoon city tour ($48, 1400 daily), a trip out to the jumping crocs at Adelaide River ($75, 1250 daily), and a full-day wildlife special that includes the jumping crocs and the Territory Wildlife Park ($110, 0730 daily). **Diving** There are many coral sites in and around Port Darwin, plus a good many boat and plane wrecks, some from the Second World War, others victims of Cyclone Tracy. High tides make visibility quite poor so diving is limited to about 3-4 days a fortnight. Contact *Cullen Bay Dive*, Marina Blvd, T8981 3049, www.divedarwin.com, for their programme. They charge from $150 for an all-inclusive 2-dive trip, $450 for the standard PADI open-water course. **Rock climbing and abseiling** *NT Xtreme*, T0410 559901, head into Litchfield for a day's taster into these sports.

**Tours from
Darwin**
*Also see page 668 for
further details of
excursions*

Aboriginal culture   As well as excursions to the Tiwi Islands, *Aussie Adventure*, T8924 1111, www.aussieadventure.com.au, run 2-day camping trips to the Peppimenarti community near Daly River ($500). **Arnhem Land** *Venture North*, T8927 5500, www.northernaustralia.com, offer 5-day 4WD safaris that look at much of the north of Kakadu and head up to Cobourg Peninsula for 3 days (Mon, Wed, $1,050). Several operators have camps or resorts in Arnhem Land that will fly you to and use as a base for exploring the region. Their packages usually include flights, accommodation, meals and a range of tours and activities. Such operators include: *Seven Spirit Bay*, T9826 2471, www.sevenspiritbay.com, *Cape Don*, T8978 5145, www.capedon.gurig.com.au, and *Davidson's Arnhemland Safaris*, T8927 5240, www.Arnhemland -safaris.com.au

Kakadu and the Top End   There are many companies offering trips of between 1 and 7 days into the park and further afield. Make sure you ask around and chat to some of the operators before deciding. Ask for details of the itinerary so you can see if the options will suit you. Prices vary but are around $120-350 per day; quality of accommodation and food mainly account for the price difference. The more expensive trips tend to cater for a mature market and are generally less physically demanding. *Odyssey*, T8948 0091,

The Tiwi Islands

Tiwi means 'we people' and the Aboriginal people of Bathurst and Melville islands do possess the strong sense of community the name implies. About 6000 people live on the islands which are run by the Tiwi Land Council, representing all of the major family clans. The Tiwi islands lie just 80 km north of Darwin yet they are thought to have had little contact with Aboriginal groups of the mainland until about 1800 and have developed distinct cultural differences, such as the use of burial totem poles, or pukunami. Macassans from Indonesia arrived from about 1700 to

collect trepang (sea slugs) and are credited with introducing steel axes, dugout canoes and playing cards to the Tiwi. There was an abortive attempt at settlement by Europeans in 1824 at Fort Dundas on Melville Island but the Tiwi had a reputation for fierceness among European explorers and after the settlement failed a few years later the islanders were left alone. A Catholic mission was established by Father Gsell in 1911 and its influence is still powerful; the islanders practice a unique blend of Catholicism and traditional Tiwi cultural beliefs.

www.odysaf.com.au, set the Top End standards for quality 4WD tours. Lasting 2-7 days their tours incorporate a strong element of Aboriginal culture and the low guide to passenger ratios make the trips informative and rewarding. Expect to pay around $300 per day. *Aussie Adventure* have a range of trips for 2-4 days, with accommodation options including camping, budget and motel. Prices are around $200 per day. Some tours include a day excursion into Arnhem Land. At the **budget** end of the market the operators offer slightly less structured tours with more basic camping and eating options. Most offer camping trips lasting into Kakadu and/or Litchfield, some venturing down to Katherine or into Arnhem Land, and all aimed squarely at the backpacker market. Expect to pay $350-450 for a 3-day trip, around $100-140 per day for longer excursions. The following local operators all use 'troop carriers' taking a maximum of 9-13 people on a trip. *Aussie Overlanders*, T8985 4255, www.aussie overlanders.com, are a relatively new company, but already have a solid reputation. *Gondwana*, T1800 242177, www.gondwana.cc, have squeezed their prices down by refusing to pay commission to agents and hostels. Excellent value, direct bookings only. Office in Mitchell St Tourist Precinct, open 0930- 1900, free internet for passengers. *Kakadu Dreams*, T8981 3266, www.kakadu dreams.com.au, are known around town as one of the main operators for whom having fun is a primary objective and they offer an unstructured itinerary. *Wilderness 4WD Adventures*, T8941 2161, www.wilderness adventures.com.au, offer similar programmes, with slightly more emphasis on wildlife, plus a 9-day one-way trip to Broome in WA via the Gibb River Rd ($1,280). If you like cycling then *Remote Outback Cycle Tours* tour (3 nights, $620), T9279 6969, www.cycletours.com.au head out roughly once a month, May-Sep As bikes go on the roof of the OKA you just cycle the best bits. **Litchfield** The best of this park can be experienced in a day trip. *Rolling Thunder*, T1800 813269, www.kakadu dreams.com.au, caters for the backpacker market, while *Darwin Day Tours*, T8924 1124, www.darwindaytours.com, generally attract the mature traveller. Both $80. **Scenic flights** *Northern Air Charter*, T8945 5444, www.flynac.com.au, offer a short flight around the city and harbour and longer flying day-tours over Kakadu ($295), Nitmiluk and the eastern Kimberley ($495). The Kakadu option reveals the scale of the park and its different habitats, and lands at Cooinda, so allowing you to get on the excellent Yellow Waters Cruise. Worth considering if you are short of time. **Turtles** *NT Wilderness Expeditions*, T1300 656071, www.gul widdi.com.au, run 2-day boat and bush trips ($275) to an offshore island as part of an on going turtle monitoring programme. Tours depart Mon, Wed, Fri-Sat, from Apr-Oct.

Northern Territory

Transport **Air** *Air North* fly to **Alice Springs** (Mon-Sat), **Broome** (daily), **Gove** (Mon, Thu-Sat), **Katherine** (Mon-Fri), **Kununurra** (daily) and **Tennant Creek** (Mon-Sat). *Qantas* fly daily to most state capitals, **Cairns**, Gove and Alice Springs. *Virgin Blue* operate daily to **Brisbane** with onward connections in QLD and NSW. **Bus** There is no state bus company, and most services are operated by *McCafferty's/Greyhound*, Mitchell St Tourist Precinct, T8941 0911. Their **Perth** service, via Kununurra and Broome, leaves daily at 0730, and the 2 **Alice Springs** buses at 0800 and 1315, stopping regularly on the Stuart Highway. The 0800 service (GX204) connects with their Townsville bus in **Tennant Creek** (30-min wait from 2155). The 1315 service (MC810) connects with the Adelaide service the following morning (1-hr wait at 0925). Their **Kakadu** service (GX871) operates daily in the dry season only, departing at 0630. Stops include the Kakadu Resort and Jabiru, terminating at Cooinda. **Backpacker buses** *Travelabout*, T9244 1200, www.travelabout.com.au, run a 14-day trip via the red centre and **Port Augusta** to Sydney. They also have trips, some 4WD, to **Broome** and on to **Perth**. *Adventure Tours*, T1300 654604, www.adventure tours.com.au, offer 6- and 10-day trips to **Alice Springs**, with options onward to **Adelaide**, Perth and **Cairns**, and an 8-day trip to Broome. Darwin is also on the *Oz Experience* circuit, T02-8356 1766, www.ozexperience.com See also under Alice Springs for other operators offering trips south. **Bicycle/4WD** *Remote Outback Cycle Tours*, T9279 6969, www.cycletours. com.au, head via the Bungles and the Gibb River Rd to Broome (10 nights, $1,730). Departs roughly once a month, May-Sep.

Directory **Airlines** *Air North*, Lancaster Dr, Darwin Airport, T8920 4000. *Garuda Indonesia*, 9 Cavenagh St, T8981 6422. *Malaysia Airlines*, Beagle House, 38 Mitchell St, T8941 3055. *Merpati Nusantara Airlines*, Level 6, Darwin Central Building, Knuckey St, T8941 1606. *Royal Brunei*, 22 Cavenagh St, T8941 0966. *Qantas*, 16 Bennett St, T8982 3316.

Banks The major banks have ATMs on Smith St, Mitchell St and Cavenagh St. Foreign exchange *American Express*, Knuckey St, open 0830-1700 Mon-Fri, 0900-1200 Sat. *Thomas Cook*, the Mall, open 0900-1700 Mon-Fri, 0900-1300 Sat. There are independent kiosks at the airport and in Mitchell St Tourist Precinct. **Bike and scooter hire** Bike hire from most hostels. *Darwin Scooter Hire*, by the Nite Markets, Mitchell St, T0418 892885. $20 for 2 hrs, $40 per day.

Campervan and car hire Most of the major hire companies are at the airport and around the north end of Smith St and Mitchell St. Local operators include *Port Rent-a-Car*, T8981 8441, www.port-rent-a-car.com.au, and *Top End 4WD & Car Hire*, T8941 2922. Note that bookings made through the VIC allow unlimited kilometres but this may not be the case if you book directly with the car hire firm. **Car sales** You might pick up a bargain at the *Backpackers Car Market*, by the Nite Markets, T0418 600830, but sales are 'as seen'. Also check out the second-hand car yards, including *Dustin's Autos* on Smith St, T8981 3397, where you'll get some sort of warranty. **Car servicing** *Phil Kerr*, 9 Harriet Pl, T8981 4630. **Communications** Internet free for research use (no email) at the *State Library*. Among many other options try the helpful *Didjworld*, Harry Chan Arc, 60 Smith St. $5.50 per hr, open 0900-2400 Mon-Sat, 1000-2000 Sun. Main **Post Office** on Cavenagh St, where **Poste Restante** (take photo ID to collect mail) is open 0830-1730 Mon-Fri with plans to open Sat morning. **Luggage store** *Luggage Locker*, shop 6, Air Raid Arcade, 35 Cavenagh St, T8941 6677. From $4 per bag, also bikes, surfboards etc. **Medical services** *Royal Darwin Hospital*, Rocklands Dr, Casuarina, T8922 8888. **Police** West La, T8999 6666. **Taxi** *City Radio*, T8981 3777, *Darwin Radio*, T131008.

Around Darwin

The Top End west of the Arnhem Land Escarpment is essentially one vast flood plain, broken only by occasional rocky plateaux. Thanks to the annual drenching of the region during the monsoon, some of the plains remain saturated all almost year acting as wildlife-rich wetlands, such as those around the Adelaide and Mary rivers. Birds, fish and crocodiles are easily seen here, particularly in the latter part of the dry season when their homes and fishing areas contract. Along stretches of the Adelaide River the magnificent estuarine crocodiles, up to 6 m long, have been 'taught' to leap vertically out of the water for dangling bait, and cruises to see this controversial but amazing phenomenon run daily. Other natural results of the summer soaking are widespread natural springs, cascading waterfalls and their plunge pools, such as those in picturesque Litchfield National Park.

Darwin to Kakadu

Just north of the dormitory suburb of Howard Springs, 30 km from Darwin, is the **Howard Springs Nature Park**, immensely popular with Darwinians at weekends. These concrete-lined springs aren't the prettiest around Darwin, but they're full of inquisitive (read 'hungry') barramundi and yellow-faced turtles, and fringed by wide lawns with plentiful picnic tables and free BBQs. ■ *Daily from 0800-2000, facilities include toilets and a kiosk.* Close to the junction of the Arnhem and Stuart highways, 40 km from Darwin, is the **Darwin Crocodile Farm**. A similar operation to Crocodylus, the farm produces croc meat and leather commercially and opens its doors to visitors to see the crocs. ■ *Daily 0900-1600, feeding tours 1400. $10, children $5.50, concessions $8. T8988 1450, www.crocfarm.co.au* Turning onto the Arnhem Highway, the settlement of **Humpty Doo** is the last opportunity for relatively cheap supplies before heading into Kakadu. After another 20 km is a turning for **Fogg Dam Conservation Reserve**, which is 10 km off the highway. Originally constructed to grow rice, the builders of Fogg Dam unwittingly created a large permanent wetland area that has become a haven for both local and migratory birds.

Darwin to the Adelaide River
Distance: 65 km

The **Window on the Wetlands** is a striking Parks and Wildlife visitor centre set on Beatrice Hill above the Adelaide River floodplain, with a first-floor deck for taking in the views of the wetlands. The centre aims to educate visitors on the wetlands environment and is worth a quick visit for the views or for information. ■ *Daily 0730-1930. Free. T8988 8188.* At the back of the centre an unsealed 2-km road leads to the wide Adelaide River and the moorings of the **Spectacular Jumping Crocodile Cruise**. This company runs one-hour cruises up and down the river, all the while enticing big, wild estuarine crocodiles ('salties') to surge up out of the water for chunks of pork dangled temptingly over the side of the boat. Small crocs can lift their entire bodies out of the water and even the big boys can manage to get over half their body length airborne in a tail-powered lunge the sight of which is quite awesome. The first cruise is often pretty full and on a larger boat, so go for one of the later trips with a smaller boat. Free tea, coffee and snake-handling while waiting for a cruise. ■ *Cruises daily on the hr every 2 hrs from 0900-1500. $22, family $55. T8988 4547, spectacular@jumpingcrocodile.com.au* Back on the highway, 3 km toward Kakadu, the larger **Adelaide River Queen** and its sister vessel offer a similar, 1½-hour cruise in more comfort but further removed from the action. ■ *Cruises daily every 2 hrs from 0900-1500 (May-Aug) and at 0900, 1100 and 1430 (Sep-Apr). $35.*

The Window on the Wetlands & the Adelaide River
Colour map 5, grid A3

Northern Territory

T8988 8144, www.jumpingcrocodilecruises.com.au, transfers from Darwin available. There's also a café serving light lunches and snacks from 0900-1630. The **Pathfinder** is a smaller vessel running one-hour trips from the same spot. ■ *Daily at 1100, 1330 and 1530. $22, family $55. T8988 8102.*

Mary River National Park (proposed)
Colour map 5, grid A3
Main turn-off 20 km from Annaburroo,
110 km from Jabiru

Protecting part of the Mary River catchment area, this park includes freshwater billabongs, and paperbark and monsoon forests. For most people who come here it's a place to catch barramundi but it also provides opportunities to see a wetlands environment full of birds and crocodiles that receives relatively few visitors. As access is by unsealed roads and 4WD tracks only, the park gets less congested than Kakadu just down the road. At **Mistake Billabong** and **Bird Billabong** there are viewing platforms or bird hides to observe from, (the latter is reached after a 1-½ km walk) and there are boat cruises on the river to get you closer to the wildlife. The park is north of the Arnhem Highway and almost all points are reached from Point Stuart Road.

Do not swim anywhere in the Mary River region as it is full of estuarine crocodiles, and do not camp or stand close to the water's edge

Sleeping There are a number of park campgrounds, including the very picturesque and popular **Shady Camp**. A quieter campsite can be found at **Couzens Lookout** on the Rockhole Rd, past the ranger station. There are good views of the river here, particularly at sunset. The area also has 2 commercial resorts with rooms, camping sites, pools, bars and bistros, and both about 35 km off the highway. **B-D** *Point Stuart Wilderness Lodge*, T8978 8914, www.adventuretours.com.au, is closer to Shady Camp, has both en suite a/c and budget fan-cooled rooms, plus a basic bunkhouse, and runs a wetlands boat cruise (2 hrs, $27.50). The slightly more luxurious **B** *Wildman River Wilderness Lodge*, T8978 8912, is in the heart of the park, has a/c rooms including breakfast and a 1-course dinner, with shared facilities and also offers river cruises (2 hrs, $39.50).

Annaburroo 50 km from Adelaide,
130 km from Jabiru

Close to the Mary River, **Annaburroo** caters both for those travelling through to Kakadu and those exploring Mary River National Park. It consists of little except for the large and friendly **B-D** *Bark Hut Inn*, T8978 8988, which has simple a/c singles, doubles and 4-bunk dorms plus large family rooms and a large en suite unit. Cheap counter meals or hot snacks are served throughout the day from 0600-2100, they cook their own muffins and pies, have a small art gallery and souvenir shop, and serve fuel at 0600-2300. **C-D** *Mary River Park*, 3 km before the pub, close to the river, T8978 8877, www.maryriverpark.com.au, has small, tidy, a/c, en suite cabins, and fan-cooled 4-bunk *YHA* dorms. There's a very basic alfresco BBQ kitchenette, and cheap meals available 0630-2130 in the simple licensed restaurant. They also run **boat cruises** on the river, daily every 2 hrs from 0900-1500 ($25, 1½ hrs), and **birdwatching tours**, taking anything from 3 hrs ($35, daily 0900 and 1500) to several days. **D-E** *Annaburroo Lodge*, opposite the inn down a 2-km unsealed road, T8978 8971, is less a lodge, more a collection of rustic chalets, cottages and bush huts clustered around the shore of the very pretty **Annaburroo Billabong**. Usually croc free, the owners supply free canoes for guests and swimming is also allowed. This is the best-value option in the region for large groups and families not equipped to camp and their small, stylish bamboo huts (a/c) are equally attractive to couples. Recommended.

Berry Springs & the Territory Wildlife Park
Colour map 5, grid A3
50 km from Darwin,
100 km from Litchfield National Park via unsealed road

A short distance west of the Stuart Highway, Berry Springs has a delightful **nature park** situated around freshwater springs. It is a great place for a swim and very popular with locals so can get crowded at weekends. There is also a small kiosk selling cheap snacks and drinks (daily 1200-1700). Next door is the main attraction of the area, the **Territory Wildlife Park**. Established by the Parks and Wildlife Commission in 1989, the park consists of flora and fauna of the tropical north set amid 1,000 acres of bushland. A bus loop (4 km) and walking paths (6 km) link the exhibits of animals in their appropriate habitat, such as wetlands, monsoon rainforest or mangroves. The highlights include the Eagle Flight Deck, when you can see birds of prey swoop down to catch a morsel of meat in mid-air, an Aquarium that has a glass tunnel so you can see huge barramundi, and various strange creatures swimming overhead, and a walk-through dome aviary. The nocturnal house is a good place to see animals such as the bilby and the park also houses the very unusual black wallaroo, found only in parts of Arnhem Land. Some of the other exhibits are looking a bit tired but the best ones make a visit well worthwhile. A shuttle-bus drives the circuit every 15 minutes but there is still a lot of walking so make sure you wear comfy shoes. Allow at least four hours, or a whole day if possible, to look around. The entry ticket allows you to leave the park and return, so you can go and have a swim and some lunch at Berry Springs, a far more appealing place than the park's lacklustre café. ■ *Daily 0830-1600, last exit 1800. $18, children and concessions $9. T8988 7200, www.territorywildlifepark.com.au Cox Peninsula Rd.* The settlement of Berry Springs itself consists of a few businesses such as a service station. The nearby caravan park **D** *Tumbling Waters*, Cox Peninsula Road (7 km west of wildlife park), T8988 6255, has pleasant, good-value cabins.

Shaded by lofty palms, this small town first acted as a service town for a supply route, and then for the Rum Jungle Uranium Mine. Now it provides facilities for students at the Batchelor College for Aboriginal tertiary education, and visitors to nearby Litchfield National Park. Part of the college is open to the public as the commercial **Coomalie Cultural Centre**, an indigenous art and craft gallery. ■ *1000-1700 Tue-Sat (Apr-Sep); 1000-1600 Tue-Fri (Oct-Mar). Awilla Rd, T8939 7404.* The other main place of interest is the **Batchelor Butterfly and Bird Sanctuary** which has two large netted enclosures and a 5-m rock waterfall with tiered swimming pools. ■ *Daily 0830-1600. $7, children $3. Meneling Rd, T8976 0199, www.butterflyfarm.net WOOFAs welcome.* Close by, on Batchelor Road, *Northern Air Charter*, T8976 0023, www.flynac.com.au, will take groups of up to five people on scenic flights over Litchfield (30 minutes, $115 per person, minimum of two).

Batchelor
Colour map 5, grid A3
100 km from Darwin, 40 km from Adelaide River

There are plans to re-open the currently closed VIC on Tarkarri Rd, hopefully with the same number, T8976 0444

Sleeping and eating As the closest town to the national park, options have been steadily on the increase over the last few years. The **B** *Rum Jungle Motor Inn*, Rum Jungle Rd, T8976 0123, big4.batchelor.nt@bigpond.com, has large, well-equipped motel rooms, the town's main public bar and serves mid-range meals in the pool-side dining room and patio from 1800-2100. Also counter meals 1200-1400. **C** *Jungle Drum Bungalows*, Meneling Rd, T8976 0555, jungledrumbunga-lows@bigpond.com, have half a dozen en suite, a/c chalets, each with enough Bali nese furniture and decoration to evoke a hint of Asia. Recommended. Their cheap, licensed, Balinese-style restaurant next to the pool serves fairly standard Aussie tucker. Open 0700-0900 and 1800-2030. Next door, the **C-E** *Butterfly and Bird Sanctuary* has 3 rooms in a relaxed, self-contained house, 2 good value a/c doubles and a 3-bed dorm. Their cheap licensed café is the best spot town for chilling out, open 0830-1600 and 1800-2030. There are several **caravan parks** in and around town. The in-town **C** *Caravillage*, Rum Jungle Rd, T8976 0166, big4.batche-lor.nt@bigpond.com, has a good range of facilities and self-contained cabins, while the **C-E** *Banyan Tree*, 12 km toward the park, T/F8976 0330, has a range of good value self-contained cabins, rooms, well-equipped on-site vans, kitchen and pool.

Northern Territory

Litchfield National Park

Colour map 5, grid A3
Wangi Falls 70 km
from Batchelor,
170 km from Darwin

This lovely park is one of the most popular in the state, thanks to its proximity to Darwin and its accessibility. It encompasses a sandstone plateau called the Tabletop Range and it is the water cascading off the range that gives Litchfield its main feature. The plateau's sandstone holds wet-season water releasing it gradually to create year-round waterfalls and rock pools, although naturally all the falls are far more impressive during the wet season. All the major sights can easily be seen in a day but an overnight camp will make the most of the experience.

Entering from Batchelor, the first stop is a field of tombstone-like **magnetic termite mounds**, built on a north-south axis to regulate the internal temperature of the mound. To regulate your own temperature take your swimming gear to the next feature, **Buley Rockholes**, a stunning series of small rock pools, that eventually flow into **Florence Falls** downstream. A 1½ km walk along the riverbank connects the two or you can drive. There is large plunge pool at the bottom of the 15-m falls and this is a quiet place to swim as you have to walk 500 m downhill to reach it. **Tolmer Falls** drop into a deep, sheer-sided gorge to a pool, but can only be viewed from above, as it is the protected habitat of orange horseshoe and ghost bats. The Tolmer Creek walk loops back to the car park from the lookout (1½ km) and is well worth doing for the views of the upper gorge. **Greenant Creek** is a quiet picnic area and the start of a 3-km return walk to Tjaetaba Falls (no swimming). The most popular falls are **Wangi Falls**, accessible by a short path. These double falls make an idyllic swimming spot, with a good walk (1½ km loop) up through tropical monsoon forest to the head of the falls. There is also a kiosk at the falls (0800-1800 May-October; 0800-1600 November-April), phones, a picnic area and campsite.

Few people visit **Walker Creek**, the last site on the road north, but this is a magical place if you like bush camping. A series of eight and secluded sites, situated beside falls and deep rock pools, are strung along 2 km of the creek and must be reached on foot. There are powered sites and an ablution block at the basic *Wangi Tourist Park*, T8978 2185, outside the park 4 km from the falls. Four-wheel drives can also get to the **Lost City**, a collection of sandstone towers. The gravel road north to Berry Springs should be sealed shortly, allowing a loop from Darwin via the Territory Wildlife Park. ■ *Park notes and a road condition report available at the entry point west of Batchelor. Camping fees from $3.30-6.60 per person payable at self-registration stations. For more information contact the park offices in Batchelor, T8976 0282 or Palmerston T8999 5511. No fuel between Batchelor and Berry Springs.*

Adelaide River (township)
Colour map 5, grid A3
115 km from Darwin,
110 km from
Pine Creek

Following the bombing of Darwin during the Second World War, Adelaide River became the base for both Australian and American military operations. Little evidence of this is left except the carefully maintained War Cemetery, the resting place of 434 allied servicemen and women and 63 civilians killed in the Top End during the war. Today, Adelaide River is not much more than a collection of roadhouses but does have a couple of good places to linger.

Mt Bundy Station
must be booked
in advance

Sleeping and eating D *Adelaide River Inn*, T8976 7047, is a very pleasant pub with a large beer garden and a pretty unusual bar adornment. Charlie the Buffalo starred in the *Crocodile Dundee* films and afterwards retired to the pub to stand proudly on the counter. The pub has motel units, caravan sites and does meals daily. The settlement has a small museum of local history in the old railway station south of the bridge and this also acts as a centre for tourist information. Daily 1000-1600 (May-Oct), Sun 1200-1700 (Nov-Apr). The road opposite the railway station leads to **A-D** *Mount Bundy Station*, T8976 7009, mt.bundy@octa4net.au This tranquil, leafy homestead area is an excellent place. It has stockmen quarters with shared kitchen and bathroom, a self-contained cottage and pool, and there are 3 traditional B&B rooms in the modern house on the hill above. The welcoming Briggs family, large sumptuous rooms and lovely balcony views make the B&B rooms memorable. Evening meals available on request.

Transport *McCafferty's/Greyhound* Darwin-bound services leave the BP roadhouse at 0950 and 1530. Their southbound buses depart at 1015 and 1505.

Daly River

Colour map 5, grid A3
110 km from Adelaide River,
170 km from Pine Creek

You don't have to spend long in the Top End to realize that the locals have a passion for fishing – especially for barramundi, the most delicious of Australian fish. The Daly is one of the Territory's best spots to catch large barramundi and hosts two major annual fishing competitions: the Barra Classic (May) and Barra Nationals (late April). There are several resorts and caravan parks on the banks of the wide, croc-infested river, catering mostly to fishermen: *Banyan Farm*, T8978 2461, *Daly River Mango Farm*, T8978 2464, www.mangofarm.com.au and *Perry's*, T8978 2452, all have a good range of accommodation and facilities. Fuel and groceries are available from the *Daly River Pub*, T8978 2418, and the *Nauiyu* Aboriginal community store. The community also operates a highly regarded arts centre, **Merrepen Arts**, known for a lively one-day arts festival and art auction, usually held in early June. The festival usually attracts thousands of people. ■ *Mon-Fri 0800-1700, Sat-Sun by appointment only. T8978 2533, merrepen@bigpond.com*

Douglas Daly

Colour map 5, grid A3
83 km from Adelaide River,
100 km from Pine Creek

The region around the upper reaches of the Daly River, known as the Douglas Daly, is a largely flat pastoral area crossed by several tributaries of the Daly including the Douglas. The most striking sight in the area is without doubt **Butterfly Gorge**, a beautiful, steep-sided series of plunge pools with excellent views from the top. Unfortunately it's only accessible via a 17-km stretch of very rough 4WD track from **Douglas Daly Hot Springs**, themselves a 7-km unsealed drive off the main through road. The springs flow into the Douglas, at this stage a shallow sandy stream winding through semi-tropical woodland. The stream can get as hot as 60°C in places so dip a toe in first and head a few yards downstream to find a cooler spot if necessary. Camping is allowed at the springs, though not at the gorge. It's well worth the visit and a day or two's stay at the isolated **C-E** *Douglas Daly Caravan Park*, T/F8978 2479, douglasdalypark@bigpond.com, one of the most relaxing and friendly parks in the Top End. Simple but spotless air-conditioned rooms come in cheap twin or pricier family options, and the facilities include a pool, bar, limited shop and café serving quality cheap meals, 0700-0900, 1200-1400 and 1600-1800. Note there are no kitchen facilities. The park is at one end of a 4-km stretch of river, called the **Esplanade**, that is dotted with rapids, hot springs, natural spas and a picturesque plunge pool known as the **Arches** (2 km). Instead of the caravan park you can choose to bushcamp at one of nine sites along this stretch, but you'll have to forego the all-important ablution block.

Pine Creek & around

Colour map 5, grid A3
Population: 500
225 km from Darwin,
160 km from Cooinda (Kakadu), 90 km from Katherine

Though much reduced in size and importance since its heyday, Pine Creek has just managed to remain a town rather than an extended roadhouse, and a surprisingly likeable one at that. One of the original 'gold-rush' towns of the 1870s, it is now the only one still remaining in the Top End. At **Gun Alley Gold Mining** you can sit comfortably under a tree and hear all about the lives of the original miners, watch the restored 1866 steam-driven crusher turn ore into manageable gravel and then pan this gravel for flecks of gold, which you can

Northern Territory

expect to find and get to keep in souvenir containers. ■ *Daily 0830-1500. $6. T8976 1221. Playford St. Allow 1½ hrs.* The town also has two museums, recounting other aspects of the region's past. Just off Main Terrace, the 1889 tin **Railway Station** has a small collection of displays and memorabilia plus, on the 200 m of remaining track, a gloriously restored 1877 steam train with passenger carriages. ■ *Daily: hrs vary but usually 0800-1300. Entry by gold coin donation.* **Pine Creek Museum**, housed in the original telegraph repeater station, concentrates on the telegraph and war eras. ■ *1100-1700 Mon-Fri, 1100-1300 Sat. $2.20, children free.* The open mine, which opened later and is now two-thirds filled with water, can be viewed from the **mine lookout** off Moule Street.

Umbrawarra Gorge
25 km unsealed
from Pine Creek

Umbrawarra Gorge is a 4-km, low-winding gorge with intensely red chunky walls and a succession of waterholes. The further you venture up, the tighter the walls get and the better the scenery. You might spot some rock wallabies or water birds, and there is also some rock art, making the effort well worthwhile. People don't usually venture too far because of the sheer difficulty. Wading, even swimming, is necessary at times and while on dry land the going can be over slippery, uneven rock surfaces. Of course if you make the effort you'll have a rock pool all to yourself. Facilities at the start of the gorge are limited to basic toilets and a camping area. Leaving Pine Creek, roughly halfway to Katherine is the turn-off to **Edith Falls**, part of Nitmiluk National Park.

4WD only in
wet season

Sleeping and eating C *Digger's Rest*, Main Terr, T8976 1442, has several modern, fully self-contained cabin-style units. Good value. The C *Pine Creek Hotel*, Moule St, T8976 1288, has motel-style units out the back and 3 separate bars, but most visitors find themselves eating next door at *Mayse's*, a long-standing deli-style café that's a popular stop for coaches. Open 0700-1900 Mon-Fri and 0700-2100 Sat-Sun, the quality of food is consistently good and the portions are generous. Recommended. Opposite, the **E** *BP Service Station*, T8976 1217, has a small camping area plus a few a/c twins and doubles in dongas. They're not particularly pretty, but clean, spacious, include linen and very good value. Also in town are a couple of site-only caravan parks, one of which, the *Lazy Lizard*, T8976 1244, is also a roadhouse and rustic tavern.

Transport *McCafferty's/Greyhound* Darwin-bound services leave the *Ah Toy's* store, Main Terr, at 0815 and 1400. Their southbound buses depart at 1130 and 1625.

Kakadu National Park and Arnhem Land

www.ea.gov.au/
parks/kakadu

Kakadu is one of Australia's great treasures – a vast area rich in landscapes, culture and wildlife. Around 80% the park is covered by open eucalypt woodland. These forested lowlands meet the South Alligator River in the middle of the park and it is this river that provides some of Kakadu's most beautiful areas – the billabongs and wetlands. The entire river system is protected within the park, from its catchment area in the stone country of the Arnhem Land plateau to the mudflats and mangroves on the coast. The wetlands areas are full of birdlife - including the jabiru stork, sea eagle, heron and grey crane - which can be seen at the Mamukala Wetlands, Anbangbang Billabong and at Yellow Waters, where you can also glide among the wildlife on a boat cruise. At the end of the dry season when the water recedes, there are impressive concentrations of wildlife at these spots. In the eastern section of the park, the escarpment towers above the floodplain, scored with secret gorges harbouring rainforest and rare animals and cascading with waterfalls in the wet season. Only a fraction of this terrain is accessible and is best seen by flying over it, but those areas of stone country you can explore are simply captivating. Some are idyllic natural features, such as the waterfalls and plunge pools of Jim Jim Falls, Twin Falls, Maguk and Gunlom, but the escarpment also contains extraordinary rock art, testifying to the inseparable nature of the spiritual and material connection between Kakadu and its indigenous people. The main sites are at Ubirr and Nourlangie, both are of outstanding natural beauty, and contain images that range from many thousands of years old to just a few decades old.

The park is managed by its Aboriginal owners and Parks Australia. Although few Aboriginal people now live in Kakadu, its a different story in Arnhem Land. About 20,000 people live in an area the size of Victoria, and only 10% are Balanda or Managa (non-indigenous people). Entry to Arnhem Land is controlled by a permit system but some areas may be visited on tours or with a 4WD. It is worth getting there to see its classic Top End scenery, some of the finest rock art in the world, and to glimpse into a part of Australia where indigenous culture remains strong.

Ins and outs

Kakadu is best seen with your own transport, though it is possible to see the park at your own pace using public transport and the local tours, and still experience much of the best that Kakadu has to offer. Many people without their own transportation choose to get on a multi-day tour from Darwin, and it is also possible to make it part of a Darwin to Katherine or Alice Springs trip (in the reverse direction also). If you do book such a tour, check exactly what is included, in terms of practicalities, subsidiary trips and itinerary. Not all tours, for instance, include Jim Jim and Twin falls. If you only have one day you should consider a scenic flight from Darwin that flies over Jim Jim and Twin falls and lands at Cooinda for the Yellow Waters Cruise. Most local tours start at either the Border Store, Jabiru or Cooinda, with most operators offering pick-ups from at least the latter two. Note that there is an entry fee to the park of $16.25 per person (valid for a week). **Bus** *McCafferty's/Greyhound* run a daily service during the dry season to Kakadu Resort, Jabiru and Cooinda, leaving at 0630. They also run a connecting tour service from Jabiru to the Border Store. There are a couple of excellent day-tours from Kakadu into the nearer parts of **Arnhem Land**, and a couple of overland multiple-day tours from Darwin up to the Cobourg Peninsula, but most trips and tours into the area involve flying from Darwin to either the Cobourg or Gove peninsula. *Qantas* fly to Gove (Nhulunbuy) daily from Darwin and Cairns, and a shuttle bus meets every flight.

Getting there & around
For details of Darwin tour operators, see page 660

Northern Territory

Northern Kakadu

From Mary River the border of **Kakadu National Park** is reached quite quickly, though there's a fair way to go before the good stuff. The first real attraction of the park is the boardwalk and lookout over the **Mamukala Wetlands** on the South Alligator floodplain. Mamukala is a tranquil place to see birdlife, but can feel a bit distant from the action – take binoculars if possible. The best time to visit these wetlands is September-October when thousands of magpie geese are concentrated here. There is a 3-km loop walk from the car park (mostly through woodland). Mamukala is 90 km from Annaburroo, and 10 km past the L *Kakadu Resort*, T8979 0166, kresort@aurora-resorts.com.au, the first of the steeply priced resort complexes inside the park's boundaries. Facilities include a bar, café (in the dry season only), expensive buffet restaurant and fuel.

Jabiru
Colour map 5, grid A3
Population: 1,200
250 km from Darwin,
220 km from
Pine Creek

Named after the black-necked stork, this small town was created in the 1970s to house and service workers from the Ranger Uranium Mine nearby. Uranium was found in Kakadu during geological surveys in the 1950s – a time when the British and Australian governments were offering rewards for uranium discoveries to feed the development of atomic weapons. It is now also home to many of the park's rangers, hospitality workers and tour operators, and has a surprisingly good range of facilities. The excellent **Bowali Visitor Centre** is the main point of park information for visitors, 5 km by road from Jabiru, or 2 km on foot. The centre features an imaginative display on the history, management,

Kakadu National Park

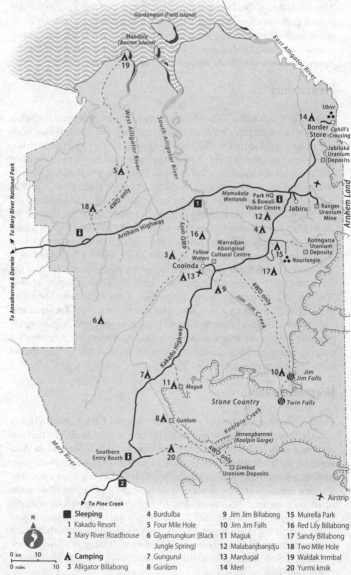

Sleeping ■

1 Kakadu Resort
2 Mary River Roadhouse

Camping ▲

3 Alligator Billabong
4 Burdulba
5 Four Mile Hole
6 Glyamungkurr (Black Jungle Spring)
7 Gungurul
8 Gunlom
9 Jim Jim Billabong
10 Jim Jim Falls
11 Maguk
12 Malabanjbanjdju
13 Mardugal
14 Merl
15 Muirella Park
16 Red Lily Billabong
17 Sandy Billabong
18 Two Mile Hole
19 Waldak Irrmbal
20 Yurmi kmik

Northern Territory

flora and fauna of the park. A small theatre shows films about Kakadu through-out the day and it is well worth trying to catch the one featuring the late Bill Neidjie, known as 'Kakadu Man' (check the timetable outside the door). Bowali has an information desk for general advice on the park and is a good place to pick up park notes if you are intending to do any walks. Walkers can also buy topographic maps here. The Marrawuddi Gallery sells a good range of Aborigi-nal arts and crafts, books and souvenirs and next door is an outdoor café. ■ *Daily 0800-1700. Free. T8938 1120.*

Sleeping and eating As the most centrally placed location for the park's sights, Jabi-ru also has the most in the way of sleeping and eating. Most striking (at least from the air) is the **L** *Gagudju Crocodile Hotel*, T8979 2800, www.holiday-inn.com, built in the shape of the ubiquitous reptile. Overall standards are the highest in the park with quite luxurious rooms and an excellent, expensive restaurant. Slightly further from the town centre is the **L-B** *Kakadu Lodge & Caravan Park*, T8979 2422, klodge@aurora-resorts.com.au The lodge rooms, close to the pool and attendant bar, are simple but comfortable and sleep up to 4 people. At $199 the cabins are some of the most expen-sive you'll set eyes on but are self-contained and well-equipped, sleeping up to 5. Facil-ities include a licensed bistro and BBQs. **B-D** *Lakeview Park*, Lakeview Dr (behind the Mobil station), T8979 3144, offers the best value within Kakadu, from the spacious self-contained 2-bedroom units and a/c doubles to the simple bush bungalows, one of which sleeps a family of 4 for just $55.

All Jabiru facilities are open year-round

    Eating The *Sports and Social Club*, Lakeside Dr, T8979 2326, serves very cheap meals from 1800-2030 Tue-Sat and 1200-1400. Their Wed '$10 steak' night is espe-cially popular and a good chance to meet some of the locals. The alfresco rear deck is surprisingly picturesque, looking out over a man-made lake. The other specials night in town is Tue when the *Plaza Takeaway*, in the main shopping centre, cooks up a curry or two at 1800-2100. Otherwise they're open for breakfasts, hot lunches and take-aways 0730-1700 Mon-Fri and 0900-1400 Sat (and Sun in the busier times of the dry season), and, during Jun-Sep, for pizzas from 1800-2100 Thu-Sat. Jabiru also has a good bakery on Gregory Pl.

Tours and activities Arnhem Land *Davidson's Arnhemland Safaris*, T8927 5240, www.arnhemland-safaris.com, have a safari camp at Mt Borradaile, halfway between Oenpelli and the Coburg Peninsula. Activities include boat cruises, rock art tours, walk-ing and fishing. Packages include charter flight from Darwin or Jabiru, meals and accommodation in safari tents. Self-drive is also an option during the dry season. **Fishing** *Kakadu Fishing Tours*, T8979 2025, take up to 3 people on very personalized trips into the wetlands. $200 for half a day if only one passenger, otherwise $120. **Ranger Uranium Mine** Departing from Jabiru airport, there are daily tours to see this huge open-cut mine and its extraction processes. Departures at 1030 and 1330 during May-Oct, also 0830 and 1500 subject to demand (75 mins, $20, children $10). Covered footwear must be worn. T8979 2411, kakair@kakair.com.au **Scenic flights** *Kakadu Air*, T8979 2411, kakair@kakair.com.au, fly both aeroplanes and helicopters out of Jabi-ru airport over the nearer parts of Arnhem Land and East Alligator Valley. Fixed-wing flights are $80 for 30 mins per person, $130 per hr, helicopter flights are around $60-75 per 10 mins. Their best value flight is the 30-min helicopter ride ($175). *North Australian Helicopters*, T8979 2444, www.northaustralianhelicopters.com.au, also offer several options including one over Jim Jim and Twin falls ($420, approx 70 mins). Minimum 2 passengers. It is also possible to fly over Kakadu from Darwin (see page 660).

See also Ubirr and Cooinda

Transport The *McCafferty's/Greyhound* dry-season service stops at **Kakadu Resort** at 1000 on its way to Jabiru, and at 1630 on its way back to Darwin. From **Jabiru**

Northern Territory

▶▶ **Kakadu's done deal**

During the 1950s uranium was found in southern Kakadu and by the 1970s high-grade deposits in northern Kakadu at Ranger, Jabiluka and Koongarra had also been discovered. The proposal to mine these areas caused such concern that the federal government began an environmental impact study in 1975. Local Aboriginal people opposed mining and the commissioners acknowledged that it was likely to result in the breakdown of traditional culture, but their report recommended that mining could proceed subject to stringent environmental protection. Under the 1976 Land Rights (NT) Act, Aboriginal ownership of Kakadu and Arnhem Land was legally recognized, with a limited veto over mining, but the Ranger Project Area was exempt from the act as were all exploration licences taken out before 1976. The Aboriginal owners could only negotiate terms of agreement with the mining companies. The first stage of Kakadu National Park was declared in 1979, with the three main uranium deposits excluded from the park area. Uranium is currently mined at an open-cut mine at Ranger, near Jabiru, where any radioactive waste is buried. Whether mining royalties paid to Aboriginal people are sufficient compensation for the impact on their culture of having land destroyed and a town built in the middle of their previously undeveloped region is a hotly disputed point. Sealed roads built for mining in the 1960s and 1970s brought the first tourists into the area, but the park's status, and the attendant visitor numbers, skyrocketed with the release of the hugely popular film Crocodile Dundee in the late 1980s. Kakadu was inscribed on the World Heritage List for natural and cultural values in three stages (1981, 1987 and 1992).

shopping centre the Darwin-bound bus heads out at 1600, the bus to Cooinda leaves at 1020, and the tour service to the **Border Store** at 0815.

Ubirr & the Border Store
Colour map 5, grid A3
Ubirr, the store and hostel are closed during the wet season

Although well off the beaten track, Ubirr is one of the most beautiful areas in the park and shouldn't be missed. The rock overhangs of Ubirr were used by Aboriginal people as campsites close to the rich food resources of the river and floodplain and as a canvas for recording those resources and their creation myths. A 1-km loop walker wanders through several rock art sites that include spirit figures and animals such as the *thylacine*, extinct in this area for several thousand years. By the Main Gallery is a short, steep track to the top of the out-crop and from here the views of the wetlands and escarpment are breathtaking; especially half an hour before sunset when golden light intensifies the green vegetation and orange-grey rock. Unfortunately hordes of chattering tour groups descend at the same time but it is still worth it.

Border Store 40 km from Jabiru, 3 km from Ubirr

The East Alligator River forms the border of **Arnhem Land** and the only way in is across Cahill's Crossing, a tidal ford that is impassable for six months of the year (permits are required to enter Arnhem Land). On the Kakadu side of the crossing is the *Border Store*, open for takeaways and a small range of expensive groceries and souvenirs, daily 0830-1730. If you intend to cross the river you'll need to check the tides chart here. Behind the shop is the **D-E** *Kakadu YHA Hostel*, T8979 2232. The hostel has 10 twins and doubles with fans and two 10-bed air conditoned dorms (no locks on doors). The kitchen is spacious and well equipped, but if you're feeling lazy put in an order by 1700 for a choice of simple meals served between 1900 and 1930. The *Merl* campground, 1 km before the border store has showers, toilets and a genera-tor zone ($5.50 per person, caravans allowed).

Northern Territory

Tours and activities Arnhem Land *Lord's*, T8979 2970, www.lords-safaris.com, runs one of the region's best tours, a day-trip that takes you to Gunbalanya (from Jabiru and Ubirr) for a look at the magnificent art site at **Injaluk Hill** ($165, maximum 9 passengers) and **Injaluk Arts and Crafts**. The rest of the day is spent exploring the spectacular rock escarpments, billabongs and wetlands of this area of Arnhem Land. Recommended. *Magela*, T8979 2114, magela@austarnet.com.au, have a small range of similar day excursions to other art sites in the area, taking a maximum of 20 passengers. *Venture North*, T8927 5500, www.northernaustralia.com 3-day 4WD tours to Cobourg Peninsula visiting **Injaluk Hill** and arts centre, and Port Essington (Tue, Thu, $705). **Boat cruise** *Guluyambi*, T8979 2411, operates boat cruises on the East Alligator River focusing on Aboriginal culture. Aboriginal guides explain the uses of some of the river plants, aspects of their culture and point out the odd croc. Cruises leave from the upstream boat ramp, 2 km from the Border Store, at 0900, 1100, 1300 and 1500 during May-Oct. Also during the wet season but you'll need to check ahead for days, times and location. **Walking** There are two good short walks close to the river. The Manngarre Walk starts from the riverside car park opposite the Border Store and passes through monsoon rainforest (1½ km loop). The more striking Bardedjilidji Walk winds through layered sandstone stacks, weathered into mushrooms shapes, caves and tunnels (2½ km). To reach this one take the riverside path from Cahills Crossing to the upstream boat ramp car park and keep walking south along the road until you reach the walk car park.

Border Store is the starting point for tours into Arnhem Land

See also Jabiru and Cooinda

Transport The *McCafferty's/Greyhound* dry season bus to **Bowali Visitor Centre**, near Jabiru, leaves the Border Store at 1300.

Central Kakadu

Nourlangie Rock is best known as a rock art site but it is also a spectacular feature of the landscape, more dramatic than Ubirr. The sheer southern wall rises at least 100 m above the plain, the orange sandstone striped with black water lines. Below this wall a walking trail leads to the most visited site, **Anbangbang rock shelter and gallery**. As recently as the 1950s this shelter contained a paperbark bed, stone scrapers, blades, used bits of ochre and burial parcels. Such items were stolen from many areas of Nourlangie in the 1970s when tourists began to arrive. The famous paintings at Anbangbang, of Namargon the lightning man and X-ray like family groups, are significant because they are among the last rock paintings done in Kakadu. Painted in 1964 by the master artist Najombolmi (also known as Barramundi Charlie) they represent the end of a tradition that began perhaps 20,000 or more years ago. Further along the path, the **Gunwarddehwardde Lookout** provides the park's best views of the escarpment, including the three pillars that are the sacred site of Namargon.

Nourlangie
12 km off the highway, 36 km from Jabiru, 45 km from Cooinda

There are many other layers of older paintings at Nourlangie, and many inaccessible sites, but if you are interested in rock art don't miss the little-visited **Nangaluwurr** site on the northern side of the rock. It requires a 2½-km return stroll through woodland to get to this overhang but it contains many fascinating paintings, such as a sailing ship, ancient hand prints and a Namandi spirit carrying dillybags to hold its victim's body parts. To get there, take the first unsealed road to the left on the road to Nourlangie. The lily-covered **Anbangbang Billabong** sits under the western face of the rock and is a picturesque place for a picnic or break, especially in the late afternoon when the wall lights up. A 2½ km walk follows the edge of the billabong but the best views are to be had from the first few picnic tables along the access road. There are also good views of the western end of Nourlangie from **Nawulandja lookout**, a large rock on the other side of the billabong (600 m climb).

Northern Territory

▶▶   **Never smile at a crocodile**

There are two species of crocodile inhabiting Australia's northern waterways. The **estuarine crocodile***, commonly known as the saltwater croc, or 'saltie', is far and away the most dangerous. Growing up to 6 m long, a big one will grab a cow or horse given the opportunity and will happily take a human for elevenses. Despite being shot on sight for decades by European pastoralists, their numbers held up well, until professional hunting started with a vengeance in the 1950s and the population soon plummeted. Protected since 1971, it was feared that they would become extinct, but they have recovered well and are now even culled in the Northern Territory. You need to start watching out for them north of Port Hedland and keep watching as far as Maryborough in Queensland. It is, unfortunately, a myth that they are only found in the sea or at the mouths of rivers. In fact they will stake territories anywhere suitable upriver, and have been found as much as 600 km inland. They are not fans of cross-country travel, however, and tend to stick to the water. A general rule of thumb for swimming in creeks and pools in the north is to get above a decent sized waterfall – though this is still no guarantee. If in any doubt whatsoever simply steer well clear of rivers, river banks and waterholes. Absence of a warning sign does not mean absence of a crocodile!*

The **freshwater crocodile** *is considerably smaller than the saltie and is not territorial. As such it tends to keep away from people and usually only attacks if trodden upon or threatened. They are not found as far west as the salties but around the Fitzroy River.*

It is easy to tell the difference between the two types of crocodile if you look at their snouts. The freshwater crocodile has a very narrow snout, tapering to a point at the end. The saltie has a much wider, chunkier snout.

Jim Jim & Twin falls
Colour map 5, grid A3
70 km off th highway, 115 km from Jabiru, 82 km from Cooinda

Due to water volume and crocodiles the falls are only open during the peak dry season

If these falls were more accessible they would probably be as famous as Uluru itself. **Jim Jim Falls** drop from a sheer 200-m cliff into a dark, tight bowl of rock and the plunge pool below. The huge boulders that lie scattered along the creek bed below the pool are all covered when the falls become a torrent in the wet season but must be clambered over to reach the falls during the dry (1 km). Often by the time Jim Jim falls are open there is just a trickle falling over the edge but the scale of the escarpment wall here is impressive enough. **Twin Falls**, a further 10 km down the track, are simply magical. The sandstone of the escarpment breaks down into soft white sand so, unlikely as it seems, the falls and their emerald-green plunge pool are fringed by a beautiful wide beach, within an amphitheatre of rock walls and bush. What makes this spot even more idyllic is that to reach it you need to swim, paddle or canoe about 1 km through the clear, cold pools of the gorge. Several operators run tours to both falls (see next page) and you can also drive yourself, although the track is 4WD only, becomes very rough towards the end and includes a ½-m deep creek crossing to get to Twin Falls. There are crocodile warning signs near both falls but park authorities go to a lot of effort to trap and remove any estuarine crocodiles before they open the area so it is generally considered safe for swimming (although you do so at your own risk). There is a bush campsite near Jim Jim Falls.

Warradjan Aboriginal Cultural Centre

Just before Cooinda, this distinctive centre is built in the shape of its namesake, the *warradjan* or pig-nosed turtle, and also represents the way Aboriginal people communicate with each other – sitting in a circle. It is one of the best centres of its kind in Australia, with attractive and innovative ways of describing the indigenous cultural environment of Kakadu. It not only explains Aboriginal uses and management of the land's resources but manages to give an insight into their way of thinking and concerns for the future. One of the highlights is a model that illustrates the complex rules and relationships of Aboriginal 'skin' groupings. A theatre shows regular videos about Kakadu and the centre also has a shop selling expensive art and craft work, souvenirs and a few drinks. ■ *Daily 0900-1700. 1 km from Gagudju Cooinda Lodge.*

Cooinda, the most southerly of the commercial centres within the park boundaries, and also the closest to Jim Jim and Twin falls, is essentially the L-D *Gagudju Cooinda Lodge*, T8979 0145, www.holiday-inn.com, with upmarket en suite air conditioned rooms grouped around the resort's swimming pool (available to all guests) and more basic budget rooms. Park facilities include fuel, basic shop, bar and expensive restaurant. **Yellow Waters Wetlands**, at the confluence of Jim Jim Creek and the South Alligator River, is a large area of billabongs, flood plains, paperbark swamps and river channels. It is one of the prettiest areas in the park but the best thing about Yellow Waters is that there are regular boat cruises that allow you to get right in among the wetlands, rather than squinting hopefully from a bird hide. It is an excellent way to see lots of birds and crocodiles at close range and the wetlands are wonderfully serene. Egrets, sea eagles, whistling kites, jacanas, pelicans and rainbow beeeaters are all commonly seen among the grass and waterlillies. There is a boardwalk (1½ km return) alongside the nearer wetlands to a platform on Home Billabong for those who want to take it all in at their own pace.

Cooinda & Yellow waters
60 km from Jabiru, 160 km from Pine Creek

During the wet season the lodge contracts its activities to the shop, fuel and minimal sleeping and eating

Tours and activities 4WD *Animal Tracks*, T8979 0145, www.kakadu.aisnet.au, is a 7 hr tour into the areas off the beaten track in a troop carrier, to see wildlife and experience something of Aboriginal culture. Information-packed, the afternoon tours culminate at sunset with damper and billy tea around a campfire. Departs daily 1300, good value at $88. Recommended. A number of tour operators pick up daily during the open-season (generally Jun-Nov) from Jabiru and Cooinda for day-tours to **Jim Jim and Twin falls**. *Kakadu Gorge and Waterfall Tours*, T8979 0111, are the only operator licensed to use canoes into Twin Falls and also have the advantage of leaving very early so their groups are often the first to arrive ($135). *Lord's*, T8979 2970, www.lords-safaris.com, runs a very similar tour, though allowing a bit longer in bed and using boogie boards instead of canoes ($130). Both supply morning tea and a simple lunch. **Boat** Yellow Waters cruises head out several times daily in the dry season, less often in the wet. Early morning and late afternoon trips are 2 hrs ($38, children $16.50), otherwise they're 1½ hrs ($33, children $15). Photographers will prefer the last cruise, while birdwatchers will benefit more earlier in the day. Free minibus transfers from the lodge leave 10-20 mins before each cruise. Prior bookings essential via the Lodge reception.

See also Jabiru and Ubirr

Transport The *McCafferty's/Greyhound* dry season service leaves Cooinda Lodge at 1430, arriving Jabiru at 1600 and **Darwin** at 1900.

Southern Kakadu

Southern Kakadu is the home of the *Jaowyn* people and is confusingly known as the Mary River area. The river forms the southwestern boundary of Kakadu but it is also part of the Mary River National Park (proposed), to the north (see page 664). The beautiful stone country of the escarpment is close to the highway here but despite its stunning beauty few, except locals, come here. The *Jaowyn* call this area *Buladjang*, the place of powerful and dangerous creation ancestor *Bula*, also translated as 'sickness country'. Jaowyn believe that if people disturb *Buladjang* country they will become unwell and their knowledge of their land has been vindicated by science. The area of sickness country

Gunlom 40 km unsealed from the highway, turn-off 10 km from Mary River

Some of the sites may be closed during the wet season, check ahead for access at this time

Northern Territory

corresponds almost exactly with areas that land surveys have shown to contain unusually high concentrations of uranium, arsenic, mercury and lead. In the 1953 a major deposit of uranium was found at Coronation Hill (*Gimbat*) and during the 1950s and 1960s a total of 13 gold and uranium mines were being worked in southern Kakadu, much to the distress and fear of the Jaowyn, until there was a world oversupply of uranium. By the 1980s, when proposals were made to mine Coronation Hill for gold, palladium and platinum, Aboriginal people had more of a political voice and after an extensive inquiry the Commonwealth government decided against mining in favour of the cultural and environmental values of the area. Most Jaowyn now live in the Katherine-Pine Creek region but continue to be involved in the management of the park.

Heading south the first attraction is **Maguk** (Barramundi Gorge), although the 12 km track to this pretty gorge is 4WD only. A 1-km walk through monsoon rainforest and paperbarks leads to a plunge pool and small waterfall. It is a fine place for a swim, you may see fish and freshwater crocodiles, and there is a bush campsite. After another 42 km, past the unexceptional **Bukbukluk Lookout**, is the turn-off for Gunlom, one of Kakadu's best camping spots. It is about 40 km to Gunlom but the unsealed road is usually fine for 2WD in the dry season (check road conditions at Bowali Visitor Centre). After 13 km on the Gunlom Road is **Yurmikmik** car park, the startpoint for several good walks. Yurmikmik lookout (2½ km from the starting point) has views over the ridge country and the Marrawal Plateau. **Motor Car Falls** (4 km from the start) drop over a high orange and black streaked sandstone wall to a large plunge pool. The falls are named after the Chevy that a miner managed to drive up the track as far as Motor Car Creek in 1946. From here the trail becomes unmarked but after crossing the bridge over the creek you can follow an old vehicle track to **Kurrundie Creek**, then drop south for 800 m to Kurrundie Falls (6 km from the start). This is another lovely plunge pool swimming spot and can make an excellent overnight walk. For more details pick up park notes from Bowali Visitor Centre and if you intend to leave the track also take a topographic map and compass. Camping is allowed at sites near Motor Car Falls and Kurrundie Falls but you must obtain a permit from Mary River Ranger Station (just north of the southern entry booth) or Bowali Visitor Centre. After walking from Yurmikmik, continue on to the comforts of **Gunlom** campground (where there are showers and toilets). One of the pleasures of camping here is that it is only a few hundred metres from a delightful plunge pool below a high dark rock wall. You can also climb to the top of the falls, from where there are great views of the South Alligator Valley and more magical green rock pools to swim in. If you have a 4WD there is one more stunning spot to find, considered one of the most beautiful gorges in the park and way off the beaten track. **Jarrangbarnmi** or Koolpin Gorge is accessible from the Gunlom Road. An unmarked trail follows the gorge of faulted and folded Kombolgie sandstone for a few kilometres, involving rock hopping, scree, rapids, rock pools and waterfalls. Access to this remote gorge is limited so a permit and access key must be obtained from the southern entry booth or Mary River ranger station.

Sleeping and eating The **C-E** *Mary River*, T8975 4564, is a recently much-improved roadhouse with very comfortable and well-equipped motel-style rooms, simple a/c donga doubles and cheap 12-bed bunkrooms. There are also caravan and camping sites. Pool and camp kitchen were planned at the time of writing. Breakfasts, fuel and hot snacks daily 0700-2300. The licensed bar serves cheap counter meals, 1200-1400 and 1800-1930 (hours can be restricted in wet season). Showers for non-residents $2.

Arnhem Land

Arnhem Land may have been the first area in Australia to be inhabited by Aboriginal people, who are thought to have arrived from southeast Asia at least 60,000 years ago. Today it is one of the last places in the country that Australian Aborigines manage to live much like they always have, continuing to maintain their cultural and spiritual ties to the land and to harvest its resources. About four times the size of Kakadu, Arnhem Land is owned by Aboriginal people, who call themselves *Yolngu*. It is beautiful country of rocky escarpment, open woodland and permanent wetlands, similar to Kakadu, and bordered by countless remote sandy beaches and the pale-blue tropical water of the Arafura Sea. Most of Arnhem Land's 18,000 Yolngu live in small communities of a few hundred people, but there is also a town, Nhulunbuy, on the Gove Peninsula in the far northeastern corner.

Getting there and around **Air** *Qantas*, T8987 1222, flies daily to Nhulunbuy from Cairns ($500 return, 1 hr 40 mins) and **Darwin** ($400 return, 1 hr 10 mins). The airport shuttle, T8987 2872, meets every flight and transfers passengers to accommodation ($7 one way). Flights to Cobourg Peninsula are usually arranged as part of an accommodation package. **Road** Most of Arnhem Land is completely inaccessible to visitors. Just 2 major tracks cross the region, and these are 4WD only and generally closed in the wet season. There are tourist facilities on the Cobourg and Gove peninsulas. Fuel is only available at the *Outback Store* at Mainoru, about 250 km from Katherine, so extra fuel must be carried. There are also 2 major river crossings: the Wilton River near Bulman Aboriginal community and Goyder River, 300 km from Nhulunbuy. Check road conditions on T1800 246199 or www.nt.gov.au/dtw **Tours** There are day-tours available from the Border Store (see page 673) into the Oenpelli region. Multi-day tours to the Cobourg Peninsula also leave from the Border Store and from Darwin (see page 660), and to the private safari camp at Mount Borradaile from Darwin and Jabiru (see page 671).

> **Ins & outs**
> *A permit (free) is required to enter Arnhem Land. Some accommodation operators will organize permits, otherwise contact the Northern Land Council in Nhulunbuy, T8987 2602, www.nlc.org.au, allowing about 2-4 weeks*

Arnhem Land is way off the beaten track (and expensive to get to) but it offers the chance to experience an ancient living culture and a landscape almost untouched by development. This is one of the finest ancient rock art sites in the world and on a guided tour you can see rock art that far surpasses the paintings at any of the public sites in Kakadu. There are also well-respected art and craft centres where you can buy the X-ray like bark paintings made in this region. Many visitors are also attracted by the superb reef and sport fishing. The most extraordinary experience of Aboriginal culture that you can have in Arnhem Land is to attend the annual **Garma Festival**, held over five days in August at a site 40 km south of Nhulunbuy. The festival celebrates and preserves traditional dance (*bunggul*), song (*manikay*), art and ceremony on Yolngu lands in northeast Arnhem Land. About 20 Yolngu clan groups and representatives from other parts of the state participate. A small number of visitors can join in the *yidaki* (didjeridu) masterclass, workshops, field trips to gather bush tucker and craft materials, and watch ceremonial dancing and bark painting. For more information see www.garma.telstra.com Festival attendance can be arranged through *World Expeditions*, T1300 720 000, www.worldexpeditions.com.au The $1,650 cost includes camping, food, activities and transfers from Nhulunbuy.

This former mission settlement just 20 km over the border sits amid magnificent wetlands and escarpment scenery. One of the main attractions of this Aboriginal community is the well-respected *Injaluk Arts and Crafts* centre, T8979 0190, where you can buy X-ray paintings on bark and paper, baskets and

> **Gunbalanya (Oenpelli)**

fabric at reasonable prices. The centre overlooks Injaluk Hill, one of the most remarkable rock art sites in the region. The caves and overhangs are covered in paintings of remarkable scale, delicacy and skill. You will need a permit to visit Gunbalanya and the art site can only be visited on a guided tour. There are regular day-tours from the Border Store and Jabiru (see pages 671 and 673 for details). Private tours of this art site ($45 per person) can also be arranged through *Injaluk Arts and Crafts* but you will need your own 4WD and to obtain a permit from the Northern Land Council in Darwin or Jabiru ($13.30).

Cobourg Peninsula
Colour map 5, grid A3

From Gunbalanya a 4WD track heads northwest out to the northern shore of the Cobourg Peninsula. The whole peninsula is preserved as **Garig Gunak Barlu National Park** (formerly Gurig) and the surrounding waters are a marine park containing dugong, turtles, dolphins, crocodiles and 250 species of fish. The park landscapes include vivid red cliffs above white beaches, dunes, grasslands, mangroves and wetland. There are no settlements as such on the peninsula, just three isolated, minimum-impact coastal resorts. Access is tightly controlled by the traditional owners under the permit system and only 15 vehicles are allowed into the park at a time. The chief delights of the peninsula are its peace, beautiful beaches, wildlife – it's particularly known as a fisherman's paradise – and its isolation. Most visitors fly in and stay at one of the resorts but you can visit the park independently if you have a 4WD vehicle equipped for remote driving and obtain a permit. Information on park walking trails and visiting Victoria Settlement can be obtained from the Black Point ranger station. There is also a cultural centre at Black Point with a display of Aboriginal, Macassan and European history of the peninsula. ■ *A permit costs $232 per vehicle and is valid for up to 5 adults for a week. To apply contact the permit officer, T8999 4814, F8999 4524 (well in advance for school holiday periods). Camping permits cost an extra $16.50 per person per night. Black Point ranger station T8979 0244.*

Sleeping and eating LL *Seven Spirit Bay Wilderness Lodge*, T9826 2471, www.sevenspiritbay.com A very luxurious and stylish resort built in open tropical style with Macassan touches, 24 units scattered among woodland. Restaurant, bar and pool and a range of activities such as guided walks, fishing, adventure safaris and sunset cruises. **LL** *Cape Don*, T8978 5145, www.capedon.gurig.com.au Accommodation in the Cape Don Lighthouse keeper's homestead, built in 1916 and still in operation. The tropical-style homestead has 5 bedrooms, housing a maximum of 12 guests. The focus of this place is fishing and their all-inclusive packages from Darwin include flights, tours and fishing charters. Closed Jan-Feb. **L** *Cobourg Beach Huts*, T8978 5145 or 1800 000871, www.cobourg.gurig.com.au 4 self-contained cabins, close to the beach, sleep up to 6. Well-equipped kitchens, but separate ablutions. Tours and dinghy hire can be arranged. Basic groceries and fuel are available at the *Garig Store*, open Mon-Sat 1600-1800. The park has 2 camping areas with showers, toilets and BBQs.

Gove Peninsula
Colour map 5, grid A3
Nhulunbuy
population: 4,000
www.ealta.org

This peninsula of perfect beaches and low rocky capes is the western gatepost of the Gulf of Carpentaria and the point at which the gulf meets the Arafura Sea. On its northern shore is **Nhulunbuy**, Arnhem Land's main town and centre for administration, industry, tourism, services, and also, as far as most visitors are concerned, indigenous culture. It's not, however, an Aboriginal town but was established in the early 1970s by *Nabalco*, to house and service workers for their bauxite mine. The Yolgnu were opposed to the mining and presented a 'bark petition' to the Commonwealth parliament in 1963, but they were defeated in the nation's first land rights case and mining proceeded. Despite mining the peninsula is still rich in wildlife and environmental beauty, as can be seen from the hide and walking trail at **Gayngaru (Town Lagoon)** which is visited by over 200 bird species. Aspects of the peninsula's culture and history are displayed at the **Buku Larrngay Mulka Art Centre and Museum** in Yirrkala, the peninsula's largest indigenous community, some 15 km south of Nhulunbuy. The centre is also well known for its important collection of historical bark paintings and as a showcase for contemporary bark paintings. There is a commercial gallery, the **Nambara Arts and Craft Centre**, 6 km from town on Melville Bay Road. Nhulunbuy has a **visitor information centre** that can help with tours, activities and details of areas you can explore with a permit. ■ *Daily 0900-1700. T8987 2255, www.ealta.org 12b Westal St (NAC building next to the airport). Permits are required to leave the town boundary, though not for the above sights: contact Dhimurru Land Management, Arnhem Rd, T8987 3992.*

Sleeping and eating L-A *Walkabout Lodge*, 12 Westal St, T8987 1777, www.walkaboutlodge.com.au, is a small beach-side resort in the centre of town. There are 40 a/c rooms, 3 bars, a restaurant and pool. **A** *Gove Peninsula Motel*, corner of Melville Bay Rd and Matthew Flinders Way, T8987 0700, www.govemotel.com 19 self-contained a/c rooms with a kitchenette, gardens and saltwater pool. The lodges take care of most of the eating, but also try the cafés *Chok's Stix* and *Gunyah*, both in Endeavour Sq.

Tours and activities Air *Northern Air Charter*, T8987 1770, www.flynac.com.au Scenic flights (Cessna) over the peninsula, from $63, 30 mins (min 3). **Boat hire** *Arnhem Boat Hire*, T8987 3181. **Diving and fishing** *Gove Diving and Fishing*, T8987 3445, www.govefish.com.au Charters, day-trips and Gove Harbour cruises. Best time for snorkelling and diving Sep-Mar. **Cultural/ecological tours** *Birds, Bees, Trees & Things*, T8987 1814, www.birdsbeestreesandthings.com.au Fishing charters, bird watching and lagoon trips. **Mining** Free tours of the mine and alumina plant, and Nambara Arts every Fri at 0830. Sleeved shirt and covered footwear required. Bookings essential, T8987 5345.

All the tours and activities are expensive. Expect to pay at least $250-300 a day for fishing, safari or cultural tours

Transport *Qantas* have daily flights to **Darwin** and **Cairns**. *Air North* fly to Darwin every Mon-Tue and Fri.

Directory Bank *Westpac*, with ATM, Endeavour Sq. **Bike, camping and sports hire** *Top Sports*, T8987 1748. **Car hire** *Kansas*, T8987 2872. **Communications** Post Office, Endeavour Sq. **Hospital** Matthew Flinders Way, T8987 0211. **Police** Matthew Flinders Way, T8987 1333.

Katherine to the 'red centre'

Though a part of the great plateau that separates the western Top End from Arnhem Land, the southwestern corner is protected not by Kakadu National Park, but by its southern state-run neighbour, Nitmiluk. The centrepiece of this park is the magnificent succession of connected gorges known collectively as Katherine Gorge. The town of Katherine sits on the banks of its namesake river a little further downstream and is the last major town on the Stuart Highway before Alice Springs in Australia's 'red centre'. There are few diversions on the long drive down, other than millions of termite mounds, though the crystal-clear springs of Mataranka and the ruddy globes of the Devil's Marbles are well worth making a stop for. The vast tracts of land either side of the highway, scrubby pastoral land and baking desert, are interrupted by just two sealed roads. From Katherine the Victoria Highway carves through the impressive bluffs of the eastern Gregory National Park before following the Victoria River to the Western Australia border.

Ins and outs

Getting there & around
Air *Air North* fly to Katherine from **Darwin** every Mon-Fri, and from **Alice Springs** and **Tennant Creek** every Sun-Fri. **Bus** 2 *McCafferty's/Greyhound* services head north along the Stuart Highway to Darwin, while 2 others go south to Alice Springs. From Katherine there is one bus a day along the Victoria Highway to WA and another from Tennant Creek along the Barkly Highway to QLD.

Katherine

Colour map 5, grid A3
Population: 11,300
310 km from Darwin,
665 km from Tennant
Creek, 510 km from
Kununurra (WA)

On the southern bank of the Katherine River, at the junction of the major routes north and west, Katherine is a service town for the pastoral industry and nearby Tindal air force base, as well as for travellers heading to Nitmiluk National Park. The town and river were named by explorer John McDouall Stuart in 1862, after a friend's daughter, but his favourable reports of the area led to the issuing of pastoral leases and dispossession of the local Jawoyn people. The Jawoyn managed to retain strong cultural links to their country but it took another century before their land ownership was legally recognized in 1989. In 1998 the entire town was flooded to the eaves. Few businesses had flood insurance so recovery has been slow but the townspeople are proud of enduring this disaster and '98 flood levels are marked all over town. The

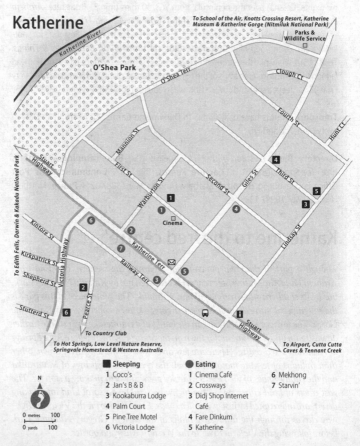

Katherine

To School of the Air, Knotts Crossing Resort, Katherine Museum & Katherine Gorge (Nitmiluk National Park)

Parks & Wildlife Service

Katherine River

O'Shea Park

O'Shea Terr

Clough Cr

Fourth St

Hunt Crt

Stuart Highway

Mannion St

First St

Second St

Giles St

Third St

Warburton St

Cinema

Lindsay St

Kintore St

Katherine Terr

Kirkpatrick St

Railway Terr

Shepherd St

Victoria Highway

Pearce St

Stutterd St

Stuart Highway

To Edith Falls, Darwin & Kakadu National Park

To Country Club

To Hot Springs, Low Level Nature Reserve, Springvale Homestead & Western Australia

To Airport, Cutta Cutta Caves & Tennant Creek

N

0 metres 100
0 yards 100

■ **Sleeping**
1 Coco's
2 Jan's B & B
3 Kookaburra Lodge
4 Palm Court
5 Pine Tree Motel
6 Victoria Lodge

● **Eating**
1 Cinema Café
2 Crossways
3 Didj Shop Internet Café
4 Fare Dinkum
5 Katherine
6 Mekhong
7 Starvin'

friendly and efficient **VIC** has information on the whole region, including the popular **Katherine Gorge**. ■ *0830-1800 Mon-Fri, 0900-1400 Sat-Sun (May-Oct); 0830-1500 Mon-Fri, 0900-1300 Sat-Sun (Nov-Apr). T8972 2650, information@krta.com.au Katherine Terr.*

On the southwest edge of Katherine, **Springvale Homestead** is one of the oldest pastoral properties in the state, built in 1879, close to natural springs. The property is now a caravan park but the small homestead still stands, although damaged by the 1998 flood, and contains a few display boards on its his - tory.■ *0800-1730. Free. Guided tour daily at 1500 (May-Oct). T8972 1355. Shadforth Rd, 8 km from town.* The new Alice Springs-Darwin railway line crosses the river by Springvale. About 3 km upstream the **Low Level Nature Reserve** is a pretty area by the low river crossing where locals swim, fish and picnic. Better for swimming though are the small clear pools of **Katherine Hot Springs**, a short distance to the north. These palm-fringed springs lie on a narrow tributary of the river and are a tepid 32°c, best experienced on a cool evening with the stars twinkling above. ■ *24 hrs. Free. Access by riverside bike path or Riverbank Drive. About 50 steps down to the river – ask at Ampol Roadhouse for a wheelchair access route.* About 1½ km from the post office is **Katherine School of the Air**, where visitors can learn how children in remote areas are educated by radio, mail and computer. The school serves 800,000 sq km of Northern Australia. Tours include listening to live radio lessons, a video and talk by school staff. ■ *Tours Mon-Fri 0900, 1000, 1100, 1300, 1400 (Mar-Nov). $5, children $2. T8972 1833. Giles St.* The **Katherine Museum** is a further 1 km past the school, in the former airport buildings. The museum has interesting displays on the early days of Katherine and the town's regular floods but the centrepiece is a De Havilland Gypsy Moth, owned by Dr Clyde Fenton, one of Australia's first 'flying doctors'. ■ *Mon-Fri 1000-1600, Sat 1000-1300, 1400-1700 (Mar-Oct) Mon-Fri 1000-1300 (Nov-Feb). Sun 1400-1700 (all year). $3.50, children $1, concessions $2.50. T8972 3945, museum@ nt-tech.com.au* The tropical **Cutta Cutta Caves**, 30 km south of Katherine, have good collections of sparkling cave decorations, including stalactites and stalagmites but are generally warm and humid. ■ *Cave tours daily at 0900, 1000, 1100, 1300, 1400 and 1500, from around Apr-Nov. $11, children $5.50.*

Sights

B *Jan's B&B*, 13 Pearce St. T8971 1005, jcomleybbaccom@yahoo.com 3 luxurious and tasteful rooms and generous living areas. Price includes cooked breakfast but is a little steep considering rooms are not en suite. Guests are, however, well looked after. **B-C** *Knotts Crossing Resort*, corner of Giles St and Cameron St, T9872 2511, www.knottscrossing.com.au Pleasant resort includes a wide range of motel rooms, self-contained units, cabins and powered sites with private en suite. Also pools, kiosk and bistro. **B** *Pine Tree Motel*, Third St, T1800 467434 and 8972 2533, pinetree@ntisp.com, is bland but comfortable with a pool and licensed bistro. The town has a plentiful supply of budget accommodation. **D** *Springvale Homestead*, Shadforth Rd (8 km from town). T8972 1355, www.travelnorth.com.au Peaceful caravan park and motel by the river with 60 a/c en suite units. Rooms are basic but great value, book early for peak season. Also pool, simple bistro and canoe hire. **D-E** *Victoria Lodge*, 21 Victoria Highway, T8972 3464, victorialodge@bigpond.com Smart and clean with doubles and small dorms. Each 2-room unit shares a living room, kitchenette and bathroom. Pool and BBQ but no other communal space.

Katherine's dedicated **backpacker hostels** are all very friendly and helpful. **D-E** *Kookburra Lodge*, Lindsay St, T8971 0257, www.kookaburrabackpackers.com.au, has 6 well-maintained units, each with a small mixed dorm, separate twin, small

Sleeping
See also Pubs below and Nitmiluk National Park on page 684

Northern Territory

kitchen and bathroom. The large lawned garden, with a pool and BBQ area, is a major plus. The larger **D-E** *Palm Court*, Third St, T8972 2722, palm_court@hotmail.com, has 20 clean and modern rooms, all en suite, including some doubles, 4- and 9-bed dorms, and facilities include internet access. Their outdoor area is more modest, though with a better pool, as are the kitchen facilities. Both hostels have overnight a/c and offer bike hire. **E** *Coco's*, First St T8971 2889, www.21first.com, has just four 4-bed single-sex rooms, and a couple of tents in the garden available if it's busy, making for an intimate, homely atmosphere. Owner Coco's long friendship with many talented local Aboriginal artists and musicians can make a few days stay here a rich experience. The town has half a dozen **caravan parks** including **C** *Low Level*, Shadforth Rd, T8972 3962, a superb shady and spacious park 5 km from town. Ensuite a/c cabins, large pool, poolside bar and great facilities. Recommended.

Eating Many of the resort complexes and sporting clubs have their own restaurants, of which the *Country Club*, T8972 1276, off Pearce St is the pick. The simple, mid-range Thai *Mekhong*, Katherine Terr, T8972 3170, is popular locally as a good spot to watch the massive road-trains passing through town with tables out front right on the corner of one of the town's main junctions. BYO, open 1800-2200 Mon-Fri. *Starvin'*, Katherine Terr, is a cheap BYO pizza and pasta joint, doubling as a pavement café by day. Open 0900-2200 Mon-Sat, 1100-2200 Sun. The unpretentious *Fare Dinkum*, Third St, serves breakfasts, sandwiches and cheap evening steaks, salads and pastas. Open 0430-1530 and 1730-2030 Mon-Sun, though from 0730 Sun. Best of the lunch cafés is the *Cinema*, with a good range of tasty but healthy breakfasts, focaccias, pastas and salads. Open 0800-1730 Mon-Fri, 0800-1400 Sat. The *Didj Shop Internet Café*, corner of Giles St and Railway Terr, is Aboriginal owned and run, and the enthusiastic owner is happy to talk about his culture and art while serving up a coffee, cake and fresh toasted sandwiches. Sofas, tables and an internet bar. Open Mon-Sat from 1000 to at least 1900, 2200 if busy, and 1000-1500 Sun. Closed Jan-Mar.

Pubs *Crossways*, Katherine Terr, T8972 1022. Large and busy pub with separate, tidy motel accommodation (**C**). Several lively bars include a shady courtyard and *Rio's* nightclub, open 2200-0430 Fri-Sat, entry $5. Cheap counter and bistro meals available 1200-1400 and 1800-2100, live cover bands most Fridays in the dry season. The usual choice for travellers is the *Katherine*, Katherine Terr, T8972 1622, katherinehotel@nt-tech.com.au, a slightly more upmarket option with a large, recently refurbished and surprisingly inclusive main bar. It's also worth checking out *RJ's* bar, just to the rear.

Shopping **Aboriginal art and music** *Coco's*, 21 First St, www.21first.com, has a huge range of didjeridoos, many crafted for serious musicians and priced 'by sound'. If you're serious about buying an instrument as opposed a cultural souvenir this should be your first stop, though you may find cheaper elsewhere. The Aboriginal owned *Didj Shop Internet Café*, Giles St, www.didj.com.au, has a modest stock of quality art and didjeridoos, and the stories behind them are related with passion and knowledge. *Katherine Art Gallery*, Katherine Terr, has the widest range. It is well worth visiting at least these 3 prior to buying. Those visiting *Manyallaluk* will find their small shop reasonably priced, and their artists no less talented than those displayed in town. **Books** *Katherine Bookshop*, Katherine Oasis, has a modest but well-chosen range of fiction, local history and culture.

Tours & activities
See also page 684
Aboriginal culture An enjoyable and joyful corroboree is held every Mon and Wed at 1900, corner of Second St and Warburton St. Dancing, didjeridoo playing, spear throwing ($15, 2½ hrs) and perhaps a bit of participation. Book at the VIC and arrive at 1830 for a good seat. *Manyallaluk*, T8975 4727, or book at VIC. Long-established Aboriginal-owned company offering a relaxed and friendly day of learning about

Aboriginal culture at the Manyallaluk community, 100 km southeast of Katherine. The day includes an interesting 'bushtucker' walk, lunch and the chance to try basket weaving, bark painting, fire lighting and spear throwing. The community gallery has excellent work at very reasonable prices. ($132 including transport, $99 self-drive). Powered and unpowered sites also available. Together with *Odyssey Safaris*, T8948 0091, www.odysaf.com.au, they also offer a 3-day, 4WD bush excursion to otherwise inaccessible country on the southern border of Arnhem Land ($990). With *Whoop Whoop*, Giles St, T/F8972 2941, you can make your own didjeridu on an excellent overnight bush trip, including selecting and cutting the tree, making the instrument and learning to play it ($220, Fri 1500 to Sat 1500). The other option is to make one in an afternoon in town ($40-100 depending on size). **Boat tours** *Crocodile Night Adventure*, T1800 089103. A short boat trip from Springvale Homestead to a campsite where guides will entice a freshwater crocodile onto the bank. Dinner by the campfire is followed by croc-spotting with your own torch (supplied) on the way back (daily 1830-2130 May-Oct, $42). **Canoes** can be hired on the same stretch of river at *Springvale Homestead* reception ($11 hr). **Kakadu** *Kookaburra Camping Safaris*, T1800 808211 or 8971 0257, www.kookaburrabackpackers.com.au, run a 3-day, 4WD bush-camping trip up through Kakadu ($360, departs 0700 twice weekly). Terminates in Darwin, or you can catch a lift back to Katherine at no extra charge.

Air *Air North* fly to **Darwin** (Sun-Mon) and to **Tennant Creek** and **Alice Springs** every Mon-Sat. *Aboriginal Air Services*, T8953 5000, operations-ca@maf.org.au, fly to **Alice Springs** at 1030 Tue and Fri, with three stops at outlying communities (6 hrs, $180). **Bus** *McCafferty's/Greyhound* Darwin-bound services leave the BP service station opposite the VIC at 0715, 1300 and 1810. Their southbound buses depart at 1330 and 1820, and the service to Perth via Kununurra leaves at 1215.

Transport
See also Tours: Kakadu, above

Banks ATMs of 3 major banks on Katherine Terr. **Bike hire** *The Bike Shop*, 16 First St, T8972 1213. $33 per day, open Mon-Fri and Sat morning. Good, if pricey, bike hire and advice. Cheaper at the two larger hostels. **Car servicing** *Master Motors*, Second St, T8971 0444. **Communications** Internet access at *Didj Shop Internet Café*, Giles St. Free 15 mins with a coffee, or for $2. **Post Office**, Katherine Terr. **Hospital** Giles St, T8973 9211. **Police** Stuart Highway, T8972 0111. **Taxi** T8972 1777. **Work** Plenty of mango-picking between Sep-Nov. Transport generally provided, expect around $10 pr hr. Contact *Employment National*, First St, T8973 1081.

Directory
Fill up with fuel before leaving Katherine

Nitmiluk National Park (Katherine Gorge)

Nitmiluk protects some of the most majestic gorge scenery in Australia, as well as dozens of waterfalls and permanent waterholes created by the rivers carving their way through the plateau. The park is owned by the *Jawoyn* people and jointly managed with the Parks and Wildlife Commission. The main feature is **Katherine Gorge**, actually a series of connected gorges that dog-leg their way across the landscape, some with sheer walls as high as 70 m. The Katherine River flows through this gorge for 13 km but unless it is very high, which happens at some point most years between January-April, each section is separated by dry rocky sections which have to be negotiated by boat-cruising visitors and canoeists alike. The most spectacular of the gorges are the long, narrow second gorge, **Katherine Canyon**, and the slightly less impressive but far less visited fifth gorge. **Aboriginal rock art** is found throughout the park, and is most easily seen on the impressive walls above the rapids between the first and second gorges. The gorges can seem like one huge waterfall when the water's flowing, but this is usually only for a few hours after local heavy rain. The Nitmiluk

Colour map 5, grid A3
30 km from Katherine via Giles St and Gorge Rd

Northern Territory

Visitors Centre is the main point of access to the park, though there is another site worth visiting, **Edith Falls**, 62 km north of Katherine (20 km off the highway). This is a picturesque series of gorges and low falls cascading into an enormous pool. There are over 130 km of great walking trails in the park, but don't visit without taking a boat cruise, or preferably hiring a canoe.

Ins & outs

Getting there There are daily services from the *BP* service station, Katherine Terr, Katherine, to the visitor centre at 0800, 1015, 1215, 1415 and 1615, calling at hostels and motels if pre-booked. Return buses every 2 hrs 0900-1700. $19 return, children $9.50. The **visitor centre** is near the first gorge, close to both the main boat jetty and caravan park. Open 0700-1900 May-Nov, otherwise 0700-1800. Café closes 1700. For info on tours, the café or the campground T8972 1253. A good range of in-depth maps and written material is available from the centre.

Around the park

All hire and tours within the park are operated by Nitmiluk Tours, T8972 1253, www.travel north.com.au

Boat cruises Flat-bottomed, 40-seater boats shuttle up the gorges on two-hour ($37), four-hour ($53) and eight-hour ($92.50, May-October only) cruises, reaching the 2nd, 3rd and 5th gorges respectively. All three options are available at 0900 then at other times during the day. Walking over rough ground is required between each gorge. Allow half an hour for the walk to jetty and queuing. While the river is running high, usually some time between December and April, **jet boats** make the 45-minute run up to the third gorge ($43). **Canoe hire** By far the best way to experience the gorges is in the single or double person canoes, available for hire from the main jetty, which should be booked in advance, especially during peak season. Expect to be able to get as far as the second gorge and back in half a day ($29.50 single, $44 double, departures at 0900 and 1300), and the third gorge in a full day ($41 single, $61 double, departure at 0900). Portage is required between gorges, as is a $20 cash deposit. If you have time the overnight camping option is well worth considering ($82 single, $122 double, $60 cash deposit). Day canoe hire is usually still available during the wet season but no overnight hire unless you join the special guided three-day canoe tours ($390). If river levels are so high that day canoe hire is not permitted, guided day-tours will be available ($44, five hours). **Helicopter** A trip to the third gorge takes 10 minutes and costs $60 per person, to the eighth gorge is 15 minutes at $90. and to the 13th gorge is 25 minutes at $150. Flights on demand, two to three passengers are required. **Swimming** May be restricted in waterholes in the dry to prevent environmental degradation, or in the river if it's running high.

Walking Although the gorges are best viewed from the water, there are walks which allow views from the rim down some of the canyons, and occasional access to the river itself. The hour-long Lookout Walk gets to the top of the first main bluff, Crocodile Rock, and is well worth the effort if you have some time to fill or you're there around sunset. To see the view down Katherine Canyon (the second gorge) you should take the slightly more challenging Butterfly Gorge Walk (12 km, four hours return). Overnight options include Smitt Walk Rock which reaches the start of the fifth gorge, and Eighth Gorge Walk. The 45-km Jatbula Trail from the visitor centre to **Edith Falls** is generally considered a four to five day walk. It is allowed in this direction only, although walkers can go as far as Crystal Falls and then retrace their steps (three to four days). For another full day's walk head out and back to the waterfall and pool at Northern Rockhole, the first major point of interest on the trail. Pick up a detailed map ($5.50) from the visitor centre. At Edith Falls itself, there is a lovely short walk, Leliyn Loop, on the plateau that circumnavigates the main pool and crosses Upper Falls with fine views and lots of swimming spots along the way.

Northern Territory

B *Maud Creek*, Gorge Rd, 6 km from the park, T8971 1814, julies@nt-tech.com.au 4 comfortable modern en suite rooms on an quiet farm property by the river. Breakfast provisions supplied in the communal kitchenette. Swimming pool. The shady *Nitmiluk Caravan Park*, T8972 1253, is adjacent to and run by the visitors centre. Powered and unpowered sites, ablutions and BBQs. Both canoeists and walkers are allowed to camp overnight in the park at designated sites. Some of these camps have toilets and water. Park camping costs are $3.30 per person and bookings must be made in advance. There is no camping available closer to the visitor centre than the 5th gorge. The licensed *café* in the visitor centre serves all-day snacks and drinks, and is also open Thu-Sat evenings 1730-2000 during May-Nov for a set BBQ ($17.50), sometimes with local live music. At **Edith Falls** there are unpowered campsites, toilets, showers, wood BBQs and a kiosk.

Sleeping & eating

Katherine to Kununurra (WA)

From Katherine the Victoria Highway heads west toward Western Australia. After 86 km is the turn-off for **Flora River Nature Park**. Canoeing and fishing is allowed on the river but no swimming as estuarine crocodiles are found here. The rare pig-nosed turtle also lives in the river. The Djarrung campground has toilets, showers, water and wood BBQs ($5 per person). For more information contact the Katherine Parks and Wildlife office, T8973 8888. The first, and usually cheapest, fuel stop is at the *Victoria River* roadhouse, T8975 0744 (open 0630-2200), 190 km from Katherine and in the midst of the spectacular eastern section of the **Gregory National Park**. The roadhouse makes an excellent base for exploring this part of the park and has motel-style, simple budget rooms (**C**) and camping sites. Cheap meals and snacks are served all day. There are a few walking trails, including the excellent **Joe Creek Walk** (see below).

Distance: 510 km

This small settlement had its beginning as a stores depot for the cattle station the size of a small country in the **Victoria River** region but is now little more than a refuelling stop on the highway and a base for trips into the **Gregory National Park**. However, if you have time a boat cruise on the Victoria River with *Max's Boat Tours*, T8975 0850, is well worth it. The 40-km cruise includes some town sights, croc-spotting and lively yarns ($55, 0800-1200 or 1600-1930). If you intend to visit the national park head for the Parks and Wildlife Commission office at the western end of town for information.

Timber Creek
Colour map 5,
grid A3
Population: 300
90 km from Victoria
River roadhouse,
230 km from
Kununurra

Sleeping and eating There are 2 characterless pubs (same owner) that have a wide range of motel, hotel rooms and caravan park sites. **C-D** *Wayside Inn*, T8975 0722, serves bar snacks 1500-2100. **C-D** *Timber Creek Hotel* also does snacks and buffet meals 1800-2000. Both pubs have swimming pools and sell fuel. There is also a supermarket open Mon-Fri 0900-1700, Sat 1000-1300.

Transport *McCafferty's/Greyhound's* WA-bound service leaves at 1520. The bus to Katherine and Darwin departs 1350.

Remote and rugged, most of Gregory is difficult to access without a 4WD. The park encompasses dramatic large-scale scenery of escarpments and flat-topped ranges above plains of open woodland. Divided into two sections, the western Gregory sector offers rough 4WD routes to explore former cattle stations and joins up with the Buchanan Highway to the south. **Limestone Gorge** is an attractive camping area with a billabong safe to swim in and a good ridge walk with views of East Baines River valley. The gorge has

Gregory
National Park
Bullita Homestead
55 km south of
Timber Creek

Northern Territory

unusual limestone karst formations, fossil stromatolites, and calcite rock that looks like a frozen waterfall. The unsealed road is often accessible by 2WD in the dry, but check road conditions at the Timber Creek park office. Back on the highway, about halfway between the two park areas is **Kuwang Lookout**, giving fine views over Stokes Range. The spectacular eastern sector of the park is a much smaller area, around the Victoria River, and accessible to two-wheeldrives. **Joe Creek Walk** (one hour loop) takes you to the escarpment wall by way of Livistonia palms and Aboriginal art. The **Escarpment Lookout** walk (1½ hour return) climbs to the top of Stokes Range for views of the valley and *Victoria River* gorge. The only campground in this sector is Sullivans Creek, by a waterhole 17 km from the Victoria River roadhouse. ■ *No park fees. Camping $2.50 per person (payable at campsite). For more information contact Parks and Wildlife Timber Creek office, T8975 0888. Beware of estuarine crocodiles in Victoria River – no swimming.*

Keep River National Park
190 km from Timber Creek, 55 km from Kununurra
There is a quarantine checkpoint at the WA border where officers

A laid-back border with WA, Keep River has more in common with the rugged landscape around Kununurra than most of the Territory scenery to the east. The park's chief attractions are the Nganalam Art Site and the long, shallow sandstone Keep River Gorge, both about 25 km off the highway and accessed by unsealed 2WD roads. The park has two campgrounds, both with toilet and picnic facilities. The one furthest from the highway, Jarrnarm (28 km), also has water. There are walking tracks and walking notes at both sites but the main walk is Keep River Gorge Walk. Due to seasonal flooding of the Keep River, parts of the park, particularly the gorge, are often closed in the wet season. ■ *For more information contact the Keep River ranger, T9167 8827.*

Katherine to Tennant Creek

Distance: 665 km   The journey south from Katherine is long, straight and mostly of little interest to those travelling through, which makes almost any stop a welcome diversion. After Mataranka the vegetation gets sparser and more stunted and population centres smaller and further apart, their hotels becoming ever more rustic.

Mataranka
Colour map 5, grid A4
105 km from Katherine, 165 km from Daly Waters

Mataranka lies just west of the thermal springs of **Elsey National Park**, a beautiful and popular oasis. The small highway town is also associated with the classic Australian novel *We of the Never Never* by Jeannie Gunn, based on her experiences as the mistress of nearby Elsey Station in the early 1900s. Mataranka has a surprisingly good range of facilities including ATMs at the pub and supermarket, an internet bureau and post office. There are two main area of springs within the park, also the headwaters of the Roper River which flows east to the Gulf of Carpentaria. **Bitter Springs** is the most natural and beautiful spring with pools of emerald-green water among a forest of palms, northeast of the township along Martin Road. Homestead Road leads to *Mataranka Homestead* and access to Rainbow Spring, feeding **Thermal Pool**. Though it doesn't appear very natural, it is located within a striking forest of tall palms and paperbarks. Rainbow Spring pumps out roughly an Olympic-size swimming pool's equivalent of water every hour at 34°C into the Waterhouse and Roper rivers, ensuring a year-round flow. A great walk is to follow the path along the riverbank from the *Mataranka Homestead* to Mataranka Falls (16 km), past swimming holes, beaches and parrots. Canoes can be hired at the campground ($6 per hour) for a 4-km canoe paddle downstream to the falls.

Sleeping and eating C *Territory Manor*, T8975 4516, on Martins Rd heading to Bitter Springs, is best place to eat in town with cheap meals available 1200-1400 and 1830-2000 on the rustic outdoor terrace. Accommodation in pleasant rammed-earth motel units, with camping grounds also available. Immediately adjacent to the Mataranka Springs is the busy **C-E** *Mataranka Homestead*, T8975 4544, with plainer motel units, self-contained cabins, some of the most depressing 'backpacker' accommodation to be found in NT, extensive lawned camping areas and a licensed bar, restaurant and takeaway. Canoe hire is available but can only be used on a 300-m section. In the centre of the town itself the **D** *Old Elsey Roadside Inn*, T8975 4512, has a small scruffy public bar and en suite, a/c motel-style rooms. Meals available 0700-2100. At the end of John Hauser Dr the Parks-run *Jalmurark campground*, T8975 4789, has extensive grassed sites, hot showers and fireplace BBQs. This is a peaceful ground without powered sites or generators. Free in the wet season, otherwise $6 per person.

Transport *McCafferty's/Greyhound* Darwin-bound services leave the Shell roadhouse at 0525 and 1045, also calling at Mataranka Homestead 15 mins earlier. The buses south to Alice Springs depart 1440 and 1930 (the homestead 15 mins later).

This tiny settlement, one of several on the highway that grew up during the Second World War, was the rail terminus for the Alice Springs line. Men, stores and equipment had to get off here and travel by road to Darwin, consequently it became a busy staging post and many units were stationed here. Now, for most people it's simply a roadhouse stop.

Larrimah
Colour map 5, grid A4
75 km from Mataranka, 90 km from Daly Waters

Sleeping and eating The **E-F** *Larrimah*, T8975 9931, has a few seriously basic bunks and cheap a/c twins, all with shared facilities. It also has caravan sites, but campers are probably better off at the roadhouse which has a pool. Breakfasts and snacks all day at the pub, main meals 1200-1400 and 1800-2000. At the northern end of town *Fran's* friendly tea room is open 0700-1700 for a chat and wide range of home-made goodies including scones, cakes and savoury pies.

Transport *McCafferty's/Greyhound* Darwin-bound services leave the BP roadhouse at 0415 and 0930. Their buses south to Alice Springs depart 1550 and 2040.

Daly Waters was a lonely telegraph repeater station until the 1930s when an enterprising couple set up a shop and aerodrome. By 1934 it had become a re-fuelling stop for *Qantas* international flights to Singapore and became an increasingly busy air and mail centre. A hotel was built for overnight stays in 1938 and the 3-km side-trip off the highway is well worth the effort to check out this, the best and friendliest of the 'Outback' pubs along this part of the Stuart Highway. Meals are cheap and satisfying, available 0630-1400 and 1830-2030, and include a 'Beef & Barra' BBQ every evening, which is often accompanied by live music. Accommodation is in simple air conditioned doubles (**D**) or en suite air conditioned cabins (**C**). Also camping and swimming pool. T8975 9927, dalywaterspub@bigpond.com

Daly Waters Hotel
Colour map 5, grid A4
270 km from Katherine, 400 km from Tennant Creek

The distinctive deep notch in the coastline of Northern Australia, dividing the Northern Territory and Queensland, is actually a shallow sea, less than 70 m deep in the middle, between Australia and Papua New Guinea. This whole area has a tiny population and few access points. The main road out to the gulf is the sealed Carpentaria Highway, from Daly Waters to the coast at Bing Bong, a port facility for mine exports. There are interesting areas of rock formations along the way but there is little else to draw visitors out to this remote coastline except

Gulf of Carpentaria
Colour map 5, grid A4
Borroloola 375 km from Daly Waters, 480 km from Barkly Highway

Northern Territory

▶▶ **What's your beef?**

The cattle stations established in the Victoria River region were some of the largest in the world. **Victoria River Downs** *was claimed by British owners Bovril Ltd in 1909 to be the largest in the world at 8,364 square miles, and there are still several of comparable size today. Another,* **Wave Hill,** *played a significant part in contemporary Aboriginal history. Until the 1960s Aborginal stockmen were working on Wave Hill station (and others) in return for rations only, working and living under disgraceful conditions. Despite attempts to extend industrial law to all Australians, pastoralists managed to lobby the government to postpone the implementation of equal wages for Aboriginal workers until 1968. Unhappy at having to wait, workers at Wave Hill went on strike for equal wages in 1966, walking off the station with their families, settling at Wattie Creek. The Wave Hill 'mob', led by Vincent Lingiari, then endured a long but successful fight for land rights, but it was the equal wages decision that has had a profound effect on the life of many Territorians. The majority of pastoralists*

claimed they could not afford to pay their Aboriginal workers equal wages and dismissed them. Workers and their families had to leave the stations, often their own traditional land, and look for work elsewhere or move to towns to receive government aid. Although it was vital that Aboriginal people earned equal pay, the unforeseen consequence of the fight was the further breakdown of Aboriginal culture.

The Victoria River region also contains Australia's best-known contemporary cattle station, **Bullo,** *made famous by Sara Henderson, author of several books about the hardships of her station life.*

Many stations have now been bought by large international companies who can better afford the exorbitant costs of mustering by helicopter and maintaining station vehicles and fences The low price of cattle today means stock is sometimes left to fend for itself in the bush for years. Much of the land bordering the highway is unfenced so keep a careful eye out for cattle wandering across the road in this region and in the Kimberley.

the excellent fishing it is known for and the appeal of Outback driving. The **D** *Heartbreak Hotel* roadhouse, T8975 9928, at **Cape Crawford** stands at the junction of the Tablelands Highway, which drops south to join the main sealed route into Queensland, the Barkly Highway, after 375 km. From Borroloola an unsealed road drops southeast to the Queensland border. It is a notorious boneshaker best suited to 4WD vehicles. Check road consitions at Borroloola.

A badly rutted route heads north from here to Roper Bar (336 km). Close to the southern route, in the Abner Ranges, is a dramatic series of sandstone columns known as the **Lost City**. These are only accessible by air; *Cape Crawford Tourism*, T8975 9611, operate helicopter flights from Cape Crawford and some flights land, offering the opportunity to walk around the rocks (April-October, $170). Continuing east the highway passes **Caranbirini Conservation Reserve** 50 km before reaching Borroloola. This is another area of sandstone rock formations by a lily-covered creek and is accessible to all vehicles.

Borroloola, on the McArthur River and the only town in this region, is on Aboriginal land and mostly services local Aboriginal communities but is actually one of the older towns in the territory, founded in the 1880s by lawless cattle drovers. The **Old Police Station** is now a fascinating museum of local history. Most of the shops and accommodation are found on the main street, Robinson Road, including the lone pub, **D** *Borroloola Hotel*, T8975 8766. **C-E** *Borroloola Holiday Village*, T8975 8742, has cabins, bunkhouse and a general store and there is also a caravan park, *McArthur River*, T8975 8734, with self-contained cabins and powered sites. Eating is limited to the pub or takeaways. **Fishing tours and scenic flights** over the Sir Edward Pellew Islands operate from Borroloola. For more information on the town and gulf region, contact the Borroloola **visitor information centre**, T8975 8799, www.grtpa.com.au, at the council complex on Robinson Road.

The **Barranyi National Park** covers North Island in the Pellew Group and is the home of the Yanuwa people. The main activities in this park are beach walking, birdwatching and turtle spotting. Access is by boat only and can be arranged with a local tour operator. From Borroloola an unsealed road drops southeast to the Queensland border at Wollogorang Station (264 km) where the **C** *Wollogorang Gulf Wilderness Lodge*, T8975 9770, has motel rooms, meals, fuel and caravan sites. Fishing, hunting and sightseeing tours are available. The road continues into Queensland, leading to Mount Isa and Mount Cairns, and is a notorious boneshaker best suited to sturdy 4WD vehicles. Check on road conditions at Borroloola.

There are small settlements or roadhouses at least every 100 km on this stretch of highway running through the prime cattle country and Aboriginal communities of the Barkly region. **Newcastle Waters** was once one of the largest cattle stations in the territory and the junction of three major overland stock routes. Cattle drovers used the station township to rest and replenish supplies just as truck drivers hauling loads of cattle now frequent the roadhouses. A few kilometres off the highway, the township is reduced to a few rusting corrugated iron buildings that once housed a pub, store, repeater station, school and post office. **Elliot**, the largest settlement between Katherine and Tennant Creek, was established as an army camp during the Second World War. The Djingili and Mudbura people of the Barkly Tablelands live in the town and on Murranji land nearby, successfully claimed in 1990. The most interesting spot to rest up is the **D-E** *Elliot Hotel*, T8969 2069, an earthy pub with a range of budget accommodation and cheap meals. All the roadhouses have caravan parks, some with alternative cabin options. Some 25 km north of Tennant Creek, the Barkly Highway heads east to Queensland (border 460 km). Passing through the heart of the pastoral Barkly Tablelands, the route is broken by only one fuel stop (after 185 km) at *Barkly Homestead*, T8964 4549, which also has a caravan park. | **Daly Waters to Tennant Creek**

Tennant Creek

Tennant Creek has an attractive setting by the McDouall (or Honeymoon) Ranges but is a fairly ordinary highway service town. It makes a useful stop for travellers, though, as it sits just south of the junction of the Barkly Highway to QLD and is a base for the beautiful Devil's Marbles, 100 km to the south. Set up as the site of an overland telegraph station in 1872, Tennant Creek stood in splendid isolation for over 50 years until gold was found in the region in 1925, kickstarting Australia's last **gold rush**. The prosperous days of mining lasted from the 1930s until the 1960s but the modern town survives mostly on government services. Almost all services lie on the highway, called Paterson Street in the town centre. The **VIC** is 1½ km off the highway, at the old mining site of Battery Hill. ■ *Daily 0900-1700 (May-Sep) Mon-Fri 0900-1700, Sat 0900-1200 (Oct-Apr)*. T8962 3388, *www.tennantcreektourism.com.au Peko Rd*. Aboriginal-owned *Anyinginyi*, Paterson Street, has a good stock of well-priced and colourful large canvases as well as smaller works, sourced from many communities in the region. | *Colour map 5, grid B4 Population: 3,500 505 km from Alice Springs, 2,000 km from Cairns (QLD)*

Northern Territory

As very little alluvial gold was ever found here, and due to the difficulty of extracting gold from the local ironstone ore, most mining has been carried out by companies rather than individuals. **Battery Hill**, named after the government battery that operated here for many years, is now an open-air museum of mining. There are daily tours of the battery and a demonstration mine under the hill. The site also includes an interesting mining museum and minerals collection. ■ *Opening hrs and contact details as for the VIC. Entry to site free. Mine tour 0730, 0930, 1400, 1530. Battery tours 1100, 1700. $13, children $6.50, concessions $11 (seniors). Both tours for $22.* **Mary Ann Dam**, 7 km north of town, was created in the 1960s as a recreational area. Well maintained, it still fulfils that role and is easily the best spot around town for a picnic. There is no access inside the **Telegraph Station**, just off the highway, 8 km north of town, but the small compound of solid stone building is in good repair and there are interpretative signs at the site.

Sleeping **C** *Bluestone*, Paterson St, T8962 2617, capefire@bigpond.com One of a handful of large motels, this has standard rooms, a pool, BBQ area and restaurant. The **D** *Goldfields*, Paterson St, T8962 2030, is plainer but is about as good value for a motel room as can be found anywhere in town. **D-E** *Tourist's Rest*, corner of Windley St and Leichhardt St, T8962 2719, www.touristrest.com.au Small, friendly backpackers with 4-bed dorms, doubles, good kitchen, lounge and sociable courtyard space. Pick-ups (24 hrs) and reasonable rates for bus travellers wanting late checkouts. Also good deals on Devils Marbles tours. The *Safari Lodge Motel*, Davidson St, T8962 2207, also has a backpacker hostel (**D-E**, YHA). At first sight a neater alternative, the facilities are less extensive and a lack of on-site staff robs it of any chance of atmosphere. There are 2 **caravan parks: D** *Outback*, T8962 2459, is the smarter with en suite cabins and is halfway along the road to the VIC; on the main road, **D-E** *Tennant Creek*, T8962 2325, also has cabins and a cheap bunkhouse.

Eating
No takeaway alcohol is available on 'Thirsty Thursdays'

The *Tennant Creek Hotel*, Paterson St, T8962 2006, has a surprisingly refined, Victorian feel, and is certainly the most characterful place to eat and drink in town. Cheap meals available 1200-1400 Mon-Sat and 1800-2100 daily. Visitors are welcome at the modern *Memorial Club*, Schmidt St, T8962 2474, but need to sign in for cheap pub-style meals. Open 1200-1400 Mon-Sat, 1800-2100 daily.

Tours & activities *Gold Fever*, T0417 873040. Self-drive fossicking tours. Metal detector, gold pan and expertise supplied and you keep what you find. Daily 0700, 1000, 1300. (3 hrs, $25). *Devils Marbles Tours*, T1300 666070, www.devilsmarbles.com.au Informative and relaxed tours of the Marbles that allow plenty of time for exploring, photos, and clambering around the rocks. Day (Mon, Wed, Fri, Sun 1100-1700, $60) or sunset tours (Tue, Thu, Sat 1300 until 90 mins after sunset, $70), including lunch or dinner. Min 2 people.

Transport **Air** *Air North* fly to Alice Springs every Mon-Sat, and to **Katherine** and **Darwin** every Sun-Mon. **Bus** *McCafferty's/Greyhound* Darwin-bound services leave the Transit Centre on Paterson St at 0320 and 2225. Their buses south to Alice Springs depart 0335 and 2245. The service to Mt Isa and Townsville (QLD) also leaves at 2225.

Directory
Fuel is similarly priced to Katherine

Banks Branches and ATMs in Paterson St. **Bike hire** *Bridgestone*, Paterson St. $5 per half day, open Mon-Fri and Sat morning. **Car servicing** *Wyatt Motors*, Irvine St, T8962 2468. **Communications** Internet at *Switch*, Paterson St. Open 0830-1700 Mon-Fri, 0900-1300 Sat. $2 for 20 mins. **Post Office**, corner of Paterson St and Memorial Dr. **Hospital** Schmidt St, T8962 4399. **Police** Paterson St, T8962 4444. **Swimming pool** Peko Rd. Daily 1000-1830 ($2.40).

The **Davenport Range National Park** lies east of the Devils Marbles, and marks the boundary between the traditional lands of the Warumungu, Alyawarre and Kaytetye people. It is also the only national park between the markedly different environments of central Australia and the Top End. These low, arid-looking ranges have many permanent waterholes, attracting lots of birdlife, and other animals. There are no tours into the park and it is a remote, rugged area suited to experienced off-roaders only. Roads may be flooded December-March. ■ *For more information contact Parks and Wildlife, Tennant Creek office, T8962 4599. Turn-off 90 km south of Tennant Creek.*

Tennant Creek to Alice Springs
*Devil's Marbles
105 km from
Tennat Creek*

The **Devils Marbles** is a vast area of bizarre-looking, gigantic granite boulders. Many seem to balance precariously on the slab below but if you look closely at the base you can see that the boulder and base are joined, and are in fact the same piece of rock that has simply eroded into these forms. There is a short loop walk by the main car park but it is worth taking the time to walk more extensively over the whole reserve and climb on top of the larger groups for good views of the plain. The boulders look wonderful at sunrise and sunset. There is a bush campsite on the eastern side of the reserve, with tables, toilets and fireplaces (BYO wood and water). ■ *No entrance or camping fees. For more information contact Parks and Wildlife, Tennant Creek office, T8962 4599. Stuart Highway. Day-tours from Tennant Creek.* Just 8 km south of the marbles is the tiny settlement of **Wauchope**, with a pub, T8964 1963, providing fuel, food and rooms. A further 26 km south, **Wycliffe Well** is another roadhouse settlement but unusually it claims regular visits from UFOs. Test your gullibility at the *Wycliffe Well Holiday Park* caravan park, T8964 1966, a roadhouse and small store. There are further services at **Barrow Creek**, site of a former telegraph station. There is also a nice old pub here, T8956 9753, but the place is now synonymous with the tragic abduction of British backpackers Falconio and Lees in 2001. **Aileron**, T8956 9703, is the last roadhouse before Alice (125 km).

Alice Springs and around

To many visitors Alice Springs is simply the town that you arrive at before visiting the 'rock', and they leave scant time to explore either the town or the region around it. It is often assumed that 'the Alice' is just up the road from Uluru so it can come as quite a surprise that Alice is actually a long, long way from the rock (435 km) and amidst the impressive MacDonnell hill ranges. Although the town is the Territory's second largest it is comparatively tiny, but its history, location and local geography combine to make it of considerable interest. Alice Springs lies in the geographical heart of Australia – a region known simply as the 'Centre' – and the locals proudly call themselves 'Centralians' rather than 'Territorians'.

*www.central
australiantourism.com*

Alice Springs

Alice Springs itself is often called 'the Alice' as if it were a phenomenon rather than a town. The southern entrance to the town is through the grand gateway of Heavitree Gap, a natural break in the Macdonnell Ranges. Once inside, neat streets, shopping malls and swimming pools appear in the middle of the Outback. A hundred years ago the only pool in town was the waterhole named Alice Springs in the Todd riverbed by the telegraph station. Winding through the town centre the sandy bed of the Todd River, lined with river red gums, is a reminder of the extremities of the region. It flows so rarely that when the locals hold their annual boating regatta they have to carry their boats downstream.

*Colour map 5, grid B4
Population: 25,000
1,490 km from Darwin,
435 km from Yulara,
1,530 km from
Adelaide*

Northern Territory

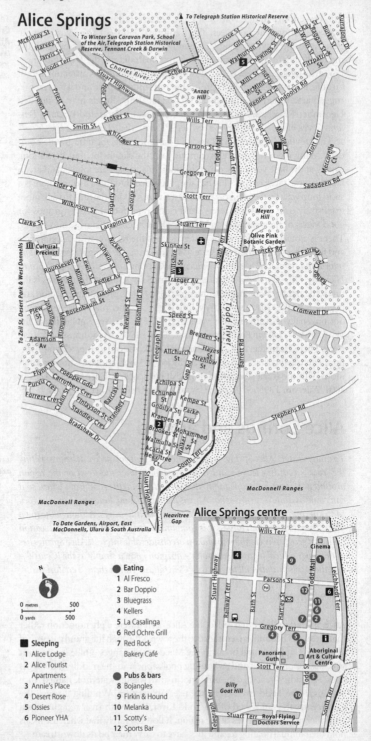

Alice Springs

To Telegraph Station Historical Reserve ▲

To Winter Sun Caravan Park, School of the Air, Telegraph Station Historical Reserve, Tennant Creek & Darwin

To Zeil St, Desert Park & West Donnells

To Date Gardens, Airport, East MacDonnells, Uluru & South Australia

Alice Springs centre

Eating
1 Al Fresco
2 Bar Doppio
3 Bluegrass
4 Kellers
5 La Casalinga
6 Red Ochre Grill
7 Red Rock Bakery Café

Sleeping
1 Alice Lodge
2 Alice Tourist Apartments
3 Annie's Place
4 Desert Rose
5 Ossies
6 Pioneer YHA

Pubs & bars
8 Bojangles
9 Firkin & Hound
10 Melanka
11 Scotty's
12 Sports Bar

N

0 metres 500
0 yards 500

Connecting Australia

In the 1860s telegraph stations linked areas of the eastern states but there was no link overland between Darwin and Adelaide, or to the rest of the world. Constructing an Overland Telegraph Line was an incredibly difficult task. The route had only been travelled by one European, John McDouall Stuart, on his third attempt. The line had to cross 3000 km of land, most of it utterly inhospitable and unknown to Europeans. In the Centre there were few places to find water and in the Top End there were deluges of it, washing away equipment and routes. In 1872 this feat was accomplished and Australia was connected to the world for the first time via underwater and overland cables from Darwin to London. Information now travelled from London in a few hours rather than the three to four months by ship. Repeater stations had to be built along the line every few hundred kilometres. These were always situated by a supply of fresh water, and while the early staff had to cope with frightening isolation, these telegraph stations later became the foundation for many settlements in the Territory. Alice Springs, Tennant Creek and Katherine all began as repeater stations.

Today the town survives as an administrative and service centre and a base for tourism. It also serves as a meeting point for Aboriginal people from many communities in the Northern Territory and South Australia. The local people are Arrernte (pronounced Arr-un-ter) who know the area as Mparntwe, a site of caterpillar dreaming. Aboriginal culture is heavily promoted in the town and there are shops full of Aboriginal art, but the divide in the black and white communities seems as deep as they lead noticeably separate lives. However, for visitors it is a convenient base for exploring the beautiful spots in the surrounding ranges and there are several fascinating sights in the town itself. The **VIC** is very helpful and has a good range of maps and park notes. ■ *0830-1730 Mon-Fri, 0900-1600 Sat-Sun. T8952 5800, visinfo@catia.asn.au Gregory Terr.*

Getting there & around
See also Transport, page 698

The **airport** is 17 km south of town. Facilities include all the main car hire companies, *Travelex* foreign exchange desk and ATM, and a tourist information and booking desk. A shuttle bus meets every flight ($10), but should be booked for departures, T1800 621188. A taxi to town will be $25-30. Many hotels and hostels also run courtesy buses. The main **coach station** is on the corner of Gregory Terr and Railway Terr and handles all state and interstate services, including *McCafferty's/Greyhound*. The **railway station** handles the *Ghan* services to and from **Adelaide**. A taxi from here will be about $10. *ASBUS*, T8952 5611, run **local buses** and single fares cost $1.40-2.40. All routes start and finish by the post office, and seem cleverly designed to miss most of the major sights. Services run approximately every 1-2 hrs 0730-1800 Mon-Fri, 0830-1230 Sat. Detailed timetables are available from the VIC. The *Alice Wanderer*, T8952 2111, is a small 'hop-on, hop-off', **tourist bus**, with commentary, that shuttles around a town centre loop. It leaves from the corner of Todd Mall and Stott Terr daily, every 70 mins 0900-1450 ($25). Stops include the Telegraph Station, School of the Air, Royal Flying Doctor Base, Cultural Precinct, and Date and Olive Pink Botanic Gardens. Pre-0900 pick-ups available.

As there is no good combination of economy with convenience, perhaps the best option is to hire a bicycle (see page 699)

Sights

Alice Springs is surrounded by many natural attractions but also has a surprising number of interesting sights in town. The difficulty will be in deciding what can be fitted in. There is a lookout at the top of **Anzac Hill** overlooking the town centre towards Heavitree Gap that is a good place to get your bearings and the **Olive Pink Botanic Garden** or **Date Gardens** are pleasantly shady green places to relieve the eye of dry red earth. ■ *Both gardens open daily and are free.*

Northern Territory

The **Telegraph Station Historical Reserve** sits above the shady banks of the Todd River. The cool stone buildings of the telegraph station have been restored to the way they looked around 1900 and reflect the self-sufficient lifestyle of the tiny community. Displays in the station buildings detail the history of the site. Scones are made for visitors in the wood-fired oven of the original kitchen (Apr-Oct only) and there is also a kiosk and pleasant picnic sites by the riverbed with free BBQs. ■ *Daily 0800-1700. $6.25, children $3.25, concessions $4.75. Free ½-hr guided tours every 45 mins. T8952 3993. The Reserve is 4 km north of town, signposted from Stuart Highway. There is a sandy walking trail beside the Todd River from town to the reserve.*

The **Alice Springs School of the Air** grew out of the 1930s Outback radio technology pioneered by the Royal Flying Doctors Service. Regular chats over the RFDS radio frequency, usually operated by women on the station, came to be known as the 'galah session' after the screechy, chattering parrots. The idea was naturally extended to giving children school lessons and in 1959 Alice Springs was the first school on-air of the sixteen schools now operating. Children who live in remote Outback areas listen to school lessons over the radio, supplemented by written material sent by post. The Alice Springs school services only 130 primary school students in an area of 1.3 million sq km. Students can hear other children in their 'class' as well as the teacher and

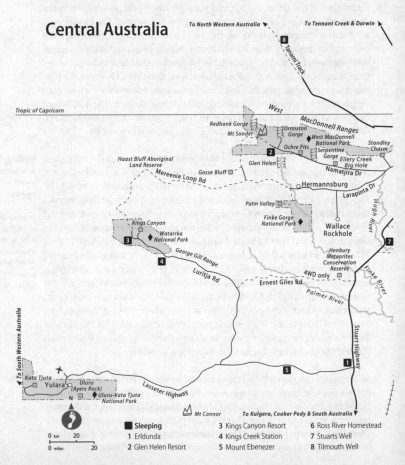

Central Australia

To North Western Australia ▼   To Tennant Creek & Darwin ▶

Tropic of Capricorn

West MacDonnell Ranges

Redbank Gorge
Mt Sonder
Ormiston Gorge
West MacDonnell National Park
Ochre Pits
Serpentine Gorge
Ellery Creek Big Hole
Standley Chasm
Namatjira Dr
Haast Bluff Aboriginal Land Reserve
Mereenie Loop Rd
Gosse Bluff
Glen Helen
Hermannsburg
Larapinta Dr
Palm Valley
Finke Gorge National Park
Wallace Rockhole
Kings Canyon
Watarrka National Park
George Gill Range
Henbury Meteorites Conservation Reserve
Luritja Rd
4WD only
Ernest Giles Rd
Palmer River
Hugh River
Finke River
Stuart Highway
Tanami Track

To South Western Australia
Kata Tjuta
Yulara
Uluru (Ayers Rock)
Uluru-Kata Tjuta National Park
Lasseter Highway
Mt Connor
To Kulgera, Coober Pedy & South Australia ▼

N

0 km 20
0 miles 20

■ **Sleeping**
1 Erldunda
2 Glen Helen Resort
3 Kings Canyon Resort
4 Kings Creek Station
5 Mount Ebenezer
6 Ross River Homestead
7 Stuarts Well
8 Tilmouth Well

this helps to allay loneliness and isolation. Visitors can watch a teacher give a lesson from the studio and listen to the children's responses, and watch a short video explaining what life is like for the students. ■ *Mon-Sat 0830-1630, Sun 1330-1630. $3.50, children $2.50. T8951 6834. 80 Head St, signposted from Stuart Highway, 3½ km north of the town centre. Bus route 3, stop 11.*

Wholly Aboriginal owned and operated, the **Aboriginal Art and Culture Centre** is a welcoming and relaxed place to learn about Aboriginal culture and chat to a few local Southern Arrernte people. The centre has an art gallery and a small museum. This is one of few places in town where an Aboriginal perspective can be heard and some of the shocking European acts of the past are documented. Didjeridu lessons are held at 1400 daily and guarantee a good laugh trying to get a sound out of the thing. The centre also runs lively and interesting morning tours that take visitors for a bush walk to learn about the relationship between the Arrernte and the landscape, followed by tea and damper, a dance performance, and a bit of boomerang and spear throwing. ■ *Daily 0800-1700. Free. Didjeridu lessons $11, 1 hr. Desert Discovery Tour $82.50, daily 0830-1230. T8952 3408, www.aboriginalart.com.au 86 Todd St.*

The **Royal Flying Doctors Service** is a much loved Australian institution. The service provides medical care for people in remote inland areas over a chunk of Australia larger than Western Europe. The Alice Springs base is one of 20 in the country that operate 45 aircraft at a cost of about $50 mn a year. Tours include a short video, a talk outside the radio control room and a stroll around a small musuem. There is also a lovely garden café and a souvenir shop. The service runs almost entirely on donations and grants so any money spent here benefits the service. ■ *Mon-Sat 0900-1600, Sun 1300-1600. Tours every ½ hr. $5.50, children $2.20. T8952 1129, www.flyingdoctor.net Stuart Terr.*

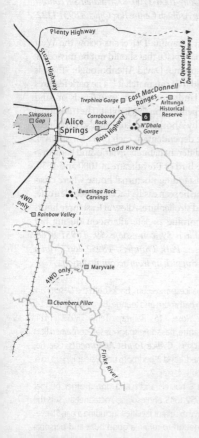

The white castellated tower of **Panorama Guth** sits above the flat streets of the town where it has been a landmark since it opened in 1975. This 360° panorama of Central Australia is the work of Dutch painter Henk Guth and the complex includes more of his landscapes and some work of the Hermannsburg school. Also an unusual collection of strange Aboriginal artefacts such as emu feather boots. ■ *Mon-Sat 0900-1700 all year, Sun 1200-1700 Mar-Nov. $5.50, $3.30. T8952 2013, 65 Hartley St.*

Just outside town is the **Cultural Precinct** which encompasses several museums and galleries. Built on the site of the town's first aerodrome, the precinct has been designed to fit around seven sites and trees sacred to

Arrernte women. Some of these sites are signposted on a path through the sculpture garden linking the buildings. The **Araluen Centre** has four galleries that show exhibitions of Aboriginal art from the Central Desert region and contemporary art by Northern Territorians. The highlight is the annual **Desert Mob** exhibition held in September featuring Central Australian Aboriginal art, which attractis buyers from all over the country. There is also a permanent exhibition on the work of Albert Namatjira, his teacher Rex Batarbee and others of the Hermannsburg School. Araluen's theatre is Alice Springs's main performing arts venue. Events listings can be picked up at the centre or the VIC. The **Museum of Central Australia** has a collection to effectively illustrate and explain the features of the Central Australian environment such as the meteorite craters of Gosse Bluff and Henbury. In the same building is the **Strehlow Research Centre**, a collection gathered by TGH (Ted) Strehlow, son of of a Hermannsburg missionary. Ted Strehlow learned Arrernte languages from his childhood playmates and later spent many years studying and recording Arrernte culture. He was entrusted with the care of 1,200 Arrernte men's sacred ceremonial objects and these along with his research are now preserved in the Research Centre. There is a display on Strehlow's life and work but most of the collection is only accessible to researchers. The Cultural Precinct also includes a small **Aviation Museum** and the **Memorial Cemetery**, where Albert Namatjira's grave can be found. **West End Café** at the Araluen Centre has drinks and snacks, daily 1030-1530. ■ *Daily 1000-1700. $7, children $4, concession $4. T8951 1120, www.nt.gov. au/dam Araluen Centre Box Office T8951 1122. Larapinta Drive, 15-min from town.*

Desert Park, 6 km west of town on Larapinta Drive, sits below the West MacDonnell Ranges. It is an extraordinary place that should not be missed by anyone. In the words of BBC wildife supremo, David Attenborough: "there is no museum or wildlife park in the world that can match it". The park features plants that are grown in their natural landscape such as woodlands or sand country, and is populated by animals dependent on that habitat. The traditional use and management of the landscape by Aboriginal people is also explained, highlighting how all desert dwellers are dependent on each other for survival. Two km of walking trails pass through different habitats, aviaries and kangaroo and emu enclosures. Highlights are the Bird of Prey theatre at 1000 and 1530, the 'Changing Heart' film, and the outstanding nocturnal house where creatures such as bilbies and thorny devils can be seen easily. Facilities include a café, picnic and BBQ area and wheelchair and stroller hire. Allow at least three hours and consider arriving in the early morning or late afternoon during hot weather. ■ *Daily 0730-1800. $18, children $9, concessions $9. T8951 8788, www.alicespringsdesertpark.com.au Desert Park Transfers, T8952 4667, run a shuttle bus to the park ($5 one way) and can pick up from accommodation.*

Sleeping

Alice has over 50 options, virtually all have a swimming pool, and most offer free airport/station pick-ups. The VIC can help track down a bed if things are busy

B *Hilltop*, 9 Zeil St, T8955 0208, www.hilltopalicesprings.com, backs onto the *Desert Park* and has great views. 2 a/c doubles with own bathroom and lounge. Bus route 1, stop 14. Of the dozens of motels **B-E** *Desert Rose*, 15 Railway Terr, T8952 1411, www.desertroseinn.com.au, is close to the centre, has some spacious self-contained flats and a couple of 4-bunk rooms for backpackers. **C** *Alice Tourist Apartments*, Gap Rd, T8952 2788, have basic but fully self-contained 1 and 2-bedroom units, sleeping up to 6. A good option for groups or families. Bus route 4, stop 7.

Backpackers are well catered for with 8 hostels and half a dozen other budget options. **D-E** *Annie's Place*, 4 Traeger Av, T8952 1545, anniesplace@octaunet.au, sets the standard. With 96 beds it's big enough to have excellent facilities, including a bar, $5 evening meals and internet café, but small enough to retain a good buzz and personal atmosphere. All 6-bed dorms and doubles are en suite and a/c. Only the small kitchen lets the side down. **D-E** *Pioneer YHA*, Parsons St, T8952 8855, alicepioneer@yhant. org.au, is the most central hostel. Once an outdoor cinema the 110 beds are split between 6-bunk, 4-bunk and double rooms. Purpose-built, a/c and good-sized communal areas around the pool. Clean and secure, but no parking. **E** *Alice Lodge*, 4 Mueller St, T8953 1975, alice_lodge@hotmail.com, is the smallest hostel in town. It's friendly, relaxed and clean. All rooms a/c, but some are in caravans. A stiff walk out, **E** *Ossies*, corner of Lindsay Av and Warburton St, T8952 2308, www.ossies.com.au, is also small with 45 beds. Cheap bunks and doubles. Light breakfast included if it isn't eaten by the resident roos. Bus route 2, stop 3. There are 8 **caravan parks** dotted around the town. None are close in but a couple are within 2 km, including the friendly **C-D** *Winter Sun*, Stuart Highway, T8952 4080. Good facilities, and all cabins have a/c.

Expensive *Bluegrass*, corner of Todd St and Stott Terr, T8955 5188. Modern Australian with a strong focus on Asia. Excellent food in a colourful, modern dining room. Open Wed-Sun, 1130-1400, 1830-2100. **Mid-range** *Kellers*, at the *Mercure* on Gregory Terr, T8952 3188, offers something different with a menu of traditional Swiss food or Indian curries in fairly bland hotel surrounds. Mon-Sat 1730-2030. *Red Ochre Grill*, Todd Mall, T8952 9614. A sophisticated brasserie-style restaurant with plenty of outdoor seating. The menu offers creative 'bush tucker' food such as a warm crocodile salad. Also open for breakfast, lunch and snacks. Daily 0630-2130. **Cheap** *Al Fresco*, Todd Mall, T8953 4944. Simple, busy place next to the cinema with a large choice of pasta dishes and a few Italian mains. Daily 1000-2100. *Bar Doppio*, Todd Mall, T8952 6525. Laid-back, hip café with fresh interesting food, excellent juices, coffee and veggie choices. Despite the name the café is BYO only. 0730-1700 Mon-Sat, Fri-Sat 1800-2100, Sun 1000-1600. Recommended. *Casalinga*, Gregory Terr, has little atmosphere but does great pizzas. Daily from 1700. *Red Rock Bakery Café*, Todd Mall, fresh bread from a tiny booth on the Mall with pavement tables. A good spot for a quick sandwich or roll.

Eating
Alice eating is pretty meaty and traditional. Most menus feature native wildlife such as kangaroo, crocodile and emu, and if you've been on a camel safari here's your chance to bite back because camel is on offer too

Alice's liveliest pub is *Bojangles*, Todd St, T8952 2873. A soothingly dim cowboy saloon with cowhide benches and solid tables. Mid-range steaks and cheaper bar meals available, and live music every night from 2000. *Firkin and Hound*, Hartley St, T8953 3033. A welcoming British-style pub that seems incongruous in Alice but is nevertheless a good place for a pint. Great cheap meals daily 1130-1430 and 1800-2100. Live cover bands Fri-Sat. *Scotty's Tavern*, Todd Mall, T8952 7131, is another locals' drinking hole with no-frills décor and clientele. The walls are lined with photos of 'characters' to look at if there aren't enough live ones about. Pub meals focus on local meat such as emu, croc, roo and camel. Live didjeridu and percussion sessions Mon, Thu. The *Sports Bar*, Todd Mall, is a popular and relaxed bar and bistro with pleasant shady tables on the Mall. The cheap bistro menu has generous meals of pasta, salads, tapas as well as the standards. Daily from 1100. Those looking for a serious late-night session generally head for the nightclub at *Melankas* on Todd St.

Pubs & bars

Cinema *Alice Springs Cinemas*, Todd Mall, T8952 4999. **Theatre** *Araluen*, Larapinta Dr, T8951 1122. **Music** Concerts are held at *Araluen* but the most common music venue in the Alice is a local pub (see above).

Entertainment

One of the world's wackier festivals, the **Henley on Todd** is a boat regatta held in the dry riverbed. Competitors race in a series of events such as the bath tub derby and BYO Boat. Boats are bottomless and worn like a skirt so competitors can carry the boat downstream. The day concludes with a pitched sea battle between ships firing flour bombs and water cannons. Held on a Sat in **late Sep**. Tickets ($10) can be purchased on the day. For more information contact the VIC or see www.henleyontodd.com.au

Festivals

Northern Territory

Shopping
Every second shop in the Todd Mall seems to sell Aboriginal art

Shop around and bargain as it is a very competitive market and quality of work varies considerably. Expect to pay a minimum of $50 for the smallest painting

For the best contemporary Aboriginal art go to *Gallery Gondwana*, 43 Todd Mall, www.gallerygondwana.com.au Other interesting galleries are *Mbantua*, 71 Gregory Terr and *Aboriginal Desart*, 87 Todd Mall. Also seek out the Aboriginal- owned galleries, *Warumpi*, 105 Gregory Terr, www.warumpi.com.au, *Papunya Tula*, 78 Todd St, and *Desart*, on the corner of Stott Terr and Bath St, www.desart. com.au **Art and crafts** *Gondwana II*, 11 Todd Mall, has high-quality Australian glass, jewellery, ceramics and paintings. **Books** New books at *Dymocks*, Alice Plaza, and *Big Kangaroo Books*, Reg Harris La, off Todd Mall. Second-hand and exchange at *Helene's*, 113 Todd St, opposite *Melankas*. **Camping and outdoor** *Alice Disposals*, Reg Harris La, off Todd Mall. Cheap equipment and clothing. *Lone Dingo Adventures*, next to the YHA, *for all the latest labels and gadgets. Also outdoor equipment hire.* **Jewellery** *Lightning Ridge Opal Mines*, 75 Todd Mall, sells opals from all Australian fields. **Market** A street market is held in Todd Mall every 2nd Sun. The stalls sell art and crafts, books, fresh produce and snacks.

Tours & excursions

4WD There are a host of companies eager to whisk travellers off into the bush, contact the VIC for a comprehensive list of these and bus tours. *Wayoutback*, T1300 551510, www.wayoutback.com.au, gets closer than most to the raw experience and have exclusive access to 2 of the major cattle stations between Yulara and Kings Canyon. Their 5-day western 'safari' is $665, max 13 people. *Sahara*, T1800-806240, www.saharatours.com.au, have bush-camping tours from 1½ to 5 days, also based around Uluru. *Adventure Tours*, T8936 1311, www.adventuretours.com.au, are one of the largest companies in the region, with a wide choice of options. There are also a number of small operators specializing in various central destinations. *Palm Valley Tours*, T8952 0033, www.palmvalleytours.com.au, run day-trips to Hermannsburg and Palm Valley ($85), while *Leigh Goldsmith* does a 350-km round trip via Rainbow Valley, Chambers Pillar and the fringes of the Simpson Desert (Full-day, $148). *Austours*, 1800 335009, austour@austourtravel.com, offer a 3-day Outback tour via Dalhousie Springsand Finke ($725). **Air** *Murray Cosson*, T8952 4625, australianoutback flights@aopa.com.au, does the usual 30-min hops, but is also available for excellent day-trips both west to Yulara and south to the Simpson Desert. Charter costs from $800 per day for the aircraft. **Bike** *Steve's Mountain Bike Tours*, T8952 1542, guide small groups up into the ranges, from $30 for 1 hr. **Bus** *AAT Kings*, T8952 1700, www.aatkings.com, and APT, T1800 891121, www.aptours.com.au, are the two big coach operators in the region, each with a comprehensive range of 'red centre' tours from 1 to 3 days. The *Alice*, T1800 669111, alicwand@ozemail.com.au, and *Emu Run*, T/F8953 7057, are more locally based and run smaller vehicles. Both cover the MacDonnell Ranges. **Horse** *Ossie's*, T8952 2308, offer trail rides including 3-hr sunset rides for $75. **Parachuting** *Pete's*, T1800-641114, www.petes parachuting.com.au, climb to over 3 km before jumping, giving lots of freefall. Tandem jumps $289.

Transport

Air *Air North* fly to Darwin via Tennant Creek and Katherine every Sun-Fri. *Aboriginal Air Services*, T8953 5000, operations-ca@maf.org.au, fly to Katherine at 0830 Mon and Thu, with three stops at outlying communities (6 hrs, $180). *Qantas* fly daily to most state capitals (not Canberra or Hobart), and also to Ayers Rock, Cairns and (Sat-Mon, Wed) Broome. **Bus** *McCafferty's/Greyhound* have several services operating out of Alice Springs. There are 2 services a day north to Tennant Creek, Katherine and Darwin at 1505 and 2100, and one south to Adelaide, departing 1030. They also run a daily service to Yulara at 0730 (arrives 1300). **Backpacker buses** Several operators head down to Adelaide via the main sights. They include *Adventure Tours*, T8936 1311, www.adventure tours.com.au (7 or 8 days) *Groovy Grape*, T1800 661177, www.groovy grape.com.au (2 days), and *Wayward*, T1800 882823, www.waywardbus.com.au (5 or 8 days). Expect to pay about $95-110 per day. *Desert Venturer*, T1800 079119, www.desertven-turer.com.au, tackle the direct rough roads to Cairns (3 days, $350), as do *Adventure*

Tours (7 days, $795). Three operators go to **Darwin**. *Remote Possibilities*, T1800 623854, www.australiaoutbacktours.com, take 2 days ($198), while *Wildway*, T1300 720777, www.wildway.com.au, take 3 ($355) and *Adventure Tours* take 6 ($625). For direct 4WD trips to **Perth** along the Outback tracks contact *Travelabout*, T1800 621200 (2½ days, $329, concessions $275). **Bicycle/4WD** If you like cycling then try to hook into a *Remote Outback Cycle Tours*, T9279 6969, www.cycletours.com.au, trip up to Darwin via Kakadu (5 nights, $790), or down to Adelaide via the Oodnadatta Track and Clare Valley (5 nights, $840). As bikes go on the roof of the OKA you just cycle the best bits. Departures roughly once a month, May-Sep. **Rail** The *Ghan*, T132147, www.gsr.com.au, leaves Alice for **Adelaide** at 1300, Tue and Fri, arriving around 2100 (from $200, concessions $100). It then carries on to **Melbourne** and **Sydney**. **Tour operators** *APT* have a daily commentated bus to **Yulara** at 0700 (5½ hrs, $99), and another, via the Mereenie Loop, to **Kings Canyon** at 0500 (4 hrs, $99).

Banks All major banks have ATMs on Todd St Mall with *Commonwealth* around the corner on Parsons St. **Bike hire** *Centre Cycles*, 13 Gregory St, T8953 2966. $16.50 per day. Open 0900-1700 Mon-Fri. 'Depots' at most hostels. **Car and 4WD hire** Local budget operators include *Boomerang*, T8955 5171, and *Outback*, T8953 5333. **Car servicing** *BP*, 73 Gap Rd, T8952 3661. **Communications** Internet cafés include *Outback Travel Shop*, near the corner of Gregory Terr and Todd St, 0800-2000 Mon-Fri, 1000-1800 Sat-Sun. $6 hr. **Post Office** Hartley St. **Hospital** *Alice Springs*, Gap Rd, T8951 7777. **Laundry** *Wash House*, Railway Terr, daily 0600-2200. **Library** corner of Leichhardt St and Stott Terr, T8950 0555. Open 1000-1700 Mon-Fri, 0900-1300 Sat, 1300-1700 Sun. Internet $6 per hr, bookings required. **Police** Parsons St, T8951 8888. **Taxi** T131008 or 8952 1877. **Work** There are often opportunities, both in town and on surrounding cattle stations. *Toddy's Backpackers*, 41 Gap Rd, T8952 1322, toddys@saharatours.com.au, is a good place to find out what's available.

Directory
Alice has the cheapest fuel along the Stuart Highway

The West MacDonnell Ranges

Standing up to 800 m above the central plain, the MacDonnells are a series of rounded, rusted hill ranges punctured by a series of gaps, gorges and chasms, some with permanent waterholes, a boon to wildlife, indigenous people and sweaty tourists alike. To the west of Alice Springs a long section of the ranges has been declared the **West MacDonnell National Park**. Entry to the park, which is free, is possible at several points between Alice Springs and Redbank Gorge.

For unsealed road conditions see www.nt.gov.au/dtw or T1800 246199

Simpsons Gap is the best spot for seeing **black-footed rock wallabies**, though the waterhole is out of bounds. There is a parks visitor information area (T8955 0310), and toilets. Rangers run nature walks here at 1000 on Saturday, Sunday and Monday for 30 minutes. A 23-km cycle path from Alice is partly cross-country. Gates are closed 2000-0500. The turn-off for **Standley Chasm** is 40 km from Alice, and the chasm itself another 9 km. This sheer gully, just a few metres across, is known for catching the sun on both sides for just a few minutes in the middle of each day. There is a takeaway and shop, toilets and shaded tables. ■ *Daily 0900-1700. $5.50, children and concessions $4.50.* Access to gaps further west is via **Namatjira Drive**.

Larapinta Drive
Simpson's Gap 24 km from Alice Springs

Access to **Ellery Creek Big Hole** is via a 2-km unsealed road. This soaring gap has a large, permanent waterhole, the first of three where swimming is allowed. Camping is also permitted ($3.30 per person) and there are basic toilets and fireplaces. **Serpentine Gorge** is a few kilometres further on. Here, several semi-permanent waterholes are strung out along a winding,

Namatjira Drive
Ellery Creek Big Hole 90 km from Alice Springs

steep-sided gorge, with an entrance straight out of *Jason and the Argonauts*. A waterhole guards this and an approach was forbidden by local Aboriginal law, except during times of extreme drought. Access isn't easy. The 3½-km drive in is unsealed and rough, and then it's another 1½-km walk. Swimming is forbidden, so a blow-up mattress with a length of string attached is required to get across – this is all well worth the effort, however. Alternatively, make the 10-minute climb up the eastern bluff to catch the grand view into the gorge and to the ranges to the south. Just before Glen Helen is the turn-off to popular **Ormiston Gorge**, 8 km down the sealed road. This has the best visitor set-up of any of the accessible gorges. The campground ($6.60 per person) has BBQs, toilets, drinking water and showers, and there is also a small parks visitor centre, open 0800-1700, T8956 7799. Swimming is allowed in the permanent waterhole. The gorge is wide and high with impressive rounded bluffs, and a colony of shy wallabies. There are several good **walks** from the campground, including the enjoyable three-hour **Ormiston Pound** loop walk. Map and walkers guides from the visitor centre.

Glen Helen &
beyond
132 km from
Alice Springs,
114 km unsealed
from Hermannsburg

The 700-km-long **Finke** is one of the Centre's principal river courses, capable of high and forceful flows, but normally a dry bed. During its more than 100-million-year existence it has cut a series of dramatic red gorges and bluffs through the landscape. One of these is **Glen Helen**, which is also important as one of the river's six permanent waterholes. Visitors who make it this far can stay at the **B-E** *Glen Helen Resort*, T8956 7489, glenhelen@ melanka.com.au They have air conditioned motel rooms and basic 4-bunk rooms and campground. Bar snacks and expensive fuel available 0700-2230, breakfast and cheap meals 0700-1530, more expensive meals in the evening. **Helicopter** tours, T9580 7177, www.helicoptergroup.com, are available. From Glen Helen the road crosses the Finke and then immediately becomes unsealed. At this point is a **lookout**, the best one easily accessible in the ranges, with extensive views to the north and the unusually craggy **Mount Sonder**. The last campground west is 20 km further on at the awesome 4WD only **Redbank Gorge**. After this the road curls south, past **Gosse Bluff**, to its western junction with Larapinta Drive and the Mereenie Loop Road (permits required, see page 646).

Hermannsburg
Colour map 5, grid B3
125 km from Alice
Springs, 195 km
unsealed from Kings
Canyon via Mereenie
Loop Rd (permits
required, see page 646

This settlement was the first Aboriginal mission in the Northern Territory, established by Lutherans in 1877, on the lands of the Western Arrente (or Aranda) people. Control of the mission lands was handed back to the original owners in 1982 under the Aboriginal Land Rights Act and is now a strong Aboriginal community with very few residents of European origin. The town is particularly well known for the skill of its artists. In the early days of the mission, the famous Aboriginal painter **Albert Namatjira** was taught how to paint European-style landscapes and quickly developed his unique style and talent. Many of Namatjira's descendants and relatives continue to paint in his distinctive style and the Hermannsburg Potters have become well regarded for their coiled pots, painted and decorated with features of the Hermannsburg landscape. **The Hermannsburg Heritage Precinct** preserves the buildings of the mission and an art gallery showing the work of Namatjira and his school. The mission is a fascinating and delightful place to explore, shaded by tall gum trees and scattered with cool whitewashed stone buildings. There is also a rustic tea room in the former Pastor's house where you can have tea and scones. Local art and the work of the Hermannsburg potters is also on display at reasonable prices. ■ *Daily 1000-1600. $4.50, children $3, concessions $3.50, includes self-guided tour and a cuppa. Art gallery $3.50. T/F8956 7402.*

Walking in the ranges

There are many well-marked walks from the various gorges, the best being at **Serpentine** and **Ormiston** in the west, and **Trephina** in the east. They vary from 10 mins to a full day, but hikers should always wear a hat and sunscreen, and carry plenty of water (4 litres a day). If doing a longer walk on your own, let someone know your plans. The **Larapinta Trail** has been marked out along the 220 km spine of the West MacDonnells, with 13 sections connecting the various accessible gorges. The easier sections are 1-3 (Alice to Standley Chasm) while sections 8-12 are more challenging (Serpentine Gorge to Redbank Gorge). Walking the trail should only be attempted during Apr-Oct and even then you should try to walk in the cool of early morning or late afternoon. The Alice Springs tourist office has a full range of maps ($2 per section) and brief guides. For transport to trail heads contact **Trek Larapinta**, T8953 2933 or **Emu Run**, T8953 7057. Long-distance walkers are strongly advised to register with the Parks & Wildlife Commission before departure, T1300 650730. Credit card details are required for a refundable deposit ($50 per person). For more advice on walking in the ranges talk to the knowledgeable staff at **Lone Dingo** in Alice Springs. They offer equipment hire and can also advise on walks run by **Central Australian Bushwalkers**, T8953 1956. Visitors can join the club's regular walks for not much more than the cost of petrol. Guided walks are conducted by **World Expeditions**, T02 9279 0188, www.worldexpeditions.com.au (8 days, $1,600 or 16 days, $3,000).

Sleeping and eating Campsites are available at $11 per site, T8956 7480. Showers, toilet and laundry are the basic facilities. Also in the town is the *Ntaria* community **supermarket**. This sells reasonably priced fuel and is open 0830-1730 Mon-Sat, 1000-1730 Sun. Their takeaway is open 0830-1700 Mon-Fri.

The course of the **Finke River**, fresh from its exertions at Glen Helen, reappears to the visitor just west of Hermannsburg. A 4WD-only track follows the course south of the town, and continues down to the Ernest Giles Road, though only the first stretch is recommended unless you are an experienced and well-equipped off-road driver. This first section heads on down to **Finke Gorge** and **Palm Valley**, which is a vibrant and permanent oasis that shelters many wonderful remnant plant species, including the *red cabbage palm*. This really is a magical place to spend a couple of nights and there is a small campground just short of the valley with facilies including toilets, water and BBQs. ■ *No entry fee and no camping fee. For more information contact Parks and Wildlife NT, T8951 8211.*

Finke Gorge National Park
Palm Valley 18 km from Hermannsburg High-clearance 4WD only

North of Alice Springs

This route heads up to **Halls Creek** in Western Australia (see page 636) and is sealed for the first 130 of its 1,030 km. This is not recommended for 2WD, and there are very few roadhouses. Travellers in any vehicle should really be very well prepared. Some 40 km into the unsealed section is **B** *Tilmouth Well*, T8956 8777, an oasis resort and roadhouse with 10 self-contained cabins, restaurant, and such diversions as an art gallery, golf course, swimming and clay-pigeon shooting. There is fuel available 100 km up the track at **Yuendumu**, and then again after a further 310 km at **Rabbit Flat**, but only from Friday to Monday.

Tanami Track
For current road conditions on the WA side T1800 013314

Westprint map available

Northern Territory

Plenty
Highway
Alice Springs 835 km
from Mt Isa via this
route, 1,210 km
via sealed roads

Westprint map
available

The short cut to Mount Isa in Queensland (see page 387) is unsealed except for the first and last 70 km or so. Again this is not really recommended for two-wheel driving, though the NT side is generally quite passable and there are a few more roadhouses along the route, around every 100-200 km or so. The first sealed section cuts through the **Central Australian Gemfields**, an area rich in semi-precious stones, particularly garnet and zircon, 140 km from Alice. Fossicking is allowed with a licence (which is free), from the Department of Mines and Energy. There is an office in Alice at 58 Hartley Street, T8951 5669. Please note that those who are part of an organized tour do not need one.

The East MacDonnell Ranges

Ross River Homestead
84 km from
Alice Springs

After visiting the West MacDonnells, the eastern ranges come across as an interesting surprise. The overall impression of ancient red rock is the same, but there is much less of the uniformity. There are many more smaller and more tortured formations that interrupt the horizon, and dense woodland crowds some of the even, wider valleys. Access is via the **Ross Highway** which leaves the Stuart Highway just south of the Heavitree Gap. After 10 km and 18 km respectively are two impressive gaps, **Emily** and **Jessie**, with semi-permanent waterholes (please note that swimming is not allowed) and a small amount of Aboriginal rock art. Both have basic toilets and picnic sites. **Corroboree Rock** is a further 30 km. This is a semi-circular, 5-m slab of weathered but resistant sandstone, standing vertically on a very small hill. It is very sacred to the Arrernte people and visitors are asked to be respectable and keep their distance. The highlight is undoubtedly the **Trephina Gorge**, which can be reached by a 8-km unsealed road, 70 km from Alice. Here visitors will find a wide watercourse which has carved-out long, low and vivid red cliffs. The approach road passes under the much higher cliffs of **Trephina Bluff**. There are several walks from the gorge campground. Camping is $3.30 per person, and facilities comprise drinking water, BBQs, fireplaces and toilets (parks office T8956 9765). The sealed highway ends at the C-E *Ross River Homestead*, T8956 9711, rrhca@ozemail.com.au, with good-value wooden cabins, basic bunk rooms and campground. Pool for guests only. Also excellent mid-range meals. Expensive fuel and snacks available 0800-1700. Recommended. Just before Ross River is the turn-off to **Arltunga Historical Reserve**, 35 km down an unsealed road. This was the site of a mini goldrush in the early 1900s and the abandoned underground mines, stone ruins and small cemetery are easily accessible. A dozen kilometres past Ross River, on a 4WD only track, is **N'Dhala Gorge**. It is best known for its cultural significance to the Arrernte people. There are thousands of rock carvings in the gorge, most engraved in the last 2,000 years, with a few as old as 10,000 years. Camping is allowed ($3.30 per person). Toilets and fireplaces, but no water.

South of Alice Springs

Fuel is available
at Maryville

It takes a special trip or an expensive tour to visit **Chambers Pillar**, a 40 m high remnant column of colourful layered sandstone. It's 150 km from the **Maryvale** turn-off near the airport. The road is unsealed the whole way, most is recommended for 4WD only, and the final 30-odd km are definitely 4WD only. If you do head this way, the **Ewaninga Rock Carvings** are about 25 km south of the airport. Several Aboriginal images, of undetermined age, have been carved into rocks on the edge of a small claypan. They can be viewed via a 20-minute loop walk.

The Stuart Highway slips through **Heavitree Gap** then takes the more or less direct route south. The turn-off to **Rainbow Valley** is 77 km from Alice, then 22 km down an unsealed road. This jagged semicircle of cliffs in the James Range are made up of clearly differentiated layers of sandstone and provide a colourful sight, particularly at sunset. Camping facilities comprise a basic toilet. The first roadhouse is at **C-E** *Stuarts Well*, T8956 0808, 90 km from Alice. Accommodation is in air conditioned motel units and a basic bunkhouse. Light meals and fuel 0630-2200. The **Henbury Metorites Conservation Reserve** is 18 km down the very poor unsealed Ernest Giles Road. The reserve encompasses 12 craters, all caused by fragments of the Henbury Meteor which crashed in from space, broke up and hit the ground about 4,700 years ago. The largest crater is 180 m across and there are walking tracks around this and several others. There are basic camping ($3.30) and picnicking facilities. **C-E** *Erldunda*, T8956 0984, 200 km south of Alice, marks the junction with the **Lasseter Highway**, the road to Uluru and King's Canyon. This is a large resort-style roadhouse, with 54 air-conditioned motel rooms and 12 backpacker rooms sleeping up to four. The pool is open to non-residents for $4. Fuel 0630-2200, takeaway 0700-2030, covered picnic tables, internet terminal.

Alice Springs to Erldunda
Erldunda 200 km from Alice Springs, 235 km from Yulara

Uluru ('Ayers Rock') and around

The grand, haunting bulk of Uluru, the country's most famous landmark, is close to the geographical centre of Australia and is often called the 'red heart'. Perhaps 'soul' would be a better word as even staunch atheists will readily acknowledge the profound feeling of spirituality it elicits, a natural cathedral rising above the surrounding bush and spinifex-covered plains. The horizon is broken only by Kata Tjuta, a more subtle and secretive formation. Beyond these huddled hills the dry plains spread further, though still not unbroken. Mount Connor, a beautifully symmetrical mesa twice the size of Uluru and sometimes mistaken for it, also stands pround on the flat landscape. A couple of hundred kilometres north, the George Gill range of hills are outliers of the MacDonnells and famous for Kings Canyon, part of the Watarrka National Park. Another of the country's most impressive sights, a walk around the rim should not be missed.

www.centralaustralian tourism.com

Northern Territory

Around 100 km from Erldunda are the first glimpses of what most travellers take to be Uluru, but is, in fact, Mount Conner, an impressive flate-topped mesa that's twice the size of 'the rock'. It is on the Curtin Springs cattle station which operates the friendly **C-D** *Curtin Springs* pub and cookhouse, T8956 2906, 160 km from Erldunda. Fuel and bar available 0700-2030. Home-cooked cheap set meals (often steaks), 0700-0900, 1200-1400, 1830-2030. Air-conditioned motel rooms and budget options, including free camping. Pool for residents only. From out front there are **camel rides**; from short ones around the yard to 1½ hours out into the desert for flora and bushtucker tours. ■ *Daily 0900, 1100-1500, 1½ hrs before sunset. Yard $3, full ride $25, children $10. T8956 7784.* There are also excellent 4WD tours from the pub out to the usually private station, which include an optional hike up Mount Connor and sunset photos from much closer than the roadside lookouts. ■ *Daily, full day 0730 ($180), half day 1330 ($90). Bookings required. T8953 4664, www.daytours-alicesprings.com.au*

Mount Connor & Curtin Springs
Colour map 5, grid B3 160 km from Erldunda, 75 km from Yulara

Yulara

Colour map 5, grid B3
435 km from Alice
Springs, 735 km
from Coober Pedy

www.ayersrock
resort.com.au

Yulara is a large and friendly resort complex, strategically built between low dunes so as not to intrude on the Uluru landscape, but with easy access to the **Uluru-Kata Tjuta National Park** in mind. It has a monopoly on accommodation in the area and the price of a bed here is high, but then so are the standards, particularly the exceptional levels of service. There are half a dozen hotels of varying styles and facilities, all built on the periphery of a loop road. Between two of these, *Emu Walk* and *Lost Camel*, is the 'resort centre' a set of shops, services and cafés surrounding a spacious, sunny courtyard. These include a good-sized supermarket (open 0830-2030), post office, bank and ATM, and art galleries and a souvenir shops. The best gallery is *Mulgara*, in *Sails* hotel. There are several **lookouts** around the resort, all with views over to Uluru with a glimpse of Kata Tjuta in the distance, the best being the one at the coach campground. The **visitors centre** is between *Desert Gardens* and *Emu Walk*, and has an extensive interpretative centre. ■ *Daily 0830-1900. T8957 7377.*

Getting there & around
See also Transport below

Airport *Quantas* operate flights to Connellan Airport (generally termed 'Ayers Rock' in published schedules), 5 km from **Yulara**, from many of the country's major cities. Hire car pick-up at the airport is available with *Thrifty*, T8956 2030, *Hertz*, T8956 2244, and *Avis*, T8956 2266. There is a free *AAT Kings* bus service between the airport and Yulara, meeting every flight. **Bus** *McCafferty's/Greyhound* run a daily service from **Alice Springs**, dropping off at each resort hotel. **Local** No 2 points in the resort are more than a 20-min walk apart, but a free minibus travels around a loop continuously, clockwise, 1030-1800 and 1830-2430, every 15 mins. **Tour operators** *AAT Kings*, T8956 2171, www.aatkings.com, and *APT*, T1800 891121, www.aptours.com.au, run one-way tours that can be used to get around the Centre.

Sleeping
Accommodation should be booked in advance at any time of year, but particularly Mar-Nov (plenty of visitors find themselves making the long journey back to Curtin Springs for the night). This even applies to campsites

All reservations for the 5,000 beds and campsite places are directed through the company office in Sydney, T02 9339 1040, www.voyages.com.au Rates can be lower for the higher budget hotels by booking special deal and combination packages. **LL** *Longitude 131°* has 15 safari tents on a sand dune overlooking Uluru, as luxurious as any 5-star hotel room. **LL** *Sails in the Desert* is the resort's 5-star flagship. The incredible suites, with Uluru views, are worth every cent of the indulgent splash-out. **LL** *Desert Gardens* is a slightly less expensive alternative to *Sails*. Rooms are less luxurious and have decidedly less character. The pool is available to all resort guests. **LL** *Emu Walk* provides the upmarket self-contained option. Apartments are extremely spacious, well-equipped and worth considering for groups or large families. **A-B** *The Lost Camel* is the smallest and newest hotel, with 90 en suite rooms. More basic than the *Gardens*, but with a lot more personality. The **A-D** *Outback Pioneer Hotel & Lodge* provides most of the budget options and the buzziest nightlife. Relatively basic but comfortable en suite double rooms vary in price and amenities, some have kitchenettes. Backpackers have the option of 4-bed or 20-bed single-sex dorms (*YHA*) where linen is not supplied. Cleanliness in rooms, kitchen and shower block, and quality of service are on a par with the rest of the resort. The pool is available to all resort guests. The **B** *Resort Campground* has the cheapest double-bed option and the few cabins also have a kitchenette, though no en suite. Camping on the grassed lawns is $13 per person for a non-powered site.

Eating
Contact hotel receptions or call T8957 7888 for restaurant bookings

The most spectacular of the resort's restaurants has the Uluru sunset as a backdrop and the stars for a ceiling. *Sounds of Silence*, is an outdoor, all-inclusive gourmet spectacular, accompanied by a didjeridoo demonstration and star talk. If $110 is not an issue, go for it. Best of the static establishments is *Winkiku*, the buffet restaurant of *Sails*, open for an **expensive** indulgent free-for-all every breakfast and dinner. Along similar lines, but

To climb or not to climb?

To many tourists a visit to Uluru means climbing to the top of the rock. Anangu do not want visitors to climb the rock and there are clear requests on the entry ticket, signs at the base of the climb and the cultural centre that ask visitors to respect their wishes. The climb follows a traditional route taken by the ancestral Mala men so it is of great spiritual significance. The Anangu also feel responsible for visitors on their land and feel sad when people die or are hurt while climbing. It is a very steep, strenuous two to

three hour walk and several people die or have to be rescued every year – at least 54 people have died attempting the climb in the past few decades. The climb is closed on very windy days or from 0800 on days when the temperature is forecast at 36°C or more. It is also sometimes closed for cultural reasons and many predict that it will be closed permanently in the future. The base walk is a far more interesting alternative offering plenty of variety and more comfortable shady terrain.

around $10 a head cheaper is the *Bough House* in the humbler surrounds of the *Outback Pioneer*. Both open 0600-1000, 1900-2200. The *Bough House* also opens for excellent and **cheap** not-so-light lunches. There is an equally good, and unsurprisingly very busy **mid-range** a là carte restaurant and café, *Gecko's*, in the resort centre. They start the day with the resort's cheapest buffet breakfast 0600-1030, serve coffee and lunches and finish with a mostly Italian evening menu. Last orders 2100. Back at the *Outback* is the cheap *Pioneer BBQ*, a grill-it-yourself affair with unlimited salad bar and tables in the bar area. The **takeaway** in the resort centre doubles as a bakery and opens 0800-2030. The *Pioneer Kitchen* at the *Outback* also serves up all the usual fast food (same hrs).

Bars The most stylish is the cocktail piano bar at *Sails*, the *Tali Bar*, but the life and soul is usually over at the *Outback* in the *Pioneer BBQ Bar*. **Cinema** Rear of the visitor centre. Fri-Sun. **Music** Live performances of 'bush music' daily from 1900 at *Pioneer BBQ*. **Entertainment**

Air There are both helicopter and light-aircraft scenic flights from Connellan airport, with resort pick-ups. Operators offer options from a 15-min Uluru flight to a grand tour that can include Kings Canyon or Mt Connor. Kata Tjuta is particularly striking from the air. The best budget options, particularly for the longer tours, are with *Ayers Rock Scenic Flights*, T8956 2345, ayersrockflights@ozemail.com.au, (30-min Uluru-Kata Tjuta flight $99). Helicopters fly lower, and have excellent visibility for wide-ranging photography. *Professional Helicopter Services*, T8956 2003, www.phs.com.au, fly over Uluru or Kata Tjuta or both (30-min Uluru-Kata Tjuta flight $180) and are the only operator cleared to land at Kings Canyon. **Bus** *AAT Kings*, T8956 2171, www.aatkings.com, have a comprehensive set of tours from the resort, including ones to **Uluru** (from $40), **Kata Tjuta** (from $75) and **Kings Canyon** (from $135). **Camel** *Frontier Camel Tours*, coach campground, T8956 2444, www.cameltours.com.au Sunset rides into the national park, includes drink and refreshments (2½ hrs, $85). **Night** *Discovery Ecotours*, T1800 803174, bookings@ecotours.com.au, have several telescopes pre-set to celestial marvels. Excellent tours ($30, children $23) nightly 2030, also 1930 Jun-Aug, 2215 Sep May. **Walking** *Anangu Tours*, T8956 2123, www.anangutours.com.au, run 2 illuminating Aboriginal-guided tours to areas around **Uluru** (see page 708). *Discovery Ecotours*, T8956 2563, bookings@ecotours.com.au, run a wider range of walking tours, including a full guided **Uluru** base walk ($83) and a *Predator* show ($22). **Tours & excursions** *Most tours do not include the $16.50 park entry fee. The central tour booking office is in the resort centre, T8957 7324*

Air *Qantas* fly daily to **Alice Springs**, **Cairns**, **Sydney** and **Perth**. They also fly to **Broome** every Sat-Mon and Wed. *Professional Helicopter Services*, T8956 2003, www.phs.com.au, fly one-way to **Kings Canyon** (approx 1 hr, $540). **Transport**

Northern Territory

Bus *McCafferty's/Greyhound* operate one bus a day to **Alice Springs**, leaving the *Outback Pioneer* at 1230 and picking up at all the other hotels. Catch this bus then change at the Luritja turn-off for the connecting service to **Kings Canyon**. **Bicycle/4WD** If you like cycling then try to hook into a *Remote Outback Cycle* tour (4 nights, $790), T9279 6969, www.cycletours.com.au, up to Alice via the MacDonnells. As bikes go on the roof of the Oka you just cycle the best bits. Departs roughly once a month, May-Sep. **Tour operators** *AAT Kings* have buses to **Kings Canyon**, daily 1340 (4 hrs, $92), and **Alice Springs**, daily 1340 (5½ hrs, $99). *APT* also go to **Kings Canyon**, leaving daily at 0500 (4 hrs, $90).

Directory   **Bank** *ANZ* branch and ATM at resort centre. **Communications** Internet kiosks at *Outback Pioneer*. **Post Office** At esort centre, open daily, 1000-1400 Sat-Sun. **Fuel** *Mobil*, cheapest west of Erldunda, open 0700-2100. **Luggage store** Free at all resort receptions. **Medical and police** Contact resort receptions.

Uluru-Kata Tjuta National Park

This national park contains an instantly car parkable Australian icon, **Uluru**. The red rock rising from the plain in the centre of the continent is also still widely known as Ayers Rock, although the name changed over a decade ago. Nearby, over the spinifex-covered plains and ancient low sand dunes lie the domes of **Kata Tjuta**, gently curving red hills leaning in closely like heads drawn together in conversation. For over 20,000 years this landscape has been revered by the Aboriginal inhabitants of the area and is now part of one of Australia's most popular national parks, receiving almost 400,000 visitors a year. The park has developed relatively recently, receiving its first tourists in the 1950s and 1960s. In 1985 the government handed the title deeds of the park to the Pitjantjatjara and Yankunytjatjara Aboriginal people, recognizing that their continual use and custodianship of the land constituted legal ownership. These people, known locally as **Anangu**, decided to lease the park back to the government and manage it jointly with Parks Australia. The park is further protected by its **World Heritage** listing, received for its outstanding natural and cultural values.

Uluru and Kata Tjuta are remarkable geological forms of great beauty but are also of profound cultural significance to the Anangu people. Many features of both landforms represent the bodies, actions and artefacts of their ancestral beings in physical form. These are related to the *Tjukurpa* (see box, page 710) and are considered sacred sites, the details of which are only disclosed to those Anangu responsible for their care. To protect this ancient but living culture the activities of visitors are subject to careful monitoring and some restrictions. ■ *National park open daily approx 1 hr before to 1 hr past sunset. T8956 2299, www.environment.gov.au $16.50 for a 3-day pass.*

Getting around   **Bicycle** Hire available at the Yulara public campground ($15 half-day, $40 for 2 days),
There is no public   T8956 2055. **Minibus** The *Uluru Express*, T8956 2152, is a quasi bus service which
transport within the   runs from the resort out to both **Uluru** ($25-35 return) and **Kata Tjuta** ($45-50 return).
national park   Minibuses run principally to allow sunrise and sunset viewing.

Uluru-Kata   The cultural centre, built in 1994, is where the Anangu teach visitors about
Tjuta Cultural   their culture, *Tjukurpa* and management of the park. The two buildings rep-
Centre   resent *Kuniya* (woma python) and *Liru* (poisonous snake), ancestral beings
The centre is a very   of the *Tjukurpa* linked to the southern side of Uluru. The entry tunnel repre-
pleasant, cool and   sents aspects of Anangu life and leads to the park information desk where
spacious place with   visitors can pick up park notes and other publications and find out more
plenty of shaded areas   about tours, events and ranger activities. The complex also includes
to picnic or rest

high-quality arts, crafts and souvenirs and a café (open from 0700) with a close view of Uluru. All businesses are Aboriginal-owned although few Anangu are visible. This is because they tend to be fairly shy and reserved people who find the attention of thousands of visitors hard to face. ■ *Daily 0700-1800 (Nov-Mar), 0700-1730 (Apr-Oct), T8956 3138. The cultural centre is 1 km from Uluru.*

Uluru is recognized as the largest monolith (or single rock) in the world and is right up there on the 'wow factor' scale. It is 3 km long and rises abruptly 340 m above the surrounding plain. It has a loaf-shape from a distance but closer up it reveals sharp vertical ridges, muscular curves, and caves eroded into evocative shapes. The beautiful form is enhanced by the deep-red colour of the rock, caused by the rusting of one of its minor constituents, iron. The colour becomes particularly rich at sunrise and sunset when light from the red end of the spectrum is reflected from the surface, making it glow as if molten. Uluru was named 'Ayers Rock' in 1873 after a South Australian politician by explorer William Gosse, the first European to climb it, but reverted to its original name when park ownership was handed back to the Anangu. It is surrounded by trees and bushes and has the feel of an oasis even in high summer. There are several walks close to the base starting from the large Mala car park, but the main facilities are concentrated at Uluru -Kata Tjuta Cultural Centre.

Uluru ('Ayers Rock')
Colour map 5, grid B3
Altitude: 863 m
20 km from Yulara

Sunrise and sunset viewing areas are clearly marked and attract hundreds of cars and coaches. Ask at the resort for sunrise and sunset times

The domes of Kata Tjuta lie to the west of Uluru, visible across 30 km of sand plains. Although they are less well known than the great rock in the distance, they are easily as beautiful, if not more so. The Anangu name means 'many heads' and there is something curiously lifelike about the smooth, high domes huddled together. Between them cool, deep valleys have the mystery and silence of a cathedral and indeed the area is sacred to Anangu men. However, the *Tjukurpa* stories of Kata Tjuta are considered men's business and cannot be revealed to the uninitiated. There are two short walks and a sunset viewing area at the western end where visitors linger over the intense red colour of the domes at the end of the day. This area has a few picnic tables and is a quieter spot than the sunset area at Uluru. Sunrise is best seen from the dune viewing area, 25 km from the Kata Tjuta turn-off, facing the southern edge of the rocks.

Kata Tjuta ('The Olgas')
Colour map 5, grid B3
Mount Olga: 1,066 m
48 km from Yulara
48 km from Uluru

The **Base Walk** at Uluru circumnavigates the entire base, combining two shorter tracks, the Mala and Mutijula walks. It is a fascinating walk allowing a close look at rock formations, rock art and waterholes passing through surprisingly lush vegetation in some areas. There are a few shelters to rest under and a drinking-water tank at the halfway point (9½ km, two to three hours). The **Mala Walk** (2 km, one hour return) focuses on the journey of the ancestral *Mala*, the wallaby. A free guided walk is conducted by a ranger every day, who explains the significance and features of Uluru. It starts from the Mala Walk sign at the Mala car park (0800 October-April, 1000 May-September). The **Mutitjulu Walk** (1 km, ½ hour) leads to a waterhole that is the home of *Wanampi*, an ancestral watersnake, and looks at the features left behind by *Kuniya*, woma python, and examples of rock art. It is accessible from the Mutijulu car park, just to the east of the main junction. The **Liru Walk** leads through mulga woodland from the cultural centre to the Mala car park (2 km one way). There are two walks at Kata Tjuta, one of which is the best in the park. The **Valley of the Winds** is a spectacular circuit

Walking in the park
All walks should be done as early as possible while it is cool and in hot weather completed by 1100. Rangers recommend that walkers carry and drink one litre of water an hour

Northern Territory

walk through the deep valleys between the western domes. The walk heads over uneven terrain to Karu Lookout, a peaceful clearing near a creek, and then swings south. Turning east again the track passes through a beautiful canyon to Karingana Lookout with views of the domes beyond. The track follows the base of the left dome back to Karu Lookout (7½ km, three hours). This track is closed beyond the first lookout from 1100 on days when the temperature is forecast at 36°C or more. The **Walpa** (Olga Gorge) **Walk** leads to the end of the narrow, high gorge and is an attractive easy walk (2½ km, one hour return). Visitors to Kata Tjuta are asked not to leave the path or climb the domes. At both Uluru and Kata Tjuta there are several rock features considered sacred sites by the Anangu that cannot be photographed or touched but these are all clearly signposted or indicated by double lines (no stopping) on the road.

Aboriginal guided walks *Anangu Tours*, T8956 2123, www.anangutours.com.au, is a company owned by the local Anangu people who lead walking tours in their own language, with an accompanying interpreter translating into English. During the walk the guides demonstrate their traditional tools and skills such as making glue, spear throwing or preparing bush food. Guides also tell the dreaming stories of Uluru specifically linked to the physical features of the rock. These fascinating, leisurely walks are one of few ways visitors can interact with the Anangu and understand something of their culture and their profound links to Uluru itself. The **Liru Walk** passes through bushland from the cultural centre to the Mala car park. The **Kuniya Walk** also starts from the cultural centre but the walk is based around the Mutitjulu waterhole and the story of the *Kuniya* python woman. It is also possible to combine these walks with a sunrise or sunset viewing. Liru Walk 0830 (Mar-Sep) 0800 (Feb, Oct) 0730 (Nov-Jan). Kuniya Walk 1530 (Mar-Oct) 1630 (Nov-Feb). $47, children $24, ($98 including sunrise, $79 including sunset). Bookings essential.

Tjukaruru Road
For unsealed road conditions see www.nt.gov.au/dtw or T1800-246199 For current road conditions on the WA side T1800-013314 Westprint map available (Gunbarrel)

This unsealed track heads west from Kata Tjuta and hits the WA border after 250 km at the *Docker River* roadhouse, T8956 7373, (open 0900-1200, 1400-1630 Monday-Friday, 0900-1100 Saturday, 1100-1200 Sunday). This is a long, remote section and shouldn't be taken lightly. It is strongly advised to travel in a well-prepared and self-sufficient convoy on the northern stretch. Once into WA, the track continues on through 280 km of spectacular country to **Warburton**. Here it splits. The notorious 4WD **Gunbarrel Highway** runs north for a further 1,025 km to Meekatharra (see page602), while the **Great Central Road** heads 425 km south to Laverton (page589). Separate permits are required for traversing Aboriginal lands in both NT and WA. Contact the Central Land Council, 31 Stuart Highway, Alice Springs, T8951 6320, for NT, and the Ngaanyatjarra Council, 8 Victoria Avenue, Perth, T9325 4630, for WA. You can also contact the *Outback Highway Development Council*, T9323 4300, www.outback-hwy.gov.au

Lasseter Highway to Kings Canyon
Distance: 165 km Fuel prices a little higher than at Yulara

The sealed **Luritja Road** connects the Lasseter Highway with the **Watarrka National Park** and **Kings Canyon**. After 65 km is the junction with the 100-km unsealed Ernest Giles Road, a 4WD 'short-cut' between Kings Canyon and Alice Springs, though it is never graded and very rough. Soon after this the red bluffs of the **George Gill Range** appear on the right-hand side. In the lee of these, 40 km short of Kings Canyon, is C *Kings Creek Station*, T8956 7474, www.kingscreekstation.com.au, where there are camping areas and canvas 'safari' cabins available, plus fuel and a takeaway 0700-1900. Also on offer are sunrise and sunset **camel tours** (one hour, $35) and **helicopter flights**.

Northern Territory

Watarrka National Park (encompassing Kings Canyon)

Enclosing the western part of the George Gill Range and its impressive western bluff, **Carmichael Crag**, Watarrka is best known for **Kings Canyon**, the upper reaches of which culminate in sheer red walls, 100 m high. Some of these are finely patterned by horizontal bedding planes and vertical water stains, others by myriad tiny cracks creating a resemblance to ancient Egyptian hieroglyphs. The ranges consist of pale Meerenie sandstone, its surface rusted everywhere to fantastically rich reds and oranges. As well as the main canyon, relentless weathering has created dozens of cool refuges from the arid plains below, such as waterholes and lush valleys like the **Garden of Eden**. These harbour rare plants such as cycads, a remnant Gondwanan species. On top of the ranges a regular grid of weaknesses have been weathered down to hundreds of beehive domes, which range from the size of a car to the size of a house. The park is named after a native cat linked to a dreaming route of the local Luritja people along Kings Creek. There is a **ranger talk and slide show** about the park, nightly at the resort from May-October. ■ *No entry fee. No camping. For more information contact Parks and Wildlife NT, T8951 8211.*

Colour map 5, grid B3 300 km from Yulara, 455 km from Alice Springs via sealed roads Best time to visit is Apr-Sep. Water, picnic tables, gas BBQs at Kings Canyon and Kathleen Springs.

Bicycle Hire available at *Kings Canyon Resort* petrol station ($12 per hr, $35 per day), T8956 7442. **Taxi** The resort (see below) runs a taxi service, taking guests to Kings Canyon (around $20 per run), Lilla (around $35) and Kathleen Springs (around $40).

Getting around

The main walk in this park, the **Kings Canyon Walk**, is superb. It begins with a climb up rock steps to the rim of the canyon. Once on the plateau the track winds through striking domes of red sandstone towards the end of the canyon. A short sidetrack leads to a lookout point giving some of the finest views on the walk. Standing on the edge of sheer rock walls you face the canyon's 100-m high south face. Returning to the main track, after a short distance steps lead down to a bridge over the **Garden of Eden**, a lush waterhole lined with palms and eucalypts, to the far side of the canyon. The track then swings south to bring you to the edge of the main wall visible from the lookout. Leaving the rim, the track passes by countless domes, sometimes called the **Lost City**, and descends to the car park (6 km, three hours). The terrain is uneven but once the rim is reached the walk is easy and flat. There is little shade so try to start the walk by 0800, earlier in summer. There is a shady short walk about halfway up **Kings Creek**, leading to a lookout point with views of the canyon walls from below (2½ km, one hour return). **Kathleen Springs**, is a similar walk, leading to a spring-fed waterhole, on terrain suitable for wheelchairs (2½ km, one hour return). It is possible to walk from Kathleen Springs to Kings Canyon on the **Giles Track** (22 km, two days) but this should only be attempted in cool weather, and walkers must register with the Overnight Walkers Scheme, T1300 650730.

Walking in Watarrka
Free track notes and maps from Kings Canyon Resort

At the end of Luritja Road is the tourist complex **LL-C** *Kings Canyon Resort*, T8956 7442, www.voyages.com.au, straddling the main road, with the reception and the more expensive hotel accommodation and restaurant on one side, and the campground, budget rooms, bar and café, internet kiosk, fuel and small expensive store (open 0700-1900) on the other. Lawned campground sites are $29 for 2 people. The kitchen facilities are meagre, crockery and cutlery is hired out at $5 a person. Also on the campground side is the **Carmichael Crag** viewing area, where champagne is served at sunset. *Carmichael's* is a buffet-style restaurant with a cocktail bar. Dinner, served 1800-2100, with a surprisingly good seafood selection, is $53 and with it the option of a $15 'wine buffet'. There are

Kings Canyon Resort
6 km from King Canyon

Reservations: T1800 817 622 or 8956 7660

Northern Territory

▶▶ What is Tjukurpa?

This Anangu word, pronounced chook-orr-pa, is often translated as 'law' or 'dreaming' but it has a much broader meaning with no equivalent in English. It refers to the creation period when ancestral beings, Tjukaritja, formed the world, but also guides daily life. The knowledge passed down by elders forms Anangu law, religion and morality, as well as explaining how people, plants, animals and the physical features of the land are related to each other and how to understand those relationships. Specific groups may be responsible for different aspects of Tjukurpa so knowledge can be restricted to initiated men or senior people. Tjukurpa is memorized and taught by song, dance, story and ceremony. To learn more about how Tjukurpa informs the past, present and future for Anangu visit the cultural centre.

also expensive buffet breakfasts, 0530-1000. The *George Gill Bar* has live music (not Tuesday) and cooks up mid-range pizzas, pasta and BBQ grills. Meals 1800-2100. The *Desert Oaks* is a cafeteria serving breakfasts, snacks and light meals, 0530-1000 and 1100-1400.

Tours
All tours can be booked via the resort reception

Air *Professional Helicopter Services*, T8956 2003, www.phs.com.au, have a couple of options from the resort, the 15-min canyon fly-over being well worth the $90 it costs. **Bus** *AAT Kings*, T8956 2171, www.aatkings.com, head out from the resort to the canyon daily, 0615 Oct-Mar, 0700 Apr Sep, returning 3½ hrs later ($40, children $20). Guided canyon walk included. **Walking** *Lilla Aboriginal Tours*, Lilla, take small groups out to the base of the ranges to learn about the local *Tjukurrpa* dreaming stories, traditional bush tucker and medicine, and to see rock art not otherwise accessible to visitors (1½ hrs, $38.50, children $27.50). Daily, early morning and late afternoon.

Transport

Air *Professional Helicopter Services* can arrange one-way options to **Yulara**. **Bus** *McCafferty's/Greyhound* offer a combined rim walk and bus trip to **Alice Springs**. Walk at 0600, bus departs 1130 (arrives 1815). **Tour operators** *AAT Kings* have one-way commentated bus tours to **Yulara**, daily 1315 (4 hrs, $92), and Alice Springs, daily 1315 (5½ hrs, $103). Similar *APT* services go to Yulara, daily 1330 (4 hrs, $90), and Alice Springs via the *Mereenie Loop*, daily 1330 (6½ hrs, $110).

The Mereenie Loop Road
Kings Canyon 195 km from Hermannsburg

For unsealed road conditions see www.nt.gov.au/dtw or T1800 246199

This unsealed road offers a northerly short-cut between Kings Canyon and Alice Springs. It can be negotiated by 2WD with care and good preparation, though trailers and caravans are never recommended. Always check on road conditions before setting out. The road passes through the **Haast Bluff Aboriginal Land Reserve**, country less flat and forbidding than along the longer sealed route, and frequently passes close to the bases of several undulating ranges. Near the far end of the road a left-turn leads to **Glen Helen** (see page 700) with an optional 4WD only side-trip to **Gosse Bluff**, a 5 km wide comet crater with tall walls. There are picnic facilities here, but no camping. The road becomes sealed just before **Hermannsburg** (see page 700). ■ *A travel permit is required for the loop. Available ($2.20) on day of travel from Kings Canyon Resort, Hermannsburg supermarket, Glen Helen Resort or the VIC in Alice Springs.*

Kulgera
75 from Erldunda, 415 km from Coober Pedy (SA)

C-E *Kulgera*, T8956 0973, is a small roadhouse on the Stuart Highway, 20 km from the border with SA. Petrol, similarly priced to Marla (SA) and Erldunda, and takeaways available 0600-2330. Motel and basic backpacker rooms. The **geographical centre** of mainland Australia is formally located 150 km to the east on the unsealed road to Finke.

South Australia

'The driest state in the driest continent' is a remark South Australians often make with a certain pride living in of such unforgiving land and with the certainty that South Australia deserves more attention than it gets. The land is so dry that most of the state is virtually uninhabitable. Two-thirds of the state's population lives in **Adelaide**, an island of easy-going sophistication where locals make the most of the climate by spending a large part of their lives at outdoor cafés. The city is surrounded by the wine regions of the **Barossa**, **McClaren Vale**, **Clare** and **Coonawarra**, all areas of fine wine and stunning scenery. To the north are the Flinders Ranges, ancient folds of weathered rock, best known for **Wilpena Pound** where a vast circle of mountains tilts at the sky like city ramparts. This area offers walking and four-wheel driving in landscape so remote and elemental that it feels almost prehistoric. Beyond the ranges in the central deserts is the opal mining town of **Coober Pedy**. The community has dealt with the desiccating heat by burrowing underground.The state stretches west to the **Nullarbor**, a flat arid plain of limestone riddled with caves and ended abruptly by the vertical Bunda cliffs. On the Eyre and Yorke peninsulas are countless secret sandy bays where whales and seals come close to shore and South Australians indulge their indefatigable passion for fishing. **Fleurieu Peninsula** points down to **Kangaroo Island**, a sanctuary of wild beauty, teeming with native animals from the perfect peaceful bays of the north coast to the rugged south coast, thrashed by winds and seas from Antarctica

South Australia

Things to do in South Australia

1   Take a trip over to **Kangaroo Island**, explore the varied coastlines and meet the prolific wildlife, especially the koalas and seals.
2   Walk up the ramparts of **Wilpena Pound** in the central Flinders Ranges, or even take a flight over them.
3   On the way across the **Nullarbor** detour to the tip of the **Eyre Peninsula**, then visit the **Head of Bight** to catch a sight of whales.
4   While in **Coorong National Park** take an early morning canoe trip out onto the water.
5   Head out to the **Clare** and **Barossa** for a wine tasting expedition
6   Explore the grand old city of **Adelaide**, especially its excellent art gallery and museums.
7   View the mysterious Blue Lake of **Mount Gambier** and explore some of the many caves and sinkholes in the surrounding area, especially those at Naracoorte.

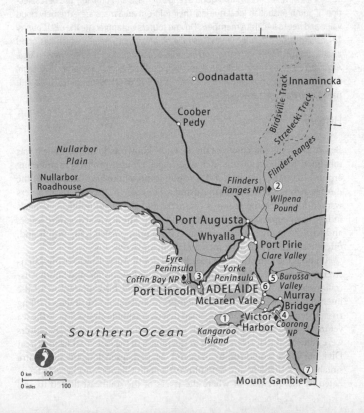

Ins and outs

Getting around **Air** *Kendell*, T131300, www.kendell.com.au, are the main airline for flights within the state, though the future of their network and schedules is subject to considerable revision following their recent sale. As ever, check availability of flights before making plans. At present they connect Adelaide with most of the major regional towns. **Bus** Premier Stateliner, T08-8415 5555, www.adelaidemetro.com.au, run or act as agents for most of the internal state bus services. Buses to most South Australian country towns leave from Adelaide's Central Bus Station.

Information The *Parks and Wildlife Service*, T8336 0924, www.environment.sa.gov.au/parks,
The South Australian supplies information on **national** and **conservation parks**, and details of visiting
Tourist Commission's and staying in them. Also check www.recsport.sa.gov.au for information on walk-
website is www.south ing, cycling **trails** and recreational **sports**. The *Environment Shop*, 77 Grenfell St,
australia.com Adelaide, T8204 1910, is another good source of parks information and passes. The **Four weeks Holiday Pass** is $18 per vehicle and covers entry to all the main parks except the Desert Parks (see page 788). As in some other states the government has seen fit to make the **internet free** to all via public libraries. Booking is usually required, and access is usually limited 1 hr. The SA Department of Transport gives reports of current **road conditions** on T1300-361033, www.transport.sa.gov.au The *Conservation Volunteers* contact point is in Adelaide, T8372 0170, adelaide@ conservationvolunteers.com.au *The Map Shop*, 6 Peel St, Adelaide, T8231 2033, www.mapshop.net.au, has the largest selection of maps in Australia, a fair few guide books, and will also offer general advice. Mail order available. The *RAA*, 41 Hindmarsh Sq, Adelaide, T8202 4600, has a good a range of maps and probably the best selection of South Australian local guides. Their fold-out area maps are extremely good value and free to RAC/RAA members. Driving tourers will appreciate the *UBD Country Towns and Street Directory: South Australia and Northern Territory*, which has good information on towns and parks, and includes a road atlas for the states. *Heysen Trail: A Walkers Guide*, by Terry Lavender, is published by Bookends in 3 volumes, $22 each. They also publish *Strolling South Australia*, also $22 (ISBN 0646376918), predominantly day-walks in the Adelaide Hills.

History

Before European settlement of the area now known as South Australia it was inhabited by about 50 distinct Aboriginal groups, probably numbering around 15,000 people. In fact this region is thought to have been one of the most heavily populated areas in Australia. However, by the early 1800s others wanted to harvest the region's resources and the life of South Australia's indigenous people was about to change forever. The first to arrive were sealers and whalers, many of whom operated from unpopulated Kangaroo Island, often stealing Aboriginal women for labour and 'company'.

At about the same time the coastline of South Australia was being extensively mapped by Matthew Flinders aboard the *Investigator*, and South Australia was becoming an important launching pad for explorations of the interior. These were inspired by attempts to understand Australia's baffling river systems. To Europeans it seemed that rivers should always flow to the sea yet in Australia they often peter out into dry salt pans or swamps. Explorers were convinced that rivers rising in the ranges of the east coast or the Great Dividing Range would run to an inland sea, perhaps making the vast centre suitable for settlement and agriculture. Captain Charles Sturt became fascinated by the question of where the rivers of the southeast flowed to and became convinced of the existence of an inland sea. In 1830 he discovered the Murray River and followed it to its mouth at Encounter Bay in South Australia, thus 'opening up' a rich, well-watered region for expansion.

As British explorers ranged over what seemed to them a wide, empty land, back at home the industrial revolution was causing fundamental change and meant chronic unemployment and poverty for the working masses. Britain's governing class considered emigration to the vast spaces of the Empire an ideal way to relieve the pressure. Although he had never been to Australia, Edward Gibbon Wakefield published a book called *Letter from Sydney* in 1829 while serving time in Newgate Prison for eloping with a schoolgirl heiress. Wakefield's book set out a persuasive theory of colonization, arguing that land in a new colony should not be given away but sold at a 'sufficient price', ensuring a constant supply of labourers because they would not be able to afford to buy land. Wakefield subsequently formed the South Australian Land Company, gaining much support from politicians and businessmen. In 1834 an Act of Parliament was passed establishing the colony of South Australia and two boatloads of colonists under the command of Captain Hindmarsh arrived in 1836 to settle at the site of Adelaide chosen by surveyor Colonel William Light.

Despite early squabbles and financial problems, the colony was a success. In the 1840s large copper deposits were found in Burra, bringing a flood of Cornish miners to the colony. Throughout the 1840s and 50s the South Australian government and its private citizens funded exploration of the interior by Eyre, Sturt and Stuart. A route from Adelaide to the northern coast was not found until Scotsman John McDouall Stuart reached Darwin on his third attempt in 1862. Stuart's achievement lead to one of the most important developments in early Australian history, construction of the Overland Telegraph Line from Port Augusta to Port Darwin through some of Australia's most arid, remote and inhospitable country. In 1872, when the line was completed and connected to an undersea cable to Britain, Australia could communicate with the rest of the world in a matter of hours instead of months.

In 1894 South Australia became only the second government in the world (after New Zealand) to grant the vote to women, and the enfranchisement was extended to all the states when they joined together following Federation in 1901. Despite this, for the next sixty years or so, South Australia was a socially and politically conservative state, known for its church-loving and temperate people. During this time South Australian Aboriginal people suffered from the same paternalistic and controlling government policies as other indigenous Australians. Things only really began to change in the 1960s and 1970s, particularly under the influence of flamboyant Labor Premier Don Dunstan. A more liberal society emerged and South Australia became the first Australian state to decriminalize homosexuality and produced some of the country's earliest Aboriginal land rights legislation.

Lack of water resources has meant that much of the state has never been settled by Europeans. The majority of people continue to live in Adelaide or near the coast and it is mostly desert land that has been handed back to its indigenous owners. Water continues to shape the state's development. The Murray River feeds vast agricultural and wine-producing districts, and Adelaide's population depends on the river for its drinking water. However the Murray is badly degraded and this is the biggest problem facing the state. Three states use the river to grow lucrative agricultural produce but South Australia is the last in line. The NSW, VIC and SA state governments are currently engaged wrangling over the issue of how to restore and share the river in the future.

▶▶ **Heysen and Mawson Trails**

Since the 1970s much effort has gone into setting up and maintaining two long-distance trails that give walkers and cyclists the opportunity to traverse much of the rural southeast of the state off-road. The impressive results are the 1,500-km walkers **Heysen Trail** and the 800-km cyclists **Mawson Trail**. The former winds its way from Parachilna Gorge in the Flinders, through those and the Lofty ranges past Adelaide to the Fleurieu Peninsula, ending at Cape Jervis. The Mawson Trail parallels the former though is less ambitious, running from Adelaide up to Blinman. The trails have been well designed, using many pre-existing back roads, walking, fire and logging trails, to weave through much of the most beautiful country in South Australia. Unsurprisingly, few people complete the trails in their entirety, but it is possible to undertake small to medium sections for those who have the time. Large sections of both routes are closed in summer due to fire bans, August to November and April to June being the most rewarding months to walk or cycle. Although the routes are reasonably well sign-posted, sensible preparation and kit is essential. For further advice and maps contact the **The** Environment Shop or **The Map Shop** in Adelaide. Also check out www.recsport.sa.gov.au

Adelaide

Colour map 1, grid B3
Population: 1,100,000

1,530 km from Alice Springs,
730 km from Melbourne,
1,415 km from Sydney,
2,624 km from Perth

Some Australians feel it's no coincidence that Adelaide rhymes with staid and it is true that there is something intrinsically 'proper' about the city. Adelaide is clean and wholesome, the streets are neat and straight, and it doesn't have the grimy organic jumble of backstreets that some of the other state capitals do. When settlers bought land in South Australia they intended to stay and the early stone civic and private buildings possess a well-crafted solidity, although these are now overshadowed by the usual collection of city centre modern office blocks and skyscrapers. Colonel Light's visionary town plan gives a sense of space to the city centre, the trees of the surrounding Park Lands and the Hills are almost always visible at the end of the street. All this well-kept tidyness doesn't mean Adelaide is dull. Actually it's one of the most liveable cities in Australia. The wonderful climate has allowed a café culture to flourish, and the arts scene is thriving, with two festivals of international standing. Public transport is plentiful and easy to use, the clean white beaches just a short tram-ride away. And if the flat, open country palls, then the spectacular steep-sided Adelaide Hills are only 20 minutes drive from the city. To top it all off the Barossa, McLaren Vale and Fleurieu Peninsula are all easy day trips.

Ins and outs

Getting there
For more details, see Transport, page 734

The **airport** is on Burbridge Rd, T8308 9211, about 8 km from the city centre, with separate domestic and international terminals, also a separate small terminal for **Emu Airways**. A taxi to the city will cost about $15, otherwise wait for the half-hourly (hourly at weekends) Transit Airport-City Bus, $7. It makes various stops around the city centre from about 0500 to 2100 (1900 weekends), but needs to be booked for departures from the city, T8381 5311. The **Central Bus Station** on Franklin St is the terminal for most interstate and state bus services. There is an adjacent taxi rank, and the free City Loop bus stops just over the road. The **Railway Station** on North Terr, between the city centre and North Adelaide, is for local services only, the Interstate Rail Terminal is 3 km to the west of the city centre, off Burbridge Rd. The Transit bus stops here ($3.50 to the city) and a taxi to the city will cost around $7.

24 hours in the city ★

Start the day early at the **Central Market**, in Gouger Street. Watch the traders set up stall and browse while there's still a bit of elbow space. Then head up to Rundle Street and have a mid-morning coffee and pastry on the pavement at *Al Fresco*. Walk down Rundle Mall, turn right onto King William, then right again onto North Terrace. Wander past the grand institutions and spend a couple of hours at the **Art Gallery**. Have lunch at the *Balaena Café* at the **SA Museum** next door. If you're feeling energetic hire a bike from the stand behind the Festival Centre and cycle along the Torrens River. If not, have a look at the Australian Aboriginal Cultures Gallery in the museum. In the late afternoon catch a tram to **Glenelg** from Victoria Square. Wander the foreshore, ice cream in hand, and look for dolphins from the jetty, then catch a taxi to **Henley Beach** and watch the sun set while having dinner at *Henley-on-Sea*. Catch a bus or taxi back to the west end of town and head for *Grace Emily* on Waymouth Street for an end of the day drink.

Getting around

Taxi stands are dotted all over the city

The city centre is compact and no 2 places are more than about a 35-min walk apart. The free City Loop **bus** service travels the full length of North Terr, and completes the loop in both directions via Light, Victoria and Hindmarsh Sq. Runs every 15 mins Mon-Fri 0800-2100, every 30 mins Sat 0830-1730 and Sun 0900-1700. North Adelaide is smaller still, and walking around it presents no difficulties. There are regular buses to all parts of the metropolitan area; pick up the detailed MetroGuide from the *Public Transport Information Office* on the corner of King William St and Currie St, T8210 1000, www.adelaidemetro.com.au They also have details of the trains to **Brighton**, **Port Adelaide** and north to **Gawler**. The tramway to **Glenelg** makes a pleasant change of transport. The heritage-listed trams run from Victoria Sq to Glenelg Jetty every 20 mins, Mon-Fri 0557-2350, Sat 0732-2355 and every 30 mins Sun 0850-2355 (30 mins). The **O-Bahn** is the fastest suburban bus service in the world and it is worth the trip out to Tea Tree Plaza just for the ride. Buses hurtle along a specially constructed concrete freeway, much of the way through *Linear Park*. Metrotickets can be bought and used on metropolitan buses, trains and trams, and come in 3 basic self-explanatory types; Multitrip, Singletrip and Daytrip. Singletrip prices vary from $1.10 to $2.90 depending on whether journeys are under or over 3 km, interpeak (0901-1500) or any time. Most bus services run from around 0730 to 2330. Metrotickets also available at many news-agents, delis, post offices and the Public Transport Information Office. Metrotickets are not valid for journeys beyond **Aldgate**.

Car Parking 1-3 hr max, ticketed street parking in city centre. Free Sun, and Sat after 1300. *EziPark*, off Grenfell St and top of Frome St, 0-30 mins free, max $8.50 Mon-Fri, $5.50 Sat-Sun. Open Mon-Thu and Sun 0630-2400, Fri-sat 0630-0300. *U-Park*, Grote St, Max $5.50 Mon-Thu 0730-1830. Open air. North Adelaide roadside parking is mostly free, though restricted to 2 hrs. Many of the roads in and around the parklands have free unrestricted parking.

Information

SA Visitor and Travel Centre is on King William St, near the Rundle Mall. T1300 655276, www.visitadelaide.on.net Mon-Fri 0830-1700, Sat-Sun 0900-1400. Informa-tion and bookings for the whole state. There is also an information kiosk at the western end of Rundle Mall which is a good place to pick up free Adelaide maps and listings brochures such as *City Scene* and *Culture Attitude*. **SA** Information, 77 Grenfell St, T8204 1900, is essentially a citizens advice office, but also has free **internet** access. The Adelaide daily newspaper, *The Advertiser*, includes 'The Guide' on Thu, a cinema and gig guide. Various free newspapers can be picked up from most bookshops, music or clothes shops: *Rip it Up* focuses on music but also has cinema and theatre listings;

South Australia

The Adelaide Review is a highbrow look at contemporary issues with book, food, art and theatre reviews; *Adelaide gt* takes a look at events in the gay community; *Kids in Adelaide* has a whats-on rundown and some good ideas; *Onion* is a magazine on club culture. Also check out www.arts.sa.gov.au for theatre, festivals, sport and events.

Sights

A stroll along the length of North Terrace is the best introduction to the heart of Adelaide

The city streets are arranged in a grid covering around one square mile just south of the Torrens River. On the other side of the river there is another grid half the size. This is North Adelaide, an oasis of genteel old homes sitting on a rise overlooking the Central Business District (CBD). In the city centre **North Terrace** is the focus of Adelaide's cultural heritage and learning. The side nearest the river is a long wide boulevard of museums and galleries, shaded by trees and interspersed with sculptures. All the great buildings of the city are here: Parliament House, Government House, the war memorials, Adelaide University, and Adelaide Hospital.

Botanic Garden & Ayers House Museum

Starting at East Terrace and heading west, cultural pilgrims will first encounter the Botanic Garden, at the eastern end of North Terrace. It makes for a tranquil retreat from the city, where you can wander around the lake and under long tunnels of wisteria or lie on the lawns under huge shady trees. It's

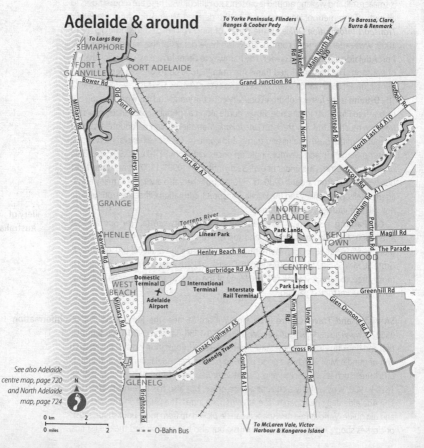

Adelaide & around

To Yorke Peninsula, Flinders Ranges & Coober Pedy

To Barossa, Clare, Burra & Renmark

To Largs Bay
SEMAPHORE
FORT GLANVILLE
PORT ADELAIDE
Bower Rd
Grand Junction Rd
Military Rd
Port Rd
P10
Tapleys Hill Rd
Port Rd A7
Main North Rd A20
Port Wakefield Rd A1
Main North Rd
Hampstead Rd
Sudholz Rd
North East Rd A10
Ascot Rd
Payneham Rd A11
Portrush Rd
GRANGE
HENLEY
Seaview Rd
Torrens River
Linear Park
NORTH ADELAIDE
Park Lands
KENT TOWN
Magill Rd
The Parade
NORWOOD
Henley Beach Rd
Burbridge Rd A6
CITY CENTRE
Domestic Terminal
International Terminal
Interstate Rail Terminal
Park Lands
Greenhill Rd
WEST BEACH
Military Rd
Adelaide Airport
Anzac Highway A5
King William Rd
Unley Rd
Glen Osmond Rd A1
Glenelg Tram
South Rd A13
Cross Rd
Belair Rd
Brighton Rd
GLENELG

See also Adelaide centre map, page 720 and North Adelaide map, page 724

N

0 km   2
0 miles   2

- - - O-Bahn Bus

To McLaren Vale, Victor Harbour & Kangaroo Island

South Australia

interesting to compare the jewel-like 19th-century Palm House and the spaceship-like conservatory housing tropical rainforest species. Also worth a look is the 'Cascade' near the Bicentennial Conservatory, a beautiful sculpture of a breaking wave, built with plates of glass. There is also a kiosk and a fine res taurant. ■ *Mon-Fri 0800-1600, Sat-Sun 0900-1600, closes 1700 during daylight saving. Free. T8222 9311. Guided tours leave from outside the kiosk Mon, Tue, Fri, Sun 1030. Bicentennial Conservatory $3.40, concessions $1.70. Open daily 1000, closing as above.*

Cross the road from the Botanical Gardens for the 19th-century Ayers House Museum at 288 North Terrace, opposite the hospital, once owned by Sir Henry Ayers, a self-made man who had emigrated from England to Australia and made his fortune from his interests in the Burra Burra copper mine. He was made premier seven times, and his house reflects the life of a high-society politician. ■ *Tue-Fri 1000-1600, Sat-Sun 1300-1600. $6, concessions $4. T8223 1234.*

National Wine Centre

This impressive new complex on the eastern edge of the Botanic Garden is a showcase for Australian Wine. More than 32,000 bottles are stored in its cellars and it also includes a working vineyard planted with 500 vines representing typical Australian varietals. There is tasting gallery and a fine restaurant, *De Castellas*, that aims to link wine varieties with complementary fresh seasonal or regional food, and lots of casual choices under $15. It operates as a wine bar Thursday-Saturday 1700-2100. A wine tourism information desk supplies detailed information on visiting each Australian wine region and, naturally, a vast selection of wines are for sale. ■ *Mon-Fri 0900-1730, Sat-Sun 1000-1730. Exhibition $11, children $6, concessions $8. Tastings from $5-20 depending on wine quality. Shop and restaurant free. T8222 9222, www.wineaustralia.com.au Corner of Botanic Rd and Hackney Rd. Short walk from Botanic Gardens stop on the free bus routes.*

Art Gallery of South Australia

Back on the north side of the road, the Art Gallery is an elegant classical-style building similar to Parliament house, built in 1898. The gallery houses one of the country's finest collections of colonial art. There are also fine collections of Rodin bronzes, Aboriginal dot paintings, Southeast Asian ceramics, modern art and European art dating from the 16th century, as well as a good café (see page 730) and art bookshop. ■ *Daily 1000-1700. Free. T8207 7075, www.artgallery.sa.gov.au Free tours run Mon-Fri 1100, 1400, Sat-Sun 1100, 1500. If you miss these times a free audioset tour describes important works.*

South Australia

South Australian Museum

For more on douglas Mawson, see page 722

Next to the Art Gallery, the main building is a duplicate of the State Library's Jervois Wing, with a long low extension tacked onto it. The museum has displays relating to natural history and anthropology. The highlights are a fascinating rainbow collection of minerals and an exhibition on the life of the Antarctic explorer **Douglas Mawson**. The exhibition includes the sled Mawson sawed in

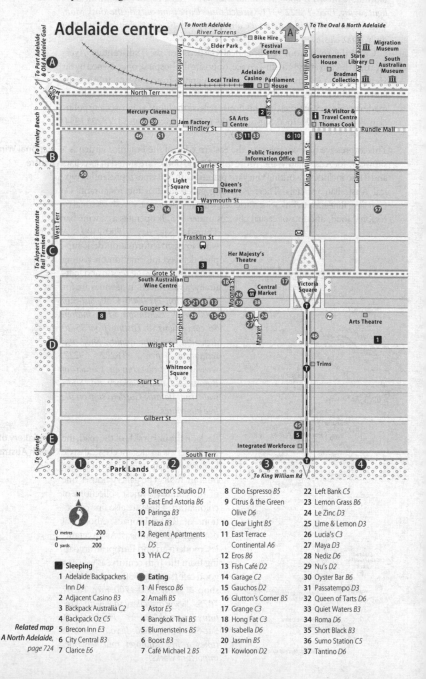

half and dragged for many miles in agony, silent film footage shot in Antarctica by Frank Hurley and many specimens collected there. The museum's flagship is the **Australian Aboriginal Cultures Gallery**, an absorbing presentation of the world's largest collection of Aboriginal artefacts, sound recordings, photographs and manuscripts. Other facilities include an excellent café (see page 657)

and bookshop, the Indigenous Information Centre and the Discovery Centre. ■ *Daily 1000-1700. Free. Discovery centre Mon-Fri 1100-1600, Sat-Sun 1000-1600. Tours of the Aboriginal Cultures Gallery Wed-Sun at 1100 and 1400 (40 mins), $10, children $7, 40 mins, book at the shop. T8207 7500, www.samuseum.sa.gov.au*

State Library The Jervois Wing on the right of this building was built in 1884 in Romanesque style and houses the **Mortlock Collection** of material on South Australia. It is a superb example of a 19th-century library, with three floors of wooden shelves, ladders and balconies opening onto a room with a vaulted timber-beamed ceiling. The modern Bastyan Wing houses the Bray Reference Library and the **Adelaide Lending Library**. There are foreign and national newspapers, (the foreign ones are shipped in by sea) and free internet access, book in advance at the helpdesk. The library also runs wonderful 'White Gloves Treasures' tours, a hands-on look at rare and important books and artifacts. ■ *Mon-Wed, Fri 0930-2000, Thu 0930-1800, Sat-Sun 1200-1700. Free. T8207 7200, www.slsa.sa.gov.au 'White Gloves Treasures', $16, 2 hrs. Book in advance T8207 7664*

Bradman Collection Cricket fans will need no introduction to Sir Donald Bradman (1908-2001), considered by some to be the greatest batsman ever. The collection of memoribilia, donated by 'the Don' himself, is housed in the The Institute, just west of the State Library. The 'Bradmania' shop might be a good place to buy presents for fans at home. ■ *Mon-Thu 0930-1800, Fri 0930-2000, Sat-Sun 1200-1700. Free. T8207 7595, www.slsa.sa.gov.au/bradman*

South Australia

▶▶ **Sir Douglas Mawson**

Long unheard of outside of Adelaide, Douglas Mawson was one of the greatest polar explorers ever to set foot on Antarctica, and as hard as tempered steel, tungsten-tipped nails. A long-term geology lecturer at University of Adelaide, Mawson led two expeditions to the frozen continent in 1911 and 1929, once declining an offer from Scott himself to join the ill-fated British expedition to the South Pole. Instead Mawson put together a team to explore some of the harshest regions of the continent. He personally led a three-man team over 400 km into uncharted territory before a crevasse claimed one of the trio and the trailing sledge, with most of the party's stores and best equipment. Losing most of their food forced them to eat their sled dogs, not knowing that the dog livers caused vitamin A poisoning. His remaining partner slid into madness then death, but

Mawson battled on for another month against appalling conditions, virtually zero rations and desperate ill health to drag himself the 160 km back to his base camp. By then the soles of his feet had come completely away and he was having to tie them back on with rags. He crawled into camp only to see his supply ship Aurora steaming out of the fast freezing bay, leaving him and a rescue team to sit out another long Antarctic winter. Incredibly, he led another expedition back to the continent and was instrumental in the organization of further Antarctic exploration. While at home in the Adelaide Hills, Mawson frequently went on geological cycle trips, and SA's long-distance cycling trail is named after him. A permanent exhibition, 'In the Footsteps of Sir Douglas Mawson', can be seen at the South Australian Museum.

Migration Museum
Just off North Terrace, heading north towards the river, is the small Migration Museum, at 82 Kintore Avenue. The museum tells the story of the many peoples who have made a new life in Australia. It sits in a small courtyard of historic brick buildings that once functioned as Adelaide's Destitute Asylum and later as a boarding school for Aboriginal children intended to separate the children from their families and culture. Though a sad and mournful place, the museum is well-curated. ■ *Mon-Fri 1000-1700, Sat-Sun 1300-1700. Entry by donation. T8207 7580, www.history.sa.giv/migra*

Linear Park
Detailed maps can be picked up from cycle shops or bike hire operator
This corridor of greenery self-contained that runs alongside the Torrens River from **West Beach**, 13 km west of the city centre, to Black Hill Conservation Park, 18 km east. A weekend cycle to the beach is a lovely way to see more of Adelaide, and bike hire is available from Elder Park, a popular picnic spot in front of the Festival Centre. ■ *Mon-Fri 0930-1700, Sat-Sun 0900-1800. $5 ½ hr, $20 day*

Jam Factory
On Morphett Street, very close to the junction with the western end of North Terrace is the Jam Factory, a working studio and gallery of contemporary craft and design. The modern building is a clever blend of style and function with a warehouse feel. A self-guided tour directs you through the superb retail shop, gallery spaces and encourages peering through studio windows. ■ *Mon-Fri 0930-1730, Sat-Sun 1000-1700. Free. T8410 0727, www.jamfactory.com.au*

Adelaide Gaol
This sturdy fortress of rock has seen 49 executions since it opened in 1841. It only closed in 1988 so walking through the empty cell blocks has a surprisingly contemporary feel to it. ■ *Mon-Fri 1100-1600. Tours Sun from 1100 to 1530, 30 mins. $5.70, children $3.50, concessions $4.60. T8231 4062. Gaol Rd is off Port Rd at the west end of North Terr. Catch bus 151, 153, 286 from North Terr.*

The National Aboriginal Cultural Institute is housed in a monumental **Tandanya** 19th-century building on Grenfell Street. Converted last century from an electricity substation, the place continues to hum with energy. Tandanya aims to promote a better understanding of Aboriginal people and culture mainly through visual and performing arts. The large gallery space houses changing exhibitions with a core of permanent works. There are daily didjeridu performances at noon. Very welcoming staff, high-quality exhibitions, a shop and café make this an excellent place to learn about Aboriginal culture, art and history. *Tandanya Café* has cheap 'bush tucker' influenced meals and live music or jam sessions at weekends. ■ *Daily 1000-1700. $4, concessions $3. T8224 3200, www.tandanya.com.au Near the intersection with East Terr.*

North Adelaide

Only a 10-minute walk north of the centre, North Adelaide is a leafy suburb full of beautiful 19th-century stone cottages. Some of Adelaide's best cafés, restaurants and pubs are clustered in this small heritage area, especially along O'Connell Street and Melbourne Street, and there's also a welcome concentration of good pubs. After walking the pedestrian-friendly streets of Colonel Light's town layout you may want to join him in admiring the view at **Light's Vision**. Head towards North Adelaide on Montefiore Road, passing the gracious **Adelaide Oval**, one of world cricketing's favourite venues. A statue of Light stands on a rise overlooking the city where he is said to have often stood while forming a picture of the city's future layout in his mind.

The Adelaide coast

Just 10 km from the city centre, and easily accessible by road, tram or bus, **Glenelg** Glenelg is Adelaide's favourite seaside playground. Known locally as 'the bay' Glenelg has a very modern feel despite some stately 19th-century civic buildings and the fact that it was the first mainland settlement in South Australia. Jetty road follows the line of the jetty and white sand beach and is the focus of the town's restaurant and night life. It also carries the immaculate 1929 trams - complete with red leather upholstery and wood panelling – all the way to King William Street in the city centre. This is a bustling seaside suburb, particularly on Sundays in summer, when it becomes thronged with swimmers, promenaders, shoppers, or diners at pavement tables. The VIC on the foreshore has guides to historic walks and cycle rides. ■ *Daily 0900-1700 summer, 1000-1600 winter, T8294 5833, www.holdfast.sa.gov.au*

Colour map 1, grid B2 Population: 14,600

The **Old Gum Tree**, where Governor Hindmarsh formally proclaimed the settlement of South Australia still stands in a reserve 15 minutes walk from the jetty. The **Bayside Discovery Centre**, in the Town Hall, has a display on the colonial history of South Australia and the early days of Glenelg. ■ *Daily 1000-1700. Free. T8179 9500.* More contemporary thrills can be had at **Rodney Fox's Shark Museum**, containing displays from Rodney's 30 years of filming Great Whites. ■ *Daily 1000-1800. $6.60, children $4.40. T8376 3373. Town Hall.*

Based at Holdfast Shores Marina, Temptation Sailing run good value day and twilight catamaran cruises. ■ *$15, 1½ hours, bookings essential. T04128 11838.* Catamarans, kayaks and windsurfers can also be hired on the beach from *Outdoor Adventure.* ■ *$10 an hr, daily Dec-Feb if over 28°c, weekends Oct, Nov, Mar, Apr if over 28°.* Bikes can be hired from *Holdfast Cycles*, 726 Anzac Highway, T8294 4537, $20 a day, $40 a week. *Beach Hire* next to the VIC, T8294 1477, also have beach gear, wave skis and snorkels. Open September to May.

South Australia

Timetables from the VIC or T8210 1000

Transport The Glenelg tram runs from Jetty Rd to **Victoria Sq** in the city every 15 mins Mon-Fri 0557-2350, Sat 0732-2355, and every 30 mins Sun 0850-1155 (30 mins, Metroticket). Tickets can be bought on board. *Torrens Transit* runs buses to **Port Adelaide** via **Henley** and **Grange** (Nos 340, 342; 40 mins) and the city (Nos 263, 264, 266; 40 mins) from Moseley St.

Glenelg to Port Adelaide From Glenelg the broad, white sand beach runs about 20 km north to the outer harbour. Almost the entire stretch is lined with beach-front housing, holiday units, and bed and breakfasts. By far the best of the beach suburbs

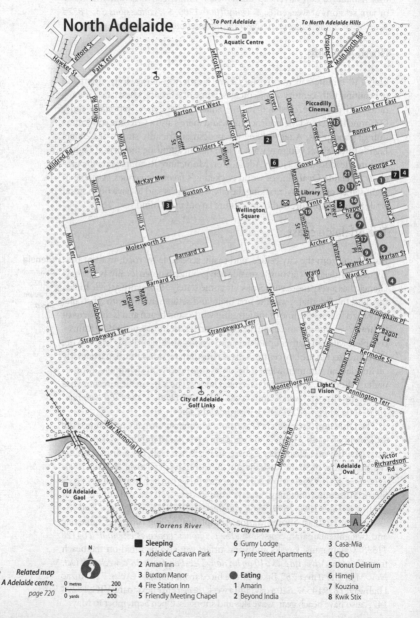

North Adelaide

To Port Adelaide   To North Adelaide Hills

Related map A Adelaide centre, page 720

Sleeping	6 Gurny Lodge	3 Casa-Mia
1 Adelaide Caravan Park	7 Tynte Street Apartments	4 Cibo
2 Aman Inn		5 Donut Delirium
3 Buxton Manor	**Eating**	6 Himeji
4 Fire Station Inn	1 Amarin	7 Kouzina
5 Friendly Meeting Chapel	2 Beyond India	8 Kwik Stix

South Australia

along here is **Henley**, which has a few restaurants and cafés encircling the small square that sits adjacent to the town jetty (see page 729). A couple of kilometres north of Henley lies **Grange** where, in between his various adventures, Captain Charles Sturt built his home, The Grange. Still there, it is now run as a Sturt museum by a private trust. ■ *Tours Fri-Sun 1300-1700. Small admission charge. T8356 8185, 800 m west on Jetty St.* **Semaphore** is a particularly good family destination with lots of cafés, a waterslide, carousel, mini steam train, public BBQs and children's playground.

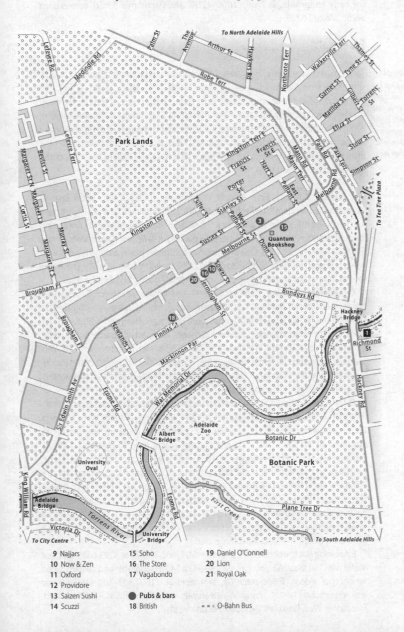

South Australia

9 Najjars	15 Soho	19 Daniel O'Connell
10 Now & Zen	16 The Store	20 Lion
11 Oxford	17 Vagabondo	21 Royal Oak
12 Providore		
13 Saizen Sushi	● **Pubs & bars**	
14 Scuzzi	18 British	▪ ▪ ▪ O-Bahn Bus

Port Adelaide
Colour map 1, grid B2
Population: 37,600
12 km from city centre

The transformation of Adelaide's neglected dockside into a buzzing, modern development is still in its infancy. There are a few dockside apartments alongside tidy heritage streets, and a busy Sunday market, but a steady influx of shops, restaurants and cafés is needed to join the few already here before the area can fully realize its potential. The town is home to a few very interesting museums, including the Maritime Museum, at 126 Lipson Street, one of Australia's best with a full-scale copy of a sailing ketch, dozens of hands-on exhibits and displays giving a real sense of what passage was like for early emigrants. ■ *Daily 1000-1700. $8.50, children $3.50, concessions $6.50. T8207 6255.*

Essentials

Sleeping
■ *On map, page 720*
Rooms become scarce during the Adelaide Festival of Arts in Mar (even years) and Womadelaide in Feb (odd years)

The upmarket hotels are concentrated on North Terr and South Terr, both pleasantly situated next to the Park Lands, although North Terr is closer to the action. The mid-range hotels and apartments are to be found in the centre of the city, between Gouger St and Hindley St, with a few interesting B&Bs on the fringes. A string of anonymous motels line Glen Osmond Rd. There are many backpackers hostels in the city centre. **North Adelaide** has many lovely B&Bs and, apart from being under the main flight path is a civilized, tranquil place to stay. Lively **Glenelg** has most of the beach-side accommodation.

City centre L-A *East End Astoria*, Vardon Av, T8224 2400, www.eastend astoria.com.au Modern, newly furnished and self-contained. Minimalist but very functional apartments with balconies. 2 bedroom appartments worth considering for groups or families. Great location. Free parking. **A-B** *Regent Apartments*, Angas St, T8224 8888, F8232 2583. One of a group of apartment blocks around the city with newly furnished fully self-contained studio and 2-bedroom balcony units. Their rates for 4 or more nights (serviced weekly) are extremely good value. Free parking.

C-D *Adjacent Casino*, Bank St, T1800 655961 or T8231 8881, 25bank@ bigblue.net.au Grim exterior, but the enthusiastic managers are working hard to shake off the hotel's equally grim reputation. Rooms are clean and tidily furnished. Good facilities and friendly, laid-back service. 'Backpacker' rooms good value. Parking $9 a day. **C-D** *YHA*, Waymouth St, T8223 2888, adelyha@chariot.net.au Very spacious, clean and efficient 240-bed 'super hostel' with lots of good facilities including cheap bike hire, though it lacks the homely familiarity of some smaller hostels. Full disabled access, including family room.

D *The Austral*, Rundle St, T8223 4660. This very happening pub has basic accommodation, though make sure you get the top floor if you actually want to sleep. **D** *City Central*, Hindley St, T8231 4049, F8231 4804. Very clean and friendly, family run hotel. All en suite. The 2 double balcony rooms need to be booked ahead. Parking $5 a day. **D** *Plaza*, Hindley St, T8231 6371. www.plazahotel.com.au Large, very clean and comfortable hotel. Full facilities including small kitchen and laundry. Extremely good value. **D-E** *Brecon Inn*, King William St, T8211 8985, breconinn@ bigpond.com Backpacker hostel associated with the adjacent *Brecknock Arms*, residents get good food/drink specials but aren't right over the pub. Very clean, if a bit small, the young enthusiastic owner goes out of his way to ensure guests have a great time. Disabled access. Recommended.

E *Adelaide Backpackers Inn*, Carrington St, T1800 247725 or 8223 6635. Efficient hostel with 100 beds. All-you-can-eat breakfast $4, free apple pie and custard. Good selection of videos. **E** *Backpack Oz*, Wakefield St, T1800 633 307. Friendly and well-run spacious hostel, sparklingly clean, vies with *Brecon Inn* as Adelaide's best. Free dinner Wed. Breakfast included. Recommended.

North Adelaide LL-B *North Adelaide Heritage Group*, T8272 1355, www.adelaide-heritage.com 20 historic properties dotted around North Adelaide, traditionally furnished with antiques and careful thought for comfort. Recommended. **B** *Tynte St Apartments*, Tynte St, T8334 7783, oldlion@majesticapartments.com.au Modern studio apartments in the heart of North Adelaide. Serviced weekly. They also have some slightly pricier apartments on Jerningham St. **B-D** *Adelaide Caravan Park*, Richmond St, T8363 1566, F8362 1989. No on-site vans, but several modern cabins 2 km from O'Connell St, just the other side of the parklands. **C** *Gurny Lodge*, Gover St, T8267 2500, gurny@hotmail.com Simple but comfortable and clean self-contained units just off O'Connell St. Good value for small groups or families wanting to stay in North Adelaide. Pleasant BBQ area. Recommended.

There are some interesting historical buildings that provide bed and breakfast accommodation, but few budget options

Glenelg A *Water Bay Villa*, 28 Broadway, T041 222 1724. Hosted B&B in an attractive stone house furnished with antiques and flowers. Cooked breakfast included. **A-C** *Sea Vista*, 52 Seaview Rd, West Beach, T8356 3975, www.seavista.com.au Comfortable, refurbished and newly furnished units in Glenelg, West Beach and Henley. Great locations with a very friendly and helpful owner. **D-E** *Glenelg Beach Resort*, 1 Moseley St, T/F8376 0007, www.glenelgbeachresort.com.au This hip backpackers hostel in a bluestone terrace has live entertainment every night, a bar, café, pool tables and Internet access. Light, freshly painted rooms, breakfast and linen included. Privacy is questionable, however, and the kitchen closes early in the evening.

There is plenty of accommodation in Glenelg, mostly of the longer-stay holiday apartment type. If this suits, call the VIC for more options

Eating out is a way of life in Adelaide. With a warm climate for many months of the year the pavements are often crowded with tables – the locals love to eat and they love to eat outside. When the weather turns cold for a couple of months many restaurants also boast roaring fires and cosy hearty food. The city's relative isolation and surrounding fertile areas mean local produce is used heavily. European and Asian immigrants have also brought much sophistication and variety to the eating scene here. The world class Central Market should not be missed, as much for its happy vibrant atmosphere as the quality of the produce. Cafés and restaurants tend to be grouped along streets so that certain streets become an eating destinations.

Eating
● On map page 720

City centre Rundle St draws the in-crowd and although there are some gems, many establishments here concentrate on style rather than substance. **Gouger St** is known for more consistent quality, with many restaurants making good use of the adjacent Central Market. On weekday lunchtimes and Fri nights, take your pick from one of the 2 cafeteria-style asian Food Markets on either side of **Moonta St** for seriously cheap food and a lively atmosphere. **Hutt St** has less choice but the wide tree-lined avenue provides a more relaxed setting.

Expensive *The Grange*, Hilton, 233 Victoria Sq, T8217 2000. Tue-Sat 1900-2130. Cchef Cheong Liew attracts superlatives and is considered by many Australians to be a national living treasure. The highly original East-West menu must be experienced by gourmets. Book 2 weeks in advance for Fri-Sat. *Nediz*, Hutt St, T8223 2618. Open Tue-Sat 0630-0900. Consistently original Australian food with Asian influences in a small and intimate modern room. *Universal Wine Bar*, Rundle St, T8232 5000. Open Mon-Sat 1200-1500, 1800-2230. Extensive international showcase wine list complements simple but very effective modern Australian cuisine.

Mid-range *Amalfi*, Frome St, T8223 1948. Open Mon-Fri 1200-1430, Sun-Thu 1730-2230, Fri-Sat 1730-2330. Contender for Adelaide's best traditional Italian restaurant, even if the menu is quite restricted. Always busy, book Fri. Recommended. *Bangkok Thai*, corner of Rundle St and Frome St, T8223 5406. Open Mon-Fri 1200-1430, daily 1730-2130. Seriously well-respected first-floor restaurant overlooking the intersection. Smart, unpretentious dining room complements the excellent food. *Citrus and The*

South Australia

Green Olive, Hutt St, T8224 0100. Open daily 0730-2130. Sophisticated and seriously good Italian influenced food and cellar. Breakfasts are pricey but highly regarded. *Fish Café*, Gouger St, T8231 2320. Fresh blue and white naval-themed restaurant with excellent seafood. Mon-Fri 1130-1500, Mon-Sat 1700-2200. *Jasmin*, Hindmarsh Sq, T8223 7837. Open Tue-Fri 1200-1430, Tue-Sat 1730-2130. Very friendly, smart Indian restaurant run by the Singh family for over 20 years. Don't be fooled by the very familiar menu, the dishes are excellent. Book ahead. Recommended. *The Oyster Bar*, East Terr, T8232 5422. Daily 1200-2400. Has over a dozen succulent options. Half price on Tue draws large eclectic crowds. *Tantino*, Hutt St, T8215 0244. Open Mon-Fri 1200-1500, daily 1800-2100. Slick and brooding design, serving full-bodied Italian fare, very popular with locals. *Tribeca*, Hutt St, T8227 2133. Open Mon-Sat 0900-2130, Sun 0900-1700. Stylish, light-filled place with excellent lunch salads. Varied breakfast menu served all day at weekends. French doors wide open on a sunny day. *Le Zinc*, Gouger St, T8212 2345. Tue-Fri 1200-1500, Tue-Sat 1800-2200. Highly regarded, French-influenced restaurant and wine bar, with a zinc wrapped bar and dark wood tables.

Cheap *Astor*, Pulteney St, T8223 2442. Food Mon-Sat 1200-1500, 1800-2030, live jazz and bar snacks Sun 1600-2000. Attractive, lively and deservedly popular pub with classy salads, sandwiches and antipasto. *Lemon Grass*, Rundle St, T 8223 6627. Mon-Fri 1200-1500, Mon-Sun 1700-2200. The middle of a trio of stylish noodle bars, with seriously cheap lunch specials. *Nu's*, Gouger St, T/F8410 2288. Tue-Fri 1200-1500, Tue-Sun 1730-2230. Rapidly growing reputation for excellent Thai food. Daily specials depend on what's good in the food markets. *Sumo Station*, Pulteney St, T8232 8477. Open Mon-Fri 1130-1500, daily 1800-2200. Curvy and colourfully designed Japanese with teppanyaki and conveyor belt sushi bar. The lunch box special for just over $10 is outstanding value. *T-Chow*, Moonta St, T8410 1413. Open daily 1200-1500, 1700-0030. One of the original market Chinese restaurants, very popular. *Wok's Happening*, Hutt St, T8232 1625. Open daily lunch and dinner. Groovy and colourful noodle bar with high quality dishes. Others around the city. *Lucia's*, just inside the Central Market. Open Mon-Thu 0730-1700, Fri 0730-2100, Sat 0730-1500. A constantly busy traditional Italian that's been going strong for over 40 years. Brilliant breakfasts, sandwiches and coffee if you haven't time for the pizza or pasta.

• On map, page 724
Some of the city's
best cafés, resturants
and pubs are to be
found on O'Connell
Street and Melbourne
Street, many with
pavement tables

North Adelaide Expensive *Cibo*, O'Connell St, T8267 2444. Mon-Fri 0730-2230, Sat 0830-2230, Sun 0900-2230. Food and service are taken very seriously at this most fashionable Italian restaurant. Eat inside cocooned by dark wood and glass doors, or on the outdoor stone patio. Also known for good coffee and pastries. *Oxford*, O'Connell St, T8267 2652. Mon-Fri 1200-1500, 1800-2200, Sat 1800-2200, Sun 1200-1500. Some of the city's best contemporary Asian and Mediterranean-influenced food is served here in elegant modern style. *Soho*, Melbourne St, T8637 0300. Open 1800-2200. Multi-award winning contemporary French cuisine, served by an equally impressive staff. Private booths create an intimate atmosphere. Bookings required.

Mid-range *Amarin*, Tynte St, T8239 0026. Tue-Fri 1200-1430, Tue-Sun 1800-2130. Simple rendered walls and exposed beam roof are the setting for excellent Thai, bookings a good idea. Special cheap lunches. *Casa-Mia*, Melbourne St, T8267 2410. Excellent service and Italian cooking have made this a longstanding locals' favourite. *Himeji*, O'Connell St, T8267 5417. Daily 1800-2230. One of the best Japanese restaurants in Adelaide. Sushi bar and traditional rooms with paper screens.

Cheap *Beyond India*, O'Connell St, T8267 3820. Open Wed-Fri 1200-1430, daily 1700-2330. Bistro-style Indian with good veggie selection. Also takeaway. *Kouzina*, O'Connell St, T8239 2655. Open daily 1700-2200. Funky Greek eatery with a strong local following. *Kwik Stix*, O'Connell St, T8239 2023, daily 1200-1430, 1700-2200. Buzzing Asian restaurant with an open kitchen and vibrant coloured walls and artwork. Great food, style and value. *Saizen Sushi*, O'Connell St, T8361 9561. Wed-Fri

1200-1430, Tue-Sun 1730-2200. Smart small sushi bar with $12 special, sushi delivered by mini rail wagon. *Providore*, Tynte St, T8239 0316. Open Mon-Fri 0900-1800, Sat 0930-1400. Healthy meals, including good range of vegan, eat in or takeaway to warm up later. Also baguettes, quiches and cakes.

Eastern and southern suburbs Expensive *Chloe's*, 36 College Rd, Kent Town, T8362 2574. Step inside this elegant and gracious villa for formal but warm service, superb modern food and an incredible 500 wine labels in the cellar. *Magill Estate*, 78 Penfold Rd, T8301 5551. Open Thu-Fri 1200-1500, Mon-Sat 1900-2130. Stylish, marble-floored restaurant with views to die for. Owners, *Penfold's*, ensure that service and cuisine are in line with their finest *Grange* vintage. Bookings required. *Melting Pot*, King William Rd, T8373 2044. Open Thu-Fri 1200-1500, Mon-Sat from 1800. French-influenced modern Australian. Highly regarded (and boy, don't they know it), weekend evening bookings required 2 weeks in advance. An exceptional wine list. **Mid-range** *Suree's Thai Kitchen*, 330 Unley Td, T8373 1133. A talented Thai chef and his Cambodian wife offer finely judged dishes in an elegant and comfortable space. *to relish*, 128 King William Rd, T8272 7944. Open all day as a café, full menu 1200-1500 and 1800-2200. Good value Italian menu. 'Mediterrasian' antipasto *bar plates* a speciality. Acid jazz DJ in the small vine-covered courtyard every Sun. Recommended. *Yellow Cello*, The Parade, Norwood, T8333 1442. Tue-Sun 0800-2400. A serious regard for quality food and service attracts many regulars. Also a wine bar with jazz on Sun nights. *Zoe's*, 164 King William Rd, T8271 6668. Traditional Greek dishes with a simple homely feel. **Cheap** *Campagnola*, 300 The Parade, T8332 2788. Open Tue-Fri, Sun 1200-1430, Tue-Sat 1800-2200. Very good value stylish Italian restaurant at café prices. Pleasant rear courtyard. *Fortuna Court*, 217 The Parade, Norwood. T8332 1272. An ordinary looking Chinese serving the best meals outside Gouger St. Thu-Tue 1200-1430, 1700-2230. *Samms*, 214 The Parade, Norwood, does the best fish and chips in the eastern suburbs. *Fish out of Water*, T8272 1996, 117 King William Rd. A healthy takeaway with salads, burgers and fish and chips so good that top Adelaide chefs have been spotted buying their dinner here.

These areas are busy suburban shopping and eating streets on arterial roads leading out of the city and are therefore noisy with traffic. The exception is King William St in Hyde Park, which is narrow and paved

Glenelg *Seafront*, 1 Moseley Sq, T8350 9555. Cool and calm mid-range café right on the foreshore, slightly tucked away from the hubbub of Jetty Rd. Modern Australian cuisine. Also with an excellent wine bar upstairs, live music or DJs every night and Wed night oyster special, $6 a dozen. Mon-Fri 1000-2200, Sat-Sun 0900-2200. Wine bar Mon-Fri 1700-0100, Sat-Sun 1500-0200. There are many Italian cafés along Jetty Rd and Moseley Sq, the most popular are the hardworking *Mama Carmela* and *Café Miramare*, next door to each other near the tram terminal on Jetty Rd. Both serve cheap pasta and pizzas daily 0900-2400.

Henley *Estia*, 255 Seaview Rd, T8353 2875. Relaxed and funky cheap Greek establishment. Cheerful waiters help generate a jolly atmosphere that frequently leads to exuberant plate smashing and dancing. Plates $2 a throw! Tue-Sun 1200-1530 and 1800-2100. *Henley on Sea*, 251 Esplanade, T8235 2250. Chef-owned mid-range brasserie with a talent for superb seafood. Simple beach-shack décor, crisp linen and attentive service in a relaxed atmosphere. Open Wed-Mon 1200-1430 and 1800-2130. Closed Mon-Tue in winter. The *Sandbar*, Henley Sq, T8353 4400, is Henley's main bar and night spot, with 80s and 90s cover bands Fri-Sat and DJs Fri-Sun. With one of the best balconies on the coast, arrive early to get a table. Open daily Oct-Apr 1500-0400, Fri-Sun in winter. $5 after 2200 Fri-Sat. *Stella*, Henley Sq, T8353 0222. Consistently good mid-range modern Mediterranean seafood, vegetarian and gourmet pizza with service to match. Open daily 1200-1530, 1730-2130.

These are all recommended

Port Adelaide *Sarah's*, 85 Dale St, T8341 2103. Excellent service combined with mid-range gourmet international vegetarian cooking. The owners encourage the 5-course 'degustation' option, which includes free corkage. Small but very popular, bookings required. Open Mon-Fri 1130-1430 when superb baguettes also available, Thu-Sat 1830-2130. Thu is curry night. Recommended.

Cafés
● *On maps,*
pages 720 & 724

Sitting in an Adelaide café people-watching is an essential part of experiencing life in this city. Italian cafes with a standard menu of pizza, pasta and pastries seem to dominate although there are a few interesting combined café and delicatessen establishments.

City centre Rundle St has become so dominated by cafés that many of the top restaurants along here have stepped into line and introduced pavement tables and all-day coffee. It's not the only place for a good coffee, however, and various corners of the city can now boast excellent cafés in more interesting locations. **East Terr** *East Terrace Continental*, T8359 2255. Laid-back casual place with lots of mags and outside tables. Very good breakfasts, light lunches and coffee. **Gouger St** *Passatempo*, T8231 6044. Popular and stylish Italian, decent pizzas, pasta, gelati and very good value full cooked breakfast. Mon-Sat 0800-2200, Sun 1030-2200. *T bar*, T8410 5522. Essential stop for tea-lovers, 130 varieties of tea and accessories for sale as well as simple breakfasts and lunches and sinfully good cakes, served in a funky red cafe. Mon-Thu 0800-1800, Fri 0800-2100, Sat 0800-1600. Recommended. **Grenfell St** *Blumensteins*, T8232 9266. An original and laid-back café that sells organic produce and groceries, cures meats, bakes sourdough bread and pizzas in its wood-fired oven and has a walk-in-fridge 'cheesery' for sales and tastings. Recommended. Open Mon-Fri 0700-2200, Sat 0800-2200, Sun 0800-2100. **Hindley St** *Short Black*, T8410 9390. Small and interestingly designed with a serious intent to serve good coffee, baguettes and snacks. 24 different chairs represent café chair design through the last century. Old black and white movies shown in winter. Open daily 0800-2400. Recommended. **Hutt St** *Isabella*, T8223 1547. Large innocuous inside and outside areas but an excellent choice for breakfast, particularly omelettes or crepes. Open Mon-Fri 0730-1800, Sat-Sun 0830-1600. *Roma*. Busy European-style café with light healthy breakfasts and fine gourmet baguettes and foccacias. Pavement tables. Open daily 0730-1700. *Queen of Tarts*, T8223 1529. Witty and friendly little neighbourhood café with mouthwatering tarts, muffins, baguettes and quiches. Also Internet access $2 for 15 min. Open Mon-Fri 0900-1700. **North Terr** *Art Gallery*, at the back of the Art Gallery of SA, T8232 4366. A modern glass room and terrace which is a cool, serene place to rest between paintings. Coffee and cakes or a mid-range modern Australian menu. Mon-Fri 1000-1630, Sat-Sun 1000-1600. *Balaena*, SA Museum. Healthy and delcious light meals are reasonably priced and served under a whale skeleton. Great place for coffee and cake too. Daily 1000-1700. **Pulteney St** *Left Bank*, T8223 3539. There's nothing special about the décor in this big café on a busy street but it's ideal for a cheap unfussy cooked breakfast. Open Mon-Fri 0700-2400, Sat-Sun 0800-2300. Rundle St *Al Fresco*, T8223 4589, a treasured local spot for a perfect coffee while watching the world go by from the pavement tables. Also gelati, pastries, foccacia. Pizzas after 1800. Practically open all hrs. *Cibo Espresso*. Heart-thumping coffee and red walls in very European 'bolt and go' bar. *Café Michael 2*, T8223 3519. Delicious reasonably priced Thai. *Clear Light*, T8223 5994. 'Wholistic' vegetarian salads, sandwiches, juices and smoothies in cool basement dining room. Mon-Sat 0900-1700. **Waymouth St** *Garage*, T8212 9577. Large old mechanics' garage gives a real warehouse feel, with wide front doors opening onto Light Sq. Mid-range dining evenings, all-day breakfast Sun. Open daily 0800-0400.

North Adelaide *Scuzzi*, O'Connell St, T8239 2233. The best of the Italian cafés on this strip, large and lively with plenty of shaded pavement tables. Licensed. Open daily Mon-Sun 0900-2300. *The Store*, Melbourne St, T8361 6999. Large licensed café and very good delicatessen. Big interesting filled rolls, light lunches, juices and smoothies. Exceptional weekend breakfasts served until late afternoon. Open daily 0700-2300. *Vagabondo*, O'Connell St, T8239 2311. Large sidewalk café, pizza, gelati, coffee, breakfast and best of all, sofas. Open Sun-Thu 0830-2200, Fri-Sat 0830-2400.

Picnic food Some of the cafés above also have impressive delicatessen sections, otherwise try the following. **City centre** If the Central Market opposite is closed, *General Organic Store* on Gouger St has a good selection of produce including wine. Open Mon-Thu to 2000, Fri to 2100. **North Adelaide** *Perryman's*, small bakery on Tynte St, for excellent pies and cakes. *Rhino's Palate Pleasers*, North Adelaide Village, O'Connell St. More than pleasing bread, cheeses, meats and gourmet sauces. *AGI Everday*, O'Connell St. Excellent supermarket with a good range of deli and takeaway-and-heat Italian and Asian dishes, open daily 0800-2200. **Norwood Par** *Eko*, at 176. Gourmet pies and pastries with an impressive range for vegetarians. *Norwood Fine Foods*, has delicious bread, cheese, meats and gourmet products. *Pasta Chef*, Woolworths Arcade, sells takeaway-and-heat pasta. Additive free and excellent value. *Vari's Grocery*, at 210. A Noah's Ark of pasta.

Common to much of South Australia, Adelaide has a seriously bad case of the 'poky' disease. The expectation of hundreds of excellent pubs is quickly dashed, but amongst the glaring majority of slot-machine filled poky pubs, there are enough good watering holes to keep most folks happy. Many pubs and bars also have very late drinking and music licences which means less money on nightclub entry fees and more on beer! The gay scene is small, with a handful of gay nights and 2 current venues, *Mars Bar* and the *Edinburgh Hotel*.

Bars & nightclubs
● On maps, pages 720 & 724

City centre *The Austral*, Rundle St, T8223 4660. Attracts a stylish crowd, with smart mid-range dining, cheap bistro and mostly free live music Fri-Sat and DJs Tue-Thu and Sun. Open to 2400 Sun-Wed, at least 0230 Thu-Sat. *Brecknock Arms*, King William St, 18231 5467. Large, popular Irish-feel pub with seriously cheap lunches and drink specials for residents at their backpackers hostel. *Crown & Anchor*, 196 Grenfell St. Lively grunge bar with a friendly atmosphere and slightly older crowd. DJs Wed-Sat, local bands Sat, open Mon-Wed to 0300, Thu-Sat to 0400. Happy hrs Wed-Sun, various times. *Crown & Sceptre*, King William St, T8212 4159. You can almost imagine *Young Ones'* Neil mouldering in one of the old armchairs here. Local live bands, almost always free, Tue-Sun, laid back fun staff and relatively cheap beer make this a popular student and backpacker haunt. Open Mon-Thu to 2400, Fri-Sat to 0230. *Enigma*, Hindley St, T8212 2313. Slightly grungy but enthusiastic and friendly bar with free internet access and seriously cheap bar meals and beer. Theme nights currently include the Gay Night with drag show on Wed and alternative bands in their upstairs bar at weekends, mostly free. Open Wed-Sat 1100-0500, Sun-Tue 1100-1700. Recommended. *Exeter*, Rundle St, T8223 2623. One of Adelaide's best pubs, its low-key style attacts a mixed crowd. Creative but simple cheap menu is excellent value for money and the wine list is unusually good. Live music Thu-Sat, DJs Tues, Sun. *Grace Emily*, Waymouth St, T8231 5500. Locals mix easily with students and backpackers in Adelaide's mellowest pub. Live acoustic, blues, country most nights. Darts and cheap pool. Open daily 1600-0200. *Planet*, 77 Pirie St, T8359 2797. Very commercial and something of a meat market, very popular with the younger crowd. *Rhino Room*, Frome St, T8227 1611. Seriously good underground club, casual yet funky, with strong theme nights drawing an eclectic crowd. Comedy Wednesday, local live bands Thu, Afro-Latin Fri and an interesting mix of cabaret and underground dance on Sat. Open 2100-0300. *Supermild*, 182 Hindley St, T8212 9699. A club with an air of a cigar lounge, caters for the late 20s-40s with anything from alternative dance to poetry readings. *Worldsend*, 208 Hindley St, T8231 9137. Laid-back pub popular with students and arty types. Live music or DJs every night, jazz on Tue, Sun. Good value restaurant and bar meals.

South Australia

North Adelaide A welcome concentration of good pubs, the following are 5 of the best in South Australia. *British*, Finnis St, T8267 2188. Wonderful, traditional drinkers' pub, that is worth going out of the way to find. Also cheap 'cook 'em yourself' steaks in the large rear atrium. Food daily 1200-1430, Mon-Thu 1800-2030, Fri-Sat 1800-2130. *Daniel O'Connell*, Tynte St, T8267 4032. Dark and cosy Irish pub with a cheap bar menu and mid-range restaurant. Lovely daytime beer garden. Live bands Tue-Wed, Fri-Sat from 2100, Irish tunes by the fire Sun 1400-1700. *Governor Hindmarsh*, 59 Port Rd, just west of North Adelaide, T8340 0744, a bastion of folk, blues and country music. *Lion*, Melbourne St, T8367 0222. Very large, wood and steel warehouse-style pub disguised by an unremarkable Victorian exterior. Pavement café tables, excellent cheap food in the 'larder', very fine expensive modern Australian dishes in the restaurant. Extensive wine list, many by the glass. Bar food daily 0900-2100. *Royal Oak*, O'Connell St, T8267 2488. The interior décor may look seriously distressed but you won't be. Funky friendly pub with excellent mid-range food, live jazz Wed, Sun evenings, band Fri and seriously fun cabaret Tue that has queues going round the block. Recommended. Food daily 1100-1500, 1700-2130.

Eastern and Southern suburbs *Finn MacCools*, corner of Norwood Pde and Osmond Terr, T8431 1822. Comfortable Irish pub with plenty of tables on the pavement. Live Irish music Fri-Sun. *The George Wine Bar*, 177 The Parade, Norwood. The glossy outdoor tiled terrace set back above the road is a very cool spot to have a drink and watch the passing parade (see also Eating). *Old Kent Town*, 76 Rundle St, Kent Town, T8362 2116. A light and open pub that attracts a big 18-25 crowd at weekends for DJs and good live music Thu-Sat.

Entertainment *SA Arts Centre*, Hindley St, T8463 5444, www.arts.sa.gov.au A good source of information on galleries, festivals, theatre, sport and events in Adelaide, they can also book tickets via *BASS*, T131246, Adelaide's premier ticket agency. **Art Galleries** Hindley Street is now the site of many artists studios and consequently a few small private galleries are opening up here. *Gallerie Australis*, T8231 4111, is in front of the *Hyatt Regency* on North Terr and specializes in the highest quality Aboriginal art, including the delicate works of Kathleen Petyarre. *Greenhill Galleries* in North Adelaide, 140 Barton Terr West, T8267 2933, is one of Australia's leading contemporary galleries. The stock includes paintings, ceramics, sculpture and glass, and exhibitions change every 3 weeks. **Cinema** *Imax*, Cinema Pl, off Rundle St, T8227 0075, 2D and 3D films daily. *Mercury*, Morphett St, T8410 0979. This arthouse cinema next to the *Jam Factory* screens the best of world cinema, short film festivals, and showcases the work of new SA filmmakers. *Palace Nova*, Rundle St, T8232 3434. Purple womb-like theatres with silver 'egg' speakers, some art releases amongst the mainstream. *Piccadilly*, O'Connell St, T8267 1500. Art deco theatre in North Adelaide showing mainstream releases. The **Botanic Gardens** also screen films on summer evenings, details www.moonlight.com.au or from *BASS*. **Theatre** *The Arts Theatre*, Angas St, T8221 5644. A wide variety of popular theatre, mostly staged by the *Adelaide Repertory*. Tickets around $20. *Festival Centre*, King William Rd, T8216 8600, is the main theatre venue in Adelaide. There is a large concert hall, the *Playhouse* which is the home of the *State Theatre Company* and *The Space* which usually shows experimental work. The other main theatres are the grand old *Her Majesty's*, 58 Grote St, T8216 8600 and Australia's oldest theatre building, *Queen's*, corner of Gilles Arcade and Playhouse Lane, T8204 9246. For details of current performances ring *BASS* or see *The Advertiser*.

Festivals Adelaide is best known for its biennial **Festival of Arts**, an event that attracts people from all over Australia and overseas. Considered by some to be second only to the Edinburgh Festival, it is held in Mar on every even year. 17 days of theatre, opera, dance, concerts, films and exhibitions, much of it held in the open. The festival also includes a Writers

Week. For details T8216 4444, www.adelaidefestival.org.au Like Edinburgh, a fringe festival has grown alongside the main one and has equalled its size. More vivacious, relaxed and silly, the **Adelaide Fringe**, is held during Feb and Mar in theatres, cafés, galleries, pubs and parks all over town (T8231 7760, www.adelaidefringe.com.au). In the fallow years of the Festival of Arts Adelaide hosts the wonderful world music festival, **Womadelaide**. For 3 days 'the sounds of the planet' resonate from Botanic Park. Over 60,000 people come to listen to more than 300 artists and wander the 'global village', a market of multicultural food and crafts, and attend artist workshops. (T8271 1488, www.womadelaide.ozemail.com.au). **Glendi Festival** is a 2-day celebration of Greek culture, food, song and dance, the biggest cultural ethnic festival in the southern hemisphere. It's held at Ellis Park every Mar (T8443 8123).

The main shopping area in Adelaide is **Rundle Mall**, 500 m of department stores, boutiques and chain stores. **Rundle St** has a few more clothes shops and some good outdoor gear outlets. Almost anything can be found in the mall or its arcades but there are also suburban shopping streets which offer quieter browsing and more unusual shops. Head down to *Trims*, King William St, for a good range of *R M Williams*, *Driza-Bone* and *Akubra* at reasonable prices. **King William Rd** in Hyde Park has very exclusive clothes boutiques and homeware shops. Have a walk down nearby tree-lined Victoria Rd for an idea of the wealth in this area. **The Parade** in Norwood is a busy stretch of the normal neighbourhood shops and cafes. Unley Rd and Glen Osmond Rd are not pedestrian friendly but **Unley Rd** has plenty of homeware and upmarket clothes shops. **Glen Osmond** Road has a small cluster of designer clearance shops, including *Ab Fab Eyewear* at No. 94, for discounted Rayban or Versace shades.

   Books Rundle St has 2 good contemporary booksellers, *Mindfield* and *Mary Martin*, and a travel/language specialist, *Europa*, all open evenings. *Adelaide Booksellers* is a very smart second-hand dealer at the western end of Rundle Mall, not far from a good branch of *Dymocks*, but for real used bargains head for *Oxfam*'s shabby but wonderful cave of a shop at 7 Hutt St, paperbacks from $1. The classiest bookshop has to be the wonderful *Imprints*, surprisingly on Hindley St. In North Adelaide, *Martin's*, O'Connell St, has a good selection of second-hand contemporary fiction from $5, while *Quantum*, Melbourne St, has a good choice of mainstream titles alongside their specialist mind, body and spirit range. Further afield, *Bookends*, 122 Unley Rd, has a great selection of second-hand books from $3, plus large comfy armchairs in which to evaluate them. *Murphy Sister's*, 240 The Parade, Norwood, has a range of gay, lesbian and feminist titles.

   Food If open look no further than the **Central Market** between Grote St and Gouger St for a vast array of fresh and gourmet food stalls under one roof. This is a lusty and vibrant market that is a pleasure for the senses. Stroll around near closing for end-of-day bargains. Open Tue, Thu 0700-1730, Fri 0700-2100, Sat 0700-1500. Chocaholics will quickly sniff out a branch of *Haigh's*. They've been giving choccy making their all since 1915 with splendid results. Factory tours just south of the parklands on Greenhill Rd, T8271 3770. See page 719 for the National Wine Centre.

   Jewellery *Metal and Stone*, 226 Grenfell St, T8227 0775, www.metaland stone.com.au Passionate and knowledgable, this small-scale craftsman takes opals, pearls and gems several steps beyond the usual. Well worth a visit. *Zu design*, 1st floor, Gays Arcade, off Adelaide Arcade. A good showcase of contemporary Australian design in silver, gold and steel. Walk right through to the workshop.

   Maps *The Map Shop*, 6 Peel St, mercator@mapshop.net.au Probably the biggest range of Australian and international maps in the country, also many guide books. Selected catalogue and ordering on the net. Staff very friendly and helpful, useful for trip planning.

   Music *Big Star*, Rundle St. Good range of alternative, indpendent and retro sounds. Second-hand section in basement.

Shopping

South Australia

Sport It is possible to play or watch almost any sport you can think of in Adelaide, contact SA Information, 77 Grenfell St, T8204 1900, for further information. The *Aquatic Centre* in North Adelaide is a large complex of leisure, slide, dive and lap pools, with sauna, spa, gymnasium and steam room. Free one-hour creche. In the adjacent parkland is an excellent childrens' playground, public BBQs and picnic areas. The car park is free and only a short walk from O'Connell St. Daily 0500-2200 in summer, Mon-Sat 0500-2200, Sun 0700-2000 in winter. General swimming admission $4.95, children/concessions $3.50, extra charges apply for other facilities. T8203 7203.

Spectator sport **Cricket** The splendid Adelaide Oval, T8300 3800, is home to the *Southern Redbacks*, during the domestic Oct-Mar season, and also the occasional venue for international matches. **Football** The *Adelaide Crows* play at the Football Park, Turner Drive, West Lakes during the Apr-Sep season. T8440 6666 for club and fixture information, *Venue Tix*, T8223 7788, for tickets. **Motor racing** The Adelaide course is partly a street circuit and is maintained so that the city can host about 3 major motor racing events a year.

Contact BASS, T131246, for details

Tours The *Adelaide Explorer*, T8364 1933 is a bus that loops around the main parts of the city centre, North Adelaide and Glenelg. $25 gets you a hop-on, hop-off day pass, renewable for $7 for each extra day. Every day at 0900, 1030, 1200, 1330 and 1500 by the corner of King William St and Rundle Mall next to *Haigh's*. *Remote Outback Cycle Tours*, T9279 6969, www.cycletours.com.au, head via the Nullarbor and Margaret River to Perth (9 nights $1,550). Departs once a month, May-Sep. Specialist gastronomic *Adelaide's Top Food & Wine Tours* include Market Adventures ($28) and Grazing on Gouger ($88), T8231 4144. Racing journalist Mal James hosts all-inclusive day and evening trips to local horse, dog and harness races. T8294 5206. *Disability Tourism*, T8294 6042, access4all@cultural tourism.com.au, offer several day-tours to the Adelaide Hills, McLaren Vale, Barossa and Clare valleys for $50-90. Glenelg and city pickups. All major coach companies offer day trips to similar locales. For personal service try a *Day Trip-it* tour with David Cooper. For a price he'll put together a day's itinerary for up to 4 people. T8341 6293, daytrip@senet.com.au

See other South Australian regions for details of excursions

Transport **Air** *Kendell* have daily flights to **Broken Hill**, **Ceduna** (not Sat), **Coober Pedy** (Sun-Wed and Fri), **Kangaroo Island**, **Mt Gambier**, **Port Lincoln** and **Whyalla**. **Emu**, T8234 3711, have several flights a day to **Kangaroo Island**. *Qantas* fly daily to all the state capitals except Canberra and Hobart, plus **Alice Springs** and, at weekends, **Kalgoorlie**. *Virgin Blue*, currently have flights to **Brisbane** and **Melbourne**, but are planning to expand coverage. Call T8381 5311 to book the **Transit Airport-City Bus** to the airport, and be sure to tell the driver which terminal you need.

Bus *Firefly*, Franklin St, T8231 1488, have good value daily buses to **Melbourne** (11 hrs, $45) and **Sydney** (24 hrs, $90). *McCafferty's/Greyhound*, Franklin St, T8212 5066, include **Alice Springs**, **Melbourne**, **Perth**, **Sydney**. Services from Central Bus Station. *Premier Stateliner*, Franklin St, T8415 5555, run or act as agents for most of the internal state services. Buses to most South Australian country towns from the Central Bus Station, www.adelaidemetro.com.au **Backpacker buses**. *Nullarbor Traveller* run excellent 9-day adventure trips to **Perth** ($891), T1800 816858, info@the-traveller.com.au *Groovy Grape*, T1800 661177, www.groovygrape.com.au, run similar trips to **Alice Springs** (7 days, $650) and **Melbourne** (3 days, $245). *Wayward*, Waymouth St, T8410 8833, also have trips to **Alice Springs** (8 days, $730) and **Melbourne** (3½ days, $265). *Heading Bush*, T1800 639933 or 8648 6655, F8648 6898, run superb 10-day 'expeditions' to **Alice Springs** ($985).

Ferry *Sealink*, King William St, T8202 8666, run ferries from **Cape Jervis** to **Kangaroo Island** at least twice a day (1½ hrs drive plus 1-hr crossing, $138 return per vehicle plus $64 per adult, $32 children, $52 concessions), they also have coach packages.

South Australia

Train The *Indian Pacific* runs to **Sydney** on Wed and Sun (26 hrs, from $176, $79 concessions), and **Perth** on Tue and Fri (39 hrs, from $283, concessions $207). The *Ghan* runs to **Alice Springs** on Mon and Thu (19 hrs, from $197, concessions $89). The *Overland* goes to **Melbourne** on Sun-Mon, Thu-Fri (11 hrs, from $57, concessions $33). The *Aussie Rail Travel Centre*, Grenfell St, T8231 4366, will help with bookings. Open Mon-Fri 0830-1700, Sat 0900-1300.

Airlines *British Airways*, North Terr, T8238 2000. *Emu Airways*, Adelaide Airport, T8234 3711. *Garuda Indonesia*, Waymouth St, T1300 365330. *Japan Airlines*, Grenfell St, T8212 2555. *Kendell Airlines*, Hindley St, T131300. *Malaysian Airlines*, North Terr, T8231 6171. *Qantas*, North Terr, T131313. *Singapore Airlines*, King William St, T131011. *United Airlines*, North Terr, T131777. *Virgin*, Pulteney St, T8306 8411. **Directory**

Banks The major banks have ATMs on all the major shopping and eating streets. *American Express*, Rundle Mall, Mon-Fri 0900-1700, Sat 0900-1200. *Thomas Cook*, Rundle Mall, Mon-Fri 0900-1700, Sat 1000-1600, Sun 1000-1400. **Bike hire** Many city centre hostels have bike hire for residents, otherwise see *Linear Park* above.

Car hire For day hire, there are several cheap options, such as *Acacia*, T8443 3313, www.acaciacarrentals.com.au, or *Koala*, T8352 7299, koalarentals@hotmail.com At the airport: *Thrifty*, T8234 4554, www.thrifty.com.au, *Budget*, T8234 4111, *Avis*, T8234 4558. **Car servicing** Many options on Pulteney St and Morphett St or try RAA-approved *Carrington Auto*, Carrington St, T8223 2362. **Communications** Internet *Enigma*, Hindley St, have free access, as does the *State Library* and *North Adelaide Library*. Main **Post Office**, King William St, Open Mon-Fri 0800-1730, Sat 0900-1230. **Poste Restante** (take photo ID to collect mail) Mon-Fri 0700-1800, Sun 0900-1300.

Medical services Chemist *Birks*, Gawler Pl, T8212 3121, daily 0900-2100. *Jeff Ramsey*, 113 O'Connell St, T8267 3224, daily 0900-2100. **Hospital**, North Terr, T8222 4000. *The Travel Doctor*, 27 Gilbert Pl, T8212 7522.

Useful numbers Police Angas St, T8207 5000. **Taxi**, T132211.

The Adelaide Hills

The eastern suburbs of Adelaide lap like an incoming tide at the base of the Adelaide Hills, part of the Mount Lofty ranges, a scenically beautiful area offering great bushwalking. Despite their proximity to the city, there is actually little development in the immediate hills, partly a result of the chain of National and Conservation Parks declared over the last century or so. The result is an amazing transition from flat urban to hilly rural within as little as a few hundred metres The best way to explore the hills is on a self-drive trip of a day or two, but take a good road map as it's easy to get lost.

www.visitadelaide hills.com.au
See also p xxx

Follow the Main North Road out of North Adelaide, but take the turn to the North East Road after a couple of kilometres. This runs up past the vast shopping complex of Modbury (the end of the line for the O'Bahn) and soon after the old, largely vanished, settlement of **Tea Tree Gully**. From here the road curves gently up the gully in between **Anstey Hill Recreation Park**, and the smaller and more accessible **Pines Park**. Once in the hills proper the road twists and turns, often dramatically, between steeply undulating hills. Soon after a reservoir are two neighbouring cellar door wineries, *Talunga* (Wednesday-Sunday 1030-1730, T8389 1233), *Chain of Ponds* (T8389 1877, chainofponds@adelaide.on.net), which also has a very lovely, fully self-contained cottage for two to six people (**B**). **The North Adelaide Hills**

South Australia

The hills smooth out slightly as the road heads through **Gumeracha** and its giant rocking horse to **Birdwood** and the **National Motor Museum**, with nearly 400 vehicles from the early steam-powered days to the present. ■ *Daily 0900-1700. $9, children $4, concessions $7. T8568 5006.* Immediately after Birdwood take the right turn to Mount Torrens. This is one of the loveliest parts of the hills and the road twists and turns through gorge bottoms to **Cudlee Creek**, near which is the **Gorge Wildlife Park**, Australia's largest privately owned wildlife collection, which features koala-cuddling sessions (if you can bear it). ■ *Daily 0800-1700, cuddles at 1130, 1330 and 1530. $9, children $5, concessions $8. T8389 2206.* Further on, past Kangaroo Creek Reservoir, follow a sign to the left for Corkscrew Road, which takes you on a spectacular drive up through **Montacute Heights** with great views. Ignore the left turn to Cherryville, but take the unsealed Moores Road shortly after to the right. Off Moores Road, is the turning for *Morialta Cottage* and *Fuzzies Farm* (see below). You can return to the city by Norton Summit Road, which descends steeply through a series of switchbacks, with great views over Morialta Conservation Park and Adelaide. The road eventually joins Magill Road into the city. Follow signs to the right off the bottom of Norton Summit Road for the three-hour loop walk to see the **Morialta Falls** in the Conservation Park, with a good chance of seeing koalas.

Sleeping and eating **B** *Morialta Cottage* is a renovated fully self-contained stone cottage with a double, 2 twins and a couple of bunks in a beautiful roadside glade just off the Heysen Trail. More than 2 people are $12 extra each per night. **F** *Fuzzies Farm*, T8390 1111, welcomes up to 4 house guests in a bunkroom. Meals with the family included, minimum one-week stay. Sounds cheap but helping out around the house and farm are a condition of your stay. Nearby the *YHA* has a timber bush hostel (**F**), advance bookings required for details and key, T8231 4219. The *Scenic Hotel*, T8390 1705, at **Norton Summit** is a gem of a pub, a pleasant 1½ km walk from Fuzzies, with an inventive mid-range menu and great views. Food served Mon-Sat 1200-2100, Sun 0900-2000 (good Sun breakfasts too). Recommended.

Mount Lofty & Cleland Conservation Park

A rewarding day's expedition is to head out to Watefall Gully. Follow the gully to the Cleland Wildlife Park and then up to the summit, returning either via the alternative Chinaman's Hat track or the 823 bus

Cleland Conservation Park covers more than 9 sq km of the southern Adelaide Hills, and includes Cleland Wildlife Park, Mount Lofty Summit and **Waterfall Gully**. Having once been the site of orchards and vegetable gardens the latter is a strange mix of native and alien plants, and has the feel of a hilly arboretum. The waterfalls running through it are spectacular after a few days rain. It really is worth making the effort to reach the summit of **Mount Lofty** to enjoy the tremendous views, though the hill can be shrouded in cloud for much of the winter. A good visitor centre, café and mid-range restaurant crown the summit, though own transport (parking fees $2 a day) or local accommodation is required to stay or dine in the evening ■ *Wed-Sun 1800-2100, book for Fri-Sat, T8339 2600.* The **YHA** has a basic stone cottage (**E**) here, booking details as for Norton Summit. Just before the summit a left turn in the road heads down to **Cleland Wildlife Park**, one of the more impressive wildlife parks in the state with most of the animals free to roam in large enclosures. ■ *Daily 0900-1700. $9.50, children $5.50, concessions $7.50, night walks $19.50, children $11.50, concessions $14.50. T8389 2206, www.cleland.sa.gov.au*

Stirling

Colour map 1, grid B3
Stirling is a great place to stop for lunch

A few kilometres south of Mount Lofty Summit, but still high in the hills, Stirling is a very leafy, small town just off the Princes Highway. The town, and its near neighbours, make a good base to explore the southern hills and, as its only a 25-minute drive from Adelaide, for many a preferred place from which to explore the city itself.

South Australia

Sleeping and eating LL *Thorngrove Manor*, Old Mount Barker Rd, T1800-251958, F8370 9950, www.slh.com/thorngro Fantasy manor built in 1985 to a medieval baroque template. Each room has its own entrance. Private evening dinners served by your personal butler come as part of the suite packages, from $500 a couple. **D-E** *Mount Lofty Railway Station*, Sturt Valley Rd, T8339 7400, www.mlrs.com.au Sleep in a 7-bed dorm waiting room or more private double-bed office and tuck into a continental breakfast out on the platform. *Pinot*, 49 Mt Barker Rd, T8339 4416. Open Mon-Fri 1100-1500, Mon, Wed-Fri 1730-2130, Sat 1000-1600, 1730-2200, Sun 1000-1600, 1730-2030. Modern Australian restaurant, lunches, mid-range evening menu. The best of the cafés by far is the *Organic Market*, Druid Av behind *National Bank* on Mt Barker Rd. Part organic food store, part café, serving spectacularly good and very reasonably priced soups, foccacias, salads, cream teas and more. Open Mon-Fri 0830-1730, 0830-1630 Sat, 1000-1630 Sun.

Some of the more interesting accommodation in the area is in and around Stirling

About 2 km from Stirling is the leafy, homely village of **Aldgate**. There's accommodation at **D** *Geoff & Hazels*, 19 Kingsland Road, T8339 8360. The owners of this small 'hostel' have three double rooms in a very comfortable eco-aware wooden annex. Warm natural hospitality and exceptionally good value. Recommended. For some pukka tucker head for *Cheers*, 200 Mount Barket Road, café serving all day breakfast, light lunches and 'International Cuisine' in the evenings. *Aldgate Café*, 6 Strathalbyn Rd, T8339 2530, is a great little cheap Italian restaurant with outdoor courtyard at the rear. Also takeaway. About 2 km down the road at tiny **Bridgewater** is the *Petaluma Bridgewater Mill*, T8339 5311, a splendid, expensive terrace and conservatory restaurant with a reputation for modern Australian cuisine with serious flair. Daily 1000-1700, lunch Thursday-Monday 1200-1430. Book at weekends to be sure of lunching on the deck where the massive waterwheel turns.

Aldgate & Waarawong Sanctuary *Aldgate 20 km from Adelaide*

Warrawong Sanctuary, 3 km from Aldgate, began as a personal attempt to give beleaguered natives a better chance of survival. Wildlife such as platypus, pademelons and potoroos can be seen on magical guided walks at dawn and dusk daily. There is also a boardwalk, mid-range restaurant and café. Rainbow lorikeets arrive for a feed in the late afternoon, a wonderful time to have a drink outside (book for lunch and dinner on weekends). Accommodation here in 'luxury-under-canvas', but as a dinner/walk/breakfast package only ($150). ■ *Gift shop and restaurant daily 0830-2200. Dawn and dusk guided walks, $22.00, children $17.50. Also 'Wetland & Rainforest Walk' 1100 and 1500 daily, $15.00 per person, concessions available. T8370 9197, www.esl.com.au*

Settled in 1839 by immigrants from northern Germany, Hahndorf has a range of fascinating colonial architecture around its centre. The town elicits mixed reactions. It overplays its German heritage and many of the fine buildings have been hijacked for a variety of gift shops and 'olde worlde' cafés. Despite this, an afternoon here can be well spent. **The Cedars**, 3 km from town on Cedars Road, is the home of the late Sir Hans Heysen, one of Australia's most celebrated painters, famous for capturing his beloved gumtrees onto canvas, and an early conservationist. The fascinating tours of his home and studio may be conducted by one of his charming family who still gather here at weekends. ■ *Shop and garden, Sun-Fri 1000-1600. $4. Guided tours Sun-Fri 1100, 1300, 1500 (1100 and 1400 Jun-Aug). $8, concessions $5.50. T8388 7277.* **Hahndorf Academy**, 68 Main Street, the largest art gallery in SA outside Adelaide, usually has a good range of local contemporary work and sells Heysen prints. They also have a small museum dedicated to the German settlers. The **Adelaide Hills Visitor Centre**, at 41 Main St, will help with booking accommodation in the hills. ■ *Daily 0900-1600, T1800 353323 or 8388 1185, F8388 1319.*

Hahndorf *Colour map 1, grid B3 Population: 1,700 25 km from Adelaide, 50 km from Murray Bridge*

South Australia

Sleeping and eating A-D *Hahndorf Resort*, 145 Main St, T1800 350143, F8388 7282. The resort is a bit kitschy, but the cabins offer the only budget accommodation. They also have camp sites. There are a couple of dozen cafés and restaurants in and around the town to choose from. *Maximilians*, 3 km from town on Onkaparinga Rd, T8388 7777. Open Wed-Fri, Sun 1200-1400, Wed-Sun 1830-2030. Mid-range central European cuisine, formal dining in a rustic farmhouse overlooking a dam and vineyards. Book at weekends. *The Stables*, 74 Main St, T8388 7988. Mon-Thu 0700-2100, Fri-Sat 0800-0100, Sun 0800-2100. Upmarket restaurant with a strong emphasis on mid-range 'bush tucker' in converted stables. Also breakfasts, coffees and light lunches. Open as an oyster and wine bar Fri-Sat. *Hahndorf Inn*, 35 Main St, T8388 7063. Best of the pubs, live cover bands Fri-Sat, good friendly service and sound mid-range pub food with a serious German slant (cheap menu lunchtimes). Food daily 0830-1100, 1130-1500, 1730-2100. *Hillstowe*, 102 Main St, T8388 1400. The second winery cellar door in the town. Wines $15-45. Beautifully converted building with lots of dark wood furniture, walls and stripped floors. Open 1000-1700 for wine and local cheese tasting, café with courtyard tables open 1200-1500.

Transport Services 163, 163F, 165, 840 and 841 are the main metropolitan buses to and from **Adelaide** (50 mins), most call at **Stirling**. Services from the Academy hourly between 0653 and 2011 Mon-Fri, 0752 and 1913 Sat, 0813 and 1813 Sun.

Fleurieu Peninsula

Don't bother with any fancy French pronounciations, South Australian's call it Floo-ree-oh

South of Adelaide, the Fleurieu Peninsula is smaller than the Eyre and Yorke Peninsulas but comprises quite diverse landscapes and towns. McClaren Vale is an unassuming wine district that quietly gets on with producing great reds. The west coast has some lovely sandy beaches, backed by ranges that edge closer to the sea as you head south to Cape Jervis. East of the cape, Victor Harbor is traditionally a beach resort for Adelaideans, although it is now attracting many visitors in winter for whale watching. Further north is Goolwa, the last of the Murray River towns, with its grand stone buildings and paddlesteamers. In the centre are gently rounded hills and valleys that have mostly been cleared for pasture and agriculture. It is pretty country to travel through, especially Strathalbyn, with a street full of historic buildings centred on the Angas River.

The McLaren Vale

McLaren Vale 40 km from Adelaide

The McLaren Vale is a lush, gently rolling stretch of countryside bounded to the north by the Adelaide outer suburbs. One of the oldest Australian wine regions west of New South Wales, the McLaren tradition begins with the English adventurer John Reynell arriving with vines bought at Cape Town, en route from Devon in 1838. The vale wineries specialized early in red wines, and the area is well known for its Grenache, Merlot and particularly Shiraz, though in recent years some wineries have been experimenting with whites such as Chardonnay and Sauvignon. The area is particularly good value with many very good wines under $20. Most of the wineries are clustered around the bustling town of McLaren Vale, which is spread along 2 km of the busy Main Road. The excellent VIC, *McLaren Vale & Fleurieu Visitor Centre*, is at the eastern end of Main Road and will help with accommodation and tour bookings. The complex also includes the pleasant *Stump Hill Café* and *McLaren Vale Regional Wine Cellar*, which offers tastings and expert advice on which wineries will suit your palate. All wine at cellar door prices and sales of wines without a cellar door. ■ *Daily 1000-1700. T8323 9944, F8323 9949, www.fleurieupeninsula.com.au*

Chapel Hill, Chapel Hill Rd, T8323 8429, open daily 1200-1700. Sited on a small hillcrest with good views over much of the vale, a converted chapel serves as the cellar door. Good reds, particularly the special edition *Vicar's Blend*. *Coriole*, Chaffeys Rd, T8323 8305, open Mon-Fri 1000-1700, Sat-Sun 1100-1700. Small family owned business with an award-winning Sangiovese, serves cheap ploughman's platters in the relaxed vine-covered rustic courtyard. Recommended. *d'Arenberg*, Osborn Rd, T8323 8206, open daily 1000-1700. Family owned since 1912, this medium-sized winery has one of the biggest ranges and some of the most respected wines in the vale. The cellar door and associated seriously expensive restaurant are in a specious renovated farmhouse. *Maglieri*, Douglas Gully Rd, T8383 2211, open daily 1000-1630. Regularly wins national and international awards. *Marienberg*, Main and Chalk Hill Rd, T8323 9666, open daily 1000-1700. Established by Australia's first female winemaker, now owned by the Hill family. The *Reserve Shiraz* is particularly sought after. In the town centre, with a good restaurant attached. *Scarpantoni*, Scarpantoni Dr, McLaren Flat, T8383 0186, open Mon-Fri 0900-1700, Sat-Sun 1100-1700. Good range, with whites unusually coming to the fore. *Wirilda Creek*, McMurtrie Rd, T8323 9688, F8323 9260, open daily 1100-1700. eco-friendly, rustic new winery built almost entirely with recycled materials.

McLaren Vale Wineries
There are over 50 wineries in the region. This is a sample of the most interesting, mostly boutique establishments

B *Belle Vue*, 12 Chalk Hill Rd, T8323 7929, www.sabnb.org.au Comfortable and modern hosted B&B in central location. **C** *Southern Vales*, 13 Chalk Hill Rd, T/F8323 8144, svbb@telstra.easymail.com.au Hosted B&B with 5 rooms, overlooks small vineyard from which owners make and share wine. Bike hire available. **D-E** *Lakeside Caravan Park*, Field St, T8323 9255, brett@chariot.net.au Well-run park between vineyards and a small lake with prolific birdlife. Clean cabins and on-site vans a 5-min walk from town.

Salopian Inn, corner of McMurtrie Rd and Willunga Rd, T8323 8769. Open Tue-Fri 1200-1430, Fri-Sat 1900-2100. Superb if expensive modern Australian cuisine in spacious freshly renovated building, pick your own wine from the cellar. Weekend booking recommended. *The Barn*, Main Rd, T8323 8618. Open daily 1200-1500, 1800-2100. Casual and cool with green filtered light from the vine-covered courtyard. Modern Australian leaning toward hearty meat flavours. Mid-range. *Limeburner's*, corner of Main Rd and Chalk Hill Rd, T8323 9666. Open daily 1200-1500, 1830-2130. Modern Australian mid-range cuisine served in a lovely light atrium-style room. Warm service and recommendations for accompanying Marienberg wines. *Oscars*, 201 Main Rd, T8323 8707. Open Mon-Sun 1200-1430, 1800-2030. Good value, laid-back pizza and pasta joint in a pleasant cottage. *Market 190*, 190 Main St, T8323 8558. Daily 0800-1800. Excellent licensed café, cooking with and selling gourmet products. Good breakfasts served until 1200 and light lunches. Recommended.

Sleeping & eating

Des's Mini Bus, T8234 8011. 1015 Tue, Fri, Sat, Sun ($36, 4½ hrs). *Outback Camel Co*, T/F8543 2280. Wine-tasting camel trek, cross country with a picnic lunch ($80, full day).

Tour operators

McLaren Vale is not the easiest of places to get to and around by private transport. There are several trains a day from **Adelaide** to **Noarlunga** and *Transit Regency Coaches*, T8381 5311, www.transitregency.com.au, operate a connecting bus service, Mon-Fri, between **Noarlunga**, **McLaren Vale** VIC, **Willunga** cemetary and **Aldinga Beach**, departing every 2-3 hrs. The **Premier Stateliner** (T8415 5555) bus from **Adelaide** to **Victor Harbor** is a more expensive option, but also stops in **McLaren Vale** and **Willunga**, 4 times a day Mon-Fri, twice on Sat, once on Sun.

Getting there and transport

Although it has fewer services than McLaren Vale, Willunga is much more attractive than its northern neighbour. The town is a major almond-growing centre and the harvest is celebrated with an Almond Blossom Festival in July.

Willunga
Colour map 1, grid B3

South Australia

There are quite a few picturesque B&Bs in Willunga, but no budget accommodation

Sleeping and eating A *Willunga House*, 1 St Peters Terr, T8556 2467, www.intertech.net.au/willungahouse This heritage-listed, elegant B&B has 4 rooms. There are antiques and brass beds, organic breakfast from the garden and local producers. **C** *McCaffrey Cottage*, 21 St James St, T8556 2539, wilson@intertech.net.au self-contained, slate-floored miner's cottage with a creek at the bottom of the garden. The **D** *Willunga*, 3-5 High St, T8556 2135, F8556 4379. This is a pleasant historic drinking pub with wide-ranging cheap menu, the 5 clean and comfortable rooms include breakfast. *Russell's Pizza*, 13 High St, T8556 2571. Locals flock to this small 1850s cottage to get their fix of Russell's cheap exquisite wood-fired pizzas and late-night tango. Open Fri and Sat only. Bookings essential. Recommended. The lively *Alma* pub, Hill St, has seriously cheap, all-you-can-eat specials every lunchtime and most evenings.

Gulf St Vincent beaches

The McClaren Vale is bordered to the west by a string of superb beaches running south from O'Sullivan Beach south to Normanville. Best of these is **Maslin Beach**, where you can dare to bare. Next is **Port Willunga**, a beautiful white sand dune-backed beach in a wide bay just to the west of Willunga. Overlooking the beach is *The Star of Greece*, a scruffy looking shack which happens to be one of the best restaurants on the peninsula, serving expensive but divine seafood (open daily 1200-1500, 1800-2100 in summer, Wednesday-Sunday 1200-1500, Friday-Saturday 1800-2100 in winter. Bookings required, T8557 7420). Continuing down the coast, **Aldinga Beach** is a long stretch of rough sand. The area is best known for the novice diving area with a reef that drops away to 21 m, 1½ km offshore, with soft coral overhangs and lots of fish. Contact *Port Noarlunga Dive and Snorkel*, 9 Salt Fleet Road, T8326 6989, for equipment hire and charter dives. Further south, though the coast is more rugged, there are good beaches and beachside café at the tiny seaside town of **Normanville**. Further toward Cape Jervis, the **Second Valley** cove is definitely worth a stop. **Yankalilla Bay** is now home to *HMAS Hobart*, scuttled here in 2001 to create an artificial reef and diving attraction.

Cape Jervis

At the the tip of the peninsula is **Cape Jervis**, the mainland port for the Kangaroo Island Sealink Ferry. About 10 km east, along the southern edge of the peninsula, is the **Deep Creek Conservation Park**, which comprises 4,500 ha of mainly stringy bark forest on steeply undulating country. The rugged coastline forms the long southern border, though it can be accessed at only a few lookout points. About a dozen walks are possible, from 1½ km to 11 km in length, and range from gentle to strenuous. Some are on sections of the Heysen Trail which runs through the full 19 km east-west length of the park. The park headquarters, T8598 0263, is at the northern border of the park. Day permits ($6 per car), camping permits ($6-18)and details of walks can all be obtained from here.

Sleeping 3 km before **Cape Jervis** is **B-E** *Cape Jervis Station*, a working historic sheep farm with various levels of accommodation in renovated farm buildings to suit most budgets. Great breakfast $10, book ahead for the set evening dinner from $20, butlered silver service an option. Licensed. Recommended. There are also 2 self-contained cottages and a homestead (**B-C**) in Deep Creek Conservation Park, privately managed and hence better equipped than standard park accommodation. Contact *Southern Ocean Retreats*, T8598 0288, capest@dove.net.au

Victor Harbor ·

Founded as a whaling centre in the the 1830s, Victor Harbor is now a holiday town, popular with families, who descend in their thousands every winter to watch **southern right whales**, so called because they were the 'right' whales to catch. Almost hunted to extinction by the early 20th century, the whales have recovered, to be joined in recent years by humpbacks. The town sprawls along a long curve of coastline interrupted by a 100-m high knoll at the western end, called The Bluff. Also good is Granite Island, linked to the shore by a 600-m long jetty. The VIC is on the Esplanade, adjacent to the causeway. ■ *Daily 0900-1700, T8552 5738, www.tourismvictorharbor.com.au*

Colour map 1, grid C3
Population: 10,500
83 km from Adelaide,
46 km from
Strathalbyn,
58 km from Cape Jervis

Sights

Most of the sights are centred on the esplanade and Granite Island but the best way to see the whole bay is on the **Cockle Train**, a steam train operated by volunteers that runs between Victor Harbor and Goolwa. The Victor Harbor to Port Elliot section runs right next to the water and passengers sometimes see whales from the train in winter. ■ *$20 return, children $11, concessions $18. Tickets can be purchased from the station, Railway Terr, on running days or T8231 4366, www.steamranger.org.au* Next door to the train station is the **South Australian Whale Centre**. This is a three-storey building full of displays about whales, dolphins, sealions and penguins, which includes a look at the days when whale watchers reached for harpoons rather than cameras, and regular updates on local sightings. ■ *Daily 1100-1630. $4.50, children $2, concessions $3.50. T8552 5644, www.sawhalecentre.com* To find out where whales are, there's a whale information line, T1900 931 223 (which costs almost $1 a minute). The rather dull local museum is opposite the VIC and called the **Encounter Coast Discovery Centre**. ■ *Daily 1300-1600 $4, children $2, concessions $3. T8552 5388.* **Granite Island** is home to a colony of about 2000 fairy penguins. Around dusk they haul themselves out of the water and waddle over to their burrows. They can be seen on a tour but are not about during the day. For two hours after dusk you can only walk across the causeway if you are taking a guided tour. ■ *Daily at dusk, 1 hr. $10, children $7, concessions $9. There are also bay cruises and tours of an undersea aquarium from Granite Island. Book all tours at the Gift Shop or T8552 7555. Penguin tours depart from the Penguin Centre on the island.*

About 15 km west of town is turning for **Newland Head Conservation Park**, which protects a range of coastal vegetation and two beautiful long sandy beaches, **Waitpinga** and **Parsons**. There's a campground with facilities and several good walks. For campground bookings T8552 3677.

Sleeping

B-E *Anchorage*, corner of Coral St and Flinders Par, T8552 5970, www.anchorage.mtx.net Wide range of accommodation in a former pub, 30 rooms plus 60 bunks in uncrowded dorms (NOMADS). Recommended. **C** *Villa Victor*, 59 Victoria St, T8552 4258. A warm welcome from overtly Scottish hosts in turn of the century cottage. Good solid breakfast, 5-min walk to town centre. **D** *Grosvenor*, corner of Ocean St and Coral St, T8552 1011. Good value doubles, expensive bunks in town centre pub. All the above are in or 5 mins walk from the town centre. 3 km to the west of town at Encounter Bay is **A** *Waves*, 10 Investigator Cres, T8552 1944, F8552 5075, with 3 modern spacious designer apartments in a great beach front setting with views from the balcony.

There is no shortage of accommodation, though it can be difficult to find somewhere in the summer holidays

Eating

Anchorage has a fresh but conservative mid-range menu in a large attractive space draped with fishing paraphernalia. Daily 0830-1000, 1200-1430, 1800-2030. *On the Rocks Bistro* on Granite Island, T8552 8311. Daily from 1000, food 1200-1500,

1800-2100. Has the best location with tables on a deck over the bay with an average mid-range seafood and steak menu. *Blue's*, Esplanade, T8552 1551, specializing in local produce, particularly seafood, this modern casual restaurant serves cheap light meals and mid-range Modern Aussie cuisine all day, Wed-Mon 1100-2100. Also available with a few hrs notice are gourmet picnic hampers at $10 a head. Recommended. There are several pubs with standard fare but the *Crown Hotel* on Ocean St, T8552 1022, has the most imaginative cheap pub meals with plenty of outdoor tables under the verandah. Daily 1200-2000. *Café Bavaria*, T8552 7505, has pavement tables opposite the esplanade park and the best coffee and cakes in town.

Transport The *Premier Stateliner* bus leaves Stuart St for stops to **Goolwa** 1125, 1355, 1755 and 1935 Mon-Fri, 1125 and 1755 Sat, 1125 Sun. The **Adelaide** service leaves 0800, 0930, 1300 and 1545 Mon-Fri, 0930 and 1545 Sat, 1545 Sun (2 hrs). *Sealink*, T8202 8688, www.sealink.com.au, operate a service to **Cape Jervis** and **Kangaroo Island**.

Directory **Banks** ATMs of 3 major banks are on Ocean St, *ANZ*, the seaside end of Coral St. **Bike Hire** *Cycle and Skate*, Victoria St, T8552 1417. $20 per ½ day. **Communications** Internet Public Library, Coral St, Tue-Thu 1000-1730, Fri 1000-1800, Sat 1000-1300. Free. **Post Office**, Ocean St.

Victor Harbor to Goolwa It may be only 17 km from Victor Harbor to Goolwa, but there's still room for a few wonderful beaches, many offering superb surfing including the very popular **Middleton Beach**. In contrast, **Horseshoe Bay**, snugly enclosed by two boulder-strewn headlands and rocky Pullen Island between their extremities, is exceptionally calm for this part of the world and popular with swimmers. It also boasts the excellent *Flying Fish Café*, T8554 3504 (open daily 0930-2000 in summer, daily in winter 0930-1700, Friday-Saturday 1800-2000). Only 500 m inland from the Bay is **Port Elliot**, a small historic town, seemingly at rest after the exertions of its days as a major port. A great alternative to staying at its larger neighbours, this small town has several B&Bs, a caravan park and the attractive **D-E** *Arnella by the Sea YHA*, North Terrace, T8554 3611. For entertainment a **drive-in cinema** shows films Friday and Saturday nights from October to April. T8554 2168.

Transport The *Premier Stateliner* bus, T8555 2211 (Goolwa agent), stops up to 4 times daily at Middleton Post Office and Port Elliot, Hotham Memorial Church. Services to **Goolwa**, **Victor Harbor** and **Adelaide**.

Goolwa
Colour map 1, grid C3
Population: 3,000
17 km from Victor Harbor,
34 km from Strathalbyn

Settled by the Europeans in the 1850s as a strategic river port due to the impossibility of navigating the shallow mouth of the Murray River, Goolwa became the final stop for cargo from Victoria and New South Wales. Supplies would then be sent by rail to Port Elliot. After several shipwrecks at Port Elliot, Victor Harbor was established as a safer port and the railway line was extended there in 1864. By the 1880s railway lines had been built from Adelaide and Melbourne to other river ports and all river trade bypassed Goolwa, leaving it to settle into the quiet existence of a small regional town. The **VIC** has information on various other water-borne activities and hire, including 1- to 5-day adventure sailing on the *Crosswind*. Their office sits to the right of the Hindmarsh Island bridge, facing the river, and is combined with the **Signal Point River Murray Interpretive Centre**, a disappointingly static but informative museum of the history and geology of the Murray River. ■ *Daily 0900-1700, $5.50, children $2.75, concessions $4.40. T8555 3488, signalpoint@alexandrina.sa.gov.au*

Sleeping A *PS Goolwa*, offshore, Barrage Rd, T8555 5525. Very comfortable hosted B&B on a replica paddle-steamer built in 1980. **B** *PS Federal*, offshore, Barrage Rd, T/F8362 6229, pgibberd@camtech.net.au Another smaller steamer built in 1902 and now converted to permanently moored self-contained accommodation. Sleeps 2. These steamers are 2 km west of the town centre. **B** *St Brigids*, Lot 1310 Broult St, T8358 5775. Century-old Baltic pine church, beautifully converted to a self-contained house on a dune just off Goolwa Beach, 4 km from town. Min 2 nights. **B-E** *Murray River Queen*, Wharf, T8555 1733, mannum@captaincook.com.au Large paddle-steamer permanently moored and run as a rather tired motel/backpackers. **C** *Dolphin Cottage*, 12 Hutchinson St, T8555 0338, prewetts@granite.net.au Self-contained modern artist's studio with mezzanine bedroom. **C** *Goolwa Cottage*, 3 Hays St, T8555 1021. Pretty, modern red-brick annex, available as hosted B&B (cooked on request). Very good value for 4 people. **D** *Corio*, Cadell St, T8555 2011. Good value clean double rooms in an old renovated stone pub. Pleasant dining area but gaming always in evidence. Mid-range pub fare with impressive salad bar. Food 1200-1400, 1800-2000.

Eating *Hector's on the Wharf*, great location on the wharf near the bridge, T8555 5885. Weatherboard café with cheap light lunches and foccacias, and limited mid-range modern Australian evening menu. Open Tue-Fri 1000-1700, Fri 1800-2000, Sat 0900-2000, Sun 0900-1700. *Whistle Stop Café*, Hay St, T8555 1171, excellent mediterranean-influenced food, cheap to mid-range, in a homely-cluttered cottage that doubles as an antique-shop. Wed-Sun 1200-1500, 1800-2030, open from 1100 for coffee and cakes. *Aquacaf*, Barrage Rd, T8555 1235. A casual and reasonably priced place for breakfast or a simple cheap lunch on the deck over the Murray. Thu-Mon 0800-1700. *Goolwa Central Health*, Cadell St, T8555 1755. A rare vegetarian café, combined with a health food shop, that does good breakfasts and cheap lunches. Mon-Fri 1000-1700, Sat 1000-1600.

Tours The Murray River bottlenecks into Lake Alexandrina at the southeastern corner of the Fleurieu Peninsula. The southern part of the lake is a long thin series of dunes now declared part of the **Coorong National Park**. Various tours to Coorong depart from the wharf, including a 6-hr 'Adventure Cruise' on the 14-m *Spirit of the Coorong*. 60-km cruise into the heart of the park, with informative walks. Wed, Sat 1000, $70 inc lunch and tea, children $46, concessions $65. T1800 442203, www.coorongcruises.com.au Coorong Experience, T8555 2222, offer 1- to 4-day charter cruises to groups.

Transport *Premier Stateliner* operate a service to **Port Elliot**, **Victor Harbor** and **Adelaide** from the bus stop on Crocker St. 0730, 0900, 1230 and 1515 Mon-Fri, 0900 and 1515 Sat, 1515 Sun. **Cycle hire** *Ampol*, T8555 3488.

The pretty little town of Strathalbyn, founded by Scottish settlers in 1839, sits on the horshoe-shaped river Angas. The town centre, which doesn't look as if it has changed much in a 100 years, is full of stately limestone buildings, shady street verandahs, gardens and tall red river gums, filled with screeching corellas. The **Old Court House Museum** was built in 1858 as a police station and the courthouse added in 1867. Victorian life is displayed in photographs and living rooms. ■ *Sat-Sun 1400-1700, $3, concessions $1.50. T8536 4038, South Terr*. The museum is just north of the **VIC**. ■ *Mon-Fri 0900-1700, Sat-Sun 1000-1600, T8536 3212, www.visitalexandrina.com*

Strathalbyn
Colour map 1, grid B3
Population: 3,000
57 km from Adelaide,
44 km from
Murray Bridge,
46 km from
Victor Harbor

Sleeping and eating **B** *Watervilla House*, 2 Mill St, T/F8536 4099, hosted B&B in a grand Victorian house, overlooking the park. The 'courtyard' and 'red' rooms are the best. Cooked breakfast included but no en suite rooms. **B** *Hamilton House*, 23 Commercial Rd, T8536 4275, olis.net.au/~hamiltonhouse. 2 en suite rooms in a charming Edwardian stone villa, friendly hosts, cooked breakfasts. **B** *The Railway Cottages*, 3-5 Parker Av, T/F 8536 4910. 2 self-contained 3-bed stone cottages with a cottage garden and picket fence. Furnished with country antiques, private and spacious. **D** *Robin Hood*, 18 High St, T8536 2608. Simple but clean and comfortable pub rooms. *Victoria on the Park*, 16 Albyn Terr, T8536 2202. Cheap pub menu in a barn-style bistro or pavement tables. Daily 1200-1430, 1800-2000. *Jack's High St Café and Bakery*, 24 High St, T8536 4147. Popular licensed lunch café. Daily 0900-1700, hot food 0900-1500.

Transport Services 843 and 830 are the main metropolitan buses from **Adelaide** (1½ hrs), also calling at **Stirling** and **Aldgate**. The daily 842 service to **Adelaide** leaves outside the Railway Station at 1855.

Kangaroo Island

Pick up a copy of the excellent Walking Trails in Kangaroo Island Parks from any parks office. Also see www.tourkangaroo island.com.au; www.kangaroo-island.au.com

Kangaroo Island, an oval shaped plateau with high rugged cliffs on the calmer north coast and long sandy beaches on the stormier south, is Australia's third largest island, approximately the size of Sussex or Long Island. Flora and fauna have thrived in this habitat, unmanaged for several thousand years. Kangaroo Island is so 'native-friendly' that some species have been deliberately introduced, such as the koala which is almost ubiquitous. Patient visitors may also see platypus, echidna and plenty of wallabies and kangaroos. Marine life is equally diverse and diving is enhanced by the 50-odd ships that have come to grief on the rocky coasts here. First charted simultaneously by Matthew Flinders and Frenchman Nicolas Baudin in 1802, sealers and escaped convicts ruled the island until official colonization began in 1836. Little freshwater and unexpectedly poor soils have, however, kept the very friendly population low, and today it numbers only 4,500. A welcome consequence is the ease with which several parks and wilderness protection areas have been declared over the last century.

Ins and outs

Getting there
There are currently no public bus or taxi services on the island

Air *Emu*, ($180) and *Kendell* (from $130) both have flights several times a day from Adelaide. *Hertz* have a shuttle bus that meets each flight and runs from the airport at Cygnet River to Kingscote only, $11 one way. Book the return journey with the driver or T8553 2390. **Ferry** *Sealink* departs at least twice a day from Cape Jervis (1½ hrs drive from Adelaide, 1 hr crossing) to Penneshaw, T8202 8688, www.sealink.com.au Petrol is 10-15 cents more expensive than on the mainland, Aldinga is often the cheapest fill-up on the way down from Adelaide.

Getting around
Driving A majority of the roads on the island are unsealed and can get very rough and corrugated from extensive use, ask at park offices about current conditions. There is also a greater chance than on the mainland of meeting animals, particulary kangaroos and wallabies, and some of the roads can look like a war zone. Care should therefore be taken, especially around dawn and dusk. Petrol is available at the western end of the island only at the *KI Wilderness Resort*, but it is around 10 cents dearer here than Kingscote, Parndana or even Vivonne Bay. 4WD hire is more expensive than 2WD, but safer and more comfortable on rough roads. Access to national parks requires a permit, currently $13 per vehicle. **Car Hire** *Hertz*, Kingscote and airport, T8553 2390, F8553 2878 and *Budget*, Kingscote, Penneshaw and airport, T8553 3133, F8553 2888. **VW Kombis** are available from *Kangaroo Island Kombi Campers*, T8553 7195, kicamp@kin.on.net ($100 per day, min 2 days). **Camper trailers** can be hired to hitch to your own vehicle, contents include kitchen, toilet, shower, table and chairs, T018 140036.

Walking There are 1-6 hr short walks near park offices but no long distance marked trails or loop walks on the island. Probably the best 2-day return trek is from the **Ravine Des Casoars** car park, down the ravine (3½ km), south along the cliff tops to **West Bay** for an overnight camp (15 km), inland 3 km along the West Bay Track, and north up the now disused road back to the car park (14 km). Any long treks must be discussed in advance with a ranger once a *Trip Intentions* form has been completed and forwarded to a parks office. Contact the Rocky River Park HQ first. Spring and Autumn are the best trekking times and 1:50,000 topographical maps can be obtained in Adelaide from either *The Map Shop* or *The Environment Shop*. The two maps covering the western end of the island are *Borda 6226-4* and *Vennachar 6226-3*

Tours Kangaroo Island is expensive to get to. If you only have 1-2 days spare for a visit you should consider taking a tour from Adelaide even if you have your own transport. Tours are also the best way to see the island if you don't have transport as getting around is very difficult. The unsealed roads even make cycling an uncomfortable option. 4WD tours do offer a more varied experience, though only for tours of 3 or more days. **Day tours** *Sealink* have various tours on large coaches, prices between $90 and $300, depending on the combination of flying/coaching and starting point. *Ferry Connections (YHA)*, T8553 1233, www.ki-ferryconnections.com, run similar tours in a smaller coach from Penneshaw from $70. **Overnight tours** Several operators offer inclusive 2-day backpacker 'bush' experiences for around $250, including *Wayward* and *Ferry Connections*. *Daniel's*, T1800 454454, danielstours@bigpond.com, are $260 but recommended. Owner-operated by an enthusiastic island resident. **Longer tours** A handful of island-based operators offer inclusive packages for small parties in 4WD vehicles. This is luxury bush-bashing so it will cost, so expect to pay around $400 per person per day and night. Try *K.I. Odysseys*, T8553 1311, www.kiodysseys.com.au, or *Rainbow Walkabouts*, 8553 5350, www.rainbowwalkabouts.com.au **Fishing and Diving** Contact *Kangaroo Island Charters*, T8553 2100, for details of various options on the 13-m *Vernita*.

Island Pass The annual Island Pass ($30 per person) includes entry and tours at Seal Bay, Kelly Hill Caves, Cape Borda, Cape Willoughby and Flinders Chase National Park. Pick one up at the Gateway Visitor Centre in Penneshaw or the Parks office in Kingscote.

Penneshaw
Colour map 1,
grid C2
Population 250
56 km from Kingscote

This very small modern township is home to the **Sealink** ferry terminal and the island's main **VIC**. It is also one of two places on the island where **fairy penguins** can be seen and walking tours go from the **Penguin Interpretative Centre** every evening. ■ *Daily in summer 2030, 2130. $6, children/concessions $4.50. T8553 1103*. The boardwalk can be trodden for free during daylight hours, but the little fellas are pretty elusive then. There is a sandy beach to the east of the ferry terminal. The helpful **Gateway Visitor Centre**, is on Howard Avenue, five minutes, walk west of town. ■ *Mon-Fri 0900-1700, Sat-Sun 1000-1600, T8553 1185, F8553 1255, www.tourkangarooisland.com.au*

Sleeping and eating A *Seaview Lodge*, Willoughby Rd, T8553 1132, www.seaviewlodge.com.au Hosted B&B in 1890s spacious and luxurious home. Licensed, expensive dinners for residents if arranged in advance. **A-B** *Seafront*, North Terr, T8553 1028, F8553 1204, www.seafront.com.au Attractive modern hotel rooms, some with ocean front balconies. Good facilities include heated pool and smart mid-range restaurant with floor to ceiling windows overlooking *Backstairs Passage*. **B-C** *The Lookout*, corner of Willoughby Rd and Ian Rd, 10 km from Penneshaw. T/F8553 1048, www.the-lookout.com.au Panoramic views from a hill 2 km from the sea. Self-contained modern weatherboard house, comfortably furnished with superb gardens. **C** *Footprints*, Flinders Terr, T8449 2488, jrluff@senet.com.au Self-contained

Book accommodation in advance as the entire island can book out at busy times

simple and fresh large cabin with good views over the beach. Sleeps 4. **D-E** *Penguin Walk YHA*, Middle Terr, T1800 018484 or 8553 1233. Range of options including doubles and self-contained accommodation. They also run island and diving tours. **E** *Penneshaw Youth Hostel*, North Terr, T8553 1284, advhost@kin.net.au Shabby hostel, but good range of hire equipment including diving gear, bikes, scooters and cars. There is a caravan park on Frenchman's Terr, T8553 1075. In the mid-range *Post Office Restaurant*, North Terr, T8553 1063, the entertainer turned chef takes up his guitar most evenings in the informal jungly courtyard. Good range of vegetarian and children's options. Open Tue-Sat 1730-2100. *Ruby Joe's*, North Terr. Good value cooked breakfasts and light lunches in wood and exposed brick café with sea-facing balcony. Entry via *Grimshaw's* shop and takeaway. Open 0800-1930.

Dudley Peninsula   Turning left just past the VIC, the unsealed Willoughby Road runs southeast with occasional beach turnoffs. The last two lead to car parks on opposite sides of the **Chapman River**, a good spot for picnicing, swimming, fishing and canoeing. Both sandy banks lead down to the beach on wide **Antechamber Bay**, but it is not very sheltered and swimming is not advised. The **Cape Willoughby Lighthouse** marks the termination of the road, some 25 km from Penneshaw. ■ *Tours daily 1000, 1100, 1230, 1315 and 1400 miniumum, 45 mins. $6.70, children/concessions $5.20. T8553 1191.* The lighthouse sits on an exposed headland with waves pounding at the base of the cliffs. Accommodation is available in two of the self-contained weatherboard keepers' cottages (**C**, T8559 7235). To the west of Penneshaw, Hog Bay Road passes **American Beach, Browns Beach** and **Island Beach** in quick succession. **Pennington Bay**

Kangaroo Island

Sleeping ■	
1 Cape Forbin Retreat	4 Kangaroo Island Wilderness Resort	7 Mudbrick House
2 Flinders Chase Farm	5 Koala Lodge	8 Nepean Bay Getaway
3 Hanson Bay Cabins	6 Lookout	9 Salt Lagoon Cottage
		10 Stranraer Homestead

South Australia

is another long white beach, the most accessible of the ones along the wilder southern coast, and popular with surfers. Nearby on the main Hog Bay Road is **C** *Salt Lagoon Cottage*, T/F8553 1136, a stone cottage, 100 m above the road overlooking Pelican Lagoon (ask for directions when booking).

American River is less a township, more a loose collection of homes and holiday accommodation along the western neck of **Pelican Lagoon**. There's no beach but the land rises away from the shore and there are some terrific views. Canoes and fishing tackle can be hired, and yacht cruises can be booked at *Rendezvous* (T8553 7150, daily 0800-1700), a shack on the wharf. Kingscote Airport is a few miles inland at tiny **Cygnet River**.

American River & Cygnet River

Sleeping and eating A-B *Kangaroo Island Lodge*, American River, T8553 7053, www.kilodge.com.au High-standard rooms, a few fully self-contained, but the best thing here is the expensive vine-covered courtyard restaurant overlooking the pool and ocean. Hearty breakfasts and imaginative cuisine using fresh local produce. Open daily 0700-0900, 1130-1400, 1800-2100. Book courtyard tables at weekends. **A-C** *Ulonga*, American River, T8553 7171, ulonga@kln.net.au Good value, self-contained units and cottage. Café serving excellent breakfasts and snacks on sail-shaded terrace overlooking the bay. Very friendly hosts. Recommended. Open Thu-Mon 0730-0930 and 1130-1430. **C** *Koala Lodge*, Cygnet River, T/F8553 9006. 2 cosy rooms in a very welcoming B&B on the main road near the airport. Surrounded by tall gums that are frequently draped in koalas. **D** *Nepean Bay Getaway*, Min Oil Rd, T/F8553 9181. Large self-contained basic farmhouse set 1 km back from the sea, superb value for groups and families.

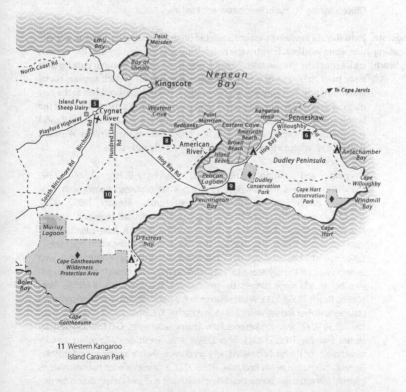

South Australia

11 Western Kangaroo
   Island Caravan Park

Kingscote

Colour map 1, grid C2
Population 1,500
60 km from
Penneshaw,
100 km from Rocky
River, 103 km from
Cape Borda

As the island's biggest town, Kingscote has the only large supermarket and a number of facilities not available elsewhere, most of which can be found along the main shopping street, Dauncey Street. The town is a good base for seeing the island. **Pelican feeding**, 1700 daily at the wharf. **Penguin tours**, leave every evening from the *Ozone*. ■ *1930 and 2030 (2100 and 2140 during daylight saving)*. *$7, children and concessions $5.50. Book at DEH, Dauncey St, 8553 2381 (open Monday-Friday 0845-1700).*

Sleeping and eating B-C *Ozone*, The Foreshore, T8553 2011, F8553 2249, www.ozonehotel.com Large pub cheerfully renovated with families in mind. Good views over Nepean Bay. 37 newly furnished rooms have access to pool, sauna and spa. Very popular cafeteria-style cheap restaurant. Food 1200-1400, 1800-2000. **C** *Queenscliffe*, Dauncey St, T8553 2254. Cheerless but traditional pub with good value en suite rooms. **D-E** *Napean Bay Tourist Park*, Brownlow, T8553 2394. Very basic but cheap cabins and lawned camping area in clean caravan park, 3 km from the town centre. **E** *Central Backpackers*, Murray St, T8553 2787. Small, basic but clean with minimal facilities. One of the best places to eat is *Bella*, Dauncey St, T8553 0400. Mid-range pastas, pizzas and interesting Italian cuisine. Open Wed-Sun 1700-2100. *Roger's Deli*, Dauncey St. The best spot for a breakfast, coffee or light lunch is this combined café, delicatessen and newsagency. Also homemade takeaway-and-heat meals. Open Sun-Wed 0800-1800, Thu-Sat 0800-2100.

Directory Banks *SA Bank* have the only ATM, on Dauncey St. **Car Servicing** *Turner Ford*, Telegraph Rd, T8553 2213. **Communications** Internet free at the Public Library, Dauncey St, T8553 2015. Open Mon 1300-1700, Tue-Fri 0930-1700. **Post Office**, Dauncey St, also in Penneshaw and Pardana.

Kingscote to Snelling Beach

Emu Bay, 17 km northwest of Kingscote on sealed roads, is a 4-km arc of pristine white sand beach with a few holiday homes clustered around the western end. From here the unsealed North Coast Road snakes through grazing land away from the sea until it reaches **Stokes Bay**, which in itself appears rocky and uninviting, but a short walk between a series of huge boulders to the east magically reveals an almost perfect long sandy beach. **Snelling Beach**, at the bottom of a narrow river valley has no facilities except toilets but is a very good swimming and fishing beach. The last beach before the parks is **Western River Cove**, where a footbridge leads to the small sandy cove.

Sleeping and eating L-A *Hannafords*, Snelling Beach, T8559 2248, bhanna@kin.net.au 3 comfortable and spacious self-contained houses with wide verandas overlooking the beach. **A** *Cape Forbin Retreat*, T8559 3219, www.capeforbinretreat.com.au Remote and eco-friendly self-contained wooden house. Perched on a hill overlooking rugged coastline. Sleeps 6. **A** *Meredith's*, west of main settlement, Emu Bay, T8553 5381, www.ki.com.au/meredith-beachside 1 self-contained 2-bedroom area and 1 hosted double room in an isolated house with stunning views of the bay. Stone terrace and sweeping lawns down to the virtually private beach. Mid-range dinners by arrangement. Recommended. **B** *Middle River*, Snelling Beach, T8553 9119, wildlife@kin.on.net 2 rustic rammed-earth self-contained cottages with river and sea views, 2 km from beach. **C** *KI Experience*, 5 km west of Stokes Bay, T8559 2277, www.kiexperience.com Luxury safari tents. **C-D** *Emu Bay Holiday Homes*, Emu Bay, T/F8553 5241, dmorris@kin.net.au Fresh, newly furnished self-contained cabins on the hill. Good views, very good value. There is a campground at Stokes Bay with toilets only, pay at *Rockpool*, T8559 2277, a simple wooden hut which serves gourmet fish and chips, burgers, excellent milkshakes and iced coffees during the day,

South Australia

expensive gourmet platters and Mediterranean dishes evenings. Licensed. Open daily, December-January 1000-2400, July-September 1430-1630, otherwise 1100-1600. May open for evenings out of peak season if booked ahead.

The **Cape Gantheaume Wilderness Protection Area** is a large dense region of mallee scrub, untouched and unmanaged. On its northern border is the **Murray Lagoon**, the largest wetland habitat on the island and home to thousands of swans, geese and ducks amongst more than 100 bird species to be found here. There is a small **Parks Office** at Murray Lagoon, with details of the accessibility of the short lagoon walks, T8553 8233. It is possible to trek around the wild coast of the Cape from **D'Estrees Bay** to **Bales Bay**, but the route is largely unmarked, there are no facilities, fresh water or return transport. Only experienced bushwalkers should consider this.

The south coast

 Seal Bay is one of the island's main attractions, where **Australian sea lions** come to rest on the long sandy beach, bordered by high dunes, after three days at sea. This colony is the last remnant of an enormous population of seals almost hunted to extinction on Kangaroo Island. A wander on the beach is only permitted with a National Parks tour guide but you can get up close. The sea lions can also be viewed from extensive boardwalks. ■ *Tours daily every 45 mins from 0900-1615 (avoid busiest time 1100-1300). $10, children/concessions $7. T8559 4207.* Further to the west is another beautiful white beach at **Vivonne Bay**, where the Harriet and Eleanor rivers flow into the sea. Swimming is safe at the western end, near the jetty, but there is a strong undertow in the rest of the bay. This is a popular surfing and fishing spot and there is a basic campground halfway down the dirt track signposted to the jetty. Petrol and supplies are available from the *Vivonne Bay Store* on South Coast Road, T8559 4285. Open daily 0800-2000 during summer, as per custom during winter. *Yurrumun Ridge*, Vivonne Bay, T8559 4297, offer horse riding, kayaking, dune buggying, and hire out sail, surf and snorkel equipment.

 Kelly Hill Caves are unusual in being buried under a series of sand dunes and, unlike true limestone, the bedrock above is porous. This has led to some weird and wonderful cave decoration which is eerily beautiful. ■ *Tours daily 1000, 1100, 1200, 1330, 1430, 1530. $7, children/concessions $5.50, 45 mins. Also 2-hr adventure caving Mon, Wed, $25-35, wear long trousers, sleeves and sturdy shoes and expect to get dirty. T8559 7231.* An excellent 18-km return hike from Kelly Hill Visitor Centre passes through the bush of the **Kelly Hill Conservation Park**, past freshwater lagoons and over steep sand dunes to reach the **Hanson Bay beach**, a superb white sandy beach, stretching away to cliffs in the distance with huge breakers rolling in from the Southern Ocean. Allow nine hours and inform a ranger of departure and return times. A little further along the South Coast Road on the left is the entrance to Hanson Bay Sanctuary. Donate $1 to walk up the driveway, wild koala sightings virtually guaranteed.

Sleeping L-C *Kangaroo Island Wilderness Resort*, South Coast Rd, T8559 7275, www.austdreaming.com.au An oasis of fine food and soft beds. Large resort with plush log cabin accommodation in the bush, from 5-star to luxurious backpacker dorms. Expensive and cheap restaurants, small shop, bottle shop and takeaway. Expensive petrol, public phone. Guests laundry. Shop and petrol 0800-2000. **A** *Stanraer Homestead*, Wheatons Rd, D'Estress Bay, T8553 8235, F8553 8226. Large traditional farmhouse on working sheep station, renovated in grand style as a very comfortable hosted B&B. Hearty breakfast, warm hospitality and fine expensive dinners using the best of local produce. Recommended. **B** *Hanson Bay Cabins*, South West River Rd, T8853 2603, F8853 2673. 3 self-contained log cabins perch on a rise with a spectacular view of the wild and

▶▶ **Tree, by gum!**

Koalas love Kangaroo Island. Their introduction from the mainland has been so successful that the island has a near epidemic of them. There are so many that they are eating themselves out of house and home. Koalas will only eat a few species of eucalyptus, one of their favourites is the manna gum, so naturally they can only expand in proportion to the area of appropriate habitat. Kangaroo Island does not have enough trees that are tasty to koalas for such a large population to remain viable. In some of the national parks the rangers have placed wide metal bands around trees to stop koalas from climbing them, thus rationing their food supply. Islanders are discussing whether to cull the population but unsurprisingly sterilization is a more popular option as they are not keen to be known as koala killers. Trees stripped bare of leaves are a sign that koalas live in the area. When trying to spot koalas look at the base of trees for bunches of leaves with freshly broken stems, as koalas drop these when feeding. On a hot day they will be low down in the tree to protect themselves from the sun and conversely on cooler days they will sit close to the top of the tree.

isolated bay. Recommended. **B** *Western KI Caravan Park*, South Coast Rd, T8559 7201. High-standard cabins (no on-site vans) surrounded by tall stands of gums. Small shop and public phone, good clean camp kitchen. **D** *The Mudbrick House*, South Coast Rd, T8559 7341. Homely self-contained house on a small eccentric farm with its own 9-hole golf course. An opportunity to see much of the island's wildlife from the marvellous fresh air loo-with-a-view. **D-E** *Flinders Chase Farm*, West End Highway, T8559 7223, chillers@kin.net.au Small wood cabins and simple dorms. Clean, leafy communal areas and friendly owners make this the best of the island's backpacker hostels.

Flinders Chase National Park
Entry $6, children & concessions $3.50

Together, the Flinders Chase National Park and the Ravine des Casoars Wilderness Protection Area constitute the largest area of untouched native bushland in Australia and cover the entire western end of the island. Set amidst stands of manna and sugar gums, **Rocky River** is the park's headquarters. ■ *Visitor Centre open daily, 0900-1700 Sep-May, 1000-1700 Jun-Aug. T8559 7235.* Park passes and accommodation must be paid for here and park rangers consulted if you plan any serious walking. Around the complex are picnic and BBQ areas, and various short bush walks where sightings of koalas and kangaroos are quite likely. One of the best walks leads through the forest to a series of boardwalks over pools. Platypus may be seen in the pools here around dawn.

From Rocky River the sealed road twists its way 15 km down to the south coast through virgin mallee bush to the small peninsula of **Cape du Couedic**, home to a large colony of **New Zealand fur seals** basking in the shadow of the impressive **Admirals Arch**. Some 6 km to the east are the equally impressive **Remarkable Rocks**. A rough unsealed road heads west from Rocky River. The right-hand turn after 7 km is the Shackle Road to Cape Borda and soon after a left turn leads the short way to **Snake Lagoon**. From the campsite a 1½-km walk heads first through thick young mallee scrub over a low limestone ridge to the Rocky River itself. At this point a boardwalk crosses the riverbed, and in the dry season there is a slim chance of seeing platypus. The path follows the shallow ravine to the ocean and a small beach. A direct return will take about 1½ hours, but a longer circular option is to follow the cliff top to the right (northwest) for 2½ km to **Sandy Beach**, take the marked track inland back to the road and use the road to return to Snake Lagoon camping ground. Allow three to four hours. The road continues for another 15 km to **West Bay**, a beautiful and particularly isolated beach bordered by two long headlands.

At **Cape Borda**, the northwesterly tip of the island, some of the highest cliffs in South Australia soar nearly vertically out of the ocean. The **Cape Borda Lighthouse**, built in 1858, has a colourful history, much of which is revealed by the daily tours and small museum. ■ *Tours daily 1100, 1230, 1315 and 1400 minimum, 45 mins. $6.50, children/concessions $5. T8559 3257.* Just to the south is the **Ravine Des Casoars**, where a steep trail winds down the ravine to a rivermouth beach with adjacent caves. Fairy penguins sometimes shelter here, but a torch is needed to see them. Nearby is a sheltered beach, hemmed in by high cliffs, at **Harveys Return**, a 25-minute walk down a very steep incline from the park campsite of the same name, where you can swim in the exceptionally clear water.

Sleeping There is a variety of simply furnished self-contained historic houses and huts at this end of the island. None have television, radio or phones. Bring your own linen and towels, or rent for $11 per person. Bookings, T8559 7235, kiparksaccom@saugov.sa.gov.au Guests who stay 5 nights or more get a free *Island Parks Pass*. The 3 cottages at **B** *Cape de Couedic* have been renovated but the usual sparse furnishing makes them feel quite stark. **C-E** *Rocky River HQ* has 2 farm cottages. The larger, May's Cottage, is traditionally furnished with woodfired stove and sleeps 6. Postman's Cottage is a single-room building with 4 bunks and small kitchen area, also with a woodfired stove. **C-F** *Cape Borda* has 2 keepers' cottages and a small 2-person store hut, known fondly as 'Chateau Woodward'. The larger cottage, Flinders Light Lodge, sleeps 6, is very spacious and has an elegant dining room. Staying in this tranquil, romantic spot is definitely recommended. Designated **camping grounds** are situated at Rocky River, Snake Lagoon, West Bay and Harveys Return (Cape Borda). Only Rocky River, with showers, has anything other than toilets and emergency water (supplies not guaranteed). Campsites must also be booked in advance.

Camping at Rocky River $15 per car, other campgrounds $6 per car

The Barossa Valley

A wide plain and soft folds of hills scattered with gum trees and neatly dressed in ribbons of green vines, the Barossa Valley has storybook church spires, small villages, grand estates and stone cottages. The Barossa is reminiscent of Europe but the clear light, the muddy green of eucalypts and the corrugated tin roofs and verandahs make this an unmistakeably Australian landscape. The Barossa is one of Australia's best wine regions and one of its oldest. The main towns, Nuriootpa and Tanunda, lie along the backbone of the valley, while picturesque Angaston is just to the east over the ranges in a small valley all its own. The area was settled by wealthy English free settlers who found the valley's soil and climate were ideal for vineyards. They were joined by Silesian Lutherans fleeing religious persecution in the 1830s. Their traditional methods of curing meats, baking and making relishes, pickles and jams have survived, along with the distinctly Lutheran architecture, and prized by visitors as much as the excellent wines.

Check www.barossa-region.org

Ins and outs

TransAdelaide Trains have an hourly service to **Gawler** from Adelaide Station. T8210 1000, www.transadelaide.com.au *Barossa-Adelaide Passenger Service* have buses twice daily from 101 Franklin St, Adelaide, stopping at **Gawler**, **Lyndoch**, **Tanunda**, **Nuriootpa** and **Angaston**. T8564 3022, www.adelaidemetro.com.au The plush *Barossa Wine Train* runs a range of pricey tours including a simple return ticket for $65. T8212 7888, info@barossawinetrain.com.au Aside from a car, the only real options for

Getting there & around
Tanunda: colour map 1, grid B3, 70 km from Adelaide, 100 km from Clare

South Australia

getting around are on foot, by bike (*Bunkhaus* for bike hire) or with a tour bus. It is possible for the energetic to walk around half a dozen wineries from Nuriootpa or Tanunda on a fair day, but cycling allows maximum flexibilty. There are daily *McCafferty's/Greyhound* **buses** from **Gawler** (at 1115) and **Nuriootpa** (at 1135) to Sydney; also to Adelaide (on request only, at 1310/1630 and 1250 respectively.

Tours Operators such as *Barossa Experience*, T8653 3248, offer day car tours, including lunch, from around $110 per person. Day bus tours can be found for as little as $39. Try *Valley Tours*, T8563 3587, or, from Adelaide, the excellent *Groovy Grape*, T1800 661177, www.groovygrape.com.au *Balloon Adventures*, T8389 3195, F8389 3220, offer weekend flights from $231, less during the week.

Wineries

'Wine is constant proof that God loves us and likes to see us happy.' Benjamin Franklin

There are over 50 wineries in the Barossa Valley, mostly clustered around Nuriootpa and Tanunda. A representative sample are mentioned below. As in most wine regions, the smaller wineries are often the most interesting and rewarding to visit, but are infrequently visited by organized tours. *Bethany*, Bethany Rd, T8563 2086, open Mon-Sat 1000-1700, Sun 1300-1700. Site of the oldest Tanunda settlement, the view over the valley is worth the trip alone. Good whites. *Elderton*, Tanunda Rd, T8562 1058, open Mon-Fri 0830-1700, Sat-Sun 1000-1600. Friendly modern winery with some superb reds. *Kaesler*, Barossa Valley Way, T8562 2711, kaesler@dove.net.au tastings daily 1000-1700, wines $10-40. Small winery in interesting 19th-century farm buildings with a fine Shiraz. *Langmeil*, Para Rd, T8563 2595, open daily 1100-1630. Site of the second Tanunda settlement, some of the smooth reds are made from their 150-year old vines. *Penfolds*, Tanunda Rd, T8568 9408, penfolds.bv@cellar-door.com.au, open Mon-Sat 1000-1700, Sun 1300-1700. Steeped in history and tradition. As well as casual tastings, the real buff can book a private *Ultimate Tasting Experience* 24 hrs in advance. *Peter Lehman*, Para Rd, T8563 2500, open Mon-Fri 0930-1700, Sat-Sun 1030-1630. Very pleasant winery with lawns and picnic areas. *Richmond Grove*, Para Rd, T8563 7303, wines $10-20, open Mon-Fri 1000-1700, Sat-Sun 1030-1630. Large winery with good Riesling. A short country walk from here runs through the next 2 wineries and past 150-year-old vines. *Rockfords*, Krondorf Rd, T8563 2720, open Mon-Sat 1100-1700. Very friendly small winery. Hand-picked grapes crushed, pressed and fermented in the traditional manner using 100-year-old equipment make some of the finest reds in the valley. Visit in Mar-Apr to see this fascinating process in full swing. *Seppelt*, Seppeltsfield, T8568 6200, open Mon-Fri 1000-1700, Sat-Sun 1100-1700. Huge, historic winery, with immaculate grounds, BBQs and picnic areas. *St Hallett*, St Hallett's Rd, T8563 7000, open daily 1000-1700. Wines by the glass. The smooth, light *Poacher's Blend* white is a bargain. *Turkey Flat*, Bethany Rd, T8563 2851, open daily 1100-1700. Very friendly small winery, their wines are extremely sought after and many sell out fast. Visit during Aug-Sep for a chance to buy the renowned *Butcher's Block* blended red.

Around the valley

On the very western edge of the Barossa, **Gawler** lies on the main highway between Nuriootpa and Adelaide. It's a good alternative choice as a base for exploring the Barossa and much better value than in the heart of the valley. The **Church Hill** area to the west of the main street, Murray Street, is a 1890s time capsule well worth spending a couple of hours strolling around. Follow the **Historic Gawler Walking Trail** signs. The **VIC** is tucked away behind Murray Street at 2 Lyndoch Road. ■ *Daily 0900-1700, T8522 6814, www.gawler.sa.gov.au*

South Australia

Sitting on the valley floor, **Tanunda** is the heart of the Barossa and has a busy and prosperous feel. Near the town centre is the site of the original 1843 settlement named Langmeil, which was on the eastern side of town, next to the North Para River. Several neat and narrow Lutheran churches survive and the quiet roads off Murray Street hide many historic houses. Leaflets on a heritage town walk can be picked up from the **Barossa Wine and Visitor Centre**. ■ *Daily 1000-1600 T8563 0600, F8563 0616, info@barossa-region.org 66-68 Murray St.*

For a great drive from Tanunda, take Bethany Road, dropping in on the *Bethany* winery. Shortly after take the right-hand turn up **Menglers Hill** and stop to admire the fantastic view at the lookout. Follow the road for a further 3 km and turn right into Tanunda Creek Road. If time allows stop in the small layby after another 3 km and take a stroll in the beautiful **Kaiser Stuhl Conservation Park**. Follow the road a further 200 m and turn left up the unsealed Pohlner Road, turning left again after a short way back onto the sealed Flaxmans Valley Road. After about 6 km turn left again and **Angaston** will appear within a couple of minutes. This is the smallest and most appealing of the three main Barossa Valley towns and offers the best eating choices.

The small town of **Lyndoch** is home to a dozen of the Barossa wineries, including the massive *Orlando*, responsible for Brits favourite, *Jacob's Creek*. The roundabout road from here to Angaston, via Williamstown and Springton, makes an extremely pleasant drive beginning almost immediately with a short detour to the **Whispering Wall** reservoir dam on Yettie Road. As the name suggests, this spectacular sweep of concrete has the acoustics of the best Greek amphitheatres (closed on days of total fire bans).

Central Barossa Valley

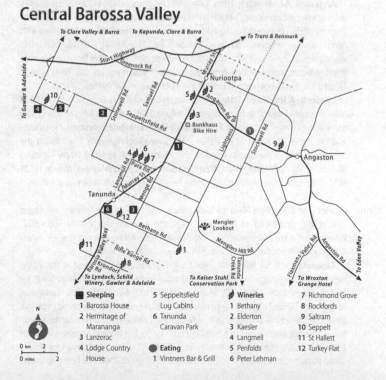

■ Sleeping	5 Seppeltsfield	🍇 Wineries	7 Richmond Grove
1 Barossa House	Log Cabins	1 Bethany	8 Rockfords
2 Hermitage of	6 Tanunda	2 Elderton	9 Saltram
Marananga	Caravan Park	3 Kaesler	10 Seppelt
3 Lanzerac		4 Langmeil	11 St Hallett
4 Lodge Country	● Eating	5 Penfolds	12 Turkey Flat
House	1 Vintners Bar & Grill	6 Peter Lehman	

South Australia

Essentials

Sleeping   **LL** *The Lodge Country House*, Seppeltsfield, T8562 8277, F8562 8344. Exquisite secluded country house a handy stroll from the winery. Expensive dinners must be pre-arranged. 2 night minimum at weekends. **B** *Wroxton Grange*, Flaxman's Valley Rd, T/F8565 3227, wroxton@dove.net.au   Large comfortable Victorian bluestone house on family vineyard. **C** *Barossa House*, Barossa Valley Way, T/F8562 4022, barossahouse@bigpond.com   3 very comfortable rooms plus warm hospitality make this exceptional value. Look no further if they have vacancies. Recommended. **C-D** *Seppeltsfield Log Cabins*, Seppeltsfield, T8562 8240. 8 comfortable self-contained cabins, some with spa, provide good value.

Gawler   **B** *Eagle Foundry*, King St, T/F 8522 3808. Guest rooms open onto the iron foundry courtyard with spa pool. *Gawler Caravan Park*, Main North Rd, T8522 3805, is just a short walk from town, and has cabins and on-site vans of varying standards.

Tanunda   There are some excellent B&Bs in Tanunda within easy walking distance from the shops and restaurants. For budget accomodation the only option is cabins or on-site vans at the caravan park. **B** *Paranook*, 6 Murray St, T8563 0208, F8563 0908. Hosted B&B in 1890s bluestone home. 2 elegant large rooms. **B** *Five Chimneys*,15 Maria St, T8563 0240. Comfortable accomodation in large federation house, spa, swimming pool. **C** *Goat Square Cottages*, 33 John St, T8359 0993, F8359 0994. Traditional German 1850s house with tiny doorways. self-contained, close to town centre. Sleeps 2-5. **D** *Tanunda*, 51 Murray St, T8563 2030, has 10 reasonable pub rooms. **D-E** *Tanunda Caravan Park*, Barossa Valley Way, T8563 2784. 10-min walk from the shopping area.

Nurioopta   **D-E** *Bunkhaus*, Barossa Valley Way, T/F8562 2260. Two 6-bed dorms, plus the best value self contained cottage in the area. Small pool, bike hire $8 a day. Friendly and knowledgable hosts. Recommended.

Angaston   **A** *Collingrove*, Eden Valley Rd, Angaston, T8564 2061, F8564 3600, www.colginrovehomestead.com.au   A museum by day, this outstanding National Trust property offers a chance to live like a rich 19th-century pastoralist. Rooms furnished with Angas family antiques. **B** *Lilac Cottage*, 19 Murray St, T0413 088 422, www.dove.net.au/~lilac   Pretty 1870s stone cottage behind a picket fence on the main street. self-contained, breakfast provisions included. **B** *Seasons*, Lot 102, Newcastle St, T8524 6380. Stylish open-plan house on a rise behind the main street.

Lyndoch   **A** *The Miners Cottage*, 6 km south on Goldfields Rd, T8524 6213, F8524 6650. This idyllic isolated stone cottage overlooking billabong, bush and swimming pool is one of the loveliest in the valley. Recommended. **B** *Kooringal Homestead*, 7 km southeast on Yettie Rd, T8524 6196, F8524 7317, www.kooringal.com   Overlooking the deep-blue water of the Barossa reservoir, this hilltop farmstead has 2 simply furnished B&B rooms. Very personable hosts. **C** *Barossa Gallery*, 8 Lyndoch Valley Highway, T8524 5191.1910 stone house with 2 guest rooms. Lovely gardens with boules on the lawn.

Eating   **Gawler**   The stylish *Café Nova* is a large Italian-style mid-range restaurant and cheap café at the south end of Murray St, near the cinema. Open daily 1000-2200. *Wheatsheaf*, 3 km east toward Lyndoch, T8522 5762. Mid-range colonial restaurant with modern Australian cuisine and the best reputation in the area.

Tanunda *1918*, 94 Murray St, T8563 0405. Traditionally the best in the valley, expensive dining in gardens of a restored villa. Some might question its value for money. Open daily 1200-1500, Mon-Sat 1830-2100, Sun 1800-2000. *Landhaus*, Bethany Rd, T8563 2191. A finely renovated and extended 1840s shepherd's cottage, this is considered one of Australia's best restaurants. Modern Australian expensive cuisine with a fine small wine list. It hardly needs saying, but book in advance. Wed-Sat 1900-2100. *Café Placebo*, 109 Murray St, T8563 1333, is a good Italian for simple cheap pasta or pizza. Mon-Tue 0900-1700, Wed-Sun 0900-2000. The best pub food is at *The Valley Hotel*, 73 Murray St, T8563 2039. Modern café-style meals in a light room, wooden french doors facing the street. *Zinfandel Tearooms*, 58 Murray St, T8563 2822. Frilly but cosy place with cooked breakfasts, wicked puddings and many German dishes. Daily 0830-1800.

Nurioopta For superb gourmet treats or a light organic lunch *Maggie Beer's Farm Shop*, Samuel Rd, T8562 4477, is unmissable. The glass fronted café hangs over a dam and foodies will hang over Maggie Beer's mouthwatering range of goodies. Open daily 1030-1700; lunch 1230-1430.

In Angaston *Vintners Bar & Grill*, Nuriootpa Rd, T8564 2488. A famous expensive Barossa restaurant, popular with winemakers and vistors. Superb cooking concentrating on local produce served in a large light room that overlooks Yalumba Vineyards. Excellent regional wine list. *Seasons of the Valley*, 6 Washington St, T8564 3688. Probably the Barossa's best café with excellent cheap regional food and wine. Also a gallery showcasing high-quality local craft and photography and a gourmet larder selling fresh pasta, sauces, homemade ice cream and other goodies. Daily 1000-1700.

Clare Valley and the Burra

A long and narrow valley in the Mount Loftus Ranges, surrounded by tall gum trees and softly rounded hills, the Clare Valley is not the biggest wine-producing area in South Australia but has more than its fair share of small 'boutique' wineries. Wine drinkers have been well catered for here since the arrival of the Jesuits in 1851. The wineries receive fewer visitors than Barossa or McClaren Vale and consequently offer a more relaxed and involved tasting experience and the the setting is also beautiful. Burra appears like a mirage out of the low bare hills some 40 km to the east of Clare. It was a very successful mining town in the mid-19th century and is the state's most interesting historic mining site. Evidence of the area's mining legacy can also be found in the picturesque settlements of Auburn and Mintaro.

Check www.clarevalley.co.au

Ins and outs

The *Mid North Passenger Service*, T8826 2346, runs daily afternoon buses from Adelaide Tue-Fri and Sun, calling at **Gawler**, **Auburn**, **Clare** and **Burra**. **Tours** *Clare Valley Tours*, T8843 8066, provide a variety of local coach and 4WD tours around the valley. *Clare Valley Experiences*, T8843 4169, david@jspace.net, run tours based around wineries, art or heritage. Minimum of 4, $55 half day, $95 full day. *The Lodge*, Penwortham, T8843 4166, lesran@telstra.easymail.com.au, can organize almost anything from winery tours, 4WD, bushwalking, to Flinders Ranges trips. Also accommodation (**C**), departures from **Clare** or **Adelaide**

Getting there & around
Clare: colour map 1, grid B3, 135 km from Adelaide, 40 km from Burra, 195 km from Port Augusta

Clare Valley Wineries

There are over 30 wineries in the Clare Valley, almost all along or just off the main highway that runs between Auburn and Clare. *Eldredge*, Spring Gully Rd, T8842 3086, wines $12-20, open daily 1100-1700. Imaginative mid-range lunches on covered deck overlooking a large dam, Thu-Sun 1200-1500. *Mt Horrocks*, The Old Railway Station, Curling St, Auburn, T8849 2202, open Sat-Sun 1000-1700. Small winery also serving cheap light lunches. *Quelltaler Estate*, Quelltaler Rd, Watervale, T8843 0003, wines $15-35, Mon-Fri 0830-1700, Sat-Sun 1100-1600. Large 1854 winery with multi-award winning wines. Refined cellar door with small museum and gallery. The *Copper Trail Shiraz* is particularly good (and expensive). *Sevenhill Cellars*, College Rd, Sevenhill, T8843 4222, open Mon-Fri 0900-1630, Sat 1000-1600. The oldest winery in the valley, set up and still run by Jesuits. *Skillogalee*, Hughes Park Rd, Sevenhill, T8843 4311, wines $15-25, open daily 1000-1700. Award-winning riesling and good shiraz. This winery stands out for its superb food served on old farmhouse verandah overlooking the vines. *Stringy Brae*, Sawmill Rd, Sevenhill, T/F8843 4313, wines $15-25, open Wed, Sat-Sun 1000-1700. Their new café *Waldie's Shed* is a lovely spot to try excellent riesling and have a cheese or antipasto platter, overlooking the dam and vines. Also 2 self-contained wooden cottages (**B**) for B&B. There are a couple of wineries in Clare that you can walk to including *Leasingham* 7 Dominic St, T8842 2785, open Mon-Fri 0900-1700, Sat-Sun 1000-1600.

Around the valley

Auburn 25 km south of Clare, 20 km from Mintaro

Auburn lies at the southern end of the Clare Valley with two wineries and a couple of very good restaurants, and acts as a base for many coming up from Adelaide. **Clare** is a bustling modern town and not as picturesque as nearby Mintaro or Burra. A **Gourmet Festival** is held in the third weekend of May, when local restauranteurs set up at cellar doors so visitors can try an entrée-sized bite as well as taste and buy wine. There is also a **Spring Garden Festival** during the first weekend in November, known as 'Roses and Riesling', when the best gardens in the district are open to the public at the most beautiful time of year.

The **Spring Gully Conservation Park** allows a closer look at the valley's wild landscape and there are walking tracks and camping sites in 400 ha of bush. Ask at the **VIC** in the Town Hall for a map. ■ *Mon-Sat 0900-1700, Sun 1000-1600. T8842 2131, F8842 1117, ask@clarevalley.com.au Main North Rd.* The **Clare Valley Riesling Trail** runs along a disused railway line for 27 km. Designed for walking or cycling, with loop trails to wineries or other places of interest. **Bike hire** from *Clare Valley Cycle Hire*, 32 Victoria Rd, T8842 2782. Book ahead in busy periods. $8 half day, $16.50 day. Delivery and pickup anywhere in the valley. If it's possible to be sick of wine tasting, extra virgin olive oil can be tasted and bought at this estate, 3 km from Clare. ■ *Daily 1030-1630.*

One of South Australia's few heritage-listed towns, **Mintaro** consists of a small huddle of 19th-century

Clare Valley

Eating
1 Brice Hill
2 Georges
3 Regalia Café Gallery

Wineries
1 Eldredge
2 Leasingham
3 Mt Horrocks
4 Quelltaler Estate
5 Sevenhill Cellars
6 Skillogalee
7 Stringy Brae

Sleeping
1 Martindale Hall
2 Thorn Park Country House
3 Trestrail

South Australia

cottages, pubs and shops which have mostly been converted into restaurants or expensive self-contained accommodation to cater for tourist demand. It is very picturesque, but temporary residents will have to travel far for any basic service. Most impressive is local **Martindale Hall**, built in 1879 by a rich young wool heir. It is now a most impressive place to spend the night (see Sleeping below). ■ *Mon-Fri 1100-1600, Sat-Sun 1200-1600. $5.50, concessions $3.80, children $2.20.*

Ringed tightly by low bare hills, Burra sits in a valley full of trees with a wide creek flowing through the centre of town. The Burra mine was just to the west and a well-preserved engine house and chimneys still stand as a reminder of how the surrounding countryside was stripped of wood in order to feed the furnaces in the late 1840s. The surviving trees line streets full of historic buildings, antique shops and old pubs, and the banks of Burra Creek are an idyllic picnic spot. The **VIC**, *Burra Visitor Centre*, is in Market Square. ■ *Daily 0900-1700, T8892 2154, bvc@capri.net.au* Much of the mining heritage of Burra can be seen on the self-conducted **Heritage Passport Trail**. The key gains access to some interesting buildings, including **Redruth Gaol**, the extensive **Unicorn Brewery Cellars**, and the **Miners' Dugouts**. The latter are all that remains of hundreds of cave-like miners' homes that peppered the banks of Burra creek from 1845 to 1860. Take a torch. ■ *24 hr access, tour $11 per person, concessions $9 (tour including four museums $20, concessions $18). Permit, key and guidebook from the VIC.* Interesting tours of a 1930s gold mine now being worked in the old style by just one man. These are run by *Mongolata Gold*. ■ *Daily 1100, 1300 at mine, $10, children $5. T8892 2233. 90 mins. Bookings essential by phone or at shop, 3 Commercial St.* There are **horse riding** trails along old stock-droving routes. *Burra Trail Rides* offer rides from one hour to three days. All food and equipment supplied except sleeping bags. Beginner riders welcome. ■ *3 hrs $44, 2 days $209, 3 days $275, T8892 2627, F8892 2557, Basin Farm, 3 km east of Burra on the road to Morgan. Bookings essential.* **Copper Ridge Wilderness Safaris** take vistors all over an outback property in an open-sided 4WD to see creek beds, hidden springs, ridges and lookouts, and wildlife. Book at the VIC.

Burra
Colour map 1, grid B3
160 km from Adelaide, 200 km from Renmark, 200 km from Port Augusta, 355 km from Broken Hill

From Burra the Barrier Highway runs all the way to Broken Hill in NSW (see p x). There are numerous small towns along the route, all with basic fuel and store facilities

Essentials

Sevenhill L *Thorn Park Country House*, College Rd, T8843 4304, F8843 4296, thornpk@capri.net.au One of the most luxurious places to stay in South Australia. Elegant and gracious with gourmet meals available to guests. The owners have thought of every indulgent detail. Recommended. **B** *Trestrail*, Sawmill Rd, T/F8842 3794. Secluded and romantic tiny stone cottage, in 40 ha of bush with outstanding views.

Auburn A *Tatehams*, Main North Rd, T8849 2030, tatehams@capri.net.au Sophisticated and thoughtfully arranged rooms, food, and wine in the beautifully renovated General Store and Stables. Expensive Asian-influenced food. Dinner Wed-Sun, bookings required. **B-C** *Rising Sun*, Main North Rd, T8849 2015, F8849 2266, rising@capri.net.au Attractive old pub with 10 rooms. This is a good place to eat with a cheap bar menu and good mid-range restaurant, daily 1200-1400, 1830-2030.

Mintaro LL-L *Martindale Hall*, 3 km from town on the Manoora road, T8843 9088, F8843 9082. A magnificent Georgian-style manor house maintained in high Edwardian manner, the hall gives a rare chance to live as the nobs once did. Those on the full package are greeted with afternoon tea, and guests are encouraged to dress up for the 5-course silver service dinner. Weekend nights are fully booked a year ahead. Recommended. For the less well-heeled amongst us the hall is a living museum, and the

Sleeping
Much of the accommodation in the Clare Valley is in the form of self-contained cottages

South Australia

grounds also make a great picnic venue. There are several self-contained historic cottages to let (**B**); contact *Magpie & Stump*, Burra St, T8843 9014, for details.

Clare A *Roscrow*, 18 Victoria Rd, T0407 602 755, F8842 2666, roscrow@capri.net.au In a quiet side street, restored 1850s stone church with pretty garden. Self-contained, sleeps up to 6. **B-C** *Bungaree Station*, 12 km north on the Yacka Rd, T8842 2677, F8842 3004, bungaree@camtech.net.au Working sheep station, established in 1841, with self-contained rooms in heritage cottages and renovated farm buildings. Warm hosts, fascinating history and beautiful grounds. Recommended. Heritage tours of the station for non-residents on request. $8, children $5. Book in advance. **D-E** *Bentleys*, Main North Rd, T8842 1700. Basic rooms in pub. Pleasant atrium, serves cheap meals from 1200-1400, 1800-2000. Big breakfast open to all 0700-0900. **D-E** *Clare*, Main North Rd, T8842 2816. Pub with 15 rooms, including many inexpensive singles, cheap meals 1200-1400, 1800-2000. The **D-E** *Clare Caravan Park* with cabins and on-site vans is on Main North Rd, a long hike south of town, T8842 2724, clarpark@rbe.net.au

Burra B The best of the old stone cottages are **C** *Burra Heritage Cottages*, Tivers Row, T8892 2461, www.weblogic.com.au/tivers 5 self-contained cosy 1850s cottages, private garden. **D** *Burra*, Market Sq, T/F8892 2389. This busy pub is in the centre of town with clean rooms upstairs. Cheap bar and dining room menus served 1200-1400, 1800-2000. **D** *Commercial*, Commercial Rd, T8892 2010. Friendly pub with neat rooms. Cheap bar menu, served daily 1200-1400, 1800-2000. **E** *Paxton Square Cottages*, Kingston St, T8892 2622, F8892 2508, rows of 32 miners' homes. Basic but good value. Kitchen, BBQ, laundry. The **E** *Caravan Park*, Bridge Terr, T8892 2442, has on-site vans and a shady position next to Burra Creek, friendly with spotless facilities.

East of Burra B Saffron Downs, 10 km east of town, T8892 2012. A working sheep station with wonderful B&B. Also unique mid-range banquets served in an hexagonal glasshouse overlooking vast plains, and in the farmhouse hall furnished with an eclectic range of Persian carpets and exotic ornaments. Superb South American, Moroccan, Middle-Eastern or Asian cuisine. Banquets Fri-Sat evening, minimum of 4, bookings essential.

Eating
Many of the area's best restaurants are outside the towns

There are a couple of restaurants complementing the winery trade efforts. *Brice Hill*, Wendouree Rd, T8842 1796, bricehil@rbe.net.au Large stylish contemporary restaurant set on 2 levels. The downstairs wine bar serves cheap dishes. Unusually food is served all day, daily 1100-2030. Recommended. *Georges*, Neagle Rock Vineyard, T8843 4020. Open Thu-Tue 1000-1700, Sat-Sun 1800-2000. Good cheap casual meals outside under sails. Licensed. *Regalia Café Gallery*, Main North Rd, Penwortham, T/F8843 4248. Swiss and Italian influenced cheap and mid-range food in colourful surroundings. Fri-Sat 1100-1400, Thu-Sat 1800-2000, Sun brunch 1000-1400.

Murray towns

Check out the website www.murray-river.net

The Murray River has carved a bright green ribbon through the flat interior deserts of South Australia, creating extensive swamp and mallee habitats and high red cliffs on many of the sharp bends. The river, which forms the boundary between New South Wales and Victoria for much of its length, was plied by paddle steamers for several decades from the mid-19th century, carrying wool, copper, grain and other mineral and agricultural produce from South Australia, New South Wales and Victoria down to the mouth of the Murray. The upper Murray in South Australia, also known in tourist brochures as Riverland, proudly boasts of prodigious wine and fruit production, but though this may be the wine capital of Australia in terms of volume, production is mostly concentrated into the vast industrial vats of only a handful of characterless wineries. Save your tasting days for the nearby Clare or Barossa valleys.

Ins and outs

Air *Kendell* have daily flights to **Renmark**. **Bus** *Murray Bridge Passenger Service*, T8415 5579, have up to 5 buses daily from **Adelaide** to **Murray Bridge**. One Mon-Fri service continues to **Tailem Bend** and on to **Meningie** and a connection from that service heads for **Mannum**. There are no connections between these and the upper river towns. *Premier Stateliner*, T8415 5555, run up to 3 buses daily from **Adelaide**, through **Gawler** and **Nuriootpa**, to **Blanchetown**, **Waikerie**, **Kingston-on-Murray**, **Barmera**, **Berri**, **Renmark** and Loxton.

Getting there & around

The main town in an agricultural area dominated by dairy farming, there's little here to excite the visitor, though there are opportunities for good value adventure activities such as go-karting, kayaking, parachuting and scenic flights. *Murray Bridge Backpackers*, has teamed up with *Groovy Grape* to offer three days of kayaking, waterskiing, and nocturnal bushwalking for $140, two nights accommodation and transfer to and from Adelaide included. *Groovy Grape* also offer a day of watersports for $65, including transport from Adelaide if required, book at the backpackers. *Murray Bridge Flying School* has reasonably priced scenic flights ($45-110) over the Murray, Coorong and Victor Harbor during whale season, T8531 1744. The VIC is on South Terrace, just to the south of main Bridge Street. ■ *Mon-Fri 0830-1730, Sat-Sun 1000-1600. T8532 6660, F8532 5288, g.braendler@rcmb.sa.gov.au*

Murray Bridge
Colour map 1, grid B3
Population: 13,500
74 km from Adelaide,
198 km from
Renmark, 360 km
from Mt Gambier

Sleeping and eating Aside from various motels there are 2 budget options. **C-E** *The Balcony*, 12 Sixth St, T8531 1411. Friendly first floor budget accommodation just off Bridge St. Great balcony, linen and free breakfast but no kitchen or laundry. **E** *Murray Bridge Backpackers*, 1 McKay Rd, T8532 6994, www.mbbackpackershostel.com.au Newer and with more facilities, though 3 km from town and beside the railway line. Almost obsessively clean, friendly family-run hostel, linen and pickups. Can also help with seasonal work, bike hire and kayaking tours.

Transport *Murray Bridge Passenger Service* buses leave from outside the VIC 1530 Mon-Fri for **Mannum**, **Tailem Bend** and **Meningie**. Services leave for **Adelaide** 0700, 0900, 1100 and 1430 Mon-Fri, also 1700 Fri, 0800 and 1530 Sat, 1700 Sun (1-1½ hrs). *McCafferty's/Greyhound* bus to **Melbourne** leaves daily (on request only) at 0900 and 2145. Buses to **Adelaide** (request only) leave at 0525 and 1700.

Though fairly charmless, little **Blanchetown** is worth a stop to see the pelicans at Lock 1, built in 1922 as the starting point of the river's lock and weir system. *Premier Stateliner* buses leave from outside the BP roadhouse at Blanchetown for stops to Renmark and Adelaide. The *McCafferty's/Greyhound* Sydney bus leaves at 1305 daily; the Adelaide bus leaves at 1200. About 50 km away is the 1,100 ha **Yookamurra Sanctuary** wildlife reserve, a haven for a diverse range of native fauna and flora. Visitors are welcome for Sunday ($12-20) and fascinating stays which include nocturnal walks Wednesday and Saturday. T8562 5011, yooka@esl.com.au

Blanchetown & Yookamurra Sanctuary
Blanchetown: Colour map 1, grid B3
60 km from Barossa,
40 km from Waikerie

Morgan was set up in 1878 as a railhead to short cut the lower Murray and speed the rich produce of the interior down to Port Adelaide. The town enjoyed over 60 years of prosperity and the line stayed open until 1969, but any hopes of cashing in on the Murray tourist traffic were dashed when the rail lines were taken up. So the town remains a backwater and ironically one of the most authentic and pleasant river towns. The **Railway Museum** has a small

Morgan
Colour map 1, grid B3
40 km from
Blanchetown, 40 km
from Waikerie, 80 km
from Burra

South Australia

▶▶ **Don't hurry on the Murray**

A visit to the Murray should really entail staying on the river and this is perfectly possible with a little planning. A couple can do this relatively economically outside of the summer peak season, and groups will find some houseboats seriously good value. A much more expensive, but more rewarding option is to book onto one of the paddle boats that offer overnight trips, such as the **Proud Mary**, *based at Murray Bridge (T8231 9472, www.proudmary.com.au, 2,- 3- and 5-night tours from Murray Bridge and Blanchetown at a little over $600 per couple per night), or* **Murray Princess** *at Mannum (T02-9206 1122, www.captaincook.com.au, 2- and 5-day cruises for around $450 per couple per night). There are hundreds of houseboats available for hire on the Murray, and anyone* keen to appreciate the river from its best vantage point should seriously consider getting out on one for a few days. Most houseboats are the size of small aircraft carriers, and have been designed to cater for groups or large families, but there are also smaller and less expensive options. A week in a 8-10 berth houseboat out of season should cost around $1,000, while a four-berth should be around $700. They are all part of the **Houseboat Hirers Association** *(T8395 0999, www.houseboat-centre.com.au), who are happy to help with choosing or booking a boat. An over-18 'captain' with driver's or boat licence is required, and a large amount of booty for deposit and bond. Boats travel an average of 7 kmph, so reckon on about 35 km a day maximum.*

collection of railway and paddle steamer memorabilia. ■ *Daily 1000-1200, 1300-1500. $2 donation, children free. T8540 2136.* On the other side of the museum is the well-preserved and massive town wharf, where loaders once worked 24 hours a day transfering produce from steamer to train. The pubs and a caravan park have accommodation. The **D** *Commercial*, T8540 2107, has the better rooms, while the **E** *Terminus*, has a preferable bar and cheap dining area with Friday night cheap specials.

Waikerie & around
Colour map 1, grid B3
Population: 5,000
100 km from the Barossa, 75 km from Renmark

This large service town has little to recommend it other than an unusual way of viewing the Murray from the air. Various climatic and geographic factors combine to make the town one of the best **gliding** spots in Australia. *Waikerie International Soaring Centre*, east on the Sturt Highway, T8541 2644, wisc@riverland.net.au, offer 20-minute scenic passenger flights for $65 and 15 minute head-spinning, stomach-churning acrobatic flights for $110. You can even go solo after a seven-day course, $228 per day includes four flights. There is on-site accommodation (**D-E**) for students.

Some 30 km from Waikerie, 3 km short of the tiny town of Kingston-on-Murray, is Banrock Station. This well-known winery was set up by the giant *BRL Hardy* in 1995, but keeps true to its original aim of preserving and regenerating local and national wetland using the profits of the winemaking. There are also informative walks through mallee, vineyards and wetland. The wonderful café on the verandah serves inventive cheap light lunches using healthy native and local produce, daily 1100-1500, book on summer weekends. ■ *Tastings 1000-1700. T8583 0299, www.banrockstation.com*

Sleeping and eating C *Jo's*, The Avenue, T/F 8541 3491, is an unremarkable but reasonable B&B within walking distance of town. The **D** *Waikerie* pub, McCoy St, T8541 3104, has a fairly creative cheap menu served in a very ordinary dining room. They have live music occasionally. The **D-E** *Waikerie Caravan Park*, Peake Terr, T8541 2651, has on-site vans and en suite cabins. The town has a wide range of deli cafés and takeaways.

Murray worries

The Murray is part of the Murray-Darling river basin, covering over 1 mn sq km, the sixth largest catchment in the world. That's 14% of Australia's surface area and twice the size of France. Its longest stretch, from the head of the Condamine in Queensland to Murray Mouth is 3,750 km long, making it the fourth longest river system in the world.

Within 20 year's of Charles Sturt's 1830 journey down the great river, confirming that it reached the southern ocean, New South Wales, Victoria and South Australia were squabbling over this valuable resource. But first the river flow had to be made predictable, so a series of great weirs and locks were put in place from the junction of the Murray and Darling down to the mouth at Lake Alexandrina. Here a barrage system was put in place to prevent the sea's salt water from getting too far upstream. Dead, sunken river red gums, nicknamed snags, were continually dredged out and the European carp introduced. Tamed, the Murray was now permanently navigable, largely salt-free and dependable amounts of water could be drawn from it for irrigation and drinking. Agriculture boomed and the system now waters about 40% of the country's produce and supplies drinking water to over a million people.

Now, though, the Darling and lower Murray are no longer crystal clear streams, but opaque and brown from sediments stirred up by the carp run-off from the adjacent land, much of it now cleared and dusty. Agricultural pollutants and diseases such as Giardia now make it too dangerous to drink directly – take care while swimming – even at the Murray's source, high in the Alps. Other rivers, such as the legendary Snowy have been diverted and ecologically sacrificed to help maintain the main flow, but even so barely 20% of the basin's run-off reaches the ocean. Native fish and crustacean populations have plummeted, thanks to the carp, unnatural water flows and the lack of wooden debris underwater. Bird populations are suffering in turn. Vast areas once nourished by periodic flooding are now either permanently underwater, creating the distinctive landscapes of 'drowned gums', or are drying out, critically damaging the rich biodiversity along the rivers' margins. Increased salination means that the water may be too salty to drink, even once treated, in as little as 20 years.

However, there is hope. Envirnomental campaigners are beginning to be heard. New South Wales, South Australia and Victoria currently limit water extraction to 1993 levels, though Queensland ducked out of the agreement, triggering an outburst of dam-building in the late 1990s to support their lucrative cotton industry. The scale of the crisis has been recognized by the media, the agricultural industry and local people alike. It is unlikely the rivers will ever return to their original state but the first tentative steps are being taken to save the river once proudly called the 'mighty Murray'.

Transport *Premier Stateliner* buses leave from outside the shell service Station for stops to **Renmark**, 1455 and 2010 Mon-Fri, 1455 Sat, 1340 and 2010 Sun. Services leave for **Adelaide** 0850, 1830 Mon-Fri, 0850 Sat, 1320 and 1720 Sun. *McCafferty's/Greyhound* bus to **Sydney** leaves (on request only) at 1335 daily; to **Adelaide** at 1100 (on request only).

Barmera sits on the shore of large **Lake Bonney**, not on the river. Donald Campbell attempted to break his own world water speed record here in 1964, but only managed to gain the Australian record with a speed of 216 mph. Would-be speedsters can hire a variety of craft in summer. Jetboats are available from the *Bluebird Café* at the eastern end of the long grassy foreshore, $50 per half hour, 0900-1800 October to April, and the *Lake Bonney Aquatic*

Barmera
Colour map 2, grid A1
Population: 1,800
29 km from Renmark,
45 km from Waikerie

South Australia

Centre, T8588 2677, daily November-May. *Riverland Leisure Canoe Tours*, Thelma Road, T8588 2053, offer a variety of guided creek and wetland tours from a single morning to two days.

Sleeping and eating D-E *Lake Bonney Holiday Park*, T8588 2234, has dozens of reasonable cabins and is good fun. *Bonneyview Winery*, on the Sturt Highway, T8588 2279, is an attractive bare-brick mid-range cellar door restaurant. Food 1200-1400 daily, 1830-2030 Fri-Sat, cellar door 1000-1500 daily. 13 km north of Barmera on the Old Coach Rd is D *Overland Corner* pub, T8588 7021, the oldest building in the area, which is worth a stop if travelling to or from Morgan. Cheap and mid-range meals available daily 1200-1400 and 1800-2000. 2 traditionally furnished bedrooms open directly onto one of the dining rooms.

Transport *Premier Stateliner* buses leave from the Travel Centre for stops to **Renmark**, 1530 and 2050 Mon-Fri, 1530 Sat, 1420 and 2050 Sun. Services leave for **Adelaide** 0810, 1755 Mon-Fri, 0810 Sat, 1240 and 1645 Sun. *McCafferty's/Greyhound* buses to **Sydney** leave (on request only) at 1410 daily, and to **Adelaide** at 1030.

Berri

Colour map 2, grid A1
Population: 7,000
18 km from Renmark,
21 km from Loxton,
61 km from Waikerie

The largest town servicing the enormous surrounding agricultural district, Berri acts as a focus for itinerant workers and backpackers looking for picking, packing and associated work. The town has few natural attractions other than the extensive grassed riverfront, where the main caravan park and houseboat moorings can be found. North of Berri, nearly opposite the awful Big Orange sign is **Wilabalangaloo**, a 100 ha native fauna and flora reserve with two good walking trails. ■ *Thu-Mon 1000-1600. $4, children $1. T8582 1804.* The **VIC**, is on Vaughan Terrace. ■ *Mon-Fri 0900-1700, Sat 0900-1130. T8582 1655, bookmark@riverland.net.au*

Sleeping and eating B-D *Berri Resort*, Riverview Dr, T8582 1411, F8582 2140, is a massive motel complex with unusually good facilities at competitive prices. The cheap food is particularly good value. E *Berri Backpackers*, on the Sturt Highway to Adelaide, T8582 3144, berribackpackers@asiaonline.net.au, has several dorms and double tree-house and tee-pee rooms as well as various outdoor and indoor games. Very busy in summer, they also act as an employment agency for those on working holidays and arrange work transport. Recommended. *Hamley House*, Berri Bypass Rd, T8582 2583. Imaginative mid-range modern Australian menu in large renovated 1930s house. Open 1200-1400, 1800-2000. Bookings required. *Dawn's Coffee Shop*, Wilson St. Good breakfasts, healthy sandwiches and light lunches, Mon 1000-1700, Tue-Fri 0800-1700, Sat 0800-1430.

Transport *Premier Stateliner* buses leave from Lyons Motors for **Renmark**, 1550 and 2110 Mon-Fri, 1550 Sat, 1440 and 2110 Sun. Services leave for **Adelaide** 0750 and 1735 Mon-Fri, 0750 Sat, 1220 and 1625 Sun. *McCafferty's/Greyhound* bus to **Sydney** at 1420 daily; to **Adelaide** at 1015.

Renmark

Colour map 2, grid A1
Population: 4,400
247 km from Adelaide, 198 km from Burra, 136 km from Mildura (Vic)

The modern town of Renmark, in the middle of a major fruit-growing area, is often bypassed by budget travellers and workers in favour of Berri, with their well set up backpacker hostels. However, it has the pick of Riverland's facilities, and makes a good base for non-working travellers exploring the Murray from Morgan up to Mildura in Victoria. The **VIC**, *Renmark Paringa Visitor Centre*, is on the riverbank opposite the *Renmark* community pub. ■ *Mon-Fri 0900-1700, Sat 0930-1600, Sun 1000-1400. T8586 6704, F8586 5444, tourist@riverland.net.au*

South Australia

The main sight is the river itself, and the best way to see it is from a paddle steamer. The lovingly-restored **PS Industry**, built in 1911, is taken out for a run by volunteers on the first Sunday of every month. ■ *Sun 1100, 1330, 1500 (90 mins). $15, concessions $12, children $7 (tea and scones included).* Book at the VIC where she is permanently moored and can also be visited during VIC hours. If the *PS Industry* is not running, the modern **Big River Rambler**, departs daily at 1400. ■ *T8595 1862. $23, tea and scones included, 2 hrs. Leaves from the town wharf, near the Post Office.*

Renmark also has one of riverland's best lookouts, **Headings Cliff**, Murtho Road, 14 km from Paringa (signposted), the view from the tower lookout is worth going out of your way to see, especially at sunrise or sunset. Sheer orange cliffs loom above a long stretch of river and trees, without a glimpse of human habitation. The 900,000 ha **Bookmark Biosphere Reserve** is a conservation area, comprising river, wetland, and mallee landscapes and largely enclosing the area around Renmark. Tours of this area are run by operators accredited by the *Bookmark Biosphere Trust*, including *Biotours SA*, T8595 3085, and *Bush and Backwaters*, T/F8586 5344, bbwaters@riverland.net.au

Sleeping B *Settler's Retreat*, Purnong St, T/F8595 5400, www.dove.net.au/ ~cammies self-contained house in 1 ha of bush, facing a creek. Catch your own dinner with yabbie pots and canoe provided. Linen supplied. **C** *Willows & Waterbirds*, 41 Murray Av, T8295 8836, elemail@senet.com.au Large self-contained and comfortable 100-year-old house, just east of the VIC. No linen supplied. **C-D** *Renmark*, Murray Av, T8586 6755, F8586 6186, mail@renmarkhotel.com.au Massive community-owned pub with 30 rooms, 37 more spacious motel rooms, balconies with river views. **D** *Chowilla Station*, Wentworth Rd, Chowilla. T/F8595 8048, chowilla@riverland.net.au 40 km north of Renmark, has shearers' quarters that sleep 25 in bunks Designed for groups but good value for 3-4 if vacant, booking exclusive to hirer with $55 min, otherwise $12pp. self-contained, no linen supplied. Also offers 4WD tours of the Bookmark Biosphere Reserve.

Accommodation in Renmark mostly consists of motels. No B&Bs but there are a few interesting self-catering options

Eating *Tower Tavern*, Jane Eliza Estate, T8586 4477. Best place in town for a lazy Sun brunch or dinner on a warm evening. Café lunches, cheap bistro menu or mid-range modern Australian cuisine. Daily 1200-1400, 1830-2030. Sun brunch 0900-1100. *Renmark Club*, Murray Av, T8586 6611. Overlooks the river. Cheap steak and schnitzel bistro meals. Seriously cheap members nights on Tue, Thu. All meals $7.50. Book for 'members nights'. Daily 1200-1330, 1800-2100. *Café Toppo Ristorante*, Murray Av, T8586 5241, is a good cheap Italian which also does takeaway pasta and sauces. Wed-Fri 1200-1700, Tue-Sat 1730-2030. *Director's Café*, 14th St, near the corner of Renmark Av, T8586 3099. A friendly place for coffee or lunch, popular with locals.

Transport Air *O'Connor Airlines*, T8723 0666, www.oconnor-airlines.com.au, have flights to Adelaide daily, Mon-Fri 1010, 1830. Sat 0845, Sun 1700 (30 mins, $143). **Bus** *Premier Stateliner* runs daily services from the Stateliner Office to **Adelaide**, Mon-Fri 0730, 1710, Sat 0730, Sun 1200, 1600 ($35, 4 hrs). Book at the VIC or T8415 5555. *McCafferty's/Greyhound* leave daily for **Sydney** at 1420, and to **Adelaide** at 1015.

Set back from a large wooded bend in the Murray, Loxton has a wide range of facilities. The **VIC** is on the central roundabout. ■ *Mon-Fri 0900-1700, Sat 0930-1230 and Sun 1300-1600, T8584 7919.* **Loxton Historical Village** is a collection of mostly authentic, transplanted shops and utility buildings, populated with second-hand dummies. ■ *Mon-Fri 1000-1600, Sat-Sun 1000-1700. $8, children $4, concessions $6. T8584 7194.*

Loxton
Colour map 2, grid B1
Population: 3,300
40 km from Renmark, 171 km from Murray Bridge

South Australia

The Southeast

Check www.thelime
stonecoast.com

*The southeast is an agricultural area of flat cleared land, gently interrupted by low ripples of hill ranges. The area is better known as the **Limestone Coast** and limestone is indeed at the core of many of its attractions. Jagged cliffs of eroding limestone run down the coast from Cape Jaffa, punctuated by sleepy crayfishing ports. The limestone caves of **Narracoorte** are a World Heritage Site, where creatures have been tumbling down sinkholes for at least 400,000 years leaving a fossil bed of overwhelming richness for palaeontologists. Limestone also lies underneath the rich red soil of the **Coonawarra** wine region and above the surface in the pretty seaport of **Robe**, most of which is built out of the stuff. **Mount Gambier** is best known for the surreal blue water of its crater lake but the city has literally been built on top of impressive limestone caves and sinkholes. The exception to the north is the stunning **Coorong National Park**.*

Ins and outs

Getting there

See also 'Mount
Gambier Transport',
page 770

Air Mount Gambier is the principal town of the southeastern area and has an airport 10 km to the north. *Kendell* and local airline *O'Connor*, T8723 0666, have up to 4 flights a day from **Adelaide** and **Melbourne**. **Bus** From Adelaide *Premier Stateliner*, T8415 5555, run services along 2 routes down to **Mount Gambier**. The coastal route leaves **Adelaide** 0815 Mon-Thu, 0745 and 1730 Fri, 1445 Sun. It stops at **Crafers***, **Murray Bridge***, **Tailem Bend***, **Meningie**, **Kingston**, **Robe**, **Beachport** and **Millicent**. The inland service leaves 0815 Mon-Sat, additionally at 1730 Thu-Fri, 1445 Sun, and calls at **Crafers***, **Murray Bridge**, **Tailem Bend***, **Coomandook***, **Coonalpyn**, **Tintinara**, **Keith**, **Bordertown**, **Padthaway***, **Naracoorte** and **Penola** (*stops on request only). **Interstate** *V~Line* have a daily service from **Melbourne** to **Mount Gambier**, T136196. **Car Hire** The larger global companies have offices at **Mount Gambier Airport** and the city.

Meningie & around

Colour map 1, grid C3
Population 400
74 km from Murray Bridge, 142 km from Kingston (SE)

On the shores of **Lake Albert**, the southern cousin of Lake Alexandrina, Meningie is a popular local stopover for sailing and fishing. It is also the nearest town to the **Coorong National Park**. The **parks office** is on the main street, Princes Highway. ■ *Mon, Wed, Fri 0900-1700, T8575 1200, www.parks.sa.gov.au* Park entry permits also available at the **VIC**, also on Princes Highway. ■ *Mon-Fri 0900-1700, T8575 1259.*

South of Meningie, 10 km down the Princes Highway, is **D-E** *Camp Coorong*, T8575 1557, a cultural and interpretative centre run by the local **Ngarrindjeri** Aboriginal people. The centre has a small cultural museum but it is the people here who make a visit memorable. There is also accommodation to suit most budgets and an excellent camp kitchen. Phone ahead. About 16 km from *Camp Coorong* is **Hack's Point**, an impressive viewpoint. On a high part of the promontory overlooking a narrow stretch of lagoon and the dunes opposite is **C-E** *Coorong Wilderness Lodge*, T8575 6001, a large fish-shaped café with wood cabins adjacent and dotted around the promontory (open Friday-Wednesday 0900-1600). The owners also offer excellent and fascinating **kayaking and bushwalking** trips over to the peninsula ($90 for a full day, over 12s only), and hire out kayaks, $15 half day, $25 full day.

Coorong National Park

This long thin park comprises the finger of dunes known as **Younghusband Peninsula**, the long series of lagoons between the peninsula and the mainland, and much of the mainland shore. Although four times more salty than the ocean, the lagoons are rich in fish and small marine animals and attract

South Australia

over two hundred species of birds, often in large flocks. The serene beauty of the park is best appreciated on foot or by boat. Various stretches of the park can be trekked, and there are many camping grounds, particularly at the southern end. It is advised to avoid driving on the peninsula. The area is of particular significance to the local Ngarrindjeri people, whose ancestors used the dune systems for their summer camps. Huge and ancient shell **middens** are easily disturbed, not to mention the remains of countless generations of people buried here.

Tours of the park *Coorong Nature Tours* run a fairly hurried but wide-ranging day-tour down the full length of the Coorong, and also into the adjacent **Messent Conservation Park**. Departs Adelaide 0630, Meningie 0830, T8574 0037, www.lm.net.au/~coorongnat They will also act as a set-down, pick-up service for long-distance **trekkers**. The **kayaking** trips from *Coorong Wilderness Lodge* are recommended. There are various boat tours available from **Goolwa** (see page 742), and scenic flights from **Murray Bridge** (see page 759).

Larry the Lobster rears up to welcome visitors to Kingston SE, one of Australia's curious collection of oversized 'sculptures' of food and animals. From the ridiculous to the sublime, Kingston also has some superb sculptures of sea creatures by Silvio Apponyi near the analemmetic sundial, on the foreshore at the northern entrance to town. *Kingston Dive & Charter*, T8767 2072, offer a variety of fishing, diving or simply cruising options on their 6-m boat, while *Cape Jaffa Charters*, T8768 5050, run scenic cruises and tailored fishing trips. The town has most amenities, a caravan park and pubs with accommodation including the jolly **D** *Royal Mail*, Hanson St, T8767 2002, offering a good menu with cheap standard pub fare daily 1200-1400, 1800-2100, and live music Saturday nights. On the road to Cape Jaffa is **Butcher's Gap Conservation Park**, designated in 1983 to protect the last remaining patch of coastal scrub between the Coorong and Robe, with interesting walks of around 1-2 hours.

Kingston SE

Sitting on the southern tip of Guichen Bay, Robe's turquoise-blue waters and sandy beaches make it a popular summer holiday spot for both South Australians and Victorians. It's long been an important crayfishing port though little remains of the port's history except many old houses built of local limestone. A brochure for a town walking tour can be obtained from the **VIC** which doubles as a library and has a display of historic photographs of Robe. ■ *Mon-Fri 0900-1700, Sat-Sun 1000-1600. T8768 2465. Mundy Terr, opposite the foreshore.* **Long Beach** is the best swimming and surfing beach although unfortunately it sometimes looks like a car park as driving on the beach is permitted. To really get out in the fresh air and see Robe the most unusual option is a **Tiger Moth** flight. Two former air force training planes are operated by Captain Boggles who takes vistors on scenic or aerobatic flights. ■ *Daily, from $60 for 10 mins, T8768 2989.*

Robe
Colour map 1,
grid C3
Population 850
41 km from Kingston
SE, 44 km
from Beachport
www.robe.sa.gov.au

Little Dip Conservation Park is a small coastal strip just south of Robe which preserves areas of sand dunes, cliffs and small salty lakes. Two loop walks wind through coastal mallee, melaleuca groves, rushes and samphire flats surrounding the lakes. The Freshwater Lake walk is about 2 km, the Big Dip and Lake Eliza walk is 5 km and daytime walkers can expect to see a host of waterbirds. At night take a torch fitted with a filter to see wombats, possums and swamp wallabies. ■ *Free entry, camping $6, pay at self-registration stations in the park. Enquiries to National Parks Office, Smillie St, T8768 2543, often closed when rangers are working in the park*

South Australia

Sleeping and eating B *Christmas and Victoria Cottages*, T8768 2216, www.robe.sa.gov.au/wilsons Fresh, country-style self-contained houses in the centre of town. **B-C** *Robe House*, 1a Hagen St, T/F8768 2770, www.robehouse.com.au This grand stone house is the oldest in town with 4 self-contained apartments of great quality, period style and value. **B- D** *Caledonian Inn*, Victoria St, T8768 2029, caled@seol.net.au Good value rooms upstairs in the 1850s stone inn with patchwork quilts and iron beds. **D** *Bowman and Campbell Cottages*, 22-26 Smillie St, T8768 2236, www.robe.sa.gov.au/bowman Old stone terrace hides modern self-contained apartments. **D-E** *Bushland Cabins*, corner of Main Rd and Nora Creina Rd, T8768 2386, bushland@seol.net.au Simple en suite cabins set in 25 acres of bush ½ km from town.

Grey Masts, 1 Smillie St, T8768 2203. Fresh and interesting mid-range food is offered in a series of simple wooden rooms hung with works by local artists. Wed-Mon 1830-2100. *Imaj*, Victoria St, T8768 2081. A vibrant and friendly place for all-day breakfasts, cheap pizza, pasta, curries, sandwiches and takeaways. Summer daily 0900-2100, Winter Wed-Mon 0900-2000. *Wild Mulberry*, 46 Victoria St, T8768 2488. Good coffee, breakfasts and lunches in a licensed café with garden tables. Daily 0800-1700.

Transport The *Premier Stateliner* service leaves the BP service station, just east of town on Victoria St, for **Adelaide** at 0956 Mon-Fri, 1326 Sat, 1626 Fri, Sun (4½ hrs). The southbound service to **Mount Gambier** leaves at 1250 Mon-Thu, 1220 and 2205 Fri, 1920 Sun (1 hr 40 mins). Local bookings T8768 2019.

Beachport
Colour map 1, grid C3
Population 450
44 km from Robe,
32 km from Millicent

Surrounded by water on three sides, it is not surprising that this is a town consumed by water activities; fishing, surfing, swimming, sailing and even floating in the salt lake, **Pool of Siloam**. With Lake George at its back, the western coast is a wild and beautiful strip where breakers attack the eroded limestone bluffs and golden beaches, best seen from **Post Office Rock** lookout on the signposted **scenic drive**. Adjacent to the rock is a superb swimming beach. Like Robe, Beachport is heavily visited at holiday times, mostly by Victorians, especially in January and at Easter. The **VIC** has information on the many local walking trails. ■ *Daily 0900-1700. Millicent Rd, T8735 8029, F8735 8309.*

Sleeping and eating **C-D** *Bompa's by the Sea*, 3 Railway Terr, T8735 8333. This big old stone ex-pub facing the foreshore has spacious, comfortable and good value rooms, the more expensive are en suite with balcony overlooking the sea. The bistro serves good simple meals from fresh ingredients, cheap lunches, afternoon snacks and mid-range dinners. Recommended. **D** *Harbourmaster's House*, Beach Rd, T8735 8197. Recently renovated budget accomodation in a limestone cottage, great location right next to the water. There are also 2 caravan parks, a post office, petrol and a couple of general stores. Takeaways from *The Green Room*, 18 Railway Terr, where you can also hire a surfboard.

Transport The *Premier Stateliner* service leaves the Rivoli Bay Deli for **Adelaide** at 0919 Mon-Fri, 1249 Sat, 1549 Fri, Sun (5 hrs). The southbound service to **Mount Gambier** leaves at 1328 Mon-Thu, 1258 and 2243 Fri, 1958 Sun (1 hr). Local bookings T8735 8122.

Millicent
& around

Millicent loses out as a tourist destination to the string of ports just to the north and as a result there's little accommodation or interesting dining here. It does, however, have a fascinating **Living History Museum** at the **Tourist Information Centre**. The museum's large collections include agricultural machinery, horsedrawn vehicles and domestic items from the 1850s to 1930s, as well as a shipwreck display and Aboriginal area with replica rock art. ■ *Mon- Fri 0900-1700, Sat-Sun 0930-1630. $5.50, concessions $4. T8733 3205, 1 Mt Gambier Rd.*

South Australia

About 13 km west of town, **Canunda National Park** is a stark and striking area for walking and four-wheel driving. The park begins with sculpted cliffs at Cape Buffon, just below **Southend**, a tiny settlement at the southern end of Rivoli Bay. *Cookie's Bushranger Tours*, T8735 6132, run 4WD tours of the park, ½ day $40, full day $95. ■ *Free entry, camping $6, pay at self-registration stations in the park. Maps and information from National Parks Office, Cape Buffon Dr, T8735 6053.* **Tantanoola Caves**, 23 km away, are home to some of Australia's most beautiful natural cave formations. ■ *Tours daily, hourly from 0915, 1200, 1315 and hourly 1400 to 1600. $7, children $4, concessions $5. T8734 4153. Wheelchair access.*

The major draw of this central agricultural town is the nearby caves, although one resident has created his very own attraction in **The Snake Pit**, which features a collection of reptilia as well as a mind-bogglingly eclectic display of everything from key fobs to cacti. ■ *Mon-Thu 1000-1700, Fri 1000-1300, Sat-Sun 1400-1700. $7.50, children $4, concessions $6. North end of Jenkins St, T8762 2059.* **The Sheep's Back Museum** has recreated all manner of scenes depicting historical wool production, and it also doubles up as the **VIC**. ■ *Daily 0900-1600. $5, children $2, concessions $4. Macdonnell St, T1800-244421.*

About 15 km south of Naracoorte is the **Naracoorte Caves National Park**, a World Heritage Site consisting of 26 separate caves, four of which are open to the public, including the fascinating **Victoria Fossil**, the cave that principally attracted World Heritage status. All the limestone caves have some excellent examples of cave decoration such as stalactites and stalagmites, but the first of over 20 **fossil beds** in the caves was found in Victoria Fossil. A natural chimney opened down to the cave, stayed open for about two hundred thousand years and closed up around 213,000 years ago according to current dating estimates. While it was open thousands of animals from over a hundred different species managed to tumble in and their bones have mixed with sediment to form a paleontologist's Chistmas pudding. ■ *Tours daily 0930-1530, Victoria Fossil 1015 and 1415. $9, children $5.50, concessions $7, multiple tours attract discounts. Novice adventure tours $22, min 4 people, advanced adventure tours $200 per group. T8762 2340, F8762 1231.* The **Wonambie Fossil Centre** displays a few megafauna fossils and also has a superb animatronic display. ■ *Daily 0900-1630. $9, children $5.50, concessions $7, includes self-guided tour of Wet Cave.*

Naracoorte
Colour map 2, grid B1
Population 4,700
260 km from Murray Bridge, 101 km from Mount Gambier

Sleeping **C** *Shepherd's Cave*, 3 km north off Sandstone Av, T8762 0246. self-contained 2-bedroom apartment in the modern home of local scrap metal and wood sculptor. Great rural setting, pool, bush walks. Good value. Recommended. **C-D** *Naracoorte*, Ormerod St, T8762 2400. Refurbished pub with 14 basic upstairs rooms and 14 motel rooms. Also mid-range menu daily 1200-1400, 1800-2030. **E** *Naracoorte Backpackers*, Jones St, T/F 8762 3835, nctebackpackers@dove.net.au Slightly tired hostel but very friendly and helpful owners make for a homely feel. They'll help find work in local wineries and agriculture, and organize transport. Bikes, linen included, tours arranged. Recommended.

Transport The *Premier Stateliner* service leaves Naracoorte Battery Service, at the eastern end of Smith St, for **Adelaide** at 0930 Mon-Sat, 1830 Fri, 1600 Sun (5 hrs). The southbound service to **Mount Gambier** leaves at 1315 Mon-Sat, 2230 Thu-Fri, 1945 Sun (75 mins). Local bookings T8762 2466.

Coonawarra wine region

Hours generally
1000-1700 daily

Of the many wineries scattered around the Southeast, over 20 are concentrated around the tiny hamlet of **Coonawarra** and along the 10-km stretch of highway south to **Penola**. *Cabernet* and *Sauvignon* were the varieties originally pioneered in the area. Most of the wineries here are small and family run. *S. Kidman*, 2 km north of Coonawarra, T8736 5070, is run by a husband and wife team on their cattle and sheep station. There are great stands of red gums here as successive owners have not cut the trees since the 1880s. In **Coonawarra** itself is the oldest of the areas wineries, *Wynns Coonawarra*, T8726 8255. Established in 1896, now owned by *Southcorp*, though still independently run. the wines are excellent and the premiums such as the *Michael Shiraz*, made from the best 1% of grapes in good years, quite stunning. South of Coonawarra *Majella* is a striking new winery producing some good reds. T8736 3055, open to 1630. *Balnaves* have won awards for their contemporary architecture and have a boardwalk area overlooking a pond that makes a great picnic spot. T8737 2946.

Penola
Colour map 2, grid C1
Population 1,200
50 km from
Naracoorte, 51 km
from Mount Gambier,
51 km from Millicent

This small agricultural town is a good base for touring caves and wineries. A five-minute walk from the centre leads to **Petticoat Lane** which has a scattering of cottages dating from the 1850s-60s. They include **Sharam's Cottage**, actually two adjacent 'slab' cottages fascinatingly preserved from around the turn of the century. On the corner of the lane is the **Mary MacKillop Penola Centre**, with displays celebrating the lives of Blessed Mary MacKillop and Friar Julian Tenison Woods, who built and taught in the stone schoolhouse on the corner of Petticoat Lane in the 1860s. ■ *Daily 1000-1600, $3.50, children free. T8737 2092.* The **VIC** is on Arthur Street. ■ *Mon-Fri 0900-1700, Sat 1000-1700, Sun 0930-1600. T8737 2855, F8737 2251.*

Sleeping and eating The town has several B&B's, but only one personally hosted, the **C** *Old Rectory*, 5 Bowden St, T8737 2684, F8737 2064. Cooked breakfast. Good value. **E** *McKays Trek Inn*, Riddoch St, T1800 626 844. A small unkempt backpackers in the centre of town. For those with transport try *Whiskas Woolshed*, Glen Yallum Rd, T8737 2428. Simple bunks in a converted shearing shed, 15 km down the Millicent Rd. There is a caravan park with budget cabins on the corner of South Terr. The best restaurant in the Coonawarra is *Pipers*, Riddoch St, T8737 3999. Superb restaurant with cheap asian lunch menu, afternoon tapas and expensive modern Australian evening dining in a beautifully restored community hall. Open daily 1100-1430, 1500-1830, 1830-2130.

Transport The *Premier Stateliner* service leaves the Penola Supermarket for **Adelaide** at 0853 Mon-Sat, 1753 Fri, 1523 Sun (5½ hrs). The southbound to **Mount Gambier** leaves at 1353 Mon-Sat, 2308 Thu-Fri, 2023 Sun (40 mins). Local bookings T8737 2166.

Mount Gambier

Colour map 2, grid C1
Population 23,000
435 km from Adelaide,
156 km from Kingston
SE, 132 km from
Hamilton (VIC)

From the volcanic slopes of the **Blue Lake**, Mount Gambier sprawls over the plain below. Though a large commercial city, its caves and volcanic crater lakes make it an unlikely tourist attraction. The very efficient **Lady Nelson Visitor & Discovery Centre** is an imaginative museum of local history and geology. ■ *Daily 0900-1700, T8724 9750, F8723 2833, www.mountgambiertourism.com.au Jubilee Highway East, look for large ship replica outside. Discovery Centre. Tours from 0900-1615. $8, children $4, concessions $7.*

The **Cave Garden** is a deep narrow sinkhole smack in the middle of the city, **Sights** surrounded by lawns and roses, and a popular lunch spot for local workers. ■ *Watson Terr. Free.* **Engelbrecht Cave** is not as impressive as the nearby Tantanoola or Narracoorte caves but it is a good opportunity to see a cave underneath a city centre. ■ *Tours daily on the hour, 1100-1500, 45 min. $5.50, children $2.50. T8725 5493, Jubilee Highway West, 1½ km from city centre, Hospital bus route goes most of the way there, North West bus loop back to town.* **Umpherston Sinkhole** is an impressively large hole in the ground, 3 km east of the city centre. Plants spill down the sides of this collapsed cave and ivy curtains reach all the way to the bottom. There used to be water in the bottom but thanks to a falling water table dry these days and there is a staircase down into the sinkhole. The garden is floodlit at night and often frequented by possums. Large gardens surrounding the sinkhole have picnic areas and BBQs. ■ *Jubilee Highway East, North East bus loop goes most of the way.* **Blue Lake** is a deep pool in the centre of an extinct volcano crater 2½ km from the city centre. It is best known for changing its grey-green winter appearance in November for luminous turquoise in summer and changing back again in March. There are several lookouts above the lake and a 4-km circular walk around the rim. ■ *Lake and pumping station tours daily on the hour 0900-1200, later in summer. $5.50, children $2. T8723 1199, John Watson Dr, South East bus loop.* The **Valley Lake** stays grey-green all year. There are some superb walks in the hills, as well as a free **Wildlife Park** next to the lake with walking trails and boardwalks. There are emus, kangaroos, wallabies, wombats, koalas and echidnas

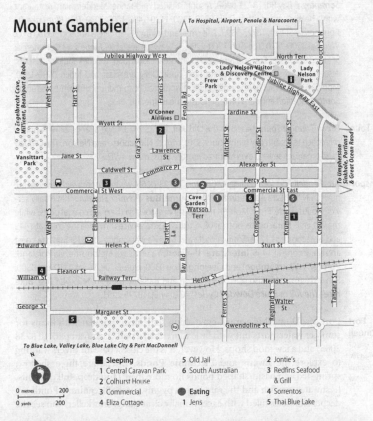

Mount Gambier

To Hospital, Airport, Penola & Naracoorte

South Australia

	Sleeping		5 Old Jail	2 Jontie's
	1 Central Caravan Park		6 South Australian	3 Redfins Seafood
	2 Colhurst House			& Grill
	3 Commercial		● Eating	4 Sorrentos
	4 Eliza Cottage		1 Jens	5 Thai Blue Lake

0 metres 200
0 yards 200

To Blue Lake, Valley Lake, Blue Lake City & Port MacDonnell

in the park, many are easily visible. **Mount Schank**, 20 minutes drive south of the city, is a perfect crater rising sharply to 158 m above the plains. Naturally there are great views for those who make the steep climb to the top, and the walk continues down into the centre.

Sleeping

There is a very good range of budget accommodation in Mount Gambier, including cheap rooms in many of the 20-odd motels and some hotels

B *Eliza*, 30 Wehl St South, T/F8725 0335. Luxurious self-contained colonial cottage with antique furniture. **C** *Colhurst House*, 3 Colhurst Pl, T8723 1309, F8723 1238. Hosted B&B in an elegant Victorian mansion. All en suite. Good value. **D-E** *The Jail*, Margaret St, T8723 0032, www.adelaide.net.au/~turnkey A prison until 1995, now a 100-bed NOMADS hostel. Twins are preferable to the crowded dorms and kitchen/bathroom facilities are thinly spread, but breakfast is included, there are seriously cheap dinners and a lively 24-hr bar. Good range of tours available. **E** *Commercial Hotel*, Commercial St West, T8725 3006. Basic but clean pub rooms with a cheap deal for backpackers. **E** *South Australian*, Commercial St West, T8725 2404. Pleasant pub with 10 clean rooms, the best deal in town for single rooms. **D-E** *Central Caravan Park*, 6 Krummel St, T8725 4427, is an easy walk to town and has very cheap clean vans and cabins, or head for the pricier but more picturesque **C-E** *Blue Lake City*, by the turn-off to Elliott Dr, T1800 676028, which has excellent facilities and couldn't be better placed for walking around the lakes area.

Eating

Redfins Seafood and Grill, 2 Commercial St West, T8725 0611. Lots of blond wood and shiny surfaces in this stylish restaurant. Mid-range seafood and steaks, and cheap foccacia, salad and pasta lunches. Also good breakfasts. Mon-Sat 0700-1500, 1800-2200. *Sorrentos*, 6 Bay Rd, T8723 0900. A sophisticated mid-range 'Mediterrasian' restaurant with a heated conservatory. Daily 0800-1100, 1130-1400, 1800-2030. *Thai Blue Lake*, 92 Commercial St East, T8723 9393. This small and sunny cheap café is not licensed so BYO. Wed-Sat 1200-1420, Tue-Sun 1700-2200. Takeaways available. *Jontie's*, 13 Commercial St East, T8723 9499. Fun and funky café with great casual food, couches and newspapers. Also joined to slick **internet** room next door. Daily breakfast and lunch 0930-1500, Mon-Sat 1730-2130. All the pubs have reasonable cheap menus, and some, including *South Australian* and *Jens* have seriously cheap specials.

Tours

Green Triangle Tours, based at the **Old Jail**, T8725 7413, have a range of well-priced day coach tours and city night tours ($10), trips to **Naracoorte** and **Nelson**. The *Old Jail* itself organizes several overnight adventure trips, many 4WD.

Transport

Air *Kendell* and local airline *O'Connor*, T8723 0666, www.oconnor-airlines.com.au, have daily flights to **Adelaide** and **Melbourne**. **Bus** *Premier Stateliner* have daily services to **Adelaide**. From Mon-Fri the 791 service goes via the main coastal ports, while the 781 is via **Naracoorte**, both at 0815 (6 hrs). Extra services on Fri via the coast at 1445 and Naracoorte at 1715. Sat, via coast at 1145, via Naracoorte at 0815. Sun, via coast and Naracoorte at 1445. **Interstate** *V~Line* run a service to **Melbourne**, via **Portland**, **Port Fairy**, **Warrnambool** and **Geelong**, Mon 0300, Mon-Fri 0820, Sat 0330 and 0800, Sun 1325 (6½ hrs). Also one to **Hamilton** and **Ballarat**. Mon-Fri 1425 (4½ hrs). **Bike hire** *The Jail* or *Bruce Dowdell Cycles*, 46 Gray St, T8725 2953.

Port MacDonnell

Colour map 2, grid C1
Population 700
30 km south of Mount Gambier

Port MacDonnell is a small crayfishing settlement, popular with locals for summer watersports but with little more than a pub, a caravan park (T8738 2085) and a few food shops. However, it is the closest base for divers wanting to explore the **Ewens** and **Piccannie Ponds**. Ewens are three shallow, spring-fed and basin-shaped ponds no more than 11 m deep, full of plants, freshwater crayfish and the rare Ewens pygmy perch. Piccaninnie Ponds are deeper sinkholes filled with exceptionally clear water. Snorkellers can see the

Chasm, a white walled entrance covered in delicate green algae, but divers can continue down into a large underwater cavern, known as The Cathedral because of its white walls of sculptured limstone. Both ponds are east of Port MacDonnell, signposted off the main highway to Nelson and Portland. Permits for Piccaninnie must be obtained from the National Parks Office, Mount Gambier. Dive and snorkel times are limited and divers must be members of the Cave Divers Association of Australia and rated at sinkhole level. Dive gear can be hired from *Smithy's Dive & Surf*, 63 Sea Parade, T8738 2225.

The Yorke Peninsula

Sticking out into the the Spencer Gulf like Jake's extra leg, the Yorke Peninsula is overwhelmingly given over to fishing and agriculture. The flat landscape, crisscrossed by uncompromisingly straight roads, can become monotonous, and most visitors quickly find their way to the swollen 'foot', known locally as the Bottom End. Copper was discovered here in 1859 and the area enjoyed a period of major importance until the price of the metal dropped in the 1920s. The relics enjoy considerable affection in the Copper Triangle towns of Kadina, Walleroo and Moonta, particularly the Cornish and Welsh heritage. A tiny area of native scrub, dubbed Innes National Park, has been given a toehold thanks to the unexpected rediscovery of the rare great western whipbird. The Park is also home to some of the best coastal scenery in South Australia.

Check out
www.yorkepeninsula.
com.au and
www.yorke
region.on.net

Ins and outs

Premier Stateliner, T8415 5555, have daily bus services from Adelaide to **Kadina**, **Wallaroo** and **Moonta**, though they don't connect with the *Yorke Peninsula Coaches*, T1800 625099, services which run a partly circular bus service as far as **Warooka** and up the eastern coast. Independent transport is essential for anyone wanting to explore the foot of the peninsula, but 4WD is not necessary. One option entails hiring a **Gipsy Waggon** at Hardwicke Bay, complete with Clydesdale horse, T8852 4455 for details.

Getting there
& around

Port Broughton is a charming small town tucked in against the sheltering elbow of Munderoo Bay. It's a quiet fishing and holiday town with not a great deal to do but relax, but a very good place to do just that. A very attractive traditional stone pub with iron lace verandahs faces West Terrace. The **D** *Port Broughton*, T8635 2004, F8635 2117, has nine basic rooms and cheap pub meals served in a pleasant cafeteria style area, daily 1200-1400, 1800-2000. The town's modern licenced *Bay Street Café*, T8635 2552, is the peninsula's best restaurant. Open Thu Sun 1000-2100 winter, 1000-2200. Bookings essential in summer. Recommended. The town is also blessed with an award winning caravan park, T8635 2188.

Port
Broughton
Colour map 1,
grid B2
Population: 1,500
45 km from Kadina,
180 km from Adelaide,
150 km from
Port Augusta

Many Cornish miners (known as 'Cousin Jacks' and 'Jennies') were attracted to what is now known as the Copper Triangle. The largest of these towns is **Kadina**, which is generally neglected by visitors in preference to its two near neighbours. It grew up as a settlement servicing the 'Walleroo' mines that opened up in 1860 and has continued on as the district's commercial centre. Dominated by grain silos and a fertilizer factory, **Walleroo** sprawls around its small central shopping street. Walleroo sprang up in 1861 and in its heyday the town had a much larger population, brass bands and a male voice choir, but has seen a steady decline since the mines closed in 1923. The legacies of the

The Copper
Triangle
150 km from Adelaide,
195 km from
Port Augusta

South Australia

Cornish and Welsh influx can still be seen and the **Heritage & Nautical Museum** has an extensive collection of local memorabilia. ■ *Wed 1030-1600, Sat-Sun and school holidays 1400-1600. $4. T8823 3015. Jetty Rd.*The third of the Copper Triangle towns, **Moonta**, has retained and exploited more of its mining heritage and has more of a buzz than its two neighbours. The **heritage drive** (the best bits of which can also be walked in half a day or so) snakes around a number of historical sites, some derelict, some still in use, testifying to the prestige of the area in its heyday.

Innes National Park
Colour map 1, grid B2
180 km from Kadina,
105 km from Edithburgh

Although the park was created in 1970 to protect a rare bird, the *great western whipbird*, it also boasts impressive coastal scenery. At the entrance the interesting new **Visitor Centre** your entry permit ($6 per car) will be provided, as well as lots of literature and the option to book accommodation in the park. ■ *Mon-Fri 0900-1630, Sat-Sun 1030-1530. T8854 3200, F8854 3299.* From here the road follows the line of the coast round to **Pondalowie Bay**, with numerous unsealed diversions to the various headlands, lighthouses and beaches. Amongst these **Cape Spencer** has impressive views over the neighbouring coast and out to sea as far as Kangaroo Island. **The Gap** is a keyhole-shaped vertical basin improbably cut into the 80-m-high cliff. **Ethel Beach** is accessible to the adventurous, and the ribcage of the park's only visible wreck can be seen rusting into the honey-coloured sand. From **West Cape** barrel-shaped breakers roll in to Surfer's Beach, often the site of surfing competitions. To the north are the first views of enclosed **Pondalowie Bay**, home to the best swimming beach. The great western whipbird is one of the many birds and animals you are unlikely to see in the park, but **emus** and **kangaroos** are here in abundance and from July to October **whales** can often be seen from Cape Spencer and West Cape. The area was also once home to those who extracted gypsum from the local salt lakes. They mostly lived in **Inneston** and much of the town can be still seen.

Sleeping and eating Many people stay at Marion Bay or further afield and day trip to the Park. There are, however, 3 alternatives (**C-D**) within the park. Several of the heritage buildings at Inneston have been converted into slightly scruffy self-contained lodges, sleeping from 6 to 10 people. Furnishings are basic and sparse, and linen is not provided, but they are very good value for groups or large families. 2-night minimum stay. The **Engineers Lodge** is the best of them with a front verandah overlooking the distant sea. Campers have access to several permitted sites. **Pondalowie Bay** has the best facilities including showers and public phone and also has a good amount of shade. Contact the Visitors Centre to book lodges or campsites. *Rhino Tavern*, Stenhouse Bay, T/F8854 4066 maintains a good value (**F**) self-contained backpackers with a variety of sized dorms, disabled access, laundry, BBQ and games area. The tavern also doubles as a general store, petrol station, takeaway, pub and pleasant cheap restaurant. This is also a good place to discuss the local swimming, fishing, surfing or snorkelling conditions with the friendly owners. Between Warooka and Point Turton is **C** *Cletta Farmhouse*, T8854 5052, a completely self-contained, isolated and recently revonated farmhouse. Make full use of the atmospheric dining room by asking the owners to come and cook. Sleeps up to 8 in very comfy beds. Recommended.

Edithburgh
Colour map 1, grid B2
Population: 500
36 km from Warooka,
39 km from Port Vincent

The peninsula's oldest town, Edithburgh sits on one of the most exposed stretches of coastline. Its *raison d'être* for beach lovers is **Sultana Point**, about 2 km south. *Troubridge Island Charter*, T8852 6290, run a 15-minute boat trip out to **Troubridge Island**, a privately owned bird sanctuary 6 km off the coast. **Fairy penguins** can be seen between March and November during the two-hour walk ($25) around the island. They also run fishing trips.

Sleeping and eating *Troubridge Island Charter* let out the picturesque old (**L**) *Lighthouse Keepers' Cottages* on Troubridge Island. The flat charge works out very reasonably for adventurous groups of up to 10 seeking a serious getaway. Own linen, food and torch required. 2-night minimum stay. **B** *Edithburgh House*, Edith St, T8852 6373, offers gourmet B&B in tasteful Victorian surroundings. No en suite, but the enthusiastic and knowledgable hosts ensure an enjoyable stay. They are also superb chefs and have a small mid-range restaurant (Mon-Sat 1830-2030). Much cheaper accommodation can be found at the divers' haunt on the foreshore *Edithburgh Lodge*, T8852 6262, and there is also a caravan park.

Transport The *Yorke Peninsula Coach*, T8852 6009 leaves Henry's Pl, Edithburgh, Mon, Wed, Fri 0705 for **Adelaide**, stopping at towns on the east coast.

The Flinders Ranges

South Australian painter Sir Hans Heysen described the Flinders Ranges as 'the bones of nature laid bare' and there is much geological truth in his observation. The forces that have shaped this region make the Flinders among the most striking and fascinating of Australian mountain ranges. Coloured bands of stone, twisted and folded layers of rock and deep jagged gorges are typically beautiful Flinders forms. In the Southern Flinders, rich farming lands and small historic towns such as **Melrose** *and* **Quorn** *rise to low forested hills. The covering of vegetation drops away in the Central Flinders to reveal the spine of the ranges among increasingly arid land dotted with the ruins of 19th-century pastoral properties. At its heart is the magnificent amphitheatre of* **Wilpena Pound**, *a feature easily as dramatic and inspirational as Uluru to the north. The Northern Flinders begins to have an outback quality as services become remote and roads rougher. The* **Gammon Ranges** *and* **Arkaroola Sanctuary** *enclose a secretive jumble of peaks and precious waterholes sheltering wildlife. The area offers suberb bushwalking and cycling on the* **Heysen** *and* **Mawson Trails**, *and peaceful bush camping, wildlife spotting and photography.*

The Flinders Ranges are only half a day's drive from Adelaide and are an essential part of any visit to South Australia. Check out www.flinders.out back.on.net

Ins and outs

Bus *Premier Stateliner* run a service from **Port Augusta** to **Quorn**, **Hawker**, **Rawnsley Park** and **Wilpena Pound**, leaving at 1310 Wed, 1600 Fri and 1140 Sun, arriving at Wilpena 2 hrs later. *OzTrax Adventures* (bookings only, T8339 6009) operate services between **Adelaide** and **Arkaroola**, via **Clare**, **Melrose** and **Wilpena**. Northbound Tue, Fri and southbound Wed and Sun. **Car** The quickest road north from Adelaide is straight up Highway One. However, there can be few less interesting 200-km stretches of Australian highway than this. Taking the route that starts with the Barrier Highway to **Gawler**, and then branches off onto B32, is much preferable, has the added bonus of threading up through the **Clare Valley**, and is actually a few km shorter. **Tours** *Wallaby Trucks* (see page 778), have a variety of short tours of the central and northern ranges. *Big Country*, T8354 4191, www.bigcountrysafaris.com.au, take small groups in 4WDs and camping out into the ranges and beyond to the Simpson Desert. *A Team Tours*, T/F8523 5077, specialize in putting together personalized tours, built around your group's time and interests.

Getting there
To check unsealed road conditions see www.transport.sa.gov .au, or T1300-361033

In the central and northern ranges accommodation becomes quite scarce, but less so than many visitors realize. Well-equipped campers will find some fantastically picturesque bush sites both in the national parks and around them. Another option is at the

Information

South Australia

Aboriginal owned and run *Iga Warta* where tents and swags are provided. Many of the cattle and sheep stations allow bushcamping and some have converted cottages or shearers' quarters to holiday accommodation. Contact *FRABS*, Hawker, T8648 4014, www.frabs.com.au, for complete details of available station accommodation.

Mount Remarkable National Park

During the fire danger season (Nov-Apr) the Heysen Trail is closed, with just a limited number of day walks available, and bush camping is not permitted anywhere in the park

Covering 16,000 ha of the Southern Flinders Ranges, the **Mount Remarkable National Park** includes some of the highest points of the Flinders south of Wilpena Pound. The park is best known for **Alligator Gorge**, a sheer-sided canyon of considerable depth that it is possible to walk through if dry. The park encloses a loop of ranges, including the Black Range on the eastern side and The Battery to the west, and is heavily forested. There are extensive views of farming plains from the high points and it's easy to spot parrots and wallabies in the shady valleys and gorges. The park can get very hot in the summer when there is a strong fire risk but in winter temperatures can drop below freezing.

Ins & outs
130 km from Clare, 60 km from Quorn

There are 3 access points to the park: **Mambray Creek**, near Port Germein, **Melrose**, and **Alligator Gorge**, near Wilmington. Those wanting to camp should base themselves at the first and last. Peak-baggers and those needing accommodation will find Melrose a good base. Park entry fees payable at self-registration stations. Day visitors $6 car, bushcamping $3.50 per person. For more information contact the ranger at Mambray Creek or see www.parks.sa.gov.au

Around the park
Emus are common but resist the temptation to feed them as they can become aggressive

The Mount Remarkable park headquarters are located at **Mambray Creek**, on the western side of the park close to the main Adelaide to Port Augusta highway (A1). Mambray Creek is also the major trailhead for walks and has the main park camping ground. This is very popular during school holidays and will be fully booked well ahead by South Australians. There are some lovely circuit walks through woodland here, all clearly signposted, particularly the demanding Mount Cavern Trail (11 km, 6 hrs) and the Hidden Gorge Trail (18 km, 7 hours) and there is also a linear day-walk to Alligator Gorge. ■ *Camping $15 per vehicle, $7.50 cycle or motorbike. Bookings required for Easter, Apr and Sep school holidays and long weekends. For bookings and information contact Parks and Wildlife SA, Mambray Creek, T8634 7068, mrnp@saugov.sa.gov.au*

Alligator Gorge is in the north of the Mount Remarkable National Park and is its most spectacular feature. From the Blue Gum Flat picnic area, a long flight of stone steps leads to the floor of the gorge at a point called the **Terraces** where the river spills over slabs of deep-red rock. A short walk leads down to the **Narrows** where the gorge walls close in to just a few metres across. *Alligator Lodge*, the former ranger's residence, is a self-contained house in bushland near the gorge that sleeps 8 ($53 for 1-4 people, $10.50 for each extra person, book at Mambray Creek, T8634 7068). Entry fees are payable at a self-registration station. The gorge is 12 km down a rough unsealed road from the turn-off, about 1 km south of Wilmington.

The oldest town in the Flinders and one of the most appealing is **Melrose**, nestled at the foot of **Mount Remarkable** itself and a favourite among walkers. Shaded by giant gums and overflown by large flocks of corellas and cockatoos, this small, quiet town is home to a string of historic buildings. From the town centre there is an easy direct walk to the summit of Mount Remarkable (six hours return), with superb views to the east for much of the ascent. This route follows the **Heysen Trail** which continues over the summit to head northwest along the spine of the Mount Remarkable Range.

Sleeping and eating in Melrose The best place to stay is **C** *Bluey Blundstone's Black-smith Shop*, T/F8666 2173. These 140-year-old buildings have been meticulously restored to what is probably well beyond their former glory. A small red-stone cottage sleeps 2 and the tin 'barn' up to 6. Breakfast included but no a/c. Recommended. Out front the old smithy leads to the cheap café which has a healthy menu with veggie options. Open Mon, Wed-Fri 1100-1600 and Sat-Sun 1000-1700. Of the hotels the old and tired **D** *North Star*, T/F8666 2110 has 8 rooms and breakfast is included. They also have free **internet** access. The **D-E** *Melrose Caravan Park* T8666 2060, F8666 2203 have 20 well-laid-out cabins and on-site vans by Willochra Creek, plus a simple backpackers house (**F**) with full facilities. They also double as the local **Tourist Information** desk and will happily arrange accommodation in the few other hotels and B&Bs in town.

Autumn and Spring are very busy and booking accommodation well in advance is essential for Easter and Oct long weekend

Transport *OzTrax Adventures* operate a bus service to **Clare** and **Adelaide** Wed, Sun 1525, and another north to **Port Augusta**, **Wilpena Pound** and on as far as **Arkaroola**, Tue, Fri 1040. Book in advance, T8339 6009. *Leisuretime Travel Melrose*, T8666 2017 run day and half-day 4WD trips into the park and onto some local private property for $95/$65.

Southern Flinders

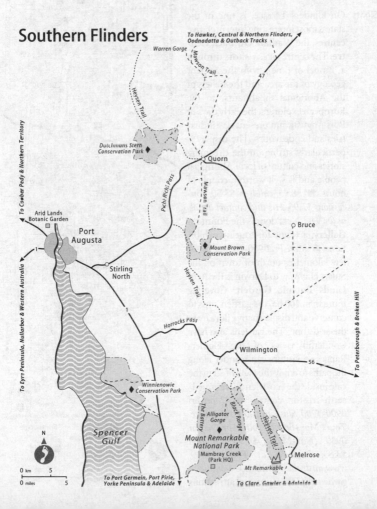

South Australia

Port Augusta

Colour map 1, grid A2
Population: 13,500
305 km from Adelaide,
465 km from Ceduna,
530 km from Coober
Pedy, 410 km from
Broken Hill (NSW)

Port Augusta lies on the fringe of South Australia's vast Outback, at the head of the Spencer Gulf. It is surrounded by arid plains relieved by the pale blue of the gulf and the ranges of the Flinders rising in the near distance. Known as the crossroads of Australia, the town forms the junction of the major road and rail routes north to Darwin and west to Perth, so many people whistle through every day. There is a high Aboriginal population, with about 4,000 Aboriginal people from the ranges and the 'lands' Aboriginal-owned territory to the west residing in the town. Some interesting sights and useful services make Port Augusta well worth a stop. The **VIC** is in the Wadlata Outback Centre and acts as a booking service for the Flinders, Outback and Northern Territory. ■ *Mon-Fri 0900-1730, Sat-Sun 1000-1600. T8641 0793, www.port augusta.sa.gov.au Flinders Terr.*

Sights   On Flinders Terrace, is one of the state's most interesting interpretative centres, the **Wadlata Outback Centre**. The centre takes visitors through a 'tunnel of time', from the ancient geology of the area and the beliefs of the Aboriginal inhabitants, to the European explorers, the early days of Port Augusta and present day industries and endeavours. The display is particularly strong on the dreaming stories and culture of local Aboriginal people and is well worth a couple of hours. ■ *$8.95, children $5.50, concessions $7.95. Hrs and contact details as for VIC.* Next door is the **Fountain Gallery**, a venue for touring exhibitions. ■ *Mon-Fri 0900-1630. Free.* A few kilometres north of town on the Stuart Highway to Darwin is the **Arid Lands Botanic Garden**. Covering more than 200 ha, the garden aims to conserve and display native flora from the arid zone. The gardens also have wonderful views of the Flinders Ranges so visitors can wander along the paths to enjoy the view or sit in the café inside the eco-friendly rammed-earth visitor centre. ■ *Mon-Fri 0900-1700, Sat-Sun 1000-1600. Free. Tours Mon-Fri at 1100 (Apr-Oct) or 0930 (Nov-Mar). $4.95, children $3.85. Bookings at T8641 1049, www.australian-aridlands-botanic-garden.org* Other unusual attractions

South Australia

Port Augusta

To Arid Lands Botanic Garden, Coober Pedy & Northern Territory

Spencer Gulf

Wadlata Outback Centre & Fountain Gallery

To Eyre Peninsula, Nullarbor & Western Australia

To School of the Air

To Royal Flying Doctor Service
To Adelaide, Broken Hill & Flinders Ranges

0 metres   200
0 yards   200

■ **Sleeping**
1 Acacia Ridge
2 Augusta
3 Big 4
4 Bluefox
5 Pastoral
6 Standpipe

● **Eating**
1 Hot Peppers
2 Ozzie's
  Coffee Lounge

include Port Augusta's two 'air' bases. **School of the Air** conducts lessons over the radio and via the internet for students who live in remote areas of the state, and the **Royal Flying Doctor Service** provides health care and emergency services to people in remote areas using light aircraft.

C *Standpipe*, corner of Stuart Highway and Highway 1, T8642 4033, standpip@ dove.net.au This large, modern motel uses the former pub hotel as its dining room. The mid-range menu includes Thai and Indian options. Meals daily from 1800. Rooms are excellent value (**D**) at weekends. Of several other anonymous motels the **D** *Acacia Ridge*, Stokes Terr, T8642 3377, has a popular, cheap dining room. The **C-E** *Augusta*, Loudon Rd, T8642 2701, is the liveliest pub at weekends when there's a $5 cover charge. The 7 hotel rooms include good value singles. The **D** *Pastoral*, 17 Stirling Rd, T8642 2818, is a shade more expensive, but has the best counter meals in town. There are a couple of dedicated backpacker hostels, including the excellent **D-E** *Bluefox*, Highway 1, T8641 2960, bluefox@dove.net.au Just 20 beds in small homely dorms plus 1 double. The facilities are mostly basic but clean, though there is a particularly comfortable garden guest lounge and spa. The owners are friendly and incredibly accommodating, offering free tours and 24-hr pick-ups whenever possible. Recommended. The closest caravan park to the town centre is the *Big 4*, corner of Highway 1 and Stokes Terr, T8642 2974. *Ozzie's Coffee Lounge* and *Hot Peppers*, both on Commercial St are good for a coffee or lunch during the day. The café at the *Arid Lands Botanic Garden* is also a good spot with more adventurous fare such as quondong pies and vegetable wraps.

Sleeping & eating

Air *Airlines of South Australia*, T8642 3100, flights to Adelaide 5 days a week and a mail run every weekend to Boulia in Queensland via Innamincka and Birdsville. Contact airport direct. **Bus** The *Premier Stateliner* depot is in Mackay St, T8642 5055. There are daily services to *Adelaide* and *Ceduna*, and a limited service to the **Flinders**. *McCafferty's/Greyhound* buses to **Perth** at 0300 on Tue, Thu and Sat; to **Adelaide** at 0245 on Wed, Fri and Sun, and daily at 0155; to **Alice Springs** at 2315 daily. **Train** The *Indian Pacific* and *Ghan* both stop at the railway station in Stirling St.

Transport

Banks Several major banks with ATMs on Commercial Rd. **Car servicing** *Fitzy's*, 15 Young St, T8642 2786, service all makes but specialize in 4WD. Pricey but thorough. **Communications** Internet at the *Library*, corner of Marryatt St and Mackay St. Mon-Fri 0900-1800, Sat 1000-1300, Sun 1400-1700 or *PZ Computers* on Church St. **Post Office** Commercial Rd. **Hospital** Hospital Rd, T8648 5500. **Outdoor hire** *Bluefox Lodge* will hire out camping equipment for trips into the Flinders. **Parks office** 9 MacKay St, T8648 5300. **Police** Commercial Rd, T8648 5020. Taxi T8642 4466.

Directory
Cheapest fuel at Woolworths, town centre

Quiet, friendly Quorn, gateway to the Flinders Ranges, has often been used as a film location for films set in the nostalgic Australian past. It was established as a railway town on the narrow-gauge line built in 1879 from Port Augusta through the **Pichi Richi Pass** to service the settlements north of Quorn and link to the Ghan train to Alice Springs. Volunteers maintaining the Pichi Richi line operate a variety of steam trains to Stirling North every weekend and some weekdays from March-December. ■ *From $25-70 return, depending on train. T8648 6598, www.portaugusta.sa.gov.au* There are some excellent walks in the low ranges to the west and south of the town. The **VIC** is on Seventh Street, which runs perpendicular to the railway station. ■ *Hours vary, if closed visit the council offices next door for information. T8648 6419, tourism@flindersrangescouncil.sa.gov.au Council T8648 6031.*

Quorn & around
Colour map 1, grid A2
Population: 1,500
41 km from Port Augusta,
67 km from Hawker

The Willochra Plain around Quorn and the country north to Hawker is littered with the stone remains of the homes and stations of 19th-century pastoralists. The most extensive ruins are those of **Kanyaka** station, 38 km north of Quorn, where 70 workers and their families lived. It is possible to wander around the site, about 1 km off the main road by Kanyaka Creek. Subtler evidence of the region's original inhabitants can be seen at **Yourambulla Caves**, where there are simple rock paintings and good views to the south and west on a 3-km loop walk, 10 km south of Hawker.

Sleeping and eating Comfortable motel rooms and a restaurant can be found at the 3-storey stone flour mill **C** *Quorn Mill Motel*, 2 Railway Terr, T8648 6016. Of the 4 pubs back-to-back down Railway Terr, the smartest is the **D** *Transcontinental*, T8648 6076. 20 clean and comfortable rooms, most with direct access to the wide balcony, and pleasant common areas. Friendly bar and surprisingly refined dining room. Cheap meals daily 1200-1400, 1800-2000. **D-E** *Criterion*, T8648 6018, has basic hotel rooms as well as 5 en suite motel rooms. **D** *Andu Lodge*, 12 First St, T8648 6655, www.headingbush.com, is one of the best-managed backpacker hostels in the country. Clean, spacious, well-organized and friendly, small dorms, 1 double. Bike hire available and pre-arranged pick-ups from Port Augusta. Recommended. Outside Quorn, north of Warren Gorge, there is stylish station accommodation at **B** *Argadells*, T8648 6210, www.argadells.com.au The old stone homestead is self-contained, sleeps 2-8 and has been furnished with elegant, country style. Bushcamping on the station is $6 per person. Guests have access to bushwalks and 4WD routes on the station. Camping is allowed at Warren Gorge, but facilities are limited to basic toilets.

Tours and activities *Wallaby Tracks*, run by *Andu Lodge*, take small minibus groups out to the central and northern Flinders for 1, 2 or 3 days ($99-300). Also pick-ups from Port Augusta and Adelaide. Their travellers get half-price flights at *Wilpena Pound Resort*.

Transport The *Premier Stateliner* bus service to **Port Augusta** leaves from the newsagency on Sixth St at 1600 Thu, Sun and 2045 Fri. The bus to **Wilpena** leaves at 1345 Wed, 1635 Fri and 1215 Sun.

Hawker
Colour map 1,
grid A3
Population: 450
89 km from
Parachilna, 54 km
from Wilpena
Pound Resort

Once a railway town, Hawker has survived thanks to its position at the junction of the highway north to Leigh Creek and the road from Port Augusta to Wilpena. With a low backdrop of the Yourambulla Range, it has some enduring heritage buildings and a few key services that make it a useful place to replenish supplies before moving on. Tourist information and petrol can be found at *Hawker Motors*, open 0730-1800. The cavernous *General Store*, over the road, seems to stock practically everything. ■ *Mon-Fri 0800-1730, Sat-Sun 0900-1700*. The solid stone post office on the main street, Wilpena Road, also houses a parks office, T8648 4244, with useful brochures and maps on the Flinders Ranges.

Sleeping and eating Hawker has an unremarkable hotel and 2 caravan parks. The *Flinders Ranges* caravan park, T8648 4266, is opposite the *Old Ghan*, T8648 4176, on Leigh Creek Rd just to the north of town. The later is a restaurant and art gallery housed in the lovely old stone railway station. Cheap traditional lunches and slightly more adventurous mid-range dinners. Open Wed-Sun, 1130-1430 and 1800-2100.

Transport The *Premier Stateliner* bus service to **Port Augusta** leaves from the shopping centre at 1515 Thu, Sun and 2000 Fri. The bus to **Wilpena** leaves at 1435 Wed, 1725 Fri and 1305 Sun.

Flinders Ranges National Park (Wilpena Pound)

The most commanding and beautiful landscapes of the Flinders Ranges are concentrated in this national park which is also a compact and accessible area. The remarkable geological formation of **Wilpena Pound**, a ring of serrated mountains, loops north to become the Heysen Range, flanked by the lower peaks of the ABC range. Creeks have cut deep gorges into the tilting red rock of the Heysen Range and score the surrounding soft valleys with dry stoney beds bordered by river red gums. It is magnificent walking country but there are also impossibly scenic drives that roll around the valleys under the walls of the pound. In spring the land is a verdant green, then in summer the lush vegetation disappears and the mountains take on a harsh red in the intense sunlight. At any time of year the royal purples, reds and golds of the ranges and ramparts of the pound are best revealed at dawn and dusk. Thriving wildlife and good bush-camping spots also make this park one of South Australia's most popular and treasured. The main **VIC** for the region, with a good range of maps and guides, is at *Wilpena Pound Resort*. ■ *Daily 0800-1800. T8648 0048, www.wilpenapound.com.au*

Wilpena Pound Resort 162 km from Port Augusta Entry to the park is $6 per vehicle for duration of stay, unless driving straight through

Bushwalking

The easiest way into the pound is to take the shuttle bus from the resort ($3.50 return approximately every 1½ hours daily). The short journey leaves an easy 1½ km walk to the lowest gap in the pound walls, **Wangarra Lookout**, via the Hills Homestead. The highest peak in the Flinders and best-known pound viewpoint is **St Mary Peak** (1,170 m). This challenging trail heads northwest outside the walls to the saddle, ascends via a sidetrack to the summit, and then descends into the pound basin to return by the Hills Homestead route (17 km, 8 hours). **Mount Ohlssen Bagge** is a good alternative to St Mary Peak, providing wonderful views over the entire pound to the Elder Range with much less effort. The trail is steep but short with some rock hopping near the top (4½ km, 3 hours return). On the southeastern edge of the pound is an enormous boulder, **Arkaroo Rock**, with 15,000-year-old Aboriginal cave paintings. A short walk leads to the rock where signs explain Adnyamathanha dreaming. It is also a good place to see the Chace Range opposite at sunset (2 ½ km, 1 hour return). To the north there are two good walks at Bunyeroo, a easy walk through the pretty, intimate **Bunyeroo Gorge** with near-permanent waterholes (7 km, 3 hours return), or the **Bunyeroo-Wilcolo Creeks** loop walk (9 km, 4 hours), through the valley and ABC Range with good views of Wilpena Pound. On the northern park border at Aroona, a favourite of painter Hans Heysen, **Red Hill** lookout gives fine views over the valley, Heysen and ABC Ranges (9 km, 4 hours return). On the eastern boundary of the park is **Wilkawillina Gorge**. This peaceful gorge is 45 km from Wilpena so it doesn't see many visitors but is well worth a visit if you have the time. There is also the chance to see a colony of rock wallabies there. The trail follows the creek bed past tranquil pools and red rock faces similar to those of Brachina Gorge (23 km, 10 hours return). For those wanting a longer walk, the section of the **Heysen Trail** (see page 716) from Parachilna Gorge to Wilpena Pound is a magnificent four to five day walk offering incredible mountain views and peaceful bush camping.

Pick up a copy of the 'Bushwalking in Flinders Ranges National Park' pamphlet for more options. Dedicated walkers should talk to staff at the park information centre where topographic maps are available

Sleeping & eating

A-C *Wilpena Pound Resort*, T8648 0004, www.wilpenapound.com.au, is just outside the northern walls of the pound, consisting of attractive low timber and mud-brick buildings by Wilpena Creek. Accommodation in either the 60 smart motel rooms or the vast camping area ($16 for 2). Some of the rooms have kitchenettes and there are

South Australia

camp BBQs, but no other kitchen facilities. Eating is in either the mid-range restaurant, the cheap, good value bar or snacks from the well-stocked shop (open 0800-1800). The shop also has an internet kiosk, ATM and sells fuel. The motel pool is available to non-room guests for $2. **B** *Merna Mora*, T8648 4717 or www.frabs.com.au, is a station just off the highway at the western end of the Moralana drive. They have 9 self-contained a/c units available, with good sunset views of the pound and each sleeping up to 6. **C-E** *Rawnsley Park Station*, T8648 0008, www.rawnsley park.com.au This property has a great location close to the southern wall of Wilpena Pound near Rawnsley Bluff and is a relaxed unsophisticated place with holiday units and a caravan park with cabins and vans. The complex also has a shop, restaurant, bike hire, and some good walking and cycling trails. **D-E** *Willow Springs* station,

Central Flinders

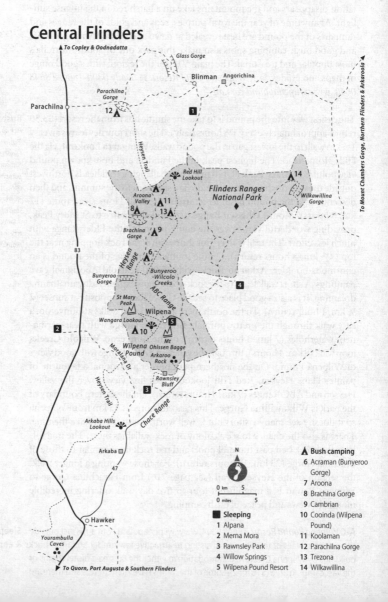

South Australia

Sleeping
1 Alpana
2 Merna Mora
3 Rawnsley Park
4 Willow Springs
5 Wilpena Pound Resort

Bush camping
6 Acraman (Bunyeroo Gorge)
7 Aroona
8 Brachina Gorge
9 Cambrian
10 Cooinda (Wilpena Pound)
11 Koolaman
12 Parachilna Gorge
13 Trezona
14 Wilkawillina

T8648 0016 or www.frabs.com.au, has 5 self-contained, converted workers' and shearers' cottages sleeping from 2 to 17. Fairly basic but very good value. There are many bush-camping areas in the park ($10 per vehicle). Some have basic toilets but most have no facilities.

Tours & activities The resort runs several half- and full-day tours to the main gorges, Blinman and Parachilna, and the peaks around Arkaba ($84 ½ day, $105 day). *Rawnsley Park* also offer similar tours for the same price and a *Skytrek* tour at *Willow Springs* station. *Skytrek* is a scenic 65-km 4WD loop route on private station land, the highlight being the lookout at Mt Caernarvon (921 m). *Balloon Adventures*, T8648 6111, take off at dawn from Jun-Oct ($165, 30 mins). Scenic flights from the resort vary from 20 mins to 2 hrs. Best option is the 30-min flight ($95, min 2 people) which includes the pound and ABC ranges.

Transport The *Premier Stateliner* bus service to **Port Augusta** leaves from the *Wilpena Pound Motel* at 1430 Thu, Sun and 1915 Fri, calling at the **Rawnsley Park** turn-off 15 mins later.

Blinman
Colour map 1, grid A3
Population: 20
Altitude: 650 m
60 km from Wilpena Pound Resort,
32 km from Parachilna

This tiny village, the prettiest in the central Flinders, is a former copper-mining town, surrounded by low hills stripped bare of trees to feed the smelter furnaces. A drive around the **Glass Gorge** loop is recommended as is the wonderful **Blinman Pools** walk from Angorichina. This is a linear walk along Parachilna and Blinman creeks, past shady gums and sheer gorge walls to two sets of pools (12 km, four hours return). **Scenic flights** are available from the village, T8648 4863, the many options including a 40-minute flight over Wilpena Pound ($95, minimum two people).

Sleeping and eating C *Blinman Hotel*, T8648 4867, dates back to 1869. It has 17 en suite, a/c doubles, some sleeping 4. All are priced equally but the smartly decorated newer rooms are much the better. Cheap but inventive pub meals are served in the modern dining room daily, 0800-1000, 1200-1400, 1800-2000. Indoor pool available for non-residents for $2. Also ask about the small, well-equipped mini-hostel (**E**) next door. C *Alpana*, T8648 4864, www.alpana-station.netfirms.com, is 6 km south and has 2 sets of 3 simple twin rooms in the shearers' quarters, each with its own bathroom. No linen but it can be hired. Each set is charged at a flat rate, so it's good value for groups or families. Spacious kitchen and lounge are shared. Run 4WD trips to Brachina and Bunyeroo Gorges or Mount Chambers Gorge ($90 a day for 2-4).

Blinman to Arkaroola
Distance 145 km via unsealed roads, 235 km via highway

The shortest route to the northern ranges from Blinman is via the rough, unsealed roads to the east, which allows a side trip to the impressive **Chambers Gorge**. Heading west via the highway you have the choice of enjoying the magnificent mountain scenery of **Glass Gorge** or the idyllic **Parachilna Gorge**, with camping spots by the riverbed. Parachilna is nothing more than a country pub, and its associated hostel but this is one of the best pubs in the state and shouldn't be missed. The traditional **L-A** *Prairie Hotel*, T8648 4844, www.prairiehotel.com.au, is relaxed and welcoming with lots of local character and wonderful distant views of the Flinders Ranges over the plain. The pub is well known for its mid-range cuisine, served all day 1000-2100, featuring various wild animals and plants. The pub also has classy earth-toned accommodation in a modern wing built to conserve and generate energy. Over the road is the **D** *Parachilna Overflow*, T8648 4844, a large hostel and cabin complex with excellent facilities. Further north the *Beltana Roadhouse* marks the central turn-off, and shortest route (8 km), to **Beltana** township, now a charming relic with old stone and tin houses which makes for an interesting wander.

South Australia

Leigh Creek, 65 km from Parachilna, is a service town for the massive open-cut coal mines nearby that feed the Port Augusta power station. About 5 km north, at **Copley**, is the turn-off to Arkaroola and the *Bush Bakery and Quandong Café*, T8675 2683, an essential stop with the best food for many kilometres. Open daily 0830-1700, Easter-November. The friendly caravan park, T8675 2288, also provides tourist information, local maps and Desert Park Passes. The pub has the last ATM for hundreds of kilometres. About 55 km east of Copley is **Iga Warta**, T8648 3737, www.igawarta.mtx.net, an environmental and cultural interpretive centre owned by a local Adnyamathanha family. It is a superb place to learn about the land and culture of the Flinders from this wonderfully warm family. Visitors can go for walks to look at bush tucker, land features or rock art sites, make wooden tools, or simply chat around a campfire. Accommodation is available in tents and swags and delicious home-made set meals are served up every breakfast, lunch and dinner. If possible ring in advance to arrange a visit but it is also okay to drop in and see what activities are on offer or camp overnight. Prices are negotiated according to requirements but expect to pay around $100 a day for camping, food and activities. Transfers can be arranged from the *Prairie Hotel* at Parachilna (see above).

The Northern Flinders Ranges

105 km from Leigh Creek, 130 km from Blinman

As the ranges approach the Outback they become appropriately more and more rugged. The **Gammon Ranges** and **Arkaroola Wilderness Sanctuary** enclose countless peaks and ranges, all with a fascinating beauty. It is wild, arid country that is difficult to access but this is part of its appeal. The rough unsealed roads mean that far fewer visitors reach this area than those drawn to the softer ranges of the Central Flinders. Only experienced walkers and 4WD vehicles will be able to penetrate its depths but the accessible waterholes and gorges are some of the most peaceful and striking in the entire ranges. The nearest **VIC** to the region is at *Leigh Creek* but the main contacts are staff at Balcanoona and Arkaroola. ■ *Mon-Fri 0900-1600, Sat-Sun 1000-1400. T8675 2723, lcvic@internode.on.net*

Gammon Ranges National Park
Colour map 1, grid A3
Most of the park is only accessible to experienced bushwalkers

The park is sandwiched between Arkaroola to the north and Nepabunna and Nantawarrina Aboriginal land to the south and also includes a corridor of land out to the saltpan of Lake Frome. Gammon means 'place of red ochre' to the Adnyamathanha people who believe Arkaroo, a giant serpent, formed the ranges, gorges and waterholes as he snaked down to drink at the salt lake, and there are painting sites and rock engravings within the park. Europeans had used the land for sheep and cattle grazing since 1857 until the park was declared about 20 years ago and have left their mark in the station buildings, tracks and hoof-damaged terrain. The park headquarters are at **Balcanoona**, where walking pamphlets, maps and advice can be obtained from the rangers. ■ *Rangers are not always available but RGS walk brochures can be collected from a box outside. Try to call ahead for advice, rangers will return all calls if the office is unattended. Note that the park is sometimes closed in order to cull feral animals. T8648 4829, www.parks.sa.gov.au*

The park's most popular walk is at **Weetootla Gorge** where there is a permanent spring and delightful pools fringed with ferns and mosses. Starting from Weetootla Trailhead the track follows Balcanoona Creek to the spring (4 km) and then continues in a loop to Grindell Hut (6 km) and back to the campground via Weetootla Gorge (18 ½ km, 7 ½ hrs). Ask the rangers for details of more rugged terrain.

South Australia

Sleeping There are bush campsites at Italowie Gap and Weetootla Gorge, both accessible by 2WD. At the Balcanoona park headquarters visitors can stay in the former **E-F** *Shearers' Quarters* which has 82-bed dorms, communal kitchen, lounge and BBQ. The Manager's Room has a double bed, private en suite and lounge. Book *Shearers' Quarters* rooms in advance as groups may book exclusive use. There are also 2 remote self-contained huts. **C** *Grindell Hut* sleeps 8 and has lovely views but is only accessible by 4WD. **D** *Nudlamutana Hut* overlooks a creek, sleeps 2-3 and is accessible by 2WD. Camping $6 per car, $3.50 walkers. Self-registration system, no bookings taken. Campers can use showers at Balcanoona for $2. Bookings for *Shearers' Quarters*, *Nudlamutana* and *Grindell Hut* to be made at the Parks Hawker office, T8648 4244.

Arkaroola encompasses much of the most rugged of the Flinders' ancient mountain ranges. There are many beautiful waterholes, especially at **Echo Camp** and **Nooldoonooldoona**, although **Bararranna** and **Arkaroola** are also lovely paces. There are also many species of birds and rare native animals such as the pretty yellow-footed rock wallaby. The former cattle station provides comfort amid a magnificent wilderness, though the extremely rocky, rough roads make even short trips slow and jolting. No bush camping is allowed in the sanctuary and the only accommodation is at **B-E** *Arkaroola Village*, T1800 676042 or 8648 4848, www.arkaroola.on.net, a tourist resort with various standards of rooms. There are also bed-only twin rooms and a self-contained hut, the *Quandong Bunkhouse* in the campground. The swimming pool is available to all guests. Cheap meals from the bar and mid-range restaurant available 0700-0900, 1200-1400, 1830-2000. Arkaroola runs the **Ridgetop Tour**, one of the best in the Flinders. This is a four hour trip in an open 4WD into the depths of the sanctuary (daily 0800, 1300, $66, children $38.50). Book at reception on arrival or call ahead during busy periods. If finances are limited don't miss the stunning **Acacia Ridge** walk. Arkaroola also has an **Observatory** to take advantage of the bright night sky. ■ *Daily after sunset. $25, 1 hr.* **Scenic flights** are available in a light aircraft over the Sanctuary, Lake Frome or Lake Eyre. ■ *Sanctuary 35-min flight $88, Arkaroola and Lake Frome 1½-hr flight $168. Minimum of 2 passengers.*

Arkaroola Wilderness Sanctuary
Colour map 1, grid A1
Arkaroola Village 30 km from Balcanoona

Coober Pedy and routes north

*South Australia north of Port Augusta and Ceduna covers over 500,000 sq km, an area about the size of France, and is a large part of Australia's true Outback. The magnificent **Flinders Ranges** cover a small part of this expanse, the rest is much flatter, much more arid and very hot. Virtually all of it is desert or semi-desert, though the eastern half is dotted with hundreds of lakes, the largest of which, **Lake Eyre**, is a lonely land-locked drainage point for a catchment area the size of the Murray-Darling basin. Despite this the lake, like all its neighbours, is usually dry, a huge saltpan filling with water perhaps twice a century. One of the few other significant ranges is the Stuart, bearer of most of the world's opals, with **Coober Pedy** perched on its edge, a mining town where they've been hungrily digging the precious stones out the ground for almost 90 years.*

Just one sealed highway cuts through the centre towards the Northern Territory, with a scant few other unsealed tracks providing access to Queensland

The Stuart Highway

From Port Augusta the main northern highway has an Outback feel almost the moment you leave the town. For most of the year the land is an unrelenting golden red, covered in a bright blue Australian sky, but after heavy rains the vegetation creates a carpet of vibrant greens, dotted with flowery yellows, purples and reds. After 175 km the community of **Pimba** and the **D-E** *Spuds* roadhouse, T8673 7473, are a welcome sight. Open 24 hours, with accommodation in 13 doubles and six singles (all air-conditioned). Pimba also marks the only junction with a sealed road before Erldunda, in the Northern Territory.

Woomera
Colour map 1, grid A2
Population: 300
7 km from Pimba
*For more information
contact the Woomera
Heritage Centre or see*
*www.powerup.com.au
/~woomera*

*Cheapest petrol
between Port Augusta
and Coober Pedy*

Once much larger, the **Woomera Prohibited Area** is chunk of desert about the size of England that extends west of Woomera to the Western Australian border and north as far as Cadney Homestead. It was surveyed and declared a prohibited area in 1946-7 to allow the British to begin missile and rocket testing here. From its beginnings till 1982 Woomera was the main residential town for those working in the various facilities in the Woomera Prohibited Area. The recent developments by *Kistler*, and the takeover of most of the facilities by *British Aerospace* has, however, rekindled interest. The sparkling, clean town now features a fascinating **Missile Park** and the **Heritage Centre**. The park is an impressive static display of a couple of dozen missiles, rockets and aeroplanes. The centre comprises a café, excellent **VIC**, 10-pin bowling alley and a small but interesting museum that recounts the history of the test facilities. ■ *Daily 0900-1700. Museum $5.30, children and concessions $3.30. T/F8673 7042.*

Sleeping and eating **C-D** *Eldo*, T8673 7867, is a large 1960s hotel with en suite a/c doubles and some budget singles. Cheap bistro and bars open daily. **D-E** *Travellers' Village*, T8673 7800, www.woomera.com Broad range of accommodation from camping and 5-berth self-contained a/c cabins to basic 2-, 3- and 4-bed backpacker rooms. Television room and camp kitchen, own linen required.

**Roxby Downs
& Andamooka**
*Colour map 1,
grid A2*
Population: 4,000
*Roxby Downs 90 km
from Pimba,
190 km from Maree*

Andamooka is a small but thriving mining town, though far smaller in scale than Coober Pedy. Off the main tourist route, the town still retains a raw edge that Coober lacks, despite the inevitable series of opal shops. Early prospectors built or dug homes from whatever came to hand and the ramshackle look of those still surviving well-suit the almost Martian landscape. Just over 30 km closer to Pimba is **Roxby Downs**, a surprisingly sophisticated town that houses and services workers of the **Olympic Dam Mine** and its support operations. ■ *Surface tours Apr-Oct. Mon, Thu, Sat 0900. 1½ hrs. Donation to Royal Flying Doctors Service. Pick-ups from Richardson Pl. T8671 8600.*

Sleeping and eating Andamooka **C** *Dukes Bottlehouse*, T8672 7007, andamookaopal@hotmail.com Good-value motel-style a/c rooms sleeping 1, 2 or 3. Book at post office. **C-D** *Opal Hotel*, T8672 7078. en suite a/c and budget rooms. There are also 2 caravan parks. *Steve's Tuckerbox*, is open for cheap lunches Fri-Sun and evening meals daily. **Roxby Downs** **C** *Roxby Downs Motor Inn*, T8671 0311. *Roxby Downs Caravan Park*, T8671 1000, has on-site vans and sites.

Glendambo
Glendambo, an extended roadhouse, is 110 km from Pimba and the last chance until Coober Pedy for fuel and supplies. The **C** *Glendambo Hotel*, T8672 1030, gtc@camtech.net.au, has a huge bar and diner built in the style of a woolshed. Cheap counter meals available daily 1200-1400, 1800-2045. Plenty of air-conditioned motel units, a bunkhouse with three 4-bunk dorms, and caravan sites. There is also a small *General Store*, open 0700-2100, with supplies including camping gear, and an all-day takeaway and café menu. From Glendambo the road enters the **Woomera Prohibited Area** and there is little of interest until the first dirt cones of the Coober Pedy opal fields.

South Australia

Coober Pedy

One of Australia's more unusual Outback towns, Coober Pedy has been settled by opal miners, many of whom live in homes underground to avoid the baking heat, adding to the alien nature of this harsh, arid landscape. Opal was 'discovered' by gold prospectors in 1915, although local Aboriginal people had long been aware of the coloured stone here, and miners soon began to descend on the area. After mining commenced local Aboriginal people dubbed the area 'kupa piti' meaning 'white man in a hole', now corrupted to Coober Pedy. The rough-and-ready community changed little until the road from Adelaide to Darwin was sealed in 1987, and then the town began to attract large numbers of tourists. Opals and tourism are big business now and though the town's edges have been smoothed considerably since the isolation of earlier days, car wrecks and junk still litter parts of the town and more eccentric locals have been known to use their explosives for more than just mining. The **VIC** is itself a mine of information. ■ *Mon-Fri 0900-1700. T8672 5298, www.opalcapitaloftheworld.com.au District Council offices, Hutchison St.*

Colour map 5, grid C4
Population. 3,500
535 km from Port
Augusta, 690 km from
Alice Springs, 730 km
from Yulara

Coober Pedy

Norton La
Chadwick Rd
To Catacomb Church
McKenzie Cl
Charnau Cl
Lemon Pl
To Jewellers Shop Rd
Seventeen Mile Rd
Edwards Rd
Umoona Rd
Stretton Rd
Underground Art Gallery
Holly Cres
To Golf Course, Oodnadatta & Dog Fence
Brewster Rd
Big Winch Lookout
Aylers St
Old Timers Mine
Crowders Gully Rd
Underground Books
Winch St
Umoona
Naylor Pl
Traeger St
Post Office Hill Rd
Hutchison St
Oliver St
Halliday Pl
Italian Club Rd
Marks Cl
Willcox St
Bean St
Saint Nicholas St
Flooring St
Wright Rd
Mines Department Rd
(Pol)
Greyhound Bus Depot
Forms Blvd
To Serbian Orthodox Church
Giles St
Eyre St
Ward St
Stuart St
Flinders St
To Alice Springs, Airport & Breakaways
To Cemetery, Woomera, Adelaide & William Creek
Stuart Highway

N
■ **Sleeping** ● **Eating**
1 Desert Cave 1 Camp Oven Kitchen
2 Mud Hut 2 John's Pizza Bar
3 Opal Cave 3 Opal Inn
4 Radeka's 4 Traces
0 metres 200
0 yards 200

There are many places in town to see former mines and dugout homes. One of the best is the **Old Timers Mine**, a mine dug by hand in around 1916. It is a warren of low curving drives, some filled with displays on early mining methods or seams of opal in situ. The trail also leads through an old style dugout and the former family home of the Goughs who still run the mine. ■ *Daily 0900-1700. $7.50, children $3.50. T8672 5555, www.oldtimersmine.com* **Umoona** is another interesting mine museum complex. Although larger and less intimate, Umoona stands out for its entrance tunnel which has an excellent display on the geology and history of the area and a good short film called 'The Story of Opal'. Guided tours include the film, mine, hand and machine dug homes and an Aboriginal Interpretative Centre. ■ *Daily 0800-1900. Tours 1000, 1200, 1400, 1600. Entrance displays free, tours $8, children $4. T8672 5288, www.umoonaopalmine.com.au Hutchison St.* There are several underground churches in the town such as

Sights

South Australia

South Australia

▶▶ Going underground

Coober Pedy is as famous for its underground living as for its opal and it certainly makes life move comfortable in a place where summer temperatures can reach 50°C in the shade. The 'dugouts' remain at about 23°C all year. They are believed to have been introduced by soldiers returning from the First World War who had discovered the advantages of life underground. About half of the locals live in dugouts which are always excavated, Hobbit-fashion, into hillsides rather than dug from shafts as vertical shafts tend to flood or fill with dust. Mining is not allowed within the town limits which extend several kilometres beyond the main street so all of the openings visible in hills

in and around town are homes. In a ridge where ten places may be visible it is likely that the hill is hiding up to 80 homes. Look for the ventilation pipes or TV aerials in the hillside rather than letterboxes as many residents don't wish to advertize their whereabouts. The swankiest homes are between the town and William Creek Road and some of these have ten bedrooms and a swimming pool. An average home takes about three weeks to create using tunnelling machines and costs about $35,000 to tunnel and furnish. The plot is a snip at about $12,000. But there's nothing like a large heap of dirt outside your home to indicate your status – the higher the pile, the larger the house inside.

the **Catacomb Church**, a hand-dug former mine that was extended into the shape of a cross and turned into a church. It has a charming simplicity that the parishioners explicitly link to the earliest days of Christianity. ■ *Visitors are welcome any time, turn off the lights when you leave. Catacomb Rd, off Hutchison St.* The **Serbian Othodox Church** is a grander affair dug by tunnelling machines with an impressive curved ceiling and unusual modern windows. ■ *Daily 1600-1700. Donation appreciated. Flinders St, off Hutchison St.*

The real attractions of Coober Pedy are simply the eccentricities of local homes, the detritus of film sets left lying around and the cone-shaped mounds of mine tailings on the barren red landscape. The best way to see the place is just to drive around a bit or take one of the tours. Start at the **Big Winch Lookout** where there are good views and some interesting homes nearby. Things to look out for are **Jewellery Shop Road**, where anyone can 'fossick' through the piles of dirt for opal, and the **Cemetery**, with Carl Bratz's keg-topped grave. The fees are cheap at the **Golf Course**. There's not a blade of grass on the 'green' and golfers take their putts on a dirt surface greased with sump oil. Note that visitors cannot enter a **mining field** unless on a guided tour. This is because the fields are riddled with 1½ million open shafts about 1-m wide and 25-m deep. The warning signs are not an exaggeration – tourists have been killed by falling down shafts while taking photos.

Sleeping

There are plenty of places to sleep 'underground' but also rooms for those who may feel claustrophobic. The underground rooms are usually airy with high ceilings but the lack of a window and natural light can feel strange

Dominating the main street is the 5-star **A** *Desert Cave Hotel*, Hutchison St, T8672 5688, www.desertcave.com.au The general facilities are indeed excellent but the 50 rooms are disappointingly bland and none are fully subterranean. The pool and spa are particularly welcome. **B-C** *Mud Hut*, St Nicholas St, T8672 3003, www.mudhutmotel.com.au 20 a/c rooms, all above ground in modern rammed-earth brick buildings, split between standard motel-style doubles and self-contained units which can sleep 6. The bar and dining room is open for breakfast and dinner. **B-E** *Radeka's*, Oliver St, T8672 5223. The 120 or so beds cover a fascinating range from the virtually fully underground suite to budget doubles and the warren of completely subterranean hostel dorms. Good bar and common rooms though the kitchen facilities are inadequate. Clean and comfortable with a Mediterranean air. Recommended. The **C-F** *Opal Cave*, Hutchison St, T8672 5028,

Opal sesame!

Opal was first discovered in Australia in 1849, in Angaston, but the trickle that at first reached Europe became far more substantial after the Coober Pedy claims began to be exploited in earnest in the late 1940s. Now over 50 percent of the world's opal comes from SA, and most of that from the Coober Pedy fields. Opals come in all shapes, sizes and hues. Value varies from opal to opal, but generally speaking a black-based opal is more valuable than a white or milky opal, red-fire opal more valuable than a green coloured opal, which is in turn a step up from a stone with blue colouring, and lastly harlequin opal, with the colouring in patches, is more valuable than pinfire opal where the coloration is in small specks. Jewellery opal is fashioned in three main ways. If sufficiently thick an opal is simply cut, polished and mounted en cabochon. This is known as **solid opal**. A **doublet** is made when a thin slice of opal will show better colouring by having a thin backing, normally of a common (uncoloured) opal or a black silica, glued to it. **Triplets** are then capped by a further layer of transparent quartz, a technique commonly found in jewellery as it enhances the inherent opal colours.

www.opalcavecooberpedy.com, manages nearly 400 beds, mostly in several 50-bed dorms with facilities varying from limited to bathroom only. They also have 4 quaint, very popular self-contained miners' homes, dug by hand in the 1930s. They are, no question, a lot more luxurious now than they were then. There are 2 large caravan parks on the outskirts of town, and another, **Riba's**, 5 km east on the William Creek Rd, T8672 5614, which has some underground sites.

Eating
The café at the Mobil station opens at 0500 ready for the first incoming buses

The expensive **Umberto's** restaurant at the *Desert Cave* provides a standard international menu but is a consistently good option. Open daily 1900-2100. The **Opal Inn**, Hutchison St, T8672 5054, is the main town pub with cheap counter meals daily, lunch and dinner. **Traces**, Hutchison St, T8672 5147, is a small but excellent Greek restaurant. Good-sized cheap meals include a melt-in-the-mouth chicken shaslick. Slightly smaller 'backpacker' portions for $8 are very good value. Daily 1600-2300. **John's Pizza Bar**, Hutchison St, does much more than just pizzas, and the **Camp Oven Kitchen**, Post Office Hill Rd, has good home-cooked meals, including breakfasts. Open 0800-1600.

Shopping

Every business in town seems to sell opal and the choice is overwhelming. However, this does mean hot competition and prices don't vary much. Shop around on Hutchison St. **Umoona**, has some of the best quality stones and settings in town and a huge range to choose from. **Opal Cave** and **Underground Art Gallery** are also worth a look.

Tours
Just about every hotel, motel and caravan park offers a day or half-day tour to the sights on the town's periphery and the Breakaways. See the VIC for a comprehensive listing

Radeka's, T8672 5223, run a lively afternoon minibus tour that also includes a spot of 'noodling' ($28, 4-5 hrs). Further afield, the **Mail Run** day tour, T8672 5558, is an excellent way to get into the deep Outback easily and safely. The Mail Run delivers mail every Mon and Thu to cattle stations on a 600-km triangle between Coober Pedy, William Creek and Oodnadatta, travelling on unsealed roads and the Oodnadatta track. There is time to stop for short walks, photos and chats with locals and there are no more than 8 passengers. Recommended ($90, 12 hrs). **Back of Beyond Tours**, T8672 5900, take small groups (minimum 5 passengers) in 4WD out to the dog fence, Anna Creek station, Williams Creek and Halligan Point on Lake Eyre. This takes a full day with lunch included (0800, 8hrs, $130). **Wrightsair**, T8672 5574, www.wrightsair.com.au, offer scenic flights over the Breakaways at sunset ($65, 30 mins). Longer options include flights to Lake Eyre, Dalhousie Springs, Uluru (Ayers Rock) and Alice Springs (day flights from $300-500). **Explore the Outback**, T1800 064 244,

South Australia

www.austcamel.com.au/explore, run 4-day camel treks from William Creek looking at ecology, history and wildlife, and sleeping under the stars in a swag. William Creek is 170 km from Coober Pedy and it is possible to be dropped off and collected by the *Mail Run* or fly there with *Wrightsair*.

Transport **Airport** Many accommodation operators offer free transfers, or contact the *Desert Cave*, T8672 5688, $6 one-way. *Kendell* operate regular flights to **Adelaide**. **Bus** *McCafferty's/Greyhound* have services from the Mobil roadhouse, north to **Alice Springs** daily at 0600 (8 hrs). Their **Adelaide** service (10½ hrs) leaves daily at 1925. **Train** The *Ghan* does stop at Manguri Station, 47 km from Coober Pedy, but you would need to pre-arrange transport from the station to Coober Pedy if coming by train.

Directory **Banks** *Westpac* ATM only in Hutchison St. **Car servicing** *Desert Traders*, Umoona Rd, *Fuel is around 5-10c* T8672 5230. Chemist *Opal Fields*, T8672 5159, Hutchison St, Mon-Fri 0900-1800, Sat *more expensive than* 0900-1400. **Communications** Internet *Radeka's* and **Post Office**, Hutchinson St. *in Port Augusta*

Coober Pedy In the desert north of Coober Pedy are the **Breakaways**, flat-topped mesas **to Marla** (hills) in a stony desert which have featured in movies such as *Mad Max III* and *The Adventures of Priscilla, Queen of the Desert*. Access is via an unsealed loop road back to Coober Pedy along the **Dog Fence**, which stretches for 5,300 km across South Australia, NSW and Queensland and was built to keep dingos out of sheep country. The **Breakaways Reserve** and Dog Fence can only be reached on unsealed roads (2WD but impassable after rain) so those without transport or in a hire car will need to take one of the many tours from town. ■ *Entry permit required from VIC or shelter at Lookout One. Signposted from Stuart Highway, 23 km north of Coober Pedy. Circuit 70 km return.*

The highway passes through the bulk of the opal fields and then out onto a 155-km stretch to the **C-E** *Cadney Homestead* roadhouse, T8670 7994, www.cadneyhomestead.com.au Accommodation is provided in self-contained units or budget cabins. Camping is free and the pool is open to non-residents. Just before the roadhouse is a rough unsealed road that leads after about 100 km to the **Painted Desert**, a series of multi-coloured mesas similar to the Breakaways but on a much grander scale. Also out here is **C** *Evelyn Downs Station*, T8670 7991, www.senet.com.au/~apttours offering B&B in the renovated shearers' quarters on this isolated pastoral lease, or the option of a full-board stay with full-on 4WD tours (from $160) included. Another 80 km further on is the **C-E** *Marla* roadhouse, T8670 7001, which has 24-hour fuel, supermarket, post office, bar and a cafeteria (open 0630-2130), air-conditioned motel rooms and budget rooms, and a pool for residents.

The Outback tracks

Desert Parks Entry to some of the outback parks and reserves (Simpson Desert, Tallaringa, Wabma Kadarbu) requires a Desert Parks Pass, covering both entry and camping (annual, $90 per vehicle). It also covers entry and camping fees for Innamincka, Lake Eyre, and Witjira parks. It's available at many outlets from Port Augusta (the Wadlata Centre) northward. For further details contact the *Parks and Wildlife Service* (hotline, T1800-816078). Note that the pass pack includes a parks booklet and all the relevant *Westprint* maps. Day passes are also available for Lake Eyre ($10 per vehicle) and day/night passes for Innamincka, Lake Eyre, and Witjira ($18).

South Australia

The unsealed Strzelecki Track follows the eastern border of South Australia, through the heart of the **Strzelecki Desert** and the **Innamincka Regional Reserve**. It is unsealed the entire way and although possible for 2WD when conditions are good, it is recommended for well-prepared 4WD vehicles only. Fuel and accommodation are available at **Innamincka**, from which other tracks fan out into the Outback of Queensland and New South Wales. The Desert Parks Pass or Innamincka day/night pass (if you're going to travel through that fast) is required to travel this track. The Desert Parks Pass lasts for a year and is $90 per vehicle, covering entry and camping fees for Innamincka, Lake Eyre, and Witjira parks. It's available at many outlets from Port Augusta (the Wadlata Centre) northward. The pass includes a parks booklet and all the relevant *Westprint* maps. Day passes are also available for *Lake Eyre* ($10 per vehicle) and day/night passes for *Innamincka, Lake Eyre,* and *Witjira* ($18). For detailed information, refer to the *Westprint* map of the Strzelecki and Birdsville.

The Strzelecki Track
No fuel is available along the 475 km from Lyndhurst to Innamincka To check unsealed road conditions see www.transport.sa. gov.au/northern or T1300-361033 Westprint map available

Innamincka, a true Outback experience and one of the most isolated communities in Australia, marks the point at which the Strzelecki Track heads over the border into Queensland, where it ceases to become a designated highway. This tiny town also marks the point where the explorers Burke and Wills finally ran out of supplies and ideas. Their graves can both be visited, though are many kilometres apart. The town is on the banks of Cooper Creek, with several large, permanent waterholes providing some pleasant camping areas and also an unexpected boat cruise aboard the **MV Cooper** ■ *Daily 0900, 1615 (2 hrs) if sufficient numbers. $25, children $15. T8675 9901 or 8675 2238.* Also along the creek are several sites of Aboriginal carvings. A day's excursion north of the town is the World Heritage area of **Coongie Lakes**, one of Australia's few arid area wetlands. Aside from camping, accommodation is provided by the legendary bush pub where the locals park their planes just outside the door, the *Innamincka Hotel,* {$44-66 double} T8675 9901. Accommodation also at *Cooper Creek Homestay,* {$70 double plus $25} T6575 9591. The *Trading Post* has fuel, groceries, maps and some camping gear.

Innamincka
Colour map 5, grid C5 475 km from Lyndhurst, 375 km from Windorah (QLD)

Marree is the biggest town on the track and boasts a historic hotel and two small roadhouses, both with cafés and basic groceries. Scenic flights are available from the town, T8675 8352. One option overflies **Lake Eyre**, another passes over the **Marree Man**, a 5-km-long detailed 'drawing' of an Aboriginal figure 70 km west of Marree, the origin of which remains a mystery. The **D** *Marree Hotel,* T8675 8344, has 20 rooms, mostly air conditoned, ranging from singles to family. Meals daily 1200-1400, 1800-2000. There are a couple of caravan parks, the **C-E** *Drovers Rest,* T8675 8371, having the best range of accommodation and facilities. Campers may prefer the grassy lawn at the *Oasis* caravan park, near the pub.

Marree
Colour map 5, grid C4 Population: 250 370 km from Coober Pedy, 520 km from Birdsville

From Marree the unsealed Birdsville Track passes east of Lake Eyre on its way north to **Birdsville**, just over the border in Queensland. It passes through **Tirari desrt** and **Sturt Stony Desert**, with a useful stop between them at **Mungerannie**, where accommodation and fuel are available. From Birdsville the **Birdsville Developmental Road** heads east to Charleville (800 km, the first 270 km of which are unsealed), and the **Eyre Developmental Road** continues north to Boulia (380 km, unsealed). None of these routes are recommended for standard vehicles. For detailed information, refer to the *Westprint* map of the Birdsville and Strzelecki (www.westprint.com.au, T03 5391 1466).

The Birdsville Track
Mungerannie 205 km from Marree, 310 from Birdsville

South Australia

Oonadatta Track
Westprint map available

The unsealed Oodnadatta Track follows a route taken by the dogged explorer, John McDouall Stuart, who first crossed Australia from Adelaide to Darwin in 1862. It was his third attempt and in 2 years of trying he only had a scant three months restocking supplies in Adelaide. Stuart is thought to have followed the advice of local Aboriginal people because the route is also an ancient Aboriginal trade route and follows a line of mound springs. The availability of water meant that the Overland Telegraph Line in the 1870s and the Central Australian Railway in 1890 also followed this route. The Oodnadatta testifies both to the detailed knowledge Aboriginal people had of their land and to tough determined European pioneers. It can be passable for 2WD and is frequently graded, though it usually gets rutted and difficult after rain. Outback driving rules apply.

Marree to William Creek
William Creek: colour map 5, grid C4
205 km from Marree,
205 km from Oodnadatta

This section first passes through a moonscape of eroded hills and mesas, by the bizarre roadside sculptures of Alberrie Creek, to the shore of Lake Eyre South. The lake is usually dry and the salty surface glitters to the horizon. About 30 km on, just past the Mound Springs, there is something of an oasis at **Coward Springs**. This former rail siding is being carefully restored by the owner, who has built a small, pleasant campground ($6 per person). A flowing bore provides the water for a novel spa bath among the reeds of a small wetlands area. Day visitors are welcome. **Lake Eyre** is usually dry, a vast salt-pan stretching as far as the eye can see. The northern and southern lakes only connect when they fill with water, something which happens perhaps twice a century (it last happened in 1974). If it does happen to be full, or nearly so, it is worth making the trip to the shores of the northern lake. There's a signposted 4WD-only track on the right about 10 km south of **William Creek**, a major overnight and refuelling stop. It consists of a pub and café and a small outdoor museum of rocket and engine parts. The bar of **D-E** *William Creek Hotel*, T8670 7880, is festooned with mementos from countless visitors, including business cards, rego plates and underwear. Accommodation in four spacious en suite, air conditioned rooms, all sleeping four, and a basic bunkhouse. No kitchen facilities. Simple counter meals available all day, the more sophisticated restaurant is open 1200-1400, 1800-2000. 4WD charters are also available at the pub. Over the road the **D** *General Store*, T8670 7746, is more of a café, open 0730-1700, with surprisingly pleasant camping areas and 20 a/c cabins out the back. Scenic flights over Lake Eyre ($135) and four-day camel safaris also operate from the miniscule settlement. Contact *Wrightsair*, T8670 7962, and *Explore the Outback*, T1800 064 244, respectively.

Oodnadatta
Population: 180
210 km from Marla

Oodnadatta was the Ghan's railhead for a few decades from 1890 until the late 1920s, though it is now difficult to imagine the hustle of transferring passengers, luggage and freight onto long camel trains for the exhausting onward journey to Alice. The spectacle is evoked to some degree in the old station, which is now a mostly photographic **museum** depicting the town's century or so of existence. A key can be picked up from the roadhouse. The frontier spirit may have gone, but this is still an evocative spot. The town has adapted well to its new clientele and the pub and roadhouse cheerfully cater for the visitors. The **D** *Transcontinental Hotel*, T8670 7804, has 6 rooms, all air conditoned with good value singles, plus a cheap self-contained house that sleeps up to 12. Cheap meals available Mon-Sat 1200-1400, 1800-2000. There is a pleasant, covered beer garden out the back and pet roos for company. Licensed to 2100 only. They also sell the Desert Parks Pass. The colourful **C-F** *Pink Roadhouse*, T8670 7822, www.biziworks.com.au/pink, is open daily 0800-1700 for fuel, repairs, supplies, snacks and takeaways. They are also a post office and run the

South Australia

caravan park which has a range of cabin-based rooms and a very basic bunk-house. Their pool is available to all town visitors. Camping is possible at the park but only on gravel. Ask at the roadhouse for pleasant, quiet places to camp close to town. There are plans afoot for a town interpretative centre and internet café to join the general store, police station and small hospital.

North of Oodnadatta a minor unsealed road continues 250 km up to **Mount Dare** where fuel and accommodation are available. A Desert Parks Pass or Witjira day/night pass is required to get this far as the road and facilities are within the **Witjira National Park**. This road is possible, but not recommended for 2WD. Mount Dare is the jump-off point for 4WD tracks heading east to Dalhousie Springs, an unusually situated hot variety, and the **Simpson Desert**, and also north to **Finke**. The eastern tracks can be followed, by thoroughly prepared parties, through this parched land all the way to Birdsville in Queensland. *Mount Dare Homestead*, T8670 7835, micscorporate@bigpond.com, near Dalhousie, has fuel, a store, a hotel, camping and homestead accommodation.

Dalhousie Springs & the Simpson Desert *For further details contact the Parks and Wildlife Service (see above) Westprint map available*

The Eyre Peninsula and the Nullarbor

*Shaped like a miniature India sitting on the eastern end of the Great Australian Bight, the Eyre Peninsula is one of Australia's forgotten corners. The interior is a huge expanse of grain fields, the results of which fill enormous silos that dominate many of the towns. The coastline, particularly the west coast, is a series of spectacular white-sand beaches, wide bays, low rocky cliffs and headlands. Unspoilt and untouched (except for the denuded interior), even in peak summer season it's almost considered rude to have to share a beach. Many of the seaside towns are remarkably similar, quiet spots where you can hunt for the big fish or the bigger wave, or camp by a beach in the middle of nowhere, though **Coffin Bay**, a small holiday village, and the lively city of **Port Lincoln** have the most to offer. Beyond the Peninsula the infamous **Nullarbor** stretches west for days. It is notoriously stark, but the well-prepared traveller who takes the time to leave the highway occasionally will be rewarded with dramatic scenery and the silence and space of the ancient plain. Southern right whales come to the Bight in winter to mate and play in the clear waters. If you are anywhere near the **Head of Bight** between June and October, a visit to see them just a few metres from the cliffs is a must.*

See www.epta.com.au

Ins and outs

Air *Kendell Air* flies to Ceduna, Port Lincoln and Whyalla from Adelaide and car hire is available in those towns. **Bus** *Premier Stateliner* operate services from **Adelaide** down the east coast of the peninsula and also across the top to **Ceduna**. *Coastlink* run the only coach service between **Port Lincoln** and **Ceduna**, though at the time of writing there was some doubt whether this service would continue to be viable. **Interstate** *McCafferty's/Greyhound* have coach services crossing the Nullarbor to **Perth**. **Car** By far the best way to see the Peninsula and the Nullarbor is in your own vehicle or on an 'adventure' tour. If travelling from **Adelaide** fuel prices take a hike at Port Augusta, and then keep increasing.

Getting there & around

Whyalla, 75 km south of Port Augusta, is the second largest city in South Australia but it doesn't feel like it. Deserted shopping streets sit at the edge of an urban sprawl that has grown up next to Australia's only operational

Port Augusta to Port Lincoln *Distance 340 km*

South Australia

steelworks. The main attraction is the **Whyalla Maritime Museum**, home to Australia's biggest landlocked ship, the *HMAS Whyalla*. ■ *Daily 1000-1600, $6, $3.30 children, under-5s free. T8645 7900. Tours every hr from 1100 to 1500.* The museum sits conveniently next to the **Whyalla Tourist Centre**. ■ *Lincoln Highway, T1800 088 589 or 8645 7900, tourist.centre@whyalla.sa.gov.au Open Mon-Fri 0900-1700, Sat 0900-1600, Sun 1000-1600.*

Some 85 km south of Whyalla is **Cowell**, home to many oyster farms and known for its locally mined, cut and polished jade, available at many outlets in the town. There are many scenic drives to the north and south, including an unsealed 20-km road to Port Gibbon, a derelict shipping port with a good clean beach, backed by massive dunes. Of the few coastal towns south of Cowell, **Tumby Bay** makes the best stop and is a cheaper sleeping alternative to nearby Port Lincoln. **Koppio Smithy Museum**, 30 km south of Tumby Bay, is worth the detour. This small turn-of-the-century settlement has been thoughtfully restored and includes a blacksmith's shop, settlers' cottage and school room. Other buildings house antique agricultural machinery and domestic appliances. ■ *School holidays, Tue-Sun 1000-1700. $4, children $1, concessions $3. T8684 4243.*

Port Lincoln

Colour map 1, grid B1
Population: 13,000
337 km from Port Augusta, 399 km from Ceduna

The prosperous fishing port of Port Lincoln sits on one of the world's largest natural harbours, protected by Boston Island. This is home to Australia's largest commercial fishing fleet and part of the wealth derived from the industry has been used to create the sophisticated **Lincoln Cove Marina**. Port Lincoln is also a major service centre for agriculture and the town's foreshore is

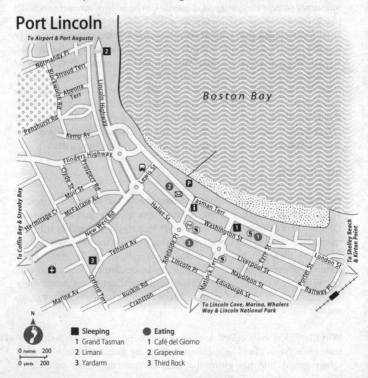

Port Lincoln

To Airport & Port Augusta

Boston Bay

To Coffin Bay & Streaky Bay

To Shelley Beach & Kirton Point

To Lincoln Cove, Marina, Whalers Way & Lincoln National Park

N

0 metres 200
0 yards 200

■ **Sleeping**
1 Grand Tasman
2 Limani
3 Yardarm

● **Eating**
1 Café del Giorno
2 Grapevine
3 Third Rock

dominated by giant wheat silos. The city has a **bus** that shuttles around three different circuits every hour and a half or so, passing the western end of Tasman Terrace on each circuit. One heads north, one passes Kirton Point, the other goes out to Lincoln Cove. T8683 3036. The enthusiastic *Visitor Information Centre* is on Adelaide Place, *T1800 629 911 or T/F8683 3544, plvic@dove.net.au* ■ *Daily 0900-1700.* Further afield, the **Lincoln National Park** has a range of interesting walks and camping facilities and is largely accessible with 2WD. ■ *Entry $6 per day/night per car. Contact the Visitor Information Centre for further details.* **Whalers Way** is a 14 km unsealed, sometimes rough, scenic drive 32 km south of Port Lincoln. The rocky coastal scenery is spectacular and encounters with kangaroos, emus or seals are likely. There are also camping areas with toilets and BBQs. Allow about five hours. ■ *Entry $17 per car. Contact the Visitor Information Centre for key and permit.*

Sleeping & eating

A-C *Marina*, 13 Jubilee Dr, Lincoln Cove, T8682 6141, lci@dove.com. Luxurious self-contained apartments overlooking the marina. Large units are exceptional value for groups. Free entry to the leisure centre. Recommended.**C-D** *Grand Tasman*, 94 Tasman Terr, T8682 2133, F8682 2936, gthotwl@camtech.net.au Centrally located pub, overlooking the sea with 26 rooms. For budget cabins try the grassy **D-E** *Kirton Point Caravan Park*, Hindmarsh St, T8682 2537. **C** *Island Towers*, 9 Island Dr, T8683 3677, F8683 3204, offord@camtech.net.au Stylish room with deck over marina waterfront. Private entrance in modern family home. **C** *Yardarm*, 14 Telford Av, T8683 0984, F8683 3637. Homely studio with private balcony.   Superb mid-range seafood can be had at *Sails*, Marina Hotel, T8682 6141. Open daily 1200-1430, Sun-Thu 1800-2030, Fri-Sat 1800-2100. Seafood lovers should also try *Moorings* in the *Grand Tasman Hotel*, T8682 2133. Inventive food in pleasant dining room on the waterfront. Open daily 1200-1400, 1800-2130. *Café del Giorno*, 80 Tasman Terr, T8683 0577. Good cheap Italian food. Open daily 1000-2200. The pick of the lunch cafés are *Grapevine*, in the Civic Centre, and *Third Rock*, Liverpool St.

Accommodation is available in the Lincoln Cove Marina, for 2 nights or more. Contact the VIC for bookings and details

Festivals

The biggest festival on the Eyre Peninsula is Tunarama, held on the foreshore and attended by 25,000 people every year. A riot of mad competitions, processions, sideshows and fish throwing. The world record in the World Champion Tuna Toss is 24.65 m, set in 1988. Huge fun and not to be missed if you are in the area at the end of Jan. Mount Dutton Bay (see below) is well worth a visit any time of year but particularly at Easter for the **Mount Dutton Bay Woolshed Craft Festival**, an event eagerly anticipated by both the local craftspeople and the thousands who attend.

Tours

Port Lincoln has become known as a place where you can 'swim' with white pointer (great white) sharks. This is possible, but very involved, expensive, and by no means guaranteed. The determined should try *Calypso Star Charter*, T8364 4428, F8332 6360, www.nbw.com.au/calypsostar, who also run fishing trips. *Tuna Farm & Boston Bay Cruise* T8682 5585, offer a range of trips on their sailing yacht *Free Spirit*, including a half-day tour to the huge local tuna farms for $30. *Out There*, T8682 6853, F8683 3177, outthere@asiaonline.net.au, have kayaking and walking tours from $15. For those without their own transport the very knowledgable Steve at *Great Australian Bight Safaris*, T/F8682 2750, www.great safariscom.au, runs a variety of 4WD tours from $50.

Transport

Air The airport is 15 km north and the only way to get there is by taxi, $20. *Kendell* have daily flights to **Adelaide**. **Bus** *Coastlink* run a bus service to **Ceduna** with several intermediate stops, leaving 1600 Mon, Wed, Fri. *Premier Stateliner* have buses to **Port Augusta** and **Adelaide** Sun-Fri 0830 and 1845, Sat 2015. Both leave from the *Stateliner* depot. T8682 1288.

South Australia

Coffin Bay & Mount Dutton Bay

Colour map 1, grid B1
Population: 450   40
km from Port Lincoln

Slung casually along a long stretch of low, bush-covered coastline and looking out over several bays, Coffin Bay is synonymous with first class oysters but the town itself remains a quiet and relaxed holiday retreat for South Australians. This is pick-your-own beach country, especially toward and beyond the much smaller Mount Dutton Bay, where a few days exploring can vanish before you know it. This is great walking country at any time of year, with three marked nature trails, from 1-5 km, leading from the Yangie Bay camping spot in the **Coffin Bay National Park** (entrance $6 per car per day/night), the only place in the park you can reach more or less entirely on sealed roads. Essentially a huge sandbar peninsula, covered with high dunes, the park's low scrub skulks around the grey skeletal remains of the Sheoak trees that once dominated the area. The signposted lookouts have spectacular views of shallow blue water and perfect empty beaches. Call in at Hulls Farm, Mount Dutton Bay, to get permission to stroll up Mount Dutton for even better panoramic views of the bays. Allow a couple of hours.

Sleeping and eating There are a couple of sleeping options at Coffin Bay. The modern, brash but comfortable **C** *Coffin Bay Hotel*, Sheppard Av, T8685 4111, F8685 4334, has 8 rooms available, a wide choice on the average mid-range menu and the best breakfast around. The historic **C-E** *Mt Dutton Bay Woolshed*, by the Mt Dutton Bay jetty, has the best location however. T/F8685 4031, www.epta.com.au. They offer B&B in very comfortable renovated shearers quarters (one unit which sleeps up to six) and also have a well equipped *NOMADS* backpacker dorm adjoining their atmospheric shearing museum. Recommended. Also a small café, open daily 0900-1700.The **E** *Coffin Bay Caravan Park*, Giles Rd, T8685 4170, has a few self-contained cabins. The other mid-range restaurant in the area is one of the best on this entire stretch of coast. The *Oysterbeds*, Coffin Bay, T8685 4000, offers very refreshing milkshakes and smoothies with its lunchtime café menu and has beautifully cooked, locally caught fish and farmed oysters on the evening menu. When warm you can sit under the sails on the front terrace overlooking the bay. Open mid-Sep to mid-May, Tue-Sun 1030-2300. Recommended.

Port Lincoln to Ceduna

Between **Elliston**, popular with surfies, and Venus Bay is the turn-off for Talia Caves, and 2 km further on is **Talia Beach**, a seemingly endless stretch of unsullied sand and dunes which makes for a magical camping spot. Situated on the northern side of a small peninsula, **Venus Bay** is home to the **Needle Eye Lookout** which gives views over the far more spectacular and very rugged southern side of the peninsula. Don't miss **Murphy's Haystacks,** a little way south of Streaky Bay (signposted). These are eroded granite outcrops (inselbergs), eerily reminiscent of England's Stonehenge.

The attractive town of **Streaky Bay** makes a good base for exploring the surrounding area, though you'll need your own transport as most of the roads are unsealed (pick up maps from the caravan park). **The Point Labatt Conservation Park** is home to Australia's only mainland breeding colony of sealions, but take binoculars as you can only see them from the top of the cliff. *Baird Bay Charter* runs tours that include snorkelling with sealions and looking for dolphins, T/F8626 5017, sealions@bigpond.com The unsealed **Westall Way Scenic Drive**, just south of Streaky Bay, is a spectacular unsealed coastal road taking in cliff scenery, rock formations and surfing beaches. **Back Beach** is known for particularly good surf. North of Streaky Bay, **Perlubie Beach**, opposite the turn-off for *Felchillo Oasis*, is a beautiful place to camp with beach shelters you can sling your hammock to and basic toilet facilities.

Sleeping and eating **C-E** *Streaky Bay Community*, 33 Alfred Terr, T8626 1008, F8626 1630, streakybayhotel.ozemail.com.au A restored and extended Victorian building with verandah, this pub has a great location overlooking the jetty. Good value budget rooms but no kitchen facilities. **D** *Streaky Bay Foreshore Tourist Park*, Wells St, T8626 1666, F8626 1788, is a council-owned caravan park with 26 cabins a 10-min walk from the pub. Well-run with good facilities, but you pay for the good beach location. The mid-range *Blue Swimmers*, Bay Rd, T8626 1988 offers modern Australian cooking using fresh local produce. Open daily 1130-1400, 1830-2100. Recommended.

Set on the wide shallow shores of Murat Bay, Ceduna services cereal growers in the surrounding area and travellers to and from the Nullarbor. The town is also famous for its local oysters and every October celebrates **Oysterfest** (T8625 3407), a wholehearted festival that includes the South Australian Oyster Opening Championship, the winner of which goes on to try their luck at national level and perhaps even the World Championships in Galway, Ireland. The **VIC** is at 58 Poynton Street, T1800 639 413, travelce@tpg.com.au ■ *Mon-Fri 0900-1730, Sat-Sun 1000-1600.*

Ceduna
Population: 4,000
465 km from Port Augusta, 400 km from Port Lincoln, 490 km from WA border

Sleeping and eating There's little other than roadhouse motels and caravan parks. On the seafront the **C-F** *Foreshore*, O'Loughlin St, T8625 2008, F8625 2854, cedunahotelmotel@ bestwestern.com.au, has a wide range of accommodation and facilities and the 5 deluxe rooms are some of the few overlooking the ocean. The laid-back **E** *Ceduna Greenacres Backpackers*, 12 Kuhlman St, T8625 3811, has small dorms and a double and includes dinner and breakfast in the price. A 10-min walk from the town centre. Most of the motels have unremarkable mid-range restaurants but try the *Cactus Café*, 52 Poynton St, T8625 2977 for Tex-Mex lunch. Open Mon-Fri 0900-1730. If you want to try the local oysters head for the *Ceduna Oyster Bar*, T8625 9086, 2 km out on the Perth road. Open Mon-Sat 0930-1800, Sun 0100-1800. ■

For a wide range of tours such as 4WD Outback trips, blue-crab fishing and whale watching contact *Sea-Dune-Ah Tours*, T/F 8625 3136, www.cedunatours.com Scuba diving gear can be hired from the *Nuyts Dive Club*, T8625 2775. **Fishing** For boat and line hire try *West Coast Boat and Equipment Hire*, 3A Park Terr, T8625 2211. For fishing trips, diving trips or boat charter contact either *Ceduna Fishing Adventures*, T/F 8625 3136, pjtaylor@tpg.com.au or *Ceduna Boat Charter*, T/F8625 2654.

Tours and activities

Air There are flights to and from **Adelaide** every day with *Kendell*. Contact *Traveland Ceduna* for bookings, T8625 2780. It shares an office with the Visitor's Centre. They can also help with bus bookings. **Bus** *Premier Stateliner* have buses to **Port Augusta** and **Adelaide** Mon-Fri 1900, Sat-Sun 1830. T8625 2279. *Coastlink* runs a coach service to **Port Lincoln** with several intermediate stops, leaving 0630 Mon, Wed, Fri. T8625 2032. *McCafferty's/Greyhound* bus to **Perth** at 0630 on Tue, Thu and Sat from outside the Pine Grove Motel; to **Adelaide** at 2055 on Tue, Thu and Sat.

Transport

South Australia

The Nullarbor

Although the coast was mapped in 1802 by Matthew Flinders, a crossing of the feared Nullarbor Plain was not attempted until Edward Eyre, John Baxter and their three Aboriginal guides set out in 1840. Baxter never made it out of the Nullarbor, as six months into the epic journey Baxter was murdered by two of the guides who then made off with most of the expedition's remaining supplies. But Eyre and his one remaining guide did make it across and into Australian history. The Eyre Highway, the only sealed road between Western

Australia and South Australia, crosses the true Nullarbor only briefly before you reach the border. The remainder of the journey is not quite as treeless and featureless as most expect and there are are plenty of excursions for those with the time and curiosity to explore.

Ins & outs **Car** Remote driving rules apply (see 218). From Adelaide take the Highway 1 out to Port Augusta and Ceduna. Penong propagevides the last reasonably priced fuel. **Bicycle** This is a punishing bike ride and not to be taken lightly, but is certainly possible. Prepare with care and inform roadhouses of your itinerary. **Train** Although the *Indian Pacific* crosses the Nullarbor on its journey between **Adelaide** and **Perth**, and purists will say this is the way to see the true plain, the trip is uncomfortable in anything but first class, and many simply find the trip monotonous. **Tours** *Nullarbor Traveller* run superb 9-day 4WD adventure trips from Adelaide to Perth ($891). 2-3 days are spent crossing the Nullarbor. T1800 816858, info@the-traveller.com.au Departures every fortnight.

The first and last real settlement is **Penong**, some 75 km west of Ceduna. A 24-hour petrol stop, grocery, caravan park and pub provide the essentials and there's an interesting stop a kilometre past the town. The 130-year-old *Woolshed* is now a rough and ready museum and craft shop that sells exquisite glassware and pottery. ■ *T8625 1105. Thu-Mon 1000-1600.* Penong is also the turn-off for **Cactus Beach**, one of Australia's best surfing spots. Experienced surfers travel from all over Australia to try their luck with the big waves off this pristine stretch of coast. Cactus beach has a caravan park, basic facilities and camping is allowed in defined areas. There are turn-offs to **Fowlers Bay** 30 km and 70 km on from Penong. Once the site of a thriving town, an equally thriving tourist area, with a shop and basic facilities, is now growing within sight of its ruins. The **D** *Fowlers Bay Caravan Park* has 20 powered sites and four on-site vans. T8625 6143. **C-E** *Nundroo*, T8625 6021, just after the second Fowlers Bay turn-off has budget accommodation and standard motel rooms. Adjacent is *Davis Motors*, the last garage until well into Western Australia, T8625 6119.

By the time you reach **C-D** *Yalata Roadhouse*, T8625 6986, 52 km beyond Nundroo, gum trees dominate and make for a stark contrast to the Nullarbor beyond. The roadhouse is Aboriginal-owned and has a good selection of art and artifacts on display and for sale. There are a small number of budget and motel rooms and camping facilities though no kitchen. Open 0800-2030. Soon after leaving Yalata the gums thin out and you hit the Nullarbor proper, cutting through the featureless bluebush 'treeless' plain close to the coastline. After 80 km you reach the turn-off to the **Head of Bight**, just 12 km off the highway, where the raw edge of the 80-m-high **Bunda Cliffs** meets the long beaches running up from the Eyre Peninsula. This is a great spot to see whales during the season (June-October). Permits $8, concessions $6, children free. T8625 6201.

The **C-E** *Nullarbor Roadhouse*, T8625 6271, is just 15 km on from the Head of Bight turning. It offers motel units and backpacker-type accommodation, a pricey restaurant, and takeaways, and the cheapest fuel before Mundrabilla. **Whale-watching flights** (in season) can be taken from here. Contact *Whale Air*, T8625 6271, F8625 6271, who also fly a 3½-hour Nullarbor Air Safari. You are now on the true Nullarbor. From here it is 180 km to the border. At the **C-E** *Border Village*, T9039 3474, are 24 motel units, eight high-standard budget cabins, a restaurant, swimming pool, and a bar.

Transport *McCafferty's/Greyhound* buses leave the *Nullabor Roadhouse* to Perth at 1000 on Tue, Thu and Sat, calling at *Border Village* at 1225. The bus to Adelaide leaves Border Village at 1225 and *Nullbor Roadhouse* at 1635.

South Australia

Tasmania

This heart-shaped island state, about the size of Ireland, is usually forgotten by mainland Australians, leftoff maps and omitted from the itineraries of visitors. There are no vast, flat plains here, no red, dusty interior, no searing heat or enormous distances to travel. Instead, much of the island is a magnificent wilderness, covered in mountains and rainforest, bordered by a dramatic coastline of cliffs and meandering peninsulas. More than a third of Tasmania is protected by a World Heritage Area, national parks, and forest reserves.The cleanest air and sea in the world, swathes of uninhabited, untouched land and a tiny population attract visitors seeking tranquil, natural beauty. Tasmania's isolation has also helped preserve many species of wildlife and flora that are now extinct on the mainland. It is a place made for adventure where almost every outdoor activity is possible, from rock climbing and kayaking to diving and bushwalking. The **World Heritage Area**, which dominates the western half of the island, includes the breathtaking **Cradle Mountain-Lake St Clair National Park**, an area traversed by the Overland Track, one of the world's best extended walks. Of course there are more sedate pleasures too – driving wonderful scenic routes, tasting the island's cheeses, wines and seafood, and exploring the ruins of the island's colonial past. Established as a major penal settlement in the early 1800s, Tasmania retains more 19th-century buildings than any other state.

Tasmania

Things to do in Tasmania

1 Take a couple of days to explore **Port Arthur** and walk out to one of the spectacular coastal cliffs, such as **Cape Huay.**

2 Test your luck and see if you can catch **Cradle Mountain** on a clear day, and if time allows pull on your boots and tackle the **Overland Track.**

3 Experience the history of **Hobart** by walking around Salamanca Place, Battery Point, and the wharves before taking a harbour cruise.

4 Brave the wild northwest coast, taking the time to meet the local **Tasmanian devils** and, who knows, maybe even the tigers!

5 Take a scenic flight out to **Port Davey** at the heart of the World Heritage-listed Wilderness Area and absorb sheer unadulterated beauty.

6 Climb **Mount Amos** for the most striking views of Wineglass Bay, the picture-perfect crescent of sand that graces part of the spectacular Freycinet Peninsula.

7 Make **Strahan** your base to see the vast Macquarie Harbour and its tributary rivers, the King and the Gordon.

Tasmania

Ins and outs

Getting there   **Air** There are daily *Qantas*, T131313, www.qantas.com.au, flights between **Melbourne** and **Hobart**, **Launceston**, **Devonport** and **Burnie** airports. Also from Sydney to Hobart. *Kendell*, T131300, www.kendell.com.au, may still offer most of these routes, plus a flight from Melbourne to King Island. *Virgin Blue*, T136789, www.virginblue.com.au, have flights from Melbourne to Launceston. *Tasair*, T6248 5088, www.tasair.com.au, fly to King Island from both **Devonport** and **Burnie**. **Ferry** *TT-Line*, T132010, www.tt-line.com.au, operate a year-round conventional car ferry, the *Spirit of Tasmania*, between Station Pier, **Port Melbourne** and **Devonport** (13 hrs). Evening sailings from **Melbourne** Mon, Wed, Fri with a morning Sun service subject to demand. Afternoon sailings from **Devonport** Tue, Thu, Sat with a late-night service Mon subject to demand. The *Spirit* goes into dry dock for around 3 weeks mid-winter. Subsidized vehicle fares from $110 return, plus driver and passenger fares from around $350 return for a hostel bunk, $450 per person for a twin-bunk cabin. Bicycles $54 return, motorbikes $76. Prices 10-30% cheaper Feb-Nov. Buffet evening meal and breakfast included. *TT-Line* also operate a vehicle catamaran service, the *Devil Cat*, from late Dec to Easter, between **Port Melbourne** and **George Town** (6 hrs). Morning sailings from Melbourne Thu, Sat and Mon. Afternoon sailings from George Town Fri, Sun and Tue. Vehicle prices as per the *Spirit*, passenger prices slightly higher than the hostel-bunk rate.

Getting around   **Air** *Par Avion*, T6248 5390, www.paravion.com.au, operate out of several airfields around the state including **Cambridge**, **Coles Bay** and **Strahan**. They specialize in national park scenic, remote stay and 'walking' flights, such as into Malaleuca for South Coast Track walkers. *Tasair*, T6248 5088, www.tasair.com.au, fly between **Hobart** and **Burnie** every Mon-Fri, and from there daily to King Island. **Bicycle** The *Launceston City Youth Hostel* hires out mountain and touring bikes, complete with panniers and camping gear. **Bus** There are 2 state-wide operators, *Redline*, T1300 360000, redline@tasredline.com.au, and *Tassie Link*, T1300 300520, www.tigerline.com.auThe former operates the main direct north-south service and northern services. The latter offers predominantly southern and west coast services and a number of 'jump-on, jump-off' passes, for example 7 days travel within a 10-day trip ($150). Their summer services run from late Dec to Easter Mon. The *YHA*, T8414 3000, travel@yhasa.org.au, offers an inclusive *Adventure Freedom Coach* pass (*Tassie Link*) plus accommodation package from $290 per person for 7 nights. **Backpacker bus** There are a couple of operators offering full-island tours, including the locally owned *Under Down Under*, T6369 5555, www.underdownunder.com.au Round island trips $415 for 5 days, $595 for 7 days. Some meals, tours and entry fees included, but not accommodation. **Vehicle hire** Cars and campervans can be hired in both cities and some major towns. The *YHA* offers inclusive car hire (*Delta*) plus accommodation packages from $318.50 per person for 7 nights (2 people). Drivers must be 21 or over. Motorbikes and fully equipped camping trailers are available just outside **Launceston**.

Tourist information   The government funded *Tourism Tasmania* website is www.discovertasmania.com For enquiries T1800-806846. Another comprehensive government website is www.tas.gov.au This has a useful index to all Tasmanian content on the world wide web. The **VICs** in Hobart, Launceston, Devonport and Burnie provide information and bookings for their local area and the rest of the state. Other offices provide information only on the local area. *Service Tasmania*, T1300-135513, www.service.tas.gov.au, provides Tasmanians with one-stop shopping for government services. It is mostly aimed at local residents but can be useful to visitors as offices usually stock regional and topographic maps, and sell national park passes. Most Tasmanian towns have a Service

Tasmania office, open Mon-Fri only. *Travelways* is an excellent free newspaper, listing all accommodation, including prices. Also online, www.travelways.com.au, but without prices. The **Conservation Volunteers** contact point is in Hobart, T6231 1779, hobart@conservationvolunteers.com.au

Maps and publications *Tasmanian Map Centre*, Hobart, T6231 9043, www.ontas.com.au/map-supplies, has the largest selection of maps in Tasmania, a fair few guides and will also offer general advice. Mail order available. The *RACT*, corner of Murray St and Patrick St, Hobart, publish a good and inexpensive fold-out map of the state. *UBD Country Towns and Street Directory: Tasmania*, has good information on towns (including Hobart) and includes a road atlas covering the whole state.

Much of the scenery of the island state is protected by **national parks**, some of which comprise the **Wilderness World Heritage Area**. They are managed by the *Parks and Wildlife Service*, T6233 6191, www.parks.tas.gov.au There is an entrance fee for all parks of $9.90 per vehicle per day, or $3.30 for pedestrians, cyclists or passengers in vehicles with 9 seats or more. Most visitors staying more than a couple of days will find it well worth while investing in a vehicle ($33) or personal ($13.20) holiday pass which covers entry for 2 months, available at any Parks and Wildlife office or station, Service Tasmania offices and many Australian travel agents. The standard park entry fees do not generally cover entrance to attractions such as caves, or park activities. Where allowed, camping fees usually apply ($4.40 per person) and operate on an honesty system, self-registration envelopes are provided near the campsites. *Forestry Tasmania*, T6233 8140, www.forestrytas.com.au, also manages vast areas of the state and provides access to many scenic locations.

National parks & state forests
There are generally no entrance fees to state forests except for specific attractions such as the Air Walk

Camping in state forests is limited but usually free

Just about every Tasmanian **adventure activity** operator is featured on the excellent website www.tasadventures.com.au *Tasmanian Expeditions*, T6334 3477, www.tasmanianexpeditions.com.au, operate a large number of supported all-inclusive trekking, cycling, rafting and canoeing trips ranging from 1-13 days including the **South Coast Track**, **Franklin River** and some excellent combinations from around $150-250 per day.

Adventure tours

History

In 1642 the Dutchman Abel Tasman became the first European to land on the coast of Van Diemen's Land (so-called until 1855), which he named after the Governor of the Dutch East India Company, but it was not until Matthew Flinders' circumnavigation in 1798 that anyone realized it was an island and not joined to the mainland. In 1803 the British authorities at Port Jackson, suspicious of French colonial intentions, sent a party to choose a place for settlement on the River Derwent. The following year Lieutenant-Colonel John Collins, who had been sent to settle what is now Victoria, removed his company of convicts, marines and civil servants to join the settlers at the Derwent River. Collins, who later became the first Governor of Tasmania, disliked the choice of town site and moved the settlement to its current position under Mount Wellington, subsequently to be known as Hobart.

The main purpose of this new colony was to contain the convicts being sent out from Britain at an ever increasing rate. Macquarie Harbour was constructed in 1821 and superseded by Port Arthur in 1830. So horrendous were conditions that some prisoners made murder pacts in order to escape their miserable existence. But, despite the infamy of these horrific penal settlements, the convict system also carried with it an ironic consequence. For

Tasmania

▶▶ **A walk on the wild side**

Tasmania has the best long-distance walking in Australia, with tracks along wild, rugged coast, through spectacular craggy mountain ranges, long white-sand beaches and thick bush and forest. For most treks walkers need to be well-prepared and entirely self-sufficient, although the popular 6-day **Overland Track** (page 864) does have basic huts. Tasmania may not be very big by Australian standards, but it's still not a good place to get lost and the **Parks and Wildlife** Service hires out EPIRBs (emergency electronic beacons) for $10 a month. The best book on walking on the island is 100 Walks in Tasmania by Tyrone T Thomas, though South West Tasmania by John

Chapman is indispensable for taking to the challenging tracks such as the **South Coast Track**. There is good information on the Parks and Wildlife website and maps can be bought or ordered from **Tasmanian Map Centre**. Tasmanian Tramp, a magazine produced by the Hobart Walking Club, publishes interesting articles on walking in Tasmania and is available at bookshops. On arrival the following all have excellent hire services and give sound advice.

Hobart Camping World, T6234 3999, jollyswagmans@bigpond.com

Launceston Launceston City Youth Hostel, T6344 9779.

Devonport Backpackers Barn, T6424 3628.

---

some, transportation resulted in opportunities, wealth and position that would have been unimaginable in class-bound British society. By the late 1830s the population of Tasmania was 43,000, 75% of whom were convicts, former convicts or children of convicts. Such an increase inevitably led to conflict with the native population, and the convicts, now armed, shot Aborigines with impunity. Those that survived were hunted down by the government or moved to Flinders Island in 1833. In this way the rich agricultural land of Tasmania was wholly possessed by free settlers and former convicts.

Economic depression in the 1840s made the convict system with its free labour and high administration costs unpopular with the new Tasmanians and transportation ceased in 1853. As Tasmanian society developed it slavishly copied British culture in all respects. The small green island's beauty was compared to Britain's, and devoted loyalty to 'Home and Crown' underpinned Tasmania's economic dependance on Britain. During the 1870s-90s the economy prospered as gold, tin and copper were found in the north and west. It was at this time that the government decided to produce hydro-electric power to support the new mining industry. Damming rivers and building power stations continued until the 1980s and was seen as vital for the development of the state.

Unlike Victoria and NSW, Tasmania did not receive large numbers of post-war migrants and the majority of the population is of British descent. However, despite popular belief that no Tasmanian Aborigines survived European invasion, Tasmania also has a strong and politically active community of about 8,000 Aboriginal people descended from inhabitants of some of the state's 300 islands, particularly those of the Furneaux group. These people, known as Pallawah, are mainly the offspring of white sealers and whalers and the Aboriginal women they abducted or were given in an attempt to form kinship ties. The Pallhwah have been fighting to prove their identity for more than a hundred years and have had some success since the 1970s, obtaining land rights, recognition of sacred sites and the return of ancestors' bones from museum collections.

Tasmania

Tasmanians are amongst the friendliest of Australians, relaxed and resourceful people who ignore the 'mainlanders' indifference to them and slights about inbreeding and get on with life. As an island people they have a sense of difference and a deep attachment that comes from the intimate knowledge possible in a small contained place. However, in some ways they have the most divided population of all Australian states. In the past Tasmania's environmental treasures, such as the rivers and forests, have been seen as resources ripe for harvesting. The industries of forestry, mining and hydro-electric power generation have shaped both the island's land and culture and the effects continue into the present. Losing some of those treasures, such as the exquisite Lake Pedder in 1972, was the genesis for Australia's green movement. Thanks to the successful campaign to save the Franklin River in the 1980s no more rivers will be dammed in Tasmania but logging (particularly woodchipping) is still a contentious issue. There are many Tasmanians who think jobs are more important than virgin forest and many 'greenies' who want to preserve the environment at any cost. Tourism is now an important part of the equation, bringing in 500,000 visitors annually, and an industry specifically based on the environmental beauty, purity and peace of the island.

Hobart

*Like most harbour cities the best way to enter Hobart is by sea. A fine white arch spans the **Derwent River** and houses spread up the surrounding foothills. The docks are lined with honey-coloured stone warehouses with the modern city buildings rising behind, framed by the imposing bluff of **Mount Wellington**. Most visitors today enter by the 'back door', through suburbia along the highway, and don't immediately see the grandeur of the city's fine Georgian architecture and harbour. The city is at its liveliest during the **Sydney to Hobart Yacht Race**. This legendary race starts in Sydney on Boxing Day when about 150 yachts head south for the four-day journey to Hobart. It is a tough challenging race so when the yachts arrive safely at Constitution Dock the sailors and the city are ready to party. A **Summer Festival** is held during January-February, incorporating the race finish and the week-long Taste of Tasmania, and there is no better time to experience the spirit of the city.*

Colour map 8, grid C1
Population: 195,000
200 from Launceston,
300 km from Strahan
www.hobartcity.com.au

Ins and outs

Air The airport is 18 km northeast of the city centre. The *Airporter Shuttle* meets every flight and makes hotel pick-ups, T0419 382240, ($8.40, children $4.20, 30 mins). A taxi will cost $25-30. **State Bus** The Transit Centre on Collins St is the main terminal for *Tassie Link*, *Tiger Line*, *Redline* and the *Airport Shuttle*.

Getting there
For more details, see Transport, page 813

Bus Most metropolitan bus services leave from outside the main post office on Elizabeth St. The *Metroshop* inside the post office has full details of all services, T132201, www.metrotas.com.au Tickets can be bought from here, from various agents including bookshop *Ellison Hawker*, or on the buses. Single tickets to city centre destinations cost $1.30. A daily multi-trip ticket, $3.40, is valid Mon-Fri from 0900 and all day Sat-Sun. A 10-day multi-trip ticket $26.50. Most buses run approximately 0800-1800, with evening services often restricted to Fri and weekends. **Ferry** The *Wrest Point Wanderer* shuttles daily around the harbour between **Wrest Point**, **Battery Point**, **Sullivans Cove**, the **Botanic Gardens** and **Bellerive**. Services about every 2 hrs, T6223 1914.

Getting around
The city centre is compact and most places of interest can be reached on foot

Tasmania

▶▶ **Great places to stay in Tasmania**

Hawley House, Port Sorrell *(page 847)*

Colville Cottage, Hobart *(page 809)*

Cradle Mountain Lodge *(page 861)*

Kabuki-by-the-sea, Swansea *(page 827)*

Maria Island Penitentiary
(page 826)

Millhouse on the Bridge, Richmond
(page 814)

Swan Haven, Bruny Island *(page 818)*

Traveller's Lodge (YHA), George Town
(page 840)

Udder Backpackers, Triabuna *(page 826)*

Information The **VIC** is called the Tasmanian Travel Centre and provides an information and booking service for the whole state. Mon-Fri 0830-1730, Sat-Sun 0900-1700. T6230 8233, tasbookings@tasvisinfo.com.au Corner of Elizabeth St and Davey St. The *Hobart Historic Walk* leaves from the VIC daily 1000-1200, Sep-May (Jun-Aug bookings only). $17, children under 12 free, concessions $15. Information and maps for national parks can be found at **Service Tasmania**, 134 Macquarie St, T1300-135513. **Disabled** A useful map for people with limited mobility is available from the city council offices, opposite the VIC on Davey St. **Tasmanian Environment Centre**, 102 Bathurst St, T6234 5566, is a useful resource centre with lots of books and information on Tasmania and noticeboards detailing walks, talks and environmental events. This is also the base for the Hobart Walking Club who often allow visitors to join their walks. **Events** can be found listed in the Hobart daily newspaper, *The Mercury*, or in *This Week in Tasmania* free at the VIC. *CentreLines* is a weekly publication listing events of interest to the gay community (also check on www.gaytas.org). **Entertainment** Music, theatre and cinema listings are published in *The Mercury* on Thu.

Sights

Tasmanian Museum & Art Gallery Just north of Franklin Square is the magnificent Tasmanian Museum and Art Gallery, the former Customs House and of unusually elaborate classical revival design with its pillars, balustrade and dome. Inside are small but significant collections of art and artefacts that display the island's fauna and flora, indigenous Australasian culture and history, the convict era and Tasmania's European heritage. The café is a good spot for a coffee and a snack. ■ *Daily 1000-1700. Free. Tours Wed-Sun 1430. T6235 0777, www.tmag. tas.gov.au 40 Macquarie St.*

Around St David's Park From Franklin Square head along Davey Street, past many fine old buildings, to **St Davids Park**. This was the original burial ground for Hobart and contains the grave of the first governor, David Collins, and many interesting plaques on a memorial wall. To the right of the park is **Parliament House**. This fine late-Georgian building was constructed by convicts around 1840 and was used as the Customs House until 1856 when Tasmania became self-governing and needed a home for its parliament. A short distance north of the park, on the corner of Murray Street and Macquarie Street, **St Davids Cathedral**, is not particularly old – its foundation stone was laid in 1868 – though both the organ and the Bishops's Throne pre-date it. The latter was made for the 1842 Westminster Abbey consecration of Francis Russell Nixon, Tasmania's first Bishop. An interesting side chapel houses a small museum notable for its collections of regimental colours and small carved stones donated by cathedrals around the British Isles and the old empire.

Tasmania

Walking on Mount Wellington

*Hobart walkers have many fine Tasmanian mountains to climb but they are fortunate to have one of the best right under (or rather above) their noses. There are two main routes to the summit. From **Fern Tree** take the Middle Track to the junction of Radfords Track and head right for The Springs. From there the Pinnacle Track climbs for 1½ km to a junction with the Organ Pipes Track. Ignore this and continue up to the Zig Zag Track. It's very steep but the views provide a good excuse to catch your breath. From the plateau a short track leads north to the summit and lookout (8 km, 3½-4 hrs). The track from **Cascades**, behind the brewery is longer but passes right underneath the spectacular dolerite columns of the Organ Pipes. Head along Old Farm Road past a vehicle barrier to Myrtle Gully Track. This is a lovely section through ferns next to a stream. After about 2 km on this track, and a steepish climb out of the gully, there is a*

junction with a rough dirt road. Turn left and continue a short distance to Junction Cabin, at the crossroads of several tracks. Take Hunters Track up to Pinnacle Road and cross the road to find the Organ Pipes Track. This is the most dramatic part of the walk, some of the pipes have vertical faces 120 m high. The track meets the Pinnacle Track, and this and the Zig Zag Track should be followed to the summit. To return by the same route makes this walk about 16 km (6½ hrs) but to descend to Fern Tree is shorter and offers more variety (12 km, 5 hrs). Both of these walks are fairly challenging and are exposed near the summit so should only be attempted in fine weather. The mountain is subject to changeable and severe weather so walkers should be prepared with adequate clothing, food and topographic map. The Mount Wellington Walk Map & Notes is widely available in Hobart.

The waterfront The area around the docks makes for a pleasant stroll. Opposite the Museum and Art Gallery is **Constitution Dock**, where many of the Sydney-Hobart yachts tie up after the race. Continue along Davey Street, past **Victoria Dock**, usually crowded with fishing boats, to Hunter Street. Turn right down **Hunter Street** passing many fine Georgian warehouses. This street was originally an island where all cargo and convicts were unloaded. In 1820 a causeway was built to the shore and land reclaimed after which the area developed into a busy industrial wharf. There are signs explaining the history of this area halfway down the street, after looking at these turn right and walk over the bridge past the docks to **Elizabeth Street Pier**. There are several excellent seafood restaurants at the pier. Continue along this area, known as Franklin Wharf, to **Brooke Street Pier** where there are several offices for companies running ferry cruises.

Battery Point Just south of the docks are the Georgian warehouses of **Salamanca Place**, opposite Princes Wharf. These warehouses have been restored and turned into galleries, studios, shops and restaurants. This is Hobart's most attractive area and a fine place to stop for a coffee or lunch. Off Salamanca Place, in Salamanca Square, is **Antarctic Adventure**, which has a room simulating a -5°C blizzard, and displays on historical exploration and modern field-camp equipment. ■ *Daily 1000-1700, $16, children $8, concessions $13. T6220 8229, www.antarctic.com.au* Heading east you'll reach **Kellys Steps** which lead behind the warehouses to **Battery Point**, a historic suburb full of former fishermen's cottages and merchant's houses. At the top of the steps turn left into McGregor Street and follow it down to **Princes Park**. Retrace your steps to McGregor Street and take the first left up Runnymede Street. This leads to **Arthurs Circus**, an unusual green surrounded by quaint cottages. Continue in the same direction to reach **Hampden Road**, the main shopping street of

Tasmania

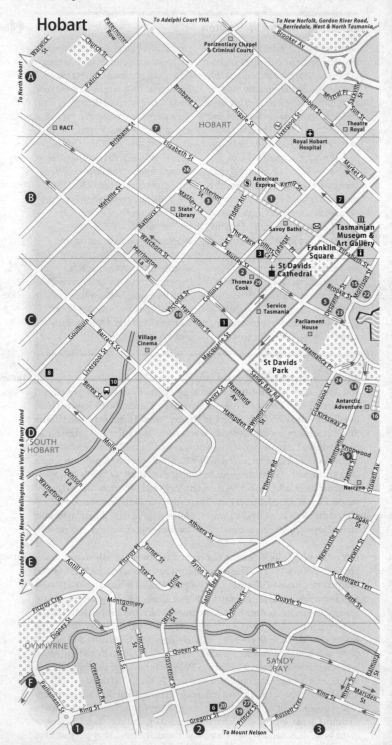

Hobart

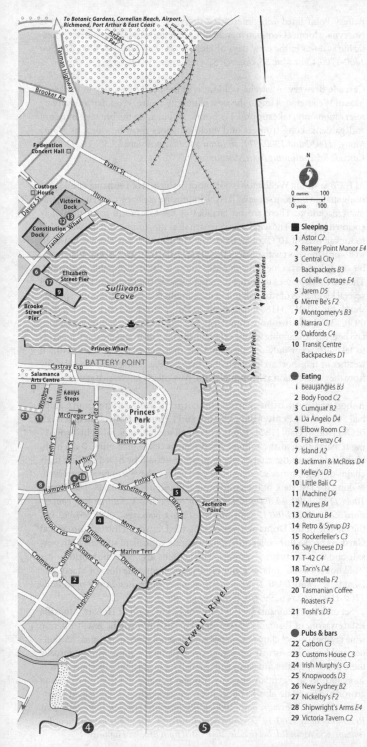

To Botanic Gardens, Cornelian Beach, Airport, Richmond, Port Arthur & East Coast

Sleeping
1 Astor C2
2 Battery Point Manor E4
3 Central City Backpackers B3
4 Colville Cottage E4
5 Jarem D5
6 Merre Be's F2
7 Montgomery's B3
8 Narrara C1
9 Oakfords C4
10 Transit Centre Backpackers D1

Eating
1 Beaujangles B3
2 Body Food C2
3 Cumquat B2
4 Da Angelo D4
5 Elbow Room C3
6 Fish Frenzy C4
7 Island A2
8 Jackman & McRoss D4
9 Kelley's D3
10 Little Bali C2
11 Machine D4
12 Mures B4
13 Orizuru B4
14 Retro & Syrup D3
15 Rockerfeller's C3
16 Say Cheese D3
17 T-42 C4
18 Taco's D4
19 Tarantella F2
20 Tasmanian Coffee Roasters F2
21 Toshi's D3

Pubs & bars
22 Carbon C3
23 Customs House C3
24 Irish Murphy's C3
25 Knopwoods D3
26 New Sydney B2
27 Nickelby's F2
28 Shipwright's Arms E4
29 Victoria Tavern C2

Tasmania

Battery Point lined with interesting domestic architecture. At No 103 is **Narryna**, a former Georgian merchant's home and now a museum of domestic life as it was in the early days of Hobart. ■ *Tue-Fri 1030-1700, Sat-Sun 1400-1700. Closed Jul. $5, children $2, concessions $3.50. T6234 2791.*

West of the centre **Cascade Brewery**, Australia's oldest, is at the head of a valley in the lee of Mount Wellington, 4 km to the west of the city centre. Weekday tours are by reservation only, take around 1½ hours, and include the brewery museum and gardens. Long trousers and enclosed shoes must be worn. ■ *Tours Mon-Fri 0930 and 1300. $11, children $4.50, concessions $7.50. T6221 8300. Cascade Rd, continuing from Macquarie St.*

Mount Wellington At 1,270 m Mount Wellington is not one of the highest of Tasmania's peaks, but rising straight up from sea-level it is the impressive centrepiece of Hobart's dramatic backdrop. There are no facilities at the top except for a thankfully enclosed lookout. The wind gets very strong at the summit and the wind-chill factor can make it 10°C colder than down in the city. The views are, however, well worth the effort with most of the city and much of the Derwent Valley visible on a clear day. One difficulty for visitors is the lack of public **transport**. There are *Metro* buses to Fern Tree and Cascades, but from here there are still several kilometres of stiff walking to the summit (see box). However, a private shuttle bus, T0417 341804, runs from 20 Davey Street and back, leaving daily 0930, 1200, 1430 (two-hour round trip, $19.80). Reckon on $50-60 for a return taxi fare. An exhilarating way of experiencing the peak – and the road down - is to take a descent-only cycling tour with *Brake Out*, T6239 1080 ($40). If weather or transport are problematic there is a reasonable view over the city from the signal station at **Mount Nelson**, particularly impressive at night.

North of the centre A short walk north of the centre, at the corner of Brisbane Street and Campbell Street, is the **Penitentiary Chapel and Criminal Courts**, all that is left of Old Hobart Gaol (1821-1963). This small site has some thought-provoking remains such as the solitary confinement cells, some only 70 cm high, built underneath the chapel where prisoners could be heard rattling their chains during Sunday services. The gaol gallows have also been preserved, making the last walk of the condemned all too imaginable. ■ *Daily tours 1000, 1130, 1300, 1430 (entrance by tour only). $7.70, children free, concessions $5.50. T6231 0911. Also daily ghost tours, bookings T0417 361392.* On the far side of the **Domain**, overlooking the Derwent, Hobart's **Botanical Gardens** hold a fine collection of native and exotic plant species, both outside and in conservatory settings. The gardens also have the world's only 'cold house', a sub-antarctic plant house containing the flora of Macquarie Island. ■ *Daily 0830-1700, to 1830 summer. Free. Restaurant open daily 1100-1500, T6234 6299, rtbg@rtbg.tas.gov.au*

Set on a tiny peninsula by the Derwent, 12 km north of Hobart, **Moorilla Estate** was one of Tasmania's first wineries and is still one of the largest, offering wine tastings of cool climate varieties such as pinot noir, merlot and chardonnay and has a fine formal restaurant overlooking the vines. More unusually there is an antiquities **museum** with a small yet fascinating collection of treasures such as an Egyptian mummy, Roman mosaics and Central American artworks. The estate also has four luxurious, modern, self-contained apartments (**L**). ■ *Wine centre daily 1000-1700, museum Wed-Sun 1000-1600, free. Restaurant daily 1200-1430 (closed Mon Jun-Aug). T6249 2949, www.moorilla.com.au 655 Main Rd, Berriedale, signposted from Brooker Highway.*

Cadbury's Factory is billed as the 'home of Cadbury'. Visitors get to see the inner workings of a chocolate-making legend. Tastings on the way round that won't make you go purple or lighter than air, plus a chance to buy lots of bargain goodies at the end. Amazingly popular, so book ahead. ■ *Tours Mon-Fri, half-hourly 0900-1100 and 1200-1330. $12.50, children $6.50, concessions $9. T6249 0333, Cadbury Rd, Claremont, 16 km north of Hobart.*

Essentials

As with the rest of Tasmania, summer is the high season in Hobart but accommodation is particularly scarce around the time of the Sydney-Hobart yacht race, so try to book well in advance for late Dec to end Jan. Many establishments offer good discounts for the winter.

A *Battery Point Manor*, 13 Cromwell St, T6224 0888. This B&B has 8 huge, individual rooms, many with harbour views, a cheerful, sunny dining room and very friendly hosts. **A** *Colville Cottage*, 32 Mona St, Battery Point, T6223 6968, www.colville cottage.com.au Traditional hosted B&B with beautiful rooms and period furnishings such as antique beds, a breakfast conservatory, and a distinguished guest living room a well as the warmest hospitality. Recommended. **A** *Jarem Waterfront*, 8 Clarke Av, Battery Point, T6223 8216. Spacious and private B&B with elegant contemporary suites in a house that projects over the water. The guest living and dining rooms and some suites have superb water views. **A-B** *Merre Be's*, 24 Gregory St, Sandy Bay, T6224 2900, www.merre bes.com.au Hosted B&B with 6 en suite rooms, comfortable period furnishings and wonderful hospitality. 3 more rooms in a similar house across the street. Continental breakfast included, cooked $5 extra.

Sleeping
■ *On map, page 808
There are also
several pubs with
good standard
accommodation,
see page 811*

B-C *Graham Court Apartments*, 15 Pirie St, 2½ km north of the city centre, T6278 1333, F6278 1087. Slightly dated but clean and homely 1-, 2- and 3-bedroom units around a garden courtyard with BBQ. Some wheelchair-friendly, good value for groups or families. Off-street parking.

C *Astor*, corner of Macquarie St and Victoria St, T6234 6611, www.astorprivate hotel.com.au Large Victorian hotel, ageing but comfortable, with doubles, twins and good value singles. Small guest lounge, continental breakfast included, some off-street parking. **C-F** *Montgomery's*, 9 Argyle St, T6231 2660, engel@south com.com.au Smart, contemporary en suite rooms, budget doubles, and excellent backpacker dorms (YHA), each with linen, heater and phone. Recommended.

D-E *Adelphi Court YHA*, 17 Stoke St, T6228 4829. Spacious and quiet hostel with 2- to 5-bed dorms and doubles facing a central courtyard with BBQ. Bus stop outside or a 20-min walk from the city centre.

E *Allport Backpackers*, 432 Elizabeth St, North Hobart, T6231 5464, allports@tassie.net.au Friendly hostel in

Tasmania

an old manor house with wide verandahs and bright, homely rooms. Cheap evening meals, parking. **E** *Central City Backpackers*, 138 Collins St, T6224 2404. A large and impersonal hostel but it's clean, warm and very central. **E** *Narrara Backpackers*, 88 Goulburn St, T6231 3191. A rabbit warren of dorms and doubles, new, clean and comfortable. Off-street parking. The owner is an experienced bushwalker who can advise on walks. **E** *Transit Centre Backpackers*, above the *Transit Centre*, Collins St, T/F6231 2400, LizK@telstra.easymail.com.au Friendly staff and a large, pleasant common and kitchen area, but the 50 beds are crowded into 6- to 10-bunk dorms. One of the closest and cheapest **caravan parks**, with on-site vans, is *Treasure Island*, 671 Main Rd, Berriedale, T6249 2379.

Self-catering *Cosy Cabins*, 13 Bayfield Street, Rosny Park, 7018, T6245 9220, www.cosycabins.com 6-berth cabins in Hobart and various locations around Tasmania (see page 862). Rates are from $65-85 for 2 persons.

Eating	**Expensive** *Elbow Room*, Despard St, T6224 4254. Lovely intimate basement dining
● *On map, page 808*	

Expensive *Elbow Room*, Despard St, T6224 4254. Lovely intimate basement dining room. Simple cooking with a mild French influence. Lunch Tue-Fri 1200-1500, dinner Tue-Sat 1800-2100. Recommended. *Kelley's*, 5 Knopwood St, T6224 7225. Some of Hobart's best seafood can be found in this small stone cottage behind Salamanca Pl. Friendly and laid-back atmosphere. Mon-Fri 1200-1500, daily 0600-2030. *Prossers on the Beach*, Beach Rd, Sandy Bay, T6225 2276. Bright, elegant first-floor room with sweeping views across the mouth of the Derwent. The seafood is excellent, and accompanied by an extensive wine list. Bookings essential in summer. Open Wed-Fri 1230-1500, Tue-Sat 1800-2130.

Mid-range *Boathouse*, Cornelian Beach, T6228 9289. Wonderful, solitary location on the lawns of this small bay. The large dining room is modern, sophisticated but relaxed and makes the best of the location. The food is an interesting medley of dishes and includes good veggie options. Superb value cheap lunches. Open daily 1200-1500, Mon-Sat 1800-2130. Recommended. *Orizuru*, tucked in beside *Mures* (see below), T6231 1790. Excellent sushi and tempura to eat-in or take away. Open Mon-Sat 1200-1430, 1800-2130. *Rockefeller's*, 11 Morrison St, T6234 3490. Casual café-bar style restaurant with a refined edge on the ground floor of this huge, partially reconstructed mill. Modern Australian menu, renowned for their diet-busting desserts. Mon-Fri 1200-1400, and Tue-Sat 1800-2200. Live jazz and tapas Sun-Mon 1800-2200. *T-42*, Elizabeth St Pier, T6224 7742. One of a cluster of good modern café-bars with plenty of outside tables on the north side of the pier. Modern Australian lunches and dinners daily 1200-1500, 1800-2200, weekend brunches from 0930. Licenced daily to 0200, DJs Fri-Sat. *Tarantella*, Gregory St, Sandy Bay, T6223 6652. Very Mediterranean feel in this unashamedly Italian restaurant. Food Fri-Sun 1200-1500, daily 1800-2100. *Toshi's*, Salamanca Sq, T6223 1230. Traditional Japanese cooking of the highest quality in a modern space on the square. Tue-Sat 1200-1430, 600-2030, Sun 1200-1500.

Cheap *Cumquat on Criterion*, 10 Criterion St, T6234 5858. Known for excellent vegetarian and vegan food, *Cumquat* also caters for meat eaters with both inventive and traditional dishes. Casual style, consistently good food and service. Mon-Fri 0800-1600. *Da Angelo*, 47 Hampden Rd, Battery Point, T6223 7011. A Hobart institution for high quality, good value Italian, handmade pasta and pizzas in an unpretentious cottage. Daily 1700-2100. *Fish Frenzy*, Elizabeth St Pier. Classy licenced fish and chip joint where you can also have a salad, glass of wine or coffee. Open Mon-Fri 1200-1500, 1730-2100, Sat-Sun 1200-2100. Recommended. *Little Bali*, 84a Harrington St, T6234 3426. Quick, cheap Indonesian food in the middle of the city in a charmingly tiny room. *Mures*, between Constitution Dock and Victoria Dock. Something of a Hobart landmark, the ground floor is a large fish and chip café and fresh fish shop, open daily 0800-2100. The first floor is a significantly more refined seafood restaurant, open daily 1200-1430,

1800-2130. *Taco's*, 41 Hampden Rd, Battery Point, T6223 5297. This place is a rare beast, a Mexican restaurant that is not tacky, although things can get lively during happy hr (1730-1900) when fishbowl margaritas are only $10. Daily 1730-2030.

North Hobart The restaurants and takeaways along the northern end of Elizabeth St don't stretch the budget and it's a lively area with plenty of choice. The best of them is mid-range *Mit Zitrone*, No 333, T6234 8113. A creative menu for serious foodies in a simple café-style room, friendly unpretentious service. Recommended. *Vanidol's*, No 353, T6234 9307, is a cheap Asian restaurant serving mostly Thai with some Indonesian and Indian dishes. BYO only, corkage $1 a head. There are several casual Asian take away or eat-in outlets including the tiny but excellent *Taste of Asia*. Only a small range of curries here, but they're cheap, tasty and the portions are substantial.

Cafés
● *On map, page 808*

Beaujangles, the Mall. French style with mags and comfy banquette to revive the shopper. Also internet access upstairs. *Island*, 171 Elizabeth St. Very laid-back city café serving uncomplicated favourites, the comfiest seats are upstairs. Open Mon-Sat 1200-2000, later Wed-Sat. *Jackman and McRoss*, 57 Hampden Rd, Battery Point, T6223 3186. This café-bakery makes the best bread in Hobart and a breakfast of fresh croissants here in the simple wooden cottage is a must, if you can get in the door. For lunch try the pies, sandwiches and tarts. Daily 0730-1700. Recommended. *Machine*, Salamanca Sq. This must be the most hip laundromat in the country with a row of gleaming silver washing machines separated by a wall of glass from a bright retro café. Great for all-day breakfasts and cakes. Open daily 0900-1800. *Retro*, Salamanca Pl, T6223 3073. In the heart of Salamanca, *Retro* is everything a café should be. Fine coffee, newspapers, dark corners and people-watching pavement tables. Daily 0900-1800. Recommended. *Say Cheese*, Salamanca Sq, T6224 2888. A café offering Tasmanian cheese and wine, ideal for a leisurely cheese platter on a sunny day. *Tasmanian Coffee Roasters*, 14 Gregory St, Sandy Bay. Relaxed small coffee shop and café which roasts and grinds its own excellent coffee. Also inexpensive sandwiches, foccaccias and cream teas. A great place to while away the morning. Open Mon-Fri 0930-1700, 1000-1400 Sat. **Takeaway** *Body Food*, 50 Murray St. A fast-food joint promoting the seductive notion of low-fat burgers and fries. Open daily 0730-2100.

Bars & clubs
● *On map, page 808*

Carbon, above the *Isobar* at the corner of Brooke St and Franklin Wharf. Nightclub with 3 bars pumping out mostly techno. Free Wed, cover charge Fri-Sat, open from 2300. Some retro on Fri. *Crescent*, corner of Burnett St and Murray St, North Hobart. Friendly, unpretentious local pub serving up Indian curries daily 1200-2000. *Customs House*, 1 Murray St, T6234 6645. Large, mildly nautical pub with a deck overlooking the harbour and separate cheap bistro. Good range of comfortably furnished rooms (**C**) including doubles and singles, a couple of en suite, and a good value family room, continental breakfast included. Meals daily 1200-1400, 1800-2030. *Irish Murphy's*, Salamanca, T6223 1119. Irish theme pub that gets very lively of a weekend with live music, mostly cover bands Wed-Sat and Irish folk Sun 1600-1900. Cheap grills and Irish pies and stews served daily 1200-1400, 1800-2100, breakfasts 0900-1130 Sat. Late licence Fri-Sat until 0200. The smaller *Knopwoods*, a couple of doors down, is plain but warm and welcoming and is the perfect pub for Salamanca. Very cheap lunches daily 1200-1400. *New Sydney*, 87 Bathurst St, T6234 4516. Friendly, unpretentious pub with live music Tue-Sun and basic dorm beds and doubles (**E**). Also a big choice of bar meals served daily. *Nickelby's*, corner Sandy Bay Rd and Gregory St, T6223 6030. Casual café-bar with an interesting international menu, including tapas and good veggie options, served daily 1200-1430, 1700-2130. A wide mix of live music Wed-Sat, when they have an 0200 licence. The outside verandah is particularly popular in summer. *Republic* (formerly the *Empire!*), Elizabeth St, North Hobart, T6234 6954. Grungy,

Tasmania

relaxed bar with sofas around the wood fires and live music every night, normally blues or jazz. Lunch Wed-Sun 1200-1400, dinners daily 1800-2200. Recommended. *Syrup*, 39 Salamanca Pl, has 2 floors of music, ranging from 60s lounge to hard house. Wed-Sat from 1800. *Shipwright's Arms*, 29 Trumpeter St, Battery Point, T6223 5551. Also known as 'Shippies', this is the yachties' choice, filled with sailing memoribilia and exuberant sailors, especially after the Sydney-Hobart. *Victoria Tavern*, 30 Murray St, is a small and welcoming city pub, similar in style to *Knopwoods*. Live music Fri, sometimes Sat. No food but customers are welcome to bring in a takeaway. Open Mon-Thu 1100-2100, Fri-Sat 1600-0230.

Entertainment Hobart boasts an international standard **Casino** at Wrest Point, T6225 0112, www.wrestpoint.com.au, 2 km south of the city centre just off Sandy Bay Rd. The complex has 4 restaurants, including a very cheap foodcourt with boardwalk tables and an expensive revolving restaurant, plus the *Blackjacks Entertainment Venue*. **Cinema** *Village*, 181 Collins St, T6234 7288, the only mainstream cinema venue in the city centre. North Hobart has the *State*, 375 Elizabeth St, T6234 6318, showing art house and festival films. **Classical** *Federation Concert Hall*, T1800 001190, home of the Tasmanian Symphony Orchestra and a performance venue. **Theatre** *Theatre Royal*, 29 Campbell St, T6233 2299, Australia's oldest theatre, now the venue for large-scale productions, opera and musicals. *Peacock Theatre*, Salamanca Arts Centre, 77 Salamanca Pl, T6234 8414. Smaller productions and experimental theatre.

Shopping
The main shopping area is on Elizabeth St Mall and its intersecting streets

Virtually all shops in the city centre are closed on Sun

Books and maps *Ellison Hawker*, 90 Liverpool St, has a good range and a very knowledgeable owner. Open daily. *Fuller's*, 140 Collins St. A large independent bookshop at the heart of Tasmanian literary life with a good café. Also holds regular readings and lectures. *Tasmanian Map Centre*, 96 Elizabeth St, T6231 9043, has Tasmania's best range of maps and guidebooks. There are also many good second-hand shops including *Hobart Bookshop*, Salamanca Sq, and *Imperial*, 138 Collins St. **Food and wine** *Lipscombe Larder*, 527 Sandy Bay Rd, T6225 1135. An Aladdin's cave of goodies, this shop combines a patisserie with bakery, and delicatessen with charcuterie. Also takeaway-and-heat meals and picnic hampers by arrangement. Open daily 0730-1930. *Tasmanian Wine Centre*, 201 Collins St. Extensive selection of Tasmanian and some national wines, tastings on Sat. Open daily 0930-1700. **Outdoor** A cluster of outdoor and adventure shops can be found on Elizabeth St, between the Mall and Melville St, including *Camping World*, T6234 3999, who have a great range of gear and hire out most essentials. **Souvenirs** *The Wilderness Shop*, Salamanca Pl, has beautiful landscape posters and Australian-made products with profits going towards protecting the Tasmanian wilderness.

Tours & activities **Air** *Tasmanian Seaplanes*, Wrest Point, T6227 8808, www.tas-seaplane.com Scenic flights over much of the south from $80, children $40 (20 mins). **Backpacker buses** There are a couple of operators offering 1- to 3-day trips. *Bottom Bits Bus*, T1800-777103, www.bottombitsbus.com, trips include a 1-day Ross and Freycinet tour ($79), and separate 3-day east and west tours ($285, including 2 nights hostel accommodation). **Boat** Several companies run harbour cruises and operate from Brooke St Pier. *The Cruise Company*, T6234 9294, has a range of reasonably priced cruises including one to catamaran manufacturer *Incat*, and another to tour the *Cadbury* chocolate factory (2 hrs, approximately $20). At Elizabeth St Pier is *Lady Nelson*, a replica of an 18th-century brig. Volunteer crews take her out for harbour cruises at weekends at a low price, T6234 3348 (2 hrs, $6). **Coach** *Gregory Omnibuses*, T6224 6169, have English double-decker buses that run an all-day 'hop-on, hop-off' service or a 1½-hr tour around the city centre (Sep-May only, $15-20). Bookings and departures from the VIC. Many companies operate day tours from Hobart (check with the VIC). One of the cheapest is operated by *Tassie Link*, (212 Main Rd, Moonah, T1300 300520), using their regular service buses. Options

Tasmania

include **Mount Field National Park, Hastings Caves** and **Freycinet National Park** ($45 for the day). Also an overnight trip to **Port Arthur**, $50 including entry fees and ghost tour, but not accommodation. Departures from Transit Centre. Their excursion coaches, *Tiger Line*, T1300-653633, www.tiger line.com.au, offer more comfort and better commentary, but are less cheap. Another major operator is *Experience Tasmania*, T6234 3336, www.experiencetas.com.au **Sailing** *Prudence Yacht Charter*, T6224 3195. Crewed or sail yourself from $40 per person per day. *Sea Dawn Charters*, T6225 4110, vinsmith@southcom.com.au A 12-m Huon pine ketch, available for charter for groups of up to 12 at $120 per hr, includes crew and refreshments. No overnight charter.

Air *Qantas* fly daily to Melbourne and Sydney, while *Tasair* hops up to Burnie every day, **Transport** Mon-Fri. The Airporter Shuttle meets all incoming flights. To book a pick-up on departure call T8381 5311. **Bus** *Tassie Link* (212 Main Rd, Moonah, T6272 7300) have 4 major routes out of the city. South through **Geeveston** (1¼ hrs, $14.90), daily, and on to **Dover**, Mon-Fri, plus an extended summer service to **Cockle Creek**, Mon, Wed and Fri. West via **Derwent Bridge** to **Strahan** (6-8 hrs, $51.70). Southeast to the **Tasman Peninsula** (2 hrs, $14.90), Mon-Sat. East via **Triabunna** and **Coles Bay** to **Bicheno**, Wed, Fri, Sun, and, in summer, Mon, and on to **St Helens**, Fri and Sun. A summer-only service heads out to **Mount Field** Mon-Sat (1 hr 20 mins, $23.50), continuing on to **Scotts Peak Dam**, Tue, Thu and Sat. Another summer service makes the route to **Derwent Bridge** a daily one. *Redline* (199 Collins St, T1300-360000) run daily direct services up the Midland Highway to **Launceston** (2¾ hrs) and Mon-Fri to **Bicheno**. *Hobart Coaches* (212 Main Rd, Moonah, T6233 4232) have Mon-Sat services to **Kettering**, **Richmond** and **New Norfolk**, tickets and info from the main post office or www.metrotas.com.au

Airline offices *Kendell Airlines*, T131300. *Qantas*, 77 Elizabeth Mall, T6237 4900. **Directory** *Tasair*, Cambridge Airport, T6248 5088. **Banks** The major banks have ATMs on Elizabeth St and the Mall. *Thomas Cook*, 40 Murray St, T6234 2699. Mon-Fri 0900-1700. *American Express*, 74 Liverpool St, T6231 2955. Mon-Fri 0845-1700. **Bike Hire** *Jim's* (also cars), 45 Burnett St, North Hobart, T6236 9779. Mountain bikes from around $20 per day. **Car Hire** All the usual operators at the airport and in the city, local companies include *Advance*, T6224 0822, www.advancecars.com.au, and *Rent-A-Bug*, T6231 0300. **Car servicing** *Blue Gum*, 431 Elizabeth St, North Hobart, T6234 2041. **Communications Internet** *Beaujangles*, Elizabeth St Mall, T6236 9980. **Main Post Office**, corner Elizabeth St and Macquarie St, open Mon-Fri 0900-1700. **Medical services** *Royal Hobart Hospital*, 48 Liverpool St, T6222 8308. *Travellers Medical and Vaccination Centre*, 270 Sandy Bay Rd, T6223 7577. **Parks and Wildlife Service** 134 Macquarie St, T1300 368 550 **Police** 31-47 Liverpool St, T6230 2111. **Taxi** T6210 1000.

Around Hobart

The southeast of Tasmania is remarkable for its jumble of convoluted islands and peninsulas. This complex maze of tiny natural harbours, secluded sandy beaches and majestic dolerite headlands makes for an almost inexhaustible playground for the adventurous. These features are concentrated in the spectacular **Tasman National Park**. *The area also contains much of historical interest. Bruny Island and the D'Entrecasteaux Channel were visited by some of the earliest European explorers,* **Richmond** *is a fine example of a Tasmanian town of the 19th century and the remains of the penal settlement* **Port Arthur** *forms the most compelling of Tasmania's historical sites. The* **far south** *has caves, mountains and forests and walkers can dip their toe into the remote southwest wilderness at Cockle Creek, all within an hour or two of Hobart.*

Tasmania

Richmond

Colour map 8, grid C4
Population: 800
Only 30 mins from
Hobart, the town
is now a popular
daytrip for visitors

The small, picturesque Georgian village of Richmond, set among rolling green hills, looks remarkably like parts of southwest England. Once an important stopping point between Hobart, Port Arthur and the east coast, Richmond was bypassed by a new causeway from Sorrell over Pitt Water in 1872 and the town died, leaving it virtually unchanged for the next century.

Richmond is best known for its **bridge**, built in 1823 by convicts and the oldest in Australia still in use. On the far side of the bridge, on a rise above the left bank of the river, is **St John's Church**, the oldest Catholic Church in the country, notable for having been designed by the great English architect Augustus Pugin in gothic revival style. On Forth Street is **Richmond Gaol**. As Richmond expanded quickly in the 1820s a large number of convicts were needed to work on constructing public buildings and as agricultural labourers. Consequently, the gaol was budilt to hold those who misbehaved, as well as bushrangers and even Aboriginal people from the local Stoney Creek tribe. The complex of solid sandstone buildings is surprisingly small but fairly complete, making the prisoners' experience here almost tangible. There are still faint marks visible in the floorboards where convicts carved draught boards to pass the time. ■ *Daily 0900-1700. $4.50, children $2. T6260 2127.*

For several
self-contained
heritage options
contact Colonial
Accommodation,
T/F6260 2750

Sleeping and eating A *Millhouse on the Bridge*, 2 Wellington St, T6260 2428, www.millhouse.com.au One of the state's finest B&Bs in a historic former millhouse overlooking Richmond Bridge. 4 large, elegant colonial-style rooms, a book-lined guest living room with open fire and pretty breakfast conservatory. Flawless style, comfort, cooking and warm hospitality. Recommended. **C** *Coachman's Rest* at the rear of *Old Time Portraits*, T6260 2630. A single, modern, self-contained chalet, cheerfully decorated and sleeping up to 4. Good value. **C-E** *Richmond Tourist Park*, 48 Middle Tea Tree Rd, T6260 2192. Cabins and vans of a very good standard. Also indoor pool, BBQs. The *Food and Wine Centre*, Bridge St, T6260 2619, is a large restaurant with plentiful garden tables. Breakfasts, lunches, cream teas and wonderful cakey desserts served daily 0830-1700. Mid-range evening meals Wed-Sat to 1930. *Prospect House*, Richmond Rd, T6260 2207, offers formal intimate dining (expensive) in a series of rooms with crisp linen and open fires, daily lunch and dinner. Bookings essential. *Richmond Arms*, Bridge St, T6260 2109. Richmond's only pub has a beautiful exterior of iron lace verandahs but the inside fails to match up to expectations. Cheap lunches daily 1200-1400, mid-range dinners 1800-2000. *Ma Foosie's*, Bridge St, provides superb cream teas and tasty homemade light lunches. Service is exceptionally friendly and efficient. Open daily 1030-1700 (closed mid-Jul to mid-Aug). Recommended.

Transport *Hobart Coaches* run 3 services a day, Mon-Fri, from Bridge St to **Hobart** at 0725, 1020 and 1645 (30 mins). *Tassie Link* have a summer service through here from the Village Store to **Triabunna** and **Swansea** (1¾ hrs, $16.40), 1655 Mon-Fri.

Directory *The Granary*, Bridge St, is a small internet café, gallery and book shop, open daily 1030-1700 in summer, otherwise Wed, Fri, Sun to Mon.

Coal Valley
wineries
& Sorrell
Colour map 8, grid C4
25 km from Hobart
75 km from Port Arthur

Most wineries only
open at weekends

This small wine region produces some good reislings and cabernets. *Meadowbank*, 699 Richmond Street, T6248 4484, is the region's flagship. Open daily 1000-1700, for tastings. The mid-range staurant serves local produce, especially seafood. Weekend performances of music, dance or poetry and also regular art exhibitions. Book lunch at weekends, especially in summer. Opposite is *Craigow*, T6248 5482, open Friday-Sunday 1200-1700 October-April. Tastings and wines by the glass. Sorrell is an unremarkable town, but notable for the wonderful **C** *Blue Bell Inn* , 26 Somerville Street, T6265 5482, bluebell@trump.net.au This 1863 building has been well cared for and exudes a luxurious but homely atmosphere. The beautifully furnished en suite rooms are good value and the mid-range menu a real treat. Meals daily 0730-0900, 1830-2030, bookings advised. Recommended.

Tasman Peninsula

Connected to its northern neighbour the Forestier Peninsula by a pinch of sand, the Tasman was selected in 1830 to become the British Empire's principal prison-within-a-prison. Macquarie Harbour had become unworkable and the Tasman Peninsula was not only close to Hobart but was easily sealed off from the rest of the island and had one of the best natural deep-water ports in Van Diemen's Land. The ruins of **Port Arthur**, the main prison settlement, now stand as Australia's main tangible symbol of its convict past and are conserved in an impressive and fascinating Historic Site. If possible, plan to spend a few days on the peninsula as it has some of the most spectacular coastal cliffs in the state and is wonderful territory for **walkers**, **climbers** and **divers** alike.

Eaglehawk Neck
88 km from Hobart
20 km from Port Arthur

Gettting there and around The main highway between Hobart and the east coast passes through the small and unremarkable service town of **Sorrell** before reaching **Dunalley,** gateway to the Forestier and Tasman Peninsulas. *Tassie Link* services stop at **Sorrell** for the **Tasman peninsula** and the east coast. Change here if heading north or south between the latter. *Tassie Link* services leave the YHA in **Port Arthur** for Sorrel and **Hobart** 0600 Mon-Fri, (0700 during school holidays), 1300 Sat, and 1300 Mon, Wed, Fri in summer (2¼ hrs, $14.90). The service calls at the Convict Bakery, **Taranna**, and Jetty Rd, **Eaglehawk Neck**, 35 and 45 mins later. Hobart-bound services from the peninsula drop off at **Sorrell** 1½ hrs after leaving Port Arthur, and east coast services leave there 0920 Wed (and Mon in summer), and 0850 Fri and Sun.

Ins & outs

Information Facilities on the peninsula are concentrated in the small service town of Nubeena, with just a store at Port Arthur that also doubles as a post office, takeaway and petrol station. The *Officer's Mess* café and restaurant at Eaglehawk Neck incorporates a small **VIC**, open daily 0900-1700, T6250 3722, eaglehawkneck@tasvisinfo.com.au The Port Arthur visitor centre doubles as a regional **VIC**, open daily 0900-1700, T6251 2329, portarth@tasvisinfo.com.au

Port Arthur is a name that evokes horror to most Australians both for its reputation as a place of abject misery for convicts and for a tragic day in 1996 when many staff and visitors were killed and wounded by a lone gunman. The penal settlement was named after Tasmania's Governor Arthur, a severe and devout man who believed that criminals suffered from a 'mental delirium' and conceived a system of punishment that would allow them to earn their own redemption.

Port Arthur Historic Site
Colour map 8, grid C5
107 km from Hobart,
206 km from Coles Bay
www.portarthur.org.au

Many visitors are surprised by the extent of the historic site which was once a busy self-sufficient working community. About 12,500 convicts served time in Port Arthur, about a sixth of all those condemned to Van Diemen's Land, and at its height during the 1840s and 1850s many thousands of people lived here including staff, soldiers and their families. Even though relatively few buildings survived the bushfires and demolitions of the two decades after Port Arthur closed in 1877, there are still more than 30 historic buildings open to visitors. Whilst the prisoners lived in abject misery, the staff and their families enjoyed the setting and facilities, and the harbour, green lawns and crumbling ruins are quite beautiful. The church,

Tasmania

gardens and Commandant's home lend the place the air of an English village and it would have been easy to forget the prisoners in later years as they were locked up in the chilling solitary confinement of the Separate Prison. Built in 1849 and modelled on Pentonville, this cruciform building drove many convicts insane and the extraordinary chapel illustrates well just how merciless this attempt at prison reform was.

The entrance fee includes an orientation tour and a short boat trip around Point Puer, where boys were kept separately from the corrupting influence of hardened crims, and the Isle of the Dead. Near the wharf, by the remains of the Broad Arrow Café, there is a poignant memorial garden dedicated to the 35 people killed here and nearby in 1996 (staff ask that visitors refrain from asking them about the incident). Allow at least half a day or more to explore the site. If staying overnight don't miss the ghost tour. If ghosts do exist there is no more likely place to find them and the guides make the stroll by lantern as terrifying as possible. There are cafes, picnic tables and a shop on site. ■ *Daily 0830-dusk. $22, children $11, concessions $17.50. Ghost tour $15.40, children $9.50, 1½ hrs. Times vary, bookings essential. T6251 2310, bookings@portarthur.org.au.*

Around the peninsula

Just north of Eaglehawk Neck is a scenic lookout over the lovely Pirates Bay and Tasman National Park. At the northern end of the bay is the **Tessellated Pavement**, a rock slab that has vertical and horizontal lines scored into it, making it look like cobblestones. **Eaglehawk Neck** itself is a scrawny bit of sand barely 50 m wide. There are some remains here of soldiers' barracks, relics of convict days when dogs were chained across the narrowest part of the peninsula to pounce on escapees. Just south of Pirates Bay are **Tasman Blowhole**, only worth seeing when there are high seas, **Tasman Arch** and **Devils Kitchen**, both high sheer cliffs skirted by boiling surf. The **Tasmanian Devil Park** focuses on wildlife rescue and rehabilitation and native animals such as devils, quolls, possums and parrots can be seen on the 900-m park walk. A bird of prey show is one of the main attractions. ■ *Daily 0900-1700. $13, children $6.60. Devil feeding daily at 1100. Kings of the Wind daily 1115. T6250 3230, www.tasmaniandevil.com.au Arthur Highway, Taranna.*

The **Tasman National Park**, along the eastern and southern edges of the peninsula, encompasses some of Tasmania's most dramatic coastal scenery and is much more accessible than the isolated southwest coast. The main walk in this area is the **Tasman Coastal Track** from Tasman's Arch to Cape Pillar (3-4 days), following the coast to the turquoise water and white sand of Fortescue Bay, then heading inland to reach the end of the cape. Alternatively start at Devil's Kitchen and walk to Tatnells Hill (four hours return), or continue to Fortescue Bay (17 km) where there are good campsites. Both of these walks include waterfalls, wildflowers and extensive cliff-top views. From Fortescue Bay there is a magnificent four-hour walk to **Cape Huay**. South of Port Arthur are yet more wonderful coastal walks. There is a track out to **Cape Raoul** along high and exposed coastal cliffs and an excellent short walk to **Mount Brown** and the sparklingly white and isolated **Crescent Bay** beach (three hours). Beach lovers will also enjoy **Lagoon Beach**, a surf beach hidden by high dunes at the north western tip of the peninsula. There is an easy 3 km walking track from Lime Bay. These walks are well marked but for more detail see the *Tasman Coastal Track Map & Notes*, available from map shops in Hobart.

Sleeping & eating

Eaglehawk Neck **C** *Lufra*, T6250 3262, gwpcon@bigpond.com, is a large, ugly pub and hotel with a position right on the neck overlooking Pirates Bay to the east. Most of the 27 basic but comfortable en suite rooms have ocean views, with room No 7 being the pick. Cheap lunches 1200-1400, mid-range and cheap evening menus, 1800-2000. **E** *Eaglehawk Neck Backpackers*, 94 Old Jetty Rd (about 1 km from highway), T6250 3248. The 2 very simple self-contained cabins, each sleep 5. Use of private internet access, bike and canoe hire, no linen. *Eaglehawk Café*, T6250 3331, Relaxed and mildly funky café by day, excellent mid-range French-influenced evening meals. Open daily.

Taranna B *Norfolk Bay Convict Station*, Arthur Highway, T6250 3487, www.convictstation.com With a peaceful waterside position on a small bay inlet, this 1838 convict outpost can claim to be Australia's first railway station. Friendly, very informative owners and 5 characterful en suite B&B rooms. Recommended. **D** *Norfolk Bayview*, Koonya, T6250 3855, norfolkbayviewbb@bigpond.com 4 simple, comfortable rooms in a secluded 'modern' family B&B home. Bush setting with balcony views to Norfolk Bay. Full cooked breakfast. Exceptionally good value.

Port Arthur A waterside walking track connects all the accommodation with the Historic Site. The **A-B** *Flag Motor Inn*, T6250 2101, portarthur@fc-hotels.com.au, has terrific views over the ruins from its twin dining rooms. En-suite motel rooms, mid-range restaurant and cheap bistro open daily 1200-1400, 1730-2000. The **D-E** *YHA*, T6250 2311, is a rambling Federation weatherboard house also immediately adjacent to the Historic Site. Clean, well-maintained with cosy common areas but quite crowded dorms. *Felons* is the excellent mid-range restaurant in the Historic Site visitor centre. Open daily 1700-2030.

Diving *Eaglehawk Dive Centre*, 178 Pirates Bay Drive, Eaglehawk Neck, T6250 3566, www.eaglehawkdive.com.au This area has Australia's best ocean cave dives, also seadragons, wrecks and kelp forests. *Eaglehawk* offers Boat dives, gear and hire, and has budget accommodation. **Walking** *Tasman Nature Guiding*, 70 Old Jetty Rd, Eaglehawk Neck, T6250 3268, brozek@southcom.com.au Guided walks from 1 hr to 1 day with a flexible and knowledgeable guide. *Tours & activities*

Banks There is an ATM in the *TAS* supermarket in Nubeena, available Mon-Sat 0800-1800, Sun 0800-1600. **Communications** Internet at the *On-Line Access Centre*, Nubeena, T6250 2858. **Post offices** in Nubeena and in the store, Port Arthur. *Directory*

Bruny Island

This relatively small hilly island is 75 km from tip to toe, but its bays and headlands manage to clock up over 400 km of coastline. It is is all but divided in two by The Neck, a thin dune-covered spit of land. Much of the north has been cleared for pasture but a large area in the south is covered in thick mixed forest and practicably inaccessible.

*Colour map 8 grid C4
Population: 600
www.bruny island.com.au*

Getting there and around A non-bookable vehicle and passenger ferry operates between Kettering and Roberts Point in the north of the island (20 mins, $21 return for cars, $3 bicycles, foot passengers free). The ferry leaves Kettering approximately hourly with the first sailings at 0650, 0745 and 0930 Mon-Sat, 0800 and 0930 Sun, and the last at 1700 and 1830. The first trips from Roberts Point are at 0715, 0825 and 1000 Mon-Sat, 0830 and 1015 Sun, and the last at 1730 and 1900. It is about a 40-min drive from central Hobart to Kettering, and 15 mins loading time should be allowed. There is no public transport on the island. *Lumeah Backpackers* (see next page), run a bus service between central Hobart hostels and Adventure Bay (leaves Hobart Mon and Wed 1200, Sat around 1400, from $25 return) and also hire out mountain bikes ($15 per day), sea kayaks ($30 for 4 hrs), plus tents and fishing gear. *Ins & outs*

Tasmania

▶▶ The 'last' Tasmanian Aborigine

Bruny Island was originally the home of the Nuenonne people. When they first came into contact with Europeans in the late 1700s the chief of the island was Mangana, now immortalized by the island's highest mountain. His daughter, Trugannini, became an ally and possibly lover of explorer George Augustus Robinson. The pair are famously painted together in Benjamin Duterrau's The Conciliation (1840), which can be seen in the Tasmanian Museum and Art Gallery in Hobart. Robinson was the government 'Conciliator' of Aborigines at a time when the last Tasmanian Aboriginals were being herded off the island by Governor Arthur's infamous 'Black Line'. In the early 1830s Trugannini helped Robinson to communicate with other tribes and persuade them to be moved to Flinders Island. Although both of their roles in this forced exile are controversial, the knowledge of Tasmanian Aboriginal people gathered by Robinson and Trugannini as they travelled around the island forms a rare and invaluable historical record. Upon her death in 1876, Trugianni went down in history as the last true Tasmanian Aborigine. Her skeleton physically remained part of history, controversially held by European institutions, until 1975 when she was cremated and her ashes scattered in the D'Entrecasteaux Channel. Most Tasmanian Aboriginal people of today are descended from Aboriginal women captured by white sealers working in the islands of Bass Strait. To learn more about Trugannini, Robinson and the history of Tasmanian Aboriginals read the The Last Frontier by historian Henry Reynolds or the recent novel, English Passengers by Matthew Knowle.

Sights & walks Much of the best of the island can only be seen on the walks or from a boat, but there are some good road lookouts. On the unsealed road that threads its way over the shoulder of **Mount Mangana** there are viewpoints to the north and south, and **Cape Bruny** is also well worth the unsealed drive. The island has a thriving **fairy penguin** and **mutton bird** rookery right on the Neck and an observation platform has been set up for visitors. Facilities are in short supply on the island, but each of the three main settlements, Alonnah, Adventure Bay and Lunawanna, have small stores selling petrol, all open daily. The main **VIC** for the island, *Bruny D'Entrecasteaux Visitor Centre* is actually by the ferry terminal in the small port of **Kettering** and has a licensed café. ■ *Daily 0900-1700, T6267 4494, kettering@tasvisinfo.com.au* There are several excellent walks around the island. The most accessible but none-the-less spectacular is the 2½-hour circuit around Grass Point and **Fluted Cape**. Slightly longer is the three-hour return walk out to **Cape Queen Elizabeth** via the beautiful rocky beach at Moorina Bay. The best day-walk is the six-hour circuit around **Labillardiere Peninsula** at the very southwest corner of the island.

Sleeping & eating

Most of the island's options are in the form of self-contained chalets or cabins

On the north part of the island there are a handful of hosted B&Bs

B *Kelly's Lookout*, Dennes Point Rd, T6260 6466, on a grassy rise looking out to the northwest has 2 comfortable B&B doubles, one with additional bunks. This is also a **café**, and information bureau. **C** *Swan Haven*, off Killora Rd, T6260 6428, swanonbruny@bigpond.com   2 light, airy B&B doubles on the upper floor of a modern, stylish house set in 20 acres of bush and beside the 'duck pond', a small natural harbour. Dinners by arrangement usually include organic salads and salmon for around $20. Recommended. **D-E** *Lumeah Backpackers*, Adventure Bay, T6293 1265, lumeah@tassie.net.au   Small, cosy and very friendly with 18 beds in 3 rooms, one of which also functions as a double. Camping also possible. Massages are available. Recommended. **D-E** *Captain James Cook Caravan Park*, T6293 1128, is 500 m east of Adventure Bay store and has cabins and on-site vans. There are a few spots where there are basic **camping** facilities, including Cloudy Bay, Jetty Beach and the south end of the Neck. Jetty Beach is for many the most picturesque but can get busy. Both water and firewood are in short supply in summer.

There is not a whole heap of eating choice on the island but what there is can be pretty good. *Rao's*, near Roberts Point, T6260 6444, is an excellent, cheap Italian restaurant with welcoming staff, beer garden and front decking overlooking Barnes Bay to Mount Wellington. Wine tasting daily 1500-1700, $6 a head, and live jazz every Sun 1230-1530. Open Wed-Sun 1000-2030, daily in summer. *Hotel Bruny*, Alonnah, T6293 1148, serves counter meals Thu-Sun 1200-1330, Thu-Sat 1800-1930, daily except Sun evening in summer. Accommodation in 2 fully self-contained units (**C**).

Tours & activities Very friendly *Bruny Island Charters*, Adventure Bay, T6293 1465, www.bruny charters.com, offer several excellent cruises in their 12-passenger boat (Oct-Apr). If time and budget allow opt for the longer trips which usually get down to the seal colony at Boreel Head (3 $85, 5 hrs $115). *Camel Tracks Australia*, just north of the Neck, T6260 6335, have short rides and longer bush and beach treks available in summer. *Lumeah* offer minibus day trips around the island for $30, and run penguin-viewing trips ($20). The best of the safer beaches are at Adventure Bay and Jetty Beach. *Inala*, T/F6293 1217, run personalized walking tours by arrangement.

Directory **Banks** No banks or ATMs on the island. **Communications** Internet at *On-Line Access Centre*, Alonnah, T6293 2036. Tue-Sat 1400-1600 and various additional times each day. Some **Post Office** services at the Adventure Bay and Alonnah stores. **Parks and Wildlife Service** T6293 1419.

Huon Valley, D'Entrecasteaux Channel and Southern Forests

To the southwest of Hobart, the Huon River snakes down from deep in the southwest to finally disgorge into the D'Entrecasteaux Channel. **Huonville** is the largest town southwest of Hobart, with lots of facilities and the 35-minute **Huon Jet Boat** ride. The *Jet Boat* office on the Esplanade doubles as a café and VIC. ■ *Jet Boat rides daily every 15 mins, 0915-0415. $50, children $32. T6264 1838, huonville@tasvisinfo.com.au* The main **Parks and Wildlife** office for the region is in Huonville. ■ *Mon-Fri 0900-1600, T6264 8460, 24 Main Rd.*

Colour map 8, grid C4
Huonville 40 km from Hobart
www.huontrail.org.au

South of Huonville the main highway splits. The route southeast passes through **Cygnet**, a charming village that makes a good lunch or overnight stop with the Tahune Wildlife Park nearby. *Red Velvet Lounge* in the main street, T6295 0466, is an alternative café with vegetarian and organic food. **B** *Cygnet Guest House* is a heritage B&B that does a hearty cooked breakfast and 5 km north of town at **D-E** *Huon Valley Backpackers* on the Channel Highway, T6295 1551, the manager helps to organize fruit-picking work (March-April) and offers day trips in the area. About 20 km further east, **Kettering** is a quiet port where most of the day's action is provided by the comings and goings of the Bruny Island ferry. The **Bruny D'Entrecasteaux Visitor Centre** is by the ferry terminal and can book accommodation or activities. ■ *Daily 0900-1700, T6267 4494, kettering@tasvisinfo.com.au* One of the best activities in the area is sea kayaking around Bruny Island and the channel. *Roaring 40s*, T6267 5000, www.tasmanianadventures.com.au, offer kayak hire ($15 per hour) and guided day trips ($110 day) from Oyster Cove Marina in Kettering. South of the Huonville the main highway continues down the west bank of the river.

Tasmania

Geeveston
Colour map 8, grid C4
Population: 800
24 km from Huonville
23 km from Dover

Established as an important timber-town back in the 1850s, Geeveston has a short, pretty main street full of weatherboard houses and is on the junction of the main highway with Arve Road which heads west into the Southern Forests. The **tourist office**, on Church Street, doubles as a **Forest and Heritage Centre**, a small museum and gallery mostly dedicated to the timber industry. ■ *Daily 0900-1700, T6297 1836, geeveston@tasvisinfo.com.au*

Sleeping and eating C *Cambridge House* Main Rd, T6297 1561, dv_potter@southcom.com.au A former mill-owner's residence dating from the 1870s, now a characterful and cheerful B&B with 2 doubles and 1 twin room, overlooking the Kermandie River. **E** *Forest House Backpackers*, Arve Rd, contact the post office for bookings, T6297 0193. Small, basic hostel but quiet and uncrowded. The owners also run, by arrangement, inexpensive half-day tours along the Arve Rd to Tahune.

Transport The *Tassie Link* service leaves from Church St to **Dover** 1925 Mon-Fri and 1625 on school days. Some additional services in summer. There are daily services to **Hobart**, from 0700 Mon-Fri, 0900 Sat and 1245 Sun.

Tahune Forest Reserve
Colour map 8, grid C3
29 km from Geeveston
Look out for the Big Tree Reserve, just off the Hartz road

Although bordered by areas of active logging, this reserve, straddling a stretch of the Huon River, protects extensive stands of mixed forest. The 20-minute return **Huon Pine Walk**, is specifically designed to allow the visitor to see several of these long-lived trees, both young and mature. The star attraction here, however, is the **Air Walk**, the longest of its kind in the world when constructed in 2001. The steel walk-way extends around a 570-m-long horseshoe, passing close to many forest giants at an elevation of between 20 and 30 m. At a far point a cantilevered extension, with a glass enclosed lookout at the end, hangs 48 m above the river. The **visitor centre** includes a café and interpretative area. ■ *Air Walk open daily 0900-1700, 0900-2200 Dec-Mar. $8, children $5.50. T6297 0068*. There are good free **camping** and picnic facilities here, including wood-fireplaces, gas BBQs, toilets and showers.

Hartz Mountains National Park
Colour map 8 grid C3
24 km from Geeveston

The Hartz Mountains form an Alpine plateau and part of the eastern border of the Wilderness World Heritage Area. The park is accessed by the snaking unsealed Hartz Road, with three car parks toward the top. The first has the main facilities, a shelter, picnic area, BBQs, toilets and water. From the **Waratah Lookout** there are great views back over the Southern Forests. From the second car park the 20-minute **Arve Falls** track is an easy and educational walk to the edge of the plateau. The park's more challenging walks are from the top car park. From here the main track leads uphill through snowgum woodland, King Billy pines, heath and cushion plants, reaching **Lake Esperance** in an hour and surmounting the main ridge at **Hartz Pass** after another hour. The pass gives some good views to the west, but the best ones are from **Hartz Peak** (1,254 m), a little under an hour further on. This is territory to be respected, however. From the pass to the peak the track is unmarked and inclement weather can bring difficulties.

Dover
Colour map 8, grid C4
Population: 500
28 km from Hastings Caves, 46 km from Cockle Creek

From Geeveston the main highway heading south stays just inland until it reaches Dover on the bay of Port Esperance. Dover has one of the more beautiful coastal settings in the south of the state, much of it on and around a small promontory and the bays either side. If clear, the backdrop is almost equally impressive, dominated by pyramidal **Adamsons Peak** to the southwest. There are picnic spots and BBQs on the foreshores of both bays.

Tasmania

Sleeping and eating C *Bayside Lodge*, Bayview Rd, T6298 1788. Small, friendly, motel-style accommodation with views over the southern bay. Continental breakfast included. The **C-D** *Dover Hotel*, T6298 1210, is a 5-min walk south of the town centre. This large pub serves cheap bistro meals daily 1200-1400, 1800-2000 restricted hrs and no Sun dinners May-Aug. The 6 basic doubles upstairs include cooked breakfast, the 5 external self-contained units do not. The small and well-maintained **C-E** *Dover Caravan Park*, T6298 1301, has cabins, on-site vans and a great spot just opposite the foreshore of the northern bay. *Woodfired Pizza and Eatery*, T6298 1905, has a great range of traditional and gourmet pizzas, also BYO. Open Wed-Thu, Sun 1600-2100, Fri-Sat 1600-2200. Recommended. On the main central junction the excellent *Gingerbread House* bakery and café serves breakfast and cheap light meals Tue-Sun 0830-1730.

Directory Banks No banks or ATMs. **Communications** Internet at *Online Access Centre*, Old School, T6298 1552. Open Tue-Sat, hrs vary but core times 1300-1500. **Post Office**, Southgate Shopping Centre.

The sealed highway continues only as far as Southport with the last shop and petrol for those heading further south. From just north of this small settlement, mostly unsealed roads head west to **Hastings Caves**, the 40-million year old chambers with extensive natural decorations. The 28°C springs feed into adult and toddlers thermal pools amid a forest setting, and support facilities include a café, BBQs and picnic areas, toilets and showers. The Parks and Wildlife Service also run adventure caving tours. ■ *Café and pool open 0900-1700 Oct-Mar, 1000-1600 Apr-Sep. Tours hourly, first 1000, last 1600 Oct-Mar, first 1100, last 1500 Apr-Sep. Full entry $13.20, children $6.60, concessions $10.45. Pool only $4.40, children $2.20, concessions $3.30. T6298 3209.* To the south are the tiny settlements of Lune River and Ida Bay. During the peak summer months **Fell's Ida Bay Railway** is in operation, taking passengers out 16 km along the peninsula between Southport Bay and Lagoon. ■ *Daily 1230 and 1415 Jan-Mar (Apr-Dec, Sun, Wed only). $20, children $10, concessions $18. T6223 5893.*

Dover to Cockle Creek
Colour map 8, grid C3/4

Australia's most southerly 'mainland' settlement is the usual exit point for those finishing the South Coast Walk, and very popular in its own right as a summer camping spot. Considering its proximity to Hobart the area is strangely unpopulated and mostly thickly forested. The only facilities beyond Southport are a couple of public phones, one at the ranger's station at Cockle Creek.

Cockle Creek
Creek 25 km from Lune River

There are two easy short walks from Cockle Creek, east to Fishers Point and west to South Cape Bay. The two-hour return walk to the **Fishers Point** first passes a life-size bronze of a baby southern right whale, a memorial to the creatures that once sheltered in Recherche Bay and a grim reminder that a favoured whalers tactic here was to wound the babies so their calls would attract the adults. The track follows the coast past Aboriginal midden sites and an old whaler's grave out to the point where the dramatic difference between sheltered and exposed coastline is readily seen. The **South Cape Bay** track, actually the last (or first) stretch of the South Coast Track, heads first over a slight rocky, wooded rise and then down onto boardwalks crossing a wide marshy buttongrass plain. This track usually takes three or four hours there and back, but most walkers will want to explore further once they emerge onto the wild and rugged stretch of coastline at the other end. Far better to pack a good lunch and allow a whole day. The track takes you to the southernmost point of Australia readily accessible by walkers.

Tasmania

Sleeping & eating At the time of writing, 2 development proposals, both for privately managed self-contained cabins, had been approved for Hastings Caves and Cockle Creek. Contact the Parks and Wildlife Office at Huonville for details. There are plans to rebuild the *Lune River YHA*, destroyed in an arson attack in late 2001, but in the meantime the *Southport Settlement*, T6298 3144, becomes an important spot this far south, providing all-in-one pub, bistro, store, takeaway, campsite and petrol stop. All open daily 0800-1800. Substantial cheap meals daily in the bistro 1200-1400, 1800-2000. A string of public **camping** areas are scattered along the few kilometres of coastal road before and at Cockle Creek, though facilities are limited to basic toilets. Camping spots are free before crossing Cockle Creek bridge as this is outside the park boundary.

Tours & activities The *Olive May*, the oldest working ketch in Australia, takes passengers on 3-hr or overnight adventure **sailing** cruises from Port Esperance. Office in Dover, T6298 1062.

Transport *Tassie Link* service comes to **Dover** Mon-Fri and in summer, goes to **Lune River** and **Cockle Creek**, Mon/Wed/Fri, leaving Dover at 1055. Services from Dover to **Hobart** (2 hrs, $14.90) leave Mon-Fri 0700 (0645 school days) and in summer Mon/ Wed/Fri 1000 and 1520. Summer service leaves Cockle Creek 1345 and Lune River 1440.

Central Tasmania

Inland Tasmania is a place of very different landscapes. In the east, the wide flat valley of the South Esk and Macquarie rivers became the natural south-north route for invading Europeans and was soon clear-cut for pasture. A spell of railway dominance has left a string of well-preserved Georgian garrison towns, including the exquisite **Ross**. *In stark contrast is the kilometre-high* **Central Plateau** *to the west, a glacier and fire scarred landscape of trout-filled lakes and boulder-strewn hills, forest and heath. The* **Great Western Tiers** *northern and eastern borders are strongly defended by spectacular dolerite ramparts hundreds of metres high. To the south, beyond the Derwent valley, is the state's oldest national park,* **Mount Field**, *displaying almost every habitat Tasmania has to offer as well as some of the state's most impressive waterfalls.*

The Midland Highway

The principal route from south to north, the A1 follows the Derwent Valley a short way from Hobart before branching north over the river at Bridgewater. Completed in 1853, the highway winds through the low hills north of the valley, passing through tiny **Brighton**, a fine collection of impressive Georgian homes, and then skirting round **Kempton**. Soon after Kempton is the main junction with the A5. From here the Midland Highway continues on past **Oatlands**, one of the original garrison towns along the route with one of the most extensive collections of historic sandstone buildings in the state. There is a small **VIC**, in the High Street, providing details of a self-guided walk. ■ *Daily 0900-1700, T6254 1212, centas@trump.net.au*

Ross & around
Colour map 8, grid B4
Population: 300
118 km from Hobart
80 km from Launceston

Also just off the highway, Ross is the smallest and best preserved of the colonial towns and villages along the route. It is also one of the prettiest villages and has a strong sense of history. There is a fine, wide central crossroads, on the corners of which are buildings informally dedicated to *Salvation, Damnation, Recreation* and *Temptation* (the Catholic church, the gaol, the town hall and the pub). The old highway heads over a beautiful 1836 sandstone bridge. Its carving was considered so fine that the convict masons were granted free pardons. Where they once laboured are now picnic spots and BBQs. The village has a **Scottish Centre**, full of all manner of things tartan, and the **Wool Centre**, an in-depth, interactive look at the industry also doubling as an excellent **VIC**. ■ *Daily 0900-1700, 1800 summer. Entry to Wool Centre by donation. Tours daily, $4.40, children $2.20, concessions $3.30. Village tours $3.30, children and concessions $2.20. T6381 5466, www.tas woolcentre.com.au* From Ross the highway heads through **Campbell Town**, another of the highway garrison towns, with a good range of facilities. The turbulent history of the highway, the destruction it caused to the Aboriginal peoples, and the many interesting characters associated with the region, are recounted in the **Heritage Highway Museum**. ■ *Daily 1000-1600. Entry free. T6381 1353.*

Sleeping and eating in Ross 4 km south, just off the main highway, is **A** *Somercoates*, T6381 5231, F6381 5356. This large sheep station, now also a B&B, has been in the same family for over 150 years and has many fascinating outbuildings, including a rusting blacksmith's that has remained untouched since the 1940s. Some of these oubuildings have been converted to pretty, rustic accommodation, self-contained but with limited kitchen facilities. Breakfast provisions. **A-B** *Colonial Cottages*, 12 Church St, T6381 5354, F6381 5408. A range of small self-contained Georgian and Victorian houses, breakfast provisions included. Also on Church St the comfortable B&B, the 1832, **B** *Ross Bakery Inn*, T6381 5246, rossbakery@ vision.net.au, has 3 en suite heritage doubles. Continental breakfast supplied by the excellent *Ross Bakery and tea-room* next door. Breads and cakes from the original wood-fired brick oven (ask to have a look), open daily 0900-1700. The friendly **C** *Man o' Ross*, Church St, T6381 5240, is the only remaining licenced pub in Ross. Pleasant front bar, beer garden, and bistro serving cheap meals daily 0730-1000, 1200-1400, 1530-2000. The comfortable double and cheap single rooms are well above usual pub standard. *Oppy's Café*, Church St, serves cheap and cheerful breakfasts, takeaways and light meals, including pancakes. Open daily 0730-2000, Thu-Tue 0800-1700 from Jun-Aug.

Central Highlands

The Lake Highway (A5), branching left off the Midland Highway 55 km north of Hobart, is the slower but more interesting of the two south to north routes. From the junction the road winds through to **Bothwell**, a small friendly town with a strong middle-of-nowhere feel to it. Bothwell was largely settled by Scottish immigrants and boasts Australia's oldest golf course. The small but fascinating **Australian Golf Museum** doubles as the **VIC**. ■ *Daily 1000-1600, 1100-1500 in winter. $3, family $5. T6259 4033.* The sparse accommodation is provided by a site-only caravan park and the **B** *Bothwell Grange*, T6259 5556, ejandrac@bigpond.com, a comfortable old B&B with 7 en suite rooms, built as a coaching inn in 1836. Internet at *Online Access Centre*, High School, Patrick Street, T6259 5549. Open Tuesday-Saturday, hours vary.

Bothwell
Colour map 8, grid B4
75 km from Hobart
50 km from Oaklands

North of Bothwell is a vast highland area, scraped more or less flat by a succession of glaciers that have left it dotted with hundreds of lakes teeming with wild rainbow trout, making it a popular destination for anglers. **Miena**, on the southern tip of **Great Lake**, is about as large a settlement of fishing shacks as you are likely to see in Australia. The only facilities are provided by the **B-D** *Great Lake Hotel* pub, 3 km further north, T6259 8163, and the **A-B** *Great Lake Chalet*, T6259 8355, just to the south (open summer only).

The Central Plateau
Colour map 8, grid B3
Miena 61 km from Bothwell,
66 km from Deloraine

The former, a pub directly on the junction of the unsealed Marlborough Highway to Bronte Park, has a range of accommodation including some self-contained units, motel-style rooms and very basic anglers' cabins, and serves cheap counter meals daily 1200-1400, 1730-1930. Guided fishing is available. Adjacent is a petrol station stocking a small range of groceries, open daily 0900-1600, later in summer.

From Miena a further 10 km of road skirts the Great Lake to **Liawenee**, at nearly 1,000 m, the entrance point to the **Central Plateau Conservation Area**. This is an inhospitable and barren landscape swept by intensely cold westerly winds, which does, however, support a wide variety of alpine flora and fauna. There is a ranger station at Liawenee with a picnic area, wood-fired BBQs and small interpretative centre, T6259 8148. Access to the plateau is almost completely restricted to 4WD. Some 20 km further north the road switchbacks up 200 m to head over a small corner of it. About 2 km after the plateau is gained there is an opportunity to see something of this alpine country at close hand. The excellent 600-m **Pencil Pine Walk** heads up to Pine Lake. The higheay then descends a wide gap in the Great Western Tiers to Golden Valley, and there are several spots to pull over and admire the views of the eastern and western bluffs and the plains and hills in the far north. This route to Deloraine is one of Tasmania's most beautiful drives on a clear day.

Transport In summer a *Tassie Link* service runs between **Launceston** and Lake St Clair via **Miena**. The northbound bus calls at Miena 1435 Mon, Wed, Fri and Sun, while the southbound service passes through earlier in the day at 1140.

The Lyell Highway
Colour map 8, grid B3
Hamilton 76 km from Hobart, 97 km from Derwent Bridge

The Lyell Highway (A10) connects Hobart and New Norfolk with Lake St Clair, the central part of the Wilderness Heritage Area, and ultimately with Strahan and the west coast. The first half of the drive is along the Derwent Valley, past ranks of low, green hills. In the midst of this pastoral country is the quiet **Hamilton**, one of Tasmania's half-dozen towns which have remained largely unchanged, at least architecturally, since their Georgian and Victorian foundations. The **C-D** *Hamilton Inn*, Tarleton Street, T6286 3204, is an old coaching inn known for its good hearty country cooking. There are also a few basic, homely rooms available, some of which are en suite. From Hamilton the route continues northwest to **Ouse**, before ascending to Tarraleah power station. The highway then threads its way past several small lakes and, 20 km from Tarraleah, the Bronte junction, where the 35-km unsealed Marlborough Highway branches off to Miena and Great Lake. At **Bronte Park**, 3 km down this road, is the **A-E** *Highland Village*, T6289 1126, bronte@netspace.net.au, an alpine-style hotel with cheap bar meals, comfortable en suite rooms, no-frills self-contained cottages and a large backpackers' hostel. There is also general store with a small range of groceries, open daily 0900-1700, petrol and post office. From Bronte Park it is 35 km to **Lake St Clair** (see page 862).

Transport *Tassie Link's* southbound services to **Hobart** stop at the **Bronte Junction** 1635 Tue, Thu, 1900 Fri, 1700 Sun plus 1310 other days in summer. Buses call at **Hamilton** 1¼ hrs later. **Derwent Bridge** and west coast services call at Hamilton 0845 Tue, Thu, 1730 Fri, 1545 Sun, plus 1000 other days in summer on request.

Comprising the triple peaks of Mount Field, this national park is home to **Russell Falls**, a beautiful series of wide graceful cascades at the base of the mountain, 1 km off the Gordon River Road (see page 857). The excellent **visitor centre** has good information on the various walking options here and throughout the southwest, and a welcome café. ■ *Daily 0830-1630, café daily 1000-1600, longer hrs in summer. T6288 1149. 6 km east of Westerway on the B61 Gordon River Rd.* From the visitor centre a 16-km unsealed road slowly winds its way up through the differing types of vegetation to the contrast of almost bare rock on the summits. Walking tracks start from various points along the way, and the road ends at over 1,000 m. From here there are superb open day walks around the Rodway Range and, if conditions allow, an exposed seven to eight hour return ridge walk up to the peak of **Mount Field West** (1,439 m) and its terrific panoramic views.

Mount Field National Park
Colour map 8, grid B3
75 km from Hobart
National Park status came in 1917, making it Tasmania's first

Sleeping and eating C *Russell Falls Holiday Cottages*, adjacent to the park entrance, T6288 1198. 2 basic but good value self-contained cottages. The **D** *National Park Hotel*, T6288 1103, on the main road just past the park turn-off, has a few rooms and serves cheap counter meals including full breakfasts if pre-ordered. There is nothing luxurious about the ageing weatherboard **E** *YHA* hostel opposite, T6288 1369, but it is clean and enthusiastically run by the friendly manager. There is also an extremely spartan option up at Lake Dobson. The park maintains a couple of cabins (**F**) up there with very little except their 4 walls, a roof, some bunks and a wood-fire. The closest shops are at Westerway, 5 km away and Maydena, 13 km to the west, where there is also some very good accommodation.

Transport *Tassie Link* run summer-only services between **national park** and **Hobart**, departing the park at 0850 and 1420 Mon, Wed, Fri, Sun, and 0750 and 1305 Tue and Thu. The morning services connect with on-going west coast buses at **Gretna**. **Scotts Peak Dam** summer services leave 0905 Tue, Thu and 1005 Sat.

The East Coast

Tasmania's eastern edge is relatively calm, dry and sunny, and is where Tasmanians come to holiday in the resort towns of Swansea, Bicheno and St Helens. Unlike the dolerite rock of other parts of the state, this area is dominated by granite, which leands it a quality of great beauty. The mountainous islands and peninsulas of **Maria Island** *and* **Freycinet National Park** *shelter and frame the coast, particularly the striking rose-coloured granite domes of the* **Hazards** *range. Granite breaks down into the cleanest and whitest beaches imaginable and the east coast harbours some of Australia's finest examples, at* **Wineglass Bay**, *the Bay of Fires and Mount William National Park. The clean sand contributes to sparkling transparent water, providing superb swimming, snorkelling and diving opportunities, notably at* **Bicheno**. *The hinterland is a mixture of cleared pastoral land and dry eucalypt forest, with tiny patches of rainforest at Wielangta and Weldborough.*

Getting there and around Tassie Link and *Redline* both have east coast services from **Hobart** and **Launceston**. Some *Tassie Link* services require a change of bus at **Bicheno**. A local ferry service (cyclists only) operates from Dolphin Sands (near Swansea) to Swanwick (5 km north of Coles Bay), in summer, T6257 0239, cutting out around 65 km for those visiting **Freycinet**. For **Port Arthur**. The southbound *Tassie Link* service drops off in **Sorrell** 1525 Wed (Mon in summer), and 1730 Fri and Sun, while the **Tasman Peninsula** service leaves there 1640 Mon-Fri, 1025 Sat and, in summer, Mon, Wed and Fri.

Ins & outs

Tasmania

Dunalley to Triabunna

This 55 km unsealed route cuts about 30 km off the bitumen alternative

Look out for log trucks on the winding road

Look for a turning just west of Copping, signposted to Kellevie or Nugent, then follow signs for the Wielangta Forest Drive. The forest is still logged so as well as areas reserved for recreation you will also see logged areas and regrowth forests. From the **Sandspit Forest Reserve** picnic area, 20 km on, there is a three-hour return walk through mixed forest directly from here, and a 15 minute rainforest walk from Robertsons Bridge, 200 m down the road. The bridge, built in the 1980s to complete the north-south route, is simply a huge pile of huge blue gum logs. **Thumbs Lookout**, 10 km further on and a 2 km detour up a steep rough, road, gives a fine view over the near coast and Maria Island. Just beyond the small highway town of Orford, is the **A-C** *Eastcoaster Resort*, T6257 1172, at Louisville Point, the jumping off point for **Maria Island**. The resort is a motel-style complex with a wide range of accommodation, restaurant and tavern. **Triabunna** is a thriving fishing port 4 km further on, the main service town for the area. There's a great tea-rooms here, *Sufi's*, and an excellent hostel 800 m from the town centre. The clean, comfortable and homely **E** *Udder Backpackers YHA*, 12 Spencer Street, T/F6257 3439, udda@southcom.com.au, has 32 beds including three twins and two doubles. Complementary biccies, organic veggies and lifts to and from the bus and Maria Island ferry. Recommended. Triabunna has a tourist office near the wharf on the Esplanade (open daily 1000-1600, T6257 4090, triabunna@tasvisinfo.com.au).

Maria Island National Park

Colour map 8, grid B/C5

This small, mountainous island, clearly visible from the mainland, has the attractions of historic ruins, quiet beaches, beautiful patterned sandstone rocks, fossil cliffs and dolerite-capped peaks. Although it has seen many settlements it is now a refuge for wildlife, such as Forester kangaroos, Bennetts wallabies and a rare little bird, the spotted pardalote, of which there are only 40 left on the island. The waters at the northern end the island are protected.

Ins & outs   **Getting there** *Tassie Link* buses will detour via **Louisville Point** if booked in advance. The *Udder Backpackers*, Triabunna, offer guests a free shuttle service between the hostel and Louisville Point. A passenger and bicycle ferry, the *Eastcoaster Express*, T6257 1589, runs between **Louisville Point** and **Darlington**, daily 1030, 1300, 1530 (25 mins). Daytrips $19, children $11, campers $22, children $14. Bookings essential. No service for 2-3 weeks, Jun-Jul.

Sights & walks   The island was a convict settlement in 1825, and again in the 1840s. The original settlement was at **Darlington** where the ferry still comes in and former convict buildings are used by visitors and rangers. The **Commissariat Store**, to the right of the jetty, provides **visitor information** and the ranger station is just to the south. There are campsites at Darlington and basic but atmospheric accommodation in the historic *Penitentiary* (**E**, recommended). Note that there are no shops or electricity on Maria Island so go prepared with food and lighting. There are some free gas BBQs and limited rainwater. ■ *Bookings required for Penitentiary, camping $4.40. T6257 1420, www.parks.tas.gov.au Ferry departs daily from the Eastcoaster Resort near Orford, T6257 1589 for bookings.*

A brochure on short day-walks is available at the Commissariat Store. The best walks are those to The Painted Cliffs and Mount Maria. The former starts from the ranger station and heads south along the shoreline, through she-oak groves and open paddocks where kangaroos may be seen grazing, then along Hopground Beach to the cliffs at the far end (two hours return). There are also rock pools near the base of the cliffs that are great for snorkelling. Note that this walk must be done within two hours of low tide. Ask the staff at the visitor information centre about tide times. The walk to the summit of **Mount Maria** (709 m) is more challenging but has lovely views of the whole island, Freycinet Peninsula and sometimes as far as Mount Wellington. The walk begins south of the ranger station, near the mouth of Counsel Creek. Almost immediately the path passes through an area of open woodland that is great for birdwatching – look out for pardalote. It is also a good spot to see wombats around dusk. The walk ascends fairly gently but the last half hour involves scrambling over large boulders (six to seven hours return). For more information purchase the *Maria Island National Park Map and Notes*, and discuss plans with a ranger.

Diving There are wonderful dive sites in the clear waters off the island, including kelp beds and sponge gardens. The best time is autumn-winter. Contact *Deep Sea Charters*, T6257 1328, in Orford for dive charters. **Kayaking** *Freycinet Adventures*, I6257 0500, coastalkayak@vision.net.au 4-day trips for experienced kayakers, Jan-Apr ($790).

Tours & activities

Swansea and around

This small settlement, on the shore of Great Oyster Bay facing the long arm of the Freycinet Peninsula, is one of the most appealing on the east coast for its great views, good facilities and relaxed feel. The main street, Franklin Street, is composed of both businesses and homes, many housed in 1850s buildings still used for their original purpose such as the council chambers and *Morris' General Store*. Just north of Swansea the Swan River flows into Moulting Lagoon, formed by the narrow strip of Nine Mile Beach stretching across the bay almost to the far side. Nine Mile Beach, the lagoon-side beach known as Dolphin Sands, and the mouth of the Swan River are fine fishing, swimming and walking spots. Most Swansea businesses provide a free town map and guide to facilities and limited **tourist information** is also available from the **Swansea Bark Mill** just north of town. The mill preserves machinery built in the 1880s to process the tannin in black wattle bark for use in leather manufacture. The machinery is still cranked up each day for visitors. There is also a small museum of local history, tea-rooms and a **Wine and Wool Centre** offering wine tastings and sales of Tasmanian wine, wool and food products. ■ *Daily 0900-1700, shorter hrs Jun-Aug. Entry to Bark Mill and Museum $5.50, children $3.25. T6257 8382, 96 Tasman Highway*. Don't miss a short walk around **Waterloo Point** for Swansea's best view of the Hazards. Just south of town is **Kate's Berry Farm**, worth a visit for its homemade jams and icecream. ■ *Daily 0800-1800, T6257 8428, signposted from Tasman Highway*. Further south are two convict-built stone bridges close to white sand swimming beaches. **Spiky Bridge** and **Spiky Beach**, are 6 km from Swansea and **Mayfield Beach** is another 8 km south. The latter has a campground and is a short walk from the **Three Arch Bridge**.

Colour map 8, grid B5
Population: 500
50 km from Triabunna
60 km from Coles Bay

B *Braeside Cottage*, 21 Julia St, T6257 8008, F6257 8889. This old stone cottage B&B has 2 traditional unfussy rooms, both with large sunroom and en suite, an English garden and views of the bay. **B** *Kabuki-by-the-Sea*, Tasman Highway, 12 km south, T/F6257 8588, www.view.com.au/kabuki Self-contained ryokan-style villas with incredible views of Great Oyster Bay and simple, homely rooms furnished with Japanese hangings and ceramics. Good standby rates (**C**). Recommended. **C** *Freycinet Waters*, 16 Franklin St, T6257 8080, www.freycinetwaters.com.au Sunny hosted B&B with 4 rooms in sea colours with sea views. Friendly hosts and a good cooked breakfast. **C** *Oyster Bay Guesthouse*, 10 Franklin St, T6257 8110, oyster.bay@bigpond.com Former coaching inn with 9 fresh, pretty en suite rooms, comfy old-fashioned guest lounge and good value

Sleeping
There is plenty of accommodation in Swansea, including some good value gems. Book ahead for October-March but prices tend not to rise for the peak summer period

Tasmania

restaurant. **C-E** *Kenmore Cabin and Tourist Park*, 2 Bridge St, T6257 8148, kenmore@ vision.net.au By the beach with a good range of self-contained cabins, on-site vans, and facilities. **E** *Swansea YHA*, 5 Franklin St, T6257 8367, yhatas@yhatas.org.au Small, hostel with 2 dorms and 2 family rooms, lounge with woodfire, kitchen and central location.

Eating   One of the best places to eat on the east coast is *Kabuki-by the-Sea*, Tasman Highway, T6257 8588. High-quality Japanese food and graceful room in a wonderful location. Also morning and afternoon Devonshire teas. Daily 1000-1600, Tue-Sat 1800-2130 (Nov-Apr), Fri-Sat 1800-2130 (May-Oct). In Swansea, *View Point*, 3 Maria St, T6257 8656, is a popular local seafood restaurant (mid-range) in a simple dining room overlooking the bay. Daily 1800-2000. *Shy Albatross* in the *Oyster Bay Guesthouse* on Franklin St, has good value pasta and seafood (cheap), aimed at families. There is also an excellent café that also does evening meals on Sat, *The Left Bank*, corner of Franklin St and Maria St. A hip, friendly place serving fresh and interesting food and Swansea's best coffee. Wed-Mon 0830-1700, Sat 0600-2030, closed Tue-Wed in winter.

Transport   The *Tassie Link* service leaves from the corner store for **Hobart** (2¾ hrs, $19.70), 1340 Wed, 1545 Fri, Sun and, in summer, 1340 Mon. Additional summer service via **Richmond**, 0600 Mon-Fri (0800 school holidays). The northbound service leaves for **Bicheno** 1050 Fri and Sun, and also on to **St Helens** 1120 Wed and, in summer, 1120 Mon. *Redline* run a 0905 Mon-Fri (0635 school Mon) service via **Campbell Town** to **Hobart** (4½ hrs). From Campbell Town there is a connecting bus to **Launceston** (total 2 hrs). Cyclists heading to **Coles Bay** during Oct-Apr might consider travelling via Nine Mile Beach and taking a boat over to the peninsula (see above for details).

Directory   **Banks** ATM in the *Corner Store*, corner of Franklin St and Victoria St, daily 0700-1900. **Bike hire** *Cherry Cycles*, Wellington St, off Maria St, T6257 8055. $22 day. **Communications** Internet at *Online Access Centre*, Primary School, T6257 8806. Open Tue-Sat, hrs vary. **Post Office**, corner of Franklin St and Arnol St.

Freycinet National Park and Coles Bay

Colour map 8
grid B5
Coles Bay 200 km
from Hobart,
120 km from Ross

One of Australia's great national parks, Freycinet is best known for **Wineglass Bay**, a perfect arc of aquamarine sea with a fine rim of white sand. The bay is hidden from view on the eastern coast of the park and the half-hour climb over a low saddle to the Wineglass Bay lookout is one of Tasmania's most popular short walks. On the western side the rugged red-granite domes of the **Hazards** range stand shoulder to shoulder between two low sandy necks. Beyond are the forests, rocky coves and remote beaches of the mountainous southern peninsula and **Schouten Island**. The park also includes a narrow coastal strip to the north, protecting the Friendly Beaches, miles of pristine white sand and sparkling clear water. Other lovely spots on the east coast of the park are **Cape Tourville** and **Sleepy Bay**, which is great for snorkelling, although beginners may prefer the more sheltered water at beautiful **Honeymoon Bay**.

Ins & outs   **Getting there and around** Coles Bay is the main access point for the park. *Coles Bay-Bicheno Coach Service*, T6257 0293, runs buses to and from **Bicheno**, some timed to connect with *Tassie Link* and *Redline* services. Departs from post office Mon-Sat 0800 all year, more services in summer (40 mins, $7.50). They also run a shuttle bus from Coles Bay via the caravan park, *Iluka* and the post office to the start of walking tracks in **Freycinet** (10 mins, $5 return), Mon-Fri 0930, Sat-Sun bookings only (returning 1000, 1350, 1550). Bookings advisable. Cyclists heading to **Swansea** during Oct-Apr might consider taking a boat over to Nine Mile Beach (see above for details).

Information Information and maps are available from the **park entry station** close to the park border. Nearby are camping and picnic areas. Campsites are allocated for the summer season by ballot although some sites are reserved for backpackers. At the time of writing an *East Coast Interpretation Centre* was planned to provide information about the natural and cultural features of the east coast. The new centre will be located close to the park border. Park open 24 hrs, entry station manned daily 0900-1700, T6257 0107, www.parks.tas.gov.au Campers should note that the park is a fuel-stove only area, fresh water is limited and rubbish must be carried out.

All walks start from the walking track car park at the end of the sealed road. The classic walk is the short walk to the Wineglass Bay lookout (one hour return). To extend this walk continue down to the beach for the **Wineglass Bay Hazards Beach circuit** (11 km, five hours). Just before reaching the beach a track off to the right leads across the swampy isthmus to Hazards Beach. Then heading north, the track continues up the beach and around the coastline back to the car park. The Hazards are under 500 m but provide wonderful views. It is possible to walk to the summit of **Mount Amos** (454 m) for the best views of Wineglass Bay and the peninsula (three hours return). Do not attempt in bad weather. These day walks can be combined for an overnight circuit walk to the summit of **Mount Graham** (579 m) along easy formed tracks and beaches.

Walking
Check with the ranger before starting overnight walks. The Freycinet National Park Map & Notes ($9) is available at the park entry station

Abseiling and climbing *Freycinet Adventures*, T6257 0500, coastalkayak@vision.net.au Hang from granite cliffs above the ocean, beginners to advanced. (Abseiling ½ day, $70, climbing from $100 day.) **Boat** *Freycinet Sea Charters*, Coles Bay jetty, T6257 0355. Flexible cruises for scenery, wildlife, fishing or diving. *Freycinet Sail Tours*, 104-0780 4084. 3-hr cruises on a 30-ft catamaran. **Flights** *Freycinet Air*, T6375 1694, Friendly Beaches Rd. Scenic flights in light aircraft over the park (30 mins, $75). **Hire** *Freycinet Rentals*, 5 Garnet Av, Coles Bay, T6257 0320. Camping gear, canoes, catamarans, dinghies, snorkels, diving gear and fishing rods. **Kayak** *Freycinet Adventures*. A tranquil way to explore the peninsula, the longer trips allowing time for walking. From ½-day ($75) to 5-day ($935) tours, twilight and moonlight trips ($45), also kayak and bike hire. **Walking** *Freycinet Experience*, T6223 7565, walk@freycinet.com.au A 4-day guided walk sleeping in luxury camps and the Friendly Beaches lodge and being fed with fine food($1,200).

Tours & activities

Coles Bay is a small fishing and holiday village just a few kilometres from the border of the Freycinet National Park. Full of holiday homes, Coles Bay has few facilities and feels remote, despite its proximity to Swansea and Bicheno. Bring plenty of cash as there are no banks or ATMs. Limited **tourist information** is available from the supermarket.

Coles Bay
Colour map 8 grid B5
198 km from Hobart, 119 km from Ross

Sleeping and eating L-A *Freycinet Lodge*, Freycinet National Park, T6257 0101. Around 60 timber cabins and the lodge are tucked unobtrusively away in bush facing Coles Bay. The lodge organizes lots of daily activities such as nocturnal wildlife walks, and has a bar and 2 restaurants open to all. **A-B** *Edge of the Bay*, 2308 Main Rd, T6257 0102, www.edgeofthebay.com.au resort 4 km from Coles Bay with the best views in the area. Elegant contemporary suites or dated but comfy self-contained cottages with wood fires. Also a good mid-range restaurant. **C-E** *Iluka Holiday Centre and YHA*, Esplanade, T6257 0115, iluka@trump.net.au A large complex with units, cabins, vans and doubles (**F**). Also a YHA hostel with 6 small dorms and 3 doubles. **F** *Freycinet Backpackers*, part of the *Coles Bay Caravan Park*, about 3 km from Coles Bay, T6257 0100. A large spartan hostel with 2 corridors of 24 twin rooms, each with bunks and heater, lockable, linen extra. One free transfer to the Wineglass Bay Track.

Much of the accommodation are self-contained holiday homes but all ranges also catered for

Book well in advance for the busy summer period, December-April

Tasmania

▶▶ **Penguin parades**

*There are fairy penguin rookeries right around the northern and eastern coasts of Tasmania with several opportunities for viewing these smallest of penguins. There are guided twilight rookery tours from several towns, including **Stanley**, **George Town** and **Bicheno**. Between Devonport and Penguin is a free penguin-watching platform at **Lillico's Beach**, just outside of Leith, and a tour to a rookery on private property 2 km east of Penguin at **Penguin Point**. The latter runs from Nov-Mar, Sun-Fri, T6437 2590. This tour is $5, but does not include transport. Others around the state range up to $15, transport included. If looking for penguins independently at free platforms, do not carry bright lights, but cover torches with your hand or red or blue material. Rug up, keep quiet and settle in just as it is getting dark. All but the largest rookeries are very quiet in winter, and one of the few opportunities to see them year-round is at Bicheno.*

Madge Malloy's, Garnet Av, T6257 0399, is a very good casual restaurant (mid-range) with super fresh seafood caught by the owners. Tue-Sat 1800-2030. Also houses a craft gallery. The excellent *Freycinet Bakery and Cafe* has all-day breakfasts, sandwiches, pizzas and of course bread. The bakery has an internet kiosk. Daily 0800-2100 Oct-Apr, 0800-1600 May-Sep.

Bicheno
Colour map 8, grid B5
Population: 700
38 km from Coles Bay
79 km from St Helens

In terms of both commerce and leisure Bicheno very much looks to the sea. There is a small commercial fleet and the town is very popular with Tasmanians for summer surf, rock and sport **fishing**. Between the headland and the small offshore Governors Island is a sheltered stretch of water known as the **Gulch**, great for snorkelling and diving. Bicheno's crystal-clear waters, at their best during autumn and winter, are said to harbour Tasmania's finest **dive sites**, including vivid sponge gardens, and spectacular granite pinnacles and boulders. The *Dive Centre*, Scuba Court, T6375 1138, sells and hires out diving ($66) and snorkelling ($22) gear, and runs boat dives ($31). Open daily 0900-1700. For those preferring to stay dry, a glass-bottomed boat heads into the Gulch every day, on the hour, weather and numbers permitting; $15, book at the VIC. As a further alternative, the **Sealife Centre** has a tired but interesting aquarium showing much of the local marine life. ■ *Daily 0900-1700. $5, children $2.50. T6375 1082. Tasman Highway*. There are **fairy penguin rookeries** right along this stretch of coast and one of the best Tasmanian penguin tours takes careful advantage of this. Tours include a visit to a small interpretative centre. ■ *Daily, all year, just after dusk. $15, children $7. Book at the VIC – well ahead in peak summer*. The **VIC** is in the centre of town where the highway meets, and briefly becomes, Burgess Street. ■ *Daily 0900-dusk, 0900-1300 winter weekends. T6375 1333*. Inland tours are provided by *Thorley's Forest Excursions*, T6375 1117, who offer night wildlife-spotting trips and half-day 4WD tours (both $35, minimum two people). Between autumn and spring whales, seals and dolphins are also known to visit the kelp beds and reefs off shore.

Sleeping B *Old Gaol Cottages*, Burgess St, T6375 1430, www.bichenogaolcottages.com 3 self-contained cottages, one the old gaol, another the stables and the third the old schoolhouse. Breakfast provisions included. Recommended. **C** *Old Tram*, T6375 1555, oldtrambb@tassie.net.au Light 1870s town house with 2 spacious, very comfortably furnished B&B rooms. Recommended. The **C** *Cabin and Tourist Park*, Tasman Highway, T6375 1117, has a range of luxury cabins, while there are on-site vans at the *East Coast Caravan Park*. The town's 2 hostels are in stark but interesting contrast. **E** *Bicheno*

Backpackers, Morrison St, T/F6375 1651, is quite simply central, modern and comfortable. The cheaper **E** *YHA*, 2 km north on the Tasman Highway, T6375 1293, is a dilapidated weatherboard building with 2 unwelcoming dorms and a scruffy kitchen. The management is very welcoming, however, and the crumbling verandah, complete with moth-eaten armchairs, is a few paces across the back lawn from a secluded beach and penguin rookery.

Eating Best of the eating is at the *Blue House*, a mobile restaurant that sets up next to the VIC daily throughout the summer. The excellent cheap meals can either be taken away or eaten at one of the few temporary tables placed out front. Recommended. There are several other evening dining options, mostly in anonymous pubs and motels. They include mid-range *Mary Harvey's Restaurant*, T6375 1430, and the French BYO *Cyrano's*, T6375 1137, both on Burgess St. *Freycinet Bakery & Café*, corner Burgess St and Tasman Highway. All-day breakfasts, inventive light lunches, great coffee. Open daily 0800-1800, to 1600 Jun-Oct. At the cheaper end of the scale, and for the best bar, try the *Beachfront Tavern* on the Tasman Highway, T6375 1111.

Transport The *Tassie Link* service leaves from four Square for **Hobart** (3½ hrs, $24.20), 1300 Wed, 1510 Fri, Sun and, in summer, 1300 Mon. One northbound service leaves for **St Helens** 1135 Wed and, in summer, Mon. Another heads for **St Marys** and **Launceston**, 1300 Wed, 1515 Fri, Sun and, in summer, 1300 Mon. *Redline* have an 0825 Mon-Fri (0600 school Mon) service via **Swansea** and **Campbell Town** to **Hobart** (5 hrs). From Campbell Town there is a connecting bus to **Launceston** (total 2½ hrs).

The Douglas Apsley National Park is a handsome park of dry eucalypt forest, river gorges and waterfalls. Tasmania's newest national park doesn't receive much attention so it has a quality of peace in the midst of its modest hidden beauty well worth seeking out. While it is very rugged, it is not an untouched wilderness. In the years since European settlement it has been used for coal mining, farming and trapping and subject to regular fires lit by trappers. What makes it unusual among forest of this type, common on the east coast, is that most of it has never been cleared. This means it has an incredible diversity of plants and animals, including rare and endangered species. Bettongs, bandicoots, quolls, bats, reptiles and over 65 species of birds also live here. A short **Lookout Track** leads to a platform above the Apsley waterhole (15-minute circuit). There is a basic campsite at the waterhole. A longer walk leads to the impressive gorge but can only be done in dry weather when water levels are low. The **Apsley Gorge Circuit** (3-4 hours return) starts from the waterhole and crosses the river, ascending a ridge, then descends to the river near the gorge. Following the river downstream for 10 mins, the track returns to the waterhole via the stream bed. Longer and overnight walks are also possible, such as the challenging 2½-day **Leeaberra Track**, traversing the park from north to south. See the *Douglas-Apsley Map and Notes* for details or talk to a ranger. ■ *For advice contact the nearest parks office, at Coles Bay, T6257 0107. Fuel stoves only Oct-Apr but recommended all year round.*

Douglas Apsley National Park
3 km north of Bicheno
7 km unsealed access

Further north, at Chain of Lagoons, the highway divides. The hilly, forested northwest branch passes through the very tidy town of **St Marys**. The limited accommodation includes the pub, **D** *St Marys Hotel*, on the corner of Story Street and Main Street, T6372 2181, and **D-E** *Seaview Farm*, 8 km away on German Town Road, T6372 2341, which has bunk rooms and en suite units. There is also a great café here, *Todd's Hall*, Storey Street, T6372 2066, which has its own theatre featuring films, bands and plays most weekends.

St Marys
Colour map 8, grid B5
45 km from Bicheno
35 km from St Helens

St Patrick's Head, nearby, is a good walk at 2 hrs return

Tasmania

St Helens
Colour map 8, grid A5
Population: 1,800
161 km from
Launceston, 117 km
from Coles Bay

St Helens has a very coastal feel despite being several kilometres from the open sea. The town straddles the point at which Georges Bay becomes the shallow inlet of Medeas Cove, and the two halves of the town are connected by the Golden Fleece Bridge. The town is best known for its **sport fishing**, with several competing operators, but can also act as a base for walkers wanting to explore the exquisite coastal scenery further north. Fishing charter companies include *Professional Charters*, T6376 3083, sportfish@vision.net.au, and *Mick Tucker's*, T6376 1511. Non-anglers with a taste for the water should not miss a sail on the *Elektra*, a 10-m catamaran. Contact *Sail St Helens*, T6372 5342. **Diving** has also become popular since the *East Coast Scuba Centre* opened on Cecila Street, T6376 1720. Boat dives from $40, equipment hire and advice. The **VIC** is toward the north end of Cecilia Street and doubles as the **History Room Museum**, an absorbing display of local Aboriginal, mining, fishing and tourism history. ■ *Mon-Fri 0900-1700, Sat 0900-1200, Sun 1000-1400. $4, children $2. T6376 1744, historyroom@hotmail.com*

Hours stated here are often restricted in the mid-Jun to mid-Sep winter season when all close on Sun

Sleeping and eating L-A *Wybalenna Lodge*, south of the bridge, T6376 1611, www.wybalennalodge.com, is one of 2 very elegant and indulgent B&Bs. Dating from 1907, Wybalenna has 5 exquisite en suite rooms, very light and white, with 2 in external garden cottages. Silver-service breakfast and, if pre-arranged, dinners in the wonderfully formal dining room (around $50 for 3 courses). **C-D** *Artnor Lodge*, 71 Cecilia St, T/F6376 1234. Cheap motel-style rooms, mostly with shared, exterior bathroom facilities. Cooked breakfast included. Good value, as is **E** *Daisy House*, Quail St, T6376 1371. Actually 2 self-contained cottages, linen included, sleeping up to 7. The small, friendly **D-E** *YHA*, 5 Cameron St, T6376 1661, yhatas@yhatas.org.au, is very clean, comfortable and homely. One double room. There are several hotel and motel restaurants in town but the best eating is in the following 3 more modest establishments. *Wok Stop*, adjacent to the VIC on Cecilia St, serves a good range of takeaway Asian curries. Open daily 1200-2100. Next door is the vibrant BYO *Milk Bar*, serving breakfasts, lunches, cakes and coffee. Open Mon-Thu 0900-1700, Fri 0900-2100 for cheap evening meals, Sat 0900-1500, Sun 1000-1400. For fish and chips or fresh shellfish head for the *Captain's Catch*, on the wharf just north of the bridge. Open Mon-Fri 1030-1600, Sat-Sun 1030-2100. There are several points along the foreshore with picnic, toilet and BBQ facilities.

Transport *Redline* run services to **Launceston** (2½ hrs) via **St Marys**, 0930 Mon, Wed, Fri, 0800 Tue, Thu, and 1630 Sun. A connecting service heads down to **Hobart** (4-5½ hrs). There is also a *Tassie Link* bus from the VIC down the east coast to **Hobart** (4¼ hrs, $35.20), 1400 Fri and Sun.

Directory Banks ATMs on Cecilia St. **Communications** Internet at *Online Access Centre*, adjacent to VIC, T6376 1116. $5 per ½ hr. Open Mon-Fri 0900-1800, Sat-Sun 1000-1400, longer hrs Jan-Feb. **Post Office**, Cecilia St. **Parks and Wildlife Office** Eagle St, 2 km north of town centre, T6376 1550.

The Northeast

Northern east coast
Mount William National Park 38 km unsealed from St Helens

To the north of St Helens, **Humbug Point** is topped by a worthwhile lookout and shelters **Binalong Bay** on its seaward side. This stretch of coast has some very popular swimming beaches. Binalong Bay marks the southern end of the legendary **Bay of Fires**, a long expanse of perfect sand, as fine and white as sugar. A road runs alongside the bay as far north as the Gardens. Just south of Mount William National Park is **Ansons Bay**, a popular local fishing shack area and Policemans Point, a camping spot.

The most northeasterly tip of Tasmania is encompassed by this remote park of beautiful coastline. Between the beaches are low headlands of granite boulders splashed with bright orange lichen. The hinterland consists of dunes, heath and woodland, covered in colourful wildflowers in spring and summer. The park also has the state's largest population of Tasmania's only kangaroo, the Forester (or eastern grey). Foresters, pademelons, wallabies, and wombats can be seen at dawn and dusk, grazing on the marsupial lawns behind Purdon Bay and around Forester Kangaroo Drive. Access to the northern end of the park is via the tiny mining town of Gladstone. **Stumpys Bay** is the main picnic and camping area with gas BBQs and fireplaces. At the southern end of the park, accessible from St Helens, it is possible to drive out to the lighthouse at **Eddystone Point** or to **Deep Creek,** where there is a smaller campsite. There is no access by public transport. The ranger station is on Musselroe Rd at the northern park border. ■ *T6357 2108. BYO drinking water.*

Mount William National Park

There are only two defined walks in the park, most walkers simply following the beaches. To walk to the summit of **Mount William** (216 m) start from the signposted car park off Forester Kangaroo Drive. This is an easy ascent on a well-defined track (one hour return) and some of the Furneaux group of islands are visible from the top. If short of time take the track from campground 4, Stumpys Bay. This leads along a fire trail to **Cobler Rocks** giving a view of the coastline south to Eddystone Point (1½ hours return). A magnificent way to see the park is to walk from **Stumpys Bay** to **Deep Creek**, along the coast (15 km, six to seven hours). An extra day could be spent exploring the northern coastline of the Bay of Fires, Abbotsbury peninsula and the bird life of Ansons Bay. For those who prefer a guided walk or a bit of comfort, there is a superb expensive alternative. *Bay of Fires Walk*, T6331 2006, www.bayoffires.com.au, take four days to walk from Stumpys Bay, staying in a comfortable bush camp and the extraordinary *Bay of Fires Lodge*, a magically secluded construction of timber and glass overlooking the ocean ($1,265 all-inclusive, November-April). Topographic maps of this area are available in Launceston and Hobart.

From St Helens the Tasman Highway heads inland to the west, winding through a succession of agricultural and forested valleys and hill passes. About 24 km out of St Helens the road slips back down to Pyengana, a tiny settlement in the George River valley. It is worth taking the left turn here to visit both the **D** *Pub in the Paddock*, T6373 6121, and the impressive **St Columba Falls**, 7 km further down the now unsealed road. The pub is an 1880s homestead, first licenced in 1901, with a cosy, rustic but smart front bar and bistro and six very good value double rooms. The narrow, stepped falls, the highest in Tasmania, are a 10-minute walk from the car park. From Pyengana the highway climbs out of the valley and up over **Weldborough Pass**, with a couple of unmarked spots to pull over and take in the views. A few kilometres on is the **Weldborough Reserve Rainforest Walk**, a lovely 15-minute circuit through the dryer sort of rainforest, dominated by giant man ferns and ancient myrtle. **Derby**, perched on the side of a deep forested valley, was for a brief period an important tin-mining town. About 6 km away in tiny **Winnaleah** is a hostel, the **E** *Merlinkei Farm YHA*, 524 Racecourse Road, T6354 2152, mervync@vision.net.au, with two large dorms on a dairy farm. They operate a pick-up service from the Tasman Highway (A3).

St Helens to Derby
*Derby 60 km from St Helens
54 km from Bridport*

Tasmania

Transport A *Redline* service runs twice a day Mon-Fri, and once on Sun, between **Launceston** and **Winnaleah**, calling at various stops including **Scottsdale** and **Derby**.

Launceston and around

*This region is one of the most populous areas of Tasmania and also encompasses diverse and spectacular countryside. **Launceston** itself is a gracious river city, notable for its lovely **Cataract Gorge** right in the heart of the city. It is an important second city and a useful base for travellers. To the north are the tame agricultural lands of the **Tamar Valley**, an expanding wine region, with a small remnant of bush at the tip, the **Narawntapu National Park**, which is known for its scores of grazing wombats. To the east is the dramatic dark plateau of **Ben Lomond**, one of few Tasmanian mountains that has a road up to the summit, albeit an alarming one. To the south of Launceston rise the **Great Western Tiers**, marking the edge of the Central Plateau and highlands. This mountain range dominates most of northern Tasmania and is both impressive and accessible, offering wonderful waterfalls and walking close to the small town of **Deloraine**.*

Launceston

Colour map 8, grid A4
Population: 100,000
173 km from Coles Bay
98 km from Hobart
278 km from Strahan

Launceston is an attractive little city of gardens and historic buildings surrounded by the hills at the head of the Tamar Valley. Established in 1806, it is Australia's oldest provincial centre and contains some of the country's best examples of Edwardian and Federation architecture. The Cataract Gorge is in the heart of the city and is surrounded by acres of parkland. The city celebrates the riches of the area with the Tamar Valley **Festival of the Senses** in mid-February. The festival celebrates food, wine, music and theatre with a three-day party in City Park. For more details see www.festivalofthesenses.com The main **VIC** is on the corner of St John Street and Paterson Street and handles bookings and information for the north of the state. ■ *Mon-Fri 0900-1700, Sat 0900-1500, Sun 0900-1200, T6336 3133, www.gatewaytas.com.au*

Ins & outs
For more details, see Transport, page 838

Getting there The **airport** is 15 km out at **Evandale**, T6391 6222. Taxi about $25. Airport Shuttle, T0500-512009, self-contained, phone for city pickups ($10, 30 mins). **State bus** The depot for *Tassie Link* is not in the centre of town so the main bus stop is outside the VIC. The *Redline* depot is at 18 Charles St, close to the river.

Getting around The main commercial district is around the junctions of Brisbane St, Charles St and St John St. **Bus** Most metropolitan bus services leave from the St John St Bus Station, between Elizabeth St and York St. The main *Metroshop* office is at 168 Wellington St, T132201, www.metrotas.com.au Tickets are available from here, various agents, or on the buses. Single tickets to city centre destinations cost $1.30. A daily multi-trip ticket, $3.40, is valid Mon-Fri from 0900 and all day Sat-Sun. Ten-day multi-trips $26.50. Most routes run daily around 0900-1800, with occasional weekend services.

Sights
The best way to see the compact city centre is on foot. The VIC has detailed self-guided tour notes

To see a sample of the city's architecture, walk east from City Park along historic Cameron Street. At the junction of St John Street is the elaborate post office and the grand, white Town Hall with its corinthian columns. Walk through the civic centre, cross Charles Street and continue along Cameron to see some wonderful terraces. Guided historic walks leave from the VIC. ■ *Mon-Fri 0945. $15, concessions $11. 2 hrs. T6331 3679.* A cruise up the Tamar is also a fine way to get acquainted with the area. Lunch cruises go down river as far as the Batman Bridge (1000, four hours, $58, children $29, concessions $53) and afternoon cruises turn around at Rosevears (1500, 2½ hours, $31, children $15.50, concessions $28). *Tamar River Cruises* leave from Home Point daily, September-May. T6334 9900.

Tasmania

Queen Victoria Museum and Art Gallery has Tasmania's finest colonial art collection, featuring the works of John Glover and Tom Roberts, and is housed in a new complex at the Inveresk Railyards on the far side of the river. The museum's natural sciences and zoology collections are housed separately in Wellington Street and if you haven't managed to spot a Tasmanian tiger in the wild they include a stuffed specimen. There is also a planetarium here projecting images of the southern sky. ■ *Daily 1000-1700. $10 for both sites, children free, concessions $9. Planetarium shows Tue-Sat 1500, $2.50 extra, children $1.50. T6323 3777, www.tmag.tas.gov.au* Also at the railyards on Sundays is the **Inveresk Market**, a community market with art, food and bric-a-brac stalls and live bands. Launceston also has several places to look at contemporary art and design. **The Design Centre of Tasmania** features Tasmania furniture, regular design exhibitions and a shop with high quality craftwork. ■ *Daily 0930-1730. $2.20. T6331 5506. City Park*. Next door is the **Wood Design Collection**, displaying what the state's finest craftspeople can do with Tasmania's beautiful timbers such as Huon and Sassafras. It was established with funding from Forestry Tasmania in 1991 and grows every second year when the best new work is selected and purchased from the Wood Design Biennial in Hobart. ■ *Mon-Fri 0930-1730. $2.20, children $1.10. T6334 6558, www.twdc.org.au* **Gallery Two**

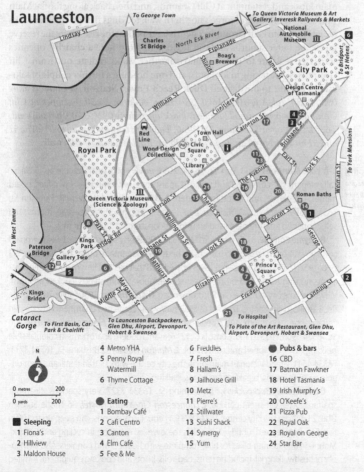

Launceston

To George Town

To Queen Victoria Museum & Art Gallery, Inveresk Railyards & Markets

Lindsay St

Charles St Bridge

North Esk River

Esplanade

National Automobile Museum

Shields

Boag's Brewery

City Park

To Bridport & St Helens

William St

Tamar St

Design Centre of Tasmania

Cimitiere St

Calneron St

Brisbane St

Red Line

Town Hall

Wood Design Collection

Civic Square

York St

Weiman St

To York Mansions

Royal Park

Library

Earl St

The Avenue

Queen Victoria Museum (Science & Zoology)

Paterson St

Charles St

Wellington St

Vincent St

St John St

Roman Baths

George St

Kings Park

Bridge Rd

Brisbane St

York St

Prince's Square

Paterson Bridge

Gallery Two

Margaret St

Bathurst St

Elizabeth St

Frederick St

Canning St

Kings Bridge

Middle St

Cataract Gorge

To First Basin, Car Park & Chairlift

To Launceston Backpackers, Glen Dhu, Airport, Devonport, Hobart & Swansea

To Hospital

To Plate of the Art Restaurant, Glen Dhu, Airport, Devonport, Hobart & Swansea

Tasmania

N

0 metres   200
0 yards   200

■ **Sleeping**
1 Fiona's
2 Hillview
3 Maldon House

4 Metro YHA
5 Penny Royal Watermill
6 Thyme Cottage

● **Eating**
1 Bombay Café
2 Cafi Centro
3 Canton
4 Elm Café
5 Fee & Me

6 Freddies
7 Fresh
8 Hallam's
9 Jailhouse Grill
10 Metz
11 Pierre's
12 Stillwater
13 Sushi Shack
14 Synergy
15 Yum

● **Pubs & bars**
16 CBD
17 Batman Fawkner
18 Hotel Tasmania
19 Irish Murphy's
20 O'Keefe's
21 Pizza Pub
22 Royal Oak
23 Royal on George
24 Star Bar

at Ritchies Mill is a private art and craft gallery in an old mill by the riverfront, and the complex also has a café, Stillwater, with an outdoor deck. ■ *Tue-Sun 1100-1600. Free. By West Tamar Bridge, at the end of Paterson St.* Art and craft of a different kind can be found at the **National Automobile Museum**, which has a collection of British and European vintage and veteran classic cars, sports cars and motorcycles. All of the cars are on loan so the collection changes regularly as the owners take their cars out for a spin or on tour. ■ *Sep-May 0900-1700, Jun-Aug 1000-1600. $8.50, $4.40 children. T6334 8888, www.tased.edu.au/ tasonline/nam 86 Cimitiere St, parking in Willis St.*

Cataract Gorge Reserve The gorge that drains the South Esk River into the Tamar is one of the most spectacular on the island, a long, wide chasm with steep sides of tiered, jumbled rock, and ridiculously accessible; the entrance is only a 10-minute walk from the city centre. The gorge extends inland for about 1 km before widening out into a huge grassed and forested natural amphitheatre at the centre of which is a wide stretch of water, First Basin. Just above this is Alexandra Suspension Bridge which allows a pleasant three-hour circular walk from the mouth of the gorge at Kings Bridge. This walk starts up the steep, winding Zig-zag Track to the First Basin, from there across the bridge to the reserve's main kiosk and restaurant at Cliff Grounds, and then back along the flat Main Track, at the base of the gorge's northern wall, to Kings Bridge. Further walks radiate out from Cliff Grounds. There is a car park at the rise where the reserve meets the outer suburbs at Basin Road, and from here a **chairlift** operates across First Basin to Cliff Grounds. Further walks radiate out from Cliff Grounds, some taking in lookouts, and one heading a further couple of kilometres upriver to the disused **Duck Reach Power Station**. ■ *Chairlift daily 0900-1630, Jul-Aug 1000-1600. $8 return, children $5.50. Facilities at Cliff Grounds comprise a small takeaway kiosk, open daily 0930-1700, a restaurant, T6331 3330, open Tue-Sun 1200-1430, Tue-Sat 1630-2000, and toilets. The 51 and 52 buses drop-off at the bottom of Basin Rd, leaving a 10-min walk.*

Sleeping
See also Bars & pubs page 837

L-A *York Mansions*, 9-11 York St, T6334 2933, www.yorkmansions.com.au 5 classically elegant self-contained and serviced apartments with antiques, open fires, board games, CD players and a cottage garden. **A-B** *Penny Royal Watermill*, Paterson St, T6331 6699, pennyroyal@vision.net.au Large complex of motel-style rooms and self-contained apartments in and around a reconstructed 1825 flour mill.

B *Thyme Cottage*, 31 Cimitiere St, T/F6331 1906. Pretty self-contained weatherboard cottage with open fires, deep bath, brass beds and handmade quilts. **B-C** *Hillview*, 193 George St, T6331 7388. Large old 1840s hosted B&B that has at different times been a vicarage, nursing home and brothel. Fresh, contemporary furnishings, cooked breakfast. Views over the city to the Tamar. Recommended. **C** *Apartments 1930s Style*, 70 Penquite Rd, 3 km from city centre, T/F6344 6953. 2 sunny self-contained apartments in a garden cottage, one 1-bedroom, one 2-bedroom. Recommended. **C** *Fiona's B&B*, 141a George St, T6334 5965, F6331 1709. Consists of 12 pleasant modern apartments in colonial-style buildings, well equipped and convenient. **C** *Maldon House*, 32 Brisbane St, T6331 3211, F6334 4641. Grand Victorian mansion in the city centre with 12 traditional and comfortable en suite rooms, breakfast provisions, parking.

E *Launceston Backpackers*, 103 Canning St, T6334 2327. Very spacious, clean but spartan hostel. Off-street parking. **E** *Launceston City Youth Hostel*, 36 Thistle St, Glen Dhu, 2 km from the city centre, T6344 9779, is equally cavernous, can sleep up to 100 in fact. The very relaxed, untidy style belies the owners' expertise in cycling and walking. Mountain and touring bikes for hire, complete with helmets and panniers. Also all manner or bushwalking kit, including tents, bed-rolls, boots and cooking equipment. All hired

Tasmania

per week at very good rates. **E** *Metro YHA*, 16 Brisbane St, T6334 4505, metrolaunceston@bidpond.com Bright and friendly modern hostel with several 8-bed dorms and 6 doubles, large living room, smallish modern kitchen and sunny rooftop terrace. Also linen, parking and bike hire. The **D-E** *Treasure Island Caravan Park*, Glen Dhu, T6344 2600, is nearly 3 km from the town centre and has cabins and on-site vans.

Eating

Expensive *Fee and Me*, 190 Charles St, T6331 3195. 4 very elegant wood-panelled dining rooms set the scene for the best dining in the state. This restaurant consistently wins prestigious awards and the fine wine cellar complements the food perfectly. Open Mon-Sat from 1900, bookings required. *Plate of the Art*, 185 Wellington St, T6334 3220. A young chef and adventurous menu combining fine food and art. Open Fri 1200-1500, Mon-Sat 1800-2100. *Stillwater*, Ritchies Mill, 2 Bridge Rd, T6331 4153. Asian-influenced, creative cooking in a lovely space on the waterfront with a mellow timber floor and old mill beams. Also breakfast and lunch café food until 1600. Daily 1800-2100.

Mid-range *Elm Café*, 168 Charles St, T6333 0600. Small rustic dining room with rough wood furniture, cream-painted stone walls and a large open fire. Very friendly staff serve an inventive variety of food from the fantastic cheap breakfasts (all day at weekends), to gourmet pizzas, tapas and fine evening cuisine. Open Tue-Sat 0930-2200, Sun-Mon 0930 1730. Recommended. *Hallam's Waterfront*, 13 Park St, T6334 0554. The city's best seafood restaurant, on the riverfront, with the look of an elegant boathouse. Daily 1130-1430, 1730-2030. *Jailhouse Grill*, 32 Wellington St, T6331 0466. Steaks and grills in an old gaol-themed dining room, includes unlimited salad bar. Open Fri 1200-1500, daily 1745-2100.

Cheap *Bombay Café*, 144 Charles St, T6334 7677. Friendly BYO Indian restaurant specializing in Kashmiri. Open Mon-Sat 1200-1400, daily 1700-2100. Opposite is the *Canton*, T6331 9448, a popular Chinese open Tue-Fri 1200-1400, daily 1700-2100. *Sushi Shack*, 134 York St. Simple good value Japanese, daily 1100-2130. For takeaways try *Hallam's Waterfront*, in Royal Park, for fish and chips by the river.

Cafés

Cafi Centro, 76 St John St, colourful contemporary café with creative salads and breads, casual meals and attentive service. Mon-Thu, Sat 0800-1800, Fri 0800-2100. *Freddies*, corner of Margaret St and Brisbane St. Hip, relaxed little café with cheap breakfasts, lunches, snacks and takeaways. Mon Fri 0800-1700. *Fresh*, 178 Charles St. Grungy café with pavement tables and interesting vegetarian food, including breakfasts, lunches, cakes and coffee. Open daily 0900-1730. *Metz*, 119 St John St. Sophisticated but unpretentious café and bar, serving Asian salads, antipasto, pasta and wood-fired pizzas. Also takeaway pizza. Open Mon-Fri 0800-2400, Sat-Sun 0900-2400. Recommended. *Pierre's*, 88 George St, has 2 long rows of tables, European style, charming formality, and a great variety of meals from breakfasts and snacks to hearty mid-range dishes. Mon-Fri 1000-2100, Sat 1000-1400, 1800-2200. *Yum*, Charles St, is a small, funky juice bar also serving light healthy lunches, cookies and coffee. Open Mon-Fri 1000-1730, Sat 1000-1600.

Bars & pubs

Batman Fawkner Inn, 35 Cameron St, T6331 7222. Historic 1822 pub, formerly the *Cornwall Hotel*. Sophisticated front bar and a range of good value accommodation (**C-D**). *Hotel Tasmania* and *Launceston Saloon*, 191 Charles St, T6331 7355. The *Saloon* is a cavernous, raucous cowboy-theme bar with very cheap meals served daily 1200-2100, DJs Wed, Fri-Sat (0300 licence) and live music Wed, Sat ($3-6 cover charge). Upstairs accommodation is in refurbished, modern and comfortable doubles, singles and family rooms (**C**). *Irish Murphy's*, corner of Brisbane St and Bathurst St, T6331 4440, launceston@irishmurphys.com.au Large Irish theme pub with lots of nooks and crannies. Very good Irish/Aussie bistro, cheap to mid-range, also bar snacks, served daily 1200-1400, 1800-2030. Live music Wed-Sun, $3 Fri-Sat after 2130. Comfortable upstairs backpacker accommodation **E**), including doubles, with guest kitchen and lounge.

Tasmania

Recommended. *O'Keefe's*, 124 George St, T6331 4015, gbeaumont@bigpond.com Another large friendly pub, popular with visitors and locals alike. Cheap salads and pastas, mid-range steaks and seafood served Mon-Sat 1200-1500, daily 1800-2030. Live cover bands Thu-Sun, acoustic Thu. Accommodation in a range of rooms from a 6-bed bunk room to singles and doubles, linen included, also guest lounge and kitchen (**E**). Recommended. *Pizza Pub*, 111 Wellington St, T6334 2322. Unremarkable, unpretentious pub that happens to specialize in cheap, filling pizzas, eat-in or takeaway. Half-price pizzas from 1730 on Tue. Also counter meals. Pizzas served Sun-Thu 1200-2400, Fri-Sat 1200-0200. *Royal Oak*, corner of Brisbane St and Tamar St, is a popular authentic wood-lined pub where many locals start their evening, cheap bistro meals daily, regular jazz club performances. *Royal on George*, 90 George St, T6331 2526. Stylish upmarket pub serving good value Asian and Mediterranean food, live music Fri-Sat, jazz on Sun. Food daily 1000-1700, 1800-2100. *Star Bar*, Charles St, T6331 9659. Café-bar and bistro with a vibrant Mexican style, terracotta floor, and sofas around the large open fire. Varied menu includes various 'plates', good veggie options and cheap snacks. Breakfasts at weekends. Food served daily 1100-2100.

Entertainment Launceston has a large student population adding liveliness to the nightlife here. Wed nights are known as 'uni night' when pubs and clubs attract big student crowds with cheap beer. The biggest and busiest club is the *CBD* on Brisbane St above the post office, Wed-Sat from 2200. A gig guide, *X-static*, is published in the city's daily newspaper, *The Examiner*, on Thu. **Cinema** *Village*, 163 Brisbane St, T6331 5066. **Theatre** *Princess*, 57 Brisbane St, T6323 3666. Popular dance, classical music and shows.

Shopping **Books** New books at *All Booked Up* and *Petrarch's*, 81 and 87 Brisbane St. Open daily. *Birchalls*, on the Mall, also has a good range. There are a couple of second-hand bookshops at 112 and 106 Elizabeth St, both with good ranges of paperback, classic and contemporary fiction. Both closed Sun. **Outdoor** *All Goods*, corner of St John St and York St. Good range of camping and walking gear, topographic and national park maps, walking and cycling guides. Open Mon-Sat, as is *Paddy Pallin*, 110 George St. Similar range of equipment with some for hire, and good bushwalking advice.

Tours & **Abseiling, climbing** *Tasmanian Expeditions*, T6334 3477, tazzie@tassie.net.au,
activities offer rock-climbing and abseiling trips into Cataract Gorge ($55 ½-day, $95 full). **Baths** The *Roman Baths*, 127 George St, T6331 2255, are open daily for serious watery pampering, massage and beauty treatment. **Beer** *Boags*, 21 Shields St, is Launceston's preferred brew over Hobart's *Cascade*, tours of the brewery Tue, Wed, Thu 1420. Free so book ahead, T6331 9311. **City** *Launceston Explorer*, does daily coach tram tours of city sights ($26, 3 hrs). Book at VIC. **Hang gliding** *Cable Hang Gliding*, Trevallyn Dam Quarry, T0419 311 198. A 200-m glide ($10). Daily 1000-1600. Several companies run day tours from Launceston. *Devils Playground*, T6343 1787, www.devilsplayground.com.au, run tours including **Cradle Mountain**, **Tamar Valley**, and **Mole Creek** ($80-120 day). *Tiger Wilderness Tours*, T6326 6515, run ½-day tours in small groups to **Tamar Valley** wineries, strawberry and lavender farms ($50).

Transport **Air** Qantas have daily flights to **Melbourne** and **Sydney** while *Virgin* Blue fly daily to **Melbourne** with onward connections to various state capitals. **Bus** *Tassie Link* have 2 main services out of the city. The west coast service leaves at 0730 Tue, Thu, 0830 Sat and, in summer, Mon, via **Sheffield**, **Gowrie Park** and **Cradle Mountain** (3½ hrs, $43.60). There are daily Cradle Mountain services in summer. The east coast service heads via **St Marys** to **Bicheno**, 0900 Wed, 0830 Fri, Sun and, in summer, 0900 Mon. A summer service heads out to **Lake St Clair** via **Miena**, 0930 Mon, Wed, Fri and Sun. *Redline* operate 3 major and 4 minor routes. There are daily services via **Deloraine**, **Devonport** and north coast towns to **Smithton**, daily services via the Midland Highway towns to **Hobart**, and separate east coast services to **St Helens** (not Sat) and **Bicheno** (Mon-Fri). They also operate local services to **Derby** and **Winnaleah** (not Sat), **George Town** (Mon-Fri), **Evandale** (Mon-Fri), and **Deloraine** and **Mole Creek** (Mon-Fri).

Banks Most major banks have ATMs on Charles St or Brisbane St. **Foreign** exchange *Thomas Cook*, 85 George St. Open Mon-Fri 0900-1715, Sat 0900-1200. **Bike hire** *City Youth Hostel* for long-term hire. **Camping trailer hire** Trailers equipped with tent, camp kitchen equipment and camp furniture. Peak rate $80 per night but good value weekly and monthly rates. Westbury Post Office, T6393 1233. **Car Hire** All the usual operators, local companies include *Advance*, T1800 030118, www.advancecars.com.au, and *Economy*, T6334 3299. **Car servicing** *Cripps Automotive*, 39 Canning St, T6331 9870. **Communications** Internet at *iCaf*, Quadrant Mall, $4 for 30 mins. **Post Office**, 107 Brisbane St. **Library** Civic Sq, T6336 2625. Mon-Fri 0930-1800, Sat 0930-1200. **Hospital** Charles St, T6348 7111. **Motorbike hire** *Tasmanian Motorcycle Hire*, Evandale, T6391 9139. Riding and touring gear also available. **Taxi** T131008 or 6331 3555.

Directory

Around Launceston

The western side of the Tamar Valley is considerably more developed than the eastern and its wineries, wetlands and waterbirds, and small museums make the valley an interesting day trip from Launceston. On the edge of the city are the **Tamar Island wetlands**. A boardwalk leads from the Visitor Interpretation Centre, just off the highway, over the wetlands and two small islands to reach Tamar Island. There are many species of waterbirds and several hides, and visitors can also watch birds from inside the visitor centre, a striking circular building overlooking the wetlands. ■ *Daily 0900-dusk. $2, children $1. www.parks.tas.gov.au* Just north, on Rosevears Drive, are two vineyards, *St Matthias* (T6330 1700) and *Strathlynn* (T6330 2388). To visit more wineries follow the blue and yellow grape signs or pick up a wine route touring guide from the VIC. There is also a good pub on Rosevears Drive, *Rosevears Waterfront Tavern*, T6394 4074. The next town beyond Rosevears is **Exeter** where there is a good **VIC**, the main one for the Tamar Valley. ■ *Daily 0900-1700 spring and summer, otherwise 1000-1600. T6394 4454, exeter@tasvisinfo.com.au* Some 20 km north is the gold-mining town of **Beaconsfield**, where magnificent brick buildings were constructed to house the world's most powerful Cornish pumping engines. The remains of these form the **Grubb Shaft Gold and Heritage Museum**, a collection of mining artefacts and machinery. ■ *Daily 1000-1600, 0930-1630 in summer. $8, children $3, concessions $6 ($2 off with voucher from VIC). T6383 1473.* At **Beauty Point**, 7 km north, is a much more successful and unusual industry, seahorse farming. *Seahorse World*, is situated in a large warehouse at the end of the wharf and aims to educate visitors on how they raise the pot-bellied seahorse. Tours lead visitors past growing tanks holding thousands of little creatures as big as an apostrophe to tanks holding six-month-old seahorses ready for sale to the aquarium market. The facility includes a waterfront café and a wine tasting centre, selling wines unavailable from cellar doors. ■ *Daily 0930-1630. $15, children $8, concessions $10. Tours every half hour from 0930, last tour at 1530. T6383 4111, www.seahorseworld.com.au* North of Beauty Point there are three access points to the **Narawntapu National Park** (see page 847). The first turn-off leads to Springlawn, the second turn-off to Badger Head. At the end of the

Launceston to Greens Beach
Greens Beach 64 km from Launceston

Tasmania

road north is **Greens Beach** where there is a caravan park (no cabins, T6383 9222) and an unsealed road continues north to **West Head**. There is a walking track around the head and a fine lookout over Badger Beach.

George Town &
Low Head
Colour map 8, grid A3
Population: 4,500
51 km from
Launceston
168 km from St Helens

Proudly boasting its claim as Australia's oldest town (anything older is now a city), George Town missed greatness by being passed over in favour of Launceston as northern Van Diemens Land's administrative capital. The modern town huddles around the small inlet of York Cove with the **Devil Cat terminal** on the south side and main Macquarie Street parallel with the north, a 10-minute walk away. Unfortunately, little remains of the town's colonial past except for a few buildings on Elizabeth Street. **The Grove** is an 1835 townhouse originally built for a port officer, which has been painstakingly restored. ■ *Daily 1000-1700, Mon-Fri 1100-1530 during Jun-Sep. $5, YHA and NT $4. T6382 1336, www.tas.quik.com.au/thegrove Elizabeth St.* The **VIC** is on Main Road, about 1 km south of the town centre. ■ *Daily 1000-1600, Jul-Aug 1000-1400. T6382 1700, georgetown@tasvisinfo.com.au* At **Low Head**, 5 km north, the well-preserved **Pilot Station** now houses a **Nautical Museum**. ■ *Daily 0800-2000. $3, children $2. T6382 1143.* There's also a **Fairy penguin** tour. ■ *Daily after dusk. $15, T0418-361860.*

Sleeping and eating The **B-D** *Pier*, Elizabeth St, T6382 1300, is an old pub, now run as a corporate hotel, but stills retaining a friendly front bar. The wide range of accommodation includes external villa and motel units, and internal doubles. Meals available daily 0700-0900, 1200-1400, 1800-2000. **B** *Belfont Cottages*, Low Head, T6382 1399. 2 small and rustic self-contained 1881 lighthouse keepers' cottages, each sleeping 4. There is similar, but more basic and larger, accommodation (**C**) at the Pilot Station, sleeping up to 8. **C** *The Grove*, has a small, self-contained, wood-panelled cottage and breakfast provisions are included. They also run a separate café, open the same hrs as the house. **D-E** *Travellers Lodge YHA*, Elizabeth St, T6382 3261, travellerslodge_yha@ hotmail.com This 1880s weatherboard house-turned-hostel has 2 6-bed dorms and 2 doubles.

Transport Bus *Redline's* Launceston services leave 21 Elizabeth St at 0900 and 1230 Mon-Fri. **Ferry** There is no public transport between the ferry terminal and Macquarie St, about a 10-min walk. **Taxi** T6382 1622. Expect to pay about $8 to get from the ferry terminal to Elizabeth St.

East of
George Town

Between George Town and Bridport sit a clutch of wineries, with *Pipers Brook* taking centre stage. T6382 7527, www.pbv.com.au Cellar door daily 1000-1700, café 1200-1500. Wines include good chardonnay and the excellent Pirie sparkling white. A self-contained farmers cottage (**B**) with a large open fire is available, sleep four. The small holiday town of **Bridport** stretches along the lower banks of the Great Forester River and then out along the coastal beaches and is a popular summer destination. These beaches stretch for many kilometres both east and west, but are generally inaccessible. *Pepper Bush Peaks*, T6352 2263, pepper@microtech, run 'cray bake' day tours to one of the very best, in St Albans Bay (from $155). Bridport is also the Tasmanian vehicular departure port for **Flinders Island** (see page 869). The **VIC** doubles as a craft shop. ■ *Daily 1000-1600, T6356 0280, Main St, near Bridport Hotel.*

Lilydale, a pretty little town close to Mount Arthur, has many art and craft studios open to the public. The **Lilydale Falls Reserve**, 3 km north of town, is a popular place for a picnic or stop at the tea-rooms and there is a short walk to two smallish falls. The reserve has campsites, fireplaces and toilets. There are also some good walking tracks at Mount Arthur.

Tasmania

Sleeping and eating in Bridport There are several sleeping options. The **C** *Bridport Hotel*, 79 Main Street, T6356 1114, has a pleasant front bar, serving cheap pub meals, looking out over the Bass Strait. The **D-E** *Seaside Lodge YHA*, is also on Main Street, though closer to the ferry wharf, T6356 1585, seasidelodge@bigpond.com Purpose-built, the hostel is modern, clean and comfortable with three double rooms and four 4-bunk dorms. A front verandah overlooks the river mouth. Recommended. There is a fish and chip café by the ferry wharf. Open Sun-Thu 0930-1900, Fri-Sat 0930-2000.

Transport The *Redline* Launceston to **Winneleah** service passes through Lilydale Tue and Thu. Westbound 1015 daily or 0800 school days, eastbound 1630 daily or 1650 school days. A service also operates on school days between Bridport and *Launceston*, leaving at 0655. Also to **Derby** and **Winnaleah**, leaving at 1740.

On a clear day the huge massif of Ben Lomond is visible from nearly 100 km away in several directions, and from the summit at Legges Tor (1,573 m) much of the island state can be seen. The flat-topped mountain, with its battlements of dark, brooding pillars, is pure Gothic fantasy. The 17-km unsealed access road skirts the forested base of the mountain for several kilometres before ascending via a road so steep, twisting and exposed it is known as Jacob's Ladder. This is one of Tasmania's most spectacular short drives, but must be negotiated with great care. For the short winter season vehicle chains are mandatory and can be hired at the rangers hut at the bottom of the road ($30 hire and fitting). There are no facilities on the mountain other than those offered by the lone pub, the **A-C** *Creek Inn*, T6390 6199, which has several double units, sleeping up to four, and a hostel-style chalet with bunk rooms and some doubles, no linen. The main ski-lodge style bar and bistro area is warm and welcoming, the hearty cheap meals are served daily, and you may be joined by baby wombats. There is a basic **camping** area with toilets and BBQs at the base of the mountain.

Ben Lomond National Park
Colour map 8, grid B5
Altitude: 1,573 m
58 km from Launceston

  Skiing There are about a dozen private lodges at the small ski village, but only the pub has public accommodation. There are nine short T-bar and poma lifts servicing the relatively shallow slopes around Legges Tor. There is usually snow from mid-July to late September. Ski hire and lessons are available in the village, T6390 6133. Expect to pay $75-90 for skis plus gear per day, and $30 for lift passes. Ski hotline: T1902-290530. **Walking** A challenging 2½-hour climb starts from the Carr Villa car park at the base of the mountain. The path climbs a scree slop to the top of the plateau and continues southeast. This walk should only be attempted in clear summer weather as the track can be very indistinct. The ski village is a further 20-minute walk down from the summit via the main tow-runs. There are no clear trails across the plateau, so day-walkers should go prepared with a detailed map and a compass.

Transport A shuttle bus, T6331 1411, operates daily during the ski season from Launceston ($22 return), leaving from outside the VIC at 0830, picking up at the park entry hut at 0915 ($11 return) for those not wanting to tackle Jacob's Ladder.

Evandale is the best-preserved small colonial town in the north of the island. The town is known for its Sunday **markets** with stalls offering homebaked goodies, plants and bric-a-brac. The annual **National Penny Farthing Championships**, during the village fair at the end of February, entices large crowds and enthusiastic racers. For more information T6391 8223. Entrants can hire old-fashioned bicycles from *Cornwall Cottage*, Scone Street. The **VIC** is at the north end of town on High Street and has a free historical museum. ■ *Daily 1000-1500, T6391 8128, evandale@tasvisinfo.com.au*

Evandale
Colour map 8, grid B4
Population: 1,000
18 km from Launceston, 64 km from Ross

Tasmania

Transport The *Redline* bus leaves Russell St for **Launceston** 0755 and 1800 Mon-Fri, with additional services 1010 Thu and 1045 Fri. There is a service to **Campbell Town** and **Bicheno** 1400 Thu, 1545 Fri and, on school days, 1400 Mon.

Launceston to Deloraine Hadspen, 10 km out of Launceston, is a small village now bypassed by the Bass Highway and best known for **Entally House**. This is a grand Georgian manor just outside the town centre, and is a rich repository of Tasmanian history and a showcase of early colonial country life. ■ *Daily 1000-1230, 1300-1700. $7.70, children free, concessions $5.50. T6393 6201. Bass Highway*. The town also boats a wonderful old pub and restaurant, the *Red Feather Inn*, Main Road, T6393 6331. Excellent food Monday-Saturday 1830-2030, bar open 1600. Recommended. Also recommended is the **C-D** *Launceston Cabin and Tourist Park*, T6393 6391, which has some superb and good value cabins, some with spa baths and wood-effect gas burners. **Westbury**, 24 km further west, is a hamlet with a very English feel, particularly around the pretty village green and two good museums. **Pearns Steamworld** is an impressive collection of steamdriven and internal combustion driven tractors and rollers. ■ *Daily 0900-1600. $4, children $1. T6393 1414. Old Bass Highway*. The **White House** is a Georgian cornershop and house, now a National Trust museum with several collections of antiques and veteran cars. ■ *Tue-Sun, Sep-Jun, 1000-1600. $7.70, children free, concessions $5.50. T6393 1171*. The **Maze and tea-room** are open October-June. ■ *Daily 1000-1600. $4.50, children $3.50. T6393 1840. Old Bass Highway*. Next door is the *White House Bakery*, still using the original 1840s brick oven to make superb bread.

Transport *Redline* have up to 6 services a day, Mon-Fri, each way between **Launceston** and **Deloraine**. All services call at **Hadspen and Westbury**.

Deloraine and around

Colour map 8, grid B3
Population: 2,200
51 km from Launceston
49 km from Devonport

Deloraine, settled in the 1830s by farmers, retains many of its early buildings but its main appeal is its position. The town is just to the north of rich pastoral river valleys rising to the impressive dark citadels of the **Great Western Tiers**. Quamby Bluff dominates, an 'island' peak, directly south of Deloraine. In clear weather the whole range can be seen from the main street. This friendly town is an ideal base for exploring the attractions of this wonderful region such as walking in the Tiers, the Liffey and Car park, and the wildlife park and caves of nearby **Mole Creek**. The area has attracted many artists and craftspeople and is known for its large, working craft fair in early November. *Artifakt*, in the main street, is a sophisticated gallery with high-quality work. The owner can advise on how to visit local artist's studios. The local tourist office (Great Western Tiers VIC) is at the top of the hill in the recently renovated **Folk Museum**, also housing a massive quilting project, Yarns, depicting the Meander Valley in silk. ■ *Daily 0900-1700. Entry fee to museum and Yarns still to be confirmed at time of writing. T6362 3471, www.deloraine.tco.asn.au*

Sleeping & eating
The craft fair can bring 20,000 people to town so book well ahead at this time

L *Calstock Country Guest House*, Lake Highway, T6362 2642, www.calstock.net A Georgian mansion and former famous horse stud, decorated with restrained English and French country elegance. Outstanding style and comfort and good meals using organic local produce. **A** *Arcoona*, East Barrack St, T6362 3443, www.arcoona.com A late-Victorian mansion restored to full splendour with 7 rooms, gardens, croquet lawns and a breakfast ballroom. The restaurant is open to non-residents, Tue-Sat 1800-2000. **B-C** *Bonney's Inn*, 19 West Par, T6362 2974, www.bonneys-inn.com A substantial 1830s coaching inn with fire rooms, decorated in traditional English style. Also a bar and evening meals for guests. **C** *Highland Rose*, 47 West Church St, T6362 2634, highlandrose.bb@bigpond.com Warm Scottish hospitality and 2 pretty rooms in a family home. **E** *Bush Inn*, Bass Highway, T6362 2365. Unfussy, friendly front bar with wood-stove and pool table. Cheap bistro meals, always including a seriously cheap roast, served daily 1200-1400, 1800-2000. Live music Sat, mostly cover bands. Large, very good value twins and doubles can include continental breakfast. Recommended. **E** *Highview Lodge*, 8 Blake St, T6362 2996. As the name suggest this YHA hostel has fantastic views of the Tiers from the large living room. Also 5 dorms and well-equipped kitchen, bike hire. 1 km from coach stop. **E** *Kev's Kumphy Corner*, opposite the *Bush*, T6362 2250. 2 very basic 10-bunk hostel dorms, pink for the girls, blue for the boys, and a kitchen that doubles as common area. *Emu Bay Brasserie*, 21 Emu Bay Rd, T6362 2067, serves interesting modern Australian cuisine (mid-range) in simple, unpretentious surroundings. Top of the list for daytime eating and always busy is the *Deloraine Deli*, 36 Emu Bay Rd, a laid-back, comfortable sort of place. Mon-Fri 0900-1700, Sat 0900-1400. Recommended.

Jahadi Outdoor Adventures, T/F6363 6172, www.jahadi.com.au An indigenous operator who offers half and full-day cultural tours of the area ($85/$110), including hands-on activities, BBQ lunch and bushtucker. *Bonneys*, T6362 2122, offer personalized day-tours in the region ($50 per person day, 2 people minimum). *Tasmanian Fly Fishing*, T6362 3441, www.tasadventures.com Lessons and fishing trips from $200 day.

Tours
Also see Mole Creek tours, page 849

The *Redline* depot is at *Tasmanian Cashworks* at the top roundabout. There are up to 6 services a day, daily, to **Launceston** and one to **Mole Creek**, 1720 Mon-Fri school days only. Services to **Devonport** leave 1100 and 1415 Mon-Fri, 1415 and 1845 Sat, 1415 and 2015 Sun. *Bonneys*, T6362 2122, is a local operator who provides bushwalker transfers, transport to Cradle Mountain ($50 per person, 2 people minimum) or any other destination in the area on request.

Transport

Banks ANZ ATM on Emu Bay Rd. **Bike Hire** *Highview Lodge YHA*. **Communications** Internet at *Online Access Centre*, 21 West Par (below library), T6362 3537. Open Mon-Fri 1000-1600, Sun 1300-1600. **Post Office**, 10 Emu Bay Rd.

Directory

Southwest of Deloraine, the Meander River flows through a flat, open valley from the foot of the Great Western Tiers where there is a wild rugged forest reserve, part of the World Heritage Area. The **Meander Forest Reserve**, about 20 minutes beyond the small farming community of Meander, offers fairly challenging long walks through magnificent country of forest, mountains, rivers and waterfalls. **Split Rock Track** starts by crossing the river on a suspension bridge then passes through beautiful myrtle forest and ferns, rising steeply to Split Rock, climbing through the two enormous sections of the rock to a loop past three waterfalls and rock overhangs (4 km, two to three hours). The longer walk to **Meander Falls** also passes through myrtle forest most of the way, climbing gradually (with one steep section) to a flat amphitheatre. The track then crosses the floor to the base of sheer dolerite cliffs and the falls (10 km, five hours). Both walks start from the car park at the end of the road. There are campsites, fireplaces and toilets near the car park although camping is permitted anywhere in the reserve for free.

Meander Valley
Topographic maps for the whole region are available from Service Tasmania in Deloraine

The area is managed by Forestry Tasmania, call the Devonport office for more information call T6424 8388

The Lake Highway heads south from Deloraine through Golden Valley, where a small community shelters below the steep sides of **Quamby Bluff** (1,226 m). From the highway, just before the settlement, Brodies Road leads to the start of a walking track to the summit. The walk is very steep, with a lot of

Golden Valley & around

Tasmania

scrambling over boulders near the summit but the reward is that most of northern Tasmania can be seen from the top (7 km, five hours return). About 3 km past the *Tiger Hill Teahouse* there is another walking track, to Quamby Bluff. Shortly afterwards a gravel road on the left is signposted to **Liffey Falls**. These are some of the loveliest of many waterfalls in the area, consisting of a series of low-stepped platforms. There is an easy walk through myrtle rainforest to the falls (45 minutes) and excellent BBQ and picnic facilities. The road continues on to the lakes of the central plateau, through a dramatic pass between **Drys Bluff** and **Projection Bluff**, high above the valley. If travelling on a clear day it is well worth travelling up to the Central Plateau for the wonderful views along this stretch of road. There is also a lovely alpine walk on the plateau not far from the pass.

Sleeping and eating **C-F** *Mountainside Accommodation*, 13185 Lake Highway, T6369 5226, offers horseback tours around the rainforest under the bluff ($25 per hour). There are large basic dorms, small cabins with 4 bunks and more comfortable self-contained cottages. Those staying in bunk rooms have use of an industrial kitchen and large hall with open fire. Just up the road is *Tiger Hill Teahouse*, T6369 5280, niecy@ireland.com The owner cooks wholesome, hearty food such as pancakes, pies and salads, local produce wherever possible. The teahouse is also a venue for performances by local artists, such as folk musicians, poets and singers, particularly at weekends. Phone for details and bookings. Thu-Sun 1000-1800 (Nov-Apr), and for events during the rest of the year. Recommended.

Devonport and around

*Devonport provides the first glimpse of Tasmania for many visitors and as a busy industrial port city it gives little indication of what is to come. However, just south of Devonport and clearly visible on a cloudless day, are the magnificent mountain ranges of the **Great Western Tiers**. The cliffs of the Tiers mark an abrupt drop from the Central Plateau to the fertile plains below. Farmers settled the area around **Sheffield** and **Mole Creek** and thought it so idyllic they named some parts of it Paradise, Promised Land and No Where Else. The fertility and gentle climate of the north coast mean it is one of the more populous areas of Tasmania but most visitors will hardly notice this. Great walking, forest, waterfalls, caves and wildlife can all be found around Devonport and the area provides easy access to Cradle Mountain. Just west of Devonport there are some small and pretty coastal towns, such as **Penguin**, on the way to the wild northwest.*

Devonport

Colour map 8, grid A3
Population: 25,000
100 km from
Launceston
50 km from Burnie

Sprawling between the mouths of the rivers Don and Mersey, Devonport is a major commercial port as well as the home dock of the Bass Strait ferry, *The Spirit of Tasmania*. It is a practical city that lacks the fine colonial architecture of Launceston and Hobart, but there is a pleasant foreshore area and it is possible to walk from the Mersey River to the Don River. From the VIC, head north past the Maritime Museum and out to Tiagarra and the lighthouse at Mersey Bluff.

Ins & outs
See also Transport
on page 846

Getting there and around **Air** *Kendell* and *Qantas* have daily flights to **Melbourne** from the small airport and *Tasair* have a daily flight to **King Island** *Fox Coaches*, T0418 142692, run a shuttle service to meet all flights. **Bus** The main interchange for local *Mersey Link* services is outside *Harris Scarfe* in Rooke St. T1300-367590, bookings

T0409-006013. The *Redline* coach depot is on Edward St, T6421 6490. **Ferry** The *TT-Line* terminal is on the eastern bank of the Mersey River, directly across from the VIC and central part of town. Ferry To get there either catch the small river ferry from just north of the terminal across to the small jetty by the VIC, or catch the *Mersey Link* bus that meets each ferry and shuttles around the hostels ($1.30). The river ferry goes every 15 mins, Mon-Fri 0800-1800, 0800-1700 Sat, and costs $1.70.

Information   The **VIC** is on Formby Rd, T6424 8176, ttic@dcc.tas.gov.au (daily 0900-1700; in summer from 0730). Devonport is a cheap place to pick up equipment for walking and camping. *All Goods* at 10 Rooke St, have a good range of trekking and camping gear. Walkers can also head for the *Backpackers Barn*, 10 Edward St, T6424 3628, for general information, advice, equipment and transport to Cradle Mountain. The *Barn* also operates as a café and travellers' rest facility with showers. A good place to spend time if waiting for the ferry to depart.

The **Maritime Museum** recounts Devonport's long connection to the sea as **Sights** both port and shipyard. This former harbourmaster's house still has its original signal mast and lookout from pre-radio days. The museum has displays on maritime and local history. ■ *Tue-Sun 1000-1600. $3, children $1. T6424 7100. Gloucester Av.* **Tiagarra** is an Aboriginal keeping place on the site of a young men's hunting ground. The museum has a fairly dusty, static display but has some interesting exhibits such as a rare stone axe and photographs of Tasmanian Aboriginals. There is also a walking track around the bluff past about a dozen fascinating rock engravings. Staff welcome visitors wanting a chat about Aboriginal culture and history and offer free beverages in the mornings. ■ *Daily 0900-1700. $3.30, children, concessions $2.20. T6424 8250. Bluff Rd.*

Devonport

Sleeping		**Eating**
1 Birchmore	2 Molly Malone's	1 Mason & Mason

Tasmania

Sleeping

Much of the accommodation in the town tends toward the functional, most of it depending primarily on business travellers

B-C *Birchmore*, Oldaker St, T6423 1336, birch@southcom.com.au 6 unfussy en suite rooms in this large period B&B. Full cooked breakfast in the pleasant conservatory dining room. **D-E** *Molly Malone's*, Best St, T6424 1898. Large Irish theme pub, with a good range of draught beers and excellent cheap lunches and evening meals, including grills, seafood and help-yourself veggie and salad bar, served daily. Live music Fri-Sat when the upstairs backpacker-style dorms aren't at their quietest. Also 5 twin rooms and 2 very good value en suite doubles. Modest kitchen and lounge facilities. *Molly's* aside, the best of Devonport's lacklustre hostels is **E** *Formby Hostel*, 16 Formby Rd, T6423 6563, a large, somewhat spartan house on the road opposite the ferry terminal with friendly managers. There is also a YHA, **F** *MacWright House*, 115 Middle Rd, T6424 5696. A reasonably homely, old-style house but a long walk from the town centre. **F** *Tasman House*, 169 Steele St, T6423 2335, is a stark, utilitarian former nurses' home with long corridors leading to 102 beds, large kitchen and living space. Linen and heaters extra. However they can help with arranging fruit picking work Mar-May. There are several caravan and cabin parks just to the north of the ferry terminal. 20 km west of town, in the tiny hamlet of Forth, is one of Tassie's best value B&Bs, **C** *The Wattles*, Pumping Station Rd, T6428 2242. A comfortable, private ground-floor apartment with 2 bedrooms and surrounded by acres of bush. Wonderfully warm hosts. Recommended.

Eating

There is a cluster of cheap restaurants around the corner of Oldaker Rd and Formby Rd

The Cove Waterfront, 17 Devonport Rd, T6424 6200. A contemporary and crisp-looking restaurant with a curved wall of glass overlooking the Mersey River. Mid-range fusion cooking with an emphasis on seafood, dishes are simply small or large. Daily 1200-1400, 1800-2100. Also a pleasant place for coffee, from 1030. *Mason and Mason*, Steele St, is easily the best café in town and the perfect place for a leisurely coffee. Also great bagels, foccaccias and cakes. Open Mon-Fri 0930-1730, Sat 0930-1600. Try *Pedro the Fisherman* on William St for fish and chips.

Transport

For Air and Ferry details, see Ins & outs

Bus *Mersey Link* services run a shuttle to the ferry terminal, pick-ups from hostels on request, and services to **Latrobe**. *Redline* run several services daily to **Launceston** and towns in between. Also daily along the north coast to **Burnie** with connecting services to **Smithton** Mon-Fri, stopping at the *Spirit* 1655 Tue, Thu, 1450 Sat and 2040 Sun. The west coast *Tassie Link* service goes from the VIC 0930 Tue, Thu, 1030 Sat and, in summer Mon, via **Sheffield**, **Gowrie Park** and **Cradle Mountain** (3½ hrs, $43.60). There are daily Cradle Mountain services in summer. Tue and Thu services pick up from the *Spirit* terminal at 0900.

Directory

Banks Most major banks have ATMs on Brooke St Mall. **Communications** Internet at *Store 44*, 6 Steward St. $4 per hr. Open Mon-Fri 0900-1730, Sat 0900-1400. **Post Office**, corner of Formby St and Stewart St. **Car hire** There are several companies in town, and it pays to shop around. At the cheaper end of the scale are *Lo-cost*, T6424 9922, and *Basic*, T6424 4757. Some operators also have offices at the ferry terminal, including *Rent-A-Bug*, T6427 9034, who hire out *VW Beetles*, and *Discount*, T6427 0888.

Around Devonport

Latrobe to Port Sorell

Latrobe, a quiet rural town with lots of antique shops and historic buildings, calls itself the 'Platypus Capital of the World'. This may be a rather extravagant claim but the little fellas can be found around dawn and dusk at **Warrawee Forest Reserve**, about 5 km south of the town. From the main street, Gilbert Street, take Hamiton Street which turns into Shale Road and leads to the reserve. Tours are conducted by the local Landcare group, T6426 2877. There is a VIC in the main street ■ *1000-1530 Mon-Fri. T6426 2693, www.latrobe.tas.gov.au* **Port Sorrell**, which sits opposite the Asbestos

Ranges and Narawntapu National Park, is a sleepy place with lovely beaches. **Hawley Beach**, just to the north, is particularly beautiful with granite rocks covered with bright orange lichen and fine pale sand.

Sleeping and eating At the end of the road that runs alongside Hawley Beach is an excellent B&B, which is a good place to stay if travelling on the Devonport ferry. **A** *Hawley House*, T6428 6221, hawley.house@tassie.net.au A large property with pretty gardens and vineyard, along with superb gourmet meals and warm hosts. Port Sorrell has a caravan park, T6428 7267, and cafes and shops at the Shearwater Shopping Centre on Pitcairn St.

This small national park just east of Devonport stretches from the low forested slopes of the Asbestos Ranges to the beaches and headlands of Bass Strait. The grassy plains of Springlawn are often referred to as Tasmania's Serengeti for the number of grazing animals commonly seen there, including Forester kangaroos, Bennetts wallabies, pademelons and wombats. The park also features a variety of heathland, lagoons, inlets and small islands in the Port Sorrell estuary. The park entrance is at Springlawn, where there is a park office and camping ground. Horseriding, waterskiing, fishing and boating are permitted at this end of the park. There is also access to the park on the road north of Beauty Point on the Tamar (see page 839). ■ *Campsites have fireplaces or BBQs, book ahead during Dec-Apr. BYO water in summer. Park office T6428 6277.* Springlawn Nature Walk is an easy and short circuit to a lagoon and bird hide, returning through the dunes (45 minutes). There are two high points that can be reached from Springlawn. **Archers Knob** (114 m), a two-hour circuit, and **Point Vision** (370 m), an easy climb through forest to see views of the coast and returning by the same path (six to seven hours return). An interesting day walk is the **Badger Head** one (18 km, six to seven hours return).

Narawntapu National Park
Colour map 8, grid A3
45 km from Devonport

There is no ferry service to the park from Port Sorrell, access is by road only

The park brochure includes a simple walking map and topographic maps are available from the usual sources

In the 1980s Sheffield hit on the idea of boosting the tourist trade by covering the walls of local businesses with murals representing historic, scenic and occupational themes. The **VIC** can provide a map detailing all the locations of the murals. It also has topographic walking maps and can be found a block behind the main street on Pioneer Crescent. ■ *Daily 0900-1700, 1000-1600 Jul-Aug. T/F6491 1036, sheffield@tasvisinfo.com.au* To the south, Mount Roland 1,234 m rises above the plains, an impressive mountain that dominates the entire district. The Roland Ranges provide some great walking, accessible from Claude Road and Gowrie Park.

Sheffield
Colour map 8, grid A3
Population: 1,000
30 km from Devonport,
60 km from Cradle Valley

Sleeping and eating **C** *Acacia*, 113 High St, T/F64912482, is a homely B&B with 3 en suite rooms. Evening meals and picnic hampers available. **D** *Sheffield Hotel*, Main St, T6491 1130. Friendly pub serving cheap meals daily 1200-1400, 1800-2000, Fri-Sat evenings only Jun-Aug. Basic but clean double and single rooms. The equally welcoming **E** *Sheffield Backpackers*, Main St, T6491 2611, innesanctum@vision.net.au, has 4 multi-bunk dorms and one twin room, a cosy lounge and kitchen. Also runs nocturnal wildlife tours. The caravan park on High St has on-site vans, T6491 2364.

Transport The west coast *Tassie Link* service leaves the *Milk Bar* for **Gowrie Park** and **Cradle Mountain** 1000 Tue, Thu, 1100 Sat and 1100 Mon, Wed, Fri, Sun in summer. **Devonport** and **Launceston** services leave 1625 Tue, Thu, 1400 Sat and, in summer, 1400 Mon, Wed, Fri and Sun. *Sheffield Minibus Charters*, T6491 2530, run walkers' drop-offs/pick-ups, including to **Cradle Mountain** and the **Walls of Jerusalem**, also service to **Devonport**.

Tassie Link services leave Gowrie Park 10 mins before or after Sheffield

Tasmania

Gowrie Park to Mole Creek

Colour map 8, grid B3
18 km from Sheffield,
42 km from Cradle Valley

For the routes see walking maps available at the Sheffield VIC

Virtually surrounded by the craggy ranges of **Mount Roland**, **Mount Van Dyke** and **Mount Claude**, **Gowrie Park** is the virtually deserted former 'hydro' town that acts as most walkers' base for climbing Mount Roland, although it is also accessible from Claude Road, a settlement just to the north. The scenery is so magnificent it is worth simply stopping here for a coffee if a steep walk doesn't appeal. To get to the Mount Roland **summit walk** (five hours return) take O'Neills Road from the highway, opposite a large map sign. Follow the road for 2 km to the car park. From the same start point it is also possible to reach the summits of Mount Van Dyke and Mount Claude. The road to Mole Creek winds around the base of Mount Claude and heads east towards a T-junction. Turn left for Mole Creek. The right-turn leads to gravel roads to the **Walls of Jerusalem National Park** and **Devils Gullet** lookout. On a fine day don't miss this lookout from which many distinctive peaks of the Overland Track are visible. Walks in the Walls of Jerusalem are only for very experienced walkers as the area is extremely isolated and exposed, but in fine weather it is possible to do a short day-walk to experience this extraordinary wilderness (see page 862).

Sleeping and eating   Some of Gowrie Park's hydro buildings are used as very basic budget accommodation by **C-F** *Weindorfers*, T6491 1385. They also have a few wood-clad cabins, usually booked well ahead in peak summer season, and several powered camp sites. Their restaurant is in a rustic timber cottage and serves wholesome, hearty meals and snacks and particularly delicious desserts. Daily 1000-2000, weekends only Jul-Sep. At the base of O'Neills Rd is a public campsite and picnic ground with toilets. On the road from Gowrie Park to Mole Creek, shortly after Moina, is the turn-off for **L-A** *Lemonthyme Lodge*, T6492 1112, www.lemonthyme.southcom.com.au, a large cosy log cabin with open fires and a fine mid-range restaurant. Accommodation is in simple rooms within the lodge (**C**), comfortable self-contained cabins or luxury suites with balcony and spa bath overlooking the forest. The lodge can arrange lots of activities and has developed several forest walks in the area.

Mole Creek & around

Stretching along the highway, known as Pioneer Drive, Mole Creek exploits a beautiful, wide valley setting with views of the massive walls of **Western Bluff** to the north, perhaps a last stronghold of the Tasmanian tiger. About 3 km east of town is a front-running candidate for Tasmania's best wildlife park, **Trowunna**, which is primarily a rehabilitation and research centre. Most of the animals roam free in the 15-ha managed area, with good sized enclosures for the Tasmanian devils and animals recuperating from injury. Entry includes a guided, very informative tour. Other tours available include nocturnal park tours, and platypus trips, outside of the park. ■ *0900-1700, 0800-2000 Jan. $12.50, children $6, concessions $10. Nocturnal and platypus tours $25 including light supper. T6363 6162, androo@vision.net.au* On a loop road behind the park, is the **Alum Cliffs Scenic Reserve**. There is a short walk to the 200-m quartzite cliffs overlooking the Mersey River gorge (2 km, 40 minutes). To the west of town two cave systems are open to the public. **Marakoopa Cave**, 12 km from Mole Creek, is a wet cave with actively growing natural decorations and supporting a diverse ecosystem of specialist creatures including glow-worms, harvestmen and anaspides. ■ *Tours daily 1000, 1115, 1300, 1430, 1600. $8.80, children $4.40, concessions $7. Both caves $13.20, $6.60 and $10.50. T6363 5181.* By contrast **King Solomon Cave** is a dry cave with extensive natural decorations. ■ *Tours hourly 1030-1230 and 1400-1600. Prices as per Marakoopa.*

Tasmania

Sleeping At one end of the long main street is **B** *Mole Creek Guesthouse*, T6363 1399, sted.mcgh@tassie.net.au tea-rooms and restaurant serving cheap, varied and inventive meals daily 0800-2000. Licenced but BYO, corkage $2. Also takeaways. They have a good range of **tourist information** in their souvenir shop, including topographical and national park maps, and walking and local guide books. 5 pleasant en suite double B&B rooms and guest lounge upstairs. Cooked breakfast. Almost next door is the is **D-E** *Mole Creek Hotel*, T6363 1102, with a pleasant tiger-decorated front bar, slightly cheaper meals, served daily 1200-1400, 1800-2000 (1900 Sun), and several basic but clean doubles and twins, including one particularly good value en suite. Guests kitchenette and lounge, continental breakfast. They also have a camping area beyond the beer garden.

Tours *Wild Cave Tours*, T6367 8142, www.wildcavetours.vetas.com.au Adventure caving in undeveloped caves, food, overalls and equipment supplied (½- and full-day tours). *Cradle Wilderness on the Edge*, T6363 1173, www.tasadventures.com 4WD trips to explore the area include Tassie Tiger Trails, Mersey Valley and Lakes, Rainforest and Waterfalls or trips can be tailored to your interests, from $55 per day. *Trowunna*, see above, can provide personalized tours, for more details see www.tasadventures.com

Transport On Mon-Fri, school days only at 0700, a *Redline* service leaves Mole Creek for **Deloraine** and **Launceston**.

The road between Devonport and Penguin passes through the large service town of Ulverstone. The **VIC** is in the main car park. ■ *Mon-Fri 0915-1530, Sat-Sun 1000-1500, T6425 2839*. From here a long detour inland, entailing about 80 km extra, takes in both **Leven Canyon** and **Gunns Plains Caves**. There are picnic areas and wood-fired BBQs at the canyon and a choice of short walks to the top of the canyon or into its heart. The Gunns Plains Caves feature an underground river and glow-worms, with tours running on the hour. ■ *Tours daily 1000-1600. $6, children $3. T6429 1388*.

Ulverstone

Eating If stopping over for lunch, the *River Arms*, just north of the main car park, is the best of the pubs, with a cheap, stylish café bar serving a good range of salads, burgers and wood-fired pizzas. Food Mon-Fri 1100-2000, Sat-Sun 1100-2100. Another good choice is *Pedros on the Wharf* which has both takeaway fish and chips and a modern mid-range seafood restaurant on the Leven River, T6425 5181.

Transport The *Redline* north coast service between **Launceston** and **Burnie** stops at 33 Victoria St, **Ulverstone** and at the Newsagency, **Penguin** up to 3 times daily. Also up to 5 daily Mon-Fri *MetroTas* service between Ulverstone and Burnie, stopping at Penguin.

Penguin, liberally dotted with representations of its namesake, doesn't actually have any of these flightless birds as residents. It seems that the town unaccountably swapped its name with nearby Sulphur Creek about 100 years ago – and got the better deal. This foreshore is one of the most picturesque on this stretch of coast with lawns ideal for walking or picnicking. The **VIC** is in the middle of town, opposite the beach. ■ *Mon-Fri 0930-1530, Sat 0900-1230, T6437 1421. Main Rd*. Penguin holds a lively craft market on the second and fourth Sunday of every month. Just inland from Penguin are the **Dial Ranges**, a series of gently rolling forested hills with some small pockets of rainforest. There are several walks in the ranges with fantastic views of the northwest coast. To reach the ranges from Penguin turn off Main Road at the railway line into Crescent Street. Turn left at the wooden Baptist chapel into Ironcliffe Road. Follow this road south for about 10 minutes until you see a left-hand turn signposted to the

Penguin & around
Colour map 8 grid A2
Population: 3,000
38 km from Devonport
18 km from Burnie

Tasmania

ranges. This road leads to the trailhead for walks to **Mount Montgomery** (two hours return), **The Gnoman**, a jagged outcrop with a sheer rock face (two hours return) and **Mount Duncan** , the highest in the range (four hours return). For an easier walk continue south on Ironcliffe Road, about 2 km past the turn-off, to **Fern Dene Reserve**. There is a picnic and BBQ area here and the half-hour walk leads to an old abandoned mine shaft, through rainforest tightly enclosed by a gully. The Dial Ranges are also the start of an 80-km walking track (recently upgraded by a local walking group) that takes you all the way to Cradle Mountain via Leven Canyon and Black Bluff. Ask at the VIC in Penguin for more details. They also have rough sketch maps of the ranges.

Sleeping and eating There is little accommodation in Penguin, but the friendly **C-D** *Beachside Tourist Park*, T6437 2785, has an enviable position at the west end of the foreshore with its own small Fairy penguin rookery just a 5-min walk away in the next bay. Their restaurant, *Monty's*, T6437 2080, shares the view and is open daily 1000-1600 for cheap light lunches including salads and pancakes, and some evenings for mid-range meals on reservation. Though small, Penguin has a good range of facilities including 2 pubs, one of which, the *Neptune Grand* has a pleasant area of outside decking looking across the road to the Bass Strait. Best spot for a coffee or cake is the friendly *Groovy Penguin*, a suitably laid-back retro-style café on Main Street. Wed-Sun 1000-1600.

The Northwest

*Because it's not on the route to anywhere and lacks a famous attraction such as Cradle Mountain or Port Arthur, the northwest is less visited than other parts. However, this is precisely the appeal of one of the most beautiful and off-the-beaten-track corners of Tasmania. A string of small towns lie on the north coast, such as the picturesque village of **Stanley** tucked under its curious promontory named 'The Nut'. The **west coast** is pounded relentlessly by howling gales and violent seas, but also boasts the cleanest air in the world at Cape Grim. **Marrawah** has a long, deserted surf beach and an opportunity to see Tasmanian devils feeding by an isolated beach hut nearby. Further south, at the mouth of the **Arthur River** mouth, it is possible to see the wild and fierce beauty of this coast with its weather-sculpted rocks and beaches littered with logs and then cruise upstream into a silent, black and pristine river bordered by rainforest.*

Ins & outs   **Getting there and around** *Kendell* and *Qantas* have daily flights to **Burnie** from Melbourne. *Tasair* have a service, Mon-Fri, from Hobart. Once on the roads much of the region is accessible only by unsealed, sometimes unsignposted, roads. Some public transport is provided by *Redline* who run daily services between **Launceston** and **Burnie**, and Mon-Fri services between Burnie and **Smithton**, via **Stanley**. *Wilderness to West Coast Tours*, T6458 3253, www.tassie.net.au/~batkins, run a superb 4WD tour around much of the top corner of the region, including the South Arthur Forests and western beaches, for $140. The trip includes a memorably delicious bush-lunch. They also offer half-day tours and overnight trips as far as Sandy Cape.

Burnie

Colour map 8, grid A2
Population: 18,000
50 km from Devonport
75 km from Stanley

An industrial city and deep-water container port, Burnie is dominated by its wharf, piled with golden pyramids of woodchips. Some Tasmanians refer to Burnie ironically as the place 'where the forest meets the sea', which is also a reference to an enormous pulp and paper mill based here. The fortunes of

Burnie are closely linked to the success of industry and visitors will notice the decaying hulks of abandoned factories along the road into town. It is, however, a friendly place with some interesting sights nearby.

Getting there Air Burnie has the state's 4th airport, though it is actually out at Wynyard. There are daily *Kendell* and *Qantas* flights to **Melbourne**, and *Tasair* have daily flights to **King Island** and. Also to Hobart, Mon-Fri. Hire car services available at airport.**Bus** *Redline* run daily services from 117 Wilson St to **Devonport** and **Launceston**.
  Information The civic centre is a square housing the art gallery, town hall, library, a pioneer village museum and the **VIC**, which has information on the whole northwest region. Open daily 0900-1700 (bookings Mon-Fri only), T6434 6111, travel@burnie.net

Ins & outs

Burnie's **Regional Art Gallery** often has impressive touring exhibitions. ■ *Mon-Fri 0900-1700, Sat-Sun 1330-1630. Free. T6431 5918.* The region's paper theme is continued at **Creative Paper**, a small papermaking operation set up to help the long-term unemployed. Tours cover the whole production process and include a go at papermaking. ■ *Mon-Fri 0900-1700. Tours 1100 and 1300. $6, children $4.50. T6430 7717. On the C112 road, off the main highway 1 km to the east of the town centre. The turn-off is within 200 m of the junction, on the right-hand side.* About 250 m further on is a left turn signposted to **Fern Glade** which is reached after another 1½ km. This small reserve is worth a visit at any time of day, but the stretch of Emu River flowing through is home to several **platypus** and there is a good chance of seeing one around dawn or dusk. ■ *Daily 0730-2000 Nov-Mar, otherwise 0730-1700.* Another 3 km on is **Lactos**, a large cheese producer responsible for the *Mersey Valley* and *Heritage* ranges. They usually have about 20 cheeses available for tasting in their small delicatessen. ■ *Mon-Fri 0900-1700, Sat-Sun 1000-1600. T6431 2566.* Near the town of Ridgely, about 10 km south of Burnie, are the **Guide Falls**, picturesque after heavy rain, and two lovely gardens. **Emu Valley Rhododendron Garden** has thousands of species of rhododendrons within its 13 ha, and **Annsleigh Gardens** is a smaller ornate English-style garden. ■ *Emu Valley open Aug-Mar, $4. T6435 1298. Annsleigh Gardens open Sep-May, $4.50. T6435 7229. Head south on Mount St (B18) for both the falls and gardens.*

Sights

B *Glen Osborne House*, 9 Aileen Cres, T6431 9866, F6431 4354. Traditional hosted B&B in a grand Victorian house with 6 en suite rooms, a large garden and tennis court. **B-C** *Apartments Downtown*, 52 Alexander St, T6432 3219, F6431 8844. 9 elegant 1930s-style self-contained apartments. Spacious, comfortable and good value. **C** *Duck House*, 26-28 Queen St, T6431 1712. 2 charming weatherboard cottages in a quiet but central street, self-contained and furnished with antiques. **D-E** *Regent*, 26 North Terr, T6431 1933. Pub on a busy road opposite the foreshore but has some good value backpacker beds and neat, clean en suite doubles. There's also a smart steakhouse restaurant, the mid-range *Mallee Grill*. The *Treasure Island* caravan park on Bass Highway west of Burnie has cabins, vans and hostel beds, T6431 1925. *Kinesis* on Mount St is a combined café and health-food shop with mostly vegetarian, organic and free-range dishes. Healthy, high-quality food in a bright, eclectic room, live music on Fri. Open Tue-Thu 0830-1800, Fri 0830-2100, Sat 0830-1600. *Rialto Gallery Restaurant*, 46 Wilmont St, T6431 7718, is a cosy place with excellent Italian and takeaway pizzas. *Weller's*, T6431 1088, on Queen St serves pricey seafood and has a good view. For something cheaper try *The Octopus* on Mount St close to the beach, selling fresh fish and the region's best fish and chips.

Sleeping & eating

Tasmania

Transport **Local Bus** *MetroTas*, T132201, www.metrotas.com.au, run various services from Cattley St. From stop C, service 60 goes approximately hourly 0740-1740, Mon-Fri, to **Wynyard**. There are also 5 daily services (70 and 74), 0838-1710 Mon-Fri, from stop D to **Penguin** and **Ulverstone**.

Long distance **Air** There are daily *Kendell* flights to and from **Melbourne** and **King Island**. **Bus** *Redline* run 1-3 services every day via the north coast towns to **Devonport** and **Launceston**, connecting there with buses to **Hobart**. Westbound services leave 1300 Mon-Fri (1500 school days) for **Wynyard**, **Stanley** and **Smithton**, stopping at some junctions for other towns and destinations. There is an additional service 1930 Fri.

Directory **Banks** Most major bank ATMs can be found on Wilson St or Catteley St. **Communications** Internet at *Online Access Centre*, 2 Spring St, T6431 9469. Open Mon, Wed, Thu 0900-1700, Tue, Fri 0900-2000, Sat 0930-1230. **Post Office**, 87 Wilson St. **Hospital** *North West Regional*, Brickport Rd, T6430 6666. Bus stop C, service 28.

Wynyard
Colour map 8, grid A2
Population: 4,500
18 km from Burnie
18 km from Boat Harbour Beach

Wynyard is a pleasant fishing village on the sheltered banks of the Inglis River, dominated by Table Cape headland just to the west. The lush green farmland and chocolate-coloured soil of the area becomes a vivid quilt of flowers in spring, particularly tulips which are grown commercially on Table Cape. The town makes the most of this display with a tulip festival in the second week of October. Wynyard is a convenient base to explore the coastal attractions further west, such as the beautiful Boat Harbour and Sisters beaches, Rocky Cape National Park or the hinterland forests. On the opposite side of the river, **Fossil Bluff** faces the ocean. These high limestone cliffs are embedded with millions of tiny shell fossils, which can be seen at low tide by wandering along the beach at the base of the cliffs. The sandy beach and rock platforms make a great spot for a picnic. Take the first right after crossing the bridge. The **VIC** is unmissable with its Tassie tiger stripes and is located at the junction of the main street, Goldie Street, and Hogg Street. ■ *Mon-Sat 0930-1630, Sun 1230-1630, T6442 4143, wynyard@tasvisinfo.com.au For more details on the Tulip Festival see www.tased.edu.au/tasonline/wyntulip*

Sleeping and eating **B** *Alexandria*, just over the bridge on Table Cape Rd, T6442 4411, alexandria@ozemail.com.au Traditional B&B in a Federation-style brick house with 5 comfy rooms. **C-E** *Hotel Federal*, 82 Goldie St, T6442 2056. Pub rooms, some en suite, including continental breakfast. Also cheap pub food and pizzas. On East beach, Old Bass Highway is the **C-E** *Wynyard Caravan Park*, T6442 1998, with a range of accommodation from cabins, on-site vans and budget doubles, small pleasant kitchen and common room and BBQs. Recommended. Even if just passing through don't miss *Coffee Art* on the corner of Moore St and Goldie St. This café, gallery and second-hand bookshop is a joyous blast of colour and originality with great coffee, and fresh homemade food. Open Fri-Tue 1030-1800. For an evening meal try the pub or *Buckaneers*, 4 Inglis St, T6442 4104, a nice spot with cheap seafood meals. Sun-Wed 0900-1900, Thu-Sat 0900-2030.

See Burnie for airport details **Transport** *Redline* buses leave Gales Auto Services, Saunders St, 1320 Mon-Fri and 1945 Fri for **Stanley** and **Smithton**. Their services to **Burnie** leave at 0810 Mon-Fri and 1600 school days. *MetroTas* buses leave Jackson St approximately hourly, 0715-1810 Mon-Fri, for Burnie.

Wynyard to Stanley
Distance 62 km

There are magnificent views of the northwest coast from Table Cape, well worth a short detour on the way west. From Wynyard, turn right at the main roundabout on Goldie Street, cross the bridge and follow Table Cape Road to the lookout. On the way back down the hill turn right into Tolleymore Road, which rejoins the Bass Highway just before the turn-off for **Boat Harbour**. This tiny community is built around one of the best beaches on the north coast and a wonderful place to stop for lunch, with a casual seafood restaurant right on the beach. Those who linger for a few days can enjoy **Sisters Beach,** a lovely 8-km swimming beach within the **Rocky Cape National Park**. This small park of coastal heathland and woodland has several caves containing vast middens of shellfish and bone that show Aboriginal people have lived in this area for more than 8,000 years. The coastline is very rugged and rocky so there are plenty of rockpools, but walking the length of the coastline is difficult. The main access points are Sisters Beach and Rocky Cape, at the western end of the park by the lighthouse, reached from Rocky Cape Road off the Bass Highway. There are several short walks to caves at each end and also a full circuit walk from Rocky Cape to Sisters Beach (25 km, eight hours). There is also a shorter circuit from Rocky Cape with great views from Tinkers Lookout in the hills and access to the coast (but not the beaches) at Cathedral Rocks (2½ hours). ■ *Day-use park only, no camping. For more information contact the Smithton parks office, T6452 4998, www.parks.tas.gov.au*

Sleeping and Eating L *Skyescape*, 282 Tolleymore Rd, Table Cape, T6442 1876. Striking, contemporary house with wonderful sea views from the Japanese-influenced guest wing (sole use), 6 acres of landscaped gardens down to the shoreline and lots of thoughtful pampering. The hosts are superb cooks and offer dinners as well as a cooked gourmet breakfast. Recommended. A *Killynaught Cottages*, 17266 Bass Highway, Boat Harbour, www.killynaught.com.au Very comfortable reproduction colonial cottages furnished with antiques beds, open fires, spas and leather couches, self-contained with breakfast provisions. B-C *Cape View Guesthouse*, Strawberry La, just off the highway above Boat Harbour, T6445 1273. Homely B&B with views over the beach, 1 sunny upstairs 2-bedroom suite and a ground floor en suite room in a family home. The hosts also own the E *Boat Harbour Beach Backpackers* and will pick-up from the highway. Simple bunk rooms and a few doubles with a small cosy common room and lots of grassy outdoor space, best In summer (no heating in sleeping rooms). C *Seaside Garden Motel* has neat, clean motel rooms and self-contained units opposite Boat Harbour beach and the *Avalon*, T6445 1111, a lively unpretentious restaurant with superb seafood and grills and friendly service. Book ahead at weekends. Recommended. *Jolly Rogers*, is right on the beach and has cheap imaginative seafood lunches. Open Wed-Sat 1000-2030, Sun 1000-1900, later in summer. Boat Harbour also has a caravan park (T6445 1253), general store, post office and petrol.

Transport The *Redline* north coast service picks up and drops off at the junctions for Rocky Cape, Boat Harbour and Table Cape. Eastbound morning services 0745, 0800 and 0803 respectively, and afternoon services 1524, 1540 and 1545 respectively on school days. Westbound services to **Stanley** and **Smithton** leave from the Table Cape junction 1328 Mon-Fri (1523 school days), calling at the Boat Harbour junction 2 mins later, and the Rocky Cape junction 15 mins after that. An additional westbound service on Fri stops at 1952, 1955 and 2005 respectively.

Stanley

Colour map 8, grid A2
Population: 600
80 km from Burnie
80 km from Arthur River

Stanley was one of the state's first settlements, the early headquarters and port for the fledgling Van Diemens Land Company (VDLC). It straddles a narrow neck of land that ends abruptly with the basalt edifice of The Nut, an imposing volcanic plug. Much of the town's small centre and busy wharf area date from Georgian and Victorian times and this combination of architecture and position makes Stanley easily the most picturesque town in the northwest, if not the

Tasmania

north, of the island. The Nut can be climbed in about 20 minutes and a 45-minute walking circuit around the top offers several sweeping lookouts. At the base of the rock, just past the old cemetary, is a Fairy penguin rookery, now built up to considerable numbers with the help of one enthusiastic guesthouse owner who has constructed dozens of rock burrows for them. A private booking agency in the Town Hall on Church Street doubles as a small **VIC**. ■ *Daily 0900-1700, T1300 656044, www.bookings.tassie.net.au*

Walking around main Church Street and Wharf Road is a must to see the town's typical weatherboard architecture. Down by the wharf the original 1842 VDLC stores now house *Stanley Artworks*, T6458 2000, a small company producing exquisite wood furniture from Tasmanian timbers. There's also a small art and ceramics gallery (open daily 1000-1800, by appointment during May-August). If a walk up The Nut (152 m) looks like it requires too much puff take the chairlift. ■ *Daily 0930-1630, $7 return, children $5. Wilderness to West Coast Tours*, T6458 3253, run evening **platypus** tours around dusk and **Fairy penguin** tours after dark (one hour, $15) for limited numbers. It is also possible to visit the local **seal** colony with *Stanley Seal Cruises*, T6458 1312. Trips at 1000, 1300 and 1500, weather permitting (1½ hours, $30). Further afield, 27 km off the main highway, is **Dip Falls** and one of Tasmania's 'Big Trees'.

Sleeping & eating **L-A** *Beachside Retreat*, 253 Stanley Highway, T6458 1350, westinlet@ozemail.com.au Striking, contemporary eco-cabins by a private beach, 2½ km from Stanley. The privacy and location makes these cabins seriously relaxing.There is also a large modern self-contained house available. **A** *Hanlon House*, 6 Marshall St, T6458 1149, www.tassie.net.au/hanlonhouse Gracious hospitality in a traditional B&B overlooking The Nut and ocean. There are spacious cosy rooms, open fires, cooked breakfasts and knowledgeable, helpful hosts. Recommended. The **C-E** *Cabin and Tourist Park*, Wharf Rd, T6458 1266, has cabins, on-site vans and an old railway building converted to a clean, comfortable and well-equipped hostel. 4-bunk dorms, twins and doubles. Recommended. *Stanley's on the Bay*, just off Wharf Rd, T6458 1404. Part of the *Stanley Village* motel (**B**), this nautically themed restaurant serves mid-range seafood and steaks with a smattering of Asian options. Open daily Sep-Jun 1800-2000. *Hurseys*, also off Wharf Rd, T6458 1103, is a combination of excellent fish and chip shop, open daily 0900-1800, café and, upstairs, a small formal expensive seafood restaurant called *Julie and Patrick's*, open daily 1800-2000.

Transport The *Redline* services call at the main store and garage, Wharf Rd. The **Smithton** bus leaves Mon-Fri at 1410 (1605 school days), and 2030 Fri. The eastbound bus leaves Mon-Fri 0715 and, on school days, also at 1455.

The South Arthur Forests Much of northwest Tasmania is covered by managed forest plantations and can be explored on roads that form a 152-km loop that takes around half a day to a day to complete, depending on lunch and walking stops. Most of the roads are unsealed but usually kept in good repair and navigable by following signs for the Forest Reserves and tiny communities, avoiding the side-roads labelled 'spurs'. Log-trucks are a common sight – and hazard – on the roads. Keep well to the left and take great care on blind corners and rises. For more information on this area contact *Forestry Tasmania*, on the corner of Nelson Street and Smith Street in Smithton, T6452 1317.

From Stanley and then Smithton the sealed B22 passes through Edith Creek and Roger River before a right turn to Trowutta and **Tayetea Bridge**. The bridge is over a particularly scenic stretch of the Arthur River and marks both the end of the sealed road and for some the start of a tremendous canoe trip right down to the river mouth. Signs from here lead to the **Milkshakes Hills Forest Reserve**. The Milkshakes are three prominent bald hills supposedly named by local loggers with vivid imaginations. A walk from the car park threads through temperate rainforest with some impressive man ferns and a few huge Stringybark gums. At **Lake Chisolm Forest Reserve** is a small tranquil lake, a 30-minute return walk from the car park, which is actually a flooded limestone sinkhole. The **Julius River Forest Reserve** has a 30-minute circular rainforest walk. On the latter part of the loop, just before the Kanunnah Bridge where the bitumen reappears, is the **Sumac Lookout** over a deep part of the Arthur River valley. Had the damming proposals of the 1970s been approved this would now be a view over a lake.

Northern west coast

Walking along the wild remote beaches of this coastline is one of the great pleasures of visiting Tasmania. Long golden beaches are littered with grey tree trunks washed down the Arthur River by floods and flung back to land by the fierce winter storms and massive seas. Waves as high as 10 m have been known and even surfers head for the more sheltered beaches such as Ann Bay.

Colour map 8, grid A1
Arthur River 80 km
from Stanley

The sealed highway ends at **Marrawah** ('marruh-wor'), a tiny settlement with most of the area's few facilities, including a pub and small store with expensive petrol, takeaway and post office, open daily 0830-1630. If heading south this is the last place to get fuel before Zeehan. To the north the unsealed road leads inland past the **Preminghana** headland (formerly Mount Cameron) to **Woolnorth**, a small VDLC town. Beyond is Cape Grim, where the air quality is said to be the cleanest in the world. The unsealed road south of Marrawah reaches the settlement of **Arthur River** after 14 km. This is the main destination for visitors to the area. Boat cruises up the river are just as impressive as the better known cruises on the Gordon River at Strahan and perhaps more peaceful. Canoe trips are also available and it is a good place to access the beautiful log-littered beaches stretching away to the south. Just south of the river is a monument marking the 'edge of the world' (there is no land westard for 15,000 km). From here the road continues past the tiny fishing shack settlements of Nelson Bay and Couta Rocks and on to Richardson Point. This is the northern edge of the **Arthur Pieman Conservation Area**, accessible only by 4WD.

A cruise up the Arthur River is a great experience, the forest reflections on a still day breathtaking. The tannin in these rivers stains the water the colour of tea and when deep the water becomes so black that it reflects perfectly. The *MV George Robinson* carries up to 50 passengers upriver for 14 km. The boat moors up for a guided walk and BBQ lunch in the midst of the rainforest at the junction of the Arthur and Frankland rivers. ■ *Daily mid-Aug to mid-May, 1000, 5 hrs. $49.50, children $22, concessions $45. T6457 1158, arthurrivercruises@bigpond.com* An alternative way to see the river is to hire canoes or kayaks from *Arthur River Canoe and Boat Hire*, Arthur River, T6457 1312. Daily hire available or they will transport kayakers upriver for expeditions lasting one, two or thee nights. *Kings Run Wildlife Tours*, Marrawah, T6457 1191, jonesking@tassie.net.au, are a small and accomodating company offering very reasonably priced personalized 4WD tours, walkers' drop-offs and pick-ups, and simply the best **Tasmanian devil** experience in the state – the chance to see wild devils feeding after dark. A couple of days' notice is required for the latter, but is an opportunity not to be missed. Owner Geoff is also happy to advise on local walks and wildlife.

Tours & activities

Tasmania

Sleeping & eating There are several self-contained options in Arthur River, contact the Stanley Booking Office for details. **C** *Glen Donald*, managed by *Kings Run*, is a simple but spacious self-contained cottage 3 km south of Marrawah. **C** *Marrawah Beach House*, 19 Beach Rd, 3 km from the pub, T/F 6457 1285. 2 isolated self-contained chalets surrounded by grazing land on a rise overlooking the sea. Bright and cheerful, they sleep 4 and are very good value. Recommended. **D** *Alert Cottage*, Arthur River, T6457 1340. Small self-contained cottage. **Camping** is allowed at a couple of spots, including Marrawah Beach and just north of Arthur River. Both camps have toilets, picnic tables and wood BBQs. The welcoming *Marrawah* pub, T6457 1102, serves cheap, hearty meals daily 1200-1330, 1800-1930, and the stores at both Marrawah and Arthur River have takeaways available.

The West Coast

Like so much of Tasmania the west coast has been shaped by the elements. Subject to the fierce gales of the 'Roaring Forties' the coast has huge seas, high rainfall and the interior is covered in dense impenetrable forest. Although Tasmanian Aboriginals are known to have lived in this area and survived on its resources, European settlers only penetrated the west for the purposes of punishment and commerce. The whole coast has just one sheltered natural harbour, though it happens to be one of Australia's biggest – over 30 km long by 10 km wide – and it was inside **Macquarie Harbour** *that colonial authorities decided to build a penal settlement, at the ends of the earth and entered through 'Hells Gate'. Later, the pretty village of* **Strahan** *was founded inside the harbour by loggers and fishermen and is now the main drawcard of the west coast for cruises up the magnificent* **Gordon River** *and to the convict ruins on* **Sarah Island**. *Just inland are the small, quiet towns of* **Queenstown**, **Rosebery**, **Zeehan** *and* **Tullah**, *established as mining and 'hydro' towns and providing routes north and east.*

Ins & outs **Getting there and around** *Tassie Link* runs one west coast bus service between Hobart and Strahan via Derwent Bridge and Queenstown, and another between Launceston and Strahan via Devonport, Cradle Mountain and Queenstown. The southern service operates Tue, Thu, Fri, Sun and, in summer, Wed. The northern runs Tue, Thu, Sat and, in summer, Mon.

Queenstown
Colour map 8, grid B2
Population: 2,600
88 km from Derwent Bridge
115 km from Cradle Valley

The startlingly bald hills of Queenstown are often compared to a lunar landscape but the devastation is unmistakably man-made. The Mount Lyell Mining Company has mined copper from these hills since 1893. The forests that once covered the area were stripped to feed the furnaces of copper smelters and the by-product of sulphurous fumes prevented any regrowth. Efforts are being made to revegetate Queenstown but the topsoil is long gone and progress is slow. However, one of the mining company's relics may ensure the town's survival. The **Abt Railway** from Queenstown to Strahan was built in the 1890s so that ore could be shipped out from the port and has now been restored for scenic trips. The restored track, locomotives and stations traverse the 35 km to Strahan through remote rainforest beside the Queen and King rivers. The train stops at several points along the route and you transfer from the steam loco to diesel-pulled carriages about midway to Strahan. ■ *Trains depart both Queenstown and Strahan about 0900. Full distance return $89, children $29, concessions $71. Singles fare about two thirds return prices. T6471 1700. Bookings essential.* There are daily tours of the surface of the Mount Lyell mine and the opportunity to descend into a modern working mine. ■ *Surface tours daily 0915, 1600. $15, children $7.50. Underground tours daily 0815, 1015, 1315. $55,*

Tasmania

maximum of 7. Bookings essential. The **VIC** is opposite the Abt Railway terminal, on the corner of Driffield Street and Orr Street, the main shopping street of Queenstown. ■ *Daily 0815-1800, shorter hrs Jun-Aug, T6471 2388.*

Sleeping and eating **B** *Penghana*, 32 The Esplanade, T6471 2560. B&B in the former mine manager's house, with 5 rooms and huge guest living areas, cooked breakfast. Motels include **C** *Gold Rush Motor Inn*, T6471 1005, which has a restaurant and some units with kitchens. **D-E** *The Empire*, 2 Orr St, T6471 1699. Basic but clean rooms and serves the town's best cheap meals daily 1200-1400, 1800-2000. The caravan park, T6471 1332, has cabins, vans and budget beds. *Dotties* at the ABT Railway terminal is a pretty country café serving sandwiches, salads and cakes, daily 0900-1730.

Options are fairly limited for both sleeping and eating

Transport The agent and departure point for Tassie Link is *Schulz Milk Bar*, at the top of Hunter St. Buses depart for **Derwent Bridge** and **Hobart** (4½ hrs, $44.70) 1415 Tue, Thu, 1645 Fri, 1445 Sun and, in summer, 0930 Wed. **Strahan** services leave 1500 Tue, Thu, 2130 Fri, 1540 Sat, 1945 Sun and, in summer, 1500 Mon and Wed. The bus via **Cradle Mountain** to **Devonport** and **Launceston** (6-6½ hrs, $52.70) leaves 1245 Tue, Thu, 1000 Sat and, in summer, 0930 Mon.

Strahan

Hugging the small bay of Risby Cove, a tiny inlet on giant Macquarie Harbour, Strahan began in the 1870s as a convenient base for those wanting to plunder the area's considerable resources, first the Huon timber cutters, the 'piners', and then the miners who ran a railway to Strahan from Queenstown. Now it is the convenient and hugely popular base for those wanting simply to see the region's quite astounding natural beauty. Pretty as it is, there is actually little to see and do in the town itself, though a stroll around the cove is always satisfying and there is a wonderful 40-minute return walk to **Hogarth Falls** from the Peoples Park. The **VIC** is on the Esplanade and incorporates a superb interactive display on the controversial aspects of local Aboriginal, convict and environmental history. ■ *Daily 1000-2000 from Nov-Apr, 1100-1800 otherwise. Interactive display $3.30, children free, concessions $2.20. T6471 7622, strahan@tasvisinfo.com.au*

Colour map 8, grid B2
Population: 700
40 km from Queenstown
80 km from Tullah

    Macquarie Harbour, Tasmania's largest natural harbour, was missed by the earliest explorers but discovered by Captain James Kelly in 1815 during his circumnavigational search for commercial resources. **Huon pine** was his major find here, a tree particularly popular with shipwrights for its bug- and worm-resistant oils. Coal was found shortly after and this combination made the harbour irresistible to the colonial authorities, who were looking for a suitably profitable site for a 'prison-within-a-prison'. A penal settlement was established on tiny **Sarah Island** in 1822, a name that was soon feared by the British Empire's convict and criminal communities. The narrow mouth of the harbour was nicknamed **Hells Gate** by the prisoners and hell it certainly was for many, leading to frequent escapes and suicides-by-proxy. The decision to relocate Tasmania's principal punishment station to Port Arthur meant closure for the settlement in 1833. Ten years later the settlement briefly re-opened as a probation station, but for 40-odd years the harbour saw little human activity other than a few piners. Today a small **fishing** fleet operates out of Strahan, and several tourist vessels use the harbour to cross from Strahan to Sarah Island and cruise up the magnificent rainforest-shrouded banks of the **Gordon River**, the western gateway to the Franklin-Gordon Wild Rivers National Park.

Tasmania

To the west of town an unsealed road threads through the **Henty Dunes** to the long **Ocean Beach**. From here it is a 8-km walk up the beach (or unsealed drive) to Macquarie Heads and a view of Hells Gate. There are basic camping and picnic facilities here. A few kilometres north of Strahan the highway also briefly touches the dunes, some of the biggest in Tasmania at up to 30 m high. *4 Wheelers*, T0419 508175, operate guided **quadbike** rides from the car park. Book in advance, driving licence required.

Sleeping & eating

Strahan Central, T6471 7612, strahancentral @trump.net.au, and Strahan Village, T6471 4200, www.strahan village.com.au manage a lot of the accommodation

L-B *Franklin Manor*, Esplanade, T6471 7311, www.franklinmanor.com.au One of 2 seriously luxurious traditional boutique hotels. Cosy guest lounges, deep-red-walled dining rooms with log fires and dark wood furniture, and 14 en suite rooms. Meals are expensive, uncomplicated but delicious, and complemented by one of the state's best wine lists. Bookings required. Recommended. **L-A** *Risby Cove*, T6471 7572, www.risby.com.au, has a wonderful dockside location with alfresco boardwalk tables overlooking the harbour. The excellent modern café serves inventive breakfasts, light lunches and mid-range evening meals daily 0700-2000, later in summer. The small complex includes a contemporary gallery and luxurious guest suites. **B** *Gordon Gateway Chalets*, Grining St, T6471 7165, www.gordongateway.com.au Exceptional self-contained cottages, studio apartments and impossibly elegant contemporary suites. Nearly all room shave harbour views. Recommended.

C-D *Hamers Hotel*, Esplanade, is part of *Strahan Village*. Accommodation is basic but comfortable. Bars and bistros are cheap and welcoming. Meals daily 1200-1400, 1730-2030. **C-D** *Sailor's Rest*, Harvey St, T6471 7237, sailorsrest@tassie.net.au Cabin park with several very comfortable, brightly furnished self-contained cabins, sleeping 2-8. Recommended. **C-D** *Wilderness Lodge*, Ocean Beach Rd, 3 km from the town centre, T6471 7142. Tired but clean and comfortable 1897 guest house with 5 twins and doubles, including continental breakfast, and 4 very private self-contained cabins in a low bush setting. The **D-E** *YHA*, Harvey St, is clean and comfy with good common facilities. Bookings through *Strahan Central*. The caravan park is opposite the police station off Innes St, T6471 7239. *Banjo's*, Esplanade, is a bakery and café serving breakfasts, light lunches and evening pizzas, daily 0600-2130. Alfresco tables overlook the harbour.

Tours & activities

Air *Seair*, T6471 7718, www.seeairac.com.au, fly 5 different scenic routes in helicopters and small seaplanes, from $70. Flights include Macquarie Harbour, Franklin-Gordon National Park and Cradle Mountain. *Wilderness Air*, T6471 7280, also operate seaplane flights into the southern part of the World Heritage Area. **Boat** *World Heritage Cruises*, T6471 7174, www.worldheritagecruises.com.au Thanks to the considerable speed of this huge catamaran, the daily tour (0900, 6 hrs, $55) provides an excellent introduction to the harbour with a run through Hells Gate, tour on Sarah Island and a walk in the rainforest up the Gordon River. Smorgasbord lunch costs extra, but is worth it. *Marine Charters*, T6471 7100, can organize personalized sightseeing and fishing tours on the harbour. **Jetboat** *Wild Rivers Jet*, T6471 7174. Trips on the hr every day up the sad but interesting King River. As much a secnic trip as a thrill ride. **Kayak** *Hells Gates Wilderness Tours*, T/F6471 7576, hellsgates@trump.net.au The best way to explore the harbour, river or nearby river, the Henty is quietly under your own steam. Hire available, including kayak, tents, mats and stoves, or join one of their half-day to 3-night tours. **Sail** *West Coast Yacht Charters*, T6471 7422, F6471 8033, manage the impressive 20-m sailing ketch *Stormbreaker*. This is taken out on a variety of sails from a crayfish dinner cruise (2½ hrs, $50) to a 2-night trip to Sarah Island and up the Gordon ($320). **Train** The *Abt Wilderness Railway*, an unusual rack and pinion type, has been restored to cover the full length of its original route from Strahan along the King and Queen rivers to Queenstown (see page 856).

Tassie Link services leave the VIC for **Queenstown**, **Derwent Bridge** and **Hobart** (5½-8 hrs, $51.70) 1130 Tue, Thu, 1600 Fri, 1400 Sun and, in summer, 0730 Wed. Buses leave for **Queenstown**, **Cradle Mountain**, **Devonport** and **Launceston** (7-8½ hrs, $59.70) 1130 Tue, Thu, 0900 Sat and, in summer, 0730 Mon.

Banks There is an ATM in the *General Store* on Innes St, open daily 0630-2000, to 2100 summer. **Bike and kayak hire** *Risby Cove*, T6471 7572. **Communications** Internet at *General Store* or the *On-line Access Centre*, adjacent to post office. Both $2.50 for 15 mins. **Post Office**, Esplanade. **Medical Centre** Esplanade, T6471 7152, open daily 0900-1700. **Parks and Wildlife Office** – adjacent to Post Office, T6471 7122.

Zeehan, just off the main highway, is a former mining town with exuberantly decorative civic buildings. The **Pioneer's Memorial Museum**, itself housed in one of these fine buildings, has an extensive display of historical photographs and documents, including a sequence of notes passed between trapped miners and their rescuers during the North Lyell Mine disaster of 1912. The mineral display is also considerable and part of it, including a collection of the beautiful red crocoite, is housed below in a mock-up mine. ■ *Daily 0830-1700, Oct-Mar to 1800. $5.50, concessions $3.30. T6471 6225.* Just south of the town is a 3-km unsealed vehicle excursion through the **Spray Tunnel**, an old access tunnel cut through simply to get a piece of mining machinery into position. The 100-m-long tunnel is wide enough for standard saloons only. From Zeehan the highway continues on to Rosebery. Just before the town there is a right-hand turn signposted to the **Montezuma Falls**. The road is 6 km long and the walk is three hours return. **Rosebery** is a mining town tightly enclosed by forested mountains, with a couple of cafés and a store with ATM facilities and petrol.

Corinna
*Colour map 8, grid B1
94 km from Strahan
76 km from Tullah*

From Zeehan the minor C249 makes its lonely way to the forested state reserve of **Corinna**, where a car ferry crosses the Pieman River (daily 0900-1900, April-September 0900-1700). There are cruises down to the mouth of the tranquil Pieman, named after an escaped convict, aboard the 1939 *MV Arcadia II*. ■ *Daily 1030, 4 hrs. 24-hr notice required Jun-Oct, min 6 people. $40, children $20. Lunch $7.70 extra but must be ordered the day before. T6446 1170.* There are also some good bushwalks around this spot and accommodation in a bunkhouse and the self-contained **C** *Retreat Cabins*, T6446 1170. From Corinna it is a further unsealed 110 km to Arthur River, skirting inland the **Arthur-Pieman Conservation Area**, with views over the Norfolk range of hills. Access to the area is by 4WD only. It is wild, beautiful, ecologically sensitive, and also important to the Aboriginal community for its cultural and historical heritage. *Wilderness to West Coast Tours*, Stanley, T6458 3253, www.tassie.net.au/~batkins, run the only overnight guided trips into the heart of the area at **Sandy Cape**.

Tullah
*Colour map 8, grid B2
61 km from Cradle Valley
94 km from Burnie*

With an exquisite position in the lee of rugged mounts Farrell and Herbert, and beside **Lake Rosebery**, Tullah is a former 'hydro' town and makes a good base for the excellent hillwalking in the area. A couple of operators now offer access to various other activities. It is also one of the main alternative bases for those wanting to visit Cradle Mountain. The best walk from the town itself is straight up **Mount Farrell**. The track starts right opposite the petrol station and the return ascent takes about three hours. **Mount Murchison** is the large mountain to the south, and the climb is comparable in length if a little more challenging. The start of the track is signposted off the road 12 km down the highway to Queenstown. Other activities include **canoe hire** and **horse-riding**, bookings via the *Tullah Chalet*. Aside from the petrol station there is a pub and small store

▶▶ **The Great Escape**

One of the more extraordinary escape attempts from Sarah Island was by the last 10 prisoners, who had been retained to complete the building of the yard's last ship. They were desperate to avert transfer to the dreaded Port Arthur and, thanks to slapdash governance, managed to steal the ship just before launch. There followed an extraordinary voyage to South America and further adventures for all the crew including recapture for some. The tale of the adventure is dramatically and hilariously told by the Round Earth Company, with audience participation, in the outdoor play 'The Ship That Never Was' Performances daily at 1730, also 2100 in January. $10, children $5, concession $7.50. Tickets and show at the tourist office.

with post office and café/takeaway, open daily 0700-1930. The small **Online Access Centre** has basic local information in addition to internet access, $5 for 30 minutes. ■ *Mon-Wed and Fri 1000-1200, Sat-Sun 1200-1400.*

Sleeping and eating Choices are limited, but the **C-E** *Tullah Chalet*, Farrell St, T6473 4121, tullahchalet@bigpond.com, has over 100 beds in rooms ranging from bunk dorms to comfortable lake-side en suite doubles. No kitchen facilities. The large ski-lodge style bar and dining room have open fires and lots of sofas. Lunches in summer, mid-range dinners daily 1800-2000. The friendly *Tullah Tavern* has cheap counter lunches and dinners available Oct-Apr, daily 1200-1400, Mon-Sat 1800-2000. The store on Farrell St has a single 'container' room available, an en suite double with lounge and basic kitchen facilities (**E**). Will sleep 4, includes continental breakfast and linen. T6473 4377.

Transport After leaving **Queenstown** the *Tassie Link* **Launceston** service calls at *Marina's Coffee Shop*, **Zeehan**, 45 mins later, *Mackrills Milkbar*, **Rosebery**, after another 30 mins and the BP station at **Tullah** in another 15 mins. From **Launceston** the bus picks up at **Tullah** 1205 Tue, Thu, 1340 Sat and, in summer, 1310 Mon.

Wilderness World Heritage Area

'If we can revise our attitudes towards the land under our feet; if we can accept a role of steward, and depart from the role of conqueror; if we can accept the view that man and nature are inseparable parts of the unified whole – then Tasmania can be a shining beacon in a dull, uniform, and largely artificial world.' Olegas Truchanus, photographer and environmentalist.

The Wilderness World Heritage Area covers one fifth of Tasmania, virtually the whole of the southwest corner, and was proposed and negotiated by the Federal Government in the early 1980s, partly as a way of blocking the state government's moves to dam the Franklin River. The region is split into a number of parks and reserves, but these mark human boundaries and do not define particularly different physical areas. It is a gloriously rugged region, covered in thick bush and low but craggy mountains that can swallow unwary or ill-prepared walkers, never to be seen again. The Wilderness is traversed by just one road and penetrated a certain way by a couple more. Other than these the only ways of really seeing region are by air or by tackling one of the great walking tracks. The **Overland** is generally regarded as the most dramatic track through the area, but not the most challenging, and so is by far the most popular. It is frequently cited as the most memorable long-distance walk in Australia.

Getting there and around *Tassie Link* run a year-round west coast service from
Hobart through **Derwent Bridge** (3 hrs, $35.50), and one from **Launceston** via
Devonport and **Cradle Mountain** (3½ hrs, $43.60). The services connect at
Queenstown. The southern service operates Tue, Thu, Fri and Sun. The northern runs
Tue, Thu, Sat. In summer there are dedicated daily services on both routes. There are also
local shuttle services between **Cradle Village** and Dove Lake, and **Derwent Bridge** and
Lake St Clair. **Overland Track** A ferry across Lake St Clair can shorten the trek by a day.
Tassie Link services with same-day **Lake St Clair** to **Cradle Mountain** connection oper-
ate Tue and Thu only, departing 1055. Change at **Queenstown**, arrives Cradle Mountain
1510. On other days overnight stops are required at Lake St Clair, Queenstown or **Strahan**. In summer *Tassie Link* run a direct bus between Lake St Clair and **Launceston** on
Mon, Wed, Fri and Sun. They offer special walkers' fares on a variety of possible routes,
such as Launceston to Cradle Mountain, Lake St Clair to Hobart for $66. **Port Davey
Track** *Tassie Link* run a Scotts Peak Dam Rd service in summer, stopping at the major
tracks (Scotts Peak Dam 3½ hrs, $58.10). Leaves **Hobart** 0730 Tue and Thu, 0845 Sat.
Departs **Scotts Peak Dam** 1130 Tue and Thu, 1230 Sat. They offer special fares for Hobart
to Scotts Peak, Cockle Creek to Hobart. **South Coast Track** *Par Avion*, T6248 5390,
www.paravion.com.au, fly daily, weather permitting, into **Malaleuca** from **Cambridge**
airport for $155. They will also bring in food parcels for those doing the *Port Davey*. Track
first. *Tassie Link* run a summer service between **Hobart** and **Cockle Creek**, Mon, Wed, Fri.

Ins & outs

The most famous and beautiful of Tasmania's mountains, Cradle Mountain is
set in a narrow ridge of jagged dolerite peaks at the northern end of the Cradle
Mountain-Lake St Clair National Park. Often wearing a balaclava of cloud, visitors must be fortunate to see the mountain on one of about 30 clear days a year.
The surrounding country of striking mountains, alpine moorland, glacial lakes
and forested valleys offers some of the most spectacular wilderness walking in
the world as well as accessible short walks. Parks and Wildlife operate a visitor
centre, about 7 km from Dove Lake, where visitors can pick up a free guide to
short walks in the area and obtain information and advice on the park. The centre also sells topographic maps, guide books and some cold-weather clothing.
The merchandise is cheaper here than elsewhere in the village and all profits are
returned to the park. ■ *Daily 0800-1700 (1800 in summer). Standard park entry
fees apply. T6492 1133, www.parks.tas.gov.au*

There are many lovely short walks in the area around the park centre and
Cradle Mountain Lodge but Dove Lake and Cradle Mountain are the main
attraction. The **Dove Lake Circuit** (6 km, two hours) stays close to the shore of
the lake and covers easy terrain accessible to all. When the mountain is visible
and the surface of the lake unruffled this is an impossibly beautiful walk and is
still worth doing, even in less than ideal conditions. There is also a more challenging **upper circuit** that allows views over the park in every direction. For the
best views a walk to **Hansons Peak** or **Marions Lookout**, on the western side of
the lake, is recommended (both about two hours return). **Crater Lake** and
Lake Lilla also make for picturesque short walks. The *Lodge* shop (open daily
0900-1700) hires out waterproof jackets and trousers by the day.

**Cradle
Mountain**
Colour map 8, grid B2
*181 km from
Launceston
91 km from Devonport*

Sleeping and eating Cradle Valley has some superb expensive accommodation but
little for those on a budget. **L-A** *Cradle Mountain Lodge*, T6492 1303, www.poresorts.
com 98 luxurious cabins with woodfires (but no TV, phone, or cooking) dotted around a
large wooden alpine lodge. The lodge has quiet reading rooms, a bar, and every conceivable facility such as massage, sauna, bike hire, internet, wilderness slide shows, guided
walks and nocturnal wildlife-spotting tours. **A** *Cradle Mountain Wilderness Village*,
T6492 1018, www.cradle village.com.au 25 attractive, modern, self-contained cabins

*Book as far in advance
as possible for the
December-Easter
period and visit
midweek in summer*

Tasmania

with satellite TV, phones and electric heating and great views of the mountain from the guest lounge and verandah bar. **C-E** *Cradle Mountain Tourist Park*, T6492 1395, www.cosycabins.com/cradle Caravan park with simple self-contained cabins, a large camping ground, basic alpine huts and a YHA backpackers with a dozen 4-bed dorms and a large warm kitchen. Bookings essential in summer, even for campsites. The national park also has some basic cabins but these will be booked out most weekends. **D** *Waldheim Cabins*, bookings T3492 1110, 4-8 berth cabins with nothing but bunks, heating and cooking facilities. No linen and no electricity except for lighting. *Cradle Mountain Lodge* has a fine-dining restaurant with excellent fresh Tasmanian produce and a walk-in wine cellar featuring state wines. The restaurant is open to all but guest bookings have priority during busy periods. There is also a great tavern bar with cheap meals, open daily 1500-2300 (winter) and 1100-2300 (summer). Further down the road is the *Cradle Mountain Wilderness Village* café with cheap meals and takeaways, daily 0800-2000 in summer, 1100-1900 winter. A limited range of groceries are available from the Lodge shop and caravan park kiosk.

Tours and activities **Scenic flights** *Seair*, T6492 1132, fly a couple of different scenic circuits out of the small airstrip. They start from $135 for a 25-min trip over Cradle Mountain. Not available in winter.

Transport *Maxwells*, T6492 1431, runs a shuttle service from the camping ground to Dove Lake daily in summer, on demand in winter. The *Tassie Link* service leaves the campsite for **Devonport** and **Launceston** 1535 Tue and Thu, 1305 Sat. There is an additional service in summer, departing 1305 Mon, Wed, Fri, Sun. All services also call at the visitors centre and airfield, check for exact times. The **Queenstown** and **Strahan** bus leaves 1125 Tue, Thu, 1300 Sat and, in summer, 1230 Mon.

Walls of Jerusalem National Park This park encloses an extraordinary area of the Central Plateau that contains over 4,000 lakes and tarns within about 480 sq km. The 'walls' are five peaks surrounding a basin, to enter which walkers must pass through the 'gates' of the old city – Herods, Damascus, Zion, Jaffa, and Ephraims. It is a fascinating alpine landscape but it is also a bleak and exposed place. The twisted pencil pines and snow gums bear witness to the harsh conditions of this park. There are few tracks and the isolation and exposure mean that only very experienced walkers should consider a visit and park rangers must be consulted. In summer it is possible to try a short day-walk. The park is usually entered from Mersey Forest Road, south west of Mole Creek. After passing lakes Parangana and Rowallan the road crosses Fish River. The left-hand turn immediately after the river leads to a parking area at the start of the walking track. Following the route past Trappers Hut and Solomons Jewels, Herods Gate and Lake Salome can be reached in about three to four hours (6 km, rising 570 m). A detailed map is essential, the *Walls of Jerusalem National Park Map & Notes* is available at Cradle Mountain and Lake St Clair park offices and other map outlets. *Tasman Bush Tours*, T6423 4965, tasmanbush@tasadventures.com, run three-day guided walks in the national park ($395 catered, $275 self-catering).

Lake St Clair
Colour map 8, grid B3
Derwent Bridge 91 km
from Queenstown
189 km from Hobart

At the southern end of the **Cradle Mountain-Lake St Clair National Park**, Lake St Clair fills a basin carved out by glaciers many thousands of years ago and lies between formidable mountain ranges covered in forest down to the shoreline. This finger lake is about 11 km long and 2 km wide and, at 167 m deep, is the deepest lake in Australia. A walking track follows the length of the shore providing tranquil views of Mount Olympus, the Traveller Range and pointy Mount Ida. However, the most leisurely way to see the lake is to take the ferry from Cynthia Bay in the south to Narcissus Bay in the north, where walkers are collected, and return. The park facilities are based at Cynthia Bay where there is a striking modern park centre with interpretative displays on the geology, history and fauna of the park. Park rangers often provide guided walks, talks and slide shows in the busy summer season. There is also a café overlooking the lake and an accommodation booking office. The **park centre** is opposite the cafe. ■ *Daily 0800-1700 Mar-Nov, 0800-1900 Dec-Feb. T6289 1172, www.parks Standard park fees apply.*

Lake St Clair is the end of the **Overland Track** for many walkers but it is also a fine walking destination for shorter walks ranging from one hour to two or three days. Walkers should be prepared for all weather conditions with warm and waterproof layers of clothing. One of the most popular walks begins with catching the ferry to **Narcissus Bay** then returning to Cynthia Bay on foot via the Overland Track along the lake shore (5-7 hours walking). On a fine day don't miss the walk to the summit of **Mount Rufus** (1,416 m), from which you can see most of the peaks of this national park as well as many in the Southwest National Park. For experienced walkers, spending a few days in the **Labyrinth and Acropolis** area is recommended, only a day's walk from Narcissus Bay. This is a high, relatively level area that has been heavily glaciated, full of lovely tarns and closely surrounded by rugged cliffs and peaks. Walking expert Tyrone T Thomas describes this area as a 'world treasure'. For details consult walking guides and topographic maps and discuss plans with staff at the park centre. The *Lake St Clair Day Walk Map* ($4) is available at the park centre.

Sleeping and eating The accommodation and café are run by *Lakeside St Clair*, T6289 1137, who have 6 stylish self-contained cabins, a small backpacker hostel and campsites. The clean, modern hostel sleeps 28 in 2-bed-heated rooms and has a large kitchen with bench seats around the wood stove. Book well in advance for Dec-Mar as there is not enough accommodation to meet demand, even for campers. The café overlooks the lake and also sells books, souvenirs and confectionary. Daily 0800-0800 Dec-Feb, 1000-1600 Mar-Nov. Nearest food shopping is the small store at Bronte Park.

   Derwent Bridge There is little in Derwent Bridge except for a pub, some cabins and a petrol station. A *Derwent Bridge Chalets*, Lyell Highway, T6289 1000, 4chalets@h130.aone.net.au 6 self-contained chalets, some with spas. **C-D** *Derwent Bridge Hotel*, Lyell Highway, T6289 1144, derwildhotel@trump.net.au 10 B&B doubles, some en suite, also 50 budget beds in twins and doubles. Linen hire for the latter $5. Log lodge-style dining area and bar with huge open stone fires. Hearty cheap breakfasts and meals, daily 0800-0930, 1200-1400, 1800-2000. Recommended. They may be able to pick up from Lake St Clair if not too busy. If unable to find budget accommodation try *Highland Village* at Bronte Park, 29 km east of Derwent Bridge.

Transport *Lakeside St Clair* ferry from **Cynthia Bay** to **Narcissus Bay** at 0900, 1230, 1500 in summer (Sep-May) and if numbers are high enough at 1000, 1400 in winter (Jun-Aug). Book during high season ($20, 30 mins one-way, $25 1½ hrs return). *Maxwells*, T6492 1431, run an on-request shuttle bus to **Derwent Bridge** ($6). The *Tassie Link* west coast service leaves Derwent Bridge 1100 Tue, Thu, 2000 Fri and 1815 Sun, calling at Lake St Clair 10 mins earlier Tue and Thu only. Additional summer service, 1230 Wed. The **Hobart** service leaves Derwent Bridge 1615 Tue, Thu, 1825 Fri and 1630 Sun, calling 10 mins earlier at Lake St Clair Tue and Thu only. Additional summer service, 1310 Mon, Wed, Fri and Sat. In summer all services call at Lake St Clair and some connect with the **Mount Field National Park** service. There is also a dedicated service direct to **Launceston** in summer, departing the lake 1330 Mon, Wed, Fri and Sun.

Tasmania

▶▶ The Overland Track

*This is the classic Tasmanian walk, through an area of alpine wilderness unlike any other in Australia. The Overland Track is about 80 km from **Dove Lake** to **Lake St Clair**, traversing a high plateau in the heart of Tasmania scoured and shaped by ice ages. In every direction lie distinctive and unusual mountain peaks and ranges, sheer columns and cliffs of dark dolerite. In fact the side trips on this walk are a peak bagger's dream, including **Mount Ossa** (1617 m), Tasmania's highest mountain. The walk winds through a varied landscape of open moorland, glacial tarns and rainforests of myrtle, deciduous beech and sassafras. There are also streams and waterfalls, stands of snow gums and native pines and flowering heath. It is undoubtedly among the finest of Australian walks and an unforgettable experience. Like most of the Tasmanian wilderness the Cradle Mountain-Lake St Clair National Park is subject to severe and changeable weather. Walkers must have warm and waterproof gear and be prepared for all conditions. Snow is not unusual in summer. The walk is best done in November-April, although February-March are the ideal months as they have relatively stable weather and are less busy than December-January when most Australians have long holidays. The colours are richest in autumn when the weather is more dicey but the leaves of the native deciduous beech turn a golden copper. The walk itself takes about five days but there are many wonderful side trips, including the unmissable **Labyrinth**, and there's always the possibility of being held up by bad weather so walkers should allow about 8-10 days. To start from Cradle Mountain is the usual route as the track is generally downhill to Lake St Clair and ends enjoyably with a ferry trip. Walkers must be entirely self-sufficient, carrying in all food, a fuel stove and camping equipment. There are basic huts along the way but a tent must be carried, as huts may be full. The standard map for this walk is the Cradle Mountain-Lake St Clair National Park Map & Notes ($9) available at the park centres at both ends. If requested, park staff can mail out an Overland Track Pack ($22) including this map, the Overland Track Walkers Notebook (describing each section and its geology, flora and fauna) and a general bushwalking guide to the World Heritage Area. It is possible to walk the Overland Track with a guide and in considerable comfort. **Craclair Tours**, run an 8-day catered walk using tents ($1,135). **Cradle Mountain Huts**, T6331 2006, www.cradlehuts.com.au, use their own private, relatively luxurious and eco-friendly cabins ($1,695, November-May).*

Franklin-Gordon Wild Rivers National Park

Travelling west from Derwent Bridge, the Lyell Highway passes right through the middle of the Franklin-Gordon Wild Rivers National Park. There are no other access points to this park except for cruises up the Gordon River from Strahan. The first stop is the **Franklin River Nature Trail** (four days return), a flat walk through rainforest to the edge of the Franklin and Surprise rivers (25-minute circuit). A few kilometres further on is the start of the **Frenchmans Cap Walking Track**. *Frenchmans Cap Walk Map and Notes* ($9) is available at the park centre at Lake St Clair where walkers can seek advice from staff on equipment and conditions. *Tasman Bush Tours*, T6423 4965, www.tasadventures.com, run a six-day walk to the summit (1,443 m) in January, March, April and November ($830 catered, $590 self-catered). Following the track for five minutes leads to the wild and renowned Franklin River. About 8 km further west is the **Donaghys Hill Wilderness Lookout**. If short of time, this is the best walk on this route; an easy route through forest, emerging onto a ridge to a lookout perched above the Franklin and Cumberland rivers with 360° views of the surrounding wilderness (2½ km, 40 minutes return). A few kilometres on there is a bridge over the **Collingwood River** and a small campsite on

Rafting the Franklin ◀◀

*The appeal of rafting the Franklin is
that it is one of the worlds few wild
rivers and carves its way through
incredibly rugged ravines and gorges. If
rapids called Churn, Cauldron and
Thunderush sound tempting contact
Rafting Tasmania, T6239 1080,*

*www.view.com.au/raftingtas Owner
Graham Mitchell was one of the first
50 people to raft the Franklin and has
done more than 100 trips. The company
runs trips lasting 4, 7 or 10 days
during November-April for 4-8
people ($1000-1700).*

the right. This is where Franklin River rafting trips usually begin. About 20 km further west the road reaches the western boundary of the World Heritage Area and just outside it are **Nelson Falls**. A 1-km boardwalk track through rainforest leads to these lovely broad falls, the rocks draped with delicate ferns and moss.

There are just two roads that significantly penetrate the World Heritage Area, the Lyell Highway and the Gordon River Road. The latter was built to service the construction of a controversial hydro-electric plant and dam. It branches off from the island's central road system at Westerway, passing **Mount Field National Park** after a few kilometres and reaching the small town of **Maydena** 13 km later. This is the last opportunity to fill the tank with relatively cheap petrol and pick up picnic supplies. **Strathgordon**, the small, former 'hydro' town, 74 km from Maydena, has a motel with café and petrol (T6280 1166, closed in winter). Just past the town a lookout affords the best view on this stretch of road, back over Lake Pedder, and 12 km from Strathgordon the road ends at **Gordon Dam**. Although it evokes mixed feelings its hard not to be impressed by the 140 m dam. *Aardvark Adventures*, T6249 4098, aardvark@tasadventures, offer an abseil down the dam ($160 day). The **visitors centre** is constructed so as to hang about 30 m above it. ■ *Daily Nov-Apr 1000-1700, May-Oct 1100-1500.*

Gordon River Road
*Colour map 8, grid C3
Gordon Dam 100 km
from Mount Field
National Park*

To get into the wilderness take the **Scotts Peak Dam Road**, 31 km past Maydena. There is also a short **Creepy Crawly Walk**, after a couple of kilometres. This 15-minute circuit is a good opportunity to see what the term 'horizontal bush' is all about. The road continues south, emerging into an open but pristine country and frequently coming close to the shore of the enlarged **Lake Pedder**. On the right the forbidding dolerite flutes of Mount Anne (1425 m), the highest peak in the southwest, and the narrow pinnacle of Lots Wife can be seen in clear weather. The **Red Knoll Lookout**, 34 km from the Gordon River Road junction, is on a small hill marking the end of the road. In clear weather the views are astounding, taking in much of the lake and the full range of the magnificent Western Arthur mountains, deep in the **Southwest National Park**.

Sleeping and eating C-E *Cockatoo Lodge*, Maydena, T6288 2293, www.tvlodge.com A range of comfortable weatherboard cottages, one operating as a hostel, and a colourful café, open daily 1800-2100. Recommended. Also free bikes, drop-off and pick-up service for walkers and 4WD day tours (around $300 per day per group). There are several great **camping** grounds much further to the west. The best along the Gordon River Road is at **Ted's Beach**, 3 km east of Strathgordon on the shore of Lake Pedder, with enclosed picnic tables, electric BBQs, sinks and water, and toilets. There are a couple toward the end of Scotts Peak Dam Road, both with wood-fireplaces and toilets. The most picturesque is at **Edgar Dam**, while the **Huon Campground** is a couple of km from Red Knoll Lookout and at the start of the **Port Davey Track**.

Tasmania

▶▶ **The Franklin River campaign**

With light bouncing off its white beach like a diamond illuminating the mountain peaks that surrounded it, Lake Pedder was described as a 'magnificent jewel'. It became a national park in 1955 but only ten years later the Hydro Electric Commission (HEC) proposed a power scheme on the Gordon River that would drown Lake Pedder under 250 sq km of water (a 'small enlargement'). Despite strident protest the HEC was allowed to go ahead and by early 1973 Lake Pedder was gone.

When rafters discovered HEC workers poking around on the Franklin river in 1976 they prepared to fight the government again. Sure enough, in 1979 the HEC recommended the damming of the lower Gordon river, thereby flooding the Franklin. After strong public dissent the government suggested an alternative dam, Gordon-above-Olga, that would save the Franklin River. A referendum was held to settle the issue but Tasmanians were only presented with two options: Gordon-below-Franklin or Gordon-above-Olga. The Tasmanian Wilderness Society conducted a huge campaign to persuade voters to write 'no dams' on their ballot paper. 45% of Tasmanians did so, but the vote for Gordon-below-Franklin was 47%. Despite the huge protest vote the Government decided not to halt the assessment process. In 1982 a new pro-dam Liberal government

quickly passed legislation approving the dam. Premier Gray called the Franklin "nothing but a brown ditch, leech-ridden, unattractive to the majority of people". Bulldozers moved into the dam site and work began.

To the conservationists, led by Launceston GP Bob Brown, this was all horribly familiar. They lobbied the Federal government and blockaded the river to oppose dam workers. On the first day of the blockade the Federal government passed a World Heritage Protection Bill and the southwest became a World Heritage Area. The blockade received huge media coverage and images of determined greenies being arrested in the rainforest flashed around the world, but the state government stood firm.

A Federal election loomed and the Labor party now promised to vigorously oppose the dam if they won. Just before the vote newspapers published a full page advert with an electrifying photograph of the Franklin: Rock Island Bend by Peter Dombrovskis, captioned 'Vote for the Franklin'. Labor won and in March 1983 passed legislation to stop construction. Premier Gray mounted a challenge in the High Court, and the case is the most important in Australian constitutional history, for it found that Commonwealth legislation had the power to override state legislation. The Franklin River remains one of the last truly wild rivers in the world.

Transport See page 861, for the *Tassie Link* summer service to Scotts Peak Dam.

Southwest National Park
Colour map 8, grid C2
The southwest has notoriously changeable weather

This 600,000 ha park is Tasmania's most wild, remote and inaccessible. It includes the rugged southern coastline shaped by seas and winds roaring in from Antarctica. The park also has temperate rainforest, glacial lakes, buttongrass plains, alpine moorlands and the most inspiring and craggy of mountain peaks and ranges. So much of the park is inaccessible that it is mostly visited only by very experienced and well-prepared bushwalkers. However, there are a few places where visitors can get a glimpse of the beauty of this wilderness. The two main tracks in the park are the Port Davey Track and the South Coast Track. **Port Davey Track** goes from Scotts Peak Dam to Melaleuca (63 km, four to five days). The route starts from Huon Campground and follows an easy but muddy path heading south through scrub, rivers and buttongrass plains, skirting the western end of the Arthur range. This walk is often combined with the South Coast Track from Melaleuca to Cockle Creek. The **South**

Tasmania

Coast Track (80 km, seven to eight days) is more varied, passing through rainforests, plains, high ridges and wild beaches. Most people fly into Melaleuca and walk east, avoiding the possiblity of being stranded for days in Melaleuca if planes are grounded by bad weather. *Par Avion* drops walkers off ($155) and will also make food drops. ■ *Park office at Mount Field National Park, T6288 1283. Fuel-stove only area.* At **Cockle Creek**, at the end of the Huon Valley Road, there are two short walks that lead to the south coast (see page 821).

Advice and information Walking in this park should not be taken lightly, walkers have died from lack of preparation and experience combined with the harsh weather conditions. A safe option is to take a guided walk. Both *Tasmanian Expeditions*, T6334 3777 and *Tasman Bush Tours*, T6424 7833, offer 9-day walks, sleeping in tents and help to carry food and equipment, for around $1300, although *Tasman Bush Tours* also offer a self-catering option at $980. See www.tasadventures.com Alternatively, fly in to Melaleuca and Port Davey; *Par Avion*, T6248 5390, www.paravion.com.au, offer flights over Federation Peak and the Arthurs combined with Port Davey boat trips as well as overnight stays of 2-3 days (½ day $190, one day $290, 2 nights $850). Another option is a longer, sea-kayaking trip with *Roaring 40s*, T6267 5000, www.tasmanian expeditions.com.au, which also includes a flight in (5 days, $1395). Flights from Cambridge airport (near Hobart) daily all year, weather permitting. Walkers considering these routes should obtain the *South Coast Walks Map and Notes* and consult Parks and Wildlife rangers. These routes and many others are also covered in *South West Tasmania* by John Chapman, a detailed walking guide. The best time for walking is Feb-Mar.

Bass Strait islands

Standing defiantly in the wild seas of the Bass Strait, battered relentlessly by the Roaring Forties, are two groups of islands. **King Island**, *the main island of the western Hunter group, is more isolated, lying more or less midway between Tasmania and Victoria. The eastern Furneaux group, of which* **Flinders Island** *is the largest, is closer to Tasmania. These remote outposts of peace and tranquility harbour plenty of wildlife and fine coastal scenery, particularly Flinders.*

King Island

King Island's flat and open plateau of lush grass feeds the cows of the commercial dairy it is best known for. Forming the western gate of Bass Strait, King Island is also a vital navigation point for ships travelling through the strait to Port Philip Bay. They are guided by the lighthouse at Cape Wickham, built after far too many ships foundered on the rocks and reefs of the island. The shipwrecks, sandy beaches, peaceful isolation and fine food attract visitors to this island, although in relatively small numbers due to its remote position. The capital is the fishing harbour of **Currie**, on the west coast. The other main towns are **Grassy** on the southeast coast, a former mining town, and **Naracoopa**, a quiet seaside village on the east coast. The **VIC** for the island is at *The Trend* shop in Currie. ■ *Daily 0900-1830, T6462 1360, www.king island.org.au Main St, Currie.*

Colour map 8, inset
Population: 1,800
King Island is 64 km
long and 27 km wide

The only way to get to the island is by air. A cargo vessel that carries vehicles does service the island but at present there are no passenger ferries. *Kendell* and *King Island Airlines*, Edwards St, Currie, T6462 1000, fly daily between the island and Melbourne *Tasair*, T6248 5577, www.tasair.com.au, operates daily from Devonport and Burnie. The airport,

Getting there & around

Tasmania

T6462 1499, is 7 km north of Currie. If you have not arranged a hire car in advance, book a taxi to pick you up, T6462 1138. There is no public transport on the island but it is pretty flat so well-suited to cycling and bike hire is available in Currie.

Sights   The island's long, isolated beaches are ideal for walking and beachcombing. Coastal birds such as short-tailed shearwaters nest in the dunes in summer and fairy penguins occupy rookeries at Grassy Harbour all year round. To see the penguins, arrive at sunset and stand quietly at a distance from the burrows. The **Lavinia Nature Reserve** in the northeast, is a refuge for birdlife, including the rare orange-bellied parrot. In the southeast, **Yarra Creek Gorge** is a remnant of the kind of bush that used to cover the island, with fern gullies and platypus. The **King Island Dairy** is known to foodies all over the world and their *Roaring Forties Blue* cheese was named cheese champion at a New York food show in 2001. Unfortunately, there are no factory tours because of food and safety regulations but it is possible to visit the fromagerie and taste or buy the produce. ■ *Mon-Fri 0900-1630, Sun 1230-1600. T6462 1348. North Rd, Loorana, 9 km north of Currie.* Another island industry is the harvesting of seaweed, employing about 100 people. Visitors can watch operations at the drying racks near Currie golf course or take a tour to learn about the industry. ■ *Tours on Sun 1000. $5, 2 hrs. T6462 1221. Bookings essential. Tours start from Currie Wharf.*

More ships have been wrecked off King Island than anywhere else in Australia. There is a shipwreck trail with explanatory signposts to some of the 70 wreck sites but only one is visible from land. The fascinating diving on the wrecks is one of the main drawcards for visitors. Some of the stories of the shipwrecks are told at the **King Island Historical Museum**, next to Currie's steel-frame lighthouse. The museum is housed in the former home of the chief lighthouse keeper. ■ *Daily 1400-1600. Entry by gold coin donation.* The island's main lighthouse is at **Cape Wickham**, on the northern tip. The 52-m white granite tower was built in 1861 and is Australia's tallest, but there are no tours or public access.

Tours &   **Bushwalking** *King Island Bush Walks*, T6461 1276, offer guided walks in Yarra Gorge
Activities   and other walks focusing on platypus and birds. **Diving** *King Island Dive Charters*, T6461 1133, based in Grassy offer shipwreck dives and reef dives to see sponges, coral and crayfish (about $100 a day). Also see www.tasmanianadventures.com.au for details of dive trips from Melbourne lasting from 4 to 7 days. **Horseriding** *King Island Trail Rides*, T6463 1147. Guided half-day rides on the beach and hinterland. **Horseracing** The King Island race club holds meetings in Dec and Jan that are the social events of the year.

Sleeping   **B** *Boomerang by the Sea*, Golf Club Rd, Currie. T6462 1288, www.bythesea.com.au 16
& eating   motel units opening onto ocean-facing verandas. Also a licensed restaurant with lots
Accommodation   of local produce and lovely sea views, daily 1800-2000. The island has one pub,
on the island is   **B-C** *Parers*, 7 Main St, Currie, T6462 1633, parers@kingisland.net.au A large complex
dominated by   with 12 motel units and a bistro open daily. **B-D** *King Island Gem*, 95 Main St, Currie.
self-contained houses   T6462 1260, www.kingislandgem.com.au A good range of budget accommodation
and units but there are   including motel rooms, A-frame houses, cabins and caravan park. **At Naracoopa**
also several motels   **C** *Baudins* on the Esplanade, T6461 1110, has attractive self-contained cottages and island produce in the colonial-themed restaurant with thatch roof and teak chairs.

Directory   **Banks** *Westpac* ATM corner of Main St and Edward St, Currie. **Bike hire** Available from the VIC. **Car Rental** *Howells Auto Rent*, 2 Meech St, Currie, T6462 1282, howellsauto@kingisland.net.au or *Cheapa Island Car Rental*, 1 Netherby Rd, Currie, T6462 1603, kimotors@kingisland.net.au **Communications** Internet at *Online Access Centre*, George St, Currie, T6462 1778. **Post Office**, Main St, Currie.

Flinders Island

Mountains, wildlife, history and its setting among a scenic jumble of islands make Flinders an appealing destination. The largest of the 54 islands in the Furneaux group, Flinders is strikingly similar to the Freycinet Peninsula with its rugged granite peaks, white crescent beaches and clear turquoise water, particularly at Killiecrankie and the **Strzelecki National Park**. Gentle rolling farmland characterizes the northern end but the east coast is hardly inhabited and is dominated by heathlands, wetlands and lagoons, often teeming with migratory birds. **Whitemark**, on the west coast, is the island's adminstrative centre. **Lady Barron**, 28 km to the south, is the main fishing port and base for diving and boat trips. Although it has fewer facilities it has a more spectacular setting within Franklin Sound with the peaks of Cape Barren Island beyond. The **VIC** is in Whitemark and is part of a gem shop on the veranda of the *Interstate* pub on Patrick Street. ■ *Mon-Fri 0830-1700, Sat 0830-1100. T6359 2160, flindersisinfo@bigpond.com The island also has 2 excellent, detailed websites; www.flinders.tco.asn.au and www.focusonflinders.com.au*

Colour map 8, inset
Population: 850

The island is 64 km long and 29 km wide

There is an Ecology Trail designed for drivers to see the highlights. Ask at the VIC for more details

Air The main way to reach the island is by air, although there is also a 8-9 hr boat trip from Bridport. *Island Airlines*, T1800 645 875, fly from **Launceston** daily ($220 return, 30 mins) and **Melbourne** (Essendon) on Mon, Wed, Fri ($330 return, 2 hrs).The airport is at Whitemark, 4 km from town. If you haven't arranged car hire from the airport book a taxi to collect you, T6359 2200. **Boat** *Southern Shipping Co*, Main St, Bridport. T6356 1753, s.ship.co@microtech.com.au Weekly service departing on Mon or Tue from **Bridport** to **Lady Barron**. Foot passengers $77 return, vehicle $372 return, (price includes driver), motorbikes $49 return, bicycles $34 return. Vehicles may have to pay an extra $100 return in wharfage charges. Also takes vehicles and foot passengers from **Port Welshpool** in Gippsland, Victoria to **Lady Barron** and **Bridport**.

Getting there
There is no public transport on the island but car hire (no bike hire) is available in Whitemark

There is little but a chapel and graveyard at **Wybalenna** but it is an important historic site. In 1830 few Aboriginal people had survived the impact of European invasion. The Governor of Tasmania, George Arthur, decided to remove those left from the Tasmanian mainland to appease terrified new settlers. A line of more than 2,000 white settlers stretched across the island and walked from one end to the other in an attempt to find every last Aboriginal person. This was known as the 'Black Line' and it was a spectacular failure, finding only two people. Eventually, though, all of the remaining tribes were visited by the 'Conciliator' George Augustus Robinson, who persuaded them to move to Wybalenna in 1834. Twelve years later only a third were left and the settlement was deemed a failure. The 45 survivors moved again to live out their days at Oyster Cove, near Hobart. Ownership of the site has recently been handed back to the Aboriginal Land Council by the Tasmanian government. Flinders Island is also an important part of the history of Aboriginal people for another reason. The lawless sealers of the 19th century, known as the 'Straitsmen', captured Tasmanian Aboriginal women to be kept as workers and 'wives' against their will.Despite the popular belief that the last indigenous Tasmanians died before 1900, the descendants of these people survived and proudly claim their Aboriginal heritage today.

At **Emita** there is an interesting museum of island history run by the Furneaux Historical Research Association. The museum holds many relics from shipwrecks, and photographs and cuttings describing the lives of local people. ■ *Sat-Sun 1300-1700. Other times by arrangement. $2, children free. T6359 2010.* **Allport and Emita beaches** nearby are popular swimming and

Around the island
Walking booklets and a Flinders topographic map are widely available in island shops

Tasmania

snorkelling spots and the only short-tailed shearwater (or muttonbird) rookery on the island is by the jetty at **Port Davies**. A road just north of **Lady Barron** links the town with Emita. This is the main route to reach the lagoons and inlets of the east coast. Logan Lagoon, Cameron Inlet and Patriarch Inlet are a birdwatcher's dream. All of these areas are frequented by thousands of water birds and migratory birds.

Strzelecki National Park, in the southwestern corner of the island, encloses a range of rounded pink and grey granite peaks rising abruptly from the plains and coastline. On the western coast, **Trousers Point** beach is an idyllic cove where the aquamarine water makes an arresting contrast against the orange lichen on the boulders that frame the beach. On the northern side of the point, sculpted limestone forms overlook the beautiful beach of **Fotheringate Bay**. Snorkelling, swimming and fishing around the beaches are popular activities but it is also a superb place for coastal and mountain bushwalking. There are picnic and camping sites at Trousers Point. The **parks office** is in Whitemark, in the *Service Tasmania* building on Lagoon Road. ■ *Office open Fri 0900-1600, T6359 2217, www.parks.tas.gov.au Standard park camping fees apply. Water supply is limited and use of fuel stoves recommended.*

There are many wonderful walks lasting just a few hours or as long as a week. Most are linear requiring walkers to retrace their steps or arrange pick-ups. The highlight for walkers will be the walk to the summit of **Mount Strzelecki** (756 m). The track passes through forest slopes and fern gullies to reach the final climb up a rocky gully to the open granite rock of the summit (6 km, five hours return). Carry food, water and both warm and wet-weather clothing as conditions can change quickly and the summit is often cold and windy. For a superb short coastal walk, a circuit around **Settlement Point** offers wonderful beaches, views and rock hopping.

Tours & activities

Bushwalking *Flinders Island Adventures*, T6359 4507, jamesluddington@bigpond.com, for guided walks or for advice on walking in the Furneaux group. This company can also arrange transport for linear walks or drop-offs for walking on Cape Barren or other islands. **4WD Tours, Boat Charters** *Flinders Island Adventures* also offer adventure tours of the island from $110 a day, also bushwalking and inter-island transport. **Diving** *Flinders Island Dive*, T6359 8429, flindersdive@yahoo.com.au A good range of trips to explore wrecks, limestone reefs and granite boulders (about $100 day). Also hire out dive and snorkelling gear. **Scenic flights** *Sinclair Air Charter*, T6359 3641.

Sleeping

C-D *Interstate Hotel*, Patrick St, Whitemark. T6359 2114, interstatehotel@trump.net.au Comfortable rooms in a restored historic pub, some with ensuite, breakfast included. The pub also has a bistro, meals available daily 1200-1400, 1800-2000. **C** *Furneaux Tavern*, T6359 3521, Franklin Par, Lady Barron. Motel-style ensuite rooms overlooking the sound, meals daily 1200-1400, 1800-2000. **C** *Yaringa*, Holloway St, Lady Barron, T6359 4522. 3 modern, self-contained cottages, clean and fresh with balconies overlooking Franklin Sound. **E** *Nunamina Hostel*, Franklin Par, Lady Barron. T6359 3617, chris_rhodes@bigpond.com Modern, comfortable hostel sleeping 12 in 2 and 3-bed rooms.

Directory

Banks *Westpac* agency, Patrick St. No ATMs on the island. **Car Hire** *Bowman Lees*, Robert St, Whitemark. T6359 2388. From $50 a day. **Communications** Internet available at *Online Access*, Lagoon Rd, Whitemark, T6359 2396. **Post Office** agency, Patrick St, Whitemark.

Background

History

"Australian history is almost always picturesque; indeed, it is also so curious and strange, that it is itself the chiefest novelty the country has to offer and so it pushes the other novelties into second and third place. It does not read like history, but like the most beautiful lies; and all of a fresh new sort, no mouldy old stale ones. It is full of surprises and adventures, the incongruities, and contradictions, and incredibilities; but they are all true, they all happened."

Mark Twain, *More Tramps Abroad*, London, 1897.

The arrival of man

From their evolution in Africa, *Homo erectus*, and then *Homo sapiens*, walked into Asia but their expansion from these strongholds to the 'new worlds' was barred by either water or ice for hundreds of thousands of years. It is true that parts of New Guinea and northwest Australia are tantalizingly close to the islands of Southeast Asia, but even during the severest of ice ages there have always been deep channels between them. It has never been possible to walk from Asia to Meganesia. Incidentally, this was one of the most profound clues to continental drifting ignored by most geologists of the early 20th century. Alfred Russell Wallace, Darwin's co-formulator of the theory of natural selection, noticed in the 1860s that these channels marked an invisible line, a threshold that heralded an incredible and inexplicable shift in types of terrestrial animal life from one landmass to the other. It is known today as *Wallace's Line*.

The idea that Aboriginal people arrived by boat is one of three relatively new concepts that have changed the traditional picture of Aboriginal history. The second is when this happened. There are no dates, not even any folk memories of the first coming of humanity to Meganesia (in geological terms the islands of Tasmania, Australia, the Torres Strait, and New Guinea), and that's because the time of first migration has been pushed back by slowly accumulating evidence to over 45,000 and possibly as much as 60,000 years ago. Finally anthropologists are now certain that Australian Aboriginals and the original New Guineans are one and the same people, separated by just a few thousand years of cultural divergence, and New Guineans were amongst the earliest and most intensive farmers on the planet.

Anthropologists have identified a general 'great leap forward' in human culture, a time when our ancestors first refined their previously clumsy stone tools, clearly invented boats, experimented with art and perhaps agriculture, and probably first became superstitious and intellectually curious. There is no geographic site as yet identified with these first cultural stirrings, but some scholars have been struck by the coincidence that these beginnings seem to coincide with humanity's first escape from its long enclosure on the Africa-Asia landmass. Tim Flannery, the Director of the South Australian Museum, has suggested that the peoples of Southeast Asia that first began their island-hopping progress toward Meganesia were perhaps the principal pioneers of the great leap. As they finally crossed Wallace's Line they encountered totally new environments and fauna for the first time in human history, and swiftly developed new technologies and social structures to exploit and interpret them to the full. Once developed, the benefits of these new cultural advances would have caused the ideas to spread rapidly, both onward with their authors and back to the Asian peoples and beyond to Europe, Africa and eventually the Americas.

Whether or not this is the case, there is little doubt that the peoples who finally crossed from Asia to Meganesia around 55,000 years ago carried with them one of the most, if not the most, technologically advanced cultures of the time. That they already had a grasp of the potential of agriculture seems likely, as some of those that settled in the northern highlands, later to become isolated as island New Guinea, had developed intensive farming systems by as much as 10,000 years ago. Population expansion amongst the early settlers in the new fertile New Guinean lands would have been exponential, and it cannot have been long before groups were heading south in search of new land.

The early Aborigines carried with them a notable firepower. Stone, bone and wooden weapons honed to perfection during the many generations of island-hopping from Asia. These hunter-gatherers had encountered, for the first time in human history, lands where they were the undisputed top predator. One of their new weapons would have been psychological, a new feeling of unbridled power, a sense of their own dominance. The Australian animals they met would have been woefully ill-prepared for such an encounter.

The few mammalian predators could not hope to compete with such a powerful new force, either in direct confrontation or for prey as the human population increased. As for the giant reptiles, the awesome *Megalania* and the giant snake *Wonambi* (6 m long with a head the size of a serving tray) were ambush predators, strictly territorial. They would have been a serious hazard to the lone hunter, but in the face of collective competition were as doomed as their mammalian counterparts. The only large Australian predator to survive to the present day is the saltwater crocodile, the feared 'saltie', probably protected by its primarily aquatic habitat.

As for the herbivores, the now vanished giants of the vast Australian plains, there can surely be little doubt that the coming of humanity was the decisive factor in the extinction of so many. On virtually every island and landmass outside of Africa-Asia a wave of faunal extinctions has followed hard on the heels of human occupation. Ecologists in both America and Australia have argued for a climate-driven cause, linking the disappearances with some phase of the last ice age, but in both cases the bulk of the fauna had previously survived dozens of ice ages and inter-glacial periods. Climate change may have weakened some species, even driven them to relatively small strongholds, but the evidence is almost overwhelming that humans, either directly or indirectly, delivered the final *coup de grace*.

An ecological crisis?

Evidence is also mounting that the coming of humanity had an extraordinarily profound effect on Australian flora. First indirectly and then, in the face of calamity, purposefully. Core samples from around Australia, but particularly in the east, seem to indicate that the now dominant **eucalypts** were surprisingly rare prior to around 60,000 years ago. These cores also sometimes show high concentrations of carbon – ash – at the point at which the gums began their ascendancy. Could this be another climate-driven coincidence? Again, some researchers think not.

A powerful, and frightening scenario may well have followed the local demise of the large herbivores. Without munching herbivores the forest undergrowth and plains brush would have proliferated, in wet times an impenetrable green morass, in the dry a huge store of kindling. Forest fires are natural, lightening-ignited phenomena on every continent, and especially common in hot and dry Australia. Massive build-ups of combustible fuel would have resulted in equally massive, and quite catastrophic fires raging through the forest and bush, deadly to the native flora and fauna, and humans alike.

In the face of this crisis the early peoples of Australia would have realized that they had to artificially keep the brush low. They would have been forced to fight fire with fire, continuously lighting small-scale blazes to prevent large-scale conflagrations. Whatever the cause, the adoption of fire for more than just cooking and heating was to have many and widespread consequences.

Most important for the first Australians was the realization that fire could have multiple uses. Not only did it prevent, life-threatening bushfires, but it was also discovered that controlled blazes had a multiplicity of uses. They could be used for offence or defence against antagonistic neighbours, or to signal distant groups or family members. They could also be used to drive and herd game to favoured trapping areas, and burn-offs encouraged new grass growth of the succulent shoots favoured by many of the Aboriginals' prey. It would also not have been lost on them how much more easily they could navigate, travel and hunt across burnt-off land.

A more-or-less constant regime of small-scale bushfires had other, less useful consequences. Crucially for the future development of Australian flora, it naturally favoured fire-resistant and fire-promoting species. Foremost amongst these are the eucalypts, the ubiquitous gum trees that once were minor players in the ecology of the continent, but are now almost all-pervading. Dry and wet rainforests have been driven back to relatively tiny refuges around Australia's eastern periphery, while the great gum woodlands have marched on triumphant.

The catch-22 of the Aboriginal's fire regime locked Australia into another ecological cul-de-sac. The total number of animals a landmass can support, its faunal biomass, depends on a number of factors. Two of these Australia already had a paucity of – water and nutrients. The fire regime would have accelerated erosion, further depleting soil nutrient levels, and would also have significantly lowered the amount of water and nutrients locked up within the plants themselves. Most obviously of all, the potential number of animals is crucially constrained by the sheer biomass of plant material available as foodstuff. With much of this being continually burned off, the amount of prey available to both humans and their competitors would have had a much reduced upper limit.

Partnership with the land

The early pioneers into each part of the continent would have had a relatively easy time of it, but once the honeymoon was over the challenges that faced the first Australians were immense. The extinction of the large herbivores and the bushfire crisis were huge blows to an already very specialized, and hence vulnerable, ecology. Without human intervention, massive bushfires could have decreased the viability of many other animal species. As it was, the introduction of the fire regime seems to have stabilized the situation and prevented further degradation of the environment. It was a fix, but a fix that stood the test of time.

As well as coping with a damaged environment and a much reduced quantity of game, most Aboriginal peoples faced challenges never previously faced by humanity. Paramount among these was the scarcity and unpredictably of water supply, and the consequent boom-and-bust fluctuations of many of the species of animals hunted for food. Paradoxically this actually seems to have resulted in a better standard of diet than that experienced by many peoples in more stable environments.

That they did so has two chief causes. The relative scarcity of food resulted in the early Australians becoming experts in everything that could possibly have nutritional value, from roots to roos, and moths to mussels. In most parts of the continent people could draw on their knowlededge of a variety of in-season fruits and animals, more than sufficient to sustain them. In the process they also discovered an extensive natural medicine chest that helped keep them healthy. That this natural larder was not over-stretched is paradoxically because of the boom-and-bust ecology. In many environments the really bad times are rare. Humans, though slow breeders, can build populations that make the most of relatively long periods of prosperity. The ENSO- (El Niño Southern Oscillation) driven Australian climate dictated the reverse pattern, with Aboriginal populations kept at the low levels sustainable in periods of drought. In times of plenty there was more than enough to go around.

This pegging of population and resultant 'abundance' of food is perhaps one of the reasons why farming was rarely employed by Aboriginal peoples. ENSO also makes farming extremely difficult, with attempts at planting crops frequently foiled by drought conditions, but one of the key factors that mitigated against Aboriginal agriculture was the lack of suitable species. It is now becoming accepted that under the experimental conditions of our early ancestors only a handful of plants and animals would have had exactly the right characteristics for domestication. In Australia all the large herbivores that may have been suitable quickly disappeared and to this day only one indigenous crop has been cultivated to any extent – the macadamia nut. The unrelated factors of no domesticated animals and continental isolation were to later combine to make the Aboriginals tragically susceptible to European diseases.

As is now widely appreciated, it is agriculture that has provided human cultures with the excess labour required to build the urban trappings of civilization. Leading a hunter-gatherer lifestyle with little incentive or opportunity for farming, the Australian peoples rarely created permanent settlements. Over much of the continent not even clothes, let alone buildings were required for warmth. Buildings were also unnecessary for either safety, keeping animals or the storage of foodstuffs. Only in the colder south were some of these trappings adopted. Here some groups built stone huts, sewed together blankets and clothes from animal skins and embarked on intensive aquaculture, building sophisticated canals and traps to catch fish and eels.

With strong parallels with the peoples in North America, the Aboriginal cultures came to place a great value on their relationship with the land. Disturbances to their environment, or deviation from the fire regime (sometimes called 'fire-stick farming'), were recognized as threats to survival, and this relationship came to be regarded as a sacred custodianship. Nomadic peoples rarely develop the concept of land ownership in the western sense, but the first Australians maintained strict territories, each carefully tended and managed by its resident people. Embarking on a journey through another group's land involved careful negotiation.

In environments as difficult as most that Australia has to offer, isolation can be lethal. Inter-tribal contact was maintained through constant trading, mostly for ochre or precious materials. These were mined in a large number of sites across Australia. There were also great regional meetings, social corroborees that usually coincided with an abundant, seasonal food source such as the bogong moths in the Victorian Alps. Over tens of thousands of years this helped maintain a remarkable consistency of culture across such a vast area.

Given such a prodigious tenure it is hardly surprising that a folk memory of the original coming to America of the ancestors' of the Aboriginal people has been lost. Aboriginal history is passed from generation to generation in the form of oral stories, part of the all-pervasive culture of 'dreaming' that also encompasses law, religion, customs and knowledge. These creation myths talk of a period when powerful ancestors, both human and animal, strode the land, creating natural features, plants, animals and peoples alike. Parts of the dreaming were also immortalized, and illustrated to younger generations through songs and dances, rock art and carvings. It is probable that Australia now has the oldest such art on the planet.

Aboriginal culture is the longest uninterrupted culture the modern world has witnessed. Over tens of thousands of years the first peoples of Australia developed unique strategies to ensure their survival in the face of some of the world's most difficult environments. They built a rich cultural heritage, a phenomenal knowledge of their land and its natural resources, prodigious internal trade routes, a carefully managed environment, and a stable population which was in harmony with that environment rather than in conflict with it.

The most significant event in Australia of the last 50 millennia was almost certainly the ending of the ice age about 9,000 years ago. Rising sea levels severed both

Background

New Guinea and Tasmania from the mainland, leaving the latter island with a population of about 5,000 people. Anthropologists now believe such a small population left the Tasmanian people vulnerable to disease, disaster and the subsequent loss of valuable cultural knowledge, contributing to the islanders' distinctive differences from mainland Aboriginal culture. At the time of first European contact with the Tasmanians they had no bone implements, no stone tools, no boomerangs, spear throwers or dingos, and no clothing. Surprisingly, in such a coastal environment, they did not eat fish and indeed reacted with horror when offered some by early European explorers. They also lacked the ability to make fire. A firestick was always kept burning and carried from place to place. If this should be extinguished a group would have to seek out another tribe possessing a firestick who were obligated to give fire, even to a traditional enemy. It is thought that Tasmanian Aboriginals may have lost knowledge when skilled individuals died unexpectedly. Ancient middens (campsites or refuse dumps) reveal that fish were eaten and bone tools such as needles used until about 3,500 years ago, indicating that later people lost the ability to sew warm skin cloaks similar to those worn in southern Australia.

Old and new worlds collide

Elsewhere around the world, other peoples were finally wrestling for mastery of their own environments. Conditions for agriculture were perfect in the 'fertile crescent', and its development enabled large-scale urban cultures for the first time. Like shock-waves, the ideas and technologies that these peoples developed spread from their Middle-eastern epicentre to Europe and many parts of Asia. These in turn fuelled population explosions that then allowed for even greater technological and agricultural advances. Fierce competition between rival empires resulted, a process that shunted populations around the vast landmass. For a variety of reasons much of the pressure was exerted on the peoples of Europe, and those in the far west were the most squeezed of all, with nowhere to go but the sea. By 1400 AD they had developed impressive maritime and military technologies. They also began to experience a growing need for raw materials and extra living space, nurtured a great thirst for personal and national wealth, and, incidentally but critically, had inherited one of the most crusading religions the world has ever seen.

It is little known that the Europeans weren't the first foreign visitors after Australia's long isolation. Macassans from the Indonesian island of Sulawesi were visiting the northern coasts by around 1500, possibly for centuries earlier. Later, following economic and political destabilization caused by the coming of the Portuguese, the Macassans became the first outsiders to regularly visit Australia, their primary purpose to harvest 'trepang', the sea slug. They also traded with the local Aborigines, and this regular contact with foreigners helped the local indigenous peoples of the Top End to cope far better with European culture, aggression and diseases when they finally began to arrive in earnest in the 1860s.

Some would argue that the first significant date in the European exploration of Australia is 1493. In that year, in one of the most breathtaking carve-ups in history, Pope Alexander VI apportioned the right of exploration of everything west of a certain meridian to the Spanish, and everything in the opposite direction to the Portuguese. The fact that the world is a sphere seems to have been overlooked and the newly encountered 'spice islands' of the far east were soon the subject of a squabble. It now seems possible that the Portuguese knew a little more about the landmass south of New Guinea than they were letting on.

Whatever the case, by the end of the 16th century the published information on the much conjectured upon *Terra Australis* (southern land) was negligible, consisting of just a few charts that clearly rely more on guesswork than actual knowledge, and a small passage written in 1598 by one Cornelius Wytfliet that begins "*The Australis Terra is the most southern of lands, and is separated from New Guinea by a narrow strait.*" In a nearly aborted voyage of discovery in 1606 the Spaniard Luis de Torres negotiated his way through this strait, and is the first European we know by name to have glimpsed the Australian mainland, even though he mistook it for a group of islands. That the certain knowledge of Torres Strait remained, for whatever reason, unavailable to the other sea-faring nations for over 150 years, had a profound effect on how the exploration of Australian shores proceeded.

This is to jump the gun, however, for we need to look at the first really important date of 1584. In that year the overbearing king of Spain, Phillip II, decided to punish the Dutch for their religious heresies by barring their ships to Lisbon, a port that had latterly come under his control. Hitherto the Dutch had done a roaring trade as the hauliers of Europe, picking up the goods the Portuguese brought back from the Far East and transporting them all over the western seaboard. Phillip, having failed to subjugate them with the sword, was now trying to cut their economic base from under them. The Dutch were nothing if not willful, however, and instead they set about fetching the goods from the Far East themselves. In 1597 the first fleet returned in triumph and in 1611 Hendrik Brouwer discovered that sailing due east from the Cape of Good Hope for 3,000 miles, and then turning north, cut about two months off the Holland-Java journey time. Five years later Dirk Hartog overshot the mark and found his namesake island off Shark Bay. A visible landmark really opened the route up, and soon the Dutch were establishing a fair picture of the west coast of what came to be called New Holland, wrecking many of their ships on it in the process.

In 1642, a generation after Torres found his strait, Dutchman Abel Tasman, failed to find it. As a result of his failure, however, he retraced his steps, properly charted the northwest coast of New Holland, headed south and found Tasmania (he called it Van Diemen's Land after his Governor-General), then west to 'discover' New Zealand. With equal enthusiasm, but less success, an English buccaneer, William Dampier, convinced the English government to fit him out a ship for exploration in 1699. Had he followed his original plan and travelled via Cape Horn rather than Good Hope, he could easily have been the one to sail into Botany Bay, but he took the traditional route, also failed to find the strait and instead sailed the now well-worn western trail.

There things stood for 70 years until Captain James Cook was sent by the English government to observe a transit of Venus in Tahiti. By now the English were very much caught up in the spirit of European exploration and he was instructed, while in the area, to check out New Zealand and, if possible, chart the hitherto unexplored east coast of New Holland. In all this he was completely successful, spending six months charting New Zealand and then sailing west as planned. This east coast was sufficiently far from the western coast that it was entirely possible the two were actually unconnected, and he named the 'new territory' New South Wales. He must have seen the Australian environment at its best and gave glowing descriptions of it in his reports to his government. His positive, though fateful and misinformed opinions were summarized in *The Voyages of Captain Cook*:

> "The industry of man has had nothing to do with any part of it, and yet we find all such things as nature hath bestowed upon it in a flourishing state. In this extensive country it can never be doubted but what most sorts of grain, fruit, roots, etc., of every kind, would flourish were they brought hither, planted and cultivated by the hands of industry; and here is provender for more cattle, at all seasons of the year, than can ever be brought into the country."

Two of the most different cultures imaginable of their day were now on an inevitable collision course.

Background

The process of colonization

No sooner had the British Empire nonchalantly claimed a large new territory than it was ignominiously turfed out of an old one. In 1782 the American colonies success-fully gained independence, thus creating all sorts of problems for the British govern-ment, not least of which was what to do with tens of thousands of convicts, who continued to be sentenced to 'transportation'. The other colonies swiftly declined to accept them, and the practice of dropping them off in West Africa was abandoned on the grounds that this simply meant a nastier death for the transportees than they could have otherwise enjoyed at the end of a noose back home.

Sir Joseph Banks, Cook's botanist on the *Endeavour*, had suggested New South Wales as early as 1779, but it wasn't until 1786 that Prime Minister William Pitt agreed to the suggestion, then formally put forward by Lord Sydney, the minister responsible for felons. The following year Arthur Phillip's 'first fleet' set out, less a grand colonial voyage than a handy solution to a pressing problem.

Botany Bay was not to Phillip's liking so he explored the harbour just to the north, Port Jackson, that had been noted, but not entered, by Cook. A quick scout round revealed that this was just the spot and Sydney Cove was duly named as the site for the new penal colony. On the 26 January 1788 the British flag was unfurled and a toast was raised to the King's health. Governor Phillip must have been a very strong-willed and fair man to have seen the colony through its first five years as well as he did. Livestock and cereals fared worse than expected and rationing was necessary for over two years, but another town was established a few miles inland and a further colony at Norfolk Island. Almost from the start con-victs were motivated by grants of land in exchange for good conduct and the local Aborigines were by and large not treated too badly, though how they really viewed this usurpation of their land can only be guessed at. They did not know that this trickle of white men was the prelude to a flood. Had they had the slight-est inkling it is likely that resistance would have been fierce, but instead a straight-forward curiosity and casual acceptance of gifts seem to have been the most common response in the first few years.

The rag-tag make-up of the early 'settlers' – the soldiers and thieves, forgers and murderers, Irish rebels and English farmers – made for an eclectic mix. Most, as the eloquent pickpocket Barrington reminds us, were unwilling pioneers:

> "True patriots we, for, be it understood,
> We left our country for our country's good.
> No private views disgraced our generous zeal,
> What urged our travels was our country's weal."

But unwilling or no, there were soon fortunes to be made. When Phillip had to resign through ill-health the government of the colony temporarily passed into the hands of the military commanders sent to guard the convicts. The military (the 'rum corps') saw this as an opportunity to really open up various trades, particularly in land, sheep and alcohol, and line their pockets in the process. Emancipated convicts with an eye for the main chance also took every advantage that came their way. For nearly 15 years Phillip's civic successors tried to bring the soldiers to heel, a period that had its dramatic conclusion with the virtual mutiny of the new economic mas-ters, and the arrest and expulsion of Governor Bligh (yes, that Bligh!) in 1806.

Two things spurred both the expansion of the New South Wales colony beyond that of a simple penal settlement, and the establishment of other Australian colo-nies. The most immediate was an expanding population of convicts, free-settlers and their offspring, all of whom required land for grazing, cultivation and speculation. The other was the possibility that the French, once more the arch enemy, would muscle in on 'British' turf. At some point the apparent potential of this vast new land sank into the minds of colonial secretaries and New South Wales governors alike. It was quickly conceived that the French should have none of this scarcely explored territory and that the British Empire should have all of it. Exploration, both publicly and privately sponsored, was encouraged.

The Blue Mountains proved an amazing obstacle, the crossing of them only accomplished after 20 years of repeated effort. Explorers elsewhere progressed more swiftly. The most important maritime explorer of his time was Matthew Flinders who arrived at Port Jackson in 1795 as a midshipman. It was Flinders, and his associate George Bass, who first demonstrated that Van Diemen's Land was separate from New South Wales, Flinders who first charted the unknown southern coasts and circumnavigated the whole continent in 1801-03, proving it at last to be one vast island. It was also Matthew Flinders who suggested the name 'Australia' for this new continent, a name that quickly caught on in preference to New Holland and became more or less official in 1817. Flinders did his work in the nick of time, for the French were indeed very interested in this new land and their explorers Nicholas Baudin and Louis de Freycinet also made many key discoveries.

The inland of Australia proved far more arduous, and was almost solely undertaken by the British or under British auspices with substantial help from indigenous recruits. There were high hopes of vast swathes of rich land in the interior, even of a substantial inland sea. The cracking of the Blue Mountains opened the way to the Bathurst Plains and beyond. By 1830 explorers such as John Oxley, Hume and Hovell, and Charles Sturt had helped give white Australians a mental picture of much of the southern and eastern parts of the continent.

Territorial conquest

For the first 40 years only a trickle of free-settlers had journeyed out with the convicts, despite the lure of free passage, but from 1830 numbers steadily increased. New South Wales slowly came to be seen as a land of opportunity and by the mid-1830s the inbound ships carried more free-settlers than convicts. Many of the new settlers had a better knowledge of agricultural and trade development than the soldiers and convicts, and better links with Britain.

Hard on the heels of the explorers were the new pastoralists, ambitious men who claimed vast areas of land on which they might prosper, largely by might rather than right. These 'squatters', given to scorn the laws and edicts of distant authorities, were a severe bane to more fair-minded colonial governments, a boon to less scrupulous ones. Farmers had quickly discovered that cattle and vegetables fared a lot more poorly than was expected in the new lands, but the more experimental soon imported strains of grain and sheep that might be better suited to the relatively arid climate. Even then the poor soil meant huge acreages were required to raise profitable quantities of wool and wheat.

Wool soon became the single most important industry in the colonies. With a large and expanding British market, hungry for every bale, the Australian sheep population simply exploded during the 1830s. Millions of them teemed over the countryside, tended by thousands of mostly convict shepherds. Wool made fortunes for hundreds of men, was the main catalyst for the Murray steamboats and later the railways, helped lay the foundation stones of new, non-penal towns, caused the felling and waste of mile upon mile of forest and scrub, and hugely aggravated conflict with the Aboriginals. Land won for the sheep was land lost to the indigenous peoples and it is estimated that an area the size of Ireland was invaded by the pastoralists every year during the 1830s.

Background

It took decades for Europeans to even begin to understand the Aboriginals' complex relationship with their land. It is ill understood even today. Most people simply didn't care and some, particularly the poor or emancipated, were happy that there were people on a rung lower than theirs. It was assumed that as the Aboriginals did not farm they had no concept or right of ownership, that since they were nomadic they could simply move out of the way, and that as their technology was inferior so was their culture and indeed so were they as people. From the very beginning there were settlers who considered them sub-human, and right up to the 1960s many Aboriginals believed themselves regarded as 'fauna'.

Today it is vigorously debated how much the early authorities were guided by the policy of *terra nullius*, the idea that Australia was an empty land, free for the taking. *Terra nullius* was a legal fiction based on the premise that land ownership was only proved by land cultivation. The colonial authorities did not think for a second that Australia was empty but rather that Aboriginal people had no legal claim upon it. At the time it seems likely that whatever angst was occurring in the minds of liberal societies and authorities in England or urban Australia, the reality on the crucial frontier was promoted by the pioneering settler, over which the authorities had little control. For many that reality was one of conflict. *Terra nullius* was immaterial, there was a future to secure and it was 'either us or them'.

Disease did a lot of the damage, with thousands of Aboriginals undoubtedly dying of smallpox and flu, syphilis and typhoid. The Europeans long association with domestic animals had fermented a rich brew of transmissable infectious diseases against which, like the native Americans before them, the native Australians had little defence. Sometimes, however, there were survivors, some of whom could not be persuaded to join a Christian mission, work as a farm hand or join the native police. Then some of the of the most intense confrontations took place. A minority of Aboriginals fought back, spearing settlers and attempting to drive them back from whence they had come. The response, both official and not, was often savage. There are known instances of whole groups being rounded up and shot wholesale as retribution for something as trivial as the death of a bullock. On the other hand some groups simply tried to maintain their existence, living off the land as their ancestors had done. Here less brutal tactics were sometimes employed by the Europeans, such as the poisoning of their waterholes.

By 1850 it was all over bar the shouting. Aboriginal peoples reached some of their lowest populations ever, driven almost entirely from Tasmania and Victoria and with hugely reduced numbers in New South Wales and South Australia. Aboriginal people in the northern regions simply had to wait longer for dispossession. By the 1870s and 1880s many had suffered a similar fate to the southerners, although they survived in greater numbers with a more intact culture. When a little later Charles Darwin's theories gained widespread notice, it was widely expected that these peoples would become extinct. Their perceived inferiority surely meant they could not survive in the face of a more 'advanced' people. It was simply a case of the 'survival of the fittest'.

Land of golden opportunity

Where the indigenous peoples had lost, the invaders had gained. The wool and grain industries were booming, coal and copper were being profitably mined, and there were many towns adopting the trappings of a civilized life. Even the convicts had for the most part outlived their usefulness and there were repeated calls for the end of transportation.

The middle of the 18th century was a landmark moment in Australian history. Wool was the bedrock of the economy of the colonies, and would remain so for another 125 years, but it was the discovery of gold that caught the world's attention.

Gold was actually discovered in the Australian colonies, mostly by shepherds and station-hands, at least as early as 1842, but during the 1840s neither the governments or squatters welcomed the social upheaval that a gold rush would bring and the knowledge of gold-bearing land was vigorously suppressed.

The Californian rushes of 1849 were the eventual trigger for the Australian finds. Some returning diggers may not have come back to the colonies with riches, but they certainly came with knowledge. Even while in the USA, many Australian diggers were casting their minds back to the foothills and geology of the Great Dividing Range, wondering at their similarity to the terrain in California. A good find meant more than a supplement to a poor income – a man could make a fortune overnight. With such prospectors abroad, public awareness of Australian gold was inevitable.

Gold was first publicly found in New South Wales in 1851 and soon after in Victoria. The discoveries created a world-wide sensation with hundreds taking passage to the colonies within days of the arrival of the news. In theory any gold found was crown property, but as with the squatters the colonial governments knew they had a flood on their hands that could only be regulated, not stopped. In a surprisingly egalitarian move both colonial governments instituted rules that opened up the new goldfields to all comers. Any gold-seeker had to buy a licence for the privilege of searching, and could select a plot of a small given size. After the easy stuff had mostly gone the system proved unworkable and heavy-handed regulation provoked a mini-revolution, but at first it had given everyone the 'fair go' that Australia has become famous for.

By the end of the decade the fledgling colony of Victoria was the richest and most populous in Australia, outshining its northern neighbour, to the latter's considerable chagrin. Both Ballarat and Bendigo could claim to be among Australia's five largest cities, and could do so for another couple of decades. The population of the colonies had more than doubled to more than a million, over half of them in Victoria, and about 80% of the gold-rush immigrants never went home, making it one of the world's largest peaceful migrations. Australia was well and truly on the map and started to attract significant investment from overseas.

Also by 1860 the transportation of convicts to the eastern colonies had finally ceased. Nearly 160,000 had made that enforced trip over the previous 60-odd years, with few returning to their homelands. The accusation is often jokingly levelled at Australians that they're all descended from thieves. In fact the number of gold-seeking immigrants between 1850 and 1860 dwarfed the number of earlier convicts. It may have been founded on a penal colony but Australia is no felon nation, it's a nation of entrepreneurs.

The next 30 years were ones of considerable consolidation in the Australian colonies. Wool had set the ball rolling, and would keep it rolling for decades, but gold was the catalyst that really sped the pace of progress. Mining corporations and agriculturalists eagerly took to the new technology of steam, fuelling Australia's own industrial revolution, and irrigation was equally enthusiastically introduced. Railways were built and telegraph lines constructed in the face of incredible physical difficulties. The urbanization of the country continued apace with huge city populations living off the vast but poorly populated agricultural regions.

Technological progress was matched by important social advances, in many cases pioneering the way for the rest of the world. Colonial governments almost competed to bring in new democratic legislation and extend free education. In 1861 about one in four European immigrants were illiterate, a figure reduced to one in forty by 1891. The unions forced a shorter working day, then a shorter working week, opening up Saturday afternoons for sport and leisure. The outdoor climate, large accessible spaces, and huge urban populations contrived to ensure that sport itself became almost a religion, and those competing successfully at international level were the new gods. By 1900 Australians were avid followers of home-grown boxers, skullers, jockeys, cricketers, athletes and footballers. Crowds at some football and cricket matches could be measured in the tens of thousands, dwarfing those in other countries. With the rise in sport came a rise in gambling, a habit Australia has never lost.

At the same time artists of the talented Heidelberg school were finally seeing the landscape in an Australian light, and interpreting it realistically for the for first time to the fascination of the largely urban population. They also led the way to a growing appreciation of indigenous flora and fauna. Bushwalking societies formed and there were moves to form reserves around outstandingly beautiful natural landmarks. These forerunners of the National Parks began to be declared in the 1870s and 1880s.

Societies very much at odds with the natural environment were also formed. A nostalgia for 'home' led groups of misguided amateur naturalists to import countless species of plants and animals in the hope that the alien landscape of Australia could be transformed into one huge English garden. Other animals were brought over as pets or for stock, and these too often escaped into the wild. Foxes were introduced, for example, so that people could participate in an authentic hunt. Today dozens of these species have gone feral, each one disturbing the native ecology to a greater or lesser degree.

That much of this progress was at the expense of the traumatized indigenous peoples and the environment they had so carefully managed went largely unnoticed and unremarked. The surviving Aboriginal population watched from the fringes, driven either to the very margins of society or out into the near-deserts of the Outback. Their cultures were almost fatally fractured and reservoirs of knowledge were disappearing fast. They were rarely actively hunted down any more, though cold-blooded massacres did occur until at least 1928, but a decline in aggression did not mean an increase in acceptance. That they would themselves soon disappear entirely still seemed entirely likely to the white population, so there was little need to include them in the future of the colonies.

The lustre wanes

In the 1890s falling global prices for the principal Australian exports coincided with the topping out of a spiralling frenzy of stock and land speculation. The combination of a drop in income with huge borrowings, loss of British investment with over-valued stock, led to an economic crash of unprecedented proportions in 1893. Soaring the highest, Victoria had the furthest to fall and Melbourne faced a crisis that saw people literally starving to death.

Just two years later a sapping drought gripped the country, decimating grain harvests and halving the sheep population by 1903. Australia has for much of its recent history been one of the world's most important grain exporters. In 1902 the usual flow was reversed with wheat being imported for the first time since the height of the gold rushes.

Its an ill-wind that blows nobody any good, however, and the crisis of the 1890s was the period when Western Australia finally became a colony of note. In 1885 Perth could have barely mustered 5,000 souls where Melbourne had over 400,000. Its initial low population meant that the effects of the drought, less significant than in the east anyway, were a relatively minor problem. A stricken and restless population in the east also provided a pool of labour and talent should the western colony become more attractive.

By the early 1890s gold was being found a few hundred miles east of Perth, and within a few years the finds were becoming fantastic, nearly rivalling the best years of Ballarat and Bendigo. A new rush was soon in full swing and by 1901 Perth, and the goldfields town of Kalgoorlie, both ranked in the country's top 10 largest cities.

Federation and nationhood

Up to about 1890 the six Australasian colonies and New Zealand had jealously guarded their independence from each other. Proud of their differences they each operated their own institutions, governments, services and military forces, united only solidly by currency, the environment and a shared heritage.

Their military forces were scant, however, and the colonies still relied heavily on the navy of the British Empire for defence. During the late 1800s other nations such as France, Germany, Japan and Russia were becoming powerful, challenging the Empire for hegemony over maritime and continental trade routes. In Australia there were very real fears that some of these powers might have designs on Australian territory, and in the late 1880s Britain pointed out that the colonies' military forces were hugely inadequate and would be far more effective if united under as single command structure.

In 1889 the prime minister of New South Wales made a bold step. He suggested that the proposed federation of armed forces be given far greater scope, that it should be widened to a political federation of the colonies. Two years later he had helped bring together a convention of delegates from most of them, including New Zealand, to draw up a draft constitution.

There things stood until the economic downturn of 1893 when Victoria in particular revived the idea, noting that an open internal market might help revive her fortunes. In that year John Quick devised a three-step strategy for federation. A poll in each state would elect delegates to another convention; this convention would then draw up a full constitution; the people of each colony would then vote on whether they would want to be included in the new Commonwealth of Australia.

The delegates first met in 1897. There were none from Queensland, which stayed ambivalent to the end, and also none from New Zealand. An economic recovery across the Tasman Sea had resulted in the view that joining with the Australian colonies was unnecessary, and they opted for political independence. In the referendums of 1898-1900 the southern states were the most enthusiastic. New South Wales was less so, but endorsed federation when promised the capital territory. Queensland's 'yes' vote was by a whisker, just 4,000 people deciding the outcome. Had it not been for the recent influx of goldminers from the eastern states to Western Australia, to a man keen on the idea, that colony might also have remained aloof.

The Commonwealth officially came into existence on 1 January 1901. Until Canberra was decided upon and built, Melbourne was the first federal capital, remaining so until 1927. The flag adopted was a well-received combination of the British Union Jack and the constellation of the Southern Cross.

Federation effectively ushered in nationhood, colonies became states, and now the relationship with the 'mother country' became more complex. On the one hand ties had never been stronger. Many who held high office in 1914 were British born, Britain was still Australia's biggest market for most of its exports, and British rather than Australian history was still considered more important in schools. On the other hand a British visitor to the new nation had to be careful not to offend local sensibilities. He or she would perhaps be called a 'pommy' (suspected to be a cockney derivative of 'immigrant' from 'pomegranate') instead of the warmer 'new chum' that had been in vogue since the gold rushes of the 1850s.

They would also have noticed signs encouraging people to 'buy Australian' and shun imported goods from the Empire and elsewhere. That they could be encouraged so was a sign of Australia's growing self-sufficiency and a renewal of confidence lost in the 1890s.

Federation also ushered in a raft of legislation that smoothed out policy across the nation. Paramount among this was the law which gave women the vote in 1902. Another piece of legislation result in the formal introduction of a 'White Australia' policy which, although in line with many nations of the day, seems shocking now and also jars given that the island continent was so manifestly 'Non-White Australia' just 115 years before. Immigration restarted in earnest in the mid-1900s, an integral part of the process being a dictation test in the European language of the immigration official's choice! In the northern regions of Australia, where the colonial frontier was still advancing, Aboriginal people were increasingly devastated by violence, disease, starvation and exploitation. Shortly before the federation the colonial governments had finally begun to worry that they were witnessing the destruction of Aboriginal people and introduced a raft of legislation to 'protect' them by confining them to certain areas away from Europeans. The Queensland Aborigines Act of 1897 meant that Aboriginal people could be forced to move to a reserve, were denied alcohol and the vote, and were paid for work under conditions and wages stipulated under the act. The state Protector was to be the legal guardian for all Aboriginal people under 21. Later amendments included the prohibition of sexual relations between Aborigines and Europeans and the need to seek permission for a mixed race marriage. This act was largely mirrored by the Aborigines Acts of WA (1905), NT (1911) and SA (1911). In NSW and Victoria, governments followed different policies, trying to get Aboriginal people off reserves, and the Tasmanian government refused to accept that it had any Aboriginal people.

Old wars, new purpose

When initiatives for peace in Europe failed after the Balkan crisis of 1914, and Britain swiftly came to the aid of its southern neighbours, Australia also quickly threw its hat in the ring with that of the Empire.

The Australian Imperial Force (AIF) were all either regular army or volunteers, but had still mustered 300,000 by the end of the First World War. They figured in many theatres of the war, the most celebrated of which has come to be known as Gallipoli. On 25 April 1915 the Anzacs (Australia and New Zealand Army Corps) constituted a large part of a force sent to win control of the banks of the Dardanelles, the narrow channel that connects the Aegean and Marmara seas. The expedition's success would open the allies supply line through the Mediterranean to the Black Sea and so to Russia.

Unfortunately the operation was compromised before it even started, with a squadron of ships trying to force the passage without silencing the Turkish guns on either flank. Pre-warned of a landing force, the Turks were well dug in and prepared. In addition the ground was hellishly difficult to attack and the Turks were tenacious and brave. The landing force did manage to create a number of toe-holds, however, and hung on to these for eight months, all the time trying not to forget the original objective.

Though forced to retreat, the chief legacy of the campaign was profound for the Australian psyche. The Anzacs were seen to display a degree of bravery, mateship and humour not expected in such an untried force. In a seminal moment for the nation its unbloodied and untested soldiers had faced the fire for the first time and had not been found wanting. It is sometimes thought that these expressions of national character were forged on the beaches of Gallipoli, but it is truer to say that it was during the campaign that foreign journalists first saw and publicised these traits that had been slowly maturing for decades. Unseen by the rest of the world, and even by many urban Australians, Australian toughness, independence and co-operation had been won on the pastoral and mining frontiers decades before.

Of the 300,000 who went to war over 50,000 were killed, a greater number than was lost by America. Many of these were the bravest, most resourceful, most inspiring men of their time. Their loss was profoundly felt, eliciting a huge outpouring of national pride and grief, given substance by literally thousands of memorials erected all over the country.

In the aftermath of victory, and the knowledge that they had played a substantial part, Australians' pride in themselves and their country increased, and they began to believe they possessed a prodigious future. E. J. Brady summarized this optimism in a huge tome, *Australia Unlimited*. Most influential politicians and commentators loudly voiced their uninformed opinions that Australia was a land of virtually unlimited resources, that could sustain a population of 100 million, perhaps half a billion. A subtext was that these people should be European, preferably British, to keep out the Asian hordes. One unusual realist, Professor Griffith Taylor, sounded several notes of caution and made the remarkably astute prediction that the population would be less than 20 million by 2000. Derided and scorned he left for America in 1928.

By the late 1920s Melbourne and Sydney could both boast over a million residents and over half a million cars travelled Australia's roads. In 1927 Canberra's Parliament House was opened to much fanfare but few spectators. One who was a poignant and tragic witness for his people was an Aboriginal street entertainer called Marvellous. After the ceremony he walked the 10 km back to Queanbeyan and bedded down, blanketless, on a dirt pathway. The night was freezing and in the morning he was found frozen to death.

Depression and consolidation

The early 1930s saw the worldwide Great Depression. This was exacerbated in Australia by large outstanding loans from Britain which the government simply stopped trying to repay. The unemployed (nearly 30% of the workforce by 1932) generally received enough food to avoid starvation, but little else. In the resulting political melee Joseph Lyons became prime minister and held the position until 1939. His right-wing United Australia Party was fiercely anti-communist, a stance which helped blind it to the ambitions of Japan and the European fascist states for a decade.

There were two events in 1932 that each added another ingredient to the mix of moods in the country. The completion of the Sydney Harbour Bridge was greeted with immense pride. This was tangible evidence of the nation's unbroken spirit and continued optimism. The other, oddly, was the visit of the English cricket team for what came to be called the 'bodyline' series. In the face of terrific talent in the Australian batting line-up, including a young Donald Bradman, the English bowlers were coached to aim for the body rather than the stumps. Relations with the 'mother country' soured considerably and the sporting wound has still not entirely healed.

The 1930s were marked by increased misery for many Aboriginal people. Influenced by popular notions of eugenics and racial purity in Europe, state governments thought that 'full bloods' would eventually die out and 'half castes' could be bred out. It was thought that if a woman of both Aboriginal and European descent took a European partner, and her children did the same, then the 'Aboriginal blood' would eventually become so diluted as to be invisible. It was also thought that if children of mixed descent with fairly pale skin could be taken from their Aboriginal mothers at an early age and raised within the white community it would give the child every material advantage and help 'half-castes' be absorbed into the community. As a result, in the Aboriginal Acts of NT (1933, 1936) WA (1936) QLD (1939) and SA (1939) provisions relating to permission to marry and sexual relations between Aboriginal people and Europeans were strengthened. The states' powers of guardianship were increasingly used to remove children of mixed descent from their mothers and rear them in missions, orphanages or foster homes. In 1937 a conference of the state government Protectors decided that, "*the destiny of the natives of aboriginal origin, but not of the full blood, lies in their ultimate absorption by the people of the Commonwealth, and it therefore recommends that all efforts be directed to that end.*" However anthropologists working with

Aboriginal people in the 1930s began to educate the rest of society about their culture, and various humanitarian groups and Aboriginal protest groups also began to agitate for a change in attitudes.

When war again broke out in 1939 the country was pitifully ill-prepared, probably less so than in 1914, but once again backed Britain to the hilt, sending troops to Europe. For the first 18 months the war seemed distant to those in Australia, with life going on as it did in the First World War. If anything, conditions for the average family improved as unemployment fell. The Japanese attack on Pearl Harbour shattered any illusion that Southeast Asia might go untouched, with waves of the Emperor's forces sweeping out across the region in an unremitting campaign of expansion. Britain, over-extended after a year of orchestrating the battle against Hitler virtually alone, was almost powerless to try to stop them. Singapore was captured and with it tens of thousands of allied troops. For the first time in 50 years invasion seemed possible.

For Australians 1942 was the most important year of the war in many ways. Japanese bombers and warships shelled Darwin, Sydney and Newcastle, but in truth it was their swan-song. In that year too, Australian troops finally halted the enemy advance on the Kokoda Trail, preventing what could have been a fatal occupation of Port Moresby in New Guinea, and the US fleet seriously bloodied the Japanese nose at the Battle of the Coral Sea. Just as courageous as Gallipoli, Kokoda also has the virtue of being a victorious campaign and by rights it should be as widely remembered as its First World War counterpart. Australians witnessed other tangible effects of war. Rationing was introduced and there were floods of fascinating newcomers in the guise of American troops, prisoners of war and European refugees.

Australia had a population of around seven million in 1939. A little under one million of these enlisted or were conscripted, of which under 40,000 were killed. It is estimated that about 500 Aborigines enlisted in the First World War and over 2,000 in the Second World War. More in the north, plus many Torres Strait Islanders, rendered valuable assistance in the defence of the country. At the close of both wars their reward was scant. Some returned only to find their ancestral lands closed to them. White Australia may have discovered a fierce wartime gusto towards its overseas enemies, but the conflicts also helped cement a deep mistrust and fear of all non-Europeans.

'White Australia'

Prime Minister Ben Chifley's Australia of the late 1940s was a careful nation. Beaten by the bomb, it was felt that Japan still had considerable potential for aggression and Australia played a leading role in garrisoning the defeated country and prosecuting its war leaders. There was a deep feeling that peace could not last. Russia and China were deemed the major new threats and it was universally felt that a large population would be the best disincentive to invasion, and defence against any such attempt.

The old 'White Australia' policy was energized once more. Chifley's chief minister for immigration, Arthur Calwell, instigated and pursued the most vigorous population programme Australia has ever seen, stating that the nation must "populate or perish". It was originally thought that the Brits, still seen as the best 'stock', could make up 90% of the numbers but this proved over-ambitious – they eventually made up around a quarter of the immigrants of the period, and some of those were unwittingly expatriated orphans. Calwell had to relax his criteria and was soon fishing in the vast refugee camp that central and southern Europe had become. However the net would be thrown no wider: those of African or Asian origin were definitely not welcome.

In continental Europe Calwell found a more enthusiastic audience, keen to escape the ravages of the war. Soon tens of thousands of Poles and Greeks, Jews and Germans, Italians and Yugoslavs were pouring into the country. All of them had to work for the government for a minimum of two years, many at large schemes such as the Snowy Mountains Hydroelectric Scheme to generate power and irrigate the inland plains. Some had to wait years before being able to properly apply their skills. Historian Phillip Knightley tells the story of one immigrant with medical experience being given the job of an ambulance driver. On witnessing a tracheotomy he suddenly cautioned the doctor "No. No. Not there. Cut here!" The doctor scornfully responded that he was following the manual of a respected international expert. "Yes," replied the driver, "but there've been developments since I wrote that."

Non-British immigrants also had to put up with a fair amount of social antagonism. 'Refos' (refugees), 'DPs' (displaced persons) and 'dagos' were taunts frequently slung at the newcomers. With sometimes only a scant grasp of English, people from the same country frequently banded together, forming distinct enclaves and giving some suburbs, particularly in Sydney and Melbourne, a decidedly international flavour. The few non-European immigrants and descendants of the earlier Chinese gold miners fared much worse, suffering at times outright racial vilification. The non-British were, however, to form the foundation of a vibrant and successful urban multi-cultural society.

In 1949 the giant of 20th-century Australian politics, Robert Menzies, strode back into the limelight, leading his new Liberal party to election victory. A staunch monarchist, he welcomed Queen Elizabeth II to Australia in 1954, the first reigning monarch to make the trip. Under Menzies the immigration policies continued apace, and between 1945 and 1973 about 3½ million people came to live in Australia. With dramatic developments in technology the 1950s saw a renewed thrust in mineral prospecting and mining. In the following decades new discoveries were repeatedly made, with a long list of metals being added to Australia's already rich list, metals such as aluminium, nickel, manganese, uranium and bauxite. Oil and black coal were also discovered in great quantities.

The post-war period, greeted initially with trepidation, had proved a boom time and the good times were neatly encapsulated by Melbourne hosting the Olympics in 1956. Television had been quickly put in place to promote the games and soon people all over the world had the opportunity of seeing, in their own homes, moving pictures of the 'land down under'.

Culture clash

There was a flip-side to all this post-war optimism, however, itself a product of the war. The Nazis had been vanquished and the Japanese firmly re-confined to their island home, but communism now stood even larger on the world stage. Although the Japanese had failed to establish a modern Asian Empire, the 'western' world became convinced that either China or the Soviets might succeed, and many Australians believed that their beloved homeland would be firmly in the sights of any nation with such ambitions.

This fear of communism had two profound effects, which between them later engendered a counter consequence of equal, if not greater, importance. Anti-communist hysteria goes a long way to explaining the firm grip that conservative governments were to have on Australian politics for a quarter of a century, with Labor Party members and supporters frequently suspected of being communist sympathizers and even spies. In 1950 Robert Menzies held a national referendum on whether the Communist Party should be banned outright and its members jailed. To the nation's credit the result was a comfortable 'no'. The other major effect of the national mood was an enthusiastic willingness to back up any Asian military efforts against the 'red tide' with practical support. The same year as the referendum saw Australian troops join those from the USA and their other allies in fighting the 'commies' in Korea. A little later, in the year of the Melbourne Olympics, the Soviet Union invaded Hungary and anti-communist fears in Australia were bolstered further by a stream of frightened refugees.

The conservative cauldron simmered on through the height of the Cold War in the late 1950s and early 1960s, thus ensuring that Australia, unlike Britain, was ready to send troops in support of another Asian crusade, this time in Vietnam. The Australian commitment was never huge in military terms, committing some 8,000 people, but Prime Minister Harold Holt's famous statement, "all the way with LBJ", neatly illustrates the depth of conservative political support. It was also an indication that Australia was shifting from British influence to follow an American lead. Although only a few troops made the journey, some of them were conscripts. This sat uneasily with much of the general public, and when conscripts started getting killed some of that public started getting visibly angry.

The nation became embroiled, for the first time in decades, in serious discussions about the direction and fitness of the government and its policies. Demonstrations against the war were organized and some marches became violent. Governments frequently clamped down hard, prompting further discussion and protests on the subject of civil liberties. Some people demonstrated simply to express their view that they had a right to demonstrate. A heady brew of general anti-establishment feeling began to ferment, particularly amongst the youth of the day, inspired by their cousins in Europe and the USA who were discovering a new independence from their 'elders and betters'.

Aboriginal people were also part of the protest movement and increasingly demanded change. In the early 1960s new legislation appeared in all states that largely removed the paternalistic and restrictive laws relating to Aboriginal people. The federal government enfranchised Aborigines of the Northern Territory (the only region under their control) and the rest of the states followed the federal lead. Previously citizenship had only been available to those who applied for it and was subject to certain conditions; in Western Australia that meant not keeping company with any Aboriginal people except the applicant's immediate family for two years before applying and after being granted citizenship. In 1967 a total of 89% of Australians voted in a referendum to allow the federal government to legislate for Aboriginal people. The ad-hoc and self-interested approach of the states was over.

The granting of rights such as equal wages had to be fought for in some cases, even when the legislation existed, and this could be the catalyst for further activism. When the Gurindji people failed to obtain equal wages from the powerful Lord Vestey of Wave Hill Station in the Northern Territory they walked off the land, led by stockman Vincent Lingiari, and decided to make a land rights claim for some of Vestey-owned land. As one of his people later said; *"We were treated just like dogs. We were lucky to get paid the fifty quid a month we were due, and we lived in tin humpies you had to crawl in and out on your knees. There was no running water. The food was bad – just flour, tea, sugar and bits of beef like the head or feet of a bullock. The Vesteys were hard men. They didn't care about blackfellas."* Just ten years earlier Lingiari and his Gurindji people would probably have been ignominiously, forcefully and quietly evicted, but this was 1966 and sections of society were prepared to listen and help. The ruling conservative Liberal-Country Party rejected the Aboriginals' claim, wary of their own land-owning voters and perhaps of the effects a positive outcome might have on future mineral exploitation. The political wind was, however, changing. The Australian people had soon had enough of the conservatives and were ready for a new broom. In 1972 they finally elected the Labor Party back into power, and with it the charismatic and energetic Gough Whitlam.

Modern Australia

There is much discussion as to when Australia really became a nation. Looking back Federation seems a likely candidate, but at the time it probably meant little to most people, and certainly nothing to its indigenous people. The return of the Anzacs from the First World War is also considered a seminal moment: they went out as boys from New South Wales, Western Australia and the othe states, but came back as Australians. There was still a profound sense of kinship with Britain, however, and many people, though born in Australia, would call themselves British and held a British passport. Another war brought with it the shocking realization that good ol' Britannia could no longer defend Australian shores, and another emotional tie was severed when Britain first lobbied to join the European Union in 1962. By then Australia knew it had to stand alone both economically and politically but, Tarzan-like, it had leaped from the British vine only to grasp desperately at the American one.

In many ways the brief tenure of Gough Whitlam as Prime Minister was the coming of age for Australia. He came to power unencumbered by decades of the politics of fear, and with a zeal to be his own man and make Australia her own nation. Within days the troops were recalled from Vietnam and conscription ended, women were legally granted an equal wage structure, 'White Australia' formally abandoned, and a Ministry of Aboriginal Affairs created. Whitlam's stated policy was "to restore to the Aboriginal people of Australia their lost power of self-determination in economic, social and political affairs". Whitlam spurned the prime ministerial Bentley, ended the old imperial honours system and dumped 'God Save the Queen' as the National Anthem. He was a political dynamo, and exacted a unprecedented work-rate from his colleagues. His policies were not everyone's cup of tea, but no one could argue that his every effort was not aimed at the betterment of Australia and Australians. In 1975 the Gurindji people were given 2,000 sq km from the Vestey leases and Whitlam flew to Wave Hill to personally hand over the deeds, symbolically pouring a handful of sand into the palm of Vincent Lingiari as he did so. Even Whitlam's sacking a few months later, a controversial affair involving the Governor-General, and consequently the British Crown, had the effect of galvanizing public opinion on the subject of republicanism. Whitlam had also permanently altered the mood of the nation, and of Australian politics.

The late 1970s and 1980s continued to be a time of rapid and shifting changes. The fledgling Green movement had failed to stop the damming of Lake Pedder in Tasmania in 1972, but did stop the similar Franklin River scheme a decade later. Sydney's first Gay and Lesbian march in 1978 was met with derision, vilification and police violence – its annual successor, the Mardi Gras, is now the biggest event of its kind in the world and Sydney's wildest party, enjoyed by gays and straights alike. Following the demise of 'White Australia', the country again opened its doors to Asian migrants, and to thousands of Vietnamese 'boat people'. Once again, the new peoples and cultures hugely enriched urban society. In 1988 the country celebrated the Bicentennial – 200 years of white settlement. Aboriginal people found little to celebrate and used the event to draw political attention to Aboriginal issues such as the high rate of Aboriginal deaths in custody, the subject of a Royal Commission enquiry throughout that year, and the question of a treaty between indigenous and non-indigenous Australians.

The 1990s was a tumultuous decade for issues involving Aboriginal people. In 1992 the High Court made what was probably the most important decision of the century in the Mabo land rights case. The court ruled that native title (or prior indigenous ownership of land) was not extinguished by the Crown's claim of possession in the Murray Islands of Torres Strait. In other words the legal fiction of *terra nullius* was overturned after 222 years, and the decision was later enshrined in the Native Title Act (1993). This was a major victory for Aboriginal people although landowners had to be able to prove a continuous relationship to the land and claims could only be made on Crown land. A land fund was suggested to buy land for the majority of Aboriginal people who were unable to claim land under the Act. Despite the limited nature of native title conservatives were horrified and lobbied hard against it.

In 1996 there was further uproar from conservatives and pastoralists when the High Court ruled in the Wik case that pastoral leases and native title could co-exist. However, as there are many different types of leaseholds, the court stated that every case would have to be decided on its own merits. This meant there was no certainty for those holding pastoral leases, covering 40% of Australia and at that time making up two-thirds of all land claims. Those bitterly opposed to land rights wanted the government to legislate to extinguish native title over pastoral leases. The Howard government responded with a 10 Point Plan to amend the Native Title Act that favoured pastoral interests and limited the powers of native title holders. Neither group was happy with the plan (it wasn't extreme enough for pastoralists) and the Australian Law Reform Commission and Labor politicians called it racially discriminatory. The Native Title Amendment Bill was passed in 1998 with the help of an independent senator.

Amid the turmoil over land rights in 1997, the Human Rights and Equal Opportunity Commission produced the report of their National Inquiry into the Separation of Aboriginal and Torres Strait Islander Children from their Families. This report, titled *Bringing Them Home*, estimated that between one in ten and one in three indigenous children were removed between 1910 and 1970. Its recommendations were compensation, counselling and an official apology. The Howard government described the report as flawed and refused to apologize or pay compensation but later announced a package to pay for counselling, family support and cultural programmes. The children who were the subject of this report are now known as the 'stolen generation'.

As Australia moved toward a new century, two campaigns aimed at moving the country in a new direction built a considerable head of steam – that for a republic and another for reconciliation. One sought to sunder further the ties with Britain, the other to build better ties between white and black Australians. Reconciliation was seen as important for the future health of the nation. A gesture that would heal the divisions between black and white and allow Australians to move into the future together. The Council for Aboriginal Reconciliation worked on a Declaration of Reconciliation that was presented to the government in 2000. In the same year there were large reconciliation marches all over the country by sections of the community who wanted to say 'sorry' for past injustices, despite the government's refusal to do so. The issue of the republic was to be decided by a 1999 national referendum. The question asked, however, was controversially worded in a way that prevented many republicans assenting to it, and the result was 'no', despite polls showing a majority in favour of a republic.

A new century

The Olympics were held in Sydney in 2000, and must be ranked as one of the greatest games ever. The Aboriginal athlete Kathy Freeman won gold in the women's 400 m track sprint, sending the nation into a frenzy of joy. Following the reconciliation movement the victory seemed, to many, serendipitous. However, the huge optimism created by the successful staging of the Olympics seemed to fizzle out with the failure of the republic and the failure to achieve any meaningful reconciliation between indigenous and non-indigenous Australians. Aboriginal people are still coming to terms with the effects of dispossession and the government policies that have affected their lives from 1788 until the present day. By almost every measure of social welfare they are less well off than non-indigenous Australians, for example the life expectancy of an indigenous person is 20 years less than other Australians, and rectifying this inequality is the great challenge of the future for all Australians.

In November 2001 the Liberal-National coalition government under John Howard was returned to power despite the unpopularity of the Goods and Services Tax introduced in 2000. The campaign was run amid the uncertainty caused by the terrorist attacks of September 11 and issues of border protection highlighted by the government's handling of the *Tampa* crisis. The *Tampa's* Norwegian captain had rescued boat people claiming to be refugees from Afghanistan but the government refused to allow the 'illegal immigrants' to land on the mainland. Since the election, border protection and the detention of asylum seekers have become even hotter issues. Asylum seekers who are refused residency may appeal the decision but while awaiting appeal they (and their children) are held in remote detention centres for as long as three years. The UN High Council for Refugees has criticized government policy on asylum seekers and detention centres, as have prominent Australians such as former conservative prime minister, Malcolm Fraser, but the government stands by its policies. This issue has affected Australia's international standing and continues to polarise Australian society today.

Politics

Although Australians are not typically political animals Australian politics are hard to ignore. This is partly because of the sheer volume of government the country bears, partly because of the colourful characters and events Australian politics seems to throw up, and partly because everyone, by law, has to vote.

Australia's head of the state is the reigning monarch of England, a throwback to when the monarch was the head of the British Empire, which the Australian colonies were very much part of. The Queen's representative in Australia, now usually Australian born, is the Governor-General, appointed by the Australian prime minister. The role is largely ceremonial, though in theory invested with considerable powers.

In practical terms the business of governing the whole country, is undertaken by the Federal ('Commonwealth') Parliament based in Canberra. Its 'lower' House of Representatives is constituted by members directly elected from electorates with approximately equally sized populations. The electorates range in size from a small city suburb to that of Kalgoorlie which encompasses most of WA and is, in fact, the largest constituency anywhere in the world. The 'upper' house, the Senate, is elected by a form of proportional representation that guarantees each state 12 members, and each territory two. The lower house formulates government policy and the upper house either vetoes or passes it. Both houses are voted for every three years.

There are two major parties which sit either side of the political fence. The Australian Labor Party (ALP) and the Liberal Party are the two chief protagonists, the ALP being the rough equivalent of the British Labour Party or American Democrats, the Liberals the equivalent of the Conservatives or Republicans. Over the last 70 years the ALP have generally polled slightly higher than the Liberals, but have usually been kept out of office by the latter's alliance with the smaller Country and National parties. The leader of the majority in the lower house forms the country's government and is its Prime Minister. In 2001 John Howard's Liberal/National coalition won their third consecutive election and are currently in office. The upper house is even more finely balanced, and here the voting system allows the smaller significant parties, the Democrats and the Greens to win more seats and so to effectively hold the balance of power.

Most of the nation's tax dollar ends up in the Commonwealth coffers. About a third of the Federal budget goes in benefit payments, about a fifth on the machinery of government and state institutions, and about a quarter is distributed as payments to individual states. A constant source of grievance between Federal and state governments is the relative proportion of each state's Federal income compared to the amount of tax its residents have paid, with bitter (and not untruthful) claims that some states subsidize the others.

In a second tier of government most states also have their own upper and lower houses, and also Governors. These too are elected on a three-year cycle, and much the same political parties vie for election. All state governments are currently ALP.

Culture

Aboriginal art and culture

From the beginning Aborigine is a Latin word meaning 'from the beginning'; the Romans used it to describe the first inhabitants of Latium and it can be used to apply to any people living in a country from its earliest period. It may seem strange that the first Australians are known by a generic name but its meaning is certainly appropriate for Australian Aboriginal people. Although anthropologists believe that Aboriginal people arrived in Australia 50,000-60,000 years ago from Southeast Asia, Aboriginal people believe that they have always been here, that they were created here by their spirit ancestors. Before Europeans arrived in Australia, Aboriginal people had no collective sense of identity. Their identity was tied to their own part of the country and to their extended family groups. Hence no name existed to describe all of the inhabitants of Australia, in the same way that until relatively recently the inhabitants of Europe would have had no conception of being 'European'.

A continent of many nations When the First Fleet arrived with its cargo of convicts in 1788 there were between 300,000 and 750,000 Aboriginal people living in Australia, who belonged to about 500 tribes or groups. It is difficult to make generalizations about Aboriginal people because each group had its own territory, its own language or dialect and its own culture. There were broad cultural similarities between these groups just as different nationalities in Europe had more in common with each other than they had with Chinese or African people for example. Naturally, neighbouring groups were more similar to each other; perhaps speaking dialects of the same language and sharing some 'Dreamtime' myths linked to territory borders such as rivers and mountains. However, if a man from Cape York had found himself transported to the Western Desert he would have been unable to communicate with the desert people. He would have found them eating unfamiliar food and using different methods to obtain it. Their art would have been incomprehensible to him and their ceremony meaningless. If he had been able to speak their language he would have found that they had a different explanation of how they came into existence and his own creation ancestors would have been unknown to them. Each group was almost like a small state or nation.

Dreaming Every traveller in Australia will encounter the concept of the 'Dreaming' or the 'Dreamtime'. These words attempt to explain a complex concept that lies at the heart of Aboriginal culture and should not be understood in the English context of something that is not real. Most Aboriginal groups believe that in the beginning the world was featureless. Ancestral beings emerged from the earth and as they moved about the landscape they began to shape it. Some of them created humans by giving birth to them or moulding them from incomplete life forms. Ancestral beings were sometimes human in form but also often animals, rocks, trees or stars, and could transform from one shape to another. Nor were they limited by their form; kangaroos could talk, fish could swim out of water. Wherever these beings went, whatever they did left its mark on the landscape. A mountain might be the fallen body of an ancestor speared to death, a waterhole may be the place a spirit emerged from the earth, a rock bar may show where an ancestor crossed a river, yellow ochre may be the fat of an ancestral kangaroo. In this way the entire continent is mapped with the tracks of the ancestor beings.

Although the time of creation and shaping of the landscape is associated with the temporal notion of 'beginning', it is important to understand that Dreaming is not part of the past. It lies within the present and will determine the future. The ancestral beings have a permanent presence in spiritual or physical form. Ancestor snakes and serpents still live in the waterholes that they created; this is why visitors are sometimes asked not to swim in certain pools, such as those below the Mitchell Falls in the Kimberley or Katherine Gorge in NT, so that these ancestors will not be disturbed. This is also why mining or development can cause great distress to Aboriginal people if the area targeted is the home of an ancestral being. The ancestors are also still involved in creation. Sexual intercourse is seen as being part of conception but new life can only be created if a conception spirit enters a woman's body. The place where this happens, near a waterhole, spring or sacred site, will determine the child's identification with a particular totem or ancestor. In this way Aboriginal people are directly connected to their ancestral world.

Aboriginal people belonged to a territory because they were descended from the ancestors who formed and shaped that territory. The ancestral beings were sources of life and powerful performers of great deeds but were also capable of being capricious, amoral and dangerous. Yet in their actions they laid down the rules for life. They created ceremony, song and designs to commemorate their deeds or journeys, established marriage and kinship rules and explained how to look after the land. In the simple forms related to outsiders, Dreaming stories often sound like moral fables. Knowledge of the land's creation stories was passed on from generation to generation, increasing in complexity or sacredness as an individual aged. With knowledge came the responsibility to look after sacred creation or resting places. Ceremonies were conducted to ensure the continuation of life forces and fertility. Aboriginal people had no idea of owning the land in the sense that it was a possession that could be traded or given away, but saw themselves as custodians of land in which humans, animals and spirits were inseparable – in fact, one and the same. Consequently Aboriginal people of one group had no interest in possessing the land of another group. Strange country was meaningless to them. To leave your country was to leave your world.

In their daily life Aboriginal people usually hunted, gathered and socialized within a small band, perhaps 50 people belonging to one or two families. These bands or clans only came together to form the whole group of several hundred people for ceremonial reasons and at places or times when food was plentiful. Group behaviour and social relations were governed by an intricate kinship system, and guided by the superior knowledge and experience of the elders. This is one of the reasons that the word 'tribe' is not used to describe groups of Aboriginal people, as a tribe by definition is led by a chief and Aboriginal society did not operate in this way. The rules of kinship are far too complicated to explain here, and also vary in different regions, but in essence the kinship system linked the whole group as family. You would call your birth mother 'mother' but you would also call your mother's sisters 'mother' and they would take on the obligations of that role. The same applied for sisters, fathers, uncles and so on. There were specific codes of behaviour for each kin relationship so you would know the appropriate way to behave towards each member of your group. For example, in

The bonds of kin

many Aboriginal societies mothers-in-law and sons-in-law were not allowed to communicate with each other. A neat solution to an age-old problem in human relations!

Kinship also determined whom an individual could marry. In one type of kinship system each person in a group belongs to one of several sections or moieties. The moiety category is inherited from the father and so contains all of an individual's patrilineal relations. That individual can only marry someone from another moiety. Kinship links also exist between people of the same totem or ancestor. People born from the goanna ancestor would be related to all other 'goannas'. Each kinship relationship carried specific responsibilities and rights such as initiating a 'son' or giving food to a 'sister', creating a strong collective society where everyone is tied to each other. By this method food and possessions are distributed equally and because of these kinship obligations it is almost impossible for an individual to accumulate material wealth. This major difference between Aboriginal culture and the dominant ethic in Australian society of Western materialism still creates problems for those trying to live in both worlds. For example a young Aboriginal footballer will often move from his close-knit rural community to Melbourne to play in the AFL, and find it very difficult to balance the material demands of his family against the demands of his team who teach him to pursue personal wealth and glory.

Environment The laws of the Dreaming provided a broad framework for spiritual and material life, but of course Aboriginal culture was not static. Although their society valued continuity above change, parts of their culture were the result of adapting to their environment. Aboriginal people have lived in Australia for so long that they have seen major environmental changes such as climate change, dramatic changes in sea level caused by the last ice age and even volcanic eruptions in southern Australia. The picture that many people have in their minds of an Australian Aboriginal is of a desert-dwelling nomad with few possessions and only a roof of stars over his head at night. Of course some people lived like this but others sewed warm skin cloaks, built bark or stone huts and lived in the same place for several seasons. The ways in which Aboriginal people differed from each other very much depended on the environment that they lived in. The wetlands of Arnhem Land were particularly rich in food resources throughout the year and were thought to have supported a large and fairly settled population. The Warlpiri people of central Australia had to range far and wide to find their food and move on quickly so as not to over-exploit the resources of a single area. Naturally, tools were developed to match the territory; boomerangs were not known to people who lived in areas of dense woodland, nor elaborate fish traps known to inland people. Conversely, Aboriginal people also changed their environment with methods such as 'fire-stick farming' (see page 875).

Hunting and gathering Aboriginal people were generally semi-nomadic rather than true nomads but they did not wander about aimlessly. They moved purposefully to specific places within their territory to find food that they knew to be ripening or abundant at certain times of the year. Their long tenure and stable society meant that they knew the qualities of every plant, the behaviour of every animal and the nature of every season intimately. Men hunted large game such as kangaroos with their toolkit of spears, clubs or boomerangs, and women gathered fruit, vegetables, seeds, honey, shellfish and small game such as lizards using their own kit of bags, bowls and digging sticks. Each gender had its own responsibilities and knowledge, including the ceremonies to ensure continuing fertility by commemorating the Dreaming. The need to 'look after country' in this way also determined their movements. Although men were generally more powerful than women, having more authority over family members and ritual, women had their own power base because of their knowledge and the reliability of the food they provided. Although hunting and gathering was labour intensive anthropologists estimate that Aboriginal people only had to spend three to five hours a day working for food, leaving plenty of time for social life and ceremony.

Ceremony and art were at the very heart of life for these were the ways in which Aboriginal people maintained their connection with the ancestors. During ceremonies the actions and movements of the ancestors would be recalled in songs and dances that the ancestors themselves had performed and handed down to each clan or group. Not only did the ancestral beings leave a physical record of their travels in the form of the landscape but also in paintings, sacred objects and sculptures that might be shown or used as part of a ceremony. Ceremonies maintained the power and life force of the ancestors thus replenishing the natural environment. Some ceremonies, such as those performed at initiation, brought the individual closer to his or her ancestors. Ceremonies performed at death made sure that a person's spirit would re-join the spiritual world. Some were public ceremonies or art forms, others were secret and restricted to those who were responsible for looking after a certain piece of country and the ancestors and stories associated with it. **Ceremony & art**

When a person painted and decorated his or her body, they did so with designs and ornaments that the ancestral beings had created. The individual was almost transformed into the ancestor, thus bringing these beings to life in the present, in the same way that carvings and paintings of spirit beings such as the Rainbow Serpent can do. Art was also a product of the kinship system as one of its obligations was the giving and receiving of goods. The value of the gift was not important in fulfilling this obligation, only the act of giving. As a result Aboriginal people were continually engaged in making material objects such as body ornaments, baskets, tools and weapons, all of which can be considered secular forms of art or craft. Of course these items also needed to be made again as they wore out. One of the features of Aboriginal art was its ephemeral nature; it existed to perform a function rather than be hoarded or kept as a perfect example of the form. Elaborate body paintings that took hours to complete could be smudged by sweat in minutes. They were also sometimes deliberately wiped off to hide or lessen the power of the ancestral image. The same applied to bark paintings which would be discarded or destroyed. Ground sculptures were often temporary, made in sand, or left to decay like the carved and painted pukunami burial poles of the Tiwi people. The most permanent forms were rock engravings and paintings but even these were eroded or painted over in time. Some Aboriginal art was like a blackboard, used to teach and then wiped clean. **Function of art**

The most immediately obvious feature of Aboriginal art is its symbolic nature. Geometric designs such as circles, lines, dots, squares or abstract designs are used in all art forms and often combine to form what seems to be little more than an attractive pattern. Even when figures are used they are also symbolic representations, an emu may be prey or an ancestral being. The symbols do not have a fixed meaning; a circle may represent a waterhole, a camping place or an event. In Aboriginal art symbols are put together to form a map of the landscape. This is not a literal map where the 'key' realtes to the topography of a piece of countryside, but rather a mythological map. Features of the landscape are depicted but only in their relation to the creation myth that is the subject of the painting. A wavy line terminating in a circle might represent the journey of the Rainbow Serpent to a waterhole. That landscape may also contain a hill behind the waterhole but if it is not relevant to the serpent's journey it will not be represented, although it may feature in other paintings related to different ancestral beings. Unlike a conventional map, scale is not consistent. The size of a feature is more likely to reflect its importance rather than its actual size or there may be several scales within a painting. Nor is orientation fixed. **A symbolic landscape**

Artistic licence As art was a means of expressing identity it follows that only those who belonged to an area of landscape and its Dreaming stories could paint those stories. No one else would know them. An artist must have the right to paint the image he has in mind and these rights are carefully guarded. This idea is refined further within the clan or group. A father and son of the same clan may know the same story but the father will be able to paint more powerful ancestral beings with more knowledge and detail, because it can take a lifetime to learn all of the knowledge connected to an ancestral being. Rights to paintings can also be established through kinship links, living in an area or taking part in ceremony. To many people Aboriginal art is recognized by its style – dots, X-ray or cross hatching – but what is painted is just as important as how it is painted. Aboriginal people working in traditional forms simply do not paint landscapes, figures or people that they are not spiritually connected to. The idea of painting a landscape simply because it is pretty is utterly foreign to Aboriginal art. Even an artist like Albert Namatjira who painted European landscape watercolours in the 1940s never painted anything but his own Arrernte land in central Australia, although he travelled widely outside it.

Interpretation How does the viewer understand the meaning of a work of Aboriginal art? Because of the use of symbols and the fact that Dreaming stories are only known to the ancestral descendants, only the painter, and perhaps his close relatives will be able to fully understand the meaning of a painting. In some areas the whole group may be able to interpret the painting. When you look at Aboriginal art in a gallery it will be labelled with the name of the artist, and often his clan or group name, dates and location but the meaning of the painting is not usually revealed. As knowledge of the creation myths illustrated relates to ownership it is not appropriate for the artists to pass on important cultural knowledge to strangers, although sometimes a very simple or limited explanation will be given to buyers. Some artists do interpret their paintings in more detail to anthropologists, land rights lawyers or art experts in order to educate non-indigenous people about Aboriginal culture. Looking at examples of Aboriginal art alongside an interpretation is the best way to comprehend the many layers of meaning possible. These can be found in art books such as the excellent *Aboriginal Art* by **Howard Morphy**.

Regional art Much of what we know about Aboriginal art and culture has been learned from groups in central and northern Australia who, although influenced by contemporary society, still maintain the system of belief they had before European contact. Even that information is limited as some groups, particularly desert people, are careful not to reveal too much detail. Although painting is the form discussed in most detail here the same information often applies to each art form. Images, symbols and designs used on a painting may well be carved into a weapon, scratched into the skin of a possum cloak or painted on a basket. Very little information is known about the culture of the Aboriginal people of the southeast, because their way of life was disrupted so rapidly when the British arrived. However, such a variety of geometrical designs were found carved into trees or wooden tools that it is thought southern people probably represented their group ancestors and land ownership in the same symbolic way. Tools were collected and held in ethnographic museum collections but often without any knowledge of where they came from, who made them or why. By the time they were recognized as works of art, an expression of identity and culture as well as functional objects, the people who made them were long gone. The oral history of surviving descendants and the writings and images produced by early colonists are the primary source of knowledge about southeastern culture. It is thought that these people believed in spirit figures of the sky, rather than spirit ancestors travelling across the earth.

After the British arrived in Australia, many Aboriginal people died from unfamiliar diseases. Those who did not were often moved off their land to missions or reserves, or killed while resisting the strangers attempting to farm or live on their land. The British acted as they did for a variety of reasons; sometimes for their own material gain, sometimes just following orders and sometimes from the genuine desire to help or protect Aboriginal people. Unfortunately the British had no understanding of Aboriginal culture and did not comprehend that separating Aboriginal people from their land was about the most destructive action possible. In unfamiliar country there was no land to look after, no reason to perform cere- mony, hand down knowledge or maintain kinship ties. In missions and reserves people had to live with groups who were perhaps recent enemies, who spoke another language, who did not share their religious beliefs. In the missions they were often forbidden to speak their own language and to practice any aspects of ceremonial life that had survived the sundering from their source. It says much for the strength of Aboriginal culture that many aspects of it still exist. Since the paternalism of the Australian government was abandoned in the 1970s and a pol- icy of self-determination implemented, many Aboriginal people from northern and central Australia have moved from government reserves back to their land to live in small remote communities. The production of art for sale in these commu- nities helps them achieve financial independence but also revives their cultural life as the art is used to instruct young people in their Dreaming. Art has always been an integral part of the life of Aboriginal people and all over Australia people con- tinue to express their Aboriginality in a variety of art forms. Aboriginal culture sur- vives but continues to change and adapt as it has for countless thousands of years.

Culture in the 21st century

When travelling across Australia it is possible to glimpse the regional variation of Aboriginal art. You may be able to see body painting at a corroborree, such as the one held regularly in Katherine (NT), and some of the world's greatest collections of rock-art in the Kimberley, Kakadu, Arnhem Land and Cape York. Few rock art galleries are accessible to the public because of the need to protect them but there are two easily accessible galleries in Kakadu and some other sites in northern Australia can be seen on guided tours. The beauty and age of the paintings make it an unforgettable experience. Most of the state museums and galleries have superb collections of both traditional and contemporary Aboriginal art and these are excellent places to learn about Aboriginal culture and art. There are also many commercial galleries. The art centres owned and run by Aboriginal communities help build self-sufficiency for Aboriginal people, offer the indigenous perspective and you may be able to see art- ists at work. Works produced for sale in Australia include bark paintings from Arnhem Land, the dot paintings, batik fabric and wood carvings of the desert regions of central Australia, baskets and didjeridus from northern Australia, and wood carv- ings and screen-printed fabric from the Tiwi Islands.

Art forms

Rock paintings and rock engravings found all over the country constitute Australia's most ancient and enduring art form. Early rock engravings in Koonalda Cave on the Nullabor have been dated to 20,000 years ago but engravings are eroded over time and it is possible that rock engravings were being made 40,000 or even 60,000 years ago. Common forms are circles, lines, and animal tracks or animal figures. Many are so ancient that Aboriginal people of the area can not explain their meaning. Rock painting can also be dated back to many thousands of years ago and was practised until the last few decades. The finest and most extensive rock-painting galleries are found in the great rocky escarpment and range country of the north. The paintings of the Arnhem Land escarpment reflect environmental changes that enable them to be dated to about 15,000 years ago. The Pre-Estuarine period dates from the last ice

Rock art

age until a rise in sea levels between 700 and 900 years ago and demonstrates drier conditions with paintings of kangaroos and boomerangs. Paintings of the Estuarine period, when the plains were inundated, include marine and Estuarine species such as barramundi and crocodiles. Paintings made after 1788 are referred to as belonging to the Contact period and these include images of ships and guns.

Painting styles have also changed over the millennia and these help to date paintings too because paintings are generally layered on top of each other. The earliest art forms are stencils, where a mouthful of ochre is spat over the hand, foot or tool to leave a reverse print on the wall. Figures in red ochre (or blood) are also some of the oldest works as red ochre lasts longer than any other colour, seeping into the rock to bond with it permanently. Some of the most intriguing figures are the red ochre Bradshaws in the Kimberley and Mimi spirits in Arnhem Land who wear elaborate ceremonial dress such as tassels and head-dresses and carry feather fans. These are known as dynamic figures for their graceful sense of movement and are thought to be 6,000-10,000 years old. Perhaps most spectacular are the finely drawn and colourful X-ray figures of the last 3,000 years, where the internal structure of a figure, such as vertebrae or stomach, is represented. Gallery walls covered in barramundi, turtles, kangaroo and other food sources are thought to be a kind of hunting magic – to ensure a successful hunt. Sorcery paintings of inverted figures are commonly found in the superb galleries around Laura-Cooktown in Cape York. Others figures, such as the Wandjina of the Kimberley, are representations of ancestral beings who 'put themselves onto the rock' as they retreated there in the Dreaming. One of the responsibilities of the custodians of a rock-art site would be to retouch the painting to keep its power bright and strong.

Bark paintings Although bark paintings are now identified with Arnhem Land and nearby islands, the only places in which this art form survives, bark was used as a painting surface in other parts of Australia. Members of Nicolas Baudin's expedition saw paintings inside Tasmanian bark shelters in 1802. This is also the form in which Europeans first saw bark paintings in Arnhem Land. The anthropologist Baldwin Spencer saw painted huts there in 1912 and commissioned the Gagadju people around Oenpelli to produce paintings on sheets of bark. The last Gagadju speaker died in 2002 but they are remembered in the name of Kakadu National Park. It is not known how long people had been producing bark paintings but it is thought that sheets may have been used in ceremony and hut walls used as a teaching tool, perhaps to instruct initiates in private. The bark comes from the stringybark tree and is stripped off in the wet season when most malleable, then scraped and uncurled by heating it over a fire. The 'canvas' is then painted upon with ochres using brushes made of bark or hair, and a fine stick. Arnhem Land barks usually depict their landscape and its creation myths in a more figurative form than art from central Australia, but still remain inherently symbolic. Paintings also differ in that they are less map-like, tending to represent the events of one place rather than the whole journey. In Western Arnhem Land, artists paint in the 'X-ray' style of their rock art. Backgrounds are often left plain, although the area inside the figure may be infilled with cross-hatching. In eastern Arnhem Land figures are represented against a background of cross-hatching within geometric segments such as diamonds. Every clan owns a design representing the creation myth of their ancestors and these are often as abstract as an elongated diamond or a line of diamonds broken by an oval. A geometric pattern may also signify many things. The same pattern could represent a flowing river or smoke from a bushfire depending on the context in which it is used. In this way the bark paintings of Arnhem Land contain incredible depth of meaning, comprehensible only to those who know the landscape and story represented.

Dot paintings

These are the most widely recognized of Aboriginal art forms, highly sought after by international collectors, but also one of the newest forms. Dot paintings are made in the western and central desert regions and relate to an older form used by desert people. In the desert there are few rock surfaces and no trees suitable for stripping off large pieces of bark so the desert people used the ground to commemorate the travels and actions of their ancestral beings. Drawings, or perhaps more correctly sculptures, were created by placing crushed plant matter and feather down on a hard-packed surface. The material would be coloured with ochre or blood. Common designs were spirals or circles and lines. These works were always ceremonial and created by old and knowledgeable men. In the 1970s many desert people were living at Papunya, a community northwest of Alice Springs. An art teacher, Geoff Bardon, encouraged local men to paint a mural on the school wall. A Honey Ant Dreaming painting was created, leading to great interest and enthusiasm from men in the community. They began painting their stories on boards, using ochres or poster paints, in the symbolic manner of ground sculptures and ceremonial body painting. Over the next few decades these paintings, increasingly on canvas using acrylic paints, were offered for sale and became incredibly successful, both in Australia and outside it. There is great diversity of colour and style in contemporary desert paintings but the qualities of symbolism and ownership discussed earlier also apply. They are popularly known as dot paintings because the background is completely filled in by areas of dots. These can represent many elements of a landscape; for example clouds, areas of vegetation, the underground chambers of a honey ants nest, or all three at once. In galleries look out for the incomparable work of **Clifford Possum Tjapaltjarri** and **Kathleen Petyarre**.

Baskets & string work

Aboriginal people all over Australia produced string and fibre from the plants in their region to make functional and ceremonial objects. These have only recently been considered works of art as non-indigenous fibre and textile work has gained in status and as the importance of these objects is increasingly understood. Fibre work is a woman's art, although men sometimes made strong ropes for fishing. Palm leaves, reeds, vines, bark, and hair were all used to make string and fibre which was then made into a variety of baskets and bags. These were primarily used to carry food collected during a day's foraging but also held personal possessions. In the tropical north the common pandanus palm is used to make strong baskets or mats woven with dried strands of palm and a bone needle. Fine narrow bags of twined pandanus are called *dilly bags*, and in Arnhem Land play an important part in ceremony and are often depicted on rock art being worn by ancestral beings. String is spun from bark or palm leaves and knotted into bags or fishing nets in Cape York, Arnhem Land and nearby islands. String was also used to made body ornaments such as belts and fringes, armbands and necklaces. Baskets and bags are still made by the women of Northern Australia and today's techniques show how new technology is adapted to continue traditional ways. Before the British arrived Aboriginal people had no steel or clay containers and therefore were not able to boil water. Fibre work was coloured by rubbing ochre into the fibre when making it or by painting the finished object with ochre. Now the fibre is dyed in boiling water but the dyes are still made by the weavers from natural sources, such as roots and grasses, with great skill and subtlety.

Works of wood

Weapons and utensils made of wood were often carved with designs that symbolized an ancestor, thus identifying the land of the owner. The beauty of these carvings carries them beyond the purely functional, as does their origin in the Dreaming. Carvings of ancestral figures were also made to be used in ceremonies such as funeral rites. The Tiwi people of Bathurst and Melville islands make wooden *pukunami* poles that are placed at the gravesite, carved and painted with symbols relevant to the deceased person. The Yolgnu of Eastern Arnhem Land placed the bones of the deceased in hollow

Background

logs, usually painted with clan designs and sometimes carved at one end, and these log coffins would stand upright in the bush. There is a moving display of 200 log coffins in the National Gallery in Canberra, created as a memorial to the Aboriginal dead in the bicentennial year. Groups in NSW carved geometric designs into living trees to mark ceremonial grounds or burial sites.

In many communities weapons are no longer made because Aboriginal people now hunt with guns. Shields and clubs are not needed, but nothing has replaced the spear, and people still make clapping sticks or carrying dishes. As well as making the pukunami poles, the Tiwi carve wonderful wooden sculptures of totemic animals and ancestral beings for sale, as do people along the coast and islands of Arnhem Land. People in central Australia also make wooden animal carvings and these are often decorated with pokerwork, a burn from a hot wire. The didjeridu is still made and used in ceremony in Arnhem Land, where it is called the *yidaki*. The didjeridu is made from a tree trunk that has been hollowed out by termites so each one is unique and the bumps and knots inside influence the sound it makes.

Contemporary Aboriginal art

The art that is produced in northern and central Australia is contemporary art. Although it has its foundation in an ancient culture, it is also shaped by the present. Contemporary art is also produced by Aboriginal people who live in the urban societies of the south and east. These people may have lost their land, language, religion and families but they still have an Aboriginal identity. The people sometimes called urban Aboriginal artists may have trained in art school and their art possesses the 'Western' quality of reflecting the experience of the individual. They are united in their experience of surviving dispossession, by their personal history and experience of being Aboriginal in a dominant non-indigenous society. Some of the common themes in their work are events of the colonial past, such as massacres, or contemporary issues that affect Aboriginal people such as the fight for land rights or the disproportionately high number of Aboriginal prisoners. Some urban artists have tried to reconnect with their past or, like the late **Lin Onus**, establish links with artists working in more traditional forms and to incorporate clan designs or symbolic elements into their work. To see powerful contemporary Aboriginal art look for the work of **Robert Campbell Jnr**, **Sally Morgan**, Lin Onus, **Gordon Bennett**, **Trevor Nikolls**, **Fiona Foley** and **Donna Leslie**.

Other Australian art

Australia was colonized during the century of Romanticism in Western Europe when interest in the natural world was at its height. Much of the earliest colonial art came from scientific expeditions and their specimens drawings. Most of these early images look slightly odd, as if even the best draughtsman found himself unable to capture the impossibly strange forms of unique Australian species such as the kangaroo. Indeed art from the whole of the first colonial century portrays Australia in a soft northern hemisphere light and in the rich colours of European landscapes. In these finely detailed landscapes the countryside was presented as romantically gothic or neatly tamed, even bucolic with the addition of cattle or a farmer at work, as seen in the work of **John Glover**, **Louis Buvelot** and **Eugene von Guérard**. In some there would also be quaint representations of a bark hut or black figure belonging to the peaceful 'children of nature'. Given the violence of what was happening to Aboriginal people at the time and the British impression that the new colony was a nasty, brutish place full of convicts, these paintings can be seen as an attempt to portray Australia as peaceful, beautiful and civilized. Things began to change in the 1880s and 1890s, by which time a majority of colonists had been born in Australia.

Increasing pride in being Australian and the influence of European Impressionism inspired Australian artists to really look at their environment and cast away conventional techniques, prompting a dramatic change in how the country was portrayed. Truth in light, colour and tone was pursued by artists such as **Arthur Streeton**, **Charles Conder**, **Tom Roberts** and **Frederick McCubbin**, who began painting *en plein air*. In their paintings bright light illuminates the country's real colours; the gold of dried grass, the smoky green of eucalypts and the deep blue of the Australian sky. These artists were known as the Heidelberg School because they painted many of their bush scenes around Heidelberg and Box Hill, just outside Melbourne. Some of Australia's most iconic and popular images were painted at this time. *Down on his luck* (1889) by Frederick McCubbin is a classic image of a bushman and his swag, staring into his campfire among gum trees. In Tom Roberts' *A break away!* (1891) a heroic lone horsemen tries to control the rush of sheep to a waterhole in drought-stricken country. The same painter's *Shearing the Rams* (1888-90) again celebrates the noble masculinity of the bush with a shearing-shed scene portraying the industry and camaraderie of the pastoral life. These paintings all represent a golden age that belie the end of the boom times in Victoria, where the economy crashed in the early 1890s, and the reality that most Australians were urban workers rather than bushmen.

After Federation in 1901 Australian landscapes became increasingly pretty and idyllic, typified by the languorous beauties enjoying the outdoors in the work of **E Phillips Fox** or **Rupert Bunny**. However, the trauma of the Great War had a cataclysmic effect on the art world and Australian artists once more followed the lead of Britain and Europe in embracing Modernism. **Margaret Preston** was influenced by the modernist focus on 'primitive' art to incorporate elements from Aboriginal art into her works, *Aboriginal flowers* (1928) and *Aboriginal Landscape* (1941). **Grace Cossington Smith** looked to Van Gogh for works such as *The Lacquer Room* (1936). **Hans Heysen** worked in the tradition of Streeton and McCubbin, glorifying the South Australian landscape with images of mighty old gum trees and the ancient folds of the Flinders Ranges, but other painters of the 1940s and 1950s were looking at the landscape differently. The Outback is presented as a harsh and desolate place in the work of **Russell Drysdale** and **Sidney Nolan**. During the Forties Nolan produced a famous series of paintings on bushranger Ned Kelly in a whimsical, naïve style in which he expressed a desire to paint the "stories which take place within the landscape" – an interesting link to Aboriginal art. Nolan belonged to a group of artists called the 'Angry Penguins', along with **Albert Tucker**, **Joy Hester** and **Arthur Boyd**. These artists worked under the patronage of John and Sunday Reed at Heide outside Melbourne, the same area that had inspired the Heidelberg School. Tucker painted the evil that the Second World War had brought to society in paintings like *The Victory Girls* (1943). Boyd worked on moral themes set among light-sodden landscapes. Other artists were portraying the alienation of urban lives, in paintings like **John Brack's** *Collins Street 5 p.m.* (1955).

During the 1960s and 70s Australian artists were influenced by the abstract movement. Artists such as **John Olsen** and **Fred Williams** still produced landscapes but in an intensely personal, emotional and unstructured way. **Brett Whiteley** painted sensous, colour-drenched Sydney landscapes and disturbing works such as the *Christie Series* (1964) in a surreal or distorted manner reminiscent of Salvador Dali or Francis Bacon. Painting became a less dominant form in this period and the following decades with many artists working in sculpture, installations, video and photography. The eighties and nineties were also marked by an intense interest in Aboriginal art, leading to its inclusion within the mainstream venues and discourse of contemporary Australian art.

The Heidelberg School & Australian Impressionism

Modernism & the Angry Penguins

Contemporary art

Background

Literature

Australia has a rich literary culture and an admirable body of national literature. Until recently this reflected only the European experience of the country, but increasingly includes Aboriginal voices and those of migrants. Awareness and exploration of the Asia-Pacific cultures of the region is also a new theme. It is not surprising that the main concern for Europeans has been the alien nature of the country they had so recently arrived in – to examine how it was different from their own country and to find both meaning and their own place within it. As in so many cultural fields it has taken a long time for an Australian identity to develop and in literature it has been primarily within the last 50 years. As questions of national identity are resolved Australian writers move towards regional and local identity. One of the features of contemporary Australian literature is the strong sense of place it conveys. The writers and poets discussed below are significant figures of Australian literature who have built up a substantial collection of work but of course there are many more fine writers. See also page 913.

A B 'Banjo' Paterson & Henry Lawson   Paterson and Lawson were both journalists of the 1890s and have done more to define the character of the Australian bushman than any other writers. Both were nationalists, although there were important differences in their work. Paterson wrote the country's most famous bush ballads such as *Waltzing Matilda*, *Clancy of the Overflow* and *The Man from Snowy River*. The latter still outsells all other volumes of Australian poetry. Paterson's was a romantic vision; brave and cheerful men on noble horses working companionably across Australia's vast land or standing firm against figures of authority. Lawson criticized Paterson in the literary journal, *The Bulletin*, for his idealism, saying "the real native outback bushman is narrow minded, densely ignorant, invulnerably thick-headed", and that heat, flies, drought and despair were missing from Paterson's poetry. Lawson was a part of the republican movement of the late 1880s and a prolific writer of poetry and prose based on the people of the bush. His well-crafted short stories present the bush in the clear light of realism and their qualities of understated style, journalistic detail, sympathy for broken characters and ironic humour mean that Lawson's stories are considered among the finest in Australian literature. His best stories are found in the collections *Joe Wilson and His Mates* and *While the Billy Boils*.

Patrick White   Patrick White detested what he saw as the emptiness and materialism at the heart of Australian life yet it inspired his visionary literature with its characters searching for meaning. He wanted to convey a transcendence above human realities, a mystery and poetry that could make an ordinary life bearable. His major novels are *The Tree of Man*, *Voss*, *Riders in the Chariot*, *The Solid Mandala*, *The Vivisector*, *Eye of the Storm* and *Fringe of Leaves*. Never very popular in Australia because of his critical eye and 'difficult' metaphysical style, White won the Nobel Prize for Literature in 1973 for *The Tree of Man* and began to receive more attention at home. His original vision, the dynamism and poetic language of his work are some of the elements that make him a giant of Australian literature.

Thomas Keneally   An energetic and prolific writer with a great store of curiosity, Keneally has ranged all over the world in subject matter yet at the core of his fiction is the individual trying to act with integrity in extreme situations. One of his most important 'Australian' novels is *The Chant of Jimmy Blacksmith*, a fictional representation of the late 19th century figure, part-Aboriginal Jimmy Governor, who married a white girl and was goaded into murder. Other subjects include Armistice negotiations (*Gossip from the Forest*), Yugoslav partisans in the Second World War (*Season in Purgatory*) and the American Civil War (*Confederates*) but Keneally's best-known novel is *Schindler's Ark*. He won the *Booker Prize* for this novel, although some complained that the book was hardly fictional, and it was made into the highly successful Spielberg film, *Schindler's List*. Keneally manages to capture historical moments vividly and is that rare kind of writer who is popular yet serious.

Contemporary poet Les Murray can be linked back to the 1890s poets Paterson and Lawson in his central theme of the bush as the source of Australian identity. Respect for pioneers, the laconic and egalitarian bush character, the shaping influence of the land and dislike for the urban life all run through his work. The city verses country theme is informed by Murray's own experience of moving between the two; he grew up on a farming property in NSW, leaving it for university and work, but later managing to buy back part of the family farm in the Bunyah district. The larger-than-life poet is often called the 'Bard of Bunyah'. Murray writes in an accessible and popular style, but is a contemplative and religious thinker of great originality. Murray's reverence for land has led to an interest in Aboriginal culture, expressed in *The Bulahdelah-Taree Holiday Song Cycle*, a series of poems echoing the style and rhythm of an Arnhem Land song cycle. Other major works include the collections *The People's Otherworld* and *Translations from the Natural World*.

Les Murray

Carey grew up in Victoria, lived for a while in Sydney, but now lives in New York. Being an expatriate writer has only focused his view of Australia, a fairly dark vision that wonders what can grow out of dispossession, violence and a penal colony. Carey is a dazzling writer who never repeats himself; each novel is entirely different in genesis, period and character. His earlier novels had magic-realist elements, such as *Bliss* in which advertising man Harry Joy is re-born several times into new realities. Other qualities include surrealism, comedy, the macabre, and a concern for truth and lies. Carey won the Booker Prize in 1988 for *Oscar and Lucinda*, a Victorian novel with echoes of George Eliot and Edmund Gosse, set in 19th-century NSW and centering on the love between two unconventional gamblers. *True History of the Kelly Gang* won Carey the Booker Prize again in 2001 for a feat of language and imagination that is simply breathtaking. Carey puts flesh on the bones of history by getting inside the mind of bushranger Ned Kelly. His other novels are *Illywhacker*, *The Tax Inspector*, *The Unusual Life of Tristan Smith*, and *Jack Maggs*.

Peter Carey

An elegant and lyrical writer, Malouf is preoccupied by the question of Australian identity. He believes writers need to create mythologies that are the means of a spiritual link between landscape and lives. Places need to be mapped by imagination to acquire meaning or belonging. His own themes are often played out against the background of his own childhood in Brisbane, a richly imagined slow and lush city of the past. In his novels characters are forced by circumstance to find a new way of seeing. *The Great World* follows the lives of Vic and Digger through Second World War prisoner of war camps to examine layers of history and identity. *An Imaginary Life* deals with the Roman poet Ovid in exile from Rome and his relationship with a wolfchild, a poetic novel that explores Australian issues of exile, place and belonging. These themes are continued in *Remembering Babylon*, set in the 1840s when a white boy who has lived with Aborigines for 16 years encounters the first settlers to reach northern Queensland. Malouf also writes poetry and short stories; forms that suit his economic yet powerfully descriptive language.

David Malouf

Tim Winton is a West Australian author who writes very successfully for both adults and children. His work is marked by a sense of place, particularly the WA coast, and a tight focus on character within an environment. Winton has said of his work "if I can get a grip on the geography, I can get a grip on the people". He certainly does so – his characters are intensely imagined and powerfully 'real', often reinforced by Winton's open

Tim Winton

Background

endings as if the rest of their lives really are still to be lived. Loneliness and self-doubt are common to his characters as they search for identity and a sense of purpose. *Cloudstreet* is a funny and affectionate tale of two very different families sharing a house in post-war Perth and the dark undercurrents of their ordinary lives. In *The Riders*, Fred Scully makes a frantic search across an alien and unfamiliar Europe for his wife. *Dirt Music* is his latest novel, a moving story of loss and loneliness set in the crayfishing towns of the west coast. Luther and Georgie belong to nowhere and nobody and are drawn together, although Luther is determined to be left alone.

Kate Grenville Grenville's novels are sharply observed, funny and sometimes gothic explorations of what makes people tick and how they create their own destiny. This writer sees Australian history as a rich source of material; full of stories still to be told, landscape to be described and ways of being 'Australian' to explore. For *Lilian's Story* Grenville was inspired by Sydney eccentric Bea Miles to write the story of an uninhibited woman who makes her own myth at a time when women are supposed to be passive. *Dark Places* is about Lilian's monstrous father and how he distorts truth and reality to justify his actions. *Joan Makes History* re-writes Australian history in the image of women. Joan imagines she is present at all the big moments of Australia's past. *The Idea of Perfection* is about two middle-aged and unattractive people drawn together because they value history and its imperfections. This novel won the Orange Prize for Fiction in 2001.

Music

Popular music Australian popular music has been heavily influenced by the British and American music scenes but has also produced exciting home-grown sounds that are distinctively Australian. The industry suffered from the 'cultural cringe' for some time – the idea that anything Australian is only any good if Britain and America think so. In the last three decades, however, Australians have embraced their own music and there have been many bands that are extremely successful in Australia but unknown outside the country. Australian musicians are limited by their tiny market – if they want to make serious money they must pursue success overseas.

Australian music first came to the notice of the rest of the world in the 1970s, when glam rock outfits **Sherbert** and the **Skyhooks** toured America. **Little River Band** did well in the US with their catchy commercial pop while punk outfit **The Saints** were simultaneously making it big in the UK. However the real success story of the decade was **AC/DC**, one of the greatest heavy-rock bands in the world. Their album *Highway to Hell* was a huge success in 1979 though they lost their lead singer Bon Scott in 1980 to a tragic rock-star death.

The 1980s was the decade of the hardworking pub rock band, the sexy funk rock of **INXS**, the stirring political anthems of **Midnight Oil**, and the working-class onslaught of **Cold Chisel**. Of these bands INXS had the most success overseas while Midnight Oil and Cold Chisel were huge at home, singing about Australian places, issues and experiences. **Men at Work** had a hit with the quirky *Down Under* and **Crowded House**, led by the master singer-songwriter and New Zealander **Neil Finn**, seduced the world with tracks like *Don't Dream It's Over*. Singer-songwriters **Richard Clapton** and **Paul Kelly** also came to prominence at this time and both continue to influence the music scene. Paul Kelly's album *Gossip* is a classic – full of finely observed stories about life in Sydney and Melbourne.

Record companies became less willing to take a chance on unproven Australian bands in the 1990s and the decade was marked by developments on the local scene. Strangely, there was a rash of success for ex-soap stars **Kylie Minogue** and **Natalie Imbruglia**, but more so in the UK than at home. Kylie even got serious when she teamed up with ex-**Birthday Party** frontman, **Nick Cave** on a track for his typically downbeat *Murder Ballads* album. Cave's dark, philosopical stylings have always gone down better in the UK and Europe than down under. **The Whitlams**, meanwhile, appealed to sophisticated punters with witty and melodic funk. At the noisier end of the spectrum **Regurgitator** appeared with an influential and original sound, **Spiderbait** and **Powderfinger** and **Savage Garden** also all made it big. The band that really caught the public imagination though was **Silverchair**, a trio of schoolboys who won a competition to record their grunge classic *Tomorrow*. Aboriginal musicians also had commercial success; look out for bands **Yothu Yindi**, **Saltwater** and **Coloured Stone**, and the soulful ballads of **Archie Roach** or energetic pop of Torres Strait Islander **Christine Anu**.

In the first few years of this decade Kylie Minogue just got bigger, Savage Garden split up but singer Darren Hayes started up a solo career. **Superjesus, Bodyjar, Even,** and **Killing Heidi** are all doing well locally.

About three million Australians a year attend classical concerts and the country has a strong classical music culture, with a dedicated national classical radio station and symphony orchestras in every state. Contemporary classical is also healthy, as demonstrated by composers such as **Peter Sculthorpe** and **Liza Lim**. Conductor **Simone Young** is considered one of the most talented conductors of her generation and was the first woman to conduct at the Vienna State Opera and the Paris Opera Bastille. She is now conducting at *Opera Australia*. Opera singer **Dame Joan Sutherland** is one of the world's best sopranos.

Country music is very popular in Australia, although highly derivative. **Slim Dusty** has represented Australian country music since 1945 and is still going strong. Younger performers include **James Blundell, Lee Kernaghan, Gina Jeffreys** and **Troy Cassar-Daley**.

Classical & country

Cinema

Although Australia produced the world's first feature film in 1906, *The Story of the Kelly Gang*, its budding film industry was soon overwhelmed by a flood of British and American films. It wasn't until the 1970s, when Australia was exploring its cultural identity, that the industry revived. Government funding commonly paid for as much as half of the production costs of a film and Australian themes were encouraged. During this period some classics were made, such as *Picnic at Hanging Rock*. Directed by **Peter Weir**. This is a story of a schoolgirls' picnic that goes horribly wrong when some of the girls disappear into the haunting and mysterious landscape, one of many Australian films to suggest that perhaps the Outback has the spiritual power that Aboriginal people believe it does. Weir went on to become a very successful Hollywood director (*Witness, Dead Poets Society, Truman Show*). *My Brilliant Career* was the beginning of brilliant careers for director **Gillian Armstrong** and actor **Judy Davis**. Davis played an independent young woman of the late-19th-century who wanted to escape from the farm and live an intellectual life. The decade was also marked by 'ocker' films made for the home audience portraying the crass, uncouth and exaggerated Australian, like *The Adventures of Barry McKenzie*.

First steps

Things changed in the 1980s when the government brought in tax incentives to encourage private investment in the film industry. Direct government funding dropped away to low levels. Naturally under these conditions the emphasis switched to profit rather than artistic merit and many big-budget commercial films were made such as *Crocodile Dundee*. In 1981 Peter Weir's *Gallipoli* was a much-loved film about the

Glamour & heroes

sacrifices and stupidity of events at Gallipoli, starring a young **Mel Gibson**. In a completely different role Gibson also starred in another successful film that year, *Mad Max II*, shot around Broken Hill in Outback NSW. Australian high-country life was romanticised in *The Man from Snowy River*, featuring a lot of handsome, rugged horsemen and spectacular scenery. In 1987 the thriller *Dead Calm* brought **Nicole Kidman** much attention and *Evil Angels* did the same for Uluru in a film about Lindy Chamberlain who claimed that a dingo took her baby from the campsite at the base of the rock in 1980. Even Meryl Streep, however, failed to master an Australian accent to play Chamberlain. Despite these big flashy films, Australian film makers also managed some interesting smaller-scale films looking at relationships, such as *Monkey Grip*, *High Tide*, *My First Wife*, and the extraordinary *Sweetie* in 1989. The first feature film directed by New Zealand born **Jane Campion**, it focuses on the sisters Sweetie and Kay in their dysfunctional suburban family life. Sweetie is perhaps the first of the freaks and misfits that would feature in films of the nineties.

Money & misfits   The industry changed again in the 1990s when the generous tax concessions of the 1980s were retracted and the country suffered through economic depression in the early years of the decade. Australian film makers had to look overseas for finance and increasingly encourage American producers to use Australian facilities and locations. The new *Fox Studios* in Sydney attracted *The Matrix*, *Star Wars Episode II* and *Mission Impossible II*. The joint finance and production arrangements made it difficult to define an 'Australian' film. Cross-fertilisation of talent and general optimism in the industry led Australian film makers to produce some bold and risk-taking films in the nineties. Issues of identity and gender came to the fore in films that weren't afraid to celebrate the daggy, the misfits or oddballs like *Strictly Ballroom*, *The Adventures of Priscilla, Queen of the Desert*, and *Muriel's Wedding*. In less subtle films, like *The Castle* or *Holy Smoke* Australians were portrayed as well-meaning but hopelessly naïve fools and bumpkins. Other films pursued more serious issues but got less attention outside the country, like *Romper Stomper*, a harrowing look at a gang of racist skinheads in Melbourne starring **Russell Crowe**, or *Dead Heart*, a confronting look at the clash of cultures in central Australia starring the ubiquitous **Bryan Brown**.

Beyond 2000   Despite the successes and attention of the 1990s, the Australian film industry still struggles against the behemoth of Hollywood. International financing is still a feature of the industry and it is difficult for distinctively Australian films to get made as they are still perceived as not very marketable outside the country. There is no shortage of suberb talent but many of the best Australian actors and directors need work overseas to get the most opportunities. Indeed at present Australian actors are better known than Australian films; Nicole Kidman, Cate Blanchett, Russell Crowe, Guy Pearce, Toni Collette, Geoffrey Rush, Judy Davis, Hugh Jackman and more are all in huge demand in Britain and America. The most recent standout film was *Moulin Rouge*, made by visionary director **Baz Luhrmann** and starring Nicole Kidman and Ewan McGregor. This love story set in the Paris of Toulouse-Lautrec is a riot of colour and music. Luhrmann has singlehandedly reinvented the musical film in *Strictly Ballroom*, *Romeo and Juliet* and *Moulin Rouge*. Other films worth looking out for are *Lantana*, an immensely sophisticated tangle of love and betrayal, and *Rabbit Proof Fence*, a film bringing alive the trauma of the 'stolen generation' in recreating the true stories of three Aboriginal girls escaping from their mission and walking thousand of miles to find their mother. *Yolngu Boy* is an interesting look at contemporary Aboriginal society, following three teenage boys in Arnhem Land as they try to exchange petrol sniffing for something better.

Language

When Europeans arrived in Australia there were about 250 Aboriginal languages and many more dialects. Many of these were as different from each other as English and Bengali. Most Aboriginal people spoke three or four languages; those of neighbouring groups, kin or birthplace. Because Aboriginal languages were oral they were easily lost. About 100 languages have disappeared since 1788, another 100 are used only by old people and will die out within 10-20 years. Only about 20 languages are commonly spoken today. Many Aboriginal people still speak several languages, of which English may be their second or third language. Aboriginal English is widely spoken; this is a form of English with the structure of Aboriginal languages or English words that do not correspond to the English meaning.

English is the official language of Australia, and it has developed a rich vocabulary all its own in its two centuries of linguistic experimentation. The words and terms listed in the glossary are mostly unique to Australia. American visitors will find a lot of unfamiliar British terms and slang words also in use (see Glossary for some common words and phrases). Unfortunately many colourful Australian phrases are gradually disappearing under the dominant influence of American television and film.

Land and environment

The shaping of the continent

There are bits of Australia that are staggeringly old. Some rocks found in the southwest date back over four billion years, a time when the world was still in its geological nappies. In fact most of that corner of the continent is made up of something called the Yilgarn Block, a vast chunk of bedrock over two billion years old, and much of the Pilbara is half as old again. The coastal areas are a little younger, and a couple of the deserts, including the great limestone Nullarbor, are composed of more recent sedimentary rocks, but most of the continent is at least a billion years old. There have been periods of excitement, such as the central faulting which created the MacDonnell Ranges, but on the whole the landscape of the west is truly ancient. It is estimated that the Finke River has more or less run its present course for a 100 million years, and a resurrected dinosaur taken back to Uluru might be curious about the visitor centre, but would be completely at home with the rock.

This ancient provenance goes a long way to explaining why Australia, compared with all the other continents, is so flat. Hundreds of millions of years of weathering have steadily taken their toll, relentlessly grinding down mountain ranges and flattening out the plains. This isn't the whole story, however. Around 250 million years ago geological activity of the faulting and folding variety pretty much ceased everywhere, except on the very periphery, as the continent began to stir. It was then part of the super-continent Gondwana, a huge landmass that broke up to become South America, Antarctica, Africa, India, and the Middle East, as well as the Australasian islands. The 'dividing' ranges that now mark Australia's east coast were formed when New Zealand made its break for independence about 90 million years ago. Those in Victoria are more recent, formed as Australia itself finally broke away from Antarctica about 40 million years ago, winning a fierce tug of war for Tasmania in the process. All this pulling and pushing helped create great vertical movement as well as horizontal. Several eastern and southern parts of the continent sank, creating huge depressions that were periodically deluged. The biggest of these depressions is the Great Artesian Basin, an area the size of South Australia centred on the junction of that state with New South Wales and Queensland. During the periods that these depressions were under water huge sheets of sediment were laid down, the other major cause of much of Australia's bewildering flatness.

If we take a broader view, however, we can see that Australia is involved in some pretty spectacular, and ongoing mountain-building. Island Australia is actually just the biggest part of a greater continent. In geological terms the islands of Tasmania, Australia, the Torres Strait, and New Guinea are one continuous mass, a super-island sometimes called Meganesia. The slightly lower areas of this landmass are usually sunk beneath sea-level, splitting the continent up as we see it today, but for ecological and human history it is important to note that this has not been the normal state of affairs for the last couple of million years. The current, slightly submerged state dates back only a few thousand years to the end of the last ice age.

Meganesia has some terrific mountains, including the central ranges of New Guinea that reach over 5,000 m and carry some of the world's last 'tropical' glaciers. The whole landmass has been heading north ever since breaking with Antarctica, and is still doing so, speeding along at about 7 cm a year. It is now crashing into the crustal plates of south Asia and the western pacific. New Guinea has been colourfully, and accurately, described as Australia's bow wave, absorbing the immense contact forces and building its highlands in the process.

The landscape

Much of the Australian landscape seems timeless; unaffected by the progress of humanity. The Anangu people of Uluru liken the visitors who climb the rock to ants, and when you first visit one of the ancient natural wonders of Australia, or roam the edges of its great deserts, it is very easy to feel like one. Much of the continent is dry, red and flat to an almost mind-boggling degree, most of it covered in low scrub or relict forests, but always somewhere over the horizon is some dramatic punctuation. This is a land where the twin forces of geology and weathering have had the time to carve almost unbelievable edifices, and the dry climate leaves many of these grand structures almost naked of vegetation. Even where the colossi of Australian geology are cloaked by vegetation you are liable to feel dwarfed. The southern forests of Australia, particularly those of Western Australia, Victoria and Tasmania boast species of gum trees that can beat almost every other tree species on the planet for height, weight and girth. An island continent, the vast interior is corralled by an almost endless coastline boasting every possible combination of beach and cliff, swamp and estuary that nature has to offer.

This is the Australia the casual visitor sees – the vibrant colours and vivid shapes, fabulous forests and sublime shores. But spare a thought for the other Australia, the land and ecology under attack from repeated human onslaughts. Huge areas of native vegetation have been cleared for agriculture, and to a small extent urbanization. There are country-sized blocks of land in Western Australia, South Australia, Victoria and New South Wales where practically nothing grows but wheat. Some soil has been improved by fertilizers, but much has been degraded. In some places the removal of trees has led to a rising of the water table, and in turn the salination of the soil, a dreadful affliction that renders the land fit for

Size matters

Australia's land mass in comparison to Western Europe

nothing but the most specialized of plants. Where the land was cleared for grazing sometimes a few trees were left but the effects of hoofed animals have been nearly as damaging, causing erosion in some areas on an unprecedented scale. Where native vegetation has been left untouched or has recovered it can now suffer dramatically from a *reduction* of human interference, that of fire management. Fuel loads build to such an extent that dramatic bushfires flare up every decade or so, many in National Parks close to city suburbs. The 'Black Christmas' of 2001 was simply the latest in a succession of such fires that have seen hectares of bush turn to ash and homes turn to cinders.

Wildlife

Wildlife is very much a part of the Australian holiday experience. The rich bio-diversity is among the most remarkable on the planet and the list of species reads like a who's who of the marvellous, the bizarre and the highly unlikely. There are over 750 bird species alone. The reason for the sheer range and wealth of bio-diversity is a result of the specialist environments within Australia in combination with millions of years of isolation. There are many myths surrounding the dangers of Australian wildlife, but provided you remain observant, cautious and have respect, your Australian wildlife experience will be a pleasant one. Try if you can to visit some of the many wildlife parks and zoos around the country to familiarize yourself with what exactly is out there, especially Taronga Zoo in Sydney, Currumbin on the Gold Coast and the Billabong Sanctuary, near Townsville. Above all try to camp in as many national parks as you can. This will inevitably result in many unexpected and memorable wild encounters. The various government conservation and environmental bodies are invaluable sources of information and have offices in most major towns and cities (listed in the travelling text).

The most famous of the marsupials are of course the **kangaroos** and **wallabies**. There are over 50 species of kangaroos, wallabies and tree kangaroos in Australia. The most well known and commonly seen are the eastern grey, western grey and the red. The eastern grey can be seen almost anywhere in NSW, Queensland and Victoria, especially along the coast. They are also the only kangaroo species present in Tasmania. The red kangaroo, which is the largest, is the one most synonymous with the outback and giving you a good punch on the nose. The tree kangaroos live deep in the bush and are notoriously shy and are therefore very seldom seen. Your encounters with these, the most famous of Australian creatures, will be frequent and highly entertaining, especially with the greys in the wildlife parks and a national park campsites around the coast. In wildlife parks they are notoriously tame and obsessed with the contents of your pockets, while in the national parks you can sit and have breakfast with them nibbling the grass nearby. Sadly 'outback' your encounters with kangaroos will most likely be of the dead variety. There are literally thousands of road kills each year involving kangaroos, since they are very inept at avoiding moving vehicles.

Marsupials

Equally famous is the **koala**. One word of advice here – koalas are not bears, never have been, never will be, and are about as closely related as Pope John Paul is to Ozzie Osborne. Koalas are not only adorable, eminently cuddly, but also incredibly well adapted to the Australian environment. How an animal can evolve to eat one of the most toxic of leaves – eucalyptus – and survive quite happily, is remarkable to say the least. But they are also notoriously stupid. They may be cute but they have a brain about the size of a walnut. Their diet also results in the slow movements and need to sleep the vast majority of the time. Coping well in captivity koalas are easily encountered in the many wildlife parks throughout the country. And there is no doubt whatsoever that being hugged by a koala is the most seminal Australian experience.

Background

Everybody loves a **wombat**. Also marsupials, there are three species: common, northern and southern hairy-nosed wombats. They are infinitely adorable creatures and, like the koala, very well adapted to the Australian environment and their specialist vegetarian diet. They are in essence somnolent, beaver-like lawn mowers, that can (and do), go where they want, when they want and generally with great success. Like sheep they are also consummate grass eaters and as a result have the largest colon in relation to size of any mammal. They also must, like the koala, sleep much of the time and are essentially nocturnal. Campsites are the best place to see them where burrows and small piles of dung will provide testimony to their presence. Another very familiar family of marsupials are the possums. There are numerous species with the most commonly encountered being the doe-eyed **brushtail possum** and the smaller **ring-tailed possum**. Both are common in urban areas and regularly show up after dusk in campsites. The best way to see them is by joining a night spotting tour, especially in Queensland, where in only a few acres of bush there may be as many as 18 different species.

Other marsupials include the delightful **quokka** (like a miniature wallaby), the Tasmanian Devil, (as the names suggests only found in Tasmania), **bandicoots** (21 species most of which are like an attractive rat with a noses like Barry Manilow), the **numbat** (endangered) and the **bilby** (with ears bigger than 'Yoda' from *Star Wars*).

Monotremes There are only three living species of monotremes in the world: the duck-billed platypus and the short-beaked echidna, both of which are endemic to Australia, and the long-beaked echidna that is found only on the islands of New Guinea. They are unique in many ways, but suffice to say, the most remarkable feature is that they are mammals that lay eggs. They have also been around for over 100 million years. The **platypus**, that most enigmatic of creatures, is living proof that nature is, and always will be, the greatest architect, and one that completely stumped zoologists of yesteryear. The duck-billed platypus is only found in rivers and freshwater lakes in eastern Australia. They live in burrows, are excellent swimmers and can stay submerged for up to ten minutes. The duck-like bill is not hard like the beak of a bird, but soft and covered in sensitive nerve endings that help to locate food. The males have sharp spurs on both hind leg ankles that can deliver venom strong enough to cause excruciating pain in humans and even kill a dog. Platypuses are best seen just before dawn.

As if the order monotremes were not weird enough, the two families within it look completely different. Although the **echidna** is in no way related to the hedgehog, it looks decidedly like one, crossed perhaps with Concorde. You will almost certainly encounter the echidna all over Australia, even in urban areas, where they belligerently go about their business and are a delight to watch. If approached they adopt the same defence tactics as hedgehogs by curling up and erecting their spines. They are immensely powerful creatures not dissimilar to small spiny tanks. They are mainly nocturnal and hunt for insects by emanating electrical signals from the long snout, before catching them with a long sticky tongue.

Birds With one of the most impressive bird lists in the world, Australia is a bird watcher's paradise and even if you are indifferent, you cannot fail to be impressed by their diversity, their colour and their calls. The most famous of Australian birds is the **Kookaburra**. They look like huge kingfishers and are indeed related. Other than their prevalence, their fearlessness and their extrovert behaviour, it is their laughing call that will remain forever in your psyche. At dawn when a family group really gets going, it can sound so much fun that you almost feel inclined to rise immediately and share the joke. About the same size as the Kookaburra is the **tawny frogmouth**. It looks like a cross between an owl and a frog, with cryptic camouflaged plumage, fiery orange eyes and a mouth the size of the Channel Tunnel. Due to its nocturnal lifestyle it is hard to observe in the wild and is best seen in zoos and wildlife parks.

From the cryptic to the colourful, Australia is famous for its psittacines – the parrot family – including parakeets, lorikeets, cockatiels, rosellas and budgerigars. There can perhaps be no better demonstration that these species should not be confined to cages than the vast outback of Australia, their true and natural domain. Out there, against oceanic skies, vast flocks roam in search of food: the **cockatoos** like ghosts against thunderclouds, the **budgerigars** like a shimmer of green and yellow in a heat haze and the **crimson rosella** like a firework in the forests. In urban areas the **rainbow lorikeet** that looks like some award-winning invention by some manic professor of colour, is a common sight (and sound), while in rural areas and forests the graceful red, white and yellow tailed **black cockatoos** are also a pleasure to behold. Others include the pink **galah**, the breathtaking **king parrot** and the evocatively named **gang-gang**.

Almost as colourful and yet remarkably obsessed by the phenomenon themselves are the bower birds. There are several species in Australia with the most notable being the beautiful, but endangered, **regent bower bird** with its startling gold and black plumage, and the **satin bower bird**. Remarkably, the latter builds a nest on the ground with an avenue of twigs decorated with objects, especially blue objects, to attract the female. A nest near an urban area can look like the ultimate in the lost and found, with anything from blue clothes pegs and sweetie wrappers to toy soldiers and flowers. A well-known bird of the bush is the **lyrebird**. Fairly unremarkable in appearance (rather like a bantam) though truly remarkable in their behaviour, they are expert mimics often fooling other birds into thinking there are others present protecting territory and humans into thinking their neighbour has the lawn mower or chainsaw out with a vengeance. Their name derives from the shape of their tail (males only), which spread out looks like the ancient Greek musical instrument.

A far larger, rarer bird of the tropical rainforest is the **cassowary**, a large flightless relative of the emu with a mantle of black hair-like plumage, colourful wattles and a strange blunt horn on its head. It is a highly specialist feeder of forest fruits and seeds and somewhat antipathetic to human disturbance, tragically, being killed regularly on the roads. Their last remaining stronghold in Australia is in Far North Queensland, especially around Mission Beach, where they are keenly protected. They are well worth seeing, but your best chance of doing so remains in wildlife sanctuaries and zoos.

Very impressive in the beak department (in fact, perhaps possessing the most remarkable of all) is the **pelican**, that large, doleful, webby white character so synonymous with a day at the beach. They are simply wonderful to watch. As well as hanging around wharfs and boat ramps for free handouts they are also regularly seen sleeping on the top of lampposts, seemingly oblivious to the chaotic urbanity beneath. Lakes and harbours are also the favourite haunt of the **black swan**, the faunal emblem of Western Australia. The Australian black swan is the only uniform black swan in the world with the other seven species being predominantly white. One interesting feature of swans is that they actually have more vertebrae in their neck than the lofty giraffe. While giraffes use that anatomy to reach leaves high up in the trees, swans use it to reach deep in to the water to sift the bottom, or to reach weed. We depart aquatic environs with a major surprise – the **fairy penguin** – the smallest penguin in the world. Like some interminably cute, chubby little pigeon in a wetsuit, they are found all along the southern coastline of Australia and without an iceberg in sight. Their scientific name 'Eudyptula' is Greek for 'good little diver'. The largest colony is on Philip Island near Melbourne where over 20,000 are known to breed in a vast warren of burrows.

From ocean to outback and small to XXL is the **emu**, the Pamela Stephenson of the outback, minus the bathers or the enhancements. With long powerful legs they are prevalent, yet quite shy, usually running off like a group of hairy basketball players on a first time shoplifting spree.

Reptiles, First up is the largest – the **crocodile**. There are two species in Australia, the saltwater
amphibians, crocodile (or 'saltie' as they are known), which is found throughout the Indo-Australian
insects & region, and the smaller freshwater crocodile, which is endemic. It is only the saltwater
arachnids crocodile that is partial to meat and could not care less whether there is a fishing rod or
a Rolex watch attached. Believe it or not the largest was measured at a fearsome 10 m
and the largest human 'feeding frenzy' occurred when one thousand Japanese soldiers
vanished in a swamp between Burma and Romree Island to escape the British during
the Second World War. By morning only 20 were left! Greatly hyped by films and television since the creation of Tarzan, there is no doubt the mighty 'saltie', is, along with the
great white shark, the most feared creature on earth. Although you will undoubtedly
encounter crocodiles in zoos, wildlife parks and crocodile farms throughout the Australia, you may also be lucky to spot one in the wild in the northern regions. Moving on
from the thoroughly dangerous department, to the relatively harmless and medium
range is the enchanting goanna, or monitor, a common sight, especially in campsites
where their belligerence is legendary. There are actually many species of **goanna** in
Australia. They can reach up to 2 m in length, are carnivores and if threatened run
towards anything upright to escape.

There are many other species of lizard that you may encounter on your travels. In
urban areas these include the **bearded dragon** (also called the water dragon) and the
blue-tongued lizard (six species), both about 50 cm in length. It is not unusual to be
out jogging in Sydney for example and have to side step one of these. They are also
commonly kept as pets. No doubt when you are in your average campsite toilet enjoying a bit of light relief, especially in the tropics, you will notice a tiny flesh-coloured lizard plastered to the roof or busy catching insects. These are **gekos**, and there are many
species in Australia, most being far more colourful and far less perverse in their choice
of habitat. They manage to cling to smooth surfaces using an adaptation, in the form of
tiny hairs on their feet called setae. On a single toe there can be over one million.

Australia has 140 species of land snake and about 32 species of sea snake. Of
these about 100 are venomous with about a dozen able to cause a human fatality. Of
the 11 most venomous snakes in the world Australia has seven of them. These
include the rather innocuous looking taipan. There are many species of frogs and
toads in Australia including the commonly seen **green tree frog**. Insects are well
beyond the scope of this handbook, but there are two arachnids, that once encountered, will almost certainly reside in your memory forever. The first is the **huntsman**
spider, a very common species seen almost anywhere in Australia, especially indoors.
Although not the largest spider on the continent, they can grow to a size that would
comfortably cover the palm of your hand. Blessed with the propensity to shock, they
are an impressive sight, do bite, but only when provoked and are not venomous. Of the
variety of glorious butterflies and moths in Australia perhaps the most beautiful is the
Ulysses blue, found in the tropics, especially in far north Queensland. They are incredibly graceful in flight and once seen, never forgotten.

Marine Although whaling was once practiced in Australia, with several species hunted to the
mammals very point of extinction, it is now thankfully whale-watching that is big business. Her-
& turtles vey Bay in Queensland is one of the most remarkable and touts itself as the whale
watching capital of the world, though there are plenty of good opportunities right
around the east, south and west coasts. Along both the eastern and western seaboards
of Australia, **humpback whales** are commonly sighted on passage between the tropics and Antarctica between the months of July and October. Occasionally they are even
seen wallowing in Sydney Harbour or breaching in the waters off the famous Bondi
Beach. The **southern right whale** is another species regularly seen in Australian
waters, likewise the **orca**, or killer whale. Several species of dolphin are present including the **bottlenose dolphin,** which are a common sight off almost any beach surfing

the waves with as much skill and delight as any human on a surfboard. There are also a few places in Australia where you can not only see wild dolphins, but also encounter them personally, including the **Tangalooma Dolphin Resort** on Moreton Island near Brisbane, **Monkey Mia** in Shark Bay, **Port Phillip** near Melbourne and **Bunbury**, just south of Perth. Another less well-known sea mammal clinging precariously to a few locales around the coast is the **dugong** or sea cow. **Shark Bay** in WA and the waters surrounding **Hinchinbrook Island** in QLD remain one of the best places to see them. Australia is also a very important breeding ground for **turtles**. The **Mon Repos** turtle rookery, near Bundaberg, QLD, is one of the largest and most important loggerhead turtle rookeries in the world. A visit there during the nesting season (October-May), when the females haul themselves up at night to lay their eggs, or the hatchlings emerge to make a mad dash for the waves, is a truly unforgettable experience.

There is no doubt that your experience of Australian wildlife will be both exciting and memorable, but the reality is that the Australian environment is in peril. The culprit, as always, is man, and in this case it is the introduction of a whole host of non-native animals which has had such a devastating impact. Species that are currently causing havoc and have done so for some time include the **rabbit**, the **fox**, the **cat** and most recently, the **cane toad**. The greatest fear is that Australia is a very fragile environment hosting many specialist species extremely antipathetic to unnatural imbalances or disturbance. Many extinct species are testament to that including the most recent and one of the most tragic, the **Thylacine**, or Tasmanian tiger lost to the world forever in the 1940s. Others currently teetering precariously on the brink, include the northern hairy-nosed wombat, the dibbler, several bandicoot species and the eastern bristlebird. But there are many others. Major efforts are being made to halt the destruction, and eco-tourism plays an important role in conservation generally, but since conservation is a drain on money not a money maker, it inevitably suffers and it does not auger well. Nowhere is this becoming more apparent than the **Great Barrier Reef**, which some scientists fear is already doomed to destruction. It is poignant perhaps that the reef is the single largest living entity on earth and has been for millions of years. Yet still, we have the ignorance and the power to destroy it.

Introduced fauna & the future

Books

Past and present NSW comes alive in **Peter Carey**'s *Oscar and Lucinda* and his memoir, *Letter to Sydney*. Also try **Murray Bail**'s gum tree fable *Eucalyptus*. Soak up the steamy lushness of QLD in the novels and stories of **David Malouf**, such as *12 Edmonstone St* or *Harland's Half Acre*. **Thea Astley**'s *The Multiple Effects of Rainshadow* explores frontier violence. For a slice of incestuous inner-city life in Melbourne during the 1970s, try **Helen Garner**'s excellent *Monkey Grip*. The classic novel of the convict experience in TAS is **Marcus Clarke**'s *For the Term of His Natural Life*, published in 1874. Tasmania's finest contemporary novelist is **Richard Flanagan**; look for *Death of a River Guide*, *The Sound of One Hand Clapping* and his latest, *Gould's Book of Fish*. **Barbara Hanrahan**'s *The Scent of Eucalyptus* evokes 1960s Adelaide with a blend of reality and fantasy. Quite charming to adult visitors, though a children's tale, is the short story *Storm Boy* by **Colin Thiele**, set in the Coorong. **Xavier Herbert**'s *Capricornia* is a classic novel of NT race relations, describing attempts to 'civilise' the thinly disguised land of Capricornia and its 'natives'. In **Robert Drewe**'s meditative *The Drowner* the son of a water diviner works to bring water to the turn of the century WA goldfields. *Benang* by **Kim Scott** is an award-winning fictional account of a man of Nyoongar and European heritage trying to cope with being bred as his family's 'first white man born'.

Australia in fiction
For a list of the best Australian writers and poets, see Literature on page 902

Background

History   Possibly the best account of the world forces that have shaped Aboriginal culture, and why it is that Europeans invaded Australia rather than an Aboriginal Captain Cook that first sailed up the Thames, is given in **Jared Diamond**'s Guns, Germs and Steel, a detailed account of how human culture has developed on all of the continents. **Richard Broome**'s *Aboriginal Australians* is a good general history of what has happenned to Aboriginal people since 1788 and how they have responded to their situation. A fascinating insight into the minds and trials of dozens of different explorers is given in *The Explorers*, edited by **Tim Flannery**, a series of excerpts from eyewitness accounts. One of the most widely read Australian histories concentrates on the detailed story of the convicts and the penal colonies they were taken to is **Robert Hughes'** *Fatal Shore*, which is exhaustive to say the least. The Aboriginal voice itself is also starting to be heard in books such as *Contested Ground*, edited by **Ann McGrath**, a state-by-state account of the experiences of Aborigines since 1788.

Culture   The classic work on Aboriginal culture is **Ronald and Catherine Berndt**'s *The World of the First Australians*. On pre-history look for the work of **Josephine Flood**. Her *Riches of Anient Australia* is a superb look at archaelogical and art sites by region, and *Archaeology of the Dreamtime* is an account of how people came to Australia and how they lived. Jennifer Issacs is a respected commentator on Aboriginal art and culture and any of her books are worth reading for detailed studies of particular art forms.Robert Hughes' *The Art of Australia* was first written in 1966 but remains an influential study of Australian art movements from 1788 to the late 1960s. The most comprehensive round-up of Australian slang can be found in *The Penguin Book of Australian Slang*, edited by **Lenie Johansen**. Those intending to drink a lot of Australian wine may find the annual *Penguin Good Australian Wine Guide* useful, by **Hooke and Kyte-Powell**.

Travelogues & memoirs   *Down Under* by American **Bill Bryson** is probably the best-selling account of a journey around Australia. Englishman **Howard Jacobson**'s *In the Land of Oz* was written more than a decade earlier but is still an amusing, perceptive and thoughtful account of travelling around some of the lesser known bits of Australia. One of the most unusual books in this over-produced genre is *Songlines* by **Bruce Chatwin**, a meditative attempt to understand the Dreaming and its song cycles or songlines across the landscape. *Tracks* by **Robyn Davidson** is highly recommended; a moving and honest account of the author's solo trip across Central Australia on camels.

Ecology, the outdoors & wildlife
The best place to find and order Australian wildlife books from afar is the Australian Geographic website, www.australian geographic.com

Tim Flannery's *Future Eaters* is a fantastic ecological history of the continent, focusing on its fauna, flora and people, and how they have shaped, and been shaped by the environment. *Feral Future* by **Tim Low** is an interesting and alarming study of the current biological invasion of Australia. The best series of walking guides is by hiker **Tyrone T. Thomas**. Those worried about getting lost may want to brush up on bush tucker with **Les Hiddins'** *Bush Tucker Field Guide*. *Safe Outback Travel* by **Jack Absalom** is a trusted manual of driving and camping advice if getting right off the beaten track. Other good wildlife books include *Birds of Australia* by **Ken Simpson**, a new and comprehensive guide that is on a par with the tried and trusted *Slater Field Guide-Australian Birds* by **Peter Slater et al** (now out of print but worth searching for). Another fine field guide is the *Field Guide to Mammals of Australia* by **Peter Menkhorst et al**.

915

Footnotes

Common Aussie words and phrases

B&S Ball	Bachelors and Spinsters Ball – young person's excuse to get as drunk as possible and get off with anything that moves
Back of Bourke	Middle of nowhere
Bananabender	Someone from Queensland
Barbie	Barbeque (BBQ)
Arvo	Afternoon
Bail up	Hold up, forcibly halt
Beauty	('Bewdy') Fantastic, wonderful (also "You beauty")
Billy	Kettle, usually non-electric
Blowies	Blow flies
Bludger	Layabout, non-worker
Bottleshop	Off-license
Bull bar/Roo bar	Extra front vehicle bumper
Bush	Generally any non-urban, non-agricultural area
Bushranger	Bush-based outlaw, eg Ned Kelly
Centralian	Someone from central Australia, eg around Alice Springs
Chips	Potato crisps
Chook	Chicken
Chunder	Vomit – 'hurl', 'spew' and 'ralph' are also used
Cobber	Friend, friendly term for non-acquaintance ("G'day cobber")
Cocky	Cockatoo, cockroach or farmer
Cray	Crayfish, lobster
Croweater	South Australian
Cyclone	Hurricane
Dag, daggy	Bit of dirty wool around sheep's backside, also uncool or silly
Digger	Goldrush miner, also soldier of the world wars
Dob in	Report on someone to the authorities
Donger	Converted shipping container used for sleeping in
Doona	Duvet
Drongo	Idiot
Dunny	Toilet
Esky	Portable cool box
Fair dinkum	Fair enough, a good show, the truth
Feral	Non-indigenous animal or person who has become 'wild'
Flush	Having plenty of money
Footy	Aussie Rules or Rugby League football
G'day	Hello (corruption of the greeting 'good day')
Give it a burl	Give it a try
Good on us/you	General term of satisfaction, endearment or thanks
Goodo	OK, Fine
Grommet	Very young surfer
Hard yakka	Hard physical work
Hot chips	Thick potato chips, french fries
Ice-block	Ice lolly (flavoured ice or ice cream on a stick)
Jackeroo/Jilleroo	Worker (usually young) on a station

Jumbuck	Sheep
Knocker/knock	Person who puts things down, to criticise
Larrikin	Mischievous person
Lay-by	Keep aside (by a shop) until paid for
Lollies	Sweets, candy
Mate	Friend, friendly term for non-acquaintance ("G'day mate")
Mob	Large number of animals or people
Moleskins	Jeans, of brushed cotton
Morning tea	Mid morning break for cake and tea
Mullet	Popular country hairstyle short on top, long at the back
No worries	Do not worry, no problem
Op-shop	Second-hand clothing shop, proceeds go to charities
Outback	Australia's interior
Park	Parking place
Pokers/pokies	Slot or gambling machines
Property	Often used to denote a large outback farm
Rego	Car registration document
Ripper	Excellent!
Sandgroper	Western Australian
Score	Secure something for free, though this has recently been hijacked by advertisers to simply mean getting a bargain ("score this for $20")
She'll be right	Everything will turn out ok, honest
Skerrick	A tiny amount
Slab	Case of beer, usually 24 bottles
Slip, slop, slap	"Slip on a t-shirt, slop on sunscreen, slap on a hat"
Smoko	Cigarette break, tea break
Snag	Sausage
Station	Often used to denote a large outback farm
Stubbie	Small bottle of beer
Stubbie holder	Keeps small bottles (or cans) of beer cold
Swag	Canvas sleeping bag and mattress, for outdoor use
Sydneysider	Someone from Sydney
TAB	State bookmakers, similar to the UK's _Tote_
Tassie	Tasmania, or a Tasmanian
Territorian	Someone from the Northern Territory
Thongs	Flip-flops (footwear)
Tinnie	Can of beer
Tucker	Food – bushtucker is gathered or hunted food
Ute	('Yoot') Utility vehicle with a flat-bed rear
Wet (the)	Northern monsoon season
Willy-willy	Small, harmless swirl of air
Yabby	Edible freshwater crustacean, like a small lobster

Index

Shorts

Advertiser's index

Maps

Map symbols

Administration
---- State border
□ Capital city
o Other city/town

Roads and travel
— Freeway
— Main highway
— Sealed road
---- Unsealed roads of variable quality
...... Footpath
⊢•▬ Railway with station

Water features
≈ River
◯ Lake
▨ Beach, dry river bed
〰 Ocean
ॴ Waterfall
〜 Reef
⬥ Ferry

Cities and towns
▫ Sight
🖪 Sleeping
➊ Eating
▭ Building
≡ Main through route
⁼ Main street
⁼ Minor street
⁼⁼⁼ Pedestrianized street
→ One way street

⌇ Bridge
∷∷ Park, garden, stadium
✦ Airport
Ⓢ Bank
🚍 Bus station
✚ Hospital
🏪 Market
🏛 Museum
ⓟ Police
✉ Post office
ℹ Tourist office
†† Cathedral, church
⬨ Petrol
@ Internet
⚲ Golf
🄿 Parking
Ⓐ Detail map
◀Ⓐ Related map

Topographical features
◯ Contours (approx), rock outcrop
⋀ Mountain
⊥⊥⊥ Escarpment
〰〰 Gorge

Other symbols
⁛ Archaeological Site
◆ National park/wildlife reserve
❈ Viewing point
⚘ Winery
⛺ Campsite
❁ Mangrove

Credits

Footprint credits

Text editor: Alan Murphy
Map editor: Sarah Sorensen

Publishers: James Dawson and
Patrick Dawson
Editorial Director: Rachel Fielding
Editorial: Ian Emery, Stephanie Lambe,
Sarah Thorowgood, Claire Boobbyer,
Felicity Laughton, Caroline Lascom
Production: Davina Rungasamy,
Emma Bryers, Mark Thomas, Jo Morgan
Cartography: Claire Benison,
Kevin Feeney, Robert Lunn
Design: Mytton Williams
Marketing and publicity:
Rosemary Dawson, La-Ree Miners
Sales: Ed Aves
Advertising: Debbie Wylde,
Lorraine Horler
Finance and administration:
Sharon Hughes, Elizabeth Taylor,
Leona Bailey
Distribution: Pam Cobb, Mike Noel

Photography credits

Front cover: Robert Harding
  Picture Library
Back cover: Darroch Donald
Inside colour section: Darroch Donald,
Philip Game

Print

Manufactured in Italy by LegoPrint

Publishing information

Australia Handbook
1st edition
© Footprint Handbooks Ltd
November 2002

ISBN 1 903471 42 7
CIP DATA: A catalogue record for this
book is available from the British Library

® Footprint Handbooks and the Footprint
mark are a registered trademark of
Footprint Handbooks Ltd

Published by Footprint Handbooks

6 Riverside Court
Lower Bristol Road
Bath BA2 3DZ, UK
T +44 (0)1225 469141
F +44 (0)1225 469461
E discover@footprintbooks.com
W www.footprintbooks.com

Distributed in the USA by

Publishers Group West

Every effort has been made to ensure that
the facts in the Handbook are accurate.
However, travellers should still obtain
advice from consulates, airlines etc about
travel and visa requirements before
travelling. The authors and publishers
cannot accept responsibility for
any loss, injury or inconvenience
however caused.

Acknowledgements

Darroch would like to thank all the staff and representatives of the many regional visitor information centres and regional tourism offices who provided invaluable advice and assistance, in particular Far North Queensland Media Representative Dion Eades and Alison Crump of Townsville Enterprise Ltd. Also a huge thanks to Sally Van Natta and Tony and Brigitte in Santa Barbara, California, for their invaluable help, valued friendship and for providing sanctuary from the rigours of the road. Also tramping companion Richard Robinson in Victoria for storing my poor, ageing van.
Also thanks to all the team at Footprint and Alan Murphy and Rachel Fielding in particular for their much appreciated patience, support and hard work. Finally a special thanks, as ever, to my mother Grace for her steadfast encouragement and support, my brother Ghill for assisting with frequent cashflow problems and for the many 'tonic' Email attachments and my partner Rebecca, who knows that although she is unable to join me on the road is always with me in my thoughts and in my heart.

Andrew and Katrina would like to thank the staff of the many tourist offices and commissions who generously gave their time to ensure that we made the best of ours. There are too many to mention, but we are particularly grateful to Karen Priest and Sascha Turner from South West WA, Kim Hadley from the Kununurra Tourist Office, and Michelle Grima and Ian Mclean from the Tasmanian Tourist Commission.
  Our thanks too to those we met along the way who helped us out and showed us genuine warmth and hospitality. Again too numerous to list fully, but special mention must be made of: Chris Ferris, Damon Hawker, Fran Wigley, Geoff and Hazel Reddall, Jeremy and Carolyn Tatchell, Joy Allen, Kenton Day, Len and Doug, Pauline McPharlin and Alistair Sawers, Sandy and Simon Watkin, Trish Fairlie, and Troy Flower.
Also thanks to the team at Footprint for their commitment, patience and passion; particularly Rachel, James, Patrick and Ro, Alan for maintaining his good humour, and La-Ree for cheerily responding to any and all questions and requests. Finally a big thanks to our friends and family: Dennis and Alexandra, whose enthusiastic support helped us to make this project possible; Bryan, Mary and Terry, for a constant ear and encouragement; Cliff for his tremendous friendship and bringing Andrew to Oz in the first place; and Flynn for keeping us sane just when sanity was at a premium.

Dr Charlie Easmon wrote the health section. His aid and development work has included: Raleigh International (Medical Officer in Botswana), MERLIN (in Rwanda his team set up a refugee camp for 12,000 people), Save the Children (as a consultant in Rwanda), ECHO (The European Community Humanitarian Office review of Red Cross work in Armenia, Georgia and Azerbaijan), board member of International Care and Relief and previously International Health Exchange. In addition to his time as a hospital physician, he has worked as a medical adviser to the Foreign and Commonwealth Office and as a locum consultant at the hospital for tropical diseases travel clinic, as well as being a specialist registrar in Public Health. He now also runs Travel Screening services (www.travelscreening.co.uk) based at 1 Harley Street.

Keep in touch

Footprint feedback

We try as hard as we can to make each Footprint Handbook as up-to-date and accurate as possible but, of course, things always change. Many people write to us - with corrections, new information, or simply comments.

If you want to let us know about an experience or adventure - hair-raising or mundane, good or bad, exciting or boring or simply something rather special - we would be delighted to hear from you. Please give us as precise information as possible, quoting the edition number (you'll find it on the front cover) and page number of the Handbook you are using.

Your help will be greatly appreciated, especially by other travellers. In return we will send you details about our special guidebook offer. Email Footprint at:
aus1_online@footprintbooks.com

or write to:
Elizabeth Taylor
Footprint Handbooks
6 Riverside Court, Lower Bristol Road
Bath BA2 3DZ UK

Footnotes

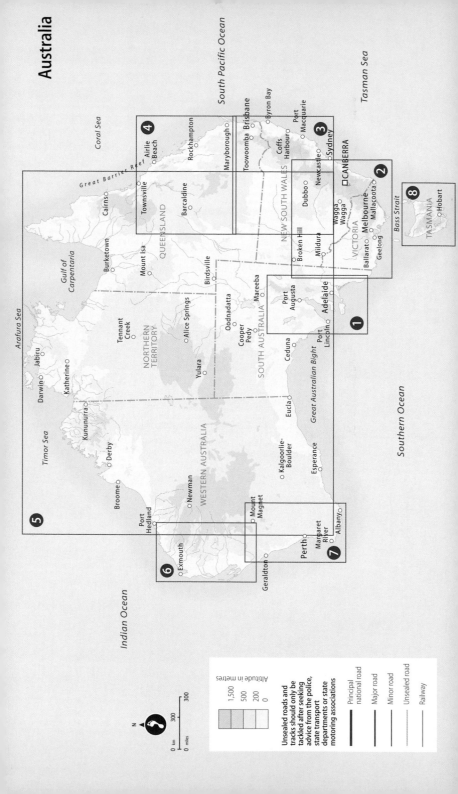

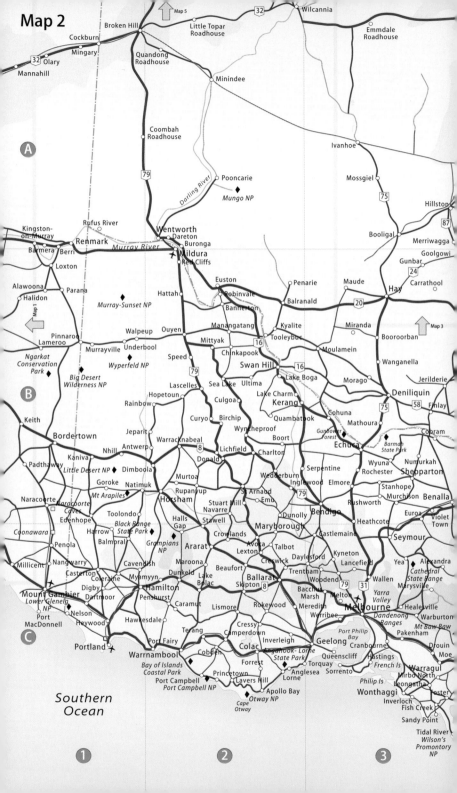

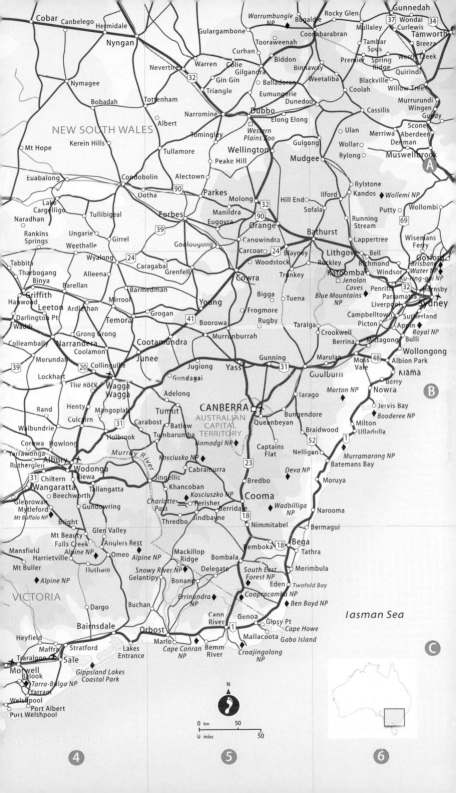

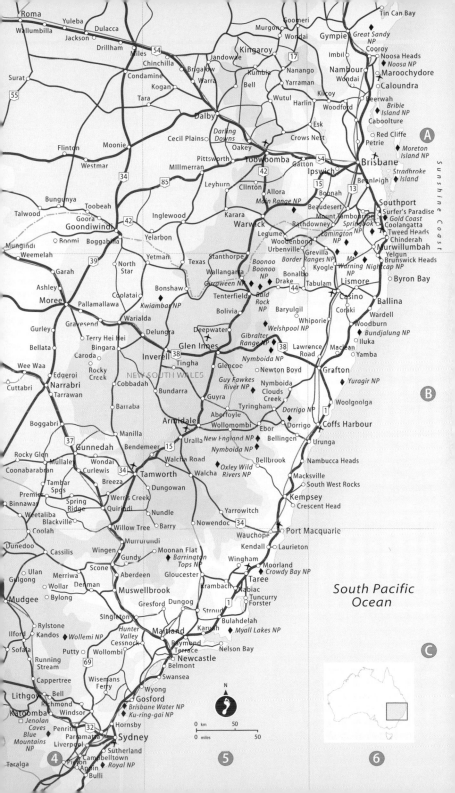

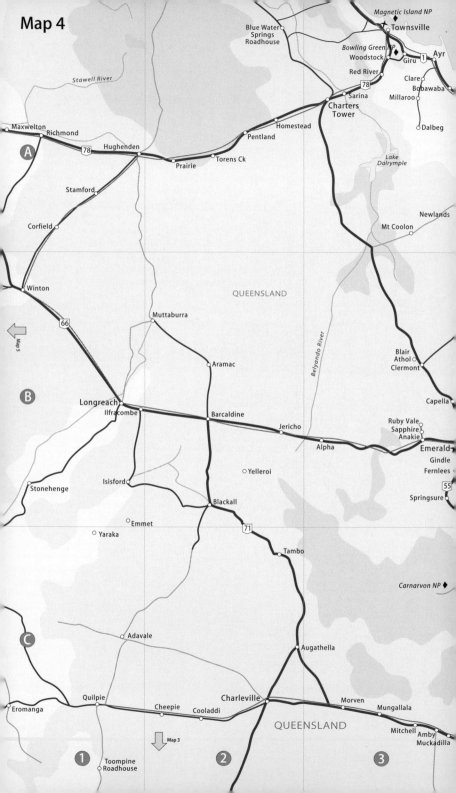

Map 4

Magnetic Island NP

Townsville

Blue Water Springs Roadhouse

Bowling Green NP

Woodstock

Giru

Ayr

Red River

Clare

Bobawaba

Sarina

Millaroo

Charters Tower

Dalberg

Homestead

Stawell River

Pentland

Maxwelton

Richmond

Hughenden

Prairie

Torens Ck

Lake Dalrymple

Stamford

Newlands

Corfield

Mt Coolon

QUEENSLAND

Winton

Muttaburra

Belyando River

Blair Athol

Clermont

Aramac

Capella

Longreach

Ilfracombe

Barcaldine

Jericho

Ruby Vale

Sapphire

Anakie

Alpha

Emerald

Gindle

Fernlees

Yelleroi

Isisford

Blackall

Springsure

Stonehenge

Emmet

Yaraka

Tambo

Carnarvon NP

Adavale

Augathella

Quilpie

Charleville

Morven

Mungallala

Eromanga

Cheepie

Cooladdi

Mitchell

Amby

QUEENSLAND

Muckadilla

Toompine Roadhouse

Map 5

Map 3

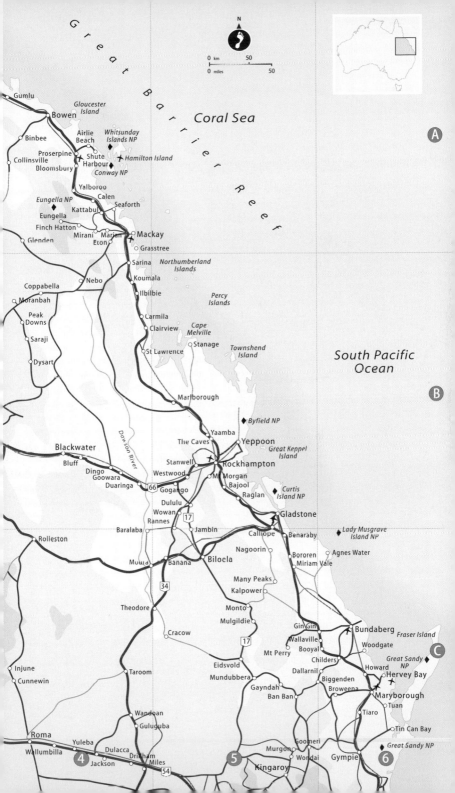

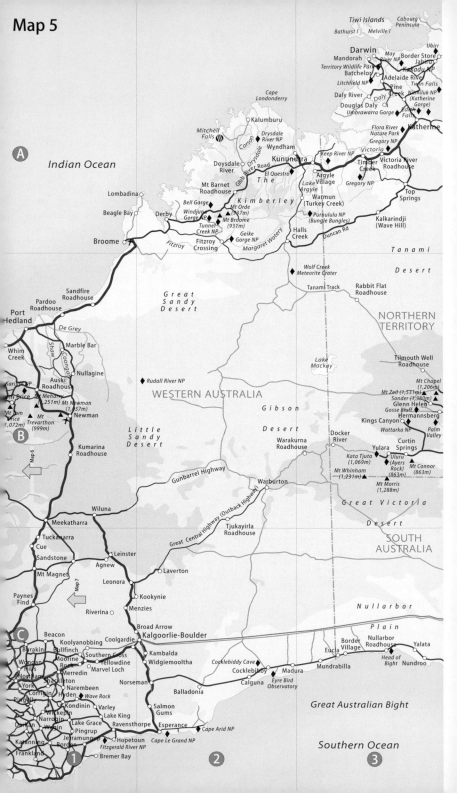

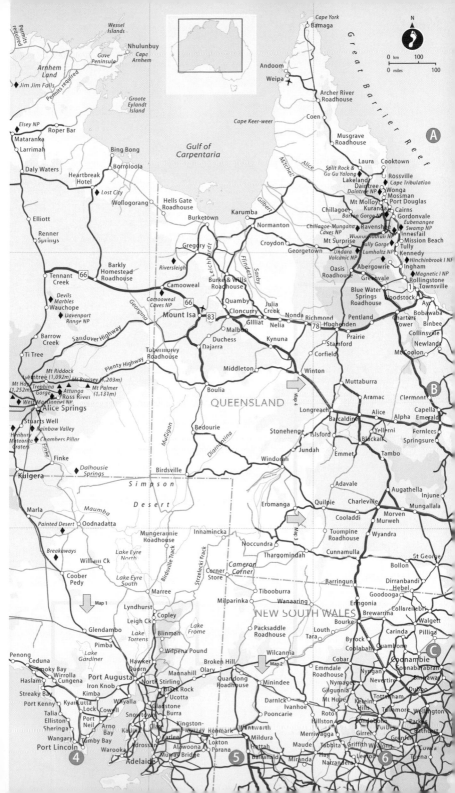

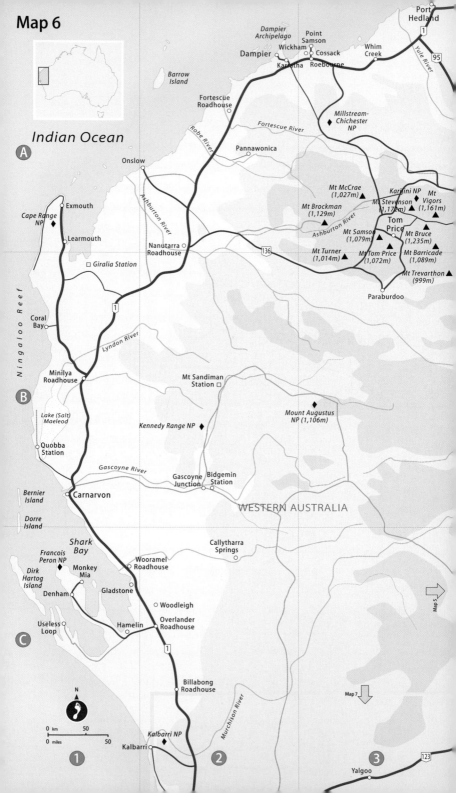

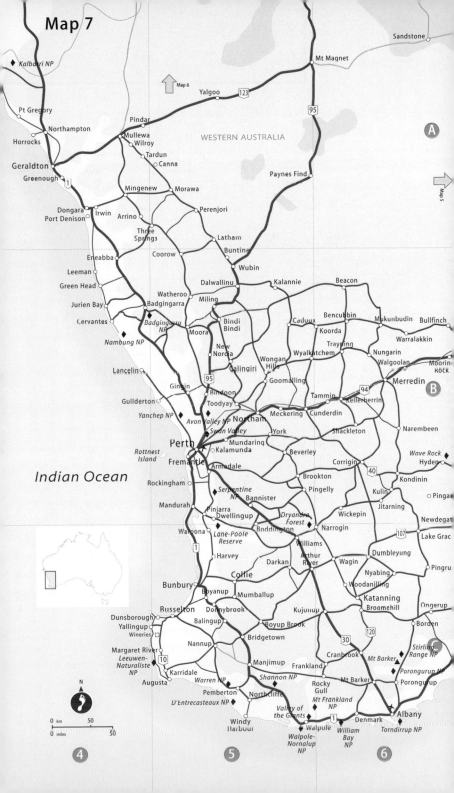

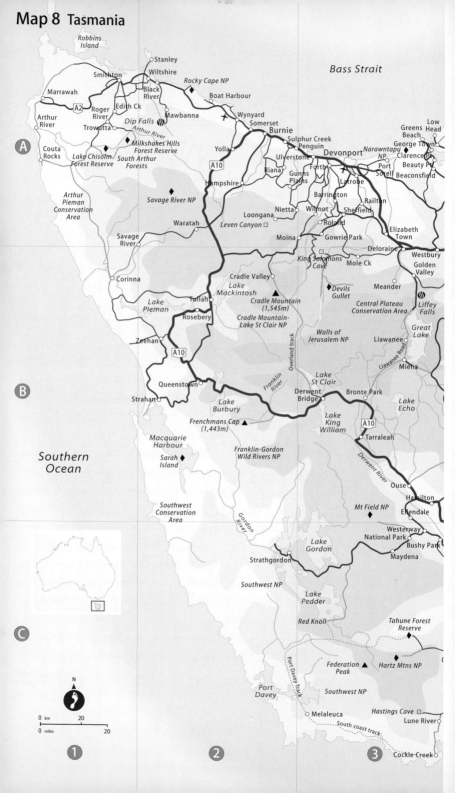

Map 8 Tasmania

Bass Strait

Robbins Island

Stanley
Wiltshire
Rocky Cape NP
Smithton
Black River
Boat Harbour
Marrawah
Roger River
Edith Ck
Mawbanna
Wynyard
Somerset
Arthur River
Trowutta
Dip Falls
Burnie
Couta Rocks
Arthur River
Milkshakes Hills Forest Reserve
Yolla
Sulphur Creek
Penguin
Devonport
Greens Beach
Low Head
George Town
Narawntapu NP
Clarence Pt
Beauty Pt

Lake Chisolm Forest Reserve
South Arthur Forests
Ulverstone
Forth
Port Sorell
Beaconsfield

Arthur Pieman Conservation Area
Hampshire
Riana
Gunns Plains
Latrobe

Savage River NP
Nietta
Barrington
Railton
Sheffield

Waratah
Leven Canyon
Wilmot
Roland
Elizabeth Town

Moina
Gowrie Park
Deloraine
Westbury

King Solomons Cave
Mole Ck
Golden Valley

Savage River
Meander

Corinna
Cradle Valley
Lake Mackintosh
Devils Gullet
Central Plateau Conservation Area
Liffey Falls

Lake Pieman
Tullah
▲ Cradle Mountain (1,545m)
Cradle Mountain-Lake St Clair NP
Walls of Jerusalem NP
Great Lake

Rosebery
Overland track
Liawanee

Zeehan
Llawanee Road
Miena

B
Queenstown
Franklin River
Lake St Clair
Derwent Bridge
Bronte Park
Lake Echo

Strahan
Lake Burbury
Lake King William
A10

Southern Ocean
Frenchmans Cap (1,443m) ▲
Franklin-Gordon Wild Rivers NP
Tarraleah

Macquarie Harbour
Sarah Island ◆
Derwent River
Ouse
Hamilton

Southwest Conservation Area
Gordon River
Mt Field NP
Ellendale

Westerway
National Park
Bushy Park

Strathgordon
Lake Gordon
Maydena

Southwest NP
Lake Pedder

Red Knoll
Tahune Forest Reserve

C
Federation Peak ▲
Hartz Mtns NP

Port Davey
Port Davey Track
Southwest NP
Hastings Cave
Lune River

N
Melaleuca
South coast track
Cockle Creek

0 km 20
0 miles 20

1　　　　　**2**　　　　　**3**

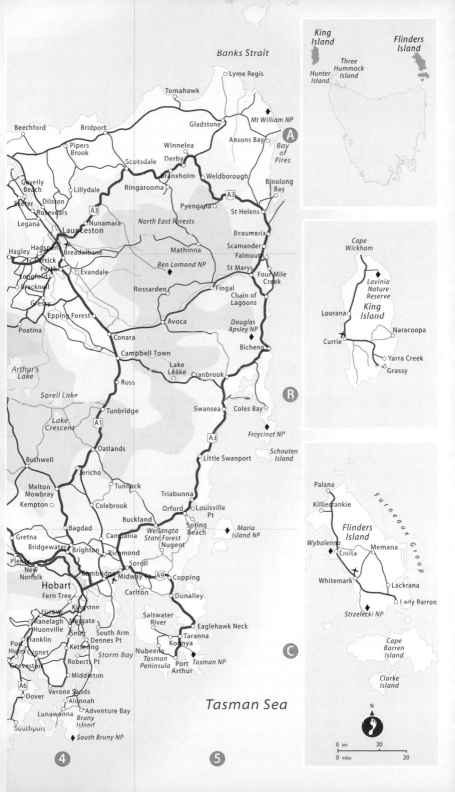

For a different view, take a Footprint